W9-AAK-369

ECONOMETRIC MODELS, TECHNIQUES, AND APPLICATIONS

ECONOMETRIC MODELS, TECHNIQUES, AND APPLICATIONS

MICHAEL D. INTRILIGATOR

Professor of Economics
University of California, Los Angeles

PRENTICE-HALL, INC., *Englewood Cliffs, New Jersey 07632*

Library of Congress Cataloging in Publication Data

INTRILIGATOR, MICHAEL D. (1938–)
Econometric models, techniques, and applications.

Bibliography: p.
Includes index.
1.–Econometrics. 2.–Econometrics–Mathematical models. I.–Title.
HB139.I57 330'.01'82 77-14564
ISBN 0-13-223255-3

© 1978 by Prentice-Hall, Inc.
Englewood Cliffs, N.J. 07632

All rights reserved. No part of this book may be reproduced in any form or by any means without permission in writing from the publisher.

Printed in the United States of America

10 9 8 7 6 5 4 3 2

PRENTICE-HALL INTERNATIONAL, INC., *London*
PRENTICE-HALL OF AUSTRALIA PTY. LIMITED, *Sydney*
PRENTICE-HALL OF CANADA, LTD., *Toronto*
PRENTICE-HALL OF INDIA PRIVATE LIMITED, *New Delhi*
PRENTICE-HALL OF JAPAN, INC., *Tokyo*
PRENTICE-HALL OF SOUTHEAST ASIA PTE. LTD., *Singapore*
WHITEHALL BOOKS LIMITED, *Wellington, New Zealand*

To Kenneth

James

William

Robert

Contents

Preface

Econometrics has come of age. It has produced a solid body of theory and, of equal importance, a host of applications both in economics and in other social sciences. In economics it has traditionally been applied to macroeconomics, but over recent years it has been applied to virtually every other field of economics including monetary economics, public finance, international trade, labor economics, and economic development. Political science, sociology, and history also have utilized econometric methods. Applications have been made to such diverse areas as education, law, health, and transportation. As a consequence, there has been a tremendous growth of interest in econometrics on the part of students as well as professional workers in economics and other social sciences.

Purpose

This book introduces and surveys the approach, techniques, and applications of econometrics. Its motivation arose largely from the observation that at least 80% of the material in most of the existing textbooks in econometrics focuses purely on econometric techniques. By contrast, practicing econometricians—or economists or social scientists performing econometric studies—typically spend 20% or less of their time and effort on econometric techniques per se; the remainder is spent on other aspects of the study, particularly on the construction of a relevant econometric model and the development of appropriate data before estimation and on the interpretation of results after estimation. The distinctive feature of this book is its balance between the econometric techniques per se, the model-building and data-collection areas, and the applications and uses of econometrics. It does not slight the techniques; rather it presents them in a logical, understandable, and usable fashion. It does, however, stress those aspects of econometrics of major importance to students and researchers interested in performing or evaluating econometric studies.

The book should enable the reader to understand and to evaluate existing econometric studies in a variety of areas. To a large extent, econometrics is not a science, defined by a narrow set of theorems, but rather an approach that can be appreciated and understood only by use. Indeed, the reader's comprehension of econometrics in practice will not be complete until he or she has performed an original econometric study, preparation for which is one of this book's basic objectives.

The book can be used as a textbook in first-year graduate or advanced undergraduate courses in econometrics. It can also be utilized as a supplementary text for courses in economic theory, economic statistics, sociometrics, engineering, public administration, policy sciences, or other social sciences. It should also be of interest to economists, statisticians, engineers, and operations-research analysts.

Prerequisites

The mathematical level has been kept as elementary as possible—an elementary knowledge of basic concepts of calculus, matrix theory, and probability and statistics would suffice. Two appendices review basic concepts—including definitions, examples, and theorems—for matrices (Appendix B) and for probability and statistics (Appendix C). These appendices are not intended as text materials but rather as convenient reviews for readers who have had some previous exposure to the general concepts, usually via previous courses in matrix theory and statistics. They also introduce the notation and some concepts not generally covered in basic courses. Introductory books on these subjects are referenced at the beginning of each appendix.

Organization

The book consists of seven major parts. *Part I* introduces the nature of econometrics and the econometric approach. It discusses some of the important objectives of econometrics in order to motivate the student—by specifically indicating what the study of econometrics may provide. *Part II* treats models and data, particularly econometric models and economic data. It provides examples of relevant models, including two prototype models that not only illustrate various aspects of models and model building but also represent a bridge to the later discussion of applications of econometrics. The discussion of data should facilitate an understanding of the nature and sources of data. *Part III* concerns the estimation of single-equation models, including discussions of multiple linear regression and problems in and extensions of the basic linear regression model. *Part IV* covers applications of the techniques developed in Part III, including applications to the household (demand functions), to the firm (production and cost functions), and to other areas. *Part V* concerns the estimation of simultaneous-equations systems, including a discussion of the identification problem, limited-information techniques, and full-information techniques. *Part VI* discusses applications of these techniques to macroeconomic models and to other areas. Finally, *Part VII* provides a discussion of three major uses of econometrics: structural analysis, forecasting, and policy evaluation.

Appendix A outlines an econometric project, which students and other readers of this book are encouraged to perform. *Appendix B* summarizes important definitions and theorems concerning matrices, while *Appendix C* summarizes the probability and statistics used in the book, including relevant statistical tables.

Distinctive Features

The distinctive features of this book are primarily the materials covered in Parts II, IV, VI, and VII.

Part II discusses those aspects of econometrics that are logically prior to estimation, namely the specification of the model and the development of data for its estimation. Remarkably enough, these aspects are generally not treated in existing econometrics textbooks.

Parts IV and VI provide case studies of the applications of econometrics to a wide variety of areas. They include traditional areas, such as the estimation of demand functions and production functions, as illustrative of single-equation estimation, and macroeconometric models, as illustrative of simultaneous-equations estimation. They also include, however, some newer areas of application of both single-equation and simultaneous-equations methods, such as monetary economics, labor economics, industrial organization, and health economics. The purpose is not to be exhaustive, but rather to select several studies illustrating the application of econometric techniques to each area and to provide references to other such studies (see, in particular, the Bibliography for Chapter 9). After having seen econometric methods applied to several areas, the reader—and especially the student—should be able to carry out an econometric project, including the specification of the model, development of data, estimation, and use, as outlined in Appendix A.

Part VII discusses the various uses to which an estimated econometric model can be put. An estimated econometric model is a very valuable product, not to be admired for its own sake, but rather to be put to use for structural analysis, forecasting, and policy evaluation. This elementary but important observation appears to have been overlooked in most existing econometrics textbooks.

The Nature of the Problems

Another distinctive feature of this book is the inclusion of problems in most chapters. These problems challenge the reader to enlarge upon the basic knowledge contained in the chapter by proving further results or developing extensions. The intent is to provide the student of econometrics with a challenge somewhat comparable to the laboratory problem facing a student in the natural sciences. The student must take the initiative and, based upon the material in the chapter, prove or discover some additional results or extension of the basic material. The problems also provide a test as to whether the material contained in the chapter has been fully comprehended.

Acknowledgments

This book is based largely on courses I have given over the last ten years at the University of California, Los Angeles; the University of Southern California; and the California Institute of Technology. My principal acknowledgment is to the students who have given me the benefit of their comments and suggestions. I have also been extremely fortunate in receiving helpful comments and suggestions from William Barger, David Belsley, Christopher Bliss, Murray Brown, Jeffrey Conner, Camilo Dagum, Otto Eckstein, Arthur Goldberger, Stephen Goldfeld, Jay Helms, Bruce Herrick, Leif Johansen, Dale Jorgenson, Linda Kleiger, Robert McNown, Jeffrey Perloff, Inga Rynell-Heller, Herman Stekler, Jack Tawil, and Victor Zarnowitz.

M. D. INTRILIGATOR

PART I

Introduction

CHAPTER 1

The Econometric Approach

1.1 What is econometrics?

To start with a definition, *econometrics* is the branch of economics concerned with the empirical estimation of economic relationships. The "metric" part of the word signifies *measurement*; and econometrics is basically concerned with measuring economic relationships. Econometrics utilizes economic theory, as embodied in an *econometric model*; facts, as summarized by *relevant data*; and statistical theory, as refined into *econometric techniques*, in order to measure and to test empirically certain relationships among economic variables, thereby giving empirical content to economic reasoning. While this definition is oriented to economics, the econometric approach is not confined exclusively to economics; it can be applied to other disciplines, especially other social sciences, such as history, political science, sociology, and psychology. It can also be applied to areas of public policy, including health, education, transportation, housing, and environmental protection.

When the term "econometrics" was first used, in the 1930s, it conveyed both the development of pure theory from a mathematical viewpoint and the empirical estimation of economic relationships. Now it signifies primarily the latter; the mathematical development of economic theory is now called *mathematical economics.*[1]

A distinction might also be drawn between econometrics and economic statistics. *Economic statistics* is concerned with descriptive statistics, including developing and refining economic data such as the national income accounts and index numbers, while econometrics utilizes these data to estimate quantitative economic relationships and to test hypotheses about them.[2]

1.2 The nature of the econometric approach

Figure 1.1 summarizes the econometric approach.[3] There are two basic ingredients in any econometric study—theory and facts. Indeed, a major accom-

[1] For expositions of mathematical economics see Intriligator (1971a) and Takayama (1974). The theory developed in mathematical economics is often a guide to the specification of an econometric model, as will be seen in Chapters 7 and 8, which include the applications of econometrics to the estimation of demand functions and production functions, respectively.

[2] See Chapter 3 for a discussion of data used in econometric studies.

[3] For a related diagram see Stone (1965) and Intriligator (1971b).

plishment of econometrics is simply that of combining these two ingredients. By contrast, a considerable amount of work in economics emphasizes one of them to the exclusion of the other. The "theory-only" school is concerned solely with purely deductive implications of certain postulate systems involving economic phenomena. Examples from mathematical economics include the neoclassical theories of demand, production, and general equilibrium. The "facts-only" school, by contrast, is concerned solely with developing and improving data on the economy. Examples from economic statistics include the collection of data at the macro level, such as the national income accounts, or at the micro level, such as individual lifetime work and income histories. Either of these extreme positions would be difficult to defend. As to the theory-only school, pure theory, by itself, has little empirical content. Furthermore, rival theories can often be developed, and the proper way to choose between them is on the basis of evidence in the form of facts, with facts guiding the development of theory. As to the facts-only school, the facts do not "speak for themselves," and to use them effectively they typically must be interpreted in terms of an underlying structure, embodied in a theory. Econometrics utilizes both theory and facts, combining them, using statistical techniques, to estimate economic relationships.

Theory is one of the basic ingredients in any econometric study, but it must be developed in a usable form. The most usable form for the purposes of econometrics, as shown in Figure 1.1, is typically that of a *model*, in particular an *econometric model*. The model summarizes the theory relevant to the system

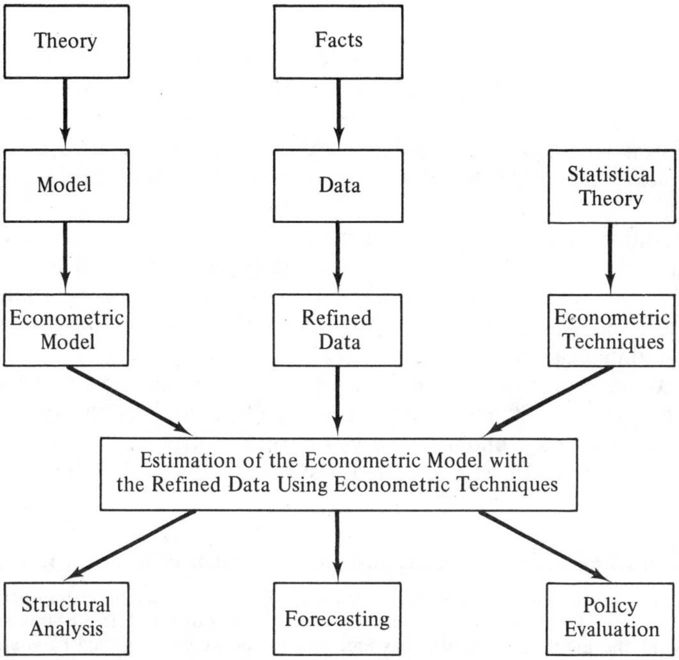

Figure 1.1 The Econometric Approach

under consideration, and it is the most convenient way of summarizing this theory for empirical measurement and testing. An important aspect of econometrics and an essential part of any econometric study is the *specification* of the model–that is, the construction and elaboration of a model that appropriately represents the phenomena to be studied. Later sections of this chapter give a few simple examples of models, and Chapter 2 discusses models in general and econometric models in particular. Chapters 7, 8, 9, 12, and 13–the "applications" chapters of this book–include many specific models that have been used in econometric studies. They should assist the reader in carrying out an original econometric study, as outlined in Appendix A.

The other basic ingredient in an econometric study is a set of *facts*, referring to events in the real world relating to the phenomena under investigation.[4] These facts lead to a set of *data*, representing observations of relevant facts. In general, however, the data have to be refined, or "massaged," in a variety of ways to make them suitable for use in an econometric study. This refinement includes various adjustments such as seasonal or cyclical adjustments, extrapolation, interpolation, merging of different data sources, and, in general, the use of other information to adjust the data. The result is a set of *refined data*. These subjects will be taken up in Chapter 3, which includes a table of data sources that should be useful in generating data for the original econometric study.

The theory has been developed in the form of an econometric model, and the facts into a set of refined data; the next and central step in the econometric approach combines these two basic ingredients. That step–the estimation of the econometric model using the refined data–requires the use of a set of *econometric techniques*. These are extensions of classical methods of statistics, particularly statistical inference (the use of sample information to infer certain characteristics of a population). Extensions of the classical methods are needed to account for certain special problems encountered in estimating an econometric model. These techniques, discussed at length in Chapters 4, 5, 6, 10, and 11–the "techniques" chapters of this book–should be used in the original econometric study.

The result of the process is an estimated econometric model, in which certain magnitudes, known as *parameters*, are estimated on the basis of relevant data. The estimated model provides a way of measuring and testing relationships suggested by economic theory. The "applications" chapters below give examples of estimated models from a variety of areas.

The econometric approach thus combines theory and facts in a particular way. From the viewpoint of theory, econometrics can be considered the application of "real-world" data to economic theory. Conversely, from the viewpoint of the facts, econometrics can be considered a systematic way of studying economic history.[5]

[4] See Section 3.1 for a discussion of quantitative representation of qualitative facts.

[5] A new approach to economic history, which uses the tools of econometrics to study such issues as the role of railroads in the economic development of the United States or the role of slavery in the antebellum South, has emerged in recent years. Called *cliometrics*, it is discussed in Section 9.6.

1.3 The purposes of econometrics

Figure 1.1 also shows the three principal purposes of econometrics: structural analysis, forecasting, and policy evaluation. Any econometric study may have one, two, or all of these purposes, which represent the "end products" of econometrics, just as "theory" and "facts" represent its "raw materials." In this sense Figure 1.1 can be thought of as a flow diagram showing schematically how the different parts of an econometric study are combined and eventually utilized.

Structural analysis is the use of an estimated econometric model for the quantitative measurement of economic relationships. It also facilitates the comparison of rival theories of the same phenomena. Structural analysis represents what might be considered the "scientific" purpose of econometrics—that of understanding real-world phenomena by quantitatively measuring, testing, and validating economic relationships. One result of this analysis may be a "feedback" influence on theory. For example, a measured relationship between the rate of inflation and the rate of unemployment, the Phillips curve, has led to various developments in the theory of unemployment.[6]

Forecasting is the use of an estimated econometric model to predict quantitative values of certain variables outside the sample of data actually observed. Forecasts may be the basis for action; for example, the purchase of raw materials and employment of additional workers in a firm may be based on a forecast that sales will increase over the subsequent two quarters.

Policy evaluation is the use of an estimated econometric model to choose between alternative policies. One approach is to introduce explicitly an objective function to be maximized by choice of policies and to regard the estimated model as a constraint in this optimization process. Another approach, often more useful to policymakers, is to simulate alternative policies and to make conditional forecasts of the future values of relevant variables under each alternative. The selection of a most desired alternative among the various possible "candidate futures" would indicate which policy should be pursued. In either case, the selection of a particular policy, combined with the effects of those outside events that have an influence on the system, leads to specific outcomes. The outcomes, in turn, lead to another "feedback relationship" connecting policy evaluation with the facts, as shown in Figure 1.1.

These three principal purposes of econometrics are closely related. The structure determined by structural analysis is used in forecasting using an econometric model, while policy evaluation using an econometric model is a type of conditional forecast. The uses and their interrelationships are discussed at greater length below, particularly in Chapters 14, 15, and 16, the "uses" chapters of this book. These discussions should guide the reader in completing an original econometric study.

[6] The original measured relationship was reported in Phillips (1958). Examples of the theoretical developments inspired, in part, by this measured relationship appear in Phelps, Ed. (1970). For a discussion of the iterative approach to modeling, with feedback from estimation to theory see Hamilton et al. (1969).

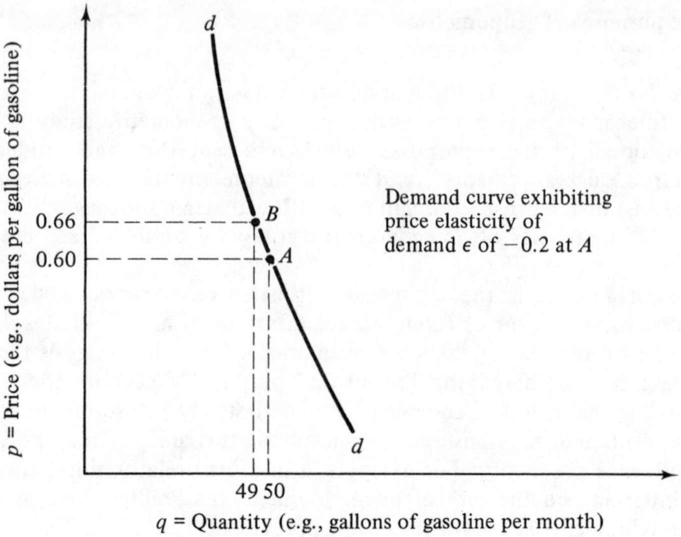

Figure 1.2 Demand Curve (e.g., for Gasoline)

1.4 An example–the demand curve and the price elasticity of demand

An example of an econometric study is the estimation of a demand curve for a particular commodity, say gasoline. The demand curve for an individual consumer, illustrated in Figure 1.2, gives the quantity he or she demands, q, in gallons per month, as a function of the price, p, in dollars per gallon:[7]

$$q = q(p) \qquad *(1.4.1)$$

The concept of a demand curve, which is the model in this example, should be familiar; it is basic to the microeconomic theory of demand and is relevant both for the individual consumer and, in the aggregate, for the market as a whole. It is also a basic component of the prototype micro model discussed in the next chapter, and it is fundamental to the discussion of applications of econometrics to households in Chapter 7.

Two points are shown on the hypothetical individual consumer demand curve of Figure 1.2. The first, A, indicates that at a price of 60 cents per gallon the particular consumer whose demand curve is represented by dd would buy 50 gallons of gasoline per month. The second, B, indicates that if everything else is the same but the price goes up to 66 cents per gallon, he or she would buy 49 gallons of gasoline per month.

[7] Note that, following a long-standing convention, the independent variable, price, is shown on the *vertical* axis while the dependent variable, quantity demanded, is shown on the *horizontal* axis, reversing the usual mathematical convention. Also note that equations will be numbered according to the section in which they appear. Thus, equation (1.4.1) is the first equation in Section 1.4. An asterisk (*) preceding an equation number, as here, indicates an important equation.

A useful measure of the responsiveness of the quantity demanded of a particular product to its price is the *price elasticity of demand*, ϵ, defined as the ratio of the relative change in quantity demanded to the relative change in price. Since the relative change in any variable z is the ratio of a change in z, say Δz, to the base level of z, that is, $\Delta z/z$, the price elasticity of demand can be written:[8]

$$\epsilon = \frac{\Delta q/q}{\Delta p/p} = \frac{p}{q}\frac{\Delta q}{\Delta p} \qquad *(1.4.2)$$

The elasticity of demand defined this way is an *arc elasticity* of demand, and it is generally negative.[9] With the data shown in Figure 1.2, the price elasticity of demand at A is approximately[10]

$$\epsilon = \frac{\Delta q/q}{\Delta p/p} = \frac{(49-50)/50}{(0.66-0.60)/0.60} = \frac{-0.02}{0.10} = -0.2. \qquad (1.4.3)$$

Thus, at A, a 10% increase in price would reduce the quantity demanded by approximately 2%, while a 5% decrease in price would increase the quantity demanded by approximately 1%.

The estimation of price elasticities of demand for particular goods or services is an example of an econometric study. It combines theory, here represented by the demand curve model, with facts, here represented by only two price-quantity pairs.[11] The technique of estimation is the arc elasticity formula (1.4.3). The resulting numerical measures of the responsiveness of quantity demanded to price are of considerable interest for purposes of structural analysis. They are

Table 1.1 Estimated Price Elasticities of Demand, United Kingdom, 1920–38

Commodity	*Price Elasticity of Demand*
Fresh milk	−0.49
Condensed milk	−1.23
Butter	−0.41
Margarine	0.01
Tea	−0.26

Source: Stone (1954), as reported in Chapter 7, Table 7.5.

[8] Section 7.2 provides a discussion of elasticity in the context of the theory of demand.

[9] Since the demand curve is downward sloping Δp and Δq are of opposite sign.

[10] In general the elasticity varies along the demand curve. The estimate, (1.4.3), approximates its value at A. The approximation becomes better the closer is the point B to A.

[11] Note that A and B were assumed to be points on the demand curve. In general, observed price-quantity pairs from a marketplace do *not* represent points on a single demand curve. For example, the demand curve may have shifted as a result of changes in income or prices of other goods. They rather represent points of intersection of demand and supply curves. This point will be developed in detail in Chapters 2, 7, and 10.

also useful for purposes of forecasting and policy evaluation, e.g., to predict next year's imports of petroleum or to set appropriate taxes on gasoline.

Table 1.1 gives some estimates of price elasticities of demand for some basic food items from the study by Stone of consumer behavior in the United Kingdom, 1920-1938.[12] According to these results the demand for condensed milk is highly responsive to price, while the demand for margarine is insensitive to its price. This study was an important one for both forecasting and policy evaluation purposes. In particular, the estimated elasticities were used to forecast the demands for various products after wartime rationing was eliminated and thereby to evaluate the policy of eliminating such wartime controls. The estimation of such elasticities will be discussed in Chapter 7.

1.5 A second example—the consumption function

The second example of an econometric study is the estimation of a consumption function, a basic component of virtually all macroeconomic models, which determines total consumption for the national economy as a function of total income. This concept will be utilized in the next chapter in the development of a prototype macro model and will also appear in Chapter 12 on macroeconometric models.

Figure 1.3 illustrates a linear consumption function, giving the dollar value of total consumption expenditure C as a function of the dollar value of national income, Y (e.g., gross national product). The consumption function is, in general, a rising curve but has a slope less than unity; i.e., added income leads to added consumption but also leads to added savings. The slope of the curve is called

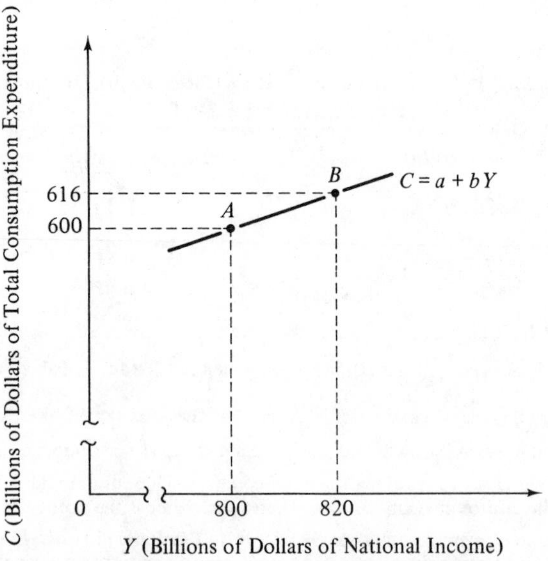

Figure 1.3 The Linear Consumption Function

[12] See Stone (1954). These results are discussed in Chapter 7, Section 7.4.

the marginal propensity to consume, MPC, and it is therefore assumed positive but less than unity. Thus, in this case of a linear consumption function

$$C = a + bY, \qquad 0 < b \equiv \text{MPC} < 1 \qquad *(1.5.1)$$

From the two points shown on Figure 1.3 the MPC can be estimated to be

$$\frac{\Delta C}{\Delta Y} = \frac{616 - 600}{820 - 800} = 0.8 \qquad (1.5.2)$$

implying that 80 cents of each dollar of added income is spent on consumption.

Measurement of the MPC exemplifies an econometric study, combining theory (of the consumption function) and data (on aggregate consumption and income) with econometric techniques [e.g., the estimate defined in (1.5.2)]. Such a measurement is important in understanding the structure of the macro economy, in forecasting future levels of aggregate income (and employment), and in analyzing policy proposals, such as monetary and fiscal policy alternatives. Estimation of MPC and other macroeconomic parameters will be discussed in Chapter 12, and the use of macroeconometric models in policy evaluation will be treated in Chapter 16.

1.6 A third example–the growth of science

The third example of an econometric type study comes from a field other than economics, illustrating the fact that the econometric approach is by no means confined to economics.

Historians of science have performed quantitative studies in which science is measured by variables such as the number of scientists and the number of papers published in scientific journals.[13] These quantitative studies have generally found that most measures of science grow at a constant proportionate rate. Letting N_t be the measure (e.g., numbers of scientists) in year t, it is found that the change in N_t from one year to the next, given as $\Delta N_t = N_{t+1} - N_t$, relative to the total N_t, is approximately constant. Thus

$$\frac{\Delta N_t}{N_t} = \text{constant} = \alpha \qquad (1.6.1)$$

e.g., a growth of 10% per year, where $\alpha = 0.1$. Consideration of the related differential equation

$$\frac{1}{N}\frac{dN}{dt} = \alpha \qquad (1.6.2)$$

leads to the exponential relationship

[13] See Price (1961, 1963).

$$N = N_0 e^{\alpha t} \tag{1.6.3}$$

where t is time and N_0 is the base number of the measure of science at time $t = 0$. This relationship is the basic hypothesis. Taking logs of (1.6.3),[14] leads to the model

$$\ln N = \ln N_0 + \alpha t \tag{1.6.4}$$

expressing a simple linear relationship between ln N and time, t. The slope coefficient α gives the rate of growth of N, while the intercept is the log of N_0, the base number at $t = 0$. This relationship is shown in Figure 1.4, where the horizontal axis, for time, is an arithmetic scale but the vertical axis, for N, is a logarithmic scale. Figure 1.4 is a convenient one for studying the growth of science. It is a particularly simple example of the econometric approach: the simple hypothesis that there is a constant growth rate of science is combined with the values taken by the measure of science at different points in time in

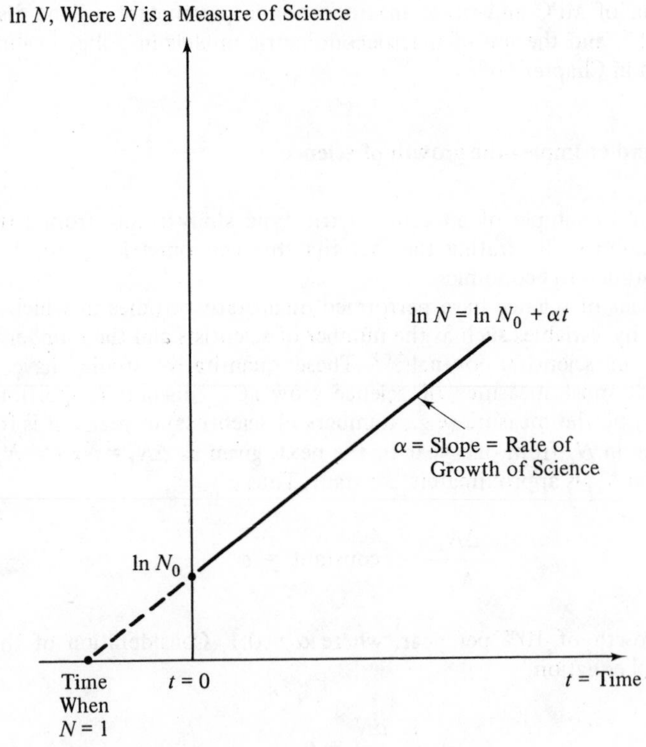

Figure 1.4 The Growth of Science

[14] Base e logs are used here and elsewhere, and "ln" means natural logarithm, i.e., log with the base e = 2.718 . . . .

order to study the structure of the process, here embodied in the estimation of the growth rate α. The estimate of α can be utilized to forecast the future levels of science, assuming that the future will be like the past.

It may be recalled that forecasting refers to the determination of values of variables outside the sample of observed data. Thus, forecasting can refer to past as well as future levels of science. One study performed in this framework considered the number of electrical engineers in the United States, measured by manpower employed in electrical engineering. As was anticipated, the growth rate was almost constant, so that plotting numbers of electrical engineers N as a function of time, t, on semilog graph paper yielded a set of points that fell very close to a straight line. This line was then projected back in time, as on Figure 1.4, to determine the time at which it hit the axis. This point is interpreted as being the time when there existed exactly *one* electrical engineer. The result of this forecast was amazingly "accurate": it turned out to be the year 1752, the year in which Benjamin Franklin flew his kite experiment! A related (tongue-in-cheek) forecast—of the year in which there was exactly one American economist—will be presented in Chapter 5, Section 5.5, as an illustration of simple linear regression.

BIBLIOGRAPHY

Hamilton, H. R., S. E. Goldstone, J. W. Milliman, A. L. Pugh, E. R. Roberts, and A. Zellner (1969), *Systems Simulation for Regional Analysis: An Application to River Basin Planning.* Cambridge: MIT Press.

Intriligator, M. D. (1971a), *Mathematical Optimization and Economic Theory.* Englewood Cliffs, N.J.: Prentice-Hall, Inc.

Intriligator, M. D. (1971b), "Econometrics and Economic Forecasting," in J. M. English, Ed., *The Economics of Engineering and Social Systems.* New York: John Wiley & Sons, Inc.

Phelps, E. S., Ed. (1970). *Microeconomic Foundations of Employment and Inflation Theory*. New York: W. W. Norton & Company, Inc.

Phillips, A. W. (1958), "The Relation Between Unemployment and the Rate of Change of Money Wages in the United Kingdom, 1861–1957." *Economica*, 25: 283–99.

Price, Derek J. de Solla (1963), *Little Science, Big Science*. New York: Columbia University Press.

Price, Derek J. de Solla (1961), *Science Since Babylon*. New Haven: Yale University Press.

Stone, R. (1965), "The Analysis of Economic Systems." *Scripta Varia*, 28: 1–88.

Stone, R. (1954), *The Measurement of Consumer's Expenditure and Behavior in The United Kingdom, 1920–1938*. Cambridge: Cambridge University Press.

Takayama, A. (1974), *Mathematical Economics*. Hinsdale, Ill.: The Dryden Press.

PART II

Models and Data

CHAPTER 2

Models and Econometric Models

2.1 What is a model?

A *model*, by definition, is any representation of an actual phenomenon such as an actual system or process. The actual phenomenon is represented by the model in order to explain it, to predict it, and to control it—purposes corresponding to the three purposes of econometrics discussed in the last chapter: structural analysis, forecasting, and policy evaluation, respectively. Sometimes the actual system is called the *real-world system* to emphasize the distinction between it and the model system that represents it.

Modeling—the art of model building—is an integral part of most sciences, whether physical or social, because the real-world systems under consideration typically are enormously complex. The system may be an electron moving in an accelerator, prices being set in various markets, or the determination of national income. In these and many other cases the real-world phenomena are so complicated that they can be treated only by means of a simplified representation—that is, via a model.

Any model represents a compromise between reality and manageability. It must be a "reasonable" representation of the real-world system and in that sense should be "realistic" in incorporating the main elements of the phenomena being represented. On the other hand it must be manageable in that it yields certain insights or conclusions not obtainable from direct observations of the real-world system. To achieve manageability usually involves various processes of idealization, including the elimination of "extraneous" influences and the simplification of processes. Clearly this process of idealization usually makes the model less "realistic", yet the process is necessary to ensure that the model system can be reasonably manipulated.

Striking the proper balance between realism and manageability is the essence of good modeling. A "good" model is both realistic and manageable. It specifies the interrelationships among the parts of a system in a way that is sufficiently detailed and explicit to ensure that the study of the model leads to insights concerning the real-world system. At the same time, however, it specifies them in a way that is sufficiently simplified and manageable to ensure that the model can be readily analyzed and conclusions can be reached concerning the real-world system. One type of "bad" model is one that is highly realistic but so complicated that it becomes unmanageable. In that case there really is no point in building the model in the first place. Another type of "bad" model goes to the other extreme: it is highly manageable but so idealized that it is unrealistic in not accounting for important components of the real-world system. In that case the process of idealization has been carried too far: influences that have been assumed away are in fact important, and/or real-world processes involve greater complexities than have been postulated in the model. This extreme may be highly dangerous in that the conclusions reached via the model may or may not be relevant to the real-world system; the trouble is that one never knows in advance whether the conclusions are or are not relevant. In this case it is certainly true that "a little bit of knowledge is a dangerous thing".

To the extent that it is impossible to convey precisely how to build a good model, modeling is partly an art and partly a science. Following certain general precepts and knowing previous modeling attempts are helpful, but it takes experience to become a good modeler.[1]

As a general rule the first models of a phenomenon are quite simple, emphasizing manageability at the cost of not treating reality in great detail. The extreme case is the so-called "black box" of Figure 2.1, where no attempt is made to re-

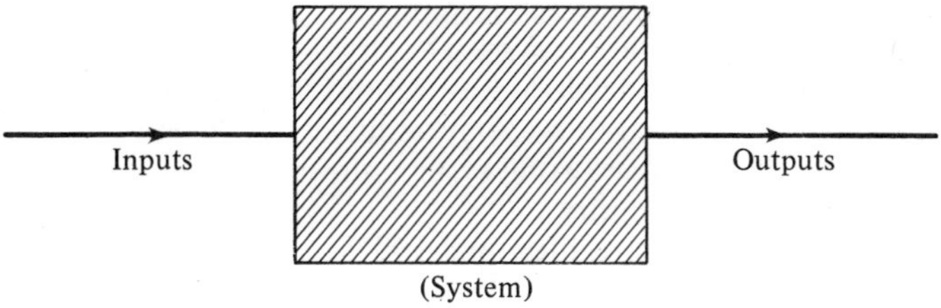

Figure 2.1 Black Box

produce reality. In this case the model treats only inputs to the system and the system outputs without considering the system itself. A black-box description of a television set, for example, would merely identify the inputs of electricity and control signals by the operator and the outputs of audio and video signals. It would treat only the inputs and outputs without attempting to analyze how the two are related.

The process of modeling usually entails starting with a black box and then elaborating on what lies "inside" the box. The initial model is a simple black-box model, which treats only inputs and outputs, sometimes called a *descriptive model.* Tracking inputs forward and outputs backward then leads to more elaborate models, eventually resulting in an *analytic model*, a "white-box" model, which explicitly treats all the interconnections between inputs and outputs. A white-box model of a television set, for example, might consist of a complete circuit diagram. The process of modeling typically entails a continuing attempt to formulate more and more analytic models, which are able to analyze more and more of the various interconnections of the real-world system. An example

[1] Appendix A describes an econometric research project that involves building a model. All readers, but especially students, are encouraged to undertake this project, a case study in formulating an original econometric model, collecting relevant data, estimating the model, and interpreting results. The discussions in the "applications" chapters of this book–Chapters 7, 8, 9, 12 and 13–should aid the reader both in understanding the process of modeling and in carrying out the research project.

is the development of models of the macroeconomy, starting with simple models, such as the one presented in Section 2.7 of this chapter, and eventually reaching highly detailed macroeconometric models, some of which will be discussed in Chapter 12.

2.2 Types of models: verbal/logical and physical models

Many types of models exist in each of the different fields to which models have been applied. Among the most important types are verbal/logical models, physical models, geometric models, and algebraic models, involving alternative forms of representation of a model.

Perhaps the simplest type of model and the one usually used first in any field of inquiry is the *verbal/logical model.* This approach uses verbal analogies, such as the metaphor and simile, and the resulting model is sometimes called a *paradigm.* Such models often treat the system "as if" it were, in some sense, purposeful. Thus in physics the "principle of least action" states that a particle in motion acts *as if* it were minimizing the energy required for its motion. This is most definitely a model in that a real-world system, the moving particle, is represented in this case by a purposeful entity.

In economics two of the earliest and still two of the best paradigms were developed by the founder of the discipline, Adam Smith.[2] The first was the pin factory. Smith used the simple operation of manufacturing pins to illustrate the concept of *division of labor*, according to which if each individual performs those tasks for which he or she has a comparative advantage, then such a division of labor can significantly increase total output. This concept is applicable at the national and international level, but the participants and processes become so numerous and their interrelations so manifold that the principle can be lost. Smith therefore used an analogy or verbal model, discussing the principle with reference to a pin factory, where it could be readily grasped. Obviously Smith was not particularly interested in pin factories per se. Rather he found in a pin factory a convenient *model* of the productive working of the entire national and international economies.

The second paradigm employed by Smith was that of the "invisible hand", an important principle in economics and one of the most important contributions of economics to the analysis of social processes. He considered a decentralized free-enterprise economy, in which each economic agent, consumer or producer, acts solely out of individual self-interest, seeking selfishly to maximize his or her own welfare. The *price system*, however, ensures that the aggregation of numerous such individual actions attains a coherent equilibrium for the economy as a whole and serves to "promote the public interest". Under the price system each agent is guided in his or her actions by a system of price signals. Thus, for example, goods and services are delivered at the appropriate time and place, their delivery being guided by the relevant prices. Smith observed that the system, in this case the total economy, acts *as if* there were an "invisible hand" directing

[2] Smith (1776)

all individual decisions for the "general welfare" of society. Again a complex process, in this case one of rationalizing all economic actions, was represented by a simple analogy.

A second type of model is the *physical model.* In certain cases the real-world system is physical and a model is obtained by appropriate scaling, up or down. Thus an airframe for a new airplane is typically tested by constructing a scaled-down version and testing it in a wind tunnel. This representation is realistic in that the influences omitted (e.g., the interior color scheme) are indeed extraneous. At the same time it is manageable in that it can be easily and inexpensively constructed and tested. Another example is an astronomer's physical model of the solar system. To consider scaling in the opposite direction, physicists sometimes use physical models of the atom, indicating protons and neutrons in the nucleus and electrons in orbit around the nucleus. Molecular biologists similarly use physical models such as those of a protein molecule or the DNA molecule. Such models are scaled-up versions of the real-world system under study and are certainly more manipulable than the actual entities under consideration.

Physical models can also be utilized to study nonphysical phenomena. Thus hydraulic models have been utilized to study macroeconomic variables, such as gross national product, aggregate consumption, aggregate investment, and the money supply, with flows of fluids representing monetary flows in the economy.[3] In general, however, the most useful of these physical models have been those relying upon electric circuits, as in the modern analog computer. The electric network may represent a wide variety of phenomena, including those from physics, engineering, and economics.[4]

2.3 Geometric models

Of enormous importance to the development of economic theory has been the third type of model, the *geometric model*, representing relationships geometrically. To appreciate its importance, thumb through almost any introductory or intermediate economic theory text; numerous diagrams of one sort or another will be found. A geometric model uses a diagram to indicate the relationships between variables. The previous chapter included three such diagrams, all of which are geometric models. For example, Figure 1.3 is a geometric model of the growth of science, indicating constant proportional growth of a measure of science.

An important economic example of a geometric model is that of price determination in a single isolated market. It is obtained by combining a market demand curve with an industry supply curve, as in Figure 2.2. The market demand curve *DD* indicates the quantity demanded of the good (or service) at alternative prices—that is, the total quantity all consumers of that product would buy at a

[3] This approach was advocated in the 1920s and 1930s by Irving Fisher.

[4] For applications of electronic analog models to economics, see Morehouse, Strotz, and Horwitz (1950), Strotz, McAnulty, and Naines (1953), Enke (1951), and Tustin (1953).

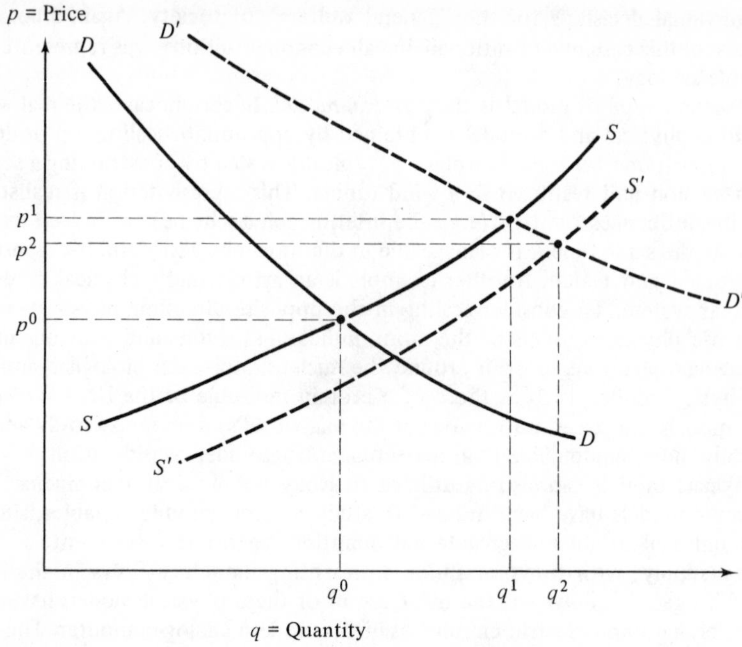

Figure 2.2 Determination of Price in a Single Market

given price, for alternative levels of that price.[5] The industry supply curve, *SS*, indicates the quantity supplied of the goods at alternative prices–that is, the total amount all producers of that product would sell at a given price, for alternative levels of that price.[6] The point at which the market demand and industry supply curves cross, (p^0, q^0), gives the equilibrium price and quantity, respectively. At this equilibrium point the buying decisions of consumers are consistent with the selling decisions of producers. Figure 2.2 thus shows the determination of equilibrium price and quantity in a single market where the curves cross.

Changes in variables other than price can be taken into account by allowing either or both curves to shift. If, for example, the income of consumers rose and/or the prices of products complementary to the product under consideration fell, the result might be a shift outward in demand, e.g., to *D'D'*. For such an outward shift of demand, at any given price more is demanded. At the old equilibrium price of p^0 there would be an excess of demand over supply, leading to

[5] The market demand curve, *DD*, of Figure 2.2 can be obtained from a set of individual household demand curves, such as *dd* of Figure 1.2, by *horizontal aggregation*, i.e., by aggregating over all possible consumers the quantities demanded at any price in order to find, at that price, the market demand. By so aggregating at each possible price, the market demand curve can be constructed.

[6] Just as the market demand curve involves (horizontal) aggregation over individual consumers, in particular, their demand curves, the industry supply curve involves (horizontal) aggregation over individual producers, in particular, their supply curves.

an unsatisfied demand and hence putting pressure on price to rise. The new equilibrium price is p^1. Supply may also shift, however, If, for example, a new manufacturing process is introduced, the supply curve may shift outward, e.g., to $S'S'$, where, at any given price, more is supplied. The new equilibrium price, with both curves having shifted, is p^2.

The basic demand-supply analysis relying upon a diagram such as Figure 2.2 is widely used in explaining how prices are determined in a single market. It is also widely used in anticipating the effects of changes, the influence of which on either the demand or the supply curve is predictable. Changes such as the imposition of an excise tax, labor-saving innovations, higher tariffs, advertising, and many others can be analyzed using this framework.

A second example of a geometric model is that of the determination of equilibrium national income. The consumption function presented in Figure 1.3, when only slightly augmented, leads to a simple model of national income determination. National income, in particular gross national product, GNP, is composed of several items of expenditure, of which the largest is consumption expenditure.[7] The consumption function determines consumption expenditure as a function of national income. The other components of GNP include investment, government expenditure, and net foreign investment. If it is assumed that these expenditures are exogenous (determined by some other mechanism), the total amount of expenditure can be shown graphically by adding to consumption, at each level of national income, this exogenous expenditure. The resulting curve, shown in Figure 2.3, can be interpreted as a demand curve for GNP, showing the total amount demanded by consumers and by other (autonomous) spending units. Since the horizontal axis is national income, the 45° line also measures national income, and it can be interpreted as the supply of GNP. The aggregate supply function is a very simple one, which states that whatever is demanded ($C + Z$) will be supplied (Y). Thus the supply equation, stating the equality of $C + Z$ and Y, is an equality and not an identity, reflecting the ability of entrepreneurs to provide whatever quantity of output is demanded. It should also be noted that only points on the 45° line are meaningful in this model, since any other point would violate the assumptions under which the supply curve is constructed. The curve and line intersect at a level of GNP that is an equilibrium level—that is, where demand equals supply. This simple geometric model conveys some of the most important aspects (but obviously not all aspects) of the determination of national income for the macroeconomy. It represents an initial model, and subsequent macroeconomic models to be presented in the next section, Section 2.7, and Chapter 12 are elaborations upon it.

Both of these models are useful in indicating the principal relationships among the major variables representing the phenomena under investigation. Because of the limited number of dimensions available, however, it is necessary to restrict geometrical models to a relatively few variables. To deal with more variables usually involves use of an algebraic, rather than a geometrical, model. The next section discusses such algebraic models and illustrates them using an algebraic version of the model of national income determination.

[7] Here "national income" refers to any measure of aggregate economic activity, including, as one special case, gross national product, or GNP.

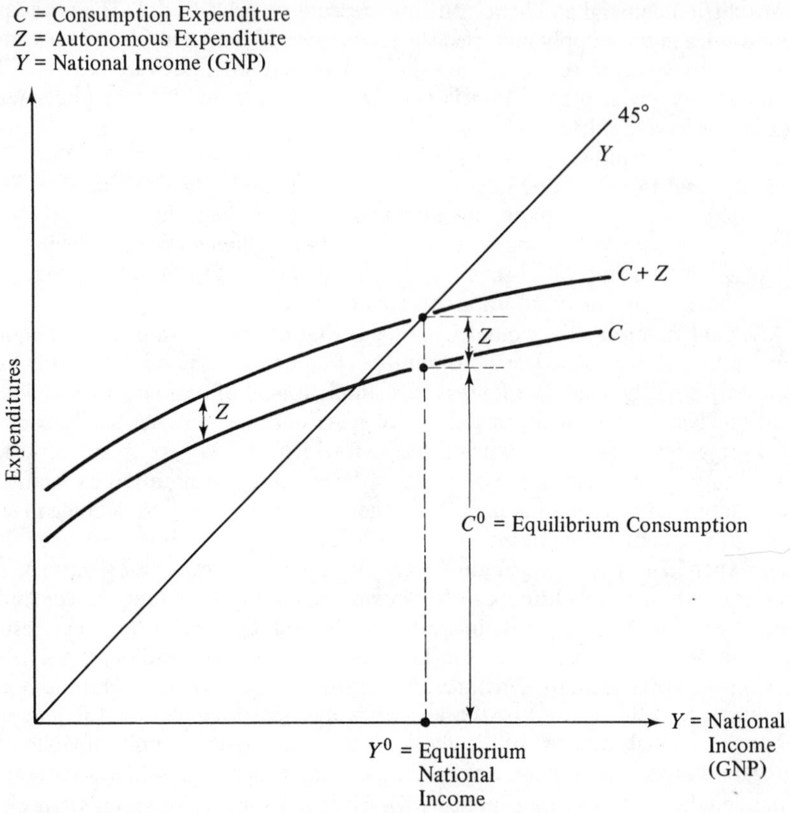

Figure 2.3 Determination of Equilibrium National Income

2.4 Algebraic models

The *algebraic model*,[8] for purposes of econometrics, is the most important type of model; it represents the real-world system by a system of equations.[9]

[8] This model and the other types are often studied using a computer. This approach may in fact involve some aspects of *all* the types of models discussed here, including verbal/logical statements, physical analogies (e.g., using hybrid digital/analog computers), graphical treatment, and algebraic expressions. In general such an approach is utilized when the phenomena become so complex and unmanageable that they cannot be treated (e.g., solved) analytically. Resort is then often made to *simulation* of the behavior of the model system under different conditions or assumptions using a computer. The "system dynamics" models of Forrester (1961, 1969, 1971) exemplify this approach. Such models have been used to study an individual firm (sales, inventories, work force, etc.), a city (population, buildings, jobs, etc.), a nation, world resource flows, and other phenomena. For a further discussion of simulation see Section 16.6

[9] Sometimes inequalities are also part of the system.

With the macroeconomic example of the determination of national income, the model shown graphically in Figure 2.3 can be expressed as the following system of two equations

$$C = C(Y) \qquad *(2.4.1)$$

$$Y = C + Z. \qquad *(2.4.2)$$

The variables of this model are consumption, C, national income, Y, and exogenous expenditure, Z. Given the consumption function $C(Y)$ and autonomous expenditure Z, the system of equations determines the equilibrium values of consumption C^0 and national income Y^0. Equation (2.4.1) is the consumption function, a behavioral relation indicating how consumers in aggregate respond to income in terms of consumption-saving decisions. Equation (2.4.2) is an equilibrium condition, stating that in equilibrium total income is the sum of consumption expenditure and exogenous expenditure. Equilibrium national income is obtained by inserting (2.4.1) into (2.4.2) and solving for Y^0 as

$$Y^0 \equiv C(Y^0) + Z. \qquad (2.4.3)$$

Equilibrium consumption is then obtained from (2.4.1) as

$$C^0 \equiv C(Y^0). \qquad (2.4.4)$$

The last two equations are written as identities because they define Y^0 and C^0, respectively. It should be noted that, so far, the model and the equilibrium obtained are exactly as in Figure 2.3, the geometric and algebraic models constituting different representations of the same model of national income determination.

There are, however, a number of advantages of the algebraic over the geometric representation of a model. One is the ease of manipulation. To illustrate this ease, differentiate both sides of the identity (2.4.3) with respect to Z to obtain

$$\frac{dY^0}{dZ} = \frac{dC}{dY^0}\frac{dY^0}{dZ} + 1. \qquad (2.4.5)$$

Collecting terms and noting that dC/dY^0 is the marginal propensity to consume, MPC, defined in equation (1.5.1) evaluated at the equilibrium level of national income,

$$\frac{dY^0}{dZ} = \frac{1}{1 - \text{MPC}}. \qquad *(2.4.6)$$

This result is known as the *multiplier*, indicating the multiple effect of a change in exogenous expenditure such as government expenditure on equilibrium national income. The multiplier depends critically on the value of the MPC. Thus, for example, an MPC of 0.8 (i.e., 80 cents out of every additional dollar of income is consumed, rather than saved) implies a multiplier of 5; that is, there is a fivefold effect on national income of a change in exogenous expenditure. In this case an increase of \$1 billion in government expenditure would lead to an increase of \$5 billion in national income. If, however, the MPC were 0.75, the multiplier would be 4, so the added \$1 billion of government expenditure would increase national income by \$4 billion. Clearly, small changes in the value of MPC can lead to large changes in the multiplier, and hence in forecasts and policy evaluations made on the basis of the model.

Another advantage of algebraic over geometric models is the ease of adding new variables and equations. This advantage will be seen in Section 2.7 in the development of the prototype macro model. Geometry by its very nature is confined to only two or three dimensions. Algebra, however, is not so confined, and the algebraic models can therefore be enlarged, disaggregated, and generalized in many ways.

The simple macroeconomic model defined by (2.4.1) and (2.4.2) illustrates the general nature of algebraic models. Such models consist of several *equations*, which may be behavioral, such as the consumption function (2.4.1), an equilibrium condition, such as the national income equilibrium condition (2.4.2), or some other type, but each such equation has a separate meaning and role in the model. The model determines values of certain variables, called *endogenous variables*, the jointly dependent variables of the model which are simultaneously determined by the relations of the model. In this case consumption and national income are the endogenous variables, which are to be explained or predicted. The model also contains other variables, called *exogenous variables*, which are determined outside the system but which influence it by affecting the values of the endogenous variables. They affect the system but are not in turn affected by it. Here exogenous expenditure is such a variable. The model also contains certain *parameters*, which are generally estimated using econometric techniques and relevant data. In this case the parameters are those appearing in the consumption function. Of course, there is a wide choice of functional forms available for an algebraic model, and the choice of a particular one depends on theoretical acceptability, plausibility, ease of estimation, goodness of fit, forecasting ability, etc.

2.5 Econometric models[10]

Typically an econometric model is a special type of algebraic model, namely a *stochastic* one that includes one or more random variables. It represents a system by a set of stochastic relations among the variables of the system.

An econometric model is either linear or nonlinear. In the linear case the model is linear in the parameters. The linearity assumption is a very important one, both for proving mathematical and statistical theorems concerning such

[10] For general discussions of economic and econometric models see Beach (1957), Suits (1963), Bergstrom (1967), Christ (1966), Ball (1968), and Kendall (1968).

models and for computing values taken by variables in such models. The macro model of the last section, defined in (2.4.1) and (2.4.2), is linear if the consumption function is of the form

$$C(Y) = a + bY. \tag{2.5.1}$$

Here a and b are the relevant parameters, b having the interpretation of the marginal propensity to consume, assumed constant here. The multiplier is then

$$\frac{dY^0}{dZ} = \frac{1}{1 - b}. \tag{2.5.2}$$

The reason for assuming linearity (in parameters) is the convenience and manageability of this assumption. In particular, the econometric techniques to be developed in Parts 3 and 5 are applicable primarily to linear models. While a considerable amount of work has been done on nonlinear models, the linear case is still the more important and common one, for which there exists a wealth of techniques and applications. Generally it is only where nonlinearity enters in an essential way that it is treated.

One should not exaggerate the importance of the linearity assumption. First, many economic relationships and relationships in other social sciences are, by their very nature, linear. The national income equilibrium condition (2.4.2), for example, is linear, as are the definitions of expenditure, revenue, cost, and profit. Second, the linearity assumption applies only to parameters, not to variables of the model. Thus the quadratic form of the consumption function

$$C(Y) = a + bY + cY^2 \tag{2.5.3}$$

while nonlinear in the variable, Y, is still linear in the parameters, in this case the parameters a, b, c.[11] Variables such as Y^n can be similarly introduced into the equation.

A third reason is that often a model can be transformed into a linear model. The logarithmic transformation can be employed in many cases. Thus, for example, the model of constant proportionate growth of Section 1.6,

$$N = N_0 e^{\alpha t} \tag{2.5.4}$$

under a logarithmic transformation becomes

$$\ln N = \ln N_0 + \alpha t \tag{2.5.5}$$

[11] Note that is this case MPC = $b + 2cY$ and the multiplier is

$$\frac{dY^0}{dZ} = \frac{1}{1 - b - 2cY^0}$$

where Y^0 is the equilibrium level of national income. Thus in this case the multiplier varies with the equilibrium level of national income.

which is linear in the parameters $\ln N_0$, the intercept, and α, the slope. Similarly, consider the constant elasticity demand function

$$q = q_0 p^{-\epsilon} I^{\eta} \tag{2.5.6}$$

where q is the quantity demanded, p is price, and I is income, q_0, ϵ, and η being parameters, the latter two being the price and income elasticities of demand, respectively. Using a logarithmic transformation

$$\ln q = \ln q_0 - \epsilon \ln p + \eta \ln I \tag{2.5.7}$$

an equation that is linear in the parameters.[12] A third example is the Cobb-Douglas production function

$$Y = AK^{\alpha}L^{\beta} \tag{2.5.8}$$

where Y is output, K is capital, L is labor, and A, α, and β are parameters. This production function can be transformed into a linear model by taking logarithms. The result is

$$\log Y = a + \alpha \log K + \beta \log L \qquad (a = \log A) \tag{2.5.9}$$

which is linear in the parameters, a, α, and β.[13]

A fourth reason not to exaggerate the linearity assumption is that any smooth function can be reasonably approximated in an appropriate range by a linear function, e.g., via a Taylor's series expansion. Consider, for example, the general production function

$$Y = F(K, L) \tag{2.5.10}$$

expressing output as a general function of capital and labor, a function that will be treated in some detail in Chapter 8. If the function is continuous, it can be approximated as a linear function in an appropriate range by simply taking the linear portion of the Taylor's series expansion. Expanding about the base levels of (K_0, L_0),

$$Y \cong F(K_0, L_0) + \frac{\partial F}{\partial K}(K_0, L_0)(K - K_0) + \frac{\partial F}{\partial L}(K_0, L_0)(L - L_0) \tag{2.5.11}$$

where the function and its partial derivatives are all evaluated at the base level. Thus in a small range around the point (K_0, L_0)

$$Y \cong a + bK + cL \tag{2.5.12}$$

[12] See the discussion in Chapter 7.

[13] See the discussion of the Cobb-Douglas production function in Chapter 8.

where, denoting the partial derivatives by marginal products, written MP_K and MP_L,

$$a = F(K_0, L_0) - MP_K(K_0, L_0)K_0 - MP_L(K_0, L_0)L_0 \quad (2.5.13)$$

$$b = MP_K(K_0, L_0) \quad (2.5.14)$$

$$c = MP_L(K_0, L_0). \quad (2.5.15)$$

Another important characteristic of an econometric model is the fact that it is stochastic, as opposed to deterministic. A *stochastic* model includes random variables, whereas a *deterministic* model does not.[14] Typically the pattern of model building involves construction initially of deterministic models and eventually, where appropriate, construction and utilization of stochastic models. Physics presents an excellent illustration of this pattern. Early models, such as those of Newtonian mechanics, are deterministic, while later models, such as those of quantum mechanics, are stochastic. Indeed, the quantum revolution in physics consisted of the revolutionary observation that one could not identify, for example, the exact location of an elementary particle but one could determine a probability distribution for its location.

To appreciate the nature of stochastic models in economics, consider again the simple macro model (2.4.1) and (2.4.2), where (2.4.1) has been replaced by the linear consumption function (2.5.1). This function specifies that, at any given level of national income Y, consumption is determined exactly as the number $a + bY$. Is this reasonable? Clearly not! Besides income many other factors can and do affect consumption, such as wealth, prices, tastes, etc. Furthermore the relationship may not be quite as simple as that given in (2.5.1), and variables may be measured inaccurately. It is therefore more reasonable to estimate C at a given level of Y, as *on average* $a + bY$. In general, consumption will fall within a certain confidence interval, i.e.,

$$C = a + bY \pm \Delta \quad (2.5.16)$$

where C is consumption at the given level of national income Y and Δ indicates the level above or below the average value such that, with a high degree of confidence, consumption falls in the defined interval. The value of Δ can be determined by assuming that C is itself a random variable with a particular density function. Because of the central limit theorem the normal distribution is typically assumed, and, in this case, C can be represented as in Figure 2.4.[15] The term "on average" generally refers to the mean value, so $a + bY$ is the mean of C. (Recall that Y is given, so $a + bY$ is just a number). The Δ can then be chosen, as illustrated, so that 90% of the distribution is included in the confidence interval (2.5.16), where each of the tails of the distribution contains 5% of the distribu-

[14] Actually there can be stochastic elements in *all* types of models, including not only the algebraic models, such as those of econometrics, but also verbal, physical, and geometric models. See Appendix C for the definition of "random variable" and other terms from statistics to be utilized here and later.

[15] See Appendix C, Section C.5, for a discussion of the central limit theorem.

tion.[16] In general, an econometric model uniquely specifies the probability distribution of each endogenous variable, given the values taken by all exogenous variables and given the values of all parameters of the model.

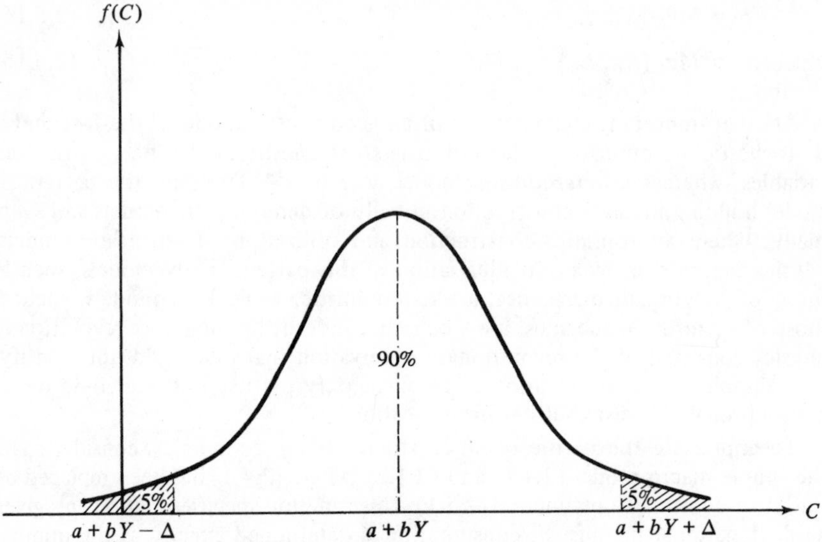

Figure 2.4 A Normal Distribution for Consumption C

So far one particular value of Y has been considered. Now consider all possible values of Y. At each level of Y, as shown in Figure 2.5, an appropriate (normal) distribution can be constructed, as in the last figure. Connecting the upper and lower levels of the 90% confidence intervals leads to a 90% confidence interval for the entire consumption function. The resulting "band," representing confidence levels for consumption, together with the point values on the function itself, representing mean values, summarize what is known about the *stochastic* (and linear) relationship between consumption and income. The deterministic (i.e., nonstochastic) case can then be interpreted as the one in which the variance of the relevant probability distribution vanishes. In that case $\Delta = 0$. The assumption of zero variance, however, is generally unwarranted, in that not all is known about the relationship. For example, relevant variables have been omitted, and even included variables may be measured subject to error.

Algebraically, the stochastic nature of the relationship is usually represented, for the consumption function as

$$C = a + bY + \epsilon \qquad *(2.5.17)$$

[16] It might be recalled that, for the normal distribution, if μ is the mean and σ is the standard deviation then $\mu \pm 1.64\sigma$ contains 90% of the distribution. For tables of the normal distribution and other distributions see Appendix C.

where ϵ is an additive *stochastic disturbance term* that plays the role of a chance mechanism. In general each equation of an econometric model, other than definitions, equilibrium conditions, and identities, is assumed to contain an additive stochastic disturbance term, as in (2.5.17).[17] The stochastic terms are unobservable random variables with certain assumed properties, e.g., means, variances, and covariances. The values taken by these variables of the model are not known with certainty; rather they can be considered random drawings from a probability distribution. The inclusion of such stochastic disturbance terms in the model is basic to the use of tools of statistical inference to estimate parameters of the model.

Econometric models can be either static or dynamic. A *static model* involves no explicit dependence on time, so time is not essential in the model. Simply adding time subscripts to variables does not convert a static model into a dynamic model. A *dynamic model* is one in which time plays an essential role, e.g., if

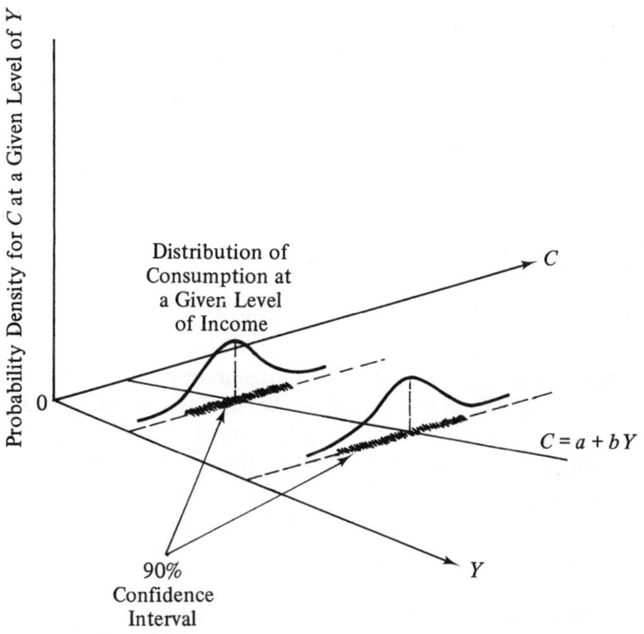

Figure 2.5 The Stochastic Relationship between Consumption and Income

[17] If the stochastic disturbance term has a variance that is always identically zero, then the model reduces to a deterministic one. The other extreme case is where the model is purely stochastic–e.g. (2.5.17) where a and b are identically zero. There are some examples of such a model in economics; one of the best known is the random walk model for the movement of prices in the stock market, as in Cootner, Ed. (1964). The econometric models to be studied, however, are usually neither deterministic nor purely stochastic; they usually have both deterministic elements [e.g., $a + bY$ in (2.5.17)] and nontrivial stochastic elements [e.g., ϵ in (2.5.17)].

lagged variables or differences of variables over time are part of the model. Thus, if any equation of the model is a difference equation, then the model is dynamic. Time also plays an essential role if variables and their time rates of change are explicitly considered, such as in a differential equation. The next two sections will treat a static model, the prototype micro model, and a dynamic model, the prototype macro model.

2.6 The prototype micro model

The first example of an econometric model–a stochastic, algebraic model–is the prototype micro model for an agricultural good. This model is a generalization of the graphical model of price determination in a single market, as in Figure 2.2. It also illustrates the advantage of algebraic over geometrical models in terms of possible generalizations to more variables. The model consists of the following three equations:

$$q^D = \gamma_1 p + \beta_1 I + \delta_1 + \epsilon^D \qquad *(2.6.1)$$

$$q^S = \gamma_2 p + \beta_2 r + \delta_2 + \epsilon^S \qquad *(2.6.2)$$

$$q^D = q^S \qquad *(2.6.3)$$

Here q^D is the quantity demanded of a particular good, q^S is the quantity supplied, p is price, I is income, r is rainfall, ϵ^D is the stochastic disturbance term for demand, and ϵ^S is the stochastic disturbance term for supply.[18]

All econometric models contain variables, which are either endogenous or exogenous; stochastic disturbance terms; and parameters in a system of structural equations. The *endogenous variables* are those variables the values for which are simultaneously determined by the model and which the model is designed to explain, in this case q^D, q^S, and p. The *exogenous variables* are variables the values for which are determined outside the model but which influence the model. From a formal standpoint the exogenous variables are assumed to be statistically independent of all stochastic disturbance terms of the model, while the endogenous variables are not statistically independent of those terms. In this case the exogenous variables are I and r. In general the exogenous variables are either historically given, policy variables, or determined by some separate mechanism.

The *stochastic disturbance terms*, in this case ϵ^D and ϵ^S, are random variables that typically are added to all equations of the model other than identities or equilibrium conditions. There are four justifications for including such a term in each nondefinitional equation. First, variables that may influence demand and supply have, in fact, been omitted from the two equations. For example, other prices or variables reflecting the distribution of income, which have been omitted, may, in fact, affect the quantity demanded. Second, the equations may be misspecified in that the particular functional forms chosen, here linear in both parameters and variables, may be incorrect. Third, the variables included may be

[18] It is possible to interpret q^D, q^S, I, and r as *logarithms* of quantity demanded, quantity supplied, income, and rainfall, respectively. In that case (2.6.1) is similar to the constant elasticity demand function (2.5.7).

measured inaccurately. Fourth, there may be basic randomness in behavior on the part of both demanders and suppliers. The stochastic terms can account for any or all of these considerations.[19]

The explicit parameters of the model are the constant coefficients that multiply the variables of the model. In this case the model contains six explicit parameters: γ_1 and γ_2, multiplying p; β_1, multiplying I; β_2, multiplying r; and δ_1 and δ_2, which may be thought of as multiplying 1. The model also contains some implicit parameters, namely those defining the probability distributions for ϵ^D and ϵ^S. These explicit and implicit parameters are the *structural parameters.* The equations of the model as given in (2.6.1) to (2.6.3) are the *structural equations.* Each has a separate meaning and identity, and the set of all structural equations, the *structural form*, is the initial stage in model building. In this model, for example, the first equation is a demand equation, the second is a supply equation, and the third is an equilibrium condition.

The demand equation (2.6.1) specifies that the quantity demanded is a linear function of price, income, and an additive stochastic disturbance term. The parameters are γ_1, β_1, and δ_1, where γ_1 is generally negative (downward sloping demand curve; i.e., the good is not a "Giffen" good) and β_1 is generally positive (added income leads to increased demand; i.e., the good is a "superior" good).[20] Given values for the parameters, income, and the stochastic disturbance term, the resulting relationship between q^D and p can be represented geometrically as a linear demand curve, *DD* in Figure 2.6. As any of these values (parameters, income, stochastic disturbance term) change, this demand curve will shift, as in Figure 2.6. Thus, for example, the demand curve will shift outward, from *DD* to *D'D'*, if income increases from I to I'.

The right-hand side of (2.6.1) includes two random variables. The first is the stochastic disturbance term ϵ^D. The second is the variable p, which is endogenous and hence influenced by both stochastic disturbance terms [see (2.6.9) below]. Thus the left-hand side, the quantity demanded, is also stochastic. In general it is assumed that the stochastic disturbance term has a zero expected value:[21]

$$E(\epsilon^D) = 0 \tag{2.6.4}$$

It therefore follows that the expected quantity demanded is

$$E(q^D) = \gamma_1 E(p) + \beta_1 I + \delta_1. \tag{2.6.5}$$

Figure 2.6 illustrates for a given level of income and a zero value of the stochastic disturbance term the (expected) quantity demanded at any given level of (expected) price.

[19] More detailed discussions of errors in variables and specification error appear below in Chapter 6.

[20] For discussions of "Giffen good" and "superior good", see Chapter 7 and Intriligator (1971).

[21] Other assumptions on the stochastic disturbance terms, involving variances and covariances, will be introduced in Chapter 4. See (4.4.2).

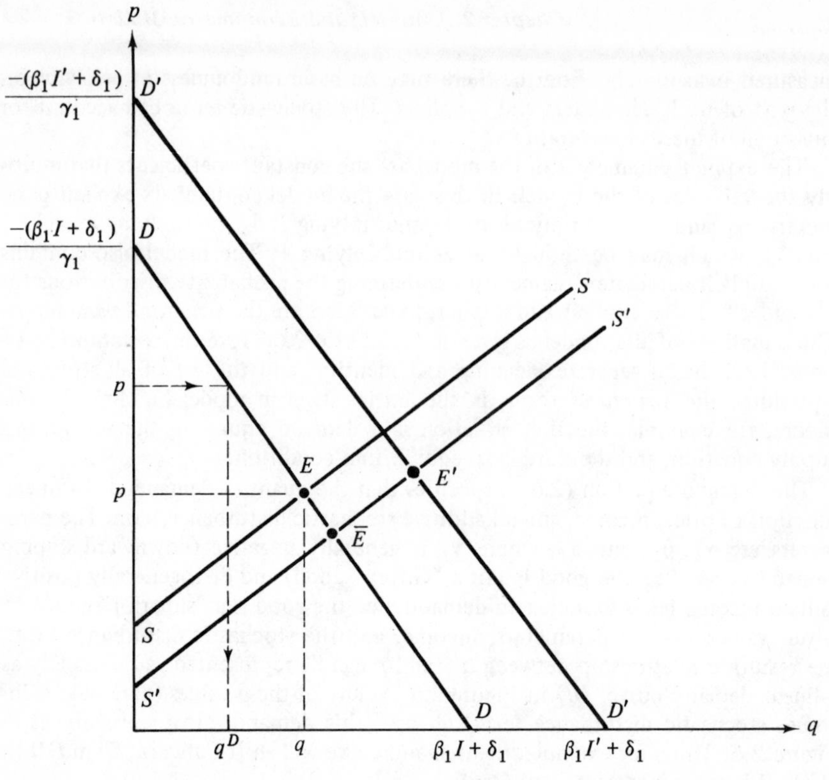

Figure 2.6 A Geometrical Representation of the Prototype Micro Model

The supply equation (2.6.2) specifies that the quantity supplied is a linear function of price, rainfall, and a stochastic disturbance term. The parameters are γ_2, β_2, and δ_2, where generally γ_2 is positive (rising supply curve) and β_2 can be either positive (in case of drought) or negative (in case of flood). Thus in drought conditions added rainfall shifts out supply, while in flood conditions added rainfall shifts in supply. Given these parameters, the levels of r, and the expected value of zero for ϵ^S, the resulting relationship is a linear supply curve, shown as SS in Figure 2.6. The supply curve will shift outward, e.g., to $S'S'$, for an increase (decrease) in rainfall, given conditions of drought (flood).

Equation (2.6.3) is the equilibrium condition, stating that demand equals supply. This equation, defining equilibrium, does not entail a stochastic disturbance term. The equilibrium values of q and p are shown at the equilibrium point E in Figure 2.6.

In general, equilibrium conditions, such as (2.6.3) and other comparable equations, such as definitions or other identities, can be eliminated. In this case letting q be the equilibrium quantity—that is, the common value of q^D and q^S—the model can be written as the two equations

$$q = \gamma_1 p + \beta_1 I + \delta_1 + \epsilon^D \qquad *(2.6.6)$$

$$q = \gamma_2 p + \beta_2 r + \delta_2 + \epsilon^S. \qquad *(2.6.7)$$

The prototype micro model then consists of these two structural equations, which determine values of the two endogenous variables q and p in terms of the exogenous variables I and r.

A convenient way of expressing this model and in fact most linear econometric models is to use vector-matrix notation.[22] In this notation the *structural form* is the set of structural equations

$$(q \quad p)\begin{pmatrix} 1 & 1 \\ \\ -\gamma_1 & -\gamma_2 \end{pmatrix} + (I \quad r \quad 1)\begin{pmatrix} -\beta_1 & 0 \\ 0 & -\beta_2 \\ -\delta_1 & -\delta_2 \end{pmatrix} = (\epsilon^D \quad \epsilon^S). \qquad *(2.6.8)$$

The row vector $(q \quad p)$ is the *vector of endogenous variables*, while $(I \quad r \quad 1)$ is the *vector of exogenous variables* (where 1 accounts for the intercepts), and $(\epsilon^D \quad \epsilon^S)$ is the *vector of stochastic disturbance terms.* The two coefficient matrices are *matrices of structural coefficients*, summarizing all parameters of the structural equations—the γ's, β's, and δ's.

The two equations (2.6.6) and (2.6.7) can be solved simultaneously by simply equating one to the other. Solving for p and then for q yields

$$p = \frac{\beta_1}{\gamma_2 - \gamma_1} I - \frac{\beta_2}{\gamma_2 - \gamma_1} r + \frac{\delta_1 - \delta_2}{\gamma_2 - \gamma_1} + \frac{\epsilon^D - \epsilon^S}{\gamma_2 - \gamma_1} \qquad *(2.6.9)$$

$$q = \frac{\gamma_2\beta_1}{\gamma_2 - \gamma_1} I - \frac{\gamma_1\beta_2}{\gamma_2 - \gamma_1} r + \frac{\gamma_2\delta_1 - \gamma_1\delta_2}{\gamma_2 - \gamma_1} + \frac{\gamma_2\epsilon^D - \gamma_1\epsilon^S}{\gamma_2 - \gamma_1}. \qquad *(2.6.10)$$

Each of these equations, called *reduced-form equations*, expresses one of the endogenous variables as a function of all exogenous variables and stochastic disturbance terms. The set of all reduced-form equations is the *reduced form*, which is used both for analysis and for estimation of the model. In vector-matrix notation it would be written

$$(q \quad p) = (I \quad r \quad 1)\begin{pmatrix} \dfrac{\gamma_2\beta_1}{\gamma_2 - \gamma_1} & \dfrac{\beta_1}{\gamma_2 - \gamma_1} \\ \dfrac{-\gamma_1\beta_2}{\gamma_2 - \gamma_1} & \dfrac{-\beta_2}{\gamma_2 - \gamma_1} \\ \dfrac{\gamma_2\delta_1 - \gamma_1\delta_2}{\gamma_2 - \gamma_1} & \dfrac{\delta_1 - \delta_2}{\gamma_2 - \gamma_1} \end{pmatrix} + \begin{pmatrix} \dfrac{\gamma_2\epsilon^D - \gamma_1\epsilon^S}{\gamma_2 - \gamma_1} & \dfrac{\epsilon^D - \epsilon^S}{\gamma_2 - \gamma_1} \end{pmatrix} \qquad *(2.6.11)$$

[22] See Appendix B for a review of matrices.

where the coefficient matrix is the *matrix of reduced-form coefficients.* The reduced form (2.6.11) could have been obtained directly from the structural form (2.6.8) by solving for the vector of endogenous variables ($q \quad p$). To obtain such a solution both sides of equation (2.6.8) would be postmultiplied by the inverse matrix[23]

$$\begin{pmatrix} 1 & 1 \\ -\gamma_1 & -\gamma_2 \end{pmatrix}^{-1} = \frac{1}{\gamma_2 - \gamma_1} \begin{pmatrix} \gamma_2 & 1 \\ -\gamma_1 & -1 \end{pmatrix} \tag{2.6.12}$$

and the result solved for ($q \quad p$).

The coefficients of the reduced-form equations summarize the comparative statics results of this model. By *comparative statics* is meant a comparison of two equilibrium values of each of the endogenous variables, where the only change that occurs is in one of the exogenous variables. Thus, for example, from (2.6.9) or (2.6.11)

$$\frac{\partial p}{\partial I} = \frac{\beta_1}{\gamma_2 - \gamma_1}. \tag{2.6.13}$$

Since the denominator is always positive ($\gamma_2 > 0$ being the slope of the supply curve and $\gamma_1 < 0$ being the slope of the demand curve), to the extent that $\beta_1 > 0$ (the good being a superior good) the partial derivative is positive. Thus a *ceteris paribus* increase in income would tend to increase the equilibrium price.[24] Similarly

$$\frac{\partial q}{\partial I} = \frac{\gamma_2 \beta_1}{\gamma_2 - \gamma_1} > 0 \tag{2.6.14}$$

For rainfall,

$$\frac{\partial p}{\partial r} = \frac{-\beta_2}{\gamma_2 - \gamma_1} \lesseqgtr 0 \tag{2.6.15}$$

$$\frac{\partial q}{\partial r} = \frac{-\gamma_1 \beta_2}{\gamma_2 - \gamma_1} \gtreqless 0 \tag{2.6.16}$$

[23] For a discussion of the concept of an inverse matrix see Appendix B, Section B.5. In general any square matrix with a nonzero determinant has an inverse. Here the determinant, given by $\gamma_1 - \gamma_2$, is nonzero. It is, in fact, negative, since $\gamma_1 < 0$ and $\gamma_2 > 0$.

[24] The expression *ceteris paribus* means other things are held equal; here the "other" things are rainfall and the stochastic disturbance terms.

where the top (bottom) sign indicates the direction of change with added rainfall under drought (flood) conditions. For example, in drought added rainfall decreases the price and increases the quantity, as shown geometrically by comparing the equilibrium at E to that at $\bar{E}$.

The comparative statics results, indicating the directions of change of each of the endogenous variables for a change in the exogenous variables, can be summarized as in Table 2.1.[25] Note that two of the signs, corresponding to shifts in the intercepts, are indeterminate. Also note that this table is simply the matrix of reduced-form coefficients in (2.6.11).

In general, economic theory stops and econometrics begins at this point, where the model and the signs of some of the relevant partial derivatives have been determined. The next logical step would be the statistical estimation of numerical values for these partial derivatives, or, what is the same thing, the estimation of the matrix of reduced-form coefficients in (2.6.11). Estimation of these reduced-form coefficients entails the use of data on the endogenous and exogenous variables and the use of econometric techniques. With numerical estimates of these coefficients it would be possible to perform *structural analysis* (e.g., test the hypotheses that price is highly responsive to income but not responsive to rainfall), to use the model for purposes of *forecasting* (e.g., forecast the price of the agricultural good next year), and to use it for purposes of *policy evaluation* (e.g., determine how policies affecting income would affect the price and quantity of the good). The estimation of the reduced-form coefficients is also usually the first step in the estimation of the structural-form coefficients.

Table 2.1 Comparative Statics of the Prototype Micro Model

Exogenous Variables \ Endogenous Variables	q	p
I	$\dfrac{\gamma_2\beta_1}{\gamma_2-\gamma_1} > 0$	$\dfrac{\beta_1}{\gamma_2-\gamma_1} > 0$
r	$\dfrac{-\gamma_1\beta_2}{\gamma_2-\gamma_1} \gtrless 0$	$\dfrac{-\beta_2}{\gamma_2-\gamma_1} \lessgtr 0$
1	$\dfrac{\gamma_2\delta_1-\gamma_1\delta_2}{\gamma_2-\gamma_1}$?	$\dfrac{\delta_1-\delta_2}{\gamma_2-\gamma_1}$?

[25] A whole theory has developed concerning comparative statics, with particular reference to the comparative statics matrix of signs. It is called *qualitative economics* and stems largely from Samuelson (1947).

2.7 The prototype macro model

The second example of an econometric model is the *prototype macro model.* This is a generalization of the graphical model of national income determination of Figure 2.3, and, like the prototype micro model, it illustrates the generalization feasible with an algebraic model. It is a prototype for the various macroeconometric models to be discussed in Chapter 12. Unlike the prototype micro model, which was a *static model* in which time played no essential role, the prototype macro model is a *dynamic model* in which time enters essentially. Specifically, one endogenous variable is specified as dependent on the value taken by another endogenous variable in the previous year.

The prototype macro model consists of the following three structural equations:

$$C_t = \gamma_1 Y_t + \beta_1 + \epsilon_t^C \qquad *(2.7.1)$$

$$I_t = \gamma_2 Y_t + \beta_2 Y_{t-1} + \beta_3 + \epsilon_t^I \qquad *(2.7.2)$$

$$Y_t = C_t + I_t + G_t. \qquad *(2.7.3)$$

Here C_t, I_t, and Y_t represent, respectively, consumption, investment, and national income, in year t, and these three variables are the endogenous variables of the model. G_t is government spending in year t, treated as exogenous, and Y_{t-1} is income of the previous year, a *lagged* endogenous variable. The variables ϵ_t^C and ϵ_t^I are stochastic disturbance terms for consumption and investment, respectively. The γ's and β's are five structural parameters to be estimated.

The first equation (2.7.1) is the consumption function as before. The second equation (2.7.2) determines investment spending on the basis of both current and lagged values of income. The case in which investment is autonomous, as in previous treatments, is the special case in which γ_2, β_2, and ϵ_t^I are all identically zero, so I_t is the constant β_3. Another important special case is that in which $\beta_2 = -\gamma_2$, where investment follows the accelerator mechanism. In that case levels of investment are based on *changes* in national income, since then

$$I_t = \gamma_2(Y_t - Y_{t-1}) + \beta_3 + \epsilon_t^I. \qquad (2.7.4)$$

The last equation of the model (2.7.3) is the equilibrium condition giving national income as the sum of consumption, investment, and government expenditure.[26]

Figure 2.7 is a flow diagram, also called an "arrow scheme", which is a common graphical method of illustrating the workings of such a model. It shows the effects of both the exogenous and the lagged endogenous variables on the current endogenous variables; it also shows the interactions among the endogenous variables. The value of current national income influences future investment, as shown by the dotted line, which would connect to income in the following year.

[26] Net foreign investment, i.e., exports less imports (the net balance of trade on current account) is either omitted altogether or included in investment I_t.

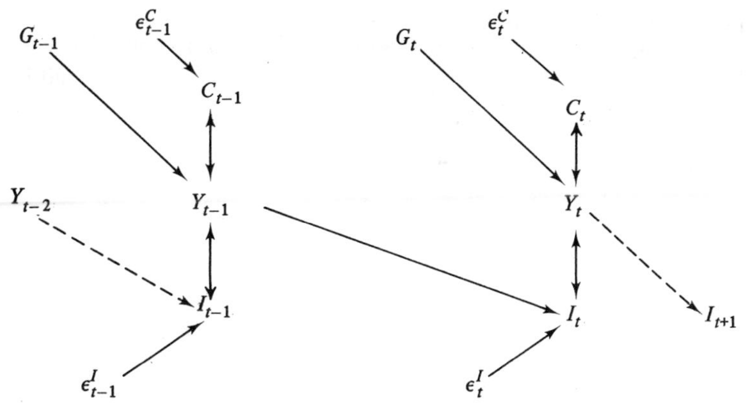

Figure 2.7 Flow Diagram of the Prototype Macro Model

Just as in the prototype micro model, the equilibrium condition can be used to eliminate one equation and one endogenous variable. In this case any one of the three endogenous variables could be eliminated. To eliminate I, equation (2.7.2) can be substituted into (2.7.3) to obtain the two structural equations, (2.7.1) and

$$Y_t = \left(\frac{1}{1-\gamma_2}\right) C_t + \left(\frac{\beta_2}{1-\gamma_2}\right) Y_{t-1} + \left(\frac{1}{1-\gamma_2}\right) G_t + \frac{\beta_3}{1-\gamma_2} + \frac{\epsilon^I_t}{1-\gamma_2} \qquad *(2.7.5)$$

The structural form is thus, in matrix notation,

$$(C_t \quad Y_t)\begin{pmatrix} -1 & \dfrac{1}{1-\gamma_2} \\ \gamma_1 & -1 \end{pmatrix} + (Y_{t-1} \quad G_t \quad 1)\begin{pmatrix} 0 & \dfrac{\beta_2}{1-\gamma_2} \\ 0 & \dfrac{1}{1-\gamma_2} \\ \beta_1 & \dfrac{\beta_3}{1-\gamma_2} \end{pmatrix} = \left(-\epsilon^C_t \quad \frac{-\epsilon^I_t}{1-\gamma_2}\right). \qquad *(2.7.6)$$

The reduced-form equations are easily obtained by substitution or by inverting the 2 × 2 matrix that postmultiplies the vector of endogenous variables, postmultiplying by this inverse in (2.7.6), and solving for $(C_t \quad Y_t)$. The result is

$$Y_t = \left(\frac{\beta_2}{1 - \gamma_1 - \gamma_2}\right) Y_{t-1} + \left(\frac{1}{1 - \gamma_1 - \gamma_2}\right) G_t + \frac{\beta_1 + \beta_3}{1 - \gamma_1 - \gamma_2} + \frac{\epsilon_t^C + \epsilon_t^I}{1 - \gamma_1 - \gamma_2} \qquad *(2.7.7)$$

$$C_t = \left(\frac{\gamma_1 \beta_2}{1 - \gamma_1 - \gamma_2}\right) Y_{t-1} + \left(\frac{\gamma_1}{1 - \gamma_1 - \gamma_2}\right) G_t + \frac{\gamma_1 \beta_3 + (1 - \gamma_2)\beta_1}{1 - \gamma_1 - \gamma_2} + \frac{\gamma_1 \epsilon_t^I + (1 - \gamma_2)\epsilon_t^C}{1 - \gamma_1 - \gamma_2}. \qquad *(2.7.8)$$

These equations determine current income and consumption as functions of lagged income and current government expenditure. In general, the *reduced-form equations* give each current endogenous variable as a function of all lagged endogenous variables, all exogenous variables, and all stochastic disturbance terms. The set of all exogenous and lagged endogenous variables is called the set of *predetermined variables*, since the lagged endogenous variables were determined in a previous period, while the exogenous variables are determined by a system other than the one under consideration. In either case they are assumed to be determined before the current endogenous variables.

Equation (2.7.7) shows the effect of a *ceteris paribus* change in current government expenditure on income as

$$\frac{\partial Y_t}{\partial G_t} = \frac{1}{1 - \gamma_1 - \gamma_2} \qquad *(2.7.9)$$

This result is known as the *impact multiplier*, since it indicates the impact of government spending on income. It is also called the *short-term multiplier*, since it shows the effect of current government spending on current income. In the special case in which investment is predetermined, for which $\gamma_2 = 0$, the impact multiplier is the same as the multiplier in (2.4.6), the reciprocal of unity less the marginal propensity to consume:

$$\left.\frac{\partial Y_t}{\partial G_t}\right|_{\gamma_2 = 0} = \frac{1}{1 - \gamma_1} = \frac{1}{1 - \text{MPC}}. \qquad (2.7.10)$$

The reduced-form equation for Y, (2.7.7), is a first-order difference equation, which may be written

$$Y_t = \pi_1 Y_{t-1} + \pi_2 G_t + \pi_3 + u_t \qquad *(2.7.11)$$

where

$$\pi_1 = \beta_2 \pi_2$$
$$\pi_2 = \frac{1}{1 - \gamma_1 - \gamma_2} \tag{2.7.12}$$
$$\pi_3 = (\beta_1 + \beta_3)\pi_2$$
$$u_t = (\epsilon_t^C + \epsilon_t^I)\pi_2.$$

If this difference equation is solved, the result, known as the *final-form* equation, will permit the calculation of all the multipliers, long- and short-term, for income.

To solve the difference equation by iteration, note that (2.7.11) implies that

$$Y_{t-1} = \pi_1 Y_{t-2} + \pi_2 G_{t-1} + \pi_3 + u_{t-1}. \tag{2.7.13}$$

Substitution of (2.7.13) into (2.7.11) yields

$$Y_t = \pi_1^2 Y_{t-2} + \pi_2(G_t + \pi_1 G_{t-1}) + \pi_3(1 + \pi_1) + (u_t + \pi_1 u_{t-1}). \tag{2.7.14}$$

Similarly, determining Y_{t-2} from (2.7.11) and inserting the result in (2.7.14) yields

$$Y_t = \pi_1^3 Y_{t-3} + \pi_2(G_t + \pi_1 G_{t-1} + \pi_1^2 G_{t-2}) + \pi_3(1 + \pi_1 + \pi_1^2) + (u_t + \pi_1 u_{t-1} + \pi_1^2 u_{t-2}). \tag{2.7.15}$$

Continuing this process of iteration back to the base year, $t = 0$, yields

$$\begin{aligned} Y_t = {} & \pi_1^t Y_0 + \pi_2(G_t + \pi_1 G_{t-1} + \pi_1^2 G_{t-2} + \cdots + \pi_1^{t-1} G_1) \\ & + \pi_3(1 + \pi_1 + \pi_1^2 + \cdots + \pi_1^{t-1}) \\ & + (u_t + \pi_1 u_{t-1} + \pi_1^2 u_{t-2} + \cdots + \pi_1^{t-1} u_1). \end{aligned} \tag*{*(2.7.16)}$$

This equation is known as the *final-form equation* for income.[27] From it all the multipliers for income, both short-term and long-term, can be calculated. Thus the impact multiplier, giving the effect on current income of a change in current government expenditure, is obtained from (2.7.16) as

$$\frac{\partial Y_t}{\partial G_t} = \pi_2 = \frac{1}{1 - \gamma_1 - \gamma_2} \tag{2.7.17}$$

as before.

[27] See Sections 2.9 and 14.5.

Consider now the effect on current income of a change in government spending in the *previous* period. From (2.7.16),

$$\frac{\partial Y_t}{\partial G_{t-1}} = \pi_2 \pi_1 . \tag{2.7.18}$$

Adding (2.7.17) and (2.7.18) gives the effect of a change in government spending over both the current and the previous period. The result is the *two-period cumulative multiplier*

$$\left.\frac{\partial Y_t}{\partial G_t}\right|_{\Delta G_{t-1}=\Delta G_t} = \pi_2(1 + \pi_1) = \frac{1 - \gamma_1 - \gamma_2 + \beta_2}{(1 - \gamma_1 - \gamma_2)^2}. \tag{2.7.19}$$

Similarly the *three-period cumulative multiplier* is

$$\left.\frac{\partial Y_t}{\partial G_t}\right|_{\Delta G_{t-2}=\Delta G_{t-1}=\Delta G_t} = \pi_2(1 + \pi_1 + \pi_1^2). \tag{2.7.20}$$

In general, the τ*-period cumulative multiplier* is the response to an increase in government expenditure over both the current and previous $\tau - 1$ periods. It is given as

$$\left.\frac{\partial Y_t}{\partial G_t}\right|_{\Delta G_{t-i}=\Delta G_t, i=1,2,\ldots,\tau-1} = \pi_2(1 + \pi_1 + \pi_1^2 + \cdots + \pi_1^{\tau-1}). \tag{2.7.21}$$

Letting τ approach infinity gives the *long-term multiplier*

$$\left.\frac{\partial Y_t}{\partial G_t}\right|_{\text{long term}} = \pi_2(1 + \pi_1 + \pi_1^2 + \cdots) = \frac{\pi_2}{1 - \pi_1} = \frac{1}{1 - \gamma_1 - \gamma_2 - \beta_2} \tag{2.7.22}$$

where use has been made both of the result on the sum of a geometric series (assuming $0 < \pi_1 < 1$) and the definitions in (2.7.12). The long-term multiplier has the interpretation of the change in income arising from a one-unit increase in government spending over not only the current period but also every past period, stretching back toward the infinite past; it is thus the response to a sustained new level in government spending. Alternatively, it can be interpreted as the change in future income arising from a permanent increase in government spending.

If β_1, β_2, and γ_1 were all positive, the impact multiplier (2.7.9) or (2.7.17) and the long-term multiplier (2.7.22) would yield the lower bound and upper bound, respectively, for all government spending multipliers, giving the effect of a unit change in government spending on income a value between

$$\frac{1}{1 - \gamma_1 - \gamma_2} \quad \text{and} \quad \frac{1}{1 - \gamma_1 - \gamma_2 - \beta_2} \tag{2.7.23}$$

depending on the number of years for which the change was implemented. Thus, to give a quantitative example, if γ_1, the marginal propensity to consume, were 0.7; γ_2, the effect of current income on investment, were 0.05; and β_2, the effect of past income on investment, were also 0.05, the impact multiplier of 4 and long term multiplier of 5 would give the bounds on all government spending multipliers. In general, the longer the "run", in the sense of the more periods over which government expenditure changes (either in the past or in the future), the larger is the multiplier.

With the estimated parameters of the model it is possible to obtain numerical values for the various multipliers (part of *structural analysis*). With these estimates it is also possible to *forecast* (e.g., forecast national income next year) and to conduct *policy evaluation* (e.g., evaluate alternative levels of government expenditure in terms of impacts on national income, consumption, and investment).

2.8 The general econometric model: structural form and reduced form[28]

The general econometric model is an algebraic, linear (in parameters) stochastic model. Assuming there are g endogenous (jointly dependent) variables y_1, $y_2, \ldots, y_g$ and k predetermined (exogenous or lagged endogenous) variables $x_1, x_2, \ldots, x_k$, the general econometric model can be written

$$\begin{aligned}
y_1\gamma_{11} + y_2\gamma_{21} + \cdots + y_g\gamma_{g1} + x_1\beta_{11} + x_2\beta_{21} + \cdots + x_k\beta_{k1} &= \epsilon_1 \\
y_1\gamma_{12} + y_2\gamma_{22} + \cdots + y_g\gamma_{g2} + x_1\beta_{12} + x_2\beta_{22} + \cdots + x_k\beta_{k2} &= \epsilon_2 \\
&\vdots \\
y_1\gamma_{1g} + y_2\gamma_{2g} + \cdots + y_g\gamma_{gg} + x_1\beta_{1g} + x_2\beta_{2g} + \cdots + x_k\beta_{kg} &= \epsilon_g
\end{aligned} \tag*{*(2.8.1)}$$

where $\epsilon_1, \epsilon_2, \ldots, \epsilon_g$ are g stochastic disturbance terms (random variables), the γ's are coefficients of endogenous variables, and the β's are coefficients of predetermined variables.[29] The system of equations is *complete* if there are as many independent equations as endogenous variables. The system of equations then jointly determines values of the endogenous variables in terms of values of the predetermined variables and values taken by the stochastic disturbance terms.

[28] For a more complete discussion of the general econometric model, including a discussion of the stochastic specification of the disturbance terms, see Chapter 10. It might be noted that the general econometric model is also referred to as "the simultaneous equations model" and "the structural equations model". Other disciplines, such as psychology and sociology, use other terms to refer to similar models, including "the linear causal scheme", "path analysis", and "dependence analysis". See Goldberger and Duncan, Ed., (1973).

[29] In some econometrics texts the roles of the γ's and β's are reversed, where the γ's are coefficients of predetermined variables and the β's are the coefficients of endogenous variables.

Each equation in (2.8.1) contains up to $g + k$ parameters, $\gamma_{1h}, \gamma_{2h}, \ldots, \gamma_{gh}$ and $\beta_{1h}, \beta_{2h}, \ldots, \beta_{kh}$, for $h = 1, 2, \ldots, g$. Of course some of these parameters may be specified as zero; that is, it may be specified that the corresponding variable, endogenous or predetermined, does not have any influence in a particular equation.[30] Intercept terms can be taken into account by specifying one of the predetermined variables, conventionally the last, x_k, to be identically unity, so $\beta_{k1}, \beta_{k2}, \ldots, \beta_{kg}$ are the intercepts.

The econometric models of the last two sections provide examples of this general formulation. In particular, (2.6.6) and (2.6.7) are the structural equations of the prototype micro model, while (2.7.1) and (2.7.5) are the structural equations of the prototype macro model.

Typically, each equation of the system (2.8.1) has an independent meaning and identity, reflecting a behavioral relation (e.g., a demand function or a consumption function), a technological relation (e.g., a production function), or some other specific relation suggested by theory for the system under study. Each equation, because it represents one aspect of the structure of the system, is called a *structural equation*, and the set of all structural equations (2.8.1) is called the *structural form.* Some equations may be deterministic, e.g., definitions, identities, and equilibrium conditions, and for these equations the stochastic disturbance terms are identically zero. In general, however, these equations can be eliminated, reducing both the number of equations and the number of endogenous variables.

The general nature of the econometric model is summarized in Figure 2.8 by a flow diagram. Values taken by the predetermined variables, together with values of stochastic disturbance terms, determine the current values of the endogenous variables. The dotted line indicates that the current values of the endogenous variables become, in the next period, the values of the lagged endogenous variables, which influence future endogenous variables. A specific illustration of such a flow diagram was presented in Figure 2.7 in connection with the prototype macro model.[31]

The structural equations may be written in either of two additional ways, which are equivalent to (2.8.1) but more compact in terms of notation. One uses summation notation, expressing the equations as

$$\sum_{h'=1}^{g} y_{h'}\gamma_{h'h} + \sum_{j=1}^{k} x_j\beta_{jh} = \epsilon_h, \qquad h = 1, 2, \ldots, g. \qquad *(2.8.2)$$

Here h' is an index of the endogenous variable, h is an index of the equation, and j is an index of the predetermined variable ($h, h' = 1, 2, \ldots, g; j = 1, 2, \ldots, k$).

[30] In fact, as discussed in Section 2.10, such zero restrictions play an important role in ensuring that the structural parameters can be estimated.

[31] See Figure 12.1 in Section 12.2 for another illustration of such a diagram. Note that arrows cannot point leftward in these diagrams, since future variables cannot influence current variables. (Note that expectations variables are current variables.)

The other uses vector-matrix notation, in which the *structural form* is written[32]

$$\underset{1\times g}{\mathbf{y}}\ \underset{g\times g}{\boldsymbol{\Gamma}} + \underset{1\times k}{\mathbf{x}}\ \underset{k\times g}{\mathbf{B}} = \underset{1\times g}{\boldsymbol{\varepsilon}} \qquad *(2.8.3)$$

In this notation **y** and **x** are row vectors of g endogenous and k predetermined variables, respectively:

$$\mathbf{y} = (y_1\ y_2\ \ldots\ y_g) \qquad (2.8.4)$$

$$\mathbf{x} = (x_1\ x_2\ \ldots\ x_k) \qquad (2.8.5)$$

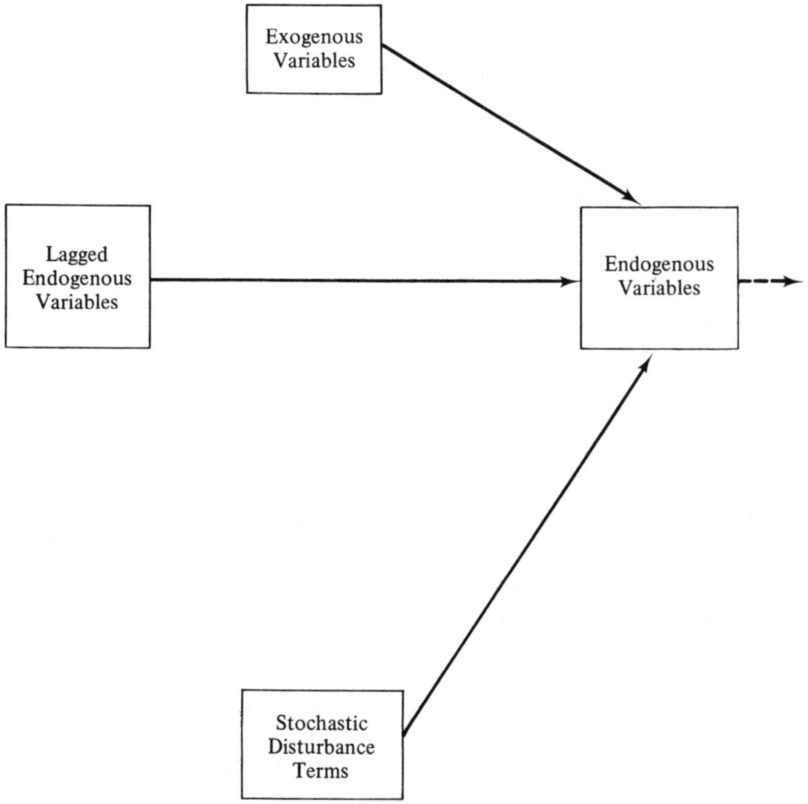

Figure 2.8 Flow Diagram of the General Econometric Model

[32] Note that vectors and matrices appear in boldface type. It might be noted that some econometrics books use the convention that all vectors are column vectors, in which case (2.8.3) would be written

$$\mathbf{y}'\boldsymbol{\Gamma} + \mathbf{x}'\mathbf{B} = \boldsymbol{\varepsilon}'$$

Here, defining **y**, **x**, and **ε** as row vectors makes it unnecessary to transpose them.

and $\boldsymbol{\varepsilon}$ is a row vector consisting of g additive stochastic disturbance terms, one for each equation:

$$\boldsymbol{\varepsilon} = (\epsilon_1 \ \ \epsilon_2 \ \ \ldots \ \ \epsilon_g). \tag{2.8.6}$$

The matrices $\boldsymbol{\Gamma}$ and $\mathbf{B}$ are the matrices of g^2 and gk structural coefficients, respectively:

$$\underset{g \times g}{\boldsymbol{\Gamma}} = (\gamma_{h'h}) = \begin{pmatrix} \gamma_{11} & \gamma_{12} & \cdots & \gamma_{1g} \\ \gamma_{21} & \gamma_{22} & \cdots & \gamma_{2g} \\ \vdots & \vdots & & \\ \gamma_{g1} & \gamma_{g2} & \cdots & \gamma_{gg} \end{pmatrix} \tag{2.8.7}$$

$$\underset{k \times g}{\mathbf{B}} = (\beta_{jh}) = \begin{pmatrix} \beta_{11} & \beta_{12} & \cdots & \beta_{1g} \\ \beta_{21} & \beta_{22} & \cdots & \beta_{2g} \\ \vdots & \vdots & & \\ \beta_{k1} & \beta_{k2} & \cdots & \beta_{kg} \end{pmatrix} \tag{2.8.8}$$

representing the complete set of coefficients of endogenous and predetermined variables, respectively. Thus, the hth columns of $\boldsymbol{\Gamma}$ and $\mathbf{B}$ contain all structural parameters in the hth equation of the system, for $h = 1, 2, \ldots, g$. The structural form in vector-matrix notation (2.8.3) is the most convenient and the most easily manipulated of the three forms of expressing the structural equations. It will generally be used throughout the remainder of this book. Both of the prototype models have been expressed in this form—in equations (2.6.8) and (2.7.6), respectively. This structural form can be written as follows:

$$(y_1 \ \ y_2 \ \ldots \ y_g) \begin{pmatrix} \gamma_{11} & \gamma_{12} & \cdots & \gamma_{1g} \\ \gamma_{21} & \gamma_{22} & \cdots & \gamma_{2g} \\ \vdots & \vdots & & \vdots \\ \gamma_{g1} & \gamma_{g2} & \cdots & \gamma_{gg} \end{pmatrix}$$

$$+ (x_1 \ \ x_2 \ \ldots \ x_k) \begin{pmatrix} \beta_{11} & \beta_{12} & \cdots & \beta_{1g} \\ \beta_{21} & \beta_{22} & \cdots & \beta_{2g} \\ \vdots & \vdots & & \vdots \\ \beta_{k1} & \beta_{k2} & \cdots & \beta_{kg} \end{pmatrix} = (\epsilon_1 \ \ \epsilon_2 \ \ldots \ \epsilon_g) \tag{2.8.9}$$

There is a trivial indeterminacy in the structural equations in that multiplying all terms in each of these equations by a nonzero constant does not change the equation. This indeterminacy is eliminated by choosing a *normalization rule*, a rule for selecting a particular numerical value for one of the nonzero structural coefficients in each equation. The most common such rule divides all coefficients of equation h by $-\gamma_{hh}$, so that

$$\gamma_{hh} = -1, \qquad h = 1, 2, \ldots, g. \tag{2.8.10}$$

According to this rule all elements along the principal diagonal of $\mathbf{\Gamma}$, the matrix of coefficients of endogenous variables, are chosen to be -1. This normalization corresponds to the usual convention of writing one endogenous variable on the left-hand side of the equation, with a coefficient of one. The prototype macro model (2.7.6) uses this normalization. Other normalization rules can be used, however. For example, the prototype micro model (2.6.8) uses the normalization $\gamma_{1h} = 1$ for $h = 1, 2$.

The structural form thus consists of g equations, each of which has an independent role and meaning in the model and which, together, determine, for given values of the parameters, the endogenous variables in terms of the predetermined variables and the stochastic disturbance terms. To the extent that every one of the equations has a stochastic disturbance term, it has been assumed that all identities, definitions, and equilibrium conditions have been removed, as was done in each of the prototype models. If the matrix of coefficients of endogenous variables $\mathbf{\Gamma}$ is nonsingular in having a nonzero determinant and hence an inverse, as will be assumed, the equation system can be solved for the endogenous variables as functions of all predetermined variables and stochastic disturbance terms. Postmultiplying (2.8.3) by the inverse of $\mathbf{\Gamma}$ yields

$$\mathbf{y\Gamma\Gamma}^{-1} + \mathbf{xB\Gamma}^{-1} = \boldsymbol{\varepsilon}\mathbf{\Gamma}^{-1} \tag{2.8.11}$$

Thus, solving for $\mathbf{y}$,

$$\mathbf{y} = -\mathbf{xB\Gamma}^{-1} + \boldsymbol{\varepsilon}\mathbf{\Gamma}^{-1} \tag{2.8.12}$$

Introducing the notation

$$\underset{k\times g}{\mathbf{\Pi}} \equiv -\underset{k\times g}{\mathbf{B}}\ \underset{g\times g}{\mathbf{\Gamma}^{-1}} \tag*{*(2.8.13)}$$

$$\underset{1\times g}{\mathbf{u}} \equiv \underset{1\times g}{\boldsymbol{\varepsilon}}\ \underset{g\times g}{\mathbf{\Gamma}^{-1}} \tag*{*(2.8.14)}$$

equation (2.8.12) can be written

$$\underset{1\times g}{\mathbf{y}} = \underset{1\times k}{\mathbf{x}}\ \underset{k\times g}{\mathbf{\Pi}} + \underset{1\times g}{\mathbf{u}} \tag*{*(2.8.15)}$$

which is the the *reduced form.* It relates each endogenous variable to all predetermined variables and stochastic disturbance terms according to

$$(y_1 \quad y_2 \ldots y_g) = (x_1 \quad x_2 \ldots x_k)\begin{pmatrix} \Pi_{11} & \Pi_{12} & \ldots & \Pi_{1g} \\ \Pi_{21} & \Pi_{22} & \ldots & \Pi_{2g} \\ \vdots & \vdots & & \vdots \\ \Pi_{k1} & \Pi_{k2} & \ldots & \Pi_{kg} \end{pmatrix} + (u_1 \quad u_2 \ldots u_g) \tag{2.8.16}$$

In summation notation the reduced form can be expressed as

$$y_h = \sum_{j=1}^{k} x_j \Pi_{jh} + u_h, \qquad h = 1, 2, \ldots, g \qquad *(2.8.17)$$

Written out in full, it states that

$$\begin{aligned} y_1 &= x_1\Pi_{11} + x_2\Pi_{21} + \ldots + x_k\Pi_{k1} + u_1 \\ y_2 &= x_1\Pi_{12} + x_2\Pi_{22} + \ldots + x_k\Pi_{k2} + u_2 \\ &\vdots \\ y_g &= x_1\Pi_{1g} + x_2\Pi_{2g} + \ldots + x_k\Pi_{kg} + u_g. \end{aligned} \qquad *(2.8.18)$$

Whether in matrix notation, summation notation, or written out in full, in the reduced form each of the endogenous variables is expressed as a linear function of the predetermined variables and stochastic disturbance terms. The reduced form thus uniquely determines the probability distributions of the endogenous variables, given the exogenous variables and given the probability distributions of the stochastic disturbance terms.

For the prototype micro model the reduced-form equations are (2.6.9) and (2.6.10) or, in vector-matrix notation (2.6.11), while for the prototype macro model the reduced-form equations are (2.7.7) and (2.7.8) or, in vector-matrix notation,

$$(Y_t \quad C_t) = (Y_{t-1} \quad G_t \quad 1)\begin{pmatrix} \dfrac{\beta_2}{1-\gamma_1-\gamma_2} & \dfrac{\gamma_1\beta_2}{1-\gamma_1-\gamma_2} \\ \dfrac{1}{1-\gamma_1-\gamma_2} & \dfrac{\gamma_1}{1-\gamma_1-\gamma_2} \\ \dfrac{\beta_1+\beta_3}{1-\gamma_1-\gamma_2} & \dfrac{\gamma_1\beta_3+(1-\gamma_2)\beta_1}{1-\gamma_1-\gamma_2} \end{pmatrix} + \left(\frac{\epsilon_t^I+\epsilon_t^C}{1-\gamma_1-\gamma_2} \quad \frac{\gamma_1\epsilon_t^I+(1-\gamma_2)\epsilon_t^C}{1-\gamma_1-\gamma_2}\right) \qquad *(2.8.19)$$

Thus, in this case, using the notation of (2.8.15),

$$\begin{pmatrix} \Pi_{11} & \Pi_{12} \\ \Pi_{21} & \Pi_{22} \\ \Pi_{31} & \Pi_{32} \end{pmatrix} = \frac{1}{1 - \gamma_1 - \gamma_2} \begin{pmatrix} \beta_2 & \gamma_1\beta_2 \\ 1 & \gamma_1 \\ \beta_1 + \beta_3 & \gamma_1\beta_3 + (1 - \gamma_2)\beta_1 \end{pmatrix} \tag{2.8.20}$$

and

$$(u_1 \quad u_2) = \left(\frac{\epsilon_t^C + \epsilon_t^I}{1 - \gamma_1 - \gamma_2} \quad \frac{\gamma_1 \epsilon_t^I + (1 - \gamma_2)\epsilon_t^C}{1 - \gamma_1 - \gamma_2} \right) \tag{2.8.21}$$

The elements of the matrix of reduced-form coefficients have a useful interpretation as *comparative statics results*, indicating the extent of change in each endogenous variable as any of the predetermined variables change. By differentiating (2.8.17)

$$\frac{\partial y_h}{\partial x_j} = \Pi_{jh}, \quad j = 1, 2, \ldots, k \quad h = 1, 2, \ldots, g \tag{*(2.8.22)}$$

Thus the jh element of the $\mathbf{\Pi}$ matrix of reduced-form coefficients is a measure of the change in the hth endogenous variable as the jth predetermined variable changes, all other predetermined variables and all stochastic disturbance terms being held constant. The estimation of the elements of the $\mathbf{\Pi}$ matrix is therefore an important part of structural analysis.

2.9 The final form

The previous section introduced the structural form and reduced form of the econometric model. If the predetermined variables include lagged endogenous variables, then it is possible to derive yet another form of the model, the final form.[33] The *final form* expresses the current endogenous variables as functions of base values and all relevant current and lagged exogenous variables and stochastic disturbance terms. It is important for structural analysis, since from it all short-term and long-term multipliers can be determined. It thus reveals the short-run and long-run comparative statics of the model.

If the system is a first-order one involving only one lag, and if the lagged endogenous variables are included first, then the vector of predetermined variables can be partitioned as

$$\mathbf{x}_t = (\mathbf{y}_{t-1} \mid \mathbf{z}_t \mid \mathbf{z}_{t-1}) \tag{*(2.9.1)}$$

$$\mathbf{x}_t = (y_{1t-1} \ldots y_{gt-1} \mid z_{1t} \ldots z_{kt} \mid z_{1t-1} \ldots z_{kt-1}). \tag{2.9.2}$$

[33] See Theil and Boot (1962).

Here $\mathbf{y}_{t-1}$ is the vector of lagged endogenous variables, $\mathbf{z}_t$ is the vector of current exogenous variables, and $\mathbf{z}_{t-1}$ is the vector of lagged exogenous variables. Partitioning the $\mathbf{B}$ matrix of (2.8.3) to conform to this partition of $\mathbf{x}$,

$$\mathbf{B} = \begin{pmatrix} \mathbf{B}_1 \\ \hline \mathbf{B}_2 \\ \hline \mathbf{B}_3 \end{pmatrix} \qquad *(2.9.3)$$

the structural form can be written

$$\mathbf{y}_t\mathbf{\Gamma} + (\mathbf{y}_{t-1} \mid \mathbf{z}_t \mid \mathbf{z}_{t-1}) \begin{pmatrix} \mathbf{B}_1 \\ \hline \mathbf{B}_2 \\ \hline \mathbf{B}_3 \end{pmatrix} = \boldsymbol{\varepsilon}_t. \qquad (2.9.4)$$

Thus

$$\mathbf{y}_t\mathbf{\Gamma} + \mathbf{y}_{t-1}\mathbf{B}_1 + \mathbf{z}_t\mathbf{B}_2 + \mathbf{z}_{t-1}\mathbf{B}_3 = \boldsymbol{\varepsilon}_t \qquad *(2.9.5)$$

The reduced form (2.8.15) then becomes

$$\mathbf{y}_t = \mathbf{y}_{t-1}\mathbf{\Pi}_1 + \mathbf{z}_t\mathbf{\Pi}_2 + \mathbf{z}_{t-1}\mathbf{\Pi}_3 + \mathbf{u}_t = (\mathbf{y}_{t-1}\ \mathbf{z}_t\ \mathbf{z}_{t-1}) \begin{pmatrix} \mathbf{\Pi}_1 \\ \mathbf{\Pi}_2 \\ \mathbf{\Pi}_3 \end{pmatrix} + \mathbf{u}_t \qquad *(2.9.6)$$

where $\mathbf{\Pi}_1$ $\mathbf{\Pi}_2$, and $\mathbf{\Pi}_3$ are submatrices of $\mathbf{\Pi}$ satisfying

$$\mathbf{\Pi}_1 = -\mathbf{B}_1\mathbf{\Gamma}^{-1}, \qquad \mathbf{\Pi}_2 = -\mathbf{B}_2\mathbf{\Gamma}^{-1}, \qquad \mathbf{\Pi}_3 = -\mathbf{B}_3\mathbf{\Gamma}^{-1} \qquad *(2.9.7)$$

and $\mathbf{u}_t$ is as in (2.8.14). The final form is obtained by solving the reduced form (2.9.6) iteratively, as in (2.7.11) to (2.7.16) for the prototype macro model, substituting for lagged endogenous variables by using the lagged form of (2.9.6). In the first iteration

$$\begin{aligned} \mathbf{y}_t &= (\mathbf{y}_{t-2}\mathbf{\Pi}_1 + \mathbf{z}_{t-1}\mathbf{\Pi}_2 + \mathbf{z}_{t-2}\mathbf{\Pi}_3 + \mathbf{u}_{t-1})\mathbf{\Pi}_1 + \mathbf{z}_t\mathbf{\Pi}_2 \\ &\quad + \mathbf{z}_{t-1}\mathbf{\Pi}_3 + \mathbf{u}_t \end{aligned} \qquad (2.9.8)$$

$$\begin{aligned} \mathbf{y}_t &= \mathbf{y}_{t-2}\mathbf{\Pi}_1^2 + [\mathbf{z}_t\mathbf{\Pi}_2 + \mathbf{z}_{t-1}(\mathbf{\Pi}_2\mathbf{\Pi}_1 + \mathbf{\Pi}_3) + \mathbf{z}_{t-2}\mathbf{\Pi}_3\mathbf{\Pi}_1] \\ &\quad + [\mathbf{u}_t + \mathbf{u}_{t-1}\mathbf{\Pi}_1] \end{aligned} \qquad (2.9.9)$$

Continuing the iteration back to the base period $t = 0$ yields

$$\begin{aligned} \mathbf{y}_t = \mathbf{y}_0\boldsymbol{\Pi}_1^t + [\mathbf{z}_t\boldsymbol{\Pi}_2 + \mathbf{z}_{t-1}(\boldsymbol{\Pi}_2\boldsymbol{\Pi}_1 + \boldsymbol{\Pi}_3) + \mathbf{z}_{t-2}(\boldsymbol{\Pi}_2\boldsymbol{\Pi}_1 + \boldsymbol{\Pi}_3)\boldsymbol{\Pi}_1 \\ + \mathbf{z}_{t-3}(\boldsymbol{\Pi}_2\boldsymbol{\Pi}_1 + \boldsymbol{\Pi}_3)\boldsymbol{\Pi}_1^2 + \ldots + \mathbf{z}_0\boldsymbol{\Pi}_3\boldsymbol{\Pi}_1^{t-1}] \\ + [\mathbf{u}_t + \mathbf{u}_{t-1}\boldsymbol{\Pi}_1 + \mathbf{u}_{t-2}\boldsymbol{\Pi}_1^2 + \ldots + \mathbf{u}_1\boldsymbol{\Pi}_1^{t-1}] \end{aligned} \qquad *(2.9.10)$$

This is the *final form*, in which each of the endogenous variables is expressed as a function of base-period values, current and lagged exogenous variables, and stochastic disturbance terms.

Equation (2.7.16) is an example of such a final-form equation. The successive coefficients of the current and lagged z's in (2.9.10), given as

$$\boldsymbol{\Pi}_2,\ (\boldsymbol{\Pi}_2\boldsymbol{\Pi}_1 + \boldsymbol{\Pi}_3),\ (\boldsymbol{\Pi}_2\boldsymbol{\Pi}_1 + \boldsymbol{\Pi}_3)\boldsymbol{\Pi}_1, \ldots \qquad *(2.9.11)$$

measure the influence on the current value of the endogenous variables of successively lagged values of the exogenous variables, starting from the current (nonlagged) exogenous variables and given as

$$\frac{\partial \mathbf{y}_t}{\partial \mathbf{z}_{t-j}} = \begin{cases} \boldsymbol{\Pi}_2 & j = 0 \\ (\boldsymbol{\Pi}_2\boldsymbol{\Pi}_1 + \boldsymbol{\Pi}_3)\,\boldsymbol{\Pi}_1^{j-1} & j = 1, 2, \ldots, t-1 \\ \boldsymbol{\Pi}_3\boldsymbol{\Pi}_1^{t-1} & j = t. \end{cases} \qquad *(2.9.12)$$

An example, in the case of the prototype macro model, is the set of equations (2.7.17), (2.7.18), and (2.7.19), giving the first three elements of the successive coefficients in (2.9.11). The estimation of these short-run and long-run multipliers is an important aspect of structural analysis, which also has major implications for forecasting and policy evaluation.

2.10 Identification of the general econometric model

An important issue in econometric model building is that of *identification.*[34] Several important approaches to the estimation of the structural equations start by estimating the reduced-form equations

$$\mathbf{y} = \mathbf{x}\boldsymbol{\Pi} + \mathbf{u} \qquad *(2.10.1)$$

from observed data on the g endogenous variables $\mathbf{y}$ and on the k predetermined variables $\mathbf{x}$. The resulting estimators are summarized by the $k \times g$ matrix $\hat{\boldsymbol{\Pi}}$.[35]

[34] See Chapter 10 for a further and a more general discussion of identification.

[35] In general "hats", as in $\hat{\boldsymbol{\Pi}}$, are used to denote estimators in econometrics. This convention differs from that in elementary statistics, where Greek letters usually designate true parameters and corresponding Roman letters designate their estimators, such as μ and m or σ and s.

This information is then used to estimate the coefficients of the endogenous and predetermined variables in the structural form

$$\mathbf{y\Gamma} + \mathbf{xB} = \boldsymbol{\varepsilon} \qquad *(2.10.2)$$

namely $\mathbf{\Gamma}$ and $\mathbf{B}$, respectively. It has been shown in (2.8.13) that

$$\mathbf{\Pi} = -\mathbf{B\Gamma}^{-1} \qquad *(2.10.3)$$

but clearly information on the estimated elements of $\mathbf{\Pi}$ is not enough to "disentangle" the effects of $\mathbf{B}$ and $\mathbf{\Gamma}$ in determining $\mathbf{\Pi}$. Trying to determine $\mathbf{B}$ and $\mathbf{\Gamma}$ from $\mathbf{\Pi}$, given (2.10.3), is like trying to determine two numbers the product of which is known to be 12. Clearly, more information is needed in order to determine $\mathbf{B}$ and $\mathbf{\Gamma}$. This is usually referred to as *a priori information*, since it precedes estimation. By contrast the information contained in (2.10.3) is called *a posteriori information*, since it is based on (and thus follows) estimation of the reduced-form equations, specifically the estimation of $\mathbf{\Pi}$.

Basically the problem of identification is that of providing enough a priori information to enable determination of structural parameters $\mathbf{B}$ and $\mathbf{\Gamma}$ from the reduced-form parameters $\mathbf{\Pi}$. With insufficient a priori information it is impossible to determine $\mathbf{B}$ and $\mathbf{\Gamma}$ from $\mathbf{\Pi}$, and this situation is called the *underidentified case* (or the *unidentified case*). In this case it is impossible to distinguish the true structural parameters from "bogus" parameters. With "just enough" information it is possible to determine uniquely (after normalization) the elements of $\mathbf{B}$ and $\mathbf{\Gamma}$, the so-called *just identified* (or exactly identified) case, in which only one set of structural parameters is consistent with the a priori information and the reduced-form parameters. With more information there would be more than one way to determine the elements of $\mathbf{B}$ and $\mathbf{\Gamma}$ from $\mathbf{\Pi}$ and the a priori information. This is the *overidentified case*, which is typically found in most econometric models.

A priori information can take several forms, but the most common is *zero restrictions.* The information in this case takes the form of zero values of certain elements of the $\mathbf{B}$ and/or $\mathbf{\Gamma}$ matrices, implying that certain variables that appear in certain equations of the model do not appear in other equations. In the prototype micro model (2.6.8), for example, the $\mathbf{B}$ matrix contains two zeros, reflecting the assumptions that demand does not depend on rainfall and supply does not depend on income, where both variables enter the model. In the prototype macro model (2.7.6), similarly, two zeros appear in the $\mathbf{B}$ matrix, reflecting the assumptions that consumption does not depend on lagged income or government expenditure.

In general, zero restrictions convey a priori information that can be used to estimate the structural form. For example, in the prototype micro model, from (2.6.11),

$$\begin{pmatrix} \Pi_{11} & \Pi_{12} \\ \Pi_{21} & \Pi_{22} \\ \Pi_{31} & \Pi_{32} \end{pmatrix} = \frac{1}{\gamma_2 - \gamma_1} \begin{pmatrix} \gamma_2\beta_1 & \beta_1 \\ -\gamma_1\beta_2 & -\beta_2 \\ \gamma_2\delta_1 - \gamma_1\delta_2 & \delta_1 - \delta_2 \end{pmatrix} \qquad (2.10.4)$$

In this case the structural parameters—the β's, γ's, and δ's—can be determined *uniquely* from the reduced-form parameters—the Π's—as

$$\gamma_1 = \frac{\Pi_{21}}{\Pi_{22}} \qquad \gamma_2 = \frac{\Pi_{11}}{\Pi_{12}}$$

$$\beta_1 = \Pi_{12}\left(\frac{\Pi_{11}}{\Pi_{12}} - \frac{\Pi_{21}}{\Pi_{22}}\right) \qquad \beta_2 = -\Pi_{22}\left(\frac{\Pi_{11}}{\Pi_{12}} - \frac{\Pi_{21}}{\Pi_{22}}\right) \qquad (2.10.5)$$

$$\delta_1 = \Pi_{31} - \Pi_{32}\frac{\Pi_{21}}{\Pi_{22}} \qquad \delta_2 = \Pi_{31} - \Pi_{32}\frac{\Pi_{11}}{\Pi_{12}}$$

This is the case of *just identification*, in which the structural parameters are given as unique functions of the reduced-form parameters.

By contrast, consider the simple demand-supply model:

$$\begin{aligned} q^D &= \gamma_1 p + \delta_1 + \epsilon^D \\ q^S &= \gamma_2 p + \delta_2 + \epsilon^S \\ q^D &= q^S. \end{aligned} \qquad (2.10.6)$$

This model may be considered the special case of the prototype micro model for which the coefficient of income in the demand equation (β_1) and the coefficient of rainfall in the supply equation (β_2) both vanish. Thus, no exogenous influences are present in either equation of the model. The reduced-form equations are

$$(q \;\; p) = \left(\frac{\gamma_2\delta_1 - \gamma_1\delta_2}{\gamma_2 - \gamma_1} \quad \frac{\delta_1 - \delta_2}{\gamma_2 - \gamma_1}\right) + \left(\frac{\gamma_2\epsilon^D - \gamma_1\epsilon^S}{\gamma_2 - \gamma_1} \quad \frac{\epsilon^D - \epsilon^S}{\gamma_2 - \gamma_1}\right) \qquad (2.10.7)$$

and so the reduced-form parameters are

$$(\Pi'_{11} \;\; \Pi'_{12}) = \frac{1}{\gamma_2 - \gamma_1}(\gamma_2\delta_1 - \gamma_1\delta_2 \quad \delta_1 - \delta_2). \qquad (2.10.8)$$

In this case knowing only Π'_{11} and Π'_{12} will *not* reveal the structural coefficients γ_1, γ_2, δ_1, and δ_2; many possible values of γ's and δ's are consistent with (2.10.8). This case is therefore one of an *underidentified* (or *unidentified*) model. The underidentification of this model is revealed also geometrically. Consider Figure 2.6 again. Suppose the initial equilibrium is at E, defined by the pair (q, p). Suppose that, because of the presence of the stochastic disturbance terms (rather than because of a shift in income), demand and supply shift to D' and S', implying the new equilibrium E', defined by (q', p'). Information on quantities and prices contained in these two equilibrium points, and, in fact, any number of such points, will not yield information on the slopes and intercepts of the demand or supply curves.

Another variant of the prototype micro model will illustrate an overidentified model. Consider the model:

$$\begin{aligned} q^D &= \gamma_1 p + \beta_1 I + \beta_1' A + \delta_1 + \epsilon^D \\ q^S &= \gamma_2 p + \beta_2 r + \beta_2' w + \delta_2 + \epsilon^S \\ q^D &= q^S \end{aligned} \tag{2.10.9}$$

where A is advertising and w is the average wage, both of which are treated as exogenous. The reduced form is

$$(q \ \ p) = (I \ \ A \ \ r \ \ w \ \ 1)\left(\frac{1}{\gamma_2 - \gamma_1}\right) \begin{pmatrix} \gamma_2\beta_1 & \beta_1 \\ \gamma_2\beta_1' & \beta_1' \\ -\gamma_1\beta_2 & -\beta_2 \\ -\gamma_1\beta_2' & -\beta_2' \\ \gamma_2\delta_1 - \gamma_1\delta_2 & \delta_1 - \delta_2 \end{pmatrix} \tag{2.10.10}$$

Thus the reduced-form parameters are

$$\begin{pmatrix} \Pi_{11}'' & \Pi_{12}'' \\ \Pi_{21}'' & \Pi_{22}'' \\ \Pi_{31}'' & \Pi_{32}'' \\ \Pi_{41}'' & \Pi_{42}'' \\ \Pi_{51}'' & \Pi_{52}'' \end{pmatrix} = \frac{1}{\gamma_2 - \gamma_1} \begin{pmatrix} \gamma_2\beta_1 & \beta_1 \\ \gamma_2\beta_1' & \beta_1' \\ -\gamma_1\beta_2 & -\beta_2 \\ -\gamma_1\beta_2' & -\beta_2' \\ \gamma_2\delta_1 - \gamma_1\delta_2 & \delta_1 - \delta_2 \end{pmatrix} \tag{2.10.11}$$

In this case some of the structural-form parameters can be determined from these reduced-form parameters in two different ways. Thus, for example, two alternative estimators of γ_2 are

$$\frac{\Pi_{11}''}{\Pi_{12}''} \quad \text{and} \quad \frac{\Pi_{21}''}{\Pi_{22}''} \tag{2.10.12}$$

and two alternative estimators of γ_1 are

$$\frac{\Pi_{31}''}{\Pi_{32}''} \quad \text{and} \quad \frac{\Pi_{41}''}{\Pi_{42}''}. \tag{2.10.13}$$

This is the case of an *overidentified* model, in which there is more than one way to infer structural parameters from reduced-form parameters.

These three cases—just identification, underidentification, and overidentification—illustrate the three possibilities for identification. In general, the problem of identification is that of combining a priori information contained in the specification of the model with a posteriori information contained in the estimation of the reduced form of the model in order to determine estimates of the structural parameters of the system. Specific conditions of identification will be discussed in Chapter 10.

PROBLEMS

2-A Using the geometric model of supply and demand shown in Figure 2.2, analyze the effects of

1. Imposition of an excise tax on the good.
2. Introduction of a labor-saving innovation in the production of the good.
3. Higher tariffs on factors used in the production of the good.
4. Advertising the good.

What other changes could be analyzed using this diagram?

2-B Generalize the prototype micro model to allow explicitly for both a tariff on factors used in the production of the good and the distribution of income, both of which are treated as exogenous. For the generalized model

1. State the structural equations and express them as a matrix equation.
2. Obtain the reduced form.
3. Obtain the matrix of comparative statics results, giving signs of the partial derivatives of each endogenous variable with respect to each exogenous variable.

2-C Consider the disequilibrium version of the prototype micro model, where the equilibrium condition that the quantity demanded equals the quantity supplied is replaced by the tâtonnement condition that the change in price is proportional to the excess of the quantity demanded over the quantity supplied. For this model obtain

1. The reduced form and comparative statics results.
2. The final form and long- and short-run multipliers.

2-D In the prototype macro model, develop the structural form, reduced form, and final form if

1. C is eliminated, so the endogenous variables are Y and I.

2. Y is eliminated, so the endogenous variables are C and I.

2-E In a model of the money market the demand for money (M^D) depends linearly on national income (Y), the interest rate (r), and population (N); the supply of money (M^S) depends linearly on national income and lagged interest rate (r_{-1}); and, in equilibrium, money demand equals money supply. National income and population are treated as exogenous, while the interest rate and stock of money (M) are treated as endogenous. All equations contain constant terms (intercepts) and are nonstochastic.

1. State the structural equations and express them as a matrix equation.
2. Obtain the reduced-form equations in matrix form.
3. What is the final-form equation for r?
4. Obtain the matrix of comparative statics results, giving signs of the partials of each endogenous variable with respect to each exogenous variable.

2-F In a certain political-economic model the proportion of votes cast for the Democratic Party (D) depends linearly on unemployment (U) and union membership (M); unemployment depends linearly on the government deficit ($G - T$) and war (W, a dummy variable, equal to 1 if war, 0 if no war); and the government deficit depends linearly on unemployment and war. D, U, and $G - T$ are treated as endogenous. All equations contain constant terms (intercepts) and are stochastic.

1. Obtain the structural form and the reduced form.
2. What hypotheses could be tested with the estimated matrices of structural and reduced-form coefficients?

2-G In a certain model of inflation and unemployment the rate of inflation (i) depends on the growth of the money supply (m), the interest rate (r), past wage increases (w_{-1}), and the government deficit (d). Unemployment (u) depends on inflation (i), the interest rate (r), current wages (w), and union membership (n). Treat i and u as endogenous.

1. Find the structural form and reduced form of this model.
2. What hypotheses could you test with the estimated model?

2-H Generalize the development of the reduced form and final form to a model including lags of both endogenous and predetermined variables up to and including those of order p. Write out the equations in both matrix and summation notation. What happens when $p \longrightarrow \infty$?

2-I In the Smithies multiplier-accelerator model savings depends linearly on current income and previous peak income while investment depends linearly on past income, previous peak income, and the difference between lagged full-capacity output and previous peak income.[36] In equilibrium savings equals investment. Assume income, savings, and investment are endogenous while all other variables are exogenous.

1. What are the structural equations of this model?
2. What is the meaning of the endogenous-exogenous assumptions?
3. What are the reduced-form equations?
4. What is the comparative statics matrix of this model?

2-J In the Kogiku model of the raw materials market, demand for raw materials depends linearly on the terms of trade for raw materials, the world index of manufacturing production, time, and a dummy variable to measure the effects of the Korean War; supply of raw materials depends linearly on the terms of trade, the lagged terms of trade, time, and the dummy variable; and, in equilibrium, demand equals supply.[37] The endogenous variables of the model are the quantity (q) and the terms of trade (p), while predetermined variables are lagged terms of trade (p_{-1}), time (t), the dummy variable (w), the world index of manufacturing production (m), and unity (1) to account for the intercepts in the two stochastic equations of the model.

1. With reference to this particular model, what do the assumptions that certain variables are endogenous and others are predetermined mean?
2. Find the structural form, the reduced form, and the final form of the model.
3. Using this model, define and contrast short-run and long-run multipliers.

2-K In the Horowitz model of the synthetic rubber market, supply of synthetic rubber (S) depends linearly on the price ratio of synthetic to natural rubber (p), natural rubber imports (M), and time (t); natural rubber imports depend linearly on the price ratio and time; and the price ratio depends linearly on the supply of synthetic rubber, the lagged price ratio (p_{-1}), and the inventory-consumption ratio (I).[38] All equations contain intercepts and additive stochastic disturbance terms. Endogenous variables of the model are S, M, and p; exogenous variables are t, I, and 1 (to account for the intercept).

1. Find the structural form and express the reduced form and final form of the model as matrix equations.
2. Using this model define and contrast short-run and long-run multipliers.

2-L In the Kaldor model of the trade cycle, savings depends on current income and lagged capital stock, investment is the change in capital stock, and the change in income is a function of the difference between savings and investment.[39]

[36] See Smithies (1957).

[37] See Kogiku (1967).

[38] See Horowitz (1963).

[39] See Kaldor (1940).

Assume that all current values of income, savings, investment, and capital stock are the endogenous variables of the model. Assume, in contrast to Kaldor, that all functions are linear.

1. Obtain the structural and reduced-form equations of the model.
2. Obtain the final-form equations for income and capital stock.
3. Obtain short-run and long-run multipliers for income.

2-M In the Harrod-Domar model of economic growth, savings at time t, S_t, is a constant proportion s of income at time t, Y_t; capital at time t, K_t, is a constant multiple β of output at time t, Y_t; investment at time t, I_t, is the change in the capital stock $(K_{t+1} - K_t)$; and, in equilibrium, savings equals investment.[40]

1. What are the structural equations and the reduced-form equations of the model? Which variables are endogenous?
2. Obtain the final-form equation for output, and show that output grows at the rate s/β–that is, at a rate given by the ratio of the savings ratio to the capital-output ratio.

2-N Gravity models are a generalization of the law of gravitational attraction, according to which the gravitational force F_{ij} attracting two point masses i and j is proportional to the product of the masses, $m_i m_j$, and inversely proportional to the square of the distance between them, d_{ij}^2. In the *generalized gravity model.*

$$F_{ij} = \gamma m_i^{\alpha_i} m_j^{\alpha_j} d_{ij}^{-\beta_{ij}} e^u$$

where u is a random variable that is normally distributed with mean 0 and variance σ^2. Using logarithms, convert this model to a linear model and indicate the values of coefficients corresponding to the law of gravitational attraction. Also show geometrically the density functions for both u and e^u.

2-O Show that by appropriate transformations of variables (e.g. logarithms, reciprocals) the following nonlinear models relating y to the explanatory variables x_1 and x_2 and the stochastic disturbance term u can be converted to models that are linear in the parameters.

1. $y = Ax_1^{\beta_1} x_2^{\beta_2} e^u$ (constant elasticity)
2. $y = \exp(\beta_0 + \beta_1 x_1 + \beta_2 x_2 + u)$ (exponential)
3. $y = (\beta_0 + \beta_1 x_1 + \beta_2 x_2 + u)^{-1}$ (reciprocal)
4. $y = [1 + \exp(\beta_0 + \beta_1 x_1 + \beta_2 x_2 + u)]^{-1}$ (logistic)

Also show that the following models are nonlinear and cannot be converted into models linear in the parameters. Obtain linear approximations for each.

[40] See Domar (1957) and Tinbergen and Bos (1962).

5. $y = Ax_1^{\beta_1} x_2^{\beta_2} + u$
6. $y = \beta_1 + \beta_2 \exp(\beta_3 x) + u$
7. $y = \beta_1 (x - \beta_2)^2 + u$

Finally determine whether the following can be converted into models that are linear in the parameters.

8. $y = \beta_0 + \beta_1 \rho^{x_1} + u, \quad o < \rho < 1$
9. $y = \exp(\beta_0 + \beta_1 x + \beta_2 x^2) + u$
10. $y = \beta_0 (e^{\beta_1 x_1} + e^{\beta_2 x_2}) + u$

BIBLIOGRAPHY

Ball, R. J. (1968), "Econometric Model Building", in *Mathematical Model Building in Economics and Industry*. London: Charles Griffin & Co., Ltd.

Beach, E. F. (1957), *Economic Models: An Exposition.* New York: John Wiley & Sons, Inc.

Bergstrom, A. R. (1967), *Selected Economic Models and Their Analysis.* New York: American Elsevier Publishing Company, Inc.

Christ, C. (1966), *Econometric Models and Methods.* New York: John Wiley & Sons, Inc.

Cootner, P. H., Ed. (1964), *The Random Character of Stock Market Prices*, Rev. Ed. Cambridge: MIT Press.

Doman, E. D. (1957), *Essays in the Theory of Economic Growth*. New York: Oxford University Press.

Enke, S. (1951), "Equilibrium among Spatially Separated Markets: Solution by Electric Analogue." *Econometrica*, 19: 40–47.

Forrester, Jay (1971), *World Dynamics*. Cambridge: Wright-Allen Press.

Forrester, Jay (1969), *Urban Dynamics*. Cambridge: MIT Press.

Forrester, Jay (1961), *Industrial Dynamics*. Cambridge: MIT Press; New York: John Wiley & Sons, Inc.

Goldberger, A. S., and O. D. Duncan, Eds. (1973), *Structural Equation Models in the Social Sciences.* New York: Seminar Press.

Horowitz, I. (1963), "An Econometric Analysis of Supply and Demand in the Synthetic Rubber Industry." *International Economic Review*, 4: 325–45.

Intriligator, Michael D. (1971), *Mathematical Optimization and Economic Theory*, Englewood Cliffs, N.J.: Prentice-Hall, Inc.

Kaldor, N. (1940), "A Model of the Trade Cycle." *Economic Journal*, 50: 78–92.

Kendall, M. G. (1968), "Introduction to Model Building and its Problems", in *Mathematical Model Building in Economics and Industry.* London: Charles Griffin & Co., Ltd.

Kogiku, K. C. (1967), "A Model of the Raw Materials Market." *International Economic Review*, 8: 116–20.

Morehouse, N. F., R. H. Strotz, and S. J. Horwitz (1950), "An Electro-Analog

Method for Investigating Problems in Economic Dynamics: Inventory Oscillations." *Econometrica*, 18: 313–28.

Samuelson, Paul A. (1947), *Foundations of Economic Analysis.* Cambridge: Harvard University Press.

Smith, Adam (1776), *The Wealth of Nations.* Edited by Edwin Cannan (1937). New York: The Modern Library.

Smithies, A. (1957), "Economic Fluctuations and Growth." *Econometrica*, 25: 1–52.

Strotz, R. H., J. C. McAnulty, and J. B. Naines, Jr. (1953), "Goodwin's Nonlinear Theory of the Business Cycle: An Electro–Analog Solution." *Econometrica*, 21: 390–411.

Suits, D., (1963), *The Theory and Application of Econometric Models.* Athens: Center of Economic Research.

Theil, H., and J. C. G. Boot (1962), "The Final Form of Econometric Equation Systems." *Review of the International Statistical Institute*, 30: 136–52, reprinted in Zellner, Ed. (1968).

Tinbergen, J., and H. C. Bos (1962), *Mathematical Models of Economic Growth.* New York: McGraw-Hill Book Company.

Tustin, A. (1953), *The Mechanism of Economic Systems.* Cambridge: Harvard University Press.

Zellner, A., Ed. (1968), *Readings in Economic Statistics and Econometrics.* Boston: Little, Brown and Company.

CHAPTER 3

Data and Refined Data

3.1 What are data?

An econometric study entails the use of data to estimate an algebraic linear stochastic model, such as those treated in the last chapter, via econometric techniques. Pure theory can treat the phenomenon or system under study only up to a certain point. That point is typically the comparative static analysis of the signs of certain partial derivatives, namely the coefficients of the reduced form. To proceed beyond this point, in particular to estimate the values of the coefficients of both the reduced form and the structural form, requires a relevant set of data on all variables of the model. Thus, for example, the prototype micro model would require data on price, quantity, income, and rainfall, while the prototype macro model would require data on national income, consumption, investment, and government spending.

The data relevant to a particular study summarize the facts concerning the phenomena under investigation. These facts may be of different types, and they may be derived from different sources, with the theory underlying the phenomena used to choose among the various alternatives. They may be fundamentally quantitative, fundamentally qualitative, or a mixture of both types. Whatever their type, source, or nature, they are expressed in a quantitative way in carrying out an econometric study. The set of all such quantitatively expressed facts is the *data* of the study.

An econometric model requires, for its estimation, data on all of the variables included in the model. Values taken by endogenous, exogenous, and, where appropriate, lagged endogenous or exogenous variables, are necessary in order to estimate the parameters of the model. Indeed, the first and often the most serious pitfall in performing an econometric study is simply lack of data. It is relatively easy to construct models of all types, sizes, etc. They can be easily manipulated in various ways, as discussed in the last chapter. Finding the data relevant to a particular model is another story, however. In general the data are either not available or not available in the form wanted. As a result various proxies are sometimes used for certain variables of the model. An example is a time trend used as a proxy for changing tastes or changing technology, as will be seen in Chapters 7 and 8. Furthermore, choices must be made on such questions as whether to express the data in the form of real or nominal quantities, total or per capita quantities, levels or first differences or percentage differences, stocks or flows, etc. Examples of these alternatives appear in Chapters 7, 8, and 9. Finally the data must sometimes be "massaged" in various ways, such as by the elimination of a trend and the use of seasonal adjustment, in order to make various series comparable and in order to focus on certain phenomena of interest. This chapter deals with the various types of data (Sections 3.2 to 3.4), problems with the data (Section 3.5), how they are "massaged" (Section 3.6), their accuracy (Section 3.7), and some major sources of data (Section 3.8).

3.2 Quantitative vs. qualitative data; dummy variables

Data can be of different types, and several distinctions can be drawn between the varieties of data available. While data, as a matter of definition, are quantitative, they may, in fact, represent either quantitative or qualitative facts. Quantitative facts, which are already expressed as numbers, lead directly to data in the form of these numbers or some suitable transformation of them. Thus the prototype micro model might, as applied to the wheat market, include data on such quantitative facts as the price of wheat, measured in dollars per bushel; the quantity of wheat, measured in (millions of) bushels per year; income, measured in (billions of) dollars per year; and rainfall, measured in inches of rain per year. Where specific measures exist for a particular set of facts, such as these measures for the facts relevant to the prototype micro model, they typically form the data. Thus, the data relevant to the prototype micro model as applied to wheat in the United States, 1961–1972, are presented in Table 3.1[1] Similarly data relevant to the prototype macro model for the United States, 1961–1972, are presented in Table 3.2.[2]

Qualitative facts, for which no numerical measure exists, can also be expressed in the form of data. Often these qualitative facts refer to either-or situations. Thus, something either happened or it did not happen, an attitude or position was adopted or it was not, etc. These qualitative facts can encompass qualitative variables (e.g., male or female, married or unmarried), qualitative shifts over time or space (e.g., war or peace time, industrialized or developing countries), or even the aggregation of quantitative facts into qualitative facts (e.g., rich or poor, rather than the quantitative level of income). These sort of qualitative facts are typically expressed as numerical data on appropriate *dummy variables.* The dummy variable takes one of two possible values, one value signifying one qualitative possibility and the other value signifying the other possibility. By convention the dummy variable customarily assumes a value of zero or unity, unity usually referring to the occurrence of an event or the presence of a characteristic, and zero referring to the nonoccurrence of the event or the absence of the characteristic.[3]

Consider, for example, the investment tax credit in the United States, which

[1] Data on rainfall are omitted here.

[2] The generation of these macroeconomic data requires considerable effort and expenditure. They are, in fact, the end products of a set of very complex estimation procedures transforming raw sources of data with differing levels of accuracy and different biases, such as tax returns and profit and loss statements, into carefully constructed estimates of the national aggregates.

[3] The dummy variable usually distinguishes only two characteristics, since it would otherwise introduce a scaling effect, with the results of the analysis depending upon the particular scale chosen for the dummy variable. See Problem 3-B.

Table 3.1. Data Relevant to the Prototype Micro Model, as Applied to the Wheat Market of the United States, 1961–1972

	Endogenous Variables		*Exogenous Variable*
Year	p *Price of Wheat ($/bushel)*	q *Quantity of Wheat (millions of bushels per year)*	I *Income (billions of dollars of GNP per year)*
1961	1.83	1235	520
2	2.04	1094	560
3	1.85	1142	589
4	1.37	1291	629
5	1.35	1316	685
6	1.63	1312	750
7	1.39	1522	790
8	1.24	1576	864
9	1.24	1460	930
1970	1.33	1352	977
1	1.34	1618	1056
1972	1.76	1545	1155

Source U.S. Bureau of the Census, *Statistical Abstract of the United States*, Washington, D.C.: U.S. Government Printing Office, various years.

Table 3.2. Data Relevant to the Prototype Macro Model, as Applied to the United States, 1961–1972

	Endogenous Variables		*Predetermined Variables*	
Year	Y *(billions of dollars of GNP per year)*	C *(billions of dollars of consumption spending per year)*	Y_{-1} *(billions of dollars of last year's GNP per year)*	G *(billions of dollars of government spending per year)*
1961	520	335	504	108
2	560	355	520	117
3	589	374	560	123
4	629	399	589	128
5	685	433	629	137
6	750	466	685	157
7	790	492	750	178
8	864	536	790	200
9	930	580	864	210
1970	977	618	930	220
1	1056	667	977	234
1972	1155	727	1056	255

Source U.S. Bureau of the Census, *Statistical Abstract of the United States*, Washington, D.C., U.S. Government Printing Office, various years.

was enacted in 1962, suspended in 1966, and reinstated in 1970. The presence of the investment tax credit can be represented by a dummy variable ITC, as shown in Table 3.3. This dummy variable might be utilized in a study of investment. Thus, the investment function of the prototype macro model of section 2.7 might be modified to

$$I_t = \gamma_2 Y_t + \beta_2 Y_{t-1} + \beta_3 + \beta_4(\mathrm{ITC})_t + \epsilon_t^I \qquad (3.2.1)$$

where ITC is the dummy variable and β_4, presumably positive, is a measure of the efficacy of the tax credit. The model might be estimated on the basis of data in Tables 3.2 and 3.3. If β_4 is estimated to be large, positive, and statistically significant, it might be concluded that the investment tax credit was important in stimulating additional investment. For the years in which the credit did not exist the investment function is

$$I_t = \gamma_2 Y_t + \beta_2 Y_{t-1} + \beta_3 + \epsilon_t^I \quad (\text{where ITC} = 0) \qquad (3.2.2)$$

while for years in which it did exist the function is

$$I_t = \gamma_2 Y_t + \beta_2 Y_{t-1} + (\beta_3 + \beta_4) + \epsilon_t^I \quad (\text{where ITC} = 1). \qquad (3.2.3)$$

Thus the investment tax credit variable ITC shifts out the investment function by increasing the intercept from β_3 to $\beta_3 + \beta_4$.

If it were assumed that the investment tax credit affected not only the intercept of the investment function but also possibly each of the slope coefficients as well, the model could be represented by the two equations

Table 3.3. The Investment Tax Credit, 1960–1972

Year	*ITC (dummy: 1 in those years in which the investment tax credit was in force; 0 for other years)*
1960	0
1	0
2	1
3	1
4	1
5	1
6	0
7	0
8	0
9	0
1970	1
1	1
1972	1

$$I_t = \gamma_2 Y_t + \beta_2 Y_{t-1} + \beta_3 + \epsilon_t^I \quad \text{(for ITC = 0)} \tag{3.2.4}$$

$$I_t = \gamma_2' Y_t + \beta_2' Y_{t-1} + \beta_3' + \epsilon_t^I \quad \text{(for ITC = 1)} \tag{3.2.5}$$

where the parameters γ_2, β_2, and β_3 refer to the situation without the investment tax credit and the corresponding parameters γ_2', β_2', and β_3' refer to the situation with the investment tax credit. In terms of the dummy variable this model can be summarized by

$$I_t = (\gamma_2 + \gamma_2''\text{ITC})Y_t + (\beta_2 + \beta_2''\text{ITC})Y_{t-1} + (\beta_3 + \beta_3''\text{ITC}) + \epsilon_t^I \tag{3.2.6}$$

where the parameters γ_2, β_2, and β_3 are as in (3.2.4), when ITC = 0. By setting ITC = 1,

$$\gamma_2' = \gamma_2 + \gamma_2'', \quad \beta_2' = \beta_2 + \beta_2'', \quad \beta_3' = \beta_3 + \beta_3''. \tag{3.2.7}$$

Estimating (3.2.6) is equivalent to estimating the two equations (3.2.4) and (3.2.5)—that is, estimating two separate investment functions, one for years when ITC = 0 and the other for years when ITC = 1. The simpler specification in (3.2.1) where only the intercept is affected is the special case for which

$$\gamma_2'' = 0, \quad \beta_2'' = 0, \quad \beta_3'' = \beta_4 \tag{3.2.8}$$

i.e., where the investment tax credit does not shift the slope coefficients, in particular, not affecting the influence of income and past income on investment. Clearly (3.2.6)—or, equivalently, (3.2.4) and (3.2.5)—is a more general specification of the model than (3.2.1) in that it subsumes the latter as one special case. Nevertheless, specifications such as (3.2.1) are often utilized simply because there are not enough data to estimate (3.2.6) or, equivalently, (3.2.4) and (3.2.5), which require adequate data for each of the two situations.

Dummy variables can also be used to distinguish among several qualitative characteristics or attributes, such as educational level, occupation, and region. If there are more than two possible characteristics or attributes, several dummy variables can be used. Suppose, for example that there are four regions to be distinguished—Northwest, Northeast, Southwest, and Southeast. These possibilities can be distinguished by the use of four dummy variables, d_1 to d_4, where d_1 is unity if Northwest, zero otherwise; d_2 is unity if Northeast, zero otherwise, etc. Alternatively these four regions can be distinguished by two dummy variables, as shown in Figure 3.1, where d_1 distinguishes North and South and d_2 distinguishes West and East. In general, then, a dummy variable is a numerical variable representing information of a quantitative type, typically showing the presence or absence of a qualitative characteristic. Use of such a numerical representation of qualitative factors facilitates the use of econometric and other quantitative methods to analyze such factors.[4]

[4] If a regression uses only dummy variables as explanatory variables, then it is equivalent to an analysis of variance, while if it includes both dummy and numerical variables as explanatory variables, then it is equivalent to an analysis of covariance. For a further discussion of dummy variables in regression analysis see Chapter 6, especially Sections 6.2 and 6.10.

d_1 (North vs. South) \ d_2 (West vs. East)	0	1
0	Northwest	Northeast
1	Southwest	Southeast

Figure 3.1 Use of Two Dummy Variables to Distinguish Four Possibilities

3.3 Time-series vs. cross-section data; pooling; microdata

Another important distinction to be drawn with reference to the data is that between time-series and cross-section data. Most data utilized in econometric model estimation are of one of these types.

Time-series data measure a particular variable during successive time periods or at different dates. The time period is often a year (i.e., annual data), but it can be a quarter, month, or week (i.e., quarterly, monthly, or weekly data). For other purposes a longer time period is used, such as two years, five years, a decade or longer. Usually the observations are successive and equally spaced in time. Examples of time-series data are given in Tables 3.1 and 3.2, presenting annual time-series data for the prototype micro model and the prototype macro model, respectively.

Cross-section data measure a particular variable at a given time for different entities. Just as the "time period" can assume different values in time-series data, the "entity" can assume different identities in cross-section data. The entities might, for example, be different countries, as in Table 3.4, which gives cross-section data relevant to the prototype macro model for selected countries. Another example, for a different entity, could be data for the prototype micro

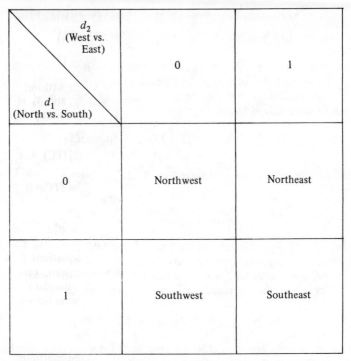

Table 3.4. Data Relevant to the Prototype Macro Model for Selected Countries, 1972

	Endogenous Variables		*Predetermined Variables*	
Country	Y *Per Capita National Income in Market Prices in 1972*	C *Per Capita Private Final Consumption Expenditure in 1972*	Y_{-1} *Per Capita National Income in Market Prices in 1971*	G *Per Capita Government Final Consumption Expenditure in 1972*
North America				
Unites States	$4984	$3143	$4580	$ 946
Canada	4235	2420	3755	826
Western Europe				
Belgium	3346	2023	2733	500
France	3403	2017	2831	423
Germany, F.R.	3769	2036	3182	664
Italy	1984	1272	1735	294
Netherlands	3165	1767	2587	528
Sweden	4669	2509	4025	1077
United Kingdom	2503	1594	2252	469
Asia-Oceania				
Australia	3426	2032	2928	167
Japan	2439	1269	1893	221

Source United Nations, Department of Economic and Social Affairs, *Monthly Bulletin of Statistics*, January 1975, 29: xxvii–xxviii, 191–7.

NOTE All figures are in per capita terms and are measured in U.S. dollars per year. Per capita consumption and per capita government spending are calculated from the National Accounts figures as percentages of gross domestic product, which are then applied to per capita national income.

model, on a statewide or countywide basis. Other cross-section data could refer to the situations of firms, industries, families, households, or individuals at a given date. Such data are frequently obtained from surveys of the entities involved, e.g., questionnaires mailed to heads of households to obtain data at the household level.

Sometimes cross-section and time-series data are merged or "*pooled*". The result could be interpreted as a cross section of time series or a time series of cross sections. An example is given in Table 3.5, which is pooled cross-section-time-series data on per capita national income in market prices for selected countries, 1969–1972. (Note that two columns of this table have already been reported in two of the columns of Table 3.4.) Any column of the table is a cross section over countries for a particular year, and any row is a time series for a particular country.

In general, cross-section and time-series data yield different estimates of a model. These data and their resulting estimates are generally not comparable.

Table 3.5. Per Capita National Income in Market Prices in Selected Countries, 1969–1972

Country \ Variable	Per Capita National Income in Market Prices (in U. S. dollars)			
	1969	*1970*	*1971*	*1972*
North America				
United States	$4139	$4289	$4580	$4984
Canada	3109	3369	3755	4235
Western Europe				
Belgium	2177	2421	2733	3346
France	2492	2550	2831	3403
Germany, F. R.	2288	2752	3182	3769
Italy	1437	1591	1735	1984
Netherlands	2013	2232	2587	3165
Sweden	3372	3736	4025	4669
United Kingdom	1829	1990	2252	2503
Asia-Oceania				
Australia	2439	2633	2928	3426
Japan	1400	1649	1893	2439

Source United Nations, Department of Economic and Social Affairs, *Monthly Bulletin of Statistics*, January 1975, 29: xxvii–xxviii. (Also reported in United Nations, *Statistical Yearbook*, annual.)

For example, it is generally found that estimated income elasticities of demand using cross-section data are greater than those obtained using time-series data. Neither estimate is "wrong", and which one to use depends on the purpose. For structural analysis, in studying certain long-run elasticities it might be appropriate to use cross-section data, while for purposes of short-run forecasting time-series data might be appropriate.[5] Sometimes, if pooled data are available, certain parameters, e.g., income elasticities, are estimated using the cross-section data, and then other parameters, e.g., price elasticities, are estimated using time-series data.[6] This approach incorporates more information in the model, avoids certain problems with the data, and can be used to construct individual behavioral equations.

Panel data (or *longitudinal data*) are a special type of pooled cross-section-time-series data in which the same cross section is sampled over time. An example is panel data on family expenditure, where certain selected families keep records of their expenditures over several years. Another is the Nielsen ratings of the popularity of television shows. Panel data are generally *microdata* pertaining to individual economic agents, such as families or firms. Most of the data available for econometric research are, however, *macrodata*, pertaining to aggregates of individual agents. Microdata are generally preferable to macrodata since they

[5] In general, time-series data usually reflect short-run behavior while cross-section data reflect long-run behavior, in particular a greater adjustment to long-run equilibrium. See Meyer and Kuh (1957). See also the discussion in Kuznets (1966) of the inappropriateness of using cross-section data to make inferences about past long-term trends.

[6] See the discussion in Section 6.2.

avoid aggregation problems and allow one to estimate models containing behavioral relations applicable to individual agents.[7] Such data are generally not available, however, since they are expensive to obtain and their publication may reveal proprietary or confidential information.

3.4 Nonexperimental vs. experimental data

A third distinction that may be drawn is that between nonexperimental and experimental data. *Nonexperimental data* are obtained typically from observations of a system not subject to experimental control. By contrast, *experimental data* are obtained from a controlled experiment—that is, a situation in which the system or process under investigation is isolated from outside influences and, to whatever extent possible, influences on the system are subject to the control of the experimenter.

It has often been stated that an important aspect of the distinction between the social sciences and the natural sciences is the type of data each utilizes. Typically data utilized in the natural sciences are experimental, resulting from controlled experiments, while in the social sciences they are nonexperimental, in which the underlying conditions are not subject to control and cannot be replicated. Although generally valid, this distinction does not apply in all cases. The laboratory natural sciences, including chemistry and physics, typically do utilize controlled experiments. A physicist, for example, performing an experiment in high-energy physics will often utilize an accelerator—a controlled environment providing experimental data that can be replicated. Astrophysicists, however, generally cannot perform laboratory experiments but must instead rely upon observations over which they have no control. The same is true, in general, of meteorologists, geologists, and classical (but not molecular) biologists.

Conversely, while social scientists—including sociologists and political scientists as well as economists—generally rely on observational, nonexperimental data, much as the astrophysicists do, some social science experiments have generated experimental data. An example is the negative income tax experiments.[8] These experiments enrolled individuals and families in a program to test the effect of direct subsidies to those with incomes below a defined poverty level. The experimenters selected sites where they could achieve some isolation of the subjects from extraneous influences and could use control groups. Other large-scale social experiments have been conducted to test the influence of health insurance for the poor and near poor and to test the influence of housing allow-

[7] Of course, conclusions of a macroeconomic type can be obtained from micro relations only via aggregation. For a discussion of the use of microdata see Orcutt et al. (1961), and Orcutt (1962), who advocate the *microanalysis* of socioeconomic systems. An example of microdata is the U.S. National Longitudinal Surveys (NLS). These surveys obtained information on a variety of economic, educational, sociological, and other variables and their influence on labor-force behavior and work attitudes for four cohorts of the U.S. civilian population: men, age 45–59; women, age 30–44; young men, age 14–24; and young women, age 14–24, where ages refer to the beginning year of the survey. The surveys were conducted over a ten-year period, from the mid 1960s to the mid 1970s, for national probability samples of approximately 5000 individuals in each of these four groups. See Parnes (1975).

[8] See Cain and Watts (1973) and Kershaw and Fair (1976).

ances. The experimental data obtained in these experiments typically relate to groups of individuals or families enrolled in specific programs, and they generally include observations over several years. Thus they yield pooled cross-section-time-series data.

3.5 Problems with the data

Although experimental data are being collected in some situations, most econometric studies must rely on nonexperimental data. The problems these data present may be referred to, in the terminology of astronomy, as problems of "bad seeing".

The first is the *degrees-of-freedom problem*—that the available data simply do not include enough observations to allow an adequate estimate of the model. In the use of nonexperimental data it is impossible to replicate the conditions that gave rise to them, so additional data points cannot be generated. In some cases the available data may be inadequate for estimating a particular model but adequate for estimating a simpler model.

Second is the *multicollinearity problem*—the tendency of the data to bunch or move together rather than being "spread out". For example, in time-series data the variables tend to exhibit the same trends, cyclical and secular, over time. With experimental data it may be possible to vary the conditions of the experiment to obtain an adequate "spread". With nonexperimental data such control does not exist, and the real-world system may involve very small independent variation in the data, and in particular a high degree of interdependence among certain variables.

Third is the *serial-correlation problem*—the fact that, when using time-series data, underlying changes occur very slowly over time. Thus conditions in time periods close together tend to be similar. To the extent that the stochastic disturbance term represents conditions relevant to the model but not explicitly accounted for in it, such as omitted variables, serial correlation manifests itself in a dependence of the stochastic disturbance term in one period on that in another period.

Fourth is the *structural-change problem*—that there may have been a discontinuous change in the real world so that the data refer to different populations. An example for times-series data is a war period, which often must be excluded as being unrepresentative.

Fifth is the *errors-in-measurement problem*—that data are measured subject to various inaccuracies and biases. In fact data are sometimes revised because of a later recognition of these inaccuracies and biases. More fundamentally, potential inaccuracies result from a lack of precise correctness in conceptualization. For example, the GNP accounts are revised from time to time on the basis of such changes in conceptualization, e.g., defining what is included in consumption. Such changes in conceptualization necessitate the massaging of the data in order to make them comparable and consistent over time.

All of these problems will be treated in detail in later chapters, particularly in Chapter 6. Because of these problems the data are usually refined in several ways.

A refinement that helps overcome one of the problems, however, may aggravate one of the others. Thus, for example, replacing annual time-series data by quarterly data increases the number of data points, but tends to aggravate both the multicollinearity and the serial-correlation problems. Eliminating "unrepresentative" data points, such as those referring to unusual periods, like war years, helps overcome the structural-change problem but aggravates both the degrees-of-freedom and the multicollinearity problems. Replacing variables by their first differences can help overcome the serial-correlation problem but it can aggravate the errors-in-measurement problem. Clearly, judicious choices must be made in obtaining relevant and usable data from a set of raw data.

3.6 "Massaging" the data

The data obtained from various sources often must be "massaged" in various ways to make them usable in an econometric study. This massaging is performed in order to obtain a consistent set of data representing comparable series, which can be used to study specific phenomena under investigation. For time-series data massaging can take a variety of forms, including interpolation, extrapolation, splicing, and smoothing.[9]

Interpolation refers to the determination of values that lie between values that are known. In time-series data, for example, data on one or more variables for a particular period may be missing. The method used to obtain values for these missing observations is that of *interpolation.* The simplest case is *linear interpolation*, where a missing point is simply a linear combination of the given data points. Thus, if x_t is an observation or an estimate of a variable at time t and x_{t+2} is an observation or estimate of the same variable at time $t + 2$, the linearly interpolated estimate at time $t + 1$, assumed equally spaced between t and $t + 2$, is given as

$$\hat{x}_{t+1} = \frac{x_t + x_{t+2}}{2} \tag{3.6.1}$$

Another method of interpolation, *exponential interpolation*, uses the geometric mean

$$\hat{x}_{t+1} = \sqrt{x_t x_{t+2}} \tag{3.6.2}$$

which is linear in the logarithms of the variables. This method is equivalent to that of fitting an exponential function between x_t and x_{t+2}, so

$$\hat{x}_{t+1} = x_t e^{\alpha t} \quad \text{where} \quad x_{t+2} = x_{t+1} e^{\alpha t} = x_t e^{2\alpha t} \tag{3.6.3}$$

where α can be calculated from

[9] See Hannan (1960), Brown (1963), Granger and Hatanaka (1964), and Anderson (1971).

$$\alpha = \frac{1}{2t} \ln \frac{x_{t+2}}{x_t}. \tag{3.6.4}$$

The choice of method depends on the characteristics of the time series under study. For example, if the series involves linear (exponential) growth, then linear (exponential) interpolation would be appropriate.

Extrapolation is a related problem, involving the prediction of points beyond the given data set. This problem can arise in using time-series data, for example, if data are available on certain variables for more periods than they are available on other variables and if one wants to use a data set longer than the shortest period for which a complete set of data is available. The techniques of extrapolation are similar to those of interpolation. For example, under linear extrapolation, given x_t and x_{t+1} observations on the variable x, the extrapolated value at time $t + 2$, given as $\hat{x}_{t+2}$, satisfies

$$\hat{x}_{t+2} - x_{t+1} = x_{t+1} - x_t \quad \text{so} \quad \hat{x}_{t+2} = 2x_{t+1} - x_t. \tag{3.6.5}$$

Under exponential extrapolation

$$\hat{x}_{t+2} = x_{t+1}e^{\alpha t} \quad \text{where} \quad x_{t+1} = x_t e^{\alpha t} \tag{3.6.6}$$

so α can be calculated from

$$\alpha = \frac{1}{t} \ln \frac{x_{t+1}}{x_t}. \tag{3.6.7}$$

Further techniques of extrapolation are discussed in Section 4.10 on prediction and in Chapter 15 on forecasting, both of which refer to the same type of problem.

Splicing refers to the problem of massaging a series in order to make it consistent when the base changes. Such a problem arises frequently in using time-series data in index form, such as a consumer price index. This index is calculated relative to certain base levels of purchases of goods and services, and these base levels are periodically revised. The series must then be spliced at this point. Usually there are some points of overlap between the old and new series, so the new series can be simply multiplied by the old series level at the point of overlap (or by an average, if there are several points of overlap). Equivalently, the old series can be divided by the (average) level of the old series at the point of overlap. If no points of overlap are reported, it is possible to extrapolate the old series to obtain one or two points of overlap in order to splice the series.

Yet another type of massaging is *smoothing*, involving eliminating trend or cycle components. A national income model using time-series data, for example, usually requires the elimination of trends and cycles–especially if national income aggregates are being related to certain "real" economic phenomena, such as real wages. Elimination of the trend–for example, the exponential time trend $e^{\alpha t}$, where α is the "average" growth rate of the variable(s) in question–might be accomplished by replacing the original data x_t by the "massaged" data $\hat{x}_t$, defined by

$$\hat{x}_t = x_t e^{-\alpha t} = \frac{x_t}{e^{\alpha t}} \tag{3.6.8}$$

in which the time trend has been eliminated. Here the trend factor $e^{\alpha t}$ has been used to deflate the original data. Similarly, cycles can be taken out by

$$\hat{x}_t = \frac{x_t}{\cos(\theta t + \varphi)} \tag{3.6.9}$$

where $\cos(\theta t + \varphi)$ has been used to deflate the original data, θ being a measure of the frequency of the cycle and φ a measure of the phase shift. Such a technique can, for example, be applied to seasonal variables in order to perform a seasonal adjustment of the data on such variables.[10]

In general, any time series, say x_t, can be decomposed into four basic components—trend, T, representing long-term movements; cycle, C, representing sinusoidal movements; seasonal, S, representing cyclical movements within a period of a year; and irregular, I, representing residual movements. A multiplicative structure of the form

$$x = T \cdot C \cdot S \cdot I \tag{3.6.10}$$

is often assumed. Various methods are then available to isolate these components.[11] The series can be adjusted after they are isolated. If, for example, T and C in (3.6.10) are represented by

$$T = e^{\alpha t} \tag{3.6.11}$$

$$C = \cos(\theta t + \varphi) \tag{3.6.12}$$

as in (3.6.8) and (3.6.9), then the series

$$\hat{x}_t = \frac{x_t e^{-\alpha t}}{\cos(\theta t + \varphi)} \tag{3.6.13}$$

is the time series adjusted for both trend and cycle. Another example is based on taking logs of (3.6.10), where

$$y_t = f(t) + u_t. \tag{3.6.14}$$

Here y_t is log x_t; $f(t)$ represents the (log of the) trend, cycle, and seasonal components; and u_t is the log of I. Equation (3.6.14) decomposes an observed time

[10] A more sophisticated approach is that of spectral analysis. See Fishman (1969) and Dhrymes (1970), and, for an application of spectral analysis to seasonal adjustment, Nerlove (1964). Yet another approach is that of Box and Jenkins (1970), as discussed in Chapter 15.

[11] See Hannan (1960) and Anderson (1971). The methods of spectral analysis, for which references are given in the previous footnote, are applicable to isolating cyclical and seasonal components.

series y_t into "signal" $f(t)$ and "noise" u_t. If the signal tends to be less erratic than the noise, then the time series can be "smoothed" by taking moving averages of the y_t, such as the two-period moving average defined by

$$y'_t = \tfrac{1}{2}(y_t + y_{t-1}). \tag{3.6.15}$$

This process of smoothing eliminates unwanted random roughness in the data.[12]

Each of the several ways of "massaging" the data entails certain difficulties or problems. There is also a danger of "overmassaging" the data, producing questionable final results. Thus "massaging" should be utilized only when it is clearly necessary.

3.7 Accuracy of economic data

Several points must be emphasized about the accuracy of economic and other social science data. First, social science data are almost never precise or exact. Just as astronomers have the problem of "bad seeing", economists and other social scientists have very imperfect measures and measuring rods of the variables they study. In fact social science data are fundamentally less accurate than physical science data, since they are subject to additional inaccuracy in the measurement and reporting of human behavior. Newspaper accounts may refer to a rise of 0.2% in the consumer price index, but the index is so imprecise that such small changes have little meaning. Similarly, national income figures such as GNP or total consumption are often reported to the billion-dollar level of accuracy (or even tenths of billions) as in Table 3.2, implying an accuracy (for large industrialized economies) of better than 1%. Because of a variety of possible sources of error, however, including observation error, roundoff and approximation error, hiding of information, and errors of computation, national income measures probably involve inaccuracies of 15 per cent or more.[13] Both the "statistical discrepancy" that is part of the national account and the revisions of the preliminary national income series into final figures are consistent with this extent of inaccuracy, but nevertheless the preliminary figures (and final figures) are often naively taken as accurate to the last tenth of a billion dollars! In the physical sciences few observations are accurate to more than five significant digits, and probably no observations are even this accurate in the social sciences. Even a relatively simple problem such as counting the population is subject to several sources of inaccuracy. The reported population of the United States of 203,211,926 on April 1, 1970, for example, is probably accurate only to the first two figures.[14] It might better be reported as 203 ± 2 million. In general two, three, or four figures of accuracy are all that can be expected of social science data. Any more is specious accuracy, and it is improper to treat these data as of greater accuracy, a point that is very frequently overlooked or mis-

[12] See Problem 3-F.

[13] See Morgenstern (1963) for a detailed account of the sources of error in economic statistics. See also Leontief (1971).

[14] The population figure is reported in the U.S. Bureau of the Census, *Statistical Abstract of the United States, 1974*, Washington, D.C.: U.S. Government Printing Office.

understood. A classic (but apocryphal) example is that of a man who, when asked the age of a river, stated that it was 3,000,021 years old because in a book published 21 years earlier its age was given as 3 million years![15]

If counting population is subject to large inaccuracies, measuring economic quantities and prices is subject to even greater ones. All items on any balance sheet or profit and loss statement of any individual or firm are subject to inaccuracy. Many are based on arbitrary accounting conventions, others are measured subject to various biases, and all are subject to reporting and other errors. Data on prices are particularly inaccurate, given various discounts, tie-in sales, quality considerations, etc., which are typically not taken into account in price statistics.[16]

A second point to be made about social science data is that they vary considerably in their accuracy. Some are relatively precise, others relatively imprecise. In the physical sciences, particularly where experimentation is possible, the differences in accuracy of measurement are indicated numerically by error brackets. Some figures may be known with an accuracy of 3%, others with an accuracy of 0.1%, and yet others with an accuracy of 10%. In the social sciences, however, these error brackets are usually not provided, so one has only indirect evidence or subjective opinion as to the precision of reported data.[17]

A third point is that the errors in accuracy of economic data are generally not symmetric. There are often biases in one direction, so the error brackets are not equal in both directions. An example is total corporate profit as derived from corporate income tax returns. To the extent that corporations bias their profits downward to avoid paying taxes, the total figure may be subject to an error of 20% on the positive side but only 1% on the negative side.

The econometrician should always keep the inaccuracies of the data in mind. If an econometric study is not satisfactory in some sense, the temptation is typically to revise the model or try a different technique. Only infrequently will the data be investigated more carefully and further refined or else alternative data be utilized, yet often the data, rather than the model or the econometric technique, may be the source of unsatisfactory performance. The alternative of improving the data or obtaining new data should be seriously considered in such a situation.

3.8 Sources of economic data

There is a wide variety of sources of economic data. Among the most useful compilations at the national level are the statistical abstracts published by various

[15] Morgenstern (1963) presents this example. He also notes that the mathematician Norbert Wiener, after reading the first edition of *On the Accuracy of Economic Observations*, remarked that "economics is a one or two digit science".

[16] See Stigler and Kendahl (1970). Griliches, Ed. (1971) provides an example of an attempt to account for quality considerations in the prices of automobiles using "hedonic" price indexes. This study illustrates both the seriousness of the problem of quality change and the difficulties involved in overcoming it.

[17] For a formal treatment of accuracy of measurement see Section 6.9 on errors in the variables.

Table 3.6. Sources of Data

Sources: International

United Nations (Annual, since 1948)
Statistical Yearbook, New York: U.N.

United Nations (Monthly)
Monthly Bulletin of Statistics, New York: U.N.

United Nations (Annual)
Demographic Yearbook, New York: U.N.

United Nations (Annual)
Compendium of Social Statistics, New York: U.N.

United Nations (Annual)
Yearbook of National Accounts Statistics, New York: U.N.

United Nations (Annual)
Yearbook of International Trade Statistics, New York: U.N.

United Nations (1966)
The Growth of World Industry, 1953–1965, New York: U.N.

UNESCO (Annual)
Statistical Yearbook, Paris: U.N.

International Labour Office (Annual)
Yearbook of Labour Statistics, Geneva: ILO

World Health Organization (Annual)
World Health Statistics Annual, Geneva: WHO

Food and Agriculture Organization (Annual)
Production Yearbook, Rome: FAO

International Monetary Fund (Monthly)
International Financial Statistics, Washington: IMF

Organization for Economic Cooperation and Development (Monthly)
Main Economic Indicators, Paris: OECD

The Institute for Strategic Studies (Annual)
The Military Balance, London: ISS

Wasserman, Paul, and Joanne Paskar (1974)
Statistics Sources, 4th Ed., Detroit: Gale Research Co.

Kendall, M. G., and A. G. Doig (1962–1968)
Bibliography of Statistical Literature, Edinburgh: Oliver & Boyd

U.S., Bureau of Economic Analysis (1973)
Long Term Economic Growth, Washington, D.C.: U.S. Government Printing Office

U.S., Bureau of Labor Statistics (Monthly)
Monthly Labor Review, Washington, D.C.: U.S. Government Printing Office

U.S., Council of Economic Advisers (Annual)
Economic Report of the President, Washington, D.C.: U.S. Government Printing Office

U.S., Board of Governors of the Federal Reserve System (Monthly)
Federal Reserve Bulletin, Washington, D.C.: U.S. Government Printing Office

American Statistics Index (Annual)
Washington, D.C.: Congressional Information Service

Various States (Annual)
Statistical Abstract (or other similar title), e.g., *California Statistical Abstract, New York State Statistical Yearbook*, published by a state agency, a university, or other organization (See Appendix to the *Statistical Abstract of the United States*)

Andriot, J. L. (1973)
Guide to U.S. Government Statistics, 4th Ed., McLean, Virginia: Documents Index

Harvey, Joan M. (1971)
Sources of Statistics, 2nd Ed., Hamden, Conn.: Linnet Books

Morton, J. E. (1972)
"A Student's Guide to American Federal Government Statistics", *Journal of Economic Literature*, 10: 371–97

Wasserman, Paul and Joanne Paskar (1974)
Statistics Sources, 4th Ed., Detroit: Gale Research Co.

National Bureau of Economic Research
Various publications, New York: NBER

Sources: United States

U.S., Department of Commerce, Bureau of the Census, (Annual, since 1878) *Statistical Abstract of the United States*, Washington, D.C.: U.S. Government Printing Office

U.S., Department of Commerce, Bureau of the Census (1976) *Historical Statistics of the United States, Colonial Times to 1970*, Washington, D.C.: U.S. Government Printing Office

U.S., Department of Commerce, Bureau of the Census (Monthly) *Business Conditions Digest*, Washington, D.C.: U.S. Government Printing Office

U.S., Bureau of Economic Analysis (Monthly) *Survey of Current Business*, Washington, D.C.: U.S. Government Printing Office

Sources: Canada

Canada, Bureau of Statistics (Annual, since 1905) *The Canada Yearbook*, Ottawa

Harvey, Joan M. (1973) *Statistics America*, Beckenham: C.B.D. Research, Ltd.

Urquhart, M. C., and K. A. H. Buckley, Eds. (1965) *Historical Statistics of Canada*, New York: Cambridge University Press

Mueller, B. (1965) *A Statistical Handbook of the North Atlantic Area*, New York: Twentieth Century Fund

Sources: Europe

Harvey, Joan M. (1972) *Statistics Europe*, 2nd Ed., Beckenham: C.B.D. Research, Ltd.

Harvey, Joan M. (1971) *Sources of Statistics*, 2nd Ed., Hamden, Conn.: Linnet Books

Kendall, M. G., and A. G. Doig (1962–1968) *Bibliography of Statistical Literature*, Edinburgh: Oliver & Boyd; Vol. 1: 1950–1958; Vol. 2, 1940–1949; Vol. 3, Pre-1940, 1962–1968

United Kingdom (Annual, since 1854) *Statistical Abstract*, London: HMSO

Sources: Other

Harvey, Joan M. (1970) *Statistics Africa*, Beckenham: C.B.D. Research, Ltd.

Harvey, Joan M. (1973) *Statistics America*, Beckenham: C.B.D. Research, Ltd.

national governments. These usually summarize the detailed studies and refer to a single year. Cross-section data can often be found within the statistical abstract for one year, while time-series data can be constructed by comparing the abstracts over several years. For example, for the United States, the *Statistical Abstract of the United States*, published annually by the U.S. Bureau of the Census, is an excellent starting point for finding data at the national and statewide levels. A companion volume, *Historical Statistics of the United States*, also published by the U.S. Department of Commerce, provides summary statistics on the United States back to colonial times. For many of the tables in the current *Statistical Abstract of the United States* comparable statistical time series are reported in *Historical Statistics of the United States.*

An excellent overall reference for data and data sources at the national and international levels is the *Statistical Yearbook*, published annually by the United Nations.

Table 3.6 summarizes some useful published sources of data for economic studies.[18] The major sources are various government agencies, which generally provide macrodata on an annual basis. In an effort to protect confidentiality, microdata pertaining to individuals or firms are generally not available or not released. Some special studies have, however, obtained such microdata.[19] As to the time period covered, certain data are now regularly reported on a quarterly, monthly, or weekly basis, but the annual period still predominates. Some private groups have generated data on specialized topics, of which perhaps the most important for the United States are business-cycle and other data compiled by the National Bureau of Economic Research.

PROBLEMS

3-A Show that a dummy variable can take any two arbitrary values, not just 0 and 1. Give an example of such a case.

3-B Show that a dummy variable distinguishing between two characteristics introduces no scaling effect, while one distinguishing between more than two characteristics introduces a scaling effect; i.e., the estimated coefficients are sensitive to the particular choice of values assumed by the dummy variable.

3-C Suppose the ITC dummy variable in (3.2.1) affects only the slope coefficient γ_2. How should the equation be specified?

3-D Suppose a study must distinguish between sex (male, female), race (white, nonwhite), and location (urban, suburban, rural).

1. How many different characteristics must be distinguished?
2. What is the minimum number of dummy variables needed to distinguish these characteristics? How could they be defined?

3-E Show how six different characteristics can be distinguished by 3, 4, 5, or 6 dummy variables.

3-F In discussing smoothing, based on (3.6.14) $y_t = f(t) + u_t$, assume u_t is a random variable for which

$$
\begin{aligned}
E(u_t) &= 0 \\
E(u_t^2) &= \text{Var}\,(u_t) = \sigma^2 \\
E(u_t u_{t+s}) &= 0, \quad s \neq 0.
\end{aligned}
$$

Consider the weighted moving average

[18] Yet other sources of data are the several large computerized data banks available through Data Resources, Incorporated, Chase Econometric Associates, the National Bureau of Economic Research, and other organizations. See, for example, Data Resources, Incorporated (1976).

[19] An example is the U.S. Census Survey summarizing microdata obtained from a 1/1000 sample and available on computer tape.

$$y_t^* = \sum_{s=-m}^{m} c_s y_{t+s}$$

where the coefficients c_s are nonnegative and normalized to sum to unity. Thus

$$y_t^* = \sum_{s=-m}^{m} c_s f(t + s) + u_t^* \quad \text{where} \quad u_t^* = \sum_{s=-m}^{m} c_s u_{t+s}.$$

Find the variance of u_t^* and prove that it is less than σ^2, the variance of u_t. What is $E(u_t^* u_{t+s}^*)$?

BIBLIOGRAPHY

Anderson, T. W. (1971), *The Statistical Analysis of Time Series.* New York: John Wiley & Sons, Inc.

Box, G. E. P., and G. M. Jenkins (1970), *Time Series Analysis; Forecasting and Control.* San Francisco: Holden-Day & Co.

Brown, R. G. (1963), *Smoothing, Forecasting and Prediction of Discrete Time Series.* Englewood Cliffs, N.J.: Prentice-Hall, Inc.

Cain, G. G., and H. W. Watts, Eds. (1973), *Income Maintenance and Labor Supply.* New York: Academic Press, Inc.

Data Resources, Incorporated (1976), *The Data Resources National Economic Information System.* Amsterdam: North-Holland Publishing Co.

Dhrymes, P. (1970), *Econometrics.* New York: Harper & Row, Publishers.

Fishman, G. S. (1969), *Spectral Methods in Econometrics.* Cambridge: Harvard University Press.

Granger, C. W. J., and M. Hatanaka (1964), *Spectral Analyses of Economic Time Series.* Princeton: Princeton University Press.

Griliches, Z., Ed. (1971), *Price Indexes and Quality Change.* Cambridge: Harvard University Press.

Hannan, E. J. (1960), *Time Series Analysis.* New York: John Wiley & Sons, Inc.

Kershaw, D. and J. Fair (1976), *The New Jersey Income-Maintenance Experiment.* New York: Academic Press, Inc.

Kuznets, S. (1966), *Modern Economic Growth.* New Haven: Yale University Press.

Leontief, W. W. (1971), "Theoretical Assumptions and Nonobserved Facts," *American Economic Review*, 61: 1–7.

Meyer, J., and E. Kuh (1957), "How Extraneous Are Extraneous Estimates?" *Review of Economics and Statistics*, 39: 380–93.

Morgenstern, O. (1963), *On the Accuracy of Economic Observations*, 2nd Ed. Princeton: Princeton University Press.

Nerlove, M. (1964), "Spectral Analysis of Seasonal Adjustment Procedures," *Econometrica*, 32: 241–86.

Orcutt, G. H. (1962), "Microanalytic Models of the United States Economy: Need and Development," *American Economic Review*, 52: 229–40.

Orcutt, G. H., M. Greenberger, J. Korbel, and A. M. Rivlin (1961), *Microanalysis of Socioeconomic Systems: A Simulation Study*. New York: Harper & Row, Publishers.

Parnes, H. S. (1975), "The National Longitudinal Surveys: New Vistas for Labor Market Research," *American Economic Review*, 65: 244–49.

Stigler, G. J., and J. K. Kindahl (1970), *The Behavior of Industrial Prices*. National Bureau of Economic Research. New York: Columbia University Press.

PART III

Single-Equation Estimation

CHAPTER 4

The Basic Linear Regression Model

4.1 The linear regression model

The problem of single-equation estimation is that of determining estimates of the parameters of the equation. If the equation is linear in these parameters, the problem of estimation is that of obtaining numerical values for the coefficients—that is, values for the parameters multiplying each of the variables of the equation and for the intercept. Given the econometric model developed in Chapter 2 and the data discussed in Chapter 3, a major problem of single equation estimation is that of estimating the parameters of each of the reduced-form equations.[1] The reduced form of an econometric model can be written, as in (2.8.15),

$$\underset{1\times g}{\mathbf{y}} = \underset{1\times k}{\mathbf{x}}\ \underset{k\times g}{\boldsymbol{\Pi}} + \underset{1\times g}{\mathbf{u}} \qquad *(4.1.1)$$

where $\mathbf{y}$ is a vector of g endogenous variables; $\mathbf{x}$ is a vector of k exogenous variables, assumed nonstochastic; $\mathbf{u}$ is a vector of g stochastic disturbance terms; and $\boldsymbol{\Pi}$ is a matrix of kg coefficients. Each column of the $\boldsymbol{\Pi}$ matrix of reduced-form coefficients contains all the parameters to be estimated in the corresponding equation, where the hth equation in the set of reduced-form equations can be written

$$y_h = \sum_{j=1}^{k} x_j \Pi_{jh} + u_h, \qquad h = 1, 2, \ldots, g \qquad *(4.1.2)$$

as in (2.8.17). The problem of estimating the k parameters in equation (4.1.2), $\Pi_{1h}, \Pi_{2h}, \ldots, \Pi_{kh}$, is one of single-equation estimation, and the problem of estimating the reduced form is that of estimating all g equations of this form.

The notation used in (4.1.2) could be utilized in all that follows, but it would be both cumbersome and tedious to carry along the index h. Instead, the h subscript will be dropped and the parameters will be written as β's rather than Π's, so the equation becomes

[1] The estimation of the structural-form equations entails certain problems—primarily the inclusion of explanatory endogenous variables—and will be discussed in Chapter 11. The reduced form does not entail these problems. Furthermore, the estimation of the reduced form is typically the first step in estimating the structural form. Thus the emphasis here is on the reduced form.

$$y = \sum_{j=1}^{k} x_j \beta_j + u. \qquad *(4.1.3)$$

This is the typical regression equation—one that is linear in the parameters $\beta_1, \beta_2, \ldots, \beta_k$ and that has an additive stochastic disturbance term u. This switch in notation will serve to remind the reader that only one of the reduced-form equations is being treated. It also is consistent with the notation used elsewhere. The problem of single-equation estimation is then that of estimating the k parameters in (4.1.3), $\beta_1, \beta_2, \ldots, \beta_k$. This equation can also be expressed in matrix notation as

$$y = \mathbf{x}\,\boldsymbol{\beta} + u = (x_1 \;\; x_2 \; \cdots x_k)\begin{pmatrix}\beta_1\\ \beta_2\\ \vdots\\ \beta_k\end{pmatrix} + u \qquad *(4.1.4)$$

where, as shown, $\mathbf{x}$ is a row vector and $\boldsymbol{\beta}$ is a column vector, each with k entries. In fact, $\mathbf{x}$ is exactly the same as before, as in (4.1.1), while $\boldsymbol{\beta}$ is one column of the $\boldsymbol{\Pi}$ matrix, and y and u are the corresponding elements of $\mathbf{y}$ and $\mathbf{u}$ respectively. It will cause no confusion to have y represent a single element of $\mathbf{y}$; it will always be clear that y is one endogenous variable while $\mathbf{y}$ is a vector of g endogenous variables. Similarly for u and $\mathbf{u}$. Of course in the special case of an econometric model with one endogenous variable, (4.1.4) is the whole reduced form; in that case $\boldsymbol{\beta}$ is the one column of the $\boldsymbol{\Pi}$ matrix.

Equation (4.1.4) or equivalently (4.1.3), specifying which variables are included, which variable is dependent (endogenous), and which variables are explanatory (exogenous), together with certain assumptions as to the distribution of the stochastic disturbance term, represents the *basic linear regression model*. It is an algebraic, linear, stochastic model, which may be static or dynamic. The case in which there are two parameters to estimate ($k = 2$) can be interpreted as that of estimating the slope and intercept of a line where β_2 is the intercept if $x_2 \equiv 1$. This case of one explanatory variable, where $k = 2$, is that of *simple linear regression*. In the more general case of one or more explanatory variable, where $k \geqslant 2$, the problem is one of *multiple linear regression.*[2] The purpose of such a regression is to estimate how two or more variables are related in order to analyze their interconnections, where one variable, the dependent or endogenous variable, is determined by one or more explanatory or exogenous variables. Estimation of the regression facilitates the analysis of the separate effects of the explanatory variables, which act together to influence the dependent variable. The estimated regression coefficients summarize quantitatively the effect of a change in any one explanatory variable on the value of the dependent variable. In particular, if $\hat{\beta}_j$ is the estimated value of the jth regression coefficient in (4.1.4), then

[2] Basic references on regression in econometrics include Christ (1966), Malinvaud (1970), Theil (1971), and Schmidt (1976). Much of this material is also presented in basic statistics books, such as Mood and Graybill (1963) and Hoel (1971). See also Williams (1959), Plackett (1960), and Draper and Smith (1966).

$$\hat{\beta}_j = \frac{\partial y}{\partial x_j}, \quad j = 1, 2, \ldots, k \tag{4.1.5}$$

is an estimate of the influence of the jth explanatory variable on y.

4.2 Data for the basic linear regression model

The econometric approach requires, in addition to an econometric model, data on its variables. These data are used to estimate the model's parameters. In the case of the general linear model (4.1.4) a sample of data takes the form of a vector of n observed values of the dependent (endogenous) variable y and a matrix of n observed values of the vector of explanatory (exogenous) variables $\mathbf{x}$, written

$$\underset{n \times 1}{\mathbf{y}} = \begin{pmatrix} y_1 \\ y_2 \\ \vdots \\ y_n \end{pmatrix}, \quad \underset{n \times k}{\mathbf{X}} = \begin{pmatrix} \mathbf{x}_1 \\ \mathbf{x}_2 \\ \vdots \\ \mathbf{x}_n \end{pmatrix} = \begin{pmatrix} x_{11} & x_{12} & \cdots & x_{1k} \\ x_{21} & x_{22} & \cdots & x_{2k} \\ \vdots & \vdots & & \\ x_{n1} & x_{n2} & \cdots & x_{nk} \end{pmatrix}. \tag*{*(4.2.1)}$$

The elements of $\mathbf{y}$ are the numbers y_i, where y_i is the value of the variable y at observation i, i being an index of observations. Here $i = 1, 2, \ldots, n$, where n is the sample size.[3] [It will always be clear from the context whether $\mathbf{y}$ is a (column) vector of n data points on one dependent variable, as in (4.2.1), or $\mathbf{y}$ is a (row) vector of g dependent variables, as in (4.1.1).] The elements of $\mathbf{X}$ are the numbers x_{ij}, where x_{ij} is the value of the variable x_j at the observation i. Equivalently, the rows of $\mathbf{X}$ are the vectors $\mathbf{x}_i$, where $\mathbf{x}_i$ consists of values taken by each of the k explanatory variables at observation i:

$$\mathbf{x}_i = (x_{i1}\ x_{i2}\ \ldots\ x_{ik}), \qquad i = 1, 2, \ldots, n. \tag{4.2.2}$$

Thus each of the n rows of the $\mathbf{X}$ matrix represents the set of observed values of all explanatory variables at a particular observation, while each of the k columns of the $\mathbf{X}$ matrix represents the set of all observed values for one explanatory variable.

It will generally be assumed that there are more data points than parameters to be estimated, so that n, the sample size, exceeds k, the number of parameters in $\boldsymbol{\beta}$, the coefficient vector to be estimated in (4.1.4). The meaning of this assumption should be clear. Consider, for example, the case of simple linear regression, in which a line is to be fitted. The basic linear regression model (4.1.4) becomes

[3] In general i will index the observation, whether the data represent a cross section or a time series. In certain contexts in which time-series data are used, however, i will be replaced by the time index t.

$$y = \beta_1 x + \beta_2 + u = (x \quad 1) \begin{pmatrix} \beta_1 \\ \beta_2 \end{pmatrix} + u \qquad *(4.2.3)$$

with suitable assumptions as to the stochastic disturbance term u. Here $k = 2$, and the parameters represent the slope (β_1) and intercept (β_2) of the line. The data of (4.2.1) become

$$\mathbf{y} = \begin{pmatrix} y_1 \\ y_2 \\ \vdots \\ y_n \end{pmatrix}, \quad \mathbf{X} = \begin{pmatrix} x_1 & 1 \\ x_2 & 1 \\ \vdots & \vdots \\ x_n & 1 \end{pmatrix} \qquad (4.2.4)$$

which can be represented as the n points (x_i, y_i) in Figure 4.1, where $n = 5$. Note that the 1's in the last column of the $\mathbf{X}$ matrix take account of the intercept term. The problem in this case is that of fitting a line through these points. Clearly, if $n = 1$, there would be only one point, and through this point an infinite number of lines could be drawn. If $n = 2$, then there is generally one unique line–two points determine a line–so the problem is not a statistical one. Only if $n > 2$ does the problem of fitting a line become a statistical one, such as the case shown for which $n = 5$.

The difference between n and k, that is, the difference between the number

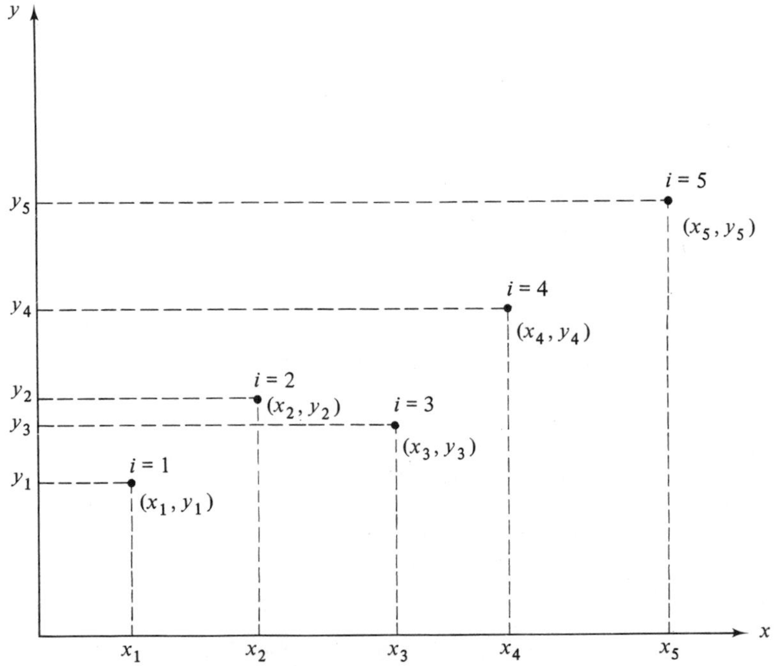

Figure 4.1 Five Data Points in the Case of Simple Linear Regression ($k = 2$, $n = 5$)

of rows and the number of columns of **X**, is referred to as the *degrees of freedom* of the problem, d.f., and the assumption that there are more data points than parameters to be estimated becomes the assumption of positive degrees of freedom.

$$\text{d.f.} = n - k > 0 \qquad *(4.2.5)$$

This is called the *degrees-of-freedom assumption.*

It will also generally be assumed that the k explanatory variables in the **X** matrix are linearly independent. The assumption states that no column of the **X** matrix can be written as a linear combination of other columns of the matrix, so that these columns are linearly independent vectors. A convenient way of writing this assumption is to require that the **X** matrix have full column rank

$$\rho(\mathbf{X}) = k \qquad *(4.2.6)$$

–that is, to require that there exists a $k \times k$ submatrix of **X** with a determinant that does not equal zero, so the columns of the **X** matrix are linearly independent. This is called the *rank assumption*. If the rank assumption is not satisfied, the data on the explanatory variables are not independent. For example, in the simplest case of Figure 4.1, if all five points had the same x-value, then the first column of the **X** matrix would be this common x value times the second column of ones, and hence the rank of the matrix would be 1, violating the rank assumption. In this case the regression line would be vertical, and the problem would not be a statistical one. Thus the rank assumption in the simplest case of one explanatory variable requires that the values taken by this variable not all "bunch up." It might be noted that the rank assumption (4.2.6) implies the degrees-of-freedom assumption (4.2.5), since if $n < k$, then the **X** matrix could not have rank k. Thus the major assumption to be made is the rank assumption.

4.3 The nature of regression analysis

Regression analysis entails the estimation of a model's parameters using data on its variables. Thus, any regression involves three basic components: The first is a model, such as the linear model of (4.1.4). The second is a set of data, such as those of (4.2.1). The third is a method of estimation–that is, a method of transforming the data, here represented by **y** and **X**, into estimators of the values of the parameters of the model, $\hat{\boldsymbol{\beta}}$. An *estimator* is simply a rule or method for combining data in order to determine the value of a parameter, and an *estimate* is a numerical value for a parameter.

There are, in fact, several possible methods of estimation. They will be illustrated here in terms of the simplest example of Figure 4.1, for which the problem is that of estimating the intercept and slope of a line from a sample of more than two data points.

Perhaps the simplest approach is the graphical one of *fitting by eye*, involving the plotting of all the points on a chart and fitting the "best" line by eye. This method can sometimes work reasonably well and in fact has been the basis of many empirical studies. Its drawbacks should, however, be obvious. It is imprecise and subjective, different individuals obtaining different estimates. Also, it is difficult or impossible to generalize to more than one independent variable. The case of two independent variables can be depicted in three dimensions, and it is possible, with some effort, to fit by eye a line between four or more points in this space. With more than two independent variables, however, the method is unworkable.

Next in order of generality and usefulness are the *naive methods*. These involve reducing the number of data points to the number of parameters to be estimated and then fitting an exact equation for the ensuing zero-degrees-of-freedom problem. There are many variants of this method, but perhaps the simplest is to take, in the simple linear regression problem of Figure 4.1, the two data points representing the lowest and highest value of the explanatory variable, points 1 and 5 in the figure, ignoring all intermediate points, and to fit a line between these two points. This method is simple, exact, and capable of generalization to higher dimensions. It was used to calculate the arc elasticity and to estimate the marginal propensity to consume in the examples of Sections 1.4 and 1.5, respectively. It does, however, ignore relevant information, specifically information contained in the other available data points. Variants of this method may even utilize all points in the sample, but they are still "naive" in eventually resulting in a problem with zero degrees of freedom. For example, one approach would be to divide the sample into two subsamples, such as one containing points 1 and 2 and another containing points 3, 4, and 5 in Figure 4.1. The mean values of x and y in each subsample would then be calculated as

$$\begin{aligned} \bar{x}_1 &= \frac{x_1 + x_2}{2}, & \bar{y}_1 &= \frac{y_1 + y_2}{2} \\ \bar{x}_2 &= \frac{x_3 + x_4 + x_5}{3}, & \bar{y}_2 &= \frac{y_3 + y_4 + y_5}{3} \end{aligned} \tag{4.3.1}$$

and a line would be fitted between the two mean points $(\bar{x}_1, \bar{y}_1)$ and $(\bar{x}_2, \bar{y}_2)$, yielding estimators

$$\hat{\beta}_1 = \frac{\bar{y}_2 - \bar{y}_1}{\bar{x}_2 - \bar{x}_1}, \qquad \hat{\beta}_2 = \frac{\bar{x}_2\bar{y}_1 - \bar{x}_1\bar{y}_2}{\bar{x}_2 - \bar{x}_1} \tag{4.3.2}$$

for the slope and intercept, respectively.[4]

In fact, two general methods will be emphasized here, since they form the basis of modern econometric techniques. The first is *least squares* and the second is *maximum likelihood*. As their names imply, they obtain estimates of the vector of parameters $\boldsymbol{\beta}$ by respectively minimizing or maximizing certain

[4] A generalization of this approach, called "Wald's method of fitting straight lines," involves dividing the observations into two groups and estimating the slope by connecting the centers of gravity of the two groups. While this method is naive in reducing the problem to one with zero degrees of freedom, it does have some value in certain situations, e.g., the errors-in-variables model of Section 6.9.

functions, which are evaluated using the data of the problem. The next two sections will develop least squares and maximum likelihood estimators in the case of simple linear regression, while Sections 4.6 and 4.7 will develop least squares and maximum likelihood estimators for the case of multiple linear regression.

4.4 Least squares: the case of simple linear regression

In the case of simple linear regression there is one explanatory variable, and the model specifies that

$$y = \beta_1 x + \beta_2 + u \qquad *(4.4.1)$$

where y is the dependent variable; x is the explanatory variable, assumed non-stochastic (fixed); u is the stochastic disturbance term; and β_1 and β_2 are the slope and intercept parameters. Indexing the variables by i over the sample and adding certain assumptions on the stochastic disturbance term yield the *basic linear regression model for simple linear regression*:

$$\begin{array}{lll} y_i & = \beta_1 x_i + \beta_2 + u_i & \text{all } i, \; i = 1, 2, \ldots, n \\ E(u_i) & = 0 & \text{all } i \\ \text{Var}\,(u_i) & = \sigma^2 < \infty & \text{all } i \\ \text{Cov}\,(u_i u_j) & = 0 & \text{all } i, j, \; i \neq j \\ \quad x_i \text{ is fixed} & & \text{all } i \end{array} \qquad *(4.4.2)$$

Here y_i and x_i represent values taken by the dependent variable and explanatory variable at the ith observation, and the parameters to be estimated on the basis of these observed sample values are β_1, β_2, and σ^2.

The stochastic assumptions in (4.4.2) concern the stochastic disturbance terms u_i, which are unobservable random variables (see Appendix C). They state that each of the stochastic disturbance terms has a zero mean, that all stochastic disturbances have the same (finite) variance, and that each pair of stochastic disturbance terms has a zero covariance. The zero mean of the stochastic disturbance terms

$$E(u_i) = 0, \qquad i = 1, 2, \ldots, n \qquad *(4.4.3)$$

is consistent with the interpretation of the u_i as *disturbance* terms, and it is called the *disturbance assumption*. According to it, "on average" the model is "correct" in that

$$E(y_i) = \beta_1 x_i + \beta_2 + E(u_i) = \beta_1 x_i + \beta_2. \qquad *(4.4.4)$$

The identical finite variance of the stochastic disturbance terms

$$\text{Var}\,(u_i) = E(u_i - E(u_i))^2 = E(u_i^2) = \sigma^2 < \infty, \qquad i = 1, 2, \ldots, n \qquad *(4.4.5)$$

is referred to as the *assumption of homoskedasticity*. By contrast, if the variances are not the same over the sample (or are infinite), then the situation is one of *heteroskedasticity*. The zero covariances of the stochastic disturbance terms

$$\begin{aligned} \text{Cov}(u_i u_j) &= E[(u_i - E(u_i))(u_j - E(u_j))] \\ &= E(u_i u_j) = 0, \quad i, j = 1, 2, \ldots, n; i \neq j \end{aligned} \tag{4.4.6}$$

is referred to as the *absence of serial correlation*. All three of these stochastic assumptions are of considerable importance, and situations in which they are not met are treated in detail in Chapter 6 on problems in the basic linear regression model.

The problem of estimation is that of obtaining estimates $\hat{\beta}_1$ and $\hat{\beta}_2$ of the parameters β_1 and β_2, given specific numerical data on the explanatory and dependent variables (x_i, y_i) for $i = 1, 2, \ldots, n$ such as in Figure 4.1, where $n = 5$. With such estimates $\hat{\beta}_1$ and $\hat{\beta}_2$, the dependent variable can be predicted as

$$\hat{y}_i = \hat{\beta}_1 x_i + \hat{\beta}_2. \tag{4.4.7}$$

The method of least squares proceeds by defining, for specific numerical estimates $\hat{\beta}_1$ and $\hat{\beta}_2$, the *residual* at observation i as

$$\hat{u}_i = y_i - \hat{y}_i = y_i - \hat{\beta}_1 x_i - \hat{\beta}_2, \quad i = 1, 2, \ldots, n. \tag*{*(4.4.8)}$$

These residuals can be interpreted as sample realizations of the stochastic disturbance terms u_i in (4.4.2). While the stochastic disturbance terms u_i in (4.4.2) are unknown and unobservable, the residuals $\hat{u}_i$ defined in (4.4.8) are based upon the estimates $\hat{\beta}_1$ and $\hat{\beta}_2$. A set of residuals is shown in Figure 4.2 for the data of Figure 4.1 and a particular (nonoptimal) choice of $\hat{\beta}_1$ and $\hat{\beta}_2$. In this case $\hat{u}_1$, $\hat{u}_2$, and $\hat{u}_3$ are negative, while $\hat{u}_4$ and $\hat{u}_5$ are positive. In general, some of the residuals will be positive and some will be negative. One way to eliminate the sign, which also turns out to be convenient in the method of analysis, is to square the residuals.[5] The process of squaring is the reason for the terminology least *squares*. Squaring each residual and adding up all the resulting squared residuals gives the *sum of squares* S for any $\hat{\beta}_1$ and $\hat{\beta}_2$:

$$S = \sum_{i=1}^{n} \hat{u}_i^2 = \sum_{i=1}^{n} (y_i - \hat{\beta}_1 x_i - \hat{\beta}_2)^2. \tag*{*(4.4.9)}$$

The method of least squares then entails minimizing the sum of squares S by choice of the parameters $\hat{\beta}_1$ and $\hat{\beta}_2$. In terms of Figure 4.2 the line is rotated about the intercept, shifting the slope $\hat{\beta}_1$, and moved up and down in a parallel fashion, shifting the intercept $\hat{\beta}_2$, until the sum of the squared residuals, which

[5] Another way to avoid the problem of residuals with different signs is to take the absolute values of the residuals [see Fisher (1961)] or to raise the absolute value to some power. These alternative approaches, however, are less tractable mathematically than the commonly used process of squaring the residuals.

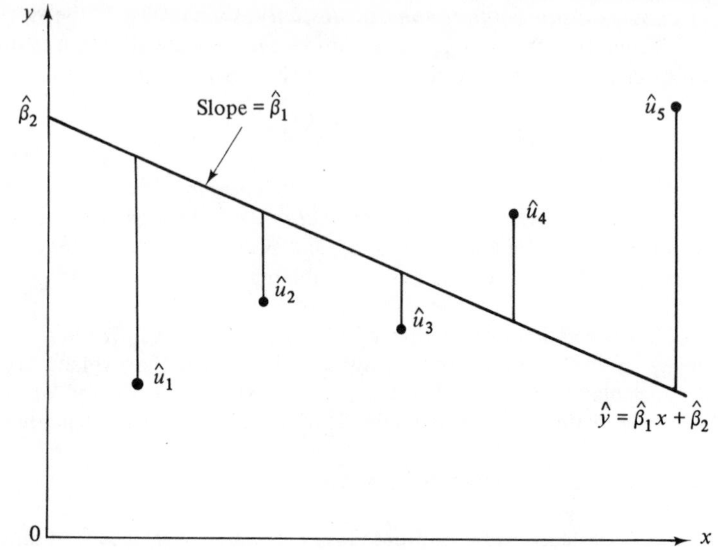

Figure 4.2 Definition of Residuals Once a Line Is Drawn.
[NOTE Compare with Figure 4.3.]

can be interpreted as the total error, is a minimum. Thus the least squares estimators are obtained as the values $\hat{\beta}_1$ and $\hat{\beta}_2$ that solve the problem:

$$\min_{\hat{\beta}_1 \hat{\beta}_2} S = S(\hat{\beta}_1, \hat{\beta}_2) = \sum_{i=1}^{n} \hat{u}_i^2 = \sum_{i=1}^{n} (y_i - \hat{\beta}_1 x_i - \hat{\beta}_2)^2. \qquad *(4.4.10)$$

The necessary and sufficient conditions for minimizing the sum of squares $S = S(\hat{\beta}_1, \hat{\beta}_2)$ are that both first-order partial derivatives vanish[6]

$$\frac{\partial S}{\partial \hat{\beta}_1} = -\sum_{i=1}^{n} 2(y_i - \hat{\beta}_1 x_i - \hat{\beta}_2)x_i = 0 \qquad (4.4.11)$$

$$\frac{\partial S}{\partial \hat{\beta}_2} = -\sum_{i=1}^{n} 2(y_i - \hat{\beta}_1 x_i - \hat{\beta}_2) = 0 \qquad (4.4.12)$$

These two equations can be written

$$\hat{\beta}_1 \sum x_i^2 + \hat{\beta}_2 \sum x_i = \sum x_i y_i \qquad *(4.4.13)$$

$$\hat{\beta}_1 \sum x_i + \hat{\beta}_2 n = \sum y_i \qquad *(4.4.14)$$

[6] See Intriligator (1971) for a discussion of necessary and sufficient conditions for minimizing or maximizing functions subject to various constraints. Here conditions (4.4.11) and (4.4.12) are both necessary and sufficient for a minimum of S, as will be shown below. Note that here the sample values (x_i, y_i) are assumed fixed and given, and the parameters $\hat{\beta}_1$ and $\hat{\beta}_2$ are chosen to minimize S.

Where, in (4.4.14), $\Sigma 1$ has been replaced by n, since all summations range from 1 to n. Note that (4.4.14) implies that the sum of the residuals is zero:

$$\Sigma \hat{u}_i = \Sigma(y_i - \hat{\beta}_1 x_i - \hat{\beta}_2) = 0 \tag{4.4.15}$$

and that (4.4.13) implies that the residuals and the values of the explanatory variable are uncorrelated:

$$\Sigma \hat{u}_i x_i = \Sigma(y_i - \hat{\beta}_1 x_i - \hat{\beta}_2)x_i = 0. \tag{4.4.16}$$

These two equations are referred to as the *normal equations* of least squares. They represent two equations in two unknowns, $\hat{\beta}_1$ and $\hat{\beta}_2$. Solving then via Cramer's rule yields[7]

$$\hat{\beta}_1 = \frac{\begin{vmatrix} \Sigma x_i y_i & \Sigma x_i \\ \Sigma y_i & n \end{vmatrix}}{\begin{vmatrix} \Sigma x_i^2 & \Sigma x_i \\ \Sigma x_i & n \end{vmatrix}} = \frac{n \Sigma x_i y_i - (\Sigma x_i)(\Sigma y_i)}{n \Sigma x_i^2 - (\Sigma x_i)^2} \tag*{*(4.4.17)}$$

$$\hat{\beta}_2 = \frac{\begin{vmatrix} \Sigma x_i^2 & \Sigma x_i y_i \\ \Sigma x_i & \Sigma y_i \end{vmatrix}}{\begin{vmatrix} \Sigma x_i^2 & \Sigma x_i \\ \Sigma x_i & n \end{vmatrix}} = \frac{\Sigma y_i \Sigma x_i^2 - \Sigma x_i \Sigma x_i y_i}{n \Sigma x_i^2 - (\Sigma x_i)^2} \tag*{*(4.4.18)}$$

and these are the unique *least-squares estimators*. They may be written in somewhat more compact notation by shifting the origin of Figure 4.2 and measuring both variables in terms of deviations from the mean values of $\bar{x}$ and $\bar{y}$, defined by

$$\bar{x} = \frac{1}{n} \Sigma x_i, \quad \bar{y} = \frac{1}{n} \Sigma y_i. \tag{4.4.19}$$

Letting $\dot{x}_i$ and $\dot{y}_i$ be deviations from mean values, defined by

$$\dot{x}_i = x_i - \bar{x}, \quad \dot{y}_i = y_i - \bar{y} \tag{4.4.20}$$

the normal equations can be written

$$\hat{\beta}_1 (\Sigma \dot{x}_i^2 + n\bar{x}^2) + \hat{\beta}_2 n\bar{x} = \Sigma \dot{x}_i \dot{y}_i + n\bar{x}\bar{y} \tag{4.4.21}$$

$$\hat{\beta}_1 n\bar{x} + \hat{\beta}_2 n = n\bar{y}. \tag{4.4.22}$$

From (4.4.22) it follows that the fitted line must pass through the mean point $(\bar{x}, \bar{y})$, so

[7] For a discussion of Cramer's rule see Appendix B, Section B.6. The two equations can also be solved via the method of substitution. See Problem 4-B.

$$\hat{\beta}_2 = \bar{y} - \hat{\beta}_1 \bar{x} \qquad *(4.4.23)$$

which gives the intercept in terms of the slope and the mean values of explanatory and dependent variables, $\bar{x}$ and $\bar{y}$, respectively. It thus remains only to obtain an expression for $\hat{\beta}_1$ from the system (4.4.21) and (4.4.22). Solving for $\hat{\beta}_1$ by Cramer's rule yields

$$\hat{\beta}_1 = \frac{\begin{vmatrix} \Sigma \dot{x}_i \dot{y}_i + n\bar{x}\bar{y} & n\bar{x} \\ n\bar{y} & n \end{vmatrix}}{\begin{vmatrix} \Sigma \dot{x}_i^2 + n\bar{x}^2 & n\bar{x} \\ n\bar{x} & n \end{vmatrix}} = \frac{\Sigma \dot{x}_i \dot{y}_i}{\Sigma \dot{x}_i^2} \qquad *(4.4.24)$$

as the estimator of the slope.[8] The estimator can be written simply as the weighted sum of the $\dot{y}_i$ or, equivalently, the weighted sum of the observations y_i on the dependent variable

$$\hat{\beta}_1 = \Sigma w_i \dot{y}_i = \Sigma w_i y_i \qquad *(4.4.25)$$

where the weights w_i are given as the deviations of the ith value of the explanatory variable from the mean value, divided by the sum of squares of such deviations

$$w_i = \frac{\dot{x}_i}{\Sigma \dot{x}_i^2} = \frac{x_i - \bar{x}}{\Sigma (x_i - \bar{x})^2}. \qquad *(4.4.26)$$

The least-squares estimators $\hat{\beta}_1$ and $\hat{\beta}_2$ from (4.4.25) and (4.4.23) and the least-squares residuals $\hat{u}_i$ from (4.4.8) can be shown geometrically for the five data points of Figure 4.1 as in Figure 4.3. Note that the total of the squared distances from the regression line to the data points, the sum of the squared residuals, is minimized. Note also that the regression line passes through the mean $(\bar{x}, \bar{y})$. Finally, note that some of the residuals are positive and some negative, with the total algebraic sum of the residuals equaling zero.

4.5 Maximum likelihood: the case of simple linear regression

The other major technique for estimating the coefficients of a regression equation is that of maximum likelihood. This section will develop maximum-likelihood estimators for the case of simple linear regression, using notation similar to that of the last section.

Consider again the basic linear regression model for one explanatory variable as in (4.4.2), which may be written using (4.4.5) and (4.4.6), as

[8] Note that division by $\Sigma \dot{x}_i^2$ is justified, since this sum does not vanish by the rank assumption, which requires that the x's not all equal $\bar{x}$.

$$\begin{aligned}
y_i &= \beta_1 x_i + \beta_2 + u_i && \text{all } i, \quad i = 1, 2, \ldots, n \\
E(u_i) &= 0, && \text{all } i \\
E(u_i u_j) &= \begin{cases} \sigma^2 & \text{if } i = j \\ 0 & \text{if } i \neq j \end{cases} && \text{all } i, j \\
x_i &\text{ is fixed,} && \text{all } i.
\end{aligned} \qquad {}^*(4.5.1)$$

The technique of least squares yielded estimators of β_1 and β_2 but did not provide an estimator of the variance σ^2. Maximum likelihood, by contrast, yields estimators of all three parameters.

In the technique of least squares no assumptions were made as to the specific form of the distribution of the stochastic disturbance terms. In maximum-likelihood estimation, by contrast, specific assumptions are made as to their distribution. Typically they are assumed to be distributed *independently, identically*, and *normally*, where[9]

$$u_i \sim N(0, \sigma^2), \qquad i = 1, 2, \ldots, n. \qquad {}^*(4.5.2)$$

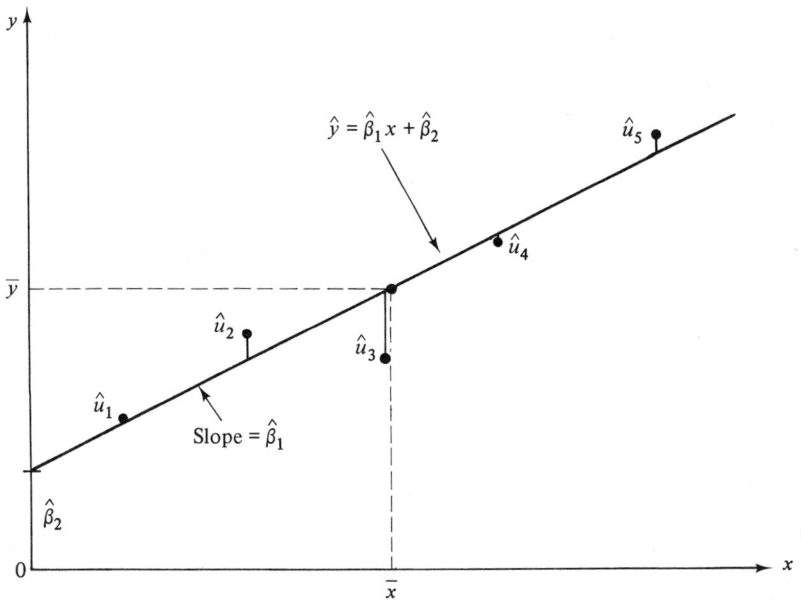

Figure 4.3 The Least-Squares Regression Line and Least-Squares Residuals

[9] A justification for the use of the normal distribution lies in the fact that the stochastic disturbance terms represent many independent additive influences, which, by the central limit theorem, are approximately normally distributed. The normal distribution is also convenient in facilitating use of classical interval estimation and hypothesis testing techniques. For discussions of both the normal distribution and the central limit theorem, see Appendix C, Section C.4.

This assumption states that the ith stochastic disturbance term is distributed as the normal distribution with zero mean and constant (finite) variance σ^2. The zero mean and constant variance assumptions are already part of (4.5.1), while the zero covariance follows from the independence of the n distributions in (4.5.2). All n stochastic disturbance terms have the same distribution, so they are distributed identically. Note in particular that the mean and variance, which define the normal distribution, and which are respectively 0 and σ^2, do not depend on i. The density function for u_i is given by[10]

$$f(u_i) = \frac{1}{\sqrt{2\pi}\,\sigma} \exp\left(-\frac{1}{2}\frac{u_i^2}{\sigma^2}\right) = \frac{1}{\sqrt{2\pi}\,\sigma} \exp\left(-\frac{1}{2}\frac{(y_i - \beta_1 x_i - \beta_2)^2}{\sigma^2}\right). \tag{4.5.3}$$

Each of these density functions refers to one observation. Since the u_i are independent, the product of these density functions over the entire sample gives the likelihood of obtaining the joint occurrence of the residuals $\hat{u}_1, \hat{u}_2, \ldots, \hat{u}_n$.

This product, called the *likelihood function L*, is given as

$$L = \prod_{i=1}^{n} f(\hat{u}_i) = (2\pi)^{-n/2}\sigma^{-n} \exp\left(-\frac{1}{2\sigma^2}\Sigma\,(y_i - \hat{\beta}_1 x_i - \hat{\beta}_2)^2\right). \qquad *(4.5.4)$$

The likelihood function, as its name implies, measures the likelihood of obtaining the sample of points actually obtained, namely the data on y_i and x_i given the values of $\hat{\beta}_1$, $\hat{\beta}_2$, and σ^2. The method of maximum likelihood calls for choosing values of parameters that will maximize this likelihood–i.e., parameters maximizing the likelihood of observing the sample that was in fact observed. The maximum-likelihood estimators are thus obtained in this case as the solutions to the problem

$$\max_{\hat{\beta}_1, \hat{\beta}_2, \sigma} L = L(\hat{\beta}_1, \hat{\beta}_2, \sigma) = \Pi f(\hat{u}_i) = (2\pi)^{-n/2}\sigma^{-n} \exp\left(-\frac{1}{2\sigma^2}\Sigma\,(y_i - \hat{\beta}_1 x_i - \hat{\beta}_2)^2\right). \qquad *(4.5.5)$$

Note that the parameters include the common variance of the stochastic disturbance term, σ^2, as well as the coefficients of the model $\hat{\beta}_1$ and $\hat{\beta}_2$. These parameters are chosen so as to maximize the likelihood function, given the data (x_i, y_i).

It is often convenient to work with the logarithm of the likelihood function, since maximizing $\ln L$ is equivalent to maximizing L, the logarithm being a strictly increasing function. Here

$$\ln L = -\frac{n}{2}\ln 2\pi - n \ln \sigma - \frac{1}{2\sigma^2}\Sigma\,(y_i - \hat{\beta}_1 x_i - \hat{\beta}_2)^2 \tag{4.5.6}$$

[10] The notation exp (z) means e^z, where e is the base of the natural logarithms.

Maximizing ln L by choice of $\hat{\beta}_1$ and $\hat{\beta}_2$ requires, since $-1/2\sigma^2$ is always negative,

$$\min_{\hat{\beta}_1, \hat{\beta}_2} \Sigma (y_i - \hat{\beta}_1 x_i - \hat{\beta}_2)^2 \qquad *(4.5.7)$$

which is exactly the same problem as that of (4.4.10), namely that of minimizing the sum of the squared residuals. Thus, under the assumptions of independent, identically, and normally distributed stochastic disturbance terms the maximum-likelihood estimators are identical to those of least squares, given above in (4.4.23) and (4.4.24). This result reinforces the importance of least squares: the least-squares estimators, under normality, maximize the likelihood of the sample. In addition to estimates of the β's, however, maximum likelihood provides estimates of σ^2, the common variance of the stochastic disturbance terms. Differentiating (4.5.6) with respect to σ yields

$$-\frac{n}{\sigma} + \sigma^{-3} \Sigma \hat{u}_i^2 = 0 \qquad (4.5.8)$$

where $y_i - \hat{\beta}_1 x_i - \hat{\beta}_2$ has been replaced by $\hat{u}_i$, the ith residual. Solving for the variance of the stochastic disturbance term yields

$$\hat{\sigma}^2 = \frac{1}{n} \Sigma \hat{u}_i^2 \qquad *(4.5.9)$$

so the maximum-likelihood estimator of the variance is the (minimized) sum of the squared residuals, divided by the size of the sample. The estimators maximizing the likelihood of the observed sample are therefore given by the least-squares estimates $\hat{\beta}_1$ and $\hat{\beta}_2$ of (4.4.23) and (4.4.24) and the estimate $\hat{\sigma}^2$ of (4.5.9).

4.6 Least squares: the case of multiple linear regression

Having treated the case of simple linear regression, in which there is only one explanatory variable, consider the more general case of multiple linear regression in which there are $k - 1$ variables and k parameters to be estimated, the last parameter being the intercept. The *basic linear regression model for multiple linear regression* can be written, by analogy to (4.4.2), as

$$\begin{aligned}
y_i &= \sum_{j=1}^{k} x_{ij}\beta_j + u_i = \mathbf{x}_i\boldsymbol{\beta} + u_i && \text{all } i,\quad i = 1, 2, \ldots, n \\
E(u_i) &= 0 && \text{all } i \\
\text{Var}(u_i) &= \sigma^2 < \infty && \text{all } i \qquad *(4.6.1) \\
\text{Cov}(u_i u_j) &= 0 && \text{all } i, j, \quad i \neq j. \\
x_{ij} &\text{ is fixed} && \text{all } i, j
\end{aligned}$$

Here y_i represents a possible value taken by the single dependent variable y at the ith observation, x_{ij} is the value of the jth explanatory variable at the ith observation, $\mathbf{x}_i$ is the corresponding vector of the k explanatory variables at the

ith observation, $\boldsymbol{\beta}$ is the $k \times 1$ vector of parameters to be estimated, and u_i is the stochastic disturbance term at the ith observation. The last parameter β_k is the intercept, and so $x_{ik} \equiv 1$ for all i. The problem is that of obtaining estimates of the $k + 1$ unknowns, namely the $k - 1$ slope coefficients $\beta_1, \beta_2, \ldots, \beta_{k-1}$, one intercept β_k, and the variance σ^2.

This basic linear model can be expressed most conveniently in matrix notation (see Appendix B). Let **y** be the $n \times 1$ vector of n values taken by the dependent variable y over the sample of n observations and let **X** be the $n \times k$ matrix of n values taken by the vector of nonstochastic explanatory variables **x** at each point in the sample, as in (4.2.1). In addition let **u** be the $n \times 1$ vector of stochastic disturbance terms at each point in the sample. Thus

$$\underset{n\times 1}{\mathbf{y}} = \begin{pmatrix} y_1 \\ y_2 \\ \vdots \\ y_n \end{pmatrix}, \quad \underset{n\times k}{\mathbf{X}} = \begin{pmatrix} x_{11} & x_{12} & \cdots & x_{1k-1} & 1 \\ x_{21} & x_{22} & \cdots & x_{2k-1} & 1 \\ \vdots & & & & \\ x_{n1} & x_{n2} & \cdots & x_{nk-1} & 1 \end{pmatrix},$$
$$\underset{n\times 1}{\mathbf{u}} = \begin{pmatrix} u_1 \\ u_2 \\ \vdots \\ u_n \end{pmatrix}, \quad \underset{k\times 1}{\boldsymbol{\beta}} = \begin{pmatrix} \beta_1 \\ \beta_2 \\ \vdots \\ \beta_k \end{pmatrix} \qquad *(4.6.2)$$

where **y** and **X** summarize the observable data, **u** summarizes the unobservable stochastic disturbance terms, and $\boldsymbol{\beta}$ summarizes the nonstochastic coefficients to be estimated.[11] The basic linear model (4.6.1) can then be written, using this matrix notation, as

$$\begin{aligned} \underset{n\times 1}{\mathbf{y}} &= \underset{n\times k}{\mathbf{X}}\ \underset{k\times 1}{\boldsymbol{\beta}} + \underset{n\times 1}{\mathbf{u}} \\ E(\mathbf{u}) &= \mathbf{0} \\ \mathrm{Cov}(\mathbf{u}) &= \sigma^2\mathbf{I} \\ \mathbf{X} \text{ is a fixed matrix, with } & \rho(\mathbf{X}) = k < n \end{aligned} \qquad *(4.6.3)$$

where **I** is the $n \times n$ identity matrix.

The first statistical assumption in (4.6.3), written as the vector equation

$$E(\mathbf{u}) = \mathbf{0} \qquad *(4.6.4)$$

is simply a statement that the means of all of the stochastic disturbance terms are zero, as in (4.6.1). It is consistent with the interpretation of **u** as a vector of stochastic *disturbance* terms. Again, "on average" the model is "correct" in that

[11] Note that **u** here is *not* the same as **u** in (4.1.1). In (4.1.1) **u** was a row vector of g disturbance terms, while here **u** is a column vector of one disturbance term over the sample of n observations. It will always be clear from the context which **u** is being used.

$$E(\mathbf{y}) = \mathbf{X}\boldsymbol{\beta} + E(\mathbf{u}) = \mathbf{X}\boldsymbol{\beta} \qquad *(4.6.5)$$

where it has been assumed that the **X** matrix and **β** vector contain fixed numbers and are therefore nonstochastic. Thus the expected values of the dependent variables are precisely the systematic portion of the model.

The second statistical assumption, which can be expressed as the matrix equation

$$\text{Cov}(\mathbf{u}) = E[(\mathbf{u} - E(\mathbf{u}))(\mathbf{u} - E(\mathbf{u}))'] = E(\mathbf{u}\mathbf{u}') = \sigma^2\mathbf{I} \qquad *(4.6.6)$$

where $\mathbf{u}'$ is the transpose of $\mathbf{u}$, when written out in full states that

$$\begin{pmatrix} \text{Var}(u_1) & \text{Cov}(u_1u_2) & \dots & \text{Cov}(u_1u_n) \\ \text{Cov}(u_2u_1) & \text{Var}(u_2) & \dots & \text{Cov}(u_2u_n) \\ \vdots & \vdots & & \vdots \\ \text{Cov}(u_nu_1) & \text{Cov}(u_nu_2) & \dots & \text{Var}(u_n) \end{pmatrix} = \begin{pmatrix} \sigma^2 & 0 & \dots & 0 \\ 0 & \sigma^2 & \dots & 0 \\ \vdots & \vdots & & \vdots \\ 0 & 0 & \dots & \sigma^2 \end{pmatrix} \qquad *(4.6.7)$$

It therefore expresses, in compact matrix notation, conditions (4.4.5) and (4.4.6). Conditions (4.4.5), the assumption of homoskedasticity, state that the stochastic disturbance terms all have the same finite variance σ^2. These conditions are implied by the assumption that the diagonal elements of the covariance matrix all equal σ^2. Conditions (4.4.6), the assumption of absence of serial correlation, state that every pair of distinct stochastic disturbance terms has a zero covariance. These conditions are implied by the assumption that all off-diagonal elements of the covariance matrix are zero. The assumption of both homoskedasticity and absence of serial correlation, as expressed in (4.6.6) or (4.6.7), is referred to as the assumption of *spherical disturbances.*

The rank condition on **X** in (4.6.3) repeats (4.2.6); it implies that the explanatory variables are independent.

Proceeding as in Section 4.4, define the *residual* at the *i*th observation as

$$\hat{u}_i = y_i - \mathbf{x}_i\hat{\boldsymbol{\beta}} = y_i - \hat{y}_i, \quad i = 1, 2, \dots, n \qquad *(4.6.8)$$

where $\hat{\boldsymbol{\beta}}$ is the vector of estimated coefficients and $\hat{y}_i$ is the predicted value of y_i, given as

$$\hat{y}_i = \mathbf{x}_i\hat{\boldsymbol{\beta}} \qquad (4.6.9)$$

The sum of squares of the residuals is then

$$S = \sum_{i=1}^{n} \hat{u}_i^2 = \sum_{i=1}^{n} (y_i - \mathbf{x}_i\hat{\boldsymbol{\beta}})^2 \qquad *(4.6.10)$$

which, according to the least-squares technique, is to be minimized by choice of $\hat{\boldsymbol{\beta}}$. In matrix notation the column vector of residuals

$$\underset{n\times 1}{\hat{\mathbf{u}}} = \underset{n\times 1}{\mathbf{y}} - \underset{n\times k}{\mathbf{X}}\ \underset{k\times 1}{\hat{\boldsymbol{\beta}}} \qquad *(4.6.11)$$

is the *residual vector*, and the sum of squares can be written

$$S = \hat{\mathbf{u}}'\hat{\mathbf{u}} = (\mathbf{y} - \mathbf{X}\hat{\boldsymbol{\beta}})'(\mathbf{y} - \mathbf{X}\hat{\boldsymbol{\beta}}) = \|\mathbf{y} - \mathbf{X}\hat{\boldsymbol{\beta}}\|^2 \qquad *(4.6.12)$$

where $\|\mathbf{y} - \mathbf{X}\hat{\boldsymbol{\beta}}\|$ is the norm of the vector $\mathbf{y} - \mathbf{X}\hat{\boldsymbol{\beta}}$.[12] Carrying out the transposition and matrix multiplication, the sum of squares is

$$S = \mathbf{y}'\mathbf{y} - 2\hat{\boldsymbol{\beta}}'\mathbf{X}'\mathbf{y} + \hat{\boldsymbol{\beta}}'\mathbf{X}'\mathbf{X}\hat{\boldsymbol{\beta}} \qquad (4.6.13)$$

where the two "cross-product" terms have been combined into the middle term on the right, since they are transposes of one another but both are scalars. The least-squares estimators are then the solution $\hat{\boldsymbol{\beta}}$ to the problem

$$\min_{\hat{\boldsymbol{\beta}}} S = S(\hat{\boldsymbol{\beta}}) = \mathbf{y}'\mathbf{y} - 2\hat{\boldsymbol{\beta}}'\mathbf{X}'\mathbf{y} + \hat{\boldsymbol{\beta}}'\mathbf{X}'\mathbf{X}\hat{\boldsymbol{\beta}} \qquad *(4.6.14)$$

which is the generalization of (4.4.10) to any $k - 1$ explanatory variables, written in matrix notation.[13] As in the simple linear regression case the necessary and sufficient conditions for minimizing S are that all first-order partial derivatives equal zero, requiring that[14]

$$\frac{\partial S}{\partial \hat{\boldsymbol{\beta}}'} = -2\mathbf{X}'\mathbf{y} + 2\mathbf{X}'\mathbf{X}\hat{\boldsymbol{\beta}} = \mathbf{0} \qquad (4.6.15)$$

[12] Recall that if $\mathbf{a}$ is any column vector, then $\|\mathbf{a}\|^2$, the square of the norm of $\mathbf{a}$, is the sum of squared elements of $\mathbf{a}$, given as

$$\|\mathbf{a}\|^2 = \mathbf{a}'\mathbf{a} = \sum_{i=1}^{n} a_i^2$$

See Appendix B, Section B.3.

[13] $k - 1$ since one parameter corresponds to the intercept, the last column of $\mathbf{X}$ being a vector of ones, as in (4.2.4).

[14] This expression is obtained by differentiating (4.6.13) with respect to the row vector $\hat{\boldsymbol{\beta}}'$. The first term on the right-hand side drops out, since it does not contain $\hat{\boldsymbol{\beta}}'$. The second term is $\hat{\boldsymbol{\beta}}'$ postmultiplied by the constant $-2\mathbf{X}'\mathbf{y}$ and, just as the derivative of a constant times b with respect to b is the constant, the derivative of $-2\hat{\boldsymbol{\beta}}\mathbf{X}'\mathbf{y}$ with respect to $\hat{\boldsymbol{\beta}}'$ is $-2\mathbf{X}'\mathbf{y}$. The third term involves both $\hat{\boldsymbol{\beta}}'$ and $\hat{\boldsymbol{\beta}}$. It is analogous to a constant times b^2, which, when differentiated with respect to b, yields 2 times the constant times b. Here the derivative of $\hat{\boldsymbol{\beta}}'\mathbf{X}'\mathbf{X}\hat{\boldsymbol{\beta}}$ with respect to $\hat{\boldsymbol{\beta}}'$ is $2\mathbf{X}'\mathbf{X}\hat{\boldsymbol{\beta}}$. Note that the derivative of a scalar with respect to a row vector, $\hat{\boldsymbol{\beta}}'$, is a column vector, as discussed in Appendix B, Section B.9. The conditions in (4.6.15) are both necessary and sufficient for minimizing S. Sufficiency follows from the fact that

$$\frac{\partial^2 S}{\partial \hat{\boldsymbol{\beta}}'^2} = 2\mathbf{X}'\mathbf{X}$$

which is a positive-definite matrix. See Appendix B, Sections B.8 and B.9. For an alternative approach see footnote 16.

This condition can be written

$$\mathbf{X}'\mathbf{X}\hat{\boldsymbol{\beta}} = \mathbf{X}'\mathbf{y} \qquad *(4.6.16)$$

and these are the *normal equations of least squares,* $\hat{\boldsymbol{\beta}}$ being the *least-squares estimator* of $\boldsymbol{\beta}$. It is possible to solve explicitly for $\hat{\boldsymbol{\beta}}$, since, from the rank condition in (4.6.3) the matrix $\mathbf{X}'\mathbf{X}$, which is a square matrix of order k, is nonsingular and therefore has an inverse.[15] Premultiplying both sides of (4.6.16) by $(\mathbf{X}'\mathbf{X})^{-1}$ yields the unique solution for $\hat{\boldsymbol{\beta}}$:

$$\hat{\boldsymbol{\beta}} = (\mathbf{X}'\mathbf{X})^{-1}\mathbf{X}'\mathbf{y} \qquad *(4.6.17)$$

This is the *least-squares estimator* for the vector of parameters $\boldsymbol{\beta}$.[16] It should be noted that (4.6.17) is a matrix generalization of the estimator (4.4.24) for simple linear regression, which could be written

$$\hat{\beta}_1 = (\Sigma\, \dot{x}_i^2)^{-1}\, \Sigma\, \dot{x}_i \dot{y}_i \qquad (4.6.18)$$

in order to emphasize the analogy between the two. The least-squares estimator can also be written

$$\hat{\boldsymbol{\beta}} = \mathbf{W}\mathbf{y}, \qquad \mathbf{W} = (\mathbf{X}'\mathbf{X})^{-1}\mathbf{X}' \qquad (4.6.19)$$

which are the analogues of (4.4.25) and (4.4.26). Here, as in the case of simple linear regression, the least-squares estimators are simply weighted averages of the observations on the dependent variables, the weights being determined by the observations on the explanatory variables.[17]

The least-squares estimator can be easily constructed using the following heuristic device: The "problem" in solving the equation

$$\mathbf{y} = \mathbf{X}\hat{\boldsymbol{\beta}} + \hat{\mathbf{u}} \qquad (4.6.20)$$

for $\hat{\boldsymbol{\beta}}$ is that the matrix multiplying it is not square—by the degrees-of-freedom

[15] For any matrix $\mathbf{X}$

$$\rho(\mathbf{X}) = \rho(\mathbf{X}'\mathbf{X})$$

and here both ranks are k. See Appendix B, Section B.4.

[16] Given the least-squares estimator $\hat{\boldsymbol{\beta}}$ in (4.6.17) it follows that the sum of squares for any estimator $\hat{\hat{\boldsymbol{\beta}}}$ can be written

$$S(\hat{\hat{\boldsymbol{\beta}}}) = (\mathbf{y} - \mathbf{X}\hat{\boldsymbol{\beta}})'(\mathbf{y} - \mathbf{X}\hat{\boldsymbol{\beta}}) + (\hat{\boldsymbol{\beta}} - \hat{\hat{\boldsymbol{\beta}}})'(\mathbf{X}'\mathbf{X})(\hat{\boldsymbol{\beta}} - \hat{\hat{\boldsymbol{\beta}}})$$

which is minimized at $\hat{\hat{\boldsymbol{\beta}}} = \hat{\boldsymbol{\beta}}$, since $(\mathbf{X}'\mathbf{X})$ is a positive-definite matrix. This approach represents an alternative proof that the estimator in (4.6.17) does indeed minimize the sum of squares.

[17] For a generalization of least squares to the case of minimizing the sum of squares subject to a set of linear inequality constraints see Appendix B, Section B.10, especially equation (B.10.26).

assumption it has more rows (n) than columns (k). To "remedy" this situation, premultiply the equation by the transpose of X to yield

$$\mathbf{X}'\mathbf{y} = \mathbf{X}'\mathbf{X}\hat{\boldsymbol{\beta}} + \mathbf{X}'\hat{\mathbf{u}} \tag{4.6.21}$$

where the matrix multiplying $\hat{\boldsymbol{\beta}}$ is now square ($k \times k$). The term $\mathbf{X}'\hat{\mathbf{u}}$ is dropped, since least squares requires that the residuals be uncorrelated with the explanatory variables. Solving for $\hat{\boldsymbol{\beta}}$ yields the least-squares estimator

$$\hat{\boldsymbol{\beta}} = (\mathbf{X}'\mathbf{X})^{-1}\mathbf{X}'\mathbf{y} \tag{4.6.22}$$

as in (4.6.17). A geometrical interpretation for dropping the term $\mathbf{X}'\hat{\mathbf{u}}$ based on their orthogonality will be presented in Section 5.1.

Given the least-squares estimator in (4.6.17), the minimized sum of squares is obtained from (4.6.12) as

$$\hat{S}(\boldsymbol{\beta}) = \hat{\mathbf{u}}'\hat{\mathbf{u}}. \tag{4.6.23}$$

But for the least-squares estimator the *least-squares-residuals vector* is given as

$$\hat{\mathbf{u}} = \mathbf{y} - \mathbf{X}\hat{\boldsymbol{\beta}} = \mathbf{y} - \mathbf{X}(\mathbf{X}'\mathbf{X})^{-1}\mathbf{X}'\mathbf{y} = (\mathbf{I} - \mathbf{X}(\mathbf{X}'\mathbf{X})^{-1}\mathbf{X}')\mathbf{y} \tag{4.6.24}$$

where $\mathbf{I}$ is the identity matrix of order n. Thus the vector of least-squares residuals is linear in the data on the dependent variables, and it may be written

$$\hat{\mathbf{u}} = \mathbf{M}\mathbf{y} \qquad *(4.6.25)$$

where

$$\mathbf{M} = \mathbf{I} - \mathbf{X}(\mathbf{X}'\mathbf{X})^{-1}\mathbf{X}'. \qquad *(4.6.26)$$

The matrix $\mathbf{M}$ appears repeatedly in regression theory. It is called the *fundamental idempotent matrix of least squares*. It is a symmetric matrix ($\mathbf{M} = \mathbf{M}'$) that is idempotent in that[18]

$$\mathbf{M}^2 = \mathbf{M}\mathbf{M} = \mathbf{M}. \tag{4.6.27}$$

These properties of $\mathbf{M}$ are used in obtaining the minimized sum of squares, from (4.6.23), as

$$\hat{S}(\hat{\boldsymbol{\beta}}) = \mathbf{y}'\mathbf{M}\mathbf{y} = \mathbf{y}'(\mathbf{I} - \mathbf{X}(\mathbf{X}'\mathbf{X})^{-1}\mathbf{X}')\mathbf{y} \qquad *(4.6.28)$$

an expression that also appears repeatedly in regression theory–e.g., in the analysis of variance for a regression that appears in the next chapter.

The next step is to show that the least-squares estimators have certain desirable properties, including linearity, unbiasedness, and minimum variance.

[18] See Problem 4-M and Appendix B, Section B.3.

The least-squares estimator is linear in $\mathbf{y}$, but $\mathbf{y}$, in turn, involves an additive stochastic term and is therefore stochastic. Thus $\hat{\boldsymbol{\beta}}$ is stochastic, representing a column vector of random variables. To calculate the mean of $\hat{\boldsymbol{\beta}}$, replace $\mathbf{y}$ from (4.6.3) in the estimator to yield

$$\hat{\boldsymbol{\beta}} = (\mathbf{X}'\mathbf{X})^{-1}\mathbf{X}'\mathbf{y} = (\mathbf{X}'\mathbf{X})^{-1}\mathbf{X}'(\mathbf{X}\boldsymbol{\beta} + \mathbf{u}) = \boldsymbol{\beta} + (\mathbf{X}'\mathbf{X})^{-1}\mathbf{X}'\mathbf{u}. \qquad *(4.6.29)$$

Taking expectations over repeated samples, assuming the same fixed matrix $\mathbf{X}$ of explanatory variables for each such sample (or allowing $\mathbf{X}$ to be determined stochastically but where the distribution determining $\mathbf{X}$ is independent of that for $\mathbf{u}$), and using the stochastic assumptions on the expectation of $\mathbf{u}$ in (4.6.3), the expectation of the last term in (4.6.29) vanishes, so, since $E(\cdot)$ is a linear operator,

$$E(\hat{\boldsymbol{\beta}}) = \boldsymbol{\beta}. \qquad *(4.6.30)$$

This remarkable result states that the average of values for $\hat{\boldsymbol{\beta}}$ that one would obtain by averaging over repeated samples is the *true* value for the vector of parameters. It states that the least-squares estimator is *unbiased*, as discussed below in Section 4.8. To analyze the variances and covariances of the least-squares estimators requires the calculation of the covariance matrix, defined as

$$\text{Cov}\,(\hat{\boldsymbol{\beta}}) = E\,[(\hat{\boldsymbol{\beta}} - E(\hat{\boldsymbol{\beta}})]\,[\hat{\boldsymbol{\beta}} - E(\hat{\boldsymbol{\beta}}))']. \qquad (4.6.31)$$

From (4.6.30)

$$E(\hat{\boldsymbol{\beta}}) = \boldsymbol{\beta} \qquad (4.6.32)$$

and from (4.6.29)

$$\hat{\boldsymbol{\beta}} - \boldsymbol{\beta} = (\mathbf{X}'\mathbf{X})^{-1}\mathbf{X}'\mathbf{u}. \qquad (4.6.33)$$

Thus

$$\text{Cov}\,(\hat{\boldsymbol{\beta}}) = E((\mathbf{X}'\mathbf{X})^{-1}\mathbf{X}'\mathbf{u}\mathbf{u}'\mathbf{X}(\mathbf{X}'\mathbf{X})^{-1}). \qquad (4.6.34)$$

Using the stochastic assumptions on the covariance of $\mathbf{u}$ in (4.6.6) and the assumption that $\mathbf{X}$ is nonstochastic, it follows that

$$\text{Cov}\,(\hat{\boldsymbol{\beta}}) = (\mathbf{X}'\mathbf{X})^{-1}\mathbf{X}'\,\text{Cov}\,(\mathbf{u})\,\mathbf{X}(\mathbf{X}'\mathbf{X})^{-1} \qquad (4.6.35)$$

where, from (4.6.6),

$$\text{Cov}\,(\mathbf{u}) = \sigma^2\mathbf{I}. \qquad (4.6.36)$$

Combining these and canceling $(\mathbf{X}'\mathbf{X})^{-1}$ and $(\mathbf{X}'\mathbf{X})$ yields

$$\text{Cov}\,(\hat{\boldsymbol{\beta}}) = \sigma^2\,(\mathbf{X}'\mathbf{X})^{-1} \qquad *(4.6.37)$$

which gives the covariance matrix of the least-squares estimators in terms of the data on the independent variables, **X**, and the common variance of the stochastic disturbance terms, σ^2. Thus the variance of any one of the estimators is the stochastic disturbance term variance times the corresponding diagonal element of the $(\mathbf{X}'\mathbf{X})^{-1}$ matrix, while the covariance of any two estimators is the stochastic disturbance term variance times the corresponding off-diagonal element of the $(\mathbf{X}'\mathbf{X})^{-1}$ matrix. The imprecision of the estimators is thus proportional to the stochastic disturbance term variance. These results will be used both to construct confidence intervals for the estimated coefficients $\hat{\boldsymbol{\beta}}$ and to prove the Gauss-Markov theorem on the optimality of least-squares estimators.

4.7 Maximum likelihood: the case of multiple linear regression

The problem of multiple linear regression is that of estimating and testing hypotheses on the coefficients of $\boldsymbol{\beta}$ of the basic linear model for $k - 1$ explanatory variables, as in (4.6.3), which can be written

$$\begin{aligned} &\underset{n\times 1}{\mathbf{y}} = \underset{n\times k}{\mathbf{X}}\ \underset{k\times 1}{\boldsymbol{\beta}} + \underset{n\times 1}{\mathbf{u}} \\ &E(\mathbf{u}) = \mathbf{0} \\ &E(\mathbf{u}\mathbf{u}') = \sigma^2\mathbf{I} \\ &\mathbf{X} \text{ is a fixed matrix, with } \rho(\mathbf{X}) = k < n. \end{aligned} \qquad *(4.7.1)$$

As in the case of simple linear regression, the method of maximum likelihood adds further specific assumptions on the distribution of the stochastic disturbance terms. Again using the normal distribution, assume the stochastic disturbance vector **u** is distributed as the multivariate normal with zero mean and covariance matrix $\boldsymbol{\Omega}$[19]

$$\mathbf{u} \sim \mathrm{N}(E(\mathbf{u}), \boldsymbol{\Omega}) = \mathrm{N}(\mathbf{0}, \sigma^2\mathbf{I}) \qquad *(4.7.2)$$

This assumption is consistent with the stochastic assumptions in (4.7.1), where the mean vector is zero

$$E(\mathbf{u}) = \mathbf{0} \qquad *(4.7.3)$$

and the covariance matrix is the scalar σ^2 times the identity matrix

$$\boldsymbol{\Omega} = \sigma^2\mathbf{I} \qquad *(4.7.4)$$

meaning homoskedasticity and absence of serial correlation as in (4.6.7). Indeed, the term "spherical disturbances" that was used in the last section to describe

[19] See Appendix C, Section C.4, for a discussion of the multivariate normal distribution. From (C.4.7), if **u** is an n-dimensional column vector, where $\mathbf{u} \sim \mathrm{N}(E(\mathbf{u}), \boldsymbol{\Omega})$, then the density function for **u** is

$$f(\mathbf{u}) = (2\pi)^{-n/2}\,|\boldsymbol{\Omega}|^{-1/2} \exp\left(-\tfrac{1}{2}\,[\mathbf{u} - E(\mathbf{u})]'\,\boldsymbol{\Omega}^{-1}\,[\mathbf{u} - E(\mathbf{u})]\right)$$

(4.6.7) refers to the fact that, assuming normally distributed stochastic terms, as in (4.7.2), the contours of equal values of the density function for **u** are spheres when $n = 3$ and hyperspheres when $n > 3$. Under these assumptions the multivariate normal density function then simplifies to

$$f(\mathbf{u}) = (2\pi)^{-n/2}\sigma^{-n} \exp\left(-\frac{1}{2\sigma^2}\mathbf{u}'\mathbf{u}\right). \tag{4.7.5}$$

The likelihood function L is $f(\hat{\mathbf{u}})$, where $\hat{\mathbf{u}}$ is the column vector of residuals for estimated values of the coefficients, as in (4.6.11). The likelihood function can therefore be written

$$L = (2\pi)^{-n/2}\sigma^{-n} \exp\left[-\frac{1}{2\sigma^2}(\mathbf{y} - \mathbf{X}\hat{\boldsymbol{\beta}})'(\mathbf{y} - \mathbf{X}\hat{\boldsymbol{\beta}})\right] \tag*{*(4.7.6)}$$

which restates (4.5.4) for the case of multiple linear regression using vector notation. Maximizing L by choice of the unknown parameters $\hat{\boldsymbol{\beta}}$ and σ is equivalent to

$$\max_{\hat{\boldsymbol{\beta}},\sigma} \ln L = -\frac{n}{2}\ln 2\pi - n\ln\sigma - \frac{1}{2\sigma^2}(\mathbf{y} - \mathbf{X}\hat{\boldsymbol{\beta}})'(\mathbf{y} - \mathbf{X}\hat{\boldsymbol{\beta}}). \tag*{*(4.7.7)}$$

The only term involving the coefficients $\hat{\boldsymbol{\beta}}$ is the last, and maximizing it is equivalent to minimizing

$$S = (\mathbf{y} - \mathbf{X}\hat{\boldsymbol{\beta}})'(\mathbf{y} - \mathbf{X}\hat{\boldsymbol{\beta}}) = \hat{\mathbf{u}}'\hat{\mathbf{u}} \tag{4.7.8}$$

which is the sum of squared residuals. Thus the maximum-likelihood estimator of the coefficients is exactly the same as the least-squares estimator (4.6.17), namely

$$\hat{\boldsymbol{\beta}} = (\mathbf{X}'\mathbf{X})^{-1}\mathbf{X}'\mathbf{y}. \tag*{*(4.7.9)}$$

Maximizing L by choice of σ calls for

$$\frac{\partial \ln L}{\partial \sigma} = -\frac{n}{\sigma} + \frac{1}{\sigma^3}\hat{\mathbf{u}}'\hat{\mathbf{u}} = 0 \tag{4.7.10}$$

so, solving for the variance,

$$\hat{\sigma}^2 = \frac{1}{n}(\hat{\mathbf{u}}'\hat{\mathbf{u}}) = \frac{1}{n}\|\hat{\mathbf{u}}\|^2 = \frac{1}{n}\mathbf{y}'\mathbf{M}\mathbf{y}. \tag*{*(4.7.11)}$$

This is the maximum-likelihood estimator of the common variance of the stochastic disturbance terms. The maximum-likelihood (and least-squares) estimator of $\boldsymbol{\beta}$ is a weighted sum of **y**, as in (4.6.19), while **y** in turn is distributed, from

(4.7.1) and (4.7.2), as **u**—that is, normally, except that it has mean $\mathbf{X\beta}$ instead of **0**. The estimators $\hat{\boldsymbol{\beta}}$ are thus also normally distributed. In particular the normality assumption in (4.7.2) implies that

$$\hat{\boldsymbol{\beta}} \sim N(\boldsymbol{\beta}, \sigma^2 (\mathbf{X}'\mathbf{X})^{-1}) \qquad *(4.7.12)$$

so that the likelihood estimators are distributed as the multivariate normal distribution with mean $\boldsymbol{\beta}$ and covariance matrix $\sigma^2 (\mathbf{X}'\mathbf{X})^{-1}$. The mean and covariance matrix were already derived in (4.6.30) and (4.6.37) for least squares. What maximum likelihood provides beyond this, under specific assumptions as to the distribution of the stochastic disturbance terms **u**, is the specific distribution of the estimators $\hat{\boldsymbol{\beta}}$. Normally distributed disturbance terms, in (4.7.2), lead to normally distributed estimators, as in (4.7.12). The results in (4.7.12) on the distribution of the estimators, specifically the variances and covariances in the covariance matrix, are useful in testing hypotheses and determining confidence intervals. To use them, however, it is necessary to know or estimate σ^2, the common variance of the stochastic disturbance terms. Usually it is not known and must be estimated. One estimator is the maximum-likelihood estimator in (4.7.11). Generally, however, this estimator is adjusted for the degrees of freedom of the problem, $n - k$, since k degrees of freedom were lost in estimating the parameters $\hat{\boldsymbol{\beta}}$. The adjusted estimator $\hat{s}^2$ is therefore defined as

$$\hat{s}^2 = \frac{1}{n-k}\hat{\mathbf{u}}'\hat{\mathbf{u}} = \frac{1}{n-k}\sum_{i=1}^{n}\hat{u}_i^2 = \frac{n}{n-k}\hat{\sigma}^2 \qquad *(4.7.13)$$

This is the estimator of σ^2 that is used in (4.7.12). Thus the estimator of the covariance matrix is

$$\widehat{\mathrm{Cov}}\,(\hat{\boldsymbol{\beta}}) = \left(\frac{1}{n-k}\sum_{i=1}^{n}\hat{u}_i^2\right)(\mathbf{X}'\mathbf{X})^{-1} \qquad *(4.7.14)$$

where the large "hat" serves as a reminder that this is an estimator of Cov $(\hat{\boldsymbol{\beta}})$, which is itself given in (4.6.37). In particular, the square roots of the diagonal elements of this matrix are used in testing hypotheses and creating confidence intervals. They are the estimated *standard errors* of the regression coefficients, where the estimated standard error of the jth coefficient is

$$\hat{s}_j = \sqrt{\left(\frac{1}{n-k}\sum_{i=1}^{n}\hat{u}_i^2\right)[(\mathbf{X}'\mathbf{X})^{-1}]_{jj}}, \quad j = 1, 2, \ldots, k. \qquad *(4.7.15)$$

This result will be used in the next chapter in a discussion, in Section 5.4, of the significance of coefficients and confidence intervals.

Another result important for tests of significance and confidence intervals, as discussed in the next chapter, is the distribution of the maximum-likelihood estimator of the variance $\hat{\sigma}^2$ in (4.7.11). The result gives the distribution of the ratio

$$\frac{n\,\hat{\sigma}^2}{\sigma^2} = (n - k)\,\frac{\hat{s}^2}{\sigma^2} \sim \chi^2\,(n - k) \tag{4.7.16}$$

–that is, the ratio is distributed as the chi-square distribution with $n - k$ degrees of freedom, justifying the previous interpretation of $n - k$ as the number of degrees of freedom.[20]

Furthermore, $\hat{\sigma}^2$ is distributed independently of $\hat{\boldsymbol{\beta}}$. From (4.7.16) it follows that, for the estimator adjusted for the degrees of freedom

$$\hat{s}^2 \sim \frac{\sigma^2}{n - k}\,\chi^2(n - k). \tag{4.7.17}$$

4.8 Properties of estimators

The estimator obtained by both least squares and maximum likelihood (the latter assuming normally distributed stochastic terms) for the vector of coefficients in a multiple linear regression is

$$\hat{\boldsymbol{\beta}} = (\mathbf{X}'\mathbf{X})^{-1}\mathbf{X}'\mathbf{y} \tag*{*(4.8.1)}$$

as in (4.6.17) and (4.7.9). The estimator obtained by maximum likelihood for the common variance of the stochastic disturbance term in (4.7.11) is

$$\hat{\sigma}^2 = \frac{1}{n}\,(\hat{\mathbf{u}}'\hat{\mathbf{u}}). \tag*{*(4.8.2)}$$

Yet a third estimator introduced in (4.7.13) is the estimator of the common variance of the stochastic disturbance term adjusted for degrees of freedom:

$$\hat{s}^2 = \frac{1}{n - k}\,(\hat{\mathbf{u}}'\hat{\mathbf{u}}) = \frac{n}{n - k}\,\hat{\sigma}^2. \tag*{*(4.8.3)}$$

These estimators satisfy certain properties, which this section will discuss, using these three specific estimators to illustrate them.

Consider a process characterized by a certain column vector of parameters $\boldsymbol{\theta}$ and resulting in a sample of n data points, summarized by the matrix $\mathbf{Z}$. An estimator $\hat{\boldsymbol{\theta}}$ of $\boldsymbol{\theta}$ is a function of the data

[20] To prove that the ratio is distributed as $\chi^2\ (n - k)$, note that $n\hat{\sigma}^2 = \hat{\mathbf{u}}'\hat{\mathbf{u}} = \mathbf{y}'\mathbf{M}\mathbf{y} = \mathbf{u}'\mathbf{M}\mathbf{u}$, where $\rho(\mathbf{M}) = n - k$. Since $\mathbf{M}$ is symmetric, there is an orthogonal matrix $\mathbf{P}$ such that $\mathbf{P}'\mathbf{M}\mathbf{P} = \mathbf{D}$, where $\mathbf{D}$ is a diagonal matrix with k zeros in the main diagonal. If $\mathbf{v} = \mathbf{P}^{-1}\mathbf{u} = \mathbf{P}'\mathbf{u}$, then $\hat{\mathbf{u}}'\hat{\mathbf{u}} = \mathbf{v}'\mathbf{D}\mathbf{v}$, which is the sum of squares of $n - k$ independent random variables, each distributed as $N(0, \sigma^2)$. Dividing by σ^2 yields the sum of $n - k$ independent standard normal variables, which defines the $\chi^2\ (n - k)$ distribution. See Appendix C, Section C.4.

$$\hat{\boldsymbol{\theta}} = \hat{\boldsymbol{\theta}}(\mathbf{Z}) \tag{4.8.4}$$

which represents a rule for estimating the true vector $\boldsymbol{\theta}$. As an example, consider a random sample of data, representing independent drawings from a population characterized by a particular density function. Suppose the numbers $Z_1, Z_2, \ldots, Z_n$ represent a random sample of n independent drawings. An estimator of the mean of the underlying distribution is the sample mean

$$m = \frac{1}{n} \sum_{i=1}^{n} Z_i \tag{4.8.5}$$

where the right-hand side states a particular functional dependence on the Z's. This is an estimator, but certainly not the only estimator. Another is simply the first observation Z_1, where all other observations are dropped.

Returning to the estimators of a multiple linear regression, the estimator $\hat{\boldsymbol{\beta}}$ is written in (4.8.1) as an explicit function of the data in the matrix $\mathbf{X}$ and the vector $\mathbf{y}$. To put $\hat{\sigma}^2$ and $\hat{s}^2$ into comparable form requires only replacing $\hat{\mathbf{u}}$ by $\mathbf{y} - \mathbf{X}\hat{\boldsymbol{\beta}}$ and $\hat{\boldsymbol{\beta}}$ by $(\mathbf{X}'\mathbf{X})^{-1}\mathbf{X}'\mathbf{y}$, yielding

$$\begin{aligned} \hat{\sigma}^2 &= \frac{1}{n}(\mathbf{y}'\mathbf{y} - \mathbf{y}'\mathbf{X}(\mathbf{X}'\mathbf{X})^{-1}\mathbf{X}'\mathbf{y}) = \frac{1}{n}\mathbf{y}'(\mathbf{I} - \mathbf{X}(\mathbf{X}'\mathbf{X})^{-1}\mathbf{X}')\mathbf{y} \\ &= \frac{1}{n}\mathbf{y}'\mathbf{M}\mathbf{y} \end{aligned} \tag*{*(4.8.6)}$$

and

$$\hat{s}^2 = \frac{1}{n-k}\mathbf{y}'(\mathbf{I} - \mathbf{X}(\mathbf{X}'\mathbf{X})^{-1}\mathbf{X}')\mathbf{y} = \frac{1}{n-k}\mathbf{y}'\mathbf{M}\mathbf{y} \tag*{*(4.8.7)}$$

where $\mathbf{I}$ is the $n \times n$ identity matrix and $\mathbf{M} = \mathbf{I} - \mathbf{X}(\mathbf{X}'\mathbf{X})^{-1}\mathbf{X}'$ is the fundamental idempotent matrix of (4.6.26).

A first property of an estimator is *linearity*. The vector of estimators $\hat{\boldsymbol{\theta}}$ is a *linear estimator* if an only if it is linear in the sample data $\mathbf{Z}$ in (4.8.4). For example, for a random sample both the sample mean (4.8.5) and the first observation are linear estimators. It is also clear that $\hat{\boldsymbol{\beta}}$ in (4.8.1) is linear in the data on the dependent variable $\mathbf{y}$. In fact, it was expressed in (4.6.19) as $\mathbf{y}$ premultiplied by a matrix of fixed weights $\mathbf{W}$. Being linear, it satisfies the principle of *superposition*: for a fixed $\mathbf{X}$, considering $\hat{\boldsymbol{\beta}}(\mathbf{y})$ as a function of $\mathbf{y}$, it follows that given two vectors $\mathbf{y}^1$ and $\mathbf{y}^2$ of data on the dependent variable,

$$\hat{\boldsymbol{\beta}}(\mathbf{y}^1 + \mathbf{y}^2) = \hat{\boldsymbol{\beta}}(\mathbf{y}^1) + \hat{\boldsymbol{\beta}}(\mathbf{y}^2). \tag{4.8.8}$$

Thus, the least-squares estimator for a sum of vectors of data on the dependent variable is the sum of the least-squares estimators for each of the separate vectors.

The estimators $\hat{\sigma}^2$ and $\hat{s}^2$, as given in (4.8.6) and (4.8.7), are clearly nonlinear estimators; in particular, they are appropriate scalars times a quadratic form in $\mathbf{y}$.

A second property of an estimator is *unbiasedness*. An estimator is *unbiased* if and only if its expected value is the true population value. Thus, the estimator $\hat{\boldsymbol{\theta}}$ is unbiased if

$$E(\hat{\boldsymbol{\theta}}) = \boldsymbol{\theta} . \qquad *(4.8.9)$$

Consider, for example, the sample mean for the random sample m in (4.8.5):

$$\begin{aligned} E(m) &= E\left(\frac{1}{n} \; \Sigma \; Z_i\right) = \frac{1}{n} \; \Sigma \; E(Z_i) \\ &= \frac{1}{n} \; \Sigma \, \mu = \frac{1}{n} \; n\mu = \mu \end{aligned} \qquad (4.8.10)$$

where μ is the mean of the underlying distribution. By the same token

$$E(Z_1) = \mu \qquad (4.8.11)$$

so both the sample mean and the first observation are unbiased estimators of the population mean.

From (4.6.30) it is clear that under appropriate assumptions (summarized in the next section) the least-squares estimator for $\hat{\boldsymbol{\beta}}$ is unbiased, in that

$$E(\hat{\boldsymbol{\beta}}) = \boldsymbol{\beta} . \qquad *(4.8.12)$$

Consider now $\hat{\sigma}^2$ and $\hat{s}^2$. Taking expectations in (4.8.2)[21]

$$E(\hat{\sigma}^2) = \frac{n - k}{n} \; \sigma^2 \qquad *(4.8.13)$$

so $\hat{\sigma}^2$ is *not* an unbiased estimation of σ^2. The estimator adjusted for degrees of freedom $\hat{s}^2$, given by

$$\hat{s}^2 = \frac{n}{n - k} \; \hat{\sigma}^2 = \frac{1}{n - k} \; \hat{\mathbf{u}}'\hat{\mathbf{u}} = \frac{1}{n - k} \; \|\hat{\mathbf{u}}\|^2 \qquad *(4.8.14)$$

[21] To prove this result, note that

$$E(\hat{\sigma}^2) = \frac{1}{n} \; E(\hat{\mathbf{u}}'\hat{\mathbf{u}}) = \frac{1}{n} E(\mathbf{u}'\mathbf{M}\mathbf{u}) = \frac{1}{n} E \text{ tr } (\mathbf{u}'\mathbf{M}\mathbf{u})$$

where $\mathbf{M} = \mathbf{I} - \mathbf{X}(\mathbf{X}'\mathbf{X})^{-1}\mathbf{X}'$, as in (4.6.26), and tr is the trace of the matrix. Since tr $(\mathbf{ABC})$ = tr $(\mathbf{BCA})$ and tr $(\mathbf{M}) = n - k$, it follows that

$$E(\hat{\sigma}^2) = \frac{1}{n} E \text{ tr } (\mathbf{M}\mathbf{u}\mathbf{u}') = \frac{1}{n} \text{ tr } (\mathbf{M}E(\mathbf{u}\mathbf{u}')) = \frac{1}{n} (n - k)\sigma^2$$

See Problems 4-I and 4-J. See Appendix B, Section B.4, for a discussion of the trace of a matrix. Here tr $(\mathbf{M})$ = tr $\mathbf{I}$ − tr $\mathbf{X}(\mathbf{X}'\mathbf{X})^{-1}\mathbf{X}' = n - k$, where tr $\mathbf{X}(\mathbf{X}'\mathbf{X})^{-1}\mathbf{X}' = k$, since, using tr $(\mathbf{ABC})$ = tr $(\mathbf{BCA})$, it is the trace of the $k \times k$ identity matrix.

is, however, an unbiased estimator, since

$$E(\hat{s}^2) = \frac{n}{n-k} E(\hat{\sigma}^2) = \sigma^2. \qquad *(4.8.15)$$

This, therefore, is the estimator that is used, e.g., in estimating the covariance matrix, as in (4.7.14), which is an unbiased estimator.

A third property of an estimator is *asymptotic unbiasedness*. Defining the *bias* of the estimator $\hat{\boldsymbol{\theta}}$ as

$$B(\hat{\boldsymbol{\theta}}) = E(\hat{\boldsymbol{\theta}} - \boldsymbol{\theta}) = E(\hat{\boldsymbol{\theta}}) - \boldsymbol{\theta} \qquad *(4.8.16)$$

an estimator is *asymptotically unbiased* if

$$\lim_{n\to\infty} B(\hat{\boldsymbol{\theta}}) = \mathbf{0} \qquad *(4.8.17)$$

–that is, as the sample size increases without limit, the expected value of the estimator equals the true population value. Considering $\hat{\sigma}^2$ again:

$$\begin{aligned} B(\hat{\sigma}^2) &= E(\hat{\sigma}^2) - \sigma^2 = \frac{n-k}{n}\sigma^2 - \sigma^2 \\ &= -\frac{k}{n}\sigma^2 \to 0 \quad \text{as } n \to \infty \end{aligned} \qquad (4.8.18)$$

Thus the limit of $B(\hat{\sigma}^2)$ is zero, so $\hat{\sigma}^2$ is an asymptotically unbiased estimator of σ^2.

A fourth property of an estimator is *efficiency*. A scalar estimator is more efficient than another if it has a smaller "spread" about the true population parameter. The *mean squared error* of $\hat{\theta}$ is defined as

$$M(\hat{\theta}) = E(\hat{\theta} - \theta)^2 \qquad *(4.8.19)$$

–an expression similar to that for variance, but where $E(\hat{\theta})$ is replaced by θ. From definitions of variance and bias it follows that

$$M(\hat{\theta}) = \text{Var}(\hat{\theta}) + [B(\hat{\theta})]^2. \qquad *(4.8.20)$$

Thus, the mean squared error is the variance in the case of an unbiased estimator. The estimator $\hat{\theta}^1$ is *at least as efficient* as $\hat{\theta}^2$ if

$$M(\hat{\theta}^1) \leqslant M(\hat{\theta}^2) \quad \text{or} \quad M(\hat{\theta}^1) - M(\hat{\theta}^2) \leqslant 0. \qquad *(4.8.21)$$

This concept of efficiency, based on mean squared error, from (4.8.20), takes account of both variance and bias, two of the undesirable properties of any estimator. As an example, consider the sample mean and first observation for a random sample, both of which are unbiased estimators. Since

$$M(m) = \text{Var}(m) = \frac{\sigma^2}{n} < \sigma^2 = \text{Var}(Z_1) = M(Z_1) \tag{4.8.22}$$

it follows that the sample mean is more efficient than the first observation.

In the vector case, defining the *co-mean squared error matrix* as

$$\mathbf{M}(\hat{\boldsymbol{\theta}}) = E[(\hat{\boldsymbol{\theta}} - \boldsymbol{\theta})(\hat{\boldsymbol{\theta}} - \boldsymbol{\theta})'] \qquad *(4.8.23)$$

the vector estimator $\hat{\boldsymbol{\theta}}^1$ is *at least as efficient as* $\hat{\boldsymbol{\theta}}^2$ if

$$\mathbf{M}(\hat{\boldsymbol{\theta}}^1) - \mathbf{M}(\hat{\boldsymbol{\theta}}^2) \text{ is negative semidefinite.} \qquad *(4.8.24)$$

To motivate this definition note that it is equivalent to stating that $\hat{\boldsymbol{\theta}}^1$ is at least as efficient as $\hat{\boldsymbol{\theta}}^2$ if the mean squared error of the linear combination $\mathbf{a}\hat{\boldsymbol{\theta}}^1$ for any nonzero row vector of weights $\mathbf{a}$, given as $\mathbf{a}\mathbf{M}(\hat{\boldsymbol{\theta}}^1)\mathbf{a}'$, is no larger than the mean squared error for the linear combination $\mathbf{a}\hat{\boldsymbol{\theta}}^2$, given as $\mathbf{a}\mathbf{M}(\hat{\boldsymbol{\theta}}^2)\mathbf{a}'$—that is, $\mathbf{a}[\mathbf{M}(\hat{\boldsymbol{\theta}}^1) - \mathbf{M}(\hat{\boldsymbol{\theta}}^2)]\mathbf{a}' \leq 0$ for any $\mathbf{a}$. A discussion of efficiency for the least-squares and maximum-likelihood estimators of parameters is given in the next section; in anticipation of that section, however, an estimator is *best* in a certain class of estimators if, and only if, it is at least as efficient as any other estimator in that class. A discussion of asymptotic efficiency is deferred until Chapter 11, Section 11.6.

A fifth property of an estimator is the large-sample property of *consistency*. The estimator $\hat{\boldsymbol{\theta}}$ is a consistent estimator of $\boldsymbol{\theta}$ if and only if, letting $|\hat{\boldsymbol{\theta}} - \boldsymbol{\theta}|$ be a scalar measure of the distance between the estimator and the true value, for any $\epsilon > 0$,

$$\lim_{n\to\infty} P(|\hat{\boldsymbol{\theta}} - \boldsymbol{\theta}| < \epsilon) = 1. \qquad *(4.8.25)$$

Here $P(\cdot)$ is the probability that this distance is less than a prescribed distance ϵ. The estimator is consistent if and only if, as the sample size increases without limit, this probability approaches unity.[22] Thus, with a sufficiently large sample a consistent estimator will have as high a probability as required of being close to the true population value. Sometimes property (4.8.25) is written in the more compact form, using the notion of a *probability limit*, as

$$\text{plim } \hat{\boldsymbol{\theta}} = \boldsymbol{\theta} \tag{4.8.26}$$

[22] Recall that the sequence a_n converges to a if and only if

$$\lim_{n\to\infty} |a_n - a| = 0$$

—that is, if and only if given any prespecified distance there is a number N such that for all $n > N$ the absolute difference $|a_n - a|$ is less than the prespecified distance. The concept of consistency is similar to this concept of convergence for a sequence, although it is phrased in terms of the probability statement of (4.8.25) because of the presence of the random variable $\hat{\boldsymbol{\theta}}$.

stating that the random variable $\hat{\boldsymbol{\theta}}$ converges in probability to the true parameter $\boldsymbol{\theta}$. The concept of a probability limit is an extremely useful one. It satisfies the properties

$$\text{plim}\,(\hat{\boldsymbol{\theta}}^1 + \hat{\boldsymbol{\theta}}^2) = \text{plim}\,\hat{\boldsymbol{\theta}}^1 + \text{plim}\,\hat{\boldsymbol{\theta}}^2 \tag{4.8.27}$$

$$\text{plim}\,(\hat{\boldsymbol{\theta}}^1 \hat{\boldsymbol{\theta}}^2) = \text{plim}\,\hat{\boldsymbol{\theta}}^1 \;\text{plim}\,\hat{\boldsymbol{\theta}}^2 \tag{4.8.28}$$

$$\text{plim}\,(\hat{\boldsymbol{\theta}}^1)^{-1} = (\text{plim}\,\hat{\boldsymbol{\theta}}^1)^{-1} \quad \text{if } \hat{\boldsymbol{\theta}}^1 \text{ is square and nonsingular} \tag{4.8.29}$$

These properties are special cases of a general *invariance property*, which states that, if plim $\hat{\boldsymbol{\theta}} = \boldsymbol{\theta}$, then, if $f(\hat{\boldsymbol{\theta}})$ is any continuous function of the estimator,

$$\text{plim}\; f(\hat{\boldsymbol{\theta}}) = f(\boldsymbol{\theta}) \tag{4.8.30}$$

Thus, any continuous function of a consistent estimator is itself a consistent estimator of the same function of the original parameters.

If an estimator "collapses" to the true population value $\boldsymbol{\theta}$ in that it is both asymptotically unbiased, its mean going to the true population value as in (4.8.17), and also asymptotically "certain," the whole distribution of the estimator falling at $\boldsymbol{\theta}$, so that

$$\lim_{n\to\infty} B(\hat{\boldsymbol{\theta}}) = \mathbf{0} \quad \text{and} \quad \lim_{n\to\infty} \text{Cov}\,(\hat{\boldsymbol{\theta}}) = \mathbf{0} \tag{4.8.31}$$

then the estimator is consistent. These conditions are, however, sufficient but not necessary for consistency.[23]

Returning to the example of the random sample, the sample mean is a consistent estimator of the population mean. In particular it is unbiased and

$$\lim_{n\to\infty} \text{Var}\,(m) = \lim \frac{\sigma^2}{n} = 0. \tag{4.8.32}$$

The first observation, however, is *not* consistent, since its variance is always equal to the population variance regardless of the sample size.

4.9 The Gauss-Markov theorem and the least-squares consistency theorem

The Gauss-Markov theorem and the least-squares consistency theorem state the optimality properties of the least-squares estimators (4.8.1), which, as has been noted in previous sections, are also maximum-likelihood estimators under

[23] For an example of an estimator that does not satisfy these properties but is nevertheless consistent see Problem 4-R. Generally, however, aside from certain special examples, consistent estimators exhibit the properties in (4.8.31).

the assumption of independent, identically, and normally distributed stochastic disturbance terms.

According to the *Gauss-Markov theorem*, under the assumptions of the basic linear regression model (4.6.3) or (4.7.1) these estimators are *linear* and *unbiased* estimators that are the *best* of all linear unbiased estimators; i.e., the estimators have minimum variance within the class of linear unbiased estimators. Sometimes the theorem is referred to as the *BLUE theorem*, where *BLUE* is an acronym for *b*est *l*inear *u*nbiased *e*stimator, and the least-squares estimators are therefore also referred to as *BLUE estimators*. To give a complete statement of the *Gauss-Markov theorem*, under the following assumptions:

$$\underset{n\times 1}{\mathbf{y}} = \underset{n\times k}{\mathbf{X}}\ \underset{k\times 1}{\boldsymbol{\beta}} + \underset{n\times 1}{\mathbf{u}} \qquad \textit{(linear model assumption)} \qquad *(4.9.1)$$

$$E(\mathbf{u}) = \mathbf{0} \qquad \textit{(disturbance assumption)} \qquad *(4.9.2)$$

$$\text{Cov}\,(\mathbf{u}) = E(\mathbf{uu}') = \sigma^2\mathbf{I} \qquad \textit{(spherical disturbances assumption)} \qquad *(4.9.3)$$

$$\mathbf{X} \text{ is fixed, with } \rho(\mathbf{X}) = k < n \qquad \textit{(nonstochastic explanatory variables and rank assumptions)} \qquad *(4.9.4)$$

the least squares estimators

$$\hat{\beta} = (\mathbf{X}'\mathbf{X})^{-1}\mathbf{X}'\mathbf{y} \qquad *(4.9.5)$$

which are well defined and unique given the rank assumption (4.9.4), are best linear unbiased estimators (BLUE). To prove this theorem, first observe that $\hat{\boldsymbol{\beta}}$ is linear in $\mathbf{y}$, as noted in (4.6.19). Second, note that $\hat{\boldsymbol{\beta}}$ is unbiased in that

$$E(\hat{\boldsymbol{\beta}}) = \boldsymbol{\beta} \qquad *(4.9.6)$$

as was shown in (4.6.30). To prove the last part of the theorem—that the least-squares estimator is the best of all linear unbiased estimators—consider the estimator

$$\hat{\hat{\boldsymbol{\beta}}} = ((\mathbf{X}'\mathbf{X})^{-1}\mathbf{X}' + \mathbf{P})\mathbf{y} \qquad *(4.9.7)$$

where $\mathbf{P}$ is a $k \times n$ nonstochastic perturbation matrix, representing a perturbation from the $\hat{\boldsymbol{\beta}}$ estimator. The estimator $\hat{\hat{\boldsymbol{\beta}}}$ becomes the least-squares estimator if and only if $\mathbf{P}$ vanishes. Thus (4.9.7) defines a whole set of estimators, which are determined once a $\mathbf{P}$ matrix is given. By construction this set consists of all estimators that are linear in $\mathbf{y}$. Under appropriate conditions the estimators in this set are unbiased. Replacing $\mathbf{y}$, using (4.9.1),

$$\hat{\hat{\boldsymbol{\beta}}} = ((\mathbf{X}'\mathbf{X})^{-1}\mathbf{X}' + \mathbf{P})(\mathbf{X}\boldsymbol{\beta} + \mathbf{u}) = \boldsymbol{\beta} + (\mathbf{X}'\mathbf{X})^{-1}\mathbf{X}'\mathbf{u} + \mathbf{PX}\boldsymbol{\beta} + \mathbf{Pu} \qquad (4.9.8)$$

and, taking expectations, all terms on the right except $\boldsymbol{\beta}$ and $\mathbf{PX}\boldsymbol{\beta}$ vanish. Thus $\hat{\hat{\boldsymbol{\beta}}}$ is unbiased if

$$\mathbf{PX} = \mathbf{0}. \tag{4.9.9}$$

Since $\mathbf{P}$ can be *any* perturbation matrix subject only to these conditions, the class of estimators defined by (4.9.8) contains all linear unbiased estimators of $\boldsymbol{\beta}$.

To show that $\hat{\boldsymbol{\beta}}$ is best (most efficient) among this class requires calculating the covariance matrix of $\hat{\hat{\boldsymbol{\beta}}}$, since efficiency is based on $\mathbf{M}(\hat{\boldsymbol{\beta}})$ and $\mathbf{M}(\hat{\hat{\boldsymbol{\beta}}})$, which here are Cov $(\hat{\boldsymbol{\beta}})$ and Cov $(\hat{\hat{\boldsymbol{\beta}}})$, respectively, since both $\hat{\boldsymbol{\beta}}$ and $\hat{\hat{\boldsymbol{\beta}}}$ are unbiased. But the covariance matrix of $\hat{\hat{\boldsymbol{\beta}}}$ is

$$\text{Cov}\,(\hat{\hat{\boldsymbol{\beta}}}) = E(\hat{\hat{\boldsymbol{\beta}}} - \boldsymbol{\beta})(\hat{\hat{\boldsymbol{\beta}}} - \boldsymbol{\beta})' = \sigma^2((\mathbf{X}'\mathbf{X})^{-1} + \mathbf{PP}') \tag{4.9.10}$$

Combining this result with Cov $(\hat{\boldsymbol{\beta}})$ from (4.6.37),

$$\text{Cov}\,(\hat{\boldsymbol{\beta}}) - \text{Cov}\,(\hat{\hat{\boldsymbol{\beta}}}) = -\sigma^2\mathbf{PP}' \tag*{*(4.9.11)}$$

This is a negative-semidefinite matrix, so from (4.8.24), $\hat{\boldsymbol{\beta}}$ is the most efficient estimator in the set of linear unbiased estimators–i.e., the best of all linear unbiased estimators, (BLUE)–completing the proof of the Gauss-Markov theorem.[24] Thus, in particular, $\hat{\beta}_j$, the jth element of $\hat{\boldsymbol{\beta}}$, is linear, unbiased, and best in that, if $\hat{\hat{\beta}}_j$ is any other linear unbiased estimator of β_j, then the variance of $\hat{\beta}_j$ is less than or equal to the variance of $\hat{\hat{\beta}}_j$.

The *least-squares consistency theorem* states that the least-squares estimators, under certain conditions, are consistent as defined in (4.8.25). The conditions guaranteeing consistency are the above conditions (4.9.1) to (4.9.4) together

[24] The efficiency of $\hat{\boldsymbol{\beta}}$ can also be shown in the normally distributed case of (4.7.1) and (4.7.2) using the *Cramer-Rao bound*. This lower bound for the covariance matrix of an unbiased (linear or nonlinear) estimator $\hat{\boldsymbol{\theta}}$ is given by

$$\mathbf{C} = -\left[E\left(\frac{\partial^2 \ln L(\mathbf{x},\boldsymbol{\theta})}{\partial\boldsymbol{\theta}^2}\right)\right]^{-1} = -\left[E\left(\frac{\partial^2 \ln L(\mathbf{x},\boldsymbol{\theta})}{\partial\boldsymbol{\theta}_r\,\partial\boldsymbol{\theta}_s}\right)\right]^{-1}$$

where $L(\mathbf{x},\boldsymbol{\theta})$ is the likelihood function and where the matrix to be inverted is called the "information matrix." $\mathbf{C}$ represents a "lower bound" for the covariance matrix in that, if $\boldsymbol{\Sigma}$ is the covariance matrix of any estimator of $\boldsymbol{\theta}$, then $\mathbf{C} - \boldsymbol{\Sigma}$ is negative semidefinite. Thus if Cov $(\hat{\boldsymbol{\theta}})$ is $\mathbf{C}$, then $\hat{\boldsymbol{\theta}}$ is most efficient in that it is at least as efficient as any other estimator of $\boldsymbol{\theta}$[See the definition in (4.8.24)]. Here the log of the likelihood function is, from (4.7.7),

$$\ln L = -\frac{n}{2}\ln 2\pi - n \ln \sigma - \frac{1}{2\sigma^2}(\mathbf{y} - \mathbf{X}\boldsymbol{\beta})'(\mathbf{y} - \mathbf{X}\boldsymbol{\beta})$$

so

$$\frac{\partial^2 \ln L}{\partial \boldsymbol{\beta}^2} = -\frac{1}{\sigma^2}(\mathbf{X}'\mathbf{X})$$

Thus

$$\mathbf{C} = \sigma^2(\mathbf{X}'\mathbf{X})^{-1} = \text{Cov}\,(\hat{\boldsymbol{\beta}})$$

implying that $\hat{\boldsymbol{\beta}}$ is most efficient since it attains the Cramer-Rao bound. For a discussion of the Cramer-Rao bound see Rao (1965).

with the assumption on the convergence of the matrix $(1/n)(\mathbf{X}'\mathbf{X})$ to a nonsingular matrix $\mathbf{Q}$ as $n \longrightarrow \infty$:[25]

$$\lim_{n\to\infty} \frac{1}{n}(\mathbf{X}'\mathbf{X}) = \mathbf{Q} \quad \text{where } \mathbf{Q} \text{ is nonsingular.} \tag*{*(4.9.12)}$$

The proof of the theorem is straightforward. First note that the least-squares estimators are unbiased (by the Gauss-Markov theorem) and hence asymptotically unbiased in that

$$\lim_{n\to\infty} E(\hat{\boldsymbol{\beta}}) = \boldsymbol{\beta} \tag{4.9.13}$$

Second, the least-squares estimator $\hat{\boldsymbol{\beta}}$ has a covariance matrix

$$\text{Cov}(\hat{\boldsymbol{\beta}}) = \sigma^2(\mathbf{X}'\mathbf{X})^{-1} = \frac{\sigma^2}{n}\left(\frac{1}{n}\mathbf{X}'\mathbf{X}\right)^{-1} \tag{4.9.14}$$

which has been written in such a way that the limit can be taken. Taking the limit as $n \to \infty$,

$$\lim_{n\to\infty} \text{Cov}(\hat{\boldsymbol{\beta}}) = \lim \frac{\sigma^2}{n}\left(\frac{1}{n}\mathbf{X}'\mathbf{X}\right)^{-1} = \lim \frac{\sigma^2}{n}\mathbf{Q}^{-1} = 0 \tag{4.9.15}$$

where $\mathbf{Q}^{-1}$ is the matrix to which $(1/n\mathbf{X}'\mathbf{X})^{-1}$ converges. It has therefore been shown that the least-squares estimator is both asymptotically unbiased and asymptotically certain. It then follows from (4.8.31) that this estimator is a consistent estimator of $\boldsymbol{\beta}$,[26]

$$\text{plim}\ \hat{\boldsymbol{\beta}} = \boldsymbol{\beta}\,. \tag{4.9.16}$$

4.10 Prediction

The Gauss-Markov theorem provides a justification for the use of least-squares estimators for purposes of prediction—that is, to estimate a value of the dependent variable for certain given levels of the explanatory variables. The *least-squares predictor* $\hat{y}$ is obtained by setting all coefficients equal to their least-squares estimators $\hat{\boldsymbol{\beta}}$, all explanatory variables at their given levels $\hat{\mathbf{x}}$, and the

[25] In general, when taking limits as $n \to \infty$, as in (4.9.12) and (4.9.15), it is necessary to include the $1/n$ factors. In the matrix $\mathbf{X}'\mathbf{X}$ each element is the sum of n terms. Thus, in order to make each such element meaningful as $n \to \infty$ it is necessary to divide it by n, as indicated.

[26] The adjusted maximum-likelihood estimator $\widehat{s^2}$ is a consistent estimator of σ^2 if $\mathbf{u}$ is distributed as the multivariate normal distribution, as in (4.7.2), or if (4.9.14) holds and the stochastic disturbance terms are independently and identically distributed.

stochastic disturbance term equal to its expected value of zero, namely

$$\hat{y} = \hat{\mathbf{x}}\hat{\boldsymbol{\beta}} \qquad *(4.10.1)$$

Such a predictor is the unique *best linear unbiased predictor* of the dependent variable y, given that $\mathbf{x} = \hat{\mathbf{x}}$. Specifically, among the class of linear and unbiased predictors, the least-squares predictor has minimum variance.[27] This variance is given by

$$\operatorname{Var}(\hat{y}) = \hat{\mathbf{x}} \operatorname{Cov}(\hat{\boldsymbol{\beta}})\hat{\mathbf{x}}' = \sigma^2 \hat{\mathbf{x}}(\mathbf{X}'\mathbf{X})^{-1}\hat{\mathbf{x}}' \qquad *(4.10.2)$$

From this result the variance of the predicted value increases with the error variance σ^2, increases with the values taken by the explanatory variables $\hat{\mathbf{x}}$, and decreases with the "spread" of the data on the explanatory variables as measured by $\mathbf{X}'\mathbf{X}$.

Assuming normally distributed stochastic disturbance terms (4.10.2) implies that the least-squares predictor $\hat{y}$ is distributed normally, as

$$\hat{y} \sim N(\hat{\mathbf{x}}\boldsymbol{\beta},\ \sigma^2 \hat{\mathbf{x}}(\mathbf{X}'\mathbf{X})^{-1}\hat{\mathbf{x}}'). \qquad *(4.10.3)$$

In terms of the standardized normal

$$\frac{\hat{y} - \hat{\mathbf{x}}\boldsymbol{\beta}}{\sqrt{\sigma^2 \hat{\mathbf{x}}(\mathbf{X}'\mathbf{X})^{-1}\hat{\mathbf{x}}'}} \sim N(0, 1). \qquad (4.10.4)$$

But, from (4.7.16), $(n - k)\,\hat{s}^2/\sigma^2$ is distributed independently as χ^2 with $n - k$ degrees of freedom. Thus the ratio

$$\frac{\dfrac{\hat{y} - \hat{\mathbf{x}}\boldsymbol{\beta}}{\sqrt{\sigma^2 \hat{\mathbf{x}}(\mathbf{X}'\mathbf{X})^{-1}\hat{\mathbf{x}}'}}}{\sqrt{\dfrac{\hat{s}^2}{\sigma^2}}} \qquad (4.10.5)$$

is distributed as the t distribution with $n - k$ degrees of freedom–i.e.,[28]

$$\frac{\hat{y} - \hat{\mathbf{x}}\boldsymbol{\beta}}{\hat{s}\sqrt{\hat{\mathbf{x}}(\mathbf{X}'\mathbf{X})^{-1}\hat{\mathbf{x}}'}} \sim t(n - k). \qquad (4.10.6)$$

From the probability statement

$$P(-t_{\epsilon/2} < t < t_{\epsilon/2}) = 1 - \epsilon \qquad (4.10.7)$$

[27] See Whittle (1963). See also Problem 4-W.
[28] See Appendix C, equation (C.4.16).

where $t_{\epsilon/2}$ is the value of the t distribution for a level of significance of $\epsilon/2$ and $n - k$ degrees of freedom, it follows that

$$P\left(-t_{\epsilon/2} < \frac{\hat{y} - \hat{\mathbf{x}}\boldsymbol{\beta}}{\hat{s}\sqrt{\hat{\mathbf{x}}(\mathbf{X}'\mathbf{X})^{-1}\hat{\mathbf{x}}'}} < t_{\epsilon/2}\right) = 1 - \epsilon. \qquad *(4.10.8)$$

Thus, a $100(1 - \epsilon)$ percent confidence interval for the prediction $\hat{y}$ is given as

$$\hat{\mathbf{x}}\hat{\boldsymbol{\beta}} \pm t_{\epsilon/2}\,\hat{s}\sqrt{\hat{\mathbf{x}}(\mathbf{X}'\mathbf{X})^{-1}\hat{\mathbf{x}}'} \qquad *(4.10.9)$$

giving an interval prediction for the mean value of the dependent variable at given levels of the explanatory variables $\hat{\mathbf{x}}$. For example, a 95% confidence interval would be given by the point prediction $\hat{\mathbf{x}}\hat{\boldsymbol{\beta}}$ plus or minus the last term in (4.10.9) with a value of t for a 0.025 level of significance. The nature of the confidence interval is illustrated in Figure 4.4 for the case of simple linear regression. Note that the confidence interval increases with the difference between the value assumed by the explanatory variable and the mean value of all observed explanatory variables. In this case the confidence interval is

$$\hat{\beta}_1\hat{x} + \hat{\beta}_2 \pm t_{\epsilon/2}\,\hat{s}\sqrt{\frac{1}{n} + \frac{(\hat{x} - \bar{x})^2}{\Sigma \dot{x}_i^2}} \qquad (4.10.10)$$

where $\bar{x}$ is the mean value for the explanatory variable and $\dot{x}_i = x_i - \bar{x}$ is the ith deviation from the mean value.[29]

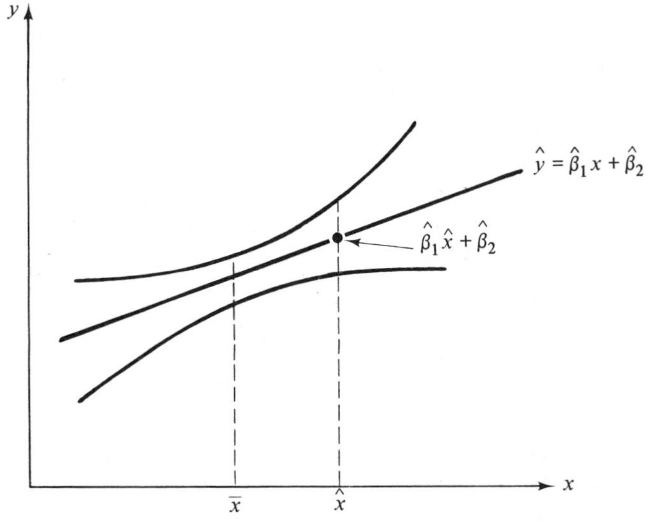

Figure 4.4 The Confidence Interval for Prediction in the Case of Simple Regression

[29] See Problem 4-X.

The interval defined in (4.10.9) is a confidence interval for the *mean* prediction. In terms of a specific value, the actual value y is related to the forecast value $\hat{y}$ by

$$y = \hat{y} + u \tag*{*(4.10.11)}$$

where u is the actual value taken by the stochastic disturbance term in the period to which the forecast refers. Thus, from the assumptions on the stochastic disturbance term

$$E(y) = E(\hat{y}) = \hat{\mathbf{x}}\boldsymbol{\beta} \tag{4.10.12}$$

$$\begin{aligned}\text{Var}(y) &= \text{Var}(\hat{y}) + \text{Var}(u) = \sigma^2\hat{\mathbf{x}}(\mathbf{X}'\mathbf{X})^{-1}\hat{\mathbf{x}}' + \sigma^2 \\ &= \sigma^2\,[1 + \hat{\mathbf{x}}(\mathbf{X}'\mathbf{X})^{-1}\hat{\mathbf{x}}'].\end{aligned} \tag{4.10.13}$$

Since y is distributed normally with the above mean and variance, following the same approach as earlier the 100 $(1 - \epsilon)$ percent confidence interval for y is given by

$$\hat{\mathbf{x}}\hat{\boldsymbol{\beta}} \pm t_{\epsilon/2}\ \hat{s}\ \sqrt{1 + \hat{\mathbf{x}}(\mathbf{X}'\mathbf{X})^{-1}\hat{\mathbf{x}}'} \tag*{*(4.10.14)}$$

where the expression multiplying $t_{\epsilon/2}$ is the *standard error of prediction*. Note that the confidence interval here for an actual value is wider than that above in (4.10.9) for the predicted (mean) value.

The confidence interval in (4.10.14) also leads to a test of the hypothesis that a new data point $(y, \mathbf{x})$ is generated by the same structure. Computing the t value for this data point as

$$t = \frac{\mathbf{x}\hat{\boldsymbol{\beta}} - y}{\hat{s}\sqrt{1 + \mathbf{x}(\mathbf{X}'\mathbf{X})^{-1}\mathbf{x}'}} \tag*{*(4.10.15)}$$

if the absolute value of t, $|t|$, computed for this observation exceeds the value t_ϵ, it would imply that, with a 100 $(1 - \epsilon)$ percent level of significance, the new observation is generated by a different structure. If, for example, it exceeds $t_{0.1}$ it would imply that, with a 90% level of significance, the new observation is generated by a different structure.

PROBLEMS

4-A The word "regression" stems from an early study relating the height of sons, S, to the height of their fathers, F, where

$$S = \beta_1 F + \beta_2.$$

The study found a *regression* toward the mean, where "regression" means a return to a previous state, in that fathers that are taller (shorter) than average tend to have sons that are also taller (shorter) than average but closer to the average height. What values for the estimates of the parameters yield this result? Prove that these values imply a regression toward the mean, and illustrate geometrically.

4-B The least-squares estimators are obtained from the normal equations.

1. Prove that the estimators in (4.4.17) and (4.4.18) can be obtained by the method of substitution—solving (4.4.13) for $\hat{\beta}_2$, inserting this result in (4.4.14), and then solving for $\hat{\beta}_1$.
2. Prove that normal equations (4.4.13) and (4.4.14) imply (4.4.21) and (4.4.22), and, by the method of substitution, show that they yield the slope estimator $\hat{\beta}_1$ in (4.4.24).

4-C Consider the weights w_i defined in (4.4.26) as the deviation of the ith value of the explanatory variable from the mean value, divided by the sum of squares of such deviations. Prove that

$$\Sigma w_i = 0, \quad \Sigma w_i^2 = \frac{1}{\Sigma \dot{x}_i^2}$$

$$\Sigma w_i \dot{x}_i = \Sigma w_i x_i = 1.$$

4-D Consider the simple linear regression model (4.4.2) estimated using the least-squares technique, where $\hat{\beta}_1$ and $\hat{\beta}_2$ are given by (4.4.24) and (4.4.23), respectively. Prove that

1. $\text{Var}(\hat{\beta}_1) = \dfrac{\sigma^2}{\Sigma \dot{x}_i^2}$.

2. $\text{Var}(\hat{\beta}_2) = \dfrac{\Sigma x_i^2}{n\, \Sigma \dot{x}_i^2} \sigma^2$.

3. $\text{Cov}(\hat{\beta}_1 \hat{\beta}_2) = -\dfrac{\bar{x}}{\Sigma \dot{x}_i^2} \sigma^2$.

where x_i is the ith observed value of the explanatory variable; $\bar{x}$ is the mean value of the x_i variables; and $\dot{x}_i$ is the deviation of x_i from $\bar{x}$, given as $x_i - \bar{x}$.

4-E Consider the simple linear regression model (4.5.1) estimated using the maximum-likelihood technique under the usual normality assumption.

1. Prove that the estimator of the slope coefficient $\hat{\beta}_1$ as given in (4.4.24) is distributed normally as

$$\hat{\beta}_1 \sim N\left(\beta_1, \frac{\sigma^2}{\Sigma \dot{x}_i^2}\right)$$

2. Show geometrically in a scatter diagram such as Figure 4.1. how the variance decreases as n increases, σ^2 decreases, or $\Sigma \dot{x}_i^2$ increases.
3. What is the distribution of the estimator of the intercept $\hat{\beta}_2$?
4. What is Cov $(\hat{\boldsymbol{\beta}})$ where $\boldsymbol{\beta} = (\beta_1 \beta_2)'$?

4-F Prove that the estimated regression coefficients for a linear regression equation with an intercept term are identical to those obtained for the same linear regression equation without an intercept term, but for which all variables are replaced by deviations from their mean values.

4-G One way of interpreting the least-squares estimators is in terms of the solutions to the problem of minimizing the variance of the estimator, given the constraint that the estimator is linear and unbiased. In the case of simple linear regression assume the slope estimator is linear and unbiased

$$\hat{\beta}_1 = \Sigma c_i y_i = \Sigma c_i (\beta_1 x_i + \beta_2 + u_i)$$
$$E(\hat{\beta}_1) = \beta_1 \Sigma c_i x_i + \beta_2 \Sigma c_i = \beta_1$$

requiring that

$$\Sigma c_i x_i = 1, \quad \Sigma c_i = 0$$

Subject to these two constraints, minimize the variance

$$\text{Var}(\hat{\beta}_1) = \sigma^2 \Sigma c_i^2$$

using the Lagrangian

$$L(\hat{\beta}_1, \lambda_1, \lambda_2) = \sigma^2 \Sigma c_i^2 + \lambda_1 (\Sigma c_i x_i - 1) + \lambda_2 (\Sigma c_i)$$

where λ_1 and λ_2 are Lagrange multipliers. Show that the resulting estimators are the least-squares estimators, where $c_i = w_i$, defined in (4.4.26). Carry out a similar proof for $\hat{\beta}_2$. (See also Problem 4-U for a generalization.)

4-H Another way of interpreting the least-squares estimators is in terms of the stochastic disturbance terms and the errors. The stochastic disturbance terms u_i in (4.6.1) are assumed to have a zero mean and are also assumed to be uncorrelated with each of the explanatory variables. Consider the related set of k equations for the residuals $\hat{u}_i$ in (4.6.8), namely

$$\Sigma \hat{u}_i = 0$$
$$\Sigma \hat{u}_i x_{ij} = 0, \quad j = 1, 2, \ldots, k - 1$$

(where $x_{ik} \equiv 1$, all i). Show that the solutions to these conditions for the parameters $\beta_1, \beta_2, \ldots, \beta_k$ are the least-squares estimators.

4-I Yet a third way of interpreting the least-squares estimators is in terms of the problem of prediction. In the case of simple linear regression, assume that the problem is to predict y at a particular level of x given as $\hat{x}$. Assume a linear and unbiased predictor

$$\hat{y} = \Sigma\, c_i y_i = \Sigma\, c_i (\beta_1 x_i + \beta_2 + u_i)$$
$$E(\hat{y}) = \beta_1\, \Sigma\, c_i x_i + \beta_2\, \Sigma\, c_i = \beta_1 \hat{x} + \beta_2$$

requiring that

$$\Sigma\, c_i x_i = \hat{x}, \quad \Sigma\, c_i = 1$$

Subject to these two constraints, minimize the variance of the prediction $\hat{y}$

$$\text{Var}(\hat{y}) = E[\hat{y} - E(\hat{y})]^2 = \sigma^2\, \Sigma\, c_i^2$$

proceeding as in Problem 4-G to show that the best linear unbiased predictors are given as

$$\hat{y} = \hat{\beta}_1 \hat{x} + \hat{\beta}_2$$

as in (4.10.1), where $\hat{\beta}_1$ and $\hat{\beta}_2$ are the least-squares estimators.

4-J Consider the multiple linear regression with two explanatory variables

$$y_i = x_{i1}\beta_1 + x_{i2}\beta_2 + \beta_3 + u_i$$

Show that if $\hat{v}_i$ are the least-squares residuals in the simple regression of y_i on x_{i2} and $\hat{w}_i$ are the least-squares residuals in the simple regression of x_{i1} on x_{i2}, then the least-squares estimator for β_1 can be obtained as the estimated slope in the simple regression of $\hat{v}_i$ on $\hat{w}_i$.

4-K Derive the normal equations of least squares for a multiple linear regression using summation notation. Using Cramer's rule solve for the least-squares estimators, and show that the results are the same as those using matrix notation.

4-L Prove that in the case of maximum-likelihood estimation for multiple linear regression, assuming homoskedasticity and absence of serial correlation, the multivariate normal density function can be written as in (4.7.5). Also prove that $\hat{\boldsymbol{\beta}}$ and $\hat{\sigma}^2$ in (4.7.9) and (4.7.11), respectively, satisfy both first- and second-order conditions for maximization of the likelihood function in (4.7.6).

4-M Consider the fundamental idempotent matrix of least squares **M**, defined in (4.6.26) as

$$\mathbf{M} = \mathbf{I} - \mathbf{X}(\mathbf{X}'\mathbf{X})^{-1}\mathbf{X}'.$$

Prove that

1. **M** is a symmetric and idempotent matrix.
2. $\mathbf{MX} = \mathbf{0}$, $\hat{\mathbf{u}} = \mathbf{Mu}$, $\hat{S}(\hat{\boldsymbol{\beta}}) = \mathbf{u}'\mathbf{Mu}$, $E(\hat{\mathbf{u}}\hat{\mathbf{u}}') = \sigma^2\mathbf{M}$.
3. $\rho(\mathbf{M}) = \text{tr}(\mathbf{M}) = n - k = \text{d.f.}$
4. $\mathbf{y}'\mathbf{My} \geqslant 0$, so **M** is positive semidefinite.
5. $\mathbf{M} = \mathbf{I} - \mathbf{XX}^+ = \mathbf{M}^+$, where $\mathbf{M}^+$ is the generalized inverse of **M**.

   (See Appendix B).

4-N An important property of maximum-likelihood estimators is that they are invariant with respect to nonsingular transformations. Illustrate this property by proving that the (biased) maximum-likelihood estimator of the standard deviation of the stochastic disturbance term, $\hat{\sigma}$, equals the square root of the (biased) maximum-likelihood estimator of the variance, $\hat{\sigma}^2$, given in (4.8.2). Show by contrast that the square root of the unbiased-estimator $\hat{s}^2$ (4.8.3) is *not* an unbiased estimator of the standard deviation.

4-O Justify each step in the proof (in footnote 21) of (4.8.13).

4-P Using the definitions of mean squared error and bias, in (4.8.19) and (4.8.16), respectively, prove that $M(\hat{\theta}) = \text{Var}(\hat{\theta}) + [B(\hat{\theta})]^2$ as in (4.8.20) by noting that

$$M(\hat{\theta}) = E(\hat{\theta} - \theta)^2 = E[(\hat{\theta} - E(\hat{\theta})) + (E(\hat{\theta}) - \theta)]^2$$

4-Q Show, using (4.7.16) that $\hat{s}^2$ is a consistent estimator of σ^2, assuming $\mathbf{u}$ is distributed as in (4.7.2).

4-R An example of an estimator that is consistent even though neither its bias nor its variance tends to zero is the estimator $\hat{\beta}^{(n)}$ of the parameter β defined as[30]

$$\hat{\beta}^{(n)} = \begin{cases} \beta & \text{with probability } 1 - (1/n) \\ n & \text{with probability } 1/n \end{cases}$$

Show that, as $n \to \infty$

1. $E(\hat{\beta}^{(n)}) \to \beta + 1 \neq \beta$
2. $\text{Var}(\hat{\beta}^{(n)}) \to \infty$
3. $P(|\hat{\beta}^{(n)} - \beta| < \epsilon) \to 1$

so that this estimator is consistent even though it is neither asymptotically unbiased nor asymptotically "certain."

4-S Consider the linear form $z = \boldsymbol{\alpha\beta}$, where $\boldsymbol{\alpha}$ is a nonzero row vector of fixed weights and $\boldsymbol{\beta}$ is the column vector of parameters in the basic linear regression model. Letting $\hat{\boldsymbol{\beta}}$ be the least-squares estimators, show, using the Gauss-Markov theorem, that

$$\hat{z} = \boldsymbol{\alpha}\hat{\boldsymbol{\beta}}$$

is the best linear unbiased estimator of z.[31]

[30] See Sewell (1969).

[31] This result implies that the minimum-variance property of least squares is preserved for any weighted combination of estimators. It also implies that it is impossible to improve upon the least-squares estimator of one of the parameters in $\boldsymbol{\beta}$ even by sacrificing precision in the estimators of all other elements of $\boldsymbol{\beta}$.

4-T Consider the simple linear model of (4.4.2).

1. Prove the Gauss-Markov theorem for this model using summation notation.
2. Show that least-squares estimators using $n_1 < n$ observations have a higher variance than those using all n observations.
3. Contrast the least-squares estimators for $n = 5$ to the naive estimators of (4.3.2) in terms of the properties of linearity, unbiasedness, efficiency, and consistency.

4-U Prove the Gauss-Markov theorem directly by constructing a linear estimator

$$\hat{\boldsymbol{\beta}} = \mathbf{Ay}$$

and minimizing elements of the covariance matrix of $\hat{\boldsymbol{\beta}}$ by choice of $\mathbf{A}$ subject to the conditions that $\hat{\boldsymbol{\beta}}$ is an unbiased estimator of $\boldsymbol{\beta}$—that is,

$$\min_{\mathbf{A}} E\,[(\hat{\boldsymbol{\beta}} - \boldsymbol{\beta})(\hat{\boldsymbol{\beta}} - \boldsymbol{\beta})'] \quad \text{subject to} \quad \mathbf{AX} = \mathbf{I}$$

4-V Under the assumptions of the Gauss-Markov theorem of Section 4.9 show that the least-squares residual vector

$$\hat{\mathbf{u}} = \mathbf{My} = (\mathbf{I} - \mathbf{X}(\mathbf{X}'\mathbf{X})^{-1}\mathbf{X}')\mathbf{y}$$

is a BLUE estimator of the stochastic disturbance vector $\mathbf{u}$, where

$$E(\hat{\mathbf{u}} - \mathbf{u}) = \mathbf{0}, \qquad \text{Cov}\,(\hat{\mathbf{u}} - \mathbf{u}) = \sigma^2\,(\mathbf{I} - \mathbf{M})$$

and where, if $\hat{\hat{\mathbf{u}}}$ is any linear unbiased estimator of $\mathbf{u}$, then

$$\text{Cov}\,(\hat{\mathbf{u}} - \mathbf{u}) - \text{Cov}\,(\hat{\hat{\mathbf{u}}} - \mathbf{u}) \quad \text{is negative semidefinite.}$$

4-W Prove that the least-squares prediction in (4.10.1) is the best linear unbiased predictor of y given $\mathbf{x} = \hat{\mathbf{x}}$. (The proof can follow that of the Gauss-Markov theorem in Section 4.9 or that of Problem 4-U.)

4-X Show for prediction with the simple linear regression model that the 100 $(1 - \epsilon)$ percent confidence level for the mean is given as in (4.10.10). What would the confidence interval be if there were error only in estimating the slope, the intercept β_2 being known? What if there were error only in estimating the intercept, the slope β_1 being known? Illustrate geometrically, as in Figure 4.4.

4-Y Assume the variables y and x depend on time t, where all three variables have mean zero. Let y_t^* and x_t^* be the detrended variables, namely the calculated residuals from the least-squares regressions of y on t and x on t, respectively. Show, for the following regressions,

$$\begin{aligned} y_t &= \beta_1 x_t + \gamma_1 t \\ &= \beta_2 x_t^* \\ &= \beta_3 x_t^* + \gamma_3 t \\ y_t^* &= \beta_4 x_t^* \\ &= \beta_5 x_t^* + \gamma_5 t \end{aligned}$$

that the least-squares estimates of the slope parameter are all equal:

$$\hat{\beta}_1 = \hat{\beta}_2 = \hat{\beta}_3 = \hat{\beta}_4 = \hat{\beta}_5.$$

Generalize to a vector of explanatory variables.

4-Z Consider the model

$$\begin{aligned} y_i &= \beta_1 x_{1i} + \beta_2 x_{2i} + u_i \\ E(u_i) &= 0 \\ E(u_i u_j) &= \begin{cases} \sigma^2 & \text{if } i = j \\ 0 & \text{if } i \neq j \end{cases} \end{aligned}$$

where all three variables have mean zero. If β_1 is estimated from the regression of y on x_1, with x_2 omitted, show that the resulting estimate is, in general, biased but has a smaller variance than the estimate obtained with x_2 included. When will the mean square error $E(\hat{\beta}_1 - \beta_1)^2$ be smaller for the regression with x_2 omitted?

BIBLIOGRAPHY

Christ, C. F. (1966), *Econometric Models and Methods.* New York: John Wiley & Sons, Inc.

Draper, N. R. and H. Smith (1966), *Applied Regression Analysis*, New York: John Wiley & Sons, Inc.

Fisher, W. D. (1961), "A Note on Curve Fitting with Minimum Deviations by Linear Programming," *Journal of the American Statistical Association*, 56: 359–62.

Hoel, P. G. (1971), *Introduction to Mathematical Statistics*, 4th Ed. New York: John Wiley & Sons, Inc.

Intriligator, M. D. (1971), *Mathematical Optimization and Economic Theory*. Englewood Cliffs, N.J.: Prentice-Hall, Inc.

Malinvaud, E. (1970), *Statistical Methods of Econometrics*. 2nd Rev. Ed. Amsterdam: North-Holland Publishing Co.

Mood, A. M., and F. A. Graybill (1963), *Introduction to the Theory of Statistics*, 2nd Ed. New York: McGraw-Hill Book Company.

Plackett, R. L. (1960), *Regression Analysis*, Oxford: Clarendon Press.

Schmidt, P. (1976), *Econometrics*. New York: Marcel Dekker, Inc.

Sewell, W. P. (1969), "Least Squares, Conditional Predictions, and Estimator Properties," *Econometrica*, 37: 39–43.

Theil, H. (1971), *Principles of Econometrics*. New York: John Wiley & Sons, Inc.

Whittle, P. (1963), *Prediction and Regulation by Linear Least Square Methods*. New York: Van Nostrand-Reinhold.

Williams, E. J. (1959), *Regression Analysis*. New York: John Wiley & Sons, Inc.

5

Extensions and Illustrations of the Basic Linear Regression Model

5.1 A geometrical interpretation of least squares

The least-squares estimators were obtained in the last chapter for the model

$$\underset{n\times 1}{\mathbf{y}} = \underset{n\times k}{\mathbf{X}}\ \underset{k\times 1}{\boldsymbol{\beta}} + \underset{n\times 1}{\mathbf{u}} \qquad *(5.1.1)$$

where $\mathbf{y}$ and $\mathbf{X}$ summarize the data on the dependent and explanatory variables, respectively. The estimators, given as

$$\hat{\boldsymbol{\beta}} = (\mathbf{X}'\mathbf{X})^{-1}\mathbf{X}'\mathbf{y} \qquad *(5.1.2)$$

can be interpreted and derived geometrically, using the concepts of vectors, distance, and orthogonality.[1] To visualize this geometrical interpretation most easily, consider the case of simple linear regression, where the problem is that of estimating the slope and intercept of a line from a sample of three observations, so the number of the data points n is 3. Then

$$\mathbf{y} = \begin{pmatrix} y_1 \\ y_2 \\ y_3 \end{pmatrix}, \quad \mathbf{X} = \begin{pmatrix} x_1 & 1 \\ x_2 & 1 \\ x_3 & 1 \end{pmatrix}, \quad \boldsymbol{\beta} = \begin{pmatrix} \beta_1 \\ \beta_2 \end{pmatrix} \qquad (5.1.3)$$

as in (4.2.3) and (4.2.4). The two column vectors of $\mathbf{X}$, each of which summarizes the three values of one of the independent variables over the sample, represent two vectors in a three-dimensional space as shown in Figure 5.1, where each axis measures values of variables at one observation. The set of all linear combinations of these two vectors, $\mathbf{X}\boldsymbol{\beta}$, for all vectors $\boldsymbol{\beta}$ is the plane P defined by the two vectors. Every vector $\mathbf{X}\boldsymbol{\beta}$ can be identified as a point in the plane, and, conversely, to each point in the plane there corresponds a $\boldsymbol{\beta}$ for which $\mathbf{X}\boldsymbol{\beta}$ is the point in question. The plane P, which is a two-dimensional subspace of three-space in this problem, is the space of all possible linear combinations of the two vectors defined by the three observations on the two independent variables. The problem treated here is, in fact, one of the simplest possible problems of regres-

[1] See Malinvaud (1970) and Wonnacott and Wonnacott (1970).

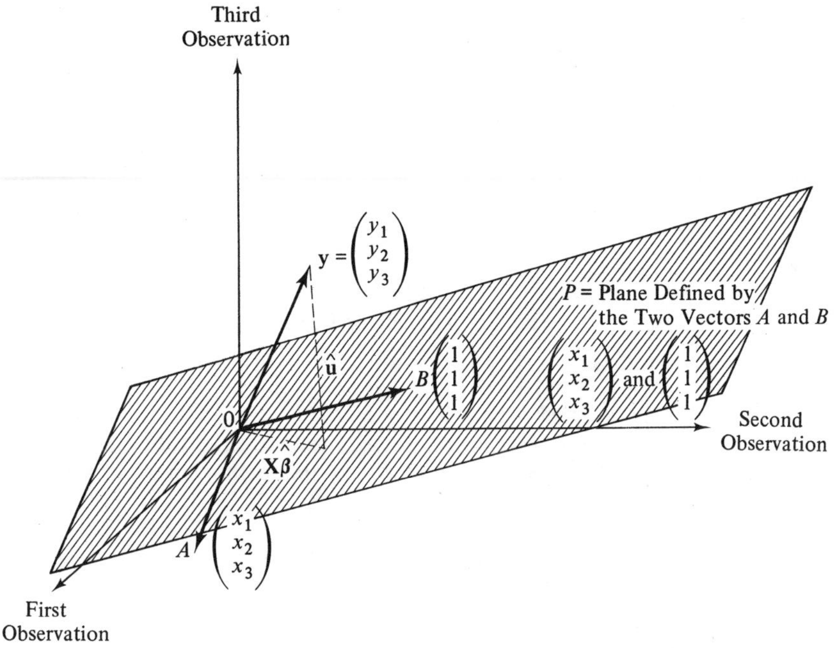

Figure 5.1 Geometrical Interpretation of Least-Squares Estimation.

[NOTE The P plane consists of all linear combinations $\mathbf{X\beta}$. $\mathbf{X\hat{\beta}}$ is the perpendicular projection of $\mathbf{y}$ on P, $\hat{\boldsymbol{\beta}}$ is the least-squares estimator, $\mathbf{u}$ is the least-squares residual vector, $\mathbf{y} - \mathbf{X\hat{\beta}}$.]

sion, with only two explanatory variables and three data points. The geometrical constructs suggested, however, apply to any regression problem. If there are k explanatory variables and n data points, then the space of data points is an n-space, and the hyperplane in this space, consisting of all linear combinations of the k column vectors in $\mathbf{X}$, given as $\mathbf{X\beta}$ for all vectors $\boldsymbol{\beta}$, is a k-dimensional subspace of the n-space, called the *parameter space* of all coefficient vectors. The complementary subset of the n-space, which contains all possible residual vectors, is the *residual space* of dimension $n - k$, the number of degrees of freedom of the problem. In Figure 5.1 the parameter space is the two-dimensional plane P and the residual space is one-dimensional—a line, shown as $\hat{\mathbf{u}}$.

The data on the dependent variable $\mathbf{y}$ define a vector, which, as shown, is generally *not* in the plane P. The problem of regression is that of finding a particular $\boldsymbol{\beta}$ vector, $\hat{\boldsymbol{\beta}}$, such that the vector $\mathbf{X\hat{\beta}}$, which lies in the plane, is closest to $\mathbf{y}$. The closest point in a plane to a point not in the plane is, however, on the perpendicular projection dropped from the point to the plane, as shown in the figure. A profile view of the triangle so formed is shown in Figure 5.2, where the residual vector is

$$\hat{\mathbf{u}} = \mathbf{y} - \mathbf{X\hat{\beta}} \qquad *(5.1.4)$$

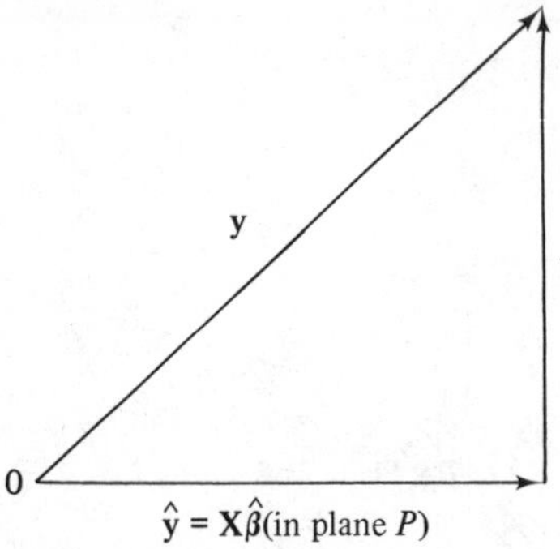

Figure 5.2 A Profile View of the Right Triangle of Figure 5.1

The fact that the residual vector $\hat{\mathbf{u}}$ is perpendicular to $\mathbf{X}\hat{\boldsymbol{\beta}}$ means that the inner product of the two vectors vanishes; i.e., the two vectors are orthogonal. The vector $\mathbf{X}\hat{\boldsymbol{\beta}}$ is, in fact, uniquely defined by this orthogonality condition, given as

$$(\mathbf{X}\hat{\boldsymbol{\beta}})'\hat{\mathbf{u}} = 0 \qquad *(5.1.5)$$

Thus

$$\hat{\boldsymbol{\beta}}'(\mathbf{X}'\hat{\mathbf{u}}) = 0 \qquad (5.1.6)$$

which, in general, requires that $\mathbf{X}'\hat{\mathbf{u}}$ vanish, as in the heuristic explanation of least squares in Section 4.6, equations (4.6.20) to (4.6.22). Thus

$$\mathbf{X}'\hat{\mathbf{u}} = \mathbf{0} \qquad *(5.1.7)$$

requiring that $\hat{\mathbf{u}}$ be orthogonal to each of the k column vectors of $\mathbf{X}$, as in Figure 5.1, where $\hat{\mathbf{u}}$ is orthogonal to both column vectors. This orthogonality condition, when combined with the definition of $\hat{\mathbf{u}}$ in (5.1.4), implies that

$$\mathbf{X}'(\mathbf{y} - \mathbf{X}\hat{\boldsymbol{\beta}}) = \mathbf{X}'\mathbf{y} - \mathbf{X}'\mathbf{X}\hat{\boldsymbol{\beta}} = \mathbf{0} \qquad (5.1.8)$$

which leads directly to the *normal equations of least squares*

$$\mathbf{X}'\mathbf{X}\hat{\boldsymbol{\beta}} = \mathbf{X}'\mathbf{y}. \qquad *(5.1.9)$$

Assuming $\mathbf{X}'\mathbf{X}$ is nonsingular, it is possible to solve for $\hat{\boldsymbol{\beta}}$ as

$$\hat{\boldsymbol{\beta}} = (\mathbf{X}'\mathbf{X})^{-1}\mathbf{X}'\mathbf{y} \qquad *(5.1.10)$$

which is the least-squares estimator in (5.1.2).

Figure 5.2, showing the right triangle formed by $\mathbf{y}$, $\mathbf{X}\hat{\boldsymbol{\beta}}$, and $\hat{\mathbf{u}}$, illustrates the decomposition of the vector $\mathbf{y}$ of observations on the dependent variable into two orthogonal components. The first is the component in the plane

$$\hat{\mathbf{y}} = \mathbf{X}\hat{\boldsymbol{\beta}} = \mathbf{X}(\mathbf{X}'\mathbf{X})^{-1}\mathbf{X}'\mathbf{y} \qquad *(5.1.11)$$

which is the *explained component*—that is, the component of $\mathbf{y}$ explained by the regression. The second is the residual vector

$$\hat{\mathbf{u}} = \mathbf{y} - \hat{\mathbf{y}} = \mathbf{y} - \mathbf{X}(\mathbf{X}'\mathbf{X})^{-1}\mathbf{X}'\mathbf{y} = (\mathbf{I} - \mathbf{X}(\mathbf{X}'\mathbf{X})^{-1}\mathbf{X}')\mathbf{y} = \mathbf{M}\mathbf{y} \qquad *(5.1.12)$$

which is the *unexplained component*—that is, the component of $\mathbf{y}$ not explained by the regression.[2] Thus

$$\mathbf{y} = \hat{\mathbf{y}} + \hat{\mathbf{u}} = \mathbf{X}\hat{\boldsymbol{\beta}} + \hat{\mathbf{u}}. \qquad *(5.1.13)$$

Figure 5.2 provides a profile view of Figure 5.1 from the perspective of the plane P (e.g., to an observer at A). Another useful perspective is that from above the plane (e.g., to an observer at $\mathbf{y}$), showing the relations between the two vectors defining the plane and the vector $\mathbf{X}\hat{\boldsymbol{\beta}}$. This perspective is shown in Figure 5.3. Using this perspective it is possible to identify geometrically the least-

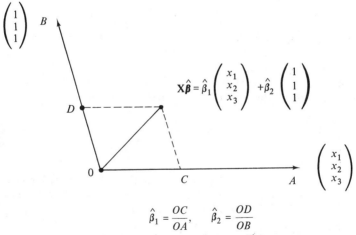

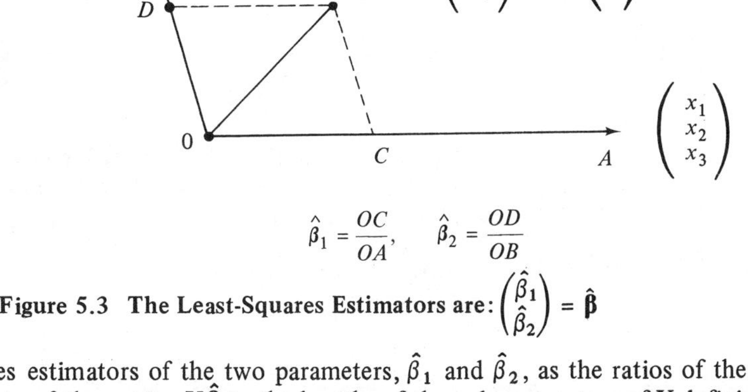

$$\mathbf{X}\hat{\boldsymbol{\beta}} = \hat{\beta}_1\begin{pmatrix} x_1 \\ x_2 \\ x_3 \end{pmatrix} + \hat{\beta}_2\begin{pmatrix} 1 \\ 1 \\ 1 \end{pmatrix}$$

$$\hat{\beta}_1 = \frac{OC}{OA}, \qquad \hat{\beta}_2 = \frac{OD}{OB}$$

Figure 5.3 The Least-Squares Estimators are: $\begin{pmatrix} \hat{\beta}_1 \\ \hat{\beta}_2 \end{pmatrix} = \hat{\boldsymbol{\beta}}$

squares estimators of the two parameters, $\hat{\beta}_1$ and $\hat{\beta}_2$, as the ratios of the components of the vector $\mathbf{X}\hat{\boldsymbol{\beta}}$ to the lengths of the column vectors of $\mathbf{X}$ defining the plane Thus the vector $\mathbf{X}\hat{\boldsymbol{\beta}}$ is obtained as the sum of two vectors, the first being $\hat{\beta}_1$ times the first column of $\mathbf{X}$ and the second being $\hat{\beta}_2$ times the second column

[2]The matrix $\mathbf{M}$ in (5.1.12) is the fundamental idempotent matrix of least squares as introduced in (4.6.26).

of **X**, where $\hat{\beta}_1$ is the estimated slope and $\hat{\beta}_2$ the estimated intercept.

With the use of simple vector geometry it has therefore been possible to derive the least-squares estimator (5.1.10), to express the least-squares residual vector as a linear combination of data on the dependent variables (5.1.12), to decompose the dependent variables into explained and unexplained components (5.1.13), and to identify the least-squares estimators geometrically, as in Figure 5.3. These results are important in understanding the meaning of the least-squares estimator. They will also be useful in developing both the multiple correlation coefficient and the analysis of variance for a regression, to be introduced in the next two sections.

5.2 Multiple correlation coefficient and coefficient of determination

Using the geometrical developments of the last section it is possible to measure the proportion of the variance of the dependent variable **y** that is explained by the regression $\hat{\mathbf{y}} = \mathbf{X}\hat{\boldsymbol{\beta}}$. Assuming that variables are measured as deviations from their mean values, the sum of squares of the elements of the $\dot{\mathbf{y}}$ vector, where $\dot{y}_i = y_i - \bar{y}$, as in (4.4.20), is the square of the norm of $\dot{\mathbf{y}}$:

$$\|\dot{\mathbf{y}}\|^2 = \dot{\mathbf{y}}'\dot{\mathbf{y}} = \sum_{i=1}^{n} (y_i - \bar{y})^2 = \sum_{i=1}^{n} \dot{y}_i^2. \qquad *(5.2.1)$$

This sum of squares, when divided by the number of degrees of freedom, given as $n - 1$, yields the variance of the dependent variable. It is often referred to as the "total sum of squares to be explained by the regression."

Measuring variables as deviations from mean values, Figure 5.4 shows the right triangle of Figure 5.2 in which $\dot{\mathbf{y}}$ is the hypotenuse and $\dot{\hat{\mathbf{y}}}$ and $\hat{\mathbf{u}}$ are the other

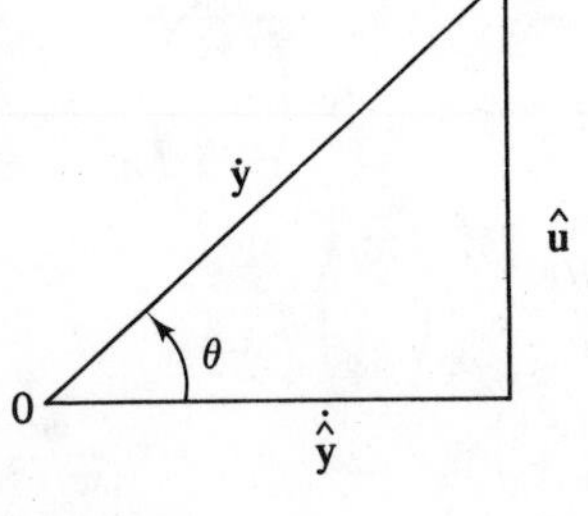

Figure 5.4 The Right Triangle of Figures 5.1 and 5.2. Where Variables are Measured as Deviations from Mean Values.

[NOTE Elements of $\dot{\mathbf{y}}$ are $y_i - \bar{y}$. Elements of $\dot{\hat{\mathbf{y}}}$ are $\hat{y}_i - \bar{y} = \mathbf{x}_i\hat{\boldsymbol{\beta}} - \bar{y}$.]

sides, where the elements of $\dot{\hat{\mathbf{y}}}$ are $\hat{y}_i - \bar{y}$. From the Pythagorean theorem, since $\|\dot{\mathbf{y}}\|^2$ is the square of the length of the hypotenuse,

$$\|\dot{\mathbf{y}}\|^2 = \|\dot{\hat{\mathbf{y}}}\|^2 + \|\hat{\mathbf{u}}\|^2 \qquad *(5.2.2)$$

where the squares of the lengths of the other sides of the right triangle are

$$\|\hat{\dot{\mathbf{y}}}\|^2 = \hat{\dot{\mathbf{y}}}'\hat{\dot{\mathbf{y}}} = \sum_{i=1}^{n} \hat{\dot{y}}_i^2 \qquad *(5.2.3)$$

$$\|\hat{\mathbf{u}}\|^2 = \hat{\mathbf{u}}'\hat{\mathbf{u}} = \sum_{i=1}^{n} \hat{u}_i^2 . \qquad *(5.2.4)$$

Thus

$$\Sigma \dot{y}_i^2 = \Sigma \hat{\dot{y}}_i^2 + \Sigma \hat{u}_i^2 \qquad *(5.2.5)$$

expressing the total sum of squares to be explained as the sum of an explained sum of squares and an unexplained sum of squares. This equation is similar to (5.1.13); while (5.1.13) expresses the decomposition into explained and unexplained components as a vector equation, (5.2.5) expresses the same decomposition in terms of the squares of the lengths of the sides of the triangle formed by the vectors. Because variables are measured as deviations from their mean values, the squared lengths, when divided by $n - 1$, have the interpretation of (sample) variances. Thus

$$\frac{1}{n-1} \sum_{i=1}^{n} \dot{y}_i^2 = \frac{1}{n-1} \sum_{i=1}^{n} \hat{\dot{y}}_i^2 + \frac{1}{n-1} \sum_{i=1}^{n} \hat{u}_i^2 \qquad (5.2.6)$$

expresses the total variance as the sum of an explained variance and an unexplained variance.

The *coefficient of determination* for a regression, R^2, is the *proportion* of the total variance that is explained by the regression. From the above this proportion can be expressed in various equivalent ways:

$$R^2 = \frac{\|\hat{\dot{\mathbf{y}}}\|^2}{\|\dot{\mathbf{y}}\|^2} = \frac{\|\dot{\mathbf{y}}\|^2 - \|\hat{\mathbf{u}}\|^2}{\|\dot{\mathbf{y}}\|^2} = 1 - \frac{\|\hat{\mathbf{u}}\|^2}{\|\dot{\mathbf{y}}\|^2}$$
$$= \frac{\hat{\dot{\mathbf{y}}}'\hat{\dot{\mathbf{y}}}}{\dot{\mathbf{y}}'\dot{\mathbf{y}}} = \frac{\Sigma \hat{\dot{y}}_i^2}{\Sigma \dot{y}_i^2} = 1 - \frac{\Sigma \hat{u}_i^2}{\Sigma \dot{y}_i^2} . \qquad *(5.2.7)$$

From the last two expressions for R^2, since a ratio of sums of squares cannot be negative,

$$0 \leqslant R^2 \leqslant 1. \qquad *(5.2.8)$$

The higher the R^2 the lower is the sum of squared errors $\|\hat{\mathbf{u}}\|^2$ relative to the total sum of squares $\|\dot{\mathbf{y}}\|^2$. In the limit when all residuals are zero, $\|\hat{\mathbf{u}}\|^2$ vanishes, $R^2 = 1$, and all of the total sum of squares is explained by the regression. At the other extreme, when all coefficients are zero, $\|\hat{\mathbf{u}}\|^2$ equals $\|\dot{\mathbf{y}}\|^2$, $R^2 = 0$, and none of the sum of squares is explained by the regression. Thus R^2 is a measure of the explanatory power of the regression—in particular, a measure of how well the model, as estimated, fits the available data. If, for example, $R^2 = 0.9$, then 90% of the variance of the dependent variables is explained by the regression, with 10% left unexplained. Some further examples of the coefficient of determination in the context of completely worked out examples of simple and multiple linear regression are given in Sections 5.5 and 5.6.

The coefficient of determination R^2 is a measure of the explanatory power of the regression, but it must be used carefully in comparing regressions. The value of R^2 can never decrease as more explanatory variables are added.[3] Furthermore, if the dependent variable is replaced by a linear combination of the dependent variable and the explanatory variables, the estimated least-squares coefficients and the least-squares residuals do not change, but R^2 will change.[4] Thus it would be inappropriate to compare the R^2 of two regression equations with different numbers of explanatory variables or with a different dependent variable. It is appropriate, however, to compare two regressions if the number of explanatory variables is fixed and if the dependent variable is the same.[5] Then the regression with the higher R^2 provides a better explanation of the phenomenon under investigation. For example, suppose that theory suggests a specific linear relation between y and the explanatory variables x_1 and x_2 but there are several ways of measuring x_1 and x_2. Comparing the values of R^2 for alternative combinations of ways of measuring the two explanatory variables would be appropriate in selecting those measures that best explain y.[6] It might also be noted that R^2 values tend to be high when using time-series data, where both dependent and explanatory variables may reflect certain underlying time trends. When using cross-section data, by contrast, R^2 values tend to be low because of both the great variability that is possible across the individual entities and the lack of a common underlying trend. An R^2 of 0.5 or higher may be acceptable with cross-section data, while a value of 0.9 or higher is usually expected with time-series data.

It is also possible to give a geometrical interpretation for the coefficient of determination. Again measuring variables as deviations from mean values, in Figure 5.4 the angle θ is that between $\dot{\mathbf{y}}$ and $\hat{\dot{\mathbf{y}}}$. From the definition of the cosine of this angle, as the ratio of the length of the adjacent side to the length of the hypotenuse

$$\cos\theta = \frac{\|\hat{\dot{\mathbf{y}}}\|}{\|\dot{\mathbf{y}}\|} \tag{5.2.9}$$

since $\|\hat{\dot{\mathbf{y}}}\|^2$ and $\|\dot{\mathbf{y}}\|^2$ are the *squared* lengths. Thus the coefficient of determination, geometrically, is the square of the cosine of the angle:

[3] See, however, the discussion below of the adjusted coefficient of determination R^2. See also Problem 5-C.

[4] See Problem 5-D.

[5] See Rao and Miller (1971).

[6] A specific example is presented in Section 8.6 on technical change, where a choice is made between alternative measures of technical change embodied in capital and labor on the basis of the R^2 of an estimated production function.

$$R^2 = \cos^2 \theta = \frac{\|\hat{\dot{\mathbf{y}}}\|^2}{\|\dot{\mathbf{y}}\|^2} \qquad *(5.2.10)$$

From this geometrical interpretation it is clear that R^2 is bounded by 0 and 1, as expressed in (5.2.8).

The *multiple correlation coefficient* R is defined as the nonnegative square root of R^2, or, equivalently,

$$R = \cos\theta \quad \text{where} \quad -\frac{\pi}{2} \leqslant \theta \leqslant \frac{\pi}{2} \quad \text{so} \quad 0 \leqslant R \leqslant 1. \qquad *(5.2.11)$$

Thus, when y lies in the plane P in Figure 5.1, so $\hat{\mathbf{u}}$ is the zero vector, it follows that $\theta = 0$, so $R = 1$ and the coefficient of determination $R^2 = 1$. At the other extreme, when y is perpendicular to the plane, so $\hat{\boldsymbol{\beta}}$ is the zero vector, it follows that $\theta = \pm\pi/2$ radians, so $R = 0$ and $R^2 = 0$. These extremes correspond, respectively, to a perfect fit (all residuals are zero) and no fit at all (all parameters are zero). From (5.2.7) it follows that the proportion of the total variance that is *un*explained is the ratio of the sums of squares of the residuals to the sums of squares of the dependent variable:

$$1 - R^2 = \frac{\Sigma\, \hat{u}_i^2}{\Sigma\, \dot{y}_i^2}. \qquad (5.2.12)$$

A related measure, the coefficient of determination adjusted for the degrees of freedom is defined as $\bar{R}^2$, where

$$1 - \bar{R}^2 = \frac{\dfrac{1}{n-k}\, \Sigma\, \hat{u}_i^2}{\dfrac{1}{n-1}\, \Sigma\, \dot{y}_i^2}. \qquad (5.2.13)$$

Here, the degrees of freedom associated with the residuals is $n - k$ (as in the calculation of $\hat{s}^2$, the unbiased estimator of σ^2, in (4.7.13)), while the degrees of freedom associated with the dependent variable is $n - 1$, and each sum of squares is deflated in (5.2.13) by the associated degrees of freedom. Thus the *adjusted coefficient of determination* is

$$\bar{R}^2 = 1 - (1 - R^2)\frac{(n-1)}{(n-k)} = R^2 - \frac{(k-1)}{(n-k)}(1 - R^2). \qquad *(5.2.14)$$

This is another measure of the goodness of fit or the explanatory power of the regression. In general $\bar{R}^2 < R^2$ (unless $k = 1$ or $R^2 = 1$, in which case $R^2 = \bar{R}^2$), and it is possible for $\bar{R}^2$ to be negative. While the (unadjusted) coefficient of determination can never decrease as added explanatory variables are taken into account, the adjusted coefficient of determination can decrease–if the reduction in $1 - R^2$ is more than offset by the increase in $(n - 1)/(n - k)$ in (5.2.14).

5.3 Analysis of variance for a regression

The division in (5.2.2) of the total sum of squares, $\|\dot{\mathbf{y}}\|^2$, into a sum of squares explained by the regression $\|\hat{\dot{\mathbf{y}}}\|^2$ and one unexplained by the regression $\|\hat{\mathbf{u}}\|^2$, leads directly to the analysis of variance for the regression. Table 5.1 summarizes the analysis of variance, where the ratio of the mean squares–in particular, the ratio of the explained to the unexplained variance–is distributed as the F distribution with $k - 1$ and $n - k$ degrees of freedom[7]

$$F = \frac{\|\hat{\dot{\mathbf{y}}}\|^2/(k-1)}{\|\hat{\mathbf{u}}\|^2/(n-k)} = \frac{R^2/(k-1)}{(1-R^2)/(n-k)} \sim F(k-1, n-k). \quad *(5.3.1)$$

This statistic tests the null hypothesis that all coefficients of the regression other than the intercept are zero,

$$H_0\colon\ \beta_1 = \beta_2 = \cdots = \beta_{k-1} = 0. \quad *(5.3.2)$$

It therefore tests the significance of the regression as a whole in testing for the existence of a linear relationship between the dependent variable and all of the explanatory variables specified by the model. If the ratio defined in (5.3.1) exceeds the $F(k - 1, n - k)$ value for a particular level of confidence, then the null hypothesis of no dependence on the explanatory variables is rejected. If so, the evidence indicates that not all regression slopes are zero, and the model therefore has some explanatory power. An example of the analysis of variance for a regression appears below in Section 5.6.

5.4 Significance of coefficients and confidence intervals

As noted in the last section, the F test performed in the analysis of variance for a regression tests the hypothesis that *all* of the coefficients in the model are zero. A related test is the test that *one* of these coefficients is zero, testing the hypothesis that the corresponding independent variable exerts no statistically significant linear influence on the dependent variable. Considering coefficient j, the null hypothesis to be tested is

$$H_0\colon\ \beta_j = 0, \qquad j = 1, 2, \ldots, k \quad *(5.4.1)$$

Assuming the stochastic disturbance terms are normally distributed, from (4.7.12) the estimated coefficients are also normally distributed:

[7] The F distribution is the ratio of two independent χ^2 (chi-square) distributions, as in (A.4.17) in Appendix A. Here, assuming a normal distribution for the stochastic disturbance term, the two sums of squares, $\|\hat{\dot{\mathbf{y}}}\|^2$ and $\|\hat{\mathbf{u}}\|^2$ are independently distributed as χ^2 distributions with $k - 1$ and $n - k$ degrees of freedom, respectively. Thus, their ratio, after dividing each by the appropriate number of degrees of freedom, is distributed as the F distribution with $k - 1$ and $n - k$ degrees of freedom. For a general F test, of which (5.3.1) is one special case, see (5.4.17).

Table 5.1. Analysis of Variance for a Regression

Source	*Sum of Squares*	*Degrees of Freedom*	*Mean Square*
Explained (by regression)	$\lVert \dot{\hat{\mathbf{y}}} \rVert^2 = R^2 \lVert \dot{\mathbf{y}} \rVert^2$	$k - 1$	$\lVert \dot{\hat{\mathbf{y}}} \rVert^2/(k - 1)$
Unexplained (residual)	$\lVert \hat{\mathbf{u}} \rVert^2 = (1 - R^2) \lVert \dot{\mathbf{y}} \rVert^2$	$n - k$	$\lVert \hat{\mathbf{u}} \rVert^2/(n - k)$
Total	$\lVert \dot{\mathbf{y}} \rVert^2 = \Sigma\, \dot{y}_i^2$	$n - 1$	

where

$\lVert \dot{\hat{\mathbf{y}}} \rVert^2 = \dot{\hat{\mathbf{y}}}'\dot{\hat{\mathbf{y}}} =$ sum of squares explained by the regression

$\lVert \hat{\mathbf{u}} \rVert^2 = \hat{\mathbf{u}}'\hat{\mathbf{u}} =$ sum of squares of error terms

$\lVert \dot{\mathbf{y}} \rVert^2 = \dot{\mathbf{y}}'\dot{\mathbf{y}} =$ total sum of squares (of deviations from the mean value)

NOTE The ratio of the mean squares tests the hypothesis that all slope coefficients vanish.

$$\hat{\boldsymbol{\beta}} \sim N(\boldsymbol{\beta}, \text{Cov}(\hat{\boldsymbol{\beta}})) = N(\boldsymbol{\beta}, \sigma^2 (\mathbf{X}'\mathbf{X})^{-1}). \qquad *(5.4.2)$$

In particular $\hat{\beta}_j$ is distributed normally with mean β_j and variance $\sigma^2 (\mathbf{X}'\mathbf{X})^{-1}_{jj}$, the jth diagonal element of the covariance matrix. Thus the ratio

$$\frac{\hat{\beta}_j - \beta_j}{\sqrt{\sigma^2 (\mathbf{X}'\mathbf{X})^{-1}_{jj}}} \qquad (5.4.3)$$

is distributed as the standardized normal with zero mean and unit variance. But from (4.7.17) $\hat{s}^2$ is distributed independently as $[\sigma^2/(n-k)]\ \chi^2(n-k)$, so the ratio

$$t = \frac{(\hat{\beta}_j - \beta_j)/\sqrt{\sigma^2 (\mathbf{X}'\mathbf{X})^{-1}_{jj}}}{\sqrt{\hat{s}^2/\sigma^2}} \qquad (5.4.4)$$

is distributed as the t distribution with $n - k$ degrees of freedom.[8] Defining the *jth standard error* as

$$\hat{s}_j = \sqrt{\hat{s}^2 (\mathbf{X}'\mathbf{X})^{-1}_{jj}} = \sqrt{\left(\frac{1}{n-k}\ \Sigma\, \hat{u}_i^2\right) (\mathbf{X}'\mathbf{X})^{-1}_{jj}} \qquad *(5.4.5)$$

it follows that

[8] See Appendix C, Equation (C.4.16). The discussion here parallels that in Section 4.10, in (4.10.6), and subsequent equations.

$$t = \frac{\hat{\beta}_j - \beta_j}{\hat{s}_j} \sim t(n - k). \qquad *(5.4.6)$$

From the probability statement

$$P(-t_{\epsilon/2} < t < t_{\epsilon/2}) = 1 - \epsilon \qquad (5.4.7)$$

it then follows that

$$P(\hat{\beta}_j - t_{\epsilon/2}\hat{s}_j < \beta_j < \hat{\beta}_j + t_{\epsilon/2}\hat{s}_j) = 1 - \epsilon \qquad (5.4.8)$$

where $t_{\epsilon/2}$ is the value of the t distribution for a level of significance $\epsilon/2$ and with $n - k$ degrees of freedom. Thus the $100(1 - \epsilon)$ percent confidence interval for the jth coefficient is given by

$$\hat{\beta}_j \pm t_{\epsilon/2}\,\hat{s}_j. \qquad *(5.4.9)$$

For example, the 95% confidence interval is given as the estimated coefficient, $\hat{\beta}_j$, plus or minus the t distribution for a 0.025 level of significance times the relevant standard error. The coefficient $\hat{\beta}_j$ is significantly different from zero, rejecting the null hypothesis in (5.4.1), whenever the confidence interval in (5.4.9) does not include the value of zero. Conversely, the coefficient is insignificant–i.e., not significantly different from zero (H_0 accepted)–whenever the confidence interval includes the value of zero. These two cases are shown in Figure 5.5.

Assuming $\hat{\beta}_j$ is positive, if the confidence interval (5.4.9) includes the origin, then solving at this point for the value of t yields the *t ratio* for the jth coefficient:

$$t_j = \frac{\hat{\beta}_j}{\hat{s}_j}. \qquad *(5.4.10)$$

Thus the t ratio is the ratio of the estimated regression coefficient to its standard error. This ratio determines the significance of the coefficient: in general the null hypothesis that β_j is zero is accepted if the absolute value $|t_j|$ is less than the value of t corresponding to a particular level of significance, and it is rejected if $|t_j|$ exceeds this value. A low t ratio implies that the coefficient is *not significant*, in that the dependent variable is not linearly dependent on the relevant explanatory variable. If, however, the t ratio exceeds the critical value (at a suitably chosen level of significance), then the coefficient is *significant*, i.e., the dependent variable does depend linearly on the relevant explanatory variable. For large degrees of freedom (e.g., $n - k > 30$) the t distribution is approximately the same as the normal distribution, and in this case a general rule of thumb is that if the t ratio exceeds 2, then the coefficient is significant. Conversely, a t ratio less than 2 in this case indicates lack of significance, i.e., a coefficient not statistically different from zero.

The t ratio in (5.4.10) used to test the hypothesis that β_j is zero will next be

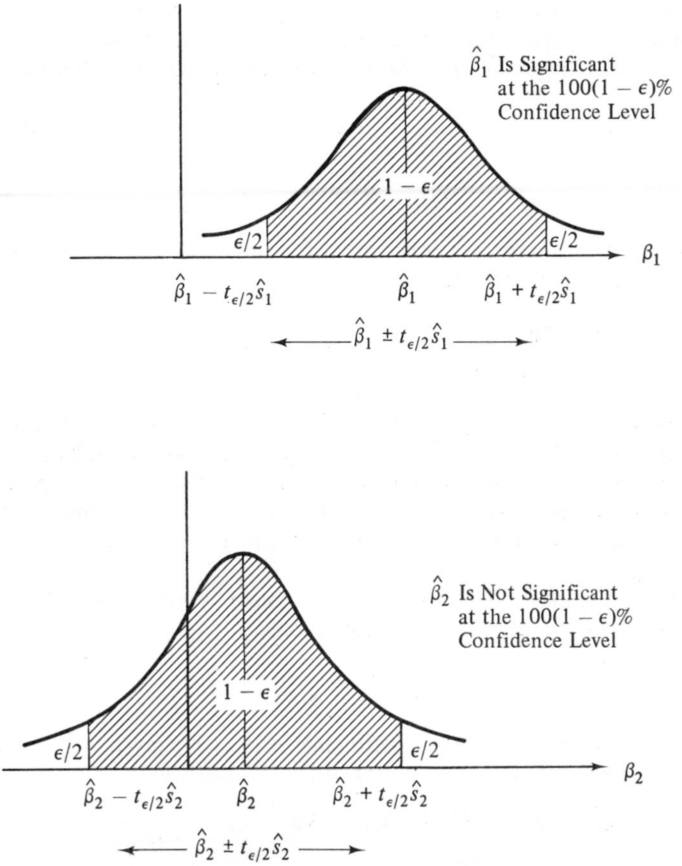

Figure 5.5 Significant and Insignificant Coefficients

successively generalized to consider more and more general hypotheses on the coefficients. As will be seen, the resulting tests will be either t or F tests.

First, consider the hypothesis that the jth coefficient is equal to a prescribed value:

$$H_0: \beta_j = \beta_j^0 \qquad *(5.4.11)$$

Assuming $\hat{\beta}_j$ exceeds β_j^0, it is possible to determine the confidence interval in (5.4.9) so as to include β_j^0:

$$\hat{\beta}_j - t_{\epsilon/2}\, \hat{s}_j = \beta_j^0 \qquad (5.4.12)$$

and, solving for t,

$$t = \frac{\hat{\beta}_j - \beta_j^0}{\hat{s}_j} \qquad *(5.4.13)$$

In general, if the absolute value of t so defined, $|t|$, exceeds the value of $t_{\epsilon/2}$ for $n - k$ degrees of freedom, then, at the $100(1 - \epsilon)$ percent level of significance the hypothesis is rejected. If $|t|$ falls below this critical value the hypothesis is accepted.

Next consider the hypothesis that the estimated coefficients satisfy a single linear restriction

$$H_0 : \boldsymbol{\alpha\beta} = c \tag{5.4.14}$$

where $\boldsymbol{\alpha}$ is a row vector of given constants and c is a given constant. From (4.10.6) a test statistic for this hypothesis is

$$t = \frac{\boldsymbol{\alpha}\hat{\boldsymbol{\beta}} - c}{\hat{s}\sqrt{\boldsymbol{\alpha}(\mathbf{X}'\mathbf{X})^{-1}\boldsymbol{\alpha}'}} \sim t(n - k). \tag{5.4.15}$$

If t exceeds $t_{\epsilon/2}$ for $n - k$ degrees of freedom at the $100(1 - \epsilon)$ percent level of significance, then H_0 is rejected–i.e., the estimated coefficients $\hat{\boldsymbol{\beta}}$ are not consistent with the linear restriction in (5.4.14). The t in (5.4.13) is the special case in which c is β_j^0 and $\boldsymbol{\alpha}$ is the jth unit vector $(0 \ldots 010 \ldots 0)$, with the one in the jth place. The denominator in (5.4.15) then reduces to the jth standard error defined in (5.4.5).

The last generalization treats the general linear hypothesis that the estimated coefficients satisfy a set of m linear restrictions:

$$H_0: \underset{m\times k}{\mathbf{A}} \; \underset{k\times 1}{\boldsymbol{\beta}} = \underset{m\times 1}{\mathbf{c}} \tag*{*(5.4.16)}$$

where $\mathbf{A}$ is a given $m \times k$ matrix with rank m and $\mathbf{c}$ is a given $m \times 1$ vector. The test for these m linear restrictions utilizes the test statistic

$$F = \frac{(\mathbf{A}\hat{\boldsymbol{\beta}} - \mathbf{c})'[\mathbf{A}(\mathbf{X}'\mathbf{X})^{-1}\mathbf{A}']^{-1}(\mathbf{A}\hat{\boldsymbol{\beta}} - \mathbf{c})}{m\hat{s}^2} \sim F(m, n - k) \tag*{*(5.4.17)}$$

which, as indicated, is distributed as the F distribution with m and $n - k$ degrees of freedom.[9] This result reduces to the previous one if $m = 1$, since then $\mathbf{A}\hat{\boldsymbol{\beta}} - \mathbf{c}$

[9] To prove (5.4.17) note that since $\hat{\boldsymbol{\beta}} \sim N(\boldsymbol{\beta}, \sigma^2(\mathbf{X}'\mathbf{X})^{-1})$, as in (5.4.2), it follows from (C.4.12) that

$$\mathbf{A}\hat{\boldsymbol{\beta}} - \mathbf{c} \sim N(\mathbf{A}\boldsymbol{\beta} - \mathbf{c}, \sigma^2\mathbf{A}(\mathbf{X}'\mathbf{X})^{-1}\mathbf{A}')$$

Thus, from (C.4.16),

$$\frac{(\mathbf{A}\hat{\boldsymbol{\beta}} - \mathbf{c})'[\mathbf{A}(\mathbf{X}'\mathbf{X})^{-1}\mathbf{A}']^{-1}(\mathbf{A}\hat{\boldsymbol{\beta}} - \mathbf{c})}{\sigma^2} \sim \chi^2(m)$$

Furthermore, this quadratic form is distributed independently of the ratio in (4.7.16)

$$(n - k)\frac{\hat{s}^2}{\sigma^2} \sim \chi^2(n - k).$$

Thus, deflating each of these expressions by its respective degrees of freedom and taking the ratio yields F in (5.4.17), which is distributed as $F(m, n - k)$.

reduces to the scalar $\boldsymbol{\alpha}\hat{\boldsymbol{\beta}} - c$ and $\mathbf{A}(\mathbf{X}'\mathbf{X})^{-1}\mathbf{A}'$ reduces to the scalar $\boldsymbol{\alpha}(\mathbf{X}'\mathbf{X})^{-1}\boldsymbol{\alpha}'$, so (5.4.17) implies

$$F = \frac{(\boldsymbol{\alpha}\hat{\boldsymbol{\beta}} - c)^2}{\hat{s}^2\boldsymbol{\alpha}(\mathbf{X}'\mathbf{X})^{-1}\boldsymbol{\alpha}'} \sim F(1, n - k). \tag{5.4.18}$$

Then, taking the square root,[10]

$$\sqrt{F} = \frac{\boldsymbol{\alpha}\hat{\boldsymbol{\beta}} - c}{\hat{s}\sqrt{\boldsymbol{\alpha}(\mathbf{X}'\mathbf{X})^{-1}\boldsymbol{\alpha}'}} \sim t(n - k) \tag{5.4.19}$$

as in (5.4.15).

Another special case of (5.4.17) tests the hypothesis that the coefficients all equal given values

$$H_0: \ \boldsymbol{\beta} = \boldsymbol{\beta}^0 \quad \text{that is,} \quad \beta_1 = \beta_1^0; \beta_2 = \beta_2^0; \ldots; \beta_k = \beta_k^0. \qquad *(5.4.20)$$

In terms of (5.4.16) this case corresponds to

$$\mathbf{A} = \mathbf{I}, \qquad \mathbf{c} = (\beta_1^0 \quad \beta_2^0 \quad \cdots \quad \beta_k^0)'. \tag{5.4.21}$$

The test statistic is then

$$F = \frac{(\hat{\boldsymbol{\beta}} - \boldsymbol{\beta}^0)'(\mathbf{X}'\mathbf{X})(\hat{\boldsymbol{\beta}} - \boldsymbol{\beta}^0)}{k\hat{s}^2} \sim F(k, n - k). \qquad *(5.4.22)$$

If $\boldsymbol{\beta}^0 = \mathbf{0}$, this test statistic tests the null hypothesis that all coefficients are zero. From (5.4.22) it follows that the set of estimates $\boldsymbol{\beta}$, satisfying

$$(\hat{\boldsymbol{\beta}} - \boldsymbol{\beta})'(\mathbf{X}'\mathbf{X})(\hat{\boldsymbol{\beta}} - \boldsymbol{\beta}) \leqslant k\hat{s}^2 F_\epsilon(k, n - k) \qquad *(5.4.23)$$

provides a 100 $(1 - \epsilon)$ percent confidence region for the complete set of coefficients. In the case of one explanatory variable, for example, the 95% confidence region is obtained as the set of pairs (β_1, β_2) satisfying the above inequality for $F_{0.05}$, which, geometrically, is an elliptical region in the (β_1, β_2) plane. More generally, inequality (5.4.23) defines an ellipsoid in the k-dimensional space of all coefficients.

Yet another special case of (5.4.17) treats the hypothesis that a certain subset of coefficients vanishes:

$$H_0: \beta_1 = 0, \ \beta_2 = 0, \ldots, \ \beta_m = 0 \tag{5.4.24}$$

where $1 \leqslant m \leqslant k$ and where coefficients can be renumbered so the hypothesis treats any set of m coefficients. In this case the F test statistic can be written

[10] See (C.4.19) in Appendix C on the relation between the F and t distributions.

$$F = \frac{(\hat{\mathbf{u}}'\hat{\mathbf{u}})_{k-m} - (\hat{\mathbf{u}}'\hat{\mathbf{u}})}{m\hat{s}^2} \sim F(m, n - k). \tag{5.4.25}$$

Here $\hat{\mathbf{u}}'\hat{\mathbf{u}}$ is the (usual) sum of squared residuals in the regression of y on all k explanatory variables, while $(\hat{\mathbf{u}}'\hat{\mathbf{u}})_{k-m}$ is the sum of squared residuals in the regression of y on the $k - m$ explanatory variables the coefficients of which are *not* part of the hypothesis (5.4.24). The test in (5.4.25) is a *partial F test*, which tests whether a subset of coefficients vanishes. The numerator gives the sum of the squared residuals when the m variables for which the coefficients vanish in (5.4.24) are omitted from the regression less the sum of squared residuals when all variables enter. If this excess is large, it means that the m variables play an important role, so their coefficients do not vanish, and the hypothesis is rejected. If the F test statistic defined in (5.4.25) exceeds a critical value of F, then the hypothesis is rejected. This partial F test becomes, at one extreme, for $m = 1$, the t test in (5.4.10), testing whether one coefficient equals zero. At the other extreme, for $m = k$, it becomes the F test in (5.4.22) for $\boldsymbol{\beta}^0 = \mathbf{0}$, testing whether all coefficients equal zero.[11] For $m = k - 1$ it becomes the F test in (5.3.1), testing whether all *slope* coefficients equal zero.

5.5 An example of simple linear regression

A few specific examples may help in understanding the results of the last chapter and this chapter. This section gives an example of simple linear regression, and the next section gives an example of multiple linear regression.

The example to be pursued here borrows from the methodology of Price in studying the history of science, as discussed in Section 1.6. Letting $N(t)$ be the number of U.S. economists at time t, and assuming a constant exponential growth of the number of economists, it follows that

$$N(t) = N_0 e^{gt}. \tag{5.5.1}$$

[11] The F test in (5.4.22) for $\boldsymbol{\beta}^0 = \mathbf{0}$ can be written

$$\frac{\hat{\boldsymbol{\beta}}'(\mathbf{X}'\mathbf{X})\hat{\boldsymbol{\beta}}}{ks^2} = \frac{\mathbf{y}'(\mathbf{I} - \mathbf{M})\mathbf{y}}{k\hat{s}^2} \sim F(k, n - k)$$

where $\mathbf{M}$ is the fundamental idempotent matrix $\mathbf{I} - \mathbf{X}(\mathbf{X}'\mathbf{X})^{-1}\mathbf{X}'$. The partial F test in (5.4.25) can be written

$$\frac{\mathbf{y}'(\mathbf{M}_{k-m} - \mathbf{M})\mathbf{y}}{m\hat{s}^2} \sim F(m, n - k)$$

where $\mathbf{M}_{k-m}$ is the idempotent matrix corresponding to the regression with $k - m$ explanatory variables. If $\mathbf{X} = (\mathbf{X}_1 \mid \mathbf{X}_2)$, where $\mathbf{X}_1$ corresponds to the m coefficients in (5.4.24) and $\mathbf{X}_2$ corresponds to the $k - m$ not in (5.4.24), then

$$\mathbf{M}_{k-m} = \mathbf{I} - \mathbf{X}_2(\mathbf{X}_2'\mathbf{X}_2)^{-1}\mathbf{X}_2'$$

Here N_0 is the number of economists in the base year ($t = 0$), and g is the growth rate of economists

$$g = \frac{1}{N}\frac{dN}{dt}. \tag{5.5.2}$$

Taking logs of (5.5.1)

$$\ln N = \ln N_0 + gt \tag{5.5.3}$$

or

$$y = a + gt \tag{5.5.4}$$

where y is $\ln N(t)$ and a is $\ln N_0$. The problem of estimating a and g in (5.5.4) from data on y and t is one of simple linear regression. Data on N, y, and t are given in Table 5.2. The least-squares estimate of the slope g is given from (4.4.25) and (4.4.26) as

$$\hat{g} = \sum w_i y_i \quad \text{where} \quad w_i = \frac{t_i - \bar{t}}{\sum (t_i - \bar{t})^2}, \quad i = 1, 2, \ldots, n \tag{5.5.5}$$

where y_i is the logarithm of the number of economists in year t_i, $\bar{t}$ is the mean of t, and w_i is the weight attached to the ith observed dependent variable in calculating the least-squares estimate g. The intercept can be estimated, from (4.4.23), as

$$\hat{a} = \bar{y} - \hat{g}\bar{t} \tag{5.5.6}$$

where $\bar{y}$ is the mean of the log of the number of economists. The relevant calculations are shown in Table 5.3. The estimated equation is found, after rounding, to be.

$$\begin{array}{llll} y = 8.766 + 0.05062t & R^2 = 0.964 & \\ \quad\;\; (0.028) \quad (0.00208) & \hat{s} = 0.0707 & \quad *(5.5.7) \\ & F = 589 & \end{array}$$

where estimated standard errors are shown in parentheses.[12] Assuming the disturbances are normal, both coefficients are highly significant in terms of the t test, and R^2 is both large and highly significant in terms of the F test [$F_{0.01}(1, 22) = 7.94$]. The estimated growth rate is $g = 0.05062$; that is, the number of U.S. economists grew, over the period, at the rate of about 5% per year. According to this estimated growth rate the number of economists doubles every 13.7 years.[13]

[12] Some studies show t values [ratios of coefficients to estimated standard errors, as in (5.4.10)] in parentheses rather than the standard errors. Here and in the applications chapters below values in parentheses will always be standard errors.

[13] If numbers grow exponentially at the rate g, then they double in $(\ln 2)/g$ years, where $\ln 2 \approx 0.693$.

Table 5.2. Number of U.S. Economists, 1950–1973

Year	*t*	*N(t)*	*y(t)* = ln *N(t)*
1950	0	6936	8.84448
1	1	7068	8.86333
2	2	7267	8.89110
3	3	7335	8.90041
4	4	7486	8.92079
5	5	7555	8.92996
6	6	8450	9.04192
7	7	8600	9.05952
8	8	9189	9.12576
9	9	10159	9.22611
1960	10	10837	9.29072
1	11	11054	9.31055
2	12	11285	9.33123
3	13	11973	9.39041
4	14	13025	9.47463
5	15	14127	9.55584
6	16	15229	9.63096
7	17	16675	9.72167
8	18	17835	9.78892
9	19	19061	9.85540
1970	20	18908	9.84734
1	21	18080	9.80256
2	22	17286	9.75765
3	23	17933	9.79440

Source: $N(t)$ = Membership in the American Economic Association. 1950–1959, *The American Economic Review*, Vol. LIX, No. 6, January 1969, *1969 Handbook of the American Economic Association.* For 1960–1973, *The American Economic Review*, Vol. LXIV, No. 5, October 1974, *1974 Directory of Members.* ln $N(t)$ is the natural logarithm of $N(t)$.

One amusing use of this estimate is to forecast *backward*, as done by Price, to determine the year t when $y = 0$ in (5.5.7). This year has the interpretation of the year in which there was exactly *one* U.S. economist. This year, $t = -173$, corresponds to the calendar year 1777. This happens to be one year after the publication of Adam Smith's *Wealth of Nations* and may therefore correspond to the year when this landmark book, which virtually started the discipline of economics, was first read in the United States. (Other explanations, also plausible and also not to be taken too seriously, are possible.)

The estimates reported in (5.5.7) can also be used to predict future numbers of economists. For example, the predicted number of economists in 1984, for which $t = 34$, is obtained, using (4.4.26), from

$$y = 8.766 + 0.05062(34) = 10.487. \tag{5.5.8}$$

By taking antilogs (e^y) the predicted number is 35,849 economists in 1984.

Table 5.3. Calculation of $\hat{g}$ and $\hat{a}$

	t_i	$t_i - \bar{t}$	$(t_i - \bar{t})^2$ $\times 10^{-2}$	$w_i = \frac{t_i - \bar{t}}{\Sigma(t_i - \bar{t})^2}$ $\times 10^3$	y_i	$w_i y_i$ $(\times 10^2)$
	0	−11.5	1.3225	−10.0000000	8.84448	−8.84448
	1	−10.5	1.1025	− 9.1304348	8.86333	−8.0926057
	2	− 9.5	.9025	− 8.2608696	8.89110	−7.3448217
	3	− 8.5	.7225	− 7.3913043	8.90041	−6.5785639
	4	− 7.5	.5625	− 6.5217391	8.92079	−5.8179065
	5	− 6.5	.4225	− 5.6521739	8.92996	−5.0473687
	6	− 5.5	.3025	− 4.7826087	9.04192	−4.3243965
	7	− 4.5	.2025	− 3.9130435	9.05952	−3.5450296
	8	− 3.5	.1225	− 3.0434783	9.12576	−2.7774052
	9	− 2.5	.0625	− 2.1739130	9.22611	−2.0056761
	10	− 1.5	.0225	− 1.3043478	9.29072	−1.2118330
	11	− 0.5	.0025	− .4347826	9.31055	−0.4048065
	12	0.5	.0025	.4347826	9.33123	0.4057057
	13	1.5	.0225	1.3043478	9.39041	1.2248361
	14	2.5	.0625	2.1739130	9.47463	2.0597022
	15	3.5	.1225	3.0434783	9.55584	2.9082991
	16	4.5	.2025	3.9130435	9.63096	3.7686365
	17	5.5	.3025	4.7826087	9.72167	4.6494943
	18	6.5	.4225	5.6521739	9.78892	5.5328678
	19	7.5	.5625	6.5217391	9.85540	6.4274348
	20	8.5	.7225	7.3913043	9.84734	7.2784687
	21	9.5	.9025	8.2608696	9.80256	8.0977670
	22	10.5	1.1025	9.1304348	9.75765	8.9091587
	23	11.5	1.3225	10.0000000	9.79440	9.79440
Sum	276	0	1150	0	224.35567	$\hat{g}$ = 5.0618775
	$\bar{t}$ = 11.5				$\bar{y}$ = 9.34815	$\hat{a} = \bar{y} - \hat{g}\bar{t}$ = 8.766037

NOTE In these computations it is extremely important to retain a large number of significant figures. Small roundoff errors can magnify enormously and create large errors in the estimates.

Similarly the predicted number of economists exceeds 80,000 in the year 2000.

A confidence interval for the predicted number can be determined using the result reported in Section 4.10. For example, for 1984, for which $t = 34$, a 95% confidence interval for y would be given, as in (4.10.10), by

$$\hat{\beta}_1 \hat{t} + \hat{\beta}_2 \pm t_{0.025}\, \hat{s} \sqrt{\frac{1}{n} + \frac{(\hat{t} - \bar{t})^2}{\Sigma \dot{t}_i^2}}$$

$$= (0.05062)(34) + 8.766 \pm (2.074)(0.0707) \sqrt{\frac{1}{24} + \frac{(34 - 11.5)^2}{1150}} \quad \textbf{(5.5.9)}$$

$$= 10.487 \pm 0.1018$$

where the t value is obtained as that for $24 - 2 = 22$ degrees of freedom. Taking antilogs, the 95% confidence interval for the number of economists in 1984 is found to be 32,377 to 39,688 economists.

5.6 An example of multiple linear regression

Consider now an example of multiple linear regression, specifically the problem of estimating one of the reduced-form equations of the prototype macro model of Section 2.7. In fact, as will be discussed in considerable detail in Chapter 11, the first step in estimating a simultaneous-equations econometric model such as the prototype macro model is usually that of estimating each of its reduced-form equations. Consider equation (2.7.7), which may be written[14]

$$Y_t = (Y_{t-1} \quad G_t \quad 1)\begin{pmatrix}\beta_1\\ \beta_2\\ \beta_3\end{pmatrix} + u_t = \beta_1 Y_{t-1} + \beta_2 G_t + \beta_3 + u_t \tag{5.6.1}$$

Here Y_t, current national income, is a linear function of lagged income Y_{t-1} and current government spending G_t. The three parameters to be estimated are the two slope parameters β_1 and β_2 and the intercept β_3. Table 3.2 provides 12 data points for the years 1961 and 1972, which can be used in the estimation of the model.

It will be assumed that all the assumptions used to derive the optimality properties of the least-squares estimators in the last chapter are applicable.[15] The least-squares estimators are then

$$\hat{\boldsymbol{\beta}} = (\mathbf{X}'\mathbf{X})^{-1}\mathbf{X}'\mathbf{y} \tag{5.6.2}$$

where $\mathbf{X}$ and $\mathbf{y}$, from Table 3.2 and the specification of the equation (5.6.1), are given as

$$\mathbf{X} = \begin{pmatrix} 0.504 & 0.108 & 1\\ 0.520 & 0.117 & 1\\ 0.560 & 0.123 & 1\\ 0.589 & 0.128 & 1\\ 0.629 & 0.137 & 1\\ 0.685 & 0.157 & 1\\ 0.750 & 0.178 & 1\\ 0.790 & 0.200 & 1\\ 0.864 & 0.210 & 1\\ 0.930 & 0.220 & 1\\ 0.977 & 0.234 & 1\\ 1.056 & 0.255 & 1 \end{pmatrix}, \qquad \mathbf{y} = \begin{pmatrix} 0.520\\ 0.560\\ 0.589\\ 0.629\\ 0.685\\ 0.750\\ 0.790\\ 0.864\\ 0.930\\ 0.977\\ 1.056\\ 1.155 \end{pmatrix} \tag{5.6.3}$$

[14] Note that the β's in (5.6.1) are not the same as the β's used in Section 2.7.

[15] In fact, one of the explanatory variables is a lagged endogenous variable, implying that these assumptions need not hold. Here this fact is not taken explicitly into account. See, however, Sections 6.7 and 11.6.

where, for convenience in the calculations, variables are measured in trillions, rather than billions, of dollars. Here[16]

$$(\mathbf{X}'\mathbf{X}) = \begin{pmatrix} 6.917464 & 1.6287 & 8.854 \\ & 0.384249 & 2.067 \\ & & 12 \end{pmatrix} \tag{5.6.4}$$

yielding the inverse matrix

$$(\mathbf{X}'\mathbf{X})^{-1} = \begin{pmatrix} 237.589 & -872.580 & -24.9995 \\ & 3240.12 & 85.7078 \\ & & 3.76564 \end{pmatrix}. \tag{5.6.5}$$

Furthermore

$$\mathbf{X}'\mathbf{y} = \begin{pmatrix} 7.436798 \\ 1.751523 \\ 9.505 \end{pmatrix} \tag{5.6.6}$$

Thus the least-squares estimators are[17]

$$\hat{\boldsymbol{\beta}} = (\mathbf{X}'\mathbf{X})^{-1}\mathbf{X}'\mathbf{y} = \begin{pmatrix} 0.940708 \\ 0.596657 \\ 0.00477692 \end{pmatrix} \tag{5.6.7}$$

The sum of the squared errors is

$$\Sigma \hat{u}_i^2 = (\mathbf{y} - \mathbf{X}\hat{\boldsymbol{\beta}})'(\mathbf{y} - \mathbf{X}\hat{\boldsymbol{\beta}}) = 0.00195961 \tag{5.6.8}$$

so an unbiased estimate of the variance of the stochastic disturbance term is

$$\hat{s}^2 = \frac{1}{n-k} \Sigma \hat{u}_i^2 = \frac{1}{9}(0.00195961) = 0.000217734. \tag{5.6.9}$$

The estimate of the covariance matrix of the estimated coefficients is thus

$$\widehat{\text{Cov}}(\hat{\boldsymbol{\beta}}) = \hat{s}^2(\mathbf{X}'\mathbf{X})^{-1} = \begin{pmatrix} 0.0517 & -0.190 & 0.00544 \\ & 0.706 & 0.0187 \\ & & 0.00082 \end{pmatrix} \tag{5.6.10}$$

[16] Since the matrix is symmetric, only elements on and above the diagonal need be reported. It should also be noted that because of roundoff error in (5.6.5) multiplying $(\mathbf{X}'\mathbf{X})$ by $(\mathbf{X}'\mathbf{X})^{-1}$ yields a matrix close to but not exactly the identity matrix.

[17] The numerical estimates reported here are, in fact, based on a more accurate $(\mathbf{X}'\mathbf{X})^{-1}$ matrix than is reported in (5.6.5); thus multiplying (5.6.5) by (5.6.6) yields estimates slightly different from (and less accurate than) those reported here. Similarly, some of the later calculations are slightly different from those that would have been obtained by hand, since some results have been rounded.

Table 5.4. Analysis of Variance for the Regression for the Reduced-Form Equation for Y in the Prototype Macro Model

Source	*Sum of Squares*	*Degrees of Freedom*	*Mean Square*
Explained (by regression)	0.46676130	2	0.23338065
Unexplained (residual)	0.00195961	9	0.000217734
Total	0.46872091	11	

NOTE The format of this table follows Table 5.1.

and the square roots of the diagonal elements of this matrix are the standard errors of the estimated coefficients.

The value of the coefficient of determination can be obtained as

$$R^2 = 1 - \frac{\Sigma \hat{u}_i^2}{\Sigma \dot{y}_i^2} = 0.9958 \tag{5.6.11}$$

where $\Sigma \dot{y}_i^2$ is the sum of squared deviations of the dependent variable (current national income) from the mean value.

The analysis of variance for the regression is shown in Table 5.4. From this table the F value for the regression is

$$F = \frac{R^2/(k-1)}{(1-R^2)/(n-k)} = \frac{0.9958/2}{0.0042/9} = 1071.85. \tag{5.6.12}$$

Comparing this value to the $F(2, 9)$ value of 4.26 at a 5% level of significance (or 8.02 at a 1% level), it is clear that the overall regression is highly significant and that the hypothesis that all coefficients are zero is overwhelmingly rejected.

All the results so far can be summarized by the estimated equation and related statistics

$$\begin{array}{llll} Y_t = 0.941 Y_{t-1} & + \; 0.597 G_t & - \; 0.00478 & R^2 = 0.996 \\ \quad\;\; (0.227) & \quad (0.840) & \quad (0.02863) & \hat{s} = 0.0148 \\ & & & F = 1072 \end{array} \tag{5.6.13}$$

where numbers have been rounded and standard errors are shown in parentheses.[18] According to (5.6.13) national income Y_t depends positively and

[18] It is appropriate to round at this stage but not earlier. Rounding off in prior calculations can significantly affect later estimates, particularly rounding off before calculating the inverse matrix. See Freund (1963).

significantly on the lagged value Y_{-1}, but insignificantly on government expenditure. A 95% confidence interval for β_1, the coefficient of Y_{-1}, can be determined, using (5.4.9), as $\hat{\beta}_1 \pm (2.262)\ (0.227455)$, where 2.262 is the t value for 9 degrees of freedom at a 0.025% level of significance. Thus

$$0.426 \leqslant \beta_1 \leqslant 1.455 \qquad \textbf{(5.6.14)}$$

provides the confidence interval for β_1.[19]

5.7 Bayesian estimation of the linear regression model

An alternative approach to the estimation of the linear regression model is that of Bayesian estimation.[20] This approach combines two types of information to make inferences about parameters, which, in the Bayesian context, are treated as random variables and hence described in terms of probabilities. The first type is prior information, reflecting the judgments of the experimenter; the second type is that contained in the sample of data actually observed. Bayesian estimation combines both, using Bayes' theorem, to obtain posterior distributions of the probabilities of the parameters. According to Bayes' theorem the posterior probabilities density function (pdf) is proportional to the prior pdf times the likelihood function:[21]

$$\text{posterior pdf} \propto (\text{prior pdf}) \times (\text{likelihood function}). \qquad \textbf{*(5.7.1)}$$

The prior pdf incorporates all prior information, while the likelihood function incorporates all sample information. The constant of proportionality is a numerical normalizing constant. The resulting posterior pdf summarizes the probability distribution for the parameters to be estimated after taking account of both prior and sample information.

The prior information typically takes the form of a probability distribution over the parameters to be estimated, the prior pdf, reflecting the experimenter's degree of belief attached to alternative values of these parameters. This information may be subjective or it may be based on previous studies. In the case in which prior information is lacking it is possible to use a diffuse prior, in which case the posterior pdf reflects mainly sample information, as represented by the likelihood function.

[19] Note that the confidence interval includes $\beta_1 = 1$, in which case the model in (5.6.1) can be written

$$\Delta Y_t = Y_t - Y_{t-1} = \beta_2 G_t + \beta_3 + u_t.$$

For a related model, which explains Y in terms of *changes* in government expenditure (and also changes in money supply), see (13.2.10), which reports one equation of the St. Louis model.

[20] See De Groot (1970), Zellner (1971a, 1971b), Barnett (1973), and Lindley (1965, 1971). See also Fienberg and Zellner, Eds. (1975) and Leamer (1977).

[21] See Appendix C, Section C.1.

The likelihood function provides a summary of the sample information, specifically a summary of how such information bears upon the problem of estimation. The likelihood function takes the form of the likelihood of alternative observations of sample values given specific sets of the parameters to be estimated.

The posterior information takes a form similar to that for prior information—that of a probability distribution over the parameters to be estimated. The posterior pdf, however, reflects both prior and sample information, as indicated in (5.7.1). It can be interpreted as a revision of the prior pdf that takes account of the information contained in the sample.

Applying the Bayesian approach to the problem of estimation of the linear regression model, consider the basic linear regression model:

$$\underset{n\times 1}{\mathbf{y}} = \underset{n\times k}{\mathbf{X}}\ \underset{k\times 1}{\boldsymbol{\beta}} + \underset{n\times 1.}{\mathbf{u}} \tag{5.7.2}$$

Assume the parameters to be estimated are summarized by the vector $\boldsymbol{\theta}$, which includes, in addition to the coefficients $\boldsymbol{\beta}$, the parameters describing the distribution of $\mathbf{u}$ [variance(s), covariances, etc.]. In the Bayesian approach it is assumed that there is a prior pdf, of the form $f(\boldsymbol{\theta})$, representing the experimenter's prior beliefs concerning the values of the parameters.

The sample information for the linear regression model is given by the data on the dependent and explanatory variables. These data are given by the matrix $\mathbf{D}$, defined as

$$\underset{n\times(k+1)}{\mathbf{D}} = (\underset{n\times 1}{\mathbf{y}} \mid \underset{n\times k}{\mathbf{X}}). \tag{5.7.3}$$

The likelihood function is then given as $L(\mathbf{D}\,|\,\boldsymbol{\theta})$, representing the likelihood of observing the data $\mathbf{D}$ given the parameters $\boldsymbol{\theta}$. In the Bayesian approach this likelihood function is emphasized, since it summarizes all the relevant information that can be obtained from the particular data set observed.

According to Bayes' theorem, if $f(\boldsymbol{\theta}\,|\,\mathbf{D})$ is the posterior pdf, namely the probability of the parameters $\boldsymbol{\theta}$ given the data $\mathbf{D}$, then from (5.7.1),

$$f(\boldsymbol{\theta}\,|\,\mathbf{D}) \propto f(\boldsymbol{\theta})L(\mathbf{D}\,|\,\boldsymbol{\theta}). \tag{5.7.4}$$

The factor of proportionality is the reciprocal of the pdf for $\mathbf{D}$, given as

$$f(\mathbf{D}) = \int f(\boldsymbol{\theta})L(\mathbf{D}\,|\,\boldsymbol{\theta})d\boldsymbol{\theta} = \int\int\cdots\int f(\boldsymbol{\theta})L(\mathbf{D}\,|\,\boldsymbol{\theta})\,d\theta_1\,d\theta_2\cdots d\theta_m \tag{5.7.5}$$

where the (multiple) integral is taken over all possible parameter vectors $\boldsymbol{\theta} = (\theta_1\ \ \theta_2\ \cdots\ \theta_m)$.[22] Thus the posterior pdf can be written[23]

[22] The case represented by (5.7.5) is one in which each of the elements of $\boldsymbol{\theta}$ is defined over an interval of values. If $\boldsymbol{\theta}$ summarizes parameters defined over a finite set of values, then

$$f(\mathbf{D}) = \sum_{\boldsymbol{\theta}} f(\boldsymbol{\theta})L(D\,|\,\boldsymbol{\theta})$$

where the sum is defined over all possible parameter vectors $\boldsymbol{\theta}$.

[23] See Appendix C, equation (C.1.12).

$$f(\boldsymbol{\theta}|\mathrm{D}) = \frac{f(\boldsymbol{\theta})L(\mathrm{D}|\boldsymbol{\theta})}{\int f(\boldsymbol{\theta})L(\mathrm{D}|\boldsymbol{\theta})\,d\boldsymbol{\theta}}. \qquad *(5.7.6)$$

This posterior distribution is a summary of all sample and prior information relevant for the estimation of $\boldsymbol{\theta}$.

While the posterior distribution $f(\boldsymbol{\theta}|D)$ is the end product of the Bayesian approach to estimation, certain summary statistics of this distribution can be used to obtain point estimates of the parameters $\boldsymbol{\theta}$. These summary statistics include various possible measures of central tendency, such as the mean (if it exists) and the mode (if the distribution is unimodal).[24] Interval estimates can be obtained from various possible measures of dispersion such as the variance (if it is finite) and the interquartile range.

To illustrate the method of Bayesian estimation, consider the problem of estimating the marginal propensity to consume, γ, for the simple consumption function

$$C = \gamma Y + \beta + \epsilon \qquad (5.7.7)$$

where C is consumption and Y is income. Suppose it is known from previous studies that γ is close to 0.75, and it is almost certain that γ lies between 0.5 and 1.0. The experimenter must choose either to take this information into account or to ignore it. The pure classical approach, as developed thus far, would totally ignore it and proceed to estimate γ on the basis of data on C and Y. One way of taking the information into account informally is to use the classical method of estimation but ignore values less than 0.5 or 1.0, perhaps reestimating using a different technique or a different sample if the estimated γ lies outside this range. The Bayesian approach, however, takes explicit and formal account of the information by postulating a specific subjective prior probability density function for γ. One such pdf might be a normal distribution with mean at 0.75 and with a variance chosen such that 0.5 and 1.0 each represent values that are two standard deviations from the mean. The Bayesian approach would then combine this prior pdf with the likelihood function, summarizing the sample information, to obtain a posterior pdf. The Bayesian approach, therefore, represents an approach to estimation based on learning from the sample, which augments past information. The classical approach, by contrast, either ignores past information or incorporates it in an ad hoc way, emphasizing instead inferences from the current sample.

[24] More typically, rather than using summary statistics relating to the distribution the entire distribution is used in conjunction with a loss function, and a specific estimator $\hat{\boldsymbol{\theta}}$ is chosen so as to minimize expected loss. If $l(\boldsymbol{\theta}, \hat{\boldsymbol{\theta}})$ is the loss function, giving the loss when estimating $\boldsymbol{\theta}$ by $\hat{\boldsymbol{\theta}}$, the estimator $\hat{\boldsymbol{\theta}}$ is chosen so as to minimize expected loss, defined as

$$\mathrm{EL}(\hat{\boldsymbol{\theta}}) = \int l(\boldsymbol{\theta},\hat{\boldsymbol{\theta}})\, f(\boldsymbol{\theta}|\mathrm{D})\, d\boldsymbol{\theta}.$$

One frequently used $l(\boldsymbol{\theta},\hat{\boldsymbol{\theta}})$ is the quadratic loss function

$$l(\boldsymbol{\theta},\hat{\boldsymbol{\theta}}) = (\boldsymbol{\theta} - \hat{\boldsymbol{\theta}})'\mathbf{Q}(\boldsymbol{\theta} - \hat{\boldsymbol{\theta}})$$

where $\mathbf{Q}$ is a given positive-semidefinite matrix.

Another problem with the classical approach, in addition to its treatment of prior information, is its use of the concept of repeated samples in order to justify concepts such as 95% levels of significance. The choice of a particular level of significance is also arbitrary in the classical approach. The Bayesian approach avoids such concepts by summarizing all evidence obtained in the sample in the likelihood function and then using this likelihood function to make inferences.

There are arguments both for and against the Bayesian approach to estimation, as opposed to the classical approach.[25] On the one hand, Bayesian approach represents a general learning model, which should aid the researcher in combining various types of information. It also combines prior and sample information in a formal way, which facilitates sensitivity analysis, testing for the influences of prior and sample information. Furthermore, it avoids the necessity of assuming repeated samples and of using arbitrary levels of significance. On the other hand, it is difficult to assess a joint density over even a moderately large number of random variables, and, while the forms taken by the prior pdf are quite flexible, the requirement that there be a prior pdf is an inflexible one. After taking these various arguments into account one might well conclude that the best course to follow is an eclectic one. Rather than siding either with the Bayesians or with those employing classical methods, it may be optimal to use the Bayesian approach if the problem is amenable to this approach (e.g., a small number of parameters, with explicit prior information) and otherwise rely upon the classical approach to estimation.

PROBLEMS

5-A Using diagrams like Figure 5.2, illustrate a case in which $\hat{\beta}_1 > 1$ and one in which $\hat{\beta}_1 < 0$.

5-B Consider the case of simple linear regression in which $n - 1$ of the data points are clustered around the point (x_0, y_0) and the last data point (x_n, y_n) is an outlier lying much further away from (x_0, y_0) than any of the other data points:

1. Show the situation in a diagram, and indicate the least-squares regression line in the diagram.
2. Prove that the least-squares regression line will be close to the line passing through (x_0, y_0) and (x_n, y_n).
3. Prove that the slope of the least-squares regression line $\hat{\beta}_1$ is more sensitive to variations in the outlier point (x_n, y_n) than to variations in any one of the points in the cluster (x_i, y_i), $i = 1, 2, \ldots, n - 1$. Specifically, assuming that the x values are fixed, calculate $\partial\hat{\beta}_1/\partial y_n$ and $\partial\hat{\beta}_1/\partial y_i$, and show that the former is larger (here $\hat{\beta}_1$ is the slope estimate for the simple linear regression). What can you conclude concerning where to spend time and effort in improving the measurement of various data points?

[25] See Zellner (1971a, 1971b) and Rothenberg (1971).

5-C Prove that whenever an additional explanatory variable enters a regression equation, the multiple correlation coefficient R^2 either increases or remains constant. Under what circumstances would R^2 remain constant?

5-D Consider the regression equation

$$\mathbf{y} = \mathbf{X}\boldsymbol{\beta} + \mathbf{u}$$

and assume that $\mathbf{y}$ is replaced by $\mathbf{y}^*$, a linear combination of $\mathbf{y}$ and the columns of the $\mathbf{X}$ matrix defined by

$$\mathbf{y}^* = a_0\mathbf{y} + \sum_{j=1}^{k} a_j\mathbf{x}_j$$

where $\mathbf{x}_j$ is the jth column of $\mathbf{X}$. Consider the new regression equation

$$\mathbf{y}^* = \mathbf{X}\boldsymbol{\beta}^* + \mathbf{u}^*$$

where $\mathbf{X}$ is the same as before.

1. Show that the least-squares estimators and residuals are changed; i.e., $\hat{\boldsymbol{\beta}} \neq \hat{\boldsymbol{\beta}}^*$, $\hat{\mathbf{u}} \neq \hat{\mathbf{u}}^*$.
2. Show that the coefficient of determination R^2 is generally different, i.e., $R^2 \neq (R^*)^2$.

5-E Verify that the multiple correlation coefficient R can be expressed as the correlation coefficient between $\mathbf{y}$ and $\hat{\mathbf{y}}$:

$$R = \frac{\text{Cov}(\mathbf{y}, \hat{\mathbf{y}})}{\sqrt{\text{Var}(\mathbf{y})\,\text{Var}(\hat{\mathbf{y}})}} = \frac{\Sigma \dot{y}_i \, \dot{\hat{y}}_i}{\sqrt{(\Sigma \dot{y}_i^2)(\Sigma \dot{\hat{y}}_i^2)}}$$

where $\hat{\mathbf{y}} = \mathbf{X}\hat{\boldsymbol{\beta}}$.

5-F Prove, in the case of the simple regression

$$\dot{y} = \beta_1 \dot{x}$$

where variables are measured as deviations from their mean values, that

$$R^2 = \hat{\beta}_1^2 \frac{\Sigma \dot{x}_i^2}{\Sigma \dot{y}_i^2} = \hat{\beta}_1^2 \frac{s_x^2}{s_y^2}$$

where s_x^2 and s_y^2 are the sample variances of x and y, respectively, given as

$$s_x^2 = \frac{1}{n-1} \Sigma \dot{x}_i^2, \quad s_y^2 = \frac{1}{n-1} \Sigma \dot{y}_i^2.$$

5-G If the y_i are not measured as deviations from mean values the multiple correlation coefficient can be obtained by noting that the total deviation of the dependent variable from its mean value can be decomposed into explained and unexplained deviations as

$$y_i - \bar{y} = (\hat{y}_i - \bar{y}) + (y_i - \hat{y}_i)$$

where $\hat{y}_i$ is the value predicted by the regression and $\bar{y}$ is the mean value. Squaring and summing, the cross-product term vanishes, so

$$\Sigma\ (y_i - \bar{y})^2 = \Sigma\ (\hat{y}_i - \bar{y})^2 + \Sigma\ (y_i - \hat{y}_i)^2$$

giving the total sum of squares as the sum of the explained and unexplained sums of squares. This equation is the same as (5.2.5) except $y_i - \hat{y}_i$ is replaced by the least-squares residual $\hat{u}_i$. The coefficient of determination is then defined as the proportion of the total sum of squares explained by the regression

$$R^2 = \frac{\Sigma\ (\hat{y}_i - \bar{y})^2}{\Sigma\ (y_i - \bar{y})^2}.$$

1. Show geometrically for simple regression in the (x, y) plane the decomposition of the total deviation into explained and unexplained deviations.
2. Prove that the cross-product term vanishes.
3. Prove that

$$R^2 = \frac{\|\mathbf{X}\hat{\boldsymbol{\beta}}\|^2 - \frac{1}{n}(\Sigma\, y_i)^2}{\|\mathbf{y}\|^2 - \frac{1}{n}(\Sigma\, y_i)^2}.$$

5-H Consider R^2 for a linear regression model that does not include an intercept term.

1. Show that $\Sigma\ \hat{u}_i$ need not vanish, so that (5.2.5) need not hold.
2. If R^2 is defined as $\|\dot{\hat{\mathbf{y}}}\|^2/\|\dot{\mathbf{y}}\|^2$, show that R^2 will always be nonnegative but that it can exceed one.
3. If R^2 is defined as $1 - (\|\hat{\mathbf{u}}\|^2/\|\dot{\mathbf{y}}\|^2)$, show that R^2 will always be less than or equal to one but that it can be negative.

5-I Consider tests of significance for estimated parameters of the dummy variable representing the investment tax credit (3.2.1).

1. Show that the t ratio $\hat{\beta}_3/\hat{s}_3$, where $\hat{s}_3$ is the standard error corresponding to β_3, tests the significance of the intercept without the tax credit.
2. Show that the t ratio $\hat{\beta}_4/\hat{s}_4$, where $\hat{s}_4$ is the standard error corresponding to β_4, tests whether there is any significant difference between the intercept with and without the tax credit.

3. Show that a test for the significance of the intercept with the tax credit would use the t ratio defined by

$$t = \frac{\hat{\beta}_3 + \hat{\beta}_4}{\sqrt{\hat{s}_3^2 + \hat{s}_4^2 + 2\,\widehat{\text{Cov}}(\hat{\beta}_3, \hat{\beta}_4)}}.$$

5-J Consider two regressions using the same k explanatory variables

$$\mathbf{y}_1 = \mathbf{X}_1\hat{\boldsymbol{\beta}}_1 + \hat{\mathbf{u}}_1, \qquad \mathbf{y}_2 = \mathbf{X}_2\hat{\boldsymbol{\beta}}_2 + \hat{\mathbf{u}}_2$$

where $\mathbf{y}_1$ and $\mathbf{X}_1$ summarize n_1 data points and $\mathbf{y}_2$ and $\mathbf{X}_2$ summarize n_2 data points. The hypothesis to be tested is the equality of the coefficients

$$H_0\colon \boldsymbol{\beta}_1 = \boldsymbol{\beta}_2$$

Combining the equations as

$$\mathbf{y} = \begin{pmatrix} \mathbf{y}_1 \\ \hline \mathbf{y}_2 \end{pmatrix} = \left(\begin{array}{c|c} \mathbf{X}_1 & \mathbf{0} \\ \hline \mathbf{0} & \mathbf{X}_2 \end{array}\right) \begin{pmatrix} \hat{\boldsymbol{\beta}}_1 \\ \hline \hat{\boldsymbol{\beta}}_2 \end{pmatrix} + \begin{pmatrix} \hat{\mathbf{u}}_1 \\ \hline \hat{\mathbf{u}}_2 \end{pmatrix} = \mathbf{X}\boldsymbol{\beta} + \mathbf{u}$$

the null hypothesis states

$$H_0\colon \mathbf{A}\boldsymbol{\beta} = \mathbf{0} \quad \text{where} \quad \mathbf{A} = (\mathbf{I} \mid -\mathbf{I}).$$

Show, using (5.4.17), that the equality of the coefficients can be tested by the ratio

$$F = \frac{(\hat{\boldsymbol{\beta}} - \hat{\hat{\boldsymbol{\beta}}})'\mathbf{X}'\mathbf{X}(\hat{\boldsymbol{\beta}} - \hat{\hat{\boldsymbol{\beta}}})/k}{(\hat{\mathbf{u}}_1'\hat{\mathbf{u}}_1 + \hat{\mathbf{u}}_2'\hat{\mathbf{u}}_2)/(n_1 + n_2 - 2k)} \sim F(k, n_1 + n_2 - 2k)$$

where $\hat{\hat{\boldsymbol{\beta}}}$ is the least-squares estimator of $\mathbf{y} = \mathbf{X}\boldsymbol{\beta} + \mathbf{u}$ subject to the constraint that $\mathbf{A}\boldsymbol{\beta} = \mathbf{0}$ and $n_1 + n_2 > 2k$.

5-K Derive the partial F test in (5.4.25) from the test of m linear restrictions in (5.4.17) in which

$$\mathbf{A} = (\mathbf{I} \mid \mathbf{0})$$

where $\mathbf{I}$ is the $m \times m$ identity matrix and $\mathbf{0}$ is a $m \times (k - m)$ matrix of zeros. Show that (5.3.1) is a special case of the partial F test for $m = k - 1$.

5-L For both the example of simple linear regression of Section 5.5 and the example of multiple linear regression of Section 5.6 show in a diagram the behavior of $\mathbf{y}$, $\hat{\mathbf{y}}$, and $\hat{\mathbf{u}}$. What conclusions can be drawn from inspection of the behavior of the residuals?

5-M For the estimated equation for national income from the prototype macro model, as presented in Section 5.6:

1. Obtain 90% confidence intervals for both the short-term and the long-term multiplier for government spending.
2. Test whether the short-term multiplier was different in the Democratic years 1965–68 than in the Republican years 1969–72.
3. Develop all partial F tests for the estimated regression coefficients.

5-N Consider the equation of the prototype macro model (5.6.1) estimated in Section 5.6. Estimate this equation using the cross-section data for selected developed countries presented in Table 3.4 and contrast the estimated parameters to those obtained in (5.6.2).

5-O One of the reduced-form equations of the prototype micro model determines price p as a function of income I and rainfall r:

$$p = \beta_1 I + \beta_2 r + \beta_3 + u = (I \quad r \quad 1)\begin{pmatrix}\beta_1\\ \beta_2\\ \beta_3\end{pmatrix} + u$$

where the notation of (2.6.9) has been simplified. Assume that over the sample the stochastic disturbance term is independently and identically distributed as $N(0, \sigma^2)$. Using the following data for wheat:

Years	*Price*	*Income*	*Rainfall*
1951–1955	2.0	2.0	2.0
1956–1960	1.8	2.2	3.2
1961–1965	1.7	2.6	2.7
1965–1970	1.3	2.9	3.3
1971–1975	1.8	3.2	3.8

do the following *without* the aid of a computer (show all calculations):

1. Obtain the least-squares estimators $(\hat{\beta}_1 \quad \hat{\beta}_2 \quad \hat{\beta}_3)' = \hat{\boldsymbol{\beta}}$ and $\text{Cov}\,(\hat{\boldsymbol{\beta}})$.
2. Find standard errors and t values for the estimated coefficients. Which, if any, are significant at the 0.90 level?
3. Find the coefficient of determination R^2 and perform an analysis of variance to test for the significance of the entire regression.
4. Forecast the price of wheat in 1976–80, assuming income is 3.5 and rainfall is 3.4. Find a 90% confidence interval for the forecasted price.

5-P Using the geometrical approach to least squares, prove and illustrate the fact that the coefficient of determination R^2 will not change if the data matrix $\mathbf{X}$ changes as long as the space defined by the columns of $\mathbf{X}$ remains the same. Give several illustrations of the types of changes in $\mathbf{X}$ that will not change the space defined by its columns.

5-Q Consider the geometrical approach to least squares.

1. Show that if $n = 3$, $k = 2$ the locus of points satisfying $S(\boldsymbol{\beta}^0) =$ constant, where $S(\boldsymbol{\beta}^0)$ is the sum of squares for the parameter vector $\boldsymbol{\beta}^0$ is a *circle* with center at the point $\hat{\mathbf{y}}$. Also show that in the parameter space (β_1, β_2) the locus of points satisfying $S(\boldsymbol{\beta}^0) =$ constant are *ellipses*. Using these ellipses illustrate 95% confidence intervals for β_1, for β_2, and for (β_1, β_2).
2. Assuming stochastic disturbance terms are normally distributed, using the F test of (5.4.22) show that in the general $n > k$ case the $100(1 - \epsilon)$ per cent confidence region for the point $\mathbf{X}\boldsymbol{\beta}^0$ is a *sphere* centered at $\hat{\mathbf{y}} = \mathbf{X}\hat{\boldsymbol{\beta}}$, with radius

$$[S(\boldsymbol{\beta}^0) - S(\hat{\boldsymbol{\beta}})]^{1/2} = [S(\hat{\boldsymbol{\beta}}) \frac{k}{n-k} F(k, n-k)]^{1/2}.$$

BIBLIOGRAPHY

Barnett, V. D. (1973), *Comparative Statistical Inference*. New York: John Wiley & Sons, Inc.

De Groot, M. (1970), *Optimal Statistical Decisions*. New York: McGraw-Hill Book Company.

Fienberg, S. E., and A. Zellner, Eds. (1975), *Studies in Bayesian Econometrics and Statistics*. Amsterdam: North-Holland Publishing Co.

Freund, R. J. (1963), "A Warning of Round-off Errors in Regression," *American Statistician* 17: 13–15.

Graybill, F. A. (1961), *An Introduction to Linear Statistical Models*. New York: McGraw-Hill Book Company.

Leamer, E. E. (1977), *Specification Searches*. New York: John Wiley & Sons, Inc.

Lindley, D. V. (1965), *Introduction to Probability and Statistics from a Bayesian Viewpoint*. New York: Cambridge University Press.

Lindley, D. V. (1971), *Bayesian Statistics: A Review*. Philadelphia: Society for Industrial and Applied Mathematics.

Malinvaud, E.(1970), *Statistical Methods of Econometrics*, 2nd Rev. Ed. Amsterdam: North-Holland Publishing Co.

Rao, P., and R. L. Miller (1971), *Applied Econometrics*. Belmont, Calif.: Wadsworth Publishing Co., Inc.

Rothenberg, T. (1971), "The Bayesian Approach in Econometrics," in M. D. Intriligator, Ed., *Frontiers of Quantitative Economics*. Amsterdam: North-Holland Publishing Co.

Scheffé, H. (1959), *The Analysis of Variance*. New York: John Wiley & Sons, Inc.

Wonnacott, R. J., and T. H. Wonnacott (1970), *Econometrics*. New York: John Wiley & Sons, Inc.

Zellner, A. (1971a), *An Introduction to Bayesian Inference in Econometrics*. New York: John Wiley & Sons, Inc.

Zellner, A. (1971b), "The Bayesian Approach in Econometrics," in M. D. Intriligator, Ed., *Frontiers of Quantitative Economics*. Amsterdam: North-Holland Publishing Co.

CHAPTER 6

Problems in the Basic Linear Regression Model

6.1 Problems–their diagnosis and their treatment

Various problems arise in empirical econometrics. Several stem from the fact that in some situations certain of the assumptions of the Gauss-Markov theorem, as presented in Section 4.9, are not met. The least-squares estimators will therefore not necessarily be the best linear unbiased estimators (BLUE). Other problems involve the basic structure of the model. This chapter treats some of the more important of these problems.[1] The approach will be very much like that of a physician curing a sick patient. The first step is that of *diagnosis*, subjecting the model, data, or estimates to appropriate tests to see if certain specific problems are, in fact, present. The second step is that of *treatment* which typically involves reformulating the model, data, or estimation technique to overcome these problems. The starting point for the diagnosis is the basic linear regression model

$$\underset{n\times 1}{\mathbf{y}} = \underset{n\times k}{\mathbf{X}}\ \underset{k\times 1}{\boldsymbol{\beta}} + \underset{n\times 1}{\mathbf{u}} \qquad *(6.1.1)$$

where, as before, $\mathbf{y}$ and $\mathbf{X}$ summarize the n data points for the dependent and the k explanatory variables, respectively. The least-squares estimator is then

$$\hat{\boldsymbol{\beta}} = (\mathbf{X}'\mathbf{X})^{-1}\mathbf{X}'\mathbf{y} \qquad *(6.1.2)$$

and this is also the maximum-likelihood estimator if the stochastic disturbance terms are normally distributed and the other assumptions of Section 4.7. are met.

Among the problems discussed in this chapter will be multicollinearity, heteroskedasticity, serial correlation, qualitative dependent variables, lagged variables, specification error, errors in the variables, and structural break. In order to keep the discussion manageable, only the most important issues are emphasized, specifically those that frequently arise in actually performing a single-equation econometric study.

[1] See also Malinvaud (1970), Theil (1971), and Goldfeld and Quandt (1972) for related discussions of these problems.

6.2 Multicollinearity

One of the assumptions made in Chapter 4 was the rank condition that

$$\rho(\mathbf{X}) = k \qquad *(6.2.1)$$

so that the columns of the $n \times k$ matrix $\mathbf{X}$ of data on the explanatory variables are linearly independent. Under this assumption it follows that $\mathbf{X}'\mathbf{X}$ is nonsingular, so it can be inverted to obtain the least-squares estimator $\hat{\boldsymbol{\beta}}$ in (6.1.2). If, however, one column of $\mathbf{X}$ is a linear combination of other columns of the matrix, then the rank condition is violated

$$\rho(\mathbf{X}) < k \qquad *(6.2.2)$$

implying that

$$|\mathbf{X}'\mathbf{X}| = 0 \qquad *(6.2.3)$$

so $\mathbf{X}'\mathbf{X}$ is a singular matrix that cannot be inverted. This situation is one of *perfect multicollinearity*, in which the normal equations of least squares (4.6.16) cannot be solved for the estimators $\hat{\boldsymbol{\beta}}$. This problem does, in fact, arise on occasion. If one of the explanatory variables is constant over the sample, then it is a multiple of the unity variable included to account for the intercept. One column of $\mathbf{X}$ is thus a multiple of another, so $\mathbf{X}'\mathbf{X}$ is singular. Another example is a case in which the data on one of the explanatory variables have been obtained by averaging over several other included explanatory variables. A third example is where dummy variables, each representing the presence or absence of a characteristic, are included in the regression, and the dummy variables include all possibilities. For example, suppose the regression includes dummy variables representing seasonal influences, where d_s is 1 if an observation is taken in season s and 0 otherwise, where $s = 1, 2, 3, 4$. If all four dummy variables d_1, d_2, d_3, and d_4 are included (as well as an intercept term), there is perfect multicollinearity. In such a case (any) one of the dummy variables must be dropped to avoid this problem of linear dependence.

A situation of perfect multicollinearity is readily identified by the inability to calculate the required inverse matrix. Following this "diagnosis" the "treatment" is clear: remove the offending explanatory variable(s)–namely those that can be expressed as linear combinations of the other explanatory variables–and estimate the model after such variables have been eliminated.

An alternative approach in this case of perfect multicollinearity would be to use all explanatory variables but to estimate not the coefficients in $\boldsymbol{\beta}$ but rather certain linear combinations of these coefficients. For example, if the first two explanatory variables, as measured, are equal, so the first and second columns of $\mathbf{X}$ are the same, then there is perfect multicollinearity. In such a case, it is possible to estimate the sum of the coefficients $\beta_1 + \beta_2$ (measuring the combined effect of the first two explanatory variables), and it is possible to estimate the other coefficients $\beta_3, \beta_4, \ldots, \beta_k$ (assuming no other linear dependencies are present), but it is impossible to distinguish β_1 from β_2; that is, it is impossible to determine the separate effects of the first two explanatory variables. More generally, with perfect multicollinearity certain linear combinations of coefficients can be estimated uniquely, even if the coefficients themselves cannot be so estimated.[2]

More typically the situation is not one of *perfect* multicollinearity but rather one of a *multicollinearity problem*, in which case $\mathbf{X}'\mathbf{X}$ is not singular but is "close to" singular in that[3]

$$|\mathbf{X}'\mathbf{X}| \approx 0. \qquad *(6.2.4)$$

In this case the data on the explanatory variables have the property that while none is an *exact* linear combination of the others, the values of one or more of them are *almost* given by such linear combinations of the values of the others. This situation, in which the explanatory variables tend to move together, arises very often in empirical studies, particularly in those using time-series data. Indeed, the problem of multicollinearity is one of the most ubiquitous, significant, and difficult problems in applied econometrics. Economic data, by their very nature, tend to move together, often reflecting common underlying factors such as trends and cycles. For example, in working with time-series macroeconomic data, the national income aggregates all tend to move together, so that

[2] More formally, with perfect multicollinearity it is possible to estimate certain linear combinations of the coefficients, given by $\mathbf{w}\boldsymbol{\beta}$, where w is a given $1 \times k$ vector of weights. Assuming the estimator of $\mathbf{w}\boldsymbol{\beta}$ is a linear estimator, of the form $\mathbf{ay}$, where $\mathbf{a}$ is a $1 \times n$ vector, for it to be unbiased

$$E(\mathbf{ay}) = \mathbf{aX}\boldsymbol{\beta} = \mathbf{w}\boldsymbol{\beta}$$

which is satisfied if

$$\mathbf{w} = \mathbf{aX}$$

This condition requires that each of the weights be a fixed linear combination of the elements of the corresponding column of $\mathbf{X}$. If w satisfies this condition for some $\mathbf{a}$, then the best linear unbiased estimator of $\mathbf{w}\boldsymbol{\beta}$ is given as $\mathbf{wz}$, where $\mathbf{z}$ is any solution of the normal equations

$$(\mathbf{X}'\mathbf{X})\mathbf{z} = \mathbf{X}'\mathbf{y}$$

While $\mathbf{z}$ need not be unique, the estimator $\mathbf{wz}$, given that $\mathbf{w} = \mathbf{aX}$, is unique, and $\mathbf{wz}$ is the unique BLUE estimator of $\mathbf{w}\boldsymbol{\beta}$. In the case without perfect multicollinearity the $\mathbf{z}$ solving the above normal equations is the unique least-squares estimator $\hat{\boldsymbol{\beta}}$; $\mathbf{a}$ can be expressed as

$$\mathbf{a} = \mathbf{w}(\mathbf{X}'\mathbf{X})^{-1}\mathbf{X}'$$

and the estimator of $\mathbf{w}\boldsymbol{\beta}$ is

$$\mathbf{wz} = \mathbf{w}\hat{\boldsymbol{\beta}} = \mathbf{w}(\mathbf{X}'\mathbf{X})^{-1}\mathbf{X}'\mathbf{y} = \mathbf{ay}.$$

Thus, in the case without perfect multicollinearity all vectors of weights w yield unique estimators.

[3] If the determinant is not zero but is very close to zero, then most computer programs will not calculate the inverse, even though it does exist. Such a situation is not one of perfect multicollinearity, but for practical purposes it can be treated as such.

including two or more of these variables among the explanatory variables in a regression equation will almost inevitably lead to a multicollinearity problem.

The problem of multicollinearity is a *sample problem* for which the sample does not provide "rich" enough information on the explanatory variables to meet the requirements of the model. If controlled experimentation were available, it might be possible to generate a "richer" data set, exhibiting greater variability in the behavior of the explanatory variables. The data used to estimate econometric models are typically nonexperimental, however, so such a richer data set generally cannot be obtained simply by choice of experimental design. Nor will additional data of the same type solve the problem; they will generally exhibit the same problem of multicollinearity.

If the value of the determinant in (6.2.4) is approximately zero, then its inverse $(\mathbf{X}'\mathbf{X})^{-1}$ will tend to have large diagonal elements—just as taking the reciprocal of a number close to zero will lead to a large value. The estimated standard errors, however, from (5.4.3), are proportional to the square roots of elements along the diagonal of the inverse matrix. The estimated standard errors will therefore typically (but not always) tend to be large, implying a lack of precision in the estimators. Equivalently, the t ratios defined in (5.4.6) will tend to be small, so that few if any of the coefficients will appear to be significantly different from zero. At the same time the R^2 may be high and the F test of (5.3.1) may very well show that the hypothesis that all coefficients are zero should be definitely rejected. If these "symptoms" occur—low t ratios coupled with a high F statistic—they indicate the presence of a multicollinearity problem. With these symptoms the set of explanatory variables does influence the dependent variable, but the separate effects of each of the individual explanatory variables cannot be distinguished. In addition, in the presence of a multicollinearity problem the estimated coefficients of certain of the explanatory variables are typically sensitive to the inclusion or exclusion of other explanatory variables, also reflecting the interrelationships present among the set of explanatory variables. The estimates also typically are sensitive to the data used in the estimation, with the addition of new data points possibly leading to large changes in parameter estimates. The estimates are thus both imprecise and unstable in the presence of a problem of multicollinearity.

The problem of multicollinearity, when viewed as a sample problem, can be considered one of a gap between the information requirements of the model, as specified, and the information provided by the sample data. It is a manifestation of the fact that the data are not rich enough in terms of independent variation of the explanatory variables to estimate adequately the model as specified. Viewing the problem this way—as one of a gap between the data required by the model as specified and the sample of data available—suggests three alternative ways to deal with multicollinearity.

One approach is to augment the sample of data by additional data or other information to facilitate the estimation of the model as specified. As already noted, additional data of the same type generally will not help. What could help are additional data of a different type, specifically data exhibiting significant differences from those that are already available. If data representing a different situation are added to the data already available, then the combined sample would exhibit less multicollinearity. For example, consider macroeconomic time-series data. Sometimes data referring to "unrepresentative" periods such as war years, years of major strike activity, or years of "credit crunch" are excluded.[4] Such exclusion of data can exclude periods in which the model is not applicable, but it can also exclude precisely the variation in the sample that can reduce the problem of multicollinearity. Clearly, some balancing is called for between excluding periods in which the data exhibit variability and excluding periods in which the model is not applicable. In general it is best to avoid the extremes of excluding all "unrepresentative" periods—for which the resulting data will exhibit a significant multicollinearity problem and will not yield precise estimators—and, at the other extreme, accepting all periods uncritically—for which the resulting data might reflect fundamentally different underlying mechanisms. The same type of considerations apply to cross-section data, e.g., the issues of whether to include both industrialized and developing economies in a cross section of national economies and of whether to include the very rich and very poor in a cross section of individuals.

Another method of augmenting the sample is to provide information directly on some of the parameters to be estimated. An example is extraneous estimates obtained from a different approach or sample. Thus, in estimating elasticities of demand, use is sometimes made of extraneous estimates of income elasticities obtained from cross-section data when estimating price elasticities from time-series data, given the multicollinearity among data on prices and income.[5] Another example is prior information on parameters—that is, restrictions on parameters imposed before estimation by theory or the results of other studies. In either case the problem of estimation, rather than that of estimating the k parameters in $\boldsymbol{\beta}$, becomes that of estimating the $k - k_1$ remaining parameters, given values for k_1 of the elements in $\boldsymbol{\beta}$. For example, using least squares the sum of squares is minimized by choice of the remaining $k - k_1$ parameters.[6]

A second approach to the treatment of the problem of multicollinearity is to scale down the model to the data available. If other data, extraneous estimates, prior information, etc. are not available, then the gap between the data and the model might be reduced by simplifying the model. Essentially the model, as specified, is asking too much of the data available. By its very nature multicollinearity means that some of the explanatory variables, as sampled, are not conveying much information over and above that conveyed by other variables. This observation suggests a simple and direct way to scale down the model: to change the specification by dropping some of the explanatory variables (as in the case of perfect multicollinearity) or to average or aggregate certain groups of

[4] See the discussion of structural break in Section 6.10.

[5] See Tobin (1950) and Stone (1954) for examples. See Meyer and Kuh (1957) for a discussion of the use of extraneous estimators.

[6] The problem can be formulated as minimizing the sum of squares subject to the k_1 linear restrictions provided by the given values of the k_1 parameters. The general problem of least squares estimation subject to linear restrictions is formulated and solved in Appendix B, Section B.10. See Problem 6-C. See also Theil and Goldberger (1961) and Theil (1963, 1971) for general approaches to mixed estimation, in which estimates reflect both prior information and sample data. For another approach in which prior information (and judgments) are modified on the basis of sample data see the discussion of Bayesian estimation in Section 5.7.

variables.[7] For example, a model of the credit markets that includes several different interest rates on different types of securities could very well lead to a problem of multicollinearity, which would be reduced by averaging the interest rates into representative long-term and short-term rates.

An obvious difficulty with this approach is knowing which specific variables to drop or average. It is generally not apparent which explanatory variables might be removed, and judicious choices must be made in respecifying the model. Simple correlation coefficients and partial correlation coefficients may help suggest candidates for exclusion, where high (absolute) values of simple correlation coefficients between two explanatory variables are suggestive that one of the variables might be omitted from the regression or that these variables might be averaged.[8]

The third approach to treating the problem is simply to recognize the multicollinearity and not try to change either the data or model. Other data, extraneous estimates, etc. may not be available to augment the sample. At the same time, if the model as specified is based on a well-developed underlying theory, then there is no justification for changing the specification. Such a change, such as omitting variables, would induce a specification error into the analysis (discussed below in Section 6.8), creating biases in all of the estimated coefficients. This specification error could lead to more problems, so that the "cure" might be worse than the "disease." The approach of "leaving things alone" is consistent with the view that multicollinearity is basically a property of the population being sampled. The fact that precise statements about the separate influences of each of the explanatory variables cannot be given, in this view, is a very real fact, and there is little or no justification for tampering with the data or specification to attempt to make estimators more precise than they really are.

Which of these three approaches to use—augmenting the data, reducing the model, or "living with" the problem—depends on the specific problem, the purpose, and, to some extent, the temperament of the investigator. For example, if the model is based directly on a well-developed theory, it would probably be inappropriate to change the specification, while if the model reflects only ad hoc and casual reasoning as to which variables might be considered relevant, then it might be appropriate to change the specification. If other data or extraneous estimates are available, they might be employed. The purpose of the study should also play a role. If the purpose is primarily forecasting, then multicollinearity may not be a serious problem; one can usually obtain good forecasts despite the presence of multicollinearity, since the same relationships among explanatory variables usually exist in the forecast period. If, however, the purpose

[7] Other approaches to changing the specification of the model include transformations of variables and the explicit consideration of relationships among the variables. In the latter case the original equation is imbedded in a system of simultaneous equations.

[8] High values of correlation coefficients indicate a linear relationship between two variables, but low values of correlation coefficients do not signify absence of multicollinearity, since multicollinearity can involve a linear relationship among *several* variables. See Chipman (1964). A more formal approach to determining which variables to average is based on principal components analysis, which identifies linear combinations of explanatory variables that tend to move together. See Theil (1971).

is structural analysis, specifically that of disentangling separate influences of explanatory variables, then multicollinearity is a very serious problem that must be addressed.

6.3 Heteroskedasticity

The problem of heteroskedasticity arises when the assumption of homoskedasticity—that the variances of the stochastic disturbance term are finite and constant over the sample—is not met. Thus, with heteroskedasticity

$$\text{Var}(u_i) \neq \text{Var}(u_{i'}), \quad i \neq i' \quad \text{or} \quad \text{Var}(u_i) = \infty \quad \text{for some } i \qquad *(6.3.1)$$

so, in contrast to assumption (4.9.5), the elements along the principal diagonal of $E(\mathbf{uu}')$ either are not equal or are infinite.

The most common form of heteroskedasticity is that in which the variances are not constant over the sample. An example is the estimation of a savings function

$$s = \beta_1 y + \beta_2 + u \qquad (6.3.2)$$

where s is family savings; y is family income; β_1 and β_2 are parameters, β_1 being the marginal propensity to save; and u is the stochastic disturbance term. Figure 6.1. shows a hypothetical scatter of cross-section observations representing family savings and income for a group of families. Clearly the variation in savings behavior is much greater for high-income than for low-income families. Low-income families do not have much to save, so they cannot differ appreciably in their levels of savings. High-income families, by contrast, exhibit wide ranges, from the penny-pinching millionaire who saves virtually all his income to the "nouveau riche" family who save virtually nothing. Clearly, a cross-section sample of data on savings and income behavior that might be used to estimate (6.3.2) does not satisfy the homoskedasticity assumption.[9] More generally, there is typically a problem of heteroskedasticity in cross-section studies in which there is a large variation in the size of the entities for which data are obtained, whether households with widely different income levels, firms with widely different scales of operation, or nations with widely different levels of output.

Heteroskedasticity has two important implications for estimation. The first is that the least-squares estimators, while still linear and unbiased (in the case of finite but differing variances), are no longer efficient, no longer providing minimum-variance ("best") estimators among the class of linear unbiased estimators.[10] The second implication is that the estimated variances of the least-squares estimators are biased, so the usual tests of statistical significance, such as the t and F tests of the last chapter, are no longer valid. It is thus important to test for and correct possible heteroskedasticity.

[9] See Prais and Houthakker (1955), as discussed in Section 7.4.

[10] The estimators exhibiting minimum variance among the linear unbiased estimators are the generalized least-squares (GLS) estimators to be introduced in Section 6.5.

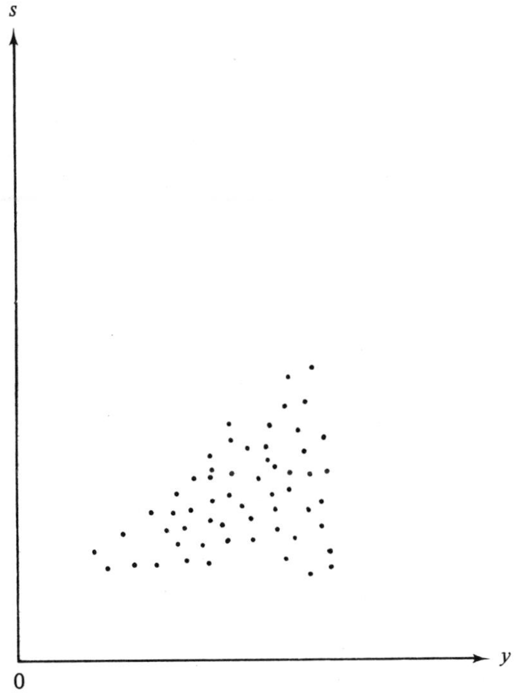

Figure 6.1 Family Savings and Family Income

A simple scatter diagram such as Figure 6.1 can help detect possible problems of heteroskedasticity. A better diagnostic test would be to compare variances in different parts of the sample. The simplest test calls for dividing the sample into two subsamples, where data are indexed in some reasonable way, e.g., by time for time-series data, or by level of some explanatory variable for cross-section data. The variance of the residual is then calculated for each of the two subsamples. If the variances differ appreciably, there is indication of heteroskedasticity. More generally, a large sample can be divided into several subsamples, variances can be calculated for each subsample, and a test can be performed to determine whether the variances are significantly different.[11]

[11] Bartlett's test for nonhomogeneity of variances utilizes a computed variance for each of p suitably chosen subsamples, $\hat{s}_j^2$, $j = 1, 2, \ldots, p$. If the underlying random variables are normally and independently distributed, then the statistic Q/l is distributed as χ^2 with $p - 1$ degrees of freedom, yielding a test of the hypothesis that there is no difference in the variances. Here

$$Q = n \log \sum_{j=1}^{p} \frac{n_j}{n} \hat{s}_j^2 - \sum_{j=1}^{p} n_j \log \hat{s}_j^2$$

$$l = 1 + \frac{1}{3(p-1)} \sum_{j=1}^{p} \left(\frac{1}{n_j} - \frac{1}{n} \right)$$

One treatment of heteroskedasticity calls for a redefinition of variables. Thus, in the estimation of family savings behavior one way to reduce the problem of heteroskedasticity is to estimate the dependence of the savings *ratio* on income, estimating

$$\frac{s}{y} = \beta_1 + \frac{\beta_2}{y} + u' \quad \text{where} \quad u' = \frac{u}{y} \tag{6.3.3}$$

rather than (6.3.2), assuming $E[(1/y)(u/y)] = 0$. It is considerably more likely that u' exhibits homoskedasticity than that u does because of the deflation by income.[12] This method often works well in simple problems of estimation. A more formal treatment is given below in Section 6.5.

Before leaving the subject of heteroskedasticity, consider the other possibility, where the error variance is infinite.[13] In such a case the probability of observing extreme values in the tails of the distribution of the calculated residuals is non-negligible. Such a problem might be indicated if, after constructing a prediction interval for the dependent variable based upon the assumption of a finite variance, for which the probability is 0.9 that the actual value will fall in the prediction interval, considerably fewer than 90% of the actual values in fact fall in this interval. Such a situation, in which the variance of the observed values of the dependent variable is constantly increasing, has in fact been observed in the stock market. Daily price changes of individual common stocks exhibit exactly such behavior, in which the standard deviation of the price changes increases approximately linearly over time. This behavior, called *Brownian motion*, is consistent with an underlying distribution of the stochastic disturbance term

---

where n_j is the number of observations in the jth subsample, $j = 1, 2, \ldots, p$, and n is the total number of observations, Σn_j. For discussions of this and other tests of heteroskedasticity, see Goldfeld and Quandt (1972).

[12] If, in the original formulation (6.3.2), the variance of the ith observation is proportional to the square of the single explanatory variable, then deflation by this variable results in a model exhibiting homoskedasticity. Thus, if in (6.3.2) the variance of the ith observation is proportional to the square of the explanatory variable,

$$\text{Var}(u_i) = \sigma^2 y_i^2$$

then, for the model expressed in terms of ratios in (6.3.3),

$$\text{Var}(u_i') = \text{Var}\left(\frac{u_i}{y_i}\right) = \frac{1}{y_i^2}\text{Var}(u_i) = \sigma^2$$

so the ratio model exhibits homoskedasticity. See, however, Madansky (1964) for a warning on the use of ratios.

[13] Mandelbrot (1963) suggests that many important economic variables, including individual incomes, firm size, and changes in speculative prices, have distributions with infinite variances. If such a variable is the dependent variable in the regression equation or is an important but omitted explanatory variable in the equation, then the variance of the stochastic disturbance term is infinite.

that possesses an infinite variance.[14] Such behavior can be analyzed by estimating the parameters of an appropriate probability distribution which exhibits an infinite variance.

6.4 Serial correlation

Another common problem in applied econometrics is serial correlation (or autocorrelation), in which the stochastic disturbance terms are not independent of one another, i.e.,

$$\text{Cov}(u_i, u_{i'}) \neq 0, \quad i \neq i' \quad \text{for some} \quad i, i'. \qquad *(6.4.1)$$

Thus, in contrast to assumption (4.9.5), the elements off the principal diagonal of the covariance matrix $E(\mathbf{uu}')$ are not all zero.[15] The problem of serial correlation is a frequent, if not typical, one when using time-series data, since in that case the stochastic disturbance terms, in part, reflect variables not included explicitly in the model, which may change slowly over time. Thus the stochastic disturbance term at one observation will be related to the stochastic disturbance terms at nearby observations. Another cause of serial correlation is the smoothing and other "massaging" of data, which results in an averaging of stochastic disturbance terms over several periods. A general cause of serial correlation is misspecification of the model, particularly the exclusion of relevant variables from the model.

As in the case of heteroskedasticity, serial correlation results both in least-squares estimators that are not efficient and in the failure of the usual statistical tests of significance. While least-squares estimators are still defined, linear, unbiased, and consistent, they no longer exhibit minimum variance.[16] There will also be a bias in the estimation of the variance of the stochastic disturbance term. Thus, as in the case of the heteroskedasticity, the t tests of the significance of coefficients and the F tests of the significance of the entire regression or of other hypotheses on regression coefficients, as derived in the last chapter, will, in general, be invalid. It is therefore important to test for serial correlation and, if found present, to correct for it.

Typically, the most important type of serial correlation is *first-order linear serial correlation*, namely the linear relation between successive stochastic disturbance terms. Such first-order serial correlation takes the form of a *Markov process* or *first-order autoregressive scheme*

$$u_i = \rho u_{i-1} + v_i, \quad \text{all } i, \quad |\rho| < 1. \qquad *(6.4.2)$$

[14] See Cootner, Ed. (1964), and Malkiel (1973).

[15] The assumption that $E(\mathbf{u}) = 0$ is still being made, so $E(\mathbf{uu}')$ is the $n \times n$ covariance matrix of $\mathbf{u}$.

[16] The minimum-variance estimators in this case, as in the case of heteroskedasticity, are the generalized least-squares (GLS) estimators to be introduced in Section 6.5. The GLS estimators are the best linear unbiased estimators in the case of nonspherical disturbances.

Here ρ is an unknown parameter and v_i is a residual stochastic disturbance term, which is assumed to satisfy the assumptions of the basic linear regression model, including absence of serial correlation:

$$E(v_i) = 0 \quad \text{all } i$$
$$E(v_i v_{i'}) = \begin{cases} \sigma_v^2 & \text{if } i = i' \\ 0 & \text{if } i \neq i' \end{cases} \quad \text{all } i, i' \qquad *(6.4.3)$$

From the original model

$$y_i = \mathbf{x}_i \boldsymbol{\beta} + u_i \qquad *(6.4.4)$$

so, lagging one period and multiplying by ρ,

$$\rho y_{i-1} = \rho \mathbf{x}_{i-1} \boldsymbol{\beta} + \rho u_{i-1}. \qquad (6.4.5)$$

Taking the difference leads to the *transformed model*:

$$y_i - \rho y_{i-1} = (\mathbf{x}_i - \rho \mathbf{x}_{i-1})\boldsymbol{\beta} + (u_i - \rho u_{i-1}) = (\mathbf{x}_i - \rho \mathbf{x}_{i-1})\boldsymbol{\beta} + v_i \qquad *(6.4.6)$$

where $u_i - \rho u_{i-1}$ has been replaced by v_i, using (6.4.2). The transformed model expresses the variable $y_i - \rho y_{i-1}$ as linear functions of the variables in $\mathbf{x}_i - \rho \mathbf{x}_{i-1}$. It is of the same form as the original model, other than the replacement of the variables by the corresponding differences, namely $y_i - \rho y_{i-1}$ and $\mathbf{x}_i - \rho \mathbf{x}_{i-1}$, and the replacement of u_i by v_i.[17] If $\rho = 1$, then the transformed model (6.4.6) implies that

$$y_i - y_{i-1} = (\mathbf{x}_i - \mathbf{x}_{i-1}) \boldsymbol{\beta} + v_i \qquad (6.4.7)$$

a model in which all variables are replaced by their *first differences*:

$$\Delta y_i = (\Delta \mathbf{x}_i) \boldsymbol{\beta} + v_i \quad \text{where} \quad \Delta z_i = z_i - z_{i-1} \qquad *(6.4.8)$$

At the other extreme, if $\rho = -1$, then (6.4.6) becomes

$$y_i + y_{i-1} = (\mathbf{x}_i + \mathbf{x}_{i-1}) \boldsymbol{\beta} + v_i \qquad (6.4.9)$$

a model in which all variables are replaced by *two-period moving averages*:[18]

$$A y_i = (A \mathbf{x}_i) \boldsymbol{\beta} + v_i \quad \text{where} \quad A z_i = \frac{z_i + z_{i-1}}{2} \qquad *(6.4.10)$$

[17] The first observation is either dropped or replaced by $\sqrt{1-\rho^2}\, y_1$ and $\sqrt{1-\rho^2}\, \mathbf{x}_1$. See footnote 46 and Problem 6-O.

[18] The first-differences and moving-average approaches have been considerably refined in the form of the *autoregressive moving-average models*. See Chapter 15 and Box and Jenkins (1970). However, while the use of first differences and moving averages has some intuitive appeal and represents a common practice, it in fact entails serious problems. From the Markov process (6.4.2), if $\rho = 1$, then

$$u_i = u_{i-1} + v_i$$

To test for first-order serial correlation consider the null hypothesis

$$H_0: \rho = 0 \tag{6.4.11}$$

for which the model with first-order serial correlation (6.4.6) reduces to the basic model. The *Durbin-Watson test* is the test of this hypothesis. It uses the *Durbin-Watson statistic* $\hat{d}$, defined by

$$\hat{d} = \frac{\sum_{i=2}^{n} (\hat{u}_i - \hat{u}_{i-1})^2}{\sum_{i=1}^{n} \hat{u}_i^2} \qquad *(6.4.12)$$

where $\hat{u}_i$ is the ith least-squares residual, $y_i - \mathbf{x}_i\hat{\boldsymbol{\beta}}$, as in (4.6.3). This statistic is the ratio of the sum of squares of successive differences of residuals to the sum of the squared residuals. Note that the sum in the numerator ranges from 2 to n because of the presence of $\hat{u}_{i-1}$, while the sum in the denominator ranges from 1 to n.[19] Carrying out the square in the numerator and recognizing that, for n large enough,

---

so, by repeatedly substituting for u_{i-j},

$$u_i = \sum_{j=0}^{\infty} v_{i-j}.$$

Thus, if v_i has variance $\sigma_v^2 > 0$ as given in (6.4.3), it follows that u_i has *infinite* variance. The restriction $|\rho| < 1$ appears in (6.4.2) to avoid such a situation. See also footnote 31 for a derivation of the means, variances, and covariances of the u_i in (6.4.2).

[19] Aside from a minor scaling factor, the Durbin-Watson statistic is a realized value of the *von Neumann ratio* defined as

$$\frac{\delta^2}{s^2} = \frac{\frac{1}{n-1}\sum_{i=2}^{n} (u_i - u_{i-1})^2}{\frac{1}{n}\sum_{i=1}^{n} u_i^2} = \frac{n}{n-1}\, d$$

–that is, as the ratio of the mean square successive difference to the variance. For large n the von Neumann ratio is approximately normally distributed, with parameters

$$E\left(\frac{\delta^2}{s^2}\right) = \frac{2n}{n-1}, \qquad \text{Var}\left(\frac{\delta^2}{s^2}\right) = \frac{4n^2(n-2)}{(n+1)(n-3)^3}$$

Thus for large n this ratio can be used, in conjunction with critical values of the normal distribution, to test for first-order serial correlation.

$$\sum_{i=2}^{n} \hat{u}_i^2 \approx \sum_{i=2}^{n} \hat{u}_{i-1}^2 \approx \sum_{i=1}^{n} \hat{u}_i^2 \tag{6.4.13}$$

it follows that $\hat{d}$ can be approximated as

$$\hat{d} \approx 2 \left(1 - \frac{\sum_{i=2}^{n} \hat{u}_i \hat{u}_{i-1}}{\sum_{i=1}^{n} \hat{u}_i^2} \right) \tag{6.4.14}$$

This approximation can motivate the use of the Durbin-Watson statistic. Suppose $\hat{u}_i$ and $\hat{u}_{i-1}$ are usually of the same sign, the case of positive first-order serial correlation. In that case $\hat{u}_i\hat{u}_{i-1}$ in (6.4.14) would tend to be positive, so

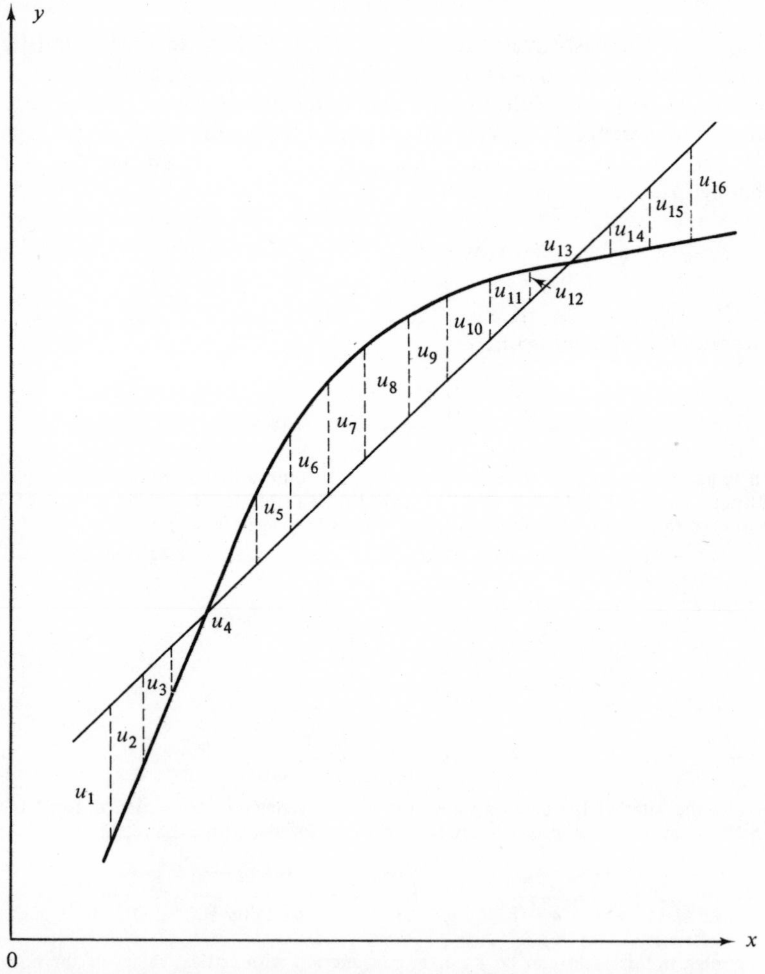

Figure 6.2 Positive First-Order Correlation When a Nonlinear Relationship Is Estimated by a Linear One

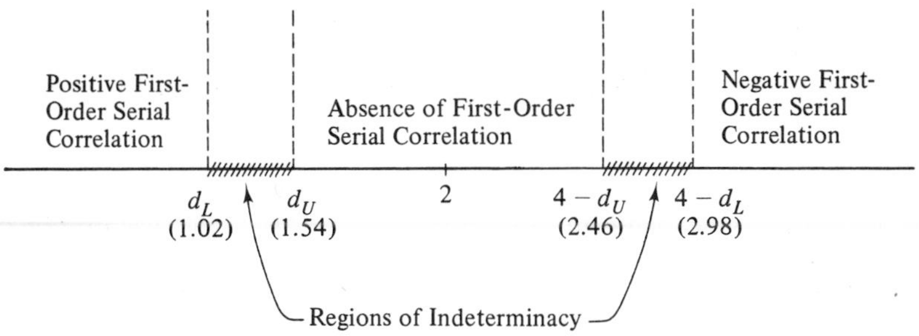

Figure 6.3 Significance Points for the Durbin-Watson Statistic d.
[NOTE Numbers refer to the $n = 25$, $k = 4$ case for a 5% level of significance; see Table C.5.5.]

$\hat{d}$ would lie significantly below 2. Conversely, if $\hat{u}_i$ and $\hat{u}_{i-1}$ are usually of the opposite sign, the case of negative first-order serial correlation, then $\Sigma\, \hat{u}_i\hat{u}_{i-1}$ would tend to be negative, so $\hat{d}$ would be significantly above 2. In the former case, the positive and negative errors tend to "bunch" together. An example is the case of estimation of a linear relationship when the actual relationship is non-linear, as shown in Figure 6.2. Note that here $\hat{u}_1$ to $\hat{u}_3$ are negative while $\hat{u}_5$ to $\hat{u}_{13}$ are positive and $\hat{u}_{14}$ to $\hat{u}_{16}$ are negative. Thus $\hat{u}_i\hat{u}_{i-1}$ will be positive for all i other than $i = 14$. Since the $\hat{u}_i$ and $\hat{u}_{i-1}$ tend to be of the same sign, the $\hat{d}$ will be significantly below 2, indicating positive first-order serial correlation. The other case, which is equally a problem, is that in which the errors tend to reverse sign from observation to observation. Such a case of negative first-order serial correlation occurs in simple linear regression if the data points are alternately above and below the regression line. The $\hat{u}_i$ then tend to reverse sign, so $\hat{d}$ will be significantly above 2, indicating negative first-order serial correlation.

Thus, if $\hat{d} \ll 2$, positive first-order serial correlation is indicated, while if $\hat{d} \gg 2$, negative first-order serial correlation is indicated. If $\hat{d} \approx 2$, the absence of first-order serial correlation is indicated. Tables of significant values of the Durbin-Watson statistic, as in Appendix C, Table C.5, are based on normally distributed disturbances and fixed explanatory variables. These tables give, for a particular sample size n and a particular number of coefficients to be estimated k, lower and upper values for d, called d_L and d_U, representing bounds on the significance level for any set of explanatory variables. For example, if $n = 25$ and $k = 4$, the values for a 5% level of significance are $d_L = 1.12$ and $d_U = 1.66$. To understand the meaning and use of these values, construct an axis for $\hat{d}$, as shown in Figure 6.3. The distribution of the statistic is symmetric about 2, so $4 - d_U$ and $4 - d_L$ are shown as significant points. If the test statistic $\hat{d}$ lies in the middle region close to 2, specifically between d_U and $4 - d_U$ (here 1.54 to 2.46) the test indicates the absence of first-order serial correlation.[20] If $\hat{d}$ lies

[20] If a lagged endogenous variable is included among the explanatory variables, then the d statistic will be biased toward 2, indicating no serial correlation even though such correlation may be present. Intuitively, this bias stems from the fact that the dependence of the error terms on lagged values is "absorbed" in the included lagged endogenous variable. The test is not conclusive and is not recommended in such a case of an included lagged endogenous variable. See also Section 6.7 and footnote 22.

significantly below 2, however, specifically below d_L (here 1.02), it indicates the presence of positive first-order serial correlation. Similarly if $\hat{d}$ lies above $4 - d_L$ (here 2.98), it indicates the presence of negative first-order serial correlation. In the two remaining regions of indeterminancy the test fails, but, in those cases, it is customary to reject the hypothesis of absence of first-order serial correlation.[21]

If first-order serial correlation is diagnosed using the Durbin-Watson test, there are two possible treatments, each involving a change in the specification of the original model. One treatment is to include other explanatory variables. To some extent the stochastic disturbance term may be representing the actions of these variables, which, if explicitly accounted for, would reduce the serial correlation. The other treatment, which is used if such additional variables are not readily available, involves estimating not the original model but the transformed model (6.4.6). To do so, however, requires an estimate of the unknown parameter ρ.

One approach to estimating the parameter ρ is to first estimate the original model (6.4.4), use these estimates to construct $\hat{u}_i$, and estimate ρ as the simple linear regression of the Markov process (6.4.2), namely[22]

[21] The regions of indeterminancy are large for small numbers of explanatory variables, leading to an inconclusive test in many situations. A test statistic has been constructed by Theil and Nagar (1971) that excludes these regions of indeterminancy. This test statistic requires, however, that each of the explanatory variables move smoothly—in particular, that the first and second differences of each explanatory variable are small in absolute value compared with the range of the variable itself. The test statistic is identical to the Durbin-Watson $\hat{d}$ of (6.4.12), and the critical value d^* is generally near d_U, usually approximately 0.06 to 0.13 higher than d_U. For example, for $n = 25, k = 4$, for a 5% level of significance d^* is 1.65 compared to 1.54 for d_U. In this case, using the Theil-Nagar test, there is no first-order serial correlation if $1.65 < d < 2.35$; positive serial correlation if $\hat{d} < 1.65$; and negative serial correlation if $\hat{d} > 2.35$, where 2.35 is obtained as $4 - d^*$. See also footnote 22.

[22] See Problem 6-F. This technique can be extended to a model with lagged endogenous variables, in which case such variables should also be included as explanatory variables in (6.4.2). See also Durbin (1970) for a large-sample test for serial correlation in such a case. The estimator in (6.4.15) is one of several possible estimators. An alternative estimator of ρ is

$$\hat{\hat{\rho}} = \frac{1 - \dfrac{\hat{d}}{2} + \left(\dfrac{k}{n}\right)^2}{1 - \left(\dfrac{k}{n}\right)^2}$$

based on the Durbin-Watson statistic $\hat{d}$, the number of parameters to be estimated k, and the number of observations n. This estimator was derived by Theil and Nagar (1971), assuming that the explanatory variables move smoothly, as discussed in the last footnote. Note that if $n \gg k$, then

$$\hat{\hat{\rho}} \approx 1 - \frac{\hat{d}}{2}$$

so $\hat{\hat{\rho}} \approx 0$ (the original model) if $\hat{d} = 2$, $\hat{\hat{\rho}} \approx 1$ (the case of first differences) if $\hat{d} = 0$, and $\hat{\hat{\rho}} \approx -1$ (the case of moving averages) if $\hat{d} = 4$. In fact, if n is sufficiently large, $1 - (\hat{d}/2)$ is a good approximation to the estimator $\hat{\rho}$ in (6.4.15), as implied by (6.4.14).

$$\hat{\rho} = \frac{\sum_{i=2}^{n} \hat{u}_i \hat{u}_{i-1}}{\sum_{i=2}^{n} \hat{u}_{i-1}^2}. \qquad *(6.4.15)$$

This estimate can be used to obtain data for the transformed model (6.4.6), which can then be estimated using usual regression techniques to obtain estimates of the parameters $\boldsymbol{\beta}$. Because of the presence of the lagged variables in (6.4.6) the estimation utilizes one less data point than in the original sample.

Another approach is a two-step procedure in which ρ is estimated by applying least squares to the equation (6.4.6) in the form

$$y_i = \rho y_{i-1} + (\mathbf{x}_i - \rho \mathbf{x}_{i-1})\boldsymbol{\beta} + v_i \qquad (6.4.16)$$

to obtain $\hat{\rho}$ as the estimated coefficient of y_{i-1}. The second step is then to estimate $\boldsymbol{\beta}$ in the transformed model (6.4.6) using this $\hat{\rho}$.[23]

Which of these approaches should be used? It is difficult to give an answer that will cover all contingencies, but, generally, the relative desirability of the various approaches is that of the order in which they have been presented. The best approach is to add relevant explanatory variables. Failing this, the next best is generally to use the simplest estimator of ρ, as given in (6.4.15). More refined estimators should be used only when necessary.

6.5 Generalized least-squares estimators; "seemingly unrelated equations"

The term "spherical disturbances" was used in Chapter 4 to indicate the assumptions of both homoskedasticity and absence of serial correlation. *Generalized least-squares estimators*, also called *GLS estimators* or *Aitken estimators*, are the best linear unbiased estimators (BLUE) of the basic linear regression model (4.7.1) when the assumption of spherical disturbances is dropped, thereby allowing for both heteroskedasticity, as discussed in Section 6.3, and serial correlation, as discussed in Section 6.4.

To allow for both heteroskedasticity and serial correlation let

$$\text{Cov}(\mathbf{u}) = E(\mathbf{u}\mathbf{u}') = \sigma^2 \boldsymbol{\Omega} \qquad *(6.5.1)$$

where $\boldsymbol{\Omega}$ is a given symmetric positive-definite matrix of order n and σ^2 is an

[23] See Durbin (1960). A related approach, that of Cochrane and Orcutt (1949), is an iterative one, which starts from an arbitrary value of $\hat{\rho}$ and minimizes the sum of squares for (6.4.6) by choice of $\hat{\boldsymbol{\beta}}$. The next step minimizes the sum of squares by choice of $\hat{\rho}$ for this $\hat{\boldsymbol{\beta}}$. This process continues until estimators $\hat{\boldsymbol{\beta}}$ and $\hat{\rho}$ are obtained that do not significantly differ from those obtained on the previous step. This process always converges, but it can converge to a local rather than a global minimum for the sum of squares. If it starts with $\hat{\rho} = 0$, then, after estimating $\hat{\boldsymbol{\beta}}$ by least squares, the next estimate of ρ is given by (6.4.15).

unknown parameter. This case reduces to spherical disturbances if $\mathbf{\Omega}$ is the identity matrix, but, more generally, allows for nonspherical disturbances. The BLUE estimator can be readily derived if it is further assumed that the stochastic disturbance term is distributed normally with mean zero and covariance matrix as in (6.5.1):

$$\mathbf{u} \sim N(0, \sigma^2\mathbf{\Omega}) \qquad *(6.5.2)$$

The estimators can then be obtained using the technique of maximum likelihood. The multivariate normal density function is

$$f(\mathbf{u}) = (2\pi)^{-n/2} |\mathbf{\Omega}|^{-1/2} \sigma^{-n} \exp\left(-\frac{1}{2\sigma^2} \mathbf{u}'\mathbf{\Omega}^{-1}\mathbf{u}\right) \qquad (6.5.3)$$

of which (4.7.5) is the special case corresponding to spherical disturbances, in which $\mathbf{\Omega}$ is the identity matrix. The log of the likelihood function is

$$\ln L = -\frac{n}{2} \ln (2\pi) - \frac{1}{2} \ln |\mathbf{\Omega}| - n \ln \sigma - \frac{1}{2\sigma^2} (\mathbf{y} - \mathbf{X}\hat{\boldsymbol{\beta}})'\mathbf{\Omega}^{-1}(\mathbf{y} - \mathbf{X}\hat{\boldsymbol{\beta}}) \qquad (6.5.4)$$

which is to be maximized by choice of $\hat{\boldsymbol{\beta}}$ and σ. Maximizing $\ln L$ by choice of $\hat{\boldsymbol{\beta}}$ requires minimization of the term

$$S(\mathbf{\Omega}) = (\mathbf{y} - \mathbf{X}\hat{\boldsymbol{\beta}})'\mathbf{\Omega}^{-1} (\mathbf{y} - \mathbf{X}\hat{\boldsymbol{\beta}}) \qquad *(6.5.5)$$

which is a weighted sum of squared residuals and cross products of residuals, the weights being the elements of the inverse matrix $\mathbf{\Omega}^{-1}$. This weighted sum of squares reduces to the ordinary sum of squared residuals S in (4.6.12) in the case of spherical disturbances. Expanding $S(\mathbf{\Omega})$

$$S(\mathbf{\Omega}) = \mathbf{y}'\mathbf{\Omega}^{-1}\mathbf{y} - 2\hat{\boldsymbol{\beta}}'\mathbf{X}'\mathbf{\Omega}^{-1}\mathbf{y} + \hat{\boldsymbol{\beta}}'\mathbf{X}'\mathbf{\Omega}^{-1}\mathbf{X}\hat{\boldsymbol{\beta}} \qquad (6.5.6)$$

as in (4.6.13). Following the same approach as in (4.6.15), the first-order conditions for minimization of $S(\mathbf{\Omega})$ are

$$\frac{\partial S(\mathbf{\Omega})}{\partial \hat{\boldsymbol{\beta}}'} = -2\mathbf{X}'\mathbf{\Omega}^{-1}\mathbf{y} + 2\mathbf{X}'\mathbf{\Omega}^{-1}\mathbf{X}\hat{\boldsymbol{\beta}} = \mathbf{0}. \qquad (6.5.7)$$

Assuming $\mathbf{X}$ is of full rank, the matrix $(\mathbf{X}'\mathbf{\Omega}^{-1}\mathbf{X})$ is nonsingular, so the estimator can be written

$$\hat{\boldsymbol{\beta}}(\mathbf{\Omega}) = (\mathbf{X}'\mathbf{\Omega}^{-1}\mathbf{X})^{-1}\mathbf{X}'\mathbf{\Omega}^{-1}\mathbf{y} \qquad *(6.5.8)$$

where $\hat{\boldsymbol{\beta}}(\mathbf{\Omega})$ is the *GLS estimator*, dependent on the matrix $\mathbf{\Omega}$. It reduces to the usual or ordinary least-squares estimator if $\mathbf{\Omega} = \mathbf{I}$, that is, in the case of spherical disturbances.[24]

As in the case of ordinary least squares it is important to analyze the distribution of the GLS estimator. In particular, the covariance matrix will provide information on standard errors that is useful in testing the significance of estimated coefficients. Using the same approach as in Section 4.6, the covariance matrix of the GLS estimator is

$$\mathrm{Cov}\,(\hat{\boldsymbol{\beta}}(\boldsymbol{\Omega})) = \sigma^2 (\mathbf{X}'\boldsymbol{\Omega}^{-1}\mathbf{X})^{-1} \qquad *(6.5.9)$$

a result which generalizes the covariance matrix for ordinary least squares in (4.6.37). To use this result, e.g., for computing standard errors and confidence intervals, it is necessary to estimate σ^2. An unbiased estimator of σ^2 is given by maximizing (6.5.4) with respect to σ and adjusting for the number of degrees of freedom as

$$\hat{s}^2(\boldsymbol{\Omega}) = \frac{1}{n-k}\,[\hat{\mathbf{u}}(\boldsymbol{\Omega})]'\boldsymbol{\Omega}^{-1}[\hat{\mathbf{u}}(\boldsymbol{\Omega})] \qquad *(6.5.10)$$

where $\hat{\mathbf{u}}(\boldsymbol{\Omega})$ is the vector of GLS residuals:[25]

$$\hat{\mathbf{u}}(\boldsymbol{\Omega}) = \mathbf{y} - \mathbf{X}\hat{\boldsymbol{\beta}}(\boldsymbol{\Omega}). \qquad (6.5.11)$$

If the stochastic disturbance terms are distributed normally, as in (6.5.2), it follows that

$$\hat{\boldsymbol{\beta}}(\boldsymbol{\Omega}) \sim N(\boldsymbol{\beta}, \sigma^2(\mathbf{X}'\boldsymbol{\Omega}^{-1}\mathbf{X})^{-1}) \qquad *(6.5.12)$$

[24] The GLS estimators can be interpreted as *weighted* least squares, obtained by minimizing $\hat{\mathbf{u}}'\mathbf{W}\hat{\mathbf{u}}$, where $\mathbf{W}$ is a positive-definite matrix of weights. Here $\mathbf{W}$ is $\boldsymbol{\Omega}^{-1}$, and the estimators in (6.5.8) are obtained as those minimizing $\hat{\mathbf{u}}'\boldsymbol{\Omega}^{-1}\hat{\mathbf{u}}$. In the case of the usual least-squares estimators $\mathbf{W}$ is the identity matrix $\mathbf{I}$.

[25] The usual least-squares estimator of σ^2,

$$\hat{s}^2 = \frac{1}{n-k}\,\hat{\mathbf{u}}'\hat{\mathbf{u}}$$

where $\hat{\mathbf{u}}$ is the vector of ordinary least-squares residuals, is no longer unbiased in the case of nonspherical disturbances. Letting $\hat{\boldsymbol{\beta}}$ be the ordinary least-squares estimator, Goldfeld and Quandt (1972) prove that the expected value of the ordinary least-squares estimator of the covariance matrix is given, in this case of nonspherical disturbances, as

$$E[\hat{s}^2(\mathbf{X}'\mathbf{X})^{-1}] = \mathrm{Cov}\,(\hat{\boldsymbol{\beta}}) + \sigma^2(\mathbf{X}'\mathbf{X})^{-1}\mathbf{X}'(\mathbf{I}-\boldsymbol{\Omega})\mathbf{X}(\mathbf{X}'\mathbf{X})^{-1} + \frac{\sigma^2}{n-k}\,\mathrm{tr}\,[(\mathbf{X}'\mathbf{X})^{-1}\mathbf{X}'(\mathbf{I}-\boldsymbol{\Omega})\mathbf{X}]\,(\mathbf{X}'\mathbf{X})^{-1}.$$

The presence of the last two terms implies that the usual t and F tests of statistical significance are not appropriate if $\boldsymbol{\Omega} \neq \mathbf{I}$.

which generalizes the result in (4.7.2). The GLS estimator, which is defined if $\boldsymbol{\Omega}$ is given, in fact satisfies all of the properties of the Gauss-Markov theorem– it is linear, unbiased, and best of all linear unbiased estimators. While the ordinary least-squares estimator is still defined, linear, and unbiased, it is no longer best (most efficient). In the nonspherical disturbances case, in which the covariance matrix is given as in (6.5.1), the GLS estimator of (6.5.8) is the BLUE estimator; in particular, it is the efficient estimator. It is also a consistent estimator.[26]

GLS may be shown to be equivalent to OLS after a suitable transformation. A mathematical result from matrix theory states that any symmetric positive-definite matrix **A** can be written as the product **P′P**, where **P** is a nonsingular matrix.[27] Since $\boldsymbol{\Omega}$ is a symmetric positive-definite matrix, so is $\boldsymbol{\Omega}^{-1}$, implying that

$$\boldsymbol{\Omega}^{-1} = \mathbf{P}'\mathbf{P} \qquad *(6.5.13)$$

where **P** is nonsingular. Inserting this result in the GLS estimator equation (6.5.8) yields

$$\hat{\boldsymbol{\beta}} = (\mathbf{X}'\mathbf{P}'\mathbf{P}\mathbf{X})^{-1}\mathbf{X}'\mathbf{P}'\mathbf{P}\mathbf{y}. \qquad (6.5.14)$$

This estimator is, however, the least-squares estimator of the transformed model[28]

$$\begin{aligned}
&\mathbf{Py} = \mathbf{PX}\boldsymbol{\beta} + \mathbf{Pu}\\
&E(\mathbf{Pu}) = \mathbf{P}E(\mathbf{u}) = \mathbf{0}\\
&E(\mathbf{Puu}'\mathbf{P}') = \mathbf{P}E(\mathbf{uu}')\mathbf{P}' = \sigma^2\mathbf{P}\boldsymbol{\Omega}\mathbf{P}' = \sigma^2\mathbf{I}\\
&\mathbf{PX} \text{ fixed, where } \rho(\mathbf{PX}) = k < n
\end{aligned} \qquad *(6.5.15)$$

Here all elements are weighted by the **P** matrix in (6.5.13), and **Pu** satisfies all the usual least-squares assumptions. Thus the ordinary least-squares technique can be applied to the data after they have been transformed as indicated in (6.5.15): **y** to **Py** and **X** to **PX**.

Since, in practice, the $\boldsymbol{\Omega}$ covariance matrix is generally not given, and is unknown and unobservable, to use the GLS estimator requires construction of an appropriate covariance matrix. It is useful here to distinguish heteroskedasticity from serial correlation.

In the case of heteroskedasticity without serial correlation, the covariance matrix is of the form

[26] See Problem 6-L. If $\boldsymbol{\Omega}$ as given or estimated is positive semidefinite, where the inverse matrix does not exist it is still possible to form an estimator, replacing $\boldsymbol{\Omega}^{-1}$ in (6.5.8) by $\boldsymbol{\Omega}^{+}$, the generalized inverse of $\boldsymbol{\Omega}$, as discussed in Appendix B, Section B.5. See Theil (1971).

[27] See Appendix B, Section B.8.

[28] From (6.5.13) it follows that $\mathbf{P}\boldsymbol{\Omega}\mathbf{P}' = \mathbf{I}$, so **P** is the modal matrix the columns of which are the characteristic vectors of the symmetric matrix $\boldsymbol{\Omega}$. See Appendix B, Section B.7.

$$\text{Cov}(\mathbf{u}) = \sigma^2 \mathbf{\Omega} = \begin{pmatrix} \sigma_1^2 & & & 0 \\ & \sigma_2^2 & & \\ & & \ddots & \\ 0 & & & \sigma_n^2 \end{pmatrix} \quad *(6.5.16)$$

where σ_i^2 is the variance of the ith stochastic disturbance term, $i = 1, 2, \ldots, n$. The inverse used in the GLS estimator is then, omitting σ^2, which cancels in (6.5.8),

$$\mathbf{\Omega}^{-1} = \begin{pmatrix} \frac{1}{\sigma_1^2} & & & 0 \\ & \frac{1}{\sigma_2^2} & & \\ & & \ddots & \\ 0 & & & \frac{1}{\sigma_n^2} \end{pmatrix} \quad *(6.5.17)$$

–that is, the matrix the diagonal elements of which are the reciprocals of the corresponding variances of the stochastic disturbance terms. This is the inverse matrix that, in theory, should be used in the GLS estimator (6.5.8) in the case of heteroskedasticity without serial correlation. If the n variances in (6.5.16) are given, this estimator can be calculated.

An interpretation can be given for the resulting estimator. Note that in this case, using (6.5.13),

$$\mathbf{\Omega}^{-1} = \mathbf{P}'\mathbf{P} \quad \text{where} \quad \mathbf{P} = \begin{pmatrix} \frac{1}{\sigma_1} & & & 0 \\ & \frac{1}{\sigma_2} & & \\ & & \ddots & \\ 0 & & & \frac{1}{\sigma_n} \end{pmatrix} \quad *(6.5.18)$$

the **P** matrix being a diagonal matrix, the diagonal elements of which are the reciprocals of the corresponding standard deviations of the stochastic disturbance terms. Using (6.5.15), it follows that both dependent and explanatory variables are weighted at each observation by the reciprocal of the standard deviation of the dependent variable (or stochastic disturbance term) at that observation. Thus GLS estimation in this case can be interpreted as OLS estimation for which the data y and **X** are replaced by the transformed data

$$\mathbf{Py} = \begin{pmatrix} y_1/\sigma_1 \\ y_2/\sigma_2 \\ \vdots \\ y_n/\sigma_n \end{pmatrix} \quad \text{and } \mathbf{PX} = \begin{pmatrix} \mathbf{X}_1/\sigma_1 \\ \mathbf{X}_2/\sigma_2 \\ \vdots \\ \mathbf{X}_n/\sigma_n \end{pmatrix} \qquad {}^*(6.5.19)$$

respectively. If the standard deviation at each observation σ_i can be assumed to be proportional to one of the explanatory variables, say x_{1i}, then the transformation called for by the GLS estimator can be realized by using appropriate ratios of variables, i.e., simple deflation by x_{1i}.[29] This was the approach utilized in equation (6.3.3). Dividing through equation (6.3.2) by income, in effect, adjusts for the variance at each observation, assuming the standard deviation of savings is proportional to income.

If the n variances in (6.5.16) are not all given, they cannot all be estimated, since it is impossible to estimate a variance for each single observation. It is possible, however, to divide the sample into various subsamples, each of which has two or more observations, to calculate a variance for each subsample as the variance of the dependent variables in the subsample, and to use the appropriate reciprocals in the GLS estimator. The inverse matrix would be

$$\mathbf{\Omega}^{-1} = \left(\begin{array}{cccc:ccc:cc} \frac{1}{\sigma_1^2} & & & & & & & & \\ & \frac{1}{\sigma_1^2} & & & & & & & \\ & & \ddots & & & & & & \\ & & & \frac{1}{\sigma_1^2} & & & & & \\ \hdashline & & & & \frac{1}{\sigma_2^2} & & & & \\ & & & & & \ddots & & & \\ \hdashline & & & & & & & \frac{1}{\sigma_3^2} & \\ & & & & & & & & \ddots \end{array}\right) \qquad (6.5.20)$$

where σ_1^2 is the variance in the first subsample, σ_2^2 is the variance in the second subsample, etc. Clearly some a priori information is required in order to choose subsamples in a reasonable way.[30]

[29] Goldfeld and Quandt (1965) compare the original to the deflated model in order to test for heteroskedasticity. See also Goldfeld and Quandt (1972).

[30] See Goldfeld and Quandt (1972).

Turning now to the case of serial correlation without heteroskedasticity, if the first-order autoregressive (Markov) process of (6.4.2) is used, the corresponding covariance matrix of the stochastic disturbance terms is

$$\sigma^2 \mathbf{\Omega} = E(\mathbf{uu}') = \sigma^2 \begin{pmatrix} 1 & \rho & \rho^2 & \cdots & \rho^{n-1} \\ \rho & 1 & \rho & \cdots & \rho^{n-2} \\ \vdots & \vdots & & & \\ \rho^{n-1} & \rho^{n-2} & & \cdots & 1 \end{pmatrix} \qquad *(6.5.21)$$

that is,

$$\text{Cov}(u_i, u_{i'}) = \sigma^2 \rho^{|i-i'|}$$

where ρ is the parameter of the Markov process ($|\rho| < 1$) and where σ^2 is defined as $\sigma_v^2/(1-\rho^2)$, σ_v^2 being given in (6.4.3).[31] Note that the covariance matrix is

[31] For the inverse of $\mathbf{\Omega}$ see Problem 6-O. To derive (6.5.21), note that, by recursive substitution in (6.4.2),

$$\begin{aligned} u_i &= \rho u_{i-1} + v_i = \rho(\rho u_{i-2} + v_{i-1}) + v_i = \cdots \\ &= v_i + \rho v_{i-1} + \rho^2 v_{i-2} + \cdots \\ &= \sum_{s=0}^{\infty} \rho^s v_{i-s}, \qquad |\rho| < 1 \end{aligned}$$

Thus, from (6.4.3),

$$E(u_i) = \Sigma \rho^s E(v_{i-s}) = 0$$

The variance of u_i is thus, since the v_i are serially uncorrelated,

$$\begin{aligned} \text{Var}(u_i) &= E(u_i^2) = E(v_i^2) + \rho^2 E(v_{i-1}^2) + \rho^4 E(v_{i-2}^2) + \cdots \\ &= (1 + \rho^2 + \rho^4 + \cdots)\sigma_v^2 = \frac{1}{1-\rho^2}\sigma_v^2 = \sigma^2 \end{aligned}$$

The covariance of u_i and u_{i-1} is

$$\begin{aligned} \text{Cov}(u_i, u_{i-1}) &= E(u_i u_{i-1}) = E[(v_i + \rho v_{i-1} + \rho^2 v_{i-2} + \cdots) \\ &\qquad (v_{i-1} + \rho v_{i-2} + \rho^2 v_{i-3} + \cdots)] \\ &= E[(v_i + \rho(v_{i-1} + \rho v_{i-2} + \cdots))(v_{i-1} + \rho v_{i-2} + \cdots)] \\ &= \rho E(v_{i-1} + \rho v_{i-2} + \cdots)^2 = \sigma^2 \rho \end{aligned}$$

Similarly

$$\text{Cov}(u_i, u_{i-2}) = E(u_i u_{i-2}) = \sigma^2 \rho^2$$

and

$$\text{Cov}(u_i, u_{i'}) = E(u_i u_{i'}) = \sigma^2 \rho^{|i-i'|}$$

completely defined by only two parameters—ρ, the Markov parameter, and σ^2, the constant error variance. The ρ parameter can be estimated as in (6.4.15), while σ^2 can be estimated as $\hat{s}^2$ in (4.6.24).

The technique of generalized least squares can be applied to systems of equations as well as to individual equations. According to the technique of "seemingly unrelated equations" it is possible to construct a GLS estimator for a system of equations.[32] Consider a system of g equations where

$$\underset{n\times 1}{\mathbf{y}_h} = \underset{n\times k_h}{\mathbf{X}_h}\ \underset{k_h\times 1}{\boldsymbol{\beta}_h} + \underset{n\times 1}{\mathbf{u}_h}, \qquad h = 1, 2, \ldots, g \tag*{*(6.5.22)}$$

Since the $\mathbf{y}_h$ are all column vectors, all g such vectors can be written as one gn column vector by "stacking" the vectors. Similarly all $\boldsymbol{\beta}_h$ can be written as one vector of length

$$k^* = \sum_{h=1}^{g} k_h,$$

and all $\mathbf{u}_h$ can be written as one vector of length gn. The entire system can thus be written in the "star" notation of "stacked" variables as

$$\underset{gn\times 1}{\mathbf{y}^*} = \underset{gn\times k^*}{\mathbf{X}^*}\ \underset{k^*\times 1}{\boldsymbol{\beta}^*} + \underset{gn\times 1}{\mathbf{u}^*} \tag*{*(6.5.23)}$$

which represents the system

$$\begin{pmatrix} \mathbf{y}_1 \\ \mathbf{y}_2 \\ \vdots \\ \mathbf{y}_g \end{pmatrix} = \begin{pmatrix} \mathbf{X}_1 & \mathbf{0} & \cdots & \mathbf{0} \\ \mathbf{0} & \mathbf{X}_2 & \cdots & \mathbf{0} \\ \vdots & & & \\ \mathbf{0} & \mathbf{0} & \cdots & \mathbf{X}_g \end{pmatrix} \begin{pmatrix} \boldsymbol{\beta}_1 \\ \boldsymbol{\beta}_2 \\ \vdots \\ \boldsymbol{\beta}_g \end{pmatrix} + \begin{pmatrix} \mathbf{u}_1 \\ \mathbf{u}_2 \\ \vdots \\ \mathbf{u}_g \end{pmatrix} \tag*{*(6.5.24)}$$

If $\boldsymbol{\Sigma}^*$ is the covariance matrix for $\mathbf{u}^*$, given as $E(\mathbf{u}^*\mathbf{u}^{*\prime})$, then the GLS estimator for all coefficients in the system is

$$\hat{\boldsymbol{\beta}}^*(\boldsymbol{\Sigma}^*) = (\mathbf{X}^{*\prime}\boldsymbol{\Sigma}^{*-1}\mathbf{X}^*)^{-1}\mathbf{X}^{*\prime}\boldsymbol{\Sigma}^{*-1}\mathbf{y}^* \tag*{*(6.5.25)}$$

which is the best linear unbiased estimator.[33] These estimators are the same as

[32] See Zellner (1962, 1963) and Zellner and Huang (1962). For a discussion of tests of hypotheses involving coefficients from different equations see Theil (1971), and for an extension to simultaneous-equations system see Section 11.7.

[33] To utilize this method it is necessary to estimate the $\boldsymbol{\Sigma}^*$ matrix. It is generally assumed that the system satisfies the conditions

$$E(\mathbf{u}_h\mathbf{u}_{h'}) = \sigma_{hh'}\mathbf{I}, \qquad \text{all } h$$

the ordinary least-squares estimators for each equation if the disturbance terms are uncorrelated between any two different equations or if the $\mathbf{X}_h$ matrices of explanatory variables are all identical.[34] If, however, the disturbance terms are correlated and the set of explanatory variables is not the same for each equation, then this method yields estimators that are asymptotically more efficient than those obtained by applying ordinary least squares to each equation individually. In fact, the gain in efficiency is greater the greater is the correlation of the residuals and the less is the correlation of the explanatory variables in the different equations of the system.

6.6 Qualitative dependent variable; logit analysis

Another problem in the basic linear regression model arises when the dependent variable is qualitative, reflecting binary choices. Examples include buy-no buy decisions, yes–no responses, and various choices between two alternatives, such as whether or not to go to college, whether or not to reside in an urban area, and whether to travel by ground or air transportation.

In such a situation a numerical dependent variable can be obtained as the computed sample relative frequencies of one of the two possible choices. For

---

so

$$\boldsymbol{\Sigma}^* = \boldsymbol{\Sigma} \otimes \mathbf{I}$$

where $\boldsymbol{\Sigma}$ is the $g \times g$ matrix

$$\boldsymbol{\Sigma} = \begin{pmatrix} \sigma_{11} & \sigma_{12} & \cdots & \sigma_{1g} \\ \vdots & & & \\ \sigma_{g1} & \sigma_{g2} & \cdots & \sigma_{gg} \end{pmatrix}$$

$\mathbf{I}$ is the identity matrix of order n, and $\boldsymbol{\Sigma} \otimes \mathbf{I}$ is the Kronecker product of the two matrices, as discussed in Appendix B (B.3.23). The estimator given by (6.5.25) is then

$$\hat{\boldsymbol{\beta}}^*(\boldsymbol{\Sigma}^*) = (\mathbf{X}^{*\prime}(\boldsymbol{\Sigma}^{-1} \otimes \mathbf{I})\mathbf{X}^*)^{-1}\mathbf{X}^{*\prime}(\boldsymbol{\Sigma}^{-1} \otimes \mathbf{I})\mathbf{y}^*$$

A two-step procedure for estimating $\boldsymbol{\Sigma}$, as proposed by Zellner, uses the vectors of residuals from the ordinary least-squares regressions of each equation, $\hat{\mathbf{u}}_h$, to construct estimates of the elements of $\boldsymbol{\Sigma}$ as

$$\hat{\sigma}_{hh} = \frac{1}{n - k_h} \hat{\mathbf{u}}_h' \hat{\mathbf{u}}_h$$

$$\hat{\sigma}_{hh'} = \frac{1}{[(n - k_h)(n - k_{h'})]^{1/2}} \hat{\mathbf{u}}_h' \hat{\mathbf{u}}_{h'}, \qquad h \neq h'$$

Thus the first step in employing this method is to estimate the covariance matrix of the residuals using the ordinary least-squares estimates of each equation. The second step is then to use this estimated covariance matrix in order to estimate all equations simultaneously using (6.5.25).

[34] See Problems 6-P and 10-B.

example, with buy-no buy decisions such a relative frequency can be obtained as the proportion of a sample of families who do buy, while with yes-no responses it could be the proportion of individuals responding yes. Assuming there are n replicated samples and that in each the relative frequency is positive and less than one, then, letting p_i be the relative frequency for the ith sample,

$$0 < p_i < 1, \qquad i = 1, 2, \ldots, n. \tag*{*(6.6.1)}$$

If the relative frequencies are influenced by variables $x_1, x_2, \ldots, x_k$, one approach to estimating the relationship would be to specify the *linear model*

$$p = \beta_1 x_1 + \beta_2 x_2 + \cdots + \beta_k x_k + u = \mathbf{x}\boldsymbol{\beta} + u \tag*{*(6.6.2)}$$

and to estimate the coefficients $\boldsymbol{\beta} = (\beta_1 \ \beta_2 \ \ldots \ \beta_k)'$ from the observed values of p_i and $\mathbf{x}_i$. With this approach it is possible, however, for a predicted value of p to be negative or larger than one, violating its interpretation as a relative frequency. Usually, therefore, an alternative specification is employed. One such alternative specification is the *logit form of regression analysis*, of the form[35]

$$\ln \frac{p}{1-p} = \mathbf{x}\boldsymbol{\theta} + \nu \tag*{*(6.6.3)}$$

This specification uses $\ln (p/(1-p))$ as the dependent variable of the regression, and it determines the effect of the k explanatory variables on this variable, as summarized by the estimated coefficients $\hat{\boldsymbol{\theta}} = (\hat{\theta}_1 \ \hat{\theta}_2 \ \ldots \ \hat{\theta}_k)'$.[36] This form is very convenient because it ensures that no matter what values are taken by the explanatory variables, the implied or predicted value of the relative frequency must be positive and less than one.

Equation (6.6.3) can be solved for the relative frequency p. Letting z be $\mathbf{x}\boldsymbol{\theta}$,

$$\ln \left(\frac{p}{1-p}\right) = \mathbf{x}\boldsymbol{\theta} + \nu = z + \nu \tag{6.6.4}$$

where the stochastic disturbance term ν can thus be interpreted as

[35] See Cox (1970) for a discussion of the logit transformation. See also Theil (1971, 1972) and Goldfeld and Quandt (1972). An axiomatic justification for the logit is based on the proposition that the variables $\mathbf{x}$ are normally distributed. Alternative assumptions on the distributions of these variables lead to other types of probability models. For a generalization of the logit transformation see McFadden (1974) and Amemiya (1975). The logit models extend to polychotomous choices, and estimation procedures are available for the case in which replicated samples are not available.

[36] The stochastic disturbance term ν in (6.6.3) exhibits heteroskedasticity, since

$$\mathrm{Var}(\nu_i) = \frac{1}{r_i p_i (1 - p_i)}$$

where r_i is the number of observations in the ith sample and p_i is the ith sample relative frequency. Thus (6.6.3) should be estimated using the GLS estimator of (6.5.8), where $\boldsymbol{\Omega}^{-1}$ can be determined from r_i and p_i.

$$\nu = \ln\left(\frac{p}{1-p}\right) - \ln\left(\frac{P}{1-P}\right) \tag{6.6.5}$$

where p is the observed relative frequency and P is the true probability. Setting $\nu = 0$, (6.6.4) implies, by taking antilogs, that

$$\frac{p}{1-p} = e^z \tag{6.6.6}$$

where $p/(1-p)$ can be interpreted as the odds in favor of the choice represented by the dependent variable. Thus

$$p = (1-p)e^z = e^z - pe^z. \tag{6.6.7}$$

Combining the terms involving p and solving yields

$$p = \frac{e^z}{e^z+1} = \frac{1}{1+e^{-z}} \tag{6.6.8}$$

which determines p as a function of z, as illustrated in Figure 6.4.[37] In particular, for estimates $\hat{\boldsymbol{\theta}}$ and predicted values $\hat{\mathbf{x}}$, the predicted p would be

$$\hat{p} = \frac{1}{1+e^{-\hat{z}}} \quad \text{where} \quad \hat{z} = \hat{\mathbf{x}}\hat{\boldsymbol{\theta}}. \tag*{*(6.6.9)}$$

As shown in Figure 6.4, no matter what value is assumed by $\hat{z}$, it is always the case that $0 < \hat{p} < 1$.

An example of this approach is the analysis of decisions to buy a particular product and how these decisions depend on income. The basic data might refer to families with particular income levels who either buy or do not buy the product. The data are converted to relative frequencies by determining the proportion who buy the product. Equation (6.6.3) is then estimated, where p is the proportion and x is the income level, with the estimated coefficient indicating the response of buying decisions to levels of income.[38]

[37] The name "logit" is based upon the logistic curve, of the form

$$y(x) = \frac{a}{1+be^{-cx}}$$

where a, b, and c are constants [$a = b = c = 1$ in (6.6.8)]. This is an S-shaped curve that is used in studying the growth of populations. In fact the logit is only one of several possible approaches to the problem of a qualitative dependent variable. Another, called the *probit form of regression analysis*, is based on the cumulative normal distribution, rather than the logistic curve, in (6.6.8). See Finney (1971).

[38] The more common measures of the responsiveness of buying decisions to levels of income, namely income elasticities, are treated in the next chapter.

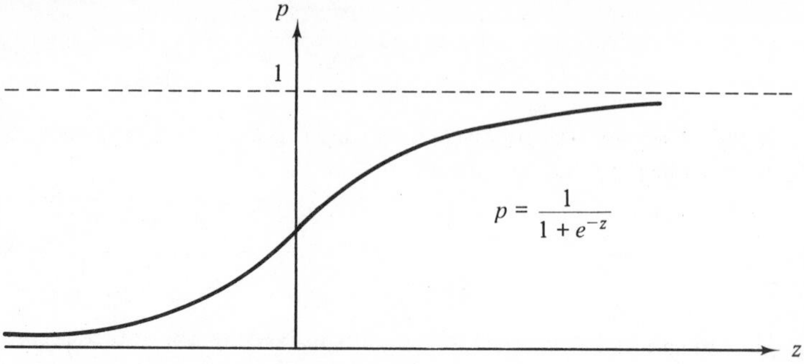

Figure 6.4 The Logit Transformation.
[NOTE As $z \to -\infty$, $p \to 0$. As $z \to \infty$, $p \to 1$.]

6.7 Lagged variables and distributed lags

Dependent variables often react to a change in one or more of the explanatory variables only after a lapse of time. This delayed reaction suggests the inclusion of lagged explanatory variables into the specification of the model, resulting in a dynamic model. In such a model, rather than an instantaneous response, there is generally a time structure of response in the gradual reaction of the dependent variable to a change in an explanatory variable.

There are several reasons why there might be a lag in the system, specifically a lapse of time between a change in an explanatory variable and a change in the dependent variable. One reason is *technical*: production requires time, and durable goods last more than one period. Thus, agricultural supply depends on lagged variables, such as lagged prices, since these variables influence decisions to plant certain crops rather than others and time must elapse between planting and harvesting. The durability of capital goods implies that current output depends, in part, on past investment decisions. A second reason is *institutional*: it takes time to respond to external events (e.g., to adjust contracts), and certain rules (e.g., the timing of payments) lead to lagged responses. A third reason is *psychological*: behavior is often based on inertia and habit, and expectations about future events are often based on past behavior. For all these reasons lagged variables often enter econometric models as explanatory variables. An example is the prototype macro model of Chapter 2, in which investment depends on both lagged and current income. The dependence on lagged income can be justified in terms of all three reasons: it takes time to produce capital goods (a technical reason), there are lags in response to external conditions (an institutional reason), and expected future output may depend on current and past income (a psychological reason). Another example is the Markov process of (6.4.2), in which the stochastic disturbance term u_i depends on the lagged term u_{i-1}, leading, in (6.4.6), to lagged variables in the transformed model.

It becomes necessary to take explicit account of lagged variables when the lag between the change in an explanatory variable and that in the dependent variable exceeds the period of observation of the variables. Thus, for example, lagged variables become increasingly important when annual models are replaced by quarterly or monthly models. They also become important when the model includes expectations variables that depend on past events.

In the simplest case of one dependent (endogenous) variable y and one explanatory (exogenous) variable x, the general relation, taking account of all possible lags over time t, is given by the *general distributed lag model*

$$y_t = f_t(x_t, x_{t-1}, x_{t-2}, \ldots) + u_t, \qquad t = 1, 2, \ldots \qquad *(6.7.1)$$

where u_t is the customary additive stochastic disturbance term. In this model all present and past values of the exogenous variable can influence the dependent variable. Thus, the effects of a change in the explanatory variable can be spread out over time, with the dependent variable gradually adjusting, over time, to a change in the explanatory variable. The "ripple effect" is much like that caused by a stone tossed in a pond.

In the linear case with time-invariant parameters the general relation becomes the *linear distributed lag model*[39]

$$y_t = \alpha + \beta_0 x_t + \beta_1 x_{t-1} + \beta_2 x_{t-2} + \cdots + u_t \qquad *(6.7.2)$$

$$y_t = \alpha + \sum_{j=0}^{\infty} \beta_j x_{t-j} + u_t \qquad *(6.7.3)$$

where α and the β's are the parameters to be estimated. The term β_j is the jth *reaction coefficient*, and it is usually assumed that

$$\lim_{j \to \infty} \beta_j = 0 \qquad (6.7.4)$$

$$\sum_{j=0}^{\infty} \beta_j = \beta < \infty. \qquad (6.7.5)$$

The vanishing of the β_j in the limit means that following a change in the explanatory variable x, the dependent variable y eventually reaches, perhaps in asymptotic fashion, a new equilibrium. If all β_j after β_m vanish, the model reduces to a *finite distributed lag*, for which the upper limit of the summation sign in (6.7.3) is m. The finiteness of the sum in (6.7.5) means that any finite change in x that persists indefinitely results in a finite change in y.

The relation between y and x in the distributed lag can be represented as in Figure 6.5. Assume x_t has been constant over a sufficiently long period so that y is constant, as shown. At $\bar{t}$ the variable x increases by a unit amount to a permanently higher level. The immediate effect is to increase y by β_0, as

[39] For surveys of distributed lag models see Griliches (1967), Dhrymes (1970), and Sims (1974).

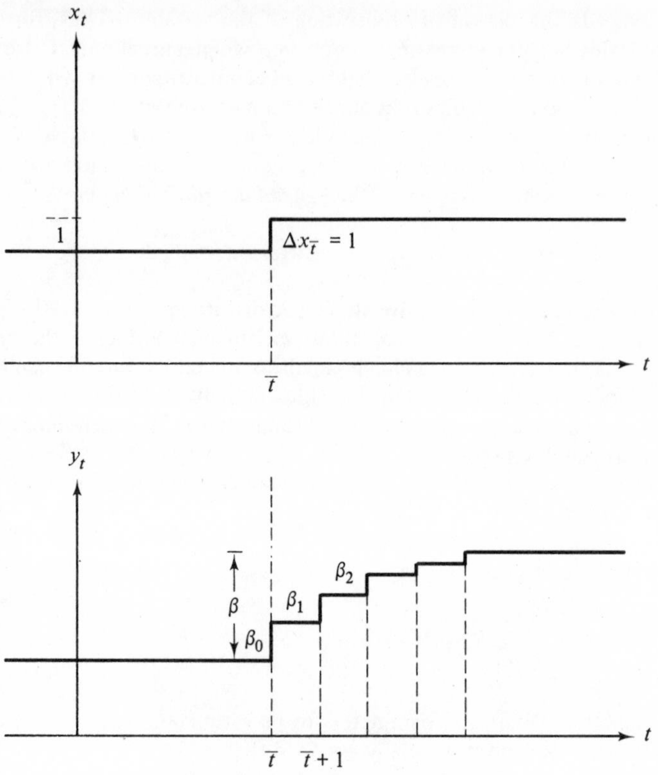

Figure 6.5 The Effect of a Permanent Change in the Explanatory Variable for a Distributed Lag Relationship

$$\Delta y_{\bar{t}} = \sum_{j=0}^{\infty} \beta_j \, \Delta x_{\bar{t}-j} = \beta_0 \, \Delta x_{\bar{t}} = \beta_0 \quad \text{since} \quad \Delta x_{\bar{t}} = 1. \tag{6.7.6}$$

The effect in the next period is to increase y by β_1, as

$$\Delta y_{\bar{t}+1} = \beta_0 \Delta x_{\bar{t}+1} + \beta_1 \, \Delta x_{\bar{t}} = \beta_1 \quad \text{since} \quad \Delta x_{\bar{t}+1} = 0. \tag{6.7.7}$$

Similarly in period $t + 2$ the increase is β_2 and, in general, in period $t + j$ the increase is β_j. Assuming, as in (6.7.4) that the β_j eventually diminish to zero, the total effect is given by

$$\Delta y = \sum_{j=0}^{\infty} \beta_j = \beta \tag{6.7.8}$$

as shown in the figure. The sum of the coefficients, β, represents the long-term effect of a change in x on y, and the gradual asymptotic approach of y to the long-term increment of β should be noted in the figure. The time shape of the adjustment in y in response to the change in x is the "signature" of the particular distributed lag under consideration. If the weights w_j are defined as

$$w_j = \frac{\beta_j}{\beta} \qquad *(6.7.9)$$

the distributed lag model can be written in normalized form as

$$y_t = \alpha + \beta \sum_{j=0}^{\infty} w_j x_{t-j} + u_t. \qquad *(6.7.10)$$

By definition the weights sum to unity, and if all the β_j are positive then so are all the weights, so that

$$w_j \geqslant 0, \qquad \sum_{j=0}^{\infty} w_j = 1. \qquad *(6.7.11)$$

From (6.7.9) the weight w_j may be interpreted as the fraction of the long-term effect β accomplished in period $t - j$.

An econometric problem arises because the distributed lag model of either (6.7.3) or (6.7.10) cannot be estimated directly, since it contains an infinite number of coefficients. No finite sample will provide adequate degrees of freedom. Two alternatives are possible in estimation. The first is to assume a finite distributed lag model in which, after a certain period, the coefficients are all zero, and to estimate the initial coefficients of the model. For example, if a finite distributed lag is assumed in which all β's beyond β_3 are zero, then the model becomes

$$y_t = \alpha + \beta_0 x_t + \beta_1 x_{t-1} + \beta_2 x_{t-2} + \beta_3 x_{t-3} + u_t \qquad (6.7.12)$$

which can be estimated directly. There are three problems, however. The first is that the choice of cutoff is somewhat arbitrary, there being generally no theoretical justification for any particular cutoff chosen. Second—as in the case of an infinite number of lags—there will generally be a multicollinearity problem, since x_t, x_{t-1}, etc. all tend to move together. The third problem is that of lack of data, since when using time-series data over a given period, each lag included implies the loss of one data point. For example, with (6.7.12) each observation requires data on y_t, x_t, x_{t-1}, x_{t-2}, and x_{t-3}. Thus ten years of data yields only seven data points.

The alternative approach is to assume a particular structure for the coefficients in (6.7.3) or (6.7.10), i.e., a maintained hypothesis, to avoid the problems encountered with direct estimation of the coefficients. The next part of this section will be devoted to a discussion of two of the most widely used of these structures, the Koyck distributed lag and the Almon distributed lag. The section concludes by discussing the estimation of models with lagged dependent variables, which frequently arise in distributed lag models.

One of the simplest and most widely used of the particular structures is the *Koyck distributed lag*, (or *geometric lag*) for which the coefficients decline geometrically:[40]

$$\beta_j = \lambda\beta_{j-1} = \lambda^2\beta_{j-2} = \cdots = \lambda^j\beta_0, \quad \text{all } j, \ 0 < \lambda < 1. \tag*{*(6.7.13)}$$

In this case the β_j form a geometric series, with each coefficient a certain proportion of the previous one, so the coefficients become successively smaller and smaller as they relate to earlier and earlier time periods. It then follows that

$$y_t = \alpha + \beta_0 x_t + \beta_0\lambda x_{t-1} + \beta_0\lambda^2 x_{t-2} + \cdots + u_t. \tag{6.7.14}$$

But, lagging one period and multiplying by λ,

$$\lambda y_{t-1} = \alpha\lambda + \beta_0\lambda x_{t-1} + \beta_0\lambda^2 x_{t-2} + \cdots + \lambda u_{t-1}. \tag{6.7.15}$$

Taking the difference leads to wholesale cancellations, resulting in

$$y_t - \lambda y_{t-1} = \alpha(1 - \lambda) + \beta_0 x_t + (u_t - \lambda u_{t-1}). \tag{6.7.16}$$

This model can thus be estimated as

$$y_t = \lambda y_{t-1} + \beta_0 x_t + \alpha(1 - \lambda) + v_t \quad \text{where} \quad v_t = u_t - \lambda u_{t-1}. \tag*{*(6.7.17)}$$

Here the lagged endogenous variable, y_{t-1}, heuristically "takes the place" of all the lagged exogenous variables $x_{t-1}, x_{t-2}, \ldots$. This model includes, as slope coefficients, only two parameters–β_0 and λ. The parameter β_0 measures the strength of the initial reaction to a change in x, while the parameter λ measures

[40] See Koyck (1954). More generally, the coefficients decline geometrically only after a certain lag, so (6.7.13) holds not for all j but only for $j \geqslant j_0$. The coefficients up to j_0 would then be estimated directly. See Problem 6-R. A related approach uses arithmetically, rather than geometrically, declining weights in a finite distributed lag model. In this case

$$y_t = \alpha + \beta \sum_{j=0}^{m} w_j x_{t-j} + u_t$$

where

$$w_j = \frac{m - j}{m + (m-1) + \cdots + 1}, \qquad j = 0, 1, \ldots, m$$

For example, for $m = 3$ the distributed lag model is

$$y_t = \alpha_0 + \beta(\tfrac{3}{6}x_t + \tfrac{2}{6}x_{t-1} + \tfrac{1}{6}x_{t-2}) + u_t.$$

the rate of decay of the distributed lag. The normalized weights for the Koyck distributed lag can be obtained as[41]

$$w_j = \frac{\beta_j}{\Sigma\,\beta_j} = \frac{\lambda^j}{\Sigma\,\lambda^j} = (1-\lambda)\lambda^j > 0, \qquad j = 0, 1, 2, \ldots \qquad \textbf{(6.7.18)}$$

The difference $1-\lambda$ is called the *speed of adjustment* of the model. A discussion of the estimation of (6.7.17) and, in general, models containing the lagged dependent variable as an explanatory variable appears later in this section.

An important example of the Koyck distributed lag is the *partial adjustment model* (or *stock adjustment model*).[42] To apply this model to capital stock growth let K_t be capital stock at time t and K_t^* be desired capital stock at time t. According to the partial adjustment model the change in capital stock (net investment) is proportional to the gap between the current desired level of capital and the past actual level:

$$K_t - K_{t-1} = \gamma(K_t^* - K_{t-1}) + \nu_t, \qquad 0 < \gamma \leqslant 1 \qquad \textbf{*(6.7.19)}$$

where ν_t is a stochastic disturbance term. Collecting terms,

$$K_t = \gamma K_t^* + (1-\gamma)K_{t-1} + \nu_t \qquad \textbf{(6.7.20)}$$

so the current capital is a weighted average of the current desired level and the past actual level of capital. If $\gamma = 1$, current and desired capital are equal, and the smaller the γ the closer is current capital to past capital. Thus γ is the *adjustment coefficient*, measuring the extent to which current capital reflects desired rather than past levels of capital.

If it is further assumed that the desired capital stock is a multiple of output, Y_t,

$$K_t^* = \delta Y_t \qquad \textbf{*(6.7.21)}$$

where δ is the desired capital-output ratio, then, combining (6.7.20) and (6.7.21) yields the *partial adjustment model*:

$$K_t = (1-\gamma)K_{t-1} + \gamma\delta Y_t + \nu_t. \qquad \textbf{*(6.7.22)}$$

[41] Recall that the sum of a geometric series can be obtained as

$$\sum_{j=0}^{\infty} \lambda^j = \frac{1}{1-\lambda}, \qquad 0 < \lambda < 1$$

Note that

$$\sum_{j=0}^{\infty} w_j = (1-\lambda)\,\Sigma\,\lambda^j = \frac{1-\lambda}{1-\lambda} = 1$$

[42] See Nerlove (1958a, b).

Here the dependent variable K_t depends on both its lagged value K_{t-1} and the current value of the explanatory variable Y_t. This equation is the same form as (6.7.17). Thus, equating coefficients of the lagged dependent variable,

$$1 - \gamma = \lambda \qquad *(6.7.23)$$

indicating why $1 - \lambda$ was earlier referred to as the "speed of adjustment"; it is simply γ. Equation (6.7.22) is equivalent to a distributed lag model of the form

$$K_t = \delta \sum_{j=0}^{\infty} \gamma(1 - \gamma)^j Y_{t-j} + u_t \quad \text{where} \quad u_t = (1 - \gamma)u_{t-1} + v_t. \qquad *(6.7.24)$$

This distributed lag model indicates the dependence of current capital stock on current and all past levels of output. In this model there is a gradual adjustment of capital stock to desired levels, with γ measuring the speed of adjustment. This model is a very useful one that has been applied to many areas, as will be seen below.[43]

A very flexible form for the distributed lag is the *Almon distributed lag* (or a *finite-length polynomial lag*).[44] In this case, starting with the finite-length distributed lag

$$y_t = \alpha + \sum_{j=0}^{m} \beta_j x_{t-j} + u_t \qquad *(6.7.25)$$

the coefficients β_j for $j = 0, 1, 2, \ldots, m$ are approximated by polynomials in the lag j of degree $l < m$

$$\beta_j = a_0 + a_1 j + a_2 j^2 + \cdots + a_l j^l = \sum_{k=0}^{l} a_k j^k. \qquad *(6.7.26)$$

When considering β_j as a function of j, this lag distribution can have a humped or even more complicated shape. With a second-degree polynomial the β's can, for example, at first rise, then fall, and with a third-degree polynomial the β's can, for example, fall, then rise, and finally fall again. In fact any complicated shape for the β's can be allowed by choosing a sufficiently high-degree polynomial. Usually, however, only polynomials of relatively low degree are employed. For example, if $m = 3$ and $l = 2$, then

[43] See Sections 7.8 and 8.5 for various applications of this model. See also Harberger, Ed. (1960) for various applications. A related model, the *adaptive expectations model*, as presented in Problem 6-R, was developed in Cagan (1956). For a generalization see Waud (1966).

[44] See Almon (1965). An even more flexible form for the lag distribution that can yield a wide range of possible shapes is the *Jorgenson distributed lag* (*rational distributed lag*), in which the normalized weights in (6.7.9) are obtained as the ratio of two polynomial functions. See Jorgenson (1966).

$$y_t = \alpha + (\Sigma a_k 0^k)x_t + (\Sigma a_k 1^k)x_{t-1} + (\Sigma a_k 2^k)x_{t-2} + (\Sigma a_k 3^k)x_{t-3} + u_t \tag{6.7.27}$$

or, equivalently,

$$y_t = \alpha + a_0 x_t + (a_0 + a_1 + a_2)x_{t-1} + (a_0 + 2a_1 + 4a_2)x_{t-2} + (a_0 + 3a_1 + 9a_2)x_{t-3} + u_t \tag{6.7.28}$$

Collecting terms,

$$y_t = \alpha + a_0(x_t + x_{t-1} + x_{t-2} + x_{t-3}) + a_1(x_{t-1} + 2x_{t-2} + 3x_{t-3}) + a_2(x_{t-1} + 4x_{t-2} + 9x_{t-3}) + u_t \tag{6.7.29}$$

The coefficients α, a_0, a_1, and a_2 can be estimated directly from this last equation, where the three combinations of lagged variables are treated as the explanatory variables. More generally the a's are obtained by estimating

$$y_t = \alpha + a_0 \left(\sum_{j=0}^{m} x_{t-j}\right) + a_1\left(\sum_{j=0}^{m} jx_{t-j}\right) + a_2\left(\sum_{j=0}^{m} j^2 x_{t-j}\right) + \cdots + a_l\left(\sum_{j=0}^{m} j^l x_{t-j}\right) + u_t \qquad *(6.7.30)$$

where the sums in parentheses are treated as the explanatory variables. Estimates of the coefficients β_j can then be obtained from the estimated a's using (6.7.26). To use this approach it is necessary to specify l, the degree of the polynomial, and m, the maximal lag.

While either of these two forms of distributed lags can be utilized to estimate the lagged relationships between y and x, the Koyck distributed lag is not only the simplest but also has the most straightforward interpretation, namely that of a stock adjustment model. If this form appears inappropriate because of the special time-delay features of the model, then the Almon distributed lag or one of the other distributed lags might be utilized. Alternatively, the Koyck distributed lag might be employed where the geometric decline in the coefficients begins only after a certain lag, allowing the first several coefficients to be estimated directly.

The estimation of the Koyck distributed lag generally involves regression with a lagged dependent variable as an explanatory variable. For example, (6.7.17) includes lagged y as an explanatory variable, while (6.7.22), based on the partial adjustment model, includes lagged K as an explanatory variable. The example presented in Section 5.6 of a multiple linear regression, based on the prototype macro model, also included a lagged dependent variable. In general such a model is of the form

$$y_t = \lambda y_{t-1} + \beta x_t + \delta + v_t, \qquad 0 < \lambda < 1 \qquad *(6.7.31)$$

as in (6.7.17), where y_t is the dependent variable, y_{t-1} is the lagged dependent variable, β (equal to β_0), is the coefficient of x_t, δ is the intercept [equal to $\alpha(1-\lambda)$], and v_t is the stochastic disturbance term. The technique that would be appropriate for estimation of this equation depends fundamentally on the assumptions made on the stochastic term v_t.[45]

If the v's are distributed independently and identically with zero mean and constant variance,

$$E(v_t) = 0 \qquad \text{all } t$$
$$E(v_t v_{t-s}) = \begin{cases} \sigma_v^2 & \text{if } s = 0 \\ 0 & \text{if } s \neq 0 \end{cases} \qquad \text{all } t, s \tag{6.7.32}$$

then least squares applied directly to (6.7.31), as in Section 5.6, is an appropriate estimation technique, yielding estimators of λ, β, and δ that are consistent, asymptotically normal, and asymptotically efficient. They are also the maximum-likelihood estimators if v_t is distributed normally. Because of the presence in (6.7.31) of the lagged dependent variable, y_{t-1}, which is not independent of v_{t-1}, however, the estimators will be biased. For example, in the simplest case in which β and δ are both zero, so

$$y_t = \lambda y_{t-1} + v_t \tag{6.7.33}$$

the least-squares estimator of λ is

$$\hat{\lambda} = \frac{\Sigma\, y_t y_{t-1}}{\Sigma\, y_{t-1}^2} \tag{6.7.34}$$

assuming y is measured as deviations from mean values. Then

$$\hat{\lambda} = \frac{\Sigma\,(\lambda y_{t-1} + v_t) y_{t-1}}{\Sigma\, y_{t-1}^2} = \lambda + \frac{\Sigma\, v_t y_{t-1}}{\Sigma\, y_{t-1}^2} \tag{6.7.35}$$

where the expectation of the last term is nonzero.

An alternative assumption on the stochastic disturbance term in (6.7.31) starts from

$$v_t = u_t - \rho u_{t-1}, \qquad 0 < \rho < 1 \tag{6.7.36}$$

as in the Koyck distributed lag model (6.7.17) for $\lambda = \rho$, and assumes that the u's are distributed independently and identically with zero mean and constant variance:

$$E(u_t) = 0 \qquad \text{all } t$$
$$E(u_t u_{t-s}) = \begin{cases} \sigma_u^2 & \text{if } s = 0 \\ 0 & \text{if } s \neq 0 \end{cases} \qquad \text{all } t, s \tag{6.7.37}$$

[45] See Liviatan (1963), Hannan (1965), and Dhrymes (1971).

While the u's are serially uncorrelated the v's are serially correlated, so (6.7.32) is not valid and least-squares estimators are inconsistent as well as biased. In this case

$$\left.\begin{aligned} E(v_t) &= 0 \\ E(v_t v_{t-s}) &= \begin{cases} \sigma_u^2 (1+\rho^2) & \text{if } s = 0 \\ -\rho\sigma_u^2 & \text{if } s = \pm 1 \\ 0 & \text{if } s \neq 0, \pm 1 \end{cases} \end{aligned}\right\} \quad \begin{aligned} &\text{all } t \\ &\text{all } s, t \end{aligned} \tag{6.7.38}$$

Thus the covariance matrix for the vector of stochastic disturbance terms v is

$$E(\mathbf{v}\mathbf{v}') = \sigma_u^2 \begin{pmatrix} 1+\rho^2 & -\rho & 0 & \cdots & 0 & 0 \\ -\rho & 1+\rho^2 & 0 & \cdots & 0 & 0 \\ \vdots & \vdots & \vdots & & & \\ 0 & 0 & 0 & \cdots & 1+\rho^2 & -\rho \\ 0 & 0 & 0 & \cdots & -\rho & 1+\rho^2 \end{pmatrix} = \mathbf{\Omega} \tag{6.7.39}$$

If ρ were known, this covariance matrix could be used to construct GLS estimators of the parameters to be estimated, λ, β, and δ. If ρ were not known, it could be estimated iteratively.[46]

A third possible specification of the stochastic disturbance terms v_t in (6.7.31) is that they follow a Markov process

$$v_t = \rho v_{t-1} + \epsilon_t, \qquad |\rho| < 1 \tag{6.7.40}$$

where the ϵ_t are distributed independently and normally with zero mean and finite variance:

$$\epsilon_t \sim N(0, \sigma_\epsilon^2). \tag{6.7.41}$$

In the simplest case (6.7.33)

$$y_t = \lambda y_{t-1} + v_t \tag{6.7.42}$$

Lagging and multiplying by ρ,

$$\rho y_{t-1} = \lambda \rho y_{t-2} + \rho v_{t-1} \tag{6.7.43}$$

so, combining these equations with (6.7.40),

[46] The iterative estimation is similar to that used in the Cochrane-Orcutt approach discussed in footnote 23. Assume an initial ρ in the interval $0 < \rho < 1$; then estimate λ, β, and γ using the GLS estimator. The residuals of (6.7.31) provide the $\hat{v}_t$, which, together with an assumed initial $\hat{u}_0$, yield a set of $\hat{u}_t$ as

$$\hat{u}_t = \rho\hat{u}_{t-1} + \hat{v}_t.$$

A new $\hat{\rho}$ can be calculated, as in (6.4.15), where $\hat{u}_i$ is replaced by $\hat{u}_t$. The process then iterates until a $\hat{\rho}$ is found for which the minimized weighted sum of squares $\hat{\mathbf{v}}'\mathbf{\Omega}^{-1}\hat{\mathbf{v}}$, using $\mathbf{\Omega}$ as defined in (6.7.39), does not vary significantly from the previous iteration.

$$y_t - \rho y_{t-1} = \lambda(y_{t-1} - \rho y_{t-2}) + \epsilon_t \tag{6.7.44}$$

or

$$y_t = (\rho + \lambda)y_{t-1} - \rho\lambda y_{t-2} + \epsilon_t \tag{6.7.45}$$

The least-squares estimator (6.7.34) thus yields

$$\hat{\lambda} = \frac{\Sigma y_t y_{t-1}}{\Sigma y_{t-1}^2} = \frac{\Sigma(\rho + \lambda)y_{t-1}^2 - \rho\lambda\Sigma y_{t-1}y_{t-2} + \Sigma\epsilon_t y_{t-1}}{\Sigma y_{t-1}^2} \tag{6.7.46}$$

$$\hat{\lambda} = \rho + \lambda - \rho\lambda\frac{\Sigma y_{t-1}\, y_{t-2}}{\Sigma y_{t-1}^2} + \frac{\Sigma\epsilon_t y_{t-1}}{\Sigma y_{t-1}^2}. \tag{6.7.47}$$

Taking probability limits,

$$\text{plim}\,\hat{\lambda} = \rho + \lambda - \rho\lambda\,\text{plim}\,\hat{\lambda} \tag{6.7.48}$$

so

$$\text{plim}\,\hat{\lambda} = \frac{\rho + \lambda}{1 + \rho\lambda} \tag{6.7.49}$$

demonstrating the lack of consistency of the estimator. The difference between the probability limit and the true value is

$$\text{plim}\,\hat{\lambda} - \lambda = \frac{\rho(1 - \lambda^2)}{1 + \rho\lambda} \tag{6.7.50}$$

and this difference can be large for high values of ρ and low values of λ. For example, if $\rho = 0.8$ and $\lambda = 0.2$, then the difference is 0.66, so the probability limit of the least-squares estimator is 0.86, while the true value of λ is 0.2. This difference underscores the fact that least squares is inappropriate in such cases of lagged dependent variables and serially correlated stochastic disturbance terms. The appropriate estimation method in this case is again GLS. Here the covariance matrix is given in (6.5.21), where σ^2 is replaced by σ_ϵ^2, and the GLS estimator (6.5.8) can be obtained if ρ is known.[47]

[47] The GLS estimators utilize the inverse of the covariance matrix, as given in Problem 6-O. The estimators are approximated by the least-squares estimator of the model utilizing the transformed data:

$$y_t - \rho y_{t-1} = \lambda(y_{t-1} - \rho y_{t-2}) + \beta(x_t - \rho x_{t-1}) + \delta(1 - \rho) + \epsilon_t$$

where y_1 and x_1 are replaced by $\sqrt{1 - \rho^2}\, y_1$ and $\sqrt{1 - \rho^2}\, x_1$, respectively. Such estimators are consistent and asymptotically efficient but biased in any finite sample. If ρ is unknown, a two-step procedure or an iterative approach such as outlined in the last footnote and footnote 23 can be employed.

6.8 Specification error

Estimators are based on both the model and the data. Thus, errors in the model and errors in the data give rise to errors in the estimators. This section treats specification error—errors in the estimators stemming from errors in formulating the model. The next section will treat errors in the variables—errors in the estimators stemming from errors in measuring the variables.

There are several types of possible errors in specifying the model. Among them are the exclusion of relevant variables, the inclusion of irrelevant variables, an incorrect form of the relationship (e.g., treating a nonlinear model as if it were linear), and an incorrect specification of the stochastic disturbance form (e.g., incorrect variances or covariances or an incorrect form of the distribution).[48] The discussion here will treat only the first two types of misspecification, relating to variable exclusion/inclusion.[49] Assume that the true model is of the form

$$\mathbf{y} = \mathbf{X}\boldsymbol{\beta} + \mathbf{u} \qquad *(6.8.1)$$

where $\mathbf{X}$ has k columns. The model that has been specified, however, is of the form

$$\mathbf{y} = \mathbf{X}_1\boldsymbol{\beta}_1 + \mathbf{u}_1 \qquad *(6.8.2)$$

where $\mathbf{X}_1$ has k_1 columns. The least-squares estimator of $\boldsymbol{\beta}_1$ in (6.8.2) is given as

$$\hat{\hat{\boldsymbol{\beta}}}_1 = (\mathbf{X}_1'\mathbf{X}_1)^{-1}\mathbf{X}_1'\mathbf{y} \qquad (6.8.3)$$

the two hats being a reminder that this is an estimator for the misspecified model. Using the true model, however, and taking expectations, assuming $\mathbf{X}$ and $\mathbf{X}_1$ are matrices of fixed numbers,

$$E(\hat{\hat{\boldsymbol{\beta}}}_1) = (\mathbf{X}_1'\mathbf{X}_1)^{-1}\,\mathbf{X}_1'\mathbf{X}\boldsymbol{\beta}. \qquad (6.8.4)$$

Each column of the matrix $(\mathbf{X}_1'\mathbf{X}_1)^{-1}\mathbf{X}_1\mathbf{X}$ here multiplying the vector of true parameters $\boldsymbol{\beta}$ is simply the least-squares regression of one of the variables in $\mathbf{X}$, the explanatory variables of the true model, on all the variables in $\mathbf{X}_1$, the explanatory variables in the misspecified model.

This formulation can be used to illustrate two important special cases—that of omitted relevant variables and that of included irrelevant variables.[50] In the former case, in which relevant variables have been omitted, the true model (6.8.1) can be written

[48] For a discussion of nonlinear models see Goldfeld and Quandt (1972).

[49] For a further discussion of specification error see Theil (1971) and Rao and Miller (1971). For an extension to simultaneous equations see Fisher (1961).

[50] In general, of course, it is possible both to omit relevant variables and to include irrelevant variables.

$$y = (X_1 \mid X_2)\begin{pmatrix}\beta_1\\ \hline \beta_2\end{pmatrix} + u = X_1\beta_1 + X_2\beta_2 + u. \qquad (6.8.5)$$

The misspecification in (6.8.2) thus is the omission of the variables in X_2. In the misspecified model only the variables in X_1 are included. The least-squares estimator of their coefficients $\hat{\hat{\beta}}_1$ will then be biased and inconsistent. Intuitively the bias and inconsistency in these estimators stem from the influences of the omitted variables X_2 on y, which are represented in part by u but also in part by $X_1\beta_1$. The included variables X_1 take account both of the influences of themselves and of the influences of the omitted variables on y.

More formally, the least-squares estimators of the coefficients of the included variables are

$$\hat{\hat{\beta}}_1 = (X_1'X_1)^{-1}X_1'y = (X_1'X_1)^{-1}X_1'[X_1\beta_1 + X_2\beta_2 + u] \qquad (6.8.6)$$

$$\hat{\hat{\beta}}_1 = \beta_1 + (X_1'X_1)^{-1}X_1'X_2\beta_2 + (X_1'X_1)^{-1}X_1'u. \qquad (6.8.7)$$

Taking expectations, the bias in estimating β_1 is

$$B(\hat{\hat{\beta}}_1) = E(\hat{\hat{\beta}}_1) - \beta_1 = (X_1'X_1)^{-1}X_1'X_2\beta_2. \qquad (6.8.8)$$

This specification bias is therefore directly proportional to the magnitudes in β_2, so that the smaller are the coefficients of the omitted variables, the smaller will be the implied bias. This bias is also smaller the smaller is the correlation between included and excluded variables, as measured by $X_1'X_2$. The specification error vanishes in the limit as either β_2 or $X_1'X_2$ approaches zero. However, in the case in which a collinear variable has been dropped, where $X_1'X_2$ is large, the bias may be substantial. The bias need also not disappear as the sample size increases, so the estimator $\hat{\hat{\beta}}_1$ is an inconsistent one. It might also be noted that the estimates of the variances of the estimated coefficients of included variables are also biased in this case of omitted relevant explanatory variables.

The obverse case is that in which irrelevant variables have been included. In that case the true model is as in (6.8.1) while the estimated model is (6.8.2), where

$$X_1 = (X \mid X_2). \qquad (6.8.9)$$

Thus the misspecified model is

$$y = (X \mid X_2)\begin{pmatrix}\beta_0\\ \hline \beta_2\end{pmatrix} + u_1. \qquad (6.8.10)$$

Since the misspecified model is still consistent with the Gauss-Markov theorem assumptions (assuming X_2 is uncorrelated with u_1), the least-squares estimators are still unbiased. To show this directly, consider the least-squares estimator of (6.8.10), which may be written in this case as

$$\begin{pmatrix} \hat{\hat{\boldsymbol\beta}}_0 \\ \hline \hat{\hat{\boldsymbol\beta}}_2 \end{pmatrix} = [(\mathbf{X} \mid \mathbf{X}_2)'(\mathbf{X} \mid \mathbf{X}_2)]^{-1}(\mathbf{X} \mid \mathbf{X}_2)'\mathbf{y} \tag{6.8.11}$$

$$= \left[\begin{pmatrix} \mathbf{X}' \\ \hline \mathbf{X}_2' \end{pmatrix} (\mathbf{X} \mid \mathbf{X}_2)\right]^{-1} \begin{pmatrix} \mathbf{X}' \\ \hline \mathbf{X}_2' \end{pmatrix} \mathbf{y} \tag{6.8.12}$$

$$= \left(\begin{array}{c|c} \mathbf{X}'\mathbf{X} & \mathbf{X}'\mathbf{X}_2 \\ \hline \mathbf{X}_2'\mathbf{X} & \mathbf{X}_2'\mathbf{X}_2 \end{array}\right)^{-1} \begin{pmatrix} \mathbf{X}'\mathbf{y} \\ \hline \mathbf{X}_2'\mathbf{y} \end{pmatrix} \tag{6.8.13}$$

Here $\hat{\hat{\boldsymbol\beta}}_0$ is the estimator from the misspecified model of the true parameters $\boldsymbol\beta$, the coefficients of $\mathbf{X}$. Using the true model (6.8.1) for $\mathbf{y}$ and taking expectations, assuming $\mathbf{X}$ and $\mathbf{X}_2$ are matrices of fixed numbers,

$$E\begin{pmatrix} \hat{\hat{\boldsymbol\beta}}_0 \\ \hline \hat{\hat{\boldsymbol\beta}}_2 \end{pmatrix} = \left(\begin{array}{c|c} \mathbf{X}'\mathbf{X} & \mathbf{X}'\mathbf{X}_2 \\ \hline \mathbf{X}_2'\mathbf{X} & \mathbf{X}_2'\mathbf{X}_2 \end{array}\right)^{-1} \begin{pmatrix} \mathbf{X}'\mathbf{X}\boldsymbol\beta \\ \hline \mathbf{X}_2'\mathbf{X}\boldsymbol\beta \end{pmatrix} \tag{6.8.14}$$

It follows that the expectation of $\hat{\hat{\boldsymbol\beta}}_0$ is the true coefficient vector[51]

$$E(\hat{\hat{\boldsymbol\beta}}_0) = \boldsymbol\beta. \tag{6.8.15}$$

Thus, in this case of included irrelevant variables, $\hat{\hat{\boldsymbol\beta}}_0$ is an unbiased estimator. It is also a consistent estimator. In addition, the estimators of the variances of the coefficients of the relevant variables are unbiased. These sample variances of the estimators of coefficients of relevant variables will tend to increase, however, as more irrelevant variables are included. The resulting influences could distort tests of significance.

The asymmetry between the results in the two cases should be noted: excluding relevant variables yields biased and inconsistent estimators, while including irrelevant variables yields unbiased and consistent estimators. Thus, in terms of bias and consistency, it is better to include too many than to include too few explanatory variables. Such practice is not generally recommended, however, because of other problems that can arise with included irrelevant variables, namely multicollinearity, inefficiency, and reduced degrees of freedom. Considerable judgment, in fact, is called for in the specification of the model, balancing between including "too few" and ' too many" variables. Theoretical justifications should be available for including each explanatory variable in the model, but it should be recognized that in a general equilibrium setting, where "everything affects everything else," theoretical considerations are not sufficient to justify including explanatory variables. In general, the best approach is to include only explanatory variables that, on theoretical grounds, *directly* influence the dependent variable and that are not accounted for by other included variables.

[51] This result follows from inverting the partitioned matrix in (6.8.14), as presented in Appendix B, equation (B.5.5). See Problem 6-X.

6.9 Errors in variables

Variables, both dependent and independent, are measured subject to error. In particular, the available data may not refer to the variable as specified (e.g., as in the use of proxy variables), or there may be systematic biases in the collection or publication of the data. If the true linear regression model is of the form

$$\mathbf{y} = \mathbf{X}\boldsymbol{\beta} + \mathbf{u} \qquad *(6.9.1)$$

where $\mathbf{y}$ represents the true values of the dependent variable and $\mathbf{X}$ represents the true values of the explanatory variables, generally none of these variables is measured without error. Rather what are observed are $\mathbf{y}_1$ and $\mathbf{X}_1$, where

$$\mathbf{y}_1 = \mathbf{y} + \mathbf{y}_E \qquad *(6.9.2)$$

$$\mathbf{X}_1 = \mathbf{X} + \mathbf{X}_E. \qquad *(6.9.3)$$

Here $\mathbf{y}_E$ is a vector and $\mathbf{X}_E$ is a matrix of random variables. It is generally assumed that $\mathbf{u}$, $\mathbf{y}_E$, and $\mathbf{X}_E$ are uncorrelated, with zero means and constant covariance matrices.

Errors in measuring $\mathbf{y}$ present no new complications, since the $\mathbf{y}_E$ errors can be merged with the additive stochastic disturbance term $\mathbf{u}$ in (6.9.1). Thus the model is of the form

$$\mathbf{y}_1 = \mathbf{X}_1\boldsymbol{\beta} + (\mathbf{v} - \mathbf{X}_E\boldsymbol{\beta}) \quad \text{where} \quad \mathbf{v} = \mathbf{u} + \mathbf{y}_E. \qquad *(6.9.4)$$

This model cannot be treated as if it were the same as the basic linear regression model, since the measured explanatory variables $\mathbf{X}_1$ are not distributed independently of the stochastic disturbance term $\mathbf{v} - \mathbf{X}_E\boldsymbol{\beta}$.

The least-squares estimator of (6.9.4) is

$$\hat{\boldsymbol{\beta}} = (\mathbf{X}_1'\mathbf{X}_1)^{-1}\mathbf{X}_1'\mathbf{y}_1 = \boldsymbol{\beta} + (\mathbf{X}_1'\mathbf{X}_1)^{-1}\mathbf{X}_1'(\mathbf{v} - \mathbf{X}_E\boldsymbol{\beta}). \qquad *(6.9.5)$$

This estimator is, in general, biased, the bias being given as

$$B(\hat{\boldsymbol{\beta}}) = E(\hat{\boldsymbol{\beta}}) - \boldsymbol{\beta} = -E[(\mathbf{X}_1'\mathbf{X}_1)^{-1}\mathbf{X}_1'\mathbf{X}_E\boldsymbol{\beta}]. \qquad *(6.9.6)$$

Taking the probability limit of (6.9.5) to check consistency,

$$\text{plim}\ \hat{\boldsymbol{\beta}} = \boldsymbol{\beta} - \text{plim}\left(\frac{1}{n}\mathbf{X}_1'\mathbf{X}_1\right)^{-1} \text{plim}\left(\frac{1}{n}\mathbf{X}_1'\mathbf{X}_E\boldsymbol{\beta}\right) \qquad (6.9.7)$$

where it has been assumed that the measured explanatory variables are uncorrelated in the probability limit with the stochastic disturbance terms

$$\text{plim}\left(\frac{1}{n}\mathbf{X}_1'\mathbf{v}\right) = \mathbf{0}. \qquad (6.9.8)$$

Replacing $\mathbf{X}_1'$ by $\mathbf{X}' + \mathbf{X}_E'$, from (6.9.3), in (6.9.7),

$$\text{plim}\,\hat{\boldsymbol{\beta}} = \boldsymbol{\beta} - \text{plim}\left(\frac{1}{n}\,\mathbf{X}_1'\mathbf{X}_1\right)^{-1}\left[\text{plim}\left(\frac{1}{n}\mathbf{X}'\mathbf{X}_E\right) + \text{plim}\left(\frac{1}{n}\,\mathbf{X}_E'\mathbf{X}_E\right)\right]\boldsymbol{\beta}\,. \quad {}^*(6.9.9)$$

Even assuming that the true values of the explanatory variables $\mathbf{X}$ are uncorrelated in the probability limit with the error matrix $\mathbf{X}_E$ (so that the first term in the bracketed expression vanishes), the second term does not vanish. Thus (6.9.9) implies that the least-squares estimators are generally inconsistent in the case of errors in explanatory variables, so in this case least-squares estimators are both biased and inconsistent.

A specific illustration of this problem in economics is the permanent-income theory of the consumption function, which is an errors-in-variables model.[52] According to this model measured income, Y_1, has a permanent (true) component, Y, and a transitory component, Y_E:

$$Y_1 = Y + Y_E. \qquad \textbf{(6.9.10)}$$

Measured consumption expenditure, C_1, similarly, has a permanent (true) component, C, and a transitory component, C_E:

$$C_1 = C + C_E. \qquad \textbf{(6.9.11)}$$

The transitory components represent accidental or chance factors, including cyclical variations. They can, however, be treated as the errors in measuring income and consumption. It is usually assumed that the errors, on average, vanish:

$$E(Y_E) = E(C_E) = 0. \qquad \textbf{(6.9.12)}$$

It is usually assumed also that the errors are correlated neither with each other nor with the permanent components:

$$\text{Cov}\,(Y,Y_E) = \text{Cov}\,(C,C_E) = \text{Cov}\,(Y_E,C_E) = 0. \qquad \textbf{(6.9.13)}$$

According to the permanent-income hypothesis,

$$C = \beta_1 Y + \beta_2 + \text{u} \qquad \textbf{(6.9.14)}$$

—that is, permanent consumption is a linear function of permanent income, where β_1 and β_2 are constant parameters and u is a stochastic disturbance term.[53] Combining (6.9.14) with (6.9.10) and (6.9.11) yields

[52] See Friedman (1957).

[53] Friedman (1957) also specified that $\beta_2 = 0$, so that β_1 is both the marginal and the average propensity to consume out of permanent income. This specification of the structural equation ensures for the normally distributed case that the model is identified—that is, that

$$C_1 = \beta_1 Y_1 + \beta_2 + (v - \beta_1 Y_E), \qquad v = u + C_E \tag{6.9.15}$$

which is a simple linear regression model of the same form as (6.9.4). In this case (6.9.9) implies that if $\hat{\beta}_1$ is the least-squares estimator of the marginal propensity to consume, β_1, then

$$\text{plim}\, \hat{\beta}_1 = \beta_1 - \frac{\sigma_E^2}{\sigma_1^2} \beta_1 = \beta_1 \left(\frac{\sigma_1^2 - \sigma_E^2}{\sigma_1^2} \right) \tag{6.9.16}$$

where σ_E^2 is the variance of the transitory component of income and σ_1^2 is the variance of the measured income. But from (6.9.10) and (6.9.13)

$$\sigma_1^2 = \sigma^2 + \sigma_E^2 \tag{6.9.17}$$

where σ^2 is the variance of permanent income. Combining with (6.9.16) yields

$$\text{plim}\, \hat{\beta}_1 = \beta_1 \frac{\sigma^2}{\sigma_1^2} = \beta_1 - \beta_1 \frac{\sigma_E^2}{\sigma^2 + \sigma_E^2} < \beta_1 . \tag{6.9.18}$$

Thus, the estimated marginal propensity to consume, $\hat{\beta}_1$, even in the probability limit systematically underestimates the true β_1. The greater the variance of transitory income, the greater will be the underestimation. Only when the variance of the transitory (error) component of income vanishes is the least-squares estimator of β_1 a consistent estimator. To solve this problem it is necessary to construct a measure of permanent income Y before estimating the consumption function.

The general problem of errors in variables can be treated in various ways. The major treatment is simply that of correcting for errors, particularly in the explanatory variables, as in the replacement of measured income by permanent income in the estimation of the marginal propensity to consume. A second approach is to determine the sensitivity of the estimated coefficients to various errors in the variables by performing several regressions for alternative assumptions regarding the errors. It would then be possible to determine an interval

---

it is possible to infer the structural parameters $[\beta_1, E(Y), \text{Var}\,(Y), \text{Var}\,(Y_E), \text{Var}\,(C_E)]$ from the observable parameters $[E(Y_1), E(C_1), \text{Var}\,(Y_1), \text{Var}\,(C_1), \text{Cov}\,(C_1, Y_1)]$. For (6.9.14) in the normally distributed case these two sets of parameters are related by

$$\begin{aligned}
E(Y_1) &= E(Y + Y_E) = E(Y)\\
E(C_1) &= E(\beta_1 Y_1 + \beta_2 + C_E) = \beta_1 E(Y) + \beta_2\\
\text{Var}\,(Y_1) &= \text{Var}\,(Y + Y_E) = \text{Var}\,(Y) + \text{Var}\,(Y_E)\\
\text{Var}\,(C_1) &= \text{Var}\,(\beta_1 Y_1 + \beta_2 + C_E) = \beta_1^2\, \text{Var}\,(Y) + \text{Var}\,(C_E)\\
\text{Cov}\,(C_1, Y_1) &= \text{Cov}\,(\beta_1 Y_1 + \beta_2 + C_E, Y + Y_E) = \beta_1\, \text{Var}\,(Y)
\end{aligned}$$

In general, then, it is not possible to solve for the six unknowns on the right $[\beta_1, \beta_2, E(Y), \text{Var}\,(Y), \text{Var}\,(Y_E), \text{Var}\,(C_E)]$ given the five observables on the left, i.e., the model is not identified. If, however, $\beta_2 = 0$, then it is possible to solve for the structural parameter unknowns from the observables (e.g., $\hat{\beta}_1 = E(C_1)/E(Y_1)$), so the model is identified. For a discussion of identification in the context of simultaneous equations estimation, where the observables are the estimates of the reduced form and the unknowns are the structural-form parameters, see Chapter 10. See also Problem 6-Y and Konijn (1962).

estimate for each coefficient, reflecting the likely range of errors in the variables. A third approach is to use Wald's method of fitting straight lines, a technique introduced as a naive method in (4.3.2) but one that yields consistent estimators in the case of errors in variables.[54] A fourth approach is to use the method of instrumental variables, provided appropriate instrumental variables are available.[55]

6.10 Structural break

The problem of structural break is one in which the data refer not to samples chosen from a single population but to samples drawn from different populations. For example, consider the model

$$\underset{n\times 1}{\mathbf{y}} = \underset{n\times k}{\mathbf{X}}\ \underset{k\times 1}{\boldsymbol{\beta}} + \underset{n\times 1}{\mathbf{u}} \tag{6.10.1}$$

and suppose the data came from two different populations, e.g., one during peacetime (n_1 observations) and the other during wartime (n_2 observations, where $n_1 + n_2 = n$). Such a situation might be indicated if the residuals in the regression were noticeably different during the war period, and, in general, an analysis of the residuals might yield information on the possibility of structural break. This information is important because it is generally desirable to use as many data points as possible to obtain efficient estimators, but it is improper to aggregate when there is evidence of structural break.

A more formal test for structural break utilizes the *Chow test* of the equality of regression coefficients when the same equation is estimated using different samples.[56] To employ this test it is necessary to divide the sample into two subsamples, based either upon extraneous information that during part of the sample certain underlying conditions were possibly different from those in another part of the sample (e.g., peacetime or wartime) or upon an analysis of the residuals. The equation is then estimated for the entire sample and one of the subsamples, and an F test is used to determine if there is a significant difference between the corresponding estimated coefficients.

To develop the test, suppose the model (6.10.1) has been estimated for the entire sample of n observations as

[54] See Wald (1940), Bartlett (1949), Durbin (1954), and Hooper and Theil (1958). This method involves grouping the sample, e.g., into three groups of approximately equal size and then obtaining an estimate of the relationship by passing a line through the means of the two end groups.

[55] See Chapter 11, Section 11.6, for a discussion of instrumental variables. Here the instrumental variables must be uncorrelated with $\mathbf{v} - \mathbf{X}_E\boldsymbol{\beta}$ in (6.9.4) but correlated with $\mathbf{X}_1$ in (6.9.3). If $\mathbf{Z}$ represents such variables, then the instrumental-variables estimator of $\boldsymbol{\beta}$ is

$$\hat{\boldsymbol{\beta}}(\mathbf{Z}) = (\mathbf{Z}'\mathbf{X}_1)^{-1}\mathbf{Z}'\mathbf{y}_1$$

which is a consistent estimator of $\boldsymbol{\beta}$.

[56] See Chow (1960) and Fisher (1970). See also Kuh (1963) for an extension to pooled cross-section time-series data using the analysis of covariance.

$$\underset{n\times 1}{\mathbf{y}} = \underset{n\times k}{\mathbf{X}}\ \underset{k\times 1}{\hat{\boldsymbol{\beta}}} + \underset{n\times 1}{\hat{\mathbf{u}}} \tag{6.10.2}$$

The sum of squares of the least-squares residuals is

$$\sum_{i=1}^{n} \hat{u}_i^2 = \hat{\mathbf{u}}'\hat{\mathbf{u}}. \tag{6.10.3}$$

Next consider the estimate of the same model using the first subsample of n_1 observations:

$$\underset{n_1\times 1}{\mathbf{y}_1} = \underset{n_1\times k}{\mathbf{X}_1}\ \underset{k\times 1}{\hat{\boldsymbol{\beta}}_1} + \underset{n_1\times 1}{\hat{\mathbf{u}}_1} \tag{6.10.4}$$

where it has been assumed that $n_1 > k$, but it is not necessary to assume that $n_2 > k$. The sum of squares for this first subsample is $\hat{\mathbf{u}}_1'\hat{\mathbf{u}}_1$. The test of the hypothesis that the n_2 observations in the second subsample are based on the same population as the first subsample of n_1 observations is the F test:

$$F = \frac{(\hat{\mathbf{u}}'\hat{\mathbf{u}} - \hat{\mathbf{u}}_1'\hat{\mathbf{u}}_1)/n_2}{(\hat{\mathbf{u}}_1'\hat{\mathbf{u}}_1)/(n_1 - k)} \sim F(n_2, n_1 - k). \tag{6.10.5}$$

This F is the percentage increase in the sum of squared residuals in going from the first subsample of n_1 observations to the pooled sample of $n = n_1 + n_2$ observations, adjusted for degrees of freedom. If F exceeds the critical value for a particular level of significance, it implies that the subsamples are drawn from different populations. Typically the test is applied to determine whether, given an initial sample, an additional set of observations is based on the same population.[57] It can also, however, be extended to the case of several subsamples in order to determine whether their aggregation is appropriate.

If there is evidence of structural break, there is the problem of treating it. One treatment is simply that of dividing the sample according to the different populations and separately estimating each subsample. Thus, in the peacetime/wartime example there would be a peacetime estimate

[57] If $n = n_1 + n_2$ exceeds $2k$, then a related statistic, given as

$$F = \frac{[\hat{\mathbf{u}}'\hat{\mathbf{u}} - (\hat{\mathbf{u}}_1'\hat{\mathbf{u}}_1 + \hat{\mathbf{u}}_2'\hat{\mathbf{u}}_2)]/k}{(\hat{\mathbf{u}}_1'\hat{\mathbf{u}}_1 + \hat{\mathbf{u}}_2'\hat{\mathbf{u}}_2)/(n_1 + n_2 - 2k)} \sim F(k, n_1 + n_2 - 2k)$$

tests the hypothesis that $\boldsymbol{\beta}_1 = \boldsymbol{\beta}_2$. Here $\hat{\mathbf{u}}_1$ and $\hat{\mathbf{u}}_2$ are, respectively, vectors of n_1 and n_2 residuals from the regressions

$$\mathbf{y}_1 = \mathbf{X}_1\hat{\boldsymbol{\beta}}_1 + \hat{\mathbf{u}}_1, \quad \mathbf{y}_2 = \mathbf{X}_2\hat{\boldsymbol{\beta}}_2 + \hat{\mathbf{u}}_2$$

and $\hat{\mathbf{u}}$ is the $n_1 + n_2$ vector of residuals from the pooled regression in (6.10.2). If F exceeds the critical value for a particular level of significance, then it implies that the subsamples are drawn from different populations. See Section 5.4, Problem 5-J, and Problem 6-Z.

$$\mathbf{y} = \mathbf{X}\boldsymbol{\beta}^{p} + \mathbf{u}^{p} \tag{6.10.6}$$

and a separate wartime estimate

$$\mathbf{y} = \mathbf{X}\boldsymbol{\beta}^{w} + \mathbf{u}^{w} \tag{6.10.7}$$

where comparable coefficients differ in the two periods. The Chow test could be used to test whether the coefficients differ significantly. If they do not differ, then the subsamples can be merged and a single set of coefficients can be estimated for the entire sample. If they do differ, however, it would be more appropriate to report the results for each subsample separately. If there are not enough data points to estimate for one of the subsamples, then just the results for the one subsample in which the coefficients can be estimated should be reported, with an indication that it would be inappropriate to merge the two subsamples.

The separate estimates for the two subsamples can be described in terms of dummy variables, as introduced in Section 3.2. Letting W be a dummy variable taking the value 1 in wartime and 0 in peacetime, the single equation

$$\mathbf{y} = \mathbf{X}(\bar{\boldsymbol{\beta}} + \bar{\bar{\boldsymbol{\beta}}}\,W) + \mathbf{u} \tag{6.10.8}$$

can be used to estimate over the whole sample. This approach leads to estimates of the $2k$ coefficients $\bar{\boldsymbol{\beta}}$ and $\bar{\bar{\boldsymbol{\beta}}}$. It is, in fact, identical to the separate estimations for each of the subsamples, since, comparing (6.10.8) to equations (6.10.6) and (6.10.7), it follows that

$$\bar{\boldsymbol{\beta}} = \boldsymbol{\beta}^{p}, \qquad \bar{\boldsymbol{\beta}} + \bar{\bar{\boldsymbol{\beta}}} = \boldsymbol{\beta}^{w}. \tag{6.10.9}$$

Using this approach, if the dummy variable applies to all coefficients, as in (6.10.8), it is equivalent to dividing the sample into two subsamples. If, however, the dummy variable applies to only some of the coefficients, then the number of coefficients to be estimated can be reduced. In the above example, if the condition of war or peace affects only s of the coefficients, then it leads to estimation of $k + s$ coefficients. In fact, it is equivalent to dividing the sample into two subsamples but requiring that $k - s$ of the coefficients be the same for each of the subsamples. The implied reduction in the number of coefficients to be estimated from $2k$ to $k + s$ can be valuable if there is a degrees-of-freedom problem. If, however, there are adequate degrees of freedom, it is generally better to divide the sample and separately estimate all $2k$ coefficients, k for each subsample. This approach can, of course, be extended to r subsamples, leading to rk coefficients to be estimated, assuming $rk < n$.

PROBLEMS

6-A Show that if all four seasonal dummy variables d_1, d_2, d_3, and d_4 are included as explanatory variables in a model that also has an intercept term, then there will be perfect multicollinearity, specifically a linear dependence in the columns of the **X** matrix.

6-B Give a geometrical interpretation of multicollinearity, following the approach of Section 5.2.

6-C One approach to multicollinearity takes account of extraneous estimates of some of the parameters. Assume the $k \times 1$ coefficient vector $\boldsymbol{\beta}$ is partitioned as

$$\begin{pmatrix} \boldsymbol{\beta}_1 \\ \hline \boldsymbol{\beta}_2 \end{pmatrix},$$

where $\boldsymbol{\beta}_1$ is given by the k_1 extraneous estimates $\bar{\boldsymbol{\beta}}_1$. Find the least-squares estimates of the $k - k_1$ remaining parameters $\hat{\boldsymbol{\beta}}_2$ by formulating the problem as one of least squares subject to the linear restrictions that $\boldsymbol{\beta}_1 = \bar{\boldsymbol{\beta}}_1$ and using the results of Appendix B, Section B.10. Generalize to the case of several linear restrictions on parameters, of the form

$$\mathbf{c} = \mathbf{A}\boldsymbol{\beta} + \mathbf{v}$$

using the formulation[58]

$$\begin{pmatrix} \mathbf{y} \\ \hline \mathbf{c} \end{pmatrix} = \begin{pmatrix} \mathbf{X} \\ \hline \mathbf{A} \end{pmatrix} \boldsymbol{\beta} + \begin{pmatrix} \mathbf{u} \\ \hline \mathbf{v} \end{pmatrix}$$

6-D Show that for the model in first differences (6.4.8):

1. There is no intercept unless the original model includes a linear time trend.
2. If the disturbances in the original model exhibit positive first-order serial correlation, then the disturbances in the first-differences model exhibit negative first-order serial correlation.

6-E Show that the Durbin-Watson statistic of (6.4.12) can be expressed as

$$\hat{d} = \frac{\hat{\mathbf{u}}'\mathbf{A}\hat{\mathbf{u}}}{\hat{\mathbf{u}}'\hat{\mathbf{u}}}$$

where **A** is the symmetric $n \times n$ matrix defined by

$$\mathbf{A} = \begin{pmatrix} 1 & -1 & 0 & \cdots & 0 & 0 & 0 \\ -1 & 2 & -1 & \cdots & 0 & 0 & 0 \\ 0 & -1 & 2 & \cdots & 0 & 0 & 0 \\ \vdots & \vdots & \vdots & & \vdots & \vdots & \vdots \\ 0 & 0 & 0 & & 2 & -1 & 0 \\ 0 & 0 & 0 & & -1 & 2 & -1 \\ 0 & 0 & 0 & & 0 & -1 & 1 \end{pmatrix}$$

[58] See Theil and Goldberger (1961) and Theil (1963, 1971).

6-F The Markov process (6.4.2) relates $\hat{u}_i$ to $\hat{u}_{i-1}$ in the case of first-order serial correlation:

1. Illustrate positive and negative first-order serial correlation geometrically in terms of the clustering of points in various quadrants of the $\hat{u}_i$, $\hat{u}_{i-1}$ plane.
2. Illustrate the Markov process using this plane.
3. Prove that $\hat{\rho}$ in (6.4.15) is the least-squares estimator of the parameter ρ in the Markov process.
4. Prove that $\hat{\rho}$ is a biased but consistent estimator of ρ.

6-G Consider the second-order autoregressive scheme

$$u_i = \rho_1 u_{i-1} + \rho_2 u_{i-2} + v_i$$

1. Find the transformed model, comparable to (6.4.6).
2. Obtain a test statistic comparable to the Durbin-Watson test statistic to test the hypothesis

$$H_0: \rho_1 = \rho_2 = 0$$

3. How could ρ_1 and ρ_2 be estimated?

6-H Consider the model

$$\begin{aligned} y_i &= \beta x_i + u_i \\ u_i &= v_i + \delta v_{i-1}, \qquad |\delta| < 1 \\ E(v_i) &= 0 \\ E(v_i v_{i'}) &= \begin{cases} \sigma_v^2 & \text{if } i = i' \\ 0 & \text{if } i \neq i' \end{cases} \end{aligned}$$

1. Show that the least-squares estimator of β is unbiased.
2. Assuming δ is known, obtain the GLS estimator of β.

6-I Show that in the *equicorrelated case*, in which the covariance matrix $\mathbf{\Omega}$ in (6.5.1) exhibits homoskedasticity (equal diagonal elements) and equal covariances (equal off-diagonal elements, which are not necessarily all zero), then the GLS estimator (6.5.8) reduces to the ordinary least-squares estimator.

6-J Assuming (6.5.1) show that

$$\begin{aligned} \text{Cov}(\hat{\mathbf{u}}) &= \sigma^2 [\mathbf{M}\mathbf{\Omega}\mathbf{M}] \quad \text{where } \mathbf{M} = \mathbf{I} - \mathbf{X}(\mathbf{X}'\mathbf{X})^{-1}\mathbf{X}' \\ \text{Cov}(\hat{\mathbf{u}}(\mathbf{\Omega})) &= \sigma^2 [\mathbf{\Omega} - \mathbf{X}(\mathbf{X}'\mathbf{\Omega}^{-1}\mathbf{X})^{-1}\mathbf{X}'] \end{aligned}$$

where $\hat{\mathbf{u}}$ is the ordinary least-squares residual vector and $\hat{\mathbf{u}}(\mathbf{\Omega})$ is the GLS residual vector of (6.5.11).

6-K Prove that if all the assumptions for the Gauss-Markov theorem other than homoskedasticity and absence of serial correlation are met, then the least-squares estimators are still linear, unbiased, and consistent but they are no longer most efficient (best).

6-L Prove the GLS version of the Gauss-Markov theorem—that the GLS estimators are BLUE—and the GLS version of the least-squares consistency theorem—that the GLS estimators are consistent (proofs can be patterned after those of Section 4.9).

6-M Prove that $\hat{s}^2(\mathbf{\Omega})$ as defined in (6.5.10) is an unbiased estimator of σ^2.

6-N In the case of heteroskedasticity develop the likelihood function and show that the GLS estimator using (6.5.16) is equivalent to that obtained by maximizing this likelihood function.

6-O Prove that if $\mathbf{\Omega}$ is given as in (6.5.21) with $\sigma^2 = 1$, then

$$\mathbf{\Omega}^{-1} = \frac{1}{1-\rho^2}\begin{pmatrix} 1 & -\rho & 0 & \cdots & 0 & 0 \\ -\rho & 1+\rho^2 & -\rho & \cdots & 0 & 0 \\ 0 & -\rho & 1+\rho^2 & \cdots & 0 & 0 \\ \vdots & \vdots & \vdots & \cdots & \vdots & \vdots \\ 0 & 0 & 0 & \cdots & 1+\rho^2 & -\rho \\ 0 & 0 & 0 & \cdots & -\rho & 1 \end{pmatrix}$$

Show that the GLS estimator is then the least-squares estimator of the transformed model

$$\mathbf{Py} = \mathbf{PX\beta} + \mathbf{Pu}$$

where here

$$\mathbf{P} = \frac{1}{\sqrt{1-\rho^2}}\begin{pmatrix} \sqrt{1-\rho^2} & 0 & 0 & \cdots & 0 & 0 \\ -\rho & 1 & 0 & \cdots & 0 & 0 \\ 0 & -\rho & 1 & \cdots & 0 & 0 \\ \vdots & \vdots & \vdots & & \vdots & \vdots \\ 0 & 0 & 0 & \cdots & 1 & 0 \\ 0 & 0 & 0 & \cdots & -\rho & 1 \end{pmatrix}$$

Give an interpretation for the transformed model.

6-P For the technique of "seemingly unrelated equations" of Section 6.5:

1. Derive the estimator $\hat{\boldsymbol{\beta}}^*$, assuming $\mathbf{\Sigma}^{-1} = (\sigma^{jj'})$, where

$$\mathbf{\Sigma}^{*-1} = \mathbf{\Sigma}^{-1} \otimes \mathbf{I} = \begin{pmatrix} \sigma^{11}\mathbf{I} & \sigma^{12}\mathbf{I} & \cdots & \sigma^{1g}\mathbf{I} \\ \vdots & \vdots & & \vdots \\ \sigma^{g1}\mathbf{I} & \sigma^{g2}\mathbf{I} & \cdots & \sigma^{gg}\mathbf{I} \end{pmatrix}$$

2. Show that if $\sigma_{jj'} = 0$ for $j \neq j'$ or if $\mathbf{X}^1 = \mathbf{X}^2 = \cdots = \mathbf{X}^g$, then the estimator reduces to the set of ordinary least-squares estimators for each equation considered alone.[59]

6-Q Obtain an equation that could be used to estimate a distributed lag model of the Koyck type:

1. In which the coefficients decline geometrically only after j_0 periods.
2. In which there are two different explanatory variables x and z for which both lag distributions are characterized by the parameter λ.
3. As in item 2 except that the two lag distributions are characterized by the two parameters λ_1 and λ_2, respectively, where $\lambda_1 \neq \lambda_2$.

6-R In the *adaptive expectations* model of capital stock growth the level of capital is set at a multiple of anticipated output Y_t^*,

$$K_t = \delta Y_t^*$$

where the change in anticipated output over time is proportional to the gap between actual and past anticipated output:

$$Y_t^* - Y_{t-1}^* = \alpha(Y_t - Y_{t-1}^*) + w_t, \qquad 0 < \alpha \leqslant 1$$

Determine for these equations an equation involving only observable magnitudes (anticipated output not being observable), and contrast it to that obtained for the partial adjustment model in (6.7.19).

6-S The partial adjustment model of (6.7.19) can be combined with the adaptive expectations model of Problem 6-R to yield the model

$$\begin{aligned} K_t^* &= \delta Y_t^* \\ K_t - K_{t-1} &= \gamma(K_t^* - K_{t-1}) + v_t, \qquad 0 < \gamma \leqslant 1 \\ Y_t^* - Y_{t-1}^* &= \alpha(Y_t - Y_{t-1}^*) + w_t, \qquad 0 < \alpha \leqslant 1. \end{aligned}$$

Combine these equations into a single equation that can be estimated. Which of the parameters δ, γ, and α can be estimated from this equation?

6-T A simple model leading to the partial adjustment model of (6.7.19) is one in which total cost is the sum of the cost of not maintaining the desired capital stock and the cost of changing capital stock. In the quadratic case

$$C = \alpha(K_t - K_t^*)^2 + \beta(K_t - K_{t-1})^2$$

where α and β are given nonnegative constants.

1. Show that the choice of K_t to minimize C yields (6.7.19).

[59] See also Problem 10-B.

2. How does the cost-minimizing choice of K_t change as $\alpha \to 0$, as $\beta \to 0$?
3. Using this approach, find a cost curve that implies the adaptive expectations model of Problem 6-R.

6-U Assume that the sales of a good in year t, Y_t, depend on the price of the good in that year, p_t, and on current and past advertising expenditures, A_t, $A_{t-1}, \ldots, A_{t-m}$. The effects of advertising on sales first increase, reach a peak, and then decrease.

1. State the general form of the model.
2. Use the Almon distributed lag to specify the lagged relationships.
3. How would you estimate the model if $m = 4$?

6-V Prove that (6.7.37) implies (6.7.38).

6-W Consider (6.7.17) with $\alpha = 0$, namely

$$y_t = \lambda y_{t-1} + \beta x_t + (u_t - \lambda u_{t-1})$$

as in (6.7.36)

1. Prove that the least-squares estimator is inconsistent.
2. Using the technique of instrumental variables, as discussed in Section 11.6, show that the estimator using x_t and x_{t-1} as instrumental variables is consistent.

6-X For the problem of specification error

1. Prove (6.8.15) by inverting the partitioned matrix in (6.8.14), using the result in Appendix B, Section B.5.
2. Prove that the inclusion of irrelevant variables $\mathbf{X}_2$, as in (6.8.10), yields inefficient estimators for the parameters of the true model (6.8.1).

6-Y Consider the identification of the errors-in-variables model, as discussed in footnote 53. Show that the model is identified if $\beta_2 = 0$. Also show that the model is identified if Var (Y_E) is known, if Var (C_E) is known, or if the ratio of these variances is known. For each case obtain the estimator for β_1.

6-Z Derive the F test in (6.10.5) using the F test on several linear restrictions in (5.4.17).

BIBLIOGRAPHY

Almon, S. (1965), "The Distributed Lag between Capital Appropriations and Expenditures." *Econometrica*, 33: 178–96.

Amemiya, T. (1975), "Qualitative Response Models." *Annals of Economic and Social Measurement*, 4: 363–72.

Bartlett, M. S. (1949), "Fitting a Straight Line when Both Variables are Subject to Error." *Biometrics*, 5: 207–12.

Box, G. E. P., and G. M. Jenkins (1970), *Time Series Analysis; Forecasting and Control.* San Francisco: Holden-Day.

Cagan, P. (1956), "The Monetary Dynamics of Hyper-Inflation" in M. Friedman, Ed., *Studies in the Quantity Theory of Money*. Chicago: University of Chicago Press.

Chipman, J. S. (1964), "On Least Squares with Insufficient Observations." *Journal of the American Statistical Association*, 59: 1078–111.

Chow, G. C. (1960), "Tests of Equality between Sets of Coefficients in Two Linear Regressions." *Econometrica*, 28: 591–605.

Cochrane, D., and G. H. Orcutt (1949), "Application of Least Square Regression to Relations Containing Autocorrelated Error Terms." *Journal of the American Statistical Association*, 44: 32–61.

Cootner, P. H., Ed. (1964), *The Random Character of Stock Market Prices.* Cambridge: The MIT Press.

Cox, D. R. (1970), *The Analysis of Binary Data*. London: Methuen & Co.

Dhrymes, P. J. (1970), *Distributed Lags*. San Francisco: Holden-Day, Inc.

Durbin, J. (1954), "Errors in Variables." *Review of the International Statistical Institute*, 22: 23–32.

Durbin, J. (1970), "Testing for Serial Correlation in Least-Squares Regression when Some of the Regressions are Lagged Dependent Variables." *Econometrica*, 38: 410–21.

Farrar, D. E., and R. R. Glauber (1967), "Multicollinearity in Regression Analysis: The Problem Revisited." *The Review of Economics and Statistics*, 49: 92–107.

Finney, D. J. (1971), *Probit Analysis*, 3rd Ed. New York: Cambridge University Press.

Fisher, F. M. (1961), "On the Cost of Approximate Specification in Simultaneous Equation Estimation." *Econometrica*, 29: 139–70.

Fisher, F. M. (1970), "Tests of Equality between Sets of Coefficients in Two Linear Regressions: An Expository Note." *Econometrica*, 38: 361–66.

Friedman, M. (1957), *A Theory of the Consumption Function*. Princeton: Princeton University Press.

Goldfeld, S. M., and R. E. Quandt (1965), "Some Tests for Homoskedasticity." *Journal of the American Statistical Association*, 60: 539–47.

Goldfeld, S. M., and R. E. Quandt (1972), *Nonlinear Methods of Econometrics.* Amsterdam: North-Holland Publishing Co.

Griliches, Z. (1967), "Distributed Lags: A Survey." *Econometrica*, 35: 16–49.

Harberger, A., Ed. (1960), *The Demand for Durable Goods*. Chicago: University of Chicago Press.

Hannan, E. J. (1965), "The Estimation of Relationships Involving Distributed Lags." *Econometrica*, 33: 206–24.

Hooper, J. W., and H. Theil (1958), "The Extension of Wald's Method of Fitting Straight Lines to Multiple Regressions." *Review of the International Statistical Institute*, 26: 37–47.

Johnston, J. (1972), *Econometric Methods*, 2nd Ed. New York: McGraw-Hill Book Company.

Jorgenson, D. (1966), "Rational Distributed Lag Functions." *Econometrica*, 34: 135–50.

Klein, L. R., and M. Nakamura (1962), "Singularity in the Equation System of Econometrics: Some Aspects of the Problem of Multicollinearity." *International Economic Review*, 3: 274–99.

Konijn, H. S. (1962), "Identification and Estimation in a Simultaneous Equations Model with Errors in the Variables." *Econometrica*, 30: 79–87.

Koyck, L. M. (1954), *Distributed Lags and Investment Analysis*. Amsterdam: North-Holland Publishing Co.

Kuh, E. (1963), *Capital Stock Growth: A Micro-Econometric Approach*. Amsterdam: North-Holland Publishing Co.

Liviatan, N. (1963), "Consistent Estimation of Distributed Lags." *International Economic Review*, 4: 44–52.

Madansky, A. (1964), "Spurious Correlation due to Deflating Variables," *Econometrica*, 32: 652–5.

Malinvaud, E. (1970), *Statistical Methods of Econometrics*, 2nd Rev. Ed. Amsterdam: North-Holland Publishing Co.

Malkiel, B. G. (1973), *A Random Walk down Wall Street*. New York: W. W. Norton & Company, Inc.

Mandelbrot, B. (1963), "New Methods in Statistical Economics." *Journal of Political Economy*, 71: 421–40.

McFadden, D. (1974), "Conditional Logit Analysis of Qualitative Choice Behavior," in P. Zarembka, Ed. *Frontiers in Econometrics*. New York: Academic Press.

Meyer, J., and E. Kuh (1957), "How Extraneous are Extraneous Estimates?" *Review of Economics and Statistics*, 39: 380–93.

Nerlove, M. (1972), "Lags in Economic Behavior," *Econometrica*, 40: 221–51.

Nerlove, M. (1958a), *Distributed Lags and Demand Analysis*. Washington, D.C.: U.S. Department of Agriculture, Agricultural Handbook 141.

Nerlove, M. (1958b), *The Dynamics of Supply: Estimation of Farmers' Response to Price*. Baltimore: The Johns Hopkins Press.

Prais, S. J., and H. S. Houthakker (1955), *The Analysis of Family Budgets*. New York: Cambridge University Press.

Rao, P., and R. L. Miller (1971), *Applied Econometrics*. Belmont, Calif.: Wadsworth Publishing Co., Inc.

Sims, C. A. (1974), "Distributed Lags," in M. D. Intriligator and D. A. Kendrick, Eds., *Frontiers of Quantitative Economics*, Vol. II. Amsterdam: North-Holland Publishing Co.

Stone, R. E. (1954), *The Measurement of Consumers' Expenditure and Behavior in the United Kingdom, 1920–1938*. New York: Cambridge University Press.

Theil, H. (1963), "On the Use of Incomplete Prior Information in Regression Analysis," *Journal of the American Statistical Association*, 58: 401–14.

Theil, H. (1971), *Principles of Econometrics*. New York: John Wiley & Sons, Inc.

Theil, H. (1972), *Statistical Decomposition Analysis*. Amsterdam: North-Holland Publishing Co.

Theil, H., and A. S. Goldberger (1961), "On Pure and Mixed Statistical Estimation in Economics." *International Economic Review*, 2: 65–78.

Theil, H., and A. Nagar (1961), "Testing the Independence of Regression Disturbances." *Journal of the American Statistical Association*, 56: 793–806.

Tobin, J. (1950), "A Statistical Demand Function for Food in the U.S.A." *Journal of the Royal Statistical Society*, Series A, 113: 113–41.

Wald, A. (1940), "The Fitting of Straight Lines if Both Variables are Subject to Error." *Annals of Mathematical Statistics*, 11: 284–300.

Waud, R. N. (1966), "Small Sample Bias due to Mis-Specification in the 'Partial Adjustment' and 'Adaptive Expectations' Models." *Journal of the American Statistical Association*, 61: 1130–52.

Zellner, A. (1962), "An Efficient Method of Estimating Seemingly Unrelated Regressions and Tests for Aggregation Bias." *Journal of the American Statistical Association*, 57: 348–68.

Zellner, A. (1963), "Estimates for Seemingly Unrelated Regression Equations: Some Exact Finite Sample Results." *Journal of the American Statistical Association*, 58: 977–92.

Zellner, A., and D. S. Huang (1962), "Further Properties of Efficient Estimators for Seemingly Unrelated Regression Equations." *International Economic Review*, 3: 300–13.

PART IV

Applications of Single-Equation Estimation

CHAPTER 7

Applications to Households; Demand Analysis

7.1 Introduction

One of the oldest and most important uses of econometrics is its application to households in the estimation of demand relationships.[1] Pioneer empirical analyses of demand, starting early in the twentieth century, led, in fact, to later studies of general issues in econometric theory.

Econometric studies of demand have involved all three of the basic objectives of econometrics discussed in Chapter 1. Virtually all involve some aspects of *structural analysis*, particularly the estimation of the impacts of prices and income on demand, as measured by elasticities of demand. Some are oriented toward *forecasting*, in particular forecasting quantities and/or prices of particular commodities in either the short-range or long-range future. Others are oriented toward *policy evaluation*, in particular, impacts of policies that may affect markets for consumer goods, such as taxes or (de)regulation. Thus, for example, from estimated demand curves it is possible to estimate the effects of excise taxes, such as the effects on the quantities demanded and the tax yield from taxes on gasoline, as in Section 1.4.

Two seminal studies, those by Wold and Jureen, and Stone, illustrate all three uses of empirical studies of demand.[2] Both utilized interwar data from the 1920's and 1930's in order to estimate demand functions for various commodities in Sweden and the United Kingdom, respectively. Each study estimated elasticities of demand, and some of these results are reported below. Each was also concerned with forecasting the pattern of demand once wartime regulations, in particular rationing, were lifted, and they both played some role in policy toward eliminating such regulations. In fact, their forecasts were remarkably accurate, considering that the data each utilized were from a much earlier period.

Section 2 of this chapter reviews the basic theory of the household, or consumer, and the demand functions derived from this theory. While the theory presented in this section is usually considered part of mathematical economics, rather than econometrics, it is included here because the specification of the econometric model is (or should be) guided by the underlying theory. Section 3 contrasts the two major types of demand studies—those of single demand

[1] Basic references for econometric studies of consumer demand are Brown and Deaton (1972), Powell (1974), Phlips (1974), Theil (1975), and Barten (1977). While "demand" can refer to the demand by firms for factors of production as well as the demand by households for goods, the discussion in this chapter is confined to the latter. For the former see Chapter 8.

[2] See Wold and Jureen (1953) and Stone (1954a).

functions and those of systems of demand functions. The next two sections present summaries of past econometric studies of single demand equations and systems of demand equations, respectively. The remaining sections treat some important econometric issues in estimating demand relationships, specifically the questions of functional form, identification, aggregation, and dynamic considerations. Included in these sections are examples from the literature of estimated demand functions. It should become clear, as a result of these summaries of past studies, that there is no single ideal model for empirical research on demand. Rather, it is necessary to "tailor make" the model to the particular phenomenon under study. The same type of conclusion will follow from the survey of empirical studies of production and cost in the next chapter, the surveys of other applications in Chapter 9, and the surveys of applications of simultaneous equations in Chapters 12 and 13.

7.2 The theory of the household

The problem of the household (or consumer), from a formal point of view, is that of choosing levels of consumption of goods (including services) so as to maximize a utility function subject to a given budget constraint.[3] Considering the simplest case of two goods, in which purchases by a single household are measured by x_1 and x_2, respectively, the problem of the household can be stated as

$$\max_{x_1, x_2} U(x_1, x_2) \quad \text{subject to} \quad p_1 x_1 + p_2 x_2 = I. \qquad *(7.2.1)$$

Here $U(x_1, x_2)$ is the utility function, p_1 and p_2 are the prices of the two goods, and I is the level of income of the household. Income and both prices are assumed to be given positive constants. The utility function is an ordinal representation of tastes in that the household prefers a bundle of goods $\mathbf{x} = (x_1, x_2)$ with a higher value of utility to a bundle with a lower value of utility.[4] The budget constraint requires that total expenditures, obtained by totaling expenditures on each of the goods, equal income. The household thus chooses among bundles that satisfy the budget constraint so as to attain the highest available level of utility.

Geometrically the problem and its solution can be depicted as in Figure 7.1. The *budget line* indicates alternative possible bundles of goods that can be purchased at the given prices and income. The curves are *indifference curves*, each of which indicates those bundles that have the same level of utility and therefore among which the consumer is indifferent. They are the level curves of the

[3] See Hicks (1946), Samuelson (1947), Intriligator (1971), and Phlips (1974) for discussions of the theory of the household.

[4] The theory described here refers to *ordinal* utility, where any monotonically increasing transformation of the utility function is a valid utility function for the household. The utility function can itself be derived from the more basic concept of a preference relation under certain conditions. See Intriligator (1971).

utility function.

In this "classical" case of smooth and smoothly varying indifference curves the solution is at the *tangency point* **x**. At this point the slope of the budget line, which is the (negative) ratio of prices, equals the slope of the indifference curve, which is called the (negative) *marginal rate of substitution.*[5] The optimal quantities demanded are then x_1 and x_2, as shown.

The *demand functions* give the dependence of the (optimal) quantities demanded on all parameters of problem (7.2.1), namely both prices and income:

$$\left.\begin{aligned} x_1 &= x_1(p_1, p_2, I) \\ x_2 &= x_2(p_1, p_2, I) \end{aligned}\right\} \quad \text{or} \quad x_j = x_j(p_1, p_2, I), \quad j = 1, 2. \qquad *(7.2.2)$$

These functions indicate the amount demanded of each of the goods at alternative combinations of prices and income.

Special cases of the demand functions, in which two of the three parameters are held constant, are also widely discussed in the literature on partial equilibrium analysis. Thus, holding p_2 and I constant in the first equation gives the *demand curve* for the first good:

$$x_1 = D_1(p_1) = x_1(p_1, \bar{p}_2, \bar{I}) \qquad *(7.2.3)$$

where the bars indicate that p_2 and I are held constant. This is the same form as equation (1.4.1), and Figure 1.2, the demand curve for gasoline, illustrates such a demand curve. Similarly the demand curve for the second good is

$$x_2 = D_2(p_2) = x_2(\bar{p}_1, p_2, \bar{I}). \qquad *(7.2.4)$$

These demand curves indicate the effect of a change in the price of a good on the quantity demanded, holding other price(s) and income constant–i.e., the *ceteris paribus* effect of a change in "own" price. If the other price(s) or income change, the result will be a shift in the demand curve. A second partial equilibrium approach holds p_1 and p_2 constant, to yield the *Engel curves*:[6]

[5] The slope of the budget line is $-p_1/p_2$. Given a continuous utility function and an indifference curve of the form $U(x_1, x_2)$ = constant, totally differentiating both sides yields

$$\frac{\partial U}{\partial x_1} dx_1 + \frac{\partial U}{\partial x_2} dx_2 = 0.$$

The marginal rate of substitution, the slope, is therefore given as

$$\text{MRS} = -\frac{dx_2}{dx_1} = \frac{\partial U/\partial x_1}{\partial U/\partial x_2}$$

Thus, at the tangency point,

$$\frac{\partial U/\partial x_1}{\partial U/\partial x_2} \equiv \text{MRS} = \frac{p_1}{p_2}.$$

[6] Named for Ernst Engel, the statistician, not to be confused with Karl Marx's collaborator Friedrich Engels.

$$\begin{aligned} \bar{p}_1 x_1 &= E_1(I) = \bar{p}_1 x_1(\bar{p}_1, \bar{p}_2, I) \\ \bar{p}_2 x_2 &= E_2(I) = \bar{p}_2 x_2(\bar{p}_1, \bar{p}_2, I) \end{aligned} \qquad *(7.2.5)$$

These Engel curves indicate the effect of a change in income on the expenditure for each good at fixed prices. If the prices change, the result will be a shift in each of the Engel curves.

The demand curves and Engel curves can be derived geometrically from the equilibrium as portrayed in Figure 7.1. Figure 7.2 indicates the derivation of the demand curve (7.2.3). If p_2 and I are held constant, the intercept on the x_2 axis of the budget line is fixed, so varying p_1 is equivalent, geometrically, to a rota-

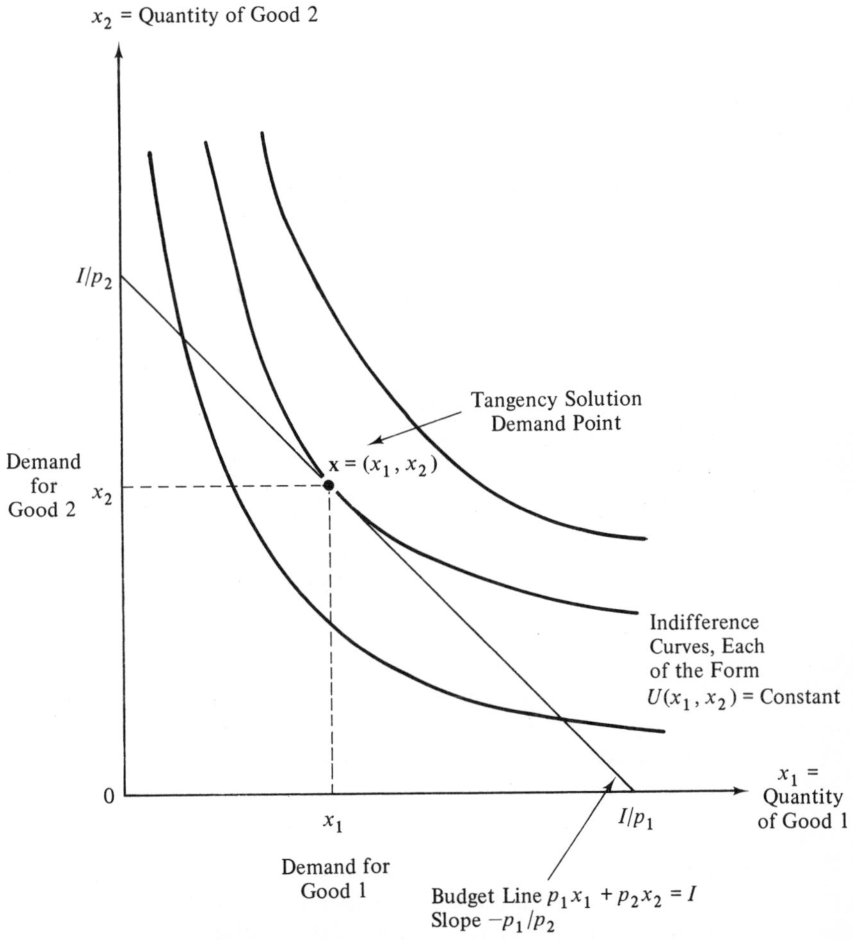

Figure 7.1 Equilibrium of the Consumer

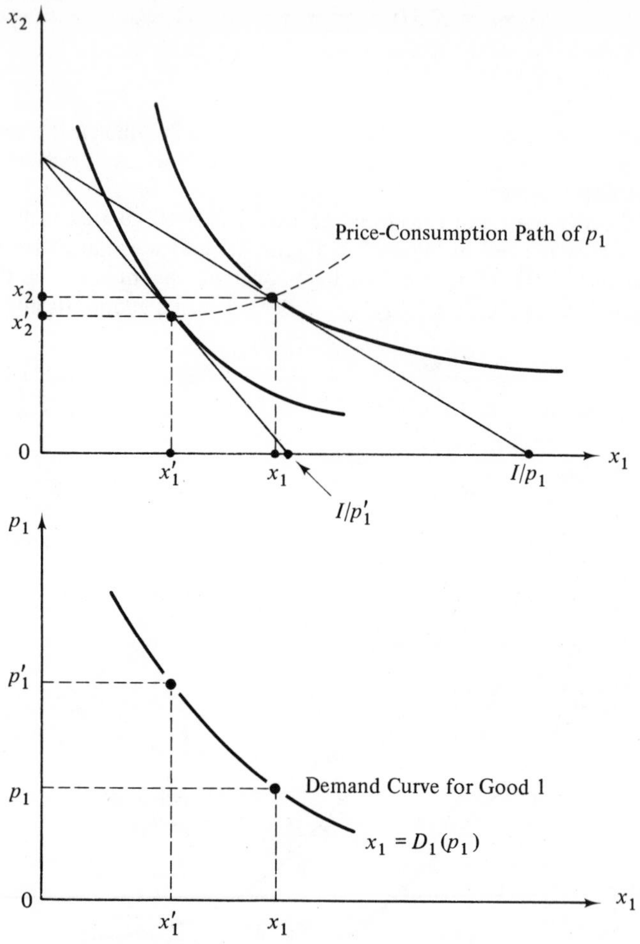

Figure 7.2 Derivation of the Demand Curve

tion of the budget line about this intercept, as shown in Figure 7.2. For each budget line there is a tangency point at which the consumer is at an equilibrium. Connecting the (x_1, x_2) pairs in the figure gives the *price-consumption path* for p_1, from which the demand curve for good 1 can be obtained, as shown. Note that if the other price p_2 or income I changes, there will be a shift in the demand curve.

The Engel curve can be similarly derived, as shown in Figure 7.3. Holding prices constant implies that the slope of the budget line is constant. Thus changing income is shown geometrically as a parallel shift of the budget line. In the figure it is assumed that $p_1 = 1$, so the horizontal intercepts of the budget lines give the two levels of income. With each budget line there is an associated equilibrium at a tangency with an indifference curve. Connecting the (x_1, x_2) pairs

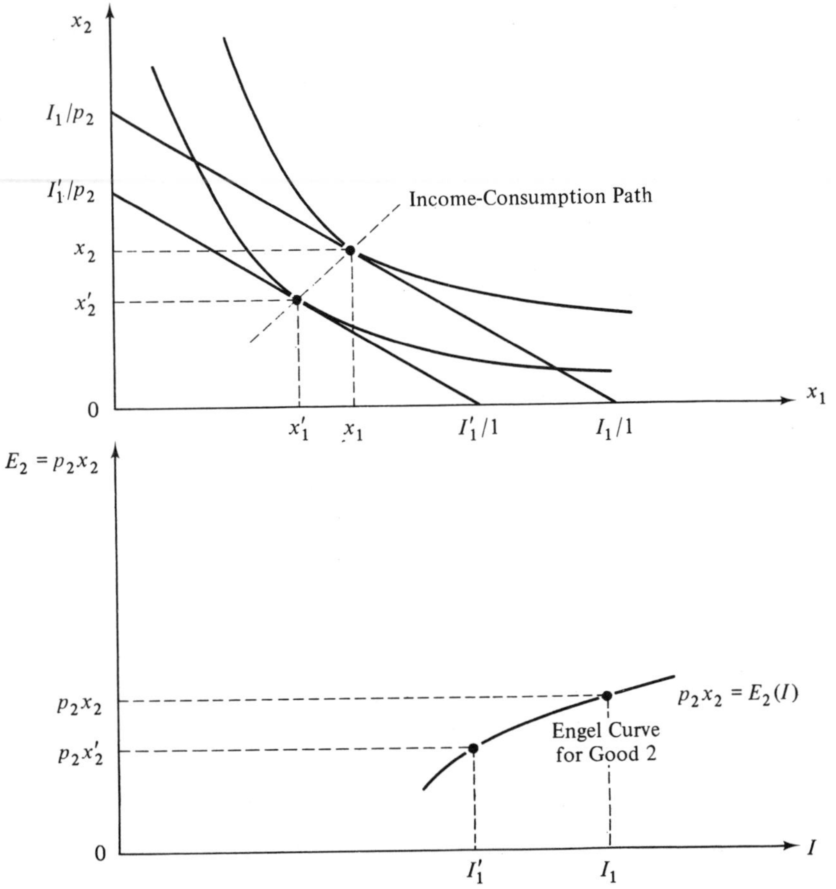

Figure 7.3 Derivation of the Engel Curve.

NOTE Here it is assumed that $p_1 = 1$.

from the figure gives the *income-consumption path*, from which the Engel curve for good 2 can be obtained, as shown. Note that a change in either price will generally lead to a shift in the Engel curve.

Engel's law refers to a property of the Engel curve for food. The law states that the proportion of income consumers spend on food decreases as their income increases. Thus, if x_2 is food, the law states that eventually the ratio p_2x_2/I decreases as I increases.

Elasticities of demand can be defined using the demand function, the demand curve, or the Engel curve. These elasticities are convenient summaries of the responsiveness of the quantity demanded to factors influencing it, in part because they are independent of the units of measurement of the good, prices, income, etc. Thus comparisons of elasticities can be made across goods, across countries, etc. The (own) *price elasticity of demand* for good j is defined as

$$\epsilon_j = \frac{\partial x_j(p_1, p_2, I)}{\partial p_j} \frac{p_j}{x_j} = \frac{\partial \ln x_j}{\partial \ln p_j} \qquad *(7.2.6)$$

giving the percentage change in the quantity demanded for a 1% change in the price of this good. Usually the price elasticity, so defined, is negative.[7] The good is said to be *price elastic* if $|\epsilon_j| > 1$ and *price inelastic* if $|\epsilon_j| < 1$. The *income elasticity of demand* for good j is

$$\eta_j = \frac{\partial x_j(p_1, p_2, I)}{\partial I} \frac{I}{x_j} = \frac{\partial \ln x_j}{\partial \ln I} \qquad *(7.2.7)$$

giving the percentage change in the quantity demand for a 1% change in income. Usually the income elasticity, so defined, is positive. The good is said to be *income elastic* if $\eta_j > 1$ and *income inelastic* if $\eta_j < 1$. In terms of elasticities, Engel's law states that food is income inelastic, i.e., that the elasticity is less than unity. Finally, the *cross price elasticities* of demand are defined as

$$\epsilon_{jj'} = \frac{\partial x_j(p_1, p_2, I)}{\partial p_{j'}} \frac{p_{j'}}{x_j} = \frac{\partial \ln x_j}{\partial \ln p_{j'}} \qquad *(7.2.8)$$

indicating the effect of a change in the price of one good on the demand for the other good. From these definitions $\epsilon_{jj} = \epsilon_j$ (the own price elasticity) and, in general, $\epsilon_{jj'} \neq \epsilon_{j'j}$ for $j \neq j'$. While the elasticities are sometimes treated as approximately constant over a limited range of variations of the variables influencing demand, in general all elasticities depend on all prices and income, so that in this case of two goods all six elasticities, ϵ_1, ϵ_2, η_1, η_2, ϵ_{12}, and ϵ_{21}, vary with p_1, p_2, and I.

Economic theory suggests that the demand functions (7.2.2) must satisfy certain restrictions. First, they must satisfy the *budget constraint*:

$$p_1 x_1(p_1, p_2, I) + p_2 x_2(p_1, p_2, I) = I \qquad *(7.2.9)$$

since they solve problem (7.2.1), which contains this constraint. Dividing both sides of this constraint by income, I, the constraint can be expressed as

$$s_1 + s_2 = 1 \qquad (7.2.10)$$

where s_1 and s_2 are the *budget shares*, defined as the proportions of income spent on each of the goods:

$$s_j = \frac{p_j x_j}{I}, \quad j = 1, 2. \qquad (7.2.11)$$

[7] Frequently the magnitude of the price elasticity of demand is reported as a positive number, referring to its absolute value and not to its sign.

It is convenient to express some of the restrictions on the demand functions in terms of these budget shares.

Second, a scaling of both prices and income, from (p_1, p_2, I) to $(\alpha p_1, \alpha p_2, \alpha I)$ does not change the basic problem (7.2.1) and hence should not change the solution as embodied in the demand functions. Thus an equiproportionate change in all prices and income should have no effect on the quantity demanded of either good:[8]

$$\begin{aligned} x_1(\alpha p_1, \alpha p_2, \alpha I) &= x_1(p_1, p_2, I) \\ x_2(\alpha p_1, \alpha p_2, \alpha I) &= x_2(p_1, p_2, I). \end{aligned} \qquad *(7.2.12)$$

These homogeneity conditions state that the demand functions are homogeneous of degree zero in all explanatory variables. It then follows from Euler's theorem on homogeneous functions that[9]

$$\begin{aligned} \frac{\partial x_1}{\partial p_1} p_1 + \frac{\partial x_1}{\partial p_2} p_2 + \frac{\partial x_1}{\partial I} I &= 0 \\ \frac{\partial x_2}{\partial p_1} p_1 + \frac{\partial x_2}{\partial p_2} p_2 + \frac{\partial x_2}{\partial I} I &= 0. \end{aligned} \qquad (7.2.13)$$

These are the *homogeneity conditions*, which should also be satisfied by the demand functions. These conditions can be expressed in elasticity form as

$$\begin{aligned} \epsilon_1 + \epsilon_{12} + \eta_1 &= 0 \\ \epsilon_{21} + \epsilon_2 + \eta_2 &= 0 \end{aligned} \qquad *(7.2.14)$$

which state that the sum of all elasticities for any good must vanish.

A third set of conditions are the *Slutsky conditions*, which are based on the comparative static effects of changing prices and income and determining the resulting changes in demand.[10] They include, first, the *negativity conditions*:

[8] These conditions are sometimes referred to as "absence of money illusion," where, for example, halving or doubling all prices and income has no effect on quantities demanded.

[9] Euler's theorem on homogeneous functions states that if $f(x_1, x_2, \ldots, x_n)$ is homogeneous of degree h, as defined by

$$f(\alpha x_1, \alpha x_2, \ldots, \alpha x_n) = \alpha^h f(x_1, x_2, \ldots, x_n), \qquad \text{all } (x_1, x_2, \ldots, x_n)$$

then

$$\sum_{j=1}^{n} \frac{\partial f}{\partial x_j} x_j = h f(x_1, x_2, \ldots, x_n).$$

[10] These conditions refer to the negative semidefiniteness and symmetry of the matrix of substitution effects in the Slutsky equation. See Intriligator (1971). The *j, k substitution effect* $(\partial x_j/\partial p_k)_{\text{comp}}$ is defined as the compensated change in the quantity demanded of good j as

$$\frac{\partial x_1}{\partial p_1} + \frac{\partial x_1}{\partial I} x_1 \leqslant 0$$
$$\frac{\partial x_2}{\partial p_2} + \frac{\partial x_2}{\partial I} x_2 \leqslant 0 \qquad *(7.2.15)$$

and second, the *symmetry condition*:

$$\frac{\partial x_1}{\partial p_2} + \frac{\partial x_1}{\partial I} x_2 = \frac{\partial x_2}{\partial p_1} + \frac{\partial x_2}{\partial I} x_1. \qquad *(7.2.16)$$

Using the budget shares defined in (7.2.11), these conditions can also be expressed in elasticity form as

$$\epsilon_1 + s_1 \eta_1 \leqslant 0$$
$$\epsilon_2 + s_2 \eta_2 \leqslant 0 \qquad *(7.2.17)$$

and

$$\frac{1}{s_2} \epsilon_{12} + \eta_1 = \frac{1}{s_1} \epsilon_{21} + \eta_2. \qquad *(7.2.18)$$

A fourth set of conditions are the *aggregation conditions* obtained by differentiating the budget constraint (7.2.9). First is the *Engel aggregation condition:*

$$p_1 \frac{\partial x_1}{\partial I} + p_2 \frac{\partial x_2}{\partial I} = 1 \qquad *(7.2.19)$$

obtained by differentiating with respect to income. It states that the sum of the marginal expenditures is unity, so that an increase in income is spent on some

---

the price of good k changes, where the compensation in income keeps the household at the same level of utility. Here the substitution effect, which enters the Slutsky equation

$$\frac{\partial x_j}{\partial p_k} = \left(\frac{\partial x_j}{\partial p_k}\right)_{\text{comp}} - \frac{\partial x_j}{\partial I} x_k, \quad \text{all } j, k$$

has been replaced by $(\partial x_j/\partial p_k) + (\partial x_j/\partial I)x_k$ in order to emphasize those changes that are, at least in principle, observable. Conditions (7.2.15) could have been written, equivalently, as

$$\left(\frac{\partial x_j}{\partial p_k}\right)_{\text{comp}} \leqslant 0 \quad \text{for } j = k.$$

See also Problem 7-H.

good(s). It is therefore also called the *"adding up" condition*. In terms of income elasticities this condition stipulates that

$$s_1\eta_1 + s_2\eta_2 = 1. \qquad *(7.2.20)$$

The second of the aggregation conditions are the *Cournot aggregation conditions*, which state that

$$\begin{aligned} p_1 \frac{\partial x_1}{\partial p_1} + p_2 \frac{\partial x_2}{\partial p_1} + x_1 &= 0 \\ p_1 \frac{\partial x_1}{\partial p_2} + p_2 \frac{\partial x_2}{\partial p_2} + x_2 &= 0 \end{aligned} \qquad *(7.2.21)$$

They can be obtained by differentiating (7.2.9) with respect to each of the prices. In terms of elasticities again:

$$\begin{aligned} \epsilon_1 + \frac{s_2}{s_1}\epsilon_{21} + 1 &= 0 \\ \frac{s_1}{s_2}\epsilon_{12} + \epsilon_2 + 1 &= 0 \end{aligned} \qquad *(7.2.22)$$

where s_1 and s_2 are again the budget shares.

The nine conditions, including the budget constraint, two homogeneity conditions, three Slutsky conditions, and three aggregation conditions, represent the principal content of the classical theory of the consumer of two goods.[11] These conditions are, however, not independent; e.g., the Slutsky symmetry condition can be derived from the other conditions. It should perhaps also be noted that the elasticities ϵ_j, $\epsilon_{jj'}$, η_j, and the budget shares s_j, in general, vary as the parameters p_1, p_2, and I change. They are *not*, in general, parameters to be estimated, although some specialized functional forms used to estimate demand functions treat certain of these as parameters, as noted below.

A good is said to be *normal* if it has a downward sloping demand curve or, equivalently, a negative own price elasticity. Otherwise it is a *Giffen good* with an upward sloping demand curve (which is not inconsistent with the basic theory but is rare). A good is said to be *superior* if it has an upward sloping Engel curve or, equivalently, a positive income elasticity. Otherwise it is an *inferior good* with a downward sloping Engel curve. From the Slutsky conditions (7.2.15)

$$\frac{\partial x_1}{\partial p_1} \leqslant -\frac{\partial x_1}{\partial I} x_1 \qquad (7.2.23)$$

[11] For the generalization to n goods see Problem 7-F. For a discussion of the modern approach to the theory of the household using duality see Problem 7-H.

so a Giffen good (for which $\partial x_1/\partial p_1 > 0$) cannot be a superior good (for which $\partial x_1/\partial I > 0$). All goods can thus be classified as belonging to one of the three types indicated in Table 7.1. Some goods are superior and hence normal, so that if income rises, more is demanded, and if price rises, less is demanded. Examples are fresh milk and butter. Other goods are normal but inferior, so that if price rises, less is demanded, but if income rises, *less* is demanded. An example is condensed milk.[12] The last type is the Giffen good, for which if income rises, less is demanded, and if price rises, more is demanded. Examples might be certain staple foods among the very poor, such as bread, corn, potatoes, or rice.[13]

Table 7.1 The Three Types of Goods

Effect of Change in Income / *Effect of Change in Own Price*	*Superior* $\frac{\partial x_1}{\partial I} > 0$	*Inferior* $\frac{\partial x_1}{\partial I} < 0$
Normal $\frac{\partial x_1}{\partial p_1} < 0$	*Normal superior good* Examples: milk, butter	*Normal inferior good* Example: Condensed milk
Giffen $\frac{\partial x_1}{\partial p_1} > 0$	X	*Giffen good* Example: Staple foods among the very poor

7.3 Single demand equations vs. systems of demand equations

The application of econometrics to the theory of the household requires, in addition to data, a specific formal econometric model. The demand functions of the last section, equations (7.2.2), can be generalized for a consumer of n goods as

$$x_j = x_j(p_1, p_2, \ldots, p_j, \ldots, p_n, I), \qquad j = 1, 2, \ldots, n. \qquad *(7.3.1)$$

These n equations indicate the quantity demanded of each of the goods as a function of all prices and income.

Econometric studies of demand include both single demand equation studies and studies of systems of demand equations. A single demand equation study would select one equation from (7.3.1) and estimate its parameters. For example, taking the first equation, and adding a stochastic term, u_1, to account for

[12] For empirical evidence on fresh milk, butter, and condensed milk see Table 7.5.

[13] Quoting Marshall (1920): "... as Sir R. Giffen has pointed out, a rise in the price of bread makes so large a drain on the resources of the poorer laboring families . . . that they are forced to curtail their consumption of meat and the more expensive farinaceous foods: and, bread, being still the cheapest food which they can get and will take, they consume more, and not less of it. But such cases are rare . . . ."

omitted variables, misspecification of the equation, and errors in measuring variables, a single demand equation study would estimate

$$x_1 = x_1(p_1, p_2, \ldots, p_n, I, u_1) \qquad {}^*(7.3.2)$$

where the reason(s) for including the stochastic disturbance term would determine both the specification of the inclusion of u_1 and the method of estimation. A specialization of this equation is represented by partial equilibrium analysis and would involve the estimation of a demand curve or an Engel curve for the first good:

$$x_1 = D_1(p_1, u_1) = x_1(p_1, \bar{p}_2, \ldots, \bar{p}_n, \bar{I}, u_1) \qquad (7.3.3)$$

$$\bar{p}_1 x_1 = E_1(I, u_1) = \bar{p}_1 x_1(\bar{p}_1, \bar{p}_2, \ldots, \bar{p}_n, I, u_1). \qquad (7.3.4)$$

An example is the estimation of the price elasticity of demand for gasoline, as in Section 1.4. Of the nine conditions on demand functions introduced in the last section, only two are applicable to the case of a single demand equation, the homogeneity condition and the negativity condition, which in this case require that

$$\sum_{k=1}^{n} \frac{\partial x_1}{\partial p_k} p_k + \frac{\partial x_1}{\partial I} I = 0 \qquad (7.3.5)$$

$$\frac{\partial x_1}{\partial p_1} + \frac{\partial x_1}{\partial I} x_1 \leqslant 0. \qquad (7.3.6)$$

(The other conditions apply to two or more demand equations.)

An econometric study of the *system* of demand equations would estimate the complete system for a single household or group of households. A stochastic term is introduced in each equation, and the budget constraint is added, so the complete system consists of the $n + 1$ equations

$$\begin{aligned} x_j &= x_j(p_1, p_2, \ldots, p_n, I, u_j), \quad j = 1, 2, \ldots, n \\ \sum_{j=1}^{n} p_j x_j &= I \end{aligned} \qquad {}^*(7.3.7)$$

The next two sections consider single demand equations and systems of demand equations, respectively. They include discussions of both functional forms and specific studies.

7.4 Single demand equations

In order to estimate either the single demand equation (7.3.2) or the system of demand equations (7.3.7) it is necessary to specify a particular functional form for the general relationship indicated. A variety of functional forms have, in fact, been utilized in both cases. This section treats single demand equations; the next treats systems of demand equations.

Perhaps the simplest functional form for a single demand equation is the linear one. Such a *linear demand equation*, that for good 1, can be written[14]

$$x_1 = a_1 + b_1 p_1 + b_2 p_2 + \cdots + b_n p_n + c_1 I + u_1 \qquad *(7.4.1)$$

where, typically, the prices $p_1, p_2, \ldots, p_n$ and income I are treated as (exogenous) explanatory variables. This equation, or special cases of it, have been estimated in various studies.

One early study, by Schultz, estimated linear demand curves for agricultural products, treating per capita consumption as a linear function of the price of the product relative to a general price index and an annual time trend. For example, the estimated equation for sugar in the United States over the period 1896-1914 was[15]

$$x_t = 92.9 - \underset{(1.01)}{3.34 p_t} + \underset{(0.15)}{0.92 t}. \qquad (7.4.2)$$

The implied price elasticity of demand, evaluated at the mean value for price and quantity, was estimated as

$$\epsilon = \frac{\partial x}{\partial p}\frac{\bar{p}}{\bar{x}} = -3.34\frac{\bar{p}}{\bar{x}} = -0.26 \qquad (7.4.3)$$

where $\bar{p}$ and $\bar{x}$ are the mean values. Some price elasticities of demand estimated by Schultz for the United States, 1915-1929 (excluding 1917 to 1921) are reported in Table 7.2. In general he found that the demands for agricultural commodities were price inelastic, all reported elasticities in the table being, in absolute value, less than unity.

Early studies also estimated linear Engel curves. Allen and Bowley, for example, estimated the following linear Engel curve from cross-section data on 112 British city families in 1926:[16]

$$E_1 = 0.47I + 62.66. \qquad (7.4.4)$$

[14]One interpretation of this equation is that it is based on taking a Taylor's series approximation for (7.3.2) and dropping all nonlinear terms. Thus

$$x_1 \approx x_1(\bar{p}_1, \bar{p}_2, \ldots, \bar{p}_n, \bar{I}) + \frac{\partial x_1}{\partial p_1}(p_1 - \bar{p}_1) + \frac{\partial x_1}{\partial p_2}(p_2 - \bar{p}_2) + \cdots + \frac{\partial x_1}{\partial p_n}(p_n - \bar{p}_n) + \frac{\partial x_1}{\partial I}(I - \bar{I}).$$

[15]See Schultz (1938). The Schultz estimates have been rounded. Numbers in parentheses are standard errors. Note that Schultz does not use income as an explanatory variable.

[16]See Allen and Bowley (1935).

Here E_1 is measured as expenditure on food, rent, and clothing and I as total expenditure. The elasticity of these expenditures with respect to total expenditure, measured at the mean values, was 0.8.

A second specification of a functional form is the *semilogarithmic demand function*:

$$x_1 = a_1 + b_1 \ln p_1 + b_2 \ln p_2 + \cdots + b_n \ln p_n + c_1 \ln I + u_1. \quad (7.4.5)$$

The Engel curve for this function was utilized by Prais and Houthakker in their study of budgets of British middle-class families in 1938.[17] Some of the income elasticities they estimated are given in Table 7.3.

Table 7.2. Estimated Price Elasticities of Demand for the United States, 1915–1929 (excluding 1917–1921)

Commodity	*Price Elasticity of Demand*
Wheat	−0.08 ± 0.04
Sugar	−0.28 ± 0.09
Potatoes	−0.31 ± 0.30
Barley	−0.42 ± 0.20
Corn	−0.48 ± 0.15
Oats	−0.54 ± 0.42
Hay	−0.62 ± 0.28

Source Schultz (1938).

NOTE The error brackets are given by the standard errors.

Table 7.3 Estimated Income Elasticities of Demand for British Middle-Class Families, 1938

Commodity	*Income Elasticity of Demand*
Margarine	0.02 ± 0.06
Butter	0.35 ± 0.04
Rice	0.41 ± 0.08
Tea	0.68 ± 0.08
Coffee	1.42 ± 0.20
Condensed milk	−0.08 ± 0.18

Source Prais and Houthakker (1955).

NOTE The error brackets are given by the standard errors.

[17] See Prais and Houthakker (1955).

The demand for margarine was found to be essentially independent of income, while that for coffee was highly dependent on income. The income elasticity of tea was significantly lower than that for coffee, suggesting that coffee was more of a luxury good than tea for middle-class British families in 1938. Condensed milk was apparently an inferior good, with a negative income elasticity, a result consistent with other studies.

A third functional form and, in fact, the one that has been the most commonly used is the *log linear* or *constant elasticity form*. It specifies the demand function as

$$x_1 = A_1 p_1^{b_1} p_2^{b_2} \cdots p_n^{b_n} I^c e^{u_1}. \tag*{*(7.4.6)}$$

Taking logarithms leads to the log linear representation

$$\begin{aligned} \ln x_1 &= a_1 + b_1 \ln p_1 + b_2 \ln p_2 + \cdots \\ &\quad + b_n \ln p_n + c \ln I + u_1 \qquad (a_1 = \ln A_1) \end{aligned} \tag*{*(7.4.7)}$$

In particular it should be evident that the demand curve will be a line when plotted on double-log graph paper, the slope of the line being b_1, where b_1 is the elasticity of demand with respect to price:

$$b_1 = \epsilon_1 = \frac{\partial \ln x_1}{\partial \ln p_1} = \frac{\partial x_1}{\partial p_1} \frac{p_1}{x_1}. \tag*{*(7.4.8)}$$

All of the coefficients are in fact elasticities, where

$$b_j = \epsilon_{1j} = \frac{\partial \ln x_1}{\partial \ln p_j} = \frac{\partial x_1}{\partial p_j} \frac{p_j}{x_1}, \qquad j = 1, 2, \ldots, n \tag*{*(7.4.9)}$$

$$c = \eta_1 = \frac{\partial \ln x_1}{\partial \ln I} = \frac{\partial x_1}{\partial I} \frac{I}{x_1} \tag*{*(7.4.10)}$$

and a defining characteristic of this specification of the demand function is that all $n + 1$ price and income elasticities are constant.

An example of the log linear specification is the Houthakker study of Engel curves.[18] He estimated the following Engel curve for food, using 1950 data for United States urban households:

$$\begin{aligned} \ln E_1 = a + \underset{(0.002)}{0.69} \ln I + \underset{(0.002)}{0.22} \ln N \end{aligned} \tag{7.4.11}$$

[18] See Houthakker (1957). Results have been rounded. Data used in this study were group means of observations of individual households in United States cities, obtained from the Survey of Consumer Expenditure conducted by the Bureau of Labor Statistics.

where E_1 is household expenditure on food, I is total household expenditures, and N is the number of persons in the household. The implied income elasticity was estimated to be 0.69, which is less than one, as expected from Engel's law. The income elasticity was estimated to be less than one for both food and housing (0.89) but greater than one for clothing (1.28) and for other items of expenditure (1.25). The elasticity of demand with respect to the number of persons in the household was estimated to be 0.22, indicating, since it is less than one, that there are economies of scale in terms of family size.[19]

A second example of the log linear specification is the later Houthakker study of demand elasticites.[20] He considered the model for commodity j:

$$\ln x_j = a_j + \epsilon_j \ln p_j + \eta_j \ln I + \delta_j t + u_j \tag{7.4.12}$$

where x_j is per capita expenditure in constant prices, p_j is relative price, I is total per capita expenditure in constant prices, and t is time. The estimated coefficients ϵ_j and η_j provide direct estimates of price and income elasticities, respectively, and the estimated δ_j provides an estimate of the trend in demand, since

$$\delta_j = \frac{\partial \ln x_j}{\partial t} = \frac{1}{x_j}\frac{\partial x_j}{\partial t}. \tag{7.4.13}$$

Some of Houthakker's results are reported in Table 7.4. Note that for all countries food is income inelastic, as implied by Engel's law. It might also be noted that the income elasticity for food in the United States fell from the earlier estimate of 0.69 in 1950 to 0.32 here. This fall in the elasticity as average incomes rise is expected and is typically found. The table similarly indicates a lower income elasticity for food for higher-income countries. It also shows that durables tend to be income elastic and nondurables tend to be income inelastic (the exceptions: rent is income elastic in the United States, Canada, and Sweden, while clothing is income elastic in France and the Netherlands, the United Kingdom being a borderline case). It might also be noted that the estimated price elasticities are not as consistent as those for income; e.g., many have the wrong sign.

[19] Note that if the Engel curve were for *per capita* expenditure and such expenditure were independent of family size, then

$$\frac{E_1}{N} = AI^c$$

so that

$$\ln E_1 = a + c \ln I + \ln N$$

where the elasticity of total household demand with respect to family size is unity. In (7.4.11) the elasticity is less than unity, implying economies of scale.

[20] Houthakker (1965a).

Table 7.4. Estimated Price and Income Elasticities of Demand for Various Countries, 1948–1959

	Food		Clothing		Rent		Durables	
Country	Price	Income	Price	Income	Price	Income	Price	Income
United States	−0.34	0.32	0.42	0.78	0.08	1.67	1.09	2.03
Canada	−0.29	0.69	−0.38	−0.09	−0.09	1.27	0.96	3.44
Belgium	−0.69	0.92	0.32	0.06	0.05	0.33	0.44	2.23
France	−0.16	0.68	0.53	1.47	−0.17	0.87	−0.15	2.53
Italy	−0.26	0.78	−0.19	0.59	−0.10	0.70	0.41	2.72
Netherlands	0.59	0.57	0.47	1.81	0.36	0.32	−2.19	1.99
Sweden	0.06	0.38	−1.81	−0.94	−0.33	1.57	0.52	2.87
United Kingdom	0.12	0.73	−0.09	1.04	−0.19	0.66	−1.46	3.01
Combined (weighted average)	0.08	0.71	−0.10	0.71	−0.29	1.29	−0.12	2.36

Source Houthakker (1965a).

NOTE Here "income" refers to total expenditure. Results have been rounded.

A third example of the log linear specification is the study by Stone of demand functions in the United Kingdom.[21] His specification was similar to (7.4.12), of the form

$$\ln x_j = a_j + \epsilon_j \ln p_j + \sum_{j'} \epsilon_{jj'} \ln p_{j'} + \eta_j \ln I + \delta_j t + u_j \tag{7.4.14}$$

where ϵ_j and η_j are elasticities as in (7.4.12), δ_j is a time trend as in (7.4.12), and $\epsilon_{jj'}$ is the cross price elasticity of demand, as in (7.2.8). The sum in (7.4.14) is taken not over all commodities, but rather over those believed, on the basis of a priori reasoning or other studies, to be related to the good as complement or substitute goods. The x_j variable is per capita consumption, and I is per capita real income, relative to a general price index. The income elasticities were estimated from a cross-section sample of household budgets in the United Kingdom, 1937-1939, and these estimates were used in estimating the remaining coefficients in (7.4.14) on the basis of time-series data for the United Kingdom over the period 1920-1938. First differences were utilized to reduce first-order serial correlation of the stochastic disturbance term u_t. Table 7.5 presents some of Stone's results for food items.

For fresh milk Stone found that demand was price inelastic and exhibited a positive income elasticity, both elasticities being approximately 0.5. Thus a 10% increase in price would reduce demand for fresh milk by 5%, and a 10% increase in income would increase demand by 5%.[22] The cross price elasticities indicate

[21] Stone (1954a). A similar specification was used in Wold and Jureen (1953).

[22] The income elasticity estimate of 0.50 for fresh milk is consistent with the range of 0.35 to 0.53 for the income elasticity of dairy produce given by Prais and Houthakker (1955) in their study of family budgets based on United Kingdom data of 1937 to 1939.

Table 7.5. Estimated Demand Elasticities for the United Kingdom, 1920–1938

Commodity	*Own Price Elasticity* ϵ_j	*Cross Price Elasticities* $\epsilon_{jj'}$	*Income Elasticity* η_j	*Trend Coefficient* δ_j	R^2 / d
Fresh milk	−0.49 (0.13)	0.73 Beef and veal (0.15) −0.23 Cream (0.07)	0.50 (0.18)	0.004 (0.004)	0.81 2.01
Condensed milk	−1.23 (0.32)	2.25 Fresh milk (0.53) 0.80 Margarine (0.23) 1.06 Tea (0.35) 0.43 Cheese (0.19)	−0.53 (0.18)	−0.047 (0.016)	0.82 1.85
Butter	−0.41 (0.13)	−0.21 Flour (0.11) 0.56 Cakes and (0.26) biscuits 0.63 Carcass meat (0.30)	0.37 (0.08)	0.040 (0.009)	0.61 1.84
Margarine	0.01 (0.17)	1.01 Butter (0.17) 1.02 Chocolate and (0.26) confectionary −0.46 Cakes and (0.31) biscuits	−0.16 (0.11)	0.016 (0.010)	0.77 1.76
Tea	−0.26 (0.07)	0.14 Coffee (0.08) 0.08 Beer (0.05)	0.04 (0.04)	0.003 (0.003)	0.56 2.15

Source Stone (1954a), reported by Phlips (1974)

NOTE Income elasticities are based on budget surveys of 1937–1939. Other elasticities are based on time-series data over the entire period.

that beef is a substitute for milk (e.g., both provide protein for the diet) and that cream is a complement for milk.[23] Increasing the price of beef, which lowers the

[23] A better measure of substitutes and complements, which is usually considered the theoretically correct measure, is the *compensated* cross price elasticities, compensated for changes in real income. The uncompensated cross price elasticities, as reported in Table 7.5, include income as well as substitution effects. Since real rather than money income is used, however, the price elasticities are closer to compensated than to uncompensated elasticities.

amount of beef demanded, increases the amount of milk demanded. Increasing the price of cream, however, lowers the amount of cream demanded but also reduces the amount of milk demanded. The trend coefficient shows a slight increase in per capita consumption after allowing for price and income effects.

The results for the other goods can be contrasted to those for fresh milk. For example, the demand for condensed milk is elastic; it is an inferior good, as also found by Prais and Houthakker; it exhibits a secular decline over time, and fresh milk, margarine, tea, and cheese are all substitutes. Butter is more like fresh milk in terms of own price and income elasticities, has a more significant positive trend, and is a complement with flour (e.g., they often go into recipes together) and a substitute for cakes and biscuits and carcass meat. The demand for margarine is highly inelastic, with a somewhat negative income elasticity. Butter and chocolate and confectionary are substitutes, while cakes and biscuits are complements. The demand for tea is price and income inelastic, and coffee and beer are substitutes. In general, demands for most commodities are both price inelastic and income inelastic; of 32 reported income elasticities 23 were in the range 0 to 1, while of 36 reported own price elasticities 26 were in the range 0 to –1.

A fourth example of the log linear specification is the study by Fox of demand functions in the United States.[24] His approach was based on the *inverse demand function*, in which the demand function is solved for price. The specification was

$$\ln p_j = \alpha_j + \beta_j \ln x_j + \gamma_j \ln I + \varphi_j \ln z_j + u_j \tag{7.4.15}$$

where z_j represents variables other than quantity and income that could lead to a shift in the demand curve. This equation can be derived from the usual log linear specification, e.g., (7.4.12), by solving for $\ln p_j$, and estimates of its parameters can be used to make inferences concerning the price and income elasticities of demand.[25] Its use reflects the assumption that quantity, rather than price, is exogenous. This assumption may be valid in agricultural markets, for which the quantity supplied depends on exogenous variables, such as climate conditions (e.g., rainfall in the prototype micro model) or lagged endogenous variables, such as the price of the previous year. Price is then determined, e.g., in commodity markets, on the basis of the available quantity (the harvest), income, and other variables, as specified in (7.4.15). Some of the implied elasticities of demand are reported in Table 7.6. In general, the estimated demands for farm products are price inelastic, as in the Schultz and Stone studies. Fox also found that those commodities that are price elastic, such as veal, chicken, apples, and sweet potatoes, tend also to be income elastic.[26] Thus such commodities are responsive

[24] See Fox (1958).

[25] See Problem 7-J.

[26] Note that Engel's law that food is income inelastic does not mean that *all* foods are income inelastic. It might also be noted that several of the results for income elasticities are consistent with those given by Prais and Houthakker (1955) for a different country (United Kingdom) over a shorter period (1937–1939) and using a different technique of estimation. For example, Prais and Houthakker report a range of 0.66 to 1.20 for income elasticities for fruit and a range of 0.40 to 0.62 for vegetables. The Prais and Houthakker estimates of income elasticities for meat, 0.44 to 0.69, are, however, lower than those estimated by Fox.

to economic factors, responding to both price and income.

Table 7.6. Estimates of Demand Elasticities for the United States, 1922–1941, Based on the Inverse Demand Function

Commodity	*Price Elasticity*	*Income Elasticity*
Pork	–0.65	1.06
Beef	–0.84	1.07
Veal	–1.22	1.59
Lamb	–0.67	0.73
Chicken	–1.61	1.71
Turkey	–0.83	0.88
Eggs	–0.34	0.49
Fluid milk	–0.67	0.50
Apples	–1.27	1.32
Oranges	–0.62	0.83
Potatoes	–0.28	0.34
Sweet potatoes	–1.30	1.15

Source: Fox (1958), as calculated by Cramer (1969).

7.5 Systems of demand equations[27]

Systems of demand functions involve the n demand equations

$$x_j = x_j(p_1, p_2, \ldots, p_n, I, u_j), \qquad j = 1, 2, \ldots, n \qquad *(7.5.1)$$

which, together with the budget equation, which the n demand equations are assumed to satisfy, form a complete system, as in (7.3.7). In such systems the variables $x_1, x_2, \ldots, x_n$, the quantities consumed of each of the goods, are typically treated as endogenous variables, while the variables $p_1, p_2, \ldots, p_n$, the prices of each of the goods, and I, the income, are typically treated as exogenous variables. The estimation of the complete system is important in identifying the interdependence among the goods, specifically the effects of changes in prices of certain goods on the demand for other goods.

Various functional forms have been employed in estimating the system (7.5.1).[28] One such functional form is the *linear system*:

$$x_j = a_j + \sum_k b_{jk} p_k + c_j I + u_j, \qquad j = 1, 2, \ldots, n \qquad *(7.5.2)$$

[27] See Brown and Deaton (1972), Powell (1974), and Barten (1977).

[28] See the references cited in the previous footnote. See also Problem 7-O for a general additive utility function that implies several possible functional forms for the system of demand functions, depending on the parameters. Note that the restrictions on demand functions imply restrictions on the parameters in (7.5.2) and (7.5.3). See Problem 7-K.

and another is the *log linear* or *constant elasticity* system for which

$$\ln x_j = a_j' + \sum_k b_{jk}' \ln p_k + c_j' \ln I + u_j', \qquad j = 1, 2, \ldots, n. \qquad *(7.5.3)$$

Each of these is a straightforward generalization of the corresponding single-equation demand function.

One of the most widely used functional forms, however, is the *linear expenditure system*, which can be written[29]

$$p_j x_j = p_j x_j^0 + \beta_j \left(I - \sum_{k=1}^{n} p_k x_k^0\right), \qquad j = 1, 2, \ldots, n$$
$$\text{where } x_j - x_j^0 > 0, \; 0 < \beta_j < 1, \; \Sigma \beta_j = 1 \qquad *(7.5.4)$$

This system can be interpreted as stating that expenditure on good j, given as $p_j x_j$, can be decomposed into two components. The first is the expenditure on a certain "base amount" x_j^0 of good j, which is the minimum expenditure to which the consumer is committed. The second is a fraction β_j of the so-called "supernumerary income," defined as the income above the "subsistence income" $\Sigma p_k x_k^0$ needed to purchase base amounts of all goods. These two components correspond, respectively, to committed and discretionary expenditure on good j. Dividing through (7.5.4) by the price p_j gives the corresponding system of demand equations:

$$x_j = x_j^0 + \frac{\beta_j}{p_j}\left(I - \Sigma p_k x_k^0\right) \qquad *(7.5.5)$$

which is hyperbolic in own price and linear in income. The demand curve can be written, again using bars to denote variables held constant, as in (7.2.3), as

$$x_j = x_j^0 (1 - \beta_j) + \beta_j \left(\bar{I} - \sum_{k \neq j} \bar{p}_k x_k^0\right) p_j^{-1} \qquad (7.5.6)$$

which, aside from the translation of the axis by the term $x_j^0 (1 - \beta_j)$, represents a hyperbola in the (x_j, p_j) plane of Figure 7.2. The Engel curve is of the form

$$E_j = \bar{p}_j x_j = \left(\bar{p}_j x_j^0 - \beta_j \Sigma \bar{p}_k x_k^0\right) + \beta_j I \qquad (7.5.7)$$

and is thus a linear relationship in the (I, E_j) plane of Figure 7.3.

The linear expenditure system is widely used for three reasons. First, it has a straightforward and reasonable interpretation as given after (7.5.4). Second, it is one of the only systems that automatically satisfies all nine theoretical restrictions

[29] See Stone (1954b, 1972), Stone, Brown, and Rowe (1965), Pollak and Wales (1969), Phlips (1974), Deaton (1975), and Barten (1977). For a generalization see Brown and Heien (1972). The original presentation of the linear expenditure system was in Klein and Rubin (1947–8), and the interpretation given below (7.5.4) was provided in Samuelson (1947–8).

in Section 9.2 on systems of demand equations. Third, it can be derived from a specific utility function.[30] The system is estimated from data on quantities x_j and prices p_j of the n goods and data on income I (or total expenditure). The parameters that are estimated are the n *base quantities* $x_1^0, x_2^0, \ldots, x_n^0$ and the n *marginal budget shares* $\beta_1, \beta_2, \ldots, \beta_n$. The linear expenditure system has been used in several empirical studies of demand, and it and the constant elasticity system are two of the most widely used specifications employed in estimating systems of demand equations.[31]

The estimation of the linear expenditure system presents certain complications because, while it is linear in the variables, it is nonlinear in the parameters, involving the product of β_j and each x_k^0 in (7.5.4) and (7.5.5). There are, in fact, several approaches to the estimation of this system. One approach determines the base quantities x_k^0 on the basis of extraneous information or prior judgments. The system (7.5.4) then implies that expenditure on each good in excess of base expenditure $(p_j x_j - p_j x_j^0)$ is a linear function of supernumerary income, so each of the marginal budget shares β_j can be estimated using the usual single-equation simple linear regression methods. A second approach reverses this procedure by first determining the marginal budget shares β_j on the basis of extraneous information or prior judgments [or Engel curve studies, which estimate the β_j from the relationship between expenditure and income, as in (7.5.7)]. It then estimates the base quantities x_k^0 by estimating the system in which the expenditure less the marginal budget share times income $(p_j x_j - \beta_j I)$ is a linear function of all prices. The total sum of squared errors—over all goods as well as all observations—is then minimized by choice of the x_k^0. A third approach is an iterative one, using the estimates of the β_j conditional on the x_k^0 (as in the first approach) and the estimates of the x_k^0 conditional on the β_j (as in the second approach) iteratively so as to minimize the total sum of squares. The process would continue, choosing β_j based on the last estimated x_k^0 and then choosing x_k^0 based on the last estimated β_j until convergence of the sum of squares is obtained. A fourth approach selects β_j and x_j^0 simultaneously by setting up a grid of possible values for the $2n - 1$ parameters (the -1 based upon the fact that the β_j sum to unity) and obtaining that point on the grid where the total sum of squares over all goods and all observations is minimized.

Estimates of the linear expenditure system for the United States, Canada, and the United Kingdom from the Goldberger and Gamaletsos study are presented in

[30] The specific utility function from which the linear expenditure system can be derived is the Stone-Geary utility function (also called the Klein-Rubin utility function) given in Problem 7-M, of which a particular case appears in Problem 7-I and a generalization appears in Problem 7-O.

[31] For the constant-elasticity system (7.5.3) see Sato (1972). Other approaches used to estimate systems of demand equations are the "indirect addilog system" of Houthakker (1965b) and the "Rotterdam system" of Theil (1967, 1975) and Barten (1968). It might be noted that there are, in general, three ways of specifying systems of demand functions. One is based on a specified utility function, as in the linear expenditure system and in Problem 7-I. Another is based on a specified indirect utility function, as discussed in Problem 7-H, such as the indirect addilog system. The third is to specify directly a form for the demand functions, such as the constant elasticity system and the Rotterdam system, which is a variant of the constant elasticity system. See Barten (1977).

Table 7.7[32] This table reports estimated base quantities, measured in units of the domestic currency, of expenditures per capita, and estimated marginal budget shares, which sum to unity. For the United States, for example, since the units of measurement are thousands of dollars, base quantities are \$330 worth of food per capita, \$140 worth of clothing, etc. According to the marginal budget shares, 8.1% of income over supernumerary income goes to food, 5.5% to clothing, etc. For all three countries the base quantities for clothing, rent, and durables were similar and significantly lower than the base quantity for food, as might be expected. Leaving aside the heterogeneous "other" category, the marginal budget shares indicate that in the United States and Canada incremental income (above supernumerary income) tends to go for rent, while in the United Kingdom such income tends to go for durables.

Table 7.8 reports, from the same study, elasticities of demand estimated at mean values for all three countries (all entries are percentages and thus should be multiplied by 10^{-2}; e.g., for the United States the income elasticity of food was estimated to be 0.35). The results for the allocation of incremental income to rent in the United States and Canada and to durables in the United Kingdom are further indicated by the high income elasticities (elasticities with respect to total expenditure). The own price elasticities (on the diagonals) are all rather low, the highest (in absolute value) own price elasticity being –0.72 for rent in Canada. According to the cross price elasticities, again leaving aside "other," in general only one price influences the demand for other goods, namely the price of food.

Table 7.7 Estimates of the Linear Expenditure System for the United States, Canada, and the United Kingdom, 1950-1961

Country / *Commodity Group*	*United States* x_j^0	*United States* β_j	*Canada* x_j^0	*Canada* β_j	*United Kingdom* x_j^0	*United Kingdom* β_j
1. Food	0.33	0.081	0.19	0.177	0.21	0.172
2. Clothing	0.14	0.055	0.09	0.029	0.08	0.130
3. Rent	0.14	0.190	0.06	0.279	0.06	0.052
4. Durables	0.15	0.096	0.07	0.133	0.06	0.269
5. Other	0.52	0.578	0.32	0.382	0.30	0.377

Source Goldberger and Gamaletsos (1970).

NOTE x_j^0 = base quantity; β_j = marginal budget share. For all countries units of measurement are thousands of U.S. dollars, where use has been made of the 1961 exchange rates of 98.73 U.S. cents per Canadian dollar and 280.27 U.S. cents per U.K. pound sterling.

There are several difficulties in actually estimating systems of demand equations, such as the linear expenditure system. One such difficulty is the multicollinearity among the prices, which all tend to move together. This difficulty is

[32] See Goldberger and Gamaletsos (1970). They obtained estimates of the linear expenditure system for 13 OECD countries. They also estimated a constant-elasticity system, using the same data, and obtained estimates of elasticities that were, in general, similar to those reported in Table 7.8 for the linear expenditure system.

Table 7.8. **Estimates from the Linear Expenditure System of Elasticities of Demand for the United States, Canada, and the United Kingdom, 1950–1961 (in percentage terms)**

Country / Elasticity / Commodity Group	*United States*						*Canada*						*United Kingdom*					
	Income Elasticity	*Price Elasticities*					*Income Elasticity*	*Price Elasticities*					*Income Elasticity*	*Price Elasticities*				
		1	2	3	4	5		1	2	3	4	5		1	2	3	4	5
1. Food	35	−13	−3	−3	−3	−12	75	−37	−7	−4	−4	−22	57	−16	−6	−5	−5	−25
2. Clothing	56	−12	−13	−5	−5	−20	29	−5	−12	−2	−2	−8	128	−39	−10	−11	−11	−57
3. Rent	154	−34	−14	−37	−15	−54	193	−35	−17	−72	−12	−57	60	−18	−6	−3	−5	−26
4. Durables	85	−19	−8	−8	−20	−30	126	−23	−11	−7	−48	−37	333	−101	−35	−29	−20	−147
5. Other	134	−30	−12	−13	−13	−66	92	−16	−8	−5	−6	−56	88	−27	−9	−8	−8	−36

Source Goldberger and Gamaletsos (1970).

NOTE All entries are percentages and thus should be multiplied by 10^{-2}. All elasticities are measured at mean values. The price elasticities are $\epsilon_{jj'}$, where j is the row category of good and j' is the column category of good (indicated by number). The circled elements along the diagonal, ϵ_{jj}, are own price elasticities, ϵ_j.

partly offset by the constraints imposed on the system by theory, as summarized in Section 7.2. Three additional difficulties, which apply both to individual demand equations and systems of demand equations, are identification, aggregation, and dynamic factors, the subjects of the next three sections of this chapter.

7.6 Identification

An important question in estimating demand relationships is that of *identification*: has the demand equation been identified and, in particular, can it be distinguished from the supply equation?[33] Consider, for example, the simple demand-supply system for a single good:

$$q^D = a - bp + u^D \quad (7.6.1)$$

$$q^S = c + dp + u^S \quad (7.6.2)$$

$$q^D = q^S \quad (7.6.3)$$

previously treated in Section 2.10. This system consists of linear demand and supply curves and an equilibrium condition equating demand to supply. The system is, in general, *not* identified, and Figure 7.4 illustrates the difficulties

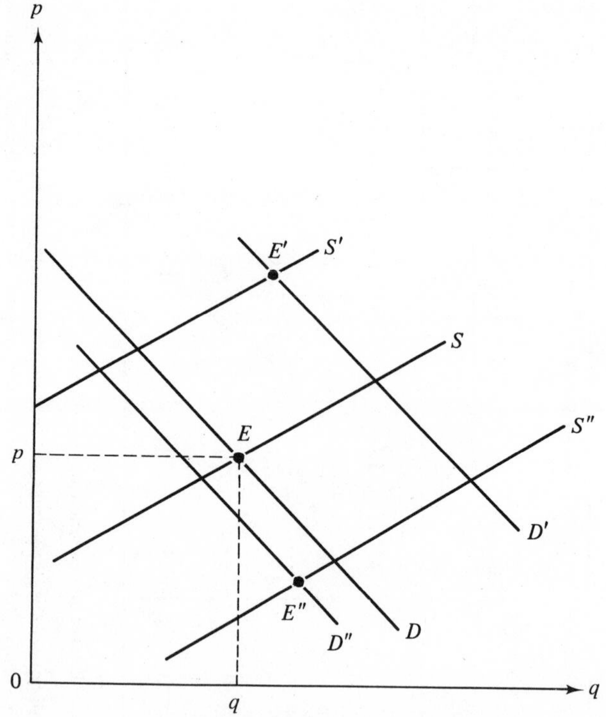

Figure 7.4 The Problem of Lack of Identification

[33] See Section 2.10 and Chapter 10.

caused by underidentification of each of the two behavioral equations of (7.6.1)-(7.6.3). Suppose D and S are the demand and supply curves, respectively, in one year. They define an equilibrium at E, consisting of q and p as quantity and price, respectively. In the next year both stochastic terms have values different from their previous values, e.g., because of changes in variables not explicitly included in the model. Such variables may include income and climate, as in the prototype micro model of Section 2.6. The result is that the demand curve shifts to D', and the supply curve shifts to S'. The new equilibrium is at E'. Similar shifts occur in the next year, leading to the quantity-price pair at E''.

Now suppose one were performing an econometric study and attempting to determine the parameters a, b, c, and d in the simple demand-supply system. Clearly one does not, in fact, know or observe the demand curves or the supply curves of Figure 7.4—they are to be determined. The data are simply the quantity-price pairs given by E, E', and E''. Fitting a curve to these points would not permit estimation of either the demand or the supply curve. Nor is the problem alleviated by more data; estimating the relationship determined by any number of data points would not provide enough information upon which to estimate the values of the four parameters in (7.6.1)-(7.6.3).

One of two approaches is generally utilized to overcome this problem of lack of identification. The first is to obtain identification by zero restrictions. This approach adds relevant variables to certain equations but not to others in order to differentiate the demand equation from the supply equation and thus to estimate each. One example is the prototype micro model of Section 2.6, which may be written

$$q = \gamma_1 p + \beta_1 I + \delta_1 + \epsilon^D \qquad (7.6.4)$$

$$q = \gamma_2 p + \beta_3 r + \delta_2 + \epsilon^S. \qquad (7.6.5)$$

This model is exactly identified, as discussed in Section 2.10, since it includes income as an exogenous variable in the demand equation that does not appear in the supply equation and it includes rainfall as an exogenous variable in the supply equation that does not appear in the demand equation. This model can be estimated from observed data on quantity, price, income, and rainfall. In terms of Figure 7.4 the identification problem is overcome because at least one of the factors causing each of the curves to shift has been explicitly included in the model. To the extent that the shifts in demand are based upon changes in income and shifts in supply are based upon changes in rainfall, the magnitude of the shifts can be taken into account from knowledge of these two exogenous variables.

A model similar to the prototype micro model was used by Fox to estimate demand for and supply of farm products.[34] His structural equations for the market for pork were

$$\ln p = \alpha_1 \ln q + \alpha_2 \ln I + u^D \qquad (7.6.6)$$

$$\ln q = \alpha_3 \ln p + \alpha_4 \ln z + u^S. \qquad (7.6.7)$$

[34] See Fox (1953).

The first equation is a constant elasticity demand function, solved for log p rather than log q, as in the inverse-demand-function approach of (7.4.15). It is the same as (7.6.4), except variables are measured in terms of logarithmic deviations from their means (so the constant term falls out) and it is solved for log p. The second equation is a supply equation giving the quantity as a log linear function of price and production (z), assumed exogenous. Fox estimated the reduced-form equations using U.S. data 1922–1941 on per capita consumption (q) and production (z) of pork, on per capita income (I), and on retail price of pork (p). He obtained the following estimated reduced-form equations:

$$\ln p = \underset{(0.10)}{0.97} \ln I - \underset{(0.11)}{0.96} \ln z, \qquad R^2 = 0.92 \tag{7.6.8}$$

$$\ln q = -\underset{(0.06)}{0.06} \ln I + \underset{(0.07)}{0.84} \ln z, \qquad R^2 = 0.91. \tag{7.6.9}$$

The structural estimates were then obtained from the relationships between the structural and reduced-form coefficients.[35] In this case the estimated structural-form equations were

$$\ln p = -1.14 \ln q + 0.90 \ln z \tag{7.6.10}$$

$$\ln q = -0.062 \ln p + 0.77 \ln z. \tag{7.6.11}$$

The implied estimates of the price and income elasticities of demand for pork are obtained by taking the reciprocals of the estimated coefficients in (7.6.10), given as

$$\epsilon = \frac{-1}{1.14} = -0.88, \qquad \eta = \frac{1}{0.90} = 1.11. \tag{7.6.12}$$

Another approach to identification utilizes relative variances. Suppose that the variance of the stochastic term for the demand equation in (7.6.1), σ_D^2, is considerably smaller than the corresponding variance for the supply equation, σ_S^2, in (7.6.2):

$$\sigma_D^2 \ll \sigma_S^2. \tag{7.6.13}$$

Then the simple demand-supply system can be depicted as in Figure 7.5. In this case estimating a line through the observed quantity-price combinations yields an approximation to the demand curve. This is the case in which the demand

[35] The reduced-form equations can be written

$$\ln p = \frac{\alpha_2}{1 - \alpha_1 \alpha_3} \ln I + \frac{\alpha_1 \alpha_4}{1 - \alpha_1 \alpha_3} \ln z$$

$$\ln q = \frac{\alpha_2 \alpha_3}{1 - \alpha_1 \alpha_3} \ln I + \frac{\alpha_4}{1 - \alpha_1 \alpha_3} \ln z$$

by solving the structural equations simultaneously and omitting the disturbances. Thus the ratio of the two coefficients of ln I yields $\hat{\alpha}_3$, while the ratio of the two coefficients of ln z yields $\hat{\alpha}_1$. The coefficient of ln I in the first equation times $1 - \hat{\alpha}_1 \hat{\alpha}_3$ yields $\hat{\alpha}_2$, while the coefficient of ln z in the second equation times $1 - \hat{\alpha}_1 \hat{\alpha}_3$ yields $\hat{\alpha}_4$.

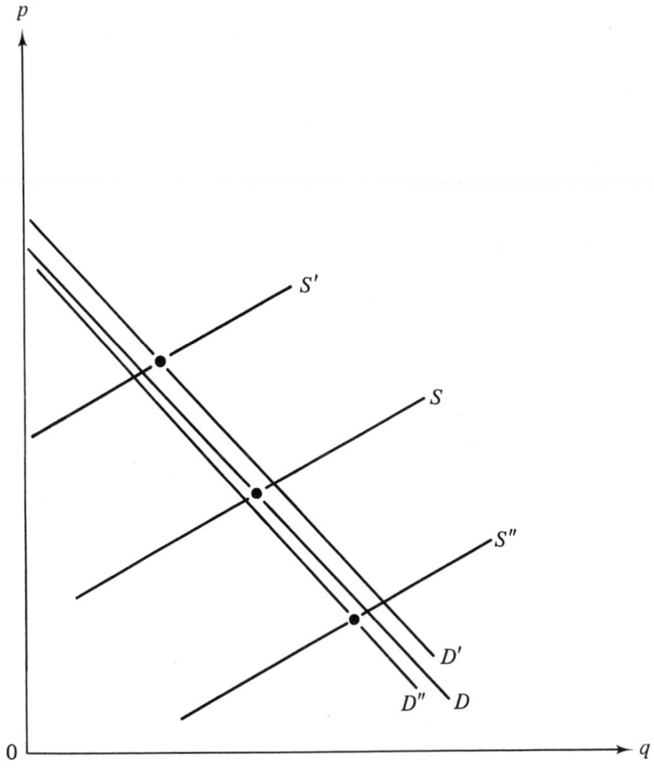

Figure 7.5 Identification Achieved via Relative Variances, where $\sigma_D^2 \ll \sigma_S^2$

curve is identified via relative variances. An example is the work of Schultz, discussed in Section 7.4, who estimated demand curves for agricultural commodities. For an agricultural commodity the variance of demand is likely to be rather low, since these commodities enter into basic foodstuffs. At the same time, the variance of supply is likely to be rather large because of the influence of weather conditions on harvests. Thus it can be argued that Schultz was, in fact, estimating demand curves, rather than supply curves or some combination of demand and supply curves, because of the relative variances.

7.7 Aggregation

Another issue in empirical work on household demand is that of aggregation.[36] The basic theory of demand, as developed in Section 7.2, refers to a single consuming unit, such as an individual or family. Empirical work, however,

[36] Basic references on aggregation are Theil (1954) and Green (1964).

usually involves market phenomena, such as the total quantity purchased in a country. The problem of aggregation is that of reconciling the two. Usually certain conditions must be met in order to overcome the problem of aggregation.

A simple example of the aggregation problem and conditions of aggregation is that of the linear demand equation (7.4.1). Considering only own price and income as explanatory variables, the equation is written for individual household h, designated by a superscript, as

$$x_1^h = a^h + b^h p_1 + c^h I^h + u_1^h, \qquad h = 1, 2, \ldots, H \tag{7.7.1}$$

where there are H households. Under what conditions can these H demand equations be aggregated into a similar demand equation for the market as a whole? Summing over the H households,

$$\Sigma\, x_1^h = \Sigma\, a^h + \Sigma\, b^h p_1 + \Sigma\, c^h I^h + \Sigma\, u_1^h \tag{7.7.2}$$

where all sums are over h, from 1 to H. The left-hand side is the aggregate quantity demanded of good 1:

$$x_1 = \Sigma\, x_1^h. \tag{7.7.3}$$

On the right-hand side the individual intercepts aggregate to a market intercept:

$$a = \Sigma\, a^h. \tag{7.7.4}$$

The price p_1 is assumed common to all, so

$$bp_1 = p_1\, \Sigma\, b^h \quad \text{where} \quad b = \Sigma\, b^h. \tag{7.7.5}$$

The aggregate stochastic term is the sum of the individual terms:

$$u_1 = \Sigma\, u_1^h. \tag{7.7.6}$$

The term that creates an aggregation problem, however, is that involving income, since both c^h and I^h, in general, vary from one household to another. If, however, it is assumed that the c^h are the same for all households,

$$c^h = c, \qquad \text{all } h \tag{7.7.7}$$

then

$$cI = \Sigma\, c^h I^h \quad \text{where} \quad I = \Sigma\, I^h \tag{7.7.8}$$

where I is aggregate income of all households. Under the assumption (7.7.7) the distribution of income will not affect aggregate demand, and the individual demand equations can be aggregated into the market demand curve:

$$x_1 = a + bp_1 + cI + u_1. \tag{7.7.9}$$

Here the assumption that the response of demand to income is the same for all households is the aggregation condition for this problem. The condition can be stated as the condition that the Engel curves are all linear, with identical slopes across households. Under this condition the market behavior of an aggregate of different households is the same as if it were the market behavior of a single representative household.

In general, aggregation conditions must be imposed in order to develop aggregate demand equations from individual household demand equations. Such conditions usually require that if an explanatory variable changes among different micro units (e.g., income), but the coefficients are the same for each such unit [as in (7.7.7)], then the macro relationship is of the same form, where the explanatory variable is the sum of the micro variables [as in (7.7.8)]. They also require that if an explanatory variable is the same for all the micro units (e.g., price), then the macro relationship is of the same linear form but the coefficient in the macro relationship is the sum of the coefficients for the micro relationships [as in (7.7.5)]. In practice, however, such aggregation conditions are usually ignored, with the totality of various individual households treated as if it were a single "representative" household. It should also be noted that there is usually an aggregation over commodities as well as households; empirical studies almost always refer to a group of individuals consuming not specific commodities but groups of commodities, as indicated in the above tables. In fact most empirical studies treat fewer than ten commodities, which clearly entails aggregation of individual commodities into broad commodity groups.

An important practical implication of the problem of aggregation involves the type of data utilized and the nature of the hypotheses being tested. To the extent that the data utilized in an econometric study are aggregate data, constructed either by the investigator or by others, such data have typically been constructed on the basis of certain assumptions, which take the role of maintained hypotheses. These assumptions are illustrated by the above conditions of aggregation. It would then be inappropriate to test for these conditions, which would, in effect, amount to testing a maintained hypothesis. Nevertheless, such studies are often conducted. The investigator must be aware of the assumptions that are built into the data and avoid testing for them. A specific example is presented in the next chapter [see (8.3.25) to (8.3.31)].

7.8 Dynamic demand analysis

So far the specifications of demand relationships have been largely static, referring to situations in which time plays no essential role. There are several ways of extending these relationships to situations in which time enters essentially—that is, to *dynamic demand functions*.

Perhaps the most straightforward of the dynamic specifications is that of a *time trend* in the demand function. An example is the log linear (constant elasticity) model (7.4.12), where δ_j is the time trend, as given in (7.4.13), with dimension (1/time). This demand function shifts out over time at the rate $100\delta_j$ percent per time period. Another example is the linear expenditure system

(7.5.4), in which the base quantitites and marginal budget shares change over time.[37]

A second approach to dynamic demand analysis involves *lagged variables*. An example is the *cobweb model*, according to which the quantity demanded depends on current price, while the quantity supplied depends on lagged price—that is, the price of a previous time period. Such a model may be a valid representation of situations in which there is a significant time lag in the production process. In such a situation, decisions to initiate production depend on the then current price, so the amount supplied, at the end of the production process, depends on the lagged price. Such an approach has been utilized in the market for certain agricultural commodities and for construction, such as house building and shipbuilding. In the simplest linear case without stochastic disturbances the model is of the form

$$q_t^D = a - bp_t \tag*{*(7.8.1)}$$

$$q_t^S = c + dp_{t-1} \tag*{*(7.8.2)}$$

where q_t^D and q_t^S are the quantities demanded and supplied, respectively, at time t, and p_t and p_{t-1} are current and lagged prices, respectively. At an equilibrium $p_t = p_{t-1} = \bar{p}$, and demand equals supply, so

$$q^D = a - b\bar{p} = c + d\bar{p} = q^S \tag{7.8.3}$$

$$\bar{p} = \frac{a - c}{b + d}. \tag{7.8.4}$$

Setting demand equal to supply in each period leads to

$$a - bp_t = c + dp_{t-1} \tag{7.8.5}$$

implying the first-order linear difference equation

$$p_t + \frac{d}{b}\, p_{t-1} = \frac{a - c}{b}. \tag*{*(7.8.6)}$$

Solving this equation yields[38]

$$p_t = \left(-\frac{d}{b}\right)^t + \bar{p}. \tag*{*(7.8.7)}$$

Thus p_t approaches $\bar{p}$ in the limit (as $t \to \infty$) provided $d < b$—that is, provided the slope of the supply curve is less than the (absolute value of the) slope of the

[37] See Stone (1966).

[38] See Allen (1959). Since (7.8.6) is a linear difference equation, its solution is the sum of a homogeneous solution (of the form m^t) and a particular solution (here the constant $\bar{p}$).

demand curve. Such a case is illustrated in Figure 7.6, where, because of the convention of setting q on the horizontal axis, the slope is relative to the *horizontal*,

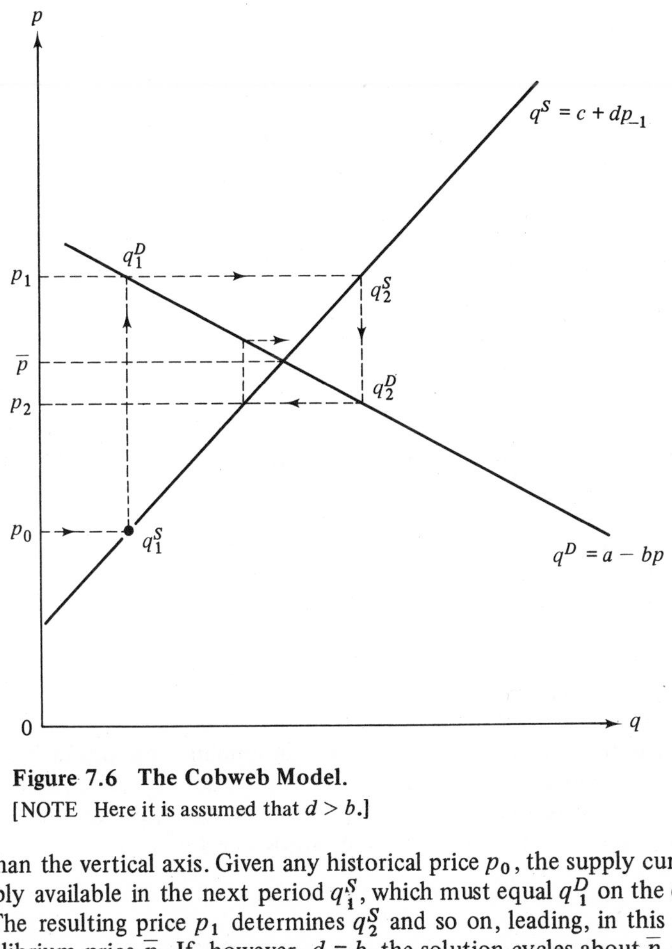

Figure 7.6 The Cobweb Model.
[NOTE Here it is assumed that $d > b$.]

rather than the vertical axis. Given any historical price p_0, the supply curve gives the supply available in the next period q_1^S, which must equal q_1^D on the demand curve. The resulting price p_1 determines q_2^S and so on, leading, in this case, to the equilibrium price $\bar{p}$. If, however, $d = b$, the solution cycles about $\bar{p}$, while if $d > b$ the solution explodes, moving further and further away from $\bar{p}$.

A third approach to dynamic demand analysis is the specification of a *distributed lag* relationship. Such a relationship is often utilized in studying the demand for consumer durables, such as houses, automobiles, and household appliances, which are goods that last more than one year. The analysis of consumer durables is usually based upon a *partial adjustment model.*[39] Letting x_t be the stock of the durable and x_t^* be the desired stock at time t, the stock adjustment model is

$$x_t - x_{t-1} = \gamma(x_t^* - x_{t-1}) + \nu_t, \quad 0 < \gamma < 1. \tag{7.8.8}$$

[39] See Section 6.7, Harberger, Ed. (1960), and Stone and Rowe (1960). See also Nerlove (1958), as discussed in Problem 7-U.

According to the model, the change in the stock of the durable good is proportional to the gap between the current desired and the past actual stock level. Here γ is the adjustment coefficient, indicating the speed of adjustment, and v_t is the stochastic disturbance term. Assuming that the desired stock is a linear function of price p and income I,

$$x_t^* = a + bp_t + cI_t \tag{7.8.9}$$

leads to

$$x_t = (1 - \gamma)x_{t-1} + a\gamma + b\gamma p_t + c\gamma I_t + v_t. \tag{7.8.10}$$

This equation is equivalent to a distributed lag model of the Koyck type, where

$$x_t = b \sum_{j=0}^{\infty} \gamma(1 - \gamma)^j p_{t-j} + c \sum_{j=0}^{\infty} \gamma(1 - \gamma)^j I_{t-j} + u_t \tag{7.8.11}$$

indicating the dependence of the current stock of the durable on current and all past levels of prices and income. The coefficients b and c are long-run coefficients, showing the impact of price and income, respectively. The coefficients $b\gamma$ and $c\gamma$ are the corresponding short-run coefficients.[40]

The stock adjustment model was used by Chow to study the demand for new automobiles in the United States.[41] Using data covering the years 1921-1953, he found that

$$\underset{}{x_t} = 0.078 - \underset{(0.047)}{0.231S_{t-1}} - \underset{(0.0026)}{0.0201p_t} + \underset{(0.0011)}{0.0117I_t}, \quad R^2 = 0.858 \tag{7.8.12}$$

where x_t is the annual purchases of new automobiles per capita, S_{t-1} is the stock of automobiles per capita at the end of the previous year, p_t is the price of automobiles relative to the consumer price index, and I_t is disposible income in constant prices per capita. The per capita stock changes according to

$$S_t - S_{t-1} = x_t - dS_{t-1} \tag{7.8.13}$$

where d is the depreciation rate. Assuming d is 0.25 yields an estimate of the adjustment coefficient, γ, of 0.48.[42] The coefficients of p_t and I_t in (7.8.12)

[40] Using a related model, which is log linear rather than linear, Stone and Rowe (1958) estimated the speed of adjustment as very small for durable household goods (0.09), small for clothing (0.27), and larger than unity for certain habit-forming goods (e.g., 1.31 for beer, 1.47 for other alcoholic beverages, and 1.20 for tobacco).

[41] See Chow (1957).

[42] The adjustment coefficient is the difference between d and the coefficient of S_{t-1} in (7.8.12). See Problem 7-W. Phlips (1974) notes that (7.8.13) should, in fact, be adjusted to allow for the depreciation of goods purchased at the beginning of year t. One simple approach is to depreciate the average stock over the year, replacing S_{t-1} on the right-hand side in (7.8.13) by $(S_t + S_{t-1})/2$. He further notes that for either specification d is restricted to values between 0 and 2.

imply that the long-run price and income elasticities of demand for new automobiles, computed at mean values, are –0.63 and 3.0, respectively.

A related but fourth approach to dynamic demand analysis is a specification based on *changes* rather than levels of the quantity demanded. An example is the Suits estimation of a demand equation for new automobiles in the United States.[43] Using data from 1929 to 1956 (excluding 1942 to 1948 as unrepresentative years of war and its aftermath), he estimated the demand function as

$$\begin{aligned}\Delta A = 0.115 &+ \underset{(0.011)}{0.106\Delta I} - \underset{(0.086)}{0.507\Delta S} - \underset{(0.088)}{0.234\Delta (p/m)} \\ &- \underset{(0.261)}{0.827PS}, \quad R^2 = 0.85.\end{aligned} \tag{7.8.14}$$

Here A is annual retail sales of new passenger automobiles, and ΔA, the change in these sales, is the dependent variable. The explanatory variables are the change in real disposable income, ΔI; the change in the stock of passenger automobiles, ΔS; the change in average retail price deflated by the average duration of automobile loans, $\Delta(p/m)$; and a dummy variable to take account of years of severe production shortages (PS). All regression coefficients are statistically significant at the 1% level. The implied elasticities of demand, evaluated at the mean values, were estimated to be 4.2 with respect to real disposable income, –3.7 with respect to the stock of automobiles, and –0.6 with respect to the deflated average retail price. The elasticities with respect to income and price were similar to those obtained by Chow, reported above, indicating a price-inelastic but income-elastic demand for new automobiles.

The demand for automobiles and other such durables can be based, in part, on the existing stock, as in the Chow and Suits studies. The Houthakker-Taylor approach to dynamic demand analysis, which is the fifth approach, extends this concept to nondurables as well.[44] It is based on the idea that consumption involves some aspect of *habit formation* or *inertia*, as individual consumers become accustomed to certain amounts of a good. This habit formation can be accounted for by an observable stock of goods in the case of certain habit-forming durables, such as stocks of books or phonograph records, which have the property that the larger the stock, other things being equal, the greater will be the demand for the good. Houthakker and Taylor extended this line of reasoning to all goods, nondurable as well as durable. In the case of nondurables, however, the stock is unobservable and is essentially a psychological construct. The model stipulates that the demand for a good, x, is a linear function of price, income, and the unobservable stock of the good:

$$x = a + bp + cI + eS + u. \tag*{*(7.8.15)}$$

This demand equation is the same as the linear demand function (7.4.1), except

[43] See Suits (1958).

[44] See Houthakker and Taylor (1970). See also Stone and Rowe (1957), Pollak (1970), and Phlips (1972, 1974) for related dynamic models.

that other prices have been omitted for simplicity (they can, in fact, be easily added) and the dependence on the stock of the good is included. The stock grows according to

$$\Delta S = x - dS \tag*{*(7.8.16)}$$

as in (7.8.13). Thus the quantities purchased at any time add to the stock, but the stock is depleted by depreciation at the rate d. This equation is the same as the one that states that the rate of change of capital stock is the (gross) rate of investment less depreciation. For durable goods the stock is observable, but for nondurable goods the analog, S, is not, so empirical estimation requires the elimination of this variable from the equation. This is accomplished by taking first differences in (7.8.15) and inserting (7.8.16) to obtain

$$\Delta x = b\Delta p + c\Delta I + e(x - dS) + \Delta u. \tag{7.8.17}$$

Now, replacing S by solving (7.8.15) for S yields

$$\begin{aligned}\Delta x = ad + (e - d)x + b\Delta p + b\,dp \\ + c\Delta I + c\,dI + (\Delta u + du).\end{aligned} \tag*{*(7.8.18)}$$

According to this equation the rate of change of demand is a linear function of the level of demand and the levels and rates of change of both price and income.

For a long-term equilibrium, x and S both remain constant over time. Denoting these long-term equilibrium levels by $\bar{x}$ and $\bar{S}$, it follows from (7.8.15) and (7.8.16) that

$$\bar{x} = a + b\bar{p} + c\bar{I} + e\bar{S} + u = d\bar{S} \tag*{*(7.8.19)}$$

where $\bar{p}$ and $\bar{I}$ represent price and income levels in the long-term equilibrium. It then follows from (7.8.15) that for deviations of the stock from its long-term level

$$x - \bar{x} = e(S - \bar{S}). \tag*{*(7.8.20)}$$

Thus the deviation of the current purchases of a good from its long-term level is proportional to the deviation of the current stock of the good from its long-term level. If the parameter e is negative, then current purchases are above the long-term level if the stock is below its long-term level; this is the situation of *stock adjustment*, e.g., for durables. If, however, e is positive, then both deviations have the same sign; this is the situation of *habit formation*. In this latter case the more of the good that is consumed the more will be purchased.

Equation (7.8.18) can be written[45]

[45] The linear demand equation

$$x_t = a + bp_t + cI_t + eS_t + u_t$$

as in (7.8.15), for which the stochastic disturbance terms follows a Markov process

$$u_t = \rho u_{t-1} + v_t$$

$$x_t = A_0 + A_1 x_{t-1} + A_2 \Delta I_t + A_3 I_{t-1} + A_4 \Delta p_t + A_5 p_{t-1} + v_t. \qquad *(7.8.21)$$

Here use is made of the definition of the first difference

$$\Delta x_t \equiv x_t - x_{t-1}. \qquad (7.8.22)$$

Thus, this specification is also that of a Koyck distributed lag model in which the current variable, demand for a good, depends on its lagged value and current values of explanatory variables.

Houthakker and Taylor estimated their model for 83 commodities using constant dollar per capita expenditure in the United States over the period 1929 to 1964 (excluding the war years 1942 to 1945). Some of their results are reported in Table 7.9.[46] In their estimations, however, I is total consumption

Table 7.9. Habit-Formation Demand Functions for the United States, 1929-1964 (excluding 1942–1945)

Coefficient / *Commodity*	*Estimates of* $x = a + bp + cI + eS$, $\Delta S = x - dS$: *b*	*c*	*e*	*d*	*Short-run Elasticities*: *Own Price*	*Income (Expenditure)*
Alcoholic beverages	–	0.011 (0.004)	1.067 (0.231)	2	–	0.29
Purchased meals	– 1.40 (0.35)	0.068 (0.017)	– 0.026 (0.012)	0	–2.27	1.61
Jewelry	– 0.026 (0.013)	0.0057 (0.0019)	0.36 (0.73)	0.92 (0.83)	–0.41	1.00
Clothing	–	0.092 (0.016)	– 0.15 (0.08)	0.12 (0.08)	–	1.14
Electricity	– 0.027 (0.014)	0.0018 (0.0008)	1.92 (0.09)	2	–0.13	0.13
Medical care	– 0.0088 (0.0026)	0.0020 (0.0008)	0.37 (0.51)	0.56 (0.56)	–0.31	0.69
Automobiles	–	0.26 (0.04)	– 0.64 (0.16)	0.16 (0.04)	–	5.46
Gasoline and oil	–	0.017 (0.003)	0.17 (0.06)	0.28 (0.07)	–	0.55

Source Houthakker and Taylor (1970).

as in (6.4.5), would imply (7.8.21) provided $e = 0$. Thus (7.8.21) can be considered a generalization of the static model with first-order serial correlation of stochastic disturbance terms. See Problem 7-T.

[46] Houthakker and Taylor (1970) also report results based on 1947–1964 data and results for other countries.

expenditure per capita, rather than income.[47] According to these results, stock adjustment (negative e) was found for automobiles, as might be expected, and also for purchased meals and clothing (although for the latter two the estimate of e is not as significant). The other goods listed exhibited habit formation (positive e), particularly electricity, alcoholic beverages, and gasoline and oil. The rates of depreciation of the stock, d, were smallest for clothing and automobiles, which are durable goods, and largest for jewelry and medical care (values of 2 were assumed for alcoholic beverages and electricity). The greatest short-run own price elasticity was for purchased meals and the least was for electricity, as might be expected. As to income elasticities, automobiles exhibited by far the greatest responsiveness to income, again indicating the demand for automobiles to be income elastic, while electricity exhibited the smallest responsiveness to income among the goods included in the table.

PROBLEMS

7-A Figure 7.2 shows the derivation of a demand curve for a normal good, and Figure 7.3 shows the derivation of an Engel curve for a superior good.

1. Show in a diagram comparable to Figure 7.2 the derivation of a demand curve for a Giffen good.
2. Show in a diagram comparable to Figure 7.3 the derivation of an Engel curve for an inferior good.
3. From the geometrical derivation show that a Giffen good must be an inferior good.

7-B The many specifications of the demand curve in various studies have included the following equations:

1. $x_1 = a - bp_1$	(linear)
2. $\ln x_1 = a - b \ln p_1$	(logarithmic or double logarithmic)
3. $x_1 = a - b \ln p_1$	(semilogarithmic)
4. $\ln x_1 = a - bp_1$	(inverse semilogarithmic)
5. $x_1 = a + b/p_1$	(linear in reciprocal)
6. $\ln x_1 = a + b/p_1$	(inverse semilogarithmic in reciprocal)

For each determine the price elasticity of demand. Which permit a *threshold level* of price above which the consumer does not purchase the good (represented by

[47] Empirical studies sometimes use total expenditure rather than total income because data on income are either not available or subject to various errors and biases. Reported elasticities with respect to total expenditure, as in Table 7.9 and some earlier tables, should, however, be approximately the same as the corresponding elasticities with respect to income, since the elasticity of total expenditure with respect to income is close to unity.

zero, negative, or undefined values of x_1)? Which permit a *saturation level*, for which the demand curve approaches an asymptote? How would the results be modified if income I were substituted for price p_1 in each equation, the sign of b changed, and the set of equations were considered alternative specifications of the Engel curve?

7-C Engel's law states that the proportion of income spent on food decreases as income increases, or, equivalently, that the demand for food is income inelastic. Prove that these two properties are equivalent.

7-D The Törnquist Engel curves are given by

$$x = \frac{\alpha I}{\alpha + \beta}, \qquad x = \alpha\left(\frac{I-\gamma}{I+\beta}\right), \qquad x = \alpha I\left(\frac{I-\gamma}{I+\beta}\right)$$

where the parameters α, β, and γ depend on prices.[48] For each, find the income elasticity and asymptote and indicate the general shape it exhibits. Why are they referred to as Engel curves for "necessities," "relative luxuries," and "luxuries," respectively?

7-E Consider the nine conditions on demand functions in the case of two goods, as summarized by equations (7.2.10), (7.2.14), (7.2.17), (7.2.18), (7.2.20), and (7.2.22). Show that they are not independent by deriving the Slutsky symmetry condition in (7.2.18) from the other conditions.

7-F For the complete system of n demand equations (7.3.7) write out, using summation notation, all the theoretical restrictions, specifically the

1. one budget constraint
2. n homogeneity conditions
3. $n + \dfrac{n(n-1)}{2}$ Slutsky conditions
4. $n + 1$ aggregation conditions

that were developed for the case of two goods in Section 7.2.

7-G Prove that[49]

$$\epsilon_{jj'} = \delta_{jj'}\,\phi\eta_j + \eta_j s_{j'}(1 - \phi\eta_j), \qquad j, j' = 1, 2, \ldots, n$$

where $\epsilon_{jj'}$ is the cross price elasticity (7.2.8), η_j is the income elasticity (7.2.7), $s_{j'}$ is the budget share (7.2.11), $\delta_{jj'}$ is the Kronecker delta ($\delta_{jj'} = 1$ if $j = j'$, 0 if $j \neq j'$), and ϕ is defined as

$$\frac{1}{\phi} = \frac{\partial \ln U^*}{\partial \ln I} = \frac{I}{U^*}\frac{\partial U^*}{\partial I} = \frac{I}{U^*}\frac{\partial^2 y^*}{\partial I^2}$$

[48] See Wold and Jureen (1953).

[49] See Frisch (1959).

where U^* is maximized utility and y^* is the Lagrange multiplier for problem (7.2.1). From this result it may be noted that if s_j is small, the own price elasticity is proportional to the income elasticity:

$$\epsilon_j = \epsilon_{jj} \approx \phi\eta_j.$$

7-H The modern approach to the theory of the household is based upon the concept of duality.[50] Inserting the demand functions (7.2.2) into the utility function (7.2.1) defines the *indirect utility function*:

$$\begin{aligned} U^* &= U^*(p_1, p_2, I) \\ &= U[x_1(p_1, p_2, I), x_2(p_1, p_2, I)] \\ &= \max_{x_1, x_2} \; U(x_1, x_2) \quad \text{subject to} \quad p_1x_1 + p_2x_2 \leqslant I \end{aligned}$$

where $U^*(p_1, p_2, I)$ is the maximum level of utility attainable at prices p_1 and p_2 and income I. Consider the minimum expenditure needed to attain a utility level U, defined as

$$E^* = E^*(p_1, p_2, U) = \min_{x_1, x_2} \; p_1x_1 + p_2x_2 \quad \text{subject to} \quad U(x_1, x_2) \geqslant U.$$

The indirect utility and expenditure functions are dual to one another in that

$$U^*[p_1, p_2, E^*(p_1, p_2, U^*)] = U^* \quad \text{and} \quad E^*[p_1, p_2, U^*(p_1, p_2, E^*)] = E^*.$$

1. Prove Roy's identity:

$$x_j = -\frac{\partial U^*/\partial p_j}{\partial U^*/\partial I} = \frac{\partial E^*}{\partial p_j}.$$

2. From these results prove the Slutsky relation:

$$\frac{\partial x_j}{\partial p_k} = \left(\frac{\partial x_j}{\partial p_k}\right)_{\text{comp}} - \left(\frac{\partial x_j}{\partial I}\right) x_j, \qquad \text{all } j, k$$

where $\partial x_j/\partial p_k$ refers to the partial derivatives of the demand function and $(\partial x_j/\partial p_k)_{\text{comp}}$ refers to the partial derivatives of the compensated demand function

$$x_j = x_j(p_1, p_2, E^*).$$

7-I Given a logarithmic utility function

$$U = \beta_1 \ln x_1 + \beta_2 \ln x_2, \qquad \beta_1, \beta_2 > 0, \; \beta_1 + \beta_2 = 1$$

[50] See Diewert (1974) and Lau (1974).

show that the demand functions are of the form

$$x_j = \frac{\beta_j I}{p_j}, \quad j = 1, 2$$

so that the expenditure on each good is a constant proportion of income. How are the demand functions modified if the normalization rule $\beta_1 + \beta_2 = 1$ is not assumed? (*Note*: Problem 7-M is a generalization of this problem.)

7-J For the inverse demand function approach in (7.4.15):

1. Show how (7.4.15) can be derived from (7.4.12).
2. How could the price and income elasticities of demand be calculated from estimates of (7.4.15)?

7-K Consider the linear and log linear systems of demand equations as given in (7.5.2) and (7.5.3). What restrictions are imposed on the *a*'s and *b*'s by the theory of the consumer? How many coefficients remain to be estimated?

7-L Verify that the linear expenditure system of demand equations (7.5.4) satisfies all theoretical restrictions, in particular the homogeneity, Slutsky, and aggregation conditions on systems of demand equations.

7-M Show that the linear expenditure system of demand equations (7.5.2) solves the problem of maximizing utility subject to a budget constraint, where the utility function is of the Stone-Geary type (or Klein-Rubin type):

$$U = \sum_{j=1}^{n} \beta_j \ln (x_j - x_j^0) \quad \text{where} \quad x_j > x_j^0, \ \text{all } j$$
$$0 < \beta_j < 1, \quad \Sigma \beta_j = 1.$$

(*Note*: Problem 7-I refers to the special case in which $n = 2$ and $x_j^0 = 0$, all j, while Problem 7-O generalizes this problem.)

7-N For the linear expenditure system of demand equations (7.5.5):

1. Obtain price and income elasticities of demand, and show that there can be neither inferior goods nor price-elastic goods (assuming $x_j > 0$).
2. Show that the budget shares s_j defined in (7.2.11) can be represented as the linear combination

   $$s_j = (1 - r)\beta_j + r s_j^*$$

   where r is the "subsistence ratio," the ratio of subsistence income to total income,

   $$r = \frac{\Sigma p_k x_k^0}{I}, \quad 0 \leqslant r \leqslant 1$$

   and s_j^* is the "subsistence budget share," the proportion of subsistence income devoted to the purchase of the base quantity of the good:

$$s_j^* = \frac{p_j x_j^0}{\sum_k p_k x_k^0}$$

3. Express the own and cross price elasticities, ϵ_j and $\epsilon_{jj'}$, as specific functions of the income elasticities η_j, the subsistence ratio r, and the budget shares s_j.

7-O Consider the general additive utility function

$$U = \sum_{j=1}^{n} \frac{\beta_j}{\alpha_j} \left(\frac{x_j - x_j^0}{\beta_j} \right)^{\alpha_j}$$

where the constant parameters satisfy $\alpha_j < 1$, $\beta_j > 0$, and $x_j^0 < x_j$.

1. What form does the utility function take in the limit as $\alpha_j \to 0$?
2. Find the demand functions implied by this utility function.
3. Show that if $x_j^0 = 0$ and all α_j are equal, then the utility function assumes the same form as the CES production function (of Section 8.3) and that if, in addition, $\alpha_j = 0$, then the form is the same as the Cobb-Douglas production function (also of Section 8.3). What are the implied demand functions in each of these cases? What are the demand functions if $x_j^0 = 0$ but α_j are not all equal (but $\alpha_j < 1$)?
4. Assume $x_j^0 > 0$ (but $x_j^0 < x_j$). Show that if $\alpha_j = 0$, then the demand functions are those of the linear expenditure system (7.5.5). What form do they take if the α_j are all equal (but not zero)?

7-P Show in a diagram analogous to Figure 7.5 that if $\sigma_S^2 \gg \sigma_D^2$, then the supply curve would be identified. In which markets would this assumption about relative variances likely be met?

7-Q Consider the estimation of elasticities as

$$\hat{\delta} = \frac{\sum p_i q_i}{\sum p_i^2}$$

where p_i and q_i here are the logarithms of price and quantity, measured as deviations from the means of the logarithms. According to the model

$$\begin{aligned} q_i^D &= \beta p_i + u_i \quad \text{where} \quad u_i \sim N(0, \sigma_u^2) \\ q_i^S &= \gamma p_i + v_i \quad \text{where} \quad v_i \sim N(0, \sigma_v^2) \\ E(u_i u_{i'}) &= E(v_i v_{i'}) = 0 \quad \text{for } i \neq i', \quad E(u_i v_{i'}) = 0, \quad \text{all } i, i'. \end{aligned}$$

Show that

$$E(\hat{\delta}) = \frac{\gamma \sigma_u^2 + \beta \sigma_v^2}{\sigma_u^2 + \sigma_v^2}$$

and indicate those circumstances in which $\hat{\delta}$ is an acceptable estimate of the price elasticity of demand.

7-R Consider the aggregation condition given in Section 7.7, stating that the Engel curves are all linear, with identical slopes across all consumers. Show that this condition is both necessary and sufficient for any redistribution of income among the consumers not to have any behavioral repercussions on aggregate demand. Illustrate geometrically.

7-S Consider the problem of aggregation for log linear demand curves. What are the conditions of aggregation in this case?

7-T Consider the homogeneity restriction for aggregate demand functions, assuming all individual demand functions exhibit homogeneity. Show that aggregate demand does not change when aggregate income and all prices change by the same proportion only if it is also assumed that all individual incomes change by the same proportion.

7-U In the Nerlove model of adaptive expectations, sellers adapt their expectations of price according to past mistakes, in that the change in expected price is proportional to the deviation between actual and expected prices in the last period.[51] Thus

$$p_t^* - p_{t-1}^* = h(p_{t-1} - p_{t-1}^*), \qquad 0 < h \leqslant 1$$

where p_t^* is the expected price in period t, p_t is the actual price in period t, and h is the expectation adjustment coefficient. Demand depends linearly on actual price

$$q_t^D = a - bp_t$$

and supply depends linearly on expected price

$$q_t^S = c + dp_t^*$$

where market clearing occurs in each period

$$q_t^D = q_t^S.$$

1. Show that the behavior of expected prices can be obtained from a Koyck distributed lag relating expected prices to actual prices.
2. Show that the model reduces to the cobweb model of (7.8.1)–(7.8.7) for $h = 1$.
3. For any h within the given bounds obtain the implied difference equation and solve it for the behavior of price over time, starting from p_0.
4. Prove that price converges to an equilibrium price $\bar{p}$ only if

$$1 - \frac{2}{h} < -\frac{d}{b}$$

[51] See Nerlove (1958). See also Section 6.7.

Compare this condition to that for convergence of the cobweb model. In particular, show that adaptive expectations can stabilize an otherwise unstable cobweb model.

5. Generalize the model to allow for stochastic disturbance terms and discuss the estimation of parameters of the model.

7-V Schultz (1938) estimated the following cobweb model for sugar:

$$p(t) = 2.34 - 1.34q^D(t) \quad \text{(demand)}$$
$$q^S(t) = 0.5 + 0.6p(t-1) \quad \text{(supply)}$$

where $p(t)$ is price at time t, $q^D(t)$ is demand at time t, and $q^S(t)$ is supply at time t.

1. What is the equilibrium price?
2. Find the time trend for the price.
3. Does the system converge to the equilibrium price?

7-W Prove that, for the Chow stock adjustment model in (7.8.12) and (7.8.13), the adjustment coefficient γ is the difference between d and the coefficient of S_{t-1} in (7.8.12).

7-X For the Houthakker-Taylor model of (7.8.15)-(7.8.22):

1. Solve for a, b, c, d, and e of (7.8.18) in terms of A_0 to A_5 of (7.8.21).
2. Show that the case $d = 2$ leads to

$$x_t = A_0 + A_1 x_{t-1} + A_2 I_t + A_4 p_t + v_t$$

as in the Koyck distributed lag. Similarly treat the case $d = -2$.

3. Show that the static model with first-order serial correlation of stochastic disturbance terms, as given in footnote 45, implies (7.8.21) provided $e = 0$.

BIBLIOGRAPHY

Allen, R. G. D. (1959), *Mathematical Economics*, 2nd Ed. London: Macmillan and Co., Ltd.

Allen, R. G. D., and A. L. Bowley (1935), *Family Expenditure*, London: P. S. King.

Barten, A. P. (1968), "Estimating Demand Equations." *Econometrica*, 36: 213–51.

Barten, A. P. (1977). "The Systems of Consumer Demand Functions Approach: A Review," in M. D. Intriligator, Ed., *Frontiers of Quantitative Economics*, Vol. III. Amsterdam: North-Holland Publishing Co.

Brown, J. A. C., and A. S. Deaton (1972), "Surveys in Applied Economics: Models of Consumer Behavior." *Economic Journal*, 82: 1143–1236.

Brown, M., and D. Heien (1972), "The S-Branch Utility Tree: A Generalization of the Linear Expenditure System." *Econometrica*, 40: 737–47.

Chow, G. C. (1957), *Demand for Automobiles in the United States*. Amsterdam: North-Holland Publishing Co.

Cramer, J. S. (1969), *Empirical Econometrics*. Amsterdam: North-Holland Publishing Co.

Deaton, A. S. (1975), *Models and Projections of Demand in Post-War Britain*. London: Chapman and Hall; New York: Halsted Press.

Diewert, W. E. (1974), "Applications of Duality Theory," in M. D. Intriligator and D. A. Kendrick, Eds., *Frontiers of Quantitative Economics*, Vol. II. Amsterdam: North-Holland Publishing Co.

Fox, K. A. (1953), *The Analysis of Demand for Farm Products*. Technical Bulletin No. 1081, U.S. Department of Agriculture, Washington, D.C.

Fox, K. A. (1958), *Econometric Analysis for Public Policy*. Ames: Iowa State College Press.

Frisch, R. (1959), "A Complete Scheme for Computing All Direct and Cross Demand Elasticities in a Model with Many Sectors." *Econometrica*, 27: 117–96.

Goldberger, A., and T. Gamaletsos (1970), "A Cross-Country Comparison of Consumer Expenditure Patterns." *European Economic Review*, 1: 357–400.

Green, H. A. J. (1964), *Aggregation in Economic Analysis: An Introductory Survey*. Princeton: Princeton University Press.

Harberger, A., Ed. (1960), *The Demand for Durable Goods*. Chicago: University of Chicago Press.

Hicks, J. R. (1946), *Value and Capital*, 2nd Ed. London: Oxford University Press.

Houthakker, H. S. (1957), "An International Comparison of Household Expenditure Patterns Commemorating the Centenary of Engel's Laws." *Econometrica*, 25: 532–51.

Houthakker, H. S. (1965a), "New Evidence on Demand Elasticities." *Econometrica*, 33: 277–88.

Houthakker H. S. (1965b), "A Note on Self-Dual Preferences," *Econometrica*, 33: 797–801.

Houthakker, H. S., and L. D. Taylor (1970), *Consumer Demand in the United States, 1929–1970*, 2nd Enlarged Ed. Cambridge: Harvard University Press.

Intriligator, M. D. (1971), *Mathematical Optimization and Economic Theory*. Englewood Cliffs, N.J.: Prentice-Hall, Inc.

Klein, L. R., and H. Rubin (1947–8), "A Constant Utility Index of the Cost of Living." *Review of Economic Studies*, 15: 84–7.

Lau, L. J. (1974), "Comments on 'Applications of Duality Theory'," in M. D. Intriligator and D. A. Kendrick, Eds., *Frontiers of Quantitative Economics*, Vol. II. Amsterdam: North-Holland Publishing Co.

Marshall, A. (1920), *Principles of Economics*, 8th Ed. London: Macmillan and Co., Ltd.

Nerlove, M. (1958), "Adaptive Expectations and Cobweb Phenomena." *Quarterly Journal of Economics*, 72: 227–40.

Phlips, L. (1972), "A Dynamic Version of the Linear Expenditure Model." *Review of Economics and Statistics*, 64: 450–58.

Phlips, L. (1974), *Applied Consumption Analysis*. Amsterdam: North-Holland Publishing Co.

Pollak, R. A. (1970), "Habit Formation and Dynamic Demand Functions." *Journal of Political Economy*, 78: 745–63.

Pollak, R. A. and T. J. Wales (1969), "Estimation of the Linear Expenditure System." *Econometrica*, 37: 611–28.

Powell, A. A. (1974), *Empirical Analytics of Demand Systems.* Lexington: Lexington Books.

Prais, S. J. and H. S. Houthakker (1955), *The Analysis of Family Budgets.* New York: Cambridge University Press.

Samuelson, P. A. (1947), *Foundations of Economic Analysis.* Cambridge: Harvard University Press.

Samuelson, P. A. (1947–8), "Some Implications of Linearity." *Review of Economic Studies*, 15: 88–90.

Sato, K. (1972), "Additive Utility Functions with Double-Log Consumer Demand Functions." *Journal of Political Economy*, 80: 102–24.

Schultz, H. (1938), *The Theory and Measurement of Demand.* Chicago: University of Chicago Press.

Stone, R. (1954a), *The Measurement of Consumers' Expenditure and Behavior in the United Kingdom, 1920–1938.* New York: Cambridge University Press.

Stone, R. (1954b), "Linear Expenditure Systems and Demand Analysis; An Application to the Pattern of British Demand." *Economic Journal*, 64: 511–27.

Stone, R. (1966), "The Changing Pattern of Consumption," in R. Stone, Ed., *Mathematics in the Social Sciences and Other Essays.* London: Chapman and Hall.

Stone, R. (1972), *A Computable Model of Economic Growth. A Programme for Growth*, Vol. 1. Cambridge: Chapman and Hall.

Stone, R., A. Brown, and D. A. Rowe (1965), "Demand Analysis and Projections for Britain: 1900–1970," in J. Sandee, Ed., *Europe's Future Consumption*, Amsterdam: North-Holland Publishing Co.

Stone, R., and D. A. Rowe (1957), "The Market Demand for Durable Goods." *Econometrica*, 25: 423–43.

Stone, R., and D. A. Rowe (1958), "Dynamic Demand Functions: Some Econometric Results." *Economic Journal*, 68: 256–70.

Stone, R., and D. A. Rowe (1960), "The Durability of Consumers' Durable Goods." *Econometrica*, 28: 407–16.

Suits, D. B. (1958), "The Demand for New Automobiles in the United States, 1929–1956." *The Review of Economics and Statistics*, 40: 273–80.

Theil, H. (1954), *Linear Aggregation of Economic Relations.* Amsterdam: North-Holland Publishing Co.

Theil, H. (1967), *Economics and Information Theory.* Amsterdam: North-Holland Publishing Co.

Theil, H. (1975), *The Theory and Measurement of Consumer Demand*, Vol. I. Amsterdam: North-Holland Publishing Co.

Wold, H., and L. Jureen (1953), *Demand Analysis.* New York: John Wiley & Sons, Inc.

Zellner, A. Ed., (1968), *Readings in Economic Statistics and Econometrics.* Boston: Little, Brown & Co.

CHAPTER **8**

Applications to Firms; Production Functions and Cost Functions

8.1 Introduction

A second important area of application of single-equation estimation is to the firm, the firm and the household constituting the two basic units of microeconomics. The firm is the basic production unit, producing goods (and services) using certain inputs called "factors of production," such as labor and capital.

The applications of econometrics to the firm include the estimation of production functions, cost curves, factor demand equations, and technical change. Each of these subjects will be treated in this chapter, following a summary of salient aspects of the theory of the firm.

8.2 The theory of the firm

The problem of the firm, from a formal point of view, is that of maximizing profits subject to a given technology.[1] Profits equal revenue minus cost; revenue is the level of output times the price of output; and cost is the sum, over all inputs, of the level of each input times the wage of each input. In the neoclassical formulation the technology is summarized by a *production function*, a technical relationship based on physical or engineering considerations indicating the (maximum) output attainable for alternative combinations of all conceivable inputs of factors of production. In the case of a firm producing a single output from two inputs, the production function can be represented as

$$y = f(x_1, x_2) \qquad *(8.2.1)$$

where y is the (maximum possible) level of output, x_1 and x_2 are the levels of the two inputs, and $f(\cdot\ \cdot)$ is a function that is generally assumed to be continuously differentiable, so that the partial derivatives are continuous. The produc-

[1] See Hicks (1946), Samuelson (1947), and Intriligator (1971). The basic assumption of profit maximization has been repeatedly challenged. For example, Baumol (1967) suggests sales (or growth of sales) maximization, Williamson (1964) suggests managerial utility maximization, and Simon (1959) suggests replacing profit maximizing by profit satisficing. Nevertheless, profit maximization is still the most widely used basic assumption for the firm, and these alternative goals frequently imply profit maximization—at least in the long run.

tion function indicates the level of output y associated with any combination of inputs (x_1, x_2).

The problem of the firm in this case of one output and two inputs can be stated as that of choosing the output and inputs so as to

$$\max_{y,x_1,x_2} \Pi = py - w_1x_1 - w_2x_2 \quad \text{subject to} \quad y = f(x_1, x_2) \tag{*(8.2.2)}$$

Here Π is profits, given as revenue (py) less cost $(w_1x_1 + w_2x_2)$, p is the price of output, and w_1 and w_2 are the wages (the prices) of the inputs. When the production function constraint is substituted into the definition of profits, the problem can be stated as the unconstrained problem

$$\max_{x_1,x_2} \Pi = pf(x_1, x_2) - w_1x_1 - w_2x_2. \tag{*(8.2.3)}$$

In the case of perfect competition, in which all three prices p, w_1, and w_2 are given parameters determined on the relevant product and factor markets, the necessary (first-order) conditions for a maximum are[2]

$$\frac{\partial \Pi}{\partial x_1} = p\frac{\partial f}{\partial x_1} - w_1 = 0 \tag{8.2.4}$$

$$\frac{\partial \Pi}{\partial x_2} = p\frac{\partial f}{\partial x_2} - w_2 = 0 \tag{8.2.5}$$

These conditions require that

$$\frac{\partial f}{\partial x_j} \equiv \text{MP}_j = \frac{w_j}{p}, \quad j = 1, 2 \tag{*(8.2.6)}$$

where the partial derivatives are the *marginal products* MP_j, the increase in output per unit increase in one input, the other input being held constant. These conditions state that the marginal product of each input must equal its real wage, namely the wage (input price) divided by the price of output. The two marginal-product conditions in (8.2.6) plus the production function in (8.2.1) form a system of three simultaneous equations that determine profit-maximizing output y and inputs x_1 and x_2.[3]

The two conditions in (8.2.6) imply that the ratio of the marginal products must equal the ratio of the wages

$$\text{MRTS}_{jk} \equiv \frac{\text{MP}_j}{\text{MP}_k} = \frac{w_j}{w_k}, \quad j, k = 1, 2 \tag{*(8.2.7)}$$

[2] For a discussion of second-order conditions see Intriligator (1971).

[3] This system can, in fact, be divided into two subsystems—the two equations in (8.2.6), determining x_1 and x_2, and the equation in (8.2.1) determining y.

where MRTS_{jk} is the *marginal rate of technical substitution* between inputs j and k, defined as the ratio of the marginal products of these inputs. In the case of two inputs, (8.2.7) gives one condition—that MRTS_{12} equal w_1/w_2.

The equilibrium of the firm can be shown geometrically as in Figure 8.1. The

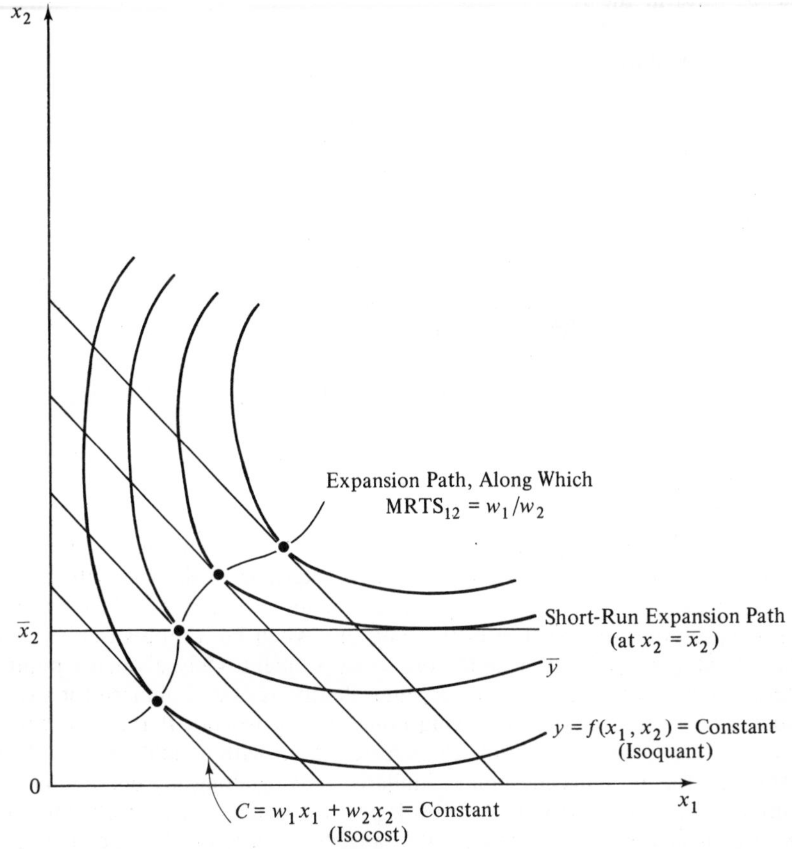

Figure 8.1 Expansion Paths for the Firm

lines are *isocosts*, defined as the locus of input combinations (x_1, x_2) for which cost C, the total payment to both inputs, is constant

$$C = w_1x_1 + w_2x_2 \equiv \text{constant.} \tag{8.2.8}$$

Totally differentiating this identity,

$$w_1dx_1 + w_2dx_2 = 0 \tag{8.2.9}$$

so the slope of the isocosts is the ratio of the wages

$$\frac{dx_2}{dx_1} = -\frac{w_1}{w_2}. \tag{8.2.10}$$

For each (positive) level of the constant in (8.2.8) an isocost is defined, and each isocost has a slope equal to the negative of the ratio of the wages of the inputs. A family of these isocosts is illustrated in the figure.

The curves in the figure are *isoquants*, each of which is the locus of input combinations for which output is fixed, i.e., level curves of the production function defined by

$$y = f(x_1, x_2) \equiv \text{constant}. \tag*{*(8.2.11)}$$

Each curve corresponds to a particular constant in this equation. Totally differentiating (8.2.11),

$$\frac{\partial f}{\partial x_1} dx_1 + \frac{\partial f}{\partial x_2} dx_2 = 0 \tag{8.2.12}$$

so the slope of any isoquant at any point is given by

$$\frac{dx_2}{dx_1} = -\frac{\partial f/\partial x_1}{\partial f/\partial x_2} = -\frac{\text{MP}_1}{\text{MP}_2} = -\text{MRTS}_{12}. \tag{8.2.13}$$

Thus the slope of the isoquant is the negative of the marginal rate of technical substitution, which generally varies as the inputs change, as shown by the change in the slope of any one of the isoquants as one input is substituted for another.

The equilibrium of the firm in the long run, when both inputs can be freely varied, is at the tangency of an isocost to an isoquant. Only at such a point is output maximized for a given cost or, equivalently, is cost minimized for a given output. The former follows by moving along any one isocost: if at any one point it crosses an isoquant it is possible to increase output with no additional cost—by moving toward the tangency point. Similarly, moving along any one isoquant, if at any one point it crosses an isocost it is possible to decrease cost while holding output constant—by moving toward the tangency point. The locus of tangency points is the set of possible equilibrium points for the firm; it is called the *expansion path* and is characterized by the equality of slopes of isocost and isoquant. From the above results on these slopes, the geometric tangency is in fact equivalent to the algebraic condition (8.2.7), stating that, for profit maximization, the marginal rate of technical substitution must equal the ratio of wages.

The possible equilibrium points along the expansion path of Figure 8.1 indicate at each such point an output, y, from the isoquant, and a level of cost, C, from the isocost. The set of all possible pairs of output and cost along the expansion path defines the *cost curve*

$$C = C(y), \tag*{*(8.2.14)}$$

in this case the long-run total cost curve, since it represents total cost

$$C = w_1x_1 + w_2x_2 \tag{8.2.15}$$

in the long-run situation in which all factor inputs can be varied freely. A *short-run cost curve* is defined using an alternative expansion path that reflects whatever factors are fixed in any particular short run. An example would be the expansion path defined by the horizontal line at $\bar{x}_2$, where the second input is fixed at this level and the first input is free to vary. The short-run cost curve defined by the output and cost along such an alternative expansion path $C_S(y)$ must satisfy

$$C_S(y) \geqslant C(y) \qquad \text{at each } y \tag{8.2.16}$$

since at all points other than those for which the two expansion paths cross the short-run situation involves producing a particular level of output y at higher cost.

Average cost curves in the long run and short run are defined by

$$\text{AC}(y) = \frac{C(y)}{y}, \qquad \text{AC}_S(y) = \frac{C_S(y)}{y} \tag*{*(8.2.17)}$$

and marginal cost curves in these cases are defined by

$$\text{MC}(y) = \frac{dC(y)}{dy}, \qquad \text{MC}_S(y) = \frac{dC_S(y)}{dy} \tag*{*(8.2.18)}$$

The various cost curves introduced here are illustrated geometrically in Figure 8.2. The upper diagram shows (total) cost curves in the long run and short run, and the lower diagram shows corresponding average and marginal cost curves in the long run and short run. Because all inputs can be freely varied in the long run, the cost at zero output is zero.

$$C(0) = 0 \tag{8.2.19}$$

In a short run, however, certain factors are fixed, and so there will be some cost at zero output—the fixed cost defined by

$$C_S(0) = \text{FC} > 0. \tag{8.2.20}$$

For example, if $C_S(y)$ represents the short-run cost curve corresponding to the short-run expansion path of Figure 8.1, then $\text{FC} = w_2\bar{x}_2$. Both long- and short-run cost curves must increase as output increases and satisfy the inequality (8.2.16). The curves will touch one another at a level of output corresponding to the crossing of the short-run and long-run expansion paths, e.g., at $\bar{y}$ in Figure 8.1, shown also in Figure 8.2. The shape of the cost curves reflects underlying assumptions concerning the technology—that initially cost increases at a decreasing rate, corresponding to increased specialization and division of labor, while at higher levels of output cost increases at an increasing rate, corresponding to managerial diseconomies in large enterprise.

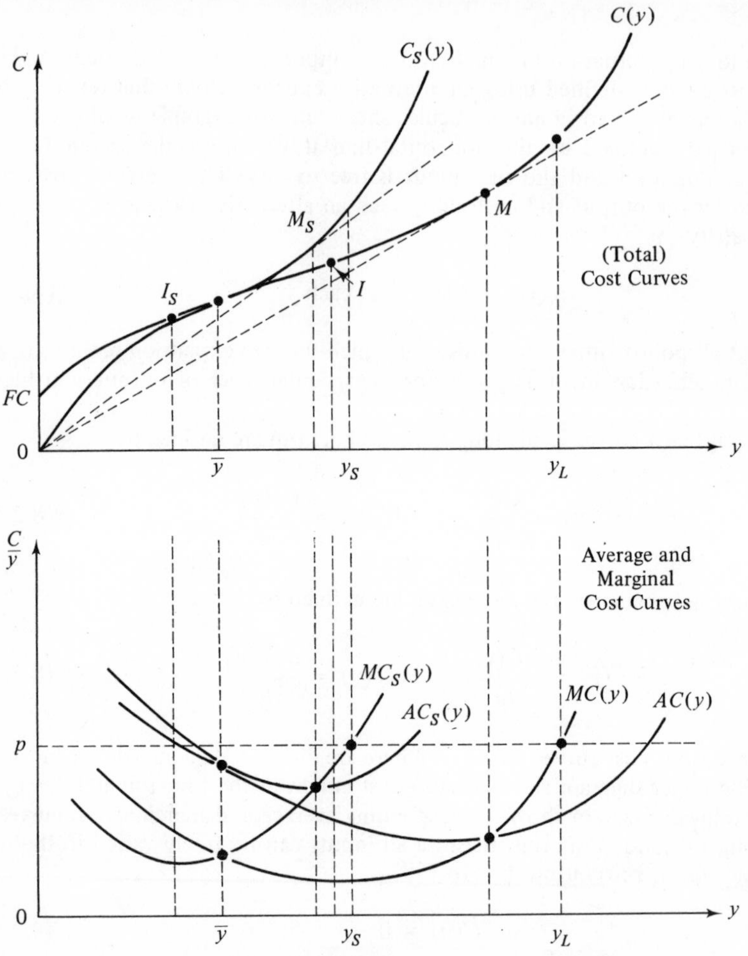

Figure 8.2 Cost Curves and Equilibrium Levels of Output

The lower diagrams show average and marginal cost curves, plotted on a separate diagram since the dimension of both, cost divided by output, differs from that of total cost. Geometrically, average cost is the slope of a ray connecting the origin and a point on the total cost curve, while marginal cost is the slope of the total cost curve itself. Thus average cost is at a minimum where the ray is tangent to the curve—at M and M_S—so at this point marginal cost and average cost are equal. The marginal cost curves reach minimum levels corresponding to inflection points of the total cost curves at I and I_S. At the point $\bar{y}$, at which the total cost curves touch, both average cost curves and both marginal cost curves give identical values.

The equilibrium of the competitive firm is also shown in Figure 8.2.[4] A given

[4] For the case of the firm in imperfect competition see Problem 8-E.

price of the product, p, is shown in the lower diagram as the horizontal line; it is in the lower diagram since p has the dimension of cost *per unit.* The equilibrium is found at that output for which the price line intersects the marginal cost and marginal cost is increasing—at y_S in the short run and y_L in the long run. Algebraically, since

$$\Pi = py - C(y) \tag*{*(8.2.21)}$$

maximizing profit by choice of output calls for choosing y so that

$$\frac{d\Pi}{dy}(y) = p - \frac{dC}{dy}(y) = p - \text{MC}(y) = 0 \tag{8.2.22}$$

Thus, a first-order condition of profit maximization is

$$p = \text{MC}(y). \tag*{*(8.2.23)}$$

The second-order condition is

$$\frac{d^2\Pi}{dy^2} = \frac{d^2C}{dy^2} = \frac{d\text{MC}(y)}{dy} \leqslant 0 \tag{8.2.24}$$

so

$$\frac{d\text{MC}(y)}{dy} \geqslant 0. \tag{8.2.25}$$

Equations (8.2.23) and (8.2.25) give, algebraically, the conditions that price equals marginal cost where marginal cost is increasing, as at y_S and y_L in Figure 8.2.

Given the optimal (profit-maximizing) output, the choice of inputs is given at that point where the corresponding isoquant intersects the relevant expansion path of Figure 8.1. The corresponding optimal inputs are x_1 and x_2, where output is given as

$$y = f(x_1, x_2). \tag{8.2.26}$$

The optimal inputs, in general, depend on both wages and output price:

$$x_j = x_j(w_1, w_2, p), \quad j = 1, 2 \tag{8.2.27}$$

This system of equations is called the system of *factor demand functions.* They are also called *derived demand functions* because they are derived from the underlying demand for the product produced by the firm. More generally, for a firm using n inputs to produce output,

$$x_j = x_j(w_1, w_2, \ldots, w_n, p), \quad j = 1, 2, \ldots, n \tag*{*(8.2.28)}$$

where w_j is the price of input j. If output price and all wages other than that of the input itself are held constant, the resulting curve

$$x_j = D_j(w_j) = x_j(\bar{w}_1, \bar{w}_2, \ldots, w_j, \ldots, \bar{w}_n, \bar{p}) \tag{8.2.29}$$

is the jth *factor demand curve*.

The optimal level of output is also a function of input wages and output price. In the two-input case

$$y = y(w_1, w_2, p) = f[x_1(w_1, w_2, p), x_2(w_1, w_2, p)] \tag{8.2.30}$$

is the *output supply function*, and in the n-input case it is

$$y = y(w_1, w_2, \ldots, w_n, p). \qquad *(8.2.31)$$

If all wages are held constant, the resulting curve

$$y = S(p) = y(\bar{w}_1, \bar{w}_2, \ldots, \bar{w}_n, p) \tag{8.2.32}$$

is the *output supply curve.* Both the factor demand functions and the output supply function are determined on the basis of the technology, as represented by the production function.

Comparative statics, as applied to the firm, is concerned with the effect of changes in input wages and output prices on the factor demand functions in (8.2.28) and on the output supply function in (8.2.31). The first-order conditions for profit maximization can be written as the identities

$$p \frac{\partial f}{\partial x_j} [x_1(w_1, \ldots, w_n, p), \ldots, x_n(w_1, \ldots, w_n, p)] \equiv w_j, \quad j = 1, 2, \ldots, n \tag{8.2.33}$$

which, together with the identities

$$y \equiv f[x_1(w_1, \ldots, w_n, p), \ldots, x_n(w_1, \ldots, w_n, p)] \tag{8.2.34}$$

$$\Pi \equiv pf[x_1(w_1, \ldots, w_n, p), \ldots, x_n(w_1, \ldots, w_n, p)] - \sum_{j=1}^{n} w_j x_j(w_1, \ldots, w_n, p) \tag{8.2.35}$$

define the equilibrium inputs, output, and profits. Differentiating these conditions with respect to wages and price gives the comparative statics results.[5] One important set of results are the *symmetry conditions*

[5] For proofs using profit and cost functions see below. For more classical proofs see Intriligator (1971), Chapter 8.

$$\frac{\partial x_j}{\partial w_k} = \frac{\partial x_k}{\partial w_j}, \quad \text{all } j, k \qquad *(8.2.36)$$

which state, for profit-maximizing inputs, that the change in the jth factor demand for a change in the kth wage is equal to the change in the kth factor demand for a change in the jth wage. For $j \neq k$, inputs j and k are *substitutes* if $\partial x_j / \partial w_k$ is positive and they are *complements* if this partial derivative is negative.

Another set of comparative statics results are the *sign conditions* on profit-maximizing inputs and output:

$$\frac{\partial x_j}{\partial w_j} < 0 \qquad *(8.2.37)$$

$$\frac{\partial x_j}{\partial p} > 0 \quad \text{for some } j \qquad *(8.2.38)$$

$$\frac{\partial y}{\partial p} > 0 \qquad *(8.2.39)$$

$$\frac{\partial y}{\partial w_j} < 0 \quad \text{for some } j \qquad *(8.2.40)$$

These conditions are analogous to the negativity of own substitution effects in the theory of the consumer. Condition (8.2.37) is that of a negatively sloped demand curve for factors, so that there can be no "Giffen factor" comparable to the Giffen good of the theory of the household. Condition (8.2.39) is that of a rising supply curve for output. The positive slope of the supply curve is also shown geometrically in Figure 8.2–raising p will clearly increase both y_S and y_L, as the optimum point moves up the marginal cost curve. In fact, the marginal cost curve in the long run above average cost is the long-run supply curve, while the marginal cost curve in the short run above average variable cost is the short-run supply curve, average variable cost being $[C_S(y) - C_S(0)]/y$. Furthermore[6]

$$\frac{\partial x_j}{\partial p} = -\frac{\partial y}{\partial w_j}, \quad \text{all } j \qquad *(8.2.41)$$

Inputs for which

$$\frac{\partial x_j}{\partial p} = -\frac{\partial y}{\partial w_j} < 0 \qquad *(8.2.42)$$

are called *inferior inputs*, for which demand decreases as output price (and

[6] This relation follows from the homogeneity of the input demand functions discussed below. See Problem 8-B.

hence output) increases or, equivalently, for which output increases when the wage of the factor increases. By (8.2.38) and (8.2.40) not all inputs can be inferior.[7]

Another set of comparative static conditions follows from the homogeneity of the factor demand equations and the output supply function. Scaling price and wages by a positive scale factor, from $(w_1, w_2, \ldots, w_n, p)$ to $(\alpha w_1, \alpha w_2, \ldots, \alpha w_n, \alpha p)$, where $\alpha > 0$, scales profits by α, from Π to $\alpha\Pi$. But maximizing $\alpha\Pi$ is equivalent to maximizing Π if $\alpha > 0$. Thus the solutions for profit-maximizing factor demands and output supply are invariant to such a change; i.e., they are homogeneous to degree zero in all wages and price:

$$x_j(\alpha w_1, \alpha w_2, \ldots, \alpha w_n, \alpha p) = x_j(w_1, w_2, \ldots, w_n, p), \qquad \text{all } j, \text{all } \alpha > 0 \tag{8.2.43}$$

$$y(\alpha w_1, \alpha w_2, \ldots, \alpha w_n, \alpha p) = y(w_1, w_2, \ldots, w_n, p), \qquad \text{all } \alpha > 0. \tag{8.2.44}$$

Euler's theorem on homogeneous functions then implies that

$$\sum_{k=1}^{n} w_k \frac{\partial x_j}{\partial w_k} + p \frac{\partial x_j}{\partial p} = 0, \qquad \text{all } j \tag*{*(8.2.45)}$$

$$\sum_{k=1}^{n} w_k \frac{\partial y}{\partial w_k} + p \frac{\partial y}{\partial p} = 0 \tag*{*(8.2.46)}$$

which are the *homogeneity conditions*. They can be expressed in elasticity form as

$$\sum_{k=1}^{n} \frac{w_k}{x_j} \frac{\partial x_j}{\partial w_k} + \frac{p}{x_j} \frac{\partial x_j}{\partial p} = 0, \qquad j = 1, 2, \ldots, n \tag*{*(8.2.47)}$$

$$\sum_{k=1}^{n} \frac{w_k}{y} \frac{\partial y}{\partial w_k} + \frac{p}{y} \frac{\partial y}{\partial p} = 0 \tag*{*(8.2.48)}$$

stating that the sum of all elasticities vanishes both for each factor demand equation and for the output supply function.

The comparative statics results (8.2.36)–(8.2.41) can be easily proven using the concepts of profit function and cost function. Profit is defined as

$$\Pi \equiv py - \sum w_j x_j \tag{8.2.49}$$

so, assuming competitive markets, inserting the output supply function (8.2.31) and the factor demand functions (8.2.28) into this identity yields

[7] Note that inferior inputs do not involve a negative marginal product; even though output increases as the level of input decreases, other inputs are also changing.

$$\Pi(w_1, w_2, \ldots, w_n, p) = py(w_1, w_2, \ldots, w_n, p) - \Sigma w_j x_j(w_1, w_2, \ldots, w_n, p). \qquad *(8.2.50)$$

This function, stating the dependence of profits on all wages and price, is called the *profit function*.[8] This function, which is defined for the long-run situation in which all inputs and outputs are freely variable, is continuous, homogeneous of degree one, convex, decreasing in each wage, and increasing in output price. Furthermore, the profit-maximizing levels of inputs and output can be expressed as the following partial derivatives of the profit function:

$$x_j = -\frac{\partial \Pi}{\partial w_j}, \quad j = 1, 2, \ldots, n \qquad *(8.2.51)$$

$$y = \frac{\partial \Pi}{\partial p}. \qquad *(8.2.52)$$

From these conditions the comparative statics results readily follow. The symmetry conditions (8.2.36) follow from the equality of the mixed second-order partial derivatives:

$$\frac{\partial x_j}{\partial w_k} = -\frac{\partial^2 \Pi}{\partial w_j\, \partial w_k} = -\frac{\partial^2 \Pi}{\partial w_k\, \partial w_j} = \frac{\partial x_k}{\partial w_j}, \quad \text{all } j, k. \qquad *(8.2.53)$$

The rising supply curve (8.2.39) follows from

$$\frac{\partial y}{\partial p} = \frac{\partial^2 \Pi}{\partial p^2} > 0 \qquad *(8.2.54)$$

where the inequality follows from the convexity of the profit function in p. Similarly the falling factor demand curve (8.2.37) follows from the convexity in w_j:

$$\frac{\partial x_j}{\partial w_j} = -\frac{\partial^2 \Pi}{\partial w_j^2} < 0, \quad \text{all } j. \qquad *(8.2.55)$$

Condition (8.2.41) follows from

$$\frac{\partial x_j}{\partial p} = -\frac{\partial^2 \Pi}{\partial p\, \partial w_j} = -\frac{\partial^2 \Pi}{\partial w_j\, \partial p} = -\frac{\partial y}{\partial w_j}, \quad \text{all } j. \qquad *(8.2.56)$$

The *cost function* is the special case of the profit function corresponding to fixed output.[9] It is given in the long-run case in which all inputs are free to vary

[8] See Diewert (1974) and McFadden and Fuss, Eds. (1977). See also Problem 8-C.

[9] See Shephard (1970) and Diewert (1974). See also Problem 8-D.

as $C(w_1, w_2, \ldots, w_n, y)$, defined as the minimum level of cost for any set of input wages $w_1, w_2, \ldots, w_n$, at a given level of output y, so that

$$C(w_1, w_2, \ldots, w_n, y) \text{ solves } \min_{x_1, x_2, \ldots, x_n} C \equiv \sum_{j=1}^{n} w_j x_j \quad \text{such that } y = f(x_1, x_2, \ldots, x_n) \qquad *(8.2.57)$$

For the cost function, the optimal factor inputs satisfy

$$x_j = \frac{\partial C}{\partial w_j} \qquad *(8.2.58)$$

where, since the cost function is concave in w_j,

$$\frac{\partial x_j}{\partial w_j} = \frac{\partial^2 C}{\partial w_j^2} < 0, \quad \text{all } j \qquad *(8.2.59)$$

as in (8.2.37). The cost curve of (8.2.14) then corresponds to the cost function with given input wages

$$C(y) = C(\overline{w}_1, \overline{w}_2, \ldots, \overline{w}_n, y). \qquad *(8.2.60)$$

Of these various functions, the ones most frequently estimated using econometric techniques are the production function (8.2.1), the cost curve (8.2.14), factor demand functions (8.2.28), and the cost function (8.2.57).

8.3 Estimation of production functions

A basic problem in applied econometrics is that of estimating the production function, representing the technological relationship between output and factor inputs.[10] In most empirical applications the production function gives output y as a function of only two homogeneous inputs–labor L and capital K:

$$y = f(L, K). \qquad *(8.3.1)$$

Data for the estimation include cross-section or time-series data on some or all three variables and related variables, such as prices and wages. Output is typically measured as value added per year, deflated for price changes in time-series studies. It can also, however, be measured as physical units of output per year or gross value of output per year. The inputs should, in theory, be measured in terms of *services* of the input per unit of time, but such data are generally not available, so they are instead typically measured by the amount of the input

[10] For surveys of production functions and their estimation see Walters (1963, 1968), Frisch (1965), Hildebrand and Liu (1965), Nerlove (1967), Solow (1967), and Ferguson (1969).

utilized or available in the production process. Labor input is typically measured as manhours employed per year, but it is also sometimes measured as number of employees. Capital input is typically measured by the net capital stock (net of depreciation), but it is also sometimes measured by the gross capital stock and by certain direct measures (e.g., number of tractors in use for agriculture). Among the other inputs that could be included in the production function are raw materials, fuel, and land. Furthermore, labor and capital can be disaggregated, e.g., into skilled and unskilled labor and, for capital, plant and equipment.

Of these variables the one that creates the most problems is the capital input. While data on output and labor are generally available, data on capital are either not available or of questionable validity. Enormously complex problems of measurement arise with respect to capital as an input to the production process. First, capital generally represents an aggregation of very diverse components, including various types of machines, plant, inventories, etc. Even machines of the same type may cause aggregation problems if they are of different vintages, with different technical characteristics, particularly different levels of productivity or efficiency. Second, some capital is rented but most is owned. For the capital stock that is owned, however, it is necessary to impute rental values to take account of capital services. Such an imputation depends, in part, on depreciation of capital. Depreciation figures are generally unrealistic, however, since they entail both tax avoidance by the firm and the creation by the tax authorities of incentives to invest via accelerated depreciation. Third, there is the problem of capacity utilization. Only capital that is actually utilized should be treated as an input, so measured capital should be adjusted for capacity utilization. Accurate data on capacity utilization are, however, difficult or impossible to obtain.[11] Other problems could be cited as well, but all these suggest that, if at all possible, the use of an explicit measure of the capital stock should be avoided, since it is virtually impossible to find data adequately representing capital stock.

To estimate the production function requires the further development of its properties, leading to the specification of an explicit functional form. In particular, it is generally assumed that the production function satisfies the properties

$$f(0,K) = f(L,0) = 0 \tag{8.3.2}$$

$$\frac{\partial f}{\partial L} \geqslant 0, \qquad \frac{\partial f}{\partial K} \geqslant 0 \tag{8.3.3}$$

$$\frac{\partial^2 f}{\partial L^2} \leqslant 0, \qquad \frac{\partial^2 f}{\partial K^2} \leqslant 0, \qquad \frac{\partial^2 f}{\partial L^2}\frac{\partial^2 f}{\partial K^2} - \left(\frac{\partial^2 f}{\partial L\,\partial K}\right)^2 \geqslant 0. \tag{8.3.4}$$

[11] One approach to capacity utilization is to assume that the percentage of capital utilized is the same as the percentage of labor utilized, and therefore to reduce total capital available by the (labor) unemployment rate. There are various problems with this approach, however. For example, to the extent that capital is owned, the cost of using unemployed capital is less than that of using unemployed labor, suggesting that labor unemployment might exceed capital unemployment.

Here (8.3.2) indicates that both factor inputs are indispensable in the production of output, (8.3.3) states that both marginal products are nonnegative, and (8.3.4) states that the Hessian matrix of second-order partial derivatives of the production function is negative semidefinite, ensuring the proper curvature of the isoquants.

The production function (8.3.1) can, in certain cases, exhibit certain *returns-to-scale* phenomena at particular points. Thus at the point (L, K) the production function exhibits local

$$\left\{\begin{array}{l}\textit{constant}\\ \textit{increasing}\\ \textit{decreasing}\end{array}\right\} \textit{returns to scale} \quad \text{if } f(\lambda L, \lambda K)\left\{\begin{array}{c} = \\ > \\ < \end{array}\right\}\lambda f(L, K), \quad \text{all } \lambda > 1. \tag{8.3.5}$$

The constant-returns-to-scale case, that in which the production function exhibits (global) constant returns to scale for all positive λ, is that in which it is positive homogeneous of degree one (sometimes called "linearly homogeneous"), satisfying

$$f(\lambda L, \lambda K) = \lambda f(L, K), \qquad \text{all } \lambda > 0, \qquad \text{all } (L, K). \qquad *(8.3.6)$$

In this case, at any levels of the inputs, scaling both inputs by the same multiplicative factor scales output by the same multiplicative factor. Then Euler's theorem on homogeneous functions implies that

$$\frac{\partial f}{\partial L} L + \frac{\partial f}{\partial K} K = f(L, K). \tag{8.3.7}$$

This condition implies, from (8.2.6), assuming perfect competition, that

$$wL + rK = pf(L, K). \qquad *(8.3.8)$$

Here the left-hand side is total income, the sum of labor income and capital income, w and r being the wages rates of labor and capital, respectively. The right-hand side is the value of output, given as output price times the level of output. Condition (8.3.8) thus states that, assuming profit maximization and perfect competition, a constant-returns-to-scale production function implies that total income equals total output. This result is sometimes called the "adding-up theorem." More generally, the production function is positive homogeneous of degree h if

$$f(\lambda L, \lambda K) = \lambda^h f(L, K), \qquad \text{all } \lambda > 0, \qquad \text{all } (L, K) \tag{8.3.9}$$

the case $h = 1$ being that of constant returns to scale. If the production function is homogeneous of degree h and $h > 1$, then it exhibits (global) increasing returns to scale, while if $h < 1$ it exhibits (global) decreasing returns to scale.[12]

[12] Of course, production functions need not be homogeneous of any degree. A local measure of returns to scale is given by the *elasticity of production* at the point (L, K):

The production function is said to be *homothetic* if it can be expressed as

$$y = F[g(L, K)] \tag{8.3.10}$$

where F is a monotonic increasing function of a single variable and g is a function that is homogeneous of degree one in L and K. The case of homogeneity of degree one of the production function, as represented by (8.3.6), is thus a special case of homotheticity. Homotheticity ensures that all isoquants, as in Figure 8.1, are "radial blowups" of a given isoquant, since the isoquants passing through a given ray from the origin all have the same slope.

Another important property of production functions, in addition to that of returns to scale, is that of the *substitutability of inputs* for one another. A local measure of such substitutability is the *elasticity of substitution* σ, defined as the ratio of the proportionate change in the ratio of factor inputs (called "factor proportions") to the proportionate change in the ratio of marginal products (the marginal rate of technical substitution at given levels of inputs):[13]

$$\sigma = \frac{d \ln (K/L)}{d \ln (\text{MP}_L/\text{MP}_K)} = \frac{d \ln (K/L)}{d \ln (\text{MRTS}_{LK})} \qquad *(8.3.11)$$

In this definition the numerator involves the ratio of capital to labor, while the denominator involves the ratio of the marginal product of labor to that of capital, ensuring that σ is nonnegative.

Assuming perfect competition and profit maximization, the ratio of the marginal products is the ratio of the factor prices, as in (8.2.7). Thus σ can, under these assumptions, be written

$$\sigma = \frac{d \ln (K/L)}{d \ln (w/r)} = \frac{d(K/L)/(K/L)}{d(w/r)/(w/r)} = \frac{(w/r)\, d(K/L)}{(K/L)\, d(w/r)} \qquad *(8.3.12)$$

The elasticity of substitution is thus a measure of how rapidly factor proportions change for a change in relative factor prices. It is therefore a measure of the curvature of the isoquants. Figure 8.3 illustrates σ by showing isoquants for each of two production functions. In this case isoquant 1 exhibits greater elasticity of substitution than isoquant 2, since the same change in relative factor prices elicits for 1 a greater change in factor proportions, shown geometrically as the change in the slope of the ray from the origin to the tangency between isocost and isoquant.

$$\epsilon(L, K) = \frac{L}{y}\frac{dy}{dL} = \frac{K}{y}\frac{dy}{dK} \quad \text{where} \quad \frac{dL}{L} = \frac{dK}{K}$$

and thus is defined for an equal proportional change in each of two inputs. See Problem 8-G.

[13] See Allen (1938)

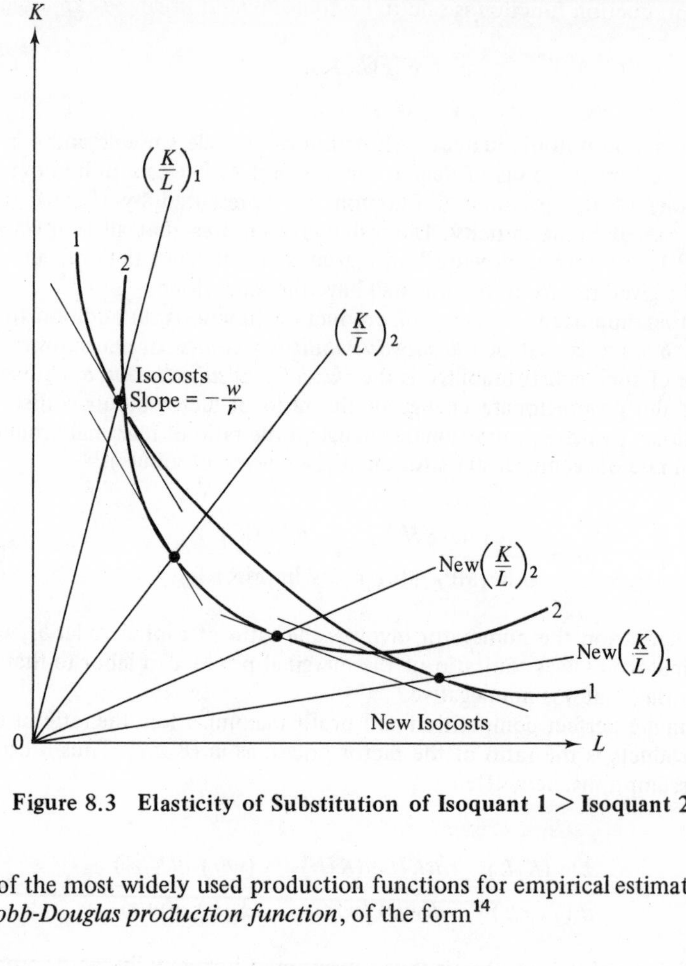

Figure 8.3 Elasticity of Substitution of Isoquant 1 > Isoquant 2

One of the most widely used production functions for empirical estimation is the *Cobb-Douglas production function*, of the form[14]

$$y = AL^{\alpha}K^{\beta} \qquad *(8.3.13)$$

where A, α, and β are fixed positive parameters. This specification is identical to that of the last chapter for constant elasticity demand functions. In this case the exponents are the elasticities of output with respect to each input:

$$\alpha = \frac{L}{y}\frac{\partial y}{\partial L}, \quad \beta = \frac{K}{y}\frac{\partial y}{\partial K}, \qquad 0 < \alpha < 1,\ 0 < \beta < 1,\ \alpha + \beta \leqslant 1. \qquad (8.3.14)$$

The constancy of these elasticities is a characteristic of the Cobb-Douglas production function, and the inequalities in (8.3.14) ensure that conditions (8.3.2)-(8.3.4) are satisfied. The sum of the elasticities is the degree of homogeneity of the function, since

$$f(\lambda L, \lambda K) = A(\lambda L)^{\alpha}(\lambda K)^{\beta} = \lambda^{\alpha+\beta}AL^{\alpha}K^{\beta} = \lambda^{\alpha+\beta}f(L, K). \qquad (8.3.15)$$

[14] See Douglas (1948) and Nerlove (1965).

The Cobb-Douglas function is linear in the logarithms of the variables. Considering cross-section studies, the Cobb-Douglas function for the ith firm, after taking logarithms and adding a stochastic disturbance term u_i to account for variations in the technical or productive capabilities of the ith firms, is[15]

$$\ln y_i = a + \alpha \ln L_i + \beta \ln K_i + u_i \qquad (a = \ln A). \qquad *(8.3.16)$$

It is assumed here that the parameters α and β (and also the prices) are the same for all firms, differences among firms being summarized by the u_i. One way of estimating the parameters a, α, and β is to estimate this equation directly, given data on output y_i, labor input L_i, and capital input K_i. Since such data are often not available, especially data on capital, the function has generally been estimated indirectly. Even if these data were available, however, a direct estimation of (8.3.16) would be a somewhat questionable procedure, since the explanatory variables $\ln L_i$ and $\ln K_i$ are endogenous variables, jointly determined with $\ln y_i$, and are not independent of the stochastic disturbance term, leading to a problem of simultaneous-equations estimation, specifically an endogenous explanatory variable. They also tend not to be independent of one another, leading to a possible problem of multicollinearity. Furthermore, the variance of the stochastic disturbance term need not be constant, leading to a problem of heteroskedasticity.

The classical approach to estimating the Cobb-Douglas production function is to assume perfect competition and profit maximization, so conditions (8.2.6) are applicable. These conditions require that marginal productivity equal the real wage:

$$\frac{\partial y_i}{\partial L_i} = \alpha \frac{y_i}{L_i} = \frac{w}{p}, \qquad \frac{\partial y_i}{\partial K_i} = \beta \frac{y_i}{K_i} = \frac{r}{p}. \qquad (8.3.17)$$

These conditions can be written

$$\alpha = \frac{wL_i}{py_i}, \qquad \beta = \frac{rK_i}{py_i}. \qquad *(8.3.18)$$

Here the common denominator is py_i, the value of output. The numerator wL_i is payments to labor, and the other numerator, rK_i, is payments to capital. Thus, these conditions require that labor's share of total income be the parameter α, while the share of capital be the parameter β. Since the total value of output equals total income (the sum of labor income and capital income),

$$py_i = wL_i + rK_i \qquad (8.3.19)$$

[15] An additive stochastic disturbance term here means that in the original formulation the stochastic disturbance is multiplicative, (8.3.13) taking the form

$$y_i = AL_i^{\alpha}K_i^{\beta}e^{u_i}$$

The multiplicative nature of this stochastic disturbance term is justified mainly by convenience.

conditions (8.3.18) and (8.3.19) require that

$$\alpha + \beta = 1. \tag{8.3.20}$$

This condition is precisely the condition that the Cobb-Douglas function exhibit constant returns to scale.

Assuming constant returns to scale, equation (8.3.16) implies that

$$\ln y_i = a + \alpha \ln L_i + (1 - \alpha) \ln K_i + u_i \tag{8.3.21}$$

which, further, implies that

$$\ln\left(\frac{y_i}{L_i}\right) = a + (1 - \alpha) \ln\left(\frac{K_i}{L_i}\right) + u_i. \tag{*(8.3.22)}$$

This equation is the production function in *intensive form*, relating output per worker to the capital-labor ratio. Estimating this equation yields an estimate of $1 - \alpha$, the elasticity of output with respect to capital, where α is the elasticity with respect to labor. Using this equation rather than (8.3.16) also reduces the problems of multicollinearity and heteroskedasticity; the use of ratios to reduce the problem of heteroskedasticity having been discussed in Section 6.3.

An alternative method of estimation, assuming constant returns to scale, perfect competition, and profit maximization, is based on the share of labor income in output. From (8.3.17) and constant returns to scale

$$\alpha = \frac{wL_i}{py_i} = s_L, \qquad \beta = 1 - \alpha \tag{*(8.3.23)}$$

where s_L is the share of labor in national income. Thus the shares yield direct estimates of both α and β under these assumptions.[16] This method requires no data on capital inputs, either in total [as in (8.3.16)] or relative to labor [as in (8.3.22)], but it does depend on the assumption of constant returns to scale and hence cannot be used to test hypotheses about returns to scale.

Assuming constant returns to scale, perfect competition, and profit maximization, the marginal-productivity equation (8.3.17) implies a log linear relation between output per worker and the real wage:

$$\ln \frac{y_i}{L_i} = \ln \frac{w}{p} - \ln \alpha. \tag{8.3.24}$$

Adding a stochastic disturbance term to this relation, to account for errors made by firms in choosing inputs so as to maximize profits, leads to a regression equation. The estimated intercept then provides an estimate of the (negative of the logarithm of the) elasticity α.

[16] With cross-section or time-series data the shares can be estimated as the *geometric* means of shares calculated for each production unit or at each time period. See Problem 8-K.

There are, then, at least four different methods of estimating the parameters of the production function, involving alternative assumptions and econometric problems.[17] The first is that of estimating *the production function itself* in log linear form, (8.3.16). This method requires no further assumptions, e.g., as to returns to scale, but it typically leads to econometric problems of simultaneity (endogenous explanatory variable), multicollinearity, and heteroskedasticity. The second method is that of estimating the *intensive production function* in log linear form, (8.3.22). This method reduces the problems of multicollinearity and heteroskedasticity, but it does require the assumption of constant returns to scale and hence cannot be used to test for increasing or decreasing returns to scale. It also has an endogenous explanatory variable. The third and fourth methods, those of *factor shares*, (8.3.23), and of the *marginal productivity relation*, (8.3.24), respectively, eliminate the simultaneity, multicollinearity, and heteroskedasticity problems, but require the assumptions of constant returns to scale, perfect competition, and profit maximization. None of these methods dominates the others. Each is appropriate in particular situations, depending upon what can be assumed and what is to be investigated.[18] The resulting para-

[17] See Walters (1963) and Nerlove (1965). A fifth method is discussed in the next footnote.

[18] A fifth method is to estimate the simultaneous system consisting of the production function and the first order conditions for profit maximization

$$y_i = AL_i^\alpha K_i^\beta e^{u_i}$$

$$\frac{\partial y_i}{\partial L_i} = \frac{\alpha y_i}{L_i} = \frac{w}{p} e^{v_i}$$

$$\frac{\partial y_i}{\partial K_i} = \beta \frac{y_i}{K_i} = \frac{r}{p} e^{w_i}.$$

Here u_i is a technical disturbance term, affecting the efficiency of the production process, and v_i and w_i are economic disturbance terms, affecting the attainment of the two profit-maximization conditions. Taking logarithms gives the linear system

$$\ln y_i = a + \alpha \ln L_i + \beta \ln K_i + u_i$$

$$\ln y_i = -\ln \alpha + \ln L_i + \ln \frac{w}{p} + v_i$$

$$\ln y_i = -\ln \beta + \ln K_i + \ln \frac{r}{p} + w_i$$

which is the structural form for a system in which $\ln y_i$, $\ln L_i$, and $\ln K_i$ are the endogenous variables and $\ln w/p$ and $\ln r/p$ are the exogenous variables (assuming perfect competition). See Marschak and Andrews (1944), Nerlove (1965), Hildebrand and Liu (1965), Zellner, Kmenta, and Dreze (1966), Griliches and Ringstad (1971), and Problem 8-I. The first method of estimation entails estimating only the first equation of this system. Estimating the complete system is generally superior to estimating only the first equation from both economic and econometric standpoints. From an economic standpoint estimating the complete system expresses the assumption that the data reflect both the behavior of the decision maker (the firm) and the technology, while the first equation reflects only the technology. From an econometric standpoint the estimator of only the first equation involves simultaneous-equations bias, so the estimators will be biased and inconsistent, as discussed in Chapter 11.

meter estimates will generally be different, and there is little evidence to suggest which estimates come closest to true values.

Table 8.1 presents some estimates of the Cobb-Douglas production function for the macroeconomy of a nation or state using time-series data and the technique of least squares, as applied to (8.3.16). The discussion of the previous section referred, however, to a single firm. Estimates of production relationships for macroeconomies, such as those of Table 8.1, are based upon the further assumption that the macroeconomic entity acts as if it were representative of the underlying microeconomic entities.[19] The index i then ranges over time.

The four alternative estimates for the United States and the two alternative estimates for New Zealand in Table 8.1 are based on alternative ways of measuring inputs and output. Douglas concluded, based on the results reported in this table and other results (some based on cross-section rather than time-series data), that production exhibits approximately constant returns to scale. He also concluded that the factors of production receive approximately the share they would receive under competitive conditions, given as the elasticity of output with respect to the factor. Later authors have questioned these conclusions, however. One criticism was based on the multicollinearity in the data used. Another was based on the condition that the total value of output equal total income (8.3.19), which creates a bias of the estimated production function toward these results.[20] To show this bias, using index numbers in (8.3.16), it follows that (ignoring the stochastic disturbance term)

$$\ln \frac{y_i}{\overline{y}_i} = \alpha \ln \frac{L_i}{\overline{L}_i} + \beta \ln \frac{K_i}{\overline{K}_i} \qquad (8.3.25)$$

where $\overline{y}_i$, $\overline{K}_i$, and $\overline{L}_i$ are base-year quantities of output, capital, and labor, respectively, for the ith firm.[21] But if y_i, K_i, and L_i do not vary appreciably from the

[19] Formally, under certain aggregation conditions, it may be possible to aggregate microeconomic production functions into macroeconomic production functions. The aggregation conditions here are comparable to those for a household, as discussed in Section 7.7. Several new issues arise here, however, with regard to aggregation. One is that of *reswitching*, where different ratios of inputs are used at different ratios of input prices. Others are *efficiency* and *technical change*, which are both affected by and affect aggregation of micro production functions into macro production functions. Also some exogeneity assumptions change (e.g., factor prices). On the general problems of aggregation see Walters (1963), Green (1964), and Problem 8-K. For a study of efficiency and aggregation see Houthakker (1955–6), who derived a macro Cobb-Douglas production function on the basis of micro fixed-coefficients (input–output) production functions [introduced in (8.3.33)], assuming a specific probability distribution (the Pareto distribution) of firms over possible values of the input coefficients. Generalizations and related approaches appear in Johansen (1972) and Sato (1975).

[20] See Cramer (1969). The bias toward constant returns to scale is an example of the practical problem stemming from the aggregation problem, as previously discussed in Section 7.7. Aggregate output is calculated from the total value of payments to factors of production, so using this value for output to test for returns to scale is questionable. Similarly, if aggregate capital data are constructed by subtracting the value of labor input from the value of output and deflating then a test of returns to scale is also questionable.

[21] The intercept drops out of the equation, since, if

$$y_i = AL_i^{\alpha}K_i^{\beta}, \qquad \overline{y}_i = A\overline{L}_i^{\alpha}\overline{K}_i^{\beta}$$

Table 8.1. Estimates of the Cobb-Douglas Production Function

Country, Time Period	Labor Elasticity α	Capital Elasticity β	Returns to Scale $\alpha + \beta$	Average Labor Share s_L
United States I 1899–1922	0.81 (0.15)	0.23 (0.06)	1.04	0.61
United States II 1899–1922	0.78 (0.14)	0.15 (0.08)	0.93	0.61
United States III 1899–1922	0.73 (0.12)	0.25 (0.05)	0.98	0.61
United States IV 1899–1922	0.63 (0.15)	0.30 (0.05)	0.93	0.61
New Zealand I 1915–1916 and 1918–1935	0.42 (0.11)	0.49 (0.03)	0.91	0.52
New Zealand II 1923–1940	0.54 (0.02)			0.54
New South Wales, Australia 1901–1927	0.78 (0.12)	0.20 (0.08)	0.98	
Victoria, Australia 1902–1929	0.84 (0.34)	0.23 (0.17)	1.07	

Source Douglas (1948).

NOTE Numbers in parentheses are standard errors.

base quantities, the ratios are close to unity, so

$$\ln \frac{y_i}{\bar{y}_i} \approx \frac{y_i}{\bar{y}_i} - 1, \ln \frac{L_i}{\bar{L}_i} \approx \frac{L_i}{\bar{L}_i} - 1, \quad \ln \frac{K_i}{\bar{K}_i} \approx \frac{K_i}{\bar{K}_i} - 1. \tag{8.3.26}$$

Thus (8.3.25) implies that

$$\frac{y_i}{\bar{y}_i} \approx \alpha \frac{L_i}{\bar{L}_i} + \beta \frac{K_i}{\bar{K}_i} + (1 - \alpha - \beta) \tag{8.3.27}$$

---

then, taking ratios,

$$\frac{y_i}{\bar{y}_i} = \left(\frac{L_i}{\bar{L}_i}\right)^{\alpha} \left(\frac{K_i}{\bar{K}_i}\right)^{\beta}.$$

Taking logarithms of this equation yields (8.3.25).

so that

$$py_i = \left(\alpha p \frac{\bar{y}_i}{\bar{L}_i}\right) L_i + \left(\beta p \frac{\bar{y}_i}{\bar{K}_i}\right) K_i + (1 - \alpha - \beta)p\bar{y}_i. \tag{8.3.28}$$

Comparing this equation to (8.3.19), however, it follows that

$$\alpha p \frac{\bar{y}_i}{\bar{L}_i} \approx w, \quad \beta p \frac{\bar{y}_i}{\bar{K}_i} \approx r, \quad (1 - \alpha - \beta)p \approx 0. \tag{8.3.29}$$

These results imply that

$$\alpha + \beta \approx 1 \tag{8.3.30}$$

which means returns to scale are approximately constant, and

$$\frac{w\bar{L}_i}{p\bar{y}_i} \approx \alpha, \quad \frac{r\bar{K}_i}{p\bar{y}_i} \approx \beta \tag{8.3.31}$$

which means that factor shares are approximately the elasticities, α and β, the shares received under competitive conditions. Thus, assuming only small variations in output and inputs, the form of the production function and the equality of the values of output and income imply that the production function exhibits approximately constant returns to scale and that factor shares are approximately the elasticities.

A second example of the Cobb-Douglas production function is the estimation by Kimbell and Lorant of a production function for physicians' services.[22] The data were obtained from an American Medical Association survey of physician activities in 1970. Altogether there were 844 observations on physicians in both solo and group practices. The estimated function is

$$\begin{aligned} \ln(py) = 2.826 &+ \underset{(0.052)}{0.255} \ln h + \underset{(0.037)}{0.708} \ln d + \underset{(0.030)}{0.302} \ln a \\ &+ \underset{(0.042)}{0.074} \ln r, \quad R^2 = 0.906. \end{aligned} \tag{8.3.32}$$

Here py is gross revenue from medical practice, a measure of output for the heterogeneous services provided by physicians; h is the average number of hours worked by (full-time) physicians in the practice; d is the number of (full-time equivalent) physicians in the practice; a is the number of (full-time equivalent) allied health personnel (e.g. nurses) employed by the practice; and r is the number of rooms used in the practice, a measure of capital input. According to these results, the elasticity of gross revenue with respect to physicians' hours is 0.255, so a 10% increase in hours would increase gross revenue by about 2.6%. The

[22] See Kimbell and Lorant (1974)

elasticity for aides implies that increasing the number of aides by one-third would increase gross revenue by about 10%. The sum of the elasticities is 1.084, which is significantly greater than unity at the 0.01 confidence level, indicating increasing returns to scale for physicians' services.

Another form of the production function is the *input-output production function*,[23]

$$y = \min\left(\frac{L}{a}, \frac{K}{b}\right), \qquad a, b > 0. \qquad *(8.3.33)$$

Here the isoquants are right-angled (L-shaped), as shown in Figure 8.4, and the production function permits no substitution between the inputs. The condition of profit maximization, given positive factor wages, is

$$\frac{L}{a} = \frac{K}{b} \qquad (8.3.34)$$

that is, operation at the vertex of the isoquants. Then

$$a = \frac{L}{y}, \qquad b = \frac{K}{y} \qquad (8.3.35)$$

so the parameters a and b are, respectively, the input of labor per unit of output and the input of capital per unit of output—the fixed proportions of inputs to output. The equations in (8.3.35) are typically used to estimate the parameters a and b, which are called "technical coefficients." The estimation is typically based on a single observation, so regression techniques are not used. The estimated production function is used in input-output studies concerned with the interrelationships among productive sectors that arise from the fact that the inputs of any one sector consist of portions of the outputs of other sectors.[24]

One of the most widely used production functions in empirical work is the *constant elasticity of substitution* (CES) production function, of the form[25]

$$y = A[\delta L^{-\beta} + (1 - \delta)K^{-\beta}]^{-1/\beta}. \qquad *(8.3.36)$$

[23] See Leontief (1951, 1966) and Chenery and Clark (1959).

[24] Let x_{ij} be the input of commodity i, as produced by sector i, that is used in the production of commodity j by sector j. If x_j is the output of sector j, then the technical coefficients comparable to (8.3.35) are given as

$$a_{ij} = \frac{x_{ij}}{x_j}, \qquad i, j = 1, 2, \ldots, n.$$

See Intriligator (1971).

[25] See Arrow, Chenery, Minhas, and Solow (1961), Brown and de Cani (1963), and Minhas (1963). Note that β here plays an entirely different role from the β in the Cobb-Douglas production function.

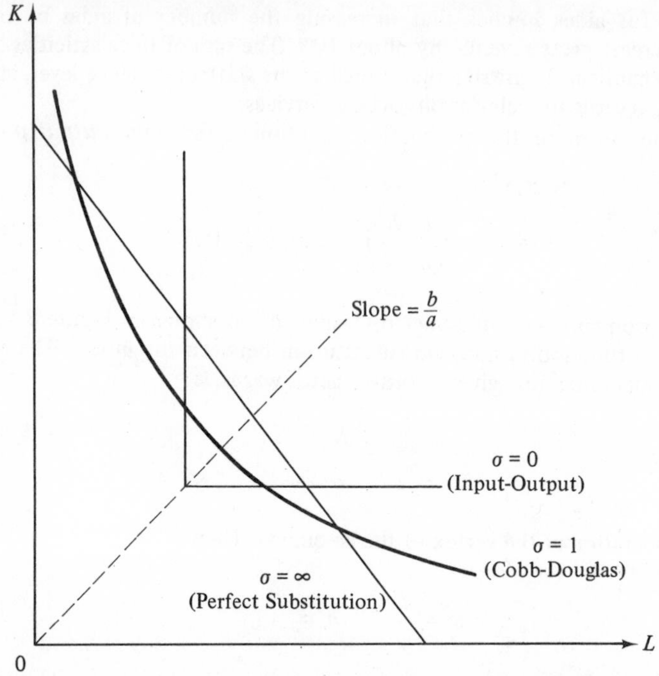

Figure 8.4 Isoquants of the CES Production Function Corresponding to Different Values of the Elasticity of Substitution, σ

The parameters defining this production function are

A: scale parameter, $A > 0$
δ: distribution parameter, $0 < \delta < 1$
β: substitution parameter, $\beta \geqslant -1$.

The name of the function is based upon the concept of the elasticity of substitution, σ, defined in (8.3.11). In general, the elasticity of substitution σ varies with K and L. Assuming σ is constant, however, and solving the resulting differential equation yields, in the constant-returns-to-scale case, precisely the CES function, where

$$\sigma = \frac{1}{1 + \beta} \qquad *(8.3.37)$$

justifying the interpretation of β as the substitution parameter. As defined in (8.3.11) σ must be nonnegative, so

$$\beta \geqslant -1. \qquad (8.3.38)$$

At the extreme value of $\beta = -1$ the CES function reduces to the linear function

$$y = A[\delta L + (1 - \delta)K] \quad \text{if} \quad \beta = -1, \text{ i.e., } \sigma = \infty. \tag*{*(8.3.39)}$$

The isoquants for this case are linear, the slope of each being $-\delta/(1-\delta)$. In this case of perfect substitution $\sigma = \infty$, meaning that certain slight changes in w/r would lead to discontinuous changes in K/L, e.g., from one boundary point to another. At the other extreme value for β, namely in the limit as β approaches ∞, from (8.3.37), σ approaches zero and, in this case, in the limit of the CES as $\beta \to \infty$, it approaches the input-output production function, as in (8.3.33):

$$y = \min\left(\frac{L}{a}, \frac{K}{b}\right) \quad \text{if} \quad \beta \to \infty, \text{ i.e., } \sigma \to 0. \tag{8.3.40}$$

In the limit as β approaches zero, σ approaches unity; this is the case of the Cobb-Douglas production function, where, taking the limit as $\beta \to 0$, the CES approaches (8.3.13)

$$y = A_0 L^{\delta} K^{1-\delta} \quad \text{if} \quad \beta \to 0, \text{ i.e., } \sigma \to 1. \tag{8.3.41}$$

Thus the CES is a family of production functions that includes, as special cases, the Cobb-Douglas, input-output, and linear production functions. The isoquants of these various cases are shown in Figure 8.4, and estimation of σ gives information on the curvature of the isoquants. It might be noted that the isoquants of the CES production function intersect the axes if $\sigma > 1$, and they are asymptotic to horizontal and vertical lines if $\sigma < 1$.[26]

The CES can be estimated by using the conditions of profit maximization (8.2.6). The marginal product of labor can be written

$$\frac{\partial y}{\partial L} = A'\left(\frac{y}{L}\right)^{1+\beta} \tag{8.3.42}$$

where A' is a constant, so setting the marginal product equal to the real wage yields

$$A'\left(\frac{y}{L}\right)^{1+\beta} = \frac{w}{p}. \tag{8.3.43}$$

Solving for output per manhour (labor productivity) y/L,

$$\frac{y}{L} = A''\left(\frac{w}{p}\right)^{1/1+\beta} \tag{8.3.44}$$

so, taking logs, and using (8.3.37):

[26] See Problem 8-N. As noted there, the case $\sigma > 1$ is excluded if both factors are essential in that output is zero if either factor input is zero—conditions (8.3.2). The case $\sigma < 1$ is consistent with factors being essential in this sense.

$$\ln\frac{y}{L} = a + \frac{1}{1+\beta}\ln\frac{w}{p} = a + \sigma\ln\frac{w}{p}, \qquad a = \ln A''. \tag{8.3.45}$$

This equation relates output per worker to the real wage, where a and σ are constants, σ being the coefficient of ln (w/p). The special case of the Cobb-Douglas for which $\sigma = 1$ was presented earlier in (8.3.24). Equation (8.3.45), with an additive stochastic disturbance term on the right-hand side, can be estimated using least-squares regression. Alternatively the equation can be solved for the real wage and the resulting equation,

$$\ln\frac{w}{p} = a' + (1+\beta)\ln\frac{y}{L} \tag{8.3.46}$$

in which the dependent and explanatory (exogenous) variables have switched roles, can be estimated to obtain $1/(1+\beta)$ as an estimate of σ. Such an estimation could, for example, utilize cross-section data on output, y, labor, L, and the real wage, w/p, assuming the real wage is exogenous and all entities in the cross section use the same underlying production function. This was the approach used by Arrow, Chenery, Minhas, and Solow, who estimated σ in (8.3.45) using cross-section data for specific industries from 19 different countries over the period 1950–1956. They found that their estimates of σ tended to cluster below unity, with 10 out of 24 industries having an estimated σ statistically different from (and below) unity. Their approach was extended by Fuchs who, using the same data, distinguished developed from less developed countries in the sample of 19 countries. He showed, using analysis of covariance, that the developed and less developed countries exhibit different intercept a in (8.3.45), but the same σ, and he reestimated σ, using a dummy variable to reflect the different intercept in the developed countries.[27] His results for σ are presented in Table 8.2, where industries are arranged in order of increasing estimated σ. The estimates tend to cluster about unity, ranging from a low of 0.658 for clay products to a high of 1.324 for grain and mill products. Only one of the estimates is statistically significantly different from unity. This one exception is glass, for which the estimated σ is significantly above unity, indicating a greater ease of substitution between capital and labor than that indicated by the Cobb-Douglas function. Since this is the only such case out of 24 industries, the Fuchs study provides justification for continued use of the Cobb-Douglas function. Various other studies also find that the estimated elasticity of substitution does not differ significantly from unity, justifying use of the Cobb-Douglas production function.[28]

The CES production function can be extended to the case of nonconstant returns to scale, but homogeneous case, for which the function can be written

$$y = A[\delta L^{-\beta} + (1-\delta)K^{-\beta}]^{-h/\beta} \tag*{*(8.3.47)}$$

where h is the degree of homogeneity of the function. This case reduces to

[27] See Fuchs (1963).

[28] See Griliches (1967), Zarembka (1970), and Griliches and Ringstad (1971). Griliches

Table 8.2. Estimates of σ, the Elasticity of Substitution for 19 Countries, 1950–1956

Industry	*Estimated Elasticity of Substitution* σ	*Industry*	*Estimated Elasticity of Substitution* σ
Clay products	0.658 (0.197)	Furniture	1.043 (0.090)
Iron and steel	0.756 (0.112)	Bakery products	1.056 (0.105)
Sugar	0.898 (0.183)	Fats and oils	1.058 (0.181)
Dairy products	0.902 (0.080)	Misc. chemicals	1.060 (0.088)
Pulp and paper	0.912 (0.175)	Ceramics	1.078 (0.125)
Nonferrous metals	0.935 (0.197)	Lumber and wood	1.083 (0.141)
Knitting mills	0.948 (0.083)	Fruit and vegetable canning	1.086 (0.098)
Leather finishing	0.975 (0.100)	Basic chemicals	1.113 (0.104)
Textile spinning	0.976 (0.104)	Tobacco	1.215 (0.208)
Metal products	1.006 (0.166)	Glass	1.269 (0.096)
Printing and publishing	1.021 (0.085)	Cement	1.308 (0.217)
Electrical machinery	1.026 (0.214)	Grain and mill products	1.324 (0.167)

Source Fuchs (1963).

(8.3.36) if $h = 1$, the constant-returns-to-scale case. The general function was estimated by Dhrymes using cross-section data on U.S. states.[29] Some of his results are shown in Table 8.3. From his results for h, most industries operate at

(1967) found only one industry (paper) out of 17 in which use of the Cobb-Douglas production function was not justified. It might be noted, however, that Nerlove (1967), in surveying over 40 papers, found conflicting estimates of the elasticity of substitution, with values ranging from 0.068 to 1.16. He concluded that the estimates are sensitive to the period under consideration and the concepts employed. In a later survey, Mayor (1969) found that studies using cross-section data obtain estimates of the elasticity of substitution close to unity while those using time-series obtain estimates considerably less than unity, clustering around one-half. Johansen (1972) attributes this difference between cross-section and time-series studies to the "putty-clay" nature of technology, according to which substitution possibilities are reduced once investment has occurred and capital is in place. Johansen suggests that the firm decides factor proportions before investment in new plant and equipment occurs and that, after this investment has occurred, subsequent decisions involve only the scale of operation. Cross-section estimates may reveal *ex-ante* substitution possibilities, before capital is in place, and so exhibit relatively high elasticities of substitution. Time-series estimates, by contrast, tend to reveal *ex-post* substitution possibilities, after capital is in place, and so exhibit relatively low elasticities of substitution. For further discussion of the putty-clay model, which distinguishes ex-ante and ex-post substitution possibilities, such as substitution possibilities ex-ante but fixed coefficients ex-post see Johansen (1959, 1972) and Bliss (1968).

[29] See Dhrymes (1965) and Kmenta (1967) and Zarembka (1970). See also Brown and de Cani (1963), where the derivation and estimation of the CES production function allowed for $h \neq 1$.

Table 8.3. Estimates of the CES Production Function for the United States

Industry	*Elasticity of Substitution σ*			*Degree of Homogeneity h*	
Machinery, except electrical	0.050	} extremes		1.029	
Rubber products	1.984	} extremes		1.092	
Textile mill products	0.936		closest to unity	0.997	} extremes
Lumber and wood products	1.109			1.218	} extremes
Furniture and fixtures	1.001	} closest to unity		1.017	
Chemicals	0.506			1.042	
Food	0.469			1.044	

Source Dhrymes (1965). Results have been rounded.

or above constant returns to scale ($h = 1$), with textile mill products exhibiting the lowest degree of homogeneity. From his results for σ, most consumer goods (e.g., textile mill products, furniture) are produced with an elasticity of substitution of approximately unity, i.e., close to the Cobb-Douglas production function. Most producer goods (e.g., machinery, chemicals), however, are produced with an elasticity of substitution significantly below unity, approaching in some cases the input-output production function. However, other studies have arrived at radically different results for certain industries. The study by Ferguson, for example, of U.S. manufacturing industries, using time-series data from the U.S. Census for 18 industries, 1949–1961, found an estimate of σ for non-electrical machinery of 1.041 (0.04), in contrast to the Dhrymes value of 0.050, and for chemicals of 1.248 (0.072), in contrast to the Dhrymes value of 0.506. Some of the other industries yielded somewhat comparable estimates, however—for example, for textile mill products [1.104 (0.44) vs. 0.936], lumber and wood [0.905 (0.067) vs. 1.109], furniture and fixtures [1.123 (0.045) vs. 1.001], and food [0.241 (0.20 vs. 0.469].[30]

It has already been noted that the Cobb-Douglas production function is a special case of the CES production function, corresponding to an elasticity of substitution of unity. Conversely the CES production function can be viewed as a generalization of the Cobb-Douglas production function to the case of a non-unitary, but constant, elasticity of substitution. For example, expanding $\ln y$ in a Taylor's series approximation of the CES around $\beta = 0$ yields[31]

[30] See Ferguson (1965) and Nerlove (1967).

[31] See Kmenta (1967). This approximation can be used to estimate the parameters of the CES production function. Using this approach, Kmenta estimated σ as 0.672 and h as 1.179. Neither of these estimates, however, was significantly different from unity, so a Cobb-Douglas production function with constant returns to scale is not ruled out by his findings. It should be noted, however, that the estimated σ is not invariant to a change in units of measurement.

$$\ln y \approx a + h\delta \ln L + h(1 - \delta) \ln K - \frac{\beta h\delta(1 - \delta)}{2} (\ln L - \ln K)^2 \qquad \textbf{(8.3.48)}$$

The first several terms on the right are those of the Cobb-Douglas production function, and the last term accounts for $\sigma \neq 1$. This approximation is better the closer the elasticity of substitution is to unity, and it reduces to the Cobb-Douglas case if $\beta = 0$.

While the CES production function represents one generalization of the Cobb-Douglas production function, the Cobb-Douglas has also been generalized in several other ways. One such way is the *transcendental production function*, of the form[32]

$$y = AL^{\alpha}K^{\beta}e^{\alpha' L + \beta' K} \qquad A > 0, \qquad \alpha', \beta' \leqslant 0. \qquad \textbf{(8.3.49)}$$

This case reduces to the Cobb-Douglas if α' and β' vanish. Taking logarithms

$$\ln y = a + \alpha \ln L + \beta \ln K + \alpha' L + \beta' K \qquad \textbf{(8.3.50)}$$

so $\ln y$ is a linear function of the inputs L and K, as well as the logarithms of the inputs $\ln L$ and $\ln K$. For this function it is possible for marginal products to rise before eventually falling. This function also permits variable elasticity of production and variable elasticity of substitution over the range of inputs.

A second approach to generalizing the Cobb-Douglas production function is the *Zellner-Revankar production function*, of the form[33]

$$ye^{cy} = AL^{\alpha}K^{\beta}, \qquad c \geqslant 0. \qquad \textbf{(8.3.51)}$$

This case reduces to the Cobb-Douglas form if $c = 0$. Taking logarithms,

$$\ln y + cy = a + \alpha \ln L + \beta \ln K. \qquad \textbf{(8.3.52)}$$

This case is essentially the obverse of the transcendental case. In the transcendental case inputs and logarithms of inputs enter on the right-hand side, while in this case output and the logarithm of output enter on the left-hand side.

A third approach to generalizing the Cobb-Douglas production function is the *Nerlove-Ringstad production function*, of the form[34]

$$y^{1 + c \ln y} = AL^{\alpha}K^{\beta}, \qquad c \geqslant 0. \qquad \textbf{(8.3.53)}$$

This case reduces to the Cobb-Douglas form if $c = 0$. Taking logarithms,

$$(1 + c \ln y) \ln y = a + \alpha \ln L + \beta \ln K \qquad \textbf{(8.3.54)}$$

so $\ln y$ and $(\ln y)^2$ appear on the left-hand side.

[32] See Halter, Carter, and Hocking (1957). Note that α' and β' are not invariant to a change in units of measurement. For a discussion of other functional forms not necessarily related to the Cobb-Douglas production function see Heady and Dillon (1961).

[33] See Zellner and Revankar (1969).

[34] See Nerlove (1963) and Ringstad (1967).

A fourth approach to generalizing the Cobb-Douglas production function is the *translog production function*, of the form[35]

$$\ln y = a + \alpha \ln L + \beta \ln K + \gamma \ln L \ln K + \delta(\ln L)^2 + \epsilon(\ln K)^2. \quad *(8.3.55)$$

This function, which is quadratic in the logarithms of the variables, reduces to the Cobb-Douglas case if the parameters γ, δ, and ϵ all vanish; otherwise it exhibits nonunitary elasticity of substitution. In general this function is quite flexible in approximating arbitrary production technologies in terms of substitution possibilities. It provides a local approximation to any production frontier.[36]

The last several production functions are extensions of the Cobb-Douglas production function. The CES production function has also been generalized in different ways. One such generalization is the two-level production function.[37] For this function factors are combined according to the CES at one level to form "higher-level" factors, which are combined again according to the CES to produce output. An example is the production function

$$y = A \left\{[\delta_1 x_1{}^{-\beta_1} + (1 - \delta_1)x_2{}^{-\beta_1}]^{-\beta/\beta_1} + [\delta_2 x_3{}^{-\beta_2} + (1 - \delta_2)x_4^{-\beta_2}]^{-\beta/\beta_2}\right\}^{-1/\beta} \quad (8.3.56)$$

Here x_1 and x_2 are combined into a "higher-level" factor, where the elasticity of substitution is $(1 + \beta_1)^{-1}$, while x_3 and x_4 are combined with an elasticity of substitution of $(1 + \beta_2)^{-1}$. The "higher-level" inputs are then combined with an elasticity of substitution of $(1 + \beta)^{-1}$. Another generalization of the CES is the *VES production function*, i.e., the variable-elasticity-of-substitution production function.[38] For this function the elasticity of substitution varies with the factor proportions (the ratio of the inputs). Such a relationship can be estimated by regressing the log of output per worker on both the real wage [as in (8.3.45)] and the capital-labor ratio.[39]

[35] "Translog" is short for "transcendental logarithmic". See Christensen, Jorgenson, and Lau (1973) and Griliches and Ringstad (1971). More generally, for n inputs, the translog function is

$$\ln y = a + \sum_{i=1}^{n} \alpha_i \ln x_i + \tfrac{1}{2} \sum_{i=1}^{n} \sum_{j=1}^{n} \gamma_{ij} \ln x_i \ln x_j$$

where x_i is the ith input and $\gamma_{ij} = \gamma_{ji}$. Note that this function is also not invariant to a change of units.

[36] It can also be applied to other frontiers, e.g., to demand functions or to price frontiers.

[37] See Sato (1967).

[38] See Sato and Hoffman (1968); see also Lu and Fletcher (1968), Revankar (1971), and Lovell (1973).

[39] See Hildebrand and Liu (1965). In most industries the coefficient of the capital-labor ratio is significant.

8.4 Estimation of cost curves and cost functions

Cost curves, based on economic theory, were developed in Section 8.2, equations (8.2.14)-(8.2.20), and illustrated in Figure 8.2. A variety of cost curves, including total, average, and marginal cost curves, have been estimated empirically for particular industries.[40]

A simple example of a total cost curve that satisfies the curvature postulated in Figure 8.2 is the *cubic cost curve*,

$$C = a_0 + a_1 y + a_2 y^2 + a_3 y^3 \qquad *(8.4.1)$$

where a_0, a_1, a_2, and a_3 are given parameters. The average cost associated with the cubic cost curve is

$$\text{AC} = \frac{a_0}{y} + a_1 + a_2 y + a_3 y^2 \qquad (8.4.2)$$

and marginal cost is given as

$$\text{MC} = a_1 + 2a_2 y + 3a_3 y^2. \qquad (8.4.3)$$

For U-shaped average and marginal cost curves, as illustrated in Figure 8.2, the parameters must satisfy the restrictions

$$a_0 \geqslant 0, \quad a_1 > 0, \quad a_2 < 0, \quad a_3 > 0, \; a_2^2 < 3a_3 a_1 \qquad (8.4.4)$$

where a_0 is the fixed cost, the cost at zero output.

Empirical studies of cost curves typically estimate a long-run cost curve using cross-sectional data on firms in the industry, specifically data on total costs, output, and other relevant variables. Assuming that the same technology applies to all firms, that observed outputs are close to planned outputs, and that firms are seeking to minimize costs at each planned output level, it follows that the cost curve estimated from a scatter diagram of cost-output points represents an estimate of the long-run cost curve. The specific curve estimated is usually an average cost curve; and taking ratios as called for in such a curve reduces problems of heteroskedasticity.[41] In the long-run case, a_0 in the cubic cost curve (8.4.1), which is fixed cost, vanishes, and so the average cost curve in this case is

$$\text{AC} = a_1 + a_2 y + a_3 y^2. \qquad (8.4.5)$$

[40] For surveys of cost curves see Johnston (1960) and Walters (1963, 1968). For cost functions see Shephard (1970).

[41] Note that if u is an additive stochastic disturbance term for the total cost curve and Var (u) = Ky^2, where K is a positive constant, then Var $(u/y) = K$; with this assumption the additive stochastic disturbance term in the average cost curve exhibits constant variance for all levels of output y.

This quadratic long-run average cost curve has been estimated for many industries.

For a wide variety of industries, including manufacturing, mining, distribution, transportation, and trade, it has been found that the long-run average cost curves are L-shaped, rather than U-shaped.[42] Thus, as illustrated in Figure 8.5,

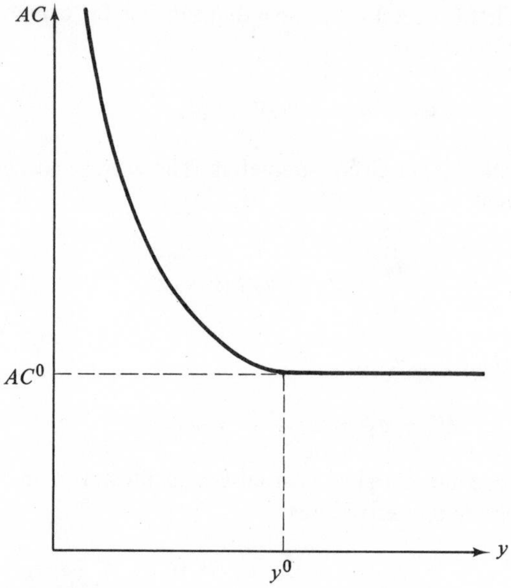

Figure 8.5 Estimated Average Cost Curve

average cost at first falls sharply (based, in part, on spreading fixed costs over more output) but then reaches or asymptotically approaches a certain minimum level AC^0 at a critical level of output, y^0, and remains flat at this level.[43] The critical level of output y^0 is the minimal efficient scale; it is the point at which there is a "knee" in the average cost curve.

Various explanations have been suggested for the L-shaped nature of the long-run average cost curve. Some are based on econometric reasoning, involving cer-

[42] See Johnston (1960), Walters (1963), Wiles (1963), and Gold (1966).

[43] In the case of a linear cost curve, of the form

$$C = a + by$$

average cost is

$$\frac{C}{y} = \frac{a}{y} + b$$

which asymptotically approaches b, marginal cost, here assumed constant.

tain biases present in the estimation or in the measurement of costs or output.[44] Others are based on economic reasoning. For example, a profit-maximizing firm would, assuming the cost curve applies to a particular plant, build new plants (until the minimum average cost level is attained) rather than move up the rising portion of the average cost curve for its existing plants. Thus the rising portion of the curve would never be observed.

Estimated cost curves have been used to study the question of economies of scale. A local measure of economies of scale is given by the *elasticity of cost*, γ, the elasticity of the cost curve with respect to output, given as

$$\gamma = \gamma(y) = \frac{y}{C(y)} \frac{\partial C(y)}{\partial y} \tag{8.4.6}$$

where factor prices are assumed given.[45] There are

$$\textit{local} \begin{Bmatrix} \textit{economies of} \\ \textit{constant returns to} \\ \textit{diseconomies of} \end{Bmatrix} \textit{scale at } y \text{ if } \gamma(y) \begin{Bmatrix} < \\ = \\ > \end{Bmatrix} 1. \tag{8.4.7}$$

Local economies of scale hold if and only if the average cost curve is decreasing, while increasing average cost is equivalent to local diseconomies of scale. Thus in Figure 8.5 there are local economies to scale up to y^0, and neither economies nor diseconomies of scale (i.e., constant returns to scale) beyond this point. The point y^0 is thus the *minimal efficient scale* (MES), i.e., the smallest output level at which average cost reaches its minimum value, or, equivalently, the smallest output for which the elasticity of cost is unity.

In the special case of a production function that is positive homogeneous of degree h, as in (8.3.9), it follows that

$$\gamma = \frac{1}{h} \tag{8.4.8}$$

so, in this case, if $h > 1$ there are economies of scale everywhere and if $h < 1$ there are diseconomies of scale everywhere. For example, in the Cobb-Douglas case γ is given as the reciprocal of the sum of the elasticities

$$\gamma = \frac{1}{\alpha + \beta} \tag{8.4.9}$$

so if this sum exceeds unity it means that there are economies of scale everywhere.

[44] There are, indeed, manifold problems in measuring cost. One is the fact that certain costs are unobservable, including the costs of capital, self-employed labor, stocks of factors, and certain other inputs.

[45] The intimate connections between cost curves and production functions is indicated by the fact that the elasticity of production, defined in footnote 12, is the reciprocal of the elasticity of cost. See Problem 8-G.

The cost function (8.2.57) gives cost as a function not only of output but also as a function of factor prices. For the Cobb-Douglas case the cost function is of the constant elasticity form, where

$$C(w, r, y) = A'(w^{\alpha} r^{\beta} y)^{1/(\alpha+\beta)}. \qquad *(8.4.10)$$

Here the elasticity of the cost function with respect to output is $1/(\alpha + \beta)$, the reciprocal of the degree of homogeneity of the production function, as in (8.4.9). Considering firm i, taking logarithms, and adding the stochastic disturbance term u_i, the elasticities α and β can be estimated from the linear model

$$\ln C_i = a' + \frac{\alpha}{\alpha + \beta} \ln w + \frac{\beta}{\alpha + \beta} \ln r + \frac{1}{\alpha + \beta} \ln y_i + u_i \qquad (8.4.11)$$

where u_i, C_i, and y_i vary with the firm, but α, β, w, and r are assumed to be the same for all firms (and hence are not subscripted). This approach provides yet another way of estimating the Cobb-Douglas production function. Nerlove estimated (8.4.11) for electricity generation, treating w, r, and y_i as exogenous.[46] In this case output can be treated as exogenous, since electric power is supplied on demand and it cannot be stored. The interest rate is exogenous, assuming competitive capital markets, and wages are exogenous since workers are unionized and wages are fixed by long-term contracts. Nerlove added another term to allow for fuel input, where the price of fuel is also exogenous, since fuel is supplied under long-term contract. He estimated the homogeneity of the production function to be approximately 1.39, indicating increasing returns to scale. Examination of the residuals suggested stratification of the sample, and after stratifying, he found that the homogeneity fell from approximately 2.5 for the smallest firms to approximately 1.0 for the largest firms. Thus he found that there are strong increasing returns to scale for the smallest firms, but approximately constant returns to scale for the largest firms, as in Figure 8.5.

Examples of general cost functions for n inputs with wages $w_1, w_2, \ldots, w_n$ are the *generalized Leontief cost function*

$$C = \left(\sum_{i=1}^{n} \sum_{j=1}^{n} b_{ij} w_i^{1/2} w_j^{1/2} \right) y \qquad (8.4.12)$$

and the *translog cost function*

$$C = \left(\alpha_0 + \sum_{i=1}^{n} \alpha_i \ln w_i + \tfrac{1}{2} \sum_{i=1}^{n} \sum_{j=1}^{n} \gamma_{ij} \ln w_i \ln w_j \right) y \qquad (8.4.13)$$

which are the cost functions related to the input-output production function (8.3.33) and the translog production function (8.3.55), respectively.[47]

[46] See Nerlove (1963).

[47] See Diewert (1974).

8.5 Estimation of factor demand equations

Another aspect of the theory of the firm is the system of factor demand equations, (8.2.28), of the form[48]

$$x_j = x_j(w_1, w_2, \ldots, w_n, p) \qquad j = 1, 2, \ldots, n. \qquad *(8.5.1)$$

This system can be estimated using alternative approaches that correspond to the estimation of consumer demand equations of the last chapter.

The partial equilibrium approach is to estimate a single equation of this system, specifically the factor demand curve for factor j, of the form

$$x_j = D_j(w_j) = x_j(\bar{w}_1, \ldots, \bar{w}_{j-1}, w_j, \bar{w}_{j+1}, \ldots, \bar{w}_n, \bar{p}). \qquad *(8.5.2)$$

Various specifications have been utilized in estimating such a factor demand curve, including the linear- and the log-linear function. The latter is of the form

$$x_j = Aw_j^{\epsilon_j}e^{u_j} \qquad (8.5.3)$$

where u_j is the stochastic disturbance term. Taking logs,

$$\ln x_j = a + \epsilon_j \ln w_j + u_j \qquad *(8.5.4)$$

where ϵ_j is the elasticity of demand for factor j.

The general equilibrium approach is to estimate the complete system, and various specifications have been used for systems of factor demand equations. One of the most common is the constant elasticity form

$$x_j = Aw_1^{\epsilon_{1j}} w_2^{\epsilon_{2j}} \ldots w_n^{\epsilon_{nj}} p^{\gamma_j} e^{u_j}, \qquad j = 1, 2, \ldots, n \qquad (8.5.5)$$

which, in log form, is the linear system

$$\ln x_j = a + \epsilon_{1j} \ln w_1 + \epsilon_{2j} \ln w_2 + \ldots$$
$$+ \epsilon_{nj} \ln w_n + \gamma_j \ln p + u_j, \qquad j = 1, 2, \ldots, n. \qquad *(8.5.6)$$

This system reduces to (8.5.3) and (8.5.4) if all wages other than that of the factor itself and output price are held constant. The ϵ_{jj} in (8.5.6) is then the same as ϵ_j in (8.5.4).

A system of factor demand equations can be derived from the first-order conditions of profit maximization, assuming a production function is given and all prices are given. Consider, for example, the case of the Cobb-Douglas production function

$$y = AL^{\alpha}K^{\beta}. \qquad *(8.5.7)$$

The first-order conditions of profit maximization require that

[48] For a survey of factor demand equations see Nadiri (1970).

$$\frac{\partial y}{\partial L} = \alpha A L^{\alpha-1} K^{\beta} = \frac{\alpha y}{L} = \frac{w}{p} \tag{8.5.8}$$

$$\frac{\partial y}{\partial K} = \beta A L^{\alpha} K^{\beta-1} = \frac{\beta y}{K} = \frac{r}{p} \tag{8.5.9}$$

where w is the given wage of labor, r is the given rental on capital, and p is the given output price. Combining these,

$$\frac{K}{L} = \frac{\beta}{\alpha}\frac{w}{r} \tag{8.5.10}$$

so the capital-labor ratio is constant. Solving this equation for K and inserting the result in (8.5.7) yields the demand for labor. Solving for L and taking logs, the demand-for-labor equation is

$$\ln L = a' - \frac{\beta}{\alpha + \beta} \ln \left(\frac{w}{r}\right) + \frac{1}{\alpha + \beta} \ln y. \tag*{*(8.5.11)}$$

This factor demand function and the comparable one for $\ln K$ (where the coefficient of $\ln (r/w)$ is $-\alpha/(\alpha + \beta)$) are of the log linear constant elasticity type, as in (8.5.6).[49] Labor demand functions of this type have been combined, by Waud, with an assumed log linear specification of a demand function for the output of the firm to explain the behavior of production-worker manhours at the two-digit level in U.S. manufacturing industry, 1954-1964.[50] Some of his findings are summarized in Table 8.4, including estimated elasticities of manhours with respect to wage, the cost of capital, and GNP (treated here as an exogenous shift variable in the demand function for output). In some industries, notably apparel, manhours are relatively insensitive to the wage or cost of capital, while in others, such as machinery, they are highly sensitive to both. In general, employment in manufacturing durables goods exhibits greater sensitivity to GNP than such employment in nondurables manufacturing. (The Durbin-Watson figures for the last two industries are quite low, however, and an alternative specification might be used in these cases.)

A related approach, the labor-requirements approach to factor demand, starts from the production function and solves it for the labor required as a function of capital and output. Thus, solving the Cobb-Douglas production function for L,

$$L = A^{-1/\alpha} K^{-\beta/\alpha} y^{1/\alpha} \tag{8.5.12}$$

so, in log form,

[49] A similar approach can be used to estimate factor demand functions using other production functions, such as the CES. See Problem 8-V.

[50] See Waud (1968).

Table 8.4 Production Worker Manhour Behavior in U.S. Manufacturing Industry, 1954–1964

	Elasticity with Respect to			
Industry	*Wage*	*Cost of Capital*	*GNP*	R^2/d
Food	−0.506 (0.145)	0.157 (0.066)	−0.036 (0.101)	0.920 2.137
Apparel	−0.287 (0.442)	0.136 (0.154)	0.796 (0.173)	0.726 1.596
Paper	−0.613 (0.345)	0.364 (0.095)	0.583 (0.152)	0.846 2.109
Chemicals	−0.654 (0.270)	0.339 (0.115)	0.690 (0.136)	0.674 1.789
Rubber and plastics	−1.334 (0.748)	0.675 (0.228)	1.400 (0.211)	0.861 1.737
Stone, clay, and glass	−1.967 (0.776)	0.445 (0.182)	1.466 (0.334)	0.574 1.505
Fabricated metals	−2.366 (0.708)	0.317 (0.124)	1.683 (0.244)	0.771 1.938
Machinery, except electrical	−2.103 (0.922)	0.995 (0.206)	2.340 (0.462)	0.791 1.399
Electrical machinery	−2.142 (0.838)	0.943 (0.217)	1.256 (0.259)	0.771 0.910

Source Waud (1968).

NOTE Coefficients of dummy variables, representing cyclical factors, which were included in these regressions, are not reported here.

$$\ln L = a_0 - \frac{\beta}{\alpha}\ln K + \frac{1}{\alpha}\ln y. \tag{8.5.13}$$

One problem with this approach is that data on capital are generally not available. Nevertheless it has been utilized, and such labor-requirement functions have been estimated.[51]

The labor-requirements approach is sometimes combined with a labor-adjustment model allowing gradual adjustment of labor input to its equilibrium level. Equation (8.5.12) is modified by interpreting the labor input as a required or desired amount of labor input at time t, designated by L_t^* and defined by

$$L_t^* = A^{-1/\alpha}K_t^{-\beta/\alpha}y_t^{1/\alpha} \tag{8.5.14}$$

[51] See Wilson and Eckstein (1964) and Kuh (1965).

where capital input and output are treated as given in the short run. The labor-adjustment equation is then typically assumed to be of the log linear form:[52]

$$\frac{L_t}{L_{t-1}} = \left(\frac{L_t^*}{L_{t-1}}\right)^{\lambda}, \quad 0 \leqslant \lambda < 1 \tag{8.5.15}$$

where λ is the adjustment coefficient. Combining the last two equations and taking logarithms yields

$$\ln L_t = (1 - \lambda) \ln L_{t-1} - \frac{\lambda}{\alpha} \ln A - \frac{\beta\lambda}{\alpha} \ln K_t + \frac{\lambda}{\alpha} \ln y_t. \qquad *(8.5.16)$$

This equation, or variants of it, have been estimated by several authors.[53]

A variant of this approach replaces the labor-requirements function by the relation of desired labor input to the wage, which is typically assumed to be of the constant elasticity form:

$$L_t^* = Aw^{\beta}. \tag{8.5.17}$$

For example, from (8.3.17) for the Cobb-Douglas production function β is -1. Combining with (8.5.15) yields, in this case,

$$\ln L_t = a_0 + a_1 \ln L_{t-1} + a_2 \ln w, \quad a_1 = 1 - \lambda, \; a_2 = \lambda\beta. \tag{8.5.18}$$

Such a function was estimated for U.S. farm workers 1911-1956 by Griliches, who obtained[54]

$$\ln L_t = a_0 + 0.77 \ln L_{t-1} - 0.10 \ln w, \quad R^2 = 0.92. \tag{8.5.19}$$

Thus the elasticity of labor demand with respect to the real wage is -0.10, and the adjustment coefficient is 0.23. The implied elasticity of desired labor with respect to the wage, the β in (8.5.17), is estimated here as -0.435.

8.6 Technical change

Technical change can be analyzed and estimated using production functions.[55] One such type of technical change is a shift in the production function over time reflecting greater efficiency in combining inputs. It is called *disem-*

[52] This labor-adjustment model is a variant of the stock adjustment model of Section 6.7. See Fair (1969).

[53] For a survey see Fair (1969). See also Nadiri and Rosen (1973) for a simultaneous equations model of employment, investment, and inventories.

[54] See Griliches (1959).

[55] See Hahn and Matthews (1964), Brown (1966), Lave (1966), Allen (1967), Nadiri (1970), Kennedy and Thirwall (1972), and Smith (1974).

bodied technical change, and it can be represented by the production function

$$y = f(L, K, t), \quad \text{i.e.,} \quad y(t) = f(L(t), K(t), t) \qquad \text{*(8.6.1)}$$

where t is time.[56] The change in output over time is given as

$$\frac{dy}{dt} = \frac{\partial f}{\partial L}\frac{dL}{dt} + \frac{\partial f}{\partial K}\frac{dK}{dt} + \frac{\partial f}{\partial t}. \qquad \text{*(8.6.2)}$$

The first two terms on the right indicate the change in output due to increased inputs of labor and capital, respectively, i.e., a movement along the production function. The last term on the right indicates the change in output due to disembodied technical change, i.e., a shift in the production function. This type of technical change is called "disembodied" because it is not embodied in the factor inputs; rather, it involves a reorganization of the inputs. It can occur with or without increases in the inputs. Dividing both sides of (8.6.2) by output y, to convert to proportionate rates of change, yields

$$\frac{1}{y}\frac{dy}{dt} = \left(\frac{L}{y}\frac{\partial y}{\partial L}\right)\frac{1}{L}\frac{dL}{dt} + \left(\frac{K}{y}\frac{\partial y}{\partial K}\right)\frac{1}{K}\frac{dK}{dt} + \frac{1}{y}\frac{\partial y}{\partial t} \qquad \text{*(8.6.3)}$$

where all terms have been expressed as proportionate rates of change. The first two terms on the right are the proportionate rates of change of the two inputs, each weighted by the elasticity of output with respect to the input. The third term is the proportionate rate of disembodied technical change.

Technical change is *neutral* (or *Hicks neutral*) if it does not change the marginal rate of substitution between the inputs. Geometrically, for a given ratio of factor prices, neutral technical change shifts the isoquants of the production function uniformly toward the origin, leaving unchanged the slope of the isoquant along any ray from the origin. Thus factor proportions remain unchanged as long as the ratio of factor prices remains unchanged. Assume, for example, that the elasticities of output with respect to labor and capital are constant and given by α and β, respectively, as in the Cobb-Douglas case. Assume further that the proportionate rate of disembodied technical change is constant at the rate m. Then (8.6.3) implies that

$$\frac{1}{y}\frac{dy}{dt} = \alpha\frac{1}{L}\frac{dL}{dt} + \beta\frac{1}{K}\frac{dK}{dt} + m \qquad \text{*(8.6.4)}$$

where m is the rate of neutral disembodied technical change. The assumption of constant elasticities is, as already noted, that of the Cobb-Douglas production function, and (8.6.4) could, in fact, be derived from such a production function with the scale parameter A increasing exponentially over time:

[56] See Solow (1957).

$$y = (A_0 e^{mt}) L^{\alpha} K^{\beta}. \tag{8.6.5}$$

Thus, taking logarithms,

$$\ln y = a_0 + \alpha \ln L + \beta \ln K + mt, \qquad a_0 = \ln A_0 \tag{8.6.6}$$

and differentiating,

$$\frac{d \ln y}{dt} = \frac{1}{y}\frac{dy}{dt} = \alpha \frac{1}{L}\frac{dL}{dt} + \beta \frac{1}{K}\frac{dK}{dt} + m \tag{8.6.7}$$

as in (8.6.4). The exponential time trend term in (8.6.5) thus accounts for neutral disembodied technical change. The rate of disembodied change, m, can be obtained from (8.6.4) as

$$m = \frac{1}{y}\frac{dy}{dt} - \alpha \left(\frac{1}{L}\frac{dL}{dt}\right) - \beta \left(\frac{1}{K}\frac{dK}{dt}\right) \tag{8.6.8}$$

–that is, as the proportionate change in output less the sum of the proportionate changes in all inputs, each such proportionate change being weighted by the elasticity of output with respect to that input. Solow used this formulation, with values of 0.65 for α and 0.35 for β, values based on relative shares, and with observed proportionate changes in y, L, and K, in order to infer the rate of disembodied technical change for U.S. nonfarm output, 1909–1949. He estimated m to be 0.015, representing a trend increase for productivity of 1.5% per year over this period.[57] He also found that the rate was about 1% per year during the 1909–1929 period and about 2% per year during the 1929–1949 period, indicating an acceleration in the rate of disembodied technical change. Over the entire period he found that technical change accounted for about 90% of the increase in output per manhour, with the increase in capital per manhour accounting for only 10%.

A related study by Aukrust for Norway, 1900–1955, excluding 1940 to 1945, obtained, as an estimate of (8.6.6):[58]

$$\ln y = \underset{}{2.62} + \underset{(0.10)}{0.76} \ln L + \underset{(0.19)}{0.20} \ln K + \underset{(0.003)}{0.018}t. \tag{8.6.9}$$

Thus he estimated elasticities with respect to labor and capital of 0.76 and 0.20,

[57] See Solow (1957). The study by Arrow, Chenery, Minhas, and Solow (1961) calculated the rate of technical change over the same period using a CES production function to be slightly higher–about 1.8% per year. Other studies yield similar estimates; e.g., Morishima and Saito (1964), using a Cobb-Douglas production function, found the rate to be about 1.5% per year over the period 1902 to 1952, while David and van de Klundert (1965), using a CES production function, found the rate to be 1.85% per year over the period 1899 to 1960.

[58] See Aukrust (1959).

respectively, and a rate of disembodied technical change (m) of 1.8% per year. Thus, with no increase in labor or capital, output would grow at the rate of 1.8% per year. Since output (real national product) grew at an average rate of 3.4% during 1948-1955, during this period over half of the growth rate is accounted for via disembodied technical change.

Another related study, by Brown, estimated the model

$$\Delta \ln y = \alpha \Delta \ln L + \beta \Delta \ln K + m \qquad \textbf{(8.6.10)}$$

obtained by taking first differences of (8.6.6).[59] He estimated this model over various historical periods, treating U.S. private domestic nonfarm output in 1929 prices as a function of manhours employed and net capital stock in 1929 prices adjusted for capital utilization. His results are presented in Table 8.5. The estimates of elasticities and returns to scale are different from those obtained by

Table 8.5 Estimates of Technical Change in the United States

Period	*Elasticity with Respect to* Labor α	Capital β	*Technical Change* m	*Returns to Scale* $\alpha + \beta$	$\bar{R}^2$ / d
1890–1960	0.325 (0.088)	0.552 (0.048)	0.0061 (0.0014)	0.877	0.887 1.49
1890–1906	0.690 (0.230)	0.416 (0.092)	0.0018 (0.0034)	1.106	0.867 1.98
1921–1939	0.383 (0.162)	0.505 (0.100)	0.0077 (0.0025)	0.888	0.928 1.81
1940–1960	0.453 (0.175)	0.489 (0.131)	0.0069 (0.0026)	0.942	0.775 1.27
1947–1960	0.659 (0.194)	0.379 (0.112)	0.0062 (0.0021)	1.038	0.891 1.90

Source Brown (1966). Results have been rounded.

Douglas, as reported in Table 8.1 for all periods other than 1947–1960. In general, the Brown results involve labor elasticities that are lower and capital elasticities that are higher than those estimated by Douglas. Technical change was highest in 1921–1939 and lowest in 1890–1906.

The discussion thus far has referred to *disembodied* technical change—that is, technical change that is not embodied in the factor inputs. By contrast, *embodied* technical change involves an augmentation in the effectiveness of factor inputs due to various possible improvements in their quality or efficiency over time. It can be represented by a *vintage model*, in which later vintages of inputs

[59] See Brown (1966).

are more effective than earlier vintages.[60] A production function incorporating both embodied and disembodied technical change was estimated by Intriligator for aggregate U.S. manufacturing output, 1929-1958.[61] Various time series for labor input were considered, involving alternative adjustments in the effectiveness of the labor force, including adjustments for the changes in working hours, education, and the age-sex composition of the labor force. For capital input, alternative rates of embodied technical change, corresponding to improvements in the technical efficiency of capital, were considered. The best estimate was

$$y = 0.869e^{\underset{(0.0026)}{0.0167}t}L^{0.862}\underset{(0.044)}{K^{0.138}}, \quad R^2 = 0.993, \quad d = 2.159 \tag{8.6.11}$$

where L refers to labor input of unchanging quality and K refers to capital input for embodied technical change of 4% annually. Thus, according to these estimates, disembodied technical change is 1.67% annually, no technical change is embodied in labor, and technical change embodied in capital amounts to 4% annually.[62]

PROBLEMS

8-A Consider the following cost curves $C(y)$, where y is output. For each, determine what conditions economic theory imposes on the coefficients, assuming fixed cost is nonnegative; average and marginal cost are both positive; and average and marginal cost initially decrease but eventually increase. For each also determine the output level at which average cost is a minimum.

1. $C = a_1 y + a_2 y^2 + a_3 y^3$ (cubic cost curve)
2. $C = a_0 + a_1 y + a_2 y^{1/2}$
3. $C = a_1 y^{a_2} e^{a_3 y}$
4. $C = a_1 y^{a_2} e^{a_3 (\log y)^2}$
5. $C = a_1 y^{1/a_2} (a_2 + a_3 y)^{-1/a_2}$

8-B Prove the comparative statics relation (8.2.41) using the production function, the homogeneity of the input demand functions, and the first-order conditions for profit maximization.

8-C For the profit function $\Pi(w_1, w_2, \ldots, w_n, p)$ defined in (8.2.50):

1. Prove that the profit function is positive homogeneous of degree one in all variables

[60] See Solow (1960, 1962) and Phelps (1962).

[61] See Intriligator (1965).

[62] Some authors have sought to explain changes in output and technology by explicitly accounting for as many influences as possible, including nonconstant returns to scale, changes in education, improvement in capital, etc. See Jorgenson and Griliches (1967).

$$\Pi(\alpha w_1, \alpha w_2, \ldots, \alpha w_n, \alpha p) = \alpha\Pi(w_1, w_2, \ldots, w_n, p), \qquad \text{all } \alpha > 0.$$

2. Prove that the demands for inputs x_j satisfy

$$x_j = -\frac{\partial \Pi}{\partial w_j} \quad \text{where} \quad \frac{\partial x_j}{\partial w_j} = -\frac{\partial^2 \Pi}{\partial w_j^2} < 0.$$

3. Prove that the supply of output y satisfies

$$y = \frac{\partial \Pi}{\partial p} \quad \text{where} \quad \frac{\partial y}{\partial p} = \frac{\partial^2 \Pi}{\partial p^2} > 0.$$

8-D For the cost function $C(w_1, w_2, \ldots, w_n, y)$ defined in (8.2.57):

1. Find the first-order conditions characterizing this function and illustrate them geometrically.
2. Prove that the cost function is positive homogeneous of degree one in all factor prices

$$C(\alpha w_1, \alpha w_2, \ldots, \alpha w_n, y) = \alpha\, C(w_1, w_2, \ldots, w_n, y), \qquad \text{all } \alpha > 0.$$

3. Prove that the demands for inputs x_j satisfy

$$x_j = \frac{\partial C}{\partial w_j} \quad \text{where} \quad \frac{\partial x_j}{\partial w_j} = \frac{\partial^2 C}{\partial w_j^2} < 0, \qquad \text{all } j.$$

8-E Consider the case of the firm in *imperfect competition*, where either output price or input prices are not given parametrically, but rather vary with the output or input levels chosen by the firm.

1. For a *monopolist* the output price falls with the level of output, since the firm faces the entire market demand curve for the product. Obtain the first-order conditions characterizing profit maximization in such a case. Illustrate geometrically.
2. For a *monopsonist* the input prices rise with the levels of input, since the firm faces the entire market supply curve for the input. Obtain the first-order conditions characterizing profit maximization in such a case. Illustrate geometrically.

8-F The production function $y = f(x_1, x_2)$ exhibits constant returns to scale if it is positive homogeneous of degree one, so

$$f(\alpha x_1, \alpha x_2) = \alpha f(x_1, x_2), \qquad \text{all } \alpha > 0$$

as in (8.3.6). Prove that if the production function exhibits constant returns to scale:

1. Marginal products and average products depend only on factor proportions $x_1/x_2 = k$.
2. The elasticity of substitution defined in (8.3.11) depends only on factor proportions, and it can be expressed in the following ways:

$$\sigma = \frac{\dfrac{\partial f}{\partial x_1}\dfrac{\partial f}{\partial x_2}}{y\dfrac{\partial^2 f}{\partial x_1\,\partial x_2}} = \frac{d\ln\left(\dfrac{y}{x_1}\right)}{d\ln\left(\dfrac{\partial f}{\partial x_1}\right)} = \frac{d\ln\left(\dfrac{y}{x_2}\right)}{d\ln\left(\dfrac{\partial f}{\partial x_2}\right)} = \frac{-g'(g-kg')}{kgg''}$$

where $k = x_1/x_2$ and $g(k) = g(x_1/x_2) = f(x_1/x_2, 1)$.
3. Real wages w_1/p and w_2/p depend only on factor proportions and there exists a *factor price frontier* $w_1/p = \varphi(w_2/p)$, where $\varphi' < 0$, $\varphi'' > 0$ and where the elasticity of w_1/p with respect to w_2/p is the relative share, i.e., the ratio of real payments to the two factors.[63]

8-G The *elasticity of production*, a local measure of returns to scale, is defined for the production function $y = f(L, K)$ as [64]

$$\epsilon = \epsilon(L, K) = \frac{L}{y}\frac{dy}{dL} = \frac{K}{y}\frac{dy}{dK} \quad \text{where} \quad \frac{dL}{L} = \frac{dK}{K}$$

It is therefore the elasticity of output with respect to an equiproportionate increase in all inputs.

1. Prove that if the production function is homogeneous of degree h, then $\epsilon = h$.
2. Prove that the elasticity of production at any point is the sum of the elasticities of output with respect to all inputs at this point:

$$\epsilon = \frac{L}{y}\frac{\partial y}{\partial L} + \frac{K}{y}\frac{\partial y}{\partial K}.$$

3. Prove that the elasticity of cost, γ, defined in (8.4.6) is the reciprocal of the elasticity of production:

$$\gamma = \frac{1}{\epsilon}.$$

8-H For the Cobb-Douglas production function (8.3.13), show that a change of units from (y, L, K) to $(c_0 y, c_1 L, c_2 K)$ changes the constant A but does not

[63] See Samuelson (1962). The factor price frontier can be defined as the locus of real wages such that the cost function is constant, for given output.

[64] See footnote 12 and Intriligator (1971). It is called the "passus coefficient" in Frisch (1965) and the "scale elasticity" in Johansen (1972).

change the exponents (elasticities) α and β. How does A change? Consider a similar change in units for other production functions, specifically the CES, transcendental, Zellner-Revankar, Nerlove-Ringstad, and translog production functions. Which parameters are invariant to a change in units?

8-I Consider the four alternative methods of estimating the Cobb-Douglas production function as discussed following (8.3.24). Assuming data y_i, L_i, K_i, and $(w/p)_i$ are available for $i = 1, 2, \ldots, n$ where n is the number of firms in a cross-section sample, determine for each method the estimator of α, the elasticity of output with respect to labor input. Give economic interpretations for these estimators, and compare them to one another.

8-J Consider the structural form defined in footnote 18 for the estimation of the Cobb-Douglas production function. Write the system as a matrix equation, and obtain the reduced form of this system. What restrictions must be placed on α and β? Show that the system is not identified. (See Chapter 10). What method(s) might be employed in estimating the elasticities α and β?

8-K A simple example of the aggregation problem, as discussed in footnote 19, is that of an industry consisting of F firms producing the same output from the same inputs of labor and capital using Cobb-Douglas production functions with different parameters. Show that for this industry there exists an aggregate Cobb-Douglas production function for which the parameters are weighted averages of those of the firms, provided aggregates of all variables are geometric means.

8-L For the Kimbell-Lorant production function for physicians services in (8.3.32), find the implied demand curve for allied health personnel as a function of the real wage of such personnel, w/p.

8-M The dependence of output on one factor input, assuming all others are held constant, is called a *product curve* (or *returns curve*). In the two-factor case, holding capital constant at K and varying labor leads to the total product, average product, and marginal product curves

$$\begin{aligned} \mathrm{TP}(L) &= f(L, \bar{K}) \\ \mathrm{AP}(L) &= \frac{1}{L} f(L, \bar{K}) \\ \mathrm{MP}(L) &= \frac{\partial f}{\partial L}(L, \bar{K}). \end{aligned}$$

Obtain these curves algebraically and geometrically for the

1. Cobb-Douglas production function.
2. Input-output production function.

8-N The isoquants of the CES production function (8.3.36) intersect the axes if $\sigma > 1$ and are asymptotic to horizontal and vertical lines if $\sigma < 1$.

1. In the case $\sigma > 1$ find the values at which the isoquants intersect the axes.
2. In the case $\sigma < 1$ find the values of the inputs defining the horizontal and

vertical lines that the isoquants approach asymptotically. Show that the assumption that factor inputs are indispensable (8.3.2) excludes the case $\sigma > 1$.

8-O For the CES production function (8.3.36), show that the relative share of labor is given as

$$s_L = \left(\frac{\delta}{1-\delta}\right)\left(\frac{L}{K}\right)^{-\beta}.$$

8-P Assuming output and both inputs are endogenous variables and output and input prices are exogenous, develop a simultaneous system of equations for the CES production function comparable to that developed for the Cobb-Douglas production function in footnote 18. What is the reduced form?

8-Q For the transcendental production function (8.3.49) show that the elasticity of substitution is

$$\sigma = 1 + \frac{1}{\dfrac{\beta}{\alpha' K} + \left(\dfrac{\beta'}{\alpha'} - \dfrac{r}{w}\right)}$$

8-R Prove by differentiating the average cost function that local economies of scale, defined in (8.4.7), hold if and only if the average cost curve is decreasing.

8-S Consider a chemical engineering process for which liquids are processed in a spherical tank. Assume that the output of the process is proportional to the volume of the tank, while the cost of the process is proportional to the surface of the tank. Letting C be cost and y be output, show, on the basis of geometrical considerations, that

$$C \sim y^{2/3}$$

so that the elasticity of the cost curve with respect to output is

$$\gamma = \tfrac{2}{3}$$

implying, by (8.4.7), economies of scale at each y.[65] Why, then, would such tanks be large, but not enormous?

8-T Consider the cost function for the Cobb-Douglas production function, as given in (8.4.10).

1. Derive this function from the conditions for profit maximization, solving explicitly for the constant term A'.
2. Show that the implied cost curve is linear in the case of constant returns to scale.

[65] See Moore (1959). See also Haldi and Whitcomb (1967) and Silberston (1972).

3. By setting marginal cost equal to price, obtain the output supply function and show that it is proportional to $p^{(\alpha+\beta)/(1-\alpha-\beta)}$. What is the shape of this supply function in the constant-returns-to-scale case?

8-U A production function implies a cost function.

1. Show for the extended CES production function (8.3.47) that the cost function is given as

$$C(w, r, y) = A' y^{1/h} [\delta^{1/(1+\beta)} w^{\beta/(1+\beta)} + (1 - \delta)^{1/(1+\beta)} r^{\beta/(1+\beta)}]^{(1+\beta)/\beta}$$

2. Show for the Zellner-Revankar production function (8.3.51) that the cost function is given as

$$C(w, r, y) = A' (w^{\alpha} r^{\beta} y e^{cy})^{1/(\alpha+\beta)}.$$

[Note that this reduces to the Cobb-Douglas cost function (8.4.10) if $c = 0$.]

8-V Consider the demand-for-labor equation (8.5.11).

1. Solve for a.
2. Prove that a comparable demand-for-labor equation for the CES production function (8.3.47) is given as

$$\ln L = a'' - \left(\frac{1}{1+\beta}\right) \ln w + \frac{1}{\beta} \ln [\delta^{1/(1+\beta)} w^{\beta/(1+\beta)} + (1 - \delta)^{1/(1+\beta)} r^{\beta/(1+\beta)}] + \frac{1}{h} \ln y$$

and solve for a''.

8-W An *engineering production function* is estimated on the basis of physical and engineering principles. An example of such a production function is that for transmission from a boiler, as determined by Smith:[66]

$$y = x_1 - \frac{a}{b + cx_2}.$$

Here y is heat output, x_1 is heat input, and x_2 is the thickness of the insulation material, where x_1 and x_2 are treated as the two inputs to the production process.

1. Determine the marginal rate of substitution between heat input and insulation material, and draw several isoquants.
2. Given w_1 and w_2 as the cost of heat input and thickness of insulation

[66] See Smith (1961). See also Chenery (1949, 1953).

material, respectively, determine the demand functions for each of the inputs.

8-X Another example of an engineering production function is that for transmission of crude oil in a pipe line, as determined by Cookenboo:[67]

$$y^a = bx_1 x_2^c.$$

Here y is the output of crude oil, x_1 is the horsepower of the transmission pump, and x_2 is the inside diameter of the pipe. As in the last problem, determine the marginal rate of substitution, draw several isoquants, and determine the demand functions for the two inputs.

BIBLIOGRAPHY

Allen, R. G. D. (1938), *Mathematical Analysis for Economists.* London: Macmillan & Co., Ltd.

Allen, R. G. D. (1967), *Macro Economic Theory.* London: Macmillan & Co., Ltd.

Arrow, K. J., H. B. Chenery, B. S. Minhas, and R. M. Solow (1961), "Capital-Labor Substitution and Economic Efficiency." *Review of Economics and Statistics*, 43: 225–35.

Aukrust, O. (1959), "Investment and Economic Growth." *Productivity Measurement Review*, 16: 35–53.

Baumol, W. J. (1967), *Business Behavior, Value and Growth*, Rev. Ed. New York: Harcourt Brace Jovanovich.

Bliss, C. (1968), "On Putty-Clay". *Review of Economic Studies*, 35: 105–32.

Brown, M. (1966), *On the Theory and Measurement of Technological Change.* New York: Cambridge University Press.

Brown, M., Ed. (1967), *The Theory and Empirical Analysis of Production.* National Bureau of Economic Research. New York: Columbia University Press.

Brown, M., and J. S. de Cani (1963), "Technological Change and the Distribution of Income."*International Economic Review*, 4: 289–309.

Chenery, H. B. (1949), "Engineering Production Functions." *Quarterly Journal of Economics*, 63: 507–31.

Chenery, H. B. (1953), "Process and Production Functions from Engineering Data," in W. W. Leontief et al., *Studies in the Structure of the American Economy.* New York: Oxford University Press.

Chenery, H. B., and P. G. Clark (1959), *Industry Economics.* New York: John Wiley & Sons, Inc.

Christensen, L. R., D. W. Jorgenson, and L. J. Lau (1973), "Transcendental Logarithmic Production Frontiers." *Review of Economics and Statistics*, 55: 28–45.

[67] See Cookenboo (1955).

Cookenboo, L. J. (1955), *Crude Oil Pipe Lines and Competition in the Oil Industry.* Cambridge, Harvard University Press.

Cramer, J. S. (1969), *Empirical Econometrics.* Amsterdam: North-Holland Publishing Co.

David, P. A., and T. van de Klundert (1965), "Biased Efficiency Growth and Capital-Labor Substitution in the U.S., 1899–1960." *American Economic Review*, 55: 357–94.

Dhrymes, P. J. (1965), "Some Extensions and Tests for the CES Class of Production Functions." *Review of Economics and Statistics*, 47: 357–66.

Diewert, W. E. (1974), "Applications of Duality Theory," in M. D. Intriligator and D. A. Kendrick, Eds., *Frontiers of Quantitative Economics*, Vol. II, Amsterdam: North-Holland Publishing Co.

Douglas, P. H. (1948), "Are There Laws of Production?" *American Economic Review*, 38: 1–49.

Fair, R. C. (1969), *The Short-Run Demand for Workers and Hours.* Amsterdam: North-Holland Publishing Co.

Ferguson, C. E. (1965), "Time Series Production Functions and Technological Progress in American Manufacturing Industry." *Journal of Political Economy*, 73: 135–47.

Ferguson, C. E. (1969), *The Neoclassical Theory of Production and Distribution.* New York: Cambridge University Press.

Frisch, R. (1965), *Theory of Production.* Dordrecht: Reidel; Chicago: Rand-McNally.

Fuchs, V. R. (1963), "Capital-Labor Substitution: A Note." *Review of Economics and Statistics*, 45: 436–8.

Gold, B. (1966), "New Perspectives on Cost Theory and Empirical Findings." *Journal of Industrial Economics*, 14: 161–94.

Green, H. A. J. (1964), *Aggregation in Economic Analysis.* Princeton: Princeton University Press.

Griliches, Z. (1959), "The Demand for Inputs in Agriculture and a Derived Supply Elasticity." *Journal of Farm Economics*, 41: 309–22.

Griliches, Z. (1967), "Production Functions in Manufacturing: Some Preliminary Results," in Brown, Ed. (1967).

Griliches, Z., and V. Ringstad (1971), *Economies of Scale and the Form of the Production Function.* Amsterdam: North-Holland Publishing Co.

Hahn, F. H., and R. C. O. Matthews (1964), "The Theory of Economic Growth: A Survey." *Economic Journal*, reprinted in American Economic Association and Royal Economic Society, *Surveys of Economic Theory*, Vol. II.

Haldi, J., and D. Whitcomb (1967), "Economies of Scale in Industrial Plants." *Journal of Political Economy*, 75: 373–85.

Halter, A. N., H. O. Carter, and J. G. Hocking (1957), "A Note on Transcendental Production Functions." *Journal of Farm Economics*, 39: 966–74.

Heady, E. O., and J. L. Dillon (1961), *Agricultural Production Functions.* Ames, Iowa: Iowa State University Press.

Hicks, J. R. (1946), *Value and Capital*, 2nd Ed. New York: Oxford University Press.

Hildebrand, G. H., and T. C. Liu (1965), *Manufacturing Production Functions in the United States, 1957.* Ithaca: New York State School of Industrial Labor Relations.

Houthakker, H. (1955–6), "The Pareto Distribution and the Cobb-Douglas Production Function in Activity Analysis." *Review of Economic Studies*, 23: 27–31.

Intriligator, M. D. (1965), "Embodied Technical Change and Productivity in the United States, 1929–1958." *Review of Economics and Statistics*, 47: 65–70.

Intriligator, M. D. (1971), *Mathematical Optimization and Economic Theory.* Englewood Cliffs, N.J.: Prentice-Hall, Inc.

Johansen, L. (1959), "Substitution vs. Fixed Production Coefficients in the Theory of Economic Growth: A Synthesis." *Econometrica*, 27: 157–76.

Johansen, L. (1972), *Production Functions.* Amsterdam: North-Holland Publishing Co.

Johnston, J. (1960), *Statistical Cost Analysis.* New York: McGraw-Hill Book Company.

Jorgenson, D. W., and Z. Griliches (1967), "Explanation of Productivity Change." *Review of Economic Studies*, **34**: 249–83.

Kennedy, C., and A. P. Thirwall (1972), "Technical Progress: A Survey." *Economic Journal*, 82: 11–72.

Kimbell, L. J., and J. Lorant (1974), "Physician Productivity and Returns to Scale." Chapter 20 in University of Southern California, Human Resources Research Center, *An Original Comparative Economic Analysis of Group Practice and Solo Fee-For-Service Practice: Final Report*, Publication No. PB 241 546. Springfield, Va.: National Technical Information Service, U.S. Department of Commerce.

Kmenta, J. (1967), "On Estimation of the CES Production Function." *International Economic Review*, 8: 180–89.

Kuh, E. (1965), "Income Distribution and Employment over the Business Cycle," in J. Duesenberry et al., Eds., *The Brookings Quarterly Econometric Model of the United States.* Amsterdam: North-Holland Publishing Co.

Lave, L. B. (1966), *Technological Change: Its Conception and Measurement.* Englewood Cliffs, N.J.: Prentice-Hall, Inc.

Leontief, W. W. (1951), *The Structure of the American Economy, 1919–1939*, 2nd Ed. New York: Oxford University Press.

Leontief, W. W. (1966), *Input-Output Economics.* New York: Oxford University Press.

Lovell, C. A. K. (1973), "Estimation and Prediction with CES and VES Production Functions." *International Economic Review*, 14: 676–92.

Lu, Y., and L. B. Fletcher (1968), "A Generalization of the CES Production Function". *Review of Economics and Statistics*, 50: 449–52.

Marschak, J., and W. H. Andrews (1944), "Random Simultaneous Equations and the Theory of Production." *Econometrica*, 12: 143–205.

Mayor, T. H. (1969), "Some Theoretical Difficulties in the Estimation of the Elasticity of Substitution from Cross-Section Data." *Western Economic Journal*, 7: 153–63.

McFadden, D., and M. Fuss, Eds. (1977), *Production Economics: A Dual Approach.* Amsterdam: North-Holland Publishing Co.

Minhas, B. S. (1963), *An International Comparison of Factor Costs and Factor Use.* Amsterdam: North-Holland Publishing Co.

Moore, F. T. (1959), "Economies of Scale: Some Statistical Evidence." *Quarterly Journal of Economics*, 73: 232–45.

Morishima, M., and M. Saito (1964), "A Dynamic Analysis of the American Economy, 1902–1952." *International Economic Review*, 5: 125–64.

Nadiri, M. I. (1970), "Some Approaches to the Theory and Measurement of Total Factor Productivity." *Journal of Economic Literature*, 8: 1137–77.

Nadiri, M. I., and S. Rosen (1973), *A Disequilibrium Model of Demand for Factors of Production.* National Bureau of Economic Research. New York: Columbia University Press.

Nerlove, M. (1963). "Returns to Scale in Electricity Supply," in C. F. Christ et al., *Measurement in Econometrics: Studies in Mathematical Economics and Econometrics in Memory of Yehuda Grunfeld.* Stanford: Stanford University Press. Reprinted in Zellner, Ed. (1968) and in Nerlove (1965).

Nerlove, M. (1965), *Estimation and Identification of Cobb-Douglas Production Functions.* Amsterdam: North-Holland Publishing Co.

Nerlove, M. (1967), "Recent Empirical Studies of the CES and Related Production Functions," in Brown, Ed. (1967).

Phelps, E. S. (1962), "The New View of Investment: A Neoclassical Analysis." *Quarterly Journal of Economics*, 76: 548–67.

Revankar, N. S. (1971), "A Class of Variable Elasticity of Substitution Production Functions," *Econometrica*, 39: 61–71.

Ringstad, V. (1967), "Econometric Analysis Based on a Production Function with Neutrally Variable Scale Elasticity." *Swedish Journal of Economics*, 69: 115–33.

Samuelson, P. A. (1947), *Foundations of Economic Analysis.* Cambridge: Harvard University Press.

Samuelson, P. A. (1962), "Parable and Realism in Capital Theory: The Surrogate Production Function." *Review of Economic Studies*, 29: 193–206.

Sato, R., and R. F. Hoffman (1968), "Production Functions with Variable Elasticity of Factor Substitution: Some Analysis and Testing." *Review of Economics and Statistics*, 50: 453–60.

Sato, K. (1967), "A Two Level Constant-Elasticity-of-Substitution Production Function." *Review of Economic Studies*, 34: 201–18.

Sato, K. (1975), *Production Functions and Aggregation.* Amsterdam: North-Holland Publishing Co.

Shephard, R. (1970), *The Theory of Cost and Production Functions.* Princeton: Princeton University Press.

Silberston, A. (1972), "Economies of Scale in Theory and Practice." *Economic Journal*, 82: 369–91.

Simon, H. (1959), "Theories of Decision-Making in Economics and Behavioral Science." *American Economic Review*, 59: 253–83.

Smith, V. K. (1974), *Technical Change, Relative Prices, and Environmental Resource Evaluation.* Baltimore: Johns Hopkins University Press.

Smith, V. L. (1961), *Investment and Production.* Cambridge: Harvard University Press.

Solow, R. M. (1957), "Technical Change and the Aggregate Production Function." *Review of Economics and Statistics*, 39: 312–20.

Solow, R. M. (1960), "Investment and Technical Progress" in K. J. Arrow, S. Karlin, and P. Suppes, Eds., *Mathematical Methods in the Social Sciences, 1959.* Stanford: Stanford University Press.

Solow, R. M. (1962), "Technical Progress, Capital Formation, and Economic

Growth." *American Economic Review, Papers and Proceedings*, 52: 76–86.

Solow, R. M. (1967), "Some Recent Developments in the Theory of Production," in Brown, Ed. (1967).

Walters, A. A. (1963), "Production and Cost Functions: An Econometric Survey." *Econometrica*, 31: 1–66.

Walters, A. A. (1968), "Econometric Studies of Production and Cost Functions." *Encyclopedia of the Social Sciences.*

Waud, R. N. (1968), "Man-hour Behavior in U.S. Manufacturing: A Neoclassical Interpretation." *Journal of Political Economy*, 76: 407–27.

Wiles, P. (1963), *Price, Cost, and Output*, Rev. Ed. New York: Praeger.

Williamson, O. E. (1964), *The Economics of Discretionary Behavior: Managerial Objectives in a Theory of the Firm.* Englewood Cliffs, N.J.: Prentice-Hall, Inc.

Wilson, T. A., and O. Eckstein (1964), "Short Run Productivity Behavior in U.S. Manufacturing." *Review of Economics and Statistics*, 46: 41–56.

Zarembka, P. (1970), "On the Empirical Relevance of the CES Production Function." *Review of Economics and Statistics*, 52: 47–53.

Zellner, A., Ed. (1968), *Readings in Economic Statistics and Econometrics.* Boston: Little, Brown and Company.

Zellner, A., J. Kmenta, and J. Dreze (1966), "Specification and Estimation of Cobb-Douglas Production Function Models." *Econometrica*, 34: 727–29.

Zellner, A., and N. Revankar (1969), "Generalized Production Functions." *Review of Economic Studies*, 36: 241–50.

CHAPTER 9

Other Applications of Single–Equation Estimation

9.1 Introduction

The technique of single-equation estimation has been applied to many areas of economics in addition to the traditional areas treated in the last two chapters. This chapter gives some examples of these "other" applications to certain traditional fields in economics, specifically monetary economics, industrial organization, labor economics, health economics, and economic history.[1]

Most fields in economics, in particular those treated in later sections of this chapter, have developed in a pattern established by many other scientific disciplines. The first works are typically discourses on various institutional or historical aspects of the field. They later lead, as a second phase, to verbal paradigms, such as analogies or case studies. The third phase often involves the use of geometrical models, such as demand and supply curves. The fourth phase is that of algebraic models, some of which are estimated using single-equation techniques. In the fifth phase, simultaneous models are developed and estimated using simultaneous-equations techniques. Current work in most fields in economics lies in the fourth phase, and some are just entering the fifth phase. This chapter reports on some of the models used and results obtained in the fourth phase, that involving single-equation estimation, in several fields (Chapter 13 reports on some results of the fifth phase for some of the same fields treated here). Space limitations preclude anything other than a cursory treatment of each of these fields. It is hoped, however, that the reader will become interested in doing further reading, for which the references given in each section and in the bibliography will serve as a guide.

9.2 The demand for money

Monetary economics is, to a large extent, concerned with the demand for and supply of money and credit; how these factors determine interest rates and other credit conditions; and how they affect and are affected by production, employment, and prices in the economy. This section treats only the demand for money.

[1] Single-equation techniques have also been applied to other areas and disciplines, including both social and natural sciences. Indeed, least-squares was first developed by Gauss in order to study planetary orbits. The bibliography to this chapter, which is organized by topic areas, includes references to econometric applications in a variety of areas. For a general reference on over 200 federally supported models in the social sciences see Fromm, Hamilton, and Hamilton (1974).

One must start with a suitable definition of "money"; the two most widely used definitions are

$$M_1 = \text{currency outside banks} + \text{demand deposits}$$

$$M_2 = \text{currency outside banks} + \text{demand deposits} \qquad *(9.2.1)$$
$$+ \text{ time deposits at commercial banks.}$$

If it can be assumed that the supply of money is set exogenously by the monetary authorities, then the single equation to be estimated is a demand equation for money.[2] Considerable work has been done on estimating such an equation.[3]

From a theoretical standpoint, the demand for money is based upon various motives for holding money rather than other assets. One is the *transactions motive*, according to which money is held because it is needed to make transactions—that is, to buy goods and services. The amount of money held is therefore assumed to depend positively on gross national product, Y. A second is the *precautionary motive*, according to which money is held because there may be an unexpected need for it in the future. The unexpected needs, by their very nature, are difficult to quantify. The cost of holding money rather than other assets can, however, be measured by the rate of return on such other assets. An asset that is similar in certain respects to money but that bears an explicit rate of return, namely an interest rate, is a bond. The interest rate, r, should therefore influence the demand for money negatively: as the interest rate rises, it becomes more "expensive" to hold money (in terms of opportunities foregone) so less money is held for precautionary reasons. A third is the *speculative motive*, according to which money is held because of a fear of capital loss in holding bonds, the expectation being that interest rates will rise in the future, so capital values will fall. The expected future interest rate, $\hat{r}$, should therefore influence the demand for money positively: as the expected future interest rate rises, it is expected that bond prices will fall, so investors will hold money rather than bonds.

Combining the factors suggested by all three motives, the demand for money equation can be written

$$M = M(Y, r, \hat{r}). \qquad *(9.2.2)$$

Here M is money balances (e.g., M_1 or M_2, perhaps deflated to real per capita terms by dividing by p, the price level, and N, the population), Y is national income (again perhaps deflated), r is the interest rate (short-term or long-term), and $\hat{r}$ is the expected interest rate (again short-term or long-term).

[2] If supply is treated as endogenous rather than exogenous, then demand for and supply of money form a system of simultaneous equations, as discussed in Section 13.2. In the single-equation approach, if the monetary authorities set the stock of money exogenously, then it would be appropriate to treat the interest rate as the dependent variable in the demand equation for money. If, however, the monetary authorities set the level of interest rates (and carry out the operations needed to maintain such a level), then it would be appropriate to treat the level of the money supply as the dependent variable in the demand equation.

[3] See Laidler (1969) for a survey.

If it is possible to separate out the transactions demand from the other two demands, if the transactions demand is proportional to national income, and if the expected future interest rate can be omitted, e.g., because it depends on the current income and interest rate, then the demand equation would take the form

$$M = kY + L(r). \qquad *(9.2.3)$$

Here k is the *Cambridge k*, giving the ratio of money utilized for transactions to national income, and $L(r)$ is the *liquidity preference function*, indicating the dependence of precautionary and speculative money balances on the interest rate. The two terms on the right-hand side of (9.2.3) are, respectively, the *transactions demand* and *asset demand* for money. The sums of money held to satisfy these demands are called, respectively, *active balances* and *passive balances.*

Another way of expressing the demand for money in (9.2.2) is

$$MV = Y \quad \text{where} \quad V = V(r, \hat{r}, Y). \qquad *(9.2.4)$$

Here V is the *velocity of money*, and equation (9.2.4) expresses the *quantity theory of money*, according to which velocity is a (stable) function of the interest rate, the expected interest rate, and income.[4]

Both of these forms of the demand equation for money have, in fact, been estimated. Equation (9.2.3) was estimated by Tobin, who distinguished active from passive balances by assuming that passive balances, $L(r)$, were zero in 1929, the year in his sample for which velocity was highest.[5] With the 1929 value of velocity, $\bar{V}$, passive balances were calculated from (9.2.3) as

$$M - \frac{1}{\bar{V}} Y = L(r). \qquad (9.2.5)$$

The left-hand side, passive balances, is, by construction, zero for 1929 and positive for other years in the sample. The right-hand side, the demand function for passive balances $L(r)$, according to the Keynesian theory of the "liquidity trap," is a negative nonlinear relationship. In particular, according to this theory, there is a floor interest rate, so, as r falls to this level, the demand for passive balances becomes infinitely elastic with respect to the interest rate. Tobin, in fact, found such a relationship.

Klein and Goldberger used a similar approach to estimate the demand for money by persons in the United States, 1929-1952, excluding 1942-1944. Their estimated demand equation is[6]

[4] See Friedman, Ed. (1956), particularly Friedman (1956). Other variables can also influence V, such as the expected rate of inflation, the expected rate of return on equities, and real balances. For an interpretation of U.S. monetary history from the viewpoint of the quantity theory of money see Friedman and Schwartz (1963).

[5] See Tobin (1947).

[6] See Klein and Goldberger (1955). They also estimated a demand for money by business. Both equations are part of a complete macroeconometric model, estimated by simultaneous-equations methods and discussed in Section 12.4.

$$M = 0.14Y + 76.03(r_L - 2.0)^{-0.84}. \qquad (9.2.6)$$
$$\qquad\qquad (16.6) \qquad\qquad (0.03)$$

Here M is the liquid assets of persons, Y is disposable income of persons, and r_L is the long-term rate of interest (the average yield on corporate bonds). The coefficient 0.14 is obtained by assuming that passive balances were zero in 1929, as in the Tobin study. The difference between the long-term rate and the rate of 2% is utilized in the demand for passive balances, assuming that the "liquidity trap" of infinitely elastic demand for money occurs at this rate. The elasticity of passive balances with respect to the excess of the interest rate over the 2% rate is estimated to be −0.84 with a standard error of 0.03.

An equation of the same form as (9.2.3) was estimated by Feige, who determined the cross-elasticities of demand between various liquid assets for a pooled cross-section, time-series sample for states of the United States, 1949–1959. His estimated demand function for demand deposits at commercial banks is[7]

$$D = \underset{(0.080)}{0.365Y} + \underset{(48)}{535r_d} - \underset{(13)}{35r_t} + \underset{(13)}{53r_s} + \cdots, \qquad \bar{R}^2 = 0.978. \qquad (9.2.7)$$

Here D is per capita commercial bank demand deposits, Y is permanent per capita personal income, r_d is the service charge on demand deposits (negative), r_t is the interest rate on commercial bank time deposits, and r_s is the interest rate on savings and loan association shares.[8] The implied elasticity with respect to both r_d and r_s is about −0.30, that with respect to r_t is 0.10, while that with respect to Y is 0.92, all elasticities estimated at mean values. He concluded that the income elasticity does not differ significantly from unity, that increases in service charges substantially reduce demand deposits, that demand deposits and commercial bank time deposits appear to be weak substitutes, and that demand deposits and savings and loan association shares appear to be complements.

Equation (9.2.4) was studied by Latané, who estimated the long-run relationship between velocity and the long-term rate of interest.[9] His specification related the reciprocal of velocity to the reciprocal of the long-term interest rate, the latter representing the capitalization factor.[10] He estimated this relationship

[7] See Feige (1969), as reported in Zellner, Ed. (1968). The • • • refers to various regional dummy variables (e.g., N.Y., defined as 1 for New York, 0 for all other states), which are omitted here. Also omitted is the interest rate on mutual savings bank deposits.

[8] "Permanent income" is income with transitory components removed. Equivalently, it is the expected permanent return on total wealth. Empirically, it is usually estimated as an exponentially weighted average of current and past levels of income. See Friedman (1957).

[9] See Latané (1954). His results, reported in (9.2.8), have been rounded. He did not report standard errors.

[10] The "capitalization factor" is the present value of a permanent stream paying $1 per year. If r is the interest rate, then the product of the present value and r is the payment, i.e.,

$$PV \cdot r = 1$$

Thus

$$\text{PV} = \frac{1}{r}$$

for the United States 1919-1952, excluding 1932, 1933, 1942, 1946, and 1947 as unrepresentative years of bank failures, war mobilization, and demobilization. His estimate, using least squares, and defining M as M_1, is

$$\frac{M}{Y} = \frac{1}{V} = 0.00743 \left(\frac{1}{r_L}\right) + 0.109, \qquad R^2 = 0.911. \tag{9.2.8}$$

Since the coefficient of $1/r_L$ is positive, the demand for money is negatively related to the rate of interest.

A follow-up study by Latané considered a linear relationship between velocity and the long-term interest rate. His estimate of this equation for the United States, 1909-1958, using least squares, is

$$\frac{Y}{M} = V = 0.77 r_L + 0.38 \tag{9.2.9}$$

Thus the demand for money function is

$$M = \frac{Y}{0.77 r_L + 0.38} \tag{9.2.10}$$

The implied elasticity of demand for money with respect to Y, Gross National Product, is 1.28, while the elasticity with respect to r_L, the long-term interest rate, is -1.71.[11]

In the studies reported thus far the demand for money is treated as a linear function of income so it cannot be determined whether there are scale economies in holding money. Several studies have, however, utilized a log linear demand function. One such study, by Bronfenbrenner and Mayer, estimated the demand for money in the United States, 1919-1956, as[12]

$$\begin{aligned} \ln \frac{M}{p} &= \underset{(0.0032)}{0.1065} - \underset{(0.0139)}{0.0928} \ln r_s - \underset{(0.0883)}{0.1158} \ln (NW) \\ &\quad + \underset{(0.0576)}{0.7217} \ln \left(\frac{M}{p}\right)_{-1} + \underset{(0.0862)}{0.3440} \ln \left(\frac{Y}{p}\right) \\ &\quad R^2 = 0.99, \quad d = 1.86. \end{aligned} \tag{9.2.11}$$

Here M/p is total deflated money balances ($M = M_1$), r_s is the short-term interest rate (commercial paper rate), NW is deflated net worth, $(M/p)_{-1}$ is lagged defla-

[11] See Latané (1960). The elasticities in his earlier article are 0.828 and -0.579, respectively.

[12] See Bronfenbrenner and Mayer (1960). Note that their specification includes income, wealth, and the interest rate as explanatory variables. To the extent that income is a return on wealth, or, equivalently, wealth is capitalized income, these variables are not independent, suggesting a possible multicollinearity problem. See Johnson (1962).

ted money balances, and Y/p is deflated GNP. All variables other than ln (NW) are statistically significant at the 1% level. The implied long-run elasticities of the demand for money are 1.24 with respect to income, −0.33 with respect to the interest rate, and −0.42 with respect to net worth.[13]

A second study using a log linear demand for money function was that of Morishima and Saito.[14] Their estimated liquidity preference function for the United States, 1902–1952, is

$$\log \frac{M}{p} = \underset{(0.035)}{1.190}\left(0.586 \log Y + 0.414 \log \frac{M_{-1}}{p} + 0.295\right) \tag{9.2.12}$$
$$\qquad - \underset{(0.061)}{0.202} \log r - \underset{(0.022)}{0.048}u - 0.650, \qquad R^2 = 0.98, d = 1.09.$$

Here M is M_2, in billions of current dollars; p is the price level (1929 = 1); Y is national income (in billions of 1929 dollars); r is the corporate bond yield; u is a dummy variable, taking the value 0 before 1941 and 1 after 1946; and "log" refers to base-10 logarithms. The dummy variable is introduced to take account of the fact that during the years 1946–1952 the Federal Reserve continued to maintain easy-money conditions by pegging the yields on government securities. If this policy had not been followed, the Treasury bill rate would most likely have risen. Long-run elasticities can be inferred from the estimated equation by setting $M/p = (M/p)_{-1}$ to obtain

$$\log \frac{M}{p} = 1.377 \log Y - 0.398 \log r - 0.095u - 0.59 \tag{9.2.13}$$

Thus the long-run elasticities of the demand for money are about 1.38 with respect to income and −0.4 with respect to the interest rate.

A somewhat different specification of the demand for money was used by B. Klein. His estimated demand function for the U.S. over the period 1880 to 1970 is[15]

$$\ln \frac{M}{pN} = \underset{(0.177)}{-13.96} + \underset{(0.025)}{1.328} \ln \frac{Y_p}{pN} - \underset{(0.018)}{0.315}(r_s - r_m) \qquad R^2 = 0.988, \; d = 1.12. \tag{9.2.14}$$

Here M is M_2, N is the total population, p is the price level, Y_p is permanent income, r_s is the short-term (four- to six-month) commercial-paper rate, and r_m is the (implicit) rate of interest on demand deposits. The "net interest rate" defined by the difference $r_s - r_m$ measures the cost of holding money rather than short-term interest-bearing notes. Note that the specification with respect to the net interest rate is semilogarithmic, in part, because this variable can be

[13] For studies using a similar log linear specification see Meltzer (1963) and Laidler (1966).

[14] See Morishima and Saito (1972). As in the case of the Klein-Goldberger model this equation is one equation from a macroeconometric model, as discussed in Section 12.3.

[15] See B. Klein (1974). He also estimated a demand function with r_s and r_m as independent variables but found that, while the coefficient of each is significant, the sum of the two coefficients is quite small and insignificant, suggesting the use of the difference $r_s - r_m$, as reported in (9.2.14).

negative. According to Klein's results the per capita real demand for money is sensitive to both real per capita permanent income and the cost of holding money.

The elasticity estimates of most of these studies are summarized in Table 9.1, which indicates that, as suggested by the underlying theory, the demand for money does depend positively on income and negatively on the interest rate. The estimates of the elasticity of demand with respect to income range from 0.828 to 1.38, but they tend to be larger than unity, suggesting diseconomies of scale in holding money. Thus, for example, increasing income by 10% increases the demand for money by more than 10%, leading to holding relatively more money and hence relatively less of an earning asset. The estimates of the elasticity of demand with respect to the interest rate range from −0.3 to −1.71, suggesting significant responsiveness of money demand to the interest rate.[16]

Table 9.1. Estimates of Elasticities of the Demand for Money in the U.S.

Study, Period \ *Elasticity*	*Short-Term Interest Rate*	*Long-Term Interest Rate*	*Income*
Latané (1954) 1919–1952, excluding 1932, 1933, 1942, 1946, 1947	–	−0.579	0.828
Latané (1960) 1909–1958	–	−1.71	1.28
Bronfenbrenner and Mayer (1960) 1919–1956	−0.33	–	1.24
Morishima and Saito (1972) 1902–1952	–	−0.40	1.38
B. Klein (1974) 1880–1970	–	–	1.33

9.3 Industrial organization

The field of industrial organization is concerned with the causes and consequences of the structure of industry. This field, as others, has progressed through various stages in its evolution. The first studies were devoted to applications of

[16] Laidler (1969) discusses several other implications of empirical studies of the demand for money, e.g., the absence of the liquidity trap. See also Goldfeld (1973) and Meyer and Neri (1975).

the basic concepts and techniques of price theory to industry, such as the model of monopolistic competition, the costs of monopoly to the economy, the analysis of advertising, and the limit price model.[17] Later works tended to be case studies of specific industries.[18]

Econometric studies of industrial organization have tended to focus on various aspects of the structure-conduct-performance (SCP) hypothesis, a basic paradigm of industrial organization.[19] According to the SCP hypothesis the structure of an industry–that is, its organizational characteristics, particularly its degree of concentration and conditions of entry–influences the conduct of firms in the industry in their decisions regarding prices, sales, employment, advertising, research and development, etc. The conduct of firms, in turn, influences performance, particularly the profits earned in the industry.

A major conclusion of the SCP paradigm is a positive relationship between concentration and profits. Concentration, a major structure variable, influences conduct, which influences profit. A specific mechanism for such an influence might be collusion: firms in more concentrated industries are more likely to engage in tacit or explicit collusion, which would presumably result in joint profit maximization. Many studies have investigated the relationship

$$\pi = \Pi(CR, \ldots) \qquad \textbf{*(9.3.1)}$$

where π is profitability, as measured, for example, by the profit rate on net worth earned in the industry, and CR is the concentration ratio, as measured, for example, by the percentage of shipments accounted for by the leading four firms in the industry.[20] The . . . in (9.3.1) represents other possible influences on profitability, aside from concentration.

An example of an estimate of (9.3.1) is the regression of Weiss for 399 United States industries in 1973:[21]

$$\underset{(0.010)}{\pi = 0.193} + \underset{(0.0002)}{0.0011CR} - \underset{(0.0001)}{0.0003GD} + \underset{(0.0002)}{0.0009K/O}, \qquad R^2 = 0.20. \qquad \textbf{(9.3.2)}$$

Here π is the price-cost margin (value of shipments less the cost of materials

[17] On the model of monopolistic competition, see Chamberlin (1933); on the costs of monopoly to the economy, see Harberger (1954); on advertising, see Dorfman and Steiner (1954); and on the limit price model, see Modigliani (1958).

[18] See, for example, the Kaysen (1956) study of United Shoe Machinery, the Adelman (1959) study of A & P, and the Caves (1962) study of air transport.

[19] For the basic structure-conduct-performance hypothesis, see Bain (1968). For surveys of quantitative studies of industrial organization, see Weiss (1971) and Phlips (1971). For a general survey of the field, see Scherer (1970). See also Section 13.3 for a simultaneous equations approach to the SCP hypothesis.

[20] Other definitions have been used for both profitability and concentration, e.g., the price-cost margin [defined below (9.3.2)] and the eight-firm concentration ratio based on value added, the latter being the percentage of value added produced by the leading eight firms in the industry.

[21] Weiss (1974). Weiss notes that the concentration-profits relationship is one of the most thoroughly tested hypotheses in economics. He reviews the results of over 80 studies of this relationship.

and payroll, all divided by the value of shipments), *CR* is the four-firm concentration ratio, *GD* is a geographic dispersion index and K/O is the fixed capital-shipments ratio. The regression coefficients for both the concentration ratio and the capital-shipments ratio are statistically significant, the t ratio for *CR* being over five. The coefficient for *CR* indicates that an increase of ten percentage points in the four-firm concentration ratio increases the price-cost margin by over one percentage point. From this regression, other regressions he estimated, and the results of other studies, Weiss concluded that concentration does lead to higher profit margins, particularly for "normal years" not subject to accelerating inflation.

Other aspects of industrial conduct and performance have also been related to concentration. Variables such as prices, wages, advertising, research and development expenditures, and productivity have been related to concentration and other variables. In the case of advertising, Comanor and Wilson estimated the following dependence of advertising on concentration for 41 consumer goods industries over the period 1954 to 1957:[22]

$$\begin{aligned} A/S = & \underset{(0.02825)}{-0.00565} + \underset{(0.0086)}{0.0118} \ln CR + \underset{(0.0132)}{0.0204} \ln G \\ & \underset{(0.0105)}{-0.0178}D - \underset{(0.0133)}{0.0154}T, \quad R^2 = 0.17. \end{aligned} \tag{9.3.3}$$

Here A/S is the advertising to sales ratio, *CR* is the four-firm concentration ratio, G is the rate of growth of sales, D is a durable-industry dummy variable, and T is a high-technical-barrier dummy variable. The negative coefficient of D indicates the association between consumer nondurables and advertising. The concentration ratio has a positive influence, but it is not significant at the 5% level. Overall, the estimated equation exhibits a lack of statistical significance of variables and a low coefficient of determination, suggesting that it is not these variables but rather others that explain advertising.

Comanor and Wilson also estimated the effects of advertising and concentration on profits. For the same sample of 41 consumer goods industries they obtained[23]

$$\begin{aligned} \pi = & \underset{(0.0119)}{0.0375} + \underset{(0.147)}{0.318}A/S - \underset{(0.000406)}{0.000065}CR + \underset{(0.0062)}{0.0107} \ln KR \\ & + \underset{(0.0151)}{0.0269} \ln G + \underset{(0.0180)}{0.0258}L, \quad R^2 = 0.52. \end{aligned} \tag{9.3.4}$$

Here π is the profit rate on stockholders' equity; A/S, *CR*, and G are as before; *KR* is capital requirements, the amount of capital required for entry at the scale of a single efficient plant; and L is a local-industry dummy variable. This estimated equation is clearly much more successful than the last in terms of both significance levels and R^2. It indicates that advertising outlays, capital require-

[22] See Comanor and Wilson (1974). See also Greer (1971).

[23] See Comanor and Wilson (1974). See also Weiss (1969).

ments, and growth of demand all have a quantitatively large and statistically significant impact on profits. Indeed, for the sample of industries treated, those industries with high advertising outlays earn, on average, a profit rate exceeding those of comparable industries by nearly four percentage points, representing a 50% increase in the profit rate. Such higher returns indicate, to some, market power, specifically the effects of advertising in establishing a barrier to the entry of new firms by promoting product differentiation. To others, however, such high returns indicate instead the effectiveness of advertising in reducing information costs.

A third regression of Comanor and Wilson relates concentration to capital requirements and economies of scale:

$$\begin{aligned} \ln CR = 3.85 &+ \underset{(0.048)}{0.244} \ln KR + \underset{(0.070)}{0.238} \ln ES \\ &- \underset{(0.245)}{0.294} L, \quad R^2 = 0.81. \end{aligned} \tag{9.3.5}$$

Here CR, KR, and L are as before, and ES is a measure of economies of scale, namely the average size of plant among the largest firms accounting for 50% of industry output, divided by total output in the relevant market. These results suggest that concentration is well explained by capital requirements and economies of scale, which may partly explain the insignificance of CR in the equation for the profit rate, (9.3.4), as due, in part, to multicollinearity.

Another area of interest in studies of industrial organization is inflation. Of particular interest is the "administered-inflation" hypothesis, according to which price increases are larger in concentrated than in unconcentrated industries. The study of this hypothesis by Weston and Lustgarten reported the following regression for 224 four-digit SIC industries over the period 1954–1970:[24]

$$\begin{aligned} \frac{p}{p_{-1}} = -1.782 &- \underset{(0.0041)}{0.0028} CR - \underset{(0.0099)}{0.0159} \frac{q}{q_{-1}} - \underset{(0.0591)}{0.1858} \frac{l}{l_{-1}} \\ &+ \underset{(0.0573)}{0.4435} \frac{m}{m_{-1}}, \quad R^2 = 0.469. \end{aligned} \tag{9.3.6}$$

Here p/p_{-1} is the relative change in the industry price from 1954 to 1970, CR is the four-firm concentration ratio, $q/(q_{-1})$ is the change in output, $l/(l_{-1})$ is the change in unit labor cost, and $m/(m_{-1})$ is the change in unit material costs. After accounting for changes in costs and output (the latter serving as a proxy for demand), any remaining influence of concentration would tend to support the administered-inflation hypothesis. The coefficient of the concentration ratio,

[24] See Weston and Lustgarten (1954). See also Weiss (1966), Phlips (1971), Dalton (1973), and Lustgarten (1974, 1975). Here "SIC" refers to the Standard Industrial Classification code for classifying different industries.

however, is insignificant (and also of the wrong sign), tending to contradict the hypothesis.[25]

Finally, another area of interest in industrial organization has been the progressiveness of industry. This interest stems, in part, from the Schumpeterian hypothesis that the more progressive and innovative firms tend to be the large firms.[26] This hypothesis suggests that concentrated industries tend to be more oriented to research and development activities than less concentrated industries. To test this hypothesis Scherer estimated the following relationship for 56 industries:[27]

$$\ln RD = \underset{}{-0.36} + \underset{(0.11)}{0.93 \ln N} + \underset{(0.24)}{0.80 \ln CR}, \qquad R^2 = 0.81. \tag{9.3.7}$$

Here RD is the number of scientific and engineering personnel by industry, N is total employment in the industry (a size variable), and CR is the four-firm concentration ratio. These results suggest that there may indeed be some truth to the Schumpeterian hypothesis, the coefficient of the concentration variable being positive, statistically significant, and reasonably large.

Single-equation studies of industrial organization have thus been used to investigate various relationships and hypotheses, most of which involve the concept of concentration. Section 13.3 below develops a simultaneous-equations model of industrial organization that integrates many of these relationships into a common framework, in part to test the importance of the concept of concentration.

9.4 Labor economics

The field of labor economics has been making increased use of single-equation estimation techniques. One branch of labor economics has been concerned with studying the economic effects of unions, in particular the effect of unionization on earnings. An example is the equation

$$w = w(U, \ldots) \tag*{*(9.4.1)}$$

where w is real wages and U is a measure of unionization. Estimates of such an equation provide a test of the hypothesis that unionization increases real wages. An example is the estimate of Lewis for 1920–1958:[28]

$$\begin{aligned}\ln w = {} & \underset{(0.056)}{0.28 \ln Q} + \underset{(0.28)}{0.77Z} + \underset{(0.32)}{0.84 \ln P} + \underset{(0.094)}{0.228U} \\ & - \underset{(1.10)}{0.16UZ} - \underset{(0.99)}{1.94U \ln P} + \text{constant}, \qquad R^2 = 0.891.\end{aligned} \tag{9.4.2}$$

[25] Weston and Lustgarten also considered various subperiods and found a positive coefficient for CR that was significant at the 5% level for 1954–1958. In one other period, 1969–1970, the coefficient was positive but insignificant; in all other subperiods it was negative.

[26] See Schumpeter (1950).

[27] See Scherer (1967). Dummy variables have been omitted. See also Comanor (1967) and Mansfield (1968a, 1968b).

[28] See Lewis (1963).

The dependent variable, ln w, is relative wages, the average hourly compensation in unionized industries (e.g., manufacturing, construction, transportation, and public utilities) relative to such compensation in nonunionized industries (e.g., agriculture, trade, finance, and service industries). The explanatory variables are ln Q, where Q is relative value of output, the national income originating in unionized industries relative to such national income originating in nonunionized industries; Z, the unemployment rate in the labor force; ln P, where P is the ratio of the actual to the expected price level, a measure of expected inflation; U, a measure of the excess of the extent of union membership in unionized over its extent in nonunionized industries; and two interaction variables. According to the estimated equation, relative wages depend positively and significantly on the relative value of output, the extent of union membership, the expected inflation, and the unemployment rate. The coefficient of the joint unionism-unemployment variable is insignificant, but that for the joint unionism-expected inflation variable is negative and significant, suggesting that unionism tends to make money wages of unionized workers rigid against movements of the general price level. Lewis calculated from this equation an estimate of the average relative wage effect of union labor relative to nonunion labor, and he found that over the entire period 1920–1958 unionism raised average wages by about 17% over nonunion labor. He also calculated this effect of unionism for several subperiods and found that it was very large during the depression period (over 25% for 1931–1933) but somewhat below the overall average estimate later (about 15% for 1955–1958).

More recently, labor economics has been concerned with characteristics of individual workers and their implications for labor-market phenomena. Such studies measure the influences of both personal characteristics of the workers (e.g., age, sex, race) and their "human capital" (e.g., years of education, on-the-job training) on employment and earnings. An example is the Bowen and Finegan study of labor-force participation.[29] They estimated the effects of both individual characteristics and labor-market variables on participation rates. Using data from the 1/1000 sample of the 1960 Census of the United States, they estimated the following labor-force participation-rate equation for the 100 largest urban areas (Standard Metropolitan Statistical Areas, or SMSA's) for "prime age" males, age 25–54:

$$\begin{aligned} L^{M}_{25\text{-}54} = {} & [\underset{(0.06)}{-0.32U} + \underset{(0.05)}{0.20IM} + \underset{(0.02)}{0.05E}] \\ & + [\underset{(0.13)}{-0.36OI} + \underset{(0.12)}{0.26S} - \underset{(0.01)}{0.03C} - \underset{(0.04)}{0.05MS} + \underset{(0.02)}{0.01NM}] + \text{constant} \\ & R^2 = 0.62. \end{aligned} \qquad \textbf{(9.4.3)}$$

The dependent variable is the percentage of males aged 25 to 54 in the civilian noninstitutional population who were in the civilian labor force (employed or unemployed) during the census week. There are two groups of explanatory variables: labor-market variables in the first bracket and control variables (i.e., indi-

[29] See Bowen and Finegan (1969).

vidual characteristics) in the second. The labor-market variables are U, unemployment (the percentage of the civilian labor force unemployed in the census week); IM, industry mix (a measure of the percentage of jobs that are expected to be held by men); and E, earnings (median income of all males working 50–52 weeks in 1959) in units of \$100. The control variables are OI, other income (mean income from nonemployment sources per recipient of any kind of income in units of \$100); S, schooling (median years of school completed); C, color (the percentage of all persons in households who are nonwhite); MS, marital status (the percentage of males in this group who are married, with wife present); and NM, net migration (of males aged 30 to 54 between 1955 and the 1960 census week, divided by the total population of the group in 1960). All coefficients, other than those for MS and NM, are statistically significant at the 5% level or better. The labor-market variables are particularly significant, with U and IM being significant at the one percent level. The unemployment rate indicates the ease with which a potential labor-force entrant might expect to find a job, and the highly significant negative coefficient indicates that high unemployment does in fact discourage some men from looking for work. Industry mix is conducive to participation, as are earnings. Some control variables also play an important role, specifically color, other income, and schooling. It should be noted in evaluating all these results, however, that some of the explanatory variables are simultaneously determined with the participation rate, leading to simultaneous-equations bias. It might have been more appropriate to estimate a complete system in which the participation rate and other variables (e.g., unemployment, earnings) are simultaneously determined as endogenous variables of the system.

A comparable regression for married women ages 14 to 54 estimated by Bowen and Finegan is

$$\begin{aligned} L_{14-54}^{MW} = {} & [\underset{(0.20)}{-0.94U} + \underset{(0.16)}{0.91IM} + \underset{(0.14)}{0.47E} - \underset{(0.30)}{0.64SF} - \underset{(0.25)}{0.75WD}] \\ & + [\underset{(0.53)}{-1.40OI} + \underset{(0.41)}{0.73S} + \underset{(0.04)}{0.08C} + \underset{(0.06)}{0.12NM} - \underset{(0.10)}{0.20IH} - \underset{(0.11)}{0.55PC}] \\ & + \text{constant}, \qquad R^2 = 0.69. \end{aligned} \tag{9.4.4}$$

Here the dependent variable is the percentage of married females aged 14 to 54 in the total population who were in the labor force during the census week. The explanatory variables are grouped, as before, into labor-market variables and control variables. Some are the same as before or only slightly redefined so as to relate to women (e.g., IM is the percentage of jobs expected to be held by women). The others are SF, supply of females (the percentage of the total civilian population 14 years old and over who are women); WD, wages of domestics (median earnings of private household workers, living out); IH, income of husbands (the median income of all men who were married with wife present); and PC, children (the percentage of all married women with one or more children under six years of age). All coefficients other than those for S, C, and IH are significant at the 5% level or better. Of very high statistical significance are the labor-market variables U and IM, as in the case of prime-age males, and the control variable PC. Comparing (9.4.4) to (9.4.3), the sign of the coefficient of the

C variable changes, with nonwhite males having a lower participation rate than white males, but nonwhite married women having a *higher* participation rate than white married women. In fact, the participation rate for nonwhite married women is about seven percentage points higher than that for white married women, even after adjusting for age, schooling, children, employment status of the husband, and other family income. It might be noted that the residuals from equations (9.4.3) and (9.4.4) are probably correlated, so that there would have been a gain in estimation efficiency if the covariances had been estimated and taken into account, as in the method of "seemingly unrelated equations."[30]

In addition to affecting participation rates, personal characteristics can also affect earnings. Several studies have analyzed the effects of personal characteristics, such as years of schooling and intellectual ability, on earnings. An example is the regression estimated by Griliches and Mason for 3000 veterans age 21–34:[31]

$$\ln Y = \underset{(0.0044)}{0.0433S} + \underset{(0.0005)}{0.0015AFQT} + \underset{(0.0479)}{0.2225C} + \ldots, \qquad R^2 = 0.173. \tag{9.4.5}$$

Here log of income is the dependent variable, S is total years of schooling, $AFQT$ is the percentile achieved on the Armed Forces Qualification Test, and C is a dummy variable for color (1 if white; 0 if nonwhite). Other explanatory variables included in the regression but not reported here are age and length of active military service. According to these results, intellectual ability, as measured by $AFQT$, has only a modest effect on earnings. The estimated coefficient of C, however, indicates that white earnings are significantly higher than black earnings, even after adjusting for years of schooling, intellectual ability, and age. For similarly situated white and nonwhite veterans, (9.4.5) implies that

$$Y_W = (e^{0.2225})Y_N \approx 1.25Y_N \tag{9.4.6}$$

where Y_W is white income and Y_N is nonwhite income. Thus, white veterans earn a premium of about 25% over comparably situated nonwhite veterans.[32]

Econometric techniques have thus been used both in studies of unionization and in studies of the influence of personal characteristics and human capital on labor-force participation and earnings. Future work in the field of labor economics will undoubtedly continue to make use of these techniques.

9.5 Health economics

The field of health economics is, broadly, the study of the allocation of re-

[30] See Section 6.5.

[31] See Griliches and Mason (1972). Results have been rounded. It might be noted that this study attempted to correct for errors of measurement in test scores by the use of instrumental variables. See Section 6.9 for a discussion of errors of measurement, and see Section 11.6 for a discussion of the instrumental-variables technique.

[32] For a discussion of labor-market discrimination, specifically differences in earnings (and employment) between similarly situated white and nonwhite workers, see Freeman (1974).

sources to the delivery of health services. In recent years there has developed a quantitative approach to this field, concentrating on the econometric estimation of certain important relationships.[33] Among the most important of these relationships are demand functions for health services and cost curves for hospitals.[34]

It is only natural that an economic study would treat demand, and the demand for health services has been the subject of numerous studies.[35] The intent of these studies is partly to determine the effects of variables included in the demand functions discussed in Chapter 7—variables such as price and income. An additional objective, however, is that of estimating the effects of variables specific to or particularly relevant to the demand for health, such as health insurance, health condition, age, sex, etc. An example of such a study is that of Newhouse and Phelps, using cross-section data on 2367 U.S. families interviewed in 1963.[36] Their analysis is limited to those individuals with positive observed quantities of the health service considered, and their estimated demand curves for hospital length of stay and physician visits are summarized in Table 9.2.[37] According to these results, disability days are the most significant explanatory variable for length of stay, while the health-status variables are the most significant explanatory variables for visits to physicians' offices.[38] The dummy variables for age are also important determinants of length of stay. For example, according to Table 9.2, everything else being equal, an individual over 65 stays in the hospital about 12 more days per year than an individual not in this age group. These age variables play no significant role in influencing visits to physicians' offices, however. The variable for color plays an important role in determining visits to physicians, with nonwhite individuals having almost two less visits per year than white individuals. This variable, however, plays no significant role for hospital length of stay. The price variables allow for the existence of health insurance in that they are the *net* price to the individual consumer, after taking account of the coinsurance rate (the percentage of the hospital or physician bill paid by the consumer).

[33] See Klarman, Ed. (1970), Perlman, Ed. (1974), and Rosett, Ed. (1975) for examples of such studies. For a survey see Feldstein (1974).

[34] A third relationship that has been treated is that of the production function for the provision of health sources. An example has already been given in the last chapter in equation (8.3.32), a production function for physicians' services, relating the gross revenue from such services to inputs of physicians, hours of physicians, allied health personnel, and rooms used in the practice. For another estimated production function for physicians' services see Reinhardt (1972).

[35] For surveys see Feldstein (1966) and Joseph (1971). For a general theoretical framework and some empirical results see Grossman (1972).

[36] See Newhouse and Phelps (1974). They also present some simultaneous-equations estimates, taking account of the endogeneity of health insurance and price.

[37] Those explanatory variables for which the t ratio of the estimated coefficient to its standard error is less than unity in both equations are not reported here. They include nonwage income if greater than \$3000, education 9–11 years, education 12 years, age 25–34, and sex.

[38] Respondents were asked whether they would characterize their health as excellent, good, fair, or poor, and responses were entered as dummy variables. Some estimates of demand functions go beyond these self-assessments of health status to include specific diagnostic or treatment categories. An example is Rosenthal (1970), who estimated elasticities of hospital length of stay with respect to average daily room charge for specific diagnostic conditions (and also age and sex). See also Yett, Drabek, Intriligator, and Kimbell (1977) for demand functions contingent upon diagnostic condition.

Table 9.2. Estimated Demand Equations for Hospital Length of Stay and Physician Office Visits

Explanatory Variables \ Dependent Variable	*Hospital Length of Stay (Days)*	*Physician Office Visits (Number)*
Price of hospital bed × hospital coinsurance rate	−0.062 (0.036)	−0.034 (0.012)
Price of office visit × physician coinsurance rate	−0.241 (0.193)	−0.054 (0.027)
Wage income/week	0.008 (0.011)	0.004 (0.002)
Nonwage income	−0.001 (0.001)	−0.76E−04 (2.71E−04)
*Education 13–15 years	−3.088 (2.998)	0.396 (0.629)
*Education 16+ years	1.029 (3.027)	−0.765 (0.638)
*Age 35–54	7.051 (5.262)	−0.815 (0.916)
*Age 55–64	10.296 (5.477)	−0.403 (0.983)
*Age 65+	12.142 (5.469)	−0.818 (0.974)
Family size	−0.451 (0.438)	−0.070 (0.119)
*White	0.743 (2.322)	1.616 (0.466)
Disability days	0.029 (0.008)	0.008 (0.004)
*Health status good	−0.256 (2.133)	1.671 (0.419)
*Health status fair	0.575 (2.396)	3.683 (0.539)
*Health status poor	−1.667 (2.646)	6.824 (0.801)
Physicians per 100,000	−0.022 (0.015)	0.006 (0.039)
Beds per 1000	0.250 (0.294)	−0.105 (0.086)
Constant	3.132 (5.910)	3.804 (1.160)
R^2	0.345	0.181
Number of observations	122	842

Source Newhouse and Phelps (1974).

*Signifies dummy variable, taking value 1 if characteristic is present, 0 if it is not.

NOTE Standard errors are shown in parentheses. Those explanatory variables for which the t ratio is less than unity for both equations have been omitted (see footnote 37). The notation −0.76E−04 means −0.000076.

The elasticities implied by the Newhouse and Phelps demand functions are reported in Table 9.3. The estimated demand functions are clearly both price and income inelastic, with all reported elasticities very small. In fact, none of the estimated price and income elasticities exceeds 0.1 in absolute value. While wage-income elasticities are positive, nonwage income is found to have no effect on demand for physician office visits. These results indicate that additional physicians per capita would increase visits and decrease length of stay, while additional hospital beds per capita would have precisely the opposite effect.

Cost curves for hospitals form the other main area of application of econometric techniques to health economics, in part because of the central role of the hospital in the delivery of health services.[39] An example is the Francisco study

[39] For surveys see Lave (1966), Mann and Yett (1968), and Hefty (1969). For a discussion of methodological issues see Feldstein (1967).

Table 9.3. Estimated Demand Elasticities

Explanatory Variables \ *Dependent Variable*	*Hospital Length of Stay*	*Physician Office Visits*
Price of hospital bed × hospital coinsurance rate	−0.10	−0.10
Price of office visit × physician coinsurance rate	−0.10	−0.06
Wage income/week	0.08	0.08
Nonwage income	−0.07	−0.01
Disability days	0.19	0.02
Physicians per 100,000	−0.28	0.13
Beds per 1000	0.13	−0.09

Source Newhouse and Phelps (1974).

of the cost curve for short-term general hospitals.[40] Using data on 4710 hospitals from the American Hospital Association annual survey for 1966, he estimated the following average-cost curve:

$$\underset{}{\text{AC}} = 46 - \underset{(0.014)}{0.25U} + \underset{(0.063)}{0.98\Sigma F} + \underset{(0.46)}{10.62D}, \qquad R^2 = 0.23. \tag{9.5.1}$$

Here AC is average cost per patient day, U is the percentage occupancy rate, ΣF is an unweighted index of facilities and services, and D is an urban dummy variable [1 for location in a Standard Metropolitan Statistical Area (SMSA); 0 otherwise]. From these results, it follows that utilization is a significant factor in lowering average cost, while added facilities and location in an urban area significantly increase average cost. Other regressions indicated that average cost does not appreciably vary with output, measured as patient days, for the entire sample of hospitals. Average cost does decrease with output, however, for small hospitals. Thus, the average-cost curve for hospitals appears to have the same L shape as the average-cost curves for various industries noted in Section 8.4.

Another example of an estimated hospital cost function is that of Lave and Lave, who used pooled cross-section, time-series data for 74 hospitals in western Pennsylvania over the period 1961–1967.[41] They obtained as one of their estimated equations:

$$\begin{aligned}\ln(\text{AC}/\overline{\text{AC}}) &= 6.670 - \underset{(0.031)}{0.357\ln(U/\bar{U})} - \underset{(0.027)}{0.006\ln(S/\bar{S})}\\ &\quad + \underset{(0.0005)}{0.031t} + \underset{(0.002)}{0.028F}, \qquad \bar{R}^2 = 0.855.\end{aligned} \tag{9.5.2}$$

[40] See Francisco (1970). Here "short-term" refers to the average length of stay of a patient in the hospital, not to be confused with "short-run" as applied to a cost curve.

[41] See Lave and Lave (1970). They tried various specifications and concluded, as did Francisco, that the average-cost curve is L shaped.

Here the dependent variable is the logarithm of the ratio of cost per patient day AC to the average of this cost per patient day for the individual hospital over the entire time period. The explanatory variables are the logarithm of the ratio of the utilization rate U (the ratio of total bed-days to available bed-days) to its average for the hospital over the period; the logarithm of the ratio of the size of the hospital S (the number of beds) to its average for the hospital over the period; time t; and a dummy variable to account for possible errors in the semi-annual data F, taking the value 0 if the observation is for the first half of the year and 1 if it is for the second half. The estimated equation implies that the cost curve can be expressed as

$$\ln \text{AC} = a_0 - 0.357 \ln U - 0.006 \ln S + 0.031t + 0.028F \qquad \textbf{(9.5.3)}$$

where the intercept, a_0, varies from hospital to hospital, depending on its average cost per patient day, utilization rate, and size. Deflating variables by the average for the individual hospital over the period was utilized precisely to account for structural differences among the hospitals, such as differences in case mix and in facilities available.

The estimated coefficients and standard errors in (9.5.2) have several implications. First, the relatively large and statistically significant coefficient of utilization, a result consistent with that obtained by Francisco, implies that marginal cost is a large percentage of average cost. The resulting substantial variation of average cost with utilization conflicts with the commonly held view that, because of the large fixed costs in a hospital, an empty bed is about as expensive as one that is utilized. Second, the small size and insignificance of the coefficient of hospital size implies that, while there may be economies of scale in providing hospital services, they are not very strong.[42] Third, there is a significant time trend, showing a substantial increase over time in average cost.[43] Finally, there is evidence of systematic underestimation of average cost during the first half of the year.

The separate econometric studies of demand for health services and cost curves for hospitals have been combined with other relationships into simultaneous-equations models of the health-care system. Several such models are discussed in Section 13.5.

9.6 Economic history; cliometrics

The "new" economic history, sometimes called *cliometrics* ("clio" referring to the muse of history), uses econometric techniques to study historical issues.[44]

[42] Both of these implications are supported by the analyses in Feldstein (1967) of 177 hospitals in England and Wales over the period 1960–1961, which explicitly accounts for case mix.

[43] Feldstein (1971) provides an analysis of the factors influencing the rising cost for hospital care over the period 1950–1966.

[44] See Conrad and Meyer (1964), Fogel (1966), Conrad (1968), Andreano, Ed. (1970), Fogel and Engerman, Eds. (1971), Wright (1971), Aydelotte, Bogue, and Fogel, Eds. (1972), Floud, Ed. (1974), McClelland (1975), Sutch (1977), and van der Wee and Klep (1977).

While in a certain sense all of econometrics is a particular, stylized way of studying history, the distinctive feature of cliometrics is that it considers issues treated by economic historians and studies them using the tools of econometrics. This section contains two examples of such studies of U.S. economic history, pertaining to railroad rate fixing before 1900 and cotton price fluctuations in the 1830s.[45]

The first study is the MacAvoy analysis of the success of railroad rate-fixing agreements before 1900.[46] Loyalty to cartel agreements is tested by estimating the relationship

$$R_T = \alpha + \beta R_0 \tag{9.6.1}$$

where R_T is the rate reported by the Chicago Board of Trade and R_0 is the official cartel rate. Complete loyalty would require that the rate changes only when the official rate changes, so that the estimated coefficients would take the values $\hat{\alpha} = 0$, $\hat{\beta} = 1$, and $R^2 = 1$. If there is cheating on the cartel agreement, however, then $\hat{\beta} < 1$ and $R^2 < 1$, since actual rates change less than official rates, and a portion of the variance in R_T is based on cheating rather than on following changes in R_0.[47] Estimates of equation (9.6.1) using weekly data for successive summer and winter seasons over the period 1871–4 indicate that $\hat{\beta}$ was not significantly different from 1 and R^2 was high, indicating success of the cartel agreement over this period. During the winter season of 1874–5, however, both $\hat{\beta}$ and R^2 fell to zero, indicating failure of the cartel agreement, perhaps because one major railroad had at that time just completed a direct line to Chicago.

The second econometric study of history is the Temin analysis of cotton price fluctuations in the U.S. during the period 1820–1859.[48] The model consists of three interrelated equations, but, because of its special structure, each of the equations can be estimated directly using ordinary least squares.[49] The first equation relates the supply of cotton Q to the U.S. price of the previous year P^A_{-1} (because the cotton was planted then) and time t (a proxy for the labor force available). The estimated equation, specified in log linear form, is

$$\log Q = \underset{}{5.37} - \underset{(0.09)}{0.05} \log P^A_{-1} + \underset{(0.002)}{0.06}t \tag{9.6.2}$$

$$R^2 = 0.96, \qquad d = 1.8.$$

The insignificance of the estimated elasticity of supply suggests that the size of the cotton crop was not responsive to price (or perhaps that the equation is misspecified). The estimated coefficient of t indicates a 6% outward shift per year in cotton supply.

[45] These studies are discussed at length in Wright (1971).

[46] See MacAvoy (1965) and the discussion in Wright (1971).

[47] This argument, in fact, depends on R_0 being exogenously set. If R_0 is based on R_T or if changes in R_T lead to changes in R_0, then the estimates $\hat{\beta} = 1$ and $R^2 = 1$ would not signify success of the cartel.

[48] See Temin (1967) and the discussion in Wright (1971).

[49] The model is a recursive one, as discussed below in Section 10.5, assuming that the covariance matrix of the stochastic disturbance terms is diagonal, so that there is no correlation between the disturbances in any two of the three equations.

The estimated demand equation is

$$\log P^B = -1.28 - \underset{(0.18)}{0.71} \log Q - \underset{(0.23)}{0.94} \log B + \underset{(0.01)}{0.03}t + \log R \qquad \textbf{(9.6.3)}$$

$$R^2 = 0.70, \quad d = 1.6$$

where P^B is the price of cotton in Britain (the primary market for U.S. cotton), B is the deflated price of bread in London, a proxy for cyclical changes in income, and R is an index of British prices (the coefficient of R is set equal to unity, since the equation is meant to explain the *relative* price of cotton). According to (9.6.3) the demand for cotton was price elastic during this period, its estimated elasticity being $-(1/0.71) = -1.4$.

The third equation, which completes the system, estimates the relationship of the U.S. price to the British price as

$$\log P^A = 0.36 + \underset{(0.09)}{1.02} \log P^B, \quad R^2 = 0.78, \quad d = 2.1. \qquad \textbf{(9.6.4)}$$

Thus the U.S. price followed the British price closely, a 10% increase in the British price raising the U.S. price by 10.2%.

Temin concluded from these and other regressions that the size of the U.S. cotton crop was not sensitive to price, but rather was determined by the growth of the labor force and random factors, such as the weather. In particular he concluded that both the price rise in 1835 and the price fall in 1838 were due to the harvest and conditions in Britain.

Other cliometric studies have treated such issues as the role of railroads in U.S. economic development, the growth of specific industries, and the economics of slavery in the U.S. South.[50]

PROBLEMS

9-A Consider the demand for (nominal) money. Construct a statistical test that would determine whether this demand function is homogeneous of degree one with respect to the price level.

9-B Using the two Latané estimates of the demand for money in (9.2.8) and (9.2.9), determine the effect of a 10% increase in the long-term interest rate on the demand for money when the initial long-term rate is 4%, 6%, or 8%. Assume income Y is not changed.

9-C Consider a stock adjustment model for money, of the form

$$M_t - M_{t-1} = \gamma(M_t^* - M_{t-1}), \qquad 0 < \gamma < 1$$

where the desired stock of money is a given function of income and the interest rate:

[50] See Fogel (1964), Fogel and Engerman (1969, 1974), and the references cited in footnote 44.

$$M_t^* = F(Y_t, r_t).$$

1. What is the equivalent Koyck distributed lag formulation of this model?
2. Show that if $M_t^* = kY_t$, where k is a constant, then the stock of money is proportional to an exponentially weighted average of all past levels of income ("permanent income"). What happens if k depends on r_t?
3. Consider the related log linear stock adjustment model

$$\frac{M_t}{M_{t-1}} = \left(\frac{M_t^*}{M_{t-1}}\right)^{\delta} \quad \text{where} \quad M_t^* = Ar_t^{\alpha} Y_t.$$

Show that ln M_t is an exponentially weighted geometric average of current and past income levels and interest rates. Show that if $\alpha = 0$, then the velocity of circulation is an exponentially weighted average of current and past rates of change of income.

9-D According to *Gresham's Law* money that is overvalued ("bad" money) tends to drive undervalued ("good") money out of circulation. In an exponential model of this process

$$N(t) = N_0 e^{-\lambda t}$$

where $N(t)$ is the number of good coins in circulation, starting from N_0 in the base year, and λ is the rate at which the undervalued money is driven out of circulation.

1. One way of estimating λ is to calculate the number in circulation at a given date and compare it to the number minted. One study found that in 1969, four years after clad copper dimes first appeared, out of 929 randomly collected dimes 26 were silver and 903 were clad copper.[51] Altogether there were 51.37×10^8 silver dimes and 67.57×10^8 clad copper dimes minted at this point. On the basis of the sample it is estimated that the number of silver dimes in circulation was

$$\frac{26}{903} \times 67.57 \times 10^8 = 1.945 \times 10^8.$$

What is the estimate of λ, the rate of disappearance of the silver dimes?
2. How would you estimate λ on the basis of n observations, given the relative numbers of each type of coin at each observation and given the total number minted of each type?

[51] See Montrol and Badger (1974).

9-E Several measures of concentration have been used in studies of industrial organization. One is the *concentration ratio*, defined as the percentage of output accounted for by the k largest firms in the industry (usually $k = 4$ or 8). Another is the *Herfindahl index*, defined as

$$H = \sum_{i=1}^{n} s_i^2$$

where s_i is the share of the ith firm in industry output (that is, x_i/x, where x_i is the output of firm i and x is total industry output) and n is the total number of firms. A third is *entropy*, defined as

$$E = -\sum_{i=1}^{n} s_i \log s_i$$

where the log usually refers to base 2 logarithms.

1. Show that

$$\frac{1}{n} \leqslant H \leqslant 1$$

and give interpretations for $H = 1/n$ and $H = 1$. Show that $1/H$ is a "numbers equivalent," giving the number of equal-sized firms with the same value of H.

2. Show that

$$0 \leqslant E \leqslant \log n$$

and give interpretations for $E = 0$ and $E = \log n$. Show that F, where $\log F = E$, is a "numbers equivalent," giving the number of equal-sized firms with the same value of E.

9-F A simple capital-theoretic model of the relation between income and years of schooling assumes that individuals choose their years of schooling S so as to maximize the discounted present value of all income.[52] This present value is given as

$$V(S) = \int_S^N e^{-rt} y(S)\, dt = y(S)\frac{1}{r}(e^{-rS} - e^{-rN})$$

where N is the age of retirement, r is the discount rate, and $y(S)$ is the relation between income and schooling. It has been assumed here that there is no income while in school and that income is constant, at $y(S)$, over the working life $N - S$.

[52] See Rosen (1977).

1. Show that the first-order condition for maximizing $V(S)$ by choice of S implies that

$$[1 - e^{-r(N-S)}]\left(\frac{y'}{y}\right) = r, \qquad \left(y' = \frac{dy}{dS}\right)$$

and given an economic interpretation to this relation.

2. Show that if N is sufficiently large, then

$$\ln y = \alpha + \beta S + u, \qquad \alpha = \ln rV, \ \beta = r$$

so that there is a semilogarithmic relation between income and schooling, where u is the stochastic disturbance term. What is the dimension of β? What is its interpretation? What is the least-squares estimator of β?

BIBLIOGRAPHY

Money

Bronfenbrenner, M., and T. Mayer (1960), "Liquidity Functions in the American Economy." *Econometrica*, 28: 810–34.

Brunner, K. (1961), "Some Major Problems in Monetary Theory." *American Economic Review, Papers and Proceedings*, 51: 47–56.

Feige, E. L. (1964), *The Demand for Liquid Assets: A Temporal Cross-Section Analysis.* Englewood Cliffs, N.J.: Prentice-Hall, Inc.

Friedman, M. (1956), "The Quantity Theory of Money: A Restatement." in Friedman, Ed. (1956).

Friedman, M. (1957), *A Theory of the Consumption Function.* Princeton: Princeton University Press.

Friedman, M. (1959), "The Demand for Money: Some Theoretical and Empirical Results." *Journal of Political Economy*, 67: 327–51.

Friedman, M., Ed. (1956), *Studies in the Quantity Theory of Money.* Chicago: University of Chicago Press.

Friedman, M., and A. Schwartz (1963), *A Monetary History of the United States, 1867–1960.* Princeton: Princeton University Press.

Goldfeld, S. (1973), "The Demand for Money Revisited." *Brookings Papers* 3: 577–638.

Johnson, H. G. (1962), "Monetary Theory and Policy." *American Economic Review*, 52: 335–84.

Keynes, J. M. (1936), *The General Theory of Employment, Interest, and Money.* New York: Harcourt, Brace & Co.

Klein, B. (1974), "Competitive Interest Payments on Bank Deposits and the Long-Run Demand for Money." *American Economic Review*, 64: 931–49.

Klein, L. R., and A. S. Goldberger (1955), *An Econometric Model of the United States, 1929–1952.* Amsterdam: North-Holland Publishing Co.

Laidler, D. (1966), "The Rate of Interest and the Demand for Money—Some Empirical Evidence." *Journal of Political Economy*, 74: 545–55.

Laidler, D. (1969), *The Demand for Money: Theories and Evidence.* Scranton: International Textbook Co.

Latané, H. A. (1954), "Cash Balances and the Interest Rate: A Pragmatic Approach." *Review of Economics and Statistics*, 36: 456–60.

Latané, H. A. (1960), "Income Velocity and Interest Rates—A Pragmatic Approach." *Review of Economics and Statistics*, 42: 445–9.

Meltzer, A. (1963), "The Demand for Money: The Evidence from the Time Series." *Journal of Political Economy* 71: 219–46.

Meyer, P. A., and T. A. Neri (1975), "A Keynes-Friedman Money Demand Function." *American Economic Review*, 65: 610–23.

Montrol, E. W., and W. W. Badger (1974), *Introduction to Quantitative Aspects of Social Phenomena.* New York: Gordon and Breach, Science Publishers, Inc.

Morishima, M., and M. Saito (1972), "A Dynamic Analysis of the American Economy, 1902–1952." In M. Morishima et al., *The Working of Econometric Models.* New York: Cambridge University Press.

Teigen, R. L. (1964), "Demand and Supply Functions for Money in the United States; Some Structural Estimates." *Econometrica*, 32: 476–509.

Tobin, J. (1947), "Liquidity Preference and Monetary Policy." *Review of Economics and Statistics*, 29: 124–31.

Zellner, A., Ed. (1968), *Readings in Economic Statistics and Econometrics.* Boston: Little, Brown and Company.

Industrial Organization

Adelman, M. A. (1959), *A & P: A Study in Price-Cost Behavior and Public Policy.* Cambridge: Harvard University Press.

Bain, J. S. (1968), *Industrial Organization*, 2nd Ed. New York: John Wiley & Sons, Inc.

Caves, R. (1962), *Air Transport and Its Regulators.* Cambridge: Harvard University Press.

Chamberlin, E. H. (1933), *The Theory of Monopolistic Competition.* Cambridge: Harvard University Press.

Comanor, W. S. (1967), "Market Structure, Product Differentiation, and Industrial Research." *Quarterly Journal of Economics*, 81: 639–57.

Comanor, W. S., and T. A. Wilson (1967), "Advertising, Market Structure, and Performance." *Review of Economics and Statistics*, 49: 423–40.

Comanor, W. S., and T. A. Wilson (1969), "Advertising and the Advantages of Size." *American Economic Review*, 59: 87–98.

Comanor, W. S., and T. A. Wilson (1974), *Advertising and Market Power.* Cambridge: Harvard University Press.

Dalton, J. A. (1973), "Administered Inflation and Business Pricing: Another Look." *Review of Economics and Statistics*, 40: 516–9.

Dorfman, R., and P. Steiner (1954), "Optimal Advertising and Optimal Quality." *American Economic Review*, 44: 826–36.

Greer, D. F. (1971), "Advertising and Market Concentration." *Southern Economic Journal*, 38: 19–32.

Harberger, A. (1954), "Monopoly and Resource Allocation." *American Economic Review*, 44: 77–87.

Kaysen, C. (1956), *U.S. vs. United Shoe Machinery Corporation.* Cambridge: Harvard University Press.

Lustgarten, S. (1974), "Administered Inflation: A Reappraisal." *Economic Inquiry*, 13: 191–206.

Lustgarten, S. (1975), *Industrial Concentration and Inflation.* Washington, D.C.: American Enterprise Institute for Public Policy Research.

Mansfield, E. (1968a), *Industrial Research and Technological Innovation.* New York: W. W. Norton & Company.

Mansfield, E. (1968b), *The Economics of Technological Change.* New York: W. W. Norton & Company.

Miller, R. A. (1969), "Market Structure and Industrial Performance: Relation of Profit Rates to Concentration, Advertising Intensity and Diversity." *Journal of Industrial Economics*, 17: 104–18.

Modigliani, F. (1958), "New Developments on the Oligopoly Front." *Journal of Political Economy*, 66: 215–32.

Phlips, L. (1971), *Effects of Industrial Concentration: A Cross Section Analysis for the Common Market.* Amsterdam: North-Holland Publishing Co.

Scherer, F. M. (1967), "Market Structure and the Employment of Scientists and Engineers." *American Economic Review*, 57: 524–31.

Scherer, F. M. (1970), *Industrial Market Structure and Economic Performance.* Chicago: Rand McNally & Company.

Schumpeter, J. (1950), *Capitalism, Socialism, and Democracy*, 3rd Ed. New York: Harper & Row.

Weiss, L. W. (1966), "Business Pricing Policies and Inflation Reconsidered." *Journal of Political Economy*, 74: 177–87.

Weiss, L. W. (1969), "Advertising, Profits, and Corporate Taxes." *Review of Economics and Statistics*, 51: 421–30.

Weiss, L. W. (1971), "Quantitative Studies of Industrial Organization." In M. D. Intriligator, Ed., *Frontiers of Quantitative Economics.* Amsterdam: North-Holland Publishing Co.

Weiss, L. W. (1974), "The Concentration-Profits Relationship and Antitrust." in H. J. Goldschmid, H. M. Mann, and J. F. Weston, Eds. *Industrial Concentration: The New Learning.* Boston: Little, Brown, and Company.

Weston, J. F., and S. H. Lustgarten, "Concentration and Wage Price Changes." in H. J. Goldschmid, H. M. Mann, and J. F. Weston, Eds., *Industrial Concentration: The New Learning.* Boston: Little, Brown, and Company.

Labor Economics

Bowen, W. G., and T. A. Finegan (1969), *The Economics of Labor Force Participation.* Princeton: Princeton University Press.

Freeman, R. B. (1974), "Labor Market Discrimination: Analysis, Findings, and Problems." In M. D. Intriligator and D. A. Kendrick, Eds., *Frontiers of Quantitative Economics*, Vol. II. Amsterdam: North-Holland Publishing Co.

Griliches, Z., and W. Mason (1972), "Education, Income, and Ability." *Journal of Political Economy*, 80: S74–103.

Lewis, H. G. (1963), *Unionism and Relative Wages in the United States.* Chicago: University of Chicago Press.

Rosen, S. (1977), "Human Capital: A Survey of Empirical Research." In M. D. Intriligator, Ed., *Frontiers of Quantitative Economics*, Vol. III. Amsterdam: North-Holland Publishing Co.

Weiss, L. W. (1966), "Concentration and Labor Earnings." *American Economic Review*, 56: 96–117.

Health Economics

Berki, S. E. (1972), *Hospital Economics.* Lexington: Lexington Books.

Evans, R. G. (1971), "'Behavioral' Cost Functions for Hospitals." *Canadian Journal of Economics*, 4: 198–215.

Feldstein, M. S. (1967), *Economic Analysis for Health Services Efficiency*. Amsterdam: North-Holland Publishing Co.

Feldstein, M. S. (1971), "Hospital Cost Inflation: A Study of Nonprofit Price Dynamics." *American Economic Review*, 51: 853–72.

Feldstein, M. S. (1974), "Econometric Studies of Health Economics." in M. D. Intriligator and D. A. Kendrick, Eds., *Frontiers of Quantitative Economics*, Vol. II. Amsterdam: North-Holland Publishing Co.

Feldstein, P. (1966), "Research on the Demand for Health Services." *Milbank Memorial Fund Quarterly*, 43: 128–65.

Francisco, E. W. (1970), "Analysis of Cost Variations Among Short-Term Hospitals." In Klarman, Ed. (1970).

Grossman, M. (1972), *The Demand for Health: A Theoretical and Empirical Investigation.* National Bureau of Economic Research, Occasional Paper No. 119. New York: Columbia University Press.

Hefty, T. R. (1969), "Returns to Scale in Hospitals: A Critical Review of Recent Research." *Health Services Research*, 4: 267–80.

Joseph, H. (1971), "Empirical Research on the Demand for Health Care." *Inquiry*, 8: 61–71.

Klarman, H. E., Ed., (1970), *Empirical Studies in Health Economics.* Baltimore: The Johns Hopkins Press.

Lave, J. R. (1966), "A Review of Methods Used to Study Hospital Costs." *Inquiry*, 2: 57–81.

Lave, L. B., and J. Lave (1970), "Hospital Cost Functions." *American Economic Review*, 60: 379–95.

Mann, J., and D. Yett (1968), "The Analysis of Hospital Costs: A Review Article." *Journal of Business*, 41: 191–202.

Newhouse, J. P., and C. E. Phelps (1974), "Price and Income Elasticities for Medical Care Services." In Perlman, Ed. (1974).

Perlman, M., Ed. (1974), *The Economics of Health and Medical Care.* International Economic Association. London: Macmillan; New York: John Wiley & Sons, Inc.

Reinhardt, U. E. (1972), "A Production Function for Physician Services." *Review of Economics and Statistics*, 54: 55–66.

Rosenthal, G. (1970), "Price Elasticity of Demand for Short-Term General Hospital Services." In Klarman, Ed. (1970).

Rosett, R. N., Ed. (1975), *The Role of Health Insurance in the Health Services Sector*, National Bureau of Economic Research.

Yett, D. E., L. J. Drabek, M. D. Intriligator, and L. J. Kimbell (1977), *A Forecasting and Policy Simulation Model of the Health Care Sector: The HRRC Prototype Microeconometric Model.* Lexington, Mass: Lexington Books.

Economic History

Andreano, R., Ed. (1970), *The New Economic History.* New York: John Wiley & Sons, Inc.

Aydelotte, W. O., A. G. Bogue, and R. W. Fogel, Eds. (1972), *The Dimensions of Quantitative Research in History.* Princeton: Princeton University Press.

Conrad, A. H. (1968), "Econometrics and Southern History." *Explorations in Entrepreneurial History*, Second Series, 6: 34–53.

Conrad, A. H., and J. R. Meyer (1964), *The Economics of Slavery and Other Studies in Econometric History.* Chicago: Aldine Publishing Co.

Floud, R., Ed. (1974), *Essays in Quantitative Economic History.* Oxford: Clarendon Press.

Fogel, R. W. (1964), *Railroads and American Economic Growth.* Baltimore: Johns Hopkins Press.

Fogel, R. W. (1966), "The New Economic History: Its Findings and Methods." *Economic History Review*, 19: 642–56.

Fogel, R. W. (1967), "The Specification Problem in Economic History." *Journal of Economic History*, 27: 283–308.

Fogel, R. W., and S. L. Engerman (1969), "A Model for the Explanation of Industrial Expansion during the Nineteenth Century: With an Application to the American Iron Industry." *Journal of Political Economy*, 77: 306–28.

Fogel, R. W., and S. L. Engerman, Eds. (1971), *The Reinterpretation of American Economic History.* New York: Harper & Row.

Fogel, R. W., and S. L. Engerman (1974), *Time on the Cross.* Boston: Little, Brown and Company.

MacAvoy, P. (1965), *The Economic Effects of Regulation: Trunk Line Railroad Cartels and the Interstate Commerce Commission Before 1900.* Cambridge: MIT Press.

McClelland, P. D. (1975), *Causal Explanation and Model Building in History, Economics, and the New Economic History.* Ithaca: Cornell University Press.

Sutch, R. (1977), "United States Economic History." In M. D. Intriligator, Ed., *Frontiers of Quantitative Economics*, Vol. III. Amsterdam: North-Holland Publishing Co.

Temin, P. (1967), "The Cause of Cotton Price Fluctuations in the 1830's." *Review of Economics and Statistics*, 49: 463–70.

Van der Wee, H., and P. M. M. Klep (1977), "Quantitative Economic History in Europe Since the Second World War: Survey, Evaluation, and Prospects." In M. D. Intriligator, Ed., *Frontiers of Quantitative Economics*, Vol. III. Amsterdam: North-Holland Publishing Co.

Wright, G. (1971), "Econometric Studies of History." In M. D. Intriligator, Ed., *Frontiers of Quantitative Economics.* Amsterdam: North-Holland Publishing Co.

Other Applications of Econometric Techniques:

Commodity or Industry Models

Cromarty, W. A. (1959), "An Econometric Model for United States Agriculture." *Journal of the American Statistical Association*, 54: 556–74.

Cummins, J.D. (1975), *An Econometric Model of the Life Insurance Sector of the U.S. Economy*. Lexington: Lexington Books.

L'Esperance, W. L. (1964), "A Case Study in Prediction: The Market for Watermelons." *Econometrica*, 32: 163–73.

Fisher, F. M., P. H. Cootner, and M. N. Baily (1972), "An Econometric Model of the World Copper Industry." *The Bell Journal of Economics and Management Science*, 3: 568–609.

Fisher, M. R. (1958), "A Sector Model—the Poultry Industry of the U.S.A." *Econometrica*, 26: 37–66.

Gerra, M. J. (1959), "An Econometric Model of the Egg Industry." *Journal of Farm Economics*, 41: 284–301.

Gollnick, H. (1957), "Demand Structure and Inventories on the Butter Market." *Econometrica*, 25: 393–422.

Hildreth, C., and F. G. Jarrett (1955), *A Statistical Study of Livestock Production and Marketing*. New York: John Wiley & Sons, Inc.

Horowitz, I. (1963), "An Econometric Analysis of Supply and Demand in the Synthetic Rubber Industry." *International Economic Review*, 4: 325–45.

Rojko, A. S. (1957), "Econometric Models for the Dairy Industry." *Journal of Farm Economics*, 39: 323–38.

Suits, D. (1955), "An Econometric Model of the Watermelon Market." *Journal of Farm Economics*, 37: 237–51.

Suits, D., and S. Koizumi (1956), "The Dynamics of the Onion Market." *Journal of Farm Economics*, 38: 475–84.

Zusman, P. (1962), "An Investigation of the Dynamic Stability and Stationary States of the United States Potato Market, 1930–1958." *Econometrica*, 30: 522–47.

Crime

Ehrlich, I. (1973). "Participation in Illegitimate Activities: A Theoretical and Empirical Investigation." *Journal of Political Economy*, 81: 521–65.

Ehrlich, I. (1975). "The Deterrent Effect of Capital Punishment: A Question of Life and Death." *American Economic Review*, 65: 397–417.

Fleisher, B. M. (1966a), "The Effect of Income on Delinquency." *American Economic Review*, 56: 118–37.

Fleisher, B. M. (1966b), *The Economics of Delinquency*. Chicago: Quadrangle Books.

McPheters, L., and W. S. Strong (1974), "Law Enforcement Expenditures and Urban Crime." *National Tax Journal*, 27: 633–44.

Phillips, L., and H. L. Votey, Jr. (1972), "An Economic Analysis of the Deterrent Effect of Law Enforcement on Criminal Activities." *Journal of Criminal Law, Criminology, and Policy Science*, 63: 336–42.

Phillips, L., H. L. Votey, Jr., and D. E. Maxwell (1972), "Crime, Youth, and the Labor Market." *Journal of Political Economy*, 80: 491–504.

Votey, H. L., Jr., and L. Phillips (1972), "Police Effectiveness and the Production Function for Law Enforcement." *Journal of Legal Studies*, 1: 423–36.

Economic Development

Adelman, I., and H. B. Chenery (1966), "Foreign Aid and Economic Development: The Case of Greece." *Review of Economics and Statistics*, 48: 1–19.

Behrman, J. R. (1972a), "Sectorial Investment Determination in a Developing Economy." *American Economic Review*, 62: 825–41.

Behrman, J. R. (1972b), "Short-Run Flexibility in a Developing Economy." *Journal of Political Economy*, 80: 292–313.

Behrman, J. R. and L. R. Klein (1970), "Econometric Growth Models for the Developing Economy." In W. A. Ellis, M. F. G. Scott, and J. N. Wolfe, Eds., *Induction, Growth, and Trade*. Oxford: Clarendon Press.

Chenery, H. B., and M. Syrquin (1975), *Patterns of Development 1950–1970*. New York: Oxford University Press.

Chenery, H. B., and L. Taylor (1968), "Development Patterns: Among Countries and Over Time." *Review of Economics and Statistics*, 50: 391–416.

Klein, L. R. (1965), "What Kind of Macroeconomic Model for Developing Economies?" *Indian Economic Journal*, 13: 313–24.

Taylor, L. (1969), "Development Patterns: A Simulation Study." *Quarterly Journal of Economics*, 83: 220–41.

UNCTAD Staff (1973), "Models for Developing Countries." In R. J. Ball, Ed. *The International Linkage of National Economic Models*. Amsterdam: North-Holland Publishing Co.

Yotopoulos, P. A., and J. B. Nugent (1976), *Economics of Development: Empirical Investigations*. New York: Harper & Row.

Education

Astin, A. W. (1968), "Undergraduate Achievement and Institutional 'Excellence'." *Science*, 161: 661–8.

Bowles, S. S., and H. M. Levin (1968), "The Determinants of Scholastic Achievement—An Appraisal of Some Recent Evidence." *Journal of Human Resources*, 3: 3–24.

Campbell, R., and B. N. Siegal (1967), "The Demand for Higher Education in the United States, 1919–1964." *American Economic Review*, 57: 482–94.

Coleman, J. S. et al. (1966), *Equality of Educational Opportunity*. Office of Education, U.S. Department of Health, Education, and Welfare. Washington, D.C.: U.S. Government Printing Office.

Freeman, R. B. (1971), *The Market for College-Trained Manpower*. Cambridge: Harvard University Press.

Energy

Balestra, P. (1967), *The Demand for Natural Gas in the United States*. Amsterdam: North-Holland Publishing Co.

Fisher, F. M. (1964), *Supply and Costs in the U.S. Petroleum Industry*. Baltimore: Johns Hopkins Press.

Jorgenson, D. W., Ed. (1976), *Econometric Studies of U.S. Energy Policy*. Amsterdam: North-Holland Publishing Co.

MacAvoy, P. W., and R. S. Pindyck (1975), *The Economics of the Natural Gas Shortage (1960–1980)*. Amsterdam: North-Holland Publishing Co.

Pindyck, R. S. (1974), "The Econometrics of Natural Gas and Oil." *Energy Modelling*. Surrey: IPC Science and Technology Press Ltd.

Steel, J. L. (1971), *The Use of Econometric Models by Federal Regulatory Agencies*. Lexington: Heath-Lexington Books.

Housing

Bailey, M. J. (1966), "Effects of Race and Demographic Factors on the Values of Single-Family Homes." *Land Economics*, 42: 215–20.

Granfield, M. (1975), *An Econometric Model of Residential Location*. Cambridge: Ballinger Publishing Co.

Kain, J. F., and J. M. Quigley (1970), "Measuring the Value of Housing Quality." *Journal of the American Statistical Association*, 65: 532–48.

Olson, E. O. (1972), "An Econometric Analysis of Rent Control." *Journal of Political Economy*, 80: 1081–1100.

Inflation

Askin, A. B. and J. Kraft (1974), *Econometric Wage and Price Models*. Lexington: Lexington Books.

Eckstein, O. and R. Brinner (1972), *The Inflation Process in the United States*. U.S. Joint Economic Committee. Washington, D.C.: U.S. Government Printing Office.

Eckstein, O. and G. Fromm (1968), "The Price Equation." *American Economic Review*, 58: 1159–83.

Goldstein, M. (1972), "The Trade-off between Inflation and Unemployment: A Survey of the Econometric Evidence for Selected Countries," *IMF Staff Papers*, 19: 647–98.

Gordon, R. J. (1972), "Inflation in Recession and Recovery." *Brookings Papers on Economic Activity* 1: 105–66.

International Trade

Adams, F. G., H. Eguchi, and F. Meyer-zu-Schlochtern (1969), *An Econometric Analysis of International Trade*. Paris: OECD.

Ball, R. J., Ed. (1973), *The International Linkage of National Economic Models*. Amsterdam: North-Holland Publishing Co.

Houthakker, H. S. and S. P. Magee (1969), "Income and Price Elasticities in World Trade." *Review of Economics and Statistics*, 51: 111–25.

Leamer, E. E. and R. M. Stern (1970), *Quantitative International Economics*. Allyn and Bacon, Inc.

Linnemann, H. (1966), *An Econometric Study of International Trade Flows*. Amsterdam: North-Holland Publishing Co.

Prachowny, M. F. J. (1969), *A Structural Model of the U.S. Balance of Payments*. Amsterdam: North-Holland Publishing Co.

Prais, S. J. (1962), "Econometric Research in International Trade: A Review." *Kyklos*, 15: 560–79.

Political Science (including Elections)

Alker, H. R. Jr. (1970), "Statistics and Politics: The Need for Causal Data Analysis." In S. M. Lipset, Ed., *Politics and the Social Sciences*. New York: Oxford University Press.

Bloom, H. S., and H. D. Price (1975), "Voter Response to Short-Run Economic Conditions." *American Political Science Review*, 69: 1240–54.

Choucri, N., and R. North (1975), *Nations in Conflict: Population, Expansion, and War*. San Francisco: W. H. Freeman.

Choucri, N., and T. W. Robinson, Eds. (1976), *Forecasting in International Relations: Theory, Methods, Problems, Prospects*. San Francisco: W. H. Freeman.

Cutright, P. (1963), "National Political Development, Its Measurement and Social Correlates." In N. W. Polsby, Ed., *Politics and Social Life: An Introduction to Political Behavior*. Boston: Houghton-Mifflin Co.

Davis, O. A., M. A. H. Dempster, and A. Wildavsky (1966), "A Theory of the Budgetary Process." *American Political Science Review*, 60: 529–47.

Hibbs, D. A. (1973), *Mass Political Violence*. New York: Wiley-Interscience.

Jackman, R. W. (1974), *Politics and Social Equality*. New York: Wiley-Interscience.

Kramer, G. M. (1971), "Short Term Fluctuations in U.S. Voting Behavior, 1896–1964." *American Political Science Review*, 65: 131–43.

Lepper, S. J. (1974), "Voting Behavior and Aggregate Policy Targets." *Public Choice*, 18: 67–81.

Tufte, E. R. (1975), "The Determinants of the Outcome of Midterm Congressional Elections." *American Political Science Review*, 69: 812–26.

Population

Adelman, I. (1963), "An Econometric Analysis of Population Growth." *American Economic Review*, 53: 314–39.

Gregory, P., et al. (1972), "A Simultaneous Equation Model of Birth Rates in the U.S." *Review of Economics and Statistics*, 54: 374–80.

Schultz, T. W., Ed. (1973), "New Economic Approaches to Fertility." *Journal of Political Economy*, Supplement 81: S1–S299.

Suits, D. B., W. Mardfin, S. Paitoonpong, and T. Yu (1975), "Birth Control in an Econometric Simulation." *International Economic Review*, 16: 92–111.

Phillips, L., H. L. Votey, Jr., and D. E. Maxwell (1969), "A Synthesis of The Economic and Demographic Models of Fertility: An Econometric Test." *Review of Economics and Statistics*, 51: 298–308.

Sociology

Blalock, H. M., Ed. (1971), *Causal Models in the Social Sciences.* Chicago: Aldine-Atherton.

Blalock, H. M., Ed. (1974), *Measurement in the Social Sciences.* Chicago: Aldine Publishing Co.

Borgatta, E. F., Ed. (1969), *Sociological Methodology 1969.* San Francisco: Jossey-Bass Publishers.

Costner, H. L., Ed. (1971), *Sociological Methodology 1971.* San Francisco: Jossey-Bass Publishers.

Costner, H. L., Ed. (1974), *Sociological Methodology 1973–1974.* San Francisco: Jossey-Bass Publishers.

Duncan, O. D. (1975), *Introduction to Structural Equation Models.* New York: Academic Press.

Goldberger, A. S., and O. D. Duncan, Eds. (1973), *Structural Equation Models in the Social Sciences.* New York: Seminar Press.

Transportation

Fisher, F. M., and G. Kraft (1971), "The Effect of the Removal of the Fireman on Railroad Accidents, 1962–1967." *The Bell Journal of Economics and Management Science*, 2: 470–94.

Griliches, Z. (1972), "Cost Allocation in Railroad Regulation." *The Bell Journal of Economics and Management Science*, 3: 26–41.

Meyer, J. R., M. J. Peck, J. Stenason, and C. Zwick (1959), *The Economics of Competition in the Transportation Industries.* Cambridge: Harvard University Press.

The Econometric Literature

Fromm, G., W. L. Hamilton, and D. E. Hamilton (1974), *Federally Supported Mathematical Models: Survey and Analysis.* National Science Foundation NSF-RA-S-74-029. Washington, D.C.: U.S. Government Printing Office.

Lovell, M. C. (1973), "The Production of Economic Literature: An Interpretation." *Journal of Economic Literature*, 11: 27–55.

PART V

Simultaneous Equations

CHAPTER **10**

The Simultaneous–Equations System and Its Identification

10.1 The simultaneous-equations system

The discussion of the last six chapters has concentrated on single equations, their estimation, and their applications. This chapter returns to the simultaneous-equations model introduced in Chapter 2 in sections 2.8 to 2.10. It is presented in its general form in this section, and the next two sections are concerned with its identification. The last section treats recursive models. In particular, this chapter develops the specification of the stochastic disturbance terms of equation (2.8.3) and the relevance of this specification for identification. The next chapter then takes up the estimation of the simultaneous-equations model, and Chapters 12 and 13 consider applications of this model.

A simultaneous-equations model determines the values of one set of variables, the *endogenous variables*, in terms of another set of variables, the *predetermined variables*. The linear simultaneous-equations model can be written in the *structural form* as the g simultaneous equations

$$\underset{1\times g}{\mathbf{y}_i}\ \underset{g\times g}{\mathbf{\Gamma}} + \underset{1\times k}{\mathbf{x}_i}\ \underset{k\times g}{\mathbf{B}} = \underset{1\times g}{\boldsymbol{\varepsilon}_i}, \qquad i = 1, 2, \ldots, n. \qquad *(10.1.1)$$

Here $\mathbf{y}_i$ is the vector of g endogenous variables at the ith observation, $\mathbf{x}_i$ is a vector of k predetermined (exogenous or lagged endogenous) variables at the ith observation, and $\boldsymbol{\varepsilon}_i$ is a vector of g stochastic disturbance terms at the ith observation. The index i ranges over the sample of observations, from 1 to n, where n is the sample size (the number of observations). The coefficient matrices to be estimated are $\mathbf{\Gamma}$ and $\mathbf{B}$, representing, respectively, coefficients of endogenous and predetermined variables.[1] The $\mathbf{\Gamma}$ matrix is square and is assumed

[1] As noted in Chapter 2 some studies reverse the role of the $\mathbf{\Gamma}$ and $\mathbf{B}$ matrices. They also frequently premultiply column vectors of variables (rather than, as here, postmultiply row vectors of variables), writing the system as (10.1.1)

$$\mathbf{B}\mathbf{y}_i + \mathbf{\Gamma}\mathbf{x}_i = \mathbf{u}_i.$$

where $\mathbf{u}_i$ is the stochastic disturbance term column vector. The notation employed in this book was chosen to be consistent with the standard notation employed in single-equation estimation. For example, if $g = 1$, choosing $\gamma_{11} = -1$, as in (10.1.2), and defining $u_i = -\epsilon_i$, equation (10.1.1) yields

$$y_i = \mathbf{x}_i\boldsymbol{\beta} + u_i$$

as in the basic linear regression model of Chapter 4, e.g., (4.6.1).

nonsingular, while **B** is generally not square. The structural form contains g equations that jointly determine, for each observation, the values of the g endogenous variables, given the k predetermined variables, the g stochastic disturbance terms, and the $g^2 + gk$ coefficients of the system.

As noted in Section 2.8, there is a trivial indeterminacy in each of the structural equations in that multiplying all terms by any nonzero constant does not change the meaning of the equation. This indeterminacy is eliminated by normalization, which usually involves choosing a specific nonzero numerical value for any one of the nonzero parameters in each equation. A frequently used normalization, as in (2.8.10), sets all diagonal elements of $\mathbf{\Gamma}$ equal to -1:

$$\gamma_{hh} = -1, \qquad h = 1, 2, \ldots, g \qquad \text{*(10.1.2)}$$

assuming $\gamma_{hh} \neq 0$. This normalization is equivalent to multiplying equation h by the constant $-1/\gamma_{hh}$. With this normalization equation h can be written, in the summation notation of (2.8.2), as

$$y_{ih} = \sum_{\substack{h'=1 \\ h' \neq h}}^{g} y_{ih'}\gamma_{h'h} + \sum_{j=1}^{k} x_{ij}\beta_{jh} - \epsilon_{ih}, \qquad h = 1, 2, \ldots, g. \qquad \text{*(10.1.3)}$$

In this form the y_{ih} plays a role comparable to the dependent variable of single-equation estimation, while the $y_{ih'}$ (for $h' \neq h$, where $\gamma_{h'h} \neq 0$) and the x_{ij} (for j, where $\beta_{jh} \neq 0$) play a role comparable to the explanatory variables of single-equation estimation. The $y_{ih'}$ are explanatory endogenous variables, and the presence of such variables distinguishes simultaneous-equations estimation from single-equation estimation.

Returning to the structural form (10.1.1), it is typically assumed that the stochastic disturbance term row vectors $\boldsymbol{\varepsilon}_i$ satisfy certain assumptions.[2] First, they are assumed to have a zero mean:

$$E(\boldsymbol{\varepsilon}_i) = \underset{1 \times g}{\mathbf{0}}, \qquad \text{all } i. \qquad \text{*(10.1.4)}$$

This assumption is a vector generalization of the comparable assumption, in (4.4.2) for the single-equation case, of the form $E(u_i) = 0$. Second, the covariance matrix of the $\boldsymbol{\varepsilon}_i$ is assumed the same at each observation:

$$\text{Cov}(\boldsymbol{\varepsilon}_i) = E(\boldsymbol{\varepsilon}_i'\boldsymbol{\varepsilon}_i) = \underset{g \times g}{\boldsymbol{\Sigma}} = \begin{pmatrix} \sigma_{11} & \sigma_{12} & \cdots & \sigma_{1g} \\ \sigma_{21} & \sigma_{22} & \cdots & \sigma_{2g} \\ \vdots & & & \\ \sigma_{g1} & \sigma_{g2} & \cdots & \sigma_{gg} \end{pmatrix}, \qquad \text{all } i \qquad \text{*(10.1.5)}$$

[2] Note that $\boldsymbol{\varepsilon}_i$ is a row vector. The summary of multivariate statistics in Appendix C refers, however, to a *column* vector of random variables (such as **u** in Chapter 4). To use the results presented in Appendix C here it is therefore necessary to transpose vectors and matrices. For example, (10.1.14) follows from (10.1.5) and (10.1.11) because of (C.3.17), when suitably transposed.

where $\boldsymbol{\Sigma}$ is a symmetric positive-definite matrix of variances and covariances. This assumption is a vector generalization of the assumption of homoskedasticity in (4.4.2), of the form Var $(u_i) = \sigma^2$. In fact, it reduces to this assumption if $g = 1$. Third, the $\boldsymbol{\varepsilon}_i$ are assumed to be uncorrelated over the sample,

$$E(\boldsymbol{\varepsilon}_i'\boldsymbol{\varepsilon}_j) = \underset{g\times g}{\mathbf{0}}, \quad \text{all } i, j, \quad i \neq j \tag*{*(10.1.6)}$$

so that each stochastic disturbance term is uncorrelated with any stochastic disturbance term (including itself) at any other point in the sample. This assumption is a vector generalization of the assumption of absence of serial correlation in (4.4.2), of the form Cov $(u_i u_j) = 0$. These assumptions are satisfied, for example, if the stochastic disturbance terms $\boldsymbol{\varepsilon}_i$ are independently and identically distributed over the sample, with a zero mean vector and a constant covariance matrix $\boldsymbol{\Sigma}$. Under these assumptions, while the stochastic disturbance terms are, by (10.1.6), uncorrelated *over the sample*, from (10.1.5) the stochastic disturbance terms *between equations* can be correlated. This latter phenomenon of correlation between stochastic disturbance terms in different equations is, in fact, the essence of the simultaneous-equation system and the principal reason why it must be estimated as a system, rather than as a set of separate single equations.

In the single-equation case specific assumptions were sometimes made as to the distribution of the stochastic disturbance terms, particularly in the derivation of maximum-likelihood estimators. The situation is similar here in dealing with simultaneous-equations systems. When additional assumptions are made as to the form of the distribution of the $\boldsymbol{\varepsilon}_i$, it is generally assumed that they are distributed independently, identically, and *normally* at each observation, so

$$\boldsymbol{\varepsilon}_i \sim \mathrm{N}(\mathbf{0}, \boldsymbol{\Sigma}). \tag*{*(10.1.7)}$$

Since it is assumed that $\boldsymbol{\Gamma}$ is a nonsingular matrix, it is possible to solve for the vector of endogenous variables $\mathbf{y}_i$ by postmultiplying (10.1.1) by $\boldsymbol{\Gamma}^{-1}$. The result is

$$\mathbf{y}_i = -\mathbf{x}_i\mathbf{B}\boldsymbol{\Gamma}^{-1} + \boldsymbol{\varepsilon}_i\boldsymbol{\Gamma}^{-1} \tag{10.1.8}$$

or

$$\underset{1\times g}{\mathbf{y}_i} = \underset{1\times k}{\mathbf{x}_i}\ \underset{k\times g}{\boldsymbol{\Pi}} + \underset{1\times g}{\mathbf{u}_i} \tag{10.1.9}$$

where

$$\underset{k\times g}{\boldsymbol{\Pi}} = -\underset{k\times g}{\mathbf{B}}\ \underset{g\times g}{\boldsymbol{\Gamma}^{-1}} \quad (\text{or } \boldsymbol{\Pi}\boldsymbol{\Gamma} = -\mathbf{B}) \tag*{*(10.1.10)}$$

and

$$\underset{1\times g}{\mathbf{u}_i} = \underset{1\times g}{\boldsymbol{\varepsilon}_i}\ \underset{g\times g}{\boldsymbol{\Gamma}^{-1}} \quad (\text{or } \mathbf{u}_i\boldsymbol{\Gamma} = \boldsymbol{\varepsilon}_i). \tag*{*(10.1.11)}$$

Equation (10.1.9) is the *reduced form*, which expresses each of the endogenous variables $\mathbf{y}_i$ as a linear function of all predetermined variables $\mathbf{x}_i$ and the stochastic disturbance terms $\mathbf{u}_i$. The coefficient matrix $\mathbf{\Pi}$, defined in (10.1.10), is known as the matrix of *reduced-form coefficients*, and $\mathbf{u}_i$, defined in (10.1.11), is known as the vector of *reduced-form stochastic disturbance terms*. The stochastic assumptions made on $\boldsymbol{\varepsilon}_i$ imply corresponding conditions on $\mathbf{u}_i$, since from (10.1.11) the reduced-form stochastic disturbance terms are linear functions of the structural equation disturbance terms. From (10.1.4) and (10.1.11) it follows that

$$E(\mathbf{u}_i) = \mathbf{0}, \qquad \text{all } i \qquad *(10.1.12)$$

so that "on average" the reduced-form model is "correct" in that

$$E(\mathbf{y}_i) = \mathbf{x}_i \mathbf{\Pi}. \qquad (10.1.13)$$

Furthermore, using (10.1.5) and (10.1.11),

$$\text{Cov}\,(\mathbf{u}_i) = E(\mathbf{u}_i'\mathbf{u}_i) = \mathbf{\Gamma}^{-1\prime}E(\boldsymbol{\varepsilon}_i'\boldsymbol{\varepsilon}_i)\mathbf{\Gamma}^{-1} = \mathbf{\Gamma}^{-1\prime}\mathbf{\Sigma}\mathbf{\Gamma}^{-1} = \mathbf{\Omega}, \quad \text{all } i \qquad *(10.1.14)$$

Here $\mathbf{\Omega}$ is the covariance matrix of $\mathbf{u}_i$. Since $\mathbf{\Sigma}$ is a symmetric and positive-definite matrix, $\mathbf{\Omega}$ is also. From the last equality in (10.1.14) it follows by premultiplying by $\mathbf{\Gamma}'$ and postmultiplying by $\mathbf{\Gamma}$ that

$$\mathbf{\Sigma} = \mathbf{\Gamma}'\mathbf{\Omega}\mathbf{\Gamma} \qquad (10.1.15)$$

showing the relation between the covariance matrix of the structural form $\mathbf{\Sigma}$ and that of the reduced form $\mathbf{\Omega}$. From (10.1.6) and (10.1.11)

$$E(\mathbf{u}_i'\mathbf{u}_j) = \mathbf{0}, \qquad \text{all } i, j, \quad i \neq j \qquad *(10.1.16)$$

so the $\mathbf{u}_i$, just as the $\boldsymbol{\varepsilon}_i$, are uncorrelated over the sample. Equations (10.1.12), (10.1.14), and (10.1.16) summarize the stochastic specification of the reduced-form equations. If it is further assumed that the structural equation stochastic disturbance terms are distributed normally, as in (10.1.7), then it follows from (10.1.11) that

$$\mathbf{u}_i \sim \text{N}(\mathbf{0}, \mathbf{\Omega}) \qquad *(10.1.17)$$

or, equivalently, from (10.1.9),

$$\mathbf{y}_i \sim \text{N}(\mathbf{x}_i\mathbf{\Pi}, \mathbf{\Omega}). \qquad *(10.1.18)$$

The observations on the endogenous and predetermined variables for both the structural-form and the reduced-form equations can be summarized by the *data matrices*

$$\underset{n\times g}{\mathbf{Y}} = \begin{pmatrix} \mathbf{y}_1 \\ \mathbf{y}_2 \\ \vdots \\ \mathbf{y}_n \end{pmatrix}, \quad \underset{n\times k}{\mathbf{X}} = \begin{pmatrix} \mathbf{x}_1 \\ \mathbf{x}_2 \\ \vdots \\ \mathbf{x}_n \end{pmatrix} \tag{10.1.19}$$

which generalize the data matrices introduced in (4.2.1) for a single equation. (These data matrices reduce to those of a single equation in (4.2.1) for the case $g = 1$, in which case the problems and methods of this part of the book, including this chapter and the next, reduce to those of estimating a single equation, as in Part III, particularly Chapter 4.) The data matrices can be written compactly as the *combined data matrix*

$$\underset{n\times(g+k)}{(\mathbf{Y} \mid \mathbf{X})} = \left(\begin{array}{ccc|ccc} y_{11} & \cdots & y_{1g} & x_{11} & \cdots & x_{1k} \\ \vdots & & & \vdots & & \\ y_{n1} & \cdots & y_{ng} & x_{n1} & \cdots & x_{nk} \end{array}\right) \tag{*10.1.20}$$

where each row gives data on all endogenous and predetermined variables at a particular observation point, and each column gives all data at every observation point on one variable of the system.

Each of the reduced-form equations (10.1.9) can be estimated as a single equation, as in Chapter 4. The coefficients of equation h, summarized by the hth column of the $\mathbf{\Pi}$ matrix

$$\underset{k\times 1}{\mathbf{\Pi}_h} = \begin{pmatrix} \Pi_{1h} \\ \Pi_{2h} \\ \vdots \\ \Pi_{kh} \end{pmatrix}, \quad h = 1, 2, \ldots, g \tag{10.1.21}$$

can be estimated, using the least-squares estimator (4.6.11) and the data in (10.1.19), as

$$\underset{k\times 1}{\hat{\mathbf{\Pi}}_h} = \underset{k\times k}{(\mathbf{X}'\mathbf{X})^{-1}} \; \underset{k\times n}{\mathbf{X}'} \; \underset{n\times 1}{\begin{pmatrix} y_{1h} \\ y_{2h} \\ \vdots \\ y_{nh} \end{pmatrix}} \tag{10.1.22}$$

where it is assumed that $\rho(\mathbf{X}) = k$, so $\mathbf{X}'\mathbf{X}$ is nonsingular. Lining up these g columns gives the entire matrix of reduced-form coefficients:

$$\hat{\Pi} = (\hat{\Pi}_1\, \hat{\Pi}_2 \cdots \hat{\Pi}_g) = (X'X)^{-1}X' \begin{pmatrix} y_{11} & y_{12} & \cdots & y_{1g} \\ y_{21} & y_{22} & & y_{2g} \\ \vdots & \vdots & & \vdots \\ y_{n1} & y_{n2} & \cdots & y_{ng} \end{pmatrix} \quad (10.1.23)$$

Thus the set of all least-squares estimators of the entire reduced-form system can be represented as [3]

$$\underset{k\times g}{\hat{\Pi}} = \underset{k\times k}{(X'X)^{-1}}\ \underset{k\times n}{X'}\ \underset{n\times g}{Y} \quad *(10.1.24)$$

Each column of this matrix, which summarizes all the estimated parameters in one of the reduced-form equations, can be written as the $(X'X)^{-1}X'$ matrix of weights times the column of the **Y** matrix corresponding to the dependent variable in that particular reduced-form equation. The estimators in (10.1.24) are the unique best linear unbiased and consistent estimators of the reduced form, since they represent least-squares estimators of each of the reduced-form equations and each of these equations satisfies the assumptions of both the Gauss-Markov theorem and the least-squares consistency theorem of Section 4.9.

The covariance matrix of the stochastic disturbance terms for the reduced-form equations Ω can be estimated using the matrix generalization of the single-equation estimator in (4.7.13) as

$$\hat{\Omega} = \frac{1}{n-k}\hat{u}'\hat{u} = \frac{1}{n-k}(Y - X\hat{\Pi})'(Y - X\hat{\Pi})$$
$$= \frac{1}{n-k} Y'[I - X(X'X)^{-1}X']Y. \quad *(10.1.25)$$

Here $\hat{u}$ is the matrix of least-squares residuals and $I - X(X'X)^{-1}X'$ is the fundamental idempotent matrix of least squares, as introduced in Section 4.6. This

[3] One might wonder whether it might be possible to use an estimate of the covariance matrix Ω to improve the efficiency of the estimator of the reduced-form coefficients by applying generalized least squares for the system of equations, namely the technique of "seemingly unrelated equations," as discussed in Section 6.5. If, however, the explanatory variables are the same for all equations, as here, where **X** summarizes the data for the explanatory variables in each equation, then the technique of seemingly unrelated equations does not improve upon the technique of ordinary least squares applied to each equation separately, as summarized in (10.1.24). See also Problems 6-P and 10-B. As noted in Problem 10-B, by stacking the stochastic disturbance terms as u^* in (6.5.23), assumptions (10.1.14) and (10.1.16) can be rewritten

$$\underset{gn\times gn}{\text{Cov}(u^*)} = \underset{g\times g}{\Omega} \otimes \underset{n\times n}{I}$$

In the single-equation case, where $g = 1$, this covariance matrix reduces to $\sigma^2 I$, as in (4.6.6). (Do not confuse the $g \times g$ matrix Ω here with the $n \times n$ matrix Ω used in GLS in Section 6.5.)

estimator is an unbiased and consistent estimator of $\mathbf{\Omega}$.[4]

Under certain conditions, to be discussed in the next sections of this chapter, the least-squares estimators of the reduced-form parameters $\mathbf{\Pi}$ and $\hat{\mathbf{\Omega}}$, given in (10.1.24) and (10.1.25), which summarize all the relevant information that can be obtained from the sample, can be used to estimate the structural-form parameters $\mathbf{\Gamma}$, $\mathbf{B}$, and $\mathbf{\Sigma}$. The specific techniques of estimation of the structural-form parameters will be presented in the next chapter.

One might wonder why the reduced-form equations were introduced at all. Why not estimate each of the structural form equations directly, using ordinary least squares?[5] This issue is treated in some detail in the next chapter, but a brief answer is that such direct estimates are generally not only biased but also inconsistent, since the structural-form equations generally include explanatory endogenous variables, as shown in (10.1.3). By contrast, the estimators of structural-form parameters that are obtained from the reduced form using the techniques to be discussed in the next chapter are generally consistent estimators.

10.2 The problem of identification[6]

The problem of identification is that of obtaining estimates of the parameters of the structural form (10.1.1), namely the coefficient matrices $\mathbf{\Gamma}$ and $\mathbf{B}$ and the covariance matrix $\mathbf{\Sigma}$ of (10.1.5), given estimates of the parameters of the reduced form (10.1.9), namely the coefficient matrix $\mathbf{\Pi}$ and the covariance matrix $\mathbf{\Omega}$ of (10.1.14). This problem can be studied prior to estimation; indeed, it was introduced in Section 2.10 before any discussion of estimation.

Since the reduced-form parameters summarize all relevant information available from the sample data, a structural equation is *identified* if and only if all parameters pertaining to it can be estimated given all the reduced-form parameters. Otherwise it is *not identified*, in which case there is no way of calculating structural parameters from the reduced-form parameters. A system of structural equations, summarized by the structural form (10.1.1), is *identified* if and only if every equation of the system is identified; if any equation is not identified, then the system is *not identified*.

A structural equation that is identified is *just identified* (or *exactly identified*) if and only if there is a unique way of calculating its parameters from the reduced-form parameters. It is *overidentified* if there is more than one way to calculate its parameters from the reduced-form parameters, leading to restrictions on the reduced-form parameters.

[4] For an approach to the derivation of (10.1.25) [and also (10.1.24)] see Problem 10-B.

[5] The "ordinary" in "ordinary least squares" distinguishes this approach from other techniques of simultaneous-equations estimation, to be introduced in the next chapter, which also utilize the basic idea of least squares.

[6] See Section 2.10, Fisher (1966), and Schmidt (1976). It might be worthwhile to reread Section 2.10, which discusses the general nature of identification and presents some simple examples. For a more general discussion of the problem of identification, treated as that of drawing inferences from observed samples to an underlying theoretical structure, see Rothenberg (1971) and Bowden (1973). Another example of the identification problem is the errors-in-variables model. See Section 6.9, especially footnote 53.

To get a "feel" for the problem of identification one might simply count the numbers of "givens" and "unknowns." The givens are the reduced-form parameters, namely the gk elements of $\mathbf{\Pi}$ and the $g(g + 1)/2$ independent elements of $\mathbf{\Omega}$.[7] The total number of givens G is thus

$$G = gk + \frac{g(g+1)}{2}. \tag{10.2.1}$$

The unknowns are the structural-form parameters, namely the g^2 elements of $\mathbf{\Gamma}$, the gk elements of $\mathbf{B}$, and the $g(g + 1)/2$ independent elements of $\mathbf{\Sigma}$. Each of the equations can be normalized, however, such as in (10.1.2), accounting for g parameters. The total number of unknowns U is therefore

$$U = g^2 + gk + \frac{g(g+1)}{2} - g. \tag{10.2.2.}$$

There is thus an excess of unknowns over givens, amounting to

$$U - G = g^2 - g = g(g - 1). \tag{10.2.3}$$

This excess implies that without additional information it is impossible to estimate structural parameters from reduced-form parameters.[8]

To demonstrate more formally that the reduced-form parameters in general are not sufficient in and of themselves to estimate the structural parameters, consider a "bogus" system of false structural parameters. Assuming $\mathbf{\Gamma}$, $\mathbf{B}$, and $\mathbf{\Sigma}$ are matrices summarizing the *true* parameters of the structural form defined by (10.1.1) and (10.1.5) consider the "*bogus*" parameters obtained by post-multiplying the system by any $g \times g$ nonsingular matrix $\mathbf{R}$:

$$\mathbf{y}_i\mathbf{\Gamma R} + \mathbf{x}_i\mathbf{BR} = \boldsymbol{\varepsilon}_i\mathbf{R}. \tag{10.2.4}$$

This bogus system is normalized in the same way that the old one was—by choosing a specific numerical value for one of the nonzero parameters in each equation, as in (10.1.2). The stochastic assumptions on the bogus system, from (10.1.4) and (10.1.5), are

[7] Since $\mathbf{\Omega}$ is a $g \times g$ symmetric matrix, it contains $g[(g + 1)/2]$ independent elements. For example,

$$= \mathbf{\Omega} \begin{pmatrix} w_{11} & w_{12} \\ w_{12} & w_{22} \end{pmatrix}$$

contains three independent elements.

[8] Note that if $g = 1$ the problem disappears, since the single equation is already the reduced form.

$$E(\boldsymbol{\varepsilon}_i\mathbf{R}) = \mathbf{0}, \qquad \text{all } i \tag{10.2.5}$$

$$\text{Cov}(\boldsymbol{\varepsilon}_i\mathbf{R}) = E(\mathbf{R}'\boldsymbol{\varepsilon}_i'\boldsymbol{\varepsilon}_i\mathbf{R}) = \mathbf{R}'\boldsymbol{\Sigma}\mathbf{R}, \qquad \text{all } i. \tag{10.2.6}$$

The matrices summarizing the parameters of this bogus system are thus

$$\bar{\boldsymbol{\Gamma}} = \boldsymbol{\Gamma}\mathbf{R}, \qquad \bar{\mathbf{B}} = \mathbf{B}\mathbf{R}, \qquad \bar{\boldsymbol{\Sigma}} = \mathbf{R}'\boldsymbol{\Sigma}\mathbf{R}. \tag{10.2.7}$$

The corresponding reduced-form parameters are given by $\bar{\boldsymbol{\Pi}}$ and $\bar{\boldsymbol{\Omega}}$, where, from (10.1.10) and (10.1.14),[9]

$$\bar{\boldsymbol{\Pi}} = -\bar{\mathbf{B}}\bar{\boldsymbol{\Gamma}}^{-1} = -\mathbf{B}\mathbf{R}\mathbf{R}^{-1}\boldsymbol{\Gamma}^{-1} = -\mathbf{B}\boldsymbol{\Gamma}^{-1} = \boldsymbol{\Pi} \tag{10.2.8}$$

$$\begin{aligned}\bar{\boldsymbol{\Omega}} &= \bar{\boldsymbol{\Gamma}}^{-1\prime}\bar{\boldsymbol{\Sigma}}\bar{\boldsymbol{\Gamma}}^{-1} = \boldsymbol{\Gamma}^{-1\prime}\mathbf{R}^{-1\prime}\mathbf{R}'\boldsymbol{\Sigma}\mathbf{R}\mathbf{R}^{-1}\boldsymbol{\Gamma}^{-1} \\ &= \boldsymbol{\Gamma}^{-1\prime}\boldsymbol{\Sigma}\boldsymbol{\Gamma}^{-1} = \boldsymbol{\Omega}.\end{aligned} \tag{10.2.9}$$

The reduced-form parameters based on the bogus estimates are thus *identical* to those based on the true estimates. The true and bogus estimates are thus *observationally equivalent*, since they yield the same reduced form.[10] Multiplication by the **R** matrix combines elements of the various equations of the structural form in a way that is permissible in the sense that it leaves unchanged the reduced form for the system. It therefore follows that if the only available information about the structural form is that of the reduced-form parameters $\boldsymbol{\Pi}$ and $\boldsymbol{\Omega}$, called *a posteriori information* and based on estimation of the reduced-form equations, then the system is not identified. In that case many different structural-form parameters, as given in (10.2.7) for alternative **R**, are consistent with the information available, and it is impossible to distinguish the true parameters $\boldsymbol{\Gamma}$, $\mathbf{B}$, $\boldsymbol{\Sigma}$ from the bogus parameters $\bar{\boldsymbol{\Gamma}}$, $\bar{\mathbf{B}}$, $\bar{\boldsymbol{\Sigma}}$ in (10.2.7). Additional information about the structural form, obtained from relevant theory or the results of other studies, must be provided in order to restrict the possible values taken in the **R** matrix in (10.2.7). Since these restrictions are imposed prior to the estimation of the reduced form, they are called a priori restrictions, which convey *a priori information.*[11] By contrast the information in (10.1.10) and (10.1.14) is *a posteriori information.*

Having assumed that each equation has been normalized by choosing a

[9] Use is made here of the result on matrices that, for two nonsingular matrices **C** and **D**,

$$(\mathbf{CD})^{-1} = \mathbf{D}^{-1}\mathbf{C}^{-1}.$$

See Appendix B, Section B.5.

[10] More precisely they are observationally equivalent in implying the same likelihood function for the observed values of the endogenous variables, given the values of the predetermined variables.

[11] In general, a priori information includes all knowledge of the system prior to parameter estimation. It therefore includes information as to which variables are included, which of the variables are endogenous and which exogenous, the form of the model, and possibly specific information as to values of variables or covariances.

specific numerical value for one of the nonzero parameters for this equation, such as in (10.1.2), this normalized system is identified if the only **R** matrix consistent with the a priori restrictions is the identity matrix

$$\mathbf{R} = \mathbf{I} = \begin{pmatrix} 1 & & & 0 \\ & 1 & & \\ & & \ddots & \\ 0 & & & 1 \end{pmatrix}. \tag{10.2.10}$$

It is then possible to distinguish each structural equation from any other equation, there being enough information so that only one set of structural coefficients could produce the estimated reduced-form parameters. Without the a priori information, but with normalization, the number of free elements in **R** is $g^2 - g$, corresponding to the excess of the number of unknowns over the number of givens in (10.2.3). Identification is achieved by adding enough a priori information to eliminate the free elements from R.

Identification is achieved by imposing a priori restrictions on the structural-form matrices $\mathbf{\Gamma}, \mathbf{B}, \mathbf{\Sigma}$. One approach to identification is to impose restrictions on the coefficient matrices $\mathbf{\Gamma}$ and **B**. The most common way of doing so is by imposing zero restrictions, equating some elements of these matrices a priori to zero. This approach, treated in the next section, is based on relevant theory or on other studies, which may suggest that certain variables do not appear in certain equations. More generally, the coefficients might be related to one another via various linear restrictions. An example of such a restriction is

$$\gamma_{11} = -\beta_{11}. \tag{10.2.11}$$

Such a restriction might occur in the prototype macro model equation for investment: under the accelerator hypothesis, the coefficient of lagged income would be the negative of that for current income, as in equation (2.7.4). Such restrictions (and zero restrictions) are treated in Section 10.4 as special cases of general linear restrictions on the coefficients.

The second approach to identification is through the imposition of restrictions on the covariance matrix $\mathbf{\Sigma}$. One way is with zero restrictions, where certain variances or covariances are assumed zero. A second way is with the relative sizes of variances or covariances. An example is an inequality restriction such as

$$\sigma_1^2 = \sigma_{11} \ll \sigma_{22} = \sigma_2^2 \tag{10.2.12}$$

which might occur in the prototype micro model if the variance of demand were much less than that of supply, as discussed in Section 7.5.

A third approach is some mixture of the above, where certain restrictions, equalities or inequalities, are imposed on $\mathbf{\Gamma}$, **B**, and $\mathbf{\Sigma}$. An example treated in Section 10.5 is that of a recursive system, in which certain zero restrictions are imposed on both $\mathbf{\Gamma}$ and $\mathbf{\Sigma}$.[12]

[12] See Fisher (1966) and Rothenberg (1971) for discussions of a more general treatment of the case in which restrictions are imposed on both coefficients and covariances.

10.3 Identification by zero restrictions in the nonstochastic case

In the nonstochastic case, in which $\boldsymbol{\Sigma}$ and $\boldsymbol{\Omega}$ do not appear as part of the problem, the structural form is

$$\mathbf{y}\,\boldsymbol{\Gamma} + \mathbf{x}\mathbf{B} = \mathbf{0} \qquad *(10.3.1)$$

and the reduced form is

$$\mathbf{y} = \mathbf{X}\boldsymbol{\Pi} \qquad *(10.3.2)$$

where the i subscript has been omitted. The relationships among the reduced-form parameters and structural-form parameters are summarized by

$$\boldsymbol{\Pi} = -\mathbf{B}\boldsymbol{\Gamma}^{-1}. \qquad *(10.3.3)$$

The problem of identification is that of using a priori information contained in the specification to determine estimates of $\boldsymbol{\Gamma}$ and $\mathbf{B}$ from estimates of the reduced-form parameters, where the latter, $\boldsymbol{\Pi}$, represents the available a posteriori information. In the case of zero restrictions the a priori information takes the form of zeros in the $\boldsymbol{\Gamma}$ and $\mathbf{B}$ coefficient matrices, representing, respectively, endogenous and predetermined variables omitted from certain equations.

Consider now, without loss of generality (since equations can be renumbered), the estimation of the first structural equation, which may be written

$$(y_1 \quad y_2 \quad \cdots \quad y_g)\begin{pmatrix}\gamma_{11}\\ \gamma_{21}\\ \vdots \\ \gamma_{g_1 1}\\ 0\\ 0\\ \vdots\\ 0\end{pmatrix} + (x_1 \quad x_2 \quad \cdots \quad x_k)\begin{pmatrix}\beta_{11}\\ \beta_{21}\\ \vdots \\ \beta_{k_1 1}\\ 0\\ 0\\ \vdots\\ 0\end{pmatrix} = 0. \qquad *(10.3.4)$$

Here only the first columns of the $\boldsymbol{\Gamma}$ and $\mathbf{B}$ matrices are indicated, corresponding to the first equation to be estimated. It is assumed that there may be zeros in both columns, and the order of the variables has been changed (that is, variables have been renumbered) so that any zeros come at the end of each of the two column vectors of parameters. In particular, of the g endogenous variables it is assumed that only g_1 enter the first equation. The remaining $g - g_1$ endogenous variables which are omitted from the equation are placed last in the row vector $(y_1 \quad y_2 \quad \cdots y_g)$, so the first column of the $\boldsymbol{\Gamma}$ matrix ends in $g - g_1$ zeros, as shown in (10.3.4). Similarly, of the k predetermined variables it is assumed that only the first k_1 enter the first equation. The remaining predetermined variables are placed last in the vector $(x_1 \quad x_2 \cdots x_k)$, so the first column of the $\mathbf{B}$ matrix ends in $k - k_1$ zeros, as shown. The first equation (10.3.4) can thus be written

$$(\gamma_{11}y_1 + \gamma_{21}y_2 + \cdots + \gamma_{g_1 1}y_{g_1}) + (\beta_{11}x_1 + \beta_{21}x_2 + \cdots + \beta_{k_1 1}x_{k_1}) = 0. \tag{10.3.5}$$

Now consider the matrix equation (10.3.3), which can be written, by post-multiplying by the $\mathbf{\Gamma}$ matrix, as

$$\mathbf{\Pi\Gamma} = -\mathbf{B}. \tag*{*(10.3.6)}$$

Considering only the first columns of $\mathbf{\Gamma}$ and $\mathbf{B}$, corresponding to the first equation of the structural form, and noting the zero values as above, the $\mathbf{\Pi}$ matrix can be partitioned so that this first equation can be represented as

$$\begin{matrix} k_1 \\ \\ k - k_1 \end{matrix} \left(\begin{array}{c|c} \mathbf{\Pi}_1 & \mathbf{\Pi}_3 \\ \hline \mathbf{\Pi}_2 & \mathbf{\Pi}_4 \end{array}\right) \begin{pmatrix} \gamma_{11} \\ \vdots \\ \gamma_{g_1 1} \\ \hline 0 \\ \vdots \\ 0 \end{pmatrix} = -\begin{pmatrix} \beta_{11} \\ \vdots \\ \beta_{k_1 1} \\ \hline 0 \\ \vdots \\ 0 \end{pmatrix} \tag*{*(10.3.7)}$$
$$\qquad g_1 \qquad g - g_1$$

where $\mathbf{\Pi}_1, \ldots, \mathbf{\Pi}_4$ are submatrices of $\mathbf{\Pi}$ corresponding to the variables included in and excluded from the first equation. The submatrix $\mathbf{\Pi}_2$, for example, is a $(k - k_1) \times g_1$ matrix. Performing the matrix multiplications leads to the two sets of equations

$$\underset{k_1 \times g_1}{\mathbf{\Pi}_1} \begin{pmatrix} \gamma_{11} \\ \vdots \\ \gamma_{g_1 1} \end{pmatrix} = -\begin{pmatrix} \beta_{11} \\ \vdots \\ \beta_{k_1 1} \end{pmatrix} \quad (k_1 \text{ equations}) \tag*{*(10.3.8)}$$

$$\mathbf{\Pi}_2 \begin{pmatrix} \gamma_{11} \\ \vdots \\ \gamma_{g_1 1} \end{pmatrix} = 0 \quad (k - k_1 \text{ equations}). \tag*{*(10.3.9)}$$

The problem of identification in this case is that of solving these equations simultaneously for the γ's and β's, given estimates of $\mathbf{\Pi}$. If, however, (10.3.9) can be solved for the γ's, then these estimates can be inserted in (10.3.8) to obtain the β's.[13] The problem thus reduces to that of solving (10.3.9) for the γ's, or, more precisely, for γ's that are unique after normalization. Multiplying both sides of (10.3.9) by a constant, say λ, does not change the equality, but will multiply the γ's by λ. Since λ can be any nonzero number, the γ's are

[13] See (10.3.19) to (10.3.24) for details.

normalized by setting one of them equal to a fixed number, usually 1 or −1, as in (10.1.2).

The system in (10.3.9) is a homogeneous system of $k - k_1$ linear equations in g_1 unknowns. This system has a nontrivial solution that is unique after normalization if and only if the coefficient matrix satisfies the rank condition

$$\rho(\mathbf{\Pi}_2) = g_1 - 1 \qquad *(10.3.10)$$

—that is, the lower left submatrix in (10.3.7) has rank equal to the number of included endogenous variables, less one.[14] This condition is known as the *rank condition of identification.* It is necessary and sufficient for identification of the first equation, and, if it holds, there exist solutions for $\gamma_{11}, \ldots, \gamma_{g_1 1}$ that are unique after normalization. Since $\mathbf{\Pi}_2$ is a $(k - k_1) \times g_1$ matrix, for the rank condition to be satisfied it is necessary that[15]

$$k - k_1 \geqslant g_1 - 1 \qquad *(10.3.11)$$

—that is, the number of *excluded* predetermined variables must be at least the number of *included* endogenous variables, less one. This condition, known as the *order condition of identification*, is necessary but not sufficient for identification. Since the order condition is easy to check—it just involves counting zeros in the relevant columns of the $\mathbf{\Gamma}$ and $\mathbf{B}$ matrices—it is usually checked first. If the order condition is not met, then the equation is *underidentified*. If the equation is identified and the order condition is met exactly, then the equation is *just identified*, while if it is met as a strict inequality, the equation is *overidentified.* Thus the equation must fall in one of the following four categories:

$$\left.\begin{array}{l}\text{overidentified}\\ \text{just identified}\\ \text{underidentified}\\ \text{unidentified}\end{array}\right\} \text{ if } \left\{\begin{array}{r}\rho(\mathbf{\Pi}_2) = g_1 - 1 \text{ and } k - k_1 > g_1 - 1\\ \rho(\mathbf{\Pi}_2) = g_1 - 1 \text{ and } k - k_1 = g_1 - 1\\ k - k_1 < g_1 - 1\\ \rho(\mathbf{\Pi}_2) < g_1 - 1 \text{ and } k - k_1 \geqslant g_1 - 1\end{array}\right. \qquad (10.3.12)$$

An underidentified equation cannot be identified, since then the $\mathbf{\Pi}_2$ matrix has too few rows to satisfy the rank condition. If $k - k_1 \geqslant g_1 - 1$, satisfying the order condition, the equation might nevertheless not be identified, since the order condition is necessary but not sufficient. The basic condition is the rank condition, which is both necessary and sufficient for identification.

The rank condition can be stated in a form that is more convenient to use than (10.3.10). Let $\mathbf{A}$ be the matrix of all structural coefficients defined as

[14] Note that (10.3.9) is a system of $k - k_1$ linear homogeneous equations in g_1 unknowns, namely $\gamma_{11}, \ldots, \gamma_{g_1 1}$. If the matrix of coefficients $\mathbf{\Pi}_2$ has rank g_1, the only solution would be the trivial solution where $\gamma_{11} = \gamma_{21} = \cdots = \gamma_{g_1 1} = 0$. If the rank were less than $g_1 - 1$, then there would be an infinite number of nontrivial solutions after normalization. It is only when the rank is $g_1 - 1$ that there exist solutions that are unique after normalization. For a discussion of solutions of system of linear equation see Appendix B, Section B.6.

[15] Recall that if $\mathbf{A}$ is an $m \times n$ matrix, then $\rho(\mathbf{A}) \leqslant \min(m, n)$, since $\rho(\mathbf{A})$ is the size of the largest nonvanishing determinant in $\mathbf{A}$. See Appendix B, Section B.4.

$$\underset{(g+k)\times g}{\mathbf{A}} = \begin{pmatrix} \boldsymbol{\Gamma} \\ \hline \mathbf{B} \end{pmatrix} = \left(\begin{array}{c|c} \gamma_{11} & \\ \vdots & \boldsymbol{\Gamma}_0 \\ \gamma_{g_1 1} & \\ \hline 0 & \boldsymbol{\Gamma}_1 \\ \hline \beta_{11} & \\ \vdots & \mathbf{B}_0 \\ \beta_{k_1 1} & \\ \hline 0 & \mathbf{B}_1 \end{array}\right) \begin{array}{l} \\ g_1 \\ \\ g - g_1 \\ \\ k_1 \\ \\ k - k_1 \end{array} \qquad (10.3.13)$$

$$\qquad\qquad\qquad\qquad 1 \quad | \quad g - 1$$

where $\boldsymbol{\Gamma}_0$, $\boldsymbol{\Gamma}_1$, $\mathbf{B}_0$, and $\mathbf{B}_1$ are submatrices forming the last $g - 1$ columns of $\boldsymbol{\Gamma}$ and $\mathbf{B}$. The condition (10.3.10) is equivalent to the condition that

$$\rho \begin{pmatrix} \boldsymbol{\Gamma}_1 \\ \hline \mathbf{B}_1 \end{pmatrix} = g - 1 \qquad *(10.3.14)$$

–that is, that the matrix of coefficients in the *other* equations that multiply variables *excluded* from the first equation have rank $g - 1$.[16]

[16] To prove the equivalence of the two rank conditions (10.3.10) and (10.3.14), note that from (10.3.3) and the definition of A in (10.3.13) that

$$\mathbf{A}\boldsymbol{\Gamma}^{-1} = \left(\begin{array}{c|c} \mathbf{I} & \mathbf{0} \\ \hline \mathbf{0} & \mathbf{I} \\ \hline -\boldsymbol{\Pi}_1 & -\boldsymbol{\Pi}_3 \\ \hline -\boldsymbol{\Pi}_2 & -\boldsymbol{\Pi}_4 \end{array}\right)$$

where the I's are identity matrices. Define $\bar{\mathbf{A}}$ as the $[(g - g_1) + (k - k_1)] \times g$ matrix

$$\bar{\mathbf{A}} = \left(\begin{array}{c|c} \mathbf{0} & \boldsymbol{\Gamma}_1 \\ \hline \mathbf{0} & \mathbf{B}_1 \end{array}\right)$$

so that

$$\bar{\mathbf{A}}\boldsymbol{\Gamma}^{-1} = \left(\begin{array}{c|c} \mathbf{0} & \mathbf{I} \\ \hline -\boldsymbol{\Pi}_2 & -\boldsymbol{\Pi}_4 \end{array}\right)$$

and defining $\bar{\boldsymbol{\Pi}}$ as the square nonsingular matrix of order $(g - g_1) + (k - k_1)$,

$$\bar{\boldsymbol{\Pi}} = \left(\begin{array}{c|c} \mathbf{I} & \mathbf{0} \\ \hline -\boldsymbol{\Pi}_4 & -\mathbf{I} \end{array}\right)$$

This condition is a convenient one to use since it does not require the computation of the inverse matrix $\mathbf{\Gamma}^{-1}$ that is used to calculate $\mathbf{\Pi}$. To check this condition all that is required is to write down the **A** matrix of all coefficients in the structural form, cross out rows in which there are nonzero entries in the first column, strike out the first column itself, and check the rank of the resulting matrix. The necessary and sufficient *rank condition of identification* is that the rank of the remaining matrix be one less than the number of endogenous variables in the *system*. The corresponding *order condition of identification* is

$$(g - g_1) + (k - k_1) \geqslant g - 1 \qquad *(10.3.15)$$

since the matrix in (10.3.14) has $(g - g_1) + (k - k_1)$ rows. This condition requires for identification that the total number of variables excluded from the equation must be at least as great as the total number of endogenous variables of the system less one.[17] Clearly some variables must be excluded; excluding no variables leads to an unidentified equation (assuming $g > 1$). If the equation is identified, then the structural coefficients of the equation can be obtained as functions of the reduced-form coefficients, and if each of the equations of the structural form is identified, then the system is identified.

A simple example of the theory of identification is the prototype micro model (2.6.8). In this case

---

it follows that

$$\bar{\mathbf{\Pi}}\bar{\mathbf{A}}\mathbf{\Gamma}^{-1} = \begin{pmatrix} \mathbf{0} & \mathbf{I} \\ \mathbf{\Pi}_2 & \mathbf{0} \end{pmatrix}$$

But, as noted in Appendix B, Section B.4, the rank of **A** is unchanged by premultiplying and postmultiplying by nonsingular matrices. Thus

$$\rho(\bar{\mathbf{A}}) = \rho(\bar{\mathbf{\Pi}}\bar{\mathbf{A}}\mathbf{\Gamma}^{-1}) = (g - g_1) + \rho(\mathbf{\Pi}_2).$$

Furthermore, from the definition of $\bar{\mathbf{A}}$,

$$\rho\begin{pmatrix} \mathbf{\Gamma}_1 \\ \mathbf{B}_1 \end{pmatrix} = \rho(\bar{\mathbf{A}}) = (g - g_1) + \rho(\mathbf{\Pi}_2).$$

Thus

$$\rho\begin{pmatrix} \mathbf{\Gamma}_1 \\ \mathbf{B}_1 \end{pmatrix} = g - 1 \quad \text{if and only if} \quad \rho(\mathbf{\Pi}_2) = g_1 - 1$$

proving the equivalence of the two conditions.

[17]Condition (10.3.15) can be obtained from (10.3.11) by adding $g - g_1$ to both sides of the inequality.

$$\mathbf{A} = \begin{pmatrix} 1 & 1 \\ -\gamma_1 & -\gamma_2 \\ \hline -\beta_1 & 0 \\ 0 & -\beta_2 \\ -\delta_1 & -\delta_2 \end{pmatrix} \tag{10.3.16}$$

where the two columns summarize the two equations of the model. Checking the order condition (10.3.11), both equations are just identified, since in each $k - k_1 = 1 = g_1 - 1$. Equivalently, for each equation $(k - k_1) + (g - g_1) = 1 = g - 1$. According to the rank condition (10.3.14) the first equation, that for demand, is identified if and only if, striking rows in which there are nonzero elements in the first column and then striking the first column itself,

$$\rho \begin{pmatrix} \Gamma_1 \\ --- \\ \mathbf{B}_1 \end{pmatrix} = \rho \begin{pmatrix} \not{1} & \not{1} \\ -\not{\gamma_1} & -\not{\gamma_2} \\ -\not{\beta_1} & \not{0} \\ \not{0} & -\beta_2 \\ -\not{\delta_1} & -\not{\delta_2} \end{pmatrix} = \rho(-\beta_2) = 1 \tag{10.3.17}$$

–that is, $\beta_2 \neq 0$. If $\beta_2 \neq 0$ there is a variable in the system of equations that does *not* enter the demand equation, namely rainfall. Similarly, the second equation is identified if and only if $\beta_1 \neq 0$, implying that there is a variable in the system, I, that is excluded from the supply equation. For this model, then, since each equation is just identified, there exist unique estimates of the structural parameters in terms of the estimated reduced-form parameters. These estimates are given in (2.10.5), and, in general, if a model is just identified, each structural coefficient can be obtained from the reduced-form coefficients by algebraic manipulations such as those in (2.10.5).

In the just-identified case, such as that of the prototype micro model, normalizing on the first element of the (first) column of the $\mathbf{\Gamma}$ matrix by setting $\gamma_{11} = -1$, as in (10.1.2), the first equation can be written

$$y_1 = (\gamma_{21}y_2 + \gamma_{31}y_3 + \cdots + \gamma_{g_1 1}y_{g_1}) + (\beta_{11}x_1 + \beta_{21}x_2 + \cdots + \beta_{k_1 1}x_{k_1}) \tag{10.3.18}$$

Here the parentheses show the dependence of the first endogenous variable on the remaining $g_1 - 1$ included explanatory endogenous variables and the k_1 included predetermined variables. With this normalization equations (10.3.8) and (10.3.9) can be written

$$\underset{k_1 \times 1}{(\mathbf{\Pi}_1^0} \;\vdots\; \underset{k_1 \times (g_1 - 1)}{\mathbf{\Pi}_1^{00})} \begin{pmatrix} -1 \\ ---- \\ \boldsymbol{\gamma}_1 \end{pmatrix} = -\boldsymbol{\beta}_1 \tag{*(10.3.19)}$$

$$\underset{(k-k_1) \times 1}{(\mathbf{\Pi}_2^0} \;\vdots\; \underset{(k-k_1) \times (g_1 - 1)}{\mathbf{\Pi}_2^{00})} \begin{pmatrix} -1 \\ ---- \\ \boldsymbol{\gamma}_1 \end{pmatrix} = \mathbf{0} \tag{*(10.3.20)}$$

where $\gamma_1 = (\gamma_{21} \quad \gamma_{31} \quad \cdots \quad \gamma_{g_1 1})'$ is the column vector of the remaining $g_1 - 1$ coefficients of endogenous variables and $\boldsymbol{\beta}_1 = (\beta_1 \quad \beta_{21} \quad \cdots \quad \beta_{k_1 1})'$ is the column vector of the k_1 coefficients of predetermined variables. Here $\boldsymbol{\Pi}_1^0$ and $\boldsymbol{\Pi}_2^0$ are simply the first column vectors of $\boldsymbol{\Pi}_1$ and $\boldsymbol{\Pi}_2$, respectively, while $\boldsymbol{\Pi}_1^{00}$ and $\boldsymbol{\Pi}_2^{00}$ are the matrices of remaining columns of $\boldsymbol{\Pi}_1$ and $\boldsymbol{\Pi}_2$, respectively. Carrying out the multiplications

$$-\boldsymbol{\Pi}_1^0 + \boldsymbol{\Pi}_1^{00}\boldsymbol{\gamma}_1 = -\boldsymbol{\beta}_1 \tag{10.3.21}$$

$$-\boldsymbol{\Pi}_2^0 + \boldsymbol{\Pi}_2^{00}\boldsymbol{\gamma}_1 = \mathbf{0} \tag{10.3.22}$$

Solving for $\boldsymbol{\gamma}_1$ from (10.3.22) and noting that $\boldsymbol{\Pi}_2^{00}$ is a square matrix—since it was assumed that this is the just-identified case, where $k - k_1 = g_1 - 1$—yields the estimator for $\boldsymbol{\gamma}_1$:

$$\hat{\boldsymbol{\gamma}}_1 = (\hat{\boldsymbol{\Pi}}_2^{00})^{-1}\hat{\boldsymbol{\Pi}}_2^0. \tag*{*(10.3.23)}$$

where $\boldsymbol{\Pi}_2^{00}$ and $\boldsymbol{\Pi}_2^0$ have been replaced by their estimated values. From (10.3.21) it then follows that the estimator for $\boldsymbol{\beta}_1$ is

$$\hat{\boldsymbol{\beta}}_1 = \hat{\boldsymbol{\Pi}}_1^0 - \hat{\boldsymbol{\Pi}}_1^{00}(\hat{\boldsymbol{\Pi}}_2^{00})^{-1}\hat{\boldsymbol{\Pi}}_2^0 \tag*{*(10.3.24)}$$

where $\hat{\boldsymbol{\Pi}}_1^0, \hat{\boldsymbol{\Pi}}_1^{00}, \hat{\boldsymbol{\Pi}}_2^0, \hat{\boldsymbol{\Pi}}_2^{00}$ are all submatrices of $\hat{\boldsymbol{\Pi}}$ in (10.1.24). These results, called the *indirect least-squares estimators*, indicate the general relationships among the estimated structural coefficients $\hat{\boldsymbol{\gamma}}_1$ and $\hat{\boldsymbol{\beta}}_1$ and the estimated reduced-form coefficients $\hat{\boldsymbol{\Pi}}$. The prototype micro model illustrates this case, where (2.10.5) indicates the form taken by these relationships.

To summarize, the necessary and sufficient condition for identification of a single equation in this nonstochastic case is the rank condition (10.3.10) or, equivalently, (10.3.14). The order condition (10.3.11) or, equivalently, (10.3.15) is necessary but not sufficient for identification. If an equation is just identified (i.e., identified and meeting the order condition exactly), it is possible to solve uniquely for its structural coefficients as functions of the reduced-form coefficients, yielding indirect least-squares estimators, as in (10.3.23) and (10.3.24).

10.4 Identification by general linear restrictions[18]

General linear restrictions on the coefficient matrices $\boldsymbol{\Gamma}$ and $\mathbf{B}$ include, as special cases, zero restrictions, as developed in the last section, and equality restrictions, such as (10.2.11). It will be assumed, however, that the covariance matrix $\boldsymbol{\Sigma}$ is unrestricted. A somewhat more compact notation will facilitate the development of identification by general linear restrictions. This notation uses the $\mathbf{A}$ matrix of all coefficients of the structural form, as in (10.3.13):

[18] See Fisher (1966).

$$\underset{(g+k)\times g}{\mathbf{A}} = \left(\frac{\mathbf{\Gamma}}{\mathbf{B}}\right) = (\mathbf{a}_1 \quad \mathbf{a}_2 \quad \cdots \quad \mathbf{a}_g) = \begin{pmatrix} \gamma_{11} & \gamma_{12} & \cdots & \gamma_{1g} \\ \vdots & \vdots & & \vdots \\ \gamma_{g1} & \gamma_{g2} & \cdots & \gamma_{gg} \\ \hline \beta_{11} & \beta_{12} & \cdots & \beta_{1g} \\ \vdots & \vdots & & \vdots \\ \beta_{k1} & \beta_{k2} & \cdots & \beta_{kg} \end{pmatrix} \quad (10.4.1)$$

Here $\mathbf{a}_h$ is the hth column vector of $\mathbf{A}$, summarizing all the coefficients in equation h, for $h = 1, 2, \ldots, g$, where

$$\mathbf{a}_h = (\gamma_{1h} \quad \gamma_{2h} \quad \cdots \quad \gamma_{gh} \mid \beta_{1h} \quad \cdots \quad \beta_{kh})'$$

In this notation the structural form can be written

$$(\mathbf{y}_i \mid \mathbf{x}_i)\mathbf{A} = (\mathbf{y}_i \mid \mathbf{x}_i)\left(\frac{\mathbf{\Gamma}}{\mathbf{B}}\right) = \boldsymbol{\varepsilon}_i, \qquad i = 1, 2, \ldots, n \quad (10.4.2)$$

and the hth equation of the structural form can be written

$$(\mathbf{y}_i \mid \mathbf{x}_i)\mathbf{a}_h = \varepsilon_{hi}, \qquad h = 1, 2, \ldots, g \quad (10.4.3)$$

This notation has already been used in (10.1.20), where data on the $g + k$ variables in (10.4.2) are summarized by an $n \times (g + k)$ matrix.

The a priori information on the hth equation of the system can be summarized as

$$\underset{r_h \times (g+k)}{\mathbf{\Phi}_h} \; \underset{(g+k)\times 1}{\mathbf{a}_h} = \underset{r_h \times 1}{\mathbf{0}} \qquad *(10.4.4)$$

—that is,

$$\begin{pmatrix} \varphi_{h_{11}} & \varphi_{h_{12}} & \cdots & \varphi_{h_{1,g+k}} \\ \varphi_{h_{21}} & \varphi_{h_{22}} & \cdots & \varphi_{h_{2,g+k}} \\ \vdots & & & \\ \varphi_{h_{r_h 1}} & \varphi_{h_{r_h 2}} & \cdots & \varphi_{h_{r_h, g+k}} \end{pmatrix} \begin{pmatrix} \gamma_{1h} \\ \vdots \\ \gamma_{gh} \\ \hline \beta_{1h} \\ \vdots \\ \beta_{kh} \end{pmatrix} = \begin{pmatrix} 0 \\ \vdots \\ 0 \end{pmatrix}$$

where $\mathbf{\Phi}_h$ is a given matrix. Each row of $\mathbf{\Phi}_h$ implies one linear restriction on $\mathbf{a}_h$, and the r_h rows of this matrix summarize all such a priori restrictions on the hth structural equation. If, for example, one row of $\mathbf{\Phi}_h$ were $(0 \quad 1 \quad 0 \quad \cdots \quad 0)$, it would impose the restriction that $\gamma_{2h} = 0$, and, in general, rows of $\boldsymbol{\Phi}_h$ that are unit vectors impose zero restrictions on the equation, requiring that certain variables be excluded from this equation. If, however, $g = 2$ and one row of $\boldsymbol{\Phi}_1$ were $(1 \quad 0 \quad 1 \quad 0 \cdots 0)$, it would impose the restriction that $\gamma_{11} = -\beta_{11}$, as in (10.2.11). Any linear equality restriction can be expressed in this way, and equation (10.4.4) imposes r_h such restrictions on the hth equation. [An example will be presented following equation (10.4.17).]

The a posteriori information on the system, of the form

$$\boldsymbol{\Pi} = -\mathbf{B}\boldsymbol{\Gamma}^{-1} \tag{10.4.5}$$

can be written

$$\boldsymbol{\Pi}\boldsymbol{\Gamma} + \mathbf{B} = \mathbf{0}. \tag{10.4.6}$$

Thus, defining $\mathbf{W}$ as the partitioned coefficient matrix and identity matrix

$$\underset{k\times(g+k)}{\mathbf{W}} = (\underset{k\times g}{\boldsymbol{\Pi}} \;\vdots\; \underset{k\times k}{\mathbf{I}}) \quad \text{where} \quad \rho(\mathbf{W}) = k \tag{10.4.7}$$

all a posteriori information can be summarized by the equation

$$\mathbf{W}\mathbf{A} = \mathbf{0}. \tag{10.4.8}$$

This equation states that

$$\mathbf{W}\mathbf{A} = (\boldsymbol{\Pi} \;\vdots\; \mathbf{I}) \begin{pmatrix} \boldsymbol{\Gamma} \\ \hline \mathbf{B} \end{pmatrix} = \boldsymbol{\Pi}\;\boldsymbol{\Gamma} + \mathbf{B} = \mathbf{0}. \tag{10.4.9}$$

In particular, for the hth equation the a posteriori information is summarized by the k restrictions in $g + k$ unknowns:

$$\underset{k\times(g+k)}{\mathbf{W}} \; \underset{(g+k)\times 1}{\mathbf{a}_h} = \mathbf{0}. \tag*{*(10.4.10)}$$

This equation summarizes all k restrictions on the coefficients of the hth equation obtained from the a posteriori information of the reduced form.

The a priori restrictions (10.4.4) and the a posteriori restrictions (10.4.10) for each equation can be combined in the single system of homogeneous equations

$$\underset{(r_h+k)\times(g+k)}{\begin{pmatrix} \boldsymbol{\Phi}_h \\ \hline \mathbf{W} \end{pmatrix}} \; \underset{(g+k)\times 1}{\mathbf{a}_h} = \underset{(r_h+k)\times 1}{\mathbf{0}}, \quad h = 1, 2, \ldots, g \tag*{*(10.4.11)}$$

which summarizes all $r_h + k$ restrictions on the hth equation. The equation is *identified* if this system of $r_h + k$ homogeneous equations in $g + k$ unknowns has a nontrivial solution. A nontrivial solution that is unique after normalization exists, however, if and only if the matrix in (10.4.11) satisfies the *rank condition*[19]

$$\rho\begin{pmatrix}\mathbf{\Phi}_h\\ \hline \mathbf{W}\end{pmatrix} = g + k - 1. \qquad *(10.4.12)$$

A condition that is equivalent to (10.4.12) is the *general rank condition of identification*[20]

$$\rho(\underset{r_h\times g}{\mathbf{\Phi}_h\mathbf{A}}) = g - 1 \qquad *(10.4.13)$$

[19] To verify this condition, note that, following the reasoning of footnote 14, (10.4.11) is a system of $r_h + k$ linear homogeneous equations in $g + k$ unknowns, namely the elements of $\mathbf{a}_h$. If the matrix of coefficients had rank $g + k$, the only solution would be the trivial solution $\mathbf{a}_h = \mathbf{0}$. If the rank were less than $g + k - 1$, then there would be an infinite number of nontrivial solutions after normalization. It is only when the rank is $g + k - 1$ that there exist solutions for the elements of $\mathbf{a}_h$ that are unique after normalization.

[20] Fisher (1966) has shown the equivalence of the two rank conditions using the concept of *column kernel*, defined as the set of column vectors transformed into the zero vector by the matrix. Thus the column kernel of the matrix $\mathbf{M}$ is the set of all column vectors $\mathbf{z}$ satisfying $\mathbf{Mz} = \mathbf{0}$. In the problem at hand, letting $\mathbf{\Psi}_h$ be

$$\begin{pmatrix}\mathbf{\Phi}_h\\ \hline \mathbf{W}\end{pmatrix},$$

suppose that $\rho(\mathbf{\Psi}_h) = g + k - 1$, but $\rho(\mathbf{\Phi}_h\mathbf{A}) \neq g - 1$. The hth column of $\mathbf{\Phi}_h\mathbf{A}$ contains only zeros because of the a priori restrictions, (10.4.4), so $\rho(\mathbf{\Phi}_h\mathbf{A}) < g - 1$. Thus there exist at least two independent column vectors in the column kernel of $\mathbf{\Phi}_h\mathbf{A}$. If these vectors are $\mathbf{v}$ and $\mathbf{w}$, then, by definition of the column kernel,

$$(\mathbf{\Phi}_h\mathbf{A})\mathbf{v} = \mathbf{0}, \quad (\mathbf{\Phi}_h\mathbf{A})\mathbf{w} = \mathbf{0}.$$

Define

$$\tilde{\mathbf{v}} = \mathbf{Av}, \quad \tilde{\mathbf{w}} = \mathbf{aW}$$

where, since $\mathbf{v}$ and $\mathbf{w}$ are independent, so are $\tilde{\mathbf{v}}$ and $\tilde{\mathbf{w}}$ [assuming $\rho(\mathbf{A}) = g$]. But

$$\mathbf{\Phi}_h\tilde{\mathbf{v}} = \mathbf{\Phi}_h\mathbf{Av} = \mathbf{0}, \quad \mathbf{\Phi}_h\tilde{\mathbf{w}} = \mathbf{\Phi}_h\mathbf{Aw} = \mathbf{0}$$

and, since, from (10.4.8), $\mathbf{WA} = \mathbf{0}$

$$\mathbf{W}\tilde{\mathbf{v}} = \mathbf{WAv} = \mathbf{0}, \quad \mathbf{W}\tilde{\mathbf{w}} = \mathbf{WAw} = \mathbf{0}.$$

Thus

$$\mathbf{\Psi}_h\tilde{\mathbf{v}} = \mathbf{0}, \quad \mathbf{\Psi}_h\tilde{\mathbf{w}} = \mathbf{0}$$

so there are at least two independent column vectors in the column kernel of $\mathbf{\Psi}_h$, implying that $\rho(\mathbf{\Psi}_h) < g + k - 1$, a contradiction. Conversely, suppose $\rho(\mathbf{\Phi}_h\mathbf{A}) = g - 1$ but $\rho(\mathbf{\Psi}_h) \neq g + k - 1$. Since, from (10.4.4) and (10.4.10), $\mathbf{\Psi}_h\mathbf{a}_h = \mathbf{0}$, it follows that $\rho(\mathbf{\Psi}_h) < g + k - 1$, so there

This is a necessary and sufficient condition for the identification of the hth equation that is preferred to (10.4.12) because it does not involve $\mathbf{W}$, making unnecessary the inversion of $\mathbf{\Gamma}$ to determine the $\mathbf{\Pi}$ in $\mathbf{W}$. From (10.4.13) and the fact that multiplying a matrix by another cannot increase its rank, it follows that a necessary condition of identification is

$$\rho(\mathbf{\Phi}_h) \geqslant g - 1 \tag*{*(10.4.14)}$$

which is the *general order condition of identification.* It is called an "order" condition even though it involves the rank of a matrix, and it is necessary, but not sufficient for identification. Since it depends only on $\mathbf{\Phi}_h$, it is easy to check. This order condition generalizes the condition (10.3.15), and it is used to define overidentified, just-identified, and underidentified equations. Thus, following the categories in (10.3.12), equation h is

$$\left.\begin{array}{l}\text{overidentified}\\ \text{just identified}\\ \text{underidentified}\\ \text{unidentified}\end{array}\right\} \quad \text{if} \quad \left\{\begin{array}{r}\rho(\mathbf{\Phi}_h\mathbf{A}) = g - 1 \text{ and } \rho(\mathbf{\Phi}_h) > g - 1\\ \rho(\mathbf{\Phi}_h\mathbf{A}) = g - 1 \text{ and } \rho(\mathbf{\Phi}_h) = g - 1\\ \rho(\mathbf{\Phi}_h) < g - 1\\ \rho(\mathbf{\Phi}_h\mathbf{A}) < g - 1 \text{ and } \rho(\mathbf{\Phi}_h) \geqslant g - 1\end{array}\right. \tag{10.4.15}$$

A necessary condition for identification, which is necessary for the general order condition to be met, is

$$r_h \geqslant g - 1 \tag*{*(10.4.16)}$$

requiring that the number of linear restrictions imposed on each equation be at least the number of endogenous variables of the system, less one.[21] For example, in a system of two equations with two endogenous variables at least one linear restriction must be imposed on each equation for the system to be

---

are at least two independent column vectors in the column kernel of $\mathbf{\Psi}_h$. Call them $\tilde{\mathbf{v}}$ and $\tilde{\mathbf{w}}$. From the definition of $\mathbf{\Psi}_h$ these vectors are in the column kernel of w. But the columns of $\mathbf{A}$ form a basis for this column kernel, so there exist two independent vectors $\mathbf{v}$ and $\mathbf{w}$ such that

$$\tilde{\mathbf{v}} = \mathbf{A}\mathbf{v}, \qquad \tilde{\mathbf{w}} = \mathbf{A}\mathbf{w}.$$

But

$$\mathbf{\Phi}_h\mathbf{A}\mathbf{v} = \mathbf{\Phi}_h\tilde{\mathbf{v}} = 0, \qquad \mathbf{\Phi}_h\mathbf{A}\mathbf{w} = \mathbf{\Phi}_h\tilde{\mathbf{w}} = 0$$

where $\tilde{\mathbf{v}}$ and $\tilde{\mathbf{w}}$ are in the column kernel of $\mathbf{\Phi}_h$, since they are in the column kernel of $\mathbf{\Psi}_h$. Thus $\mathbf{v}$ and $\mathbf{w}$ are two independent vectors of the column kernel of $\mathbf{\Phi}_h\mathbf{A}$, implying that $\rho(\mathbf{\Phi}_h\mathbf{A}) < g - 1$, a contradiction. Thus the equivalence of the two rank conditions is proved.

[21] The reason for subtracting one here and earlier is that, because of the homogeneity of the equation, subtracting less than one means structural estimators are not defined, while subtracting more than one means that the estimators are not unique after normalization. See footnotes 14 and 19.

identified, as was illustrated in Section 2.10. If this condition is violated the equation is *underidentified* and therefore not identified. If there are no a priori restrictions, so $r_h = 0$, the equation can be identified only if $g = 1$, in which case the reduced form and the structural form are equivalent. This is the single-equation case treated earlier.

The rank and order conditions derived in the last section are special cases of (10.4.13) and (10.4.14), corresponding to the case in which the restrictions on coefficients are all zero restrictions. Thus, for example, (10.3.15), which states, as an order condition, that the total number of variables excluded from the equation (i.e., the total number of zero restrictions) must be no less than $g - 1$, is the special case of (10.4.14) in which all rows of $\mathbf{\Phi}_h$ are unit vectors, so

$$\rho(\mathbf{\Phi}_h) = r_h = (g - g_h) + (k - k_h) \geqslant g - 1 \tag{10.4.17}$$

and $h = 1$, referring to the first equation.

An example should help clarify the nature of the general conditions of identification. Suppose $g = 3$ and $k = 4$, so, in the normalized case,

$$\mathbf{A} = \begin{pmatrix} -1 & \gamma_{12} & \gamma_{13} \\ \gamma_{21} & -1 & \gamma_{23} \\ \gamma_{31} & \gamma_{32} & -1 \\ \hline \beta_{11} & \beta_{12} & \beta_{13} \\ \beta_{21} & \beta_{22} & \beta_{23} \\ \beta_{31} & \beta_{32} & \beta_{33} \\ \beta_{41} & \beta_{42} & \beta_{43} \end{pmatrix}. \tag{10.4.18}$$

Assume the a priori restrictions are given by

$$\gamma_{21} = \beta_{11} = \beta_{32} = \gamma_{23} = \beta_{23} = 0, \qquad \beta_{13} = \beta_{33} \tag{10.4.19}$$

Considering now the first equation, involving coefficients summarized by the first $\mathbf{A}$ column vector $\mathbf{a}_1$, all a priori restrictions for this equation can be written in the form

$$\mathbf{\Phi}_1 \mathbf{a}_1 = \mathbf{0} \tag{10.4.20}$$

where

$$\mathbf{\Phi}_1 = \begin{pmatrix} 0 & 1 & 0 & 0 & 0 & 0 & 0 \\ 0 & 0 & 0 & 1 & 0 & 0 & 0 \end{pmatrix}. \tag{10.4.21}$$

Since

$$\mathbf{\Phi}_1 \mathbf{A} = \begin{pmatrix} \gamma_{21} & -1 & \gamma_{23} \\ \beta_{11} & \beta_{12} & \beta_{13} \end{pmatrix} \tag{10.4.22}$$

it is clear, by inspection, that, barring special coincidences,

$$\rho(\mathbf{\Phi}_1) = 2 = g - 1, \qquad \rho(\mathbf{\Phi}_1 \mathbf{A}) = 2. \tag{10.4.23}$$

Thus this equation is just identified. For the second equation

$$\mathbf{\Phi}_2 = (0 \quad 0 \quad 0 \quad 0 \quad 0 \quad 1 \quad 0), \qquad \rho(\mathbf{\Phi}_2) = 1 < g - 1, \qquad r_2 = 1 < g - 1 \tag{10.4.24}$$

so this equation is underidentified and hence not identified.[22] For the third equation

$$\mathbf{\Phi}_3 = \begin{pmatrix} 0 & 1 & 0 & 0 & 0 & 0 & 0 \\ 0 & 0 & 0 & 0 & 1 & 0 & 0 \\ 0 & 0 & 0 & 1 & 0 & -1 & 0 \end{pmatrix}, \qquad \rho(\mathbf{\Phi}_3) = 3, \quad \rho(\mathbf{\Phi}_3 \mathbf{A}) = 2 \tag{10.4.25}$$

so this equation is overidentified. Thus, in this example, the first equation can be estimated directly from the reduced form, which yields unique estimators of the structural coefficients of this equation; the second equation cannot be estimated from the reduced form; and the third equation can be estimated in more than one way from the reduced form. Because one equation is not identified, the system is not identified.

In any econometric project involving simultaneous equations the identification of the system is of crucial importance. If an equation is just identified then it can be estimated from the least-squares estimates of the reduced form, using the technique of indirect least squares. If an equation is overidentified then there are several techniques that can be used in its estimation, as discussed in the next chapter. If, however, any equation is underidentified then it cannot be estimated, and it is not possible to infer structural coefficients for this equation from reduced-form estimates. In such a case the system might be respecified to avoid underidentified equations. In general, ordinary least squares applied to just-identified or overidentified equations leads to biased and inconsistent estimators, while ordinary least squares applied to underidentified equations yields bogus estimators. The next section, however, summarizes one type of simultaneous-equations system for which ordinary least squares does provide estimators with desirable properties—the recursive system.

10.5 Recursive systems

An important type of simultaneous-equations system is the *recursive system*, in which the endogenous variables and the structural equations can be arranged in such an order that $\mathbf{\Gamma}$, the matrix of coefficients of endogenous variables, is a triangular matrix and $\mathbf{\Sigma}$, the matrix of variances and covariances of stochastic disturbance terms, is a diagonal matrix.[23] Thus in this case

[22] Note that either test would be adequate to show that this equation is underidentified. It fails on both tests, each of which is necessary.

[23] See Wold (1954, 1960, 1964). In Wold's terminology a model that is not recursive is *interdependent*. He argues against such models both philosophically on the basis of a unilateral flow of causation and econometrically on the basis of the difficulties of estimation of interdependent models.

$$\Gamma = \begin{pmatrix} \gamma_{11} & \gamma_{12} & \gamma_{13} & \cdots & \gamma_{1g} \\ 0 & \gamma_{22} & \gamma_{23} & \cdots & \gamma_{2g} \\ 0 & 0 & \gamma_{33} & \cdots & \gamma_{3g} \\ \vdots & & & \ddots & \\ 0 & 0 & 0 & & \gamma_{gg} \end{pmatrix} \tag{10.5.1}$$

$$\Sigma = \begin{pmatrix} \sigma_1^2 & 0 & \cdots & 0 \\ 0 & \sigma_2^2 & & \\ \vdots & & \ddots & \\ 0 & & & \sigma_g^2 \end{pmatrix} \tag{10.5.2}$$

The first set of conditions, on the coefficient matrix, requires that the structural equations can be expressed such that no equation includes those endogenous variables included in higher-numbered equations. The second set of conditions, on the covariance matrix, requires that all covariances between the stochastic disturbance terms in any two different equations vanish. It should be noted that the first set of conditions, on the coefficients, is not, by itself, adequate. The conditions on the covariances are also essential for the system to be recursive.

Under the assumptions (10.5.1) and (10.5.2) on a recursive system the system of equations can then be written, using the usual normalization of diagonal elements, as

$$\begin{aligned} y_1 &= \sum_{j=1}^{k} \beta_{j1} x_j - \epsilon_1 \\ y_2 &= \gamma_{12} y_1 + \sum_{j=1}^{k} \beta_{j2} x_j - \epsilon_2 \\ y_3 &= \gamma_{13} y_1 + \gamma_{23} y_2 + \sum_{j=1}^{k} \beta_{j3} x_j - \epsilon_3 \\ &\vdots \\ y_g &= \sum_{h=1}^{g-1} \gamma_{hg} y_h + \sum_{j=1}^{k} \beta_{jg} x_j - \epsilon_g \end{aligned} \tag{10.5.3}$$

Thus each endogenous variable can be explained in terms of the predetermined variables, stochastic disturbance term, and *lower*-numbered endogenous variables. The assumption that the covariance matrix of the $\boldsymbol{\varepsilon}$'s, the $\boldsymbol{\Sigma}$ matrix, is diagonal ensures that contemporaneous stochastic disturbance terms are uncorrelated. Each equation therefore stands alone, and its stochastic disturbance term does not "contaminate" the other equations of the system. Every endogenous variable is predetermined with respect to higher-numbered equations in that the direction of flow of impulses is only from lower-numbered to higher-numbered equations. This unidirectional flow is illustrated in Figure 10.1 in an arrow diagram. All the predetermined variables and ϵ_1 determine y_1. Then y_1, all the predetermined variables, and ϵ_2 determine y_2. Then y_1, y_2, all the predetermined variables, and ϵ_3 determine y_3.

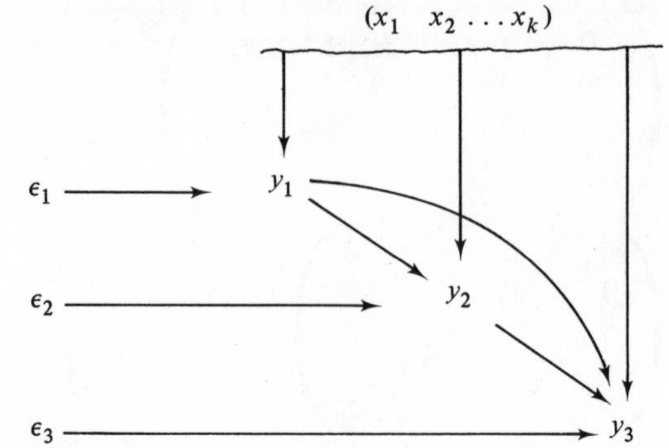

Figure 10.1 Unilateral Flow for a Recursive Model

Recursive models are always exactly identified. That is, with the zero restrictions in $\mathbf{\Gamma}$ and $\mathbf{\Sigma}$ given in (10.5.1) and (10.5.2) it is always possible to infer the nonzero structural coefficients from the reduced-form coefficents. The normalized system contains $g[(g+1)/2] - g$ coefficients to be estimated in $\mathbf{\Gamma}$, gk in $\mathbf{B}$, and g in $\mathbf{\Sigma}$, and the reduced form contains the usual number of $gk + g[(g+1)/2]$ parameters, as in (10.2.1). The number of givens and unknowns is therefore the same

$$G = U = \frac{g(g+1)}{2} + gk. \tag{10.5.4}$$

For example, if $g = 2$ and $k = 3$, the number of unknowns and givens is 9. In this case, from (10.1.15)

$$\begin{pmatrix} \sigma_1^2 & 0 \\ 0 & \sigma_2^2 \end{pmatrix} = \begin{pmatrix} -1 & 0 \\ \gamma_{12} & -1 \end{pmatrix} \begin{pmatrix} \omega_1^2 & \omega_{12} \\ \omega_{12} & \omega_2^2 \end{pmatrix} \begin{pmatrix} -1 & \gamma_{12} \\ 0 & -1 \end{pmatrix} \tag{10.5.5}$$

where the ω's are elements of the $\mathbf{\Omega}$ matrix, assumed known or estimated. From (10.5.5) it follows that

$$\begin{aligned} \sigma_1^2 &= \omega_1^2 \\ \gamma_{12} &= \frac{\omega_{12}}{\omega_1^2} \\ \sigma_2^2 &= \omega_2^2 - \frac{\omega_{12}^2}{\omega_1^2} \end{aligned} \tag{10.5.6}$$

where ω_1^2 and ω_2^2 are variances of the reduced-form stochastic disturbance terms. But from (10.1.10)

$$\begin{pmatrix} \pi_{11} & \pi_{12} \\ \pi_{21} & \pi_{22} \\ \pi_{31} & \pi_{32} \end{pmatrix} \begin{pmatrix} -1 & \gamma_{12} \\ 0 & -1 \end{pmatrix} = - \begin{pmatrix} \beta_{11} & \beta_{12} \\ \beta_{21} & \beta_{22} \\ \beta_{31} & \beta_{32} \end{pmatrix} \tag{10.5.7}$$

so, solving for the remaining unknowns, the β's,

$$\begin{aligned} \beta_{11} &= \pi_{11}, & \beta_{12} &= \pi_{12} - \gamma_{12}\pi_{11} \\ \beta_{21} &= \pi_{21}, & \beta_{22} &= \pi_{22} - \gamma_{12}\pi_{21} \\ \beta_{31} &= \pi_{31}, & \beta_{32} &= \pi_{32} - \gamma_{12}\pi_{31} \end{aligned} \tag{10.5.8}$$

where γ_{12} is given in (10.5.6). These results summarize the indirect least-squares estimators for the structural parameters, given the reduced-form coefficients. The coefficients of the first equation are the reduced-form coefficients (since this equation contains only one endogenous variable), while the coefficients of the second equation are obtained using the recursive nature of the system from the coefficients obtained for the first equation and the reduced-form coefficients for the second equation. The first equation is of the form

$$y_1 = \beta_{11}x_1 + \beta_{21}x_2 + \beta_{31}x_3 - \epsilon_1 \tag{10.5.9}$$

and the β's are the reduced-form coefficients

$$\beta_{11} = \pi_{11}, \quad \beta_{21} = \pi_{21}, \quad \beta_{31} = \pi_{31}. \tag{10.5.10}$$

The second equation is of the form

$$y_2 = \gamma_{12}y_1 + \beta_{12}x_1 + \beta_{22}x_2 + \beta_{32}x_3 - \epsilon_2 \tag{10.5.11}$$

so, replacing y_1 from (10.5.9) and (10.5.10),

$$y_2 = \gamma_{12}(\pi_{11}x_1 + \pi_{21}x_2 + \pi_{31}x_3) + \beta_{12}x_1 + \beta_{22}x_2 + \beta_{32}x_3 - \epsilon_2 \tag{10.5.12}$$

$$y_2 = (\gamma_{12}\pi_{11} + \beta_{12})x_1 + (\gamma_{12}\pi_{21} + \beta_{22})x_2 + (\gamma_{12}\pi_{31} + \beta_{32})x_3 - \epsilon_2 \tag{10.5.13}$$

Equating the terms in parentheses to the coefficients of the second reduced-form equation yields

$$\beta_{12} = \pi_{12} - \gamma_{12}\pi_{11}, \quad \beta_{22} = \pi_{22} - \gamma_{12}\pi_{21}, \quad \beta_{32} = \pi_{32} - \gamma_{12}\pi_{31} \tag{10.5.14}$$

as in (10.5.8). The nine results in (10.5.6) and (10.5.8) give the normalized structural coefficients as explicit functions of the reduced-form coefficients, illustrating the identification and indirect least-squares estimators that are always guaranteed for recursive systems.

PROBLEMS

10-A Prove that the least-squares estimator $\hat{\mathbf{\Pi}}$ given in (10.1.24) is both an unbiased and a consistent estimator of $\mathbf{\Pi}$ and that the estimator $\hat{\mathbf{\Omega}}$ given in (10.1.25) is both an unbiased and a consistent estimator of $\mathbf{\Omega}$.

10-B The star notation of Section 6.5 and 11.7 can be used to derive the estimator of the reduced-form system. In this notation the reduced form is

$$\underset{gn\times 1}{\mathbf{y}^*} = \underset{gn\times gk}{\mathbf{X}^*}\ \underset{gk\times 1}{\mathbf{\Pi}^*} + \underset{gn\times 1}{\mathbf{u}^*}$$

where $\mathbf{y}^*$ and $\mathbf{u}^*$ are as in (6.5.23), $\mathbf{X}^*$ is as in (11.7.14), in the next chapter, and $\mathbf{\Pi}^*$ is obtained by stacking the columns of the $\mathbf{\Pi}$ matrix. The stochastic assumptions in (10.1.12), (10.1.14), and (10.1.16) can be written

$$E(\mathbf{u}^*) = \mathbf{0}$$
$$\text{Cov}\,(\mathbf{u}^*) = \mathbf{\Omega} \otimes \mathbf{I}.$$

1. Show that the GLS estimators of the column vectors constituting $\mathbf{\Pi}^*$ are given by the columns of $\hat{\mathbf{\Pi}}$ in (10.1.24).
2. Show that if $\hat{\mathbf{\Pi}}^*$ is the GLS estimator of $\mathbf{\Pi}^*$, then

$$\text{Cov}\,(\hat{\mathbf{\Pi}}^*) = \mathbf{\Omega} \otimes (\mathbf{X}'\mathbf{X})^{-1}$$

3. Assuming normality

$$\mathbf{u}^* \sim N(\mathbf{0}, \mathbf{\Omega} \otimes \mathbf{I})$$

show that the maximum-likelihood estimator of $\mathbf{\Pi}^*$ is the GLS estimator $\hat{\mathbf{\Pi}}^*$ and that the maximum-likelihood estimator of $\mathbf{\Omega}$ is the same as (10.1.25) except for the usual division by n rather than $n - k$. Also show that $\hat{\mathbf{\Pi}}^*$ is distributed normally, where

$$\hat{\mathbf{\Pi}}^* \sim N[\mathbf{\Pi}^*, \mathbf{\Omega} \otimes (\mathbf{X}'\mathbf{X})^{-1}]$$

10-C Give examples of a priori restrictions relating coefficients to one another, such as (10.2.11), for several specific demand functions and production functions.

10-D Determine the identification of the

1. Kogiku model of Problem 2-J.
2. Horowitz model of Problem 2-K.

10-E A macroeconomic model is of the form

$$C = \alpha_1 + \alpha_2 Y + \alpha_3 W + u_1$$
$$I = \beta_1 + \beta_2 Y + \beta_3 Y_{-1} + \beta_4 r + u_2$$
$$Y = C + I + G$$

where C, I, and Y are endogenous; Y_{-1}, W, r, and G are predetermined; and u_1 and u_2 are stochastic, where W is wealth and r is the interest rate.

1. Determine the reduced-form equations.
2. Determine the identification of the model both without and with the hypothesis that investment satisfies the acceleration hypothesis $\beta_3 = -\beta_2$.

10-F A structural model of a firm using a Cobb-Douglas production function takes the form

$$\begin{aligned}
(1)\ \ln y &= a_1 + \alpha_1 \ln L + \beta_1 \ln K \\
(2)\ \ln w &= a_2 + \alpha_2 \ln L + \beta_2 \ln K \\
(3)\ \ln r &= a_3 + \alpha_3 \ln L + \beta_3 \ln K
\end{aligned}$$

where equation (1) is the log linear production function and equations (2) and (3) jointly determine the inputs of labor and capital given the factor prices.[24] Assuming that the endogenous variables are $\ln y$, $\ln L$, and $\ln K$ and that the exogenous variables are $\ln w$ and $\ln r$, obtain the reduced form, show that each equation is just identified, and indicate how the structural parameters can be estimated from the reduced-form parameters. How do the results change if stochastic disturbance terms are added to the right-hand sides of all three equations?

10-G The Suits model of the watermelon market treats the demand for and supply of watermelons using the two equations:[25]

$$P = a_0 + a_1 \frac{X}{N} + a_2 \frac{Y}{N} + a_3 F$$

$$X = b_0 + b_1 \frac{P}{W} + b_2 P_{-1} + b_3 C_{-1} + b_4 T_{-1}$$

Here the first equation is a demand equation, relating price, P, to per capita quantity (demanded), X/N; per capita income, Y/N; and freight costs, F. The second equation is a crop supply schedule, relating the harvest, X, to price relative to the farm wage rate, P/W; lagged price, P_{-1}; lagged price of cotton, C_{-1}, and lagged price of other vegetables, T_{-1}. The endogenous variables are P and X.

1. Show the cobweb behavior of price and quantity in a diagram.
2. Obtain the reduced form and the final form.
3. Determine the identification of the model.

10-H Given the structural equations

$$(y_1\ \ y_2\ \ y_3)\begin{pmatrix} -1 & \gamma_{12} & 0 \\ 0 & -1 & \gamma_{23} \\ \gamma_{31} & \gamma_{32} & -1 \end{pmatrix} + (x_1\ \ x_2\ \ x_3\ \ x_4)\begin{pmatrix} \beta_{11} & 0 & \beta_{13} \\ \beta_{21} & \beta_{22} & 0 \\ \beta_{31} & 0 & 0 \\ \beta_{41} & \beta_{42} & \beta_{43} \end{pmatrix} = (\epsilon_1\ \ \epsilon_2\ \ \epsilon_3)$$

[24] See the related system in footnote 18 of Chapter 8.

[25] See Suits (1955). The model has been somewhat simplified.

1. Determine the identification of the model, analyzing, for each equation, the order and rank conditions.
2. For all exactly identified equations show specifically how the structural parameters can be estimated from the reduced-form parameters.
3. For all overidentified equations show several ways in which structural parameters can be estimated from the reduced-form parameters.

10-I Answer the same questions as in the previous problem for the following **Γ**, **B** matrices:

1. $$\mathbf{\Gamma} = \begin{pmatrix} -1 & \gamma_{12} & 0 \\ \gamma_{21} & -1 & 0 \\ \gamma_{31} & 0 & -1 \end{pmatrix}, \quad \mathbf{B} = \begin{pmatrix} \beta_{11} & \beta_{12} & \beta_{13} \\ 0 & \beta_{22} & 0 \\ 0 & 0 & \beta_{33} \\ 0 & \beta_{42} & \beta_{43} \\ \beta_{51} & 0 & 0 \\ \beta_{61} & \beta_{62} & \beta_{63} \end{pmatrix}$$

2. $$\mathbf{\Gamma} = \begin{pmatrix} -1 & \gamma_{12} & \gamma_{13} & \gamma_{14} \\ \gamma_{21} & -1 & \gamma_{23} & \gamma_{24} \\ 0 & 0 & -1 & \gamma_{34} \\ 0 & 0 & \gamma_{43} & -1 \end{pmatrix}, \mathbf{B} = \begin{pmatrix} 0 & 0 & 0 & \beta_{14} \\ \beta_{21} & 0 & 0 & \beta_{24} \\ 0 & \beta_{32} & \beta_{33} & 0 \\ 0 & \beta_{42} & \beta_{43} & 0 \\ \beta_{51} & \beta_{52} & \beta_{53} & \beta_{54} \end{pmatrix}$$

10-J In a certain model of the steel industry the endogenous variables are shipments (S), price (p), and imports (M), while the predetermined variables are lagged price (p_{-1}), time (t), inventory (I), and unity (1). The equations of the model are

$$\begin{aligned} S &= f_1(p, M, t) \\ p &= f_2(S, p_{-1}, I) \\ M &= f_3(p, t) \end{aligned}$$

where all equations are linear and contain intercepts. Show that the model is not identified and respecify it to yield a related model that is identified.

10-K In the following macroeconomic model the endogenous variables are

ΔY = change in national income

ΔS = change in private spending

ΔW = change in the wage rate

U = unemployment rate

and the predetermined variables are

ΔG = change in government spending

ΔM = change in money supply

ΔW_{-1} = lagged change in the wage rate

The model states that

$$\begin{aligned}
\Delta Y &= \Delta S + \Delta G \\
\Delta S &= \alpha_1 \, \Delta Y + \alpha_2 \, \Delta M + \epsilon_1 \\
\Delta W &= \beta_1 \, \Delta Y + \beta_2 U + \beta_3 \, \Delta W_{-1} + \epsilon_2 \\
U &= \gamma_1 \, \Delta Y + \gamma_2 \, \Delta W + \epsilon_3
\end{aligned}$$

1. Obtain the reduced form (first eliminate the nonstochastic equation).
2. Analyze the identification of the model.
3. Discuss the implications of the estimated model for monetary and fiscal policies that would promote low unemployment without large wage increases.

10-L Show that for identification by general linear restrictions in the over-identified case as defined in (10.4.15) the number of "excess" restrictions, given by

$$\rho(\mathbf{\Phi}_h) - (g - 1) = \rho(\mathbf{\Phi}_h) - \rho(\mathbf{\Phi}_h \mathbf{A})$$

represents the number of restrictions imposed on the hth column of the $\mathbf{\Pi}$ matrix.

10-M Suppose $\mathbf{\Sigma}$ can be expressed as

$$\mathbf{\Sigma} = \sigma^2 \mathbf{I}$$

where σ^2 is the only unknown parameter in the covariance matrix. Prove that the system is identified if $g = 1$ and if $g = 2$ but not if $g > 2$.

10-N Consider the demand-supply model

$$\begin{aligned}
q &= \gamma_1 p + \delta_1 + \epsilon^D \\
q &= \gamma_2 p + \delta_2 + \epsilon^S
\end{aligned}$$

where Cov $(\epsilon^D, \epsilon^S) = 0$ and Var $(\epsilon^S) = K$ Var (ϵ^D). Assume that K is known, so the covariance matrix

$$\mathbf{\Sigma} = \begin{pmatrix} \sigma^2 & 0 \\ 0 & K\sigma^2 \end{pmatrix}$$

contains only one unknown parameter, σ^2, the variance of demand. Prove that the system is identified.

10-O A recursive model is one in which $\mathbf{\Gamma}$ is triangular and $\mathbf{\Sigma}$ is diagonal.

1. Prove that a recursive model is always identified by showing that the only admissible transformation matrix $\mathbf{R}$ as in (10.2.7) is the identity matrix.
2. Show by using the $\mathbf{R}$ matrix that the triangular nature of $\mathbf{\Gamma}$ and the diagonal nature of $\mathbf{\Sigma}$ are each, by themselves, not sufficient to identify the system.

10-P Show that the following models are recursive. For each depict the unilateral direction of flow in an arrow diagram.

1. The Cobweb model of Section 7.7.
2. The Walrasian tâtonnement model of Problem 2-C.

10-Q A generalization of the recursive system is the *block recursive* system, in which the system is recursive in certain subsets of variables. In this case $\boldsymbol{\Gamma}$ is block triangular and $\boldsymbol{\Sigma}$ is block diagonal:

$$\boldsymbol{\Gamma} = \begin{pmatrix} \boldsymbol{\Gamma}_{11} & \boldsymbol{\Gamma}_{12} & \cdots & \\ \mathbf{0} & \boldsymbol{\Gamma}_{22} & & \\ & & \ddots & \\ \mathbf{0} & & & \boldsymbol{\Gamma}_{qq} \end{pmatrix}, \quad \boldsymbol{\Sigma} = \begin{pmatrix} \boldsymbol{\Sigma}_{11} & \mathbf{0} & & \mathbf{0} \\ \mathbf{0} & \boldsymbol{\Sigma}_{22} & & \mathbf{0} \\ & & \ddots & \\ \mathbf{0} & \mathbf{0} & & \boldsymbol{\Sigma}_{qq} \end{pmatrix}$$

Here $\boldsymbol{\Gamma}_{11}$ and $\boldsymbol{\Sigma}_{11}$ are square matrices of the same order, $\boldsymbol{\Gamma}_{22}$ and $\boldsymbol{\Sigma}_{22}$ are square matrices of the same order (but not necessarily the same order as $\boldsymbol{\Gamma}_{11}$), and so on. Each equation is then identified with respect to other equations in its own block. Determine the identification of such a model.[26]

10-R A general definition of identification states that a model is *identified* if and only if its parameters can be obtained from knowledge of the likelihood function. Using the likelihood function for the simultaneous-equations model, as given in (11.8.9), prove that

1. The reduced-form model is identified.
2. In the absence of a priori information the structural form is not identified. [In particular show that the bogus parameters in (10.2.7) yield the same likelihood function as the true parameters.]

10-S Consider the identification of the first equation of the simultaneous-equations system. Assume that specific numerical values are given for g_1' of the $g_1 - 1$ explanatory endogenous variables and for k_1' of the k_1 included exogenous variables. Given this additional information obtain the rank and order conditions of identification.

10-T Consider the model

$$\sum_{j=0}^{p} \mathbf{y}_{t-j}\boldsymbol{\Gamma}_j + \sum_{j=0}^{q} \mathbf{x}_{t-j}\mathbf{B}_j = \mathbf{u}_t$$

$$\sum_{j=0}^{r} \mathbf{u}_{t-j}\mathbf{C}_j = \boldsymbol{\varepsilon}_t$$

$$E(\boldsymbol{\varepsilon}_t) = \mathbf{0}$$

[26] See Ando, Fisher, and Simon (1963) and Fisher (1965).

$$E(\boldsymbol{\varepsilon}'_{t-\tau}\boldsymbol{\varepsilon}_t) = \begin{Bmatrix} \mathbf{0} & \tau \neq 0 \\ \boldsymbol{\Sigma} & \tau = 0 \end{Bmatrix} \quad \text{all } t$$

Obtain the reduced form and final form of this system.

BIBLIOGRAPHY

Ando, A., F. M. Fisher, and H. A. Simon (1963), *Essays on the Structure of Social Science Models*. Cambridge: MIT Press.

Bowden, R. (1973), "The Theory of Parametric Identification." *Econometrica*, 41: 1069–74.

Duesenberry, J. S., G. Fromm, L. R. Klein, and E. Kuh, Eds. (1965), *The Brookings Quarterly Econometric Model of the United States*. Chicago: Rand McNally & Co.; Amsterdam: North-Holland Publishing Co.

Fisher, F. M. (1966), *The Identification Problem in Econometrics*. New York: McGraw-Hill Book Company.

Fisher, F. M. (1965), "Dynamic Structure and Estimation in Economy-wide Econometric Models," in Duesenberry, Fromm, Klein, and Kuh, Eds. (1965).

Rothenberg, T. (1971), "Identification in Parametric Models." *Econometrica*, 38: 577–91.

Schmidt, P. (1976), *Econometrics*. New York: Marcel Dekker, Inc.

Suits, D. B. (1955), "An Econometric Model of the Watermelon Market." *Journal of Farm Economics*, 37: 237–51.

Wold, H. (1954), "Causality and Econometrics." *Econometrica*, 22: 162–77.

Wold, H. (1960), "A Generalization of Causal Chain Models." *Econometrica*, 28: 443–63.

Wold, H. (1964), *Econometric Model Building: Essays on the Causal Chain Approach*. Amsterdam: North-Holland Publishing Co.

CHAPTER **11**

Estimation of Simultaneous–Equations Systems[1]

11.1 Introduction

The simultaneous-equations system to be estimated is

$$\underset{1\times g}{\mathbf{y}_i}\ \underset{g\times g}{\mathbf{\Gamma}} + \underset{1\times k}{\mathbf{x}_i}\ \underset{k\times g}{\mathbf{B}} = \underset{1\times g}{\boldsymbol{\varepsilon}_i}, \qquad i = 1, 2, \ldots, n \qquad *(11.1.1)$$

as in (10.1.1). Here $\mathbf{y}_i$ and $\mathbf{x}_i$ are, respectively, vectors of g endogenous and k predetermined variables and $\boldsymbol{\varepsilon}_i$ is the vector of g stochastic disturbance terms, one for each of the g equations of the system. The subscript i refers to the observation number, indexing the n observations.

Several stochastic assumptions are made on $\boldsymbol{\varepsilon}_i$, as in (10.1.4)-(10.1.6). First is the *disturbance assumption* that the stochastic disturbance terms have a zero mean in each period:

$$E(\boldsymbol{\varepsilon}_i) = \mathbf{0}, \qquad \text{all } i. \qquad *(11.1.2)$$

Second is the *homoskedasticity assumption* that these stochastic disturbances have a constant (and finite) covariance matrix:

$$\text{Cov}(\boldsymbol{\varepsilon}_i) = E(\boldsymbol{\varepsilon}_i'\boldsymbol{\varepsilon}_i) = \underset{g\times g}{\mathbf{\Sigma}}, \qquad \text{all } i \qquad *(11.1.3)$$

where $\mathbf{\Sigma}$ is a symmetric positive-definite matrix of variances and covariances. Third is the *absence-of-serial-correlation assumption* that the stochastic disturbance terms are uncorrelated over the sample, implying that

$$E(\boldsymbol{\varepsilon}_i'\boldsymbol{\varepsilon}_{i'}) = \mathbf{0}, \qquad \text{all } i, i', \ i \neq i'. \qquad *(11.1.4)$$

The n observations on each of the g endogenous variables can be summarized by the data matrix

[1] General references on the estimation of simultaneous-equations systems include Christ (1966), Dhrymes (1970), Malinvaud (1970), Theil (1971), Madansky (1976), and Schmidt (1976). For discussions of Bayesian estimation of simultaneous-equations systems see Zellner (1971), Morales (1971), and Harkema (1971).

$$\underset{n\times g}{\mathbf{Y}} = \begin{pmatrix} \mathbf{y}_1 \\ \mathbf{y}_2 \\ \vdots \\ \mathbf{y}_n \end{pmatrix} = \begin{pmatrix} y_{11} & y_{12} & \cdots & y_{1g} \\ y_{21} & y_{22} & \cdots & y_{2g} \\ \vdots & & & \\ y_{n1} & y_{n2} & \cdots & y_{ng} \end{pmatrix} \qquad *(11.1.5)$$

where $\mathbf{y}_i$ is the vector of data on all g endogenous variables at observation i. Similarly the n observations on each of the k predetermined variables can be summarized by the data matrix

$$\underset{n\times k}{\mathbf{X}} = \begin{pmatrix} \mathbf{x}_1 \\ \mathbf{x}_2 \\ \vdots \\ \mathbf{x}_n \end{pmatrix} = \begin{pmatrix} x_{11} & x_{12} & \cdots & x_{1k} \\ x_{21} & x_{22} & \cdots & x_{2k} \\ \vdots & & & \\ x_{n1} & x_{n2} & \cdots & x_{nk} \end{pmatrix} \qquad *(11.1.6)$$

where $\mathbf{x}_i$ is the vector of data on all k predetermined variables at observation i. Using these data matrices, which were previously introduced in (10.1.19), the simultaneous equations system can be written

$$\underset{n\times g}{\mathbf{Y}}\ \underset{g\times g}{\mathbf{\Gamma}} + \underset{n\times k}{\mathbf{X}}\ \underset{k\times g}{\mathbf{B}} = \underset{n\times g}{\mathbf{E}} \qquad *(11.1.7)$$

where $\mathbf{E}$ is here the $n \times g$ matrix, each row of which is the $\boldsymbol{\varepsilon}_i$ vector of stochastic disturbance terms in (11.1.1). This system is the generalization of the single-equation model to g endogenous variables. It reduces to the single-equation model if $g = 1$, in which case the matrix $\mathbf{Y}$ collapses to the column vector $\mathbf{y}$; the matrix $\mathbf{\Gamma}$ collapses to a single element, which may be chosen as -1 to normalize the equation; the matrix $\mathbf{B}$ collapses to the column vector $\boldsymbol{\beta}$; and the matrix $\mathbf{E}$ collapses to the column vector $-\mathbf{u}$, so

$$\mathbf{y}(-1) + \mathbf{X}\boldsymbol{\beta} = -\mathbf{u} \qquad (11.1.8)$$

or

$$\mathbf{y} = \mathbf{X}\boldsymbol{\beta} + \mathbf{u} \qquad (11.1.9)$$

as in Chapters 4–6.

The problem of simultaneous equation estimation is that of using the matrices $\mathbf{Y}$ and $\mathbf{X}$ to estimate the parameters of the system (11.1.7), namely the coefficient matrices $\mathbf{\Gamma}$ and $\mathbf{B}$ and the matrix $\mathbf{\Sigma}$ of covariances of $\boldsymbol{\varepsilon}_i$ in (11.1.3). Some of these coefficients may be specified a priori, as discussed in the last chapter with reference to the identification of the system. In fact, the case that will be emphasized here is the normalized system in which some of the coefficients are specified to be zero—the case of zero restrictions as discussed in Section 10.3.

As noted in the last chapter, each of the equations can be normalized, and a convenient normalization is the one introduced in (10.1.2), which sets each of the n elements along the principal diagonal of the $\mathbf{\Gamma}$ matrix equal to -1:

$$\gamma_{hh} = -1, \quad h = 1, 2, \ldots, g \tag{11.1.10}$$

Solving equation h for y_{ih} then yields

$$y_{ih} = \sum_{\substack{h'=1 \\ h' \neq h}}^{g} y_{ih'} \gamma_{h'h} + \sum_{j=1}^{k} x_{ij} \beta_{jh} - \varepsilon_{ih}, \quad h = 1, 2, \ldots, g \tag{11.1.11}$$

as in (10.1.3). Here h is an index of the equation, h' is an index of the endogenous variables, and j is an index of the exogenous variables, as in (2.8.2).[2] In this formulation, also, the simultaneous equations-system collapses to the single-equation model if $g = 1$, in which case the first summation on the right vanishes and the h subscripts can be dropped.

Consider, without loss of generality, the first equation of the system ($h = 1$), and assume that the a priori restrictions on the coefficients are all zero restrictions. The variables can be renumbered, if necessary, so that only the first g_1 endogenous variables ($g_1 < g$) and only the first k_1 exogenous variables ($k_1 < k$) are included in the equation, the other $(g - g_1) + (k - k_1)$ variables having zero coefficients. The first equation can then be written

$$y_{i1} = \sum_{h'=2}^{g_1} y_{ih'} \gamma_{h'1} + \sum_{j=1}^{k_1} x_{ij} \beta_{j1} - \epsilon_{i1} \tag{11.1.12}$$

Introducing the vectors

$$\mathbf{Y}_{i1} = (y_{i2} \;\; y_{i3} \;\; \cdots \;\; y_{ig_1}), \qquad \mathbf{X}_{i1} = (x_{i1} \;\; x_{i2} \;\; \cdots \;\; x_{ik_1}) \tag{11.1.13}$$

for the included explanatory variables and introducing

$$\boldsymbol{\gamma}_1 = (\gamma_{21} \;\; \gamma_{31} \;\; \cdots \;\; \gamma_{g_1 1})', \quad \boldsymbol{\beta}_1 = (\beta_{11} \;\; \beta_{21} \;\; \cdots \;\; \beta_{k_1 1})' \tag{11.1.14}$$

for the nonzero coefficients, equation (11.1.12) can be written

$$y_{i1} = \underset{1\times(g_1-1)}{\mathbf{Y}_{i1}} \; \underset{(g_1-1)\times 1}{\boldsymbol{\gamma}_1} + \underset{1\times k_1}{\mathbf{X}_{i1}} \; \underset{k_1 \times 1}{\boldsymbol{\beta}_1} - \epsilon_{i1} \tag*{*(11.1.15)}$$

Here the subscript 1 indicates "included in the first equation." Thus $\mathbf{Y}_{i1}$ is the vector of $g_1 - 1$ explanatory endogenous variables included in the first equation; $\mathbf{X}_{i1}$ is the vector of k_1 exogenous variables included in the first equation; ϵ_{i1} is the stochastic disturbance term included in the first equation; and $\boldsymbol{\gamma}_1$ and $\boldsymbol{\beta}_1$ are,

[2] The discussion here and below refers to "exogenous" rather than "predetermined" variables. Lagged endogenous variables as explanatory variables were treated in the single-equation context in Section 6.7, and they will be treated in the simultaneous-equations context in Section 11.6.

respectively, the $g_1 - 1$ coefficients of explanatory endogenous and k_1 coefficients of exogenous variables included in the first equation.

The data on all variables of the system, summarized by the **Y** and **X** matrices in (11.1.5) and (11.1.6), can be divided into data on the variables indicated in (11.1.15). Thus, the matrix of data on the endogenous variables **Y** can be partitioned into

$$\underset{n\times g}{\mathbf{Y}} = (\underset{n\times 1}{\mathbf{y}_1} \;\vdots\; \underset{n\times(g_1-1)}{\mathbf{Y}_1} \;\vdots\; \underset{n\times(g-g_1)}{\mathbf{Y}_2}) \qquad *(11.1.16)$$

where $\mathbf{y}_1$ is the column vector of data on the dependent endogenous variable (the one on which this equation has been normalized), $\mathbf{Y}_1$ is the matrix of data on the $g_1 - 1$ explanatory endogenous variables in $\mathbf{Y}_{i1}$, and $\mathbf{Y}_2$ is the matrix of data on the $g - g_1$ excluded endogenous variables. Similarly, the matrix of data on the exogenous variables **X** can be partitioned into

$$\underset{n\times k}{\mathbf{X}} = (\underset{n\times k_1}{\mathbf{X}_1} \;\vdots\; \underset{n\times(k-k_1)}{\mathbf{X}_2}) \qquad *(11.1.17)$$

where $\mathbf{X}_1$ is the matrix of data on the k_1 included exogenous variables in $\mathbf{X}_{i1}$ and $\mathbf{X}_2$ is the matrix of data on the $k - k_1$ excluded exogenous variables.

In terms of the data matrices, equation (11.1.15) can be represented as

$$\underset{n\times 1}{\mathbf{y}_1} = \underset{n\times(g_1-1)}{\mathbf{Y}_1}\;\underset{(g_1-1)\times 1}{\boldsymbol{\gamma}_1} + \underset{n\times k_1}{\mathbf{X}_1}\;\underset{k_1\times 1}{\boldsymbol{\beta}_1} + \underset{n\times 1}{\boldsymbol{\varepsilon}_1} \qquad *(11.1.18)$$

where $\boldsymbol{\varepsilon}_1$ is the negative of the vector of n stochastic disturbance terms for the first equation. The subscript ones serve as a reminder that this is the first equation of the system. This equation can be obtained from the system (11.1.7) and the partitioning of the variables in (11.1.16) and (11.1.17) as

$$(\mathbf{y}_1 \;\vdots\; \mathbf{Y}_1 \;\vdots\; \mathbf{Y}_2)\begin{pmatrix} -1 & \cdots \\ \boldsymbol{\gamma}_1 & \cdots \\ \mathbf{0} & \cdots \end{pmatrix} + (\mathbf{X}_1 \;\vdots\; \mathbf{X}_2)\begin{pmatrix} \boldsymbol{\beta}_1 & \cdots \\ \mathbf{0} & \cdots \end{pmatrix} = (-\boldsymbol{\varepsilon}_1 \;\vdots\; \cdots) \qquad (11.1.19)$$

—that is, as

$$-\mathbf{y}_1 + \mathbf{Y}_1\boldsymbol{\gamma}_1 + \mathbf{X}_1\boldsymbol{\beta}_1 = -\boldsymbol{\varepsilon}_1 \qquad (11.1.20)$$

Since only the first equation is being considered, only the first columns of $\boldsymbol{\Gamma}$, **B**, and **E** are shown in (11.1.19). The first column of $\boldsymbol{\Gamma}$ is as shown because of the normalization ($\gamma_{11} = -1$), the definition of $\boldsymbol{\gamma}_1$ in (11.1.14), and the zero restrictions. Similarly the first column of **B** is as shown because of the definition of $\boldsymbol{\beta}_1$ in (11.1.14) and the zero restrictions. The first column of the **E** matrix is written here $-\boldsymbol{\varepsilon}_1$, where the change in sign allows the stochastic disturbance terms to be added, as shown in (11.1.18).[3]

Equation (11.1.18) is the basic equation to be used in developing several of the estimators of the simultaneous-equations system. It represents the first equation of the system, with the subscript 1 serving as a convenient reminder that it is the first equation. More generally the hth equation can be represented as

$$\mathbf{y}_h = \mathbf{Y}_h \boldsymbol{\gamma}_h + \mathbf{X}_h \boldsymbol{\beta}_h + \boldsymbol{\varepsilon}_h, \quad h = 1, 2, \ldots, g \qquad *(11.1.21)$$

where $\mathbf{y}_h$ is the column vector of data on the dependent endogenous variable, $\mathbf{Y}_h$ is the matrix of data on the $g_h - 1$ explanatory endogenous variables, $\mathbf{X}_h$ is the matrix of data on the included exogenous variables, and $\boldsymbol{\varepsilon}_h$ is the negative of the hth column of $\mathbf{E}$ in (11.1.7).

An example of the form specified in (11.1.18) or (11.1.21) is the consumption function from the prototype macro model of Section 2.7, of the form

$$C = \gamma_1 Y + \beta_1 + \epsilon^C \qquad *(11.1.22)$$

as in (2.7.1), where γ_1 is the marginal propensity to consume and β_1 is the intercept. This equation is already of the form (11.1.18), where C, consumption, is the normalized endogenous variable; Y, income, is the single explanatory endogenous variable in this equation; and 1 is the single exogenous variable included in this equation. The complete system, of which this is one equation, is the system of two equations given by

$$(C \quad Y)\begin{pmatrix} -1 & \gamma_3 \\ \gamma_1 & -1 \end{pmatrix} + (Y_{-1} \quad G \quad 1)\begin{pmatrix} 0 & \beta_4 \\ 0 & \beta_5 \\ \beta_1 & \beta_6 \end{pmatrix} = (-\epsilon^C \quad -\epsilon^Y) \qquad *(11.1.23)$$

as in (2.7.6), where Y_{-1} is lagged income and G is government expenditure.[4] Using the results of the last chapter, the first equation, that for consumption, as given by (11.1.22), is identified if

$$\rho\begin{pmatrix} \beta_4 \\ \beta_5 \end{pmatrix} = 1 \qquad (11.1.24)$$

which is satisfied if either β_4 or β_5 does not vanish. This equation excludes a total of two variables, so

$$(g - g_1) + (k - k_1) = 2 > 1 = g - 1 \qquad (11.1.25)$$

implying that the equation is overidentified.

[3] Here $\boldsymbol{\varepsilon}_1$ is the $n \times 1$ negative of the first column of E, not to be confused with the row vector $\boldsymbol{\varepsilon}_i$ in (11.1.1) for $i = 1$.

[4] Here γ_3 and $\beta_4, \beta_5, \beta_6$ simplify the notation of (2.7.6).

A variant of this model is one in which the lagged variable Y_{-1} does not appear, so in this variant the structural form is

$$(C \quad Y) \begin{pmatrix} -1 & \gamma_3' \\ \gamma_1' & -1 \end{pmatrix} + (G \quad 1) \begin{pmatrix} 0 & \beta_5' \\ \beta_1' & \beta_6' \end{pmatrix} = (-\epsilon^{C'} \quad -\epsilon^{Y'}) \qquad *(11.1.26)$$

The first equation is the variant consumption function

$$C = \gamma_1' Y + \beta_1' + \epsilon^{C'} \qquad (11.1.27)$$

which is similar in form to (11.1.21) and where γ_1' and β_1' are again the marginal propensity to consume and intercept, respectively. In this case, however, the first equation excludes a total of one variable and so (assuming $\beta_5' \neq 0$) this equation is just identified. Note that the form of the consumption function is the same for both models, but, because of a change in the other equation of the model, the original consumption function is overidentified while the variant consumption function is just identified.

The methods of estimation to be introduced will be illustrated using both the overidentified original consumption function (11.1.22) and the just-identified variant consumption function (11.1.27). In both cases the parameters to be estimated are the marginal propensity to consume (γ_1 or γ_1') and the intercept (β_1 or β_1'). In both cases the stochastic disturbance term (ϵ^C or $\epsilon^{C'}$) will be assumed to satisfy the conditions (11.1.2) to (11.1.4). The data for the estimation of the original consumption function in the prototype macro model (11.1.23) would be summarized by the data matrices

$$\left(\begin{array}{c|c|} C_1 & Y_1 \\ C_2 & Y_2 \\ \vdots & \vdots \\ C_n & Y_n \end{array}\right), \quad \left(\begin{array}{c|cc} 1 & Y_0 & G_1 \\ 1 & Y_1 & G_2 \\ \vdots & \vdots & \vdots \\ 1 & Y_{n-1} & G_n \end{array}\right) \qquad (11.1.28)$$

as in (11.1.16) and (11.1.17). In this case, as shown by the partitions, there are no excluded endogenous variables, and lagged Y and G are the excluded predetermined variables.

11.2 Naive, limited-information, and full-information approaches

There are three alternative approaches to estimating the simultaneous-equations system in (11.1.1) or (11.1.7) using the data in (11.1.5) and (11.1.6). They are the naive approach, the limited-information approach, and the full-information approach. These approaches differ, as their names indicate, in the amount of information utilized in the estimation process.

The *naive approach* expresses each equation of the system in the form of (11.1.18) and estimates it as a single equation using the technique of least squares. The approach is identical to that discussed earlier under single-equation estimation, where the explanatory endogenous variables $\mathbf{Y}_1$ and included exogenous variables $\mathbf{X}_1$ constitute the set of $g_1 - 1 + k_1$ explanatory variables. In fact, this approach is called "naive" for precisely this reason: it ignores information as to which of the explanatory variables in the equation under consideration are endogenous and which are exogenous. In this approach they are all lumped together as explanatory variables. Moreover, no use is made of information on variables that are included in the system but are excluded from the equation being estimated. They are ignored altogether, and all explanatory variables are used to estimate the parameters. For example, in the prototype macro model consumption function (11.1.22) the naive approach would estimate the parameters γ_1 and β_1 as the slope and intercept of a simple linear regression of C on Y. In this case and in general, the resulting estimators are biased and inconsistent because of the inclusion of endogenous variables among the set of explanatory variables. This approach, called *ordinary least squares* (OLS), is developed in Section 11.3.

The *limited-information approach* estimates one equation at a time, estimating (11.1.18) as does OLS, but unlike OLS it distinguishes between explanatory endogenous variables $\mathbf{Y}_1$ and included exogenous variables $\mathbf{X}_1$. It also uses information as to which variables, both endogenous and exogenous, are included in the other equations of the system but excluded from the equation being estimated, given as $\mathbf{Y}_2$ and $\mathbf{X}_2$. Thus it utilizes all identifying restrictions pertaining to the equation. The information required is limited, however, to the variables included in or excluded from the equation being estimated. This approach does not require information as to the specification of the other equations of the system—in particular, the identifying restrictions on these other equations. The limited-information approach leads to estimators of (11.1.18) for coefficients $\boldsymbol{\gamma}_1$ of the $g_1 - 1$ explanatory endogenous variables and coefficients $\boldsymbol{\beta}_1$ of the k_1 included exogenous variables. Comparing this equation to the system conveys information as to the $g - g_1$ excluded endogenous variables and the $k - k_1$ excluded exogenous variables. In the consumption function of the prototype macro model (11.1.22) the coefficients are estimated given the information that Y is an explanatory endogenous variable and that Y_{-1} and G are excluded predetermined variables. While the variant consumption function (11.1.27) would result in the same naive OLS estimators as the original consumption function, the limited-information estimators would generally differ, since the excluded predetermined variables are Y_{-1} and G for the original consumption function but only G for the variant consumption function. The limited-information approach includes several specific estimators, of which *indirect least squares (ILS)* is presented in Section 11.4 and *two-stage least squares (2SLS)* and *k-class estimators*, including *limited-information maximum likelihood (LIML)*, are presented in Section 11.5. These estimators can be expressed as *instrumental variable estimators (IV)*, for particular choices of instrumental variables, as discussed in Section 11.6.

The *full-information approach* estimates the entire system of simultaneous equations in (11.1.1) [or (11.1.7) or (11.1.21) for all h] simultaneously in "one fell swoop," using all information available on each of the equations of the system. It estimates all structural parameters of the system, namely $\mathbf{\Gamma}$, $\mathbf{B}$, and $\mathbf{\Sigma}$, given the model and all identifying restrictions on each equation of the system. For the prototype macro model it would lead to estimators of (11.1.23), including the γ_1 and γ_3 elements of $\mathbf{\Gamma}$; the $\beta_1, \beta_4, \beta_5$, and β_6 elements of $\mathbf{B}$; and the three independent elements of $\mathbf{\Sigma}$, σ_{11}, σ_{22}, and σ_{12}. The variant model would result in different estimators because it entails a different specification for one of the equations of the model. The full-information approach includes two specific estimators, of which *three-stage least squares (3SLS)* is presented in Section 11.7 and *full-information maximum likelihood (FIML)* is presented in Section 11.8.

There are, therefore, several different estimators available for simultaneous-equations systems. All, however, are extensions of the two basic techniques of single-equation estimation: least squares and maximum likelihood. As indicated by their names, ordinary least squares, two-stage least squares, and three-stage least squares are extensions of the least-squares technique to simultaneous-equations estimation. Similarly, limited-information maximum likelihood and full-information maximum likelihood are extensions of the maximum-likelihood technique to simultaneous-equations estimation. The choice of a particular technique, in particular the small-sample properties of estimators, is discussed in Section 11.9.

11.3 Ordinary least squares and least-squares bias

The naive approach to estimating the parameters of a system of simultaneous equations is that of *ordinary least squares (OLS)*. This approach applies least squares to each equation of the model separately, ignoring the distinction between explanatory endogenous and included exogenous variables. It also ignores all information available concerning variables not included in the equation being estimated. It will be shown that this approach leads to biased and inconsistent estimators.

The equation to be estimated, the first equation of the system, (11.1.18), can be written

$$\mathbf{y}_1 = \mathbf{Y}_1 \boldsymbol{\gamma}_1 + \mathbf{X}_1 \boldsymbol{\beta}_1 + \boldsymbol{\varepsilon}_1 = (\mathbf{Y}_1 \mid \mathbf{X}_1)\begin{pmatrix} \boldsymbol{\gamma}_1 \\ \hline \boldsymbol{\beta}_1 \end{pmatrix} + \boldsymbol{\varepsilon}_1 = \mathbf{Z}_1 \boldsymbol{\delta}_1 + \boldsymbol{\varepsilon}_1 \qquad *(11.3.1)$$

Here $\mathbf{Z}_1$ lumps together data on all $(g_1 - 1 + k_1)$ included explanatory variables whether endogenous or exogenous:

$$\underset{n\times(g_1-1+k_1)}{\mathbf{Z}_1} = (\underset{n\times(g_1-1)}{\mathbf{Y}_1} \mid \underset{n\times k_1}{\mathbf{X}_1}) \qquad *(11.3.2)$$

and $\boldsymbol{\delta}_1$ is a vector summarizing all coefficients to be estimated in the equation:

$$\underset{(g_1-1+k_1)\times 1}{\boldsymbol{\delta}_1} = \begin{pmatrix} \boldsymbol{\gamma}_1 \\ \hline \boldsymbol{\beta}_1 \end{pmatrix} \begin{matrix} g_1 - 1 \\ k_1 \end{matrix} . \qquad *(11.3.3)$$

The ordinary least-squares estimators of the coefficients are obtained in the same way they were for the single-equation model in Chapter 4. Applying equation (4.6.17) to (11.3.1) yields the estimator

$$\hat{\boldsymbol{\delta}}_{1\,\mathrm{OLS}} = (\mathbf{Z}_1'\mathbf{Z}_1)^{-1}\mathbf{Z}_1'\mathbf{y}_1 \qquad *(11.3.4)$$

where the inverse exists if $\mathbf{Z}_1$ has rank $g_1 - 1 + k_1$. In terms of the original notation the *OLS estimators* can be written

$$\begin{pmatrix} \hat{\boldsymbol{\gamma}}_1 \\ \hline \hat{\boldsymbol{\beta}}_1 \end{pmatrix}_{\mathrm{OLS}} = \left(\begin{array}{c|c} \mathbf{Y}_1'\mathbf{Y}_1 & \mathbf{Y}_1'\mathbf{X}_1 \\ \hline \mathbf{X}_1'\mathbf{Y}_1 & \mathbf{X}_1'\mathbf{X}_1 \end{array}\right)^{-1} \begin{pmatrix} \mathbf{Y}_1' \\ \hline \mathbf{X}_1' \end{pmatrix} \mathbf{y}_1. \qquad *(11.3.5)$$

While the OLS estimators are readily calculated and are utilized extensively, they do have certain limitations. For single-equation models the Gauss-Markov theorem in Section 4.9 established that least-squares estimators are unbiased, and it was also shown in Section 4.9 that they are consistent estimators. The proofs of both unbiasedness and consistency in the single-equation case relied, however, on the assumption that the explanatory variables were fixed numbers and hence statistically independent of the stochastic disturbance terms. This assumption is not valid here, however. In (11.3.1) the $\mathbf{Y}_1$ are *endogenous* variables, which are *not* statistically independent of the stochastic disturbance terms, even in the probability limit. The result is that in a system of simultaneous equations the OLS estimators are *biased* and also generally *inconsistent* estimators.[5] The biased and inconsistent nature of OLS estimators can be easily demonstrated by substituting $\mathbf{Z}_1\boldsymbol{\delta}_1 + \boldsymbol{\varepsilon}_1$ for $\mathbf{y}_1$ in (11.3.4), leading to

$$\hat{\boldsymbol{\delta}}_1 = (\mathbf{Z}_1'\mathbf{Z}_1)^{-1}\mathbf{Z}_1'(\mathbf{Z}_1\boldsymbol{\delta}_1 + \boldsymbol{\varepsilon}_1) = \boldsymbol{\delta}_1 + (\mathbf{Z}_1'\mathbf{Z}_1)^{-1}\mathbf{Z}_1'\boldsymbol{\varepsilon}_1 \qquad (11.3.6)$$

Taking expectations,

$$E(\hat{\boldsymbol{\delta}}_1) = \boldsymbol{\delta}_1 + E[(\mathbf{Z}_1'\mathbf{Z}_1)^{-1}\mathbf{Z}_1'\boldsymbol{\varepsilon}_1]. \qquad (11.3.7)$$

In the single-equation case the term corresponding to $E[(\mathbf{Z}_1'\mathbf{Z}_1)^{-1}\mathbf{Z}_1'\boldsymbol{\varepsilon}_1]$ vanishes because the explanatory variables are nonstochastic fixed numbers (or, stochastic but statistically independent of any of the stochastic disturbance terms). Here, however, $\mathbf{Z}_1$ includes endogenous variables, $\mathbf{Y}_1$, which are stochastic and not independent of the stochastic disturbance term. Thus $E[(\mathbf{Z}_1'\mathbf{Z}_1)^{-1}\mathbf{Z}_1'\boldsymbol{\varepsilon}_1]$ does not vanish, implying that the OLS estimators are biased:

$$E(\hat{\boldsymbol{\delta}}_1) \neq \boldsymbol{\delta}_1. \qquad *(11.3.8)$$

This bias does not vanish even in the limit as $n \to \infty$, so the OLS estimators are also asymptotically biased. Nor does it vanish in the probability limit, so the OLS estimators are inconsistent:

[5] See Haavelmo (1943, 1947). A simultaneous system in which least squares is appropriate, however, is a recursive system as discussed in Section 10.5 and below in Section 11.8.

$$\text{plim}\,(\hat{\boldsymbol{\delta}}_1) = \boldsymbol{\delta}_1 + \text{plim}\left(\frac{1}{n}\,\mathbf{Z}_1'\mathbf{Z}_1\right)^{-1}\left(\frac{1}{n}\,\mathbf{Z}_1'\,\boldsymbol{\varepsilon}_1\right) \neq \boldsymbol{\delta}_1. \qquad *(11.3.9)$$

In terms of the original coefficients and data the OLS estimators are

$$\begin{pmatrix}\hat{\boldsymbol{\gamma}}_1\\ \hline \hat{\boldsymbol{\beta}}_1\end{pmatrix}_{\text{OLS}} = \begin{pmatrix}\boldsymbol{\gamma}_1\\ \hline \boldsymbol{\beta}_1\end{pmatrix} + \left(\begin{array}{c|c}\mathbf{Y}_1'\,\mathbf{Y}_1 & \mathbf{Y}_1'\,\mathbf{X}_1\\ \hline \mathbf{X}_1'\,\mathbf{Y}_1 & \mathbf{X}_1'\,\mathbf{X}_1\end{array}\right)^{-1}\begin{pmatrix}\mathbf{Y}_1'\\ \hline \mathbf{X}_1'\end{pmatrix}\boldsymbol{\varepsilon}_1 \qquad (11.3.10)$$

In general, the expectation of the second term on the right does not vanish, even in the probability limit, since the explanatory endogenous variables are not independent of the stochastic disturbance term. The bias is given by

$$\begin{aligned} B\begin{pmatrix}\hat{\boldsymbol{\gamma}}_1\\ \hline \hat{\boldsymbol{\beta}}_1\end{pmatrix}_{\text{OLS}} &= E\left[\begin{pmatrix}\hat{\boldsymbol{\gamma}}_1\\ \hline \hat{\boldsymbol{\beta}}_1\end{pmatrix} - \begin{pmatrix}\boldsymbol{\gamma}_1\\ \hline \boldsymbol{\beta}_1\end{pmatrix}\right] \\ &= E\left[\left(\begin{array}{c|c}\mathbf{Y}_1'\mathbf{Y}_1 & \mathbf{Y}_1'\mathbf{X}_1\\ \hline \mathbf{X}_1'\mathbf{Y}_1 & \mathbf{X}_1'\mathbf{X}_1\end{array}\right)^{-1}\begin{pmatrix}\mathbf{Y}_1'\\ \hline \mathbf{X}_1'\end{pmatrix}\boldsymbol{\varepsilon}_1\right]\end{aligned} \qquad *(11.3.11)$$

and this bias does not vanish, even asymptotically.

The consumption function of the prototype macro model (11.1.22) can be used to illustrate the OLS estimators. Using (11.3.5),

$$\begin{pmatrix}\hat{\gamma}_1\\ \hat{\beta}_1\end{pmatrix}_{\text{OLS}} = \begin{pmatrix}\Sigma\, Y_i^2 & \Sigma\, Y_i\\ \Sigma\, Y_i & n\end{pmatrix}^{-1}\begin{pmatrix}\Sigma\, C_i\,Y_i\\ \Sigma\, C_i\end{pmatrix} \qquad (11.3.12)$$

leading to the OLS estimator of the slope, the marginal propensity to consume, as

$$\hat{\gamma}_{1\,\text{OLS}} = \frac{\Sigma\,\dot{C}_i\,\dot{Y}_i}{\Sigma\,\dot{Y}_i^2} \qquad (11.3.13)$$

in this case of simple linear regression. Here $\dot{C}_i$ and $\dot{Y}_i$ are the ith deviations of consumption and income from their mean values, as defined by

$$\dot{C}_i = C_i - \bar{C}, \quad \bar{C} = \frac{1}{n}\,\Sigma\, C_i \qquad (11.3.14)$$

$$\dot{Y}_i = Y_i - \bar{Y}, \quad \bar{Y} = \frac{1}{n}\,\Sigma\, Y_i \qquad (11.3.15)$$

In terms of these deviations the structural equations can be written

$$\dot{C}_i = \gamma_1 \dot{Y}_i + \epsilon_i^C \tag{11.3.16}$$

$$\dot{Y}_i = \gamma_3 \dot{C}_i + \beta_4 \dot{Y}_{i-1} + \beta_5 \dot{G}_i + \epsilon_i^Y. \tag{11.3.17}$$

Using (11.3.16), the OLS estimator of γ_1 can be written

$$\hat{\gamma}_{1\text{OLS}} = \gamma_1 + \frac{\Sigma\, \epsilon_i^C\, \dot{Y}_i}{\Sigma\, \dot{Y}_i^2} \tag{11.3.18}$$

which is of the same form as the general expression (11.3.10). Taking expectations, as in (11.3.11), the bias in the estimation of the marginal propensity to consume is

$$B(\hat{\gamma}_{1\text{OLS}}) = E\left(\frac{\Sigma\, \epsilon_i^C\, \dot{Y}_i}{\Sigma\, \dot{Y}_i^2}\right) > 0. \tag{11.3.19}$$

The bias is positive, as can be readily seen from the structural equations. Suppose that there were a positive ϵ_i^C at observation i. The result from (11.3.16) would be a larger $\dot{C}_i$ at this observation than would be expected. But a larger $\dot{C}_i$ would, from (11.3.17), assuming $\gamma_3 > 0$, lead to a larger Y_i than would be expected. Thus a positive ϵ_i^C implies a larger Y_i than would be expected. Similarly a negative ϵ_i^C implies a smaller $\dot{Y}_i$ than would be expected. The expectation of the ratio in (11.3.19) is therefore positive, so the OLS estimator of γ_1 is biased upward:

$$E(\hat{\gamma}_{1\text{OLS}}) > \gamma_1 \tag{11.3.20}$$

overstating the marginal propensity to consume. At the same time OLS understates β_1, the intercept, as illustrated in Figure 11.1, where the OLS estimate of the slope is biased upward, but the OLS estimate of the intercept is biased downward, as compared to the true consumption function. The inclusion of an explanatory endogenous variable leads to this bias.

The OLS overstatement of the marginal propensity to consume is not corrected by taking a larger sample, so the OLS estimator is inconsistent as well as biased. From (11.3.18), in general

$$\text{plim}\, \hat{\gamma}_{1\text{OLS}} = \gamma_1 + \frac{\text{plim}\, \frac{1}{n}\, \Sigma\, \epsilon_i^C\, \dot{Y}_i}{\text{plim}\, \frac{1}{n}\, \Sigma\, \dot{Y}_i^2} > \gamma_1 \tag{11.3.21}$$

so that the OLS estimator generally overstates the true marginal propensity to consume even in the limit, as the sample size grows without bound.[6]

[6] See Problem 11-C for certain special conditions under which the OLS estimator of γ_1' in the variant model is consistent.

While OLS yields estimators that are biased and inconsistent, it should not be totally rejected as an estimation technique for simultaneous-equations systems. As will be seen in Section 11.9, the OLS estimators tend to exhibit both efficiency and insensitivity to specification error. Furthermore, as little is known concerning the finite-sample properties of any estimator, OLS may be as good as any other method of estimation, even the consistent estimators to be presented later in this chapter. In fact, as will be seen in the next two chapters, OLS is indeed used in estimating several specific simultaneous-equations systems.

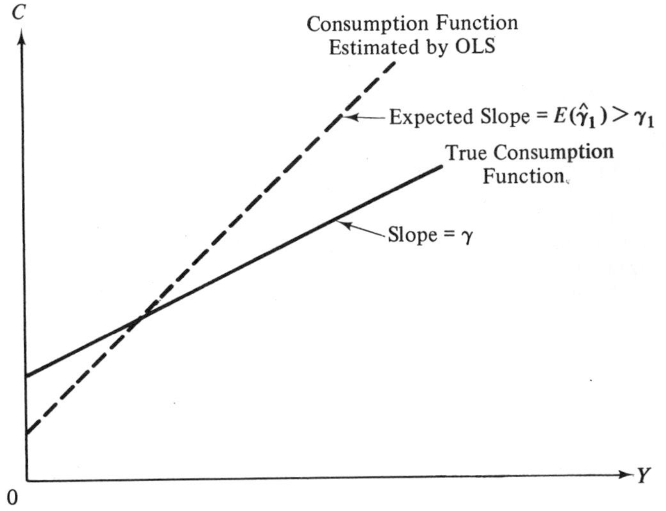

Figure 11.1 Least-Squares Bias in Estimating the Consumption Function by OLS

11.4 Indirect least squares

Indirect least squares (ILS) is a limited-information technique that can be used to obtain consistent estimators of a just-identified equation, as discussed in Section 10.3. In the just-identified case the structural parameters are uniquely determined from the reduced-form parameters, so the estimated reduced-form parameters can be used to infer estimated structural parameters indirectly, leading to the name "indirect least squares."

This approach involves two steps. The first is the estimation of the reduced-form parameters $\mathbf{\Pi}$ using least squares. The second, which is possible if and only if the equation is just identified, is the estimation of structural-form parameters $\mathbf{\Gamma}$ and $\mathbf{B}$ using the relationships between these parameters and the reduced-form parameters and the identifying restrictions. If the equation is overidentified, the ILS method will not work and either OLS or other approaches, discussed in the next sections, must be employed. It will be seen, however, that these other approaches, which apply both to just-identified and overidentified equations, typically are equivalent to ILS in the just-identified case.

The ILS method starts by estimating the reduced form, which is

$$\underset{n\times g}{\mathbf{Y}} = \underset{n\times k}{\mathbf{X}}\ \underset{k\times g}{\mathbf{\Pi}} + \underset{n\times g}{\mathbf{U}} \tag{11.4.1}$$

where

$$\mathbf{\Pi} = -\mathbf{B}\mathbf{\Gamma}^{-1} \tag*{*(11.4.2)}$$

$$\mathbf{U} = \mathbf{E}\mathbf{\Gamma}^{-1} \tag*{*(11.4.3)}$$

as in (10.1.10) and (10.1.11). The least-squares estimator of the matrix of reduced-form coefficients $\mathbf{\Pi}$ is given by

$$\underset{k\times g}{\hat{\mathbf{\Pi}}} = \underset{k\times k}{(\mathbf{X}'\mathbf{X})^{-1}}\ \underset{k\times n}{\mathbf{X}'}\ \underset{n\times g}{\mathbf{Y}} \tag*{*(11.4.4)}$$

as in (10.1.24), where $\mathbf{X}$ and $\mathbf{Y}$ are the data matrices of (11.1.5) and (11.1.6). This estimator is equivalent to estimating each equation of the reduced form separately via least squares, since each column of $\hat{\mathbf{\Pi}}$ is the common matrix of weights $(\mathbf{X}'\mathbf{X})^{-1}\mathbf{X}'$ times the column of the $\mathbf{Y}$ matrix corresponding to the dependent variable in that particular reduced-form equation.

Now consider one just identified equation. The $\mathbf{Y}$ matrix can be partitioned as in (11.1.16), corresponding to the one dependent endogenous variable $\mathbf{y}_1$, the $g_1 - 1$ explanatory endogenous variables $\mathbf{Y}_1$, and the $g - g_1$ excluded endogenous variables $\mathbf{Y}_2$. The $\mathbf{X}$ matrix can be similarly partitioned as in (11.1.17), corresponding to the k_1 included exogenous variables $\mathbf{X}_1$ and the $k - k_1$ excluded variables $\mathbf{X}_2$. The reduced form (11.4.1) can then be written

$$\Big(\underset{n\times 1}{\mathbf{y}_1}\ \Big|\ \underset{n\times(g_1-1)}{\mathbf{Y}_1}\ \Big|\ \underset{n\times(g-g_1)}{\mathbf{Y}_2}\Big) = \Big(\underset{n\times k_1}{\mathbf{X}_1}\ \Big|\ \underset{n\times(k-k_1)}{\mathbf{X}_2}\Big)\left(\begin{array}{c|c|c} \mathbf{\Pi}_1^0 & \mathbf{\Pi}_1^{00} & \mathbf{\Pi}_3 \\ \hline \mathbf{\Pi}_2^0 & \mathbf{\Pi}_2^{00} & \mathbf{\Pi}_4 \end{array}\right)_{\substack{\\ 1 \quad g_1-1 \quad g-g_1}}$$

$$+ \Big(\underset{n\times 1}{\mathbf{u}_0}\ \Big|\ \underset{n\times(g_1-1)}{\mathbf{u}_1}\ \Big|\ \underset{n\times(g-g_1)}{\mathbf{u}_2}\Big) \tag*{*(11.4.5)}$$

where the stochastic disturbance terms have been partitioned in the same way as $\mathbf{Y}$, corresponding to the dependent, explanatory, and excluded endogenous variables. The matrix of reduced-form coefficients $\mathbf{\Pi}$ has been partitioned here into six submatrices in order to carry out the matrix multiplication, as in (10.3.7), (10.3.19), and (10.3.20). Its columns have been divided to correspond to the one dependent endogenous variable, the $g_1 - 1$ explanatory endogenous variables, and the $g - g_1$ excluded endogenous variables. Its rows have been divided to correspond to the k_1 included exogenous variables and $k - k_1$ excluded exogenous variables. Thus, for example, the submatrix $\mathbf{\Pi}_2^{00}$ is a $(k - k_1) \times (g_1 - 1)$ matrix. If the equation to be estimated is just identified, then $k - k_1 = g_1 - 1$, so $\mathbf{\Pi}_2^{00}$ is a square matrix.

The relations between the structural-form and reduced-form parameters, (11.4.2), may be written

$$\mathbf{\Pi\Gamma} = -\mathbf{B}. \tag{*(11.4.6)}$$

For the first equation, involving only the first columns of $\mathbf{\Gamma}$ and $\mathbf{B}$, using the normalization and zero restrictions, and using the partitioned $\mathbf{\Pi}$ matrix in (11.4.5),

$$\begin{pmatrix} \mathbf{\Pi}_1^0 & \mathbf{\Pi}_1^{00} & \mathbf{\Pi}_3 \\ \mathbf{\Pi}_2^0 & \mathbf{\Pi}_2^{00} & \mathbf{\Pi}_4 \end{pmatrix} \begin{pmatrix} -1 \\ \boldsymbol{\gamma}_1 \\ \mathbf{0} \end{pmatrix} = -\begin{pmatrix} \boldsymbol{\beta}_1 \\ \mathbf{0} \end{pmatrix}. \tag{*(11.4.7)}$$

Writing out the resulting two sets of equations, where elements of $\mathbf{\Pi}$ are replaced by the estimators $\hat{\mathbf{\Pi}}$ in (11.4.2) and the structural coefficients of the first equation are replaced by their estimators $\hat{\boldsymbol{\gamma}}_1$ and $\hat{\boldsymbol{\beta}}_1$,

$$-\hat{\mathbf{\Pi}}_1^0 + \hat{\mathbf{\Pi}}_1^{00}\hat{\boldsymbol{\gamma}}_1 = -\hat{\boldsymbol{\beta}}_1 \qquad (k_1 \text{ equations}) \tag{11.4.8}$$

$$-\hat{\mathbf{\Pi}}_2^0 + \hat{\mathbf{\Pi}}_2^{00}\hat{\boldsymbol{\gamma}}_1 = \mathbf{0} \qquad (k - k_1 \text{ equations}). \tag{11.4.9}$$

As already noted, if the equation to be estimated is just identified, then $\hat{\mathbf{\Pi}}_2^{00}$ is a square matrix. Assuming it is nonsingular, (11.4.9) can be solved for $\hat{\boldsymbol{\gamma}}_1$, as in (10.3.23), as

$$\hat{\boldsymbol{\gamma}}_1 = (\hat{\mathbf{\Pi}}_2^{00})^{-1}\hat{\mathbf{\Pi}}_2^0. \tag{11.4.10}$$

From this result and (11.4.8) it follows that $\hat{\boldsymbol{\beta}}_1$ can be obtained, as in (10.3.24), as

$$\hat{\boldsymbol{\beta}}_1 = \hat{\mathbf{\Pi}}_1^0 - \hat{\mathbf{\Pi}}_1^{00}(\hat{\mathbf{\Pi}}_2^{00})^{-1}\hat{\mathbf{\Pi}}_2^0. \tag{11.4.11}$$

These are the *indirect least-squares (ILS) estimators*, which may be written

$$\begin{pmatrix} \hat{\boldsymbol{\gamma}}_1 \\ \hat{\boldsymbol{\beta}}_1 \end{pmatrix}_{\text{ILS}} = \begin{pmatrix} (\hat{\mathbf{\Pi}}_2^{00})^{-1}\hat{\mathbf{\Pi}}_2^0 \\ \hat{\mathbf{\Pi}}_1^0 - \hat{\mathbf{\Pi}}_1^{00}(\hat{\mathbf{\Pi}}_2^{00})^{-1}\hat{\mathbf{\Pi}}_2^0 \end{pmatrix}. \tag{*(11.4.12)}$$

These estimators use the least-squares estimators of reduced-form coefficients, (11.4.4), plus the identifying restrictions to obtain estimators of the structural parameters for one just-identified equation of the simultaneous-equations system. They are the first of several limited-information estimators to be considered.

The ILS estimators are generally biased estimators, as are the OLS estimators, but unlike the OLS estimators, ILS estimators are consistent, where

$$\text{plim}\begin{pmatrix}\hat{\gamma}_1\\ \hline \hat{\beta}_1\end{pmatrix}_{\text{ILS}} = \begin{pmatrix}\gamma_1\\ \hline \beta_1\end{pmatrix}. \tag{11.4.13}$$

The consistency of the ILS estimators follows from the fact that, as indicated in Section 4.8, continuous functions of consistent estimators are also consistent estimators. The ILS estimators are obtained, however, as continuous functions of the reduced-form estimators $\hat{\Pi}$, as summarized in (11.4.12), and the reduced-form estimators themselves are consistent from the least-squares consistency theorem of Section 4.9.[7]

The ILS estimator can be illustrated using the variant consumption function (11.1.27), which is a just-identified equation. The structural form, from (11.1.26), is

$$C = \gamma_1' Y + \beta_1' + \epsilon^{C'} \tag{11.4.14}$$

$$Y = \gamma_3' C + \beta_5' G + \beta_6' + \epsilon^{Y'} \tag{11.4.15}$$

The reduced form is obtained readily by inserting Y from (11.4.15) in (11.4.14) and solving for C and then Y to yield

$$C = \Pi_1' + \Pi_2' G + u^{C'} \tag{11.4.16}$$

$$Y = \Pi_3' + \Pi_4' G + u^{Y'} \tag{11.4.17}$$

where

$$\Pi_1' = \frac{\beta_1' + \gamma_1' \beta_6'}{1 - \gamma_1' \gamma_3'}, \quad \Pi_2' = \frac{\gamma_1' \beta_5'}{1 - \gamma_1' \gamma_3'}, \quad u^{C'} = \frac{\epsilon^{C'} + \gamma_1 \epsilon^{Y'}}{1 - \gamma_1' \gamma_3'} \tag{11.4.18}$$

$$\Pi_3' = \frac{\beta_6' + \gamma_3' \beta_1'}{1 - \gamma_1' \gamma_3'}, \quad \Pi_4' = \frac{\beta_5'}{1 - \gamma_1' \gamma_3'}, \quad u^{Y'} = \frac{\gamma_3' \epsilon^{C'} + \epsilon^{Y'}}{1 - \gamma_1' \gamma_3'} \tag{11.4.19}$$

But the reduced form can be written, following (11.4.5), as

[7] While continuous functions of consistent estimators are consistent, continuous functions of unbiased estimators need not be unbiased, and continuous functions of efficient estimators need not be efficient. Thus, even though the reduced-form estimators $\hat{\Pi}$ are unbiased and efficient by the Gauss-Markov theorem of Section 4.9, the ILS estimators are, in general, neither unbiased nor efficient. It should also be noted that since $\hat{\gamma}_{1\,\text{ILS}}$, the ILS estimator of γ_1, is consistent, the continuous transformation $(1 - \hat{\gamma}_{1\,\text{ILS}})^{-1}$, the estimator of the multiplier, is also a consistent estimator (but not necessarily an unbiased or efficient estimator). It might further be noted that another property that holds over continuous transformations is that of maximum likelihood. Thus if the reduced-form estimators $\hat{\Pi}$ are maximum-likelihood estimators, which they are if the structural- and reduced-form stochastic disturbance terms are normally distributed, then the ILS estimators in (11.4.12) are also maximum-likelihood estimators.

$$(C \mid Y \mid \quad) = (1 \mid G)\begin{pmatrix} \Pi_1' & \Pi_3' & \\ \Pi_2' & \Pi_4' & \end{pmatrix} + (u^{C'} \mid u^{Y'} \mid \quad) \tag{11.4.20}$$

where the order of the exogenous variables has been adjusted so the exogenous variable excluded from the consumption function, G, appears last. Following (11.4.7) for the relations between the reduced-form and structural-form coefficients:

$$\begin{pmatrix} \Pi_1' & \Pi_3' & \\ \Pi_2' & \Pi_4' & \end{pmatrix}\begin{pmatrix} -1 \\ \gamma_1' \end{pmatrix} = -\begin{pmatrix} \beta_1' \\ 0 \end{pmatrix} \tag{11.4.21}$$

Thus

$$-\Pi_1' + \Pi_3'\gamma_1' = -\beta_1' \tag{11.4.22}$$

$$-\Pi_2' + \Pi_4'\gamma_1' = 0 \tag{11.4.23}$$

where here $\mathbf{\Pi}_1^0$ reduces to Π_1'; $\mathbf{\Pi}_2^0$ reduces to Π_2'; $\mathbf{\Pi}_1^{00}$ reduces to Π_3'; and $\mathbf{\Pi}_2^{00}$ reduces to Π_4'. From (11.4.12) the ILS estimators are

$$\begin{pmatrix} \hat{\gamma}_1' \\ \hat{\beta}_1' \end{pmatrix}_{\text{ILS}} = \begin{pmatrix} \hat{\Pi}_4'^{-1}\hat{\Pi}_2' \\ \hat{\Pi}_1' - \hat{\Pi}_3'\hat{\Pi}_4'^{-1}\hat{\Pi}_2' \end{pmatrix} \tag{11.4.24}$$

so that

$$\hat{\gamma}_{1\,\text{ILS}}' = \frac{\hat{\Pi}_2'}{\hat{\Pi}_4'} \tag{11.4.25}$$

$$\hat{\beta}_{1\,\text{ILS}}' = \hat{\Pi}_1' - \frac{\hat{\Pi}_2'\hat{\Pi}_3}{\hat{\Pi}_4'}. \tag{11.4.26}$$

In this simple example these estimators can also be readily obtained directly from (11.4.18) and (11.4.19) by solving for γ_1' and β_1'.

Using the least-squares estimators of the two simple linear regression equations that constitute the reduced form (11.4.16) and (11.4.17), the ILS estimator of the marginal propensity to consume is

$$\hat{\gamma}_{1\,\text{ILS}}' = \frac{\hat{\Pi}_2'}{\hat{\Pi}_4'} = \frac{\Sigma\,\dot{C}_i\dot{G}_i/\Sigma\,\dot{G}_i^2}{\Sigma\,\dot{Y}_i\dot{G}_i/\Sigma\,\dot{G}_i^2} = \frac{\Sigma\,\dot{C}_i\dot{G}_i}{\Sigma\,\dot{Y}_i\dot{G}_i} \tag{11.4.27}$$

where $\dot{C}_i$, $\dot{Y}_i$, and $\dot{G}_i$ represent deviations from mean values. This result can be contrasted with the OLS estimator, which is the same for the variant consumption function as for the original consumption function. From (11.3.13)

$$\hat{\gamma}'_{1\,\text{OLS}} = \frac{\Sigma \dot{C}_i \dot{Y}_i}{\Sigma \dot{Y}_i^2}. \tag{11.4.28}$$

The OLS estimator is biased and inconsistent, while the ILS estimator is biased but consistent. The consistency of the ILS estimator can be readily seen, since, using (11.4.16) and (11.4.17) in (11.4.27),

$$\hat{\gamma}'_{1\,\text{ILS}} = \frac{\Sigma \dot{C}_i \dot{G}_i}{\Sigma \dot{Y}_i \dot{G}_i} = \frac{\Pi'_2 + \left(\frac{1}{n}\,\Sigma u_i^{C'} \dot{G}_i\right) / \left(\frac{1}{n}\,\Sigma\, \dot{G}_i^2\right)}{\Pi'_4 + \left(\frac{1}{n}\,\Sigma u_i^{Y'} \dot{G}_i\right) / \left(\frac{1}{n}\,\Sigma\, \dot{G}_i^2\right)}. \tag{11.4.29}$$

In any finite sample the expectation of $\hat{\gamma}'_{1\,\text{ILS}}$ need not be $(\Pi'_2/\Pi'_4) = \gamma'_1$, since the expectation of a ratio is not, in general, the ratio of the expectations. Thus

$$E(\hat{\gamma}'_{1\,\text{ILS}}) \neq \gamma'_1. \tag{11.4.30}$$

Taking the probability limit, however, the probability limit of a ratio is the ratio of the probability limits, so, since both $\text{plim}\,(1/n)\,\Sigma u_i^{C'} \dot{G}_i$ and $\text{plim}\,(1/n)\,\Sigma u_i^{Y'} \dot{G}_i$ vanish,

$$\text{plim}\,(\hat{\gamma}'_{1\,\text{ILS}}) = \gamma'_1 \tag{11.4.31}$$

demonstrating the consistency of this indirect least-squares estimator.[8]

The indirect least-squares approach provides consistent estimators, but it is defined only for just-identified equations. This estimator is not defined in the overidentified case such as the original consumption function of the prototype macro model. The methods to be introduced in the next two sections are limited-information approaches for which estimators are defined in both the overidentified and the just-identified cases. As already noted, however, these estimators are generally equivalent to the indirect least-squares estimator in the just-identified case.

11.5 Two-stage least squares and *k*-class estimators[9]

The last two sections have introduced OLS estimators, which are generally biased and inconsistent, and ILS estimators, which are biased but consistent and defined only for just-identified equations. This section presents a limited-

[8] A comparable approach for $\hat{\gamma}'_{1\,\text{OLS}}$ shows that it is inconsistent as well as biased. See Problem 11-E.

[9] For the initial development of two-stage least squares, see Theil (1961) and Basmann (1957, 1959, 1960). Basmann has referred to the technique as a "generalized classical linear" (GCL) estimator. See the next two sections for related presentations of two-stage least squares. For an extension to nonlinear estimation see Kelejian (1971) and Amemiya (1974).

information technique that can be used to estimate either an overidentified or an identified equation from a system of simultaneous equations—the technique of two-stage least squares (2SLS) and its generalization to k-class estimators.

Several formulations of the 2SLS estimator will be presented in this section and the next two sections. The first formulation will provide both a motivation for the estimator and a rationale for its name.

Consider the (first) equation to be estimated, as presented previously in (11.1.18), of the form

$$\mathbf{y}_1 = \mathbf{Y}_1 \boldsymbol{\gamma}_1 + \mathbf{X}_1 \boldsymbol{\beta}_1 + \boldsymbol{\varepsilon}_1 \tag{11.5.1}$$

The "problem" in applying least squares directly to estimate this equation is the presence of explanatory endogenous variables, $\mathbf{Y}_1$, which are correlated with the stochastic disturbance terms, $\boldsymbol{\varepsilon}_1$, even in the probability limit. If these variables could be replaced by related variables that are uncorrelated, in the probability limit, with the stochastic disturbance terms, the resulting estimator would be consistent. The method of two-stage least squares accomplishes this by using the estimated reduced form to replace explanatory endogenous variables by their estimated values. Thus, $\mathbf{Y}_1$ is replaced in (11.5.1) by $\hat{\mathbf{Y}}_1$, the estimated values of each of the explanatory endogenous variables at each observation using the reduced form. The least-squares estimator of the resulting equation, which is the same as the OLS estimator in (11.3.5) other than $\mathbf{Y}_1$ being replaced by $\hat{\mathbf{Y}}_1$, is the *two-stage least-squares (2SLS) estimator*, of the form

$$\begin{pmatrix} \hat{\boldsymbol{\gamma}}_1 \\ \hline \hat{\boldsymbol{\beta}}_1 \end{pmatrix}_{2SLS} = \left(\begin{array}{c|c} \hat{\mathbf{Y}}_1'\hat{\mathbf{Y}}_1 & \hat{\mathbf{Y}}_1'\mathbf{X}_1 \\ \hline \mathbf{X}_1'\hat{\mathbf{Y}}_1 & \mathbf{X}_1'\mathbf{X}_1 \end{array}\right)^{-1} \begin{pmatrix} \hat{\mathbf{Y}}_1' \\ \hline \mathbf{X}_1' \end{pmatrix} \mathbf{y}_1. \tag{*(11.5.2)}$$

This first formulation of the 2SLS estimator indicates that it yields estimators of all coefficients of one equation of the system, given data on the dependent endogenous variable $\mathbf{y}_1$, data on the included exogenous variables $\mathbf{X}_1$, and estimated values of the explanatory endogenous variables $\mathbf{Y}_1$. These estimated values are determined, themselves, from the estimated reduced-form coefficients and the data on all exogenous variables of the system. Thus the estimator depends on all exogenous variables, not just those included in the equation to be estimated.

The rationale for the name "two-stage least squares" is indicated by (11.5.2). Least-squares regression is, indeed, done in two stages. The first stage uses least squares to estimate the reduced form in order to calculate the $\hat{\mathbf{Y}}_1$ in (11.5.2). The second stage uses least squares once again to estimate the structural-form equation, as seen in (11.5.2), which is a least-squares estimator for which $\mathbf{Y}_1$ in (11.5.1) has been replaced by $\hat{\mathbf{Y}}_1$. Thus 2SLS involves two stages, each of which entails the least-squares estimation of g equations—those of the reduced form in the first stage and those of the structural form in the second stage.[10]

[10] The ILS estimator also involves two steps, but only the first step, the estimation of the reduced form in (11.4.4), involves least squares. The second step involves algebraic manipulations of the reduced-form estimators to obtain structural-form estimators, as in (11.4.12).

The formulation of the 2SLS estimator in (11.5.2) uses $\hat{\mathbf{Y}}_1$, and it will be important to specify more formally the computation of these estimates of the explanatory endogenous variables. The reduced form is

$$\mathbf{Y} = \mathbf{X\Pi} + \mathbf{u} \qquad *(11.5.3)$$

and the least-squares estimators of the reduced-form coefficients $\hat{\mathbf{\Pi}}$ are given as

$$\hat{\mathbf{\Pi}} = (\mathbf{X}'\mathbf{X})^{-1}\mathbf{X}'\mathbf{Y} \qquad *(11.5.4)$$

as in (11.4.4). In this first of the two stages all exogenous variables are treated as the explanatory variables in each of the g least-squares regressions, one for each endogenous variable. The $\hat{\mathbf{\Pi}}$ estimator consists of g columns, each representing the estimators of the coefficients in one such regression. The estimates of the endogenous variables $\hat{\mathbf{Y}}$ are obtained from the estimated $\hat{\mathbf{\Pi}}$ and data on all exogenous variables of the model $\mathbf{X}$ as

$$\hat{\mathbf{Y}} = \mathbf{X}\hat{\mathbf{\Pi}} = \mathbf{X}(\mathbf{X}'\mathbf{X})^{-1}\mathbf{X}'\mathbf{Y}. \qquad *(11.5.5)$$

Furthermore

$$\mathbf{Y} = \mathbf{X}\hat{\mathbf{\Pi}} + \hat{\mathbf{u}} = \hat{\mathbf{Y}} + \hat{\mathbf{u}} \qquad *(11.5.6)$$

where $\hat{\mathbf{u}}$ is the matrix of reduced-form residuals. Following the usual partitioning based on those variables included in or excluded from the equation to be estimated, as in (11.4.5), equation (11.5.6) can be written

$$(\mathbf{y}_1 \mid \mathbf{Y}_1 \mid \mathbf{Y}_2) = (\mathbf{X}_1 \mid \mathbf{X}_2)\begin{pmatrix} \hat{\mathbf{\Pi}}_1^0 & \hat{\mathbf{\Pi}}_1^{00} & \hat{\mathbf{\Pi}}_3 \\ \hat{\mathbf{\Pi}}_2^0 & \hat{\mathbf{\Pi}}_2^{00} & \hat{\mathbf{\Pi}}_4 \end{pmatrix} + (\hat{\mathbf{u}}_0 \mid \hat{\mathbf{u}}_1 \mid \hat{\mathbf{u}}_2). \qquad *(11.5.7)$$

Solving for the variables of interest, the explanatory endogenous variables in the equation to be estimated,

$$\mathbf{Y}_1 = \mathbf{X}_1\hat{\mathbf{\Pi}}_1^{00} + \mathbf{X}_2\hat{\mathbf{\Pi}}_2^{00} + \hat{\mathbf{u}}_1 = \hat{\mathbf{Y}}_1 + \hat{\mathbf{u}}_1. \qquad (11.5.8)$$

Thus $\hat{\mathbf{Y}}_1$, the matrix of estimated values of the explanatory endogenous variables in (11.5.2), is given as the linear combination of the exogenous variables

$$\hat{\mathbf{Y}}_1 = \mathbf{X}_1\hat{\mathbf{\Pi}}_1^{00} + \mathbf{X}_2\hat{\mathbf{\Pi}}_2^{00}. \qquad *(11.5.9)$$

Furthermore, from (11.5.5) and (11.5.7),

$$\begin{aligned} \hat{\mathbf{Y}} = (\hat{\mathbf{y}}_1 \mid \hat{\mathbf{Y}}_1 \mid \hat{\mathbf{Y}}_2) &= \mathbf{X}\hat{\mathbf{\Pi}} = \mathbf{X}(\mathbf{X}'\mathbf{X})^{-1}\mathbf{X}'\mathbf{Y} \\ &= \mathbf{X}(\mathbf{X}'\mathbf{X})^{-1}\mathbf{X}'(\mathbf{y}_1 \mid \mathbf{Y}_1 \mid \mathbf{Y}_2) \end{aligned} \qquad (11.5.10)$$

so that $\hat{\mathbf{Y}}_1$ can be expressed as the linear function of the actual $\mathbf{Y}_1$, namely

$$\hat{\mathbf{Y}}_1 = \mathbf{X}(\mathbf{X}'\mathbf{X})^{-1}\mathbf{X}'\mathbf{Y}_1. \tag{11.5.11}$$

The $\hat{\mathbf{Y}}_1$ can be also expressed as the actual $\mathbf{Y}_1$ less the relevant reduced-form residuals:

$$\hat{\mathbf{Y}}_1 = \mathbf{Y}_1 - \hat{\mathbf{u}}_1 \tag{11.5.12}$$

where $\hat{\mathbf{u}}_1$ can be expressed in terms of the fundamental idempotent matrix of least squares (4.6.26) as

$$\hat{\mathbf{u}}_1 = (\mathbf{I} - \mathbf{X}(\mathbf{X}'\mathbf{X})^{-1}\mathbf{X}')\mathbf{Y}_1 = \mathbf{M}\mathbf{Y}_1. \tag{11.5.13}$$

The $\hat{\mathbf{Y}}_1$ in (11.5.2) has thus been expressed in three equivalent ways in (11.5.9), (11.5.11), and (11.5.12).

The last formulation of $\hat{\mathbf{Y}}_1$, in (11.5.12), indicates that it can be obtained from the data on explanatory endogenous variables $\mathbf{Y}_1$ by subtracting the relevant estimated reduced-form residuals $\hat{\mathbf{u}}_1$ in order to "purge" the variables of their statistical dependence on the stochastic term. The 2SLS estimator can then be interpreted in terms of the original equation. Combining (11.5.1) and (11.5.12),

$$\mathbf{y}_1 = (\hat{\mathbf{Y}}_1 + \hat{\mathbf{u}}_1)\boldsymbol{\gamma}_1 + \mathbf{X}_1\boldsymbol{\beta}_1 + \boldsymbol{\varepsilon}_1. \tag{11.5.14}$$

Thus,

$$\mathbf{y}_1 = \hat{\mathbf{Y}}_1\boldsymbol{\gamma}_1 + \mathbf{X}_1\boldsymbol{\beta}_1 + \mathbf{v}_1 \qquad *(11.5.15)$$

where

$$\mathbf{v}_1 = \hat{\mathbf{u}}_1\boldsymbol{\gamma}_1 + \boldsymbol{\varepsilon}_1. \qquad *(11.5.16)$$

The 2SLS estimator is the least-squares estimator of (11.5.15), which is of exactly the same form as (11.5.1), but in which explanatory endogenous variables are replaced by values estimated from the reduced form.

Combining (11.5.2) and (11.5.12) yields the second formulation of the 2SLS estimator.

$$\begin{pmatrix} \hat{\boldsymbol{\gamma}}_1 \\ \hline \hat{\boldsymbol{\beta}}_1 \end{pmatrix}_{2SLS} = \left(\begin{array}{c|c} \mathbf{Y}_1'\mathbf{Y}_1 - \hat{\mathbf{u}}_1'\hat{\mathbf{u}}_1 & \mathbf{Y}_1'\mathbf{X}_1 \\ \hline \mathbf{X}_1'\mathbf{Y}_1 & \mathbf{X}_1'\mathbf{X}_1 \end{array}\right)^{-1} \begin{pmatrix} \mathbf{Y}_1' - \hat{\mathbf{u}}_1' \\ \hline \mathbf{X}_1' \end{pmatrix} \mathbf{y}_1. \qquad *(11.5.17)$$

To obtain this estimator, $\hat{\mathbf{Y}}_1$ in (11.5.2) is replaced by $\mathbf{Y}_1 - \hat{\mathbf{u}}_1$ from (11.5.12). The upper left submatrix in the partitioned matrix to be inverted is then

$$\hat{\mathbf{Y}}_1'\hat{\mathbf{Y}}_1 = (\mathbf{Y}_1' - \hat{\mathbf{u}}_1')(\mathbf{Y}_1 - \hat{\mathbf{u}}_1) = \hat{\mathbf{Y}}_1'\mathbf{Y}_1 = \mathbf{Y}_1'\mathbf{Y}_1 - \hat{\mathbf{u}}_1'\hat{\mathbf{u}}_1 \tag{11.5.18}$$

where the last two equalities follow from

$$\hat{\mathbf{u}}_1'\mathbf{Y}_1 = \mathbf{Y}_1'\hat{\mathbf{u}}_1 = \hat{\mathbf{u}}_1'\hat{\mathbf{u}}_1 = \mathbf{Y}_1'\mathbf{M}\mathbf{Y}_1 \tag{11.5.19}$$

using the fact that the **M** matrix in (11.5.13) is both symmetric and idempotent. The upper right submatrix in the partitioned matrix to be inverted is

$$\hat{\mathbf{Y}}_1'\mathbf{X}_1 = (\mathbf{Y}_1' - \hat{\mathbf{u}}_1')\mathbf{X}_1 = \mathbf{Y}_1'\mathbf{X}_1 \tag{11.5.20}$$

where the last equality follows from the fact that **MX** must vanish.[11] Comparing the 2SLS estimator in (11.5.17) to the OLS estimator in (11.3.5), the only difference is the correction of the explanatory endogenous variables $\mathbf{Y}_1$ using the reduced-form least-squares residuals $\hat{\mathbf{u}}_1$. Thus, in this formulation the $\mathbf{Y}_1$ are "purged" of their endogenous nature by netting out the $\hat{\mathbf{u}}_1$ residuals.

It has been stated previously that the 2SLS estimator is defined only for an equation that is just identified or overidentified. This fact can be inferred from the two formulations of the 2SLS estimator in (11.5.2) and (11.5.17). The matrix to be inverted is of the order $g_1 - 1 + k_1$, and for the equation to be just identified or overidentified it is necessary that it fulfill the order condition $k - k_1 \geqslant g_1 - 1$ or, equivalently,

$$g_1 - 1 + k_1 \leqslant k. \tag{11.5.21}$$

But the matrix to be inverted in (11.5.2) and (11.5.17) consists of combinations of the elements of the **X** matrix, where $\hat{\mathbf{Y}}_1 = \mathbf{Y}_1 - \hat{\mathbf{u}}_1$ represents, from (11.5.9), linear combinations of **X**. The matrix to be inverted thus cannot have rank larger than that of the original **X** matrix, namely k. Thus, if condition (11.5.21) is not met, in which case the equation is underidentified, the matrix cannot be inverted, so the 2SLS estimator is not defined. It is generally assumed that the matrix does, in fact, have full rank and hence can be inverted if the equation is just identified or overidentified.

It has also been stated previously that the 2SLS estimator reduces to ILS in the just-identified case. To show this it suffices to express the equation to be estimated in terms of the reduced-form coefficients. Thus combining (11.5.15) and (11.5.9),

$$\mathbf{y}_1 = (\mathbf{X}_1\hat{\mathbf{\Pi}}_1^{00} + \mathbf{X}_2\hat{\mathbf{\Pi}}_2^{00})\,\boldsymbol{\gamma}_1 + \mathbf{X}_1\boldsymbol{\beta}_1 + \mathbf{v}_1. \tag{11.5.22}$$

Collecting terms,

$$\mathbf{y}_1 = \mathbf{X}_1(\hat{\mathbf{\Pi}}_1^{00}\boldsymbol{\gamma}_1 + \boldsymbol{\beta}_1) + \mathbf{X}_2\hat{\mathbf{\Pi}}_2^{00}\boldsymbol{\gamma}_1 + \mathbf{v}_1. \tag{11.5.23}$$

The 2SLS estimator is the least-squares estimator of this equation, which can be written

[11] Recall that, from Section 4.6,

$$\mathbf{MX} = [\mathbf{I} - \mathbf{X}(\mathbf{X}'\mathbf{X})^{-1}\mathbf{X}']\mathbf{X} = \mathbf{X} - \mathbf{X} = \mathbf{0}.$$

$$\mathbf{y}_1 = (\mathbf{X}_1 \;\vdots\; \mathbf{X}_2)\begin{pmatrix}\hat{\mathbf{\Pi}}_1^{00}\boldsymbol{\gamma}_1 + \boldsymbol{\beta}_1 \\ \hline \hat{\mathbf{\Pi}}_2^{00}\boldsymbol{\gamma}_1\end{pmatrix} + \mathbf{v}_1$$

$$= \mathbf{X}\begin{pmatrix}\hat{\mathbf{\Pi}}_1^{00}\boldsymbol{\gamma}_1 + \boldsymbol{\beta}_1 \\ \hline \hat{\mathbf{\Pi}}_2^{00}\boldsymbol{\gamma}_1\end{pmatrix} + \mathbf{v}_1 \tag{11.5.24}$$

The least-squares estimation of this equation yields

$$\begin{pmatrix}\hat{\mathbf{\Pi}}_1^{00}\hat{\boldsymbol{\gamma}}_1 + \hat{\boldsymbol{\beta}}_1 \\ \hline \hat{\mathbf{\Pi}}_2^{00}\hat{\boldsymbol{\gamma}}_1\end{pmatrix} = (\mathbf{X}'\mathbf{X})^{-1}\mathbf{X}'\mathbf{y}_1 = \begin{pmatrix}\hat{\mathbf{\Pi}}_1^{0} \\ \hline \hat{\mathbf{\Pi}}_2^{0}\end{pmatrix} \tag{11.5.25}$$

–that is, it is simply the first column of the estimated matrix of reduced-form coefficients. This equality always holds for 2SLS estimators of $\boldsymbol{\gamma}_1$ and $\boldsymbol{\beta}_1$. If, however, the equation is just identified, then $\hat{\mathbf{\Pi}}_2^{00}$ will be square, and, assuming it is nonsingular, solving for $\hat{\boldsymbol{\gamma}}_1$ and $\hat{\boldsymbol{\beta}}_1$ yields

$$\hat{\boldsymbol{\gamma}}_1 = (\hat{\mathbf{\Pi}}_2^{00})^{-1}\hat{\mathbf{\Pi}}_2^{0} \tag{11.5.26}$$

$$\hat{\boldsymbol{\beta}}_1 = \hat{\mathbf{\Pi}}_1^{0} - \hat{\mathbf{\Pi}}_1^{00}(\hat{\mathbf{\Pi}}_2^{00})^{-1}\hat{\mathbf{\Pi}}_2^{0}. \tag{11.5.27}$$

These are precisely the ILS estimators in (11.4.10) and (11.4.11).[12]

Finally, it has been previously stated that the 2SLS estimators are consistent estimators. In general 2SLS estimators are biased, as are OLS estimators, but, unlike the OLS estimators, they are consistent. The problem in OLS was the inclusion of $\mathbf{Y}_1$ as explanatory variables, which led to an inconsistent estimator. In 2SLS, however, the $\mathbf{Y}_1$ have been replaced by $\hat{\mathbf{Y}}_1$, which consists of linear combinations of exogenous variables. Since the full set of explanatory variables are either exogenous ($\mathbf{X}_1$) or linear combinations of exogenous variables ($\hat{\mathbf{Y}}_1$), the explanatory variables are uncorrelated in the probability limit with the stochastic disturbance terms, ensuring consistency. To show this more formally consider (11.5.15), which may be written

$$\mathbf{y}_1 = (\hat{\mathbf{Y}}_1 \;\vdots\; \mathbf{X}_1)\begin{pmatrix}\boldsymbol{\gamma}_1 \\ \hline \boldsymbol{\beta}_1\end{pmatrix} + \mathbf{v}_1 = \hat{\mathbf{Z}}_1\boldsymbol{\delta}_1 + \mathbf{v}_1. \qquad *(11.5.28)$$

In this notation the 2SLS estimator is

[12] While the estimates in the case of a just-identified equation are the same for both ILS and 2SLS, the 2SLS method also yields information on asymptotic standard errors, which is not available using ILS. See the next section for a discussion of these asymptotic standard errors. See, in particular, the estimator of the variance σ_1^2 in (11.6.35) and the asymptotic covariance matrix in (11.6.37).

$$\begin{pmatrix} \hat{\gamma}_1 \\ \hline \hat{\beta}_1 \end{pmatrix}_{2SLS} = \hat{\delta}_{1\,2SLS} = (\hat{Z}_1'\hat{Z}_1)^{-1}\hat{Z}_1'y_1 \qquad *(11.5.29)$$

where $\hat{Z}_1$ summarizes the data on estimated explanatory endogenous variables and included exogenous variables:

$$\underset{n\times(g_1-1+k_1)}{\hat{Z}_1} = (\underset{n\times(g_1-1)}{\hat{Y}_1} \;\vdots\; \underset{n\times k_1}{X_1}) \qquad *(11.5.30)$$

as in (11.3.2), but where Y_1 is replaced by $\hat{Y}_1$. From (11.5.28) and (11.5.29)

$$\hat{\delta}_{1\,2SLS} = \delta_1 + (\hat{Z}_1'\hat{Z}_1)^{-1}\hat{Z}_1'v_1. \qquad (11.5.31)$$

Taking expectations,

$$E(\hat{\delta}_{1\,2SLS}) = \delta_1 + E[(\hat{Z}_1'\hat{Z}_1)^{-1}\hat{Z}_1'v_1] \qquad (11.5.32)$$

where the second term in general does not vanish, given the definition of $\hat{Z}_1$ in (11.5.30) and the definition of v_1 in (11.5.16). Thus the 2SLS estimator is generally biased:

$$E(\hat{\delta}_{1\,2SLS}) \neq \delta_1. \qquad (11.5.33)$$

Returning to the proof of consistency, (11.5.31) can be written

$$\hat{\delta}_{1\,2SLS} = \delta_1 + \left(\frac{1}{n}\hat{Z}_1'\hat{Z}_1\right)^{-1}\left(\frac{1}{n}\hat{Z}_1'v_1\right) \qquad (11.5.34)$$

where the $1/n$ factors, as usual, ensure the meaningfulness of the elements of the matrices shown, each element of which is the sum of n terms. Assuming for the set of explanatory variables

$$\text{plim}\left(\frac{1}{n}\hat{Z}_1'\hat{Z}_1\right) = Q_1 \qquad (11.5.35)$$

where Q_1 is a nonsingular matrix, it follows that

$$\text{plim}\ \hat{\delta}_{1\,2SLS} = \delta_1 + Q_1^{-1}\ \text{plim}\left(\frac{1}{n}\hat{Z}_1'v_1\right). \qquad (11.5.36)$$

Thus the 2SLS estimator is consistent if

$$\text{plim}\left(\frac{1}{n}\hat{Z}_1'v_1\right) = \begin{pmatrix} \text{plim}\ \frac{1}{n}\hat{Y}_1'\varepsilon_1 \\ \text{plim}\ \frac{1}{n}X_1'\varepsilon_1 \end{pmatrix} = 0 \qquad (11.5.37)$$

where $\boldsymbol{\varepsilon}_1$ has replaced $\mathbf{v}_1$, since plim $[(1/n)\hat{\mathbf{Z}}_1'\hat{\mathbf{u}}_1] = \mathbf{0}$. The bottom expression vanishes since the $\mathbf{X}_1$ are exogenous and hence are uncorrelated with the stochastic disturbance terms in the probability limit. The top expression is, from (11.5.9),

$$\text{plim}\ \frac{1}{n}\ \hat{\mathbf{Y}}_1'\boldsymbol{\varepsilon}_1 = \text{plim}\ \frac{1}{n}\ (\hat{\boldsymbol{\Pi}}_1^{00\prime}\mathbf{X}_1' + \hat{\boldsymbol{\Pi}}_2^{00\prime}\mathbf{X}_2')\boldsymbol{\varepsilon}_1 = \mathbf{0} \qquad (11.5.38)$$

since both $\mathbf{X}_1$ and $\mathbf{X}_2$ are uncorrelated with $\boldsymbol{\varepsilon}_1$ in the probability limit. Thus 2SLS provides a consistent estimator:

$$\text{plim}\ \hat{\boldsymbol{\delta}}_{1\,2\text{SLS}} = \boldsymbol{\delta}_1. \qquad (11.5.39)$$

Another way of proving consistency of the 2SLS estimator is based on the *k*-class estimator to be introduced later in this section and the instrumental-variables interpretation of this estimator to be presented in the next section.

The 2SLS estimator, given by (11.5.2), (11.5.17), and (11.5.29), is thus a consistent estimator, which is defined for overidentified and just-identified equations and which reduces to the ILS estimator in the just-identified case. As already noted, the technique is called "two-stage least squares," since it uses two distinct least-squares sets of regressions. The first set of regressions, the *first stage*, is the estimation of the coefficients of the reduced form, as given in (11.5.4). These estimators summarize a set of *g* least-squares regressions, one for each of the reduced-form equations. In each such regression one of the endogenous variables is treated as the dependent variable, and all exogenous variables of the complete model are treated as the explanatory variables.[13] The second set of regressions, the *second stage*, also constitutes *g* least-squares regressions, each of which represents the estimation of the parameters of one of the structural equations. Each such equation is expressed in a form similar to that used in (11.5.15) for the first such equation, where $\hat{\mathbf{Y}}_1 = \mathbf{Y}_1 - \hat{\mathbf{u}}_1$ represents the estimated values of the explanatory endogenous variables, as obtained from the results

[13] In general, the estimation in the first stage is that of the *unrestricted* reduced form not taking explicit account of overidentifying restrictions, which restrict the reduced-form coefficients. In a large econometric model, however, it may be the case that the total number of exogenous variables in the system exceeds the total number of data points available, so that there are insufficient degrees of freedom to estimate the unrestricted first-stage reduced-form equations. In such a case there are several ways to redefine the first-stage equations to obtain a set of equations that can be estimated. One is to select only those exogenous variables that are most closely related to the endogenous variable in the equation, excluding from each equation those exogenous variables believed to be unimportant on the basis of a priori considerations. An example is the partitioning of the model into certain submodels, each involving a particular set of variables, where the only exogenous variables entering the reduced-form equation for any particular endogenous variable are those of the submodel in which the variable appears, as in the Brookings model. See Fisher (1965a) and Section 12.6. An alternative approach is to replace the set of all exogenous variables by the leading principal components of such variables, as discussed in Kloek and Mennes (1960), Amemiya (1966b), Dhrymes (1970), Malinvaud (1970), and Mitchell (1971). A third approach uses certain instrumental variables; see the references cited in footnotes 21 and 22. See also Klein (1973).

of the first stage. The result of this second-stage estimation is a set of estimated coefficients for each of the structural equations, the 2SLS estimators.

As noted for (11.5.17) the difference between the OLS estimator and the 2SLS estimator is the fact that in 2SLS the reduced-form residuals $\hat{\mathbf{u}}_1$, as defined in (11.5.13), are netted out from $\mathbf{Y}_1$ to determine $\hat{\mathbf{Y}}_1$. These residuals are zero if the reduced form is estimated exactly, so in this special case $\mathbf{Y}_1 = \hat{\mathbf{Y}}_1$ and the OLS and 2SLS estimates are identical. In this case the coefficient of determination R^2 for each of the relevant reduced-form equations (those for $\mathbf{Y}_1$) is unity. At the opposite extreme, if the values of R^2 for the relevant reduced-form equations are close to zero, then the data on the explanatory endogenous variables are replaced by what are essentially disturbance terms, so the 2SLS estimators are largely meaningless. Thus the method of two-stage least squares works poorly if the R^2 values in the first stage are "too small," i.e., close to zero, while it is only negligibly different from OLS if the R^2 values in the first stage are "too large," i.e., close to unity. It is only in the case of "intermediate" values of R^2 in the first stage that the 2SLS estimators make sense.[14]

The 2SLS estimator can be illustrated using the consumption function of the prototype macro model (11.1.22). In this overidentified equation there is one explanatory endogenous variable Y. The 2SLS estimators are obtained as the least-squares estimators of

$$C = \gamma_1 \hat{Y} + \beta_1 + v^C \tag{11.5.40}$$

where $\hat{Y}$ is the estimated value of Y. This estimated value is obtained by estimating the reduced-form equation for Y:

$$Y = \Pi_3 + \Pi_4 G + \Pi_5 Y_{-1} + u^Y \tag{11.5.41}$$

yielding $\hat{\Pi}_3$, $\hat{\Pi}_4$, and $\hat{\Pi}_5$, and determining $\hat{Y}_i$ as

$$\hat{Y}_i = \hat{\Pi}_3 + \hat{\Pi}_4 G_i + \hat{\Pi}_5 Y_{i-1} \tag{11.5.42}$$

The 2SLS estimators of (11.5.40) are then

[14] It is possible to define a coefficient of determination for the second stage of 2SLS as

$$R^2_{2SLS} = 1 - \frac{\hat{\boldsymbol{\varepsilon}}_1' \hat{\boldsymbol{\varepsilon}}_1}{\dot{\mathbf{y}}_1' \dot{\mathbf{y}}_1}$$

where $\dot{\mathbf{y}}_1$ represents deviations from mean values, $\hat{\boldsymbol{\varepsilon}}_1$ represents the residuals in the estimation of (11.5.15), given as

$$\hat{\boldsymbol{\varepsilon}}_1 = \mathbf{y}_1 - (\hat{\mathbf{Y}}_1 + \hat{\mathbf{u}}_1)\hat{\boldsymbol{\gamma}}_1 - \mathbf{X}_1 \hat{\boldsymbol{\beta}}_1 = \mathbf{y}_1 - \hat{\mathbf{y}}_1$$

and $\hat{\boldsymbol{\gamma}}_1$ and $\hat{\boldsymbol{\beta}}_1$ are the 2SLS estimators. The R^2_{2SLS} so defined cannot exceed unity, but it can be negative. It therefore does not have the usual interpretation of R^2 as the proportion of variance explained by the regression. See Problem 11-H.

$$\hat{\gamma}_{1\,2SLS} = \frac{\Sigma \dot{C}_i \dot{\hat{Y}}_i}{\Sigma \dot{\hat{Y}}_i^2} \tag{11.5.43}$$

$$\hat{\beta}_{1\,2SLS} = \overline{C} - \hat{\gamma}_1 \overline{\hat{Y}} \tag{11.5.44}$$

where $\overline{C}$ and $\overline{\hat{Y}}$ are mean values and $\dot{C}$ and $\dot{\hat{Y}}$ are deviations from these mean values.

For the variant consumption function the reduced form for Y is

$$Y = \Pi_3' + \Pi_4' G + u^{Y'} \tag{11.5.45}$$

as in (11.4.17), and the least-squares estimators of this equation are

$$\hat{\Pi}_4' = \frac{\Sigma \dot{Y}_i \dot{G}_i}{\Sigma \dot{G}_i^2} \tag{11.5.46}$$

$$\hat{\Pi}_3' = \overline{Y} - \hat{\Pi}_4' \overline{G} \tag{11.5.47}$$

where $\overline{Y}$ and $\overline{G}$ are mean values and $\dot{Y}_i$ and $\dot{G}_i$ are deviations from mean values. The 2SLS estimators are then given as in (11.5.43) and (11.5.44), where

$$\hat{Y}_i = \hat{\Pi}_3' + \hat{\Pi}_4' G_i. \tag{11.5.48}$$

Thus, $\dot{\hat{Y}}_i = \hat{\Pi}_4' \dot{G}_i$, implying that

$$\Sigma \dot{C}_i \dot{\hat{Y}}_i = \hat{\Pi}_4' \, \Sigma \dot{C}_i \dot{G}_i \tag{11.5.49}$$

$$\Sigma \dot{\hat{Y}}_i^2 = \hat{\Pi}_4'^2 \, \Sigma \dot{G}_i^2. \tag{11.5.50}$$

Then, from (11.5.43) and (11.5.46),

$$\hat{\gamma}'_{1\,2SLS} = \frac{1}{\hat{\Pi}_4'} \frac{\Sigma \dot{C}_i \dot{G}_i}{\Sigma \dot{G}_i^2} = \frac{\Sigma \dot{C}_i \dot{G}_i}{\Sigma \dot{Y}_i \dot{G}_i} \tag{11.5.51}$$

which is the same estimator as the ILS estimator in (11.4.27), as would be expected in this case of a just-identified equation.

A general class of limited-information estimators can be introduced as an extension of the two-stage least-squares estimator in (11.5.17). Letting k be a scalar parameter, which may be either a fixed number or a number determined by the sample, the *k-class estimator* of the structural parameters in the equation to be estimated is[15]

[15] See Theil (1961, 1971). Do not confuse the k here with the total number of exogenous variables in the system of structural equations.

$$\begin{pmatrix} \hat{\gamma}_1 \\ \hline \hat{\beta}_1 \end{pmatrix}_k = \left(\begin{array}{c|c} Y_1'Y_1 - k\hat{u}_1'\hat{u}_1 & Y_1'X_1 \\ \hline X_1'Y_1 & X_1'X_1 \end{array}\right)^{-1} \begin{pmatrix} Y_1' - k\hat{u}_1' \\ \hline X_1' \end{pmatrix} y_1 \qquad *(11.5.52)$$

where $\hat{\mathbf{u}}_1$ is the reduced-form residuals for $\mathbf{Y}_1$. This definition of an entire class of estimators may be motivated by an inspection of (11.5.17) and a comparison of this formulation of the 2SLS estimator with the OLS estimator in (11.3.5). The only differences between these estimators is the subtraction of $\hat{\mathbf{u}}_1'\hat{\mathbf{u}}_1$ in the upper left submatrix of the matrix to be inverted in (11.5.17) and the subtraction of $\hat{\mathbf{u}}_1$ in the upper submatrix of the second matrix on the right in (11.5.17). But the scalar k in the k-class estimator multiplies both of these terms. Thus if $k = 0$ the k-class estimator is the OLS estimator, while if $k = 1$ the k-class estimator is the 2SLS estimator. The k class interpolates between these by allowing k to be any scalar, and it extends the estimators to other possible k values that may not lie between 0 and 1.

A general result on k-class estimators states that if k satisfies

$$\text{plim}\,(k - 1) = 0 \qquad (11.5.53)$$

then the k-class estimator is consistent:[16]

$$\text{plim}\begin{pmatrix} \hat{\gamma}_1 \\ \hline \hat{\beta}_1 \end{pmatrix}_k = \begin{pmatrix} \gamma_1 \\ \hline \beta_1 \end{pmatrix}. \qquad (11.5.54)$$

The consistency result for 2SLS, in (11.5.39), is the special case for which $k = 1$.[17]

[16] See Problem 11-J for an approach to proving this result using the method of instrumental variables, to be introduced in the next section.

[17] Another estimator of the k class that is consistent since it satisfies (11.5.53) is the *limited-information maximum-likelihood (LIML) estimator*. This estimator is obtained by maximizing the likelihood function for an individual equation subject only to the a priori restrictions imposed on the equation, without requiring information as to the specification of other equations of the system (other than information on variables in the entire system but not in the particular equation being estimated). In this case $k = \hat{l}$, the smallest root of the polynomial equation

$$|\mathbf{R}_1 - l\mathbf{R}| = 0$$

where $\mathbf{R}_1$ and $\mathbf{R}$ are defined as

$$\mathbf{R}_1 = \begin{pmatrix} y_1' \\ \hline Y_1' \end{pmatrix} \mathbf{M}_1 (y_1 \mid Y_1)$$

$$\mathbf{R} = \begin{pmatrix} y_1' \\ \hline Y_1' \end{pmatrix} \mathbf{M} (y_1 \mid Y_1)$$

11.6 Instrumental variables

The method of instrumental variables (IV) is a general approach to estimating a single equation in a system of equations, and all of the estimators introduced so far can be interpreted as IV estimators for particular choices of instrumental variables.[18] Consider once again the first structural equation, which can be expressed

$$\mathbf{y}_1 = \mathbf{Z}_1\boldsymbol{\delta}_1 + \boldsymbol{\varepsilon}_1 = (\mathbf{Y}_1 \mid \mathbf{X}_1)\begin{pmatrix}\boldsymbol{\gamma}_1 \\ \hline \boldsymbol{\beta}_1\end{pmatrix} + \boldsymbol{\varepsilon}_1 \qquad *(11.6.1)$$

as in (11.3.1), where $\mathbf{Z}_1$ lumps together data on all included explanatory variables, whether endogenous or exogenous, and $\boldsymbol{\delta}_1$ summarizes all coefficients to be estimated:

$$\mathbf{Z}_1 = (\mathbf{Y}_1 \mid \mathbf{X}_1), \qquad \boldsymbol{\delta}_1 = \begin{pmatrix}\boldsymbol{\gamma}_1 \\ \hline \boldsymbol{\beta}_1\end{pmatrix} \qquad *(11.6.2)$$

A heuristic explanation of the OLS estimator, following the approach out-

---

and where $\mathbf{M}_1$ and $\mathbf{M}$ are the idempotent matrices

$$\mathbf{M}_1 = \mathbf{I} - \mathbf{X}_1(\mathbf{X}_1'\mathbf{X}_1)^{-1}\mathbf{X}_1'$$
$$\mathbf{M} = \mathbf{I} - \mathbf{X}(\mathbf{X}'\mathbf{X})^{-1}\mathbf{X}'$$

This technique, which is also called *least variance ratio (LVR)* and *limited-information single equation (LISE)*, is a limited-information technique that yields consistent estimators, since plim $(\hat{l} - 1) = 0$. The LIML technique can be used to estimate any just identified or over-identified equation, and, as in the case of 2SLS, it reduces to ILS in the just-identified case. One advantage of the LIML technique over 2SLS and other members of the k class is its invariance to the choice of normalization—that is, the choice of which included endogenous variable is to be the dependent variable. It is the only member of the k class with this property.

Assuming normally distributed stochastic terms, the LIML estimator is asymptotically normally distributed, and it has the same limiting distribution as 2SLS. It has the asymptotically efficient property of minimum variance in the class of all estimators with the same a priori information. (See also footnote 20.)

While LIML is of historical importance, having been used to estimate several major econometric models in the 1950's, it has not been used in recent work and thus is not stressed here. Other reasons for not stressing it here are the findings in studies of exact finite-sample distributions of estimators that LIML has no finite moments and the findings in Monte Carlo studies that the LIML as an estimator exhibits erratic and highly unstable behavior. For references to these studies see footnote 36. For a further discussion of LIML see Theil (1971).

[18] See Sargan (1958), Brundy and Jorgenson (1971, 1973, 1974), and Madansky (1976). See also the next section, e.g., equation (11.7.28), for the application of instrumental variables to the entire system of equations.

lined in Section 4.6 [in (4.6.20)-(4.6.22)], is based on premultiplying (11.6.1) by $\mathbf{Z}_1'$ to make the matrix multiplying $\boldsymbol{\delta}_1$ square, yielding

$$\mathbf{Z}_1'\mathbf{y}_1 = \mathbf{Z}_1'\mathbf{Z}_1\boldsymbol{\delta}_1 + \mathbf{Z}_1'\boldsymbol{\varepsilon}_1. \tag{11.6.3}$$

Dropping the term $\mathbf{Z}_1'\boldsymbol{\varepsilon}_1$ and solving the resulting "normal equations" yields the OLS estimator

$$\hat{\boldsymbol{\delta}}_{1\,\text{OLS}} = (\mathbf{Z}_1'\mathbf{Z}_1)^{-1}\mathbf{Z}_1'\mathbf{y}_1 \tag{11.6.4}$$

as in (11.3.4). In the single-equation context of Chapter 4 dropping the term corresponding to $\mathbf{Z}_1'\boldsymbol{\varepsilon}_1$ was justified because the explanatory variables were exogenous and hence uncorrelated with the stochastic disturbance term. In the simultaneous-equations context, however, dropping this term cannot be so justified, since the explanatory endogenous variables in $\mathbf{Z}_1$ are not statistically independent of $\boldsymbol{\varepsilon}_1$. They are correlated with the $\boldsymbol{\varepsilon}$'s, even in the probability limit.

Suppose, however, that there exists a set of $g_1 - 1 + k_1$ variables (the same number as in $\mathbf{Z}_1$) that are uncorrelated with $\boldsymbol{\varepsilon}_1$ but, at the same time, correlated with $\mathbf{Z}_1$. Such variables are *instrumental variables*, and data on them are summarized by the $n \times (g_1 - 1 + k_1)$ matrix $\mathbf{W}_1$, where the subscript again refers to the first equation. Then premultiplying (11.6.1) by $\mathbf{W}_1'$ yields

$$\mathbf{W}_1'\mathbf{y}_1 = \mathbf{W}_1'\mathbf{Z}_1\boldsymbol{\delta}_1 + \mathbf{W}_1'\boldsymbol{\varepsilon}_1. \tag{11.6.5}$$

Dropping $\mathbf{W}_1'\boldsymbol{\varepsilon}_1$, since the variables in $\mathbf{W}_1$ were assumed uncorrelated with $\boldsymbol{\varepsilon}_1$, and solving for $\boldsymbol{\delta}_1$ yields

$$\hat{\boldsymbol{\delta}}_{1\,\text{IV}} = \hat{\boldsymbol{\delta}}_1(\mathbf{W}_1) = (\mathbf{W}_1'\mathbf{Z}_1)^{-1}\mathbf{W}_1'\mathbf{y}_1. \tag*{*(11.6.6)}$$

This is the *instrumental-variables (IV) estimator*, which, as indicated by the functional relationship $\hat{\boldsymbol{\delta}}_1(\mathbf{W}_1)$, depends on the choice of instruments and the data on these instruments.

The IV estimator is extremely useful, since it represents a whole class of estimators, each defined by $\mathbf{W}_1$, the matrix of data on the instrumental variables. As already noted, all of the estimators introduced so far are members of this class and can be interpreted as IV estimators for particular choices of $\mathbf{W}_1$. For example, the OLS estimator is

$$\hat{\boldsymbol{\delta}}_{1\,\text{OLS}} = \hat{\boldsymbol{\delta}}_1(\mathbf{Z}_1) = (\mathbf{Z}_1'\mathbf{Z}_1)^{-1}\mathbf{Z}_1'\mathbf{y}_1 \tag*{*(11.6.7)}$$

where $\mathbf{Z}_1$ itself is used for data on the instrumental variables (although this choice of instrumental variables is not one that satisfies the assumption of independence of the stochastic disturbance term). The example given in (11.3.13) of the OLS estimator of the marginal propensity to consume for the prototype macro model consumption function is of this form. This estimator may be written

$$\hat{\gamma}_{1\,\mathrm{OLS}} = (\Sigma\, \dot{Y}_i^2)^{-1}\, \Sigma\, \dot{Y}_i \dot{C}_i \tag{11.6.8}$$

to emphasize that it is of same form as (11.6.7), where Y_i is the explanatory variable (comparable to $\mathbf{Z}_1$) and C_i is the dependent variable (comparable to $\mathbf{y}_1$). Other examples of estimators developed in previous sections will be similarly shown to be of the same form as the IV interpretation of the estimator.

In the case of a just-identified equation the number of instrumental variables $g_1 - 1 + k_1$ is equal to the number of exogenous variables in the system k. In this case all exogenous variables can be used as the instrumental variables, so $\mathbf{W}_1$ is simply $\mathbf{X}$, and the indirect least-squares estimator can be written

$$\hat{\boldsymbol{\delta}}_{1\,\mathrm{ILS}} = \hat{\boldsymbol{\delta}}_1(\mathbf{X}) = (\mathbf{X}'\mathbf{Z}_1)^{-1}\mathbf{X}'\mathbf{y}_1. \tag*{*(11.6.9)}$$

The example given in (11.4.29) of the ILS estimator of the marginal propensity to consume for the variant consumption function is of this form. This estimator may be written

$$\hat{\gamma}'_{1\,\mathrm{ILS}} = (\Sigma\, \dot{G}_i \dot{Y}_i)^{-1}\, \Sigma\, \dot{G}_i \dot{C}_i \tag{11.6.10}$$

to emphasize that it is of the same form as (11.6.9), where G_i is the exogenous variable (comparable to $\mathbf{X}$), Y_i is again the explanatory endogenous variable (comparable to $\mathbf{Z}_1$), and C_i is again the dependent variable (comparable to $\mathbf{y}_1$).

The OLS and ILS estimators have thus been expressed as IV estimators. The 2SLS estimator can also be so expressed as an IV estimator. To understand the IV formulation of 2SLS note first that the only variables that must be treated via appropriate instrumental variables are the explanatory endogenous variable $\mathbf{Y}_1$ since the included exogenous variables $\mathbf{X}_1$ can be used as their own instrumental variables. In the 2SLS approach the explanatory endogenous variables are replaced by their estimated values $\hat{\mathbf{Y}}_1$, which can serve as instrumental variables. The choice of instrumental variables for 2SLS is thus given by $(\hat{\mathbf{Y}}_1 \mid \mathbf{X}_1)$, consisting of the estimated values of the $g_1 - 1$ explanatory endogenous variables and the actual values of the k_1 included exogenous variables. This choice of instrumental variables, from (11.5.30), can be written

$$\mathbf{W}_{1\,\mathrm{2SLS}} = (\hat{\mathbf{Y}}_1 \mid \mathbf{X}_1) = \hat{\mathbf{Z}}_1. \tag*{*(11.6.11)}$$

Thus the 2SLS estimator can be written as the IV estimator

$$\hat{\boldsymbol{\delta}}_{1\,\mathrm{2SLS}} = \hat{\boldsymbol{\delta}}_1(\hat{\mathbf{Z}}_1) = (\hat{\mathbf{Z}}_1'\mathbf{Z}_1)^{-1}\hat{\mathbf{Z}}_1'\mathbf{y}_1. \tag*{*(11.6.12)}$$

By (11.5.18) and (11.5.19), however,

$$\hat{\mathbf{Z}}_1'\mathbf{Z}_1 = \hat{\mathbf{Z}}_1'\hat{\mathbf{Z}}_1 \tag{11.6.13}$$

leading to the 2SLS estimator as presented previously in (11.5.29):

$$\hat{\delta}_{1\,2SLS} = (\hat{Z}_1'\hat{Z}_1)^{-1}\hat{Z}_1'y_1. \tag*{*(11.6.14)}$$

The example given in (11.5.43) of the 2SLS estimator of the marginal propensity to consume for the prototype macro model consumption function is of this form. This estimator may be written

$$\hat{\gamma}_{1\,2SLS} = (\Sigma\,\dot{\hat{Y}}_i^2)^{-1}\,\Sigma\,\dot{\hat{Y}}_i\dot{C}_i \tag{11.6.15}$$

to emphasize that it is of the same form as (11.6.14), where $\hat{Y}_i$ is the estimated explanatory endogenous variable (comparable to $\hat{Z}_1$) and C_i is again the dependent variable (comparable to y_1).

It will prove useful to develop yet another formulation of the 2SLS estimator using the IV approach. To derive this formulation note that

$$\hat{Y}_1 = X(X'X)^{-1}X'Y_1 \tag{11.6.16}$$

as previously shown in (11.5.11), and that

$$X_1 = X(X'X)^{-1}X'X_1 \tag{11.6.17}$$

which follows from

$$(X_1 \mid X_2) = X = X(X'X)^{-1}X'X = X(X'X)^{-1}X'(X_1 \mid X_2) \tag{11.6.18}$$

by dropping X_2 from the first and last expressions. The equalities in (11.6.16) and (11.6.17) can be combined as

$$W_{1\,2SLS} = \hat{Z}_1 = (\hat{Y}_1 \mid X_1) = X(X'X)^{-1}X'(Y_1 \mid X_1) = X(X'X)^{-1}X'Z_1 \tag{11.6.19}$$

which is the matrix of estimated values obtained from a regression of all explanatory variables Z_1 on all exogenous variables X. This is the instrumental-variables data matrix used in 2SLS. Thus the 2SLS estimator can be written

$$\hat{\delta}_{1\,2SLS} = \hat{\delta}_1(X(X'X)^{-1}X'Z_1) = [Z_1'X(X'X)^{-1}X'Z_1]^{-1}Z_1'X(X'X)^{-1}X'y_1 \tag*{*(11.6.20)}$$

where X consists of data on all exogenous variables and Z_1 consists of data on all explanatory variables, both endogenous and exogenous, in the equation. Thus this formulation of the 2SLS estimator involves only actual data matrices.

The 2SLS estimator in (11.6.20) can also be interpreted as the estimator obtained if all exogenous variables are used as instrumental variables, as in the ILS estimator of (11.6.9), but the GLS estimator of (6.5.8) is employed. Thus, premultiplying (11.6.1) by X',

$$X'y_1 = X'Z_1\delta_1 + X'\varepsilon_1 \tag*{*(11.6.21)}$$

where

$$\text{Cov}(\mathbf{X}'\boldsymbol{\varepsilon}_1) = E(\mathbf{X}'\boldsymbol{\varepsilon}_1\boldsymbol{\varepsilon}_1'\mathbf{X}) = \sigma_1^2(\mathbf{X}'\mathbf{X}). \qquad *(11.6.22)$$

Using the inverse of this covariance matrix for the GLS estimator,

$$\hat{\boldsymbol{\delta}}_{1\,2SLS} = [\mathbf{Z}_1'\mathbf{X}(\mathbf{X}'\mathbf{X})^{-1}\mathbf{X}'\mathbf{Z}_1]^{-1}\mathbf{Z}_1'\mathbf{X}(\mathbf{X}'\mathbf{X})^{-1}\mathbf{X}'\mathbf{y}_1 \qquad *(11.6.23)$$

which is precisely the 2SLS estimator in (11.6.20). Thus the 2SLS estimator has the additional interpretation as the GLS estimator of the equation after having used all exogenous variables as instrumental variables. This interpretation will be important in the next section, since the three-stage least-squares estimator uses a similar approach–applying GLS after having used all exogenous variables as instrumental variables–but where the system as a whole, rather than only one equation of the system, is estimated.

To complete this summary of IV interpretations of various estimators, consider the k-class estimator of (11.5.52). This estimator is an IV estimator for which the data on the instruments are given by

$$\mathbf{W}_1 = (\mathbf{Y}_1 - k\hat{\mathbf{u}}_1 \mid \mathbf{X}_1). \qquad (11.6.24)$$

Here the instrumental variables for the explanatory endogenous variables are their measured values less k times the reduced-form residuals for these variables, as in (11.5.52), while the included exogenous variables serve as their own instrumental variables. Thus the k-class estimator is

$$\hat{\boldsymbol{\delta}}_{1k} = \hat{\boldsymbol{\delta}}_1(\mathbf{Y}_1 - k\hat{\mathbf{u}}_1 \mid \mathbf{X}_1) = \left[\begin{pmatrix}\mathbf{Y}_1' - k\hat{\mathbf{u}}_1' \\ \hline \mathbf{X}_1'\end{pmatrix}(\mathbf{Y}_1 \mid \mathbf{X}_1)\right]^{-1} \begin{pmatrix}\mathbf{Y}_1' - k\hat{\mathbf{u}}_1' \\ \hline \mathbf{X}_1'\end{pmatrix}\mathbf{y}_1. \qquad *(11.6.25)$$

As noted in the last section, this estimator reduces to OLS if $k = 0$, in which case $\mathbf{W}_1 = \mathbf{Z}_1$, as in (11.6.7). It reduces to 2SLS if $k = 1$, in which case $\mathbf{W}_1 = \hat{\mathbf{Z}}_1 = (\hat{\mathbf{Y}}_1 \mid \mathbf{X}_1)$, as in (11.6.11).

The instrumental-variable estimator is a consistent estimator under certain conditions. The general IV estimator of (11.6.6) can be combined with the first equation (11.6.1) to yield

$$\begin{aligned}\hat{\boldsymbol{\delta}}_{1\,IV} &= (\mathbf{W}_1'\mathbf{Z}_1)^{-1}\mathbf{W}_1'\mathbf{y}_1 = (\mathbf{W}_1'\mathbf{Z}_1)^{-1}\mathbf{W}_1'(\mathbf{Z}_1\boldsymbol{\delta}_1 + \boldsymbol{\varepsilon}_1) \\ &= \boldsymbol{\delta}_1 + (\mathbf{W}_1'\mathbf{Z}_1)^{-1}\mathbf{W}_1'\boldsymbol{\varepsilon}_1\end{aligned} \qquad (11.6.26)$$

so that

$$\text{plim}\,\hat{\boldsymbol{\delta}}_{1\,IV} = \boldsymbol{\delta}_1 + \text{plim}\left(\frac{1}{n}\mathbf{W}_1'\mathbf{Z}_1\right)^{-1}\text{plim}\left(\frac{1}{n}\mathbf{W}_1'\boldsymbol{\varepsilon}_1\right). \qquad *(11.6.27)$$

Assume that the instrumental variables are asymptotically uncorrelated with the stochastic disturbance terms, so

$$\operatorname{plim}\left(\frac{1}{n}\mathbf{W}_1'\boldsymbol{\varepsilon}_1\right) = \mathbf{0} \qquad \text{*(11.6.28)}$$

and that they are asymptotically correlated with the $\mathbf{Z}_1$'s so

$$\operatorname{plim}\left(\frac{1}{n}\mathbf{W}_1'\mathbf{Z}_1\right) = \mathbf{Q}_1 \qquad \text{*(11.6.29)}$$

where $\mathbf{Q}_1$ exists and is nonsingular. Under these two assumptions on $\mathbf{W}_1$, from (11.6.27) it follows that $\hat{\boldsymbol{\delta}}_{1\,\text{IV}}$ is a consistent estimator:

$$\operatorname{plim}\hat{\boldsymbol{\delta}}_{1\,\text{IV}} = \boldsymbol{\delta}_1 . \qquad \text{*(11.6.30)}$$

Thus if a set of instruments were available that satisfied these two assumptions, it would yield a consistent estimator. Of the specific estimators introduced thus far the OLS estimator is not consistent, because it fails to satisfy (11.6.28), while the 2SLS estimator is consistent, since both conditions are satisfied. The k-class estimator is consistent if condition (11.5.53) is met.

The asymptotic covariance matrix is defined for an estimator $\hat{\boldsymbol{\delta}}_1$ as

$$\begin{aligned}\lim \operatorname{Cov}(\hat{\boldsymbol{\delta}}_1) &= \frac{1}{n}\operatorname{plim}\,[n(\hat{\boldsymbol{\delta}}_1 - \boldsymbol{\delta}_1)(\hat{\boldsymbol{\delta}}_1 - \boldsymbol{\delta}_1)'] \\ &= \frac{1}{n}\operatorname{plim}\left\{[\sqrt{n}\,(\hat{\boldsymbol{\delta}}_1 - \boldsymbol{\delta}_1)]\,[\sqrt{n}\,(\hat{\boldsymbol{\delta}}_1 - \boldsymbol{\delta}_1)']\right\}\end{aligned} \qquad \text{*(11.6.31)}$$

that is, as $1/n$ times the limiting covariance matrix of $\sqrt{n}\,(\hat{\boldsymbol{\delta}}_1 - \boldsymbol{\delta}_1)$. For the IV estimator, using (11.6.26), this definition implies that

$$\lim \operatorname{Cov}(\hat{\boldsymbol{\delta}}_{1\,\text{IV}}) = \frac{1}{n}\operatorname{plim}\left[\left(\frac{1}{n}\mathbf{W}_1'\mathbf{Z}_1\right)^{-1}\left(\frac{1}{n}\mathbf{W}_1'\boldsymbol{\varepsilon}_1\,\boldsymbol{\varepsilon}_1'\mathbf{W}_1\right)\left(\frac{1}{n}\mathbf{Z}_1'\mathbf{W}_1\right)^{-1}\right] \qquad \text{*(11.6.32)}$$

or, since

$$E(\boldsymbol{\varepsilon}_1\boldsymbol{\varepsilon}_1') = \sigma_{11}\mathbf{I} = \sigma_1^2\mathbf{I} \qquad \text{*(11.6.33)}$$

$$\lim \operatorname{Cov}(\hat{\boldsymbol{\delta}}_{1\,\text{IV}}) = \frac{1}{n}\sigma_1^2\operatorname{plim}\left[\left(\frac{1}{n}\mathbf{W}_1'\mathbf{Z}_1\right)^{-1}\left(\frac{1}{n}\mathbf{W}_1'\mathbf{W}_1\right)\left(\frac{1}{n}\mathbf{Z}_1'\mathbf{W}_1\right)^{-1}\right]. \qquad \text{*(11.6.34)}$$

The variance of the first equation, σ_1^2, can be estimated as

$$\hat{\sigma}_1^2 = \frac{1}{n}\hat{\boldsymbol{\varepsilon}}_1'\hat{\boldsymbol{\varepsilon}}_1 = \frac{1}{n}(\mathbf{y}_1 - \mathbf{Z}_1\hat{\boldsymbol{\delta}}_1)'(\mathbf{y}_1 - \mathbf{Z}_1\hat{\boldsymbol{\delta}}_1) \qquad *(11.6.35)$$

where $\hat{\boldsymbol{\delta}}_1$ is the IV estimator and $\hat{\boldsymbol{\varepsilon}}_1$ is the vector of residuals in the estimation of the first equation when using this estimator.[19] Using these results, the asymptotic covariance matrix for the 2SLS estimator is given as

$$\lim \text{Cov}\,(\hat{\boldsymbol{\delta}}_{1\,2\text{SLS}}) = \frac{1}{n}\sigma_1^2 \operatorname{plim}\left(\frac{1}{n}\hat{\mathbf{Z}}_1'\hat{\mathbf{Z}}_1\right)^{-1} = \frac{1}{n}\sigma_1^2 \operatorname{plim}\left[\frac{1}{n}\begin{pmatrix}\hat{\mathbf{Y}}_1'\mathbf{Y}_1 & \mathbf{Y}_1'\mathbf{X}_1 \\ \mathbf{X}_1'\mathbf{Y}_1 & \mathbf{X}_1'\mathbf{X}_1\end{pmatrix}\right]^{-1} \qquad *(11.6.36)$$

or using (11.6.19), as[20]

$$\lim \text{Cov}\,(\hat{\boldsymbol{\delta}}_{1\,2\text{SLS}}) = \frac{1}{n}\sigma_1^2 \operatorname{plim}\left[\left(\frac{1}{n}\mathbf{Z}_1'\mathbf{X}\right)\left(\frac{1}{n}\mathbf{X}'\mathbf{X}\right)^{-1}\left(\frac{1}{n}\mathbf{X}'\mathbf{Z}_1\right)\right]^{-1}. \qquad *(11.6.37)$$

The variance σ_1^2 can be consistently estimated as $\hat{\sigma}_1^2$ in (11.6.35), using the 2SLS estimator for $\hat{\boldsymbol{\delta}}_1$. The resulting consistent estimator of the asymptotic covariance matrix can be used to construct asymptotic tests of hypotheses and interval estimates for structural parameters, as in Chapter 5. For example, asymptotic standard errors, given as the square roots of the diagonal elements of the asymptotic covariance matrix, can be used to construct asymptotic *t*-tests of statistical significance. While these tests apply only asymptotically, finite-sample approximations are frequently used in applications of the 2SLS approach for given n, $\mathbf{Z}_1$, and $\mathbf{X}$ in (11.6.37) and with σ_1^2 estimated by $\hat{\sigma}_1^2$ in (11.6.35) using the 2SLS estimator for $\hat{\boldsymbol{\delta}}_1$. This practice is supported by the results of Monte Carlo studies, as discussed in Section 11.9.

[19] Note that no correction is made for degrees of freedom (which would change the denominator to $n - g_1 + 1 - k_1$), since this estimator is primarily relevant only asymptotically, as $n \to \infty$.

[20] The 2SLS estimator is asymptotically efficient within the class of all estimators that use the same a priori restrictions for a single equation, but, as discussed in the next section, it is not asymptotically efficient relative to the full-information technique of three-stage least squares. [See (11.7.27) and footnote 30.] The asymptotic efficiency of 2SLS is based upon the fact that, assuming the stochastic disturbance terms at each observation are independently and identically (but not necessarily normally) distributed, the 2SLS estimators are asymptotically normally distributed [that is, the estimator $\sqrt{n}(\hat{\boldsymbol{\delta}}_{1\,2\text{SLS}} - \boldsymbol{\delta}_1)$ is asymptotically normal] with mean given by the true vector of parameters and with an asymptotic covariance matrix given by (11.6.37). See Malinvaud (1970) and Theil (1971). The asymptotic covariance matrix of (11.6.37) is also that of the *k*-class estimator if

$$\operatorname{plim} \sqrt{n}(k - 1) = 0.$$

For example, it is the asymptotic covariance matrix for the LIML estimator discussed in footnote 17.

The major problem in using the instrumental-variables technique is simply that of obtaining a suitable set of instrumental variables that are both sufficiently uncorrelated with the stochastic disturbance terms and sufficiently correlated with the relevant explanatory variables. Furthermore, when there is choice of such instrumental variables, the estimates are usually very sensitive to the particular instrumental variables chosen, leading to a genuine problem of choice of such variables.[21]

It might be noted that while the estimators defined thus far can be applied to simultaneous-equations models with lagged endogenous variables, they generally fail to satisfy any desired properties in such a case. They will certainly fail to satisfy these properties if the stochastic disturbance terms exhibit serial correlation. In that case past disturbances, which influence the lagged endogenous variables, also influence current disturbances, so the lagged endogenous variables will be correlated with current endogenous variables, leading to biased and inconsistent estimators.

Several techniques have been proposed for such a case, one of which is the technique of *iterative instrumental variables* (IIV).[22] This technique starts with the predicted values from the least-squares estimates of the restricted reduced form, i.e., the reduced form taking account of all overidentifying restrictions, which impose restrictions on reduced-form parameters. These predicted values are then used as instruments for the estimation of the structural form, and the process iterates, such that at each stage of the estimation instrumental variables calculated from the restricted reduced form of the previous stage are used to estimate the structural parameters. This process continues until convergence is achieved—that is, until parameter estimates cease to vary significantly upon iteration.

11.7 Three-stage least squares

The estimators introduced thus far have all been estimators of a single equation from a system of simultaneous equations. By contrast the technique of three-stage least squares (3SLS) and that of full-information maximum likelihood (FIML), to be presented in the next section, are full-information estimation techniques, which estimate all parameters of the structural equations simultaneously.[23] As its name implies, 3SLS can be considered an extension of 2SLS. In fact, the first two of the three stages of 3SLS are those of 2SLS, the first stage being the estimation of all reduced-form coefficients using the least-squares estimator, the second stage the estimation of all structural coefficients

[21] For discussions of the choice of instrumental variables see Fisher (1965b), Mitchell and Fisher (1970), Mitchell (1971), and Brundy and Jorgenson (1971, 1973, 1974).

[22] See Lyttkens (1970), Dutta and Lyttkens (1974), and Brundy and Jorgenson (1971, 1973, 1974). For other approaches to estimating a system with lagged endogenous variables and serial correlation see Sargan (1961), Amemiya (1966a), Fair (1970, 1972), Dhrymes and Erlat (1974), Dhyrmes, Berner, and Cummins (1974), and Hatanaka (1976).

[23] The 3SLS estimator was developed by Zellner and Theil (1962). See also Sargan (1964), Theil (1971), and Madansky (1976).

by applying 2SLS to each of the structural equations. The third stage is then the generalized least-squares estimation of all of the structural coefficients of the system, using a covariance matrix for the stochastic disturbance terms of the structural equations that is estimated from the second-stage residuals. Using the information contained in this covariance matrix has the effect of improving efficiency. In fact, in terms of properties of estimators, the 3SLS technique is an improvement over 2SLS, since, while both are consistent, 3SLS is asymptotically more efficient than 2SLS. Thus the basic rationale for 3SLS, as opposed to 2SLS, is its use of information on the correlation of the stochastic disturbance terms of the structural equations in order to improve asymptotic efficiency.

The 3SLS technique can be viewed as an extension of the GLS approach of Section 6.5 to the estimation of a system of simultaneous equations. It can also, however, be viewed as an extension of the method of "seemingly unrelated equations," also presented in Section 6.5, to a system of equations in which explanatory endogenous variables are present in some or all of the equations.[24] If there are no explanatory endogenous variables in the system (e.g., if $\mathbf{\Gamma}$ is diagonal), then 3SLS reduces to "seemingly unrelated equations," while if $g = 1$ it reduces to GLS.

In order to develop the 3SLS estimator it is convenient to use the star notation, as in Section 6.5. The hth equation of the system, which contains g_h endogenous and k_h exogenous variables, can be written as in (11.1.21):

$$\underset{n\times 1}{\mathbf{y}_h} = \left(\underset{n\times(g_h-1)}{\mathbf{Y}_h} \;\middle|\; \underset{n\times k_h}{\mathbf{X}_h}\right)\begin{pmatrix}\boldsymbol{\gamma}_h\\ \hline \boldsymbol{\beta}_h\end{pmatrix} + \underset{n\times 1}{\boldsymbol{\varepsilon}_h} \qquad *(11.7.1)$$

$$= \underset{n\times(g_h-1+k_h)}{\mathbf{Z}_h}\;\underset{(g_h-1+k_h)\times 1}{\boldsymbol{\delta}_h} + \boldsymbol{\varepsilon}_h, \qquad h = 1, 2, \ldots, g$$

where $\boldsymbol{\delta}_h$ summarizes all the coefficients to be estimated in the equation. It will be assumed that all identities have been eliminated and that all equations are either just identified or overidentified. The star notation basically involves "stacking" the vectors, so that a series of column vectors is written as one "stacked" column vector. The g vectors of dependent endogenous variables and

[24] The following table indicates the relations between 3SLS, 2SLS, and "seemingly unrelated equations."

	No explanatory endogenous variables	*Explanatory endogenous variables*
Estimate a single equation from a system of equations	Estimation of a reduced-form equation using least squares (Section 4.6)	2SLS and k-class estimators (Section 11.5)
Estimate all equations of a system simultaneously	"Seemingly unrelated equations" (Section 6.5)	3SLS (Section 11.7)

stochastic disturbance terms are stacked to form the column vectors of *gn* elements:

$$\underset{gn\times 1}{\mathbf{y}^*} = \begin{pmatrix} \mathbf{y}_1 \\ \hline \mathbf{y}_2 \\ \hline \vdots \\ \hline \mathbf{y}_g \end{pmatrix}, \qquad \underset{gn\times 1}{\boldsymbol{\varepsilon}^*} = \begin{pmatrix} \boldsymbol{\varepsilon}_1 \\ \hline \boldsymbol{\varepsilon}_2 \\ \hline \vdots \\ \hline \boldsymbol{\varepsilon}_g \end{pmatrix} \qquad *(11.7.2)$$

the star serving as a reminder that these are the stacked vectors. Similarly the g vectors of coefficients are stacked to form the column vector of k^* coefficients:

$$\underset{k^*\times 1}{\boldsymbol{\delta}^*} = \begin{pmatrix} \boldsymbol{\delta}_1 \\ \hline \boldsymbol{\delta}_2 \\ \hline \vdots \\ \hline \boldsymbol{\delta}_g \end{pmatrix} \qquad *(11.7.3)$$

where k^* is the total number of coefficients to be estimated, given as

$$k^* = \sum_{h=1}^{g} (g_h - 1 + k_h) \qquad *(11.7.4)$$

The vector $\boldsymbol{\delta}^*$ thus contains all coefficients to be estimated. The matrices of explanatory variables are summarized in the star notation by the single matrix

$$\mathbf{Z}^* = \left(\begin{array}{c|c|c|c} \mathbf{Z}_1 & \mathbf{0} & \cdots & \mathbf{0} \\ \hline \mathbf{0} & \mathbf{Z}_2 & \cdots & \mathbf{0} \\ \hline \vdots & \vdots & & \\ \hline \mathbf{0} & \mathbf{0} & \cdots & \mathbf{Z}_g \end{array}\right) \qquad *(11.7.5)$$

$$= \left(\begin{array}{c|c|c|c|c|c} \mathbf{Y}_1 & \mathbf{X}_1 & \multicolumn{2}{c|}{\mathbf{0}} & \cdots & \mathbf{0} \\ \hline \multicolumn{2}{c|}{\mathbf{0}} & \mathbf{Y}_2 & \mathbf{X}_2 & \cdots & \mathbf{0} \\ \hline \multicolumn{2}{c|}{\vdots} & \multicolumn{2}{c|}{\vdots} & & \vdots \\ \hline \multicolumn{2}{c|}{\mathbf{0}} & \multicolumn{2}{c|}{\mathbf{0}} & \cdots & \mathbf{Y}_g \quad \mathbf{X}_g \end{array}\right)$$

in which each matrix along the "principal diagonal" of matrices contains all data on explanatory variables in one equation. In this star notation all g equations of the system can be written

$$\underset{gn \times 1}{\mathbf{y}^*} = \underset{gn \times k^*}{\mathbf{Z}^*} \underset{k^* \times 1}{\boldsymbol{\delta}^*} + \underset{gn \times 1}{\boldsymbol{\varepsilon}^*} \qquad *(11.7.6)$$

and the problem of estimation is that of estimating $\boldsymbol{\delta}^*$ given the data summarized by $\mathbf{y}^*$ and $\mathbf{Z}^*$.

In the single-equation case the assumptions on the stochastic disturbance terms in (4.5.1) were conveniently represented by a matrix equation in (4.6.3). The same is true here, and the star notation facilitates the statement of the assumptions on the stochastic disturbance terms for the simultaneous-equations system. Thus the disturbance assumption (11.1.2) can be written

$$E(\boldsymbol{\varepsilon}^*) = \mathbf{0} \qquad *(11.7.7)$$

which can be considered the generalization of (4.6.4) to the case of simultaneous-equations systems. The homoskedasticity assumption (11.1.3) and the absence of serial correlation assumption (11.1.4) can be written

$$\text{Cov}(\boldsymbol{\varepsilon}^*) = E(\boldsymbol{\varepsilon}^*\boldsymbol{\varepsilon}^{*\prime}) = \begin{pmatrix} \sigma_{11}\mathbf{I} & \sigma_{12}\mathbf{I} & \cdots & \sigma_{1g}\mathbf{I} \\ \sigma_{21}\mathbf{I} & \sigma_{22}\mathbf{I} & \cdots & \sigma_{2g}\mathbf{I} \\ \vdots & & & \\ \sigma_{g1}\mathbf{I} & \sigma_{g2}\mathbf{I} & \cdots & \sigma_{gg}\mathbf{I} \end{pmatrix} = \boldsymbol{\Sigma} \otimes \mathbf{I} \qquad *(11.7.8)$$

where $\boldsymbol{\Sigma} \otimes \mathbf{I}$ is the Kronecker product of these matrices.[25] This is the generalization of (4.6.6) to the case of simultaneous equations. In this expression the covariance matrix has been partitioned into blocks, where each block is an element of the $\boldsymbol{\Sigma}$ matrix times the $n \times n$ identity matrix. In the case of a single equation ($g = 1$) the Kronecker product reduces to $\sigma^2\mathbf{I}$, which is the covariance matrix in this case, as in (4.6.6). Each block is a diagonal matrix, reflecting the independence among noncontemporaneous disturbances. The contemporaneous disturbances can, however, be correlated, as reflected in the elements of $\boldsymbol{\Sigma}$. For example, the matrix $\sigma_{11}\mathbf{I}$ represents the covariance matrix for the first equation. The equal diagonal elements of this block represent the constant variance of the stochastic disturbance terms of the first equation at each observation, while the zero off-diagonal elements of this block represent the assumption of absence of correlation between the disturbance terms of the first equation at different observations. The matrix $\sigma_{12}\mathbf{I}$, referring to the first and second equations, is also a diagonal matrix, where the equal diagonal elements represent the assumption of constant covariance at corresponding observations for the first and second equations, and where the zero off-diagonal elements indicate the assumption that the stochastic disturbance terms of the first and second equations are uncorrelated at different observations.

The star notation can be used to state some of the estimators previously introduced. For example, the OLS estimator is readily expressed in this notation as

[25] For a definition of the Kronecker product of matrices and a summary of its properties see (B.3.19) in Appendix B.

$$\hat{\boldsymbol{\delta}}^*_{\text{OLS}} = (\mathbf{Z}^{*\prime}\mathbf{Z}^*)^{-1}\mathbf{Z}^{*\prime}\mathbf{y}^* \qquad *(11.7.9)$$

This estimator summarizes the OLS estimator of each equation, of the form

$$\hat{\boldsymbol{\delta}}_{h_{\text{OLS}}} = (\mathbf{Z}_h'\mathbf{Z}_h)^{-1}\mathbf{Z}_h'\mathbf{y}_h, \quad h = 1, 2, \ldots, g \qquad (11.7.10)$$

in the star notation.

The 2SLS estimator can be expressed using the star notation as

$$\hat{\boldsymbol{\delta}}^*_{\text{2SLS}} = (\hat{\mathbf{Z}}^{*\prime}\hat{\mathbf{Z}}^*)^{-1}\hat{\mathbf{Z}}^{*\prime}\mathbf{y}^* \qquad *(11.7.11)$$

—that is, as the same estimator as OLS except for the replacement of explanatory variables by their estimated values. Here $\hat{\mathbf{Z}}^*$ is

$$\hat{\mathbf{Z}}^* = \begin{pmatrix} \hat{\mathbf{Y}}_1 \;\; \mathbf{X}_1 & \mathbf{0} & \cdots & \mathbf{0} \\ \mathbf{0} & \hat{\mathbf{Y}}_2 \;\; \mathbf{X}_2 & \cdots & \mathbf{0} \\ \vdots & \vdots & & \vdots \\ \mathbf{0} & \mathbf{0} & \cdots & \hat{\mathbf{Y}}_g \;\; \mathbf{X}_g \end{pmatrix}$$

$$= \begin{pmatrix} \hat{\mathbf{Z}}_1 & \mathbf{0} & \cdots & \mathbf{0} \\ \mathbf{0} & \hat{\mathbf{Z}}_2 & \cdots & \mathbf{0} \\ \vdots & \vdots & & \vdots \\ \mathbf{0} & \mathbf{0} & \cdots & \hat{\mathbf{Z}}_g \end{pmatrix} \qquad *(11.7.12)$$

representing the estimated values of all explanatory endogenous variables and the actual values of all exogenous variables in each of the equations of the model. Using (11.6.19), however,

$$\hat{\mathbf{Z}}^* = \mathbf{X}^*(\mathbf{X}^{*\prime}\mathbf{X}^*)^{-1}\mathbf{X}^{*\prime}\mathbf{Z}^* \qquad (11.7.13)$$

where $\mathbf{X}^*$ is defined as

$$\underset{gn\times gk}{\mathbf{X}^*} = \begin{pmatrix} \mathbf{X} & \mathbf{0} & \cdots & \mathbf{0} \\ \mathbf{0} & \mathbf{X} & \cdots & \mathbf{0} \\ \vdots & \vdots & & \vdots \\ \mathbf{0} & \mathbf{0} & & \mathbf{X} \end{pmatrix} = \underset{g\times g}{\mathbf{I}} \otimes \underset{n\times k}{\mathbf{X}}. \qquad (11.7.14)$$

Thus the 2SLS estimator can be expressed as

$$\hat{\boldsymbol{\delta}}^*_{\text{2SLS}} = [\mathbf{Z}^{*\prime}\mathbf{X}^*(\mathbf{X}^{*\prime}\mathbf{X}^*)^{-1}\mathbf{X}^{*\prime}\mathbf{Z}^*]^{-1}\mathbf{Z}^{*\prime}\mathbf{X}^*(\mathbf{X}^{*\prime}\mathbf{X}^*)^{-1}\mathbf{X}^{*\prime}\mathbf{y}^*. \qquad *(11.7.15)$$

This estimator is of exactly the same form as (11.6.23) except for the use of starred variables. The 2SLS estimator can also be written, using the properties of the Kronecker product, as[26]

$$\hat{\boldsymbol{\delta}}^*_{2SLS} = \{\mathbf{Z}^{*\prime}[\mathbf{I} \otimes \mathbf{X}(\mathbf{X}'\mathbf{X})^{-1}\mathbf{X}']\mathbf{Z}^*\}^{-1}\mathbf{Z}^{*\prime}[\mathbf{I} \otimes \mathbf{X}(\mathbf{X}'\mathbf{X})^{-1}\mathbf{X}']\mathbf{y}^*. \quad *(11.7.16)$$

The problem with the 2SLS estimator of the system, as given in (11.7.11), (11.7.15), and (11.7.16), is the same as that encountered in OLS for one equation of the system, namely the correlation between explanatory variables, specifically the explanatory endogenous variables in $\mathbf{Z}^*$ [shown explicitly as $\mathbf{Y}_1, \mathbf{Y}_2, \ldots, \mathbf{Y}_g$ in (11.7.5)], and the stochastic disturbance term $\boldsymbol{\varepsilon}^*$. The OLS estimator in (11.7.9) takes no account of the distinction between explanatory endogenous and included exogenous variables and is biased and inconsistent. The 2SLS estimator in (11.7.11) and (11.7.15) takes account of this distinction in each equation, but it does not take account of the possible correlation between explanatory endogenous variables of one equation and the stochastic disturbance terms in all other equations. This correlation between stochastic disturbance terms in different equations, leading to the correlation of dependent endogenous variables with stochastic disturbances in other equations, is represented by the blocks of the covariance matrix (11.7.8) that lie off the principal diagonal of matrices. For example, the block $\sigma_{12}\mathbf{I}$, as previously noted, refers to the correlation between the first and second equations, which results in a correlation of the first endogenous variable $\mathbf{y}_1$ with the contemporaneous stochastic disturbance term of the second equation $\boldsymbol{\varepsilon}_2$. If these off-diagonal blocks of the covariance matrix all vanish—that is, if $\boldsymbol{\Sigma}$ in (11.1.3) is diagonal—then there is no way to improve upon the 2SLS estimator. If, however, these off-diagonal blocks do not vanish, then it is possible to improve upon the asymptotic efficiency of 2SLS by taking explicit account of this interequation correlation. This improvement in asymptotic efficiency is incorporated in the 3SLS estimator.

The 3SLS estimator is a GLS estimator of the entire system in (11.7.6) that takes explicit account of the covariance matrix in (11.7.8). GLS was used earlier in this chapter in (11.6.21)-(11.6.23), where it was shown that 2SLS is equivalent to using all exogenous variables as instrumental variables and estimating the resulting equation using GLS. The 3SLS estimator follows exactly the same approach for the entire system of equations. Using all exogenous variables as instruments implies that the equation to be estimated is obtained from (11.7.6) by premultiplying by $\mathbf{X}^{*\prime}$, the matrix defined by

$$\mathbf{X}^{*\prime} = \begin{pmatrix} \mathbf{X}' & \mathbf{0} & \cdots & \mathbf{0} \\ \mathbf{0} & \mathbf{X}' & \cdots & \mathbf{0} \\ \vdots & \vdots & & \vdots \\ \mathbf{0} & \mathbf{0} & \cdots & \mathbf{X}' \end{pmatrix} \quad *(11.7.17)$$

[26] Note that for the product of Kronecker products

$$(\mathbf{A}_1 \otimes \mathbf{B}_1)(\mathbf{A}_2 \otimes \mathbf{B}_2)(\mathbf{A}_3 \otimes \mathbf{B}_3) = (\mathbf{A}_1\mathbf{A}_2\mathbf{A}_3) \otimes (\mathbf{B}_1\mathbf{B}_2\mathbf{B}_3).$$

yielding

$$\mathbf{X}^{*\prime}\mathbf{y}^{*} = \mathbf{X}^{*\prime}\mathbf{Z}^{*}\boldsymbol{\delta}^{*} + \mathbf{X}^{*\prime}\boldsymbol{\varepsilon}^{*}. \qquad *(11.7.18)$$

This is the system obtained by premultiplying each equation by $\mathbf{X}'$, using all exogenous variables as instrumental variables in each equation of the system. It as the systems analogue of (11.6.21). The GLS estimator of this equation is the 3SLS estimator

$$\hat{\boldsymbol{\delta}}^{*}_{3SLS} = \{\mathbf{Z}^{*\prime}\mathbf{X}^{*}[\mathrm{Cov}\,(\mathbf{X}^{*\prime}\boldsymbol{\varepsilon}^{*})]^{-1}\mathbf{X}^{*\prime}\mathbf{Z}^{*}\}^{-1} \cdot \mathbf{Z}^{*\prime}\mathbf{X}^{*}[\mathrm{Cov}\,(\mathbf{X}^{*\prime}\boldsymbol{\varepsilon}^{*})]^{-1}\mathbf{X}^{*\prime}\mathbf{y}^{*}. \qquad *(11.7.19)$$

The covariance matrix, however, from (11.7.8), is

$$\mathrm{Cov}\,(\mathbf{X}^{*\prime}\boldsymbol{\varepsilon}^{*}) = \mathbf{X}^{*\prime}\,\mathrm{Cov}\,(\boldsymbol{\varepsilon}^{*})\mathbf{X}^{*} = \mathbf{X}^{*\prime}(\boldsymbol{\Sigma} \otimes \mathbf{I})\mathbf{X}^{*} \qquad *(11.7.20)$$

which is the systems analogue of (11.6.22). Thus the 3SLS estimator can be written

$$\hat{\boldsymbol{\delta}}^{*}_{3SLS} = \{\mathbf{Z}^{*\prime}\mathbf{X}^{*}[\mathbf{X}^{*\prime}(\boldsymbol{\Sigma} \otimes \mathbf{I})\mathbf{X}^{*}]^{-1}\mathbf{X}^{*\prime}\mathbf{Z}^{*}\}^{-1} \cdot \mathbf{Z}^{*\prime}\mathbf{X}^{*}[\mathbf{X}^{*\prime}(\boldsymbol{\Sigma} \otimes \mathbf{I})\mathbf{X}^{*}]^{-1}\mathbf{X}^{*\prime}\mathbf{y}^{*} \qquad *(11.7.21)$$

which is the systems analogue of (11.6.23). This estimator is of the same form as the 2SLS estimator in (11.7.15), except for the insertion of $\boldsymbol{\Sigma} \otimes \mathbf{I}$ between $\mathbf{X}^{*\prime}$ and $\mathbf{X}^{*}$ in two places. Thus the 3SLS estimator can be interpreted as taking all the 2SLS results, summarized in (11.7.15), and "correcting" them for the covariance matrix $\boldsymbol{\Sigma}$. In this interpretation the 3SLS estimator is precisely the technique of "seemingly unrelated equations," as discussed in Section 6.7, applied to the set of all second-stage equations of 2SLS. The resulting estimator is both consistent and asymptotically more efficient than the 2SLS estimators, since it takes explicit account of the covariances in $\boldsymbol{\Sigma}$. If all equations were just identified or the covariance matrix $\boldsymbol{\Sigma}$ were diagonal, then the 3SLS estimator would reduce to the 2SLS estimator.[27]

All components of the 3SLS estimator other than the covariance matrix are obtained directly from the data. Thus $\mathbf{Z}^{*}$ is defined by (11.7.5), $\mathbf{X}^{*}$ by (11.7.14), and $\mathbf{y}^{*}$ by (11.7.2). If $\boldsymbol{\Sigma}$ is given, then it is used as given. Typically, however, $\boldsymbol{\Sigma}$ is not given, and it must be estimated. This is the rationale for referring to a "three-stage" estimator. The result of the first two stages, the 2SLS estimates, yield the information, in the residuals, needed to estimate the covariance matrix. In particular, $\boldsymbol{\Sigma}$ is estimated as

$$\hat{\boldsymbol{\Sigma}} = (\hat{\sigma}_{hh'}) \text{ where } \hat{\sigma}_{hh'} = \frac{1}{n}\hat{\boldsymbol{\varepsilon}}'_h\hat{\boldsymbol{\varepsilon}}_{h'} = \frac{1}{n}(\mathbf{y}_h - \mathbf{Z}_h\hat{\boldsymbol{\delta}}_h)'(\mathbf{y}_{h'} - \mathbf{Z}_{h'}\hat{\boldsymbol{\delta}}_{h'}) \qquad h, h' = 1, 2, \ldots, g \qquad *(11.7.22)$$

[27] See Problem 11-L.

and is assumed nonsingular.[28] Here $\hat{\boldsymbol{\delta}}_h$ and $\hat{\boldsymbol{\delta}}_{h'}$ are the 2SLS estimates that are the relevant column-vector components of (11.7.15). The first two stages are performed in the 3SLS technique only to provide estimates of $\boldsymbol{\Sigma}$; no other use is made of the 2SLS estimates of coefficients $\hat{\boldsymbol{\delta}}_h = \hat{\boldsymbol{\delta}}_{h\,2SLS}$.

Another way of stating the 3SLS estimator is based on using (11.7.14) so as to express the covariance matrix in (11.7.20) as

$$\text{Cov}\,(\mathbf{X}^{*\prime}\boldsymbol{\varepsilon}^*) = \mathbf{X}^{*\prime}(\boldsymbol{\Sigma} \otimes \mathbf{I})\mathbf{X}^* = (\mathbf{I} \otimes \mathbf{X}')(\boldsymbol{\Sigma} \otimes \mathbf{I})(\mathbf{I} \otimes \mathbf{X}) \qquad (11.7.23)$$

so that[29]

$$\text{Cov}\,(\mathbf{X}^{*\prime}\boldsymbol{\varepsilon}^*) = \boldsymbol{\Sigma} \otimes (\mathbf{X}'\mathbf{X}) \qquad *(11.7.24)$$

Combining (11.7.21) and (11.7.24), the 3SLS estimator can be written, replacing $\boldsymbol{\Sigma}$ by $\hat{\boldsymbol{\Sigma}}$, as

$$\hat{\boldsymbol{\delta}}^*_{3SLS} = \left\{\mathbf{Z}^{*\prime}[\hat{\boldsymbol{\Sigma}}^{-1} \otimes \mathbf{X}(\mathbf{X}'\mathbf{X})^{-1}\mathbf{X}']\mathbf{Z}^*\right\}^{-1}\mathbf{Z}^{*\prime}[\hat{\boldsymbol{\Sigma}}^{-1} \otimes \mathbf{X}(\mathbf{X}'\mathbf{X})^{-1}\mathbf{X}']\mathbf{y}^*. \qquad *(11.7.25)$$

This statement of the 3SLS estimator, if compared to the 2SLS estimator of (11.7.16), indicates that the 3SLS differs from the 2SLS estimator only in taking explicit account of the estimate of the covariance matrix $\hat{\boldsymbol{\Sigma}}$.

The 3SLS estimator is thus given by (11.7.25) or, equivalently, (11.7.21) with $\boldsymbol{\Sigma}$ replaced by $\hat{\boldsymbol{\Sigma}}$ and where $\hat{\boldsymbol{\Sigma}}$ is estimated from (11.7.22). It is the estimator obtained by using all exogenous variables as instrumental variables and then applying GLS to the whole system, where the 2SLS estimates are used to obtain an estimate of the relevant covariance matrix. The three stages of 3SLS are thus: *first*, estimation of the reduced form, as in (11.5.4); *second*, estimation of each structural equation via 2SLS as in (11.7.15); *third*, GLS estimation of the system after having used all exogenous variables as instrumental variables, as in (11.7.21), where the covariance matrix is estimated from the residuals of the 2SLS estimates, as in (11.7.22). This estimator is both consistent, in that

$$\text{plim}\ \hat{\boldsymbol{\delta}}^*_{3SLS} = \boldsymbol{\delta}^* \qquad *(11.7.26)$$

and asymptotically more efficient than 2SLS, in that

$$\lim \text{Cov}\,(\hat{\boldsymbol{\delta}}^*_{3SLS}) - \lim \text{Cov}\,(\hat{\boldsymbol{\delta}}^*_{2SLS}) \text{ is negative semidefinite.} \qquad *(11.7.27)$$

In the last section it was shown that several single-equation estimators could be interpreted as instrumental-variables estimators for particular choices of instrumental variables. The same interpretation can be given the various systems

[28] Note that $\hat{\sigma}_1^2$ in (11.6.35) is identical to $\hat{\sigma}_{11}$ in (11.7.22). See also footnote 33 in Chapter 6, Section 6.5, and (11.8.13) in the next section.

[29] See footnote 26.

estimators presented here. Given the system in star notation (11.7.6), the instrumental-variables (IV) estimator of $\boldsymbol{\delta}^*$, by analogy to (11.6.6), is

$$\hat{\boldsymbol{\delta}}^*_{IV} = \hat{\boldsymbol{\delta}}^*(\mathbf{W}^*) = (\mathbf{W}^{*\prime}\mathbf{Z}^*)^{-1}\mathbf{W}^{*\prime}\mathbf{y}^* \qquad *(11.7.28)$$

where $\hat{\boldsymbol{\delta}}^*(\mathbf{W}^*)$ shows the functional dependence of the estimator on $\mathbf{W}^*$, the matrix of data on instrumental variables. Thus the OLS estimator in (11.7.9) corresponds to the IV estimator for which $\mathbf{W}^*$ is simply the set of all explanatory variables $\mathbf{Z}^*$:

$$\hat{\boldsymbol{\delta}}^*_{OLS} = \hat{\boldsymbol{\delta}}^*(\mathbf{Z}^*) = (\mathbf{Z}^{*\prime}\mathbf{Z}^*)^{-1}\mathbf{Z}^{*\prime}\mathbf{y}^* \qquad *(11.7.29)$$

which is the systems analogue of (11.6.7). The 2SLS estimator in (11.7.11), (11.7.15), and (11.7.16) is the IV estimator for which

$$\mathbf{W}^*_{2SLS} = \hat{\mathbf{Z}}^* = \mathbf{X}^*(\mathbf{X}^{*\prime}\mathbf{X}^*)^{-1}\mathbf{X}^{*\prime}\mathbf{Z}^* = [\mathbf{I} \otimes \mathbf{X}(\mathbf{X}'\mathbf{X})^{-1}\mathbf{X}']\mathbf{Z}^* \qquad *(11.7.30)$$

where, for example, in (11.7.16)

$$\hat{\boldsymbol{\delta}}^*_{2SLS} = \hat{\boldsymbol{\delta}}^*\left([\mathbf{I} \otimes \mathbf{X}(\mathbf{X}'\mathbf{X})^{-1}\mathbf{X}']\mathbf{Z}^*\right). \qquad *(11.7.31)$$

Finally the 3SLS estimator in (11.7.25) is the IV estimator for which

$$\mathbf{W}^*_{3SLS} = [\boldsymbol{\Sigma}^{-1} \otimes \mathbf{X}(\mathbf{X}'\mathbf{X})^{-1}\mathbf{X}']\mathbf{Z}^* \qquad *(11.7.32)$$

so that

$$\hat{\boldsymbol{\delta}}^*_{3SLS} = \hat{\boldsymbol{\delta}}^*\left([\boldsymbol{\Sigma}^{-1} \otimes \mathbf{X}(\mathbf{X}'\mathbf{X})^{-1}\mathbf{X}']\mathbf{Z}^*\right). \qquad *(11.7.33)$$

For the general IV estimator, using (11.7.6) and (11.7.28),

$$\begin{aligned} \hat{\boldsymbol{\delta}}^*_{IV} &= (\mathbf{W}^{*\prime}\mathbf{Z}^*)^{-1}\mathbf{W}^{*\prime}(\mathbf{Z}^*\boldsymbol{\delta}^* + \boldsymbol{\varepsilon}^*) \\ &= \boldsymbol{\delta}^* + (\mathbf{W}^{*\prime}\mathbf{Z}^*)^{-1}\mathbf{W}^{*\prime}\boldsymbol{\varepsilon}^* \end{aligned} \qquad *(11.7.34)$$

so that

$$\text{plim}\ \hat{\boldsymbol{\delta}}^*_{IV} = \boldsymbol{\delta}^* + \text{plim}\left(\frac{1}{n}\mathbf{W}^{*\prime}\mathbf{Z}^*\right)^{-1} \text{plim}\left(\frac{1}{n}\mathbf{W}^{*\prime}\boldsymbol{\varepsilon}^*\right) \qquad *(11.7.35)$$

which is the systems analogue of (11.6.27). Assuming the instrumental variables are asymptotically uncorrelated with the stochastic disturbance terms

$$\text{plim}\left(\frac{1}{n}\mathbf{W}^{*\prime}\boldsymbol{\varepsilon}^*\right) = \mathbf{0} \qquad *(11.7.36)$$

and that they are asymptotically correlated with the $\mathbf{Z}^*$'s

$$\text{plim}\left(\frac{1}{n}\mathbf{W}^{*\prime}\mathbf{Z}^{*}\right) = \mathbf{Q}^{*} \qquad *(11.7.37)$$

where $\mathbf{Q}^*$ exists and is nonsingular, the IV estimator is consistent:

$$\text{plim}\ \hat{\boldsymbol{\delta}}^{*}_{\text{IV}} = \boldsymbol{\delta}^{*}. \qquad *(11.7.38)$$

The two conditions for consistency are systems analogues for (11.6.28) and (11.6.29), and they are satisfied for 2SLS and 3SLS, which are both consistent estimators, but not for OLS, which is generally not consistent.

The asymptotic covariance matrix for the IV estimator, from its definition in (11.6.31) and $\hat{\boldsymbol{\delta}}^{*}_{\text{IV}} - \boldsymbol{\delta}^{*}$, as given in (11.7.34), is given as

$$\lim \text{Cov}\,(\hat{\boldsymbol{\delta}}^{*}_{\text{IV}}) = \frac{1}{n}\,\text{plim}\left[\left(\frac{1}{n}\mathbf{W}^{*\prime}\mathbf{Z}^{*}\right)^{-1}\left(\frac{1}{n}\mathbf{W}^{*\prime}\boldsymbol{\varepsilon}^{*}\boldsymbol{\varepsilon}^{*\prime}\mathbf{W}^{*}\right)\left(\frac{1}{n}\mathbf{Z}^{*\prime}\mathbf{W}^{*}\right)^{-1}\right] \qquad (11.7.39)$$

which is the systems analogue of (11.6.32). From (11.7.8), however,

$$\lim \text{Cov}\,(\hat{\boldsymbol{\delta}}^{*}_{\text{IV}}) = \frac{1}{n}\,\text{plim}\left\{\left(\frac{1}{n}\mathbf{W}^{*\prime}\mathbf{Z}^{*}\right)^{-1}\left[\frac{1}{n}\mathbf{W}^{*\prime}(\boldsymbol{\Sigma}\otimes\mathbf{I})\mathbf{W}^{*}\right]\left(\frac{1}{n}\mathbf{Z}^{*\prime}\mathbf{W}^{*}\right)^{-1}\right\} \qquad *(11.7.40)$$

which is analogous to (11.6.34). This result yields as the asymptotic covariance matrix for 2SLS, using (11.7.31),

$$\begin{aligned}\lim \text{Cov}\,(\hat{\boldsymbol{\delta}}^{*}_{\text{2SLS}}) = \frac{1}{n}\,\text{plim}\Bigg(&\left\{\frac{1}{n}\mathbf{Z}^{*\prime}[\mathbf{I}\otimes\mathbf{X}(\mathbf{X}'\mathbf{X})^{-1}\mathbf{X}']\mathbf{Z}^{*}\right\}^{-1}\\ &\cdot\left\{\frac{1}{n}\mathbf{Z}^{*\prime}[\boldsymbol{\Sigma}\otimes\mathbf{X}(\mathbf{X}'\mathbf{X})^{-1}\mathbf{X}']\mathbf{Z}^{*}\right\}\\ &\cdot\left\{\frac{1}{n}\mathbf{Z}^{*\prime}[\mathbf{I}\otimes\mathbf{X}(\mathbf{X}'\mathbf{X})^{-1}\mathbf{X}']\mathbf{Z}^{*}\right\}^{-1}\Bigg)\end{aligned} \qquad *(11.7.41)$$

which generalizes (11.6.37) to the entire system. The covariance matrix $\boldsymbol{\Sigma}$ can be consistently estimated as $\hat{\boldsymbol{\Sigma}}$ in (11.7.22), where $\hat{\boldsymbol{\delta}}_h$ and $\hat{\boldsymbol{\delta}}_{h'}$ are the 2SLS estimators. The result in (11.7.40) also yields as the asymptotic covariance matrix for 3SLS, using (11.7.33),[30]

$$\lim \text{Cov}\,(\hat{\boldsymbol{\delta}}^{*}_{\text{3SLS}}) = \frac{1}{n}\,\text{plim}\left(\left\{\frac{1}{n}\mathbf{Z}^{*\prime}[\boldsymbol{\Sigma}^{-1}\otimes\mathbf{X}(\mathbf{X}'\mathbf{X})^{-1}\mathbf{X}']\mathbf{Z}^{*}\right\}^{-1}\right) \qquad *(11.7.42)$$

[30] As in footnote 20, assuming the stochastic disturbance terms at each observation are independently and identically (but not necessarily normally) distributed the 3SLS estimator is asymptotically normally distributed [that is, the estimator $\sqrt{n}(\hat{\boldsymbol{\delta}}^{*}_{\text{3SLS}} - \boldsymbol{\delta}^{*})$ is asymptotically normal] with mean given by the true vector of parameters and with an asymptotic covariance matrix given by (11.7.42). If there are no restrictions on $\boldsymbol{\Sigma}$, then the asymptotic

The covariance matrix $\boldsymbol{\Sigma}$ can again be consistently estimated as $\hat{\boldsymbol{\Sigma}}$ in (11.7.22), but where $\hat{\boldsymbol{\delta}}_h$ and $\hat{\boldsymbol{\delta}}_{h'}$ are now the 3SLS estimators. These are the two asymptotic covariance matrices used in (11.7.27), which states that 3SLS is asymptotically more efficient than 2SLS. They can also be used for constructing (asymptotic) tests of significance and confidence intervals, as discussed following (11.6.37).

11.8 Full-information maximum likelihood

The other major full-information technique is that of full-information maximum likelihood (FIML).[31] In this approach the likelihood function for the entire system is maximized by choice of all system parameters, subject to all a priori identifying restrictions. The resulting estimators are consistent and asymptotically efficient.[32] They also have the same asymptotic properties as 3SLS, including the same asymptotic covariance matrix. A major advantage of FIML over 3SLS, however, is that with this technique it is possible to use in the estimation process a wide range of a priori information, pertaining not only to each equation individually but also to several equations simultaneously, such as constraints involving coefficients of different structural equations and certain restrictions on the error structure. The major disadvantage of FIML, however, is that it is difficult and expensive to compute, involving the estimation of rather awkward simultaneous nonlinear equations, which usually must be computed via iteration.

It is convenient to use the star notation of the previous section in developing the FIML estimator. In this notation all g equations of the simultaneous system, after normalization, can be written

$$\underset{gn\times 1}{\mathbf{y}^*} = \underset{gn\times k^*}{\mathbf{Z}^*}\ \underset{k^*\times 1}{\boldsymbol{\delta}^*} + \underset{gn\times 1}{\boldsymbol{\varepsilon}^*} \qquad *(11.8.1)$$

distribution of the 3SLS estimator is identical to that of full-information maximum likelihood. In particular, the asymptotic distribution is normal and the asymptotic covariance matrix (11.7.42) is asymptotically efficient in that it attains the asymptotic Cramer-Rao bound of the full-information maximum-likelihood estimator. See footnote 32; footnote 24, in Chapter 4; and Rao (1965). For further discussions of asymptotic efficiency see Malinvaud (1970), Theil (1971), and Rothenberg (1974).

[31] See Sargan (1964), Fisk (1967), Theil (1971), and Madansky (1976). For an instrumental-variable interpretation see Hausman (1975). For extensions to nonlinear econometric systems see Eisenpress and Greenstadt (1966), Chow (1973), and Jorgenson and Laffont (1974).

[32] The FIML estimator $\hat{\boldsymbol{\delta}}^*_{\text{FIML}}$ is asymptotically normally distributed, and it is asymptotically efficient in that it attains the asymptotic Cramer-Rao bound. In particular, given any estimator $\hat{\boldsymbol{\delta}}^*$ that is asymptotically normally distributed, lim Cov $(\hat{\boldsymbol{\delta}}^*_{\text{FIML}})$ − lim Cov $(\hat{\boldsymbol{\delta}}^*)$ is negative semidefinite, where the asymptotic covariance matrix of the FIML estimator is identical to that for 3SLS, as given in (11.7.42). See Rothenberg and Leenders (1964), Madansky (1964, 1976), Sargan (1964), and Rothenberg (1974).

as in (11.7.6). The vector of all stochastic disturbances in all equations $\boldsymbol{\varepsilon}^*$ is assumed to satisfy the properties

$$E(\boldsymbol{\varepsilon}^*) = \mathbf{0} \qquad *(11.8.2)$$

$$\text{Cov}(\boldsymbol{\varepsilon}^*) = \boldsymbol{\Sigma} \otimes \mathbf{I} \qquad *(11.8.3)$$

as in (11.7.7) and (11.7.8). The FIML technique is one of maximum likelihood, however, and maximum likelihood always requires a specific assumption as to the form of the distribution of the stochastic disturbances. If it is again assumed that the stochastic disturbances are distributed normally,

$$\boldsymbol{\varepsilon}^* \sim N(\mathbf{0}, \boldsymbol{\Sigma} \otimes \mathbf{I}) \qquad *(11.8.4)$$

then the logarithm of the likelihood function is given by

$$\ln L(\boldsymbol{\varepsilon}^*) = -\frac{gn}{2} \ln 2\pi - \tfrac{1}{2} \ln |\boldsymbol{\Sigma} \otimes \mathbf{I}| - \tfrac{1}{2}(\mathbf{y}^* - \mathbf{Z}^*\boldsymbol{\delta}^*)'(\boldsymbol{\Sigma}^{-1} \otimes \mathbf{I})(\mathbf{y}^* - \mathbf{Z}^*\boldsymbol{\delta}^*) \qquad *(11.8.5)$$

This is the likelihood function of the $\boldsymbol{\varepsilon}^*$ disturbance vector, but what is needed is the likelihood function of the endogenous variables $\mathbf{y}^*$, since the objective is to choose values of parameters so as to maximize the likelihood of observing the values given by $\mathbf{y}^*$. But, letting $L(\mathbf{y}^*)$ be the likelihood function for $\mathbf{y}^*$,

$$\ln L(\mathbf{y}^*) = \ln L(\boldsymbol{\varepsilon}^*) + \ln \left| \frac{\partial \boldsymbol{\varepsilon}^*}{\partial \mathbf{y}^*} \right| \qquad (11.8.6)$$

since the transformation of variables from $\boldsymbol{\varepsilon}^*$ to $\mathbf{y}^*$ multiplies the likelihood function by the determinant of the relevant Jacobian matrix.[33] It is convenient to simplify this expression for the likelihood function in order to obtain a form such that the first-order conditions of maximization characterize the estimators of the system parameters, as given by $\boldsymbol{\delta}^*$ and $\boldsymbol{\Sigma}$. One such simplification applies to the determinant of the Jacobian matrix in (11.8.6). From (11.7.2) it follows that

[33] The likelihood function for the endogenous variables $\mathbf{y}^*$ can be obtained from the likelihood function for the stochastic disturbance terms $\boldsymbol{\varepsilon}^*$ as

$$L(\mathbf{y}^*) = L(\boldsymbol{\varepsilon}^*) \left| \frac{\partial \boldsymbol{\varepsilon}^*}{\partial \mathbf{y}^*} \right|$$

where the last term is the determinant of the Jacobian matrix of all first-order partial derivatives of elements of $\boldsymbol{\varepsilon}^*$ with respect to elements of $\mathbf{y}^*$. This result on "change of variables" follows from the calculus of several variables, and it is discussed in standard texts on analysis, such as Rudin (1964), Apostol (1974), and Hoffman (1975).

$$\left|\frac{\partial \boldsymbol{\varepsilon}^*}{\partial \mathbf{y}^*}\right| = \left|\begin{pmatrix} \boldsymbol{\Gamma} & \mathbf{0} & \cdots & \mathbf{0} \\ & \boldsymbol{\Gamma} & \cdots & \mathbf{0} \\ & & \ddots & \vdots \\ & & \cdots & \boldsymbol{\Gamma} \end{pmatrix}\right| = |\boldsymbol{\Gamma}|^n \tag{11.8.7}$$

since, while elements below the principal diagonal of $\boldsymbol{\Gamma}$ matrices may be nonzero, reflecting lagged endogenous variables, all elements above the principal diagonal must be zero, reflecting the fact that future variables do not influence present ones. These zeros ensure that the determinant of the Jacobian is the nth power of the (positive value of the) determinant of $\boldsymbol{\Gamma}$. Another simplification is the replacement of $-\frac{1}{2}\ln|\boldsymbol{\Sigma} \otimes \mathbf{I}|$ in (11.8.5) by $-(n/2)\ln|\boldsymbol{\Sigma}|$, since

$$-\tfrac{1}{2}\ln|\boldsymbol{\Sigma} \otimes \mathbf{I}| = -\tfrac{1}{2}\ln|\boldsymbol{\Sigma}|^n = -\frac{n}{2}\ln|\boldsymbol{\Sigma}|. \tag{11.8.8}$$

The relevant likelihood function is then

$$\begin{aligned}\ln L(\mathbf{y}^*) = -\frac{gn}{2}\ln 2\pi - \frac{n}{2}\ln|\boldsymbol{\Sigma}| + n\ln|\boldsymbol{\Gamma}| \\ -\tfrac{1}{2}(\mathbf{y}^* - \mathbf{Z}^*\boldsymbol{\delta}^*)'(\boldsymbol{\Sigma}^{-1} \otimes \mathbf{I})(\mathbf{y}^* - \mathbf{Z}^*\boldsymbol{\delta}^*).\end{aligned} \tag*{*(11.8.9)}$$

This likelihood function is maximized by choice of the parameters. It is convenient to consider first the choice of elements of the covariance matrix $\boldsymbol{\Sigma}$, where it is assumed that there are no a priori restrictions on $\boldsymbol{\Sigma}$. The last term in (11.8.9) can be written

$$\begin{aligned}-\tfrac{1}{2}(\mathbf{y}^* - \mathbf{Z}^*\boldsymbol{\delta}^*)'(\boldsymbol{\Sigma}^{-1} \otimes \mathbf{I})(\mathbf{y}^* - \mathbf{Z}^*\boldsymbol{\delta}^*) = \\ -\tfrac{1}{2}\sum_{h=1}^{g}\sum_{h'=1}^{g}\sigma^{hh'}(\mathbf{y}_h - \mathbf{Z}_h\boldsymbol{\delta}_h)'(\mathbf{y}_{h'} - \mathbf{Z}_{h'}\boldsymbol{\delta}_{h'})\end{aligned} \tag{11.8.10}$$

where superscripted elements $\sigma^{hh'}$ are those of the inverse of the covariance matrix and subscripted elements $\sigma_{hh'}$ continue to be those of the matrix itself:

$$\boldsymbol{\Sigma} = (\sigma_{hh'}), \qquad \boldsymbol{\Sigma}^{-1} = (\sigma^{hh'}). \tag{11.8.11}$$

Using (11.8.10), the first-order conditions for a maximum by choice of elements of the (inverse of the) covariance matrix are[34]

$$\frac{\partial \ln L(\mathbf{y}^*)}{\partial \sigma^{hh'}} = \frac{n}{2}\sigma_{hh'} - \tfrac{1}{2}(\mathbf{y}_h - \mathbf{Z}_h\boldsymbol{\delta}_h)'(\mathbf{y}_{h'} - \mathbf{Z}_{h'}\boldsymbol{\delta}_{h'}) = 0. \tag{11.8.12}$$

[34] For the first term on the right see Problem 11-O.

These conditions lead to the FIML estimator of the elements of the covariance matrix:

$$\hat{\boldsymbol{\Sigma}} = (\hat{\sigma}_{hh'}) \quad \text{where} \quad \hat{\sigma}_{hh'} = \frac{1}{n}(\mathbf{y}_h - \mathbf{Z}_h\hat{\boldsymbol{\delta}}_h)'(\mathbf{y}_{h'} - \mathbf{Z}_{h'}\hat{\boldsymbol{\delta}}_{h'}) \qquad h, h' = 1, 2, \ldots, g. \tag*{*(11.8.13)}$$

These estimators were previously used in the 3SLS estimator in (11.7.22). Using them, the estimate of $\boldsymbol{\Sigma} \otimes \mathbf{I}$ is

$$\hat{\boldsymbol{\Sigma}} \otimes \mathbf{I} = \frac{1}{n}(\mathbf{y}^* - \mathbf{Z}^*\hat{\boldsymbol{\delta}}^*)(\mathbf{y}^* - \mathbf{Z}^*\hat{\boldsymbol{\delta}}^*)'. \tag{11.8.14}$$

Inserting this result in (11.8.9), the matrices in the last term cancel, yielding

$$\ln L(\mathbf{y}^*) = -\frac{gn}{2}\ln 2\pi - \frac{n}{2}\ln|\hat{\boldsymbol{\Sigma}}| + n\ln|\boldsymbol{\Gamma}| - \frac{n}{2}. \tag{11.8.15}$$

The FIML estimators of the coefficients are then obtained by maximizing this likelihood function by choice of $\boldsymbol{\delta}^*$ subject to all a priori restrictions. In the unrestricted case the first-order conditions are

$$\frac{\partial \ln L(\mathbf{y}^*)}{\partial \boldsymbol{\delta}^*} = -\frac{n}{2}\frac{\partial \ln|\hat{\boldsymbol{\Sigma}}|}{\partial \boldsymbol{\delta}^*} + n\frac{\partial \ln|\boldsymbol{\Gamma}|}{\partial \boldsymbol{\delta}^*} = \mathbf{0} \tag*{*(11.8.16)}$$

where $\hat{\boldsymbol{\Sigma}}$ depends on $\hat{\boldsymbol{\delta}}^*$, as given in (11.8.13). This is the system of nonlinear equations that must be solved for the FIML estimators $\hat{\boldsymbol{\delta}}^*_{\text{FIML}}$. Since $|\boldsymbol{\Gamma}|$ is a function of the coefficient of endogenous variables in all equations, the system of nonlinear equations in unknown coefficients is particularly awkward to solve. For example, for the coefficient $\gamma_{hh'}$,

$$\frac{\partial \ln|\boldsymbol{\Gamma}|}{\partial \gamma_{hh'}} = \gamma^{hh'} \tag{11.8.17}$$

where $\gamma^{hh'}$ is the (h, h') element of $\boldsymbol{\Gamma}^{-1}$, involving all elements of $\boldsymbol{\Gamma}$ in a nonlinear fashion. Similarly the partial derivatives of $\ln|\hat{\boldsymbol{\Sigma}}|$ are nonlinear in the parameters. Thus, the system is very difficult to solve.[35]

The difficulties of solving for FIML estimators vanish in the recursive case where $\boldsymbol{\Gamma}$ is triangular and $\boldsymbol{\Sigma}$ is diagonal. Since $\boldsymbol{\Gamma}$ is triangular, the system can be normalized so that $|\boldsymbol{\Gamma}|$ is simply unity. Thus, in this case $\boldsymbol{\delta}^*$ is estimated from

[35] Rothenberg and Leenders (1964) have proposed a linearized version of the system with the same asymptotic properties as FIML that is much simpler to compute. It might be noted that for computation of the FIML estimator it is necessary that n, the number of data points, exceed the sum of the number of exogenous variables k and the number of endogenous variables g. See Klein (1971) and Sargan (1975).

$$\frac{\partial \ln |\hat{\Sigma}|}{\partial \delta^*} = 0 \tag{11.8.18}$$

since $\ln |\Gamma|$ vanishes in (11.8.16). But here, since Σ is diagonal,

$$\begin{aligned}\ln |\hat{\Sigma}| &= \sum_{h=1}^{g} \ln \hat{\sigma}_{hh} = \sum_{h=1}^{g} \ln \frac{1}{n} (\mathbf{y}_h - \mathbf{Z}_h\hat{\boldsymbol{\delta}}_h)'(\mathbf{y}_h - \mathbf{Z}_h\hat{\boldsymbol{\delta}}_h) \\ &= \sum_{h=1}^{g} \ln \frac{1}{n} (\mathbf{y}_h'\mathbf{y}_h - 2\hat{\boldsymbol{\delta}}_h'\mathbf{Z}_h'\mathbf{y}_h + \hat{\boldsymbol{\delta}}_h'\mathbf{Z}_h'\mathbf{Z}_h\hat{\boldsymbol{\delta}}_h)\end{aligned} \tag{11.8.19}$$

so, differentiating with respect to $\hat{\boldsymbol{\delta}}_h$,

$$\frac{\partial \ln |\hat{\Sigma}|}{\partial \hat{\boldsymbol{\delta}}_h'} = \sum_{h=1}^{g} \frac{1}{\hat{\sigma}_{hh}} \frac{1}{n} (-2\mathbf{Z}_h'\mathbf{y}_h + 2\mathbf{Z}_h'\mathbf{Z}_h\hat{\boldsymbol{\delta}}_h) = 0 \tag{11.8.20}$$

leading to the estimators

$$\hat{\boldsymbol{\delta}}_h = (\mathbf{Z}_h'\mathbf{Z}_h)^{-1}\mathbf{Z}_h'\mathbf{y}_h, \quad h = 1, 2, \ldots, g. \tag{11.8.21}$$

These are, of course, the OLS estimators of each of the equations of the system (11.7.1), as presented in (11.3.4). Thus, in the case of a recursive system, the OLS estimators are also the FIML estimators and hence are consistent and asymptotically efficient. They are also unbiased if the model does not include lagged endogenous variables. OLS "works" in this case because, assuming Γ is triangular and Σ is diagonal, the variables in each equation are not correlated with the stochastic disturbance term in that equation.

11.9 Monte Carlo studies of small-sample properties of estimators

While all of the estimators presented so far, other than OLS, have the property of consistency, and some are asymptotically efficient, these properties are asymptotic ones, referring to large samples. Applied econometric studies, however, typically utilize small samples, as will be seen in the next two chapters, and the large-sample properties of consistency and asymptotic efficiency provide no direct information about the small-sample properties of the various estimators. There is thus a real problem of choosing among these estimators.

One way of studying the small-sample properties of estimators is to utilize the Monte Carlo approach.[36] This approach virtually turns the problem on its

[36] For surveys of various Monte Carlo studies see Cragg (1967) and Smith (1973). Another approach is to determine the exact finite-sample distribution of the estimators, as discussed by Basmann (1961, 1963, 1974), and Richardson (1968). Yet a third approach is to study approximations of the estimators for finite samples, as in Nagar (1959, 1962), Kadane (1971), Sargan and Mikhail (1971), and Anderson and Sawa (1973).

head: instead of estimating unknown parameters using a specific technique, known parameters, which are chosen beforehand, are estimated using different techniques. The resulting comparisons between estimated and true parameters are used to make inferences about the different techniques. This approach thus simulates the process of estimating parameters using a controlled setting, in which the true parameter values are known. The Monte Carlo approach has been applied not only to the choice of alternative estimators but also to the influence of sample size, multicollinearity, and other factors on the various possible estimators. It provides a type of "laboratory" in which "controlled experiments" on econometric estimators can be studied. As with most laboratory results, however, there can arise the issue of their applicability to "real-world" phenomena. In particular, an important issue in the Monte Carlo approach to simultaneous-equations estimation is whether the results for certain specific models can, in fact, be applied to models in general. Such an application should be made only after extensive testing and systematic treatment of various possible changes in the formulation of the model.

The Monte Carlo approach starts by postulating a specific simultaneous-equations model and assigns numerical values to all parameters, including not only the coefficient matrices $\mathbf{\Gamma}$ and $\mathbf{B}$ but also the covariance matrix $\mathbf{\Sigma}$. Numerical values are also specified for the values of all exogenous variables $\mathbf{X}$. From the reduced-form equations, the implied values of reduced-form coefficients $\mathbf{\Pi} = -\mathbf{B}\mathbf{\Gamma}^{-1}$ and the assumed values of exogenous variables $\mathbf{X}$, together with a sample of reduced-form disturbances $\mathbf{u}$ generate a sample of data on the endogenous variables $\mathbf{Y}$ via

$$\mathbf{Y} = \mathbf{X}\mathbf{\Pi} + \mathbf{U} \tag{11.9.1}$$

Both $\mathbf{X}$ and $\mathbf{\Pi}$ are known; all that is needed to generate $\mathbf{Y}$ is $\mathbf{U}$. But $\mathbf{u}$ is a random variable that, under the usual normality assumptions, is distributed normally as

$$\mathbf{u} \sim N(\mathbf{0},\mathbf{\Omega}) \tag{11.9.2}$$

where $\mathbf{\Omega}$ is known, since

$$\mathbf{\Omega} = \mathbf{\Gamma}^{-1\prime}\mathbf{\Sigma}\mathbf{\Gamma}^{-1} \tag{11.9.3}$$

and both $\mathbf{\Gamma}$ and $\mathbf{\Sigma}$ are known. Random numbers are used to generate a particular sample of values for the reduced-form disturbances $\mathbf{u}$ that are consistent with the known distribution in (11.9.2). The sample size is in the range typically used in an actual econometric study, e.g., 15-50 observations. From this sample for $\mathbf{u}$ equation (11.9.1) yields a sample of values for all endogenous variables $\mathbf{Y}$. Thus the result is a sample of data $\mathbf{Y}$ and $\mathbf{X}$, as in (11.1.5) and (11.1.6), and this sample of data is used to estimate values of structural-form parameters using various alternative estimators. The process of selecting $\mathbf{u}$ and generating a sample for $\mathbf{Y}$ is then replicated, e.g. 50-200 times, leading to a series of samples of data, each of a given size, and a series of alternative estimates, each referring to a particular estimation technique. The resulting estimates can then be compared to the known true values of the parameters.[37]

Various criteria are used in the comparison of estimates to the true values of parameters. Letting θ be the known true value of a parameter and $\hat{\theta}_j$ be the estimated value at the jth replication, the mean estimate of this parameter is

$$\bar{\hat{\theta}} = \frac{1}{N} \sum_{j=1}^{N} \hat{\theta}_j \tag{11.9.4}$$

where N is the total number of replications. The *bias* is then estimated numerically as

$$B = \bar{\hat{\theta}} - \theta \tag{11.9.5}$$

where $\bar{\hat{\theta}}$ is taken as a sample measure of $E(\hat{\theta})$. The bias is one important criterion used in evaluating the small-sample properties of estimators. Another criterion is the *variance*, defined as

$$V = \frac{1}{N} \sum_{j=1}^{N} (\hat{\theta}_j - \bar{\hat{\theta}})^2 \tag{11.9.6}$$

measuring the dispersion of the estimates about their mean value. A third criterion is the *mean square error* defined as

$$M = \frac{1}{N} \sum_{j=1}^{N} (\hat{\theta}_j - \theta)^2 \tag{11.9.7}$$

measuring the dispersion of the estimates about the true value.[38] These criteria are related by

$$M = V + B^2 \tag{11.9.8}$$

[37] The use of tables of random numbers and replication are the hallmarks of the Monte Carlo technique of simulation by random sampling. To give one example of many that illustrate the application of the Monte Carlo technique and one that is completely different from that presented in this section, consider the problem of approximating the area enclosed by a complicated two-dimensional figure. A Monte Carlo approach to this problem would be to enclose the object in a square and to choose units so that the sides of the square are both of length one, so the square has unit area. A table of uniformly distributed random numbers would then be used to select a random point in the square (as a pair of fractional numbers), and this process of random selection would be replicated many times. The limiting fraction of times the randomly chosen points fall in the figure rather than outside it would then approximate its area (in the units of the square). For a discussion of the Monte Carlo technique see Hamersley and Handscomb (1964) and Naylor, Ed. (1969).

[38] Sometimes the square root of the mean square error, the root mean square error, RMS, is used instead of M. Thus

$$\text{RMS} = \sqrt{M} = \sqrt{V + B^2}.$$

so that only two of these three criteria are independent. For example, a particular biased estimate may show a smaller mean square error than a rival unbiased estimate if it more than compensates for the bias by a smaller variance. In addition to these criteria, Monte Carlo studies have used others, such as the median and mode (in addition to the mean) as measures of central tendency; the range, interquartile range, and mean sum of absolute deviations (in addition to the variance and mean squared error) as measures of dispersion; and various higher-order sample moments as measures of skewness and other characteristics of the shape of the distribution of the estimators.

The Monte Carlo studies of small-sample properties of estimators have treated OLS, 2SLS, *k*-class estimators, IV, 3SLS, FIML, and other estimators. The results of these studies are not definitive, since differences between estimators are often not large and the results often vary more significantly with the choice of model and the choice of values for the exogenous variables and elements of the covariance matrix than with the choice of a particular estimator. In terms of actual econometric studies, the data frequently exhibit such inaccuracy and/or the specification of the model is so uncertain that any reasonable rounding off of results would tend to eliminate the differences among the rival estimators. Indeed, in certain applications it is expected that the estimates vary considerably more both over the likely range of data points (e.g., adding or deleting certain data points) and over the likely range of specifications (e.g., adding or deleting an explanatory variable, endogenous or exogenous, in an equation of the model) than over the range of possible estimation techniques.[39] Nevertheless, some guidelines can be drawn from the Monte Carlo studies concerning the choice of estimator.

Starting with the naive and inconsistent technique of OLS, the Monte Carlo studies generally indicate that the OLS estimates have the largest bias among the estimators considered. On the other hand, OLS generally retains the Gauss-Markov property of minimum variance, albeit about a biased mean. The large bias, however, usually more than offsets the small variance, so OLS estimates usually exhibit the largest mean squared error of any technique. Despite these problems the technique still has the advantage of simplicity and low variance and might still be utilized, particularly in preliminary work. OLS is also appropriate if the model is recursive or approximately recursive. More generally, it may be conjectured that OLS is appropriate if the matrix of coefficients of endogenous variables $\mathbf{\Gamma}$ is sparse, containing many zeros. Such sparseness frequently arises as the size of the model increases, since the total number of endogenous variables usually increases faster than the number of such variables appearing in a typical equation of the model.[40]

Of the various possible limited-information estimators, e.g., those of the *k*-class, the 2SLS estimator generally performs best in terms of both bias and mean squared error. It is also usually more stable than the others; in particular, it is not greatly affected by specification errors. Furthermore, it is also generally

[39] For a specific application plus a discussion of this point see Denton and Kuiper (1965).

[40] For a discussion of the conjecture that OLS may be appropriate when $\mathbf{\Gamma}$ is sparse see Smith (1973). Both Mosbaek and Wold (1970) and Smith (1973) found that OLS tends to improve relative to the limited-information estimators as the size of the model increases. See also Klein (1960) for a discussion of the use of OLS.

easily and inexpensively computed.[41] On the other hand, the 2SLS estimator is significantly affected by multicollinearity. Nevertheless, the 2SLS estimator is generally the best available limited-information estimator.

The full-information techniques, specifically 3SLS and FIML, generally provide the most desirable estimators in terms of both bias and mean squared error when the model is correctly specified and the variables are correctly measured. FIML is, however, extremely sensitive to both specification error and measurement error. A slight misspecification or measurement error can change the results so as to make the FIML estimator less desirable than the limited-information estimators. Such a sensitivity to specification error and measurement error may be expected in this approach, where, because of its computation via a system of nonlinear equations, an error in one equation or in one variable will propagate throughout the whole system in the process of estimation. By contrast, the limited-information approach, which estimates only one equation at a time, confines a misspecification in one equation to that particular equation and confines an error in measurement in one variable to those equations containing that particular variable. In addition to this sensitivity to error, the full-information estimators, particularly FIML, are, as already noted, computationally more complicated than other estimators and hence more costly to use. Furthermore, both FIML and 3SLS require a much larger sample size than the limited-information estimators.

The results of the Monte Carlo studies thus suggest that the 2SLS estimator, while not ideal, is a good compromise choice among the group of various estimators. Thus, 2SLS avoids the bias (and inconsistency) of OLS while, at the same time, it avoids the sensitivity to specification error and measurement error (and the cost) of 3SLS and FIML. Of course other estimators may be more appropriate under certain circumstances. If, for example, the model is nearly recursive, then the 2SLS approach may not be necessary and OLS may be appropriate. OLS may also be appropriate if the first-stage R^2 values are either "too small" or "too large," as discussed in Section 11.5. At the other extreme, if correlations between stochastic disturbance terms in different equations are important and specification errors and sample size are not a problem, then it may be appropriate to improve upon the 2SLS estimates by using the 3SLS approach. Barring such special circumstances, 2SLS is both reasonable and appropriate as an estimation technique. It is, therefore, not at all surprising that 2SLS has emerged as the most widely used technique for estimating simultaneous-equations systems, such as those discussed in the next two chapters.

[41] Studies of the exact finite-sample distribution of estimators, while limited to very small simultaneous systems of two or three endogenous variables, suggest that for 2SLS the number of finite moments is, at most, equal to the number of independent overidentifying restrictions for the equation, higher-order moments generally failing to exist. For example, no finite moments exist if the equation is just identified. Comparisons of estimators involving such moments, e.g., a comparison of the bias for estimators with no finite first moments, are meaningless. See Smith (1973) and Basmann (1974).

PROBLEMS

11-A Show that if the simultaneous-equations system includes a definitional equation, then the covariance matrix $\mathbf{\Sigma}$ in (11.1.3) is positive semidefinite rather than positive definite. Will excluding all definitional equations ensure that $\mathbf{\Sigma}$ is positive definite?

11-B Express conditions (11.1.2) to (11.1.4) on the stochastic disturbance term for the prototype macro model in (11.1.23).

11-C Consider (11.3.21) for the variant model (11.1.26) in which Y_{i-1} does not appear, so $\beta_4 = 0$. By using the reduced-form equation for $\dot{Y}_i$ show that the OLS estimator is consistent if any of the following conditions hold:

$$\gamma_1'\gamma_3' = 1$$

$$\text{Var}(G) = \infty$$

$$\text{Var}(\epsilon^{C'}) = 0 \quad \text{and} \quad \text{Cov}(\epsilon^{Y'}\epsilon^{C'}) = 0$$

11-D Show that the OLS estimators of each equation of a recursive model, in which $\mathbf{\Gamma}$ is triangular and $\mathbf{\Sigma}$ is diagonal, are consistent.

11-E Using (11.4.16) and (11.4.17) as in (11.4.29), show that the OLS estimator of the marginal propensity to consume for the variant model (11.4.28) is both biased and inconsistent.

11-F Consider the prototype micro model of Section 2.6, which takes the form

$$(q \quad p)\begin{pmatrix} -1 & -1 \\ \gamma_1 & \gamma_2 \end{pmatrix} + (I \quad r \quad 1)\begin{pmatrix} \beta_1 & 0 \\ 0 & \beta_2 \\ \delta_1 & \delta_2 \end{pmatrix} = (\epsilon^D \quad \epsilon^S)$$

where the stochastic disturbance terms are distributed normally:

$$(\epsilon^D \quad \epsilon^S) \sim \mathrm{N}\left[(0 \quad 0), \begin{pmatrix} \sigma_D^2 & \sigma_{SD} \\ \sigma_{SD} & \sigma_S^2 \end{pmatrix}\right]$$

1. Obtain the OLS estimators of both equations and show that they are inconsistent by demonstrating that the explanatory endogenous variable is correlated with the stochastic disturbances in both equations. Find explicit expressions for $E(p_i\epsilon_i^D)$ and $E(p_i\epsilon_i^S)$.
2. Obtain the ILS estimators of both equations and determine their distribution.
3. Show that if $\beta_2 = 0$, then consistent estimation of the demand equation is impossible.

11-G For the 2SLS approach to estimation:

1. Show that the elements of $\mathbf{v}_1$, as defined in (11.5.16), have zero mean, exhibit constant variance, and are uncorrelated.

2. Show that the 2SLS estimators do not exist if $n < k$.
3. Show that the 2SLS estimators satisfy the orthogonality conditions

$$\mathbf{X}_1'\hat{\boldsymbol{\varepsilon}}_1 = \mathbf{X}_1'(\mathbf{y}_1 - \mathbf{Y}_1\hat{\boldsymbol{\gamma}}_1 - \mathbf{X}_1\hat{\boldsymbol{\beta}}_1) = \mathbf{0}$$

where $\hat{\boldsymbol{\varepsilon}}_1$ is the vector of 2SLS residuals. How many conditions does this represent?
4. Show that the sum of the 2SLS residuals vanishes.

11-H Prove that the R^2_{2SLS} for the second stage of 2SLS, as defined in footnote 14, cannot exceed unity but can be negative. Under what conditions will it be negative?

11-I Prove that the ILS estimator expressed as an instrumental-variable estimator in (11.6.9) is the same as the ILS estimator in (11.4.12).

11-J Using the interpretation of the k-class estimator as an instrumental-variable estimator in (11.6.25) and the conditions for an instrumental-variable estimator to be consistent in (11.6.28) and (11.6.29), prove that the k-class estimator is consistent if

$$\text{plim}\,(k - 1) = 0$$

as in (11.5.53). Also prove that the k-class estimator has the same asymptotic covariance matrix as 2SLS, given in (11.6.36), if

$$\text{plim}\,\sqrt{n}\,(k - 1) = 0$$

as in footnote 20.

11-K Prove that the estimator $\hat{\sigma}_1^2$ in (11.6.35) is a consistent estimator of σ_1^2 if $\hat{\boldsymbol{\delta}}_1$ is the 2SLS estimator. Also prove that $\hat{\hat{\sigma}}_1^2$ obtained as in (11.6.35) but where $\mathbf{Z}_1$ is replaced by $\hat{\mathbf{Z}}_1$ (and $\hat{\boldsymbol{\delta}}_1$ is the 2SLS estimator) is not a consistent estimator of σ_1^2

11-L Prove that the 3SLS estimator in (11.7.21) and the 2SLS estimator in (11.7.16) are identical if either

1. All equations are just identified, or
2. The error term of any one equation is contemporaneously uncorrelated with the error term of any other equation, i.e., $\boldsymbol{\Sigma}$ is diagonal.

11-M Prove that the 3SLS estimator can be written

$$\hat{\boldsymbol{\delta}}^*_{3SLS} = [\hat{\mathbf{Z}}^{*\prime}(\boldsymbol{\Sigma}^{-1} \otimes \mathbf{I})\hat{\mathbf{Z}}^*]^{-1}\hat{\mathbf{Z}}^{*\prime}(\boldsymbol{\Sigma}^{-1} \otimes \mathbf{I})\mathbf{y}^*$$

and, from this expression, show that the 3SLS estimator is defined only if each equation of the system is either overidentified or just identified.

11-N Prove that the 3SLS estimator is asymptotically more efficient than 2SLS, (11.7.27), using the asymptotic covariance matrices in (11.7.41) and (11.7.42).

11-O Prove that if $\mathbf{\Sigma}$ is the symmetric matrix $(\sigma_{hh'})$ and its inverse is $(\sigma^{hh'})$, then

$$\frac{\partial \ln |\mathbf{\Sigma}^{-1}|}{\partial \sigma^{hh'}} = \sigma_{hh'}$$

as was used in (11.8.12) and (11.8.17)

11-P Prove that ILS estimators are equivalent to FIML estimators if the model is just identified.

11-Q Consider the following simultaneous-equations system:

$$(y_1 \quad y_2)\begin{pmatrix} -1 & \gamma_2 \\ \gamma_1 & -1 \end{pmatrix} + (x_1 \quad x_2 \quad x_3)\begin{pmatrix} \beta_1 & 0 \\ 0 & \beta_2 \\ 0 & \beta_3 \end{pmatrix} = (\epsilon_1 \quad \epsilon_2)$$

where there are no intercepts, since all variables are measured as deviations from mean values. In this system the first equation is overidentified and the second equation is just identified. Given data $y_{i1}, y_{i2}, x_{i1}, x_{i2}, x_{i3}$ for $i = 1, 2, \ldots, n$, construct, using summation notation,

1. The OLS estimator of the first equation.
2. The ILS estimator of the second equation.
3. The 2SLS and k-class estimators of the first equation.
4. The IV estimator of the first equation.
5. The 3SLS estimator of both equations.

11-R An equation widely used in applied econometrics is the constant elasticity equation

$$y = Ax_1^{\alpha_1} x_2^{\alpha_2} \cdots x_k^{\alpha_k} e^u$$

where y is the dependent variable, the x's are explanatory variables, A and the α's are parameters, and u is a stochastic disturbance term.

1. Why is the equation called a "constant elasticity" equation? Interpret the elasticities in the case of demand equations and in the case of a production function.
2. Assume $k = 2$ and assume the x's are exogenous. Given a sample of n data points on y, x_1, and x_2, show specifically how you would estimate the parameters of the model.
3. Again assume $k = 2$ and that x_1 is exogenous, but now suppose x_2 is endogenous. How would you now estimate the parameters of the model, given a sample of n data points? [Make whatever assumptions you feel appropriate as to the specification of additional equation(s) of the model.]

11-S In a model of the money market the demand for money depends on the interest rate and population, while the interest rate depends on the quantity of money, the discount rate, and excess reserves. Assume the money market is in equilibrium, the demand for money equaling the quantity of money. Assume the quantity of money (M) and the interest rate (r) are endogenous, while population (N), the discount rate (d), and excess reserves (R) are exogenous. Each equation of the model (other than the equilibrium condition) is linear and stochastic but contains no intercept, variables being measured in terms of deviations from their mean values.

1. Express the structural equations and reduced-form equations as matrix equations, and determine the identification of each of the structural equations, analyzing both order and rank conditions.
2. For each relevant equation obtain the following estimators:

   OLS = ordinary least squares

   ILS = indirect least squares

   2SLS = two-stage least squares

   in terms of data on each of the variables of the model: M_t, r_t, N_t, d_t, R_t for $t = 1, 2, \ldots, T$. Which estimators are identical? Which one(s) would you use?

11-T For the Kogiku model of the raw materials market, as presented in problem 2-J:

1. Examine the order and rank conditions for each of the structural equations.
2. Develop alternative estimators for each of the structural equations, based on the estimators presented in this chapter. Which one(s) would you use?

11-U For the Horowitz model of the synthetic rubber market, as presented in problem 2-K:

1. Examine the order and rank conditions for each of the structural equations.
2. Develop alternative estimators for each of the structural equations, based on the estimators presented in this chapter. Which one(s) would you use?

11-V A subject of some debate in the economics literature is whether growth in the money supply is a cause or an effect of inflation. Outline a simultaneous-equations model econometric project that could shed some light on this issue and discuss how such a model might be estimated.

BIBLIOGRAPHY

Amemiya, T. (1966a), "Specification Analysis in the Estimation of Parameters of a Simultaneous Equation Model with Autoregressive Residuals." *Econometrica*, 34: 283–306.

Amemiya, T. (1966b), "On the Use of Principal Components of Independent

Variables in Two-Stage Least Squares Estimation." *International Economic Review*, 7: 283–303.

Amemiya, T. (1974), "The Nonlinear Two-Stage Least Squares Estimator." *Journal of Econometrics*, 2: 105–10.

Anderson, T. W., and T. Sawa (1973), "Distribution of Estimates of Coefficients of a Single Equation in a Simultaneous System and their Asymptotic Expansions." *Econometrica*, 41: 683–714.

Apostol, T. M. (1974), *Mathematical Analysis*, 2nd Ed. Reading, Mass.: Addison-Wesley Publishing Co.

Basmann, R. L. (1957), "A Generalized Classical Method of Linear Estimation of Coefficients in a Structural Equation." *Econometrica*, 25: 77–83.

Basmann, R. L. (1959), "The Computation of Generalized Classical Estimates of Coefficients in a Structural Equation." *Econometrica*, 27: 72–81.

Basmann, R. L. (1960), "On the Asymptotic Distribution of Generalized Linear Estimators." *Econometrica*, 28: 97–108.

Basmann, R. L. (1961), "A Note on the Exact Finite Sample Frequency Functions of Generalized Classical Linear Estimators in Two Leading Over-identified Cases." *Journal of the American Statistical Association*, 56: 619–36.

Basmann, R. L. (1963), "A Note on the Exact Finite Sample Frequency Functions of Generalized Classical Linear Estimators in a Leading Three Equation Case." *Journal of the American Statistical Association*, 58: 161–71.

Basmann, R. L. (1974), "Exact Finite Sample Distributions for Some Econometric Estimators and Test Statistics: A Survey and Appraisal," in M. D. Intriligator and D. A. Kendrick, Eds., *Frontiers of Quantitative Economics*, Vol. II. Amsterdam: North-Holland Publishing Co.

Berndt, E. R., B. H. Hall, R. E. Hall, and J. A. Hausman (1974), "Estimation and Inference in Nonlinear Structural Models." *Annals of Economic and Social Measurement*, 3: 653–65.

Brundy, J. M., and D. W. Jorgenson (1971), "Efficient Estimation of Simultaneous Equations by Instrumental Variables." *Review of Economics and Statistics*, 53: 207–24.

Brundy J. M., and D. W. Jorgenson (1973), "Consistent and Efficient Estimation of Systems of Simultaneous Equations," in P. Zarembka, Ed., *Frontiers in Econometrics*. New York: Academic Press.

Brundy J. M., and D. W. Jorgenson (1974), "The Relative Efficiency of Instrumental Variables Estimators of Systems of Simultaneous Equations." *Annals of Economic and Social Measurement* 3: 679–700.

Chow, G. (1973), "On the Computation of Full Information Maximum Likelihood Estimates for Nonlinear Equation Systems." *Review of Economics and Statistics*, 55: 104–9.

Christ, C. F. (1966), *Econometric Models and Methods*. New York: John Wiley & Sons, Inc.

Cragg, J. (1967), "On the Relative Small-Sample Properties of Several Structural-Equation Estimators." *Econometrica*, 35: 89–110.

Denton, F. T., and J. Kuiper (1965), "The Effect of Measurement Errors on Parameter Estimates and Forecasts: A Case Study Based on Canadian Preliminary National Accounts." *Review of Economics and Statistics*, 47: 198–206.

Dhrymes, P. J. (1970), *Econometrics: Statistical Foundations and Applications*. New York: Harper & Row

Dhrymes, P. J., R. Berner, and D. Cummins (1974), "A Comparison of Some Limited Information Estimators for Dynamic Simultaneous Equations Models with Autocorrelated Errors." *Econometrica*, 42: 311–32.

Dhrymes, P. J., and H. Erlat (1974), "Asymptotic Properties of Full Information Estimation in Dynamic Autoregressive Simultaneous Equation Model." *Journal of Econometrics*, 2: 247–60.

Dutta, M., and E. Lyttkens (1974), "Iterative Instrumental Variables Method and Estimation of a Large Simultaneous System." *Journal of the American Statistical Association*, 69: 977–86.

Eisenpress, H., and J. Greenstadt (1966), "The Estimation of Nonlinear Econometric Systems." *Econometrica*, 34: 851–61.

Fair, R. C. (1970), "The Estimation of Simultaneous Equation Model with Lagged Endogenous Variables and First Order Serially Correlated Errors." *Econometrica*, 38: 507–16.

Fair, R. C. (1972), "Efficient Estimation of Simultaneous Equations with Autoregressive Errors by Instrumental Variables." *Review of Economics and Statistics*, 54: 444–9.

Fisher, F. M. (1965a), "Dynamic Structure and Estimation in Economy-Wide Econometric Models," in J. S. Duesenberry, G. Fromm, L. R. Klein, and E. Kuh, Eds., *The Brookings Quarterly Econometric Model of the United States*. Chicago: Rand-McNally & Company; Amsterdam: North-Holland Publishing Co.

Fisher, F. M. (1965b), "The Choice of Instrumental Variables in the Estimation of Economy-Wide Econometric Models." *International Economic Review*, 6: 245–74.

Fisk, P. R. (1967), *Stochastically Dependent Equations*. London: Charles Griffen & Co., Ltd.

Goldfeld, S. M., and R. E. Quandt (1968), "Nonlinear Simultaneous Equations: Estimation and Prediction." *International Economic Review*, 9: 113–46.

Goldfeld, S. M., and R. E. Quandt (1972), *Nonlinear Methods in Econometrics*. Amsterdam: North-Holland Publishing Co.

Haavelmo, T. (1943), "The Statistical Implications of a System of Simultaneous Equations." *Econometrica*, 11: 1–12.

Haavelmo, T. (1947), "Methods of Measuring the Marginal Propensity to Consume." *Journal of the American Statistical Association*, 42: 105–22.

Hammersley, J. M., and D. C. Handscomb (1964), *Monte Carlo Methods*. New York: John Wiley & Sons, Inc.

Harkema, R. (1971), *Simultaneous Equations: A Bayesian Approach*. Rotterdam: Universitaire Pers.

Hatanaka, M. (1976), "Several Efficient Two-Step Estimators for the Dynamic Simultaneous Equation Model with Autoregressive Disturbances." *Journal of Econometrics*, 4: 189–204.

Hausman, J. A. (1975), "An Instrumental Variable Approach to Full Information Estimators for Linear and Certain Nonlinear Econometric Models." *Econometrica*, 43: 727–38.

Hoffman, K. (1975), *Analysis in Euclidean Space*. Englewood Cliffs, N.J.: Prentice-Hall, Inc.

Jorgenson, D. W., and J. J. Laffont (1974), "Efficient Estimation of Nonlinear Simultaneous Equations with Additive Disturbances." *Annals of Economic and Social Measurement*, 3: 615–40.

Kadane, J. B. (1971), "Comparison of k-Class Estimators when the Disturbances are Small." *Econometrica*, 39: 723–37.

Kelejian, H. H. (1971), "Two Stage Least Squares and Econometric System Linear in Parameters but Nonlinear in the Endogenous Variables." *Journal of the American Statistical Association*, 66: 373–4.

Klein, L. R. (1960), "Single Equation vs. Equation System Methods of Estimation in Econometrics." *Econometrica*, 28: 866–71.

Klein, L. R. (1969), "Estimation of Interdependent Systems in Macroeconometrics." *Econometrica*, 37: 171–92.

Klein, L. R. (1971), "Forecasting and Policy Evaluation Using Large-Scale Econometric Models: The State of the Art," in M. D. Intriligator, Ed., *Frontiers of Quantitative Economics*. Amsterdam: North-Holland Publishing Co.

Klein, L. R. (1973), "The Treatment of Undersized Samples in Econometrics." in A. A. Powell and R. A. Williams, Eds., *Econometric Studies of Macro and Monetary Relations*. Amsterdam: North-Holland Publishing Co.

Kloek, T., and L. B. M. Mennes (1960), "Simultaneous Equation Estimation Based on Principal Components of Predetermined Variables." *Econometrica*, 28: 45–61.

Lyttkens, E. (1970), "Symmetric and Asymmetric Estimation Methods," in Mosbaek and Wold, Eds. (1970).

Madansky, A. (1964), "On the Efficiency of Three-Stage Least Squares Estimation." *Econometrica*, 32: 51–6.

Madansky, A. (1976), *Foundation of Econometrics*. Amsterdam: North-Holland Publishing Co.

Malinvaud, E. (1970), *Statistical Methods of Econometrics*, 2nd Rev. Ed. Amsterdam: North-Holland Publishing Co.

Mitchell, B. (1971), "Estimation of Large Econometric Models by Principal Component and Instrumental Variable Methods." *Review of Economics and Statistics*, 53: 140–6.

Mitchell, B., and F. M. Fisher (1970), "The Choice of Instrumental Variables in the Estimation of Economy-Wide Econometric Models: Some Further Thoughts." *International Economic Review*, 11: 226–34.

Morales, J. A. (1971), *Bayesian Full Information Structural Analysis*. Berlin. Springer-Verlag.

Mosbaek, E. J., and H. O. Wold, Eds. (1970), *Interdependent Systems: Structure and Estimation*. Amsterdam: North-Holland Publishing Co.

Nagar, A. L. (1959), "The Bias and Moment Matrix of the General k-Class Estimators of the Parameters in Simultaneous Equations." *Econometrica*, 27: 575–95.

Nagar, A. L. (1962), "Double k-Class Estimators of Parameters in Simultaneous Equations and their Small Sample Properties." *International Economic Review*, 3: 168–88.

Naylor, T. H., Ed. (1969), *The Design of Computer Simulation Experiments*. Durham, N.C.: Duke University Press.

Rao, C. R. (1965), *Linear Statistical Inference and Its Applications*. New York: John Wiley & Sons, Inc.

Rothenberg, T. J. (1974), *Efficient Estimator with A Priori Information*. New Haven: Yale University Press.

Rothenberg, T. J., and C. T. Leenders (1964), "Efficient Estimation of Simultaneous Equation Systems." *Econometrica*, 32: 57–76.

Rudin, W. (1964), *Principles of Mathematical Analysis.* New York: McGraw-Hill Book Company.

Sargan, J. D. (1958), "The Estimation of Economic Relationships Using Instrumental Variables." *Econometrica*, 26: 393–415.

Sargan, J. D. (1961), "The Maximum Likelihood Estimations of Economic Relationships with Autoregressive Residuals." *Econometrica*, 29: 414–26.

Sargan, J. D. (1964), "Three-Stage Least Squares and Full Information Maximum Likelihood Estimates." *Econometrica*, 32: 77–81.

Sargan, J. D. (1975), "Asymptotic Theory and Large Models." *International Economic Review*, 16: 75–91.

Sargan, J. D., and W. M. Mikhail (1971), "A General Approximation to the Distribution of Instrumental Variable Estimates." *Econometrica*, 39: 131–69.

Schmidt, P. (1976), *Econometrics*. New York: Marcel Dekker, Inc.

Smith, V. K. (1973), *Monte Carlo Methods*. Lexington: Lexington Books.

Theil, H. (1961), *Economic Forecasts and Policy*, 2nd Ed. Amsterdam: North-Holland Publishing Co.

Theil, H. (1971), *Principles of Econometrics*. New York: John Wiley & Sons, Inc.

Zellner, A. (1971), *An Introduction to Bayesian Inference in Econometrics*. New York: John Wiley & Sons, Inc.

Zellner, A., and H. Theil (1962), "Three Stage Least Squares: Simultaneous Estimation of Simultaneous Equations." *Econometrica*, 30: 54–78.

PART VI

Applications of Simultaneous-Equations Estimation

CHAPTER 12

Applications to Macroeconometric Models

12.1 The nature of macroeconometric models

The earliest and still one of the most important applications of econometric techniques is to macroeconometric models.[1] Such models generally utilize a Keynesian framework for the determination of national income (usually measured as Gross National Product) and its components, consumption and investment, as well as other macroeconomic variables such as those listed in Table 12.1.[2] Such models are utilized for all three purposes of econometrics–structural analysis (e.g., determination of multipliers), forecasting (e.g., forecasting GNP over the next eight quarters), and policy evaluation (e.g., analyzing the impact of government expenditure and taxation programs), as will be seen in Chapters 14-16.

The nature of macroeconometric models can be perhaps easiest understood in terms of the prototype macro model of Chapter 2, of the form

$$C = \gamma_1 Y + \beta_1 + \epsilon^C \tag{12.1.1}$$

$$I = \gamma_2 Y + \beta_2 Y_{-1} + \beta_3 + \epsilon^I \tag{12.1.2}$$

$$Y = C + I + G. \tag{12.1.3}$$

The first equation is a consumption function, according to which consumption (C) is determined as a linear function of current national income (Y). The second equation is an investment function, according to which investment is determined as a linear function of current and lagged national income.[3] Both equations are stochastic, where the stochastic disturbance terms, the ϵ's, are included to represent omitted variables influencing consumption and investment, misspecifi-

[1] For surveys of macroeconometric models see Nerlove (1966), Fromm (1973), Wynn and Holden (1974), and Samuelson (1975). For a presentation of macroeconomics from the perspective of macroeconometric models see Evans (1969) and Kuh and Schmalensee (1972). For a summary overview of macroeconometric models see Figure 12.3 and Table 12.12 on page 454.

[2] Most of these variables are aggregates of corresponding micro variables, such as individual household consumption and individual firm investment. For a discussion of the problem of aggregating micro relationships into macro ones see Section 7.7.

[3] Net foreign investment, exports less imports, is omitted here. The consumption function and investment function have generated considerable interest in their own right. For surveys of econometric studies of the consumption function see Ferber (1962), Suits (1963), and Malinvaud (1970). For surveys of studies of the investment function see Eisner and Strotz (1963), Meyer and Glauber (1964), Bridge (1971), and Jorgenson (1971, 1974).

cation of these two behavioral relationships, and errors in measuring the included variables. By contrast, the last equation is an equilibrium condition, defining national income as the sum of consumption, investment, and government expenditure (G), and is therefore nonstochastic. These three equations determine values of the three current endogenous variables—C, I, and Y—given values of the

Table 12.1. Macroeconomic Variables

GNP and Its Components
- Gross National Product (GNP)
- Consumption
  - Nondurable
  - Durable
- Investment
  - Fixed plant and equipment investment
  - Inventory accumulation
  - Residential construction
- Government
  - Federal
  - State and local
- Net foreign investment
  - Exports
  - Imports

Income
- Disposable income
- Corporate profits
- Income of unincorporated enterprises

Prices, Wages, Interest Rates
- Implicit price deflator for GNP
- Consumer price index (CPI)
- Nonfarm wage rate
- Short-term interest rate
- Long-term interest rate

Employment, Unemployment
- Employment
- Unemployment
- Labor force
- Unemployment rate
- Participation rate

Production
- Index of production
- Production in various sectors

Assets
- Capital stock
- Financial assets

NOTE: See Table 16.1 for macroeconomic policy variables.

one lagged endogenous variable Y_{-1} and the one exogenous variable G.

This model is a prototype of macroeconometric models because all such models generally contain the same basic elements as this one: a consumption function or a group of such functions, an investment function or a group of such functions, and a national income equilibrium condition or a group of such conditions. They generally involve a greater degree of disaggregation than is indicated in the prototype model, however. The prototype macro model disaggregates national income into only three components, two of which are determined endogenously in the model. The macroeconometric models to be discussed below typically further disaggregate these two components. Thus consumption may be disaggregated into consumption of goods and consumption of services, while consumption of goods may be itself further disaggregated into durables (e.g., automobiles) and nondurables (e.g., food). Similarly, investment may be disaggregated into business fixed plant investment, inventory accumulation, and residential construction. Income may itself be disaggregated into various components such as labor income and capital income, while output may be disaggregated by production sector. The macroeconometric models also involve more equations and variables by including certain factors not treated explicitly in the prototype model, which focuses exclusively on national income variables. Among these are prices, wages, interest rates, employment, and unemployment, as indicated in Table 12.1.[4]

The next sections of this chapter will summarize seven different macroeconometric models of the United States economy: the Klein interwar and Morishima-Saito models, two "small" models of less than ten stochastic equations; the Klein-Goldberger and the Wharton models, two "medium-size" models of between ten and 100 equations; and the Brookings model, the MPS model, and the DRI model, three "large" models of more than 100 equations. The last two sections survey various macroeconometric models that have been developed for the U.S., including the seven presented in the earlier sections, and trends in macroeconometric model construction.

12.2 The Klein interwar model

The Klein interwar model was developed by Lawrence R. Klein to analyze the economy of the United States during the period between World Wars I and II, 1921-1941.[5] It is a particularly interesting model, both because it is simple enough to be treated fully, being only slightly larger than the prototype macroeconometric model, and also because it has been used to study policy pursued during the Depression years. The variables of the model are summarized in Table 12.2. The six endogenous variables are simultaneously determined by the model. Of the four exogenous variables, one is clearly determined outside the

[4] See also problem 12-A for how some of these variables can enter a macroeconometric model.

[5] See Klein (1950). This model is also called "Klein Model I" in Goldberger (1964), Christ (1966), and Theil (1971). A larger model in Klein (1950), called "Klein Model III," includes 15 equations, of which 12 are stochastic.

system–time, t. The remaining three are government variables, controlled by government economic policy, and therefore treated as exogenous. The model, as estimated via ordinary least squares using annual data on the U.S. economy, 1921-1941, is presented in Table 12.3. The first three equations are the estimated behavioral equations for consumption, investment, and private wages; the last three equations are identities, for income, profits, and net investment.

Table 12.2. Variables of the Klein Interwar Model

6 Endogenous Variables		*4 Exogenous Variables*	
Y	= Output	G	= Government nonwage expenditure
C	= Consumption	W_G	= Public wages
I	= Investment (net)	T	= Business Taxes
W_P	= Private Wages	t	= Time
Π	= Profits		
K	= Capital stock (at year end)		

NOTE All variables other than K and t are flows, measured in billions of dollars of 1934 purchasing power per year. K, a stock, is measured in billions of 1934 dollars. Time, t, is measured as annual deviations (positive or negative) from 1931.

Table 12.3. The Estimated Klein Interwar Model

(1) $C = 16.79 + 0.800(W_P + W_G) + 0.020\Pi + 0.235\Pi_{-1}$

(2) $I = 17.78 + 0.231\Pi + 0.546\Pi_{-1} - 0.146K_{-1}$

(3) $W_P = 1.60 + 0.420(Y + T - W_G) + 0.164(Y + T - W_G)_{-1} + 0.135t$

(4) $Y = C + I + G$

(5) $\Pi = Y - W_P - T$

(6) $K = K_{-1} + I$

Source Klein (1950).

The interactions of the variables of the model are shown in a flow diagram in Figure 12.1, which follows the approach of Figure 2.8 and can be considered a generalization of Figure 2.7, which represented the prototype macro model in a similar way. Note that in this type of diagram no arrows can point to either lagged endogenous variables or exogenous variables.

This model is clearly only slightly larger than the prototype macro model. Like the prototype model, it includes a single consumption function. In the Klein interwar model, however, consumption in (1) depends not on total income but rather on the components of income–wage income and profit income. Total wage income, the sum of private and government wages, has an associated marginal propensity to consume of 0.8; that is, every dollar of additional wage income increases consumption by 80 cents. By contrast, the marginal propensity to consume out of profit income, either current or lagged, is considerably smaller—0.02 for current profits and 0.23 for lagged profits. The low marginal propensity to consume out of current profit income makes it plausible to include lagged profit income, while the high marginal propensity to consume out of wage income makes it plausible to exclude lagged wage income as a determinant of current consumption expenditure.

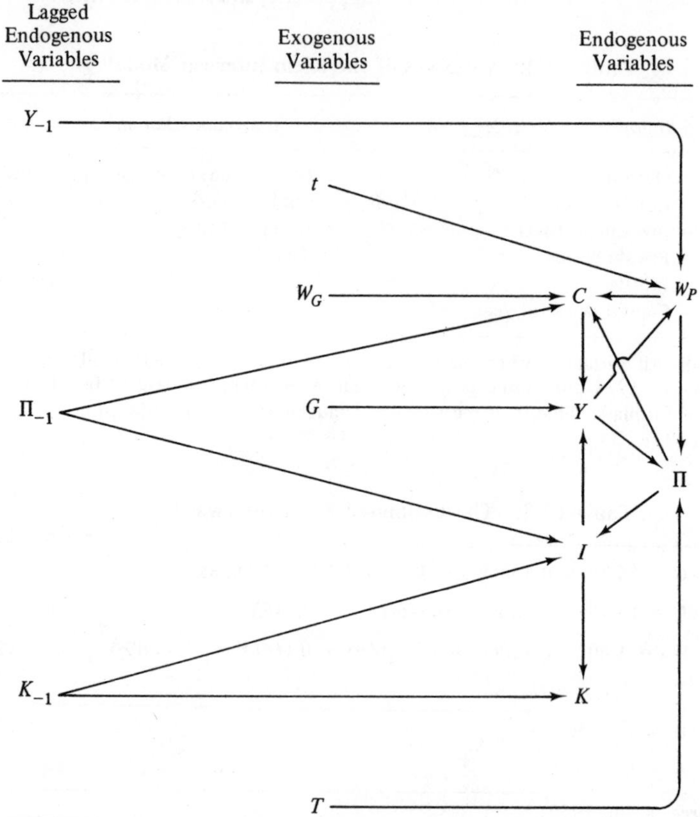

Figure 12.1 Flow Diagram of the Klein Interwar Model [NOTE The dependence of W_P on current and lagged W_G and T is not shown here.]

The investment function of the model (2) is also only a slight elaboration of that of the prototype model. It takes account, as in the consumption function, of the various types of income, but relies upon current and lagged *profit* income rather than current and lagged total income, since profits are more important for investment than wages. The last term is the depreciation term, suggesting that 15% of capital depreciates each year and must be replaced.

The third equation of the model (3), that for private wages, has no counterpart in the prototype model, because the latter does not treat the separate wage and profit components of income. According to the Klein interwar model private wages depend on current and lagged income and on a time trend, which is a proxy for increased union strength during the period. This equation may be considered a private demand-for-labor equation, since it determines the wage bill paid by private industry.

The remaining equations of the Klein interwar model are three identities, thereby completing the model, which involves six equations and six endogenous variables. Equation (4) is the national income identity, as in the prototype model. Equation (5) defines total profits of the private sector as the difference between revenue–here, for the national economy–total output, and cost, represented here by private wages and taxes. Finally equation (6) defines net investment as the change in capital stock.

The reduced form of the model is presented in Table 12.4, where endogenous variables have been ordered in such a way that those with included lagged values

Table 12.4. The Reduced Form of the Klein Interwar Model

$$\mathbf{y} = \mathbf{y}_{-1}\mathbf{\Pi}_1 + \mathbf{z}\mathbf{\Pi}_2$$

where

$$\mathbf{y} = (\Pi \quad Y \quad K \quad C \quad W_P \quad I)$$

$$\mathbf{y}_{-1} = (\Pi \quad Y \quad K \quad C \quad W_P \quad I)_{-1}$$

$$\mathbf{z} = (W_G \quad T \quad G \quad t \quad W_{G-1} \quad T_{-1})$$

$$\hat{\mathbf{\Pi}}_1 = \begin{pmatrix} 0.863 & 1.489 & 0.746 & 0.743 & 0.626 & 0.746 \\ -0.063 & 0.174 & -0.015 & 0.189 & 0.237 & -0.015 \\ -0.164 & -0.283 & 0.816 & -0.098 & -0.119 & -0.184 \\ 0 & 0 & 0 & 0 & 0 & 0 \\ 0 & 0 & 0 & 0 & 0 & 0 \\ 0 & 0 & 0 & 0 & 0 & 0 \end{pmatrix}$$

$$\hat{\mathbf{\Pi}}_2 = \begin{pmatrix} -0.224 & 0.614 & -0.052 & 0.666 & -0.162 & -0.052 \\ -1.281 & -1.484 & -0.296 & -0.188 & -0.204 & -0.296 \\ 1.119 & 1.930 & 0.259 & 0.671 & 0.811 & 0.259 \\ -0.052 & 0.143 & -0.012 & 0.155 & 0.195 & -0.012 \\ 0.063 & -0.174 & 0.015 & -0.189 & -0.237 & 0.015 \\ -0.063 & 0.174 & -0.015 & 0.189 & 0.237 & -0.015 \end{pmatrix}$$

Source Theil and Boot (1962).

appear first.[6] Since lagged C, W_P, and I do not appear in the model the coefficients of the lagged variables are zero, giving the last three rows of zeros in the coefficient matrix $\hat{\mathbf{\Pi}}_1$ for the lagged endogenous variables. From $\hat{\mathbf{\Pi}}_2$ a billion-dollar increase in government expenditure in the current period increases income by \$1.930 billion, private wages by \$0.811 billion, consumption by \$0.671 billion, and investment by \$0.259 billion, the circled figures. The balanced-budget income multiplier for government spending (where the change in G is

[6] See Theil and Boot (1962).

offset by the change in T) is 1.930 − 1.484 = 0.446. The implied long-run multipliers for maintained changes in values of three of the exogenous variables are given in Table 12.5. Thus the long-run balanced-budget income multiplier is 2.323 − 1.569 = 0.754, of which 0.446 occurs in the first year.

Table 12.5. Long-Run Multipliers for the Klein Interwar Model

	Π	Y	K	C	W_P	I
W_G	−0.192	0.536	−1.024	0.536	−0.271	0
T	−1.237	−1.569	−6.564	−0.569	−0.333	0
G	0.965	2.323	5.123	1.323	1.358	0

Source Theil and Boot (1962).

In addition to this type of structural analysis, the Klein interwar model has been used both for forecasting and for policy evaluation. It was not very successful in predicting postwar phenomena, however, as compared to various naive models, which tended to work as well or better.[7] This lack of predictive ability may, however, be attributed to the change in the structure of the U.S. economy resulting from World War II. The model has also been used for policy evaluation, specifically the evaluation of policy choices during the Depression.[8] This model is therefore useful as an exploratory model for all three purposes of econometrics—structural analysis, forecasting, and policy evaluation. A deficiency of the model, however, which prevents its use for anything more than exploratory work, is its use of highly aggregated variables and its failure to consider factors other than those of national income determination, such as production, economic growth and financial factors. These deficiencies have been remedied in later models.

12.3. The Morishima-Saito model

The Morishima-Saito model of the U.S. economy over the period 1902–1952 (excluding 1941–1945) is a model of long-term growth.[9] It has been used both for structural analysis and for policy evaluation, particularly for the study of the relative effectiveness of monetary and fiscal policy. The variables of the model are summarized in Table 12.6. The model was estimated using annual data. The variables Y, C, I, B, and K are measured in billions of dollars of 1929 purchasing power; population variables N and L are measured in millions of persons; the price level p is an implicit deflator for NNP, an index number with 1929 as the

[7] Christ (1951).

[8] See van den Bogaard and Theil (1959) and Chapter 16.

[9] See Morishima and Saito (1972). Other models of long-term growth are the Valavanis and Hickman and Coen models described in Section 12.9.

base year; the wage rate w is an average of earnings per worker, in thousands of current dollars; the corporate bond yield r is in percent per annum; the hours worked per person h is in thousands of hours; cash balances M are in billions of current dollars; and time is measured as annual deviations from 1927.

Table 12.6. Variables of the Morishima-Saito Model

9 Endogenous Variables	*6 Exogenous Variables*
Y = Net national output (national income)	I = Investment (gross)
C = Consumption	B = Trade balance
D = Capital consumption allowances	M = Cash balances
K = Capital stock (at year end)	N = Population 15 and over
L = Employment	t = Time (1927: 0)
p = Price level (1929: 1)	u = Dummy variable (0 before 1941; 1 after 1946)
w = Wage rate	
r = Corporate bond yield	
h = Hours worked per person per year	

NOTE The notations for L and N have been reversed from those used by Morishima and Saito in order to be consistent with their use elsewhere in this book.

The model, in log linear form (using base-10 logarithms) was estimated using two-stage least squares and the resulting estimated model is presented in Table 12.7. In this table the numbers in parentheses are standard errors, the coefficients of determination $\bar{R}^2$ are adjusted for degrees of freedom, and the Durbin-Watson statistics are given as d.

The first equation (1) is an estimated consumption function, determining consumption per capita as a function of its lagged value, per-capita income, and real cash balances. Since the relationship is linear in the logs of the variables, the coefficients are elasticities. For example, the elasticity of consumption (per capita) with respect to income (per capita) is estimated to be 0.349. Given an observed average propensity to consume at the sample means of 0.924, the estimated marginal propensity to consume at the sample mean for this nonlinear consumption function is 0.322, implying a multiplier of 1.47.[10]

The second equation (2) is a liquidity preference function determining real cash holdings per dollar of income as a function of its lagged value, income, the interest rate, and the dummy variable.[11] The estimation of this equation proceeds via two steps—first estimating the bracketed term, accounting for income and lagged cash balances, and then estimating the rest of the equation accounting for the interest rate and the dummy variables.

The third equation (3) is a production function of the log-linear Cobb-Douglas type, with constant returns to scale, as discussed in Section 8.3, e.g. (8.3.21). It determines output as a function of manhours of labor, adjusted for utilization via the employment ratio, and capital. A time trend accounts for technological

[10] Note that the elasticity is $(Y/C)\,(dC/dY) = 0.349$, so $dC/dY = (0.349)(0.924) = 0.322$ and the multiplier is $[1 - (dC/dY)]^{-1} = 1.47$.

[11] This equation was discussed earlier in Section 9.2.

Table 12.7. The Estimated Morishima-Saito Model

Consumption Function:

$$(1)\quad \log\frac{C}{N} = \underset{(0.054)}{0.349}\log\frac{Y}{N} + \underset{(0.036)}{0.160}\log\frac{M}{pN} + \underset{(0.079)}{0.460}\log\frac{C_{-1}}{N_{-1}} + 0.007$$

$\bar{R}^2 = 0.98, \quad d = 2.14$

Liquidity Preference Function:

$$(2)\quad \log\frac{M}{p} = \underset{(0.035)}{1.190}\left(0.586\log Y + 0.414\log\frac{M_{-1}}{p} + 0.295\right) \underset{(0.061)}{-0.202}\log r - \underset{(0.022)}{0.048}u - 0.650$$

$\bar{R}^2 = 0.98, \quad d = 1.09$

Production Function:

$$(3)\quad \log Y = 0.824\log hL + 0.176\log K_{-1} + \underset{(0.00041)}{0.00633}t + \underset{(0.017)}{0.052}u - 0.242655$$

$\bar{R}^2 = 0.93, \quad d = 0.71$

Relative-Share Equation:

$$(4)\quad \frac{wL}{pY} = 0.824 \quad\text{or}\quad \log\frac{wL}{pY} = \underset{(0.027)}{-0.084}$$

Wage-Determination Equation:

$$(5)\quad \log\frac{w}{h} = \underset{(0.019)}{1.006}\log\frac{w_{-1}}{h_{-1}} + \underset{(0.217)}{0.456}\left(\frac{1}{5}\log\frac{p}{p_{-1}} + \frac{4}{5}\log\frac{p_{-1}}{p_{-2}}\right) + \underset{(0.171)}{0.188}\log\frac{L}{0.57N} + 0.017$$

$\bar{R}^2 = 0.99, \quad d = 1.94$

Hours-Worked Equation:

$$(6)\quad \log h = \underset{(0.016)}{-0.282}\log\frac{w_{-1}}{p_{-1}h_{-1}} + \underset{(0.056)}{0.343}\log\frac{L}{0.57N} + 0.324$$

$\bar{R}^2 = 0.91, \quad d = 1.07$

Depreciation Equation:

$$(7)\quad \log D = \underset{(0.085)}{1.593}\log K_{-1} - 2.817$$

$\bar{R}^2 = 0.89, \quad d = 0.14$

Identities:

(8) $Y = C + I - D + B$

(9) $K = K_{-1} + I - D$

Source Morishima and Saito (1972).

NOTE "log" means base 10 logarithms.

change, which is estimated to add about 0.6% per year to output. The significant coefficient of the dummy variable indicates a shift in the production function from the prewar to the postwar period. The input coefficients imply elasticities of output with respect to labor of 0.824 and with respect to capital of 0.176.

The fourth equation (4) is a relative-share equation, giving labor's share of national income. This equation is derived from the production-function equation by equating the marginal product of labor to the real wage, as in (8.3.23). According to this estimate, labor earns 82.4% of national income.

The fifth equation (5) is a wage-determination equation determining hourly earnings as a function of its lagged value, the current and lagged rate of price change, and the employment ratio, here given as $L/0.57N$, where $0.57N$ is an estimate of the employable population, that is, 57% of the total population.

The sixth equation (6) is an hours-worked equation, determining hours worked as a function of lagged real hourly earnings and the employment ratio.

The last estimated equation (7) is a depreciation equation determining capital consumption allowances as a function of the lagged capital stock.

The remaining two equations are identities. Equation (8) is the national income accounting identity, and equation (9) is the identity relating the change in capital stock to net investment.

While the Morishima-Saito model and the Klein interwar model contain some common components, e.g., a consumption function and the definitional relation between capital stock and investment, they differ fundamentally in the phenomena they are intended to represent. The Klein interwar model is a representation of short-run national income determination, with each one of its equations representing either income or one of the expenditure or income components of income. The Morishima-Saito model, by contrast, is a representation of long-run economic growth and related factors. The production function in this model measures and projects long-run growth of output, the other equations being present primarily in order to determine the labor and capital components of this function. Given the focus on long-run growth, represented formally in the model by the production function, some deficiencies might be noted. First, constant returns to scale are assumed, whereas the possibility of nonconstant returns to scale would have a significant bearing on the issue of long-term growth. Second, investment is treated as exogenous, whereas its endogenous nature and resulting implications for capital formation and output would be important in analyzing growth. Third, only disembodied technical change is treated, whereas economic growth may be related to qualitative changes in the inputs of labor and capital.

The implications of the estimated Morishima-Saito model for structural analysis and policy evaluation will be discussed in Chapters 14 and 16, respectively. It might simply be noted here, however, that it implies various multipliers for the effect of investment (which includes government spending) and cash balances on both income and employment. These multipliers tend to support the Keynesian concept that fiscal policy is relatively more effective than monetary policy in reducing unemployment when the rate of unemployment is high.[12]

12.4 The Klein-Goldberger model

The Klein-Goldberger model is a "medium size" econometric model of the U.S. economy for the period 1929–1952, excluding the war years 1942–1945.[13] It consists of 20 equations, of which 15 are stochastic and 5 are identities. It contains 34 variables, of which 20 are endogenous and 14 are exogenous. Table 12.8 summarizes these variables. The model has been extremely important

Table 12.8 Variables of the Klein-Goldberger Model

20 Endogenous Variables	*14 Exogenous Variables*
5 Income	Government expenditure
Consumption	4 Direct taxes
Gross private investment	Indirect tax
Depreciation	5 Population and labor force
Imports	Hours worked
Corporate saving	Excess reserves
Corporate surplus	Import prices
Private employees	
Capital stock	
2 Liquid assets	
3 Prices	
2 Interest rates	

in influencing the construction of most of the later models, as will be seen in Figure 12.3 on page 452.

From the table it is clear that the Klein-Goldberger model involves a greater degree of disaggregation than the "small" models treated in previous sections. Thus, five categories of income, five of population and labor force, four of direct tax, three prices, two liquid assets, and two interest rates are included in the model. The model includes lags of up to five years, cumulated investment, and time trends. It makes use of the Koyck distributed lag, and it contains several nonlinear equations.

The Klein-Goldberger model was estimated using 20 annual observations from the periods 1929–1941 and 1946–1952; the war years were excluded because it was believed they did not conform to the economic structure described by the

[12] For a debate over the relative effectiveness of monetary and fiscal policy see Ando and Modigliani (1965) and Friedman and Meiselman (1965).

[13] See Klein and Goldberger (1955).

model. All variables representing stocks and flows of goods were measured in billions of dollars of 1939 purchasing power. The method of estimation was limited-information maximum likelihood. It might be noted that when the model was reestimated using the same data but using the technique of ordinary least squares, the resulting estimates were not very different.[14]

The Klein-Goldberger model treats both real and monetary phenomena, with most but not all behavioral equations in real terms. Of these it is generally more successful in representing real phenomena, particularly the components of demand in GNP other than investment. A major problem with investment is that the model lumps together inventory investment with fixed business investment, precluding a detailed study of inventory cycles. The model tends, in fact, to be dominated by consumer demand elements, reflecting its Keynesian origins. Thus, production is treated in a cursory way, and the entire monetary portion of the model, dealing with prices and interest rates, is generally inadequate.[15] Later models have sought to remedy these deficiencies.

One study, by Adelman and Adelman, compared the long-term behavior of the Klein-Goldberger model to actual trends and cycles in the U.S. economy.[16] It simulated the performance of the model over time, from 1952 to 2052, with and without additive random shocks, given as artificially generated random numbers in the behavioral and technological equations. Without the random shocks a linearized version of the model exhibited, over the long run, simple linear growth trends for each of its variables, assuming the exogenous variables follow linear trends. With the addition of the exogenous normally distributed additive random shocks (with variances equal to the residual variances exhibited over the sample), the resulting simulated series exhibited business cycles similar in length, amplitude, and timing to those actually observed for the U.S. economy. In fact, the simulated cycles conformed remarkably well to the usual pattern of lead-lag relationships over the cycle, as formulated and estimated by the National Bureau of Economic Research, and to other measures, such as the mean duration of the cycle and the mean lengths of the expansion and contraction phases. This result supports the validity of the model with the additive random shocks as a representation of the U.S. economy. It is also consistent with the view that cycles represent a response of the economy to exogenous random shocks.

12.5 The Wharton model

The Wharton model is a "medium size" macroeconometric model of the U.S. economy, a descendant of the Klein-Goldberger model but differing from the

[14] Fox (1958). Where there was a substantial discrepancy, such as when the same coefficient had a different sign, the OLS estimators tended, on the basis of economic considerations, to be superior to the LIML estimators. It might also be noted that it was impossible to estimate the reduced form of the model, since the number of predetermined variables exceeded the number of observations. Klein and Goldberger therefore restricted the predetermined variables to those that on the basis of a priori considerations seemed most important to "capture the spirit of simultaneity."

[15] See Goldberger (1959).

[16] See Adelman and Adelman (1959). See also Hickman, Ed. (1972).

previous models in three important respects.[17] First, it is estimated using quarterly rather than annual data, the original estimates of the model being based on 68 observations from the first quarter of 1948 to the last quarter of 1964, usually written 1948.1-1964.4. Second, unlike the previous models, it was designed explicitly for developing forecasts of the future of the economy, particularly national income components and unemployment. Third, it involves a greater degree of disaggregation, a better treatment of accounting identities, and a better integration of the monetary sector than the previous models.

The Wharton model consists of 76 equations, of which 47 are stochastic and 29 are identities. The original version contains 118 variables, of which 76 are endogenous and 42 are exogenous.[18] Table 12.9. summarizes these variables.

Table 12.9. Variables of the Wharton Model

76 Endogenous Variables	*42 Exogenous Variables*
5 Output	2 Output
2 Sales	Income
4 Income	Consumption anticipations
5 Consumption	Farm fixed investment
5 Fixed investment	Farm inventories
4 Depreciation	2 Investment anticipations
Exports	Depreciation
3 Imports	2 Government purchases
2 Corporate profits	Interest payments
Dividends	2 Social Security contributions
2 Retained earnings	Housing starts
Cash flow	Population
Inventory valuation adjustment	5 Labor force
Rent and interest payments	2 Wage bill
3 Taxes	7 Prices
Transfer payments	Discount rate
4 Labor force	Net free reserves
2 Hours worked	Time
2 Wage bill	6 Dummy variables
2 Unemployment rate	Productivity trend
6 Capital stocks	Index of world trade
3 Inventories	Statistical discrepancy
Unfilled orders	
Index of capacity utilization	
10 Prices	
2 Wage rates	
2 Interest rates	

From the table it is clear that this model is considerably more disaggregated than previous ones. For example, while all the previous models involved only single

[17] See Evans and Klein (1967, 1968), Evans (1969), and Evans, Klein, and Saito (1972). See also Figure 12.3.

[18] A later version is slightly larger. See Table 12.12.

aggregate measures of consumption and investment expenditure, the Wharton model involves five different categories of consumption expenditure and five different categories of investment expenditure. It disaggregates the economy into manufacturing and nonmanufacturing sectors, the latter including regulated industry, trade, and finance. Production relationships in the model are of the Cobb-Douglas type. The treatment of supply conditions, the inclusion of the effects on prices of unit labor costs, and the endogenous determination of capacity utilization are among the main distinguishing features of the model. It further includes a small monetary sector. The exogenous components include governmental variables and variables relating to the farm sector. Also included as exogenous variables are consumption and investment anticipations, population, and a productivity trend. The policy variables of the model include government expenditures, social security contributions, the discount rate, and net free reserves.

The Wharton model and most of the later macroeconometric models are quarterly rather than annual models, involving variables and data defined over a three-month period. Estimation of such a model, rather than an annual model, gives a much finer and more complete description of both interrelationships among variables and the types of lag structures present in the system. Thus, for example, certain short-term business-cycle phenomena that would not appear in an annual model can be identified using a quarterly model. Quarterly models are particularly useful for analyzing and forecasting short-term macroeconomic phenomena.

The Wharton model contains lags of up to nine quarters, and it uses the Almon distributed lag in the investment function to account for the lags between investment decisions and capital goods expenditures. The model uses first differences for some variables but absolute levels of others. It also contains time trends and six dummy variables relating to periods of war, strikes, supply shortages, and credit conditions. It contains nonlinear relationships, specifically for the Phillips curve relating the unemployment rate and money wage adjustment.

The Wharton model was estimated using the technique of two-stage least squares. It was built primarily for forecasting purposes and is used on a continuing basis for projecting ahead eight quarters under alternative assumptions regarding the exogenous variables, particularly government policy. In the opinion of the authors, it is "as simple a model as one can build to give realistic quarterly forecasts and have broad enough scope to include most of the economic variables that seem to be relevant to general business and government policy decisions at the macroeconomic level."[19] In fact, the forecasts, when combined with judgments of experts, in the form of "add factors," as will be discussed in Chapter 15, represent some of the best forecasts available for gross national product and its components. This model frequently provides more accurate forecasts than not only the smaller models but even also the larger models.

There are several variants of the Wharton model, which constitute related econometric models. The first is the Wharton Mark III model.[20] This model contains 201 endogenous and 104 exogenous variables in 67 stochastic equations and 134 identities. It entails more detailed elaborations of the financial sector;

[19] Evans and Klein (1967), p. 4.

[20] See McCarthy (1972) and Duggal, Klein, and McCarthy (1974).

the nonmanufacturing sector (into regulated, commercial, government, mining, and agriculture sectors); and prices, price-wage behavior, and labor demand. It makes extensive use of distributed lag analysis in investment and other areas. This model involves 25 policy instruments as opposed to the 7 policy instruments of the original Wharton model, with considerably more detailed treatment of both monetary variables and fiscal policy variables, particularly tax rates.

Another related model is the Wharton Annual and Industry Forecasting model.[21] It yields more disaggregated forecasts of both quantities and prices than the original Wharton model. It provides annual long-term forecasts of up to ten years on an industry basis, in contrast to the original model, which provides quarterly short-term forecasts of up to eight quarters for the aggregate economy. The Annual and Industry Forecasting model utilizes input-output information, and it explicitly accounts for eight aspects of the economy–namely, final demand, input–output, labor requirements, sector wage, sector price, final demand price, income payments, and financial factors.

A third related model is the Wharton III Anticipations model.[22] In this model anticipations variables are added to several of the structural equations: consumer anticipations, measured on an eight-point index, influence purchases of automobiles and other consumer durables; housing starts influence residential construction; and investment anticipations influence plant and equipment investment by manufacturing industry and by regulated and mining industry.

12.6 The Brookings model

The Brookings model was, at the time of its construction in the early 1960's, the largest and most ambitious macroeconometric model of the U.S. economy.[23] It is a highly disaggregated quarterly model, involving, in the "standard" version, 176 endogenous and 89 exogenous variables.[24] A major goal in building a model of this size was that of advancing the state of the art in model building both via disaggregation and via the inclusion of sectors not treated in previous models. The resulting model, in representing the detailed structure of the economy, has been used both for structural analysis of cycles and for growth and policy evaluation.

The Brookings model was estimated using seasonally adjusted quarterly data from 1949 to 1960, amounting to approximately 60 observations. The reader may well wonder how so large a model, involving so many explanatory variables, could have been estimated from a sample of this size. Statistical estimation in

[21] See Preston (1972, 1975).

[22] See Adams and Duggal (1974).

[23] See Duesenberry, Fromm, Klein, and Kuh, Eds. (1965, 1969), Fromm, Ed. (1971) and Fromm and Klein, Eds. (1975). More than 30 economists at various universities and research organizations collaborated in the development of the model, with individual specialists working on particular sectors. For a critique of the Brookings model see Basmann (1972).

[24] Other versions have more than 200 endogenous variables and allow for further expansion up to over 400 endogenous variables, depending on the disaggregation of the producing sectors. For the sizes of several different versions see Table 12.12.

this case appears to violate the fundamental degrees-of-freedom assumption. The model was estimated using econometric techniques, however, because of its approximately block recursive structure.[25] The model was divided into various interacting blocks, and two-stage least squares (and limited-information maximum likelihood) was then used to make consistent estimates of the individual equations within each major block of equations. The entire model was then re-estimated to take account of the interactions among the blocks, and the resulting estimated model was the one used for policy simulation experiments.

The approximately block recursive nature of the model and the interconnections among the major blocks are indicated in Figure 12.2. The initial simultaneous

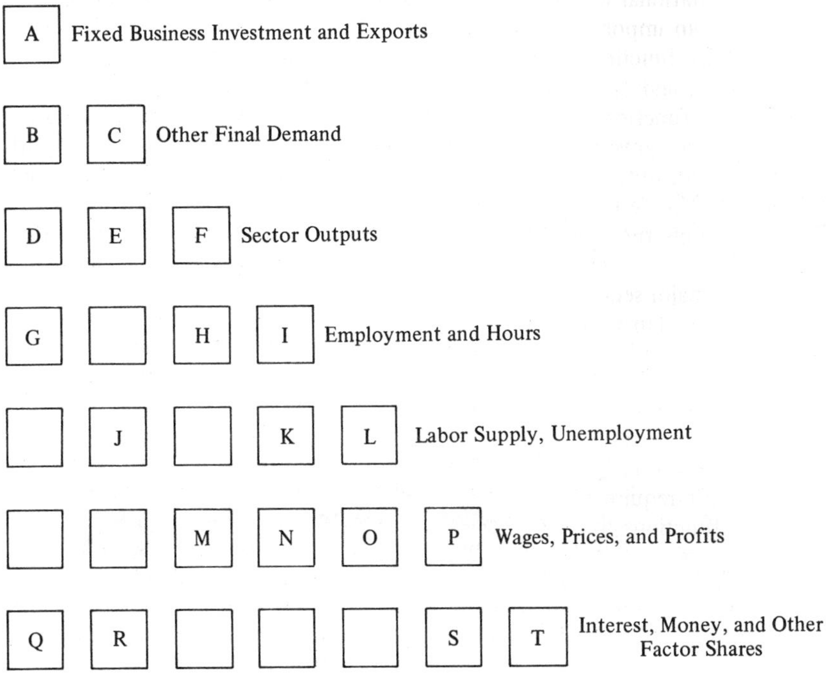

Figure 12.2 Interconnections Among the Blocks of the Brookings Model

block, in A, is that for fixed business investment and exports. The next block is for other final demand, which depends on itself (i.e., variables in this block depend on the variables in this block), in C, and on fixed business investment and exports, in B. Next come the individual sector outputs, which depend on

[25] See Fisher (1965) and the discussion in Klein (1971). Recall that the nature of a recursive model from Section 10.5 is one in which the coefficient matrix is triangular and the covariance matrix is diagonal. Here these properties are assumed for *blocks* of variables in both matrices, as indicated in Problem 10-Q. The block recursive structure was a particularly convenient one to use, since it enabled the individual specialists who collaborated in developing the model to concentrate on their own specific areas of expertise.

themselves and on the previous two blocks. The next block, for employment and hours, depends on itself, sector outputs, and fixed business investment and exports, but *not* on other final demand, as indicated by the unlettered block. The remaining blocks are labor supply and unemployment; wages, prices, and profits; and interest, money, and other factor shares, as shown.

To give a simplified version of the model, block A starts with an investment function giving fixed business investment as a function of lagged output, lagged capital stock, lagged interest rate, and investment anticipations. Also in block A are exports, which depend on external factors, treated as exogenous. Since all explanatory variables in equations in this block are predetermined, the block can be readily estimated.

Blocks B and C involve other final demands, specifically the other components of GNP and national income measures themselves. Included are a consumption function and an import function, each of which depends on disposable income; an investment function for residential construction, which depends on past housing starts; and an inventory investment function, which depends on gross output. These functions, together with the fixed business investment and exports of block A and government spending, treated as exogenous, simultaneously determine GNP, output, disposable income, consumption, investment, exports, and imports. The dependence on fixed business investment and exports is given in block B, while the simultaneous interaction among these variables is given in block C.

The next major sector is sector outputs. The outputs of the producing sectors are assumed to depend on fixed business investment (block D), on other components of GNP (block E), and on themselves (block F). The dependence on components of GNP and on themselves reflects production of goods as final goods and as intermediate goods, respectively.

Continuing this simplified version of the model, employment and hours are determined on the basis of themselves, sector outputs, and fixed business investment via labor requirements functions. These functions can be interpreted as production functions that have been solved for labor inputs as functions of outputs and capital levels. Such solutions indicate the dependence of labor inputs on sector outputs and fixed business investment, here summarized by blocks H and G, respectively. Block I gives the simultaneous interdependence of labor inputs on one another.

Labor supply, which, when combined with labor requirements, gives unemployment, is determined in blocks J, K, and L. Labor supply depends on GNP and its components, in block J; demand for labor, in block K; and itself, in block L. It also depends on exogenous factors relating to population.

Wages, prices, and profits are determined in blocks M, N, O, P. Prices are obtained on the basis of a markup equation, marking up on the basis of labor cost per unit of output, and hence involving output in block M and labor in block N. Wages are obtained on the basis of a Phillips-curve type of relationship, involving unemployment in block O. The simultaneous interaction among prices, wages, and profits is estimated in block P.

Rounding out the simplified model is a liquidity preference equation, giving the interest rate as a function of investment, in block Q, and output, in block R. The relationships between money and prices and other factor shares and profits are treated in block S. Finally, block T treats the simultaneous relationships among interest, money, and other factor shares.

The simplified version of the model conveys an impression of its approach, but it obviously cannot do full justice to its rich detail. The model is highly disaggregated, including detailed treatment of investment components, employment-output relations, and price-wage behavior. It also includes coverage of sectors that often had been excluded in earlier econometric models, such as the financial sector, residential construction, agriculture, and government. Its treatment of production in the sector output blocks is highly detailed, involving estimation of input-output relations for seven producing sectors:

Durable manufacturing
Nondurable manufacturing
Trade
Regulated industry (e.g., utilities)
Construction
Agriculture
All other (mining, finance, insurance, services)

It includes anticipation variables, such as fixed business investment anticipations and an index of consumer intentions to buy. For the government sector, it estimates receipts and expenditures in some detail. Its treatment of labor force includes marriage and participation rates. Its disaggregation and coverage thus make it one of the most ambitious models estimated for a national economy.

The model structure utilizes a large number of lagged endogenous variables, with lags up to eight quarters, and relatively few exogenous variables, leading to a reliance on autoregressive explanations of certain variables. The exogenous variables are primarily population, certain government expenditures, and certain instruments of monetary control. Within any block the predetermined variables of that block, including lagged endogenous variables from prior blocks, are used as instrumental variables to estimate that block. Certain linear combinations of current and lagged exogenous and endogenous variables from later blocks are then used, together with the predetermined variables of that block, as the instrumental variables in the final estimation of the system.

The focus of the Brookings model has been policy evaluation with emphasis on the analysis of business cycles and short-run stabilization policies. It has also been useful, however, for long-term studies, such as capital accumulation and population growth. It has been used to study fiscal and monetary policy, using policy simulation experiments. One such study, for example, analyzed the impact of the tax cut of 1964 using the Brookings model.[26] Perhaps the most important outcome of the Brookings model, however, was its role in integrating various sectors of the economy, methodologies, and data into a single unified framework and its influence in these respects on later models, estimation approaches, and data banks.

[26] See Fromm and Taubman (1968) and Chapter 16.

12.7 The MPS model

The MPS model is the public version of an econometric model of the U.S. economy developed by the Federal Reserve Board, MIT, and the University of Pennsylvania.[27] The official version, called the FMP model (for Federal Reserve, MIT, and Pennsylvania), is used for forecasting and policy evaluation by the Federal Reserve System. The public version is called the MPS model (for MIT, Pennsylvania, and the Social Science Research Council). It was previously called the FRB-MIT model.

The MPS model is a large-scale quarterly econometric model involving over 100 equations. Its main focus, as might be expected of an econometric model due, in part, to the Federal Reserve Board, is in estimating the impacts of alternative monetary policies.[28] The model includes six major blocks of equations, as summarized in Table 12.10.

Table 12.10. Equations of the MPS Model

	Stochastic Equations	*Nonstochastic Equations*	*Total Equations*
Final demand	24	20	44
Distribution of income	5	21	26
Tax and transfer	12	9	21
Labor market	3	10	13
Prices	10	22	32
Financial sector	21	14	35
Total	75	96	171

NOTE This listing refers to Version 4.1 of the Federal Reserve-MIT-Penn Model, dated April 15, 1969.

The final demand sector treats consumption, investment in plant and equipment, housing, state and local government expenditure (treated as endogenous variables), inventory investment, and imports. The investment portion of this sector involves highly nonlinear functional forms.

The financial sector of this model is the most detailed of any econometric model, including attempts to treat aspects of the operation of commercial banks, commercial loan markets, savings and loan associations, and mutual savings banks.

Among the fiscal policy variables explicitly considered in this model are components of Federal government purchases of goods and services, transfer payments, and rates and other parameters of the Federal tax system. On the monetary side the model treats the money supply, the monetary base, the basic short-term interest rate, the discount rate, and reserve ratios.

[27] See Rasche and Shapiro (1968), de Leeuw and Gramlich (1968, 1969), Ando and Modigliani (1969), Ando, Modigliani, and Rasche (1972), and Ando (1974).

[28] See Section 13.2 for a discussion of some equations of the model relating to money demand and supply.

The specification of the model makes extensive use of distributed lags, nonlinear equations, intercept shifts, and corrections for first-order autocorrelation. The model also allows for alternative specification of various equations.

The model, as estimated from quarterly postwar data, has been used to analyze the workings of certain sectors of the economy, particularly the financial, investment, and housing sectors. It has also been used for short-run forecasting, given projected values of all exogenous variables, values of lagged endogenous variables, and estimates of all parameters. Its most important use, however, is by the Federal Reserve Board for evaluating alternative monetary and fiscal policies.

12.8 The DRI model

The DRI model, developed by Data Resources, Inc., is one of the largest models of the U.S. economy.[29] It is a highly disaggregated model that was influenced by the Brookings model, the Wharton model, and other earlier models.

The 1976 DRI model includes 718 endogenous variables and 170 exogenous variables. Of the endogenous variables, however, about half are not central to the model's mechanism, but rather are based upon the breakdown by industry. Table 12.11 presents a profile of the seven broad sectors of the model, indicating the degree of structural detail in each sector. Clearly this model, in at least several sectors, involves a considerable degree of disaggregation. In particular, the industry sector, the financial system, and the final GNP demands all involve a high degree of disaggregation. The industry sector is based on an input-output model of 51 industries, with interindustry relations summarized by relevant input–output coefficients that are automatically corrected for systematic trend and cycle factors.

The DRI model includes several other unique features. One such feature is a flow-of-funds model for the household and nonfinancial corporate sectors that is fully simultaneous with the income–expenditure flows. A second feature is a detailed stage-of-processing model of the inflation process, with which it is possible to trace the impacts of changes in the prices of basic and raw materials, such as world oil or food, through later stages of production to the retail level. A third feature is the inclusion of demographic and supply considerations affecting potential output and determining the composition, by age, sex, and race, of employment and unemployment. A fourth feature is a wholly endogenous and behavioral state and local government sector, which responds to macro conditions, demographic factors, and financial conditions of the sector's budget.

An example of one equation from the DRI model is that for consumer purchases of automobiles, one of the 14 categories of consumer spending in the consumption sector of the model. This equation illustrates how day-to-day use

[29] See Eckstein, Green, and Sinai (1974) and Data Resources, Inc. (1976). Data Resources, Inc. maintains a large integrated computerized data bank, which it provides to subscribers in industry and government on a time-shared basis. The DRI model is based on this data bank, and it represents a service provided subscribers. Other commercial ventures that also provide subscribers access to large data banks and various models using these data include Chase Econometrics Associates, Inc., and Wharton Econometric Forecasting Associates, Inc., providing the Chase model and the various Wharton models. See Table 12.12.

Table 12.11. Equations of the DRI Model

	Stochastic Equations	*Nonstochastic Equations*	*Total Equations*
I. Final GNP demands	66	110	176
Consumption	14	24	38
Investment	22	44	66
Government	11	20	31
Foreign	19	22	41
II. Incomes	11	20	31
III. Financial	103	99	202
Monetary and reserve aggregates	8	15	23
Interest rates	23	1	24
Commercial bank loans	5	3	8
Stock prices, price expectations, misc.	9	2	11
Flow-of-funds; households	20	18	38
Flow-of-funds; nonfinancial corporations	24	48	72
Flow-of-funds and mortgage activity	14	12	26
IV. Supply, capacity, operating rates	6	4	10
V. Employment, unemployment, and the labor force	9	1	10
VI. Prices, wages, and productivity	56	25	81
VII. Industry	128	80	208
Production	51	24	75
Investment	48	20	68
Capital stock	0	32	32
Employment	29	4	33
Total	379	339	718

Source Eckstein, Green, and Sinai (1974). Eckstein, Ed. (1976), and private communication from Otto Eckstein (1976).

and annual rethinking have added significant elements to the basic theoretical structure provided by textbook macroeconomics. The equation, as estimated by 2SLS using data from 1956.1 to 1976.2 is

$$\begin{aligned}\text{CDMV\&P72/N16\&} = {} & \underset{(0.51)}{2.66} + \underset{(0.020)}{0.154}(.6(\text{YD} + \text{YSURNW} - \text{VG})/\text{PC} + .4(\text{YD}_{-1} \\ & + \text{YSURNW}_{-1} - \text{VG}_{-1})/\text{PC}_{-1})/\text{N16\&} - \underset{(0.45)}{2.01}\Big(\sum_{t=-1}^{-4} \text{KREGCARS}_t/4/\text{N16\&}\Big) \\ & - \underset{(0.90)}{2.00}(\text{JCOSTCAR/PC}) + \underset{(0.036)}{0.118}\Big(\sum_{t=0}^{-4} \alpha_t \text{JATTC}_t\Big) - \underset{(0.45)}{2.14}(\text{CDTPIL}_{-1}/ \\ & \text{YD}_{-1}) - \underset{(36.7)}{214.1}(\text{I/N16\&}) + \underset{(0.62*10^{-6})}{3.30*10^{-6}}\text{DMY1} + \underset{(0.037)}{0.121}\text{DMY2}\end{aligned} \qquad \textbf{(12.8.1)}$$

$\bar{R}^2 = 0.944 \quad d = 0.989.$

The variable CDMV&P72 is consumer spending on motor vehicles and parts in 1972 dollars (including net used cars and tires and parts); N16& is population 16 years of age and older (the driving-age population, used to calculate purchases per capita); (YD + YSURNW – VG)/PC is a measure of income pertinent to auto purchases. It is disposable income plus nonwithheld personal income tax surcharge less transfer payments, deflated by the implicit deflator for personal consumption expenditures. KREGCARS is the stock of registered cars; JCOSTCAR/PC is a measure of the relative price of owning and operating a car, where JCOSTCAR = (.7PCDMV&P + .3PCNGAS) (.06/4 + RCIC/400) and PC, PCDMV&P, PCNGAS are the implicit deflators for total consumption, consumption of motor vehicles and parts, and consumption of gasoline, respectively, .06/4 is the quarterly depreciation rate, and RCIC is the finance rate on installment credit auto loans; JATTC is the Michigan Survey Index of Consumer Sentiment, representing consumer confidence; DMY1 is an auto industry strike dummy; and DMY2 is a dummy for anticipatory buying before large, announced price increases. A bridge equation relates consumer spending on new automobiles to total auto spending. Other relations translate new car purchases into unit domestic retail sales and unit domestic foreign sales, and into outlays for parts and tires.

The DRI model is reestimated each year to take advantage of data revisions and new research findings. The model has been used for all three purposes of econometrics. It has been used for structural analysis to evaluate various multipliers and elasticities. Its detailed structure describes many economic processes, including cyclical factors and financial conditions, and it is sufficiently disaggregated that both macro effects of micro changes and micro effects of macro changes can be analyzed in detail. The model has been used for short-run forecasting, providing quarterly forecasts of up to twelve quarters of both the main macroeconomic variables and detailed components. Dynamic simulations using the model have covered up to a fifteen-year period. The model has also been used for policy evaluation, to estimate the impacts of various monetary and fiscal policies on unemployment, price stability, and economic growth.[30] Its highly detailed structure and its inclusion of numerous detailed policy levers make it very useful for analyzing the implications of various policy packages.

12.9 A survey of macroeconometric models of the U.S. economy

Earlier sections of this chapter have treated, in various degrees of detail, seven macroeconometric models of the U.S. economy. There have been many other macroeconometric models of the U.S. and other countries. Figure 12.3 illustrates the connections between these models in terms of a "family tree," and Table 12.12 provides a tabular survey of such models of the U.S. economy, including those discussed previously.[31]

The first macroeconometric model was the *Tinbergen model* of U.S. business

[30] See Eckstein, Ed. (1976), for structural-analysis and policy-evaluation studies using the DRI model.

[31] See Nerlove (1966), Fromm (1973), Fromm and Klein (1974, 1976), Christ (1975),

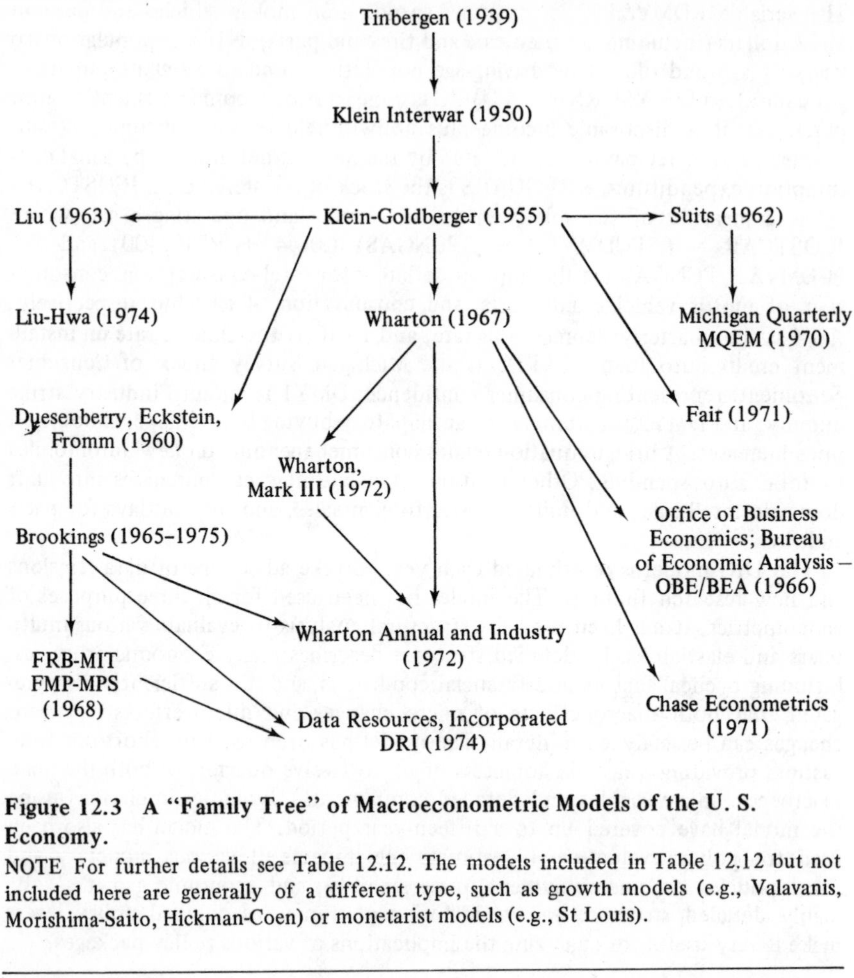

Figure 12.3 A "Family Tree" of Macroeconometric Models of the U. S. Economy.

NOTE For further details see Table 12.12. The models included in Table 12.12 but not included here are generally of a different type, such as growth models (e.g., Valavanis, Morishima-Saito, Hickman-Coen) or monetarist models (e.g., St Louis).

Fromm and Klein, Eds. (1976), and Greenberger, Crenson, and Crissey (1976). See also the symposium in the *International Economic Review*, June 1974, October 1974, and February 1975. Related econometric models have been used to study regional economies, international and interregional trade, and economic development (see the bibliography for Chapter 9). Various econometric models have also been developed for other national economies. For example, see Klein et al. (1961), Ball and Burns (1968), Surrey (1971), Worswick and Blackaby, Eds., (1974), and Renton, Ed. (1975), for models of the United Kingdom; Klein and Shinkai (1963), Ueno (1963), and Ichimura et al. (1964) for models of Japan; Helliwell et al. (1969) and Brown (1970) for models of Canada; Evans (1970) for a model of Israel; Agarwala (1970) for a model of India; Sylos-Labini (1974) for a model of Italy; Behrman (1975) for models of Latin American economies; and Nugent (1974, 1975) for a model of Central American economies. See Ball, Ed. (1973), Waelbroeck (1975), and Hickman and Lau (1976) for surveys of such models, which now exist for most industrialized nations and several developing economies. In the Netherlands the construction and use of econometric models dates back to Tinbergen's work, and econometric models have played an important role in government forecasting and policymaking, specifically in forecasting growth rates and setting certain wage rates.

cycles in the period 1919–1932. This model was quite influential in three respects. First, it influenced future research by developing a quantitative approach to the subject of business-cycle analysis. Second, it fostered the further development and use of econometrics. Third, it was partly responsible for the later work on problems of estimation of a simultaneous-equations system.[32]

The next two econometric models, the *Klein interwar* and *Klein-Goldberger models*, have been treated in previous sections. The pervasive influence of the Klein-Goldberger model on later models is clearly seen in Figure 12.3.

The *Valavanis model* is an unusual model in treating long-term economic growth over an extended period—from 1869 to 1953. The size of the model and the types of variables used are similar to those of the Klein-Goldberger model but in this one, because of the focus on long-term growth, such variables as those of population and labor force, the employment rate, and the birth rate are treated as *endogenous*, to be explained by the model. The exogenous variables include the money supply, the value of land, net immigration, the death rate, the percentage of the labor force that is unionized, standard hours, and time.

The *Duesenberry-Eckstein-Fromm model* is a quarterly model of the United States economy in recession, emphasizing tax and transfer payments. It was influenced by the Klein-Goldberger model but is not a direct descendant. It, in turn, influenced the development of both the Brookings model and the DRI model, being a model of quarterly movements in GNP.

The *Suits model* is based on an expanded version of the Klein-Goldberger model, where variables of the model are replaced by first differences. This model influenced the later Michigan quarterly model, the MQEM model.

The *Liu model* is an exploratory model of effective demand in the postwar economy, starting with the first quarter of 1947. By comparison to the Klein-Goldberger model it entails somewhat greater disaggregation (e.g., four consumption variables plus consumer durables and three investment variables). It also has a monetary sector, involving five liquid assets, five interest rates, and, as exogenous variables, excess reserves relative to required reserves and the discount rate. It influenced the development of the later Liu-Hwa model.

The *Morishima-Saito, Brookings,* and *Wharton models* have been discussed in previous sections. Figure 12.3 indicates the influence of the Wharton and Brookings models on later ones, and Table 12.12 summarizes several variants of the Brookings model.

The *BEA model* (formerly called the *OBE model*) is a quarterly model based upon an early version of the Wharton model and developed by the Bureau of Economic Analysis (formerly the Office of Business Economics) in the U.S. Department of Commerce. In size and general structure this model is roughly similar to the original Wharton model, but it emphasizes the government sector, while the Wharton model emphasizes the private sector. The BEA model includes three sectors: the output market, for components of GNP; the labor market, for hours, wage rate, labor force, and labor income; and prices, for price deflators for GNP components and the wage rate. The short-run employment function included in the model converges to the Cobb-Douglas production function at full

[32] Criticism of the Tinbergen study by Haavelmo and others led to the postwar development of simultaneous-equations estimation techniques.

Table 12.12. A Tabular Survey of Macroeconometric Models of the U.S. Economy

Model, Reference	*Time Interval, Period, Technique*	*Number of Variables*		*Number of Equations*	
		Endogenous	*Exogenous*	*Stochastic*	*Nonstochastic*
Tinbergen Tinbergen (1939)	1919–32 Annual; OLS	50	14	32	18
Klein Interwar Klein (1950)	1920–41 Annual; OLS	6	4	3	3
Klein-Goldberger Klein and Goldberger (1955)	1929–41, 1946–52 Annual; LIML	20	14	15	5
Valavanis Valavanis (1955)	1869–1953 Annual; LIML	20	7	12	8
Duesenberry, Eckstein, Fromm Duesenberry, Eckstein, Fromm (1960)	1947.3–1959.2 Quarterly; OLS	28	11	10	18
Suits Suits (1962)	1947–1960 Annual; OLS	33	21	16	17
Liu Liu (1963)	1947.1–1959.4 Quarterly; OLS, 2SLS	36	16	19	17
Morishima-Saito Morishima and Saito (1972)	1902-40, 1946–52 Annual; 2SLS	9	6	7	2
Brookings Duesenberry et al., Eds. (1965, 1969) Fromm and Taubman (1968) Fromm, Ed. (1971) Fromm and Klein, Eds. (1975)	1949–1960 Quarterly; 2SLS LIML	(a) 176 (b) 226 (c) 216 (d) 167	89 218 105 117	101 119 156 81	75 107 60 86
Wharton Evans and Klein (1967, 1968) Evans (1969) Evans, Klein, and Saito (1972)	1948.1–1964.4 Quarterly; 2SLS	(a) 76 (b) 88	42 43	47 51	29 37
Wharton, Mark III McCarthy (1972) Duggal, Klein and McCarthy (1974)	1953.3–1970.1 Quarterly; OLS, 2SLS	201	104	67	134

Table 12.12. *(continued)*

Model, Reference	*Time Interval, Period, Technique*	*Number of Variables*		*Number of Equations*	
		Endogenous	*Exogenous*	*Stochastic*	*Nonstochastic*
Wharton Annual and Industry Preston (1972, 1975)	1954–1969 Annual; OLS, 2SLS	346	90	155	191
Wharton III Anticipations Adams and Duggal (1974)	1953.3–1970.1 Quarterly	202	92	79	123
Office of Business Economics/Bureau of Economic Analysis (OBE/BEA) Liebenberg, Hirsch, and Popkin (1966) Liebenberg, Green, Green, Liebenberg, and Hirsch (1972) Hirsch, Grimm, and Narasimham (1974)	1954.1–1971.4 Quarterly; OLS	98	83	58	40
Federal Reserve Board/ MIT-Penn-SSRC (FMP/MPS) Rasche and Shapiro (1968) de Leeuw and Gramlich (1968, 1969) Ando and Modigliani (1969) Ando, Modigliani, and Rasche (1972) Ando (1974)	1958–1965 Quarterly; OLS, IV	171	119	75	96
St. Louis Andersen and Jordan (1968) Andersen and Carlson (1970, 1974)	1953.1–1968.4 Quarterly; OLS	9	4	5	4
Michigan Quarterly (MQEM) Hymans and Shapiro (1970, 1974)	1954.1–1970.4 Quarterly; OLS, IV	59	63	35	24

Table 12.12. (*continued*)

Model, Reference	*Time Interval, Period, Technique*	*Number of Variables*		*Number of Equations*	
		Endogenous	*Exogenous*	*Stochastic*	*Nonstochastic*
Fair Fair (1971, 1974)	1956.1–1973.2 Quarterly; 2SLS	19	20	14	5
Chase Econometrics Evans (1974)	Quarterly; OLS	150	100	125	25
Hickman-Coen Hickman, Coen, and Hurd (1975) Hickman and Coen (1976)	1924–1940, 1949–1966 Annual	170	115	50	120
Liu-Hwa Liu and Hwa (1974)	1954.01–1971.12 Monthly	131	27	51	80
Data Resources Incorporated (DRI) Eckstein, Green, and Sinai (1974) Eckstein, Ed. (1976) Data Resources Inc. (1976)	1956.1–1976.2 Quarterly; OLS, 2SLS	718	170	379	339

NOTE 1957.3 refers to the third quarter of 1957; 1954.01 refers to the first month of 1954.

capacity. The policy variables of the model include various tax rates and monetary policy variables. This model is used for short-term forecasting and policy evaluation in the Department of Commerce and other government agencies, including the Council of Economic Advisors.

The *FMP/MPS model*, which is also used extensively for policy evaluation, was discussed in Section 12.7.

The *St. Louis model*, developed at the Federal Reserve Bank of St. Louis, runs counter to the trend of developing ever larger and nonlinear economic models. It utilizes a small linear model of five reduced-form equations to study alternative monetary and fiscal policies. It also runs counter to most of the other models by emphasizing monetary aggregates, using a monetarist perspective, in assessing monetary and fiscal impacts on national income, employment, prices and interest rates. Its three exogenous variables are change in the money stock (M_1), change in Federal expenditures at high employment levels, and potential full-employment output. The money supply, however, is the principal driving force of this model.[33]

The *Michigan quarterly econometric model (MQEM)* was influenced by the Suits model, which had been used earlier at Michigan. It is, however, a direct

[33] See Section 13.2 for a discussion of part of the model.

descendant of a small quarterly model developed in the late 1960's at the Council of Economic Advisers for use in forecasting. The model is a medium-size nonlinear one designed primarily for short-term prediction. It consists of six main blocks—wages and prices, productivity and employment, expenditures, income flows, interest rates, and output composition—which form an integrated and interdependent system. The model is used for policy analysis as well as forecasting.

The *Fair model* is a short-run quarterly forecasting econometric model that is small by comparison to other quarterly models, consisting of 14 stochastic equations and 5 identities. It comprises three sectors—the monthly housing starts sector, the money GNP sector, and the price-employment-labor force sector. It explicitly allows for disequilibrium in the housing sector and makes use of the concept of "excess labor" to explain employment. The model also provides direct estimates of potential GNP. Included as exogenous variables are expectations with regard to both consumer buying and plant and equipment investment. The estimation technique accounts for both the first-order serial correlation and the simultaneity that are present. A unique aspect is that when this model is used to forecast, no use is made of subjective add factors to adjust intercept terms.[34]

The *Chase Econometrics model*, constructed in 1970, is a large-scale quarterly model used for short-term forecasting. The model as a whole has not been published, but several estimated equations have been.[35] One such equation is that for new passenger car sales, which may be compared to the comparable equation in the DRI model (12.8.1). The equation for the Chase Econometrics model is

$$\begin{aligned} C_{\mathrm{NCS}} = {} & 7.43 + \underset{(0.0052)}{0.0141} \sum_{i=0}^{4} (0.6)^i (\mathrm{DI} - \mathrm{TR})_{-i} \\ & + \underset{(3.72)}{4.83} \sum_{i=0}^{4} (0.6)^i (Y_{\mathrm{DIST}})_{-i} - \underset{(0.114)}{0.422} \sum_{i=0}^{4} (\mathrm{CRED})_{-i} \\ & - \underset{(0.0336)}{0.0975} \left(\frac{P_{\mathrm{CAMP}}}{P_{\mathrm{CI}}}\right) - \underset{(0.084)}{0.565}\mathrm{UN} + \underset{(0.339)}{0.883} d_{\mathrm{ASTR}} \\ & - \underset{(0.0196)}{0.0196} \sum_{i=0}^{4} (0.6)^i (K_{\mathrm{NCS}})_{-i-1}, \quad \bar{R}^2 = 0.923, \quad d = 1.46. \end{aligned} \tag{12.9.1}$$

Here C_{NCS} is new passenger car sales (millions), DI is personal disposable income (billions of constant dollars), TR is transfer payments (billions of constant dollars), Y_{DIST} is the ratio of nonwage personal income to wages and salaries (a measure of income distribution), CRED is a credit-rationing variable (a measure of the degree to which loans are not available to consumers and small business),

[34] See Chapter 15, especially Sections 15.3 and 15.6.

[35] See Evans (1974). Also reported there are estimated equations for single-family housing starts and demand deposits.

P_{CAMP}/P_{CI} is the ratio of the average monthly payment for new cars to the consumer price index, UN is the unemployment rate, d_{ASTR} is a dummy variable for auto strikes, and K_{NCS} is the stock of new cars. The summations from 0 to 4 take account of explanatory variables over the current and previous quarters, including four quarters earlier, where $(0.6)^i$ discounts the influence of these lagged values. Among the important features of the overall model is the explicit inclusion of credit rationing (as in the above equation) and capacity utilization; a distributed lag pattern for the effect of income on consumption, in which initially the weights rise, reach a plateau, and then eventually fall; and various nonlinearities and asymmetries (e.g., prices rise much more easily than they fall). The forecasts produced by this model, which are among the most accurate available for national income components, are provided to subscribers of Chase Econometrics Associates, Inc.

The *Hickman-Coen model* is an annual model of long-term growth. It is used for medium-range and long-range prediction purposes, specifically for predictions of the annual time paths of major macroeconomic variables, such as actual and potential GNP, labor force, unemployment, wages, and prices over a 10 year horizon. These predictions are made under alternative assumptions concerning government policies and demographic and technological trends. The model thus emphasizes long-run growth factors rather than short-run cyclical phenomena. Among its distinguishing features are interrelated firm demand functions for labor and capital; discrimination among concepts of potential full-employment, and capacity output; an integrated cost, production, and pricing framework; a search-theory approach to unemployment; a long-run model of housing in a disequilibrium framework; and a high proportion of logarithmic behavioral functions (e.g., Cobb-Douglas production functions) and partial adjustment hypotheses. Policy simulations with the model imply that a sustained exogenous increase in federal expenditure (or reduction in tax receipts) can permanently reduce unemployment, with most of the reduction accomplished within five years. Expansionary monetary policy (an increase in unborrowed reserves), by contrast, will reduce unemployment temporarily, but after two or three years the unemployment rate returns to approximately its original level.

The *Liu-Hwa model* is a monthly model of national income determination that is intended for forecasting and policy analysis. It disaggregates the production sector into private nonfarm and general government components and makes use of the CES production function. It includes 12 policy instruments, the values of which, together with lagged endogenous and exogenous variables, generate monthly forecasts of GNP and its components. It is the first major monthly econometric model.

The last and largest of these models is the *DRI model*, discussed in Section 12.8.

12.10 Trends in macroeconometric model construction

It should be apparent in considering their evolution over time, as summarized in the tabular survey, that macroeconomic models have tended to increase in size, as measured, for example, by the number of stochastic equations. They have also tended to increase in scope and complexity. This change can be easily understood in terms of a rational choice of scale, reflecting size, scope, and complexity. A rational choice would seek the point at which the marginal benefit of added scale (measured in terms, for example, of more accurate or more complete forecasts) equals the marginal cost of added scale (measured in terms, for example, of the added cost of data collection and information processing), as illustrated in Figure 12.4. The successive models of the tabular survey were developed, how-

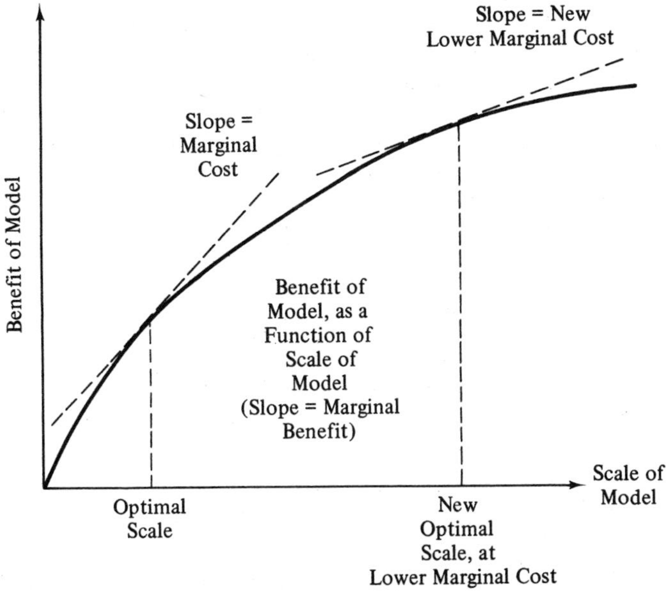

Figure 12.4 Increase of Model's Optimal Scale with a Fall in the Marginal Cost

ever, during decades in which the marginal cost of added scale fell precipitously as a result of the advent of computers to perform the necessary calculations, library programs for econometric routines, and readily available or even computerized data banks.[36] This change over time is depicted in Figure 12.4: the fall in the marginal cost of scale has led to an overall increase in scale.

Another trend in macroeconometric model construction has been the attempt to combine several distinct models into a larger integrated model. One aspect of this trend is the inclusion of input-output models into macroeconometric models.[37] Another is the attempt to link together several national macroecono-

[36] In terms of the basic ingredients of an econometric model, as given in Figure 1.1, the econometric techniques and data have become much more readily available and reasonably standardized. As a result, the remaining basic ingredient—the economic model—has become a major focus of attention in recent years.

[37] Examples include the Brookings model, the Wharton Annual and Industry model, and the DRI model. See Fisher, Klein, and Shinkai (1965), Fromm and Klein (1969), and Kresge (1969) for the Brookings model and Preston (1975) for the DRI model.

metric models into a global model that can treat international trade as well as national economic phenomena.[38] A third aspect is the attempt to relate microeconomic behavior, of individual agents, to macroeconomic phenomena.[39]

A third trend in macroeconometric model construction has been the tendency to rely more and more upon nonlinear rather than linear models. While many phenomena represented in such models are linear or can be approximated by linear relationships, some are inherently nonlinear. Thus, for example, all value terms represent the product of price and quantity; production relationships are typically nonlinear; and ratios, such as those of prices to an average price level, are frequently included in such models. Modern econometric models usually include such nonlinearities. They must therefore be solved by nonlinear techniques. For example, obtaining the reduced form from the structural form involves solving a system of nonlinear equations.[40]

The uses of the models discussed in this chapter for purposes of structural analysis, forecasting, and policy evaluation will be the topics of Chapters 14, 15, and 16. Chapter 13 will treat some applications of simultaneous-equations models in fields other than the macroeconomy.

PROBLEMS

12-A Consider the following nine-equation macroeconomic model:

1. $C_t = \alpha_{11} Y_t + \alpha_{21} + \epsilon_{1t}$ (consumption function)
2. $I_t = \alpha_{12} Y_t + \alpha_{22} Y_{t-1} + \alpha_{32} r_t + \alpha_{42} K_{t-1} + \alpha_{52} + \epsilon_{2t}$ (investment function)
3. $M_t = \alpha_{13} Y_t + \alpha_{23} r_t + \alpha_{33} + \epsilon_{3t}$ (money supply, demand)
4. $L_t = \alpha_{14} w_t + \alpha_{24} Y_t + \alpha_{34} K_t + \alpha_{44} + \epsilon_{4t}$ (employment function)
5. $p_t - p_{t-1} = \alpha_{15}(w_t - w_{t-1}) + \alpha_{25}(M_t - M_{t-1}) + \alpha_{35} + \epsilon_{5t}$ (price change function)
6. $w_t - w_{t-1} = \alpha_{16}(p_t - p_{t-1}) + \alpha_{26} U_t + \alpha_{36} U_{t-1} + \alpha_{46} + \epsilon_{6t}$ (Phillips curve)
7. $Y_t = C_t + I_t + G_t$ (national income identity)
8. $U_t = N_t - L_t$ (unemployment identity)
9. $K_t - K_{t-1} = I_t - \alpha_{42} K_{t-1}$ (capital stock identity)

[38] Project LINK represents such an attempt. It has the goal of developing such linkages, through import and export equations, of econometric models of the United States, Canada, Japan, Western European nations, and other economies, which account for over half of world trade. See Ball, Ed. (1973), and Johnson and Klein (1974).

[39] For microsimulation models in which linkages between participants occur via markets see Feldstein and Friedman (1976) and Yett, Drabek, Intriligator, and Kimbell (1975, 1977).

[40] The Gauss-Seidel technique is typically used to solve such a nonlinear system for the reduced-form equations. This technique starts from an initial trial solution (e.g., past values of the endogenous variables) and iterates toward the solutions for the endogenous variables by correcting discrepancies at each stage. The process continues until the change in solution values from one iteration to the next is less than a preassigned degree of accuracy, e.g., a percentage change of less than 0.001 in absolute value. See Fromm and Klein (1969) and Klein and Evans (1969).

where the nine endogenous variables are

Y = national income
C = consumption
I = investment
K = capital stock
L = employment
U = unemployment
w = wage rate
p = price level
r = interest rate

and the three exogenous variables are

G = government expenditure
M = money supply
N = labor force.

1. Show the interrelationships of the model in a flow diagram (arrow diagram) covering the periods $t - 1$, t, and $t + 1$ (stochastic disturbance terms can be omitted).
2. Formulate the structural form as a matrix equation. Indicate by partitioning the coefficient matrix the clustering of variables.

12-B Consider the following macroeconomic model:

$$C_t = a + bY_t + cC_{t-1}$$
$$Y_t = C_t + I_t$$
$$I_t = I_0 \lambda^t$$

where the consumption function includes a term representing habit formation and where investment grows exogenously, λ being the (positive) growth factor.

1. Solve for the time path for C_t.
2. Show that, for equilibrium values, the long-run marginal propensity to consume is given by

$$\text{MPC}_L = \frac{b}{1 - c/\lambda} = \frac{\lambda b}{\lambda - c}$$

3. Show that the equation for consumption is equivalent to the Koyck distributed lag formulation:

$$C_t = \frac{a}{1 - c} + b \sum_{j=0}^{\infty} c^j Y_{t-j}.$$

4. Evans estimated the following consumption function for the U.S., 1929–1962 (excluding 1942–1946), using annual data in constant dollars:[41]

$$C_t = \underset{(0.041)}{0.280Y_t} + \underset{(0.052)}{0.676C_{t-1}}.$$

Estimate the short-run and long-run marginal propensity to consume (assume $\lambda = 1.02$, corresponding to 2% growth per year), and give 95% confidence intervals for both.

12-C Consider the following model for investment:

1. $I_t = K_t - K_{t-1} + D_t$
2. $D_t = \delta K_{t-1}$
3. $K_t - K_{t-1} = (1 - \lambda)(K_t^* - K_{t-1})$
4. $K_t^* = \alpha Y_t + \beta \left(\frac{w}{r}\right)_t$

where equation 1 identifies gross investment as the change in the capital stock (net investment) plus depreciation; equation 2 stipulates that depreciation is proportional to the existing capital stock; equation 3 is the stock adjustment hypothesis; and equation 4 relates desired capital to output and the wage-rental ratio.

Assuming Y and w/r can be treated as exogenous, show that it is impossible to determine unique parameter estimates for α, β, δ, and λ, but that it is possible to determine the ratio α/β uniquely. If δ were available from extraneous information, show specifically how α, β, and λ could be estimated.

12-D For the Klein interwar model of Table 12.3:

1. Find the dimensions (units of measurement) of each estimated coefficient.
2. Using the order condition, investigate the identification of each equation.

12-E Construct a flow diagram such as that in Figure 12.1 for the Morishima-Saito model.

12-F For the Morishima-Saito model of Table 12.7:

1. Using the order condition, investigate the identification of each equation.
2. Find the reduced-form equations.

12-G Develop a formal model structure of the type outlined as a "simplified version" of the Brookings model of Section 12.6. For each block of equations find the reduced form and determine the identification of each equation.

[41] See Evans (1969), Section 3.3.

BIBLIOGRAPHY

Adams, F. G., and V. G. Duggal (1974), "Anticipations Variables in an Econometric Model: The Anticipations Version of Wharton Mark IV." *International Economic Review*, 15: 267–84.

Adelman, I., and F. Adelman (1959), "The Dynamic Properties of the Klein-Goldberger Model." *Econometrica*, 27: 596–625, reprinted in Zellner, Ed. (1968).

Agarwala, R. (1970), *An Econometric Model of India, 1948-61*. London: Frank Cass & Co.

Andersen, L. C., and K. M. Carlson (1970), "A Monetarist Model for Economic Stabilization." *Federal Reserve Bank of St. Louis Review*, 52: 7–25.

Andersen, L. C., and K. Carlson (1974), "St. Louis Model Revisited." *International Economic Review*, 15: 305–27.

Andersen L. C., and J. L. Jordan (1968), "Monetary and Fiscal Actions: A Test of their Relative Importance in Economic Stabilization." *Federal Reserve Bank of St. Louis Review*, 50: 11–23.

Ando, A. (1974), "Some Aspects of Stabilization Policies, the Monetarist Controversy, and the MPS Model." *International Economic Review*, 15: 541–71.

Ando, A., and F. Modigliani (1965), "The Relative Stability of Monetary Velocity and the Investment Multiplier." *American Economic Review*, 55: 693–728, and "Rejoinder," 55: 786–90.

Ando, A., and F. Modigliani (1969), "Econometric Analysis of Stabilization Policies." *American Economic Review*, 59: 296–314.

Ando, A., F. Modigliani, and R. Rasche (1972), "Equations and Definitions of Variables for the FRB-MIT-Penn Econometric Model, November, 1969," in Hickman, Ed. (1972).

Ball, R. J., Ed. (1973), *The International Linkage of National Economic Models*. Amsterdam: North-Holland Publishing Co.

Ball, R. J., and T. Burns (1968), "An Econometric Approach to Short-Run Analysis of the United Kingdom Economy, 1955–1966." *Operational Research Quarterly*, 19: 225–56.

Basmann, R. L. (1972), "The Brookings Quarterly Econometric Model: Science or Number Mysticism?" in K. Brunner, Ed., *Problems and Issues in Current Econometric Practice*. Columbus: College of Administrative Science, Ohio State University.

Behrman, J. R. (1975), "Econometric Modeling of National Income Determination in Latin America, with Special Reference to the Chilean Experience." *Annals of Economic and Social Measurement*, 4: 461–88.

Bridge, J. L. (1971), *Applied Econometrics*. Amsterdam: North-Holland Publishing Co.

Brown, T. M. (1970), *Specification and Uses of Econometric Models*. London: Macmillan & Co., Ltd.

Christ, C. F. (1951), "A Test of an Econometric Model of the United States, 1921–1947." *Conference on Business Cycles*, New York National Bureau of Economic Research, Inc.

Christ, C. F. (1966), *Econometric Models and Methods*, New York: John Wiley & Sons, Inc.

Christ, C. F. (1975), "Judging the Performance of Econometric Models of the U.S. Economy." *International Economic Review*, 16: 54–74.

Data Resources, Incorporated (1976), *The Data Resources National Economic Information System*. Amsterdam: North-Holland Publishing Co.

de Leeuw, F., and E. M. Gramlich (1968), "The Federal Reserve-M.I.T. Econometric Model." *The Federal Reserve Bulletin*, 54: 11–40.

de Leeuw, F., and E. M. Gramlich (1969), "The Channels of Monetary Policy." *Federal Reserve Bulletin*, 55: 472–91.

Duesenberry, J. S., O. Eckstein, and G. Fromm (1960), "Simulation of the United States Economy in Recession." *Econometrica*, 28: 749–809.

Duesenberry, J. S., G. Fromm, L. R. Klein, and E. Kuh, Eds. (1965), *The Brookings Quarterly Econometric Model of the United States*. Chicago: Rand-McNally & Company; Amsterdam: North-Holland Publishing Co.

Duesenberry, J. S., G. Fromm, L. R. Klein, and E. Kuh, Eds. (1969), *The Brookings Model: Some Further Results*. Chicago: Rand-McNally & Company.

Duggal, V. G., L. R. Klein, and M. D. McCarthy (1974), "The Wharton Model Mark III: A Modern IS-LM Construct." *International Economic Review*, 15: 572–94.

Eckstein, O., Ed. (1976), *Parameters and Policies in the U.S. Economy*. Amsterdam: North-Holland Publishing Co.

Eckstein, O., E. W. Green, and A. Sinai (1974), "The Data Resources Model: Uses, Structure, and Analysis of the U.S. Economy." *International Economic Review*, 15: 595–615.

Eisner, R., and R. Strotz (1963), "Determinants of Business Investment," in Commission on Money and Credit. *Impacts of Monetary Policy*. Englewood Cliffs, N.J.: Prentice-Hall, Inc.

Evans, M. K. (1969), *Macroeconomic Activity: Theory, Forecasting and Control; An Econometric Approach*. New York: Harper & Row.

Evans, M. K. (1970), "An Econometric Model of the Israeli Economy 1952–1953." *Econometrica*, 38: 624–60.

Evans, M. K. (1974), "Econometric Models" in W. F. Butler, R. A. Kavesh, and R. B. Platt, Eds. *Methods and Techniques of Business Forecasting*. Englewood Cliffs, N.J.: Prentice-Hall, Inc.

Evans, M. K., and L. R. Klein (1967), *The Wharton Econometric Forecasting Model*. Philadelphia: Economics Research Unit, Wharton School, University of Pennsylvania.

Evans, M. K., and L. R. Klein (1968), *The Wharton Econometric Forecasting Model*, 2nd Enlarged Ed. Philadelphia: Economics Research Unit, Wharton School, University of Pennsylvania.

Evans, M. K., L. R. Klein, and M. Saito (1972), "Short Run Prediction and Long Run Simulation of the Wharton Model," in B. G. Hickman, Ed. (1972).

Fair, R. C. (1971), *A Short-Run Forecasting Model of the United States Economy*. Lexington: Heath Lexington Books.

Fair, R. C. (1974), "An Evaluation of a Short-Run Forecasting Model." *International Economic Review*, 15: 285–303.

Feldstein, M., and B. Friedman (1976), "The Effect of National Health Insurance on the Price and Quantity of Medical Care," in R. Rosett, Ed., *The Role of Health Insurance in the Health Services Sector*. New York: National Bureau of Economic Research.

Ferber, R. (1962), "Research on Household Behavior." *American Economic Review*, 52: 19–63.

Fisher, F. M. (1968), "Dynamic Structure and Estimation in Economy-Wide Econometric Models," in Duesenberry et al., Eds. (1965).

Fisher, F. M., L. R. Klein, and Y. Shinkai (1965), "Price and Output Aggregation in the Brookings Econometric Model," in Duesenberry et al., Eds. (1965).

Fox, K. A. (1958), *Econometric Analysis for Public Policy*. Ames: Iowa State University Press.

Friedman, M., and D. Meiselman (1965), "Reply to Ando and Modigliani and to De Prano and Mayer." *American Economic Review*, 55: 753–85.

Fromm, G. (1973), "Implications to and from Economic Theory in Models of Complex Systems." *American Journal of Agricultural Economics*, pp. 259–71.

Fromm, G., Ed. (1971), *Tax Incentives and Capital Spending*. Amsterdam: North-Holland Publishing Co.

Fromm, G., and L. R. Klein (1969), "Solutions of the Complete System," in Duesenberry et al., Eds. (1969).

Fromm, G., and L. R. Klein (1973), "A Comparison of Eleven Econometric Models of the United States." *American Economic Review*, **63**: 385–93.

Fromm, G., and L. R. Klein, Eds. (1975), *The Brookings Model: Perspective and Recent Developments*. Amsterdam: North-Holland Publishing Co.

Fromm, G., and L. R. Klein (1976), "The NBER/NSF Model Comparison Seminar: An Analysis of Results." *Annals of Economic and Social Measurement.*

Fromm, G., and P. Taubman (1968), *Policy Simulations with an Economic Model*. Amsterdam: North-Holland Publishing Co.

Goldberger, A. S. (1959), *Impact Multipliers and Dynamic Properties of the Klein-Goldberger Model*. Amsterdam: North-Holland Publishing Co.

Goldberger, A. S. (1964), *Econometric Theory*. New York: John Wiley & Sons, Inc.

Green, G. R., in association with M. Liebenberg and A. A. Hirsch (1972), "Short- and Long-Term Simulations with the OBE Econometric Model," in Hickman, Ed. (1972).

Greenberger, M., M. A. Crenson, and B. L. Crissey (1976), *Models in the Policy Process: Public Decision Making in the Computer Era*. New York: Russell Sage Foundation.

Helliwell, J. F., L. H. Officer, H. T. Shapiro, and J. A. Stewart (1969), *The Structure of RDX1*. Ottawa: Bank of Canada.

Hickman, B. G., Ed. (1972), *Econometric Models of Cyclical Behavior*. National Bureau of Economic Research. New York: Columbia University Press.

Hickman, B. G., and R. M. Coen (1976), *An Annual Growth Model of the U.S. Economy*. Amsterdam: North-Holland Publishing Co.

Hickman, B. G., R. M. Coen, and M. D. Hurd (1975), "The Hickman-Coen Annual Growth Model: Structural Characteristics and Policy Responses." *International Economic Review*, 16: 20–37.

Hickman, B. G., and L. J. Lau (1976) "Pacific Basin National Econometric Models: A Survey and Evaluation of Linkage Feasibility." *Explorations in Economic Research*, 3: 199–252.

Hirsch, A. A., B. T. Grimm, and G. L. V. Narasimham (1974), "Some Multiplier and Error Characteristics of the BEA Quarterly Model." *International Economic Review*, 16: 616–31.

Hymans, S. H., and H. T. Shapiro (1970), *The DHL III Quarterly Econometric Model of the U.S. Economy*. Research Seminar in Quantitative Economics, University of Michigan.

Hymans, S. H., and H. T. Shapiro (1974), "The Structure and Properties of the Michigan Quarterly Econometric Model of the U.S. Economy." *International Economic Review*, 15: 632–53.

Ichimura, S., L. R. Klein, S. Koizumi, K. Sato, and Y. Shinkai (1964), "A Quarterly Econometric Model of Japan, 1952–59." *Osaka Economic Papers*, 12: 19–44.

Johnson, K., and L. R. Klein (1974), "LINK Model Simulations of International Trade: An Evaluation of the Effects of Currency Realignment." *Journal of Finance*, 29: 617–30.

Jorgenson, D. W. (1971), "Econometric Studies of Investment Behavior: A Review." *Journal of Economic Literature*, 9: 1111–47.

Jorgenson, D. W. (1974), "Investment and Production: A Review" in M. D. Intriligator and D. A. Kendrick, Eds., *Frontiers of Quantitative Economics*, Vol. II. Amsterdam: North-Holland Publishing Co.

Klein, L. R. (1950), *Economic Fluctuations in the United States, 1921-1941*. Cowles Commission Monograph No. 11. New York: John Wiley & Sons, Inc.

Klein, L. R., R. J. Ball, A. Hazlewood, and P. Vandome (1961), *An Econometric Model of the United Kingdom*. Oxford: Basil Blackwell.

Klein, L. R., and M. K. Evans (1969), *Econometric Gaming*. New York: Macmillan.

Klein, L. R., and A. S. Goldberger (1955), *An Econometric Model of the United States, 1929-1952*. Amsterdam: North-Holland Publishing Co.

Klein, L. R., and Y. Shinkai (1963), "An Econometric Model of Japan, 1930–59." *International Economic Review*, 4: 1–28.

Kresge, D. T. (1969), "Price and Output Conversion: A Modified Approach," in Duesenberry et al., Eds. (1969).

Kuh, E. and R. Schmalensee (1972), *An Introduction to Applied Macroeconomics*. Amsterdam: North-Holland Publishing Co.

Liebenberg, M., G. Green, and A. Hirsch (1971), "The Office of Business Economics 1970 Quarterly Econometric Model." Washington, D.C.: U.S. Department of Commerce, Econometrics Branch.

Liebenberg, M., A. A. Hirsch, and J. Popkin (1966), "A Quarterly Econometric Model of the United States: A Progress Report." *Survey of Current Business*, 46: 13–39.

Liu, T. C. (1963), "An Exploratory Quarterly Econometric Model of Effective Demand in the Post-War U.S. Economy." *Econometrica*, 31: 301–48.

Liu, T. C., and E. C. Hwa (1974), "Structure and Applications of a Monthly Econometric Model of the U.S. Economy." *International Economic Review*, 15: 328–65.

Malinvaud, E. (1970), *Statistical Methods of Econometrics*. Second Revised Edition. Amsterdam: North-Holland Publishing Co.

McCarthy, M. D. (1972), *The Wharton Quarterly Econometric Forecasting Model, Mark III*. Philadelphia: Economics Research Unit, University of Pennsylvania.

Meyer, J. R. and R. R. Glauber (1964), *Investment Decisions, Economic Forecasting, and Public Policy*. Boston: Graduate School of Business Administration, Harvard University.

Morishima, M., and M. Saito (1972), "A Dynamic Analysis of the American Economy, 1902–1952," in M. Morishima et al., *The Working of Econometric Models*. New York: Cambridge University Press.

Nerlove, M. (1966), "A Tabular Survey of Macroeconometric Models." *International Economic Review*, 7: 127–75.

Nugent, J. B. (1974), *Economic Integration in Central America: Empirical Investigations*. Baltimore: Johns Hopkins University Press.

Nugent, J. B. (1975), "Policy Oriented Macroeconometric Models for Development and Planning." *Annals of Economic and Social Measurement*, 4: 509–29.

Preston, R. S. (1972), *The Wharton Annual and Industry Forecasting Model*. Philadelphia: Economics Research Unit, Wharton School, University of Pennsylvania.

Preston, R. S. (1975), "The Wharton Long Term Model: Input-Output Within the Context of a Macro Forecasting Model." *International Economic Review*, 16: 3–19.

Rasche, R. H., and H. Shapiro (1968), "The FRB-MIT Econometric Model: Its Special Features and Implications for Stabilization Policies." *American Economic Review*, 58: 123–49.

Renton, G. A., Ed. (1975), *Modelling the Economy*. London: Heinemann.

Samuelson, P. A. (1975), "The Art and Science of Macro-Models," in Fromm and Klein, Eds. (1975).

Suits, D. B. (1962), "Forecasting and Analysis with an Econometric Model." *American Economic Review*, 52: 104–32.

Suits, D. B. (1963), "The Determinants of Consumer Expenditure: A Review of Present Knowledge" in Commission on Money and Credit. *Impacts of Monetary Policy*. Englewood Cliffs, N.J.: Prentice-Hall, Inc.

Surrey, M. J. C. (1971), *The Analysis and Forecasting of the British Economy*. National Institute of Economic and Social Research, Occasional Paper No. 25.

Sylos-Labini, P. (1974), *Trade Unions, Inflation, and Productivity*. Lexington: Lexington Books.

Theil, H. (1971), *Principles of Econometrics*. New York: John Wiley & Sons, Inc.

Theil, H., and J. C. G. Boot (1962), "The Final Form of Econometric Equation Systems." *Review of the International Statistical Institute*, 30: 136–52, reprinted in Zellner, Ed. (1968).

Tinbergen, J. (1939), *Statistical Testing of Business Cycle Theories*. Vol. 1: *A Method and Its Application to Investment Activity*. Vol. 2: *Business Cycles in the United States of America, 1919–1932*. Geneva: League of Nations.

Tinbergen, J. (1959), *Selected Papers*. Amsterdam: North-Holland Publishing Co.

Ueno, H. (1963), "A Long-Term Model of the Japanese Economy, 1920–1958." *International Economic Review*, 4: 171–93.

Valavanis, S. (1955), "An Econometric Model of Growth, U.S.A., 1869–1953." *American Economic Review*, 45: 208–21.

van den Bogaard, P. J. M., and H. Theil (1959), "Macrodynamic Policy-Making: An Application of Strategy and Certainty Equivalence Concepts to the Economy of the United States, 1933–36." *Metroeconomica*, 11: 149–67.

Waelbroeck, J. (1975), "Survey of Foreign Models," in G. Fromm and L. R. Klein, Eds. (1975).

Worswick, G. D. N., and F. T. Blackaby, Eds. (1974), *The Medium Term: Models of the British Economy*. London: Heinemann.

Yett, D. E., L. Drabek, M. D. Intriligator, and L. J. Kimbell (1975), "A Microeconometric Model of the Health Care System in the United States." *Annals of Economic and Social Measurement*, 4: 407–33.

Yett, D. E., L. Drabek, M. D. Intriligator, and L. J. Kimbell (1977), *A Forecasting and Policy Simulation Model of the Health Care Sector: The HRRC Prototype Microeconometric Model*. Lexington: Lexington Books.

Zellner, A., Ed. (1968), *Readings in Economic Statistics and Econometrics*. Boston: Little, Brown and Company.

CHAPTER **13**

Other Applications of Simultaneous-Equations Estimation

13.1 Introduction

While macroeconometric models are the oldest and most widely known application of simultaneous-equations estimation, they are by no means the only application. In fact, as noted in Chapter 9, in many fields of economics (and also in other social sciences) use is now being routinely made of single-equation estimation techniques, and several are beginning to make use of simultaneous-equations techniques. This chapter surveys some other applications of simultaneous-equations techniques in the recognition that most if not all are highly preliminary and will undoubtedly be superseded by later work.[1] Yet other applications of simultaneous-equations techniques, to demand and production, have already been mentioned in Chapters 7 and 8.

13.2 Simultaneous-equations models of money demand and supply

Section 9.2 treated several single-equation estimates of the demand equation for money based upon the assumption that the supply of money is exogenous. If money supply is treated as endogenous, then the demand for and supply of money become a simultaneous system of equations, of the form

$$M^D = M^D(Y, r, \hat{r}, \ldots) \qquad *(13.2.1)$$

$$M^S = M^S(Y, r, \hat{r}, \ldots) \qquad *(13.2.2)$$

$$M^D = M^S = M \qquad *(13.2.3)$$

Here equation (13.2.1), that for demand, is like (9.2.2), based upon the transactions and asset (precautionary and speculative) demands for money. Equation

[1] For a bibliography of other applications, including some applications of simultaneous-equations techniques in economics and other social sciences, see the "Other Applications of Econometric Techniques" section of the bibliography in Chapter 9. See in particular Goldberger and Duncan, Eds. (1973), cited there, which presents simultaneous-equations models in a variety of fields, including models of scholastic achievement, demographic changes, and congressional constituency representation.

(13.2.2), that for supply, includes the same variables as that for demand—national income Y; the interest rate r; and the expected interest rate $\hat{r}$, assuming that the monetary authorities are responsive to these factors. Equation (13.2.3) is the equilibrium condition, equating demand and supply. The . . . in the demand and supply equations indicates that other variables can enter both equations. In fact, without either the inclusion of other variables, or the exclusion of some of the variables shown in one of the equations, neither equation of the model would be identified, assuming identifications via zero restrictions. In the form presented in (13.2.1) to (13.2.3) there is no way, empirically, to differentiate the demand equation from the supply equation. Thus, one of the first issues raised in estimating a simultaneous-equations model of money demand and supply is that of identification. Has a demand equation in fact been identified? A supply equation? This issue also arises in evaluating the demand for money equations reported in Section 9.2, as does the problem of simultaneous-equations bias.

Several studies have treated simultaneous demand for and supply of money equations. One, by Teigen, considered the model[2]

$$M^D = M^D(Y, r_s Y, M_{-1}) \tag{13.2.4}$$

$$M^S = M^* f(r_s - r_d) \tag{13.2.5}$$

$$M^D = M^S = M. \tag{13.2.6}$$

The demand function specifies the demand for money as a function of income, the product of the short-term rate of interest and income, and lagged money stock.[3] The inclusion of lagged money stock allows for a lagged response or partial adjustment to equilibrium. The supply function determines the supply of money as the product of the maximum potential money stock based upon reserves supplied by the Federal Reserve System, M^*, and a function $f(\cdot)$ of the difference between r_s, the short-term interest rate, and r_d, the discount rate. The maximum potential money stock is related to reserves by the identity

$$M^* \equiv \frac{1}{\rho(1 - c - h)} R \tag{13.2.7}$$

where R represents reserves, ρ is the (weighted average) reserve ratio, c is the currency ratio, and h is the demand deposit ratio. Finally the last equation is the equilibrium condition, equating the demand for and the supply of money.

The endogenous variables of this model are M, the money stock (measured as M_1), and r_s, the short-term rate of interest (the rate on 4- to 6-month prime commercial paper). The exogenous variables are Y, national income (in money terms), and r_d, the discount rate.[4]

[2] See Teigen (1964). Another model treating the supply of as well as the demand for money is presented in Brunner and Meltzer (1964). Some of the macroeconometric models of Chapter 12 also include simultaneous monetary submodels. See below for the FMP/MPS model.

[3] Several seasonal and structural shift dummy variables are also included.

[4] In fact Teigen considered a somewhat larger model in which national income, Y, is endo-

Teigen estimated this model using quarterly data with 49 observations over the period 1946.4 to 1959.4–i.e., the fourth quarter of 1946 to the fourth quarter of 1959. The technique of estimation was two-stage least squares. His results for demand and supply, respectively, were[5]

$$\begin{aligned} M = \underset{(0.0126)}{0.0618Y} - \underset{(0.0007)}{0.0025r_sY} + \underset{(0.0728)}{0.6860M_{-1}} + \underset{(4.9783)}{23.0600} + \cdots \\ R^2 = 0.992, \quad d = 1.885 \end{aligned} \tag{13.2.8}$$

$$\begin{aligned} M = M^*(\underset{(0.0159)}{0.0751}(r_s - r_d) + \underset{(0.0068)}{0.8522} + \cdots) \\ R^2 = 0.726, \quad d = 1.536. \end{aligned} \tag{13.2.9}$$

All signs agree with prior expectations, all coefficients are at least three times their standard errors, and the Durbin-Watson statistics indicate no significant serial correlation. The implied short-run elasticity of demand (evaluated at mean values) with respect to the interest rate is –0.0168 and with respect to income is 0.1613. The corresponding long-run elasticities are –0.0538 and 0.5130, respectively. The estimated elasticity of *supply* with respect to the interest rate is 0.1950.

Teigen also found that all of the elasticities appear to have declined significantly in the postwar period, as compared to the prewar years, even though interest rates were very low in the 1930's.[6] This finding casts doubt upon the liquidity-trap hypothesis of high elasticity of demand at low interest rates. Teigen, however, saw it as reflecting a change in the role of money, with the asset demand for money declining in the postwar years as a result of the advent of newer forms of liquid asset-holding.

Another model that might be considered in this context is the St. Louis "monetarist" model.[7] This model is constructed on the foundation of the modern quantity theory of money, where monetary impacts are treated through their effects on changes in the stock of money. The model leads to predictions of GNP (and other variables, such as employment and prices) based on the supply of money. A major equation of the model, as estimated over the period 1952.1 to 1968.2, is

---

genous, and an additional equation determines Y on the basis of its lagged value, exogenous expenditure, and net worth. Since this equation contains no monetary variables, however, the larger system can be divided into a real system, namely the equation for national income, and a monetary system, the equations for money demand and supply, reported here.

[5] The omitted variables are the seasonal and structural shift dummy variables. The equation for Y is also omitted here.

[6] His estimates of the demand elasticities for the prewar years were –0.091 with respect to the interest rate and 0.443 with respect to income.

[7] See Andersen and Jordan (1968). For a more complete monetarist model see Andersen and Carlson (1970).

$$\Delta Y_t = 2.28 + (\underset{(0.62)}{1.54}\,\Delta M_t + \underset{(0.45)}{1.56}\,\Delta M_{t-1} + \underset{(0.45)}{1.44}\,\Delta M_{t-2} + \underset{(0.65)}{1.29}\,\Delta M_{t-3})$$
$$+ (\underset{(0.27)}{0.40}\,\Delta E_t + \underset{(0.20)}{0.54}\,\Delta E_{t-1} - \underset{(0.23)}{0.03}\,\Delta E_{t-2} - \underset{(0.26)}{0.74}\,\Delta E_{t-3}) \qquad \textbf{(13.2.10)}$$
$$\bar{R}^2 = 0.60, \quad d = 1.78$$

Here ΔY_t is the change in GNP at time (quarter) t, ΔM_{t-i} is the change in the money supply i quarters earlier, and ΔE_{t-i} is the change in government high-employment expenditures i quarters earlier. This equation was used to study short-term policy impacts of monetary and fiscal variables. It is considered here because it may be considered a reduced-form equation of a larger (unspecified) system in that it relates a key endogenous variable to current and past policy variables, treated as exogenous. The estimated equation suggests that monetary variables are more important than fiscal variables in explaining subsequent changes in GNP. It implies that monetary policy has a larger, a more predictable, and a faster effect on economic activity than fiscal policy. Thus, for example, the t ratios for the change in the money supply are all larger than the corresponding ratios for the change in government expenditure, two of the coefficients of the change in government expenditure are of the wrong sign, and two of these coefficients are statistically insignificant.[8] These results, which cast some doubt upon fiscal policy relative to monetary policy, have led to considerable discussion of the economic and econometric justification for the model.[9] The outcome of this discussion appears to be a widely held belief that a small, single, reduced-form equation such as (13.2.10) may be valuable for purposes of short-term prediction, but not for structural analysis or policy evaluation involving long-term considerations.

A structural macroeconometric model that might also be considered here is the Federal Reserve Board-MIT-Pennsylvania-Social Science Research Council (FMP/MPS) model.[10] This model, as pointed out in the last chapter, is a large nonlinear quarterly macroeconometric model of the U.S. economy over the post-Korean War period. As noted there, this model places considerable emphasis on the role of money in the economy, with the goal of improving understanding of monetary and fiscal stabilization policies. One portion of the model, comprising the demand for and supply of money and their interaction in determining both the equilibrium stock of money and the equilibrium short-term interest rate, will be the focus of the discussion here.[11] It is in this monetary sector that policy decisions of the Federal Reserve, such as changes in the discount rate and reserve requirements, have their initial impacts.

One version of the monetary sector of the FMP model, which jointly deter-

[8] The sum of the coefficients for changes in the money supply is large (5.83) and statistically significant (t = 7.25), while that for changes in government expenditure is small (0.17) and statistically insignificant (t = 0.54).

[9] See, for example, Davis (1969) and de Leeuw and Kalchbrenner (1969).

[10] See de Leeuw and Gramlich (1968, 1969), Rasche and Shapiro (1968), Ando and Modigliani (1969), Ando, Modigliani, and Rasche (1972), and Ando (1974).

[11] See Modigliani, Rasche, and Cooper (1970), Cooper and Fischer (1972), and Cooper (1974).

mines demand deposits (the major component of the stock of money) and the short-term rate of interest (the Treasury bill rate), was estimated as [12]

$$\frac{M_d^D}{Y} = \underset{(0.00038)}{-\,0.00212 r_s} - \underset{(0.00206)}{0.00428 r_t} + \underset{(0.0156)}{0.0542} + \underset{(0.0383)}{0.0046}\frac{Np}{Y} + \underset{(0.079)}{0.833}\frac{M_{d_{-1}}}{Y}$$

$$R^2 = 0.999 \quad d = 2.01 \tag{13.2.11}$$

$$\begin{aligned}\frac{\text{FR}}{\bar{D}_{-1}} = {} & \underset{(0.001)}{0.001} - \underset{(0.00058)}{0.00204 S_2} - \underset{(0.00049)}{0.00237 S_3} - \underset{(0.00084)}{0.00223 S_4} - \underset{(0.00051)}{0.00122 r_s} \\ & + \underset{(0.00060)}{0.00144 d} + \underset{(0.079)}{0.646}(1 - \delta)\frac{\Delta\text{RU}}{\bar{D}_{-1}} - \underset{(0.096)}{0.502\delta}\frac{\Delta\text{CL}}{\bar{D}_{-1}} \\ & + \underset{(0.079)}{0.394}\frac{\text{RL}}{\bar{D}_{-1}} + \underset{(0.044)}{0.705}\frac{\text{FR}_{-1}}{\bar{D}_{-1}}\end{aligned} \tag{13.2.12}$$

$$R^2 = 0.952 \quad d = 2.09$$

$$D \equiv \frac{\text{RU} - \tau T - \text{FR}}{\delta} \tag{13.2.13}$$

$$M_d^S = J^S(\lambda D - \text{Mg}) \tag{13.2.14}$$

$$M_d^D = M_d^S = M_d \tag{13.2.15}$$

where all variables are defined below.

The first two equations were estimated on the basis of data over the period 1955.1 to 1966.4. Equation (13.2.11) explains the demand for demand deposits held by the public M_d^D, relative to Gross National Product Y. The explanatory variables are the short-term rate of interest (Treasury bill rate) r_s; the rate on savings deposits r_t; population N; the price level p; and the lagged value $M_{d_{-1}}/Y$. All of the t-values, other than that for Np/Y, the reciprocal of real per capita income, exceed two in absolute value.

The inclusion of the lagged value means that this equation can be interpreted as that of a partial adjustment model or, equivalently, a Koyck distributed lag. The partial adjustment model takes the form

$$\Delta M = \gamma(M^* - M_{-1}) \tag{13.2.16}$$

where M^*, desired money stock, depends on r_s, r_t, and Np/Y. Thus, if M^*/Y is linear in these three variables, then

$$\frac{M}{Y} = \gamma\left(a_0 - a_1 r_s - a_2 r_t + a_3\frac{Np}{Y}\right) + (1 - \gamma)\frac{M_{-1}}{Y} \tag{13.2.17}$$

[12] See Cooper (1974), Table 1-5, p. 58. The notation has been slightly changed to be consistent with the earlier discussion. The result reported here used ordinary least squares. Cooper also reports results using a "somewhat ad hoc two-step least squares estimator."

The speed-of-adjustment coefficient γ is estimated in (13.2.11) as about 17% per quarter.

Equation (13.2.12) explains the ratio of free reserves FR to a four-quarter moving average of demand deposits ending with the previous quarter $\bar{D}_{-1}$. The explanatory variables are several seasonal dummy variables S_2, S_3, and S_4; the short-term rate of interest r_s; the discount rate d; the required reserve ratio against demand deposits δ; the change in unborrowed reserves ΔRU (where RU is total reserves less borrowings from the Federal Reserve and the Federal Funds market); the change in commercial loans ΔCL; released reserves RL; and the lagged value $\text{FR}_{-1}/\bar{D}_{-1}$.[13] Aside from the constant term, all t-values exceed two in absolute value. The speed-of-adjustment coefficient for this equation is much higher than that for the last, amounting to about 30% per quarter.

The remaining equations are identities completing the system. According to the reserve identity (13.2.13), member bank deposits D are given as a ratio. The numerator is unborrowed reserves, RU, less reserves required against time deposits (given as the product of the required reserve ratio on time deposits τ, and time deposits T) and also less free reserves (unborrowed reserves less required reserves). The denominator is the required reserve ratio on demand deposits, δ. Equation (13.2.14) gives the relation between the supply of demand deposits held by the public M_d^S and total member deposits D in terms of three corrections that must be made: the first for seasonal factors, summarized by J^S; the second for the fact that not all banks are members of the Federal Reserve System, summarized by λ, the ratio of demand deposits to member bank deposits (which, in the larger FMP model, depends on both seasonal variables and a secular trend); and the third for the existence of U.S. Treasury deposits, summarized by U.S. Treasury deposits at all commercial banks Mg. The last equation (13.2.15) is the equilibrium condition that the demand for demand deposits equal the supply of demand deposits.

The system defined by these equations is shown schematically in Figure 13.1, with arrows labeled by equation numbers indicating causal flows among the endogenous variables. On the supply side, the short-term interest rate influences free reserves, which influence demand deposits at member banks. They, in turn, influence the total supply of demand deposits. On the demand side, the short-term rate of interest influences the total demand for demand deposits. The equilibration of the money market determines both the total demand deposits (the major part of the money supply) and the short-term rate of interest (the Treasury bill rate).[14] The effects of various lagged endogenous variables ($M_{d_{-1}}$, FR_{-1}, $\bar{D}_{-1}$), exogenous variables (Y, r_t, ΔCL, . . .), and policy variables (d, δ, τ, . . .) are indicated in equations (13.2.11) to (13.2.15).

[13] Released reserves, RL, is defined as

$$\text{RL} \equiv -(\Delta\delta D_{-1} + \Delta\tau T_{-1})$$

where $\Delta\delta$ and $\Delta\tau$ are the changes in the required reserve ratios on demand and time deposits, respectively, and D_{-1} and T_{-1} are lagged demand and time deposits, respectively.

[14] The remaining part of the money supply, currency, is entirely controlled by its demand, which is determined by the short-term rate of interest, consumer expenditure, and its lagged value.

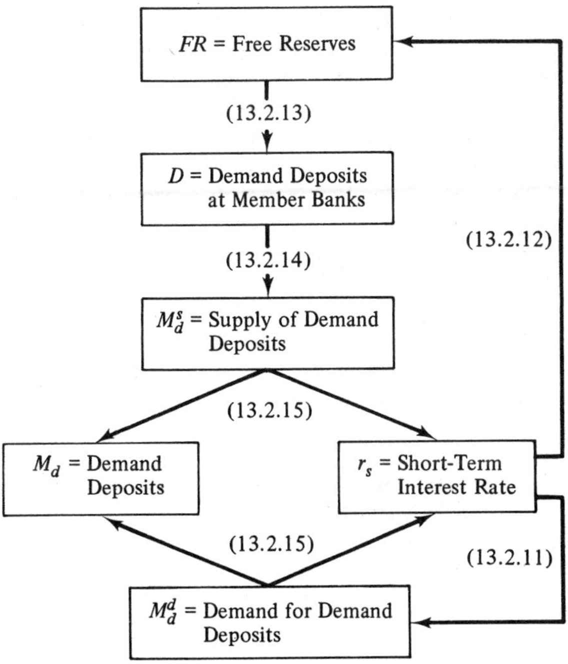

Figure 13.1 Relationships among Endogenous Variables in the Monetary Sector of the FMP Model
Source Based upon Cooper (1974).

Predictions using this model were compared to actual values of demand deposits and the Treasury bill rate over the period 1955.1 to 1968.1, which includes the entire sample period for the estimation plus five postsample quarters.[15] In general, the simulation tracks the actual behavior quite well.

The larger model, of which the above is one portion, includes various linkages between the monetary sector and the real economy, including the effects of interest rates on investment, the effect of credit rationing, and a wealth effect. The estimated FMP model implies that both monetary and fiscal policies exert significant influences on the economy and that there is a long lag before the effects of monetary policy are realized.

13.3 A simultaneous-equations model of industrial-organization relationships[16]

Section 9.2 presented several estimated equations indicating the effect of concentration on industrial-organization variables, such as profit, advertising, and price change. Each can be considered a single equation from a larger and simul-

[15] See Cooper (1974).

[16] This section is based upon Intriligator, Weston, and De Angelo (1975). See also Mueller

taneous model of industrial-organization relationships. Such a larger model can be considered a representation, using an econometric model, of the structure-conduct performance (SCP) paradigm, which, as presented in Section 9.2, is a main source for single-equation studies of industrial organization. To the extent that these single-equation studies analyze pairwise relationships between concentration and variables such as profit, advertising, and price change, they individually either ignore or implictly assume the validity of other aspects of the SCP paradigm. A logical next step in the development of the field would therefore appear to be the integration of these previous individual studies into a larger system of equations to explain, to predict, and even to control industrial-organization relationships.

A simultaneous-equations model of industrial organization that represents a simplified version of the SCP paradigm and can test the role played by concentration is summarized in Tables 13.1 and 13.2. Table 13.1 summarizes the six

Table 13.1. Variables of the Simultaneous-Equations Model of Industrial Organization

ENDOGENOUS VARIABLES

Structure Module:

(1) CR = Concentration ratio
(2) ΔN = Relative change in number of firms

Conduct Module:

(3) K/L = Capital-labor ratio
(4) A/S = Advertising-sales ratio

Performance Module:

(5) Δp = Relative change in price
(6) Π = Profit rate on net worth

EXOGENOUS VARIABLES

Underlying-Considerations Module:

ϵ_p = Price elasticity of demand (negative)
ϵ_I = Income elasticity of demand
MES = Minimum efficient size (weighted average of the total asset size class)

Factors External to a Particular Industry:

w = Real wage
g = Growth in the value of shipments
Δc = Relative change in direct costs

(1967), Grabowski and Mueller (1970), Greer (1971), Phillips (1974), and Comanor and Wilson (1974) for discussions of econometric approaches to industrial organization.

endogenous and six exogenous variables of the model. Industry structure is represented by two variables: concentration, measured by the four-firm concentration ratio based on the value of shipments (CR), and entry, measured by the relative change in the number of firms (ΔN, defined as N/N_{-1}). Conduct, involving the decisions of the firm, is represented by two variables: capital intensity, measured by the capital-labor ratio (K/L), and advertising, measured by the advertising-sales ratio (A/S). Performance, involving the social performance of the industry, is also represented by two variables: price change, measured by the relative change in price (Δp, defined as p/p_{-1}) and profit, measured by the net profit rate on net worth (Π).

Table 13.2. The Simultaneous-Equations Model of Industrial Organization

Structure:

$$(1)\quad \text{CR} = f_1(\underset{+}{K/L}, \underset{+}{A/S}, \underset{+}{\Pi}; \underset{+}{\epsilon_p}, \underset{-}{g})$$

$$(2)\quad \Delta N = f_2(\underset{-}{\text{CR}}, \underset{-}{A/S}, \underset{+}{\Pi}; \underset{-}{\text{MES}})$$

Conduct:

$$(3)\quad K/L = f_3(\underset{+}{\text{CR}}; \underset{+}{w})$$

$$(4)\quad A/S = f_4(\underset{+}{\text{CR}}, \underset{+}{\Pi}; \underset{-}{\epsilon_p})$$

Performance:

$$(5)\quad \Delta p = f_5(\underset{+}{\text{CK}}, \underset{-}{K/L}; \underset{+}{\Delta c})$$

$$(6)\quad \Pi = f_6(\underset{+}{\text{CR}}, \underset{+}{A/S}; \underset{+}{\text{MES}}, \underset{+}{g}, \underset{+}{\epsilon_I})$$

NOTE Explanatory variables appearing before the semicolon are specified to be endogenous; those appearing after it are specified to be exogenous. Expected signs appear below each explanatory variable.

The exogenous variables fall into two categories. First are those factors that may be treated as "underlying considerations," specifically, price and income elasticities of demand (ϵ_p and ϵ_I) and the minimum efficient size (MES). Second are factors that are endogenous to the overall economy but are treated as exogenous for any particular industry, namely the real wage (w), the growth in the value of shipments (g), and the relative change in direct costs (Δc). The real wage is assumed to be set by aggregate labor markets, which cut across all industries. As to the growth in shipments and the change in direct costs, they reflect considerations that are, from an input-output standpoint, respectively, "downstream" and "upstream" from any particular industry. If the data permitted, an expanded model would treat some of these exogenous variables as endogenous.

The six equations of the model and the expected signs of coefficients of all variables of the model are specified in Table 13.2. It is by no means claimed that the model is either definitive or exhaustive. Rather it is an attempt to represent the SCP paradigm. The variables included and relationships indicated were chosen on the basis of three considerations—their roles in the SCP paradigm, their use in previous studies, and the availability of relevant and usable data.[17]

Data used in the estimation of the model were obtained for 381 four-digit SIC (Standard Industrial Classification) manufacturing industries for the 1963-1966 period.[18] A linear version of the model was then estimated using both ordinary least-squares (OLS) and two-stage least-squares (2SLS) techniques. The results of this estimation are given in Table 13.3, which gives both OLS and 2SLS regression coefficients and standard errors.

Several findings emerge from estimation of this model, particularly the 2SLS coefficient and (asymptotic) standard errors. One set of findings concerns the several two-way relationships of the model, in which one variable both influences and is influenced by another. The first is that between the capital-labor ratio and the concentration ratio: K/L exerts a statistically significant positive influence on CR, and CR exerts a statistically significant positive effect on K/L. As to CR and the advertising-sales ratio, while CR exerts a positive influence of borderline statistical significance on A/S, the A/S variable exerts no statistically significant influence on CR. The relationship between CR and the profit rate Π has been a major implication of the SCP paradigm. The estimated model, however, indicates that CR exerts no statistically significant influence on the profit rate, while the reverse feedback, that of Π on CR, shows a positive influence of borderline significance. The fourth and last of the two-way relationships is that between A/S and Π. According to the estimates in Table 13.3, A/S exerts a statistically significant positive influence on Π, while Π exerts a positive influence of borderline statistical significance on A/S.

A second set of findings concerns the one-way relationships of the estimated model, specifically the lack of a statistically significant influence of CR on either ΔN or Δp.

A third set of findings relates to the role of concentration. This construct has played a central role in the SCP literature, but the results suggest that while concentration does have some place in industrial-organization relationships, it perhaps does not occupy the central place it has assumed as a result of an inadequately tested acceptance of the SCP paradigm. Concentration has no significant influence on entry. Nor does it have a significant influence on the two conduct variables of decisions of the firm with regard to capital intensity and advertising or on the two performance variables of the change in price and the profit rate. Even the central doctrine of the SCP paradigm that concentration leads to higher profitability is not supported by the evidence. Furthermore, concentration can-

[17] For a detailed discussion of each of the equations of the model, see Intriligator, Weston, and De Angelo (1975). It might be noted that the model includes no measures of research and development, in part because data in this area are quite weak. For example, most data concern *inputs*, e.g., numbers of scientists and engineers employed [as in equation (9.3.7)], rather than *outputs* of research and development activities.

[18] Data sources include the Bureau of the Census, *Annual Survey of Manufacturers*, the Department of Commerce *Profiles, 1958-1968*, and data provided by the Office of Economic Analysis of the Department of Commerce, the Federal Reserve Board, and the Internal Revenue Service.

Table 13.3. The Industrial Organization Simultaneous Model, Estimated for 381 Four-Digit Manufacturing Industries

(1) (2SLS)
$$\mathrm{CR} = \underset{(0.23)}{-0.298} + \underset{(0.41)}{1.26K/L} - \underset{(3.39)}{2.59A/S} + \underset{(4.62)}{9.75\Pi} - \underset{(0.032)}{0.037g} - \underset{(0.95)}{1.03\epsilon_p}$$

(1′) (OLS)
$$\mathrm{CR} = \underset{(0.06)}{0.132} + \underset{(0.144)}{0.745K/L} + \underset{(0.75)}{1.42A/S} + \underset{(0.89)}{2.24\Pi} + \underset{(0.017)}{0.004g} - \underset{(0.74)}{0.074\epsilon_p} \qquad R^2 = 0.117,\ F = 9.97$$

(2) (2SLS)
$$\Delta N = \underset{(0.0015)}{0.007} + \underset{(0.0027)}{0.002\mathrm{CR}} + \underset{(0.029)}{0.054\Pi} - \underset{(0.027)}{0.067A/S} - \underset{(0.0000005)}{0.000002\ \mathrm{MES}}$$

(2′) (OLS)
$$\Delta N = \underset{(0.0005)}{0.009} + \underset{(0.00051)}{0.005\mathrm{CR}} + \underset{(0.008)}{0.014\Pi} - \underset{(0.007)}{0.016A/S} - \underset{(0.0000002)}{0.000001\mathrm{MES}} \qquad R^2 = 0.065,\ F = 6.56$$

(3) (2SLS)
$$K/L = \underset{(0.016)}{-0.106} + \underset{(0.076)}{0.176\mathrm{CR}} + \underset{(0.011)}{0.046w}$$

(3′) (OLS)
$$K/L = \underset{(0.014)}{-0.093} + \underset{(0.016)}{0.037\mathrm{CR}} + \underset{(0.006)}{0.062w} \qquad R^2 = 0.283,\ F = 74.72$$

(4) (2SLS)
$$A/S = \underset{(0.010)}{-0.013} + \underset{(0.014)}{0.020\mathrm{CR}} + \underset{(0.196)}{0.283\Pi} - \underset{(0.053)}{0.127\epsilon_p}$$

(4′) (OLS)
$$A/S = \underset{(0.004)}{-0.025} + \underset{(0.003)}{0.010\mathrm{CR}} + \underset{(0.054)}{0.504\Pi} - \underset{(0.051)}{0.121\epsilon_p} \qquad R^2 = 0.237,\ F = 39.00$$

(5) (2SLS)
$$\Delta p = \underset{(0.042)}{0.848} - \underset{(0.101)}{0.036\mathrm{CR}} + \underset{(0.184)}{0.157K/L} + \underset{(0.27)}{2.56\Delta C}$$

(5′) (OLS)
$$\Delta p = \underset{(0.020)}{0.861} - \underset{(0.015)}{0.034\mathrm{CR}} + \underset{(0.044)}{0.065K/L} + \underset{(0.22)}{2.46\Delta C} \qquad R^2 = 0.272,\ F = 46.90$$

(6) (2SLS)
$$\Pi = \underset{(0.004)}{0.043} + \underset{(0.014)}{0.025\mathrm{CR}} + \underset{(0.171)}{0.450A/S} + \underset{(0.000002)}{0.000002\mathrm{MES}} + \underset{(0.001)}{0.003g} + \underset{(0.099)}{0.200\epsilon_I}$$

(6′) (OLS)
$$\Pi = \underset{(0.002)}{0.052} + \underset{(0.0027)}{0.002\mathrm{CR}} + \underset{(0.038)}{0.393A/S} + \underset{(0.000002)}{0.000006\mathrm{MES}} + \underset{(0.001)}{0.003g} + \underset{(0.084)}{0.203\epsilon_I} \qquad R^2 = 0.311,\ F = 33.87$$

not itself be explained on the basis of considerations such as advertising. These findings concerning the influence and role of the concentration ratio in the system pose serious questions about its central role in the literature on industrial organization.

A fourth set of findings relates to the role of advertising. The evidence points to a mixed answer to the question of whether advertising is a barrier to entry. Advertising does appear to reduce entry, but, at the same time, it appears to have no statistically significant effect on concentration. Thus, advertising may create a barrier to the entry of new firms without changing the degree of concentration in the industry.

A fifth set of findings relates to the two techniques of estimation, OLS and 2SLS. Comparing the estimates obtained using OLS with those obtained using 2SLS indicates the effect of the estimation technique. Three important shifts take place in moving from OLS to 2SLS estimates. The influence of advertising on concentration is positive and significant using OLS but negative and no longer significant using 2SLS. In the advertising equation, the influence of concentration and profits on advertising intensity is significant using OLS but not using 2SLS. A third switch occurs in the profit equation, where MES is no longer significant using 2SLS. Thus, the method of estimation does have an important effect on the estimated model, and certain of the results of previous studies using OLS are called into question.

Several conclusions emerge from this study. First, it is possible to specify and estimate a simultaneous-equations model of industrial organization. Second, the OLS and 2SLS techniques provide different estimates, casting some doubt upon previous single-equation studies. Third, the SCP paradigm may be improperly giving too much weight to concentration as an explanatory variable for industry conduct and performance.

13.4 A simultaneous-equations model in labor economics

The field of labor economics, like that of industrial organization, has begun to make use of simultaneous-equations models and techniques to treat the joint determination of relevant labor-market variables. An example is the Ashenfelter-Heckman model of family labor supply.[19] The endogenous variables of the model are ΔR_h, the change in the labor supply of the husband; ΔR_w, the change in the labor supply of the wife; and ΔF, the change in total income. The exogenous variables are ΔW_h, the change in the wage rate of the husband, and ΔW_w, the change in the wage rate of the wife. One equation of the model is the identity

$$\Delta F_k \equiv \Delta(R_{hk} W_{hk}) + \Delta(R_{wk} W_{wk}) + \Delta Y_k \tag{13.4.1}$$

where ΔY_k is the change in nonlabor income and k is an index of the observation of a particular family. The other two equations of the model take the form

$$\Delta R_{ik} = S_{ih}\, \Delta W_{hk} + S_{iw}\, \Delta W_{wk} + \beta_i\, \Delta F_k + \epsilon_{ik}, \qquad i = h, w \tag{13.4.2}$$

[19] See Ashenfelter and Heckman (1974). For other studies see Cain and Watts, Eds. (1973).

where i indicates husband or wife; S_{ih}, S_{iw}, and β_i are the parameters to be estimated; and ϵ_{ik} are the stochastic disturbance terms.[20] The disturbances ϵ_{hk} and ϵ_{wk} are expected to be correlated in that the labor-supply decisions of the husband and the wife in any particular family are likely to be interrelated. Furthermore, ΔF_k is expected to be correlated with both of these stochastic disturbances. The system is therefore estimated via three-stage least squares. Estimates of the two behavioral equations of the system for husbands and wives aged 25 to 54 for 100 metropolitan areas in 1960 are given by

$$\Delta R_h = \underset{(0.043)}{0.106}\,\Delta W_h + \underset{(0.067)}{0.127}\,\Delta W_w - \underset{(0.067)}{0.102}\,\Delta F \tag{13.4.3}$$

$$\Delta R_w = \underset{(0.067)}{0.127}\,\Delta W_h + \underset{(0.273)}{1.233}\,\Delta W_w - \underset{(0.177)}{0.886}\,\Delta F \tag{13.4.4}$$

For these estimates the constraint that $S_{wh} = S_{hw}$ in (13.4.2), as implied by basic theory, has been imposed.[21] The estimated substitution effect for husbands, $\hat{S}_{hh} = 0.106$, is statistically different from zero, but it implies the very small value of 0.06 for the substitution elasticity (evaluated at the means). Thus, the labor supply of husbands is not very responsive to the husband's wage. For wives, however, the substitution effect, $\hat{S}_{ww} = 1.233$, is much larger than that for husbands, and it implies the relatively large substitution elasticity (again evaluated at the means) of 1.154. Thus, the labor supply of wives is highly responsive to wives' wages. The estimated cross effect is positive, indicating that husbands' labor supply responds positively to wives' wages (and wives' labor supply responds positively to husbands' wages). The negative β coefficients, $\hat{\beta}_h = -0.102$ and $\hat{\beta}_w = -0.886$, imply that leisure is a normal good, but $\hat{\beta}_h$ is not statistically significant.

13.5 Simultaneous-equations models of the health system

As noted in Chapter 9, health economics, like several other fields of economics, has evolved from nonquantitative studies to quantitative studies of single relationships in the health-care system, and work has already begun on formulating, estimating, and utilizing simultaneous-equations models of the entire health-care system. Such models promise to play an important role in analysis, forecasting, and policy formulation for this important and complex system.

An initial attempt to estimate a small (six-equation) econometric model of the U.S. health-care system, primarily for teaching purposes, was that of Feldstein.[22] Early quantitative work in health economics was concerned with

[20] Equation (13.4.2) is a discrete difference version of the Slutsky decomposition relating the effects of changes in wages and nonlabor income. See Ashenfelter and Heckman (1974) and Section 7.2, especially equation (7.2.14).

[21] This constraint is the symmetry condition of consumer theory, as in equation (7.2.14). Here this theory has been extended to labor-supply decisions.

[22] See Feldstein (1967).

certain ratios, such as the physician-population ratio, and the Feldstein model was influenced by this approach. The variables of the model are summarized in Table 13.4, and, of the six endogenous variables, five are such ratios. The exo-

Table 13.4. Variables of the Feldstein Model of the Health-Care System

Endogenous Variables (per 1000 population, except for MS)		
INS	=	Number of persons with health insurance
GP	=	Number of general practitioners
SPEC	=	Number of medical specialists
BA	=	Number of available short-term general hospital beds
ADM	=	Number of admissions to short-term general hospitals
MS	=	Mean duration of stay per case in short-term general hospitals
Exogenous Variables		
AGE	=	Percentage of persons aged 65 and over
INC	=	Percentage of families with incomes under $2000
URB	=	Percentage of persons living in urban communities
MAR	=	Percentage of married females in the population
P_{-1}	=	Previous utilization of available beds

Source Feldstein (1967).

genous variables are certain major demographic, economic, and health variables. The model relates these variables to one another and to lagged values of the variables. The model, as estimated with a modified form of two-stage least squares, utilizing cross-section data pertaining to states, is given in Table 13.5. The model reduces to constant ratios if the explanatory variables are set at fixed levels. For example, the second equation explains the number of general practitioners per 1000 population as a function of insurance, income, and previous levels of physicians. Holding these explanatory variables constant yields a fixed number of general practitioners per 1000 population. The model attempts to explain this ratio and other ratios in terms of certain broad underlying considerations and past values. It should be emphasized, however, that the intent was to illustrate the application of econometric techniques to the health-care system rather than to simulate the system in detail. The model was developed to serve as a methodological prototype, not to provide detailed estimates of structural parameters of a complete model of the health-care system.

The second example of a simultaneous-equations model of the health-care system is the 47-equation macroeconometric model of Yett, Drabek, Intriligator, and Kimbell.[23] The endogenous variables can perhaps best be described in terms of the institutions and manpower explicitly included.

[23] See Yett, Drabek, Intriligator, and Kimbell (1972, 1974). The model is called the "macro-

Table 13.5. Estimated Equations of the Feldstein Model of the Health-Care System

$$\text{INS} = 0.322\text{AGE} - 0.209\text{INC} - 0.224\text{URB} + 0.283\text{INS}_{-1} + 5.715$$
$$\text{GP} = 0.258\text{INS} + 0.255\text{INC} + 0.972\text{GP}_{-1} - 1.882$$
$$\text{SPEC} = 0.288\text{INS} - 0.157\text{BA} + 0.159\text{AGE} - 0.327\text{INC} + 0.712\text{SPEC}_{-1} + 2.934$$
$$\text{BA} = 0.249\text{INS} + 0.127\text{GP} - 0.187\text{SPEC} + 0.081\text{INC} - 0.112\text{URB} + 0.159\text{P}_{-1} + 0.616\text{BA}_{-1} - 1.397$$
$$\text{ADM} = 0.641\text{BA} - 0.053\text{AGE} - 0.118\text{URB} + 0.561\text{MAR} + 2.249$$
$$\text{MS} = 0.186\text{INS} + 0.026\text{GP} + 0.229\text{BA} + 0.190\text{URB} - 1.559\text{MAR} + 5.955$$

Source Feldstein (1967).

The inpatient institutions treated in the model are

1. Voluntary and proprietary short-term hospitals
2. State and local governmental hospitals
3. Federal and nonfederal short-term general hospitals
4. Skilled nursing homes

The endogenous variables for each are patient days provided and number of beds. In addition the model includes, as endogenous variables, the daily service charges for 1 and 4 and the occupancy rate for 1, 2, and 4.

The outpatient institutions treated in the model are

5. Outpatient clinics of short-term voluntary and proprietary hospitals
6. Outpatient clinics of short-term state and local governmental hospitals
7. Outpatient clinics of federal and nonfederal short-term general hospitals
8. Offices of medical specialists in private practice
9. Offices of surgical specialists in private practice

The endogenous variable for each is patient visits. The model also includes, as endogenous variables, the price per visit for 5, 8, and 9.

The types of manpower treated in the model are

10. Medical specialist physicians in private practice

econometric model" to distinguish it from the "microeconometric model" of the same group, which is based on the behavior of individual consumers and providers of health services. For a discussion of the microeconometric model see Yett, Drabek, Intriligator, and Kimbell (1970, 1975, 1977). For the conceptualization of another econometric model of the health-care system see Feldstein and Kelman (1970), and for other microsimulation models of the system see Feldstein, Friedman, and Luft (1972) and Feldstein and Friedman (1976). Other simultaneous-equations models that deal with portions of the health-care system are the Feldstein (1971a) model of hospitals, the Feldstein (1971b) model of the Medicare system, the Fuchs and Kramer (1972) model of physicians' services, and the Benham (1971) model of the market for registered nurses.

11. Surgical specialist physicians in private practice
12. Other specialists in private practice
13. Physicians employed by hospitals
14. Hospital interns and residents
15. Registered nurses
16. Practical nurses
17. Allied health professionals
18. Nonmedical labor

The endogenous variable for each is the number active or employed. In addition, the model includes, as endogenous variables, the annual wage for 15, 16, and 17.

The exogenous and standardizing variables of the model include demographic variables (total population, proportion of the population age 65 and over), economic variables (per capita income, Consumer Price Index), insurance variables (private health insurance, Medicare and Medicaid expenditures), and health manpower variables (stocks of registered nurses and practical nurses).

The basic mechanism of the model is that of demand and supply, as applied to inpatient institutions to yield patient days and daily service charges, to outpatient institutions to determine patient visits and prices per visit, and to health manpower categories to determine numbers employed and wage rates. The model is not an equilibrium one, however. It allows both for inequality of demand and supply and for lags in the process of adjustment to equilibrium.

The model was estimated using primarily 1970 cross-sectional data on states. The estimated model has been used for various purposes, including forecasts of health services and health manpower and simulation of certain changes in a state health-care system. Among the changes simulated using the model are a redistribution of physicians to "shortage" areas and a reduction in the rate of construction of new hospital beds. The model has been able to reveal both primary and secondary consequences of such changes—for example, the magnitude of increase of outpatient visits resulting from reduced bed construction. Through this type of simulation, the estimated model and other estimated models of the health-care system can reveal the consequences of various policy changes. They can therefore provide an important vehicle for health-care planners to use in evaluating policy alternatives.

PROBLEMS

13-A Show that a linear version of the Teigen model in (13.2.4), (13.2.5), and (13.2.6) is an identified model.

13-B Prove that, if M^*/Y is linear in the variables r_s, r_t, and Np/Y, then (13.2.14) implies (13.2.15). Also state the equivalent Koyck distributed lag model.

13-C Using the order condition of identification, discuss the identification of the simultaneous-equations model of industrial organization presented in Tables 13.1 and 13.2.

13-D For the Ashenfelter-Heckman model of Section 13.4 construct a statistical test of the condition that $S_{wh} = S_{hw}$.

13-E Using the order condition of identification discuss the identification of the Feldstein model of the health-care system, as reported in Table 13.5.

BIBLIOGRAPHY

Money

Andersen, L. C., and K. M. Carlson (1970), "A Monetarist Model for Economic Stabilization." *Federal Reserve Bank of St. Louis Review*, 52: 7–25.

Andersen, L. C., and J. L. Jordan (1968), "Monetary and Fiscal Actions: A Test of Their Relative Importance in Economic Stabilization." *Federal Reserve Bank of St. Louis Review*, 50: 11–24.

Ando, A. (1974), "Some Aspects of Stabilization Policies, the Monetarist Controversy, and the MPS Model." *International Economic Review*, 15: 541–71.

Ando, A. and F. Modigliani (1969), "Econometric Analysis of Stabilization Policies." *American Economic Review*, 59: 693–728.

Ando, A., F. Modigliani, and R. Rasche (1972), "Equations and Definitions of Variables for the FRB-MIT-Penn Econometric Model," in B. Hickman, Ed. *Econometric Models of Cyclical Behavior.* National Bureau of Economic Research. New York: Columbia University Press.

Brunner, K., and A. Meltzer (1964), "Some Further Evidence on Supply and Demand Functions for Money." *Journal of Finance*, 19: 240–83.

Cooper, J. P. (1974), *Development of the Monetary Sector, Prediction, and Policy Analysis in the FRB-MIT-Penn Model.* Lexington, Mass.: Lexington Books.

Cooper, J. P., and S. Fischer (1972), "Simulation of Monetary Rules in the FRB-MIT-Penn Model." *Journal of Money, Credit, and Banking*, 4: 384–96.

Davis, R. G. (1969), "How Much Does Money Matter? A Look at Some Recent Evidence," *Monthly Review*, Federal Reserve Bank of New York, 51: 119–31.

de Leeuw, F., and E. M. Gramlich (1968), "The Federal Reserve-MIT Econometric Model." *Federal Reserve Bulletin*, 54: 11–40.

de Leeuw, F., and E. M. Gramlich (1969), "The Channels of Monetary Policy," *Federal Reserve Bulletin*, 55: 472–91.

de Leeuw, F., and J. Kalchbrenner (1969), "Monetary and Fiscal Actions: A Test of Their Relative Importance in Economic Stabilization—Comment." *Federal Reserve Bank of St. Louis Review*, 51: 6–11. (Followed by "Reply" by L. C. Andersen and J. L. Jordan, 51: 12–16.)

Goldfeld, S. M. (1966), *Commercial Bank Behavior and Economic Activity.* Amsterdam: North-Holland Publishing Co.

Modigliani, F., R. H. Rasche, and J. P. Cooper (1970), "Central Bank Policy, the Money Supply, and the Short-Term Rate of Interest." *Journal of Money, Credit, and Banking*, 2: 166–218.

Rasche, R. H., and H. T. Shapiro (1968), "The FRB-MIT-Econometric Model: Its Special Features." *American Economic Review, Papers and Proceedings*, 58: 123–49.

Teigen, R. L. (1964), "Demand and Supply Functions for Money in the United States: Some Structural Estimates." *Econometrica*, 32: 477–509.

Industrial Organization

Comanor, W. S., and T. A. Wilson (1974), *Advertising and Market Power*. Cambridge: Harvard University Press.

Grabowski, H., and D. C. Mueller (1970), "Industrial Organization: The Role and Contribution of Econometrics." *American Economic Review*, 60: 100–5.

Greer, D. F. (1971), "Advertising and Market Concentration." *Southern Economic Journal*, 38: 19–32.

Intriligator, M. D., J. F. Weston, and H. De Angelo (1975), "An Econometric Test of the Structure-Conduct-Performance Paradigm in Industrial Organization." Paper presented at the Econometric Society Third World Congress, Toronto.

Mueller, D. C. (1967), "The Firm's Decision Process: An Econometric Investigation." *Quarterly Journal of Economics*, 81: 58–87.

Phillips, A. (1974), "Industrial Concentration and Public Policy," in H. J. Goldschmid, H. M. Mann, and J. F. Weston, Eds. *Industrial Concentration: The New Learning*. Boston: Little, Brown and Company.

Labor Economics

Ashenfelter, O., and J. Heckman (1974), "The Estimation of Income and Substitution Effects in a Model of Family Labor Supply." *Econometrica*, 42: 73–86.

Cain, G. and H. Watts, Eds. (1973), *Income Maintenance and Labor Supply: Econometric Studies.* Chicago: Markham Press.

Health Economics

Benham, L. (1971), "The Labor Market for Registered Nurses: A Three Equation Model." *Review of Economics and Statistics*, 53: 246–52.

Feldstein, M. S. (1967), "An Aggregate Model of the Health Care Sector." *Medical Care*, 5: 369–81

Feldstein, M. S. (1971a), "Hospital Cost Inflation: A Study in Non-Profit Price Dynamics." *American Economic Review*, 61: 853–72.

Feldstein, M. S. (1971b), "An Econometric Model of the Medicare System." *Quarterly Journal of Economics*, 85: 1–20.

Feldstein, M. S., and B. Friedman (1976), "The Effect of National Health Insurance on the Price and Quantity of Medical Care," in R. Rosett, Ed., *The Role of Health Insurance in the Health Services Sector*. New York: National Bureau of Economic Research.

Feldstein, M. S., B. Friedman, and H. Luft (1972), "Distributional Aspects of National Health Insurance Benefits and Finance." *National Tax Journal*, 25: 497–510.

Feldstein, P. J., and S. Kelman (1970), "A Framework for an Econometric Model of the Medical Care Sector," in H. E. Klarman, Ed. *Empirical Studies in Health Economics*, Baltimore: The Johns Hopkins Press.

Fuchs, V. R., and M. J. Kramer (1972), *Determinants of Expenditures for Physicians' Services in the United States, 1948–68*. Rockville, Md.: National Center for Health Services Research and Development, U.S. Department of Health, Education, and Welfare.

Yett, D. E., L. J. Drabek, M. D. Intriligator, and L. J. Kimbell (1970), "The Development of a Microsimulation Model of Health Manpower Demand and Supply," in *Proceedings and Report of Conference on a Health Manpower Simulation Model*, Vol. 1. Washington, D.C.: Bureau of Health Manpower Education, Public Health Service.

Yett, D. E., L. J. Drabek, M. D. Intriligator, and L. J. Kimbell (1972), "Health Manpower Planning: An Econometric Approach." *Health Services Research*, 7: 134–47.

Yett, D. E., L. J. Drabek, M. D. Intriligator, and L. J. Kimbell (1974), "Econometric Forecasts of Health Services and Health Manpower," in M. Perlman, Ed., *The Economics of Health and Medical Care*. International Economic Association, London: Macmillan.

Yett, D. E., L. J. Drabek, M. D. Intriligator, and L. J. Kimbell (1975), "A Microeconometric Model of the Health Care System in the United States." *Annals of Economic and Social Measurement*, 4: 407–33.

Yett, D. E., L. J. Drabek, M. D. Intriligator, and L. J. Kimbell (1977), *A Forecasting and Policy Simulation Model of the Health Care Sector: The HRRC Prototype Microeconometric Model*. Lexington, Mass: Lexington Books.

PART VII

The Uses of Econometrics

CHAPTER **14**

Structural Analysis

14.1 The uses of econometrics

This chapter begins the final part of this book, consisting of three chapters on the uses of econometrics. The models, data, and estimation techniques of econometrics, as well as several applications, have been developed in previous parts of the book. At this point it is therefore appropriate to assess the significance and impact of these developments. To perform such an assessment it is necessary to return to the ideas developed in Chapter 1 on the nature of the econometric approach, particularly the purposes of econometrics as displayed in Figure 1.1. The three purposes identified there–structural analysis, forecasting, and policy evaluation–will be treated in the present three chapters. They correspond, respectively, to the descriptive, predictive, and prescriptive uses of econometrics.

In developing not only structural analysis but also forecasting and policy evaluation, it is convenient to use a particular format for the econometric model. This format, similar to that developed in Section 2.9, expresses the structural form as

$$\underset{1\times g}{\mathbf{y}_t}\ \underset{g\times g}{\mathbf{\Gamma}} + \underset{1\times g}{\mathbf{y}_{t-1}}\ \underset{g\times g}{\mathbf{B}_1} + \underset{1\times k}{\mathbf{z}_t}\ \underset{k\times g}{\mathbf{B}_2} = \underset{1\times g}{\boldsymbol{\varepsilon}_t}\,. \qquad *(14.1.1)$$

Here $\mathbf{y}_t$ is a vector of g current endogenous variables of the model, $\mathbf{y}_{t-1}$ is a vector of the same g endogenous variables in the previous period, $\mathbf{z}_t$ is a vector of k exogenous variables, and $\boldsymbol{\varepsilon}_t$ is a vector of g stochastic disturbance terms. Taken together, $\mathbf{y}_{t-1}$ and $\mathbf{z}_t$ are the predetermined variables of the system, which can be written

$$\underset{1\times g}{\mathbf{y}_t}\ \underset{g\times g}{\mathbf{\Gamma}} + \underset{1\times(g+k)}{(\mathbf{y}_{t-1} \mid \mathbf{z}_t)} \underset{(g+k)\times g}{\begin{pmatrix}\mathbf{B}_1\\ \hline \mathbf{B}_2\end{pmatrix}} = \underset{1\times g}{\boldsymbol{\varepsilon}_t}\,. \qquad (14.1.2)$$

The partitioned matrix of coefficients of predetermined variables is the **B** matrix used previously; here the matrix is partitioned to take explicit account of lagged endogenous and exogenous variables.[1]

[1] Note that the **B** matrix in (14.1.2) is of order $(g + k) \times g$ rather than $k \times g$ as earlier because of the explicit inclusion of lagged endogenous variables. Also note that lagged exogenous variables are not accounted for explicitly here, whereas they are in equation (2.9.4). These variables can be taken into account by including them within $\mathbf{z}_t$.

Assuming $\mathbf{\Gamma}$ is nonsingular, the reduced form can be written

$$\mathbf{y}_t = \mathbf{y}_{t-1}\mathbf{\Pi}_1 + \mathbf{z}_t\mathbf{\Pi}_2 + \mathbf{u}_t \qquad *(14.1.3)$$

where the coefficient matrices and reduced-form stochastic disturbance terms are given as

$$\mathbf{\Pi}_1 = -\mathbf{B}_1\mathbf{\Gamma}^{-1}, \quad \mathbf{\Pi}_2 = -\mathbf{B}_2\mathbf{\Gamma}^{-1}, \quad \mathbf{u}_t = \boldsymbol{\varepsilon}_t\mathbf{\Gamma}^{-1}. \qquad *(14.1.4)$$

The final form can be obtained by iteration, using the reduced form, as

$$\mathbf{y}_t = \mathbf{y}_0\mathbf{\Pi}_1^t + \sum_{j=0}^{t-1} \mathbf{z}_{t-j}\mathbf{\Pi}_2\mathbf{\Pi}_1^j + \sum_{j=0}^{t-1} \mathbf{u}_{t-j}\mathbf{\Pi}_1^j. \qquad *(14.1.5)$$

Here each of the g endogenous variables is expressed as a linear function of base values of all endogenous variables ($\mathbf{y}_0$), current and lagged values of all exogenous variables ($\mathbf{z}_t, \mathbf{z}_{t-1}, \ldots, \mathbf{z}_1$), and current and lagged values of all reduced-form stochastic disturbance terms ($\mathbf{u}_t, \mathbf{u}_{t-1}, \ldots, \mathbf{u}_1$).

14.2 The nature of structural analysis

One of the major purposes of performing an econometric study is that of using the estimated econometric model for structural analysis. By *structural analysis* is meant an investigation of the underlying interrelationships of the system under consideration in order to understand and to explain relevant phenomena. Structural analysis involves the quantitative estimation of the interrelationships among the variables of the system.

The basic step in structural analysis is the estimation of the coefficients of the system, in particular $\mathbf{\Gamma}$, $\mathbf{B}_1$, and $\mathbf{B}_2$ in the structural form (14.1.1); $\mathbf{\Pi}_1$ and $\mathbf{\Pi}_2$ in the reduced form (14.1.3); and $\mathbf{\Pi}_1^t$, $\mathbf{\Pi}_2$, $\mathbf{\Pi}_2\mathbf{\Pi}_1$ $\mathbf{\Pi}_2\mathbf{\Pi}_1^2, \ldots,$ in the final form (14.1.4).

In addition to the estimation of the coefficient matrices themselves, structural analysis is concerned with the interpretation of certain coefficients or combinations of coefficients. Three important ways of interpreting the coefficients are the comparative statics results, the elasticities, and the multipliers. These will be the subjects of the next sections of this chapter.

Another aspect of structural analysis is the testing of rival theories. An example is the CES production function of Section 8.3. The estimation of this function, in particular the estimate of σ, the elasticity of substitution, can be considered a test of rival theories, in particular the Cobb-Douglas and input-output production functions. If $\sigma = 1$, the CES reduces to the Cobb-Douglas case, while if $\sigma = 0$, it reduces to the input-output case. An econometric measurement of σ, together with its estimated standard error, would allow a statistical test of the hypothesis that $\sigma = 1$ or that $\sigma = 0$. Thus if σ is not significantly different from 0, the input-output production function may be accepted as a simpler but adequate theory, while if σ is not significantly different from 1, the Cobb-Douglas form of the function may be so accepted.

14.3 Comparative statics

The comparative statics technique is one of the most useful techniques of economic analysis.[2] It involves the comparison of two equilibrium points of a system of equations describing the phenomenon under consideration. The two equilibrium points typically involve equilibrium before and after displacement by a change in one of the parameters of the system of equations.

Consider the following system of g independent and consistent (i.e., mutually compatible) equations in g variables $y_1, y_2, \ldots, y_g$ involving m parameters $\alpha_1, \alpha_2, \ldots, \alpha_m$:

$$\begin{aligned} f^1(y_1, y_2, \ldots, y_g; \alpha_1, \alpha_2, \ldots, \alpha_m) &= 0 \\ f^2(y_1, y_2, \ldots, y_g; \alpha_1, \alpha_2, \ldots, \alpha_m) &= 0 \\ &\vdots \\ f^g(y_1, y_2, \ldots, y_g; \alpha_1, \alpha_2, \ldots, \alpha_m) &= 0. \end{aligned} \qquad *(14.3.1)$$

If the g functions of $f^1, f^2, \ldots, f^g$ are sufficiently smooth and independent, this system can be solved to obtain a set of equilibrium values for the variables, each of which can be treated as a differentiable function of the parameters of the system:[3]

$$\begin{aligned} y_1^0 &= y_1^0(\alpha_1, \alpha_2, \ldots, \alpha_m) \\ y_2^0 &= y_2^0(\alpha_1, \alpha_2, \ldots, \alpha_m) \\ &\vdots \\ y_g^0 &= y_g^0(\alpha_1, \alpha_2, \ldots, \alpha_m). \end{aligned} \qquad *(14.3.2)$$

Inserting these equilibrium values in the original set of equations yields the identities:

$$\begin{aligned} f^1(y_1^0, y_2^0, \ldots, y_g^0; \alpha_1, \alpha_2, \ldots, \alpha_m) &\equiv 0 \\ f^2(y_1^0, y_2^0, \ldots, y_g^0; \alpha_1, \alpha_2, \ldots, \alpha_m) &\equiv 0 \\ &\vdots \\ f^g(y_1^0, y_2^0, \ldots, y_g^0; \alpha_1, \alpha_2, \ldots, \alpha_m) &\equiv 0. \end{aligned} \qquad *(14.3.3)$$

Now consider the effect of a change in one of the parameters, say α_l, on the

[2] For a general discussion of the theory of comparative statics see Samuelson (1947), Intriligator (1971), and Kalman and Intriligator (1973).

[3] The smoothness and independence assumptions are the conditions on the Jacobian matrix required for the application of the implicit function theorem. See the references listed in Chapter 11, footnote 32.

equilibrium values of the variables. Differentiating each of the identities in (14.3.3) with respect to α_l yields

$$\sum_{j=1}^{g} \frac{\partial f^i}{\partial y_j^0} \frac{\partial y_j^0}{\partial \alpha_l} + \frac{\partial f^i}{\partial \alpha_l} = 0, \qquad i = 1, 2, \ldots, g. \tag{14.3.4}$$

Solving for the effect of a change in every α_l on y_j^0 yields, in matrix notation,

$$\underset{g \times m}{\frac{\partial \mathbf{y}^0}{\partial \boldsymbol{\alpha}}} = - \underset{g \times g}{\left(\frac{\partial \mathbf{f}}{\partial \mathbf{y}}\right)^{-1}} \underset{g \times m}{\left(\frac{\partial \mathbf{f}}{\partial \boldsymbol{\alpha}}\right)} \qquad *(14.3.5)$$

where

$$\frac{\partial \mathbf{y}^0}{\partial \boldsymbol{\alpha}} = \begin{pmatrix} \frac{\partial y_1^0}{\partial \alpha_1} & \cdots & \frac{\partial y_1^0}{\partial \alpha_m} \\ \vdots & & \\ \frac{\partial y_g^0}{\partial \alpha_1} & \cdots & \frac{\partial y_g^0}{\partial \alpha_m} \end{pmatrix} \quad \frac{\partial \mathbf{f}}{\partial \mathbf{y}} = \begin{pmatrix} \frac{\partial f^1}{\partial y_1} & \cdots & \frac{\partial f^1}{\partial y_g} \\ \vdots & & \\ \frac{\partial f^g}{\partial y_1} & \cdots & \frac{\partial f^g}{\partial y_g} \end{pmatrix}, \tag{14.3.6}$$

$$\frac{\partial \mathbf{f}}{\partial \boldsymbol{\alpha}} = \begin{pmatrix} \frac{\partial f^1}{\partial \alpha_1} & \cdots & \frac{\partial f^1}{\partial \alpha_m} \\ \vdots & & \\ \frac{\partial f^g}{\partial \alpha_1} & \cdots & \frac{\partial f^g}{\partial \alpha_m} \end{pmatrix}$$

Equation (14.3.5) expresses the change in the equilibrium levels of each endogenous variable as each of the parameters of the model varies. The effect of a change in any one parameter, α_l, on the equilibrium value of any of the variables, y_j^0, is then given as

$$dy_j^0 = \frac{\partial y_j^0}{\partial \alpha_l} d\alpha_l, \quad j = 1, 2, \ldots, g; \; l = 1, 2, \ldots, m \tag{14.3.7}$$

where $\partial y_j^0 / \partial \alpha_l$ is the jl element of the matrix $\partial \mathbf{y}^0 / \partial \boldsymbol{\alpha}$ in (14.3.5).

The econometric model is a special case of this system of equations, and so the comparative statics developments are applicable to it. The structural form (14.1.1) is a special case of (14.3.1) for which the f^i functions are linear and the g endogenous variables $y_1, y_2, \ldots, y_g$ are determined on the basis of a certain set of parameters. The parameters include not only the coefficients of the system, embodied in the $\boldsymbol{\Gamma}$, $\mathbf{B}_1$, and $\mathbf{B}_2$ matrices, but also the exogenous and lagged endogenous variables $\mathbf{z}$ and $\mathbf{y}_{-1}$ and the parameters determining the stochastic disturbance terms (e.g., the elements of the covariance matrix). The equilibrium values of the endogenous variables in general all change as any one of these parameters varies.

The comparative statics results can be illustrated most easily in the case of a single-equation model with one exogenous variable where the stochastic disturbance term is set equal to its expected value of zero, in which case the structural form (14.1.1) is

$$y\gamma + y_{-1}\beta_1 + z\beta_2 = 0. \tag{14.3.8}$$

The reduced form is then

$$y = -y_{-1}\frac{\beta_1}{\gamma} - z\frac{\beta_2}{\gamma}. \tag{14.3.9}$$

The effect of a change in the coefficient of the endogenous variable γ is then

$$\frac{\partial y}{\partial \gamma} = y_{-1}\frac{\beta_1}{\gamma^2} + z\frac{\beta_2}{\gamma^2} = -\frac{y}{\gamma} \tag{14.3.10}$$

a result that could have been obtained either by differentiating (14.3.9) or alternatively from (14.3.5), since here

$$f(y;\ \gamma, \beta_1, \beta_2, y_{-1}, z) = y\gamma + y_{-1}\beta_1 + z\beta_2 = 0 \tag{14.3.11}$$

so

$$\frac{\partial y}{\partial \gamma} = -\left(\frac{\partial f}{\partial y}\right)^{-1}\frac{\partial f}{\partial \gamma} = -(\gamma)^{-1}y = -\frac{y}{\gamma}. \tag{14.3.12}$$

Thus the change in the equilibrium value of y stemming from a change in γ is proportional to y, the factor of proportionality being $-1/\gamma$. Once the model is estimated and a value of γ is obtained, (14.3.10) can be used to test the sensitivity of the equilibrium value of the endogenous variable to a change in its parameter. The other comparative statics results, obtained either from (14.3.5) or from differentiating (14.3.9), are

$$\begin{aligned} \frac{\partial y}{\partial \beta_1} &= -\frac{y_{-1}}{\gamma}, & \frac{\partial y}{\partial \beta_2} &= -\frac{z}{\gamma} \\ \frac{\partial y}{\partial y_{-1}} &= -\frac{\beta_1}{\gamma}, & \frac{\partial y}{\partial z} &= -\frac{\beta_2}{\gamma} \end{aligned} \tag{14.3.13}$$

Consider now once again the prototype macro model of Chapter 2, Section 2.7. The reduced-form equation for national income can be written

$$Y = \left(\frac{\beta_2}{1-\gamma_1-\gamma_2}\right) Y_{-1} + \left(\frac{1}{1-\gamma_1-\gamma_2}\right) G + \frac{\beta_1+\beta_3}{1-\gamma_1-\gamma_2} \tag{14.3.14}$$

as in (2.7.7), where the stochastic disturbance terms have been dropped for simplicity. One of the comparative statics results

$$\frac{\partial Y}{\partial G} = \frac{1}{1 - \gamma_1 - \gamma_2} \tag{14.3.15}$$

has been discussed earlier as the *multiplier*, indicating the changes in the equilibrium level of national income as government expenditure changes. Another result is

$$\frac{\partial Y}{\partial Y_{-1}} = \frac{\beta_2}{1 - \gamma_1 - \gamma_2} \tag{14.3.16}$$

indicating how the equilibrium level of national income changes as national income of the previous year changes.

There are, however, also the comparative statics results obtained by changing the parameters of the model. Changing the intercept of the consumption function, β_1, or the intercept of the investment function, β_3, has the same effect on equilibrium national income, given as

$$\frac{\partial Y}{\partial \beta_1} = \frac{\partial Y}{\partial \beta_3} = \frac{1}{1 - \gamma_1 - \gamma_2} \tag{14.3.17}$$

which, of course, is the same as the multiplier. Thus the multiplier can be more generally interpreted as the effect on national income of any change in one of its autonomous components, whether consumption (β_1), investment (β_3), or government expenditure (G).

The effect of a change in the marginal propensity to consume, γ_1, is given as

$$\frac{\partial Y}{\partial \gamma_1} = \frac{Y}{1 - \gamma_1 - \gamma_2} \tag{14.3.18}$$

and the same value is obtained for the change in equilibrium national income as the marginal propensity to invest out of current income γ_2 changes. Finally, the effect of a change in β_2, the coefficient of lagged income in the investment equation, is given as

$$\frac{\partial Y}{\partial \beta_2} = \frac{Y_{-1}}{1 - \gamma_1 - \gamma_2} \tag{14.3.19}$$

These results summarize the comparative statics for equilibrium national income in the prototype macro model. Similar results can be obtained for other models, including the macroeconometric models of Chapter 12. The estimated coefficients of the model, together with relevant (current) values of the variables, could then be used to obtain numerical estimates of all comparative statics results. Such results summarize the interaction between elements of the model, specifically the effect of changes in coefficients of the system and in exogenous and lagged endogenous variables on equilibrium values of all endogenous variables. They provide insight into the quantitative importance of influences contained in the model. They are also useful for purposes of forecasting and policy evaluation.

14.4 Elasticities

It is often convenient to express the comparative statics results of structural analysis in the form of elasticities. Assume, as in (14.3.2), that

$$y_j^0 = y_j^0\,(\alpha_1, \alpha_2, \ldots, \alpha_m), \quad j = 1, 2, \ldots, g \qquad \text{*(14.4.1)}$$

expresses the equilibrium value of the jth endogenous variable as a function of the m parameters of the model. Then the elasticity of y_j^0 with respect to α_l is given as

$$\epsilon_{jl} = \frac{\alpha_l}{y_j^0}\,\frac{\partial y_j^0}{\partial \alpha_l}, \qquad j = 1, 2, \ldots, g;\ l = 1, 2, \ldots, m. \qquad \text{*(14.4.2)}$$

An advantage of this representation is that it provides a dimensionless measure of the sensitivity of y_j to changes in α_l. The value of elasticity thus does not depend on the units in which y_j and α_l are measured.

Since the elasticity can be written

$$\epsilon_{jl} = \frac{\partial \log y_j^0}{\partial \log \alpha_l} = \frac{\alpha_l}{y_j^0}\,\frac{\partial y_j^0}{\partial \alpha_l} \qquad \text{*(14.4.3)}$$

it can be interpreted as the *proportionate* change in the variable y_j^0 given a unit *proportionate* change in the parameter α_l, all other parameters held fixed.

The comparative statics results of the last section can be expressed in elasticity form. Thus, for the single-equation model (14.3.8) the effect of a change in γ, as in (14.3.12), can be written in elasticity form as

$$\epsilon_{y\gamma} = \frac{\gamma}{y}\,\frac{\partial y}{\partial \gamma} = -\,1. \qquad (14.4.4)$$

Thus, for example, a 10% increase in γ, holding all other parameters constant, would decrease the equilibrium y by 10%. The results in (14.3.13) can be written, in elasticity form, as

$$\begin{aligned} \epsilon_{y\beta_1} &= -\,\frac{\beta_1}{\gamma}\left(\frac{1}{y/y_{-1}}\right), & \epsilon_{y\beta_2} &= -\,\frac{\beta_2}{\gamma}\left(\frac{1}{y/z}\right) \\ \epsilon_{yy_{-1}} &= -\,\frac{\beta_1}{\gamma}\left(\frac{1}{y/y_{-1}}\right), & \epsilon_{yz} &= -\,\frac{\beta_2}{\gamma}\left(\frac{1}{y/z}\right) \end{aligned} \qquad (14.4.5)$$

Thus the elasticity with respect to β_1 is the same as the elasticity with respect to y_{-1}, both being proportional to the reciprocal of the proportionate change in y (given as y/y_{-1}). Similarly $\epsilon_{y\beta_2}$ and ϵ_{yz} are the same, both proportional to the reciprocal of the ratio y/z.

For the prototype macro model, as in (14.3.14),

$$\epsilon_{YG} = \frac{1}{1 - \gamma_1 - \gamma_2}\left(\frac{G}{Y}\right), \quad \epsilon_{YY_{-1}} = \frac{\beta_2}{1 - \gamma_1 - \gamma_2}\left(\frac{Y}{Y_{-1}}\right)^{-1} \tag{14.4.6}$$

so the elasticity with respect to government expenditure is proportional to the fraction of national income spent by the government, while the elasticity with respect to previous national income is inversely proportional to the growth in national income. For changes in the marginal propensity to consume

$$\epsilon_{Y\gamma_1} = \frac{\gamma_1}{1 - \gamma_1 - \gamma_2} \tag{14.4.7}$$

so this elasticity is independent of Y—at any level of national income a 1% increase in the marginal propensity to consume raises equilibrium national income by a percentage increase equal to the product of the marginal propensity to consume and the multiplier.

A model that is linear in the logarithms of the variables entails constant elasticities, as indicated in (14.4.3). Earlier chapters have considered such models. An example is the constant elasticity demand function of Section 7.4, of the form

$$x_1 = Ap_1^{b_1}p_2^{b_2}\cdots p_n^{b_n}I^c. \tag{14.4.8}$$

Taking logarithms,

$$\begin{aligned}\log x_1 &= a + b_1 \log p_1 + b_2 \log p_2 + \cdots \\ &\quad + b_n \log p_n + c \log I \qquad (a = \log A)\end{aligned} \tag{14.4.9}$$

so

$$\epsilon_{x_1 p_j} = \frac{\partial \log x_1}{\partial \log p_j} = b_j, \quad j = 1, 2, \ldots, n_j; \; \epsilon_{x_1 I} = \frac{\partial \log x_1}{\partial \log I} = c. \tag{14.4.10}$$

Another example is the Cobb-Douglas production function of Section 8.3, of the form

$$y = AL^{\alpha}K^{\beta}. \tag{14.4.11}$$

Again, taking logarithms,

$$\log y = a + \alpha \log L + \beta \log K \qquad (a = \log A) \tag{14.4.12}$$

so

$$\epsilon_{yL} = \frac{\partial \log y}{\partial \log L} = \alpha, \qquad \epsilon_{yK} = \frac{\partial \log y}{\partial \log K} = \beta. \tag{14.4.13}$$

For such log linear models are exponents of the original multiplicative specification are the elasticities, assumed constant. Estimation of the parameters immediately yields the constant elasticities.

Some specific numerical estimates of such elasticities have been presented in earlier chapters, including Chapters 1, 7, and 8. Some additional estimates of income elasticities of demand for different categories of consumer goods in the United Kingdom 1920-1938 and the Netherlands 1921-1939 and 1948-1958 as estimated by Stone and Barten, respectively, are summarized in Table 14.1.

Table 14.1. Income Elasticities of Demand

	United Kingdom, 1920–1938		*Netherlands, 1921–1939, 1948–1958*	
Category of Consumer Goods	*Income Elasticity*	*Standard Error*	*Income Elasticity*	*Standard Error*
Margarine	–0.16	0.11	–	–
Bread	–0.05	0.04	0.12	0.06
Milk/dairy products	0.50	0.18	0.57	0.13
All food	0.53	0.04	0.67	0.16
Fish	0.88	0.07	0.88	0.41
Vegetables	0.93	0.14	0.84	0.17
Textiles and clothing	–	–	1.84	0.12
Meals away from home	2.39	0.18	–	–

Sources Stone (1954) for the United Kingdom, Barten (1964) for the Netherlands.

According to this table, for the United Kingdom margarine was close to if not an inferior good, while meals away from home was a good with a very high income elasticity: a 10% increase in income would have reduced margarine consumption by 1.6% and would have increased meals away from home by about 24%. The elasticities were reasonably similar in both countries and were, in fact, identical for fish—in both countries a 10% increase in income would have increased consumption of fish by 8.8%, although there was a much larger confidence interval for this estimate in the Netherlands than in the United Kingdom, for which the standard error is considerably smaller. The income elasticity for all food was 0.53 in the United Kingdom and 0.67 for the Netherlands. This particular elasticity is of considerable interest, since it indicates the responsiveness of a major item of expenditure to income. *Engel's law*, which states that as income increases the proportion of income spent on food decreases, implies that this elasticity should be less than unity, as obtained. It has also been estimated for other countries and periods, e.g., as 0.677 for France, 0.782 for Italy, 0.574 for the Netherlands, 0.381 for Sweden, 0.728 for the United Kingdom, 0.689 for

Canada, and 0.319 for the United States for the period 1948–1959.[4]

While the constant elasticity log linear models are convenient in yielding direct estimates of elasticities, it is frequently important to calculate elasticities for other models, specifically linear models. In a linear model the estimated coefficients are slopes, and the related elasticities vary with the point at which they are evaluated. Usually they are evaluated and reported at mean values for the variables. For example, for the single-equation model (14.3.8), the elasticity of y with respect to z is defined as

$$\epsilon_{yz} = \frac{z}{y}\,\frac{\partial y}{\partial z}. \tag{14.4.14}$$

Using (14.3.9) this elasticity can be obtained from estimates of β_2 and γ, by evaluating it at mean values of the variables:

$$\hat{\epsilon}_{yz} = -\frac{\bar{z}}{\bar{y}}\,\frac{\hat{\beta}_2}{\hat{\gamma}} \tag{14.4.15}$$

where $\bar{z}$ and $\bar{y}$ are mean values of the variables and $\hat{\beta}_2$ and $\hat{\gamma}$ are estimates of the parameters of the equation.

14.5 Multipliers: impact, interim, and long-run

The most common way of developing the structural analysis of an econometric model is in terms of multipliers. The multipliers can be recognized as special cases of the comparative statics results corresponding to changes in each of the exogenous variables of the model. Thus the (single) multiplier of the prototype macro model is given as

$$\frac{\partial Y}{\partial G} = \frac{1}{1 - \gamma_1 - \gamma_2} \tag{14.5.1}$$

indicating the effect of a change in government expenditure on equilibrium national income. In fact this is usually referred to as an *impact multipler*, since it indicates the impact of a change in a current value of an exogenous variable on the current value of an endogenous variable. For the general reduced form (14.1.3) the $k'g'$ *impact multiplier* is given as

$$\frac{\partial y_{t,g'}}{\partial z_{t,k'}} = (\mathbf{\Pi}_2)_{k'g'}, \qquad g' = 1, 2, \ldots, g; \quad k' = 1, 2, \ldots, k \tag{14.5.2}$$

–that is, as the $k'g'$ element of the $\mathbf{\Pi}_2$ matrix. Since

[4] See Houthakker (1965).

$$\mathbf{\Pi}_2 = -\mathbf{B}_2\mathbf{\Gamma}^{-1} \tag{14.5.3}$$

once either the reduced form or the structural form is estimated, all the impact multipliers can be determined. Of course, if g is even moderately large, the problem of numerically inverting $\mathbf{\Gamma}$ in (14.5.3) can be very laborious, suggesting the value of using the estimated reduced form directly. As long as $\mathbf{\Gamma}^{-1}$ is easy to compute, however, there are advantages in terms of efficiency in estimating the structural form, due to use of prior information.

The interim and long-term multipliers of a model are obtained from the final form of the econometric model. For the prototype macro model of Section 2.7, for which the final form for Y is (omitting stochastic disturbance terms)

$$Y_t = Y_0\Pi_1^t + \sum_{j=0}^{t-1} G_{t-j}\Pi_1^j\Pi_2 + \sum_{j=0}^{t-1} \Pi_1^j\Pi_3 \tag{14.5.4}$$

as in (2.7.16), the two-period cumulative multiplier is

$$\left.\frac{\partial Y_t}{\partial G_t}\right|_{\Delta G_{t-1}=\Delta G_t} = \Pi_2(1 + \Pi_1) \tag{14.5.5}$$

as in (2.7.19), and the three-period cumulative multiplier is

$$\left.\frac{\partial Y_t}{\partial G_t}\right|_{\Delta G_{t-2}=\Delta G_{t-1}=\Delta G} = \Pi_2(1 + \Pi_1 + \Pi_1^2) \tag{14.5.6}$$

as in (2.7.20). These are both *cumulative interim multipliers*, obtained by treating equal changes in the exogenous variables over two or more periods. More generally, the τ-period cumulative multiplier is

$$\left.\frac{\partial Y_t}{\partial G_t}\right|_{\tau} = \Pi_2(1 + \Pi_1 + \Pi_1^2 + \cdots + \Pi_1^{\tau-1}) \tag{14.5.7}$$

as in (2.7.21). Taking the limit, as $\tau \to \infty$, yields the long-term multiplier

$$\left.\frac{\partial Y_t}{\partial G_t}\right|_{L} = \Pi_2(1 + \Pi_1 + \Pi_1^2 + \cdots) = \frac{\Pi_2}{1 - \Pi_1} \tag{14.5.8}$$

as in (2.7.22), assuming $0 \leqslant \Pi_1 < 1$.

More generally, for the final form of the general econometric model, as given in (14.1.5), the $k'g'$ *τ-period cumulative multiplier* is given as

$$\left.\frac{\partial y_{t,g'}}{\partial z_{t,k'}}\right|_{\tau} = \sum_{j=0}^{\tau-1} (\mathbf{\Pi}_2\mathbf{\Pi}_1^j)_{k'g'} = [\mathbf{\Pi}_2(\mathbf{I} + \mathbf{\Pi}_1 + \cdots + \mathbf{\Pi}_1^{\tau-1})]_{k'g'} \qquad *(14.5.9)$$

Setting $\tau = 1$ yields the *impact multipliers* as in (14.5.2). Finite values of τ larger than 1 yield the *cumulative interim multipliers*, indicating the change in each endogenous variable as each exogenous variable experiences a sustained increase over a period of τ periods.[5] Taking the limit as $\tau \to \infty$ yields the *long-term multipliers*,

$$\left.\frac{\partial y_{t,g'}}{\partial z_{t,k'}}\right| = [\mathbf{\Pi}_2(\mathbf{I} - \mathbf{\Pi}_1)^{-1}]_{k'g'} \qquad *(14.5.10)$$

assuming the power series in (14.5.9) converges.[6] This long-term multiplier measures the effect on the endogenous variable g' when the exogenous variable k' experiences a sustained change in every period. The next sections explore some examples of multiplier analysis.

14.6 An example of multiplier analysis: the Suits study

Three specific examples of multiplier analysis are discussed in this and the next two sections in order to indicate the nature of this approach to structural analysis. They are the Suits, Goldberger, and Morishima-Saito analyses. Each relates to a particular macroeconometric model of the United States economy, as presented in Chapter 12.

The Suits analysis of the U.S. economy was based on a 33-equation model of the real economy using first differences of most variables.[7] Some multipliers for government actions are indicated in Table 14.2. The first line indicates that an additional \$1 billion in government purchases from firms in 1960 would have increased GNP by \$1.304 billion and would have increased total employment by

[5] These multipliers can be estimated directly, from estimates of $\mathbf{\Pi}_1$ and $\mathbf{\Pi}_2$, or indirectly, via simulating the response of the endogenous variables to changes in the exogenous variables. The simulation approach is particularly useful for nonlinear models. See Howrey and Klein (1972) and Friedman (1975).

[6] The power series in (14.5.9) called a *Neumann expansion*, converges if $\lim_{\tau\to\infty} \mathbf{\Pi}_1^\tau = \mathbf{0}$ or, equivalently, if all characteristic roots of $\mathbf{\Pi}_1$ have modulus less than unity. See Nikaido (1972). Note that (14.5.10) could have been obtained directly from (14.1.3) by noting that in the long run $\mathbf{y}_t = \mathbf{y}_{t-1}$, so

$$\mathbf{y}_t = \mathbf{y}_t\mathbf{\Pi}_1 + \mathbf{z}_t\mathbf{\Pi}_2 + \mathbf{u}_t.$$

Solving for $\mathbf{y}_t$,

$$\mathbf{y}_t = \mathbf{z}_t\mathbf{\Pi}_2(\mathbf{I} - \mathbf{\Pi}_1)^{-1} + \mathbf{u}_t(\mathbf{I} - \mathbf{\Pi}_1)^{-1}$$

implying (14.5.10).

[7] Suits (1962). The Suits model was estimated in 1954 dollars using data from 1947–1960.

89,000. The second line indicates the effects of an additional $1 billion in federal wages used to hire 0.2 million new workers. Clearly such an increase in federal spending would have had a greater effect on GNP than federal purchases from firms and a much greater effect on total employment, which increased by 0.263 million, the added 0.063 million new workers being employed in the private sector. (It might be noted, however, that the more effective of these two

Table 14.2. Multipliers for the Suits Model

Exogenous Change \ *Endogenous Variable Affected*	*National Income (GNP)*	*Employment*
Federal purchases from firms	1.304	0.089
Federal wages (each $1 billion in Federal wages is used to hire 0.2 million new workers)	1.692	0.263
Federal personal income tax shift	−1.119	−0.076

Source Suits (1962). Dollar figures in 1954 dollars; employment figures in millions.

policies for causing increases in employment in the private sector is federal purchase from firms.) The last line indicates the effects of a federal personal income tax shift–increasing the personal income tax by $1 billion would have lowered GNP by 1.119 billion and employment by 76,000 workers. This last multiplier can perhaps best be understood in terms of its reciprocal. To increase employment by one million workers would have required a reduction in the federal personal income tax of (1/0.076) or $13.2 billion.

Any particular combination of policies could be analyzed using the multipliers of Table 14.2 and other related multipliers. Thus, for example, an increase in federal purchases from firms of $2 billion, coupled with additional federal wages of $0.5 billion and an upward shift in the personal tax schedule of $1.3 billion, would have produced a total change in gross national product (Y) of

$$\Delta Y = (2 \times 1.304) + (0.5 \times 1.692) + [1.3 \times (-1.119)] \cong 2 \qquad \textbf{(14.6.1)}$$

–that is, of about $2 billion. Such a change would have produced a total change in employment (N) of

$$\Delta N = (2 \times 0.089) + (0.5 \times 0.263) + [1.3 \times (-0.076)] = 0.211 \qquad \textbf{(14.6.2)}$$

–that is, of approximately 211,000 workers.

14.7 A second example of multiplier analysis: the Goldberger study

The second example of multiplier analysis is the Goldberger study of impact and long-run multipliers for the Klein-Goldberger model.[8] Goldberger calculated the reduced form of the model and interpreted the coefficients as impact multipliers, giving the change in each of the endogenous variables as any of the predetermined variables of the model changed, as summarized above in equation (14.5.2). Some of his impact multipliers are summarized in Table 14.3. The first

Table 14.3. Impact Multipliers for the Klein-Goldberger Model

Exogenous Change \ *Endogenous Variable Affected*	*National Income (GNP)*	*Employment*
Government expenditures	1.39	0.61
Government wages	1.78	0.34
Wage taxes	−0.76	−0.34
Corporate taxes	−0.15	−0.07

Source Goldberger (1959). Figures have been rounded. The row for government wages was obtained by adding the government wage bill and government expenditure multipliers.

item in the table is the change in GNP given a change in government expenditure on goods and services. The value of this multiplier–1.39–is similar to that found by Suits in Table 14.2. The multiplier giving the effect of government wages on GNP–1.78–is also similar to that of Suits. It was obtained by adding the multiplier for the government wage bill, 0.39, to the multiplier for government expenditures, 1.39, since the wage-bill multiplier is based on holding government expenditures constant.

Two tax multipliers are shown in Table 14.3: those for wage taxes and for corporate taxes. The wage-tax multiplier is lower in absolute value for the Klein-Goldberger model than for the Suits model, but it is much larger than the corporate-tax multiplier. The two tax multipliers may be combined with the expenditure multipliers to determine the alternative possible effects of government policy within a fixed budget surplus or deficit. Thus, according to this model, increasing both government expenditure and wage taxes by \$1 billion would have increased GNP by \$0.63 billion. Increasing government wage expenditure and corporate taxes by \$1 billion, however, would have increased GNP by \$1.24 billion.

[8] See Goldberger (1959). For a discussion of the Klein-Goldberger model see Section 12.4 and Klein and Goldberger (1955).

Table 14.3 also shows multiplier effects on employment. Government expenditures in this model have a multiplier effect of 0.61 on employment, so an additional $1 billion in government expenditure would have created 610,000 new jobs. The multiplier is larger here than in the Suits model, in part because the period covered extends back further (to 1929) and hence involves smaller average wage payments.

Government wages have a smaller multiplier effect on employment than government expenditures, and the value is equal to the multiplier for wage taxes. Thus lowering wage taxes by $1 billion would have had the same effect on employment as increasing government wages by $1 billion. The employment multiplier for corporate taxes is extremely small; i.e., the level of employment is not sensitive to the level of corporate taxes.

Goldberger also calculated cumulative interim multipliers for the Klein-Goldberger model, and some of his estimates are presented in Table 14.4. A sustained unit increase in government expenditure has the initial multiplier of 1.39, as in Table 14.3, but increases rapidly over the next several years to reach almost 5.0. It then declines somewhat, having overshot the long-term value. Similar multiplier buildups over time in the first several years are indicated for employment.

Table 14.4. Interim Multipliers for the Klein-Goldberger Model

	Response to a Sustained Unit Increase in Government Expenditure in Year 0		*Response to a Sustained Unit Increase in Wage Taxes in Year 0*	
Year	*National Income*	*Employment*	*National Income*	*Employment*
0	1.39	0.61	–0.68	–0.30
1	2.81	1.21	–1.20	–0.53
2	3.88	1.63	–1.44	–0.62
3	4.57	1.84	–1.53	–0.65
4	4.89	1.90	–1.54	–0.64
5	4.92	1.84	–1.53	–0.62
6	4.75	1.69	–1.51	–0.61

Source Goldberger (1959). Figures have been rounded.

Somewhat comparable patterns emerge for the cumulative interim multipliers in response to a sustained unit increase in wage taxes, the initial values differing from those of Table 14.3 because of the assumption here that tax rates are given. It might be noted that this model is highly aggregated, so that the effects on particular labor sectors or industries cannot be determined.

14.8 A third example of multiplier analysis: the Morishima-Saito study

The third example of multiplier analysis is that of the Morishima-Saito model.[9] A major purpose in estimating this model was, in fact, to perform one key structural analysis. Morishima and Saito were interested in testing the Keynesian contention that fiscal policy was relatively more effective than monetary policy in conditions of high unemployment. They found that while full employment can be achieved by promoting aggregate demand via either monetary or fiscal policy, monetary policy tends to have the same effect on employment regardless of the level of unemployment, while fiscal policy tends to have a greater effect on employment the larger is the unemployment rate. Thus their findings for the relevant multipliers tend to support the Keynesian contention.

The multiplier indicating the effect of real gross investment (including government expenditure) on income, dY/dI, was approximately 1.35 in the most recent periods of full employment but approximately 1.40 in periods of 10–15% unemployment.[10] The multiplier indicating the effect of real cash balances on income, dY/dM, where M is real cash balances, was approximately 0.25 in both of these periods.[11] A measure of the relative effectiveness of fiscal versus monetary policy is the ratio of the multipliers, which may be interpreted as the marginal rate of substitution of monetary policy for fiscal policy:[12]

$$\text{MRS}_{\text{MI}} = \frac{dY/dI}{dY/dM} = \frac{dM}{dI}. \tag{14.8.1}$$

This marginal rate of substitution was estimated to be approximately 5.4 for the most recent periods of full employment and approximately 5.6 for periods of 10–15% unemployment. Thus, as Keynes contended, Morishima and Saito found that public investment policy becomes relatively more important than monetary policy in increasing income and employment during periods of high unemployment.

These three studies of multipliers are illustrative of structural analysis, indicating the responsiveness of endogenous variables of the model to predetermined

[9] For a discussion of the Morishima-Saito model see Section 12.3 and Morishima and Saito (1972).

[10] See Morishima and Saito (1972), Figure 3.

[11] See Morishima and Saito (1972), Figure 5. Note that M is *real* cash balances, since this is one of the variables of the model. To find the multiplier indicating the effect of nominal cash balances it is necessary to correct for the impact of money on prices. Morishima and Saito report an estimated multiplier of nominal cash balances on nominal income of 0.355 for the period 1929–1952.

[12] An alternative measure of the relative effectiveness would be the ratio of elasticities. Morishima and Saito estimated the fiscal elasticity to be 0.27 over the period 1929–1952 and the monetary elasticity to be 0.23 over the same period.

variables. Of central importance for purposes of both forecasting and policy analysis in the macroeconomic models is the responsiveness of such key endogenous variables as national income and employment to important government policy variables, such as government expenditure and taxes. The next two chapters discuss the use of these multipliers for purposes of forecasting and policy evaluation.

PROBLEMS

14-A Develop the comparative statics results for the prototype micro model.

14-B Construct confidence intervals for the income elasticities presented in Table 14.1, and determine for which categories of consumer goods the elasticities in the United Kingdom and the Netherlands show no statistically significant difference.

14-C Consider the Klein interwar model as presented in equations (12.2.1)–(12.2.6).

1. Find numerical values of all relevant multipliers, short-run and long-run.
2. Obtain numerical comparative statics results.

14-D Prove that Engel's law implies that the income elasticity of demand for food must be less than unity.

14-E Consider the following macroeconometric model:

$$C = a + b(Y - T)$$

$$I = c + dY_{-1}$$

$$T = eY$$

$$Y = C + I + G$$

which is based on that presented by Suits (1962). Here C, I, T, and Y are the four endogenous variables: consumption, investment, tax revenue, and national income, respectively; and Y_{-1} and G are predetermined: last-period income and government expenditure, respectively.

1. Find equilibrium values of the endogenous variables if the last-period income is $\bar{Y}_{-1}$ and current government expenditure is $\bar{G}$.
2. Using a table, trace out the implications over three periods of time for changes in each of the endogenous variables, given a unit increase in government expenditures in the base period.
3. Similarly trace out the implications over time of a unit increase in both government expenditure and taxes in the base period (assume the marginal tax yield of e is constant, but that tax revenue increases by 1 by a shift in the intercept of the tax-yield equation).

14-F Using the multipliers of Table 14.2, consider the following policies for the U.S.

1. An increase in federal purchases from firms of \$10 billion combined with a federal personal income tax shift of \$10 billion.
2. An increase in federal wages of \$10 billion combined with a federal personal income tax shift of \$10 billion.

Contrast the effect of these policies on GNP and total employment. Note that they both have the same (zero) impact on the federal deficit. What can be concluded about the use of the federal deficit as a measure of the impact of the federal government on the economy?

14-G Assume the U.S. federal government wants to increase employment by two million workers in order to reach "full employment." Using Table 14.2, show geometrically the alternative combinations of changes in federal purchases from firms and federal personal income tax shift that will reach full employment. Similarly show the combinations of changes in federal wages and income tax shift that will reach full employment. Determine the implications of several alternative combinations on each diagram for the federal deficit. Can full employment be attained with no additional federal deficit? If so, how?

BIBLIOGRAPHY

Barten, A. P. (1964), "Consumer Demand Functions under Conditions of Almost Additive Preferences." *Econometrica*, 32: 1–38.

Friedman, B. M. (1975), *Economic Stabilization Policy: Methods in Optimization*. Amsterdam: North-Holland Publishing Co.

Goldberger, A. S. (1959), *Impact Multipliers and Dynamic Properties of the Klein-Goldberger Model*. Amsterdam: North-Holland Publishing Co.

Houthakker, H. S. (1965), "New Evidence on Demand Elasticities." *Econometrica*, 33: 277–288.

Howrey, E. P., and L. R. Klein (1972), "Dynamic Properties of Nonlinear Econometric Models." *International Economic Review*, 13: 599–618.

Intriligator, M. D. (1971), *Mathematical Optimization and Economic Theory*. Englewood Cliffs, N.J.: Prentice-Hall, Inc.

Kalman, P. J., and M. D. Intriligator (1973), "Generalized Comparative Statics, with Application to Consumer and Producer Theory." *International Economic Review*, 14: 473–86.

Klein, L. R., and A. S. Goldberger (1955), *An Econometric Model of the United States Economy, 1929-1952*. Amsterdam: North-Holland Publishing Co.

Morishima, M., and M. Saito (1972), "A Dynamic Analysis of the American Economy, 1902–1952," in M. Morishima et al., Eds., *The Working of Econometric Models*. New York: Cambridge University Press.

Nikaido, H. (1972), *Introduction to Sets and Mappings in Modern Economics.* Amsterdam: North-Holland Publishing Co.

Samuelson, P. A. (1947), *Foundations of Economic Analysis.* Cambridge: Harvard University Press.

Stone, R. (1954), *The Measurement of Consumers' Expenditure and Behavior in the United Kingdom, 1920–1938.* New York: Cambridge University Press.

Suits, D. B. (1962), "Forecasting and Analysis with an Econometric Model." *American Economic Review*, 52: 104–32, reprinted in Zellner, Ed. (1968).

Zellner, A., Ed. (1968), *Readings in Economic Statistics and Econometrics.* Boston: Little, Brown and Company.

CHAPTER 15

Forecasting

15.1 The nature of forecasting[1]

One of the major objectives of econometrics is *forecasting*, by which is meant the prediction of values of certain variables outside the available sample of data–typically, a prediction for other times or places. It will generally be assumed that the forecast is quantitative, explicit, and unambiguous, and therefore verifiable in that there are conceivable outcomes that would validate or refute it. Examples include, in addition to forecasts of economic phenomena, forecasts of demographic, political, meteorological, astronomical, and many other phenomena. More specific examples include forecasts of national income and its components, population, election outcomes, the weather, and eclipses.

Forecasting is closely related to policy evaluation. In fact, most methods of policy evaluation rely upon a specific type of forecast–one that is conditional upon adoption of a policy (or, more generally, alternate policies). This subject will be discussed at length in the next chapter.

Assuming the vector of variables $\mathbf{y}$ is to be forecast, the problem of forecasting is typically that of predicting values for $\mathbf{y}$ at the future time $T + h$, given the T observations, $\mathbf{y}_1, \mathbf{y}_2, \ldots, \mathbf{y}_T$, and, possibly, observations of certain other variables.[2] The time T is often taken to be the present, and the positive time interval h is called the *forecast horizon*. A *point forecast* would be

$$\hat{\mathbf{y}}_{T+h} \qquad *(15.1.1)$$

representing a prediction of the values of $\mathbf{y}$ at time $T + h$. To the extent that the true values of the variables at this time, $\mathbf{y}_{T+h}$, are determined according to a probability distribution, the point forecast (15.1.1) is generally taken to be the expected value of the distribution as estimated at time T from the data $\mathbf{y}_1, \mathbf{y}_2, \ldots, \mathbf{y}_T$. This expected value can be bracketed by the *forecast interval*–for example, the 90% confidence interval

$$[\bar{\hat{\mathbf{y}}}_{T+h}, \bar{\bar{\hat{\mathbf{y}}}}_{T+h}]_{0.90} \qquad *(15.1.2)$$

[1] See Theil (1961, 1966), Mincer, Ed. (1969), Stekler (1970), Klein (1971). Intriligator (1971), and Evans (1974). For general discussions of various approaches to business forecasting see Chambers, Mullich, and Smith (1971) and Butler, Kavesh, and Platt, Eds. (1974).

[2] Forecasting can, however, also apply to the period *before* the sample–predicting the value of $\mathbf{y}$ at time $T-h$. Examples are the prediction of the first electrical engineer in the U.S. by Price, in Section 1.6, and the similar prediction for economists in Section 5.5. It can also apply to cross-section analyses, e.g., predictions for one family or for one nation on the basis of data of other families or other nations. Sometimes these are referred to as "ex-post simulations" or "ex-post predictions," to distinguish them from predictions of the future.

defined by

$$P(\bar{\hat{y}}_{T+h} \leqslant y_{T+h} \leqslant \bar{\bar{\hat{y}}}_{T+h}) = 0.90. \qquad *(15.1.3)$$

This forecast interval is illustrated in Figure 15.1 for the scalar case of predicting a single variable y. Because of the greater uncertainty in the more distant future, the forecast interval "fans out" over time.[3] The rate at which the interval fans out determines what constitutes a "short-term" as opposed to a "long-term" forecast. Thus a short-term economic forecast might involve a forecast horizon of one quarter or one year, whereas a short-term weather forecast might involve

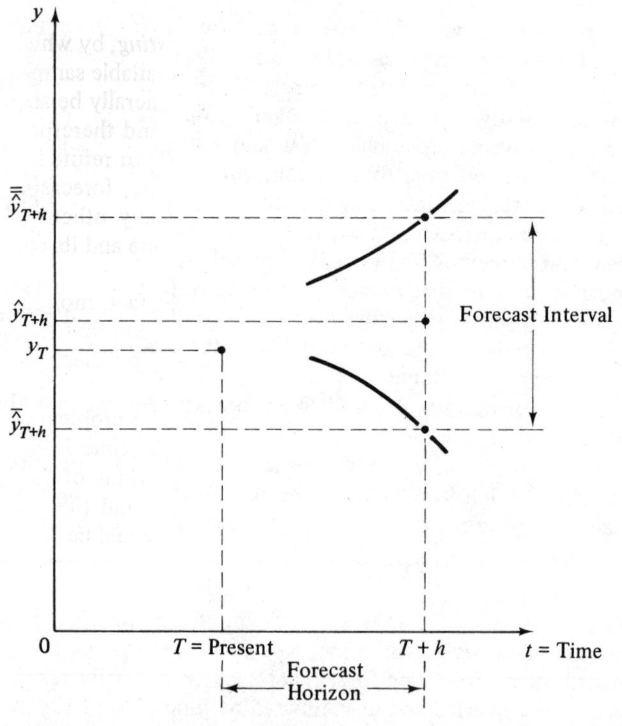

Figure 15.1 The Point Forecast and the Interval Forecast.

[3] From (4.10.12) a $100(1-\epsilon)$ percent confidence interval for the predicted $\hat{y}$ is

$$\hat{y} \pm t_{\epsilon/2}\hat{s}\sqrt{\frac{1}{n} + \frac{(\hat{x} - \bar{x})^2}{\Sigma \dot{x}_j^2}}$$

where $\hat{x}$ is the predicted value of the explanatory variable, $\bar{x}$ is the mean value of this variable over the sample, and $\dot{x}_j$ is the deviation from the mean value. Thus, as $\hat{x} - \bar{x}$ becomes larger—that is, as the value of the explanatory variable moves away from the mean value observed in the sample—the confidence interval widens, as shown in Figure 15.1. See also Problem 15-A.

a forecast horizon of one day. Similarly a long-term forecast in economics might be of the order of five years, whereas one in meteorology might be one week. The time scale for economic forecasts is much longer than that for weather forecasts, since the confidence interval for weather forecasts fans out much more rapidly. The time scale is then measured in appropriate units, e.g., quarters of a year for economic forecasts and days for weather forecasts. Given these units, the shortest short-term forecast is $\hat{\mathbf{y}}_{T+1}$, while $\hat{\mathbf{y}}_{T+h}$ for sufficiently large h would represent a long-term forecast.

Another type of forecast based on the probability distribution of y_{T+h} is the *probability forecast*, which reports the probability of a certain statement as to the future value of the variable. An example is

$$P(\mathbf{y}_{T+h} \geqslant \mathbf{y}^0) = \alpha \qquad \text{*(15.1.4)}$$

where $\mathbf{y}^0$ is specified and α is the probability forecast. An example is a weather forecast giving the probability of rain. Such forecasts have not been utilized in economics as extensively as point forecasts and interval forecasts, but they may well be more extensively used in the future as the methodology for their construction and evaluation is developed.

15.2 Alternative approaches to forecasting

There are several different approaches to forecasting. This section introduces approaches other than the econometric approach, and the next section presents the econometric approach. It will be shown, however, that the econometric approach includes as special cases several of the approaches to be presented here.

The oldest approach to forecasting is that of *expert opinion*, based on the informed judgment of experts acquainted with the phenomena in question. An important special case is that of *anticipation surveys*, such as surveys of capital investment anticipations or consumption anticipations, where decision makers themselves are asked to forecast their own future actions. In general, the factors relevant to the forecast, such as anticipations surveys, budgets, sales and credit conditions, are not considered in the context of an explicit framework in this approach. Rather, these factors are weighted and evaluated subjectively by the expert.

A modern variant of the method of expert opinion, the *Delphi method*, pools the judgments of a panel of experts in order to obtain forecasts.[4] Each of the experts is consulted and then their forecasts are presented, in summary statistical

[4] See Helmer (1966), North and Pyke (1969), and Dalkey et al. (1972). The Delphi method has also been applied to areas other than forecasting, including the quantification of both social goals and subjective uncertainty. A specific example of the pooling of expert opinion (but without the revision of forecasts that is part of the Delphi methodology) is the American Statistical Association–National Bureau of Economic Research consensus forecast of GNP and its components published quarterly by the NBER in *Explorations in Economic Research*. This ASA-NBER "consensus" forecast is the median of the forecasts produced by over 40 regular forecasters, most of whom use an informal GNP model rather than a formal econometric model. See Zarnowitz (1969) and Su and Su (1975).

form, to all. This presentation of responses is usually done anonymously and without face-to-face contact (e.g., via mail questionnaire) in order to avoid problems of small-group interaction, which might create certain biases in the outcome. The experts are then asked to revise their forecasts on the basis of the summary of all the forecasts and perhaps additional information. This process is repeated until the group of experts reaches a consensus.

A more formal approach is *persistence forecasting*, based on the assumption that the system has a certain momentum, with the future replicating the past. The simplest type is the *status quo* forecast, which predicts that the present value of the variable will continue through time into the future. Assuming a single variable to be forecast, the *status quo* forecast is the point forecast

$$\hat{y}_{T+1} = y_T \qquad *(15.2.1)$$

also called the "Naive I" forecast. An example is the forecast that tomorrow's weather will be identical to today's, a forecast that tends to be valid a very high fraction of the time.

Another simple type of persistence forecast predicts the same change from one period to the next:

$$\hat{y}_{T+1} - y_T = y_T - y_{T-1} \quad \text{or} \quad \hat{y}_{T+1} = 2y_T - y_{T-1} \qquad *(15.2.2)$$

also called the "Naive II" forecast, while yet another predicts the same proportionate change

$$\frac{\hat{y}_{T+1} - y_T}{y_T} = \frac{y_T - y_{T-1}}{y_{T-1}} \quad \text{or} \quad \hat{y}_{T+1} = y_T + \frac{y_T}{y_{T-1}}(y_T - y_{T-1}). \qquad (15.2.3)$$

A general form for most persistence forecasts is the *autoregressive model*, yielding the forecast of the distributed lag form:

$$\hat{y}_{T+1} = \sum_{j=0}^{\infty} a_j\, y_{T-j} \qquad *(15.2.4)$$

Here the forecasted value is obtained as a weighted linear combination of all past values of the variable. The coefficients a_j may be specified a priori, as in (15.2.1) and (15.2.2), or they may be estimated statistically.[5]

[5] Mincer and Zarnowitz (1969) and Klein (1971) argue that this purely autoregressive model should be used as a standard of reference in evaluating forecasts. Note that in (15.2.1) $a_0 = 1$ and $a_j = 0$, for all $j > 0$, while in (15.2.2) $a_0 = 2$, $a_1 = -1$, and $a_j = 0$ for all $j > 1$. Statistical estimation of the more general integrated autoregressive moving-average (ARIMA) model in the variable y_t and with disturbance term ϵ_t

$$\phi_p(L)\,\Delta^d y_t = \theta_q(L)\epsilon_t$$

is discussed in Box and Jenkins (1970), and Pindyck and Rubinfeld (1976). In this ARIMA

A related approach to forecasting is *trend extrapolation*, based on simple functions of time.[6] An example is the linear trend

$$y_t = a + bt \qquad *(15.2.5)$$

for which the forecasted value at $T + 1$ is

$$\hat{y}_{T+1} = a + b(T + 1) \qquad *(15.2.6)$$

where a and b are either postulated or estimated statistically. In fact this model is a special case of the persistence forecast (15.2.2) based on a constant absolute change from one period to the next, where

$$\hat{y}_{T+1} - y_T = y_T - y_{T-1} = b. \qquad (15.2.7)$$

Similarly the exponential trend

$$y_t = Ae^{\alpha t} \qquad (15.2.8)$$

yielding the forecast

$$\hat{y}_{T+1} = Ae^{\alpha(T+1)} \qquad (15.2.9)$$

is a special case of (15.2.3) where the prediction is based on a constant relative change, given by

---

model L is the lag operator ($LZ_t = Z_{t-1}$), p and q are the order of the polynomial operators ϕ and θ in the lag operator, and d is the order of the difference. Thus the left-hand side is the polynomial function ϕ_p of order p of the lagged (L) difference of degree d (Δ^d) of y_t, and the right-hand side is the polynomial function θ_q of the lagged ϵ_t. The model is specified by (p, d, q), where p is the order of the autoregressive operator ϕ_p and q is the order of the moving-average operator θ_q of the model. If $p = 0$ and $q \neq 0$, the model reduces to a pure moving-average process, e.g.,

$$y_t - y_{t-1} = \epsilon_t + \theta_1\epsilon_{t-1} + \theta_2\epsilon_{t-2} + \beta$$

for $(p, d, q) = (0, 1, 2)$. If $p \neq 0$ and $q = 0$, the model reduces to a pure autoregressive process, e.g.,

$$(y_t - y_{t-1}) + \varphi_1 (y_{t-1} - y_{t-2}) = \epsilon_t + \beta$$

for $(p, d, q) = (1, 1, 0)$. If $p = q = 0$, the model reduces to a *random walk*, e.g.,

$$y_t - y_{t-1} = \epsilon_t + \beta$$

for $(p, d, q) = (0, 1, 0)$.

[6] See also Section 3.6. It might be noted that in several areas it has been found that trend extrapolation provides more accurate forecasts than anticipations surveys. See Ferber (1953, 1958), Modigliani and Weingartner (1958), and Okun (1962).

$$\frac{\hat{y}_{T+1} - y_T}{y_T} = \frac{y_T - y_{T-1}}{y_{T-1}} = e^{\alpha} - 1. \tag{15.2.10}$$

Taking logarithms of (15.2.8),

$$\ln y_t = \ln A + \alpha t \tag*{*(15.2.11)}$$

so the forecast at time $T + h$ can be written

$$\ln \hat{y}_{T+h} = \ln A + \alpha(T + h) \tag{15.2.12}$$

where α is the proportionate rate of change in y. This is the model used for forecasting the growth of science in Sections 1.6 and 5.5. For example, the model as used to forecast backward in time predicted that $y = 1$ when

$$\ln \hat{y}_{T+h} = \ln A + \alpha(T + h) = 0 \tag*{*(15.2.13)}$$

—that is, when the horizon h was equal to h^*, where

$$T + h^* = -\frac{\ln A}{\alpha} \tag{15.2.14}$$

obtained from estimates of A and α.

Yet another approach to forecasting is the method of *leading indicators*. To use this approach a forecast for y is based on a related variable x, the leading indicator, where y at time t depends on x at the previous time $t - \theta$. Thus

$$y_t = f(x_{t-\theta}). \tag{15.2.15}$$

The predicted value of y at time $T + h$ is thus

$$\hat{y}_{T+h} = f(x_{T+h-\theta}). \tag{15.2.16}$$

In fact, this method is almost exclusively applied not to *levels* of variables but rather to their *rates of change*. In particular, the model

$$\Delta y_{T+h} = g(\Delta x_{T+h-\theta}) \tag*{*(15.2.17)}$$

is used to predict turning points, where, for example, a downturn in one variable signals the eventual downturn of another variable. The leading indicators are selected on the basis of their record in predicting (leading) past turning points. Examples of leading indicators for the general level of economic activity include hours worked per week, new incorporations, business failures, wholesale prices, new orders, and construction contracts, all of which generally lead overall economic activity by approximately six months. Thus a downturn in several of these indicators signals a downturn in overall business conditions in six months time.[7] Another example is the money supply, where a change in the rate of growth of the money supply generally leads to a change in the rate of growth of national income in nine to twelve months.[8]

15.3 The econometric approach to forecasting; short-term forecasts

The econometric approach to forecasting is based on the reduced-form equations introduced in Section 14.1:

$$\mathbf{y}_t = \mathbf{y}_{t-1}\mathbf{\Pi}_1 + \mathbf{z}_t\mathbf{\Pi}_2 + \mathbf{u}_t. \qquad *(15.3.1)$$

Here $\mathbf{y}_t$ is a vector of g endogenous variables to be forecast; $\mathbf{z}_t$ is a vector of k exogenous variables; $\mathbf{y}_{t-1}$, the lagged endogenous variables, and $\mathbf{z}_t$ together are the predetermined variables; and $\mathbf{u}_t$ is a vector of g stochastic disturbance terms. The coefficient matrices are estimated as $\hat{\mathbf{\Pi}}_1$ and $\hat{\mathbf{\Pi}}_2$, numerical matrices with g^2 and kg elements, respectively. These estimated reduced-form coefficient matrices can be obtained directly from an estimate of the reduced form, or indirectly from the estimated structural form, as in (14.5.3). The time period involved in the lag in (15.3.1) should depend on the system under consideration and, as indicated at the end of Section 15.1, should depend on how rapidly the forecast interval "fans out."

The model in (15.3.1), ideally, is based upon some underlying theory as embodied in the structural-form equations. Sometimes the data are used to help specify the model, in particular to select the exogenous variables, e.g., via an analysis of correlations of variables. The most likely result of this approach, however, will be either spurious correlation (e.g., the correlation of the birth rate with the stork population) or the regression of a variable on itself (e.g., the regression of investment on savings). Such an approach might lead to good fits, including high R^2 values, but generally does not lead to good forecasts.

Given the econometric model, summarized by the estimated reduced-form equations, a *short-term forecast* of values taken by all endogenous variables in the next period is given as[9]

[7] See Moore, Ed. (1961), Moore and Shiskin (1967) and Hymans (1973). In practice the leading indicators predict virtually all the true turns, but they also predict false turns. The principal way of treating this problem of false turns is to pool the leading indicators. See Shiskin (1967) for an index of leading series. Another way of pooling is via a *diffusion index*, representing the percentage of the group of indicators that is rising. Since the diffusion index is like a first difference, when it turns up it signals a future rise in general business conditions. See Alexander (1958), and Alexander and Stekler (1959). Yet another approach is by a *composite index*, which takes into account the size as well as the direction of changes in the component series. See Moore (1969, 1973).

[8] See Friedman (1960) and Friedman and Schwartz (1963). Note that the change in growth of national income can involve a change in the price level and/or real income.

[9] See Theil (1966) and Klein (1971).

$$\hat{\mathbf{y}}_{T+1} = \mathbf{y}_T\hat{\mathbf{\Pi}}_1 + \hat{\mathbf{z}}_{T+1}\hat{\mathbf{\Pi}}_2 + \hat{\mathbf{u}}_{T+1} \qquad *(15.3.2)$$

This prediction of the next-period values of the endogenous variables consists of two systematic components and one judgmental component.

The first systematic component in (15.3.2), $\mathbf{y}_T\hat{\mathbf{\Pi}}_1$, indicates the dependence on current values of the endogenous variables, which are weighted by the estimated coefficients in $\hat{\mathbf{\Pi}}_1$. This term summarizes the systematic dependence of each of the endogenous variables on previous values of all endogenous variables due to factors such as serial correlation, constant growth processes, or distributed lag phenomena. In many instances a very good forecast can be obtained on the basis only of lagged values, as in the case of persistence forecasting.

The second systematic component in (15.3.2) is $\hat{\mathbf{z}}_{T+1}\hat{\mathbf{\Pi}}_2$, based upon a prediction of the future values of the exogenous variables, $\hat{\mathbf{z}}_{T+1}$, and the estimated coefficients, $\hat{\mathbf{\Pi}}_2$. This term reflects the dependence of the endogenous variables on exogenous variables of the model. Since the $\mathbf{z}_T$ are exogenous variables, they are themselves determined on the basis of factors not explicitly treated in the econometric model, so it is reasonable that these variables must be forecast on the basis of factors other than those of the model itself. One important case is that in which the $\mathbf{z}_{T+1}$ are themselves forecasts from another econometric model. For example, several major corporations forecast their sales, employment, etc. on the basis of an econometric model specific to their company or industry. Such a model typically treats major macroeconomic variables, such as personal income or investment expenditure, as exogenous. In order to predict corporate sales, therefore, it is necessary to use forecasts of the major macroeconomic variables, which are obtained as forecasts of the endogenous variables of a macroeconometric model, e.g., one of those discussed in Chapter 12. The macroeconometric model itself contains certain exogenous variables, some of which are predicted on the basis of anticipations surveys of consumer behavior and capital spending decisions. In addition to the output of another econometric model and anticipations surveys, the future values of the exogenous variables $\hat{\mathbf{z}}_{T+1}$ are sometimes obtained on the basis of expert opinion or extrapolations of past trends in these variables.[10]

The third component in (15.3.2) is the judgmental component $\hat{\mathbf{u}}_{T+1}$, called "add factors," which can be interpreted as estimates of the future values of the disturbance terms or, alternatively, as adjustments of the intercepts in each of the reduced-form equations. These add factors round out the econometric forecast—the first component in (15.3.2) summarizes the effects of past endogenous variables; the second component summarizes the effects of all other included exogenous variables; and the third component, the add factors, summarizes the effects of all other factors, including variables omitted from the model. The add factors are based on judgments of factors not explicitly included in the model. For example, in a macroeconometric model there may be no explicit account taken of strike activity, but if major union contracts are expiring and a strike appears likely in the forecast period, the forecasts of production should be appropriately revised downward. Many other factors may not have been in-

[10] For example, the z_{T+1} might be obtained from an autoregressive model for the z's comparable to that for the y's in (15.2.4). See Problem 15-E.

cluded in the model because their occurrence is rare or because data are difficult to obtain, but this does not mean that they must be overlooked in formulating a forecast. Indeed, it would be inappropriate to ignore relevant considerations simply because they were omitted from the model. In this sense forecasting with an econometric model is not simply a mechanical exercise but rather a blending of objective and subjective considerations. The subjective considerations, embodied in the add factors, generally improve significantly on the accuracy of the forecasts made with an econometric model.

While the add factors reflect judgmental considerations, choices of values for $\hat{\mathbf{u}}_{T+1}$ can be guided not only by relevant factors that have been omitted from the model but also by past residuals in estimating the model and past errors in forecasts. These residuals and errors are clues not only to omitted variables but also to errors in measurement of coefficients and systematic biases in forecasting exogenous variables. Thus, for example, if the recent features of the system are different from those over the entire sample and it is expected that these features will continue into the forecast period, or if the past residuals or forecast errors exhibit positive serial correlation (or a cyclical pattern), then it might be appropriate to use the recent residuals or forecast errors to construct add factors. One such approach would use add factors in such a way that the computed values of the endogenous variables at the most recent observation, as adjusted by the add factors, are the same as the observed value. Another would use add factors such that an average of the last several forecast errors vanishes.[11]

The econometric forecast in (15.3.2) is called an *ex-ante forecast* because it is a true forecast, made before the event occurs. By contrast, an *ex-post forecast*, made after the event, would replace the predicted values of the exogenous variables $\hat{\mathbf{z}}_{T+1}$ by their actual values $\mathbf{z}_{T+1}$ and would replace the add factors $\hat{\mathbf{u}}_{T+1}$ by the zero expected values of the stochastic disturbance terms. Thus the ex-post forecast is

$$\hat{\hat{\mathbf{y}}}_{T+1} = \mathbf{y}_T\hat{\mathbf{\Pi}}_1 + \mathbf{z}_{T+1}\hat{\mathbf{\Pi}}_2. \qquad (15.3.3)$$

The relation between the ex-ante forecast $\hat{\mathbf{y}}_{T+1}$ and the ex-post forecast $\hat{\hat{\mathbf{y}}}_{T+1}$ is

$$\hat{\hat{\mathbf{y}}}_{T+1} = \hat{\mathbf{y}}_{T+1} + (\mathbf{z}_{T+1} - \hat{\mathbf{z}}_{T+1})\hat{\mathbf{\Pi}}_2 - \hat{\mathbf{u}}_{T+1} \qquad (15.3.4)$$

so $\hat{\hat{\mathbf{y}}}_{T+1}$ can be obtained from $\hat{\mathbf{y}}_{T+1}$ after observing $\mathbf{z}_{T+1}$ by correcting both for the errors in predicting the exogenous variables $\mathbf{z}_{T+1} - \hat{\mathbf{z}}_{T+1}$ and for the add factors $\hat{\mathbf{u}}_{T+1}$. The ex-post forecast is useful in focusing on the explicitly estimated parts of the forecast, specifically the estimated coefficient matrices $\hat{\mathbf{\Pi}}_1$ and $\hat{\mathbf{\Pi}}_2$, and eliminating the influence of the other elements of the ex-ante forecast, namely $\hat{\mathbf{z}}_{T+1}$ and $\hat{\mathbf{u}}_{T+1}$, which are generally not explicitly estimated. For example, it is possible to replicate ex-post forecasts, but not ex-ante forecasts.

Another variant on the econometric forecast in (15.3.2) is the *stochastic forecast*. The forecast in (15.3.2) is a *deterministic forecast* in that it is based upon specific values for the current endogenous and future exogenous variables, for the coefficients, and for the future stochastic disturbance terms. All of these

[11] See Klein (1971) and Haitovsky, Treyz, and Su (1974).

(with the possible exception of the current endogenous variables–which may be measured subject to error) are subject to uncertainty. In a stochastic forecast this uncertainty is indicated via the forecast interval (15.1.2) or the probability forecast (15.1.4). One approach to developing such forecasts is to use available estimates of the parameters of the distribution of the coefficients and the stochastic disturbance terms, particularly estimated variances and covariances, together with judgments or statistical inferences as to the distribution of the variables, to determine a probability distribution for $\hat{\mathbf{y}}_{T+1}$. This probability distribution can be described using the forecast interval or the probability forecast. Another approach is the Bayesian one, in which judgments on prior probabilities, together with the likelihood function, would imply posterior (forecast) probabilities.[12]

Yet a third approach is the Monte Carlo technique of stochastic simulation in which a set of alternative forecasts is prepared based on repeated random drawings using the distributions of the parameter estimates and stochastic disturbance terms. This set of forecasts can be described in terms of either the forecast interval (e.g., 90% of the forecasts fall within a certain range) or the probability forecast (e.g., the percent of the forecasts that exceed a certain level.)[13]

Returning to the ex-ante deterministic forecast of (15.3.2), the various approaches to forecasting introduced in the last section can all be interpreted in terms of this econometric forecast. The expert-opinion forecast is the special case in which there is no systematic part, so the forecast can be represented as the purely judgmental one

$$\hat{\mathbf{y}}_{T+1} = \hat{\mathbf{u}}_{T+1} \tag{15.3.5}$$

where $\hat{\mathbf{\Pi}}_1 = \mathbf{0}$ and $\hat{\mathbf{\Pi}}_2 = \mathbf{0}$. In persistence forecasting the first systematic component $\mathbf{y}_T\hat{\mathbf{\Pi}}_1$ is emphasized, since it reflects dependence on past values of the same variables. For example, the *status quo* forecast

$$\hat{\mathbf{y}}_{T+1} = \mathbf{y}_T \tag{15.3.6}$$

corresponds to the case $\hat{\mathbf{\Pi}}_1 = \mathbf{I}, \hat{\mathbf{\Pi}}_2 = \mathbf{0}, \hat{\mathbf{u}}_{T+1} = \mathbf{0}$.[14] Other persistence forecasts, such as the autoregressive model of (15.2.4), can be represented using (15.3.2) by simply adding terms for $\mathbf{y}_{T-2}$, $\mathbf{y}_{T-3}$, etc. Trend extrapolation can be

[12] See Problem 15-C. For a discussion of the Bayesian approach to estimation see Section 5.7. For a discussion of analytical computations of forecast intervals see Goldberger, Nagar, and Odeh (1961).

[13] See Klein (1971), Evans, Klein, and Saito (1972), and Fromm, Klein, and Schink (1972). In the simplest case this approach takes the two systematic components of (15.3.2) and adds to it values for $\mathbf{u}_{T+1}$ obtained from repeated random drawings from a distribution with the stochastic characteristics of $\mathbf{u}$, e.g., $N(\mathbf{0},\Sigma)$, where Σ is either estimated or assumed. The result is a sample of values for $\hat{\mathbf{y}}_{T+1}$ that can be used to construct forecast intervals or probability forecasts.

[14] In this case the reduced form can be written

$$\mathbf{y}_t - \mathbf{y}_{t-1} = \mathbf{u}_t$$

explained in terms of (15.3.2) either by lagged endogenous variables or by including time as an exogenous variable. Leading indicators can be represented in the econometric approach using lagged exogenous variables.[15] Anticipation variables can be directly included in the model, and their inclusion usually leads to improved forecasts.

There are, in fact, several advantages of econometric forecasts, as in (15.3.2), over alternative approaches to forecasting. First, the econometric approach provides a useful structure in which to consider various possible factors, such as past values of the variables to be forecast, values of related variables, and other factors. Second, it is broad enough to allow for treatment of many different considerations, including a synthesis of various systematic and judgmental factors. Third, it leads to forecasts of related variables that are consistent with one another, since they all must satisfy the requirements of the model, particularly its identities. Fourth, it leads to forecasts that are explicitly conditional on predicted values of future exogenous variables $\hat{\mathbf{z}}_{T+1}$, add factors $\hat{\mathbf{u}}_{T+1}$, coefficient matrices $\hat{\mathbf{\Pi}}_1$ and $\hat{\mathbf{\Pi}}_2$, and current values of endogenous variables $\mathbf{y}_T$. It is therefore possible to analyze the relative importance of each of these elements of the forecast individually and to test the sensitivity of the forecast to changes in each, particularly in the light of new data. Fifth, it is possible to replicate a related forecast—the ex-post forecast of (15.3.3). Sixth, and perhaps most important, it has a good record for accuracy, compared to other approaches, such as those of Section 15.2, each of which can be interpreted as emphasizing one aspect of the econometric forecast but excluding its other aspects. Indeed, the best forecasts generally combine an econometric model that includes leading indicators, anticipations data, and time-series analysis with judgmental factors, represented by add factors, as discussed in Sections 15.5 and 15.6.

15.4 Long-term forecasts

Long-term forecasts are those for which the forecasting horizon, h in (15.1.1), exceeds some prespecified level, h_0. Thus the long-term point forecast is

$$\hat{\mathbf{y}}_{T+h}, \qquad h > h_0 \qquad *(15.4.1)$$

---

so the first differences of the endogenous variables are random variables. This model and the implied status quo forecasts work quite well for certain complex systems in which change is influenced by a multitude of random causal factors. An example is the motion of molecules in a gas, called *Brownian motion*, in which each molecule moves randomly. At the macroscopic level, weather conditions also generally change according to this model, so one of the best weather forecasts is the status quo forecast that tomorrow's weather will be the same as today's. An example closer to economics is the behavior of prices in the stock market. Studies of these prices, as discussed in Cootner, Ed. (1964), Granger and Morgenstern (1970), Fama (1971), and Malkiel (1973), indicate that they change over time, from a statistical standpoint, in a way very much like the molecules in a gas—according to Brownian motion. Thus the best predictors of tomorrow's prices are today's prices.

[15] Note that lagged exogenous variables can appear in $\mathbf{z}_t$. See Problem 15-F.

consisting of predicted values of all endogenous variables h periods ahead. The level h_0 depends primarily on the nature of the variables being forecast, specifically the rate at which the forecast interval (15.1.2) "fans out" over time. It also depends on the purpose of the forecast. Thus, for example, in forecasting national income aggregates for certain purposes long-term forecasts might be of the order of eight years, while for other purposes they might be of the order of eight quarters. Customarily, however, in this context long-term forecasts refer to horizons in excess of five years.

Long-term forecasts can be obtained by developing a succession of short-term forecasts—that is, by iterating the forecasts obtained from the reduced form, as in (15.3.2). Equivalently, they can be obtained from the final-form equations of Section 14.2. Using this approach, the long-term forecasts can be written

$$\hat{\mathbf{y}}_{T+h} = \mathbf{y}_T \hat{\mathbf{\Pi}}_1^h + \sum_{j=0}^{h-1} \hat{\mathbf{z}}_{T+h-j} \hat{\mathbf{\Pi}}_2 \hat{\mathbf{\Pi}}_1^j + \sum_{j=0}^{h-1} \hat{\mathbf{u}}_{T+h-j} \hat{\mathbf{\Pi}}_1^j. \qquad *(15.4.2)$$

In this formulation the long-term forecasts are explicitly conditional on the current values of the endogenous variables $\mathbf{y}_T$; forecasts of future values of the exogenous variables up to and including time $T + h$, $\hat{\mathbf{z}}_{T+1}, \hat{\mathbf{z}}_{T+2}, \ldots, \hat{\mathbf{z}}_{T+h}$; add factors for all these future periods, $\hat{\mathbf{u}}_{T+1}, \hat{\mathbf{u}}_{T+2}, \ldots, \hat{\mathbf{u}}_{T+h}$; and the estimated coefficient matrices $\hat{\mathbf{\Pi}}_1$ and $\hat{\mathbf{\Pi}}_2$. It is therefore possible to analyze the effects of changes in these considerations on the long-term forecasts. The corresponding ex-post long-term forecast is

$$\hat{\hat{\mathbf{y}}}_{T+h} = \mathbf{y}_T \hat{\mathbf{\Pi}}_1^h + \sum_{j=0}^{h-1} \mathbf{z}_{T+h-j} \hat{\mathbf{\Pi}}_2 \hat{\mathbf{\Pi}}_1{}^j \qquad (15.4.3)$$

and stochastic forecasts can be constructed as in the short-term forecast case.

15.5 Forecast accuracy

Given a forecast, whether short-term or long-term, interest centers both on its impact for action and on its accuracy. The former will be the subject of the next chapter, on policy evaluation. As will be developed in some detail there, forecasts can have significant impacts on the system. The present section will consider forecast accuracy.

Various errors must be taken into account in any study of the accuracy of econometric forecasts.[16] First, there is the inaccuracy in the model, which is a simplification of reality and hence omits certain influences and simplifies others. Second, there is the inaccuracy of the data used in the estimation of the model, as discussed in Section 3.7. Third, there is the inaccuracy or bias present in the method of estimation, to which must be added possible errors of computation, e.g., round-off error. Fourth there are errors in the forecasts of the exogenous variables and in the add factors. Finally, there are possible inaccuracies in the

[16] See Morgenstern (1963).

"actual" data to which the forecast is compared. Of course, some may be offsetting, leading to spurious accuracy in the forecast.

There are several possible measures of the accuracy of a forecast. For simplicity only short-run ex-ante deterministic forecasts are treated here, but similar approaches can be used for studying the accuracy of long-term forecasts.

The absolute error $\hat{\mathbf{e}}_{T+1}$ of the short-term forecast in (15.3.2) is given by combining this equation with (15.3.1):

$$\hat{\mathbf{e}}_{T+1} = \mathbf{y}_{T+1} - \hat{\mathbf{y}}_{T+1} = (\mathbf{y}_T\mathbf{\Pi}_1 + \mathbf{z}_{T+1}\mathbf{\Pi}_2 + \mathbf{u}_{T+1}) - (\mathbf{y}_T\hat{\mathbf{\Pi}}_1 + \hat{\mathbf{z}}_{T+1}\hat{\mathbf{\Pi}}_2 + \hat{\mathbf{u}}_{T+1}). \quad \text{*(15.5.1)}$$

Combining terms, $\hat{\mathbf{e}}_{T+1}$ can be expressed as

$$\hat{\mathbf{e}}_{T+1} = \mathbf{y}_T(\mathbf{\Pi}_1 - \hat{\mathbf{\Pi}}_1) + \mathbf{z}_{T+1}(\mathbf{\Pi}_2 - \hat{\mathbf{\Pi}}_2) + (\mathbf{z}_{T+1} - \hat{\mathbf{z}}_{T+1})\hat{\mathbf{\Pi}}_2 + (\mathbf{u}_{T+1} - \hat{\mathbf{u}}_{T+1}) \quad \text{*(15.5.2)}$$

The equation has been arranged in this fashion because each term in the decomposition of the error has a meaning. The first consists of the errors due to incorrect estimation of the coefficient matrix $\mathbf{\Pi}_1$, these errors being weighted by $\mathbf{y}_T$. The second consists of the errors in estimating the coefficient matrix $\mathbf{\Pi}_2$, these being weighted by the *true* values of the future exogenous variables $\mathbf{z}_{T+1}$. The third consists of the errors in forecasting these future exogenous variables, weighted by the *estimated* coefficient matrix $\hat{\mathbf{\Pi}}_2$. The fourth consists of the errors in the disturbance terms, where $\hat{\mathbf{u}}_{T+1}$ are the add factors. All four terms, but particularly the last, can be based, in part, on a change in economic structure over time, which can be a major source of forecast error. Of course, some of these errors can and generally will be offsetting.

The error $\hat{\mathbf{e}}_{T+1}$ is a random variable, since $\hat{\mathbf{\Pi}}_1$, $\hat{\mathbf{\Pi}}_2$, and $\mathbf{u}_{T+1}$ are all random variables. Taking expectations, if the coefficient matrices $\hat{\mathbf{\Pi}}_1$ and $\hat{\mathbf{\Pi}}_2$ are unbiased estimators, then, assuming $\mathbf{z}_{T+1}$ and $\mathbf{u}_{T+1}$ are deterministic.

$$E(\hat{\mathbf{e}}_{T+1}) = (\mathbf{z}_{T+1} - \hat{\mathbf{z}}_{T+1})\mathbf{\Pi}_2 - \hat{\mathbf{u}}_{T+1} \quad (15.5.3)$$

since $\mathbf{u}$ is assumed to have a zero mean. Thus the expected error consists of the error in predicting the exogenous variables, weighted by the *true* coefficient matrix $\mathbf{\Pi}_2$, minus the add factors. The forecast $\hat{\mathbf{y}}_{T+1}$ is an *unbiased forecast* if the absolute error defined in (15.5.1) has a zero expectation:

$$E(\hat{\mathbf{e}}_{T+1}) = \mathbf{0}. \quad (15.5.4)$$

In this case the mean values of actual and forecast values coincide:

$$E(\mathbf{y}_{T+1}) = E(\hat{\mathbf{y}}_{T+1}). \quad (15.5.5)$$

From (15.5.3) the forecast is unbiased if

$$\hat{\mathbf{u}}_{T+1} = (\mathbf{z}_{T+1} - \hat{\mathbf{z}}_{T+1})\mathbf{\Pi}_2 \qquad (15.5.6)$$

which implies that unless the exogenous variables are forecast without error (or $\mathbf{\Pi}_2 = \mathbf{0}$), not including add factors or, equivalently, setting them equal to zero will result in biased forecasts.

A convenient way of showing geometrically the accuracy of forecasts in the case of a forecast of a single variable is given in Figure 15.2.[17] The actual per-

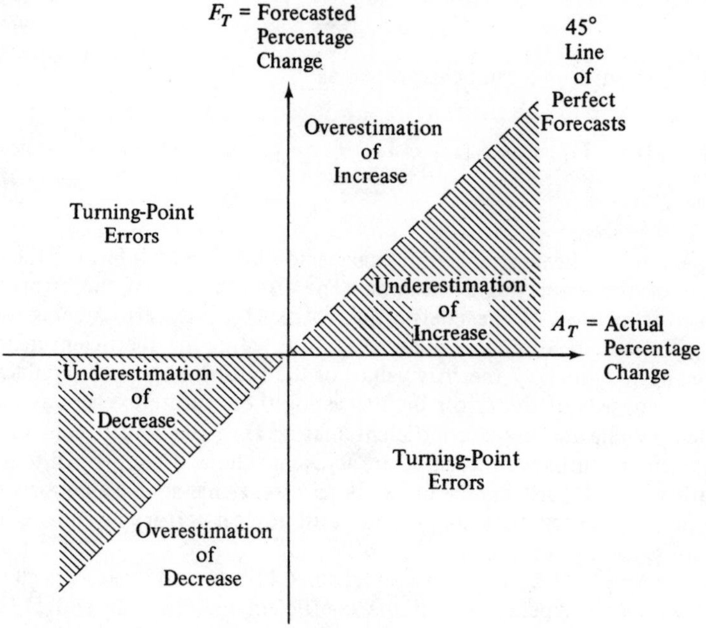

Figure 15.2 Forecasted vs. Actual Percentage Change

centage change, shown on the horizontal axis, is

$$A_T = \left(\frac{y_{T+1} - y_T}{y_T}\right) 100 \qquad (15.5.7)$$

and the forecasted percentage change, shown on the vertical axis, is

$$F_T = \left(\frac{\hat{y}_{T+1} - y_T}{y_T}\right) 100 \qquad (15.5.8)$$

In this figure the 45-degree line is the *line of perfect forecasts*, for which the

[17] See Theil (1961, 1966).

actual and forecasted percentage changes are equal. The first quadrant contains points for which an increase was forecasted and for which the increase actually occurred, and the third quadrant contains points for which a decrease was forecasted and for which the decrease actually occurred. The second and fourth quadrants contain the *turning-point errors*, i.e., incorrect forecasts of the direction of change: in the second quadrant an increase was forecasted but the variable actually decreased in value, and in the fourth quadrant a decrease was forecasted but the variable actually increased in value.

A series of forecasted percentage and actual changes (A_T, F_T) for different variables or different periods can be depicted as a scatter of points as in Figure 15.2. It is generally found, however, for many different variables and for many different periods, that most of these points fall in the shaded cone between the line of perfect forecasts and the actual percentage increase axis, the cone of *underestimation of change*. For example, out of 210 forecasts, using the Netherlands macroeconometric model over the period 1953 to 1962, 59% involved an underestimation of change, 26% involved an overestimation of change, and 15% involved turning-point errors.[18] Such a systematic *underestimation* of change is a general finding for most forecasts.[19] Thus, a forecast of 3% increase might, for certain variables, involve, on average, an actual increase of 5%. Typically, in terms of the above definitions of A_T and F_T,

$$|A_T| > |F_T| \tag{15.5.9}$$

In the case of positive y_T, where y_{T+1} and $\hat{y}_{T+1}$ both exceed y_T, (15.5.9) implies that y_{T+1} exceeds $\hat{y}_{T+1}$—that is, actual levels exceed forecasted levels. Then (15.5.2) implies that

$$y_T(\Pi_1 - \hat{\Pi}_1) + \mathbf{z}_{T+1}(\mathbf{\Pi}_2 - \hat{\mathbf{\Pi}}_2) + (\mathbf{z}_{T+1} - \hat{\mathbf{z}}_{T+1})\hat{\mathbf{\Pi}}_2 + (u_{T+1} - \hat{u}_{T+1}) > 0 \tag{15.5.10}$$

Taking expectations, this inequality implies, on average, that

$$\hat{u}_{T+1} < (\mathbf{z}_{T+1} - \hat{\mathbf{z}}_{T+1})\hat{\mathbf{\Pi}}_2 \tag{15.5.11}$$

in contrast to (15.5.6), where equality holds for unbiased forecasts. In the simplest case of a single exogenous variable, where $\hat{\Pi}_2 > 0$, inequality (15.5.11) is based on both the underestimation of the future value of the exogenous variable ($\hat{\mathbf{z}}_{T+1} < \mathbf{z}_{T+1}$) and the underestimation of the add factor, e.g., its absence.

One possible explanation of the systematic underestimation of change is that all forecasting methods are based on some explicit or implicit model, and all models involve, in their simplification of reality, an assumption that certain rele-

[18] See Theil (1966).

[19] In estimating regression equation

$$F_T = bA_T + \nu_T \quad \text{where } E(\nu_T) = 0, \quad E(A_T\nu_T) = 0$$

it is generally found that $0 < b < 1$, so turning-point errors are avoided, but the forecast underestimates change. See Theil (1961, 1966) and Mincer and Zarnowitz (1969).

vant variables either do not change or are accounted for in the stochastic disturbance term. To the extent that these variables actually do change and to the extent that they affect the forecasted variable, the result of this simplification is the observed systematic underestimation of change. The result is a *conservative bias* in forecasting, shading both upward and downward forecasts below their true magnitudes.[20] This bias is reinforced by hedging in forecasts (e.g., adjusting add factors toward zero) so as to avoid taking extreme positions.

An algebraic measure of the overall accuracy of several forecasts is the *inequality coefficient.*[21] If F_{Ti} and A_{Ti} are forecast and actual percent changes, respectively, for period (or variable) i, ranging from 1 to m, then the inequality coefficient for this set of forecasts is

$$U_T = \frac{\sqrt{\frac{1}{m}\sum_{i=1}^{m}(A_{Ti} - F_{Ti})^2}}{\sqrt{\frac{1}{m}\sum_{i=1}^{m}A_{Ti}^2}} \qquad *(15.5.12)$$

Here the numerator is the root mean square error in the forecast, while the denominator is the root mean square error assuming zero forecasted change. The case of perfect forecasts is that in which $U = 0$. If $F_{Ti} = 0$, so the forecasted percent change were zero, meaning a status quo forecast for all variables in question, then $U = 1$. The case of $U = 1$ is therefore equivalent to a status quo forecast. Of course U can exceed unity, in which case the forecasts are, in an overall sense, worse than *status quo* forecasts. More generally, if

$$F_{Ti} = kA_{Ti} \qquad (15.5.13)$$

where k is a constant greater than zero (i.e., turning-point errors are avoided) but less than unity (i.e., there is a systematic underestimation of change), then

$$U_T = 1 - k \qquad (15.5.14)$$

For example, if forecasted percentage changes are all 75% of the actual percentage changes, then $U_T = 0.25$.

The inequality coefficient can be decomposed into several terms, reflecting the different causes of inaccuracy. To perform such a decomposition it is convenient to consider the square of (15.5.12). The square of the numerator can be written

[20] Of course, shading downward movement means *overstating* the value of the variable. See Figure 15.2. In fact, however, the underestimation of change applies primarily to upswings. There is a general tendency to miss turning points and/or slightly overestimate downswings.
[21] See Theil (1961, 1966). See also Mincer (1969) and Evans, Haitovsky, and Treyz (1972).

$$\frac{1}{m}\sum_{i=1}^{m}[(A_{Ti} - \bar{A}) - (F_{Ti} - \bar{F}) + (\bar{A} - \bar{F})]^2 \tag{15.5.15}$$

where A and F are the mean actual and forecasted percentage changes, respectively. Squaring the terms in the bracket leads to the expression

$$U_T^2 = \frac{1}{\frac{1}{m}\sum A_{Ti}^2}[(\bar{A} - \bar{F})^2 + (s_A - s_F)^2 + 2(1 - r)s_A s_F] \qquad *(15.5.16)$$

where s_A and s_F are the standard deviations of A and F, respectively, and r is the correlation coefficient between A and F. In this expression the square of the inequality coefficient is decomposed into three terms. The first is the squared difference in the means, a measure of the bias—that is, the unequal central tendencies of the actual and forecasted percentage changes. The second is the squared difference between standard deviations, a measure of their unequal variation. The third involves the correlation coefficient and is a measure of their imperfect covariation. This last term represents a nonsystematic random error that cannot be avoided. The first two terms, however, represent systematic errors that should be avoided.

15.6 Forecasting experience with macroeconometric models

Econometric models have been used for forecasting macroeconomic variables such as those listed in Table 12.1, starting with the early macroeconometric models. This experience has yielded knowledge as to what variables econometric models generally forecast accurately, what types of models have the best forecasting abilities, and what are the best approaches to forecasting.

The prototype macro model first introduced in Section 2.7 and later referred to in connection with the macroeconometric models of Chapter 12 can be used to illustrate the nature of forecasting with such models. The reduced-form equation of the prototype model for national income is

$$Y_t = \Pi_1 Y_{t-1} + \Pi_2 G_t + \Pi_3 + u_t \tag{15.6.1}$$

as in (2.7.7). A short-term forecast of national income, e.g., national income next year, is then

$$\hat{Y}_{T+1} = \hat{\Pi}_1 Y_T + \hat{\Pi}_2 \hat{G}_{T+1} + \hat{\Pi}_3 + \hat{u}_{T+1} \tag{15.6.2}$$

which is of the same form as (15.3.2). This ex-ante deterministic point forecast is conditional upon the current value of national income Y_T; predicted future government expenditure $\hat{G}_{T+1}$; the estimated coefficients $\hat{\Pi}_1$, $\hat{\Pi}_2$, and $\hat{\Pi}_3$; and the predicted future disturbance term $\hat{u}_{T+1}$. The comparable long-term forecast is obtained from the final-form equation for national income, yielding the forecast for Y at time $T + h$ of

$$\hat{Y}_{T+h} = \hat{\Pi}_1^h Y_T + \hat{\Pi}_2(\hat{G}_{T+h} + \hat{\Pi}_1 \hat{G}_{T+h-1} + \hat{\Pi}_1^2 \hat{G}_{T+h-2} + \cdots + \hat{\Pi}_1^{h-1} \hat{G}_{T+1})$$
$$+ \hat{\Pi}_3(1 + \hat{\Pi}_1 + \hat{\Pi}_1^2 + \cdots + \hat{\Pi}_1^{h-1}) \qquad \textbf{(15.6.3)}$$
$$+ (\hat{u}_{T+h} + \hat{\Pi}_1 \hat{u}_{T+h-1} + \hat{\Pi}_1^2 \hat{u}_{T+h-2} + \cdots + \hat{\Pi}_1^{h-1} \hat{u}_{T+1})$$

which is of the same form as (15.4.2). This forecast is conditional upon the current value of national income, all predicted future values for government expenditures up to the time horizon, the estimated coefficients, and all predicted future disturbance terms up to the time horizon.

The forecasts in (15.6.2) and (15.6.3), which are the short-term and long-term forecasts of national income from the prototype macro model, are themselves prototypes of the forecasts obtained using macroeconometric models. Such forecasts typically determine the forecasted value as a sum of systematic and judgmental factors. The first set of systematic factors includes the lagged endogenous variables of the model, particularly lagged values of the variable being forecast, here represented by Y_T, the current value of national income in both (15.6.2) and (15.6.3). The second set of systematic factors includes the exogenous variables of the model, which must themselves be forecast or obtained from some source other than the model itself. They are represented by $\hat{G}_{T+1}$ in (15.6.2) and by $\hat{G}_{T+1}, \hat{G}_{T+2}, \ldots, \hat{G}_{T+h}$ in (15.6.3). In general, the exogenous variables can include both policy variables, such as government expenditure here, and nonpolicy exogenous variables, such as variables representing population and the foreign sector. More generally, both sets of systematic factors—lagged endogenous variables and policy and nonpolicy exogenous variables—can contain many variables, specifically all the lagged endogenous and exogenous variables of the model.

The last elements of the forecast are the judgmental factors, namely the add factors, represented by $\hat{u}_{T+1}$ in (15.6.2) and $\hat{u}_{T+1}, \hat{u}_{T+2}, \ldots, \hat{u}_{T+h}$ in (15.6.3). They can be interpreted either as adjustments of the intercepts or as future values of the stochastic disturbance term. For the interpretation as an adjustment of the intercepts note in (15.6.2) that $\hat{u}_{T+1}$ is added to $\hat{\Pi}_3$. (The fact that it is "added to" the intercept led to the terminology "add factor.") More generally, an econometric forecast typically includes forecasts of all endogenous variables of the model, so there would be add factors for each of these variables. These add factors reflect the judgment of the forecaster concerning factors not specifically included in the model. The forecast also depends on the estimated coefficients of the model, represented in (15.6.2) and (15.6.3) by $\hat{\Pi}_1$, $\hat{\Pi}_2$, and $\hat{\Pi}_3$. More generally, all estimated reduced-form coefficients are used in generating forecasts of all endogenous variables of the model.

The fact that the forecast is explicitly conditional means that it is possible to investigate the sensitivity of the forecast to alternative assumptions. For the short-term forecast in (15.6.2) it is possible to vary the forecasted level of government expenditure $\hat{G}_{T+1}$ to determine alternative forecasts for $\hat{Y}_{T+1}$, each conditional on a particular level of $\hat{G}_{T+1}$. It is also possible to consider alternative add factors $\hat{u}_{T+1}$—for example, one add factor if there will be a major strike and another if there will be no strike. For the long-term forecast (15.6.3) it is possible to vary not only the levels of government expenditure but also the timing of these expenditures. If, for example, the model were a quarterly model, it would be possible to determine the impacts of shifting government expenditure within the fiscal year, such as increasing it in the two quarters before an election and decreasing it in the quarter following the election.

An early study of forecasting using an estimated econometric model was Christ's study of forecasts generated by the Klein interwar model of the United States economy.[22] Christ tested the predictive performance of this model by modifying it to fit data for 1946 and 1947 and predicting values of endogenous variables for 1948. He compared these structural forecasts with two "naive" forecasts, specifically the status quo forecast and the constant-percentage-change forecast, (15.2.1) and (15.2.3), respectively. He found that the naive forecasts tended, in fact, to be more accurate than the structural forecasts in a majority of cases. This finding was valid even when the econometric forecasts were ex-post forecasts, as in (15.3.3), in which the data on the explanatory variables were the actual observations of these variables.

Christ utilized a similar test for the Klein-Goldberger model.[23] He found that, for forecasts of endogenous variables for 1951 and 1952, the status quo forecasts were generally more accurate than ex-post structural forecasts. In other respects as well, the Klein-Goldberger model was not successful as a forecasting model. It failed to call turning points correctly, even during the estimated period. One problem with the model in terms of forecasting was its investment equation, which combines inventories with fixed business investment, leading to an understatement of investment in the 1951-52 period.[24] The model also performed poorly on prices, overestimating the price rises of 1951-52. While, unlike other forecasts, it correctly forecasted the rise in activity in 1953, it overstated the price and wage rises for 1954.

Later forecasts using econometric models have performed better than these very early forecasts. It has, in fact, been found that forecasts using econometric models are superior to those based on simple extrapolation techniques. For forecasts from the Netherlands model over the period 1953-62, for example, the values of the inequality coefficient U of (15.5.12) tend to range between 0.4 and 0.7.[25] The best forecasts were those for wage levels, for which $U = 0.29$, and for employment, for which $U = 0.30$. At the other extreme, the worst forecasts were those for inventory accumulation, for which $U = 1.04$. While this result ($U > 1$) means that forecasts of this variable were, on average, worse than those obtained by status quo forecasts, it was the only variable out of over twenty for which this was true. It was also found that the inequality coefficients tended to rise in years of rapid expansion and to fall in years of relative stagnation; that turning points tended to be relatively well predicted; and that, as already noted, there was a systematic tendency to underestimate change.[26]

[22] Christ (1951). See Section 12.2 for a discussion of the Klein interwar model.

[23] See Christ (1956). The naive forecasts were better for six out of fourteen cases in 1951 and ten out of fourteen cases in 1952. See Section 12.4 for a discussion of the Klein-Goldberger model.

[24] See Goldberger (1959).

[25] See de Wolff and van den Beld (1963) and de Wolff (1967).

[26] Similar findings for the United States appear in Zarnowitz (1967) and Moore (1969), who found that most forecasts of GNP and its components are more accurate than simple trend

More recent experience with forecasting using an econometric model has indicated the importance and value of add factors. These add factors, reflecting expert judgment on factors not included in the model, generally improve significantly on model performance. Forecasts with such subjective adjustments have generally been more accurate than those obtained from the purely mechanical application of the econometric model, including ex-post forecasts.[27] Combining an econometric model with expert opinion in this way utilizes the best features of each. It combines the explicit objective discipline of the formal econometric model and regression estimators with the implicit subjective expertise of individual experts intimately aware of the real-world system. The econometric model provides a useful starting place for formulating the forecast, it identifies those factors for which judgmental decisions must be made, and it provides a framework that ensures that the forecast is internally consistent. The add factors take account of special circumstances and knowledge not embodied in the formal model, which can substantially improve forecasting performance. They can also take account of revisions and updating of the data, which represent the main links between information on the real-world system and information contained in the model.

Experience with macroeconometric models has also indicated that such models are generally capable of generating accurate forecasts of certain variables but much less accurate forecasts of others. In general, as might be expected, smooth slow-moving variables are more accurately predicted than those that exhibit high variance and large fluctuations from period to period.[28] Thus, for example, the forecasting performance for variables such as consumption expenditure and wage income has been very good because these variables tend to exhibit stable patterns of growth with only small variations over time. By contrast, forecasts of variables such as inventory investment, profit income, and short-term interest rates, all of which exhibit large variations over time, have generally been only fair or even poor. Furthermore, the forecast error tends to increase the longer the forecast horizon. Short-term forecasting is comparatively easy, especially if the model includes lagged variables. Real and nominal gross national product, for example, can be forecast up to three quarters ahead with a root mean square error of less than 1% and up to six quarters with an error of less than 2%.[29] Medium-term and especially long-term forecasts, however, have

---

extrapolation, particularly for short-term forecasts, and that there is a systematic tendency to underestimate change.

[27] See Evans, Haitovsky, and Treyz (1972), Haitovsky and Treyz (1972), McNees (1973, 1974), Haitovsky, Treyz, and Su (1974), Fromm and Klein (1973, 1976), and Christ (1975), who found that forecasts incorporating add factors were generally better than those without such factors. See also Evans (1974) and Stekler (1976). Econometric forecasts with add factors are also generally superior—at least for the short-term—to purely judgmental forecasts that do not use an econometric model at all, although Christ (1975) comments that ex-ante econometric forecasts are, on average, no better than the heavily judgmental ASA-NBER consensus forecasts described in footnote 4. See also Moore (1969) and Zarnowitz (1972). For the view that forecasts from one model, the Fair model, do not require add factors see Fair (1974).

[28] See Christ (1975) and Fromm and Klein (1976).

[29] See Christ (1975). The root mean square error of forecasts up to τ periods ahead is defined as

much larger errors, with the forecasts deteriorating significantly as the horizon increases.[30]

On the types of models that have the best forecasting abilities, one major issue has been the proper extent of disaggregation and size of the model. Small models of less than ten endogenous variables, such as the Klein interwar model and the St. Louis model; medium-size models of between ten and one hundred such variables, such as the Klein-Goldberger and Wharton model; and large models of more than one hundred endogenous variables, such as the Wharton Mark III, Chase Econometrics, and DRI models, have all been used for purposes of forecasting major macroeconomic phenomena.[31] While there have been some exceptions, there has been a tendency to build and use larger models as the data bases have increased and the costs of data retrieval and computation have fallen.

There are several reasons for using larger models, specifically the medium size and large models, for purposes of forecasting.[32] First, a fundamental problem with small, highly aggregated models is that they simply do not provide forecasts for variables of interest. For example, it is usually important to disaggregate investment into components and to treat explicitly increases in inventories, which are generally more volatile than the other components and which, to some extent, play the role of a leading indicator. Second, the medium- and large-scale models include many important variables and relationships that must be taken into account when dealing with a complex system such as the determination of national income and related phenomena. It is important, for example, to be specific about exogenous variables that influence the system in order both to allow explicitly for their influence and to test the sensitivity of the forecast to alternative assumptions regarding such variables.[33] In a small model these variables are taken into account only through the stochastic disturbance terms and add factors, but this may put too heavy a burden on such factors. The larger models can take cognizance of these variables explicitly and reserve the add factors for unusual or nonquantitative factors. Third, the medium-size and large models provide a better framework in which to use expert judgment, in the form of add factors, than the small models. The larger models pinpoint the issues and

---

$$\text{RMSE} = \sqrt{\frac{1}{T}\sum_{i=1}^{T}(\hat{y}_{T+i} - y_{T+i})^2}$$

where $\hat{y}_{T+i}$ is the forecast value of the variable y at time $T+i$ and y_{T+i} is the actual value at time $T+i$.

[30] Christ (1975) notes that the root mean square error for nine econometric models of the U.S. economy typically doubles or triples in going from forecasts of one quarter ahead to forecasts of five quarters ahead. He concludes: "These econometric models are at best only approximations to the economy as it existed when they were built and estimated; they do not state fundamental immutable laws of human behavior" (p. 64).

[31] See Table 12.12 for a summary of these models. Sometimes other measures are used for the size of an econometric model, such as the number of stochastic equations and the total number of variables (endogenous and exogenous).

[32] See Klein (1971) and Fromm and Schink (1973). The latter presents evidence that larger models tend to provide more accurate predictions than smaller models.

[33] While the measure of the size of the model suggested earlier involved only the number of endogenous variables, in general, models with many endogenous variables also have many exogenous variables. (See Table 12.12.)

can make effective use of detailed expert judgment. For example, experts can give informed judgments not only on overall government expenditure but also on its various components. It may therefore be predicted with a high degree of confidence that greater use will be made in the future of medium-size and large econometric models, combined with expert judgment in the form of add factors, for the purpose of forecasting macroeconomic (and other) phenomena.

PROBLEMS

15-A Consider the problem of forecasting a single endogenous variable where the only exogenous variable is time, representing a time trend. The reduced form is

$$y_t = a + bt + u_t, \qquad u_t \sim N(0, \sigma^2)$$

and the long-term forecast is

$$\hat{y}_{T+h} = \hat{a} + \hat{b}(T + h).$$

1. Show that this long-term forecast is consistent with (15.4.2).
2. Prove that the variance of $\hat{y}_{T+h}$ is Var $(y_{T+h}) = (T + h)^2 \sigma^2$, as in Figure 15.1, where the forecast interval fans out as h increases.
3. Use the result on variance to construct 90% and 95% confidence intervals for $\hat{y}_{T+h}$.

15-B In the leading-indicators approach to forecasting, certain variables lead other variables over time, in that they turn upward or downward before these other variables, as in (15.2.17). In terms of an econometric model, the only explanatory variables are lagged exogenous variables, so the reduced-form equation, which explicitly treats lagged as well as current exogenous variables, reduces to

$$\mathbf{y}_t = \mathbf{z}_{t-1}\mathbf{\Pi}_3 + \mathbf{u}_t$$

where the z's lead the y's.

1. Obtain short-term and long-term forecasts using this model.
2. How would you use this model to predict turning points?

15-C Expert opinion has been interpreted in this chapter in terms of the selection of a specific value, or set of values, for the stochastic disturbance term. Another way to introduce such opinion is to use the Bayesian approach to the revision of probabilities, where the probabilities are forecast probabilities. State the Bayes theorem and interpret it in terms of expert opinion. Give a specific example of such an approach, e.g., to forecasting the future unemployment rate.

15-D Obtain the long-term forecast using the final-form equations, where the iteration is carried back to the base-period vector of endogenous variables $\mathbf{y}_0$ rather than the current-period vector y_T in (15.4.2). When would this be used rather than (15.4.2)? What is the ex-post forecast for this case?

15-E Consider the distributed lag model for predicting future values of exogenous variables

$$\hat{\mathbf{z}}_{t+1} = \sum_{j=0}^{\infty} \mathbf{z}_{t-j}\mathbf{F}_j$$

where the $\mathbf{F}_j$ form a sequence of $k \times k$ matrices.

1. Obtain short-run and long-run forecasts.
2. Obtain these forecasts in the special case of the Koyck distributed lag, as discussed in Section 6.7.

15-F Consider an econometric model that includes in its structural equations specific consideration of various lagged endogenous and exogenous variables:

$$\sum_{i=0}^{p} \mathbf{y}_{t-i}\mathbf{\Gamma}_i + \sum_{j=0}^{q} \mathbf{z}_{t-j}\mathbf{B}_j = \mathbf{u}_t$$

where $\mathbf{\Gamma}_0, \mathbf{\Gamma}_1, \ldots, \mathbf{\Gamma}_p$ and $\mathbf{B}_0, \mathbf{B}_1, \ldots, \mathbf{B}_q$ are $p+q+2$ matrices of constant terms.[34]

1. Find the reduced form and final form.
2. Obtain for this model both short-term and long-term forecasts of all endogenous variables $\mathbf{y}$. Identify those factors upon which both forecasts are explicitly conditional.

15-G Suppose two forecasts are available for y_{T+1}, given as $\hat{y}^1_{T+1}$ and $\hat{y}^2_{T+1}$. Assume further that if $\hat{e}^j_{T+1}$ is the error using forecast j, where

$$\hat{e}^j_{T+1} = y_{T+1} - \hat{y}^j_{T+1}, \quad j = 1, 2$$

then

$$E(\hat{e}^j_{T+1}) = \mathbf{0}, \quad j = 1, 2$$
$$\text{Var}(\hat{e}^j_{T+1}) = \sigma_j^2 \quad j = 1, 2$$
$$\text{Cov}(\hat{e}^1_{T+1}\, \hat{e}^2_{T+1}) = \rho\sigma_1\sigma_2.$$

Let $\hat{y}_{T+1}$ be a weighted average of the two forecasts:

[34] See Klein (1971).

$$\hat{y}_{T+1} = \alpha\hat{y}^1_{T+1} + (1 - \alpha)\hat{y}^2_{T+1}$$

implying the forecast error[35]

$$\hat{e}_{T+1} = y_{T+1} - \hat{y}_{T+1} = \alpha\hat{e}^1_{T+1} + (1 - \alpha)\hat{e}^2_{T+1}.$$

1. Find the error variance for the average forecast, Var $(\hat{y}_{T+1})$.
2. Find the weight α that minimizes Var $(\hat{y}_{T+1})$ and show that, using this,

$$\text{Var}(\hat{e}_{T+1}) \leqslant \min[\text{Var}(\hat{e}^1_{T+1}), \text{Var}(\hat{e}^2_{T+1})].$$

   Under what conditions will equality hold?
3. Show that the weight α can be negative, and provide an interpretation for a negative α.

15-H Consider a loss function reflecting the cost of an incorrect decision stemming from an error in a forecast. A general form for the loss function for the short-term forecast at period T is

$$L_T = L(y_{T+1} - \hat{y}_{T+1}) = L(\hat{e}_{T+1})$$

where y_{T+1} is the actual value, $\hat{y}_{T+1}$ is the forecast value, and the forecast error is

$$\hat{e}_{T+1} = y_{T+1} - \hat{y}_{T+1}$$

Generally it is assumed that the loss function $L(\cdot)$ satisfies

$$L(0) = 0$$
$$L' > 0$$
$$L(\hat{e}_{T+1}) = L(-\hat{e}_{T+1}).$$

1. Show that if $L(\cdot)$ is the absolute value function

$$L_T^{(1)} = a|\hat{e}_{T+1}|$$

   then an appropriate measure of the inaccuracy of N forecasts is the mean absolute error

$$\text{MAE} = \frac{1}{N}\sum_T |\hat{e}_{T+1}|.$$

2. Show that if $L(\cdot)$ is quadratic

[35] See Granger and Newbold (1977).

$$L_T^{(2)} = a\hat{e}_{T+1}^2$$

then an appropriate measure of the inaccuracy of N forecasts is the mean square error

$$\text{MSE} = \frac{1}{N}\sum_T \hat{e}_{T+1}^2 .$$

3. Generalize to the loss function

$$L_T^{(k)} = a\,|\hat{e}_{T+1}|^k$$

which includes $L_T^{(1)}$ and $L_T^{(2)}$ as special cases corresponding to $k = 1$ and $k = 2$, respectively.[36]

15-I One approach to trend extrapolation uses the *logistic curve*

$$y(t) = \frac{c}{1 + ae^{-bt}}, \qquad a, b, c, > 0 \qquad t \geqslant 0$$

a curve that, starting from $c/(1 + a)$, rises at first at an increasing rate, then at a decreasing rate, asymptotically approaching the value of c.

1. At what time does the logistic reach an inflection point? Draw the curve.
2. At what time does the logistic reach 90% of c?
3. Show that the logistic curve satisfies the differential equation

$$\frac{1}{y}\frac{dy}{dt} = b\left(1 - \frac{y}{c}\right).$$

15-J The *adaptive expectations* approach to forecasting changes the forecast from one period to the next by an amount proportional to the most recently observed forecast error, as in[37]

$$\hat{y}_{T+1} - \hat{y}_T = \eta(y_T - \hat{y}_T).$$

1. Show that the solution to this difference equation in $\hat{y}_T$ is

$$\hat{y}_{T+1} = \eta \sum_{j=0}^{\infty} (1 - \eta)^j y_{T-j+1}$$

which is a distributed lag of the Koyck type.

[36] See Sims (1967).

[37] See Cagan (1956) and Nerlove (1958).

2. What do the model and its solution reduce to when $\eta = 1$? When $\eta = 0$?

15-K In Price's study of the effect of World War II on science in the United States, he found that if $A(t)$ is the number of abstracts in the physics journals at time t, then A was increasing exponentially at the rate α in the years prior to 1941.

$$A = A_0 e^{\alpha t} \quad \text{or} \quad \frac{\dot{A}}{A} = \alpha \qquad \text{for } t < 1941.$$

During the war years the rate fell to

$$\frac{\dot{A}}{A} = \beta < \alpha \qquad \text{for } 1941 \leqslant t \leqslant 1945$$

and, after the war, the rate went back to the prewar rate:

$$\frac{\dot{A}}{A} = \alpha \qquad \text{for } t > 1945.$$

1. Show on diagrams A as a function of time and $\ln A$ as a function of time.
2. Find an expression for the number of abstracts in the postwar period.
3. What is the gap between the actual number of physics abstracts and the number there would have been if the prewar rate had continued throughout?
4. At what time will the gap exceed a prespecified number of abstracts $\bar{A}$?

15-L Using the estimated Klein interwar model from section 12.2 and data from the *Statistical Abstract of the United States*, forecast total output for the 1940's and 1950's. Plot your results on a diagram as in Figure 15.2 and discuss your findings.

15-M Consider the following variant of inequality coefficient (15.5.12)[38]

$$\bar{U}^2 = \frac{\Sigma (F_t - A_t)^2}{\Sigma (A_t - A_{t-1})^2}.$$

1. To what naive forecast does this inequality coefficient compare the forecast?
2. Decompose $\bar{U}'$ into constituent elements, as in (15.5.16).
3. Letting $A_t = F_t + \epsilon_t$ where ϵ_t is the forecast error, relate the reciprocal of $\bar{U}$ to the Durbin-Watson statistic of Section 6.4.

[38] See Theil (1966).

BIBLIOGRAPHY

Alexander, S. S. (1958), "Rate of Change Approaches to Forecasting: Diffusion Indexes and First Differences." *Economic Journal*, 68: 288–301.

Alexander, S. S., and H. O. Stekler (1959), "Forecasting Industrial Production: Leading Series versus Autoregression." *Journal of Political Economy*, 67: 402–9.

Box, G. E. P., and G. M. Jenkins (1970), *Time Series Analysis; Forecasting and Control*. San Francisco: Holden-Day, Inc.

Butler, W. F., R. A. Kavesh, and R. B. Platt, Eds. (1974), *Methods and Techniques of Business Forecasting*. Englewood Cliffs, N.J.: Prentice-Hall, Inc.

Cagan, P. (1956), "The Monetary Dynamics of Hyperinflation," in M. Friedman, Ed., *Studies in the Quantity Theory of Money*. Chicago. The University of Chicago Press.

Chambers, J. C., S. K. Mullich, and D. D. Smith (1971), "How to Choose the Right Forecasting Technique." *Harvard Business Review*, July–August, 49: 45–74.

Christ, C. (1951), "A Test of an Econometric Model for the U.S. 1921–1947." *Conference on Business Cycles*. New York: National Bureau of Economic Research.

Christ, C. (1956), "Aggregate Econometric Models: A Review Article." *American Economic Review*, 46: 385–408.

Christ, C. F. (1975), "Judging the Performance of Econometric Models of the U.S. Economy." *International Economic Review*, 16: 54–74.

Cootner, P., Ed. (1964), *The Random Character of Stock Market Prices*. Cambridge: The MIT Press.

Dalkey, N. C., et al. (1972), *Studies in the Quality of Life; Delphi and Decision-Making*. Lexington, Mass.: Lexington Books.

de Wolff, P. (1967), "Macroeconomic Forecasting," in Wold et al. (1967).

de Wolff, P., and C. A. van den Beld (1963), "Ten Years of Forecasts and Realizations." Paper presented at the Ottawa Meeting of the International Statistical Institute, reported in C. A. van den Beld, "Short-Term Planning Experience in the Netherlands," in Hickman, Ed. (1965).

Evans, M. K. (1974), "Econometric Models." in Butler, Kavesh, and Platt, Eds. (1974).

Evans, M. K., Y. Haitovsky, and G. I. Treyz (1972), "An Analysis of the Forecasting Properties of U.S. Econometric Models," in Hickman, Ed. (1972).

Evans, M. K., L. R. Klein, and M. Saito (1972), "Short-Run Prediction and Long-Run Simulation of the Wharton Model," in Hickman, Ed. (1972).

Fair, R. C. (1974), "An Evaluator of a Short-Run Forecasting Model." *International Economic Review*, 15: 285–303.

Fama, E. F. (1971), "Efficient Capital Markets: A Review of Theory and Empirical Work," in M. D. Intriligator, Ed., *Frontiers of Quantitative Economics*. Amsterdam: North-Holland Publishing Co.

Ferber, R. (1953), *The Railroad Shippers Forecast*. Bureau of Economic and Business Research: University of Illinois.

Ferber, R. (1958), *Employers' Forecasts of Manpower Requirements: A Case Study*. Bureau of Economic and Business Research: University of Illinois.

Friedman, M. (1960), *A Program for Monetary Stability*. New York: Fordham University Press.

Friedman, M., and A. Schwartz (1963), *A Monetary History of the United States, 1867–1960*. Princeton, N.J.: Princeton University Press.

Fromm, G., and L. R. Klein (1973), "A Comparison of Eleven Econometric Models of the United States." *American Economic Review*, 63: 385–93.

Fromm, G., and L. R. Klein (1976), "The NBER/NSF Model Comparison Seminar: An Analysis of Results." *Annals of Economic and Social Measurement*, 5: 1–28.

Fromm, G. S., L. R. Klein, and G. R. Schink (1972), "Short- and Long-Term Simulations with the Brookings Model." in Hickman, Ed. (1972).

Fromm, G., and G. R. Schink (1973), "Aggregation and Econometric Models." *International Economic Review*, 14: 1–32.

Goldberger, A. S. (1959), *Impact Multipliers and the Dynamic Properties of the Klein Goldberger Model*. Amsterdam: North-Holland Publishing Co.

Goldberger, A. S., A. L. Nagar, and H. S. Odeh (1961), "The Covariance Matrices of Reduced-Form Coefficients and of Forecasts for a Structural Econometric Model." *Econometrica*, 29: 556–73.

Granger, C. W. J., and O. Morgenstern (1970), *Predictability of Stock Market Prices*. Lexington, Mass.: Heath Lexington Books.

Granger, C. W. J., and P. Newbold (1977), *Forecasting Economic Time Series*. New York: Academic Press.

Haitovsky, Y., and G. Treyz (1972), "Forecasts with Quarterly Econometric Models: Equation Adjustments and Benchmark Predictions: The U.S. Experience." *Review of Economics and Statistics*, 44: 317–25.

Haitovsky, Y., G. Treyz, and V. Su (1974), *Forecasts with Quarterly Macroeconometric Models*. National Bureau of Economic Research. New York: Columbia University Press.

Helmer, O. (1966), *Social Technology*. New York: Basic Books.

Hickman, B. G., Ed. (1972), *Econometric Models of Cyclical Behavior*. National Bureau of Economic Research. New York: Columbia University Press.

Howry, E. P., L. R. Klein, and M. D. McCarthy (1974), "Notes on Testing the Predictive Performance of Econometric Models." *International Economic Review*, 15: 336–83.

Hymans, S. H. (1973), "On the Use of Leading Indicators to Predict Cyclical Turning Points." *Brookings Papers on Economic Activity*, 2: 339–75.

Intriligator, M. D. (1971), "Econometrics and Economic Forecasting," in J. M. English, Ed., *The Economics of Engineering and Social Systems*. New York: John Wiley & Sons, Inc.

Klein, L. R. (1971), *An Essay on the Theory of Economic Prediction*. Chicago: Markham Publishing Co.

Klein, L. R. (1971), "Forecasting and Policy Evaluation Using Large Scale Econometric Models: The State of the Art," in M. D. Intriligator, Ed., *Frontiers of Quantitative Economics*. Amsterdam: North-Holland Publishing Co.

Malkiel, B. G. (1973), *A Random Walk Down Wall Street*. New York: Norton Publishing Co.

McNees, S. K. (1973), "The Predictive Accuracy of Econometric Forecasts." *New England Economic Review*, September/October 3–27.

McNees, S. K. (1974), "How Accurate are Economic Forecasts?" *New England Economic Review*, November/December, 2–39.

Mincer, J., Ed. (1969), *Economic Forecasts and Expectations: Analysis of Forecasting Behavior and Performances.* National Bureau of Economic Research. New York: Columbia University Press.

Mincer, J., and V. Zarnowitz (1969), "The Evaluation of Economic Forecasts," in Mincer, Ed. (1969).

Modigliani, F., and H. Weingartner (1958), "Forecasting Uses of Anticipatory Data on Investment and Sales." *Quarterly Journal of Economics*, 72: 23–54.

Moore, G. H. (1969), "Forecasting Short-Term Economic Changes" *Journal of the American Statistical Association*, 64: 1–22.

Moore, G. H. (1973), "Economic Indicator Analysis during 1969–72" in *Nations and Households in Economic Growth.* New York: Academic Press.

Moore, G. H., Ed. (1961), *Business Cycle Indicators.* National Bureau of Economic Research. Princeton, N.J.: Princeton University Press.

Moore, G. H., and J. Shiskin (1967), *Indicators of Business Expansions and Contractions.* New York: National Bureau of Economic Research.

Morgenstern, O. (1963), *On the Accuracy of Economic Observations*, 2nd Ed. Princeton, N.J.: Princeton University Press.

Nerlove, M. (1958), "Adaptive Expectations and Cobweb Phenomena." *Quarterly Journal of Economics*, 73: 227–40.

North, H. Q., and D. L. Pyke (1969), "'Probes' of the Technological Future." *Harvard Business Review*, May–June 47: 68.

Okun, A. M. (1962), "The Predictive Value of Surveys of Business Intentions." *American Economic Review*, 52: 218–25.

Pindyck, R. S., and D. L. Rubinfeld (1976), *Econometric Models and Economic Forecasts.* New York: McGraw-Hill Book Company.

Shiskin, J. (1967), "Reverse Trend Adjustment of Leading Indicators." *Review of Economics and Statistics*, 49: 45–9.

Sims, C. A. (1967), "Evaluating Short-Term Macroeconomic Forecasts: The Dutch Performance." *The Review of Economics and Statistics*, 49: 225–36.

Su, V., and J. Su (1975), "An Evaluation of the ASA/NBER Business Outlook Survey Forecasts." *Explorations in Economic Research*, 2: 588–618.

Stekler, H. O. (1970), *Economic Forecasting.* New York: Praeger Publishers.

Theil, H. (1961), *Economic Forecasts and Policy*, 2nd Ed. Amsterdam: North-Holland Publishing Co.

Theil, H. (1966), *Applied Economic Forecasting.* Amsterdam: North-Holland Publishing Co.

Wold, H. et al. (1967), *Forecasting on a Scientific Basis.* Proceedings of an International Summer Institute.

Zarnowitz, V. (1967), *An Appraisal of Short-Term Economic Forecasts.* National Bureau of Economic Research, Occasional Paper No. 104. New York: Columbia University Press.

Zarnowitz, V. (1969), "The New ASA-NBER Survey of Forecasts by Economic Statisticians." *The American Statistician*, 23: 12–16.

Zarnowitz, V. (1972), "Forecasting Economic Conditions. The Record and the Prospect," in V. Zarnowitz, Ed., *The Business Cycle Today.* New York: National Bureau of Economic Research.

CHAPTER **16**

Policy Evaluation

16.1 The nature of policy evaluation

The final objective of econometrics, and perhaps its most important potential use, is that of *policy evaluation*. This objective refers to a situation in which a decision maker must choose one policy, called a "plan," from a given set of alternative policies. An important example is national macroeconomic planning, in which government decision makers must choose among alternative fiscal, monetary, and other policies that affect the national economy. Another example is corporate capital planning, in which corporate decision makers must choose among alternative investment projects. An example at the international level would be an international development fund, the officials of which must choose among alternative development projects.

Policy evaluation is closely related to forecasting, and just as in the case of forecasting, it will be assumed here that the policy choice is quantitative, explicit, and unambiguous. In fact, forecasting and policy evaluation are interrelated in a feedback system: A forecast must be based, in part, on assumptions concerning the actions of the relevant decision makers. Conversely, policy evaluation must be based, in part, on forecasts of the effects of policy choices. The forecaster and decision maker are indeed often combined in the same person (or agency or office), responsible for both forecasting and policy evaluation.

Just as the forecasting use of econometrics distinguishes between short-term and long-term forecasts, the policy evaluation use also distinguishes between short-term and long-term policy. In general, short-term policy is concerned, for macroeconometric models, with stabilization of the economy within a period of one or two years. Long-term policy, by contrast, is concerned with the pattern of growth over longer periods. A basic issue in policy evaluation, in fact, is the *time horizon* of the plan—the issue of how far ahead policy is to be formulated and how far ahead the effects of various policies are to be studied in order to evaluate the plan.[1] As in the last chapter, the relevant time unit depends on the subject matter. For example, in some contexts an annual period is reasonable, while in others a quarter would be a more appropriate unit.

The type of policy evaluation to be stressed here is that of short-term policy

[1] A related basic issue is the *frequency* of the plan—i.e., how often the plan is revised. The traditional annual plan revised annually has been replaced in many corporations by a three- to five-year plan revised either annually or every six months. Some macroeconometric forecasts (and corresponding policies) extend over six to eight quarters and are revised each quarter. Such a plan is called a *rolling plan*.

evaluation, namely that of choosing a policy at time T given the course of events up to and including time $T - 1$. The analysis can, however, be generalized to long-term policy, which is the choice of a policy for times $T, T+1, T+2, \ldots, T+h$, where h is the time horizon of the plan.

Assuming the vector of variables $\mathbf{r}$ summarizes the policy variables to be chosen by the decision maker, the problem of policy evaluation in the short run is that of choosing optimal values for these variables during the current period T, *the short-term optimal policy*:

$$\mathbf{r}_T^*. \qquad *(16.1.1)$$

A *long-term optimal policy* would be summarized by the sequence of current and future values of policy variables:

$$\mathbf{r}_T^*, \mathbf{r}_{T+1}^*, \ldots, \mathbf{r}_{T+h}^* \qquad *(16.1.2)$$

where h is the time horizon of the plan.

While the methodologies to be presented here can be applied to any problem of policy evaluation, whether at the corporate, regional, national, or international level, they are most frequently applied to the evaluation of national economic policy. Some of the policy variables in this area, including fiscal, monetary, and other policy variables, are summarized in Table 16.1. These policy variables together with the (endogenous) variables of Table 12.1 and appropriate nonpolicy exogenous variables (e.g., demographic variables) constitute the variables of a relevant macroeconometric model for national economic policy evaluation, such as those of Chapter 12.

16.2 Alternative approaches to policy evaluation

The last chapter explored several different approaches to forecasting, and corresponding approaches exist for policy evaluation. Furthermore, just as the last chapter showed that the econometric approach includes several of these approaches as special cases, so too in the area of policy evaluation the various approaches can be considered special cases of the econometric approach.

Expert opinion is the traditional approach to forecasting and it is also the traditional approach to policy evaluation. Indeed, in most areas of policy, the responsibility for selection of a particular policy alternative is assigned to particular individuals selected on the basis of their expertise. Thus, national fiscal policy decisions in the United States are the responsibility of the executive and legislative branches. The President is advised by an Office of Management and Budget, and the Congress is advised by Budget Committees. The individuals in these organizations are chosen on the basis of their expertise, and their judgments influence, to a significant extent, the fiscal policy of the nation. Policy decisions in other areas are also based on expert opinion. Thus major corporations, municipalities, and nonprofit organizations frequently have planning departments staffed by experts responsible for policy evaluation.

The *Delphi method* can be employed for policy evaluation, using an approach

Table 16.1. Policy Variables for the National Economy

Fiscal Policy:

- Nondefense purchases
- Defense purchases
- Transfer payments
- Effective individual income tax rate
- Value of the standard deduction in the individual income tax
- Effective corporate tax rate
- Investment tax credits
- Depreciation tax lives
- Social insurance tax rates
- Social insurance taxable bases
- Excise tax rates
- Grants in aid to local authorities
- Government employment

Monetary Policy:

- Unborrowed reserves
- Required reserve ratio on demand and time deposits
- Discount rate
- Ceiling rates on certain types of deposits

Other Policy:

- Minimum wage rates
- Government wage rates
- Regulation of certain prices (e.g., certain natural resources, transportation)
- Import quotas
- Antitrust policy

NOTE See Table 12.1 for corresponding endogenous variables for the national economy.

similar to that used for forecasting.[2] Opinions of a panel of experts can be merged to obtain a consensus on policy choices. In fact this method is similar to the approach that delegates responsibility for policy to a committee, the principal difference being that the Delphi method involves no face-to-face contact.[3]

Persistence forecasting also has an analogue in the area of policy evaluation—that of continuation of the status quo with certain gradual changes, an approach sometimes referred to as *disjointed incrementalism*.[4] Decision makers using this approach analyze marginal changes rather than global ones. An example is

[2] See the discussion of the Delphi method in Section 15.2.

[3] *Indicative planning*, as utilized in France, can be interpreted as a type of Delphi approach to policy. In this approach to planning, individual enterprises submit their plans to a ministry, which formulates a consistent set of estimates for the future course of the economy. These estimates are transmitted back to the individual enterprises, which modify their plans accordingly. The "self-fulfilling prophecy" element in indicative planning is similar to the iteration toward a consensus in the Delphi approach. On French-type planning see Hickman, Ed. (1965).

[4] See Braybrooke and Lindblom (1963) and Lindblom (1965, 1968).

budgeting.[5] Under disjointed incrementalism decision makers do not decide on an entirely new budget each year. Rather, small changes are made from budget levels of the previous year, with only certain items being closely scrutinized. This approach to policy exemplifies *satisficing*, as opposed to optimizing, behavior. Rather than overall optimizing, e.g., creating an entire budget *de novo*, decision makers "satisfice," recognizing the inherent limitations on their capabilities in complex situations. The decision makers do not examine all possible courses of action but rather they search out satisfactory courses that attain certain aspiration levels.[6]

16.3 Policy evaluation using an econometric model

In the econometric approach to policy evaluation an estimated econometric model is combined with explicit or implicit information on objectives of policy to evaluate policy alternatives.[7] As shown in Figure 1.1, this evaluation aids in the selection of a desired policy. The chosen policy, together with external events, some of which are inherently stochastic, determine the outcomes, which become the facts to be utilized in future econometric analyses.

Several alternative ways in which an estimated econometric model can be used for policy evaluation are discussed in this chapter. This section develops a framework for treating policy evaluation. This framework and the various approaches to policy evaluation can be perhaps most readily understood in the case of a macroeconometric model, but they are, in fact, applicable to any econometric model that includes policy decisions as predetermined variables.

Consider the structural form of the econometric model as formulated in Section 14.1, but in which the exogenous variables are shown explicitly:

$$\underset{1\times g}{\mathbf{y}_t}\,\underset{g\times g}{\boldsymbol{\Gamma}} + \underset{1\times g}{\mathbf{y}_{t-1}}\,\underset{g\times g}{\mathbf{B}_1} + \underset{1\times k}{\mathbf{z}_t}\,\underset{k\times g}{\mathbf{B}_2} + \underset{1\times l}{\mathbf{r}_{t-1}}\,\underset{l\times g}{\mathbf{A}} = \underset{1\times g}{\boldsymbol{\varepsilon}_t}, \qquad t = 1, 2, \ldots, \tag{*16.3.1}$$

Here $\mathbf{y}_t$ is a vector of g endogenous variables, $\mathbf{y}_{t-1}$ is a vector of g lagged endogenous variables, $\mathbf{z}_t$ is a vector of k exogenous variables, and $\boldsymbol{\varepsilon}_t$ is a vector of g stochastic disturbance terms, as before. The vector $\mathbf{r}_{t-1}$ represents l added exogenous variables that are subject to the control of the policy maker. Values of such variables at time $t-1$ influence the system at time t, as shown in the structural form (16.3.1).[8] The policy variables in $\mathbf{r}_{t-1}$ are also called *instruments*, and Table 16.1 summarizes some of these variables for macroeconometric

[5] See Davis, Dempster, and Wildavsky (1966a, 1966b) and Wildavsky (1964).

[6] See Simon (1955, 1959) and March and Simon (1958).

[7] Basic references on policy evaluation using an econometric model are Theil (1964), Hickman, Ed. (1965), Fox, Sengupta, and Thorbecke (1966), Klein (1971, 1977), Naylor (1971), Powell and Williams, Eds. (1973), and Eckstein, Ed. (1976). See also Greenberger, Crenson, and Crissey (1976).

[8] Allowing for a lag in the influence of policy variables is convenient but not essential in this formulation.

models. The current endogenous variables in $\mathbf{y}_t$ are also called *targets*, for which the policy maker has certain goals, and Table 12.1 summarizes some of these variables for macroeconometric models.[9]

The structural form can be solved for the values of the current endogenous variables if the $\mathbf{\Gamma}$ matrix is nonsingular. The resulting reduced form is

$$\mathbf{y}_t = -\mathbf{y}_{t-1}\mathbf{B}_1\mathbf{\Gamma}^{-1} - \mathbf{z}_t\mathbf{B}_2\mathbf{\Gamma}^{-1} - \mathbf{r}_{t-1}\mathbf{A}\mathbf{\Gamma}^{-1} + \boldsymbol{\varepsilon}_t\mathbf{\Gamma}^{-1} \qquad (16.3.2)$$

determining the endogenous variables as functions of lagged values, exogenous variables, policy variables, and stochastic disturbance terms.

Given this formulation of the econometric model, there are at least three alternative approaches to evaluating policy: the *instrument-targets approach*, the *social-welfare-function approach*, and the *simulation approach*, developed in the next three sections. For all three approaches it is assumed that the coefficients have been estimated to be $\hat{\mathbf{\Gamma}}$, $\hat{\mathbf{B}}_1$, $\hat{\mathbf{B}}_2$, and $\hat{\mathbf{A}}$. It is also assumed that the exogenous variables at the future time $T+1$ have been estimated to be $\hat{\mathbf{z}}_{T+1}$ by some mechanism other than that of the model itself, such as those discussed in the last chapter. Finally, it is assumed that the stochastic disturbance terms take certain values $\hat{\boldsymbol{\varepsilon}}_{T+1}$, based on information and judgment about factors not explicitly included in the model, as in the case of add factors discussed in the last chapter. The resulting structural form is

$$\mathbf{y}_{T+1}\hat{\mathbf{\Gamma}} + \mathbf{y}_T\hat{\mathbf{B}}_1 + \hat{\mathbf{z}}_{T+1}\hat{\mathbf{B}}_2 + \mathbf{r}_T\hat{\mathbf{A}} = \hat{\boldsymbol{\varepsilon}}_{T+1} \qquad *(16.3.3)$$

and the corresponding reduced form is

$$\mathbf{y}_{T+1} = -\mathbf{y}_T\hat{\mathbf{B}}_1\hat{\mathbf{\Gamma}}^{-1} - \hat{\mathbf{z}}_{T+1}\hat{\mathbf{B}}_2\hat{\mathbf{\Gamma}}^{-1} - \mathbf{r}_T\hat{\mathbf{A}}\hat{\mathbf{\Gamma}}^{-1} + \hat{\boldsymbol{\varepsilon}}_{T+1}\hat{\mathbf{\Gamma}}^{-1}. \qquad *(16.3.4)$$

These two systems of equations are basic to the econometric approach to policy evaluation.

A simple specific example is again the prototype macro model, in which the reduced-form equation for national income can be written

$$Y_t = \Pi_1 Y_{t-1} + \Pi_2 G_t + \Pi_3 + u_t. \qquad (16.3.5)$$

Treating government spending G as a policy variable, and assuming G_{T+1} is related to G_T, e.g., via trend extrapolation, the equation can be written for period $T+1$, using estimates $\hat{\Pi}_1$, $\hat{\Pi}_2$, $\hat{\Pi}_3$, and $\hat{u}_{T+1}$, as

$$Y_{T+1} = \hat{\Pi}_1 Y_T + \hat{\Pi}_2' G_T + \hat{\Pi}_3 + \hat{u}_{T+1}. \qquad *(16.3.6)$$

This is a simple example of the reduced form in (16.3.4)—the endogenous variable being a linear function of its lagged value and the one policy variable.

[9] For a discussion of specific instruments and targets (goals) of economic policy in nine Western countries see Kirschen and Morrisens (1965). Targets include full employment, price stability, an improved balance of payments, and expansion of production, while instruments include public finance, money, and credit, exchange rate policy, direct controls, and institutional framework policies. See also Kirschen et al. (1964).

16.4 The instruments-targets approach

A first approach to policy evaluation using an estimated econometric model is the *instruments-targets* approach, developed by Tinbergen.[10] This approach is based on two assumptions. The first is that there exist certain desired levels for each of the endogenous variables of the model (16.3.3), given as

$$\mathbf{y}^0_{T+1} \quad *(16.4.1)$$

These are the fixed "targets" of policy. The second assumption is that there are enough policy variables, in particular that the number of policy variables, called "instruments," exceeds or equals the number of endogenous variables:

$$l \geqslant g \quad *(16.4.2)$$

The difference $l - g$ is then called the *policy degrees of freedom.*

Consider first the problem with zero policy degrees of freedom, for which $l = g$, so $\mathbf{A}$ in (16.3.1) is a square matrix. Assume further that the estimated coefficient matrix $\hat{\mathbf{A}}$ is nonsingular, so that its inverse $\mathbf{A}^{-1}$ exists. Postmultiplying the estimated structural form (16.3.3) by $\mathbf{A}^{-1}$ and solving for the optimal values of policy instruments yields

$$\mathbf{r}^*_T = -\mathbf{y}^0_{T+1}\hat{\mathbf{\Gamma}}\hat{\mathbf{A}}^{-1} - \mathbf{y}_T\hat{\mathbf{B}}_1\hat{\mathbf{A}}^{-1} - \hat{\mathbf{z}}_{T+1}\hat{\mathbf{B}}_2\hat{\mathbf{A}}^{-1} + \hat{\boldsymbol{\varepsilon}}_{T+1}\hat{\mathbf{A}}^{-1} \quad *(16.4.3)$$

This equation gives optimal values for the instruments, $\mathbf{r}^*_T$ as linear functions of the desired values of target variables $\mathbf{y}^0_{T+1}$ (and also of the current values of target variables $\mathbf{y}_T$, the forecasted values of exogenous variables $\hat{\mathbf{z}}_{T+1}$, and the values of the stochastic disturbance terms $\hat{\boldsymbol{\varepsilon}}_{T+1}$). This equation indicates the basic interdependence of policies and objectives. In general, optimal values for each instrument depend on values of all target variables. Only in special circumstances will one instrument correspond to one target variable.[11]

From equation (16.4.3), the sensitivities of the optimal values of each of the variables to the desired values of each of the target variables can be readily determined. These sensitivities are summarized by

$$\frac{\partial \mathbf{r}^*_T}{\partial \mathbf{y}^0_{T+1}} = -\hat{\mathbf{\Gamma}}\hat{\mathbf{A}}^{-1} \quad (16.4.4)$$

which gives the impact of a change in any $\mathbf{y}^0_{T+1}$ on any $\mathbf{r}^*_T$.[12] Similarly the impacts of $\mathbf{y}_T$, $\hat{\mathbf{z}}_{T+1}$, and $\hat{\boldsymbol{\varepsilon}}_{T+1}$ on r^*_T can be determined from (16.4.3).

[10] See Tinbergen (1952, 1954, 1956). See also Hansen (1958).

[11] See Problem 16-B.

[12] Do not confuse the elements of (16.4.4) with multipliers. Multipliers usually give the multiple effect of policy variables on endogenous variables, whereas the elements of (16.4.4) give the sensitivities of optimal policy variables to changes in the target endogenous variables. See Section 16.6 for a discussion of policy multipliers.

In the case of a problem with positive policy degrees of freedom a similar approach can be utilized. In such a case $l - g$ of the policy variables can be specified a priori at convenient levels. The remaining problem is then one with zero policy degrees of freedom, which can be solved as in (16.4.3).

In the case of the prototype macro model $l = g = 1$, so given a desired target value for the endogenous variable Y^0_{T+1} the implied optimal value for the instrument variable G^*_T is given by solving (16.3.6) for G_T:

$$G^*_T = \frac{Y^0_{T+1} - \hat{\Pi}_1 Y_T - \hat{\Pi}_3 - \hat{u}_{T+1}}{\hat{\Pi}'_2}. \tag{16.4.5}$$

Thus

$$\frac{\partial G^*_T}{\partial Y^0_{T+1}} = \frac{1}{\hat{\Pi}'_2} \tag{16.4.6}$$

showing how a change in desired national income is translated into a change in the optimal level of government expenditure.[13]

The instruments-targets approach to policy evaluation has been utilized in the Netherlands by the Central Planning Bureau. Short-term stabilization policy has been formulated on the basis of an estimated econometric model and target values of endogenous variables.[14] Another example of use of the instruments-targets approach is the setting of target growth rates by international development funds of the UN and other organizations. In this case, capital transfers, treated as the instruments, can be computed on the basis of the target growth rates.

The instruments-targets approach has three serious difficulties. One is that it assumes there are no tradeoffs among the targets, but rather specifies fixed values for each. The second is that it is doubtful that policymakers would or perhaps even could reveal specific target choices. The third is that of a shortage of independent instruments. The first difficulty (but not the other two) is overcome by the social-welfare-function approach discussed in the next section.

16.5 The social-welfare-function approach; optimal control

A second approach to policy evaluation using an estimated econometric model such as (16.3.3) is via a *social welfare function*, as developed by Theil.[15] This approach relaxes the assumptions of the instruments-targets approach. Rather than assuming specific desired targets for each endogenous variable, as in (16.4.1), it assumes the existence of a social welfare function, determining a

[13] As in the last footnote, do not confuse this partial derivative with the multiplier $\partial Y_T/\partial G_T$, showing the effect of government expenditure on the level of national income.

[14] See Hickman, Ed. (1965).

[15] See Theil (1961, 1964, 1965).

scalar measure of performance on the basis of both endogenous and policy variables:[16]

$$W = W(\mathbf{y}_{T+1}, \mathbf{r}_T). \qquad *(16.5.1)$$

The endogenous variables $\mathbf{y}_{T+1}$ affect welfare directly, while the policy variables $\mathbf{r}_T$ can affect welfare if, for example, there are costs associated with use of such variables. With this approach it is not necessary to make the policy degrees-of-freedom assumption of the instruments-targets approach.

The social welfare function can incorporate information about tradeoffs in objectives that the target levels in (16.4.1) do not allow. Thus, holding welfare constant and taking a total differential,

$$dW = \sum_{g'=1}^{g} \frac{\partial W}{\partial y_{g',T+1}} dy_{g',T+1} + \sum_{l'=1}^{l} \frac{\partial W}{\partial r_{l',T}} dr_{l',T} = 0 \qquad (16.5.2)$$

indicating joint changes in the current endogenous variables and policy variables for which welfare does not change. In particular, if only $y_{1,T+1}$ and $y_{2,T+1}$ change, it follows that

$$\left.\frac{dy_{1,T+1}}{dy_{2,T+1}}\right|_{W=\text{constant}} = \frac{\partial W/\partial y_{2,T+1}}{\partial W/\partial y_{1,T+1}}. \qquad (16.5.3)$$

This expression gives the tradeoff between the first and second endogenous variables. If they change according to (16.5.3), then welfare W does not change.

The social welfare function may or may not be based on the existence of certain desired values of endogenous (and policy) variables. If such desired values do exist, given by $\overset{0}{\mathbf{y}}_{T+1}$ and $\overset{0}{\mathbf{r}}_T$, respectively, then the social welfare function is often assumed to be quadratic, of the form

$$W = -\tfrac{1}{2}(\mathbf{y}_{T+1} - \overset{0}{\mathbf{y}}_{T+1})\mathbf{E}(\mathbf{y}_{T+1} - \overset{0}{\mathbf{y}}_{T+1})' - \tfrac{1}{2}(\mathbf{r}_T - \overset{0}{\mathbf{r}}_T)\mathbf{F}(\mathbf{r}_T - \overset{0}{\mathbf{r}}_T)' \qquad *(16.5.4)$$

where $\mathbf{E}$ and $\mathbf{F}$ are given constant positive-definite symmetric matrices.[17] In this case the maximum value of W is attained when the variables are at their desired levels:

[16] Do not confuse this Theil social welfare function, a function of levels of endogenous and policy variables, with a Bergson-type social welfare function, a function of individual levels of utility. The approach here makes no explicit reference to or connection with individual utility functions.

[17] The $\frac{1}{2}$ factors are included here simply for the sake of convenience. In differentiating the quadratic form the factors of 2 cancel the factors of $\frac{1}{2}$. It might be noted that the quadratic form is a convenient one that may be a reasonable approximation in a limited range around the values under consideration. In some instances, however, particularly away from the values under consideration, it may be inappropriate. Sometimes piecewise quadratic forms, each relevant in a particular range, are used to overcome this problem. See Friedman (1975).

$$\mathbf{y}_{T+1} = \mathbf{y}^0_{T+1}, \quad \mathbf{r}_T = \mathbf{r}^0_T \tag{16.5.5}$$

in which case $W = 0$.

Returning to the general welfare function of (16.5.1), the social-welfare-function approach to policy evaluation involves the choice of policy variables $\mathbf{r}_T$ so as to maximize the value of social welfare subject to the constraints of the basic estimated econometric model–i.e.,

$$\max_{\mathbf{r}_T} W(\mathbf{y}_{T+1}, \mathbf{r}_T) \quad \text{subject to} \quad \mathbf{y}_{T+1}\hat{\mathbf{\Gamma}} + \mathbf{y}_T\hat{\mathbf{B}}_1 + \hat{\mathbf{z}}_{T+1}\hat{\mathbf{B}}_2 + \mathbf{r}_T\hat{\mathbf{A}} = \hat{\boldsymbol{\varepsilon}}_{T+1}. \tag{*16.5.6}$$

If $\hat{\mathbf{\Gamma}}$ is nonsingular, so the reduced form of the econometric model is

$$\mathbf{y}_{T+1} = -\mathbf{y}_T\hat{\mathbf{B}}_1\hat{\mathbf{\Gamma}}^{-1} - \hat{\mathbf{z}}_{T+1}\hat{\mathbf{B}}_2\hat{\mathbf{\Gamma}}^{-1} - \mathbf{r}_T\hat{\mathbf{A}}\hat{\mathbf{\Gamma}}^{-1} + \hat{\boldsymbol{\varepsilon}}_{T+1}\hat{\mathbf{\Gamma}}^{-1} \tag{16.5.7}$$

then this problem, which is one of classical programming, can be solved by the method of substitution.[18] Solving for $\mathbf{y}_{T+1}$ from the constraint, and inserting this value in the social welfare function, the problem becomes that of the unconstrained maximization of

$$W = W(-\mathbf{y}_T\hat{\mathbf{B}}_1\hat{\mathbf{\Gamma}}^{-1} - \hat{\mathbf{z}}_{T+1}\hat{\mathbf{B}}_2\hat{\mathbf{\Gamma}}^{-1} - \mathbf{r}_T\hat{\mathbf{A}}\hat{\mathbf{\Gamma}}^{-1} + \hat{\boldsymbol{\varepsilon}}_{T+1}\hat{\mathbf{\Gamma}}^{-1}, \mathbf{r}_T). \tag{16.5.8}$$

Using the chain rule, maximizing by choice of $\mathbf{r}_T$ requires that

$$\frac{\partial W}{\partial \mathbf{r}_T} = \hat{\mathbf{A}}\hat{\mathbf{\Gamma}}^{-1}\frac{\partial W}{\partial \mathbf{y}_{T+1}}. \tag{*16.5.9}$$

These are the first-order necessary conditions for maximizing the social welfare function subject to the constraints of the estimated econometric model.

In the quadratic case with certain desired levels of both endogenous and policy variables, for which the social welfare function is given in (16.5.4), the first-order necessary conditions (16.5.9) require that

$$\mathbf{F}(\mathbf{r}_T - \mathbf{r}^0_T)' = \hat{\mathbf{A}}\hat{\mathbf{\Gamma}}^{-1}\mathbf{E}(\mathbf{y}_{T+1} - \mathbf{y}^0_{T+1})'. \tag{16.5.10}$$

Solving for $\mathbf{r}_T$ yields, since $\mathbf{E}$ and $\mathbf{F}$ are symmetric matrices and $\mathbf{F}$ is nonsingular, the optimal values of the policy variables:

$$\mathbf{r}^*_T = \mathbf{r}^0_T + (\mathbf{y}_{T+1} - \mathbf{y}^0_{T+1})\mathbf{E}(\hat{\mathbf{\Gamma}}')^{-1}\hat{\mathbf{A}}'\mathbf{F}^{-1}. \tag{*16.5.11}$$

Thus the policy variables are optimally determined by starting at the desired levels and adjusting according to the deviations of the endogenous variables from their desired levels. This result is referred to as a *linear decision rule*, since it gives the optimal values for the policy variables as linear functions of the endogenous variables of the problem. A linear decision rule always results from

[18] See Intriligator (1971) for a discussion of classical programming.

maximizing a quadratic (social welfare) function subject to a linear (econometric) model.[19]

In the case of the prototype macro model, the social-welfare-function approach problem becomes

$$\max_{G_T} W(Y_{T+1}, G_T) \quad \text{subject to} \quad Y_{T+1} = \hat{\Pi}_1 Y_T + \hat{\Pi}_2' G_T + \hat{\Pi}_3 + \hat{u}_{T+1}. \tag{16.5.12}$$

Assuming, for example, a quadratic welfare function, where Y_{T+1}^0 is the desired level of national income and G_T^0 is the desired level of government expenditure, of the form

$$W = -\tfrac{1}{2}e(Y_{T+1} - Y_{T+1}^0)^2 - \tfrac{1}{2}f(G_T - G_T^0)^2 \tag{16.5.13}$$

the optimal government expenditure is given as

$$G_T^* = G_T^0 - \frac{e}{f}\Pi_2'(Y_{T+1} - Y_{T+1}^0). \tag{16.5.14}$$

Thus the optimal policy adjusts the desired level of government expenditure by a linear function of the difference between actual and desired national income. This type of policy, for which the corrective action is proportional to and of opposite sign to the error, here given as $Y_{T+1} - Y_{T+1}^0$, is called *proportional stabilization policy.*[20]

Van den Bogaard and Theil used the social-welfare-function approach in order to study policies that the United States might have pursued in the Great Depres-

[19] See van Eijk and Sandee (1959), Holt, Modigliani, Muth, and Simon (1960), Holt (1962), and Theil (1964). In addition to a linear decision rule, problems involving a quadratic objective function and linear constraints generally exhibit *certainty equivalence*, in that the solution to the problem of maximizing expected welfare can be obtained by replacing random variables by their expected values. This result provides a justification for replacing the stochastic disturbance terms in the basic econometric model by their expected values of zero.

[20] See Phillips (1954, 1957) for a comparison of three types of policy, *proportional stabilization policy*, for which

$$A(t) = -kE(t)$$

where A is the action at time t, E is the error (actual level less desired level), and k is a constant; *derivative stabilization policy*, for which

$$A(t) = -k\frac{dE(t)}{dt}$$

and *integral stabilization policy*, for which

$$A(t) = -k\int_{t_0}^{t} E(\tau)\, d\tau.$$

sion.[21] The econometric model they employed was the Klein interwar model, introduced in Section 12.2. Their objective function was of the quadratic type

$$W = -\tfrac{1}{2}(\mathbf{y}_{T+1} - \mathbf{y}^0_{T+1})(\mathbf{y}_{T+1} - \mathbf{y}^0_{T+1})' - \tfrac{1}{2}(\mathbf{r}_T - \mathbf{r}^0_T)(\mathbf{r}_T - \mathbf{r}^0_T)' \qquad (16.5.15)$$

as in (16.5.4), where here the **E** and **F** matrices of (16.5.4) are both identity matrices. The endogenous variables $\mathbf{y}_{T+1}$ were consumption per capita, investment per capita, and a distribution variable giving the relation of profits to private wages. The target values of these variables $\mathbf{y}^0_{T+1}$ were their 1929 levels, the intent being to bring the depression to an end by restoring these endogenous variables to their predepression levels. The policy (instrument) variables $\mathbf{r}_T$ were government wages, business taxes, and government expenditure on goods and services.[22] The target values of these variables $\mathbf{r}^0_T$ were obtained by simple extrapolation of time trends established over the period 1920–1932. The period under consideration was the first administration of President Roosevelt, extending from 1933 to 1936, and the objective function minimizes the expected value of the sum of the squares of the deviations of endogenous variables and policy variables from desired or target levels over the entire four-year period.

Van den Bogaard and Theil solved for the optimal behavior of the instruments given the objective function and the estimated model. They found the largest deviations between optimal and actual values for government expenditure on goods and services. For example, government expenditure should have been approximately \$14 billion in 1933, approximately \$5 billion higher than its actual value, and \$13 billion in 1936, \$3 billion higher than its actual value, all money magnitudes being in dollars of 1934 purchasing power. While optimal levels of business taxes were higher than actual levels, in part because of the inclusion of a target for the distribution of income, optimal national income exhibits an even greater deviation from realized levels, so tax *rates* are optimally *reduced*. Government wages are optimally somewhat higher than actual levels in 1933 but lower in the later years, optimal government wages being over \$1 billion *lower* than the realized figure of approximately \$7 billion for 1936.

The social-welfare-function approach can be extended to the determination of long-term optimal policy over the time period from T to $T + h$, as in (16.1.2), via *optimal control.*[23] In this approach an objective function for the entire time period is chosen and maximized by choice of time paths for the policy instruments subject to the constraint of the estimated econometric model in each period. An example of such an objective function, to be maximized by choice of $\mathbf{r}_T, \mathbf{r}_{T+1}, \ldots, \mathbf{r}_{T+h}$, is

[21] See van den Bogaard and Theil (1959). Other examples of the use of the social welfare function appear in van Eijk and Sandee (1959), Fromm and Taubman (1968), and Fromm (1969a, b).

[22] It might be noted that monetary variables, which Friedman and Schwartz (1963) found to be of crucial importance in explaining the Great Depression, were ignored here.

[23] See Pindyck (1973) and Klein (1977). For the mathematical theory of optimal control over continuous time, see Intriligator (1971).

$$W = -\frac{1}{2} \sum_{t=T+1}^{T+h+1} [w_u(u_t - u_t^0)^2 + w_i(i_t - i_t^0)^2] \qquad (16.5.16)$$

where u_t is the rate of unemployment at time t, u_t^0 is the target rate of unemployment, i_t is the rate of inflation at time t, and i_t^0 is the target rate of inflation.[24] The weights w_u and w_i determine the importance of the unemployment goal relative to the inflation goal. Optimal policies for this example might include time paths for monetary policy variables, fiscal policy variables, and other policy variables, as in Table 16.1. This approach determines the optimal timing as well as the optimal level for such policy variables.

The problem with the social-welfare-function approach, whether of the short-run form, as in (16.5.1), or of the long-run optimal control form, as in (16.5.16), is that the parameters and even the specific form of the objective function are not known and cannot be elicited from policymakers in any practical way. Thus alternative approaches that do not rely upon the specification of an explicit objective function (or explicit targets) would be useful. One such approach is that of policy simulation, described in the next section.

16.6 The simulation approach

A third approach to policy evaluation using an estimated econometric model is *simulation.*[25] This approach avoids the necessity of assuming either the existence of desired levels of endogenous variables, as in the instruments-targets approach, or the existence of a well-defined objective function to be maximized, as in the social-welfare-function approach.

In general, *simulation* refers to the determination of the behavior of a system via the calculation of values from an estimated model of the system.[26] The model is assumed to be sufficiently explicit so that it can be programmed for numerical study, typically using a computer. The system's numerical behavior is then determined (simulated) under different assumptions in order to analyze its response to a variety of alternative inputs. Each simulation run is an experiment performed on the model, determining values of endogenous variables for alternative assumptions regarding the policy variables, other exogenous variables, stochastic disturbance terms, and values of parameters.[27]

In a *simulation run* data on the values of the policy and other exogenous variables, together with estimated values of parameters and stochastic disturbance

[24] Note that the sum in (16.5.16) ranges from $T + 1$ to $T + h + 1$ because of the one-period lag in the effect of policy variables, which range from T to $T + h$. The short-run single-period case here corresponds to $h = 0$. Also note that (16.5.9) gives each period equal weight. Alternative weights might be treated, e.g., discounting future periods.

[25] See Fromm and Taubman (1968), Naylor, Wertz, and Wonnacott (1968), Fromm (1969a, b), Naylor (1971), Klein (1971), Howrey and Kelejian (1971), Treyz (1972), Powell and Williams, Eds. (1973), Duggal (1975), and Eckstein, Ed. (1976).

[26] See Orcutt (1960), Shubik (1960), Clarkson and Simon (1960), Orcutt et al. (1961), Naylor et al. (1968), Naylor (1970), and Naylor, Ed. (1971).

[27] The stochastic disturbance terms can be either specified a priori at given levels (e.g.,

terms, are used to calculate the values of the endogenous variables from the equations of the model. The simulation run can, in fact, take several forms. A *historical simulation* refers to the computation of estimated values of endogenous variables for the sample actually observed, using historical values of exogenous variables (as in ex post forecasts) and estimated parameters. These simulated values can then be compared to actual values in order to determine whether the model accurately "tracks" the historical period. A failure to "track" should suggest that the model be reformulated.[28] A second type of simulation is a *projection*, which forecasts values of endogenous variables beyond the sample, as discussed in the last chapter. The third type of simulation, the one emphasized here, is a *policy simulation*, which determines values of the endogenous variables for alternative assumed sets of values of policy variables, corresponding to the alternative policies that are under consideration.

For purposes of policy simulation it is most convenient to use the reduced form

$$\mathbf{y}_{T+1} = -\mathbf{r}_T\hat{\mathbf{A}}\,\hat{\mathbf{\Gamma}}^{-1} - \mathbf{y}_T\hat{\mathbf{B}}_1\hat{\mathbf{\Gamma}}^{-1} - \hat{\mathbf{z}}_{T+1}\hat{\mathbf{B}}_2\hat{\mathbf{\Gamma}}^{-1} + \hat{\boldsymbol{\varepsilon}}_{T+1}\hat{\mathbf{\Gamma}}^{-1} \qquad (16.6.1)$$

which expresses the future values of endogenous variables as linear functions of current policy variables, current endogenous variables, future exogenous variables, and future stochastic disturbance terms.[29] Specific estimated values are assumed: for the coefficient matrices $\hat{\mathbf{A}}$, $\hat{\mathbf{B}}_1$, $\hat{\mathbf{B}}_2$, $\hat{\mathbf{\Gamma}}$; for the future exogenous variables $\hat{\mathbf{z}}_{T+1}$; and for stochastic disturbance terms $\hat{\boldsymbol{\varepsilon}}_{T+1}$. The values assumed for the coefficient matrices are based on estimates of the system, while the future values assumed for the exogenous variables and stochastic disturbance terms are based on results of other models or on extrapolations of trends.

The simulation approach uses this estimated reduced-form system to provide policymakers with a "menu" of alternatives from which they can pick a desired alternative. The "menu" can be presented as in Table 16.2, where the option numbers simply index the set of alternative policies.[30] The policymakers would then select a particular alternative $\mathbf{r}_T^*$, $\mathbf{y}_{T+1}^*$ according to their preferences, which may depend on both the policy variables and the endogenous variables.[31] Conceptually, the result is similar to that of the earlier approaches, but operationally it is quite different. The difference arises from the fact that it does not

---

their expected values of zero) or chosen via random drawings from a distribution with the appropriate characteristics (here, the means and covariances). The latter case is that of *Monte Carlo analysis.* Section 11.10 used this type of analysis to study small-sample properties of estimators, but it can also be applied, as here, to the study of alternative policy choices in an estimated stochastic model.

[28] Various measures of accuracy can be employed, some of which have been discussed in the previous chapter. See especially Section 15.5.

[29] If the model is nonlinear then the solution for the endogenous variables is usually obtained using an iterative solution technique, such as the Gauss-Seidel algorithm. The Brookings, Wharton, and MPS models discussed in Chapter 12 all use this approach. See Chapter 12, footnote 40.

[30] The table can be extended to consider entire time paths for both policy and endogenous variables, e.g., $\mathbf{r}_T^1, \mathbf{r}_{T+1}^1, \mathbf{r}_{T+2}^1, \ldots$, and $\mathbf{y}_{T+1}^1, \mathbf{y}_{T+2}^1, \mathbf{y}_{T+3}^1, \ldots$ for option number 1.

[31] Alternative simulations could, in fact, be developed depending on alternative assumptions

require the policymaker to state either specific targets or an entire social welfare function; rather, it requires only that he or she choose a policy, given the implications of each alternative policy option.

Table 16.2. Simulated Effects of Alternative Policy Options

Option Number	*Current Policy*	*Future Endogenous Variables*
1	$\mathbf{r}_T^1$	$\mathbf{y}_{T+1}^1$
2	$\mathbf{r}_T^2$	$\mathbf{y}_{T+1}^2$
3	$\mathbf{r}_T^3$	$\mathbf{y}_{T+1}^3$
.	.	.
.	.	.
.	.	.

One way to interpret the simulation approach is that of experimentation within the model system. Rather than "trying out" alternative policies in the real world, the simulation approach "tries out" these alternatives within the model system. The results of these experiments, specifically the implied future values of endogenous variables, indicate to the policymaker the implications of each alternative policy. In this interpretation the estimated econometric model serves as a type of "laboratory" for policy alternatives. Just as a wind tunnel is used to test alternative configurations of aerodynamic bodies, an estimated econometric model is used to test alternative configurations of policy choices. The alternative outcomes can each be regarded as a type of controlled experiment in the model system, where controlled experimentation in the real-world system is virtually impossible.[32]

The method of policy simulation frequently uses *policy multipliers*. For the linear model (16.6.1) the policy multipliers can be obtained as

$$\frac{\partial \mathbf{y}_{T+1}}{\partial \mathbf{r}_T} = -\hat{\mathbf{A}}\hat{\mathbf{\Gamma}}^{-1} \tag{16.6.2}$$

giving the effect on each of the endogenous variables of a change in any of the policy variables. The total effect on the endogenous variable g' of a change in each of the l policy variables can then be obtained by summing the separate effects of each of the policy variables, as in

as to the predicted future values of exogenous variables $\hat{\mathbf{z}}_{T+1}$. For example, different contingencies can be assumed for consumer or investment behavior in simulating a macroeconometric model. Such alternative simulations represent a substitute for explicit probabilistic forecasts.

[32] Simulation can be based, as here, on an estimated econometric model. It can, however, also be used in other contexts, such as the system dynamics models of Forrester, cited in Chapter 2. For an application to a regional analysis see Hamilton et al. (1969).

$$\Delta y_{g',T+1} = \sum_{l'=1}^{l} \frac{\partial y_{g',T+1}}{\partial r_{l',T}} \Delta r_{l',T} \tag{16.6.3}$$

If the model is large, so the computation of $\hat{\Gamma}^{-1}$ in (16.6.2) is cumbersome, or if the model is nonlinear then the policy multipliers can be obtained from the computation of two dynamic simulations. One is a "base run" using anticipated or status quo values of all exogenous variables and all policy variables. The other uses the same values for all exogenous variables and all policy variables, except that one policy variable is augmented by a unit amount. The differences in the resulting values for the endogenous variables for the two simulations can then be attributed to the particular policy variable that was changed. These differences can be interpreted as the policy multipliers, showing the effects on the endogenous variables, over time, of unit policy changes.[33] The overall effects of a set of policy changes can then be obtained by summing the separate effects of each, where each effect is the product of the corresponding change in the policy variable and the relevant policy multiplier, as in (16.6.3).

In the case of the prototype macro model the simulation approach would be based on solving

$$Y_{T+1} = \hat{\Pi}_1 Y_T + \Pi_2' G_T + \hat{\Pi}_3 + \hat{u}_{T+1} \tag{16.6.4}$$

for Y_{T+1}, future national income, given alternative values of government expenditure G_T and perhaps also alternative values of Y_T and $\hat{u}_{T+1}$ and alternative assumptions regarding the coefficients $\hat{\Pi}_1$, $\hat{\Pi}_2'$, and $\hat{\Pi}_3$. The single policy multiplier in this case is

$$\frac{\partial Y_{T+1}}{\partial G_T} = \hat{\Pi}_2'. \tag{16.6.5}$$

Of course, this example is highly simplified. Simulation becomes relatively more valuable as an approach when the system is large, complex, and nonlinear.

One advantage of the simulation approach is that it facilitates a synthesis of subjective judgmental factors on the part of decision makers and objective analysis using an estimated econometric model, as in the add factors of the last chapter. Subjective considerations enter at several points in the simulation approach. First, the particular set of alternative policies to be investigated is chosen largely on the basis of subjective factors. Second, the simulation itself includes add factors to take account of expert judgment, as represented by $\hat{\varepsilon}_{T+1}$, the values taken by the stochastic disturbance terms. Finally, the choice of a

[33] See Fromm and Taubman (1968), Klein (1971), Christ (1975), and Fromm and Klein (1976). They found that the major econometric models of the U.S. economy in the 1960's implied a multiplier for government nondefense purchases on nominal GNP of between 1.9 and 2.8 after two years; that is, each billion-dollar increase of government purchases increased nominal GNP by between \$1.9 billion and \$2.8 billion after two years. The multipliers for monetary policy were much less consistent, ranging between 4.0 and 14 for the two-year effect of an increase in unborrowed reserves on nominal GNP. For a simulation study of monetary rules using the FMP/MPS model see Cooper and Fischer (1972).

specific policy based on the various simulated results of alternative policies involves subjective judgments, which need not be made explicit, concerning the objectives of policy.

Three examples of the simulation approach involved use of the Brookings model of the U.S. economy to study fiscal and monetary policy. Klein analyzed the income tax cut of 1964, Fromm and Taubman analyzed the excise tax cut of 1965 and Fromm analyzed monetary and fiscal policy.[34] Klein solved the Brookings model for time paths of endogenous variables both with the tax rates prevailing in 1963 (the status quo) and with the new tax rates after the 1964 cut. These two solutions were then compared to determine the various impacts of the tax cut. Fromm and Taubman used the Brookings model to compare the situation that would have prevailed without the excise tax cut of 1965 to the situation with the tax cut. Excise taxes were considered in the context of taxes on broad commodity classes, and alternative assumptions were made as to how much of the tax cut was "absorbed" by producers and how much was "passed on" to consumers. Fromm used the Brookings model to analyze two fiscal policies (government purchase of durables and changes in federal personal income tax rates) and four monetary policies (changes in the discount rate, in the demand deposit reserve ratio, in the time deposit reserve ratio, and in unborrowed reserves). All three analyses were useful retrospective studies of how monetary and fiscal policies affect the economy.[35] While these studies were not used to *plan* policy, a similar methodology has been employed to determine the impacts of alternative policies *prior* to the choice of a particular policy. In fact, policy simulations conducted in and out of government have been a principal method of deriving and testing economic policies.

16.7 The econometric approach to policy evaluation

Estimated econometric models, particularly large, disaggregated, and dynamic models, may in the future be of considerable importance in the formulation and evaluation of policy.[36] As the basic ingredients of econometrics—data and models—are further developed and improved, and as econometric techniques

[34] See Klein (1969), Fromm and Taubman (1968), and Fromm (1969). For an econometric analysis of the 1968 tax surcharge using the Wharton model see Klein (1974).

[35] A related historical type of study uses simulation to analyze how various alternative policies might have affected the economy. Klein (1971), for example, reports on two studies of the 1929–1933 era involving simulation of alternative monetary and fiscal policies in the Great Depression. These studies indicated that simple monetary and fiscal policies could have substantially mitigated the Great Depression, a finding consistent with those of van den Bogaard and Theil (1959) discussed in the last section. Klein also mentions studies of disarmament and currency revaluation using estimated econometric models.

[36] See Holt (1965), Kuh (1965), Klein (1971, 1977). Klein (1977) argues that the macroeconometric models that are the most useful for policy formation are stochastic, dynamic, disaggregated models that explicitly treat both the foreign sector and the process of price-level determination. He further argues that forecast accuracy is essential for establishing the credibility of the model, but that forecast accuracy should not be overemphasized by excluding structural elements in the model, as in some of the small macroeconometric models and in forecasts based on autoregressive moving-average models.

are further refined, there will become available estimated econometric models encompassing many of the areas in which policy choices must be made. Such areas include not only the traditional macroeconomic phenomena of Tables 12.1 and 16.1 but also important sectors such as transportation, housing, and health.

The particular way in which the econometric models can aid in formulating and evaluating alternative policies will probably involve a mixture of some or all of the elements of policy evaluation treated in previous sections of this chapter. To the extent that specific goals and policy variables can be identified, the instruments-targets approach would be useful. To the extent that some explicit objective function can be determined or elicited from policymakers, the social welfare function or optimal-control approach would be useful. To the extent that policymakers seek answers to "what if" type questions, the simulation approach would be useful. Expert opinion on goals, parameters, and forecasts of related variables would be useful. The approach therefore will probably be an eclectic one, involving both objective and subjective factors.

The econometric approach to policy evaluation is indicated in a highly idealized fashion in Figure 16.1. The process might begin with a policymaker–

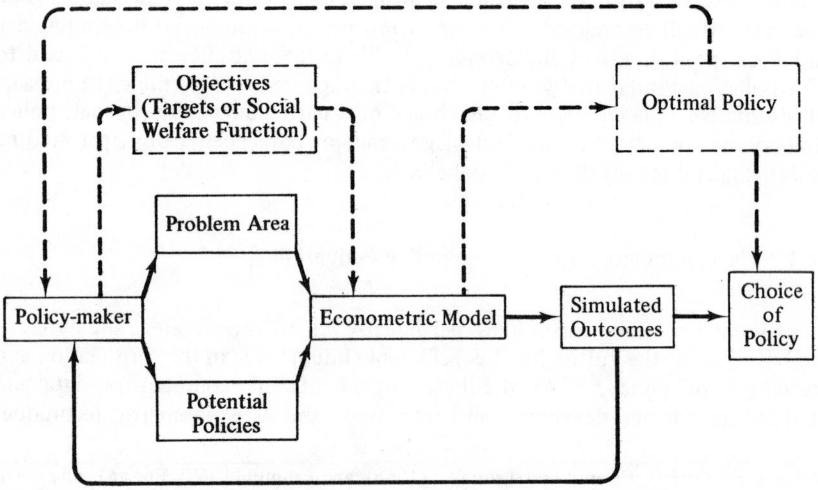

Figure 16.1 The Econometric Approach to Policy Evaluation

for example, a government official. The policymaker (with staff assistance) would identify a particular issue or problem area that is both of concern and subject to influence by policy. Some potential policies bearing on the problem area would also be identified.

The problem area and policy alternatives would then be considered within the structure of an econometric model. The estimated model would be used to obtain simulated outcomes–typically in the form of a series of time paths for relevant variables, each of which is conditional on a particular choice of policy. A status quo simulation would project the likely course of relevant variables in the event no action is taken, and the other simulations would each employ one of the possible policy alternatives. The series of simulations would indicate both the likely effects of alternative policy choices and the sensitivity of the system to the various policy alternatives, as measured, for example, by multipliers or elasticities.[37] The simulations, if based on a sufficiently comprehensive model, would indicate not only the direct and immediate consequences of alternative policies, but also their indirect effects in other areas and their long-term consequences.

The simulated outcomes would be communicated to the policymaker, who might, in their light, revise either the problem area or the potential policies, If so, the process would be iterated. Eventually, guided by the simulated outcomes, the policymaker would choose a specific policy alternative. For example, after identifying the outcome that appears most desirable, the policy that led to this outcome might be adopted. Of course, actually carrying out a specific policy usually entails a complex process of implementation.

The dotted paths indicate that if the policymaker were able to formulate objectives in the form either of targets or of a social welfare function, the econometric model could be used to determine optimal policy for these objectives. Here also the process could be iterated, with the policymaker eventually choosing a specific policy, guided by the optimal policy implied by the objectives and model.

A few specific examples will illustrate this approach. In the first, a policymaker responsible for health is concerned with the problem of access to medical care. Various potential policies, in the form of alternative systems of health insurance, additional medical school enrollments, neighborhood health centers, etc. are under consideration. Each can be evaluated using an econometric model of the health-care system, such as presented in Section 13.5, to determine simulated outcomes–in particular, the access of various groups classified by income, region, etc. to medical care. In fact, alternative features of various health insurance systems, such as coinsurance, deductibles, and alternative plans to expand medical school enrollments, can be separately treated and the simulated outcomes of each determined. Various "hybrid" schemes, involving different features of different systems, as well as other programs, can then be evaluated in order to help the policymaker choose an overall policy in this area.

A second example is the analysis of alternative energy policies, including various taxes on energy use, import and export duties, pricing policies, direct controls, and development of new energy sources. An estimated econometric model with sufficient detail as to energy demand and supply could be used to simulate the impacts of alternative policies, both singly and in various combined programs.[38] The resulting simulations could aid policy planners in selecting among alternative policy combinations.

The econometric approach of Figure 16.1 might also be applied in other areas of policy, such as transportation, education, housing, and the environment, where policies have traditionally been chosen with little or no understanding of their potential impacts, particularly secondary and long-run impacts. In these and in many other areas an estimated econometric model might play a significant

[37] See Klein (1971) and Eckstein, Ed. (1976).

[38] See, for example, MacAvoy and Pindyck (1975) and Jorgenson, Ed. (1976).

role in aiding and improving policy choices. Clearly, such an approach would encounter many problems of data collection, estimation, implementation, etc. If, however, these problems can be overcome, then the future of policy evaluation could very well be based on simulation or optimization using an estimated econometric model, with close links being formed between policymakers and econometricians.

PROBLEMS

16-A Formulate long-term optimal policy, as in (16.1.2), using the instruments-targets approach of Section 16.4. Obtain the sensitivities

$$\frac{\partial r^*_{T+h'}}{\partial y^0_{T+h''}}, \qquad h', h'' = 1, 2, \ldots, h$$

comparable to those of (16.4.4).

16-B In general, optimal instruments in the instruments-targets approach depend on *all* targets. Under what conditions will one instrument (or a subset of instruments) be determined entirely on the basis of one target (or a subset of targets)? Construct a macroeconometric model that yields "matching" behavior, in which fiscal policy is used for an employment objective and monetary policy is used for a price-stability objective.

16-C Consider the instruments-targets approach in each of the following cases. For each describe the nature of the optimal policy.

1. $\hat{\mathbf{\Gamma}}$ and $\hat{\mathbf{A}}$ are diagonal.
2. $\hat{\mathbf{\Gamma}}$ and $\hat{\mathbf{A}}$ are triangular.
3. $\hat{\mathbf{\Gamma}}$ and $\hat{\mathbf{A}}$ are block diagonal.
4. $\hat{\mathbf{\Gamma}}$ and $\hat{\mathbf{A}}$ are block triangular.

16-D Generalize the developments of the instruments-targets, social-welfare-function, and simulation approaches to the case of an econometric model containing lagged endogenous variables with lags up to and including those of order p.

16-E Consider in the estimated Klein interwar model in equations (12.2.1)-(12.2.6) that G, W, and T are policy variables.

1. Assuming there are three target variables, Y, C, and W_p, illustrate the targets-instruments approach.
2. Assuming a quadratic objective function in output and private wages, illustrate the social-welfare-function approach.
3. Use the model to simulate the effects of alternative policy choices.

BIBLIOGRAPHY

Braybrooke, D., and C. E. Lindblom (1963), *A Strategy of Decision*. New York: Free Press.

Christ, C. F. (1975), "Judging the Performance of Econometric Models of the U.S. Economy." *International Economic Review*, 16: 54-74.

Clarkson, G. P. E., and H. A. Simon (1960), "Simulation of Individual and Group Behavior." *American Economic Review*, 50: 920–932.

Cooper, J. P., and S. Fischer (1972). "Simulation of Monetary Rules in the FRB-MIT-Penn Model." *Journal of Money, Credit, and Banking*, 4: 384–96.

Davis, O., M. A. H. Dempster, and A. Wildavsky (1966a), "On the Process of Budgeting: An Empirical Study of Congressional Appropriation." *Papers on Non-Market Decision Making*, 1966: 63–132.

Davis, O. A., M. A. H. Dempster, and A. Wildavsky (1966b), "A Theory of the Budgetary Process." *American Political Science Review*, 60: 529–47.

Duesenberry, J. S. et al., Eds. (1969), *The Brookings Model: Some Further Results*. Amsterdam: North-Holland Publishing Co.; Chicago: Rand McNally & Company.

Duggal, V. (1975), "Fiscal Policy and Economic Stabilization," in Fromm and Klein, Eds. (1975).

Eckstein, O., Ed. (1976), *Parameters and Policies in the U.S. Economy*. Amsterdam: North-Holland Publishing Co.

Fox, K. A., J. K. Sengupta, and E. Thorbecke (1966), *The Theory of Quantitative Economic Policy, with Applications to Economic Growth and Stabilization*. Amsterdam: North-Holland Publishing Co.; Chicago: Rand McNally & Company.

Friedman, B. M. (1975), *Economic Stabilization Policy: Methods in Optimization*. Amsterdam: North-Holland Publishing Co.

Friedman, M., and A. Schwartz (1963), *A Monetary History of the United States, 1867-1960*. Princeton, N.J.: Princeton University Press.

Fromm, G. (1969a), "An Evaluation of Monetary Policy Instruments." in Duesenberry et al., Eds. (1969).

Fromm, G. (1969b), "Utility Theory and the Analysis of Simulation Output Data," in T. H. Naylor, Ed. *The Design of Computer Simulation Experiments*. Durham, N.C.: Duke University Press.

Fromm, G., and L. R. Klein, Eds. (1975), *The Brookings Model: Perspective and Recent Developments*. Amsterdam: North-Holland Publishing Co.

Fromm, G., and L. R. Klein (1976), "The NBER/NSF Model Comparison Seminar: An Analysis of Results." *Annals of Economic and Social Measurement*, 5: 1–28.

Fromm, G., and P. Taubman (1968), *Policy Simulations with an Econometric Model*. Amsterdam: North-Holland Publishing Co.

Greenberger, M., M. Crenson, and B. Crissey (1976), *Models in the Policy Process*. New York: Russell Sage Foundation.

Hamilton, H. R. et al. (1969), *Systems Simulation for Regional Analysis*. Cambridge: MIT Press.

Hansen, B. (1958), *The Economic Theory of Fiscal Policy*. London: George Allen & Unwin, Ltd. (originally published in Swedish in 1955).

Hickman, B. G., Ed. (1965), *Quantitative Planning of Economic Policy*. Washington, D.C.: The Brookings Institution.

Holt, C. C. (1962), "Linear Decision Rules for Economic Stabilization and Growth." *Quarterly Journal of Economics*, 76: 20–45.

Holt, C. C. (1965), "Quantitative Decision Analysis and National Policy: How Can We Bridge the Gap? in B. G. Hickman, Ed. (1965).

Holt, C. C., F. Modigliani, J. F. Muth, and H. Simon (1960), *Planning Production, Inventories, and Work Force*. Englewood Cliffs, N.J.: Prentice-Hall, Inc.

Howrey, E. P. and H. H. Kelejian (1971), "Simulation versus Analytical Solution: the Case of Econometric Models," in Naylor, Ed. (1971).

Intriligator, M. D. (1971), *Mathematical Optimization and Economic Theory*. Englewood Cliffs, N.J.: Prentice-Hall, Inc.

Jorgenson, D. W., Ed. (1976), *Econometric Studies of U.S. Energy Policy*. Amsterdam: North-Holland Publishing Co.

Kirschen, E. S., and L. Morrisens (1965), "The Objectives and Instruments of Economic Policy," in Hickman, Ed. (1965).

Kirschen, E. S. et al., (1964), *Economic Policy in Our Time*. Amsterdam: North-Holland Publishing Co.

Klein, L. R. (1969), "An Econometric Analysis of the Tax Cut of 1964," in Duesenberry et al., Eds. (1969).

Klein, L. R. (1971), "Forecasting and Policy Evaluation Using Large Scale Econometric Models: The State of the Art," in M. D. Intriligator, Ed., *Frontiers of Quantitative Economics*. Amsterdam: North-Holland Publishing Co.

Klein, L. R. (1974), "An Econometric Analysis of the Revenue and Expenditure Control Act of 1968–1969," in W. L. Smith and J. M. Culbertson, Eds., *Public Finance and Stabilization Policy*. Amsterdam: North-Holland Publishing Co.

Klein, L. R. (1977), "Economic Policy Formation through the Medium of Economic Models," in M. D. Intriligator, Ed., *Frontiers of Quantitative Economics*, Vol. III. Amsterdam: North-Holland Publishing Co.

Kuh, E. (1965), "Econometric Models: Is a New Age Dawning?" *American Economic Review*, 55: 362–369.

Lindblom, C. E. (1965), *The Intelligence of Democracy: Decision Making Through Mutual Adjustment*. New York: Free Press.

Lindblom, C. E. (1968), *The Policy-Making Process*. Englewood Cliffs, N.J.: Prentice-Hall, Inc.

MacAvoy, P. W., and R. S. Pindyck (1975), *The Economics of the Natural Gas Shortage (1960–1980)*. Amsterdam: North-Holland Publishing Co.

March, J. G., and H. Simon (1958), *Organizations*. New York: John Wiley & Sons, Inc.

Naylor, T. H. (1970), *Computer Simulation Experiments*. New York: John Wiley & Sons, Inc.

Naylor, T. H. (1971), "Policy Simulation Experiments with Macroeconometric Models: The State of the Art," in M. D. Intriligator, Ed., *Frontiers of Quantitative Economics*. Amsterdam: North-Holland Publishing Co.

Naylor, T. H., Ed. (1971), *Computer Simulation Experiments with Models of Economic Systems*. New York: John Wiley & Sons, Inc.

Naylor, T. H., J. L. Balintfy, D. S. Burdick, and K. Chu (1968), *Computer Simulation Techniques*. New York: John Wiley & Sons, Inc.

Naylor, T. H., K. Wertz, and T. H. Wonnacott (1968), "Methods for Evaluating the Effects of Economic Policies Using Simulation Experiments." *Review of the International Statistical Institute*, 36: 184–200.

Orcutt, G. H. (1960), "Simulation of Economic Systems." *American Economic Review*, 50: 893–907.

Orcutt, G. H., M. Greenburger, J. Korbel, and A. M. Rivlin (1961), *Microanalysis of Socioeconomic Systems: A Simulation Study*. New York: Harper & Row.

Phillips, A. W. (1954), "Stabilization Policy in a Closed Economy." *Economic Journal*, 64: 290–323.

Phillips, A. W. (1957), "Stabilization Policy and the Time-Forms of Lagged Responses." *Economic Journal*, 67: 265–77.

Pindyck, R. (1973), *Optimal Planning for Economic Stabilization*. Amsterdam: North-Holland Publishing Co.

Powell, A. A., and R. A. Williams, Eds. (1973), *Econometric Studies of Macro and Monetary Relations*. Amsterdam: North-Holland Publishing Co.

Shubik, M. (1960), "Simulation of the Industry and the Firm." *American Economic Review*, 50: 908–919.

Simon, H. (1955), "A Behavioral Model of Rational Choice." *Quarterly Journal of Economics*, 69: 99–118.

Simon, H. (1959), "Theories of Decision Making in Economics and Behavioral Science." *American Economic Review*, 49: 253–83.

Theil, H. (1961), *Economic Forecasts and Policy*, 2nd Ed. Amsterdam: North-Holland Publishing Co.

Theil, H. (1964), *Optimal Decision Rules for Government and Industry*. Chicago: Rand McNally & Company; Amsterdam: North-Holland Publishing Co.

Theil, H. (1965), "Linear Decision Rules for Macrodynamic Policy Problems." in B. G. Hickman, Ed. (1965).

Tinbergen, J. (1952), *On the Theory of Economic Policy*. Amsterdam: North-Holland Publishing Co.

Tinbergen, J. (1954), *Centralization and Decentralization in Economic Policy*. Amsterdam: North-Holland Publishing Co.

Tinbergen, J. (1956), *Economic Policy: Principles and Design*. Amsterdam: North-Holland Publishing Co.

van den Bogaard, P. J. M., and H. Theil (1959), "Macrodynamic Policy-Making: An Application of Strategy and Certainty Equivalence to the Economy of the United States, 1933–36." *Metroeconomica*, 11: 149–67, reprinted in Zellner, Ed. (1968).

van Eijk, C. J., and J. Sandee (1959), "Quantitative Determination of an Optimum Economic Policy." *Econometrica*, 27: 1–13.

Wildavsky, A. (1964), *The Politics of the Budgetary Process*. Boston: Little, Brown and Company.

Zellner, A., Ed. (1968), *Readings in Economic Statistics and Econometrics*. Boston: Little, Brown and Company.

Appendices

APPENDIX A

An Econometric Project

A.1 The nature of the econometric project

A basic purpose of this book is to prepare its readers to carry out their own econometric study. The econometric project is a case study in formulating an original econometric model, collecting data relevant to the model, using econometric techniques to estimate the model, and interpreting the results obtained. It is strongly suggested that all readers, but especially students, actually carry out such a study. As noted in the Preface, econometrics, to a large extent, is best learned by actually doing an econometric study. Only then will the "uninitiated" learn the power as well as the pitfalls of the econometric approach. This Appendix will guide the student in carrying out an econometric project.

As in any econometric study the "raw materials" are a model and a relevant set of data. These are the topics of the next two sections. Section 4 then treats estimation of the model, and Section 5 summarizes what to include in the write-up of the paper, which is most clearly and succinctly expressed in the style of an article in a scholarly journal.

A.2 The model

The model and the data are the starting points of an econometric project. The first step in formulating a model is to select a topic of interest and to consider the model's scope and purpose. In particular thought should be given to the objectives of the study, what boundaries to place on the topic, what hypotheses might be tested, what variables might be predicted, and what policies might be evaluated. Close attention must be paid, however, to the availability of adequate data: it is all too easy to design an ambitious project that fails for lack of data. In particular the model must involve *causal* relations among *measurable* variables. The most useful type of model in this context is typically a simultaneous-equations model, as discussed in Sections 2.8–2.10 and treated extensively in Chapters 10–13.

The topic selected can be either economic or noneconomic. It could be a particular market (e.g., the market for aerospace engineers, the market for pharmacists, the onion market, the markets for professional football seats and players), a process (economic development, political development, inflation), demographic phenomena (birth rates, death rates), environmental phenomena (water quality, air quality), political phenomena (elections, voting behavior of legislatures), some combination of these, or some other topic. Some topics that have been studied in student econometric papers are:[1]

Air Pollution and Population
Automobile Accidents and Driver Control Actions
Birth Rates, Death Rates, and Economic Growth in Developing Economies
Consumer Credit and "Truth in Lending"
Demand for and Supply of Higher Education
Differential Growth in U.S. Cities
Discrimination in Retail Food Markets
Divorce Rates, Birth Rates, and Female Participation in the Labor Force
Economic and Social Determinants of Infant Mortality in the United States
The Effect of Noise on School Achievement
The Effect of Unemployment on Crime
Elections and Money
Factors Affecting Baseball Attendance
Medical School Applications
Mental Health Hospitals in the United States
Police Expenditure and the Deterrence of Crime
The Relationship between Exports and Growth in Less Developed Countries
Unionization and Strike Activities
Violent Crimes in the United States

Perhaps the best choice of a topic is one that the student has prior experience in or knowledge of, e.g. one that may have been the subject of another course or that otherwise has been of previous interest. Of course, the previous literature on the subject should be identified and studied. Good sources are card catalogs and various indexes of the periodic literature.[2] The relevant literature should indicate, or at least suggest, a model and also hypotheses to be tested, variables to be forecast, and policies to be evaluated. It can also be a useful guide to relevant data.

All variables of the model should be defined, and the student should indicate for each whether it is being treated as endogenous or exogenous. If possible, these assumptions should be justified. To ensure that the model is both interesting and manageable it should contain at least two or three endogenous variables, three or

[1] For published papers on various topics see the bibliographies for Chapters 9 and 13, especially the last section of the bibliography for Chapter 9, "Other Applications of Econometric Techniques." See also the bibliographies for Chapters 7, 8, and 11 for more "standard" econometric studies.

[2] For economic studies see the American Economic Association, *Index of Economic Articles*. This index includes a classification by subject. For the general social science literature since 1973 see the *Social Sciences Citation Index*, which not only classifies articles by subject but also lists them by cited author. This index is extremely useful in identifying articles, given only the names of any individual author(s) who has worked on the topic.

four exogenous variables, and, if time-series data are used, one lagged endogenous variable. For purposes of this project, however, the number of variables should probably be limited to no more than four endogenous and eight exogenous variables. The model should then be formulated as a set of algebraic, linear, stochastic equations and a corresponding verbal statement of the meaning of each equation. If appropriate, all identities, equilibrium conditions, definitions, and other nonstochastic equations might then be eliminated. The resulting structural equations should be expressed as a matrix equation. From this structural form, the reduced form and, if appropriate, the final form should be determined and presented, both as sets of equations and as matrix equations.[3] This development of the model can follow that of Sections 2.6 and 2.7 on the prototype micro model and prototype macro model, respectively.

The expected signs of all structural and reduced-form coefficients should be given, and they should be utilized to analyze the comparative statics properties of the model, as in Figure 2.6. All relevant multipliers, short-run and long-run, should also be identified and discussed.

The last step in the development of the model is to investigate its identification. Both order and rank conditions of identification should be checked for each structural equation, and the model adjusted, if necessary, so as to ensure that all equations are either exactly identified or overidentified.[4] For all exactly identified equations it should be shown explicitly how the structural parameters can be inferred from reduced-form parameters, as in equations (2.9.18) for the prototype micro model.

A.3 The data

Data form an essential ingredient in any econometric study, and obtaining an adequate and relevant set of data is an important and often critical part of the econometric project. Data should be available for all variables of the model, both endogenous and exogenous.

Good starting points for the acquisition of relevant data are the various national and international statistical abstracts or yearbooks. National *Statistical Abstracts*, *Statistical Yearbooks*, or *Statistical Handbooks*, published annually by the United States, Canada, United Kingdom, and many other countries, provide both summary statistics and references to primary sources. The United Nations *Statistical Yearbook* provides a wealth of data on member countries, as do statistical yearbooks of other international organizations. Various almanacs and other reference works also abound in statistics. These sources contain data on so many topics that they may suggest a topic for the econometric project; to this end, Tables A.1 and A.2 summarize the contents of recent issues of the

[3] The reduced form should generally be a system of equations different from the structural form. If it is the same, not enough interactions among endogenous variables have been incorporated in the model, which should be reformulated to allow for such interactions.

[4] This adjustment is necessary, since the estimation technique to be employed, two-stage least squares, requires that all structural equations be exactly identified or overidentified.

Table A.1. Contents of a Recent *Statistical Abstract of the United States*

Section

1. Population
2. Vital Statistics, Health, and Nutrition
3. Immigration and Naturalization
4. Education
5. Law Enforcement, Federal Courts, and Prisons
6. Geography and Environment
7. Public Lands, Parks, Recreation, and Travel
8. Federal Government Finances and Employment
9. State and Local Government Finances and Employment
10. Social Insurance and Welfare Services
11. National Defense and Veterans Affairs
12. Labor Force, Employment, and Earnings
13. Income, Expenditures, and Wealth
14. Prices
15. Elections
16. Banking, Finance, and Insurance
17. Business Enterprise
18. Communications
19. Energy
20. Science
21. Transportation–Land
22. Transportation–Air and Water
23. Agriculture
24. Forests and Forest Products
25. Fisheries
26. Mining and Mineral Products
27. Construction and Housing
28. Manufactures
29. Distribution and Services
30. Foreign Commerce and Aid
31. Outlying Areas Under the Jurisdiction of the United States
32. Comparative International Statistics
33. Federal Administrative Regions and States
34. Metropolitan Area Statistics

Statistical Abstract of the United States and the United Nations *Statistical Yearbook*, respectively. Table 3.6 in Chapter 3 provides an overall summary of sources of data.

Table A.2. Contents of a Recent United Nations *Statistical Yearbook*

Section

World Summary
Population
Manpower
Agriculture
Forestry
Fishing
Industrial Production
Mining, Quarrying
Manufacturing
Construction
Energy
Internal Trade
External Trade
Transport
Communications
Consumption
Balance of Payments
Wages and Prices
National Accounts
Finance
Public Finance
Development Assistance
Health
Housing
Education
Science and Technology

Data can be either time-series or cross-section. For this project it is probably best not to pool data of the two types. Also it is best to avoid too-small data sets, e.g., less than ten observations.

The data should be examined and, if necessary, refined to make them suitable for the purposes of the model. For time-series data it may be necessary to use seasonal adjustment or perhaps to eliminate certain trends. For both time-series and cross-section data consideration should be given to whether to divide the data or perhaps exclude certain observations. Thus in time-series data it may (or may not) be appropriate to exclude war years or years of recession. In a cross section of nations it may be inappropriate in an economic study to include all countries that are UN members; rather, the developed countries might be treated as one group and the developing countries as another. Dividing the data this way into subsamples not only leads to more homogeneous data sets but also facilitates the study by allowing comparative analyses. Thus, for a study using the UN data, a comparison of results for developed and developing countries would facilitate structural analysis (e.g., finding the greatest differences between the results from the two subsamples), forecasting (e.g., using current information on developed countries as proxies or predictions for future values of variables in developing countries), and policy evaluation (e.g., mapping out policies for developing countries that would enable them to follow the lead–or avoid the mistakes–of the developed countries).

A.4 Estimation of the model

After both model and data have been developed the next step is to utilize econometric techniques to estimate the model. Since the model utilizes several equations to determine values of several endogenous variables, the appropriate technique is one of simultaneous-equations estimation. Among these techniques, one of the most widely used is that of two-stage least squares (2SLS), as discussed in Section 11.5, which is recommended unless there are reasons for using another technique.

The model is most conveniently, quickly, and inexpensively estimated using a computer, and virtually all computer centers have library source programs for multiple linear regression.[5] Such a source program makes computer programming unnecessary, and typically the only cards that must be prepared are the control cards and the data cards, in the appropriate format.

To use a library multiple linear regression program to perform 2SLS, each of the two stages is estimated separately. In the first stage each of the reduced-form equations is estimated. The resulting estimates of the reduced form are used in

[5] Examples of library source programs for multiple linear regression are those in SPSS, BMD, ESP, TSP, and TROLL. Of these SPSS or BMD may be the most convenient to use. See Nie et al. (1975) for SPSS and Dixon, Ed. (1973) for BMD. Several library programs are also available for 2SLS, such as TSP, ESP, and TROLL, but they generally do not print the results of the first stage, namely the estimated reduced-form equations. For this reason use might be made of both the 2SLS source program for the structural-form equations and the ordinary multiple linear regression source program for the reduced-form equations.

the second stage. They are also of interest in their own right: they are quantitative estimates of the comparative statics of the model, giving for each endogenous variable the magnitudes of change associated with changes in each of the exogenous and lagged endogenous variables.

To prepare for the second stage, the estimated parameters of the reduced form are used to determine calculated values of endogenous variables from the reduced form. Some programs provide these estimates, but with a relatively small model and data set this calculation can be done easily with a small calculator.

The second stage is then completed by using the library source program for multiple linear regression once again to estimate each of the structural equations, replacing actual values of explanatory endogenous variables by their calculated values.[6]

The outputs of this estimation thus include both estimated reduced-form equations (as in Section 5.6) and estimated structural equations.

A.5 What to include in the write-up

Unless there are reasons for doing otherwise, the best style to use in the final write-up of the econometric project is that of an article in a scholarly journal, a style that is both clear and succinct.[7] It should include the following:

a) *Title page.*

b) An *abstract*, of less than one page, giving a description of the topic, a concise specification of the model, the nature of the data used, the method of estimation, and the most important conclusions.

c) An *introductory section*, stating the nature and objectives of the topic; a general description of the scope of the model; and what can be done with the estimated model in terms of structural analysis (e.g., hypotheses to be tested), forecasting (which variables are to be forecasted for what periods), and/or policy evaluation (which policies are to be evaluated and in what way).

d) A section on *previous literature*, in particular the approaches and results of previous studies of this topic or related topics.

e) A section on *the model*, including definitions and discussion of each of the variables, a statement as to which are endogenous and which are exogenous, formulations of the structural form, the reduced form, and the final form; the expected signs of coefficients; the comparative statics of the model; and a deter-

[6] This approach will yield the 2SLS estimates of the structural-form equations but it will not yield the correct standard errors or t-values, since the estimate of the variance of the stochastic disturbance term is based on the sum of squares of the $\hat{v}_1$ from (11.5.15) rather than the correct sum of squares of the $\hat{\epsilon}_1$ from (11.5.14), as in (11.6.35). (See Problem 11-K). To obtain the standard errors and t-values requires either correcting the $\hat{v}_1$, using (11.5.16), or using a 2SLS source program, as in the last footnote.

[7] For examples of such articles, which might be considered models for econometric papers, see the articles in Zellner, Ed. (1968), in Hooper and Nerlove, Eds. (1970), and in journals such as *Econometrica*, the *Review of Economics and Statistics*, the *International Economic Review*, and the *Journal of Econometrics*. See, in particular, the articles cited in Chapters 7, 8, 9, 12, and 13.

mination of the identification of the model. This section should also include both a clear statement of stochastic and other assumptions being made concerning the model and a discussion of the likely consequences of violations of these assumptions.

f) A section on *the data*, including a table of all data used, a complete description of their nature, their sources, refinements used, and their possible biases or other possible weaknesses.

g) A section on the *estimated model*, including estimates of the reduced form and the structural form; related statistics, such as standard errors and t statistics, and a discussion of which coefficients are significant at the 0.05 and 0.01 levels; R^2 for each reduced-form regression equation; if relevant, a Durbin-Watson test for first-order serial correlation and a discussion of possible serial correlation and its correction; a test for homoskedasticity and a discussion of possible heteroskedasticity and its correction; and a discussion of possible multicollinearity and its correction.

h) A section on *econometric results*, including signs and magnitudes of estimated coefficients and their comparisons to predicted or theoretical signs and magnitudes. This section can also include implications for future econometric research, particularly how the model might be reformulated in future studies.

i) A section on *uses of the estimated model*, including structural analysis (relevant multipliers and elasticities and the results of tests of hypotheses), forecasts (forecasted values and, if possible, their comparison to actual values), policy evaluation (comparisons of alternative policies, measurements of impacts of policies, etc.).

j) A section on *overall conclusions*, including major results and suggestions for future studies.

k) A *bibliography*, including complete citations of all items referred to in the paper.

BIBLIOGRAPHY

American Economic Association (various years), *Index of Economic Articles*. Homewood, Ill.: Richard D. Irwin.

Dixon, W. F., Ed. (1973) *BMD: Biomedical Computer Programs*, Berkeley, Cal.: University of California Press.

Hooper, J. W., and M. Nerlove, Ed. (1970), *Selected Readings in Econometrics from Econometrica*. Cambridge Mass.: MIT Press.

Nie, N. H., et al. (1975), *SPSS: Statistical Package for the Social Sciences*, 2nd Ed. New York: McGraw-Hill Book Company.

Social Sciences Citation Index (Annual plus updates since 1973). Philadelphia: Institute for Scientific Information.

Zellner, A., Ed. (1968), *Readings in Economic Statistics and Econometrics*. Boston: Little, Brown and Company.

APPENDIX B

Matrices[1]

B.1 Basic definitions and examples

A *matrix* is a rectangular array of real numbers.[2] The size of the array, called the *order* of the matrix, is indicated by the number of rows and columns. The matrix **A** is of order $m \times n$ if

$$\underset{m\times n}{\mathbf{A}} = \begin{pmatrix} a_{11} & a_{12} & \cdots & a_{1n} \\ a_{21} & a_{22} & \cdots & a_{2n} \\ \vdots & & & \\ a_{m1} & a_{m2} & \cdots & a_{mn} \end{pmatrix} = (a_{ij}) \qquad *(\text{B.1.1})$$

so the matrix has m rows and n columns and contains *mn elements*. Here i is an index of the rows ($i = 1, 2, \ldots, m$), j is an index of the columns ($j = 1, 2, \ldots, n$), and a_{ij} is the typical element of the matrix. If $m = n = 1$, then the matrix reduces to a *scalar* (an ordinary real number). If m or n equals unity, then the matrix is a *vector*, a $1 \times n$ *row vector* if $m = 1$ and an $m \times 1$ *column vector* if $n = 1$. Generally scalars are represented by lower-case letters (e.g., k), vectors are represented by boldface lower-case letters (e.g., $\mathbf{x}$), and matrices are represented by boldface capital letters (e.g., $\mathbf{A}$). If $m = n$, so that the number of rows equals the number of columns, then the matrix is *square*, in which case the elements for $i = j$, starting with the upper left (1, 1) element and ending with the lower right (n, n) element are the elements of the *principal diagonal*.

[1] This appendix summarizes relevant definitions, examples, and properties of matrices for those who already have some familiarity with matrices. It is *not* intended as a way to learn matrices but rather as a review of concepts. Good introductions to matrices are Hadley (1961), Horst (1963), and Graybill (1969). Sections of this appendix not generally covered in standard texts or courses are the Kronecker product of matrices (B.3.21)–(B.3.24); the generalized inverse of a matrix, (B.5.9)–(B.5.12); least-squares fits to systems of equations, (B.6.10)–(B.6.21); matrix derivatives, (B.9.1)–(B.9.4); and the theory of mathematical programming using matrices, (B.10.1)–(B.10.26). The format of this appendix is similar to one in Intriligator (1971).

[2] All matrices here are composed of real numbers. In other disciplines, such as physics, matrices with complex numbers are also used.

Some examples of vectors and matrices used in econometrics are the column vector **y** of n observed values of a dependent variable:

$$\underset{n\times 1}{\mathbf{y}} = \begin{pmatrix} y_1 \\ y_2 \\ \vdots \\ y_n \end{pmatrix} = (y_i), \quad i = 1, 2, \ldots, n \tag{B.1.2}$$

the column vector $\boldsymbol{\beta}$ of k coefficients of explanatory variables:

$$\underset{k\times 1}{\boldsymbol{\beta}} = \begin{pmatrix} \beta_1 \\ \beta_2 \\ \vdots \\ \beta_k \end{pmatrix} = (\beta_j), \quad j = 1, 2, \ldots, k \tag{B.1.3}$$

the matrix **X** of n observed values of each of k explanatory variables:

$$\underset{n\times k}{\mathbf{X}} = \begin{pmatrix} x_{11} & x_{12} & \cdots & x_{1k} \\ x_{21} & x_{22} & \cdots & x_{2k} \\ \vdots & & & \\ x_{n1} & x_{n2} & \cdots & x_{nk} \end{pmatrix} \tag{B.1.4}$$

$$= (\mathbf{x}_i) = (x_{ij}), \quad i = 1, 2, \ldots, n; \; j = 1, 2, \ldots, k$$

where $\mathbf{x}_i$ is the row vector of values taken by each of the k variables at observation i:

$$\underset{1\times k}{\mathbf{x}_i} = (x_{i1} \quad x_{i2} \quad \cdots \quad x_{ik}), \quad i = 1, 2, \ldots, n \tag{B.1.5}$$

and the square matrix $\boldsymbol{\Omega}$ of covariances of stochastic disturbance terms

$$\underset{n\times n}{\boldsymbol{\Omega}} = \begin{pmatrix} \omega_{11} & \omega_{12} & \cdots & \omega_{1n} \\ \omega_{21} & \omega_{22} & \cdots & \omega_{2n} \\ \vdots & & & \\ \omega_{n1} & \omega_{n2} & \cdots & \omega_{nn} \end{pmatrix} = (\omega_{ii'}), \quad i, i' = 1, 2, \ldots, n \tag{B.1.6}$$

where $\omega_{ii'}$ is the ii' covariance and ω_{ii} is the ith variance (see Appendix C for definitions of variance and covariance).

B.2 Some special matrices

The *zero matrix* is a matrix for which all elements are zero:

$$\underset{m\times n}{\mathbf{0}} = (a_{ij}) \quad \text{where} \quad a_{ij} = 0, \quad i = 1, 2, \ldots, m; \; j = 1, 2, \ldots, n \qquad \text{*(B.2.1)}$$

For example,

$$(0), \quad (0 \quad 0), \quad \begin{pmatrix} 0 & 0 \\ 0 & 0 \end{pmatrix}$$

are all zero matrices. A zero matrix need not be square.

The *identity matrix* is a square matrix for which all elements along the principal diagonal are unity, and all other (off-diagonal) elements are zero:

$$\underset{n\times n}{\mathbf{I}} = (\delta_{ij}) \quad \text{where} \quad \delta_{ij} = \begin{Bmatrix} 1 \\ 0 \end{Bmatrix} \quad \text{if} \quad i \begin{Bmatrix} = \\ \neq \end{Bmatrix} j, \quad i, j = 1, 2, \ldots, n \qquad \text{*(B.2.2)}$$

and where δ_{ij} is called the *Kronecker delta*. For example,

$$(1), \quad \begin{pmatrix} 1 & 0 \\ 0 & 1 \end{pmatrix}, \quad \begin{pmatrix} 1 & 0 & 0 \\ 0 & 1 & 0 \\ 0 & 0 & 1 \end{pmatrix}$$

are all identity matrices. The columns of the identity matrix are *unit column vectors*, where

$$\mathbf{e}_1 = \begin{pmatrix} 1 \\ 0 \\ 0 \\ \vdots \\ 0 \end{pmatrix}, \quad \mathbf{e}_2 = \begin{pmatrix} 0 \\ 1 \\ 0 \\ \vdots \\ 0 \end{pmatrix}, \quad \text{etc.} \qquad \text{(B.2.3)}$$

are all unit vectors.

A *unity column vector* is a vector, all elements of which are unity:

$$\underset{n\times 1}{\mathbf{i}} = \begin{pmatrix} 1 \\ 1 \\ \vdots \\ 1 \end{pmatrix}. \qquad \text{(B.2.4)}$$

A *diagonal matrix* is a square matrix for which all elements off the principal diagonal are zero.

$$\underset{n\times n}{\mathbf{D}} = (d_{ij}) \quad \text{where} \quad d_{ij} = 0 \quad \text{if} \quad i \neq j, \quad i, j = 1, 2, \ldots, n. \qquad \text{(B.2.5)}$$

For example,

$$\begin{pmatrix} 2 & 0 \\ 0 & -3 \end{pmatrix}$$

and any identity matrix are diagonal matrices. If all elements on the diagonal matrix are equal, then the matrix is a *scalar matrix*.

A *triangular matrix* is a square matrix for which all elements on one side of the principal diagonal are zero:

$$\underset{n\times n}{\mathbf{T}} = (t_{ij}) \quad \text{where} \quad t_{ij} = 0 \quad \text{if} \quad i > j \quad \text{or if} \quad i < j, \quad i,j = 1, 2, \ldots, n. \tag{B.2.6}$$

For example,

$$\begin{pmatrix} 6 & -1 \\ 0 & 8 \end{pmatrix}$$

and any diagonal matrix are triangular matrices.

A *permutation matrix* is a square matrix for which each row and each column contain a one, all other elements being zero. For example,

$$\begin{pmatrix} 1 & 0 \\ 0 & 1 \end{pmatrix}, \quad \begin{pmatrix} 0 & 1 \\ 1 & 0 \end{pmatrix}, \quad \begin{pmatrix} 0 & 1 & 0 \\ 1 & 0 & 0 \\ 0 & 0 & 1 \end{pmatrix}$$

are permutation matrices, as are all the identity matrices. Altogether there are $n! = n(n-1)(n-2)\cdots(2)(1)$ permutation matrices of order n, of which one is an identity matrix.

A *partitioned matrix* is one that has been divided into submatrices of appropriate orders. For example,

$$\underset{m\times n}{\mathbf{A}} = \left(\begin{array}{c|c} \mathbf{A}_{11} & \mathbf{A}_{12} \\ \hline \mathbf{A}_{21} & \mathbf{A}_{22} \end{array}\right) \begin{array}{l} m_1 \\ m - m_1 \end{array} \quad \begin{array}{c} \\ \text{columns: } n_1 \mid n-n_1 \end{array} \tag{B.2.7}$$

where $\mathbf{A}_{11}$ is an $m_1 \times n_1$ matrix, $\mathbf{A}_{12}$ is an $m_1 \times (n - n_1)$ matrix, etc., is a partitioned matrix.

A *block diagonal matrix* can be partitioned in such a way that the only nonzero submatrices form a "principal diagonal" of square submatrices. Thus

$$\mathbf{A} = \left(\begin{array}{c|c|c|c} \mathbf{A}_{11} & \mathbf{0} & & \mathbf{0} \\ \hline \mathbf{0} & \mathbf{A}_{22} & & \mathbf{0} \\ \hline & & & \\ \hline \mathbf{0} & \mathbf{0} & & \mathbf{A}_{qq} \end{array}\right) \tag{B.2.8}$$

where each of the q submatrices $\mathbf{A}_{11}, \mathbf{A}_{22}, \ldots, \mathbf{A}_{qq}$ is square (but not necessarily of the same order) is a block diagonal matrix.

A *block triangular matrix* can be partitioned in such a way that only zero elements lie above or below a "principal diagonal" of submatrices. For example, both a triangular matrix and a block diagonal matrix are block triangular matrices.

B.3 Matrix relations and operations

Two matrices are *equal* iff they are of the same order and corresponding elements are equal:[3]

$$\mathbf{A} = \mathbf{B} \quad \text{iff} \quad a_{ij} = b_{ij}, \qquad i = 1, 2, \ldots, m;\ j = 1, 2, \ldots, n. \qquad ^*\textbf{(B.3.1)}$$

Similarly, two matrices can satisfy various forms of *inequalities* if they are of the same order and if all corresponding elements satisfy the inequality. Thus

$$\mathbf{A} \leqslant \mathbf{B} \quad \text{iff} \quad a_{ij} \leqslant b_{ij}, \qquad i = 1, 2, \ldots, m;\ j = 1, 2, \ldots, n. \qquad \textbf{(B.3.2)}$$

For example,

$$(2 \quad 6) \leqslant (5 \quad 8)$$

The *addition of two matrices* of the same order involves adding corresponding elements:

$$\mathbf{A} + \mathbf{B} = \mathbf{C} \quad \text{iff} \quad c_{ij} = a_{ij} + b_{ij}, \qquad i = 1, 2, \ldots, m;\ j = 1, 2, \ldots, n \qquad ^*\textbf{(B.3.3)}$$

For example,

$$\begin{pmatrix} 2 & 0 \\ 1 & 3 \end{pmatrix} + \begin{pmatrix} 8 & 2 \\ -1 & 0 \end{pmatrix} = \begin{pmatrix} 10 & 2 \\ 0 & 3 \end{pmatrix}$$

Properties of matrix addition include[4]

$$\begin{aligned} &\text{(i) } \mathbf{A} + \mathbf{B} = \mathbf{B} + \mathbf{A} \\ &\text{(ii) } \mathbf{A} + (\mathbf{B} + \mathbf{C}) = (\mathbf{A} + \mathbf{B}) + \mathbf{C} \\ &\text{(iii) } \mathbf{A} + \mathbf{0} = \mathbf{0} + \mathbf{A} = \mathbf{A} \end{aligned} \qquad ^*\textbf{(B.3.4)}$$

The *multiplication of a matrix by a scalar* involves multiplying all elements of the matrix by the scalar:

$$k\mathbf{A} = \mathbf{B} \quad \text{iff} \quad b_{ij} = ka_{ij}, \qquad i = 1, 2, \ldots, m;\ j = 1, 2, \ldots, n. \qquad ^*\textbf{(B.3.5)}$$

[3] The expression "iff" means "if and only if," signifying a definition or an equivalence.

[4] Most of the important theorems on matrices are summarized by these "properties" statements containing subentries (i), (ii), etc., such as (B.3.4), (B.3.6), and (B.3.8). The reader might test his or her understanding of this material by proving these properties. For help in the proofs see Hadley (1961).

For example,

$$6\begin{pmatrix}1 & 0\\ 2 & -1\end{pmatrix} = \begin{pmatrix}6 & 0\\ 12 & -6\end{pmatrix}$$

Properties of scalar multiplication include

(i) $k\mathbf{A} = \mathbf{A}k$
(ii) $k(\mathbf{A} + \mathbf{B}) = k\mathbf{A} + k\mathbf{B}$
(iii) $(k + l)\mathbf{A} = k\mathbf{A} + l\mathbf{A}$
(iv) $(kl)\mathbf{A} = k(l\mathbf{A})$ ***(B.3.6)**
(v) $(-1)\mathbf{A} = -\mathbf{A}$ *(negative of a matrix)*
(vi) $\mathbf{A} + (-1)\mathbf{B} = \mathbf{A} - \mathbf{B}$ *(matrix subtraction)*

The *multiplication of two matrices* requires that the number of columns of the matrix on the left equal the number of rows of the matrix on the right. Elements of the product are then obtained by multiplying elements of a row of the left matrix by corresponding elements of a column of the right matrix and adding all such products:

$$\underset{m\times r}{\mathbf{A}}\ \underset{r\times n}{\mathbf{B}} = \underset{m\times n}{\mathbf{C}} \quad \text{iff} \quad c_{ij} = \sum_{k=1}^{r} a_{ik}b_{kj}, \qquad i = 1, 2, \ldots, m; j = 1, 2, \ldots, n. \qquad \textbf{*(B.3.7)}$$

For example,

$$(a_{11} \quad a_{12})\begin{pmatrix}b_{11} & b_{12}\\ b_{21} & b_{22}\end{pmatrix} = (a_{11}b_{11} + a_{12}b_{21} \quad a_{11}b_{12} + a_{12}b_{22})$$

$$\begin{pmatrix}2 & 1\\ 0 & 5\end{pmatrix}\begin{pmatrix}8 & -1\\ 2 & 3\end{pmatrix} = \begin{pmatrix}18 & 1\\ 10 & 15\end{pmatrix}, \quad \begin{pmatrix}8 & -1\\ 2 & 3\end{pmatrix}\begin{pmatrix}2 & 1\\ 0 & 5\end{pmatrix} = \begin{pmatrix}16 & 3\\ 4 & 17\end{pmatrix}$$

In general, **AB** does *not* equal **BA**, even if both are defined, so matrix multiplication is generally noncommutative. It is therefore essential to indicate the intended order of multiplication, using the concepts of *premultiplication*, i.e., multiplication on the left, and *postmultiplication*, multiplication on the right. Thus the matrix product **AB** means **A** is postmultiplied by **B** or, equivalently, **B** is premultiplied by **A**.

Properties of matrix multiplication include

(i) $\mathbf{A}(\mathbf{B} + \mathbf{C}) = \mathbf{AB} + \mathbf{AC}$
(ii) $(\mathbf{A} + \mathbf{B})\mathbf{C} = \mathbf{AC} + \mathbf{BC}$
(iii) $\mathbf{A}(\mathbf{BC}) = (\mathbf{AB})\mathbf{C}$
(iv) $k(\mathbf{AB}) = \mathbf{A}(k\mathbf{B})$ ***(B.3.8)**
(v) $\mathbf{A0} = \mathbf{0A} = \mathbf{0}$
(vi) $\mathbf{AI} = \mathbf{IA} = \mathbf{A}$
(vii) $\mathbf{II} = \mathbf{I}$
(viii) $\mathbf{00} = \mathbf{0}$

Premultiplication by a permutation matrix permutes the rows of a matrix, while postmultiplication by a permutation matrix permutes the column of a matrix. For example,

$$\begin{pmatrix} 0 & 1 \\ 1 & 0 \end{pmatrix} \begin{pmatrix} 2 & 4 \\ 6 & 1 \end{pmatrix} = \begin{pmatrix} 6 & 1 \\ 2 & 4 \end{pmatrix}$$

$$\begin{pmatrix} 2 & 4 \\ 6 & 1 \end{pmatrix} \begin{pmatrix} 0 & 1 \\ 1 & 0 \end{pmatrix} = \begin{pmatrix} 4 & 2 \\ 1 & 6 \end{pmatrix}$$

Powers of a matrix are obtained by repeated multiplication:

$$\mathbf{A}^t = \mathbf{A}\mathbf{A}^{t-1}, \qquad t = 1, 2, \ldots \tag*{*(B.3.9)}$$

Properties of powers of a matrix include

$$\begin{aligned} &\text{(i) } \mathbf{A}^0 = \mathbf{I} \\ &\text{(ii) } \mathbf{A}^t\mathbf{A}^s = \mathbf{A}^{t+s} \\ &\text{(iii) } (\mathbf{A}^t)^s = \mathbf{A}^{ts} \\ &\text{(iv) } \mathbf{I}^t = \mathbf{I} \end{aligned} \tag*{*(B.3.10)}$$

The matrix **A** is *idempotent* iff

$$\mathbf{A}^2 = \mathbf{A} \tag*{*(B.3.11)}$$

Examples of idempotent matrices are

$$\begin{pmatrix} 6 & 10 \\ -3 & -5 \end{pmatrix}$$

any identity matrix, and any square zero matrix [see (B.3.8) (vii) and (viii)]. If **A** is idempotent, then

$$\mathbf{A}^t = \mathbf{A} \qquad \text{for all } t \geqslant 1 \tag*{(B.3.12)}$$

An *inner product* (or *scalar product, dot product*) of two vectors is a row vector times a column vector, yielding a scalar:

$$\underset{1\times n}{\mathbf{w}}\ \underset{n\times 1}{\mathbf{x}} = \sum_{j=1}^{n} w_j x_j. \tag*{*(B.3.13)}$$

For example,

$$(1 \quad 3) \begin{pmatrix} 2 \\ -1 \end{pmatrix} = -1$$

In fact, all the elements of the product of two matrices, as defined in (B.3.7), are inner products of the appropriate row vector of the left-hand matrix times the appropriate column vector of the right-hand matrix. If the inner product of the two vectors vanishes, then the vectors are *orthogonal*. For example,

$$(4 \quad 6) \quad \text{and} \quad \begin{pmatrix} 3 \\ -2 \end{pmatrix}$$

are orthogonal.

An *outer product* of two vectors is a column vector times a row vector, yielding a matrix:

$$\underset{n\times 1}{\mathbf{x}}\ \underset{1\times n}{\mathbf{w}} = \begin{pmatrix} x_1w_1 & \cdots & x_1w_n \\ \vdots & & \vdots \\ x_nw_1 & \cdots & x_nw_n \end{pmatrix} \tag{B.3.14}$$

The *transpose* $\mathbf{A}'$ of a matrix $\mathbf{A}$ is obtained by interchanging rows and columns. Thus,

$$\underset{n\times m}{\mathbf{A}'} = (a_{ji}) \quad \text{iff} \quad \underset{m\times n}{\mathbf{A}} = (a_{ij}),\quad i = 1, 2, \ldots, m;\ j = 1, 2, \ldots, n. \qquad {}^*\text{(B.3.15)}$$

For example,

$$\begin{pmatrix} 4 & 2 & 3 \\ 8 & 0 & -1 \end{pmatrix}' = \begin{pmatrix} 4 & 8 \\ 2 & 0 \\ 3 & -1 \end{pmatrix}$$

Properties of the transpose include

$$\begin{aligned} &\text{(i) } (\mathbf{A}')' = \mathbf{A} \\ &\text{(ii) } (k\mathbf{A})' = k\mathbf{A}' \\ &\text{(iii) } (\mathbf{A} + \mathbf{B})' = \mathbf{A}' + \mathbf{B}' \\ &\text{(iv) } (\mathbf{AB})' = \mathbf{B}'\mathbf{A}' \\ &\text{(v) } \mathbf{A}'\mathbf{A} = \mathbf{0} \text{ implies } \mathbf{A} = \mathbf{0} \end{aligned} \qquad {}^*\text{(B.3.16)}$$

The square matrix $\mathbf{A}$ is *symmetric* iff $\mathbf{A} = \mathbf{A}'$. For example,

$$\begin{pmatrix} 8 & 2 \\ 2 & -6 \end{pmatrix}$$

any diagonal matrix, and the covariance matrix $\mathbf{\Omega}$ in (B.1.6) are all symmetric matrices. If $\mathbf{A}$ is symmetric of order n, then it contains $n(n + 1)/2$ independent elements. The square matrix $\mathbf{A}$ is *skew-symmetric* iff $\mathbf{A} = -\mathbf{A}'$. For example,

$$\begin{pmatrix} 0 & 5 \\ -5 & 0 \end{pmatrix}$$

is skew-symmetric. If $\mathbf{A}$ is skew-symmetric of order n, then it contains $n(n - 1)/2$ independent elements, since all elements on the principal diagonal must be zero.

Given the $n \times 1$ column vector $\mathbf{x}$, the *sum of squares* is the inner product of the vector with itself:

$$\mathbf{x}'\mathbf{x} = \sum_{j=1}^{n} x_j^2 = \|\mathbf{x}\|^2. \tag{B.3.17}$$

Here $\|\mathbf{x}\|$, the square root of the sum of squares, is the *norm* of $\mathbf{x}$, a measure of the "length" of the vector. The vector $\mathbf{x}$ is *normalized* iff $\|\mathbf{x}\| = 1$. The *scatter matrix* is the outer product of the vector with itself:

$$\mathbf{x}\mathbf{x}' = \begin{pmatrix} x_1^2 & x_1x_2 & \cdots & x_1x_n \\ \vdots & & & \\ x_nx_1 & & \cdots & x_n^2 \end{pmatrix} \tag{B.3.18}$$

which is a symmetric matrix. For example, if $\mathbf{x} = \binom{3}{1}$, then

$$\mathbf{x}'\mathbf{x} = 10, \quad \|\mathbf{x}\| = \sqrt{10}, \quad \text{and} \quad \mathbf{x}\mathbf{x}' = \begin{pmatrix} 9 & 3 \\ 3 & 1 \end{pmatrix}.$$

The elements on the principal diagonal of the scatter matrix are the squares of the elements of the vector, while elements off the principal diagonal are cross products of elements of the vector.

The square matrix $\mathbf{A}$ is *orthogonal* iff each column (row) vector of $\mathbf{A}$ is normalized and orthogonal to any other column (row) vector, so that

$$\mathbf{A}\mathbf{A}' = \mathbf{A}'\mathbf{A} = \mathbf{I}. \tag*{*(B.3.19)}$$

Examples of orthogonal matrices include any permutation matrix and the matrix

$$\begin{pmatrix} \dfrac{3}{\sqrt{10}} & \dfrac{2}{\sqrt{40}} \\[2ex] \dfrac{1}{\sqrt{10}} & \dfrac{-6}{\sqrt{40}} \end{pmatrix}$$

The square matrix $\mathbf{A}$ is *decomposable* iff there exists a permutation matrix $\mathbf{P}$ such that

$$\mathbf{P}'\mathbf{A}\mathbf{P} = \left(\begin{array}{c|c} \mathbf{A}_{11} & \mathbf{A}_{12} \\ \hline \mathbf{0} & \mathbf{A}_{22} \end{array}\right) \tag{B.3.20}$$

where $\mathbf{A}_{11}$ and $\mathbf{A}_{22}$ are square matrices. For example,

$$\begin{pmatrix} 0 & 2 & 0 \\ 0 & -8 & 0 \\ 1 & 3 & 5 \end{pmatrix}$$

is decomposable into

$$\left(\begin{array}{c|cc} 5 & 1 & 3 \\ \hline 0 & 0 & 2 \\ 0 & 0 & -8 \end{array}\right)$$

using the permutation matrix

$$\begin{pmatrix} 0 & 1 & 0 \\ 0 & 0 & 1 \\ 1 & 0 & 0 \end{pmatrix}.$$

A matrix that is not decomposable is *indecomposable* (or *connected*). The $n \times n$ matrix **A** is indecomposable iff for every pair of indices (i, j) there exists a set of indices $j_1, j_2, \ldots, j_l$ such that

$$a_{ij_1} a_{j_1 j_2} \cdots a_{j_l j} \neq 0, \qquad i,j = 1, 2, \ldots, n.$$

The *Kronecker product* of a matrix with a matrix involves multiplying each element of the matrix on the left by the entire matrix on the right, using the rule (B.3.5) for multiplying a matrix by a scalar.[5] Thus

$$\underset{m \times n}{\mathbf{A}} \otimes \underset{p \times q}{\mathbf{B}} = \underset{mp \times nq}{\left(\begin{array}{c|c|c|c} a_{11}\mathbf{B} & a_{12}\mathbf{B} & \cdots & a_{1n}\mathbf{B} \\ \hline a_{21}\mathbf{B} & a_{22}\mathbf{B} & \cdots & a_{2n}\mathbf{B} \\ \hline \vdots & & & \\ \hline a_{m1}\mathbf{B} & a_{m2}\mathbf{B} & \cdots & a_{mn}\mathbf{B} \end{array}\right)} \qquad *(\text{B.3.21})$$

For example if **A** is the identity matrix of order 2 and **B** is a 2×2 matrix with elements (b_{ij}), then

$$\mathbf{I} \otimes \mathbf{B} = \left(\begin{array}{cc|cc} b_{11} & b_{12} & & \\ & & \multicolumn{2}{c}{\mathbf{0}} \\ b_{21} & b_{22} & & \\ \hline & & b_{11} & b_{12} \\ \multicolumn{2}{c|}{\mathbf{0}} & & \\ & & b_{21} & b_{22} \end{array}\right) \qquad (\text{B.3.22})$$

while if **A** is a 2×2 matrix with elements (a_{ij}) and **B** is the identity matrix of order 2, then

$$\mathbf{A} \otimes \mathbf{I} = \left(\begin{array}{cc|cc} a_{11} & 0 & a_{12} & 0 \\ 0 & a_{11} & 0 & a_{12} \\ \hline a_{21} & 0 & a_{22} & 0 \\ 0 & a_{21} & 0 & a_{22} \end{array}\right). \qquad (\text{B.3.23})$$

[5] See Theil (1971), Section 7.2.

Properties of the Kronecker product of two matrices include

$$\begin{aligned}
&\text{(i) } (\mathbf{A} + \mathbf{B}) \otimes \mathbf{C} = \mathbf{A} \otimes \mathbf{C} + \mathbf{B} \otimes \mathbf{C}\\
&\text{(ii) } \mathbf{A} \otimes (\mathbf{B} + \mathbf{C}) = \mathbf{A} \otimes \mathbf{B} + \mathbf{A} \otimes \mathbf{C}\\
&\text{(iii) } \mathbf{A} \otimes (\mathbf{B} \otimes \mathbf{C}) = (\mathbf{A} \otimes \mathbf{B}) \otimes \mathbf{C}\\
&\text{(iv) } (\mathbf{A} \otimes \mathbf{B})' = \mathbf{A}' \otimes \mathbf{B}'\\
&\text{(v) } (\mathbf{A} \otimes \mathbf{B})(\mathbf{C} \otimes \mathbf{D}) = \mathbf{AC} \otimes \mathbf{BD}
\end{aligned} \qquad *(\text{B.3.24})$$

assuming all matrix sums and products are defined.

B.4 Scalar-valued functions defined on matrices

The *trace* of a square matrix of order n is the sum of the n elements on its principal diagonal:

$$\operatorname{tr}(\mathbf{A}) = \sum_{i=1}^{n} a_{ii}. \qquad *(\text{B.4.1})$$

For example,

$$\operatorname{tr}\begin{pmatrix} 2 & 1 \\ 3 & 8 \end{pmatrix} = 10$$

and the trace of the scatter matrix (B.3.18) is the sum of squares (B.3.17).

Properties of the trace of a square matrix include:

$$\begin{aligned}
&\text{(i) } \operatorname{tr}(\mathbf{I}) = n, \quad \operatorname{tr}(\mathbf{0}) = 0\\
&\text{(ii) } \operatorname{tr}(\mathbf{A}') = \operatorname{tr}(\mathbf{A})\\
&\text{(iii) } \operatorname{tr}(\mathbf{AA}') = \operatorname{tr}(\mathbf{A}'\mathbf{A}) = \sum_{i=1}^{n}\sum_{j=1}^{n} a_{ij}^2\\
&\text{(iv) } \operatorname{tr}(k\mathbf{A}) = k \operatorname{tr}(\mathbf{A}) \qquad *(\text{B.4.2})\\
&\text{(v) If } \mathbf{A} \text{ and } \mathbf{B} \text{ are of the same order, } \operatorname{tr}(\mathbf{A} + \mathbf{B}) = \operatorname{tr}(\mathbf{A}) + \operatorname{tr}(\mathbf{B})\\
&\text{(vi) If } \mathbf{AB} \text{ and } \mathbf{BA} \text{ are both defined, } \operatorname{tr}(\mathbf{AB}) = \operatorname{tr}(\mathbf{BA})\\
&\text{(vii) If } \mathbf{ABC}, \mathbf{BCA}, \text{ and } \mathbf{CAB} \text{ are all defined, } \operatorname{tr}(\mathbf{ABC}) = \operatorname{tr}(\mathbf{BCA}) = \operatorname{tr}(\mathbf{CAB})\\
&\text{(viii) } \operatorname{tr}(\mathbf{A} \otimes \mathbf{B}) = \operatorname{tr}(\mathbf{A}) \operatorname{tr}(\mathbf{B})
\end{aligned}$$

The *determinant* of a square matrix of order n is the sum of the $n!$ signed terms, each of which is the product of n elements of the matrix—one from each row and one from each column:

$$|\mathbf{A}| = \det(\mathbf{A}) = \sum_{\substack{\text{all } n! \\ \text{permutations} \\ (i_1, \ldots, i_n)}} \operatorname{sgn}(i_1, \ldots, i_n) a_{1i_1} a_{2i_2} \cdots a_{ni_n} \qquad *(\text{B.4.3})$$

where $\operatorname{sgn}(i_1, \ldots, i_n)$ is $\begin{Bmatrix} +1 \\ -1 \end{Bmatrix}$ if the permutation $i_1, \ldots, i_n$ is $\begin{Bmatrix} \text{even} \\ \text{odd} \end{Bmatrix}$; i.e., obtained by an $\begin{Bmatrix} \text{even} \\ \text{odd} \end{Bmatrix}$ number of interchanges from $(1, 2, \ldots, n)$. For example, if $n = 2$, since $\operatorname{sgn}(1, 2) = 1$ and $\operatorname{sgn}(2, 1) = -1$,

$$\begin{vmatrix} a_{11} & a_{12} \\ a_{21} & a_{22} \end{vmatrix} = a_{11}a_{22} - a_{12}a_{21}.$$

Properties of the determinant include

(i) $|\mathbf{I}| = 1$, $|\mathbf{0}| = 0$
(ii) $|\mathbf{A}| = |\mathbf{A}'| = (-1)^n|-\mathbf{A}| = (\lambda)^{-n}|\lambda\mathbf{A}|$
(iii) $|\mathbf{AB}| = |\mathbf{BA}|$, assuming both products are defined (if $\mathbf{A}$ and $\mathbf{B}$ are square and of the same order $|\mathbf{AB}| = |\mathbf{A}|\,|\mathbf{B}|$)
(iv) If $\mathbf{A}$ is diagonal or triangular, $|\mathbf{A}| = a_{11}a_{22}\cdots a_{nn}$
(v) If $\mathbf{A}$ is orthogonal, then $|\mathbf{A}| = \pm 1$
(vi) If any row (column) of $\mathbf{A}$ is a nontrivial linear combination of all the other rows (columns) of $\mathbf{A}$, then $|\mathbf{A}| = 0$. [In particular, if two rows (or columns) of $\mathbf{A}$ are identical, or a row (or column) contains only zero, then $|\mathbf{A}| = 0$.] *(B 4.4)
(vii) If $\mathbf{B}$ results from $\mathbf{A}$ by interchanging two rows (or columns), then $|\mathbf{B}| = -|\mathbf{A}|$
(viii) If $\mathbf{B}$ results from $\mathbf{A}$ by multiplying one row (or column) by k, then $|\mathbf{B}| = k|\mathbf{A}|$
(ix) $|\mathbf{A} \otimes \mathbf{B}| = |\mathbf{A}|^n|\mathbf{B}|^m$ if $\mathbf{A}$ is square of order m and $\mathbf{B}$ is square of order n

The *kth-order leading principal minor* of the square matrix $\mathbf{A}$ is the determinant of the $k \times k$ matrix consisting of the first k rows and columns of $\mathbf{A}$:

$$M_k = \begin{vmatrix} a_{11} & \cdots & a_{1k} \\ \vdots & & \vdots \\ a_{k1} & \cdots & a_{kk} \end{vmatrix} \qquad \text{(B.4.5)}$$

A *kth-order principal minor* of the square matrix $\mathbf{A}$ of order n is the kth-order leading principal minor of $\mathbf{P}'\mathbf{AP}$, where $\mathbf{P}$ is a permutation matrix; and the *kth-order trace*, α_k, is the sum of all $n!/[k!(n-k)!]$ possible kth-order principal minors. Thus

$$\begin{aligned} \alpha_1 &= a_{11} + a_{22} + \cdots + a_{nn} = \operatorname{tr}(\mathbf{A}) \\ \alpha_2 &= \begin{vmatrix} a_{11} & a_{12} \\ a_{21} & a_{22} \end{vmatrix} + \begin{vmatrix} a_{11} & a_{13} \\ a_{31} & a_{33} \end{vmatrix} + \cdots \\ &\cdots \\ \alpha_n &= |\mathbf{A}| \end{aligned} \qquad \text{(B.4.6)}$$

The *i, j minor* of a square matrix is the determinant of the $(n-1) \times (n-1)$ matrix obtained by deleting the ith row and jth column of $\mathbf{A}$:

$$M_{ij} = \begin{vmatrix} a_{11} & \cdots & a_{1j} & \cdots & a_{1n} \\ \vdots & & & & \vdots \\ a_{i1} & \cdots & a_{ij} & \cdots & a_{in} \\ \vdots & & & & \vdots \\ a_{n1} & \cdots & a_{nj} & \cdots & a_{nn} \end{vmatrix}. \qquad \text{(B.4.7)}$$

The i, j cofactor of a square matrix is the same as the i, j minor if $i+j$ is even and the negative of the i, j minor if $i+j$ is odd:

$$C_{ij} = (-1)^{i+j}M_{ij}, \qquad i = 1, 2, \ldots, n;\ j = 1, 2, \ldots, n. \qquad \text{(B.4.8)}$$

The cofactors can be used to evaluate a determinant via the *expansion by cofactors*:

$$|\mathbf{A}| = \sum_{i=1}^{n} a_{ij}C_{ij}, \quad \text{any } j,\ j = 1, 2, \ldots, n \quad \text{(any column)}$$

$$|\mathbf{A}| = \sum_{j=1}^{n} a_{ij}C_{ij}, \quad \text{any } i,\ i = 1, 2, \ldots, n \quad \text{(any row)} \qquad \text{(B.4.9)}$$

The *rank* of any matrix **A**, written $\rho(\mathbf{A})$, is the size of the largest nonvanishing determinant contained in **A**.[6] For example,

$$\rho\begin{pmatrix} 2 & 3 \\ 8 & 6 \end{pmatrix} = 2, \qquad \rho\begin{pmatrix} 3 & 6 \\ 2 & 4 \end{pmatrix} = 1$$

Properties of the rank of a matrix include

(i) $0 \leqslant \rho(\mathbf{A}) = \text{integer} \leqslant \min(m, n)$, where **A** is an $m \times n$ matrix
(ii) $\rho(\mathbf{I}) = n,\ \rho(\mathbf{I}) = n,\ \rho(\mathbf{0}) = 0,\ \rho(\mathbf{P}) = n$
(iii) $\rho(\mathbf{A}) = \rho(\mathbf{A}') = \rho(\mathbf{A}'\mathbf{A}) = \rho(\mathbf{A}\mathbf{A}')$
(iv) If **A** and **B** are of the same order, $\rho(\mathbf{A} + \mathbf{B}) \leqslant \rho(\mathbf{A}) + \rho(\mathbf{B})$
(v) If **AB** is defined, $\rho(\mathbf{AB}) \leqslant \min\,[\rho(\mathbf{A}), \rho(\mathbf{B})]$
(vi) If **A** is diagonal, $\rho(\mathbf{A})$ = number of nonzero elements ***(B.4.10)**
(vii) If **A** is idempotent, $\rho(\mathbf{A}) = \text{tr}\,(\mathbf{A})$
(viii) The rank of a matrix is not changed if one row (column) is multiplied by a nonzero constant or if such a multiple of one

[6] Equivalently the rank is the (maximum) number of linearly independent rows (or columns) of **A**, where $\mathbf{a}_1, \mathbf{a}_2, \ldots, \mathbf{a}_n$ is a set of *linearly independent* vectors iff

$$\sum_{j=1}^{n} k_j\mathbf{a}_j = \mathbf{0} \text{ implies } k_1 = k_2 = \cdots = k_n = 0$$

See Hadley (1961) for a discussion of linear independence and other topics in linear algebra.

row (column) is added to another row (column)
(ix) $\rho(\mathbf{A} \otimes \mathbf{B}) = \rho(\mathbf{A})\rho(\mathbf{B})$ if **A** and **B** are square

A square matrix of order n is *nonsingular* iff it is of full rank:

$$\rho(\mathbf{A}) = n \quad \text{or equivalently} \quad |\mathbf{A}| \neq 0 \tag{B.4.11}$$

Otherwise, it is singular ($|\mathbf{A}| = 0$). The rank of a matrix is unchanged by premultiplying or postmultiplying by a nonsingular matrix. Thus, if there are nonsingular matrices **E** and **F** for which

$$\mathbf{EAF} = \left(\begin{array}{c|c} \mathbf{I} & \mathbf{0} \\ \hline \mathbf{0} & \mathbf{0} \end{array}\right) \tag{B.4.12}$$

where **I** is the identity matrix of order k, then $\rho(\mathbf{A}) = k$.

B.5 Inverse and generalized inverse matrices

If **A** is a square, nonsingular matrix of order n, then a unique inverse matrix $\mathbf{A}^{-1}$ of order n exists, where

$$\mathbf{AA}^{-1} = \mathbf{A}^{-1}\mathbf{A} = \mathbf{I} \tag*{*(B.5.1)}$$

The inverse matrix can be computed as

$$\mathbf{A}^{-1} = \frac{(C_{ij})'}{|\mathbf{A}|} = \frac{((-1)^{i+j}M_{ji})}{|\mathbf{A}|} \tag{B.5.2}$$

where (C_{ij}) is the matrix of cofactors, and its transpose $(C_{ij})'$ is called the *adjoint matrix*. For example, if

$$\mathbf{A} = \begin{pmatrix} 2 & 3 \\ 1 & 3 \end{pmatrix}$$

then

$$A^{-1} = \frac{1}{3}\begin{pmatrix} 3 & -1 \\ -3 & 2 \end{pmatrix}' = \begin{pmatrix} 1 & -1 \\ -\frac{1}{3} & \frac{2}{3} \end{pmatrix}$$

Properties of the inverse matrix include

(i) $\mathbf{I}^{-1} = \mathbf{I}$
(ii) $(\mathbf{A}^{-1})^{-1} = \mathbf{A}$, $(\mathbf{A}')^{-1} = (\mathbf{A}^{-1})'$, $|\mathbf{A}^{-1}| = |\mathbf{A}|^{-1} = 1/|\mathbf{A}|$
(iii) $(\mathbf{AB})^{-1} = \mathbf{B}^{-1}\mathbf{A}^{-1}$, assuming both **A** and **B** are nonsingular and of the same order
(iv) $\mathbf{A}^{-1} = \mathbf{A}'$ iff **A** is orthogonal, in which case $\mathbf{A}^{-1}$ and $\mathbf{A}'$ are also orthogonal *(B.5.3)

(v) Given the diagonal matrix $\mathbf{D} = (d_j\delta_{ij})$, $\mathbf{D}^{-1} = (d_j^{-1}\delta_{ij})$, where δ_{ij} is the Kronecker delta of (B.2.2)
(vi) If $\mathbf{A}$ is nonsingular and symmetric, then so is $\mathbf{A}^{-1}$
(vii) $(\mathbf{A} \otimes \mathbf{B})^{-1} = \mathbf{A}^{-1} \otimes \mathbf{B}^{-1}$ if $\mathbf{A}$ and $\mathbf{B}$ are square and nonsingular

For the partitioned matrix

$$\mathbf{A} = \left(\begin{array}{c|c} \mathbf{A}_{11} & \mathbf{A}_{12} \\ \hline \mathbf{A}_{21} & \mathbf{A}_{22} \end{array}\right) \tag{B.5.4}$$

assuming $\mathbf{A}_{22}$ and $\mathbf{B} = \mathbf{A}_{11} - \mathbf{A}_{12}\mathbf{A}_{22}^{-1}\mathbf{A}_{21}$ are nonsingular:

$$\mathbf{A}^{-1} = \left(\begin{array}{c|c} \mathbf{B}^{-1} & -\mathbf{B}^{-1}\mathbf{A}_{12}\mathbf{A}_{22}^{-1} \\ \hline -\mathbf{A}_{22}^{-1}\mathbf{A}_{21}\mathbf{B}^{-1} & \mathbf{A}_{22}^{-1}(\mathbf{I} + \mathbf{A}_{21}\mathbf{B}^{-1}\mathbf{A}_{12}\mathbf{A}_{22}^{-1}) \end{array}\right). \tag{B.5.5}$$

In particular, the inverse of a block diagonal matrix is also block diagonal.

If $\mathbf{A}$ is a nonnegative square matrix, then $(\mathbf{I} - \mathbf{A})$ has a nonnegative inverse iff all principal minors of $(\mathbf{I} - \mathbf{A})$ are positive. Then the inverse of $(\mathbf{I} - \mathbf{A})$ can be written as the expansion

$$(\mathbf{I} - \mathbf{A})^{-1} = \mathbf{I} + \mathbf{A} + \mathbf{A}^2 + \cdots \tag{B.5.6}$$

Two square matrices of the same order, $\mathbf{A}$ and $\mathbf{B}$, are *similar* iff there exists a nonsingular matrix $\mathbf{M}$ such that

$$\mathbf{B} = \mathbf{M}^{-1}\mathbf{A}\mathbf{M}. \qquad *(\text{B.5.7})$$

Properties of similar matrices $\mathbf{A}$ and $\mathbf{B}$ include

(i) $\text{tr}(\mathbf{A}) = \text{tr}(\mathbf{B})$
(ii) $|\mathbf{A}| = |\mathbf{B}|$ *(B.5.8.)
(iii) $\rho(\mathbf{A}) = \rho(\mathbf{B})$
(iv) $\mathbf{B}^t = \mathbf{M}^{-1}\mathbf{A}^t\mathbf{M}$, where $\mathbf{B}^t$ is the tth power of $\mathbf{B}$ as in (B.3.10)

Given the square or nonsquare matrix $\mathbf{A}$ of order $m \times n$ the *generalized inverse matrix* $\mathbf{A}^+$ of order $n \times m$ is the matrix satisfying the properties[7]

$$\begin{aligned} \mathbf{A}\mathbf{A}^+\mathbf{A} &= \mathbf{A} \\ \mathbf{A}^+\mathbf{A}\mathbf{A}^+ &= \mathbf{A}^+ \\ \mathbf{A}\mathbf{A}^+ &= (\mathbf{A}\mathbf{A}^+)', \quad \text{that is,} \quad \mathbf{A}\mathbf{A}^+ \text{ is symmetric} \\ \mathbf{A}^+\mathbf{A} &= (\mathbf{A}^+\mathbf{A})', \quad \text{that is,} \quad \mathbf{A}^+\mathbf{A} \text{ is symmetric.} \end{aligned} \qquad *(\text{B.5.9})$$

If $\mathbf{A}$ is square and nonsingular, then $\mathbf{A}^+$ is unique and is given by $\mathbf{A}^{-1}$, so $\mathbf{A}^+$ is,

[7] See Theil (1971), Section 6.6.

indeed, a generalization of the concept of an inverse matrix. If **A** is square but singular, then there is no inverse matrix, but a generalized inverse exists. If **A** is not square, a unique generalized inverse also exists. For example,

$$\mathbf{0}^+ = \mathbf{0}'$$

$$(\mathbf{B} \quad \mathbf{0})^+ = \begin{pmatrix} \mathbf{B}^{-1} \\ \\ \mathbf{0} \end{pmatrix} \qquad \text{if } \mathbf{B} \text{ is square and nonsingular}$$

$$\left(\begin{array}{c|c} \mathbf{B} & \mathbf{0} \\ \hline \mathbf{0} & \mathbf{0} \end{array}\right)^+ = \left(\begin{array}{c|c} \mathbf{B}^{-1} & \mathbf{0} \\ \hline \mathbf{0} & \mathbf{0} \end{array}\right) \qquad \text{if } \mathbf{B} \text{ is square and nonsingular}$$

Properties of the generalized inverse include

(i) $\mathbf{A}^{++} = \mathbf{A}$
(ii) $(\mathbf{A}^+)' = (\mathbf{A}')^+$
(iii) $\mathbf{AA}^+, \mathbf{A}^+\mathbf{A}, \mathbf{I} - \mathbf{AA}^+, \mathbf{I} - \mathbf{A}^+\mathbf{A}$ are all idempotent matrices ***(B.5.10)**
(iv) $\rho(\mathbf{A}^+) = \rho(\mathbf{A})$
(v) $\mathbf{A} = \mathbf{A}^+$ if **A** is idempotent and symmetric

If **A** is $m \times n$, where $m > n$ and $\rho(\mathbf{A}) = n$, then

$$\mathbf{A}^+ = (\mathbf{A}'\mathbf{A})^{-1}\mathbf{A}' \qquad \textbf{*(B.5.11)}$$

where the inverse exists by reason of (B.4.10) (iii). In this case, using (B.5.10) (iii),

$$\mathbf{I} - \mathbf{AA}^+ = \mathbf{I} - \mathbf{A}(\mathbf{A}'\mathbf{A})^{-1}\mathbf{A}' \qquad \textbf{(B.5.12)}$$

is an idempotent matrix.

B.6 Systems of linear equations; solutions and least-squares fits

The system of m linear equations in n unknowns

$$\begin{aligned} a_{11}x_1 + a_{12}x_2 + \cdots + a_{1n}x_n &= b_1 \\ a_{21}x_1 + a_{22}x_2 + \cdots + a_{2n}x_n &= b_2 \\ \cdots \\ a_{m1}x_1 + a_{m2}x_2 + \cdots + a_{mn}x_n &= b_m \end{aligned} \qquad \textbf{(B.6.1)}$$

is summarized by the matrix equation

$$\underset{m \times n}{\mathbf{A}} \ \underset{n \times 1}{\mathbf{x}} = \underset{m \times 1}{\mathbf{b}} \qquad \textbf{*(B.6.2)}$$

where $\mathbf{A} = (a_{ij})$ is the $m \times n$ coefficient matrix, $\mathbf{x} = (x_j)$ is the column vector of variables, and $\mathbf{b} = (b_i)$ is the column vector of constants, $i = 1, 2, \ldots, m$; $j = 1, 2, \ldots, n$. The system can also be written in summation notation as

$$\sum_{j=1}^{n} a_{ij}x_j = b_i, \qquad i = 1, \ldots, m. \tag{B.6.3}$$

An example of such a system is

$$\begin{aligned} 2x_1 + 3x_2 &= 7 \\ x_1 + 4x_2 &= 6 \end{aligned}$$

which can be summarized by the matrix equation

$$\begin{pmatrix} 2 & 3 \\ 1 & 4 \end{pmatrix} \begin{pmatrix} x_1 \\ x_2 \end{pmatrix} = \begin{pmatrix} 7 \\ 6 \end{pmatrix}.$$

The system of linear equations can have a unique solution, a nonunique solution, or no solution. A solution exists iff

$$\rho(\mathbf{A}) = \rho(\mathbf{A} \mid \mathbf{b}) = r \tag{*B.6.4}$$

and, if a solution exists, it is unique iff $r = n$. If a solution exists, but $r < n$, then $n - r$ of the variables can be assigned arbitrary values, with the remaining r variables then being uniquely determined.

If the coefficient matrix is square (the number of equations equals the number of unknowns) and nonsingular (the equations are independent), so that

$$m = n = \rho(\mathbf{A}) \tag{*B.6.5}$$

then the solution is unique. The solution can be obtained in this case by premultiplying the matrix equation by the inverse matrix as

$$\mathbf{x} = \mathbf{A}^{-1}\mathbf{b}. \tag{*B.6.6}$$

For example, the solution to the above equation is

$$\begin{pmatrix} x_1 \\ x_2 \end{pmatrix} = \begin{pmatrix} 2 & 3 \\ 1 & 4 \end{pmatrix}^{-1} \begin{pmatrix} 7 \\ 6 \end{pmatrix} = \begin{pmatrix} 2 \\ 1 \end{pmatrix}.$$

The solution can also be obtained from *Cramer's rule*:

$$x_j = \frac{|\mathbf{A}_j|}{|\mathbf{A}|}, \qquad j = 1, 2, \ldots, n \tag{B.6.7}$$

where $\mathbf{A}_j$ is obtained from $\mathbf{A}$ by replacing the jth column of $\mathbf{A}$ by $\mathbf{b}$. In the above example the unique solutions are

$$x_1 = \frac{\begin{vmatrix} 7 & 3 \\ 6 & 4 \end{vmatrix}}{\begin{vmatrix} 2 & 3 \\ 1 & 4 \end{vmatrix}} = 2, \qquad x_2 = \frac{\begin{vmatrix} 2 & 7 \\ 1 & 6 \end{vmatrix}}{\begin{vmatrix} 2 & 3 \\ 1 & 4 \end{vmatrix}} = 1.$$

Unique solutions can exist, however, even if $m \neq n$. For example, if

$$\begin{pmatrix} 2 \\ 8 \end{pmatrix} x_1 = \begin{pmatrix} 6 \\ 24 \end{pmatrix}$$

then $x_1 = 3$.

A case in which solutions exist but are nonunique is the *homogeneous* case in which the vector of constants is zero. For this case a necessary and sufficient condition for nontrivial solutions to exist is that the coefficient matrix be of less than full row rank. In this case, therefore, from (B.6.4)

$$\mathbf{b} = \mathbf{0} \quad \text{and} \quad \rho(\mathbf{A}) = r < n. \qquad \text{*(B.6.8)}$$

The solution is nonunique in that $n - r$ of the variables can be assigned arbitrary values. An example is

$$\begin{pmatrix} 2 & 4 \\ 3 & 6 \end{pmatrix} \begin{pmatrix} x_1 \\ x_2 \end{pmatrix} = \mathbf{0}$$

where $n - r = 1$. Setting x_1 equal to the arbitary value c, all solutions are of the form

$$\begin{pmatrix} x_1 \\ x_2 \end{pmatrix} = \begin{pmatrix} c \\ -c/2 \end{pmatrix}.$$

In general, in this homogeneous case, if $\rho(\mathbf{A}) = n - 1$, then the solution is unique up to a factor of proportionality. Since $\rho(\mathbf{A}) \leqslant \min(m, n)$, another case in which nonunique solutions exist is that in which the number of equations is less than the number of unknowns and the rank condition is satisfied, so that $m < n$, but $\rho(\mathbf{A}) = \rho(\mathbf{A} \mid \mathbf{b})$. For example, if

$$\begin{pmatrix} 2 & -3 & 1 \\ 8 & 2 & 0 \end{pmatrix} \begin{pmatrix} x_1 \\ x_2 \\ x_3 \end{pmatrix} = \begin{pmatrix} 2 \\ 4 \end{pmatrix}$$

then, setting x_1 equal to the arbitrary value c, all solutions are of the form

$$\begin{pmatrix} x_1 \\ x_2 \\ x_3 \end{pmatrix} = \begin{pmatrix} c \\ 2 - 4c \\ 8 - 14c \end{pmatrix}.$$

No solutions exist if $\rho(\mathbf{A}) < \rho(\mathbf{A} \mid \mathbf{b})$. Some examples are

$$\begin{pmatrix} 2 \\ 3 \end{pmatrix} x_1 = \begin{pmatrix} 6 \\ -1 \end{pmatrix}, \quad \begin{pmatrix} 2 & 4 \\ 3 & 6 \end{pmatrix} \begin{pmatrix} x_1 \\ x_2 \end{pmatrix} = \begin{pmatrix} 6 \\ 10 \end{pmatrix}$$

$$\begin{pmatrix} 1 & 2 & -3 \\ 2 & 4 & -6 \end{pmatrix} \begin{pmatrix} x_1 \\ x_2 \\ x_3 \end{pmatrix} = \begin{pmatrix} 4 \\ 6 \end{pmatrix}$$

where $m > n$, $m = n$, and $m < n$, respectively.

Geometrically, each linear equation represents a hyperplane in Euclidean n-space, E^n, the space of all n-tuples of real numbers. If all m hyperplanes intersect at a point, then this point is the unique solution to the system of linear equations. If they intersect to form a line (plane, etc.), then all points on this line (plane, etc.) are solutions, and one (two, more) of the variables can be assigned arbitrary values. If they do not intersect (e.g., parallel lines in the plane E^2), no solution exists. A homogeneous equation represents a hyperplane passing through the origin, so, unless nonunique solutions exist, the only solution is the unique but trivial solution at the origin.

When there are more equations than unknowns, the system of linear equations is rewritten as

$$\underset{n\times 1}{\mathbf{y}} = \underset{n\times k}{\mathbf{X}}\ \underset{k\times 1}{\boldsymbol{\beta}} \qquad \text{*(B.6.9)}$$

where $\mathbf{X}$ is an $n \times k$ coefficient matrix, $\boldsymbol{\beta}$ is a $k \times 1$ vector of unknowns, and $\mathbf{y}$ is an $n \times 1$ vector of constants.[8] It is assumed that n, the number of equations, exceeds k, the number of unknowns. One approach to "solving" this system is that of *least-squares fit*. This approach minimizes the sum of squared deviations between elements of $\mathbf{y}$ and elements of $\mathbf{X}\boldsymbol{\beta}$, given as[9]

$$S = \|\mathbf{y} - \mathbf{X}\boldsymbol{\beta}\|^2 = (\mathbf{y} - \mathbf{X}\boldsymbol{\beta})'(\mathbf{y} - \mathbf{X}\boldsymbol{\beta}) = \operatorname{tr}(\mathbf{y} - \mathbf{X}\boldsymbol{\beta})(\mathbf{y} - \mathbf{X}\boldsymbol{\beta})'. \qquad \text{*(B.6.10)}$$

The solution for $\boldsymbol{\beta}$ to the problem of minimizing S is

$$\hat{\boldsymbol{\beta}} = \mathbf{X}^{+}\mathbf{y} \qquad \text{*(B.6.11)}$$

where $\mathbf{X}^{+}$ is the generalized inverse matrix defined in (B.5.9). If the $\mathbf{X}$ matrix has maximal rank, then, from (B.5.11),

$$\mathbf{X}^{+} = (\mathbf{X}'\mathbf{X})^{-1}\mathbf{X}' \qquad [\text{when } \rho(\mathbf{X}) = k]. \qquad \text{*(B.6.12)}$$

In this case

$$\hat{\boldsymbol{\beta}} = (\mathbf{X}'\mathbf{X})^{-1}\mathbf{X}'\mathbf{y}. \qquad \text{*(B.6.13)}$$

Both the solution in (B.6.11) and the solution in the special case in (B.6.13) corresponding to a coefficient matrix of maximal rank are called the *least-squares estimators* of $\boldsymbol{\beta}$.

In the maximal-rank case, since

$$\mathbf{y} - \mathbf{X}\hat{\boldsymbol{\beta}} = \mathbf{y} - \mathbf{X}(\mathbf{X}'\mathbf{X})^{-1}\mathbf{X}'\mathbf{y} = [\mathbf{I} - \mathbf{X}(\mathbf{X}'\mathbf{X})^{-1}\mathbf{X}']\mathbf{y} \qquad \text{*(B.6.14)}$$

[8] This switch in notation will ensure that the notation here is consistent with that in the text, particularly Chapter 4. The switch replaces $\mathbf{A}$ by $\mathbf{X}$, $\mathbf{x}$ by $\boldsymbol{\beta}$, and $\mathbf{b}$ by $\mathbf{y}$, so $\mathbf{Ax} = \mathbf{b}$ is replaced by $\mathbf{X}\boldsymbol{\beta} = \mathbf{y}$.

[9] See (B.4.2), property (iii).

where $\mathbf{I} - \mathbf{X}(\mathbf{X}'\mathbf{X})^{-1}\mathbf{X}'$ is a symmetric and idempotent matrix, the sum of squares S in (B.6.10) can be written

$$S = (\mathbf{y} - \mathbf{X}\hat{\boldsymbol{\beta}})'(\mathbf{y} - \mathbf{X}\hat{\boldsymbol{\beta}}) = \mathbf{y}'[\mathbf{I} - \mathbf{X}(\mathbf{X}'\mathbf{X})^{-1}\mathbf{X}']\mathbf{y} = \mathbf{y}'\mathbf{M}\mathbf{y}. \quad \text{*(B.6.15)}$$

The $\mathbf{M}$ matrix, here defined as $[\mathbf{I} - \mathbf{X}(\mathbf{X}'\mathbf{X})^{-1}\mathbf{X}']$, is the *fundamental idempotent matrix of least squares*. It satisfies the properties

$$\begin{aligned} &\text{(i) } \mathbf{M} = \mathbf{M}' \\ &\text{(ii) } \mathbf{M} = \mathbf{M}^2 \\ &\text{(iii) } \rho(\mathbf{M}) = \operatorname{tr}(\mathbf{M}) = n - k \\ &\text{(iv) } \mathbf{M}\mathbf{X} = \mathbf{0} \end{aligned} \quad \text{*(B.6.16)}$$

More generally, consider the *weighted* sum of squared deviations, $S(\mathbf{W})$ defined as

$$S(\mathbf{W}) = (\mathbf{y} - \mathbf{X}\boldsymbol{\beta})'\mathbf{W}(\mathbf{y} - \mathbf{X}\boldsymbol{\beta}) \quad \text{(B.6.17)}$$

where $\mathbf{W}$ is a symmetric nonsingular matrix of weights.[10] Then the *weighted least-squares estimator* is given as

$$\hat{\boldsymbol{\beta}} = (\mathbf{P}\mathbf{X})^{+}\mathbf{P}\mathbf{y} \quad \text{(B.6.18)}$$

where $\mathbf{P}$ is a nonsingular matrix that satisfies[11]

$$\mathbf{P}'\mathbf{P} = \mathbf{W}. \quad \text{(B.6.19)}$$

In particular, if $\mathbf{PX}$ is of full rank, then

$$\hat{\boldsymbol{\beta}} = [(\mathbf{P}\mathbf{X})'(\mathbf{P}\mathbf{X})]^{-1}(\mathbf{P}\mathbf{X})'\mathbf{P}\mathbf{y} \quad \text{(B.6.20)}$$

leading to

$$\hat{\boldsymbol{\beta}} = [\mathbf{X}'\mathbf{W}\mathbf{X}]^{-1}\mathbf{X}'\mathbf{W}\mathbf{y} \quad \text{(B.6.21)}$$

which is the weighted least-squares estimator under the full-rank condition.

B.7 Linear transformations and characteristic roots and vectors

Any $m \times n$ matrix $\mathbf{A}$ represents a linear transformation from Euclidean n-space to Euclidean m-space in that, given any vector $\mathbf{x} \in E^n$, there exists a unique vector $\mathbf{y} \in E^m$ such that[12]

[10] The matrix W is usually assumed to be positive definite, a property defined below in Section B.8. The weighted sum of squares in (B.8.1) is a quadratic form, as defined in (B.8.1).

[11] From (B.8.2) (vii) below, if W is positive definite, then such a matrix always exists.

[12] E^n is Euclidean n-space, the space of all n-tuples of real numbers, here treated as the space of all n-dimensional column vectors.

$$\mathbf{y} = \mathbf{A}\mathbf{x} = \mathbf{A}(\mathbf{x}). \qquad *(\text{B.7.1})$$

The transformation is linear, since

$$\mathbf{A}(\mathbf{x}^1 + \mathbf{x}^2) = \mathbf{A}\mathbf{x}^1 + \mathbf{A}\mathbf{x}^2 \qquad *(\text{B.7.2})$$

$$\mathbf{A}(k\mathbf{x}^1) = k\mathbf{A}(\mathbf{x}^1) \qquad *(\text{B.7.3})$$

where $\mathbf{x}^1$ and $\mathbf{x}^2$ are vectors in E^n and k is any scalar. A property of such linear transformations is

$$\mathbf{A}(\mathbf{0}) = \mathbf{0}. \qquad (\text{B.7.4})$$

A *characteristic vector* for a square matrix, $\mathbf{A}$, is a nonzero vector $\mathbf{x}$, which, when transformed by $\mathbf{A}$, yields the same vector except for a scale factor

$$\mathbf{A}\mathbf{x} = \lambda\mathbf{x} \qquad *(\text{B.7.5})$$

where the scale factor λ is a *characteristic root* of $\mathbf{A}$. Since the above equation can be written

$$(\mathbf{A} - \lambda\mathbf{I})\mathbf{x} = \mathbf{0} \qquad (\text{B.7.6})$$

which is a homogeneous system of equations, a necessary condition for nontrivial solutions, from (B.6.8), is that the coefficient matrix be of less than full rank, so

$$|\mathbf{A} - \lambda\mathbf{I}| = 0. \qquad (\text{B.7.7})$$

The resulting equation for λ is the *characteristic equation*. If $\mathbf{A}$ is an $n \times n$ matrix, the characteristic equation is an nth-order polynomial equation in λ:

$$|\mathbf{A} - \lambda\mathbf{I}| = (-\lambda)^n + \alpha_1(-\lambda)^{n-1} + \cdots + \alpha_{n-1}(-\lambda) + \alpha_n = 0 \qquad (\text{B.7.8})$$

where α_k is the kth-order trace of $\mathbf{A}$, $k = 1, \ldots, n$, as in (B.4.6). For example, in the 2×2 case

$$\begin{aligned} |\mathbf{A} - \lambda\mathbf{I}| &= \begin{vmatrix} a_{11} - \lambda & a_{12} \\ a_{21} & a_{22} - \lambda \end{vmatrix} \\ &= \lambda^2 - (a_{11} + a_{22})\lambda + (a_{11}a_{22} - a_{12}a_{21}) \qquad (\text{B.7.9}) \\ &= 0. \end{aligned}$$

The solution to the characteristic equation consists of n roots, $\lambda_1, \lambda_2, \ldots, \lambda_n$ which are not necessarily all distinct or real. To each of these characteristic roots there corresponds a characteristic vector that is determined up to a constant. For example, if

$$\mathbf{A} = \begin{pmatrix} 6 & 10 \\ -2 & -3 \end{pmatrix}$$

the characteristic equation is $\lambda^2 - 3\lambda + 2 = 0$, yielding $\lambda_1 = 1, \lambda_2 = 2$. The characteristic vector corresponding to λ_1 is

$$\mathbf{x}^1 = \begin{pmatrix} c \\ -c/2 \end{pmatrix}$$

while that corresponding to λ_2 is

$$\mathbf{x}^2 = \begin{pmatrix} c \\ -\frac{2}{5}c \end{pmatrix}$$

where c is any constant. Constants are often eliminated by normalizing the vectors, and the normalized characteristic vectors for this example are, respectively

$$\begin{pmatrix} 2/\sqrt{5} \\ -1/\sqrt{5} \end{pmatrix} \quad \text{and} \quad \begin{pmatrix} 5/\sqrt{29} \\ -2/\sqrt{29} \end{pmatrix}$$

Properties of characteristic roots $\lambda_1, \lambda_2, \ldots, \lambda_n$ of any square matrix **A** include

(i) $\sum_{j=1}^{n} \lambda_j = \text{tr}(\mathbf{A}) = \alpha_1$

(ii) $\prod_{j=1}^{n} \lambda_j = |\mathbf{A}| = \alpha_n$

(iii) $\lambda_j = d_j$ if **A** is the diagonal matrix $(d_j \delta_{ij})$

(iv) $\lambda_j = 1$ or -1 if **A** is orthogonal

(v) $\lambda_j = 1$ or 0 and $\rho(\mathbf{A}) = \Sigma \lambda_j$ if **A** is an idempotent matrix ***(B.7.10)**

(vi) If **A** and **B** are similar matrices, then they have the same characteristic roots

(vii) λ_j^t are the characteristic roots of $\mathbf{A}^t$ if λ_j are the (nonzero) characteristic roots of **A** and t is any positive integer (or any integer if **A** is nonsingular)

Properties of the characteristic roots $\lambda_1, \lambda_2, \ldots, \lambda_n$ and vectors for any *symmetric* matrix **A** include

(i) $\rho(\mathbf{A})$ = the number of nonzero characteristic roots

(ii) The characteristic roots λ_j are all real

(iii) Any two characteristic vectors $\mathbf{x}_j$ and $\mathbf{x}_{j'}$ corresponding to distinct characteristic roots λ_j and $\lambda_{j'}$ are orthogonal, so $\mathbf{x}_j' \mathbf{x}_{j'} = 0$

(iv) If $\mathbf{x}_j$ is a characteristic vector of **A** corresponding to the characteristic root λ_j, then $\mathbf{x}_j' \mathbf{A} \mathbf{x}_j = \lambda_j$ **(B.7.11)**

(v) **A** is similar to a diagonal matrix $\mathbf{\Lambda}$, the diagonal elements of which are the characteristic roots of **A**, so $\mathbf{M}^{-1}\mathbf{A}\mathbf{M} = \mathbf{M}'\mathbf{A}\mathbf{M} = \mathbf{\Lambda}$. Here **M** is the *modal matrix*, an orthogonal matrix the columns of which are the normalized characteristic vectors of **A**.

To give an example, if

$$\mathbf{A} = \begin{pmatrix} 6 & 2 \\ 2 & 3 \end{pmatrix} \quad \text{then} \quad \lambda_1 = 7, \quad \lambda_2 = 2, \quad \text{and} \quad \mathbf{M} = \frac{1}{\sqrt{5}} \begin{pmatrix} 2 & 1 \\ 1 & -2 \end{pmatrix}$$

where $\mathbf{M}'\mathbf{AM} = \begin{pmatrix} 7 & 0 \\ 0 & 2 \end{pmatrix} = \mathbf{\Lambda}$.

B.8 Quadratic forms

Given a square symmetric matrix **A** and a column vector **x**, the *quadratic form* of **A** is[13]

$$\begin{aligned} Q_{\mathbf{A}}(\mathbf{x}) &= \mathbf{x}'\mathbf{A}\mathbf{x} \\ &= \sum_{i=1}^{n} \sum_{j=1}^{n} a_{ij} x_i x_j \\ &= a_{11}x_1^2 + a_{22}x_2^2 + \cdots + a_{nn}x_n^2 + 2a_{12}x_1x_2 + 2a_{13}x_1x_3 \\ &\quad + \cdots + 2a_{n-1\ n}x_{n-1}x_n \end{aligned} \qquad *(\text{B.8.1})$$

For example, if

$$\mathbf{A} = \begin{pmatrix} 1 & 3 \\ 3 & 4 \end{pmatrix} \quad \text{then} \quad Q_{\mathbf{A}}(\mathbf{x}) = x_1^2 + 4x_2^2 + 6x_1x_2$$

while if **D** is the diagonal matrix $(d_j \delta_{ij})$, then $Q_{\mathbf{D}}(\mathbf{x})$ is

$$\sum_{j=1}^{n} d_j x_j^2,$$

the weighted sum of squares.

The quadratic form $Q_{\mathbf{A}}(\mathbf{x})$ is *positive definite* iff $Q_{\mathbf{A}}(\mathbf{x}) > 0$ for all $\mathbf{x} \neq \mathbf{0}$; is *negative definite* iff $Q_{\mathbf{A}}(\mathbf{x}) < 0$ for all $\mathbf{x} \neq \mathbf{0}$; is *positive semidefinite* iff $Q_{\mathbf{A}}(\mathbf{x}) \geqslant 0$ for all **x** and $Q_{\mathbf{A}}(\mathbf{x}) = 0$ for some $\mathbf{x} \neq \mathbf{0}$; is *negative semidefinite* iff $Q_{\mathbf{A}}(\mathbf{x}) \leqslant 0$ for all **x** and $Q_{\mathbf{A}}(\mathbf{x}) = 0$ for some $\mathbf{x} \neq \mathbf{0}$; and otherwise is *indefinite*. Sometimes

[13] The assumption that **A** is symmetric is not restrictive, since

$$Q_{\mathbf{A}}(\mathbf{x}) = \mathbf{x}'\mathbf{A}\mathbf{x} = \Sigma\Sigma a_{ij}x_ix_j = \Sigma\Sigma \tfrac{1}{2}(a_{ij} + a_{ji})x_ix_j$$

It will always be assumed that the matrix of the quadratic form is symmetric.

the related matrix **A** is described as positive definite (etc.) if $Q_{\mathbf{A}}(\mathbf{x})$ is positive definite (etc.). Thus, for example, a diagonal matrix the diagonal elements of which are all positive (negative) is a positive (negative) definite matrix. If, for the diagonal matrix, all diagonal elements are nonnegative (nonpositive) and at least one is zero, then the matrix is positive (negative) semidefinite. Another example is an idempotent matrix, which must be positive semidefinite.

Properties of quadratic forms for the symmetric matrix **A** include

(i) **A** is positive definite iff all characteristic roots of **A** are positive or, equivalently, iff all leading principal minors of **A** are positive
(ii) **A** is negative definite iff all characteristic roots of **A** are negative or, equivalently, iff all leading principal minors of **A** alternate in sign from negative to positive
(iii) **A** is positive (semi) definite iff $-\mathbf{A}$ is negative (semi) definite
(iv) If **A** is positive (negative) definite, then **A** is nonsingular, $\mathbf{A}^{-1}$ exists, and $\mathbf{A}^{-1}$ is positive (negative) definite
(v) If **A** is positive (negative) definite and **P** is nonsingular, then $\mathbf{P}'\mathbf{A}\mathbf{P}$ is positive definite
(vi) If **A** is of order $m \times n$ and $\rho(\mathbf{A}) = n < m$, then $\mathbf{A}'\mathbf{A}$ is positive definite (and nonsingular), while $\mathbf{A}\mathbf{A}'$ is positive semidefinite ***(B.8.2)**
(vii) If **A** is a positive definite matrix, then there exists a nonsingular matrix **P** such that $\mathbf{P}'\mathbf{P} = \mathbf{A}$ and $\mathbf{P}\mathbf{A}^{-1}\mathbf{P}' = \mathbf{I}$. There is also a unique (lower) triangular matrix **T** such that $\mathbf{A} = \mathbf{T}\mathbf{T}'$
(viii) If $\mathbf{x} = \mathbf{M}\mathbf{y}$, where **M** is the modal matrix of (B.7.11) (v), then, from the diagonalization of a symmetric matrix

$$Q_{\mathbf{A}}(\mathbf{x}) = \mathbf{x}'\mathbf{A}\mathbf{x} = \mathbf{y}'\mathbf{\Lambda}\mathbf{y} = \sum_{j=1}^{n} \lambda_j y_j^2$$

so the quadratic form can always be written as a weighted sum of squares, the weights being the characteristic roots.

B.9 Matrix derivatives

It is possible to differentiate matrices or to differentiate with respect to matrices.

Differentiating a vector or matrix with respect to a scalar yields a vector or matrix of derivatives. Thus

(i) If $\mathbf{x} = (x_1, x_2, \ldots, x_n)'$, then

$$\frac{d\mathbf{x}}{dt} = \left(\frac{dx_1}{dt}, \frac{dx_2}{dt}, \ldots, \frac{dx_n}{dt}\right)'$$

(ii) If $\mathbf{A} = (a_{ij})$, then

$$\frac{d\mathbf{A}}{dt} = \left(\frac{da_{ij}}{dt}\right) \qquad *(B.9.1)$$

(iii) $\dfrac{\partial \mathbf{AB}}{\partial t} = \mathbf{A}\dfrac{\partial \mathbf{B}}{\partial t} + \dfrac{\partial \mathbf{A}}{\partial t}\mathbf{B}$

(iv) $\dfrac{\partial \mathbf{A}^{-1}}{\partial t} = -\mathbf{A}^{-1}\dfrac{\partial \mathbf{A}}{\partial t}\mathbf{A}^{-1}$. In particular, letting $\mathbf{A}^{-1} = (a^{gh})$,

$$\frac{\partial a^{gh}}{\partial a_{ij}} = (-a^{gi}a^{jh})$$

where, in all cases, t is a scalar on which some or all of the elements of the vector or matrix depend.

Differentiating a scalar with respect to a column (row) vector yields a row (column) vector.[14] Examples of such derivatives include:

(i) If $y = f(\mathbf{x})$, where $\mathbf{x} = (x_1, x_2, \ldots, x_n)'$, then

$$\frac{\partial y}{\partial \mathbf{x}} = \left(\frac{\partial f}{\partial x_1}, \frac{\partial f}{\partial x_2}, \ldots, \frac{\partial f}{\partial x_n}\right)$$

which is the *gradient vector* $\partial f(\mathbf{x})/\partial \mathbf{x}$

(ii) Given the linear form (inner product) $\mathbf{cx}$,

$$\frac{\partial \mathbf{cx}}{\partial \mathbf{x}} = \mathbf{c} \qquad *(B.9.2)$$

(iii) Given the quadratic form $\mathbf{x}'\mathbf{Ax}$,

$$\frac{\partial \mathbf{x}'\mathbf{Ax}}{\partial \mathbf{x}} = 2\mathbf{x}'\mathbf{A}$$

(iv) Given the bilinear form $\mathbf{wAx}$,

$$\frac{\partial \mathbf{wAx}}{\partial \mathbf{w}} = \mathbf{Ax}, \qquad \frac{\partial \mathbf{wAx}}{\partial \mathbf{x}} = \mathbf{wA}$$

Differentiating a scalar with respect to an $m \times n$ matrix yields an $n \times m$ matrix. Examples of such derivatives include:

[14] This convention follows Intriligator (1971), Appendix B.

(i) Given the quadratic form $\mathbf{x}'\mathbf{A}\mathbf{x}$,

$$\frac{\partial \mathbf{x}'\mathbf{A}\mathbf{x}}{\partial \mathbf{A}} = \mathbf{x}\mathbf{x}'$$

(ii) Given the bilinear form $\mathbf{w}\mathbf{A}\mathbf{x}$,

$$\frac{\partial \mathbf{w}\mathbf{A}\mathbf{x}}{\partial \mathbf{A}} = \mathbf{x}\mathbf{w}$$

(iii) Given the bilinear form $\mathbf{w}\mathbf{A}\mathbf{x}$, where $\mathbf{A}$ is square and nonsingular and where $\mathbf{C} = \mathbf{A}^{-1}$, *(B.9.3)

$$\frac{\partial \mathbf{w}\mathbf{C}^{-1}\mathbf{x}}{\partial \mathbf{C}} = -\mathbf{C}^{-1}\mathbf{x}\mathbf{w}\mathbf{C}^{-1}$$

(iv) If tr $(\mathbf{A})$ = trace of $\mathbf{A}$, then

$$\frac{\partial \operatorname{tr}(\mathbf{A})}{\partial \mathbf{A}} = \mathbf{I}$$

(v) If $|\mathbf{A}|$ = determinant of $\mathbf{A}$, then

$$\frac{\partial |\mathbf{A}|}{\partial \mathbf{A}} = |\mathbf{A}|\mathbf{A}^{-1}$$

$$\frac{\partial \ln |\mathbf{A}|}{\partial \mathbf{A}} = \mathbf{A}^{-1} \qquad \text{(assuming } |\mathbf{A}| > 0\text{)}$$

Differentiating a vector with respect to a vector yields a matrix. Examples of such derivatives include:

(i) $\partial \mathbf{A}\mathbf{x}/\partial \mathbf{x} = \mathbf{A}$
(ii) If $(\partial f/\partial \mathbf{x})$ is the gradient vector, then

$$\frac{\partial}{\partial \mathbf{x}}\left(\frac{\partial f}{\partial \mathbf{x}}\right) = \frac{\partial^2 f}{\partial \mathbf{x}^2} = \frac{\partial^2 f}{\partial x_i \partial x_j}$$

which is the *Hessian matrix* (a symmetric matrix)

(iii) If $\mathbf{g} = \mathbf{g}(\mathbf{x}) = [g_1(\mathbf{x}), g_2(\mathbf{x}), \ldots, g_m(\mathbf{x})]$, where $\mathbf{x} = (x_1, x_2, \ldots, x_n)$, then *(B.9.4)

$$\frac{\partial \mathbf{g}}{\partial \mathbf{x}}(\mathbf{x}) = \left(\frac{\partial g_i}{\partial x_j}\right)$$

which is the *Jacobian matrix*.

B.10 Mathematical programming[15]

The problem of mathematical programming is that of choosing the column vector $\mathbf{x} = (x_1, x_2, \ldots, x_n)'$ within the set X in Euclidean n-space E^n so as to

$$\max_{\mathbf{x}} F(\mathbf{x}) \quad \text{subject to} \quad \mathbf{x} \in X \subset E^n. \qquad \text{*(B.10.1)}$$

A problem of minimization, e.g., that of minimizing $G(\mathbf{x})$, can be formulated as one of maximizing $-G(x)$.

A global maximum is defined as a point $\mathbf{x}^0$ for which

$$\mathbf{x}^0 \in X \quad \text{and} \quad F(\mathbf{x}^0) \geqslant F(\mathbf{x}) \qquad \text{for all } \mathbf{x} \in X. \qquad \text{*(B.10.2)}$$

Such a global maximum always exists, by the Weierstrass theorem, if the function $F(\cdot)$ is continuous and the set X is closed and bounded. A local maximum is defined as $\mathbf{x}^0$ for which

$$\mathbf{x}^0 \in X \quad \text{and} \quad F(\mathbf{x}^0) \geqslant F(x) \quad \text{for all } \mathbf{x} \in X, \text{where } \mathbf{x} \in N_\epsilon(\mathbf{x}^0) \quad \text{*(B.10.3)}$$

and where $N_\epsilon(\mathbf{x}^0)$ is an ϵ-neighborhood of $\mathbf{x}^0$. A local maximum is thus a maximum relative to "nearby" points. Clearly a global maximum is a local maximum, but not necessarily vice versa.

In the unconstrained case, when the set X is the entire space E^n, so the problem is

$$\max_{\mathbf{x}} F(\mathbf{x}) \qquad \text{*(B.10.4)}$$

a first-order necessary condition for $\mathbf{x}^0$ to be a local maximum of $F(\mathbf{x})$ is that the gradient vector defined in (B.9.2) (i) vanish:

$$\frac{\partial F}{\partial \mathbf{x}}(\mathbf{x}^0) = \mathbf{0} \qquad \text{*(B.10.5)}$$

so that the point is a *stationary point* at which all first-order partial derivatives vanish. A second-order necessary condition is that the Hessian matrix defined in (B.9.4) (ii), evaluated at this point, be negative definite or negative semidefinite:

$$\frac{\partial^2 F}{\partial \mathbf{x}^2}(\mathbf{x}^0) \text{ negative definite or negative semidefinite.} \qquad \text{*(B.10.6)}$$

[15] See Intriligator (1971), especially Chapters 2 and 3.

Sufficient conditions for $\mathbf{x}^0$ to be a local maximum are

$$\frac{\partial F}{\partial \mathbf{x}}(\mathbf{x}^0) = \mathbf{0}$$

$$\frac{\partial^2 F}{\partial \mathbf{x}^2}(\mathbf{x}^0) \text{ negative definite.} \qquad *(\text{B.10.7})$$

An example is the problem of least squares, as in (B.6.10), where the problem is one of minimizing the sum of squares. The problem is

$$\max_{\boldsymbol{\beta}} - S(\boldsymbol{\beta}) = -(\mathbf{y} - \mathbf{X}\boldsymbol{\beta})'(\mathbf{y} - \mathbf{X}\boldsymbol{\beta}) = -\mathbf{y}'\mathbf{y} + 2\boldsymbol{\beta}'\mathbf{X}'\mathbf{y} - \boldsymbol{\beta}'\mathbf{X}'\mathbf{X}\boldsymbol{\beta} \qquad (\text{B.10.8})$$

and the first-order conditions state that

$$\frac{\partial S}{\partial \boldsymbol{\beta}'} = 2\mathbf{X}'\mathbf{y} - 2(\mathbf{X}'\mathbf{X})\boldsymbol{\beta} = \mathbf{0}. \qquad (\text{B.10.9})$$

The second-order sufficiency condition is met, since, assuming $\rho(\mathbf{X}) = k$,

$$\frac{\partial^2 S}{\partial \boldsymbol{\beta}'^2} = -2(\mathbf{X}'\mathbf{X}) \text{ negative definite.} \qquad (\text{B.10.10})$$

Solving for the vector $\boldsymbol{\beta}$ that minimizes $S(\boldsymbol{\beta})$ from (B.10.9) yields

$$\hat{\boldsymbol{\beta}} = (\mathbf{X}'\mathbf{X})^{-1}\mathbf{X}'\mathbf{y} \qquad (\text{B.10.11})$$

as in (B.6.13).

In the classically constrained case the set X is defined by a set of m equality constraints, so

$$X = \left\{\mathbf{x} \mid \mathbf{g}(\mathbf{x}) = \mathbf{b}\right\}. \qquad (\text{B.10.12})$$

Here

$$\mathbf{g}(\mathbf{x}) = \begin{pmatrix} g_1(x_1, x_2, \ldots, x_n) \\ g_2(x_1, x_2, \ldots, x_n) \\ \vdots \\ g_m(x_1, x_2, \ldots, x_n) \end{pmatrix}, \quad \mathbf{b} = \begin{pmatrix} b_1 \\ b_2 \\ \vdots \\ b_m \end{pmatrix} \qquad (\text{B.10.13})$$

and $n > m$; that is, there are more variables to choose than there are constraints.

Thus the problem can be stated:[16]

$$\max_{\mathbf{x}} F(\mathbf{x}) \quad \text{subject to} \quad \mathbf{g}(\mathbf{x}) = \mathbf{b}. \qquad *(B.10.14)$$

A classical approach to solving this problem is the *method of Lagrange multipliers*. It utilizes a row vector of m additional new variables,

$$\boldsymbol{\lambda} = (\lambda_1 \lambda_2 \cdots \lambda_m) \qquad (B.10.15)$$

one for each constraint. These variables are called *Lagrange multipliers* and they are used to define a Lagrangian function

$$L(\mathbf{x}, \boldsymbol{\lambda}) = F(\mathbf{x}) + \boldsymbol{\lambda}[\mathbf{b} - \mathbf{g}(\mathbf{x})] \qquad *(B.10.16)$$

where the last term is the inner product of a row vector and a column vector. A necessary first-order condition for solving (B.10.4) are then the $n + m$ conditions[17]

$$\begin{aligned} \frac{\partial L}{\partial \mathbf{x}} &= \frac{\partial F}{\partial \mathbf{x}} - \boldsymbol{\lambda} \frac{\partial \mathbf{g}}{\partial \mathbf{x}} = \mathbf{0} \qquad (n \text{ conditions}) \\ \frac{\partial L}{\partial \boldsymbol{\lambda}} &= \mathbf{b} - \mathbf{g}(\mathbf{x}) = \mathbf{0} \qquad (m \text{ conditions}). \end{aligned} \qquad *(B.10.17)$$

Thus, at the solution $\mathbf{x}^0$ the constraint $\mathbf{g}(\mathbf{x}^0) = \mathbf{b}$ is met and, in addition,

$$\frac{\partial F}{\partial \mathbf{x}}(\mathbf{x}^0) = \boldsymbol{\lambda} \frac{\partial \mathbf{g}}{\partial \mathbf{x}}(\mathbf{x}^0). \qquad (B.10.18)$$

As an example, suppose the sum of squares $S(\boldsymbol{\beta})$ in (B.10.8) is to be minimized subject to the m linear constraints[18]

$$\mathbf{A}\boldsymbol{\beta} = \mathbf{c} \qquad (B.10.19)$$

where $\mathbf{A}$ is a given $m \times k$ matrix of rank m and $\mathbf{c}$ is a given $m \times 1$ vector. The Lagrangian for this problem of least squares subject to linear constraints is

$$L = -\mathbf{y}'\mathbf{y} + 2\boldsymbol{\beta}'\mathbf{X}'\mathbf{y} - \boldsymbol{\beta}'\mathbf{X}'\mathbf{X}\boldsymbol{\beta} + \boldsymbol{\lambda}(\mathbf{c} - \mathbf{A}\boldsymbol{\beta}). \qquad (B.10.20)$$

Using the conditions in (B.10.17),

[16] It is assumed that the constraints are independent in that $\rho(\partial \mathbf{g}/\partial \mathbf{x}) = m$, where $\partial \mathbf{g}/\partial \mathbf{x}$ is the Jacobian matrix of (B.9.4) (iii).

[17] For a discussion of the second-order conditions see Intriligator (1971).

[18] See Theil (1971).

$$\frac{\partial L}{\partial \boldsymbol{\beta}'} = 2\mathbf{X}'\mathbf{y} - 2\mathbf{X}'\mathbf{X}\boldsymbol{\beta} - \mathbf{A}'\boldsymbol{\lambda}' = \mathbf{0} \qquad (k \text{ conditions})$$
$$\frac{\partial L}{\partial \boldsymbol{\lambda}} = \mathbf{c} - \mathbf{A}\boldsymbol{\beta} = \mathbf{0} \qquad (m \text{ conditions}). \tag{B.10.21}$$

From the first set of conditions

$$\boldsymbol{\beta} = (\mathbf{X}'\mathbf{X})^{-1}(\mathbf{X}'\mathbf{y} - \tfrac{1}{2}\mathbf{A}'\boldsymbol{\lambda}') \tag{B.10.22}$$

so, using the constraint,

$$\mathbf{A}(\mathbf{X}'\mathbf{X})^{-1}\mathbf{X}'\mathbf{y} - \tfrac{1}{2}\mathbf{A}(\mathbf{X}'\mathbf{X})^{-1}\mathbf{A}'\boldsymbol{\lambda}' = \mathbf{c}. \tag{B.10.23}$$

This equation may be solved for $\boldsymbol{\lambda}'$ as

$$\boldsymbol{\lambda}' = 2[\mathbf{A}(\mathbf{X}'\mathbf{X})^{-1}\mathbf{A}']^{-1}[\mathbf{A}(\mathbf{X}'\mathbf{X})^{-1}\mathbf{X}'\mathbf{y} - \mathbf{c}]. \tag{B.10.24}$$

Finally, inserting this value in (B.10.22) yields

$$\hat{\hat{\boldsymbol{\beta}}} = (\mathbf{X}'\mathbf{X})^{-1}\mathbf{X}'\mathbf{y} - (\mathbf{X}'\mathbf{X})^{-1}\mathbf{A}'[\mathbf{A}(\mathbf{X}'\mathbf{X})^{-1}\mathbf{A}']^{-1}[\mathbf{A}(\mathbf{X}'\mathbf{X})^{-1}\mathbf{X}'\mathbf{y} - \mathbf{c}]. \tag{B.10.25}$$

This is the least-squares estimator subject to the additional linear constraints that $\mathbf{A}\boldsymbol{\beta} = \mathbf{c}$. In terms of the ordinary estimator $\hat{\boldsymbol{\beta}}$ in (B.10.11),

$$\hat{\hat{\boldsymbol{\beta}}} = \hat{\boldsymbol{\beta}} - (\mathbf{X}'\mathbf{X})^{-1}\mathbf{A}'[\mathbf{A}(\mathbf{X}'\mathbf{X})^{-1}\mathbf{A}']^{-1}[\mathbf{A}\hat{\boldsymbol{\beta}} - \mathbf{c}]. \tag{B.10.26}$$

If $\hat{\boldsymbol{\beta}}$ satisfies the constraints, then $\hat{\hat{\boldsymbol{\beta}}} = \hat{\boldsymbol{\beta}}$. More generally, the difference between the estimators $\hat{\hat{\boldsymbol{\beta}}} - \hat{\boldsymbol{\beta}}$ is a linear function of the amounts by which the ordinary estimator fails to satisfy the constraints, $\mathbf{A}\hat{\boldsymbol{\beta}} - \mathbf{c}$.

BIBLIOGRAPHY

Graybill, F. A. (1969), *Introduction to Matrices with Applications in Statistics*, Belmont, Calif.: Wadsworth Publishing Co., Inc.

Hadley, G. (1961), *Linear Algebra*. Reading, Mass.: Addison-Wesley Publishing Co., Inc.

Horst, P. (1963), *Matrix Algebra for Social Scientists*. New York: Holt, Rinehart, & Winston.

Intriligator, M. D. (1971), *Mathematical Optimization and Economic Theory*. Englewood Cliffs, N.J.: Prentice-Hall, Inc.

Theil, H. (1971), *Principles of Econometrics*. New York: John Wiley & Sons, Inc.

APPENDIX C

Probability and Statistics[1]

C.1 Probability

The concept of probability underlies the whole field of statistics and thus also econometrics, which is based upon statistical foundations.[2] Consider the *sample space* S, the set of all possible outcomes of a (conceptual) experiment, and let the subsets $A, B, \ldots$ of S represent possible *events*. The *probability* of an event is defined as a real-valued function mapping the subsets of S into the closed interval $[0, 1]$ on the real line, where $P(A)$ is the probability of event A. The probabilities, which can be interpreted either as the real-valued function or values taken by this function, satisfy the following three axioms:

$$0 \leqslant P(A) \leqslant 1 \tag*{*(C.1.1)}$$

$$P(\emptyset) = 0, \qquad P(S) = 1 \tag*{*(C.1.2)}$$

$$P(A \cup B) = P(A) + P(B) - P(AB) \tag*{*(C.1.3)}$$

The first fundamental axiom (C.1.1) states that the probability of any event is a nonnegative real number not larger than unity. A probability of zero means the event is essentially impossible, while a probability of one means the event is essentially certain. The second axiom (C.1.2) states that the empty set $\emptyset$ is impossible and that the entire set S is certain in that some event must occur and S includes all possible events. The third axiom (C.1.3) states that the probability of a union of two events is the sum of the probabilities of each taken individually less the probability of the joint event that both occur, where $P(AB) = P(A \cap B)$. Thus, in particular, if the two events are disjoint ($A \cap B = \emptyset$), the probability of the union of the two events is the sum of the probabilities of the separate events.[3]

There are several possible interpretations of probability. The classical examples

[1] Basic references on statistics are Cramer (1946), Wilks (1962), Fisz (1963), and Rao (1965). Good introductory books are Fraser (1958), Hoel (1971), and Mood, Graybill and Boes (1974).

[2] Basic references on probability are Fisz (1963) and Feller (1968).

[3] More generally, given a finite or infinite sequence of disjoint subsets A_i of S,

$$P\left(\bigcup_{i=1}^{n} A_i\right) = \sum_{i=1}^{n} P(A_i) \quad \text{where} \quad A_i \cap A_j = \emptyset \text{ for } i \neq j$$

of coin tossing or rolling dice suggest a *relative-frequency* interpretation, where

$$P(A) = \frac{\text{number of times } A \text{ occurs}}{\text{total number of trials}} = \frac{N(A)}{N}. \qquad \textbf{*(C.1.4)}$$

This relative-frequency interpretation is meaningful and real. It usually, however, makes sense only in the context of rather stylized experiments of the sort described and utilized almost exclusively by statisticians, such as tossing coins, rolling dice, or selecting colored balls out of urns. For the purposes of social science research, and particularly econometrics, a more reasonable interpretation of probability is that of *limiting relative frequency*, where, using the notation of (C.1.4),

$$P(A) = \lim_{N \to \infty} \frac{N(A)}{N}. \qquad \textbf{*(C.1.5)}$$

One therefore imagines a whole series of experiments in which the limiting (asymptotic) ratio of the number of times A occurs to the total number of trials is the probability of A. To give an example, a statement such as "The probability that GNP will be between \$1400 and \$1700 billion next year is 0.9" means that if all the conditions for the next year could be replicated many times and GNP were calculated for each replication, 90% of the replications would involve a level of GNP between \$1400 and \$1700 billion.

A third interpretation of probability, which has been used in social science and even in econometrics, is that of *subjective degree of belief*. Under this interpretation each individual forms his or her own assessment of the likelihood of events, and the probability is a measure of this assessment.[4] Thus a higher probability of an event means a greater belief that the event will occur. Economic forecasts are sometimes based on such probabilities. With this interpretation the statement "The probability that GNP will be between \$1400 and \$1700 billion next year is 0.9" means that the individual making the statement would be indifferent between betting that GNP next year will fall in this range or betting that a randomly selected digit in a table of random digits will be a number other than zero.

Given a set of probabilities, under any of the interpretations given here there is defined a *calculus of probabilities*. Thus, for example, *conditional probabilities* are defined as

$$P(A \mid B) = \frac{P(AB)}{P(B)}. \qquad \textbf{*(C.1.6)}$$

Since

$$P(AB) = P(A \mid B)\,P(B) = P(B \mid A)\,P(A) \qquad \textbf{(C.1.7)}$$

it follows that

[4] See Savage (1954), Raiffa (1968), and De Groot (1969).

$$P(B \mid A) = \frac{P(B)P(A \mid B)}{P(A)}. \qquad \textbf{(C.1.8)}$$

If the events $B_1, B_2, \ldots, B_n$ form a mutually exclusive and exhaustive set of events–i.e.,

$$P(B_iB_j) = 0 \qquad \text{for } i \neq j \qquad \textbf{(C.1.9)}$$

$$P\left(\bigcup_{i=1}^{n} B_i\right) = 1 \qquad \textbf{(C.1.10)}$$

then it follows that

$$P(A) = \sum_{i=1}^{n} P(B_i)P(A \mid B_i). \qquad \textbf{(C.1.11)}$$

Thus (C.1.8) implies that

$$P(B_i \mid A) = \frac{P(B_i)P(A \mid B_i)}{\Sigma\, P(B_i)P(A \mid B_i)}. \qquad \textbf{*(C.1.12)}$$

This result, known as *Bayes' theorem*, forms the foundation of Bayesian statistics, which involves yet another interpretation of probabilities.[5] Interpret $P(B_i \mid A)$ in (C.1.12) as the probability of the ith hypothesis B_i, given the observation, event A. According to Bayes' theorem this probability is obtained as the product of the *prior probability* of the hypothesis $P(B_i)$ times the *likelihood* of the observation A, given the hypothesis, $P(A \mid B_i)$, normalized by dividing by the sum of all such products of likelihoods and prior probabilities. The result is the *posterior probability* $P(B_i \mid A)$–that is, the probability after observing the event A. Bayes' theorem thus represents a rule for generating posterior probabilities from prior probabilities and likelihoods. If the prior probability is interpreted as a subjective degree of belief, the posterior probability combines this subjective belief with objective information on an observed event, A, to determine a hybrid subjective-objective probability. The rule can be used again and again, however, at each stage taking account of the prior probability, which has taken the past observations into account, and the current observations. The limit of this process is an objective probability, independent of the initial subjective degree of belief (unless the prior belief is held with certainty). It can be interpreted as a limiting relative frequency as in (C.1.5). Thus Bayes' theorem (C.1.12) represents a bridge between two interpretations of probability.

[5] For a discussion of the Bayesian approach to econometrics see Section 5.7.

C.2 Random variables; distribution and density functions

A *random variable* is a real-valued function defined on a sample space. If S is the sample space, the space of all possible events, the random variable X is a mapping from S into the real line:

$$X: S \to E. \qquad *(C.2.1)$$

For example, if S consists of the events heads (H) and tails (T) obtained by tossing a coin, one possible random variable defined on this sample space would be

$$X(H) = 1, \quad X(T) = 0 \qquad (C.2.2)$$

but, of course, many other random variables could be defined on this sample space. Usually the problem suggests a convenient choice of random variable. Thus, if the sample space consists of all possible values of GNP, the random variable may be defined simply as the value taken by GNP. Thus, for example, for a GNP of \$1500 billion

$$X(\$1500 \text{ billion}) = 1500. \qquad (C.2.3)$$

The term "random variable" can apply to either the function, as in (C.2.1), or the values taken by the function. In the latter interpretation the random variable can be finite or countable. Thus the head-tail example of (C.2.2) defines a finite random variable, while the GNP example defines a countable random variable, since the values assumed by the random variable include all the positive integers. Continuous random variables are also possible, where the values assumed by the random variable define a continuum of points on the real line. In fact, the emphasis below, corresponding to that in econometrics, will be on continuous random variables.[6]

Given a random variable X, the *distribution function* $F(x)$ is defined as

$$F(x) = P(-\infty < X \leqslant x) \qquad *(C.2.4)$$

—that is, as the probability that the values assumed by the random variable are less than or equal to the value x. For example, for the random variable defined by (C.2.2), if the coin is a fair coin,

$$F(x) = \begin{Bmatrix} 0 \\ \frac{1}{2} \\ 1 \end{Bmatrix} \text{ for } \begin{Bmatrix} x < 0 \\ 0 \leqslant x < 1 \\ 1 \leqslant x \end{Bmatrix} \qquad (C.2.5)$$

Since $F(x)$ is a probability, it must satisfy

$$0 \leqslant F(x) \leqslant 1, \quad \text{all } x \qquad (C.2.6)$$

[6] For discussions of discrete statistics see the basic references of the first footnote. See also the next footnote.

where, taking limits,

$$\lim_{x\to-\infty} F(x) = F(-\infty) = 0, \qquad \lim_{x\to\infty} F(x) = F(\infty) = 1. \tag{C.2.7}$$

The distribution function is nondecreasing in that

$$F(x) \geqslant F(x') \quad \text{if} \quad x \geqslant x' \tag{C.2.8}$$

so, assuming the random variable is continuous and $F(x)$ is a differentiable function

$$\frac{dF(x)}{dx} \geqslant 0, \qquad -\infty < x < \infty. \tag{C.2.9}$$

Geometrically, then, the distribution function is a curve that is nonnegative, "starting" at zero and "ending" at unity, nowhere falling in value.

Given a differentiable distribution function $F(x)$, the *density function* $f(x)$ is defined as the derivative of $F(x)$ evaluated at x:

$$f(x) = \lim_{\Delta x\to 0} \frac{F(x+\Delta x) - F(x)}{\Delta x} = \frac{dF(x)}{dx} \geqslant 0, \qquad -\infty < x < \infty. \tag*{*(C.2.10)}$$

The *probability element* is defined as

$$dF(x) = f(x)\,dx = P(x < X \leqslant x + dx) \geqslant 0. \tag*{*(C.2.11)}$$

Integrating the probability element from a to b, where $a < b$,[7]

$$\int_a^b dF(x) = \int_a^b f(x)\,dx = F(b) - F(a) = P(a < X \leqslant b) \tag*{*(C.2.12)}$$

so the definite integral of the density function has the interpretation of a probability. Taking the limit as $a \to -\infty$,

$$\int_{-\infty}^{b} f(x)\,dx = F(b) = P(-\infty < X \leqslant x) \quad \text{so} \quad \int_{-\infty}^{x} f(\xi)\,d\xi = F(x) \tag*{*(C.2.13)}$$

expressing the relation between the distribution and density function in integral form, the relation having been previously expressed in differential form in (C.2.10). Taking the limit as $b \to \infty$, using (C.2.7),

$$\int_{-\infty}^{\infty} f(\xi)\,d\xi = 1. \tag{C.2.14}$$

[7] Integrals are used here and below because of the emphasis on *continuous* rather than discrete distributions. In the discrete case the integrals would be replaced by summation signs with appropriate limits.

Geometrically, then, the density function is a curve that is nonnegative, can rise above unity, can fall in value, but has "under" it a unit area. Any function $f(x)$ satisfying these conditions can be interpreted as a density function. The relation between distribution and density function is illustrated in Figure C.1. When $F(x)$ is "flat," $f(x)$ is zero, and when $F(x)$ reaches an inflection point, $f(x)$ is at a

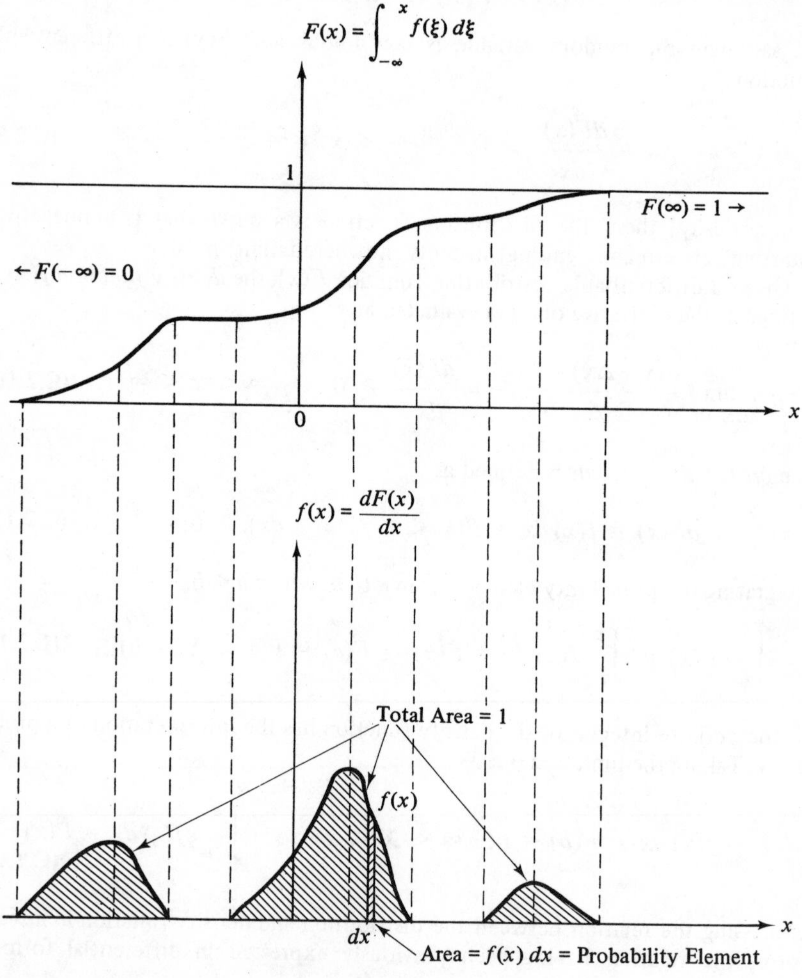

Figure C.1 Distribution and Density Functions

maximum. The total shaded area "under" $f(x)$ is unity. Note that $f(x)$ is *not* a probability, even though $f(x)\,dx$, the probability element, is.

The correspondence between the distribution function and the axioms of probability should be clear. Thus (C.2.6) corresponds to (C.1.1), and (C.2.7) corresponds to (C.1.2). Finally, by the definition of the definite integral,

$$F(x) = \int_{-\infty}^{y} f(\xi)\, d\xi + \int_{y}^{x} f(\xi)\, d\xi = P(X \leqslant y) + P(y < X \leqslant x) = P(X \leqslant x) \tag{C.2.15}$$

corresponding to (C.1.3).

The concepts introduced thus far refer to a *single* random variable, the *univariate* case. They can be extended readily, however, to the *multivariate* case. In the multivariate case there are m real-valued functions defined on the sample space, so

$$\mathbf{X}: S \rightarrow E^m. \qquad \text{*(C.2.16)}$$

Thus the *m-dimensional random variable* (or m-vector valued random variable) $\mathbf{X}$ maps the sample space S into Euclidean m-space, the space of all m-tuples of real numbers.[8] The random variable is summarized by the column vector

$$\underset{m \times 1}{\mathbf{X}} = \begin{pmatrix} X_1 \\ X_2 \\ \vdots \\ X_m \end{pmatrix} = (X_1 \quad X_2 \quad \cdots \quad X_m)' \tag{C.2.17}$$

where X_j is the jth random variable, $j = 1, 2, \ldots, m$. The *distribution function* is then

$$F(\mathbf{x}) = F(x_1, x_2, \ldots, x_m) = P(-\infty < X_1 \leqslant x_1, -\infty < X_2 \leqslant x_2, \ldots, -\infty < X_m \leqslant x_m) \qquad \text{*(C.2.18)}$$

–that is the probability that each of the m random variables is less than the corresponding given value. This definition reduces to (C.2.4) in the *univariate case*, the special case in which $m = 1$; and the *bivariate case* is that for which $m = 2$. As before, since $F(\mathbf{x})$ is a probability,

$$0 \leqslant F(\mathbf{x}) \leqslant 1. \tag{C.2.19}$$

Generalizing (C.2.7),

$$F(x_1, x_2, \ldots, x_m) = 0 \quad \text{if any } x_j = -\infty, \quad j = 1, 2, \ldots, m \tag{C.2.20}$$

$$F(x_1, x_2, \ldots, x_m) = 1 \quad \text{if all } x_j = \infty, \quad j = 1, 2, \ldots, m. \tag{C.2.21}$$

Assuming differentiability of $F(\mathbf{x})$, generalizing (C.2.9),

$$\frac{\partial F}{\partial x_j}(\mathbf{x}) \geqslant 0, \quad j = 1, 2, \ldots, m. \tag{C.2.22}$$

[8] For discussions of *multivariate statistics*, the study of multivariate random variables, see Anderson (1958), Kendall and Stuart (1958), Graybill (1961), and Rao (1965). See also Scheffé (1959) and Searle (1971).

The *density function* is $f(\mathbf{x})$, defined as

$$f(\mathbf{x}) = \frac{\partial^m F}{\partial x_1 \, \partial x_2 \cdots \partial x_m} \qquad (\mathbf{x}) \geqslant 0 \qquad \text{*(C.2.23)}$$

so the *probability element* is

$$\begin{aligned} dF(\mathbf{x}) &= f(x_1, x_2, \ldots, x_m)\, dx_1\, dx_2 \cdots dx_m \\ &= P(x_j < X_j < x_j + dx_j,\ j = 1, 2, \ldots, m) \geqslant 0. \end{aligned} \qquad \text{*(C.2.24)}$$

Integrating the probability element,

$$\int_{-\infty}^{b_m} \cdots \int_{-\infty}^{b_1} f(x_1, x_2, \ldots, x_m)\, dx_1\, dx_2 \cdots dx_m = F(b_1, b_2, \ldots, b_m) \qquad \text{*(C.2.25)}$$

Thus the relation between the density function and the distribution function can be written in integral form:

$$\int_{-\infty}^{x_m} \cdots \int_{-\infty}^{x_1} f(\xi_1, \xi_2, \ldots, \xi_m)\, d\xi_1\, d\xi_2 \cdots d\xi_m = F(x_1, x_2, \ldots, x_m) \qquad \text{*(C.2.26)}$$

an alternate form to the differential form of (C.2.23). From (C.2.21)

$$\int_{-\infty}^{\infty} \cdots \int_{-\infty}^{\infty} f(\xi_1, \xi_2, \ldots, \xi_m)\, d\xi_1\, d\xi_2 \cdots d\xi_m = F(\infty, \infty, \ldots, \infty) = 1. \qquad \text{(C.2.27)}$$

Furthermore, from the definition of the probability element (C.2.24),

$$\begin{aligned} \int_{a_m}^{b_m} \cdots \int_{a_1}^{b_1} & f(\xi_1, \xi_2, \ldots, \xi_m)\, d\xi_1\, d\xi_2 \cdots d\xi_m \\ &= F(b_1, b_2, \ldots, b_m) - F(a_1, a_2, \ldots, a_m) \qquad \text{*(C.2.28)} \\ &= P(a_j < X_j < b_j,\ j = 1, 2, \ldots, m). \end{aligned}$$

Geometrically the multivariate case can be illustrated in the bivariate case $m = 2$, as the three-dimensional density function surface $f(x_1, x_2)$. This surface has, at any point (x_1, x_2), a nonnegative value, and the total volume enclosed by the surface is unity, i.e.,

$$f(x_1, x_2) \geqslant 0, \qquad \int_{-\infty}^{\infty} \int_{-\infty}^{\infty} f(\xi_1, \xi_2)\, d\xi_1\, d\xi_2 = 1. \qquad \text{(C.2.29)}$$

Given a partition of the random variable $\mathbf{X}$ as

$$\mathbf{X} = \begin{pmatrix} \mathbf{X}_1 \\ \hdashline \mathbf{X}_2 \end{pmatrix} \begin{matrix} p \\ \\ m-p \end{matrix} \tag{C.2.30}$$

where $\mathbf{X}_1$ is a column vector of p elements and $\mathbf{X}_2$ is a column vector of $m - p$ elements ($p < m$), the *marginal distribution function* of $\mathbf{X}_1$ is defined as

$$F_1(\mathbf{x}_1) = F_1(x_1, x_2, \ldots, x_p) = F(x_1, x_2, \ldots, x_p, \infty, \infty, \ldots, \infty) \tag{C.2.31}$$

and the *marginal density function* of $\mathbf{X}_1$ is defined as

$$f_1(\mathbf{x}_1) = f_1(x_1, x_2, \ldots, x_p) = \frac{\partial^p F_1(x_1, x_2, \ldots, x_p)}{\partial x_1\, \partial x_2 \cdots \partial x_p}. \tag{C.2.32}$$

The set of random variables $\mathbf{X}_1$ is *statistically independent* of the set $\mathbf{X}_2$ if

$$F(\mathbf{x}) = F(\mathbf{x}_1 | \mathbf{x}_2) = F_1(\mathbf{x}_1)F_2(\mathbf{x}_2) \quad \text{so} \quad f(\mathbf{x}) = f_1(\mathbf{x}_1)f_2(\mathbf{x}_2) \tag{C.2.33}$$

In particular, the set $X_1, X_2, \ldots, X_m$ is *mutually independent* if

$$F(x_1, x_2, \ldots, x_m) = F_1(x_1)F_2(x_2) \cdots F_m(x_m) \tag{C.2.34}$$

where $F_j(x_j)$ is the marginal distribution function of X_j. The *conditional density* of $\mathbf{X}_1$ given $\mathbf{X}_2$ is

$$f(\mathbf{x}_1 | \mathbf{x}_2) = \frac{f(x_1, x_2, \ldots, x_m)}{f_2(x_{p+1} x_{p+2} \cdots x_m)} = \frac{f(\mathbf{x})}{f_2(\mathbf{x}_2)}. \tag{C.2.35}$$

If $\mathbf{X}_1$ and $\mathbf{X}_2$ are statistically independent, then

$$f(\mathbf{x}) = f_1(\mathbf{x}_1)f_2(\mathbf{x}_2) \quad \text{so} \quad f(\mathbf{x}_1 | \mathbf{x}_2) = f_1(\mathbf{x}_1). \tag{C.2.36}$$

C.3 Mean, variance, covariance, and other moments; sample measures

Given a univariate random variable, the mean of the random variable is defined as

$$\mu = \int_{-\infty}^{\infty} x f(x)\, dx. \qquad \text{*(C.3.1)}$$

This definition may be motivated by noting that the mean is obtained by taking any value x, "weighting" it by the probability element $f(x)\,dx$, and adding (integrating) over all such x. Geometrically the mean is the center of gravity of the density function $f(x)$, the point where a template cut out in the shape of $f(x)$ "just balances." It is a measure of central tendency. In the multivariate case the *jth mean* of **X** is defined as

$$\mu_j = \int_{-\infty}^{\infty} \cdots \int_{-\infty}^{\infty} x_j f(x_1, x_2, \ldots, x_m)\, dx_1\, dx_2 \cdots dx_m, \quad j = 1, 2, \ldots, m \qquad *(C.3.2)$$

and $\boldsymbol{\mu}$ is the column vector of all m of these means:

$$\underset{m \times 1}{\boldsymbol{\mu}} = (\mu_1, \mu_2, \ldots, \mu_m)'. \qquad (C.3.3)$$

Geometrically, the mean $\boldsymbol{\mu}$ is the center of gravity of the density function $f(x_1, x_2, \ldots, x_m)$, located where the surface defined by this function "just balances."

Returning to the univariate case, the *variance* of the random variable is defined as

$$\text{Var}(x) = \sigma^2 = \int_{-\infty}^{\infty} (x - \mu)^2 f(x)\, dx \geqslant 0. \qquad *(C.3.4)$$

Here deviations of x from the mean μ are squared to eliminate the sign, weighted by the probability element, and summed over all possible x values. The variance is a measure of the dispersion of the distribution. In the multivariate case the *jth variance* of **X** is

$$\text{Var}(x_j) = \sigma_j^2 = \sigma_{jj}$$
$$= \int_{-\infty}^{\infty} \cdots \int_{-\infty}^{\infty} (x_j - \mu_j)^2 f(x_1, x_2, \ldots, x_m)\, dx_1\, dx_2 \cdots dx_m \geqslant 0,$$
$$j = 1, 2, \ldots, m \qquad *(C.3.5)$$

so there are m such variances, measuring the dispersion in each coordinate direction. The jj' covariance of **X** is defined in this case as

$$\text{Cov}(x_j x_{j'}) = \sigma_{jj'}$$
$$= \int_{-\infty}^{\infty} \cdots \int_{-\infty}^{\infty} (x_j - \mu_j)(x_{j'} - \mu_{j'})\, f(x_1, x_2, \ldots, x_m) \qquad *(C.3.6)$$
$$dx_1\, dx_2 \cdots dx_m, \quad j, j' = 1, 2, \ldots, m$$

so the variance is the special case corresponding to $j = j'$—that is, $\sigma_{jj} = \sigma_j^2$. The matrix of all variances and covariances is the *covariance matrix* of **X**:

$$\underset{m\times m}{\text{Cov}(\mathbf{x})} = \boldsymbol{\Sigma} = \begin{pmatrix} \sigma_{11} & \sigma_{12} & \cdots & \sigma_{1m} \\ \sigma_{21} & \sigma_{22} & \cdots & \sigma_{2m} \\ \vdots & & & \\ \sigma_{m1} & \sigma_{m2} & \cdots & \sigma_{mm} \end{pmatrix} = \begin{pmatrix} \sigma_1^2 & \sigma_{12} & \cdots & \sigma_{1m} \\ \sigma_{21} & \sigma_2^2 & \cdots & \sigma_{2m} \\ \vdots & & & \\ \sigma_{m1} & \sigma_{m2} & \cdots & \sigma_m^2 \end{pmatrix} \quad \text{*(C.3.7)}$$

where the elements along the principal diagonal are the m variances and the other elements are the covariances proper. Clearly from the definition (C.3.6)

$$\sigma_{jj'} = \sigma_{j'j}, \quad j, j' = 1, 2, \ldots, m \quad \text{(C.3.8)}$$

so the covariance matrix is a symmetric matrix. It is also a positive-semidefinite matrix.[9] It contains m variances and $m(m-1)/2$ independent covariances, thus containing altogether $m(m+1)/2$ independent elements. For example, if $m = 2$, the three elements

$$\begin{pmatrix} \sigma_1^2 & \sigma_{12} \\ & \sigma_2^2 \end{pmatrix} \quad \text{(C.3.9)}$$

define the covariance matrix, the missing element equaling σ_{12}.

The definitions introduced thus far can be expressed in terms of *expectations*, where in the multivariate case the expectation of a given function of $\mathbf{X}$, say $\varphi(\mathbf{x})$, is defined as

$$E[\varphi(\mathbf{x})] = \int_{-\infty}^{\infty} \cdots \int_{-\infty}^{\infty} \varphi(x_1, x_2, \ldots, x_m) f(x_1, x_2, \ldots, x_m)\, dx_1\, dx_2 \cdots dx_m. \quad \text{*(C.3.10)}$$

The jth mean of X is then given as

$$\mu_j = E(x_j), \quad j = 1, 2, \ldots, m \quad \text{*(C.3.11)}$$

so in vector notation the column vector of means (C.3.3) is

$$\boldsymbol{\mu} = (\mu_1\ \mu_2\ \cdots\ \mu_m)' = E(\mathbf{x}). \quad \text{*(C.3.12)}$$

The *jth variance* of $\mathbf{X}$ is

$$\text{Var}(x_j) = \sigma_j^2 = E(x_j - \mu_j)^2 = \sigma_{jj}, \quad j = 1, 2, \ldots, m \quad \text{*(C.3.13)}$$

and the *jj′ covariance* of $\mathbf{X}$ is

$$\text{Cov}(x_j x_{j'}) = \sigma_{jj'} = E(x_j - \mu_j)(x_{j'} - \mu_{j'}), \quad j, j' = 1, 2, \ldots, m \quad \text{*(C.3.14)}$$

[9] For the definition of "positive semidefinite," see Appendix B, Section B.8.

Thus the *covariance matrix* can be expressed in matrix notation as

$$\mathbf{\Sigma} = E(\mathbf{x} - \boldsymbol{\mu})(\mathbf{x} - \boldsymbol{\mu})' = \text{Cov}(\mathbf{x}) = (\sigma_{jj'}) \qquad \text{*(C.3.15)}$$

where $(\mathbf{x} - \boldsymbol{\mu})'$ is the row vector obtained by transposing the column vector $(\mathbf{x} - \boldsymbol{\mu})$.

The expectation operator $E(\cdot)$ defined by (C.3.10) satisfies the linearity property that for any given $(r \times 1)$-column vector $\mathbf{a}$ and any given $r \times m$ matrix $\mathbf{B}$

$$E(\mathbf{a} + \mathbf{Bx}) = \mathbf{a} + \mathbf{B}E(\mathbf{x}) = \mathbf{a} + \mathbf{B}\boldsymbol{\mu}. \qquad \text{*(C.3.16)}$$

In particular the expectation of a weighted sum of random variables $E(\mathbf{bx})$, where $\mathbf{b}$ is a given row vector of weights, is the weighted sum of the expectations $\mathbf{b}E(\mathbf{x})$—that is, $\mathbf{b}\boldsymbol{\mu}$. By contrast the covariance operator of (C.3.15) satisfies

$$\text{Cov}(\mathbf{a} + \mathbf{Bx}) = \mathbf{B}\,\text{Cov}(\mathbf{x})\mathbf{B}' = \mathbf{B\Sigma B}' \qquad \text{*(C.3.17)}$$

so Cov $(\cdot)$ is not a linear operator. In particular the variance of a weighted sum of random variables Var $(\mathbf{bx})$ is the quadratic form $\mathbf{b}$ Cov $(\mathbf{x})\mathbf{b}'$—that is, $\mathbf{b\Sigma b}'$.[10] In the univariate case the variance of a linear function of the random variables, Var $(a + bx)$, is given by b^2 Var (x).

If X_j and $X_{j'}$ are statistically independent, as in (C.2.32), then

$$E(x_j x_{j'}) = E(x_j)E(x_{j'}) \quad \text{and} \quad \sigma_{jj'} = 0. \qquad \text{(C.3.18)}$$

Thus if the random variables $X_1, X_2, \ldots, X_m$ are mutually independent, as in (C.2.33), then the covariance matrix Cov $(\mathbf{x})$ is a diagonal matrix, since then $\sigma_{jj'} = 0$ for $j \neq j'$. While independence implies zero covariance, the converse is *not* true: zero covariance does not necessarily imply that random variables are statistically independent. Variables with a zero covariance are *uncorrelated*, and statistical independence is sufficient but not necessary for variables to be uncorrelated.

The j, j' *correlation coefficient* of $\mathbf{X}$ is

$$\rho_{jj'} = \frac{\sigma_{jj'}}{\sigma_j \sigma_{j'}}, \qquad -1 \leqslant \rho_{jj'} \leqslant 1, \quad j, j' = 1, 2, \ldots, m. \qquad \text{(C.3.19)}$$

If the random variables X_j and $X_{j'}$ are uncorrelated, then $\rho_{jj'} = 0$, since then $\sigma_{jj'} = 0$.

Moments can be defined in terms of expectations. The $(h_1, h_2, \ldots, h_m)$ moment about the point x^0 is defined as

$$E(x_1 - x_1^0)^{h_1}(x_2 - x_2^0)^{h_2} \cdots (x_m - x_m^0)^{h_m} \qquad \text{*(C.3.20)}$$

[10] For the definition of "quadratic form" see Appendix B, Section B.8.

$$= \int_{-\infty}^{\infty} \cdots \int_{-\infty}^{\infty} (x_1 - x_1^0)^{h_1} \cdots (x_m - x_m^0)^{h_m} f(x_1 \cdots x_m) dx_1 \cdots dx_m$$

The first mean μ_1 is then the $(1, 0, \ldots, 0)$ moment about the origin, and, in general, the jth mean is the $(0, 0. \ldots, 1, \ldots, 0)$ moment about the origin. The first variance is the $(2, 0, \ldots, 0)$ moment about the mean, and the $(1, 2)$ covariance is the $(1, 1, 0, \ldots, 0)$ moment about the mean. Given a density function $f(x_1 \cdots x_m) = f(\mathbf{x})$, all the moments are defined; conversely, given all the moments, the density function is defined. Sometimes *statistics* is defined as simply the study of moments. The moments are convenient ways of summarizing a distribution; e.g., means provide measures of central tendency, variances measure dispersion, covariances measure the degree to which variables move together, etc. There is, in fact, a one-to-one unique correspondence between a probability density function and a moment generating function, where the *moment generating function* is defined as

$$M_{\mathbf{X}}(\mathbf{t}) = E(e^{t_1 X_1 + \cdots + t_m X_m}) = \int_{-\infty}^{\infty} \cdots \int_{-\infty}^{\infty} e^{t_1 x_1 + \cdots + t_m x_m} f(x_1 \cdots x_m)\, dx_1 \cdots dx_m \quad \text{(C.3.21)}$$

assuming the integral converges. This function "generates" moments in that, for example,

$$\left.\frac{\partial M_{\mathbf{X}}(\mathbf{t})}{\partial t_j}\right|_{\mathbf{t}=0} = E(x_j) = \mu_j \quad \text{(C.3.22)}$$

The one-to-one correspondence implies that a distribution is completely characterized by its moments. In particular, if, given two random variables **X** and **Y**, with the same moment generating functions

$$M_{\mathbf{X}}(t) = M_{\mathbf{Y}}(t) \quad \text{for all } t \quad \text{(C.3.23)}$$

then **X** and **Y** have the same distribution.

Sample measures can be defined in terms of data points. Assuming a sample of n observations of the form $\mathbf{x}_1, \mathbf{x}_2, \ldots, \mathbf{x}_n$, where each sample point is an $m \times 1$ vector, these data can be expressed as the *data matrix*

$$\underset{n \times m}{\mathbf{X}} = \begin{pmatrix} \mathbf{x}_1' \\ \mathbf{x}_2' \\ \vdots \\ \mathbf{x}_n' \end{pmatrix} = (x_{ij}), \quad i = 1, 2, \ldots, n; \; j = 1, 2, \ldots, m \quad \text{(C.3.24)}$$

where j is an index of the variable and i is an index of the data point. Each sample point is a row of the data matrix. The jth *sample mean* is defined as

$$\bar{x}_j = \frac{1}{n} \sum_{i=1}^{n} x_{ij} \tag{C.3.25}$$

and the *sample mean vector* is

$$\bar{\mathbf{x}} = (\bar{x}_1, \bar{x}_2, \cdots, \bar{x}_m). \tag{C.3.26}$$

The *j*th *sample variance* is

$$s_j^2 = \frac{1}{n} \sum_{i=1}^{n} (x_{ij} - \bar{x}_j)^2 = s_{jj} \tag{C.3.27}$$

and the j, j' *sample covariance* is

$$s_{jj'} = \frac{1}{n} \sum_{i=1}^{n} (x_{ij} - \bar{x}_j)(x_{ij} - \bar{x}_{j'}). \tag{C.3.28}$$

The *sample covariance matrix* is then

$$S = \begin{pmatrix} s_1^2 & s_{12} & \cdots & s_{1m} \\ s_{21} & s_2^2 & \cdots & s_{2m} \\ \vdots & & & \\ s_{m1} & s_{m2} & \cdots & s_m^2 \end{pmatrix} = (s_{jj'}) \tag{C.3.29}$$

the j, j' *sample correlation coefficient* is

$$r_{jj'} = \frac{s_{jj'}}{s_j s_{j'}} \tag{C.3.30}$$

and the *sample correlation matrix* is

$$\mathbf{R} = (r_{jj'}). \tag{C.3.31}$$

C.4 Some specific distributions

This section treats some specific distributions that are used in econometrics, including the normal, lognormal, multivariate normal, χ^2, t, and F distributions. Tables for most of these distributions are given in the next section.

One of the most widely used distributions is the *normal distribution*. The univariate random variable X is distributed as the normal distribution with mean μ and variance σ^2, written

$$X \sim N(\mu, \sigma^2) \tag{*C.4.1}$$

if the density function is of the form[11]

$$f(x) = \frac{1}{\sqrt{2\pi}\,\sigma} \exp\left(-\frac{1}{2}\frac{(x-\mu)^2}{\sigma^2}\right), \qquad -\infty < x < \infty. \qquad *(C.4.2)$$

The familiar smooth symmetric bell shape of this continuous distribution is illustrated in Figure C.2. The mean of the distribution is μ and the variance is σ^2, and these two parameters

$$E(x) = \mu, \qquad \text{Var}(x) = \sigma^2 \qquad *(C.4.3)$$

completely characterize the normal distribution. For the *standard normal distribution* $X \sim N(0, 1)$; that is, the mean is zero and the variance is unity.

An important justification for the wide use of the normal distribution is the *central limit theorem*. According to this theorem, whenever the outcome of an event depends on the superposition of many independent random variables, the distribution of outcomes converges stochastically to the normal distribution; i.e., as the number of independent random variables increases without limit, the probability of observing any arbitrary deviation from normality approaches zero. More specifically, if $[X_i]$ form a sequence of independent random variables distributed identically with mean μ and finite variance σ^2, then the sample mean converges to the normal distribution defined by these parameters; i.e.,[12]

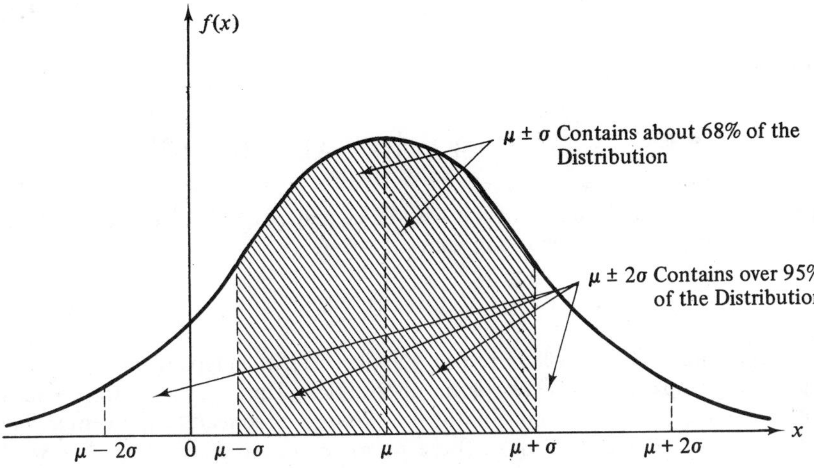

Figure C.2 The Normal Density Function

[11] The expression "exp (z)" means e^z, where e is the base of the natural logarithms.

[12] The theorem can be generalized to allow each observation to come from a different probability distribution, provided the random variables are independent and have variances that are approximately equal. This result is useful in econometrics, since it provides a justification for normally distributed stochastic disturbance terms, assuming they represent the superposition of many independent stochastic terms.

$$\bar{X}(r) = \frac{1}{r}\sum_{i=1}^{r} x_i \to N\left(\mu, \frac{\sigma^2}{r}\right) \quad \text{as } r \to \infty. \qquad *(C.4.4)$$

Note that the limiting expectation of $\bar{X}(r)$ is μ, the mean of the random variable.[13]

A random variable, the logarithm of which is normally distributed, is said to have the *lognormal distribution*

$$\log X \sim N(\mu, \sigma^2). \qquad (C.4.5)$$

The density function for the lognormal distribution, unlike that for the normal distribution, is asymmetric, exhibiting a long tail in the positive direction. It is defined only for positive values of X. A justification for the lognormal distribution is provided by the central limit theorem, according to which the geometric mean of independent identically distributed positive random variables converges stochastically to the lognormal distribution.

A multivariate generalization of the normal distribution is the *multivariate normal distribution*. The m-dimensional (column vector) random variable $\mathbf{X}$ is distributed as the multivariate normal with mean vector $\boldsymbol{\mu}$ and covariance matrix $\boldsymbol{\Sigma}$ (where $\boldsymbol{\Sigma}$ is symmetric and positive definite), written

$$\mathbf{X} \sim \mathbf{N}(\boldsymbol{\mu}, \boldsymbol{\Sigma}) \qquad *(C.4.6)$$

if the density function is of the form

$$f(\mathbf{x}) = (2\pi)^{-m/2}\,|\boldsymbol{\Sigma}|^{-1/2} \exp\left[-\tfrac{1}{2}(\mathbf{x} - \boldsymbol{\mu})'\boldsymbol{\Sigma}^{-1}(\mathbf{x} - \boldsymbol{\mu})\right] \qquad *(C.4.7)$$

where $|\boldsymbol{\Sigma}|$ is the determinant of the covariance matrix and $\boldsymbol{\Sigma}^{-1}$ is the inverse of this matrix, known as the *precision matrix*.[14] Here

$$E(\mathbf{x}) = \boldsymbol{\mu}, \qquad \text{Cov}(\mathbf{x}) = \boldsymbol{\Sigma} \qquad *(C.4.8)$$

which generalize (C.4.3), where the $m + [m(m + 1)/2]$ independent parameters in $\boldsymbol{\mu}$ and $\boldsymbol{\Sigma}$ completely characterize this distribution. The set of all vectors $\mathbf{x}$ such that $(\mathbf{x} - \boldsymbol{\mu})'\boldsymbol{\Sigma}^{-1}(\mathbf{x} - \boldsymbol{\mu})$ = constant is the *ellipsoid of concentration* centered at $\boldsymbol{\mu}$. In the two-variable case ($m = 2$) the bivariate normal density function is of the form

[13] This result is consistent with the law of large numbers which states that plim $\bar{X}(r) = \mu$; that is, for any $\epsilon > 0$, $\lim_{r\to\infty} P(|\bar{X}(r) - \mu| < \epsilon) = 1$.

[14] Note that the term in the exponential function is, other than the factor $-\frac{1}{2}$, a quadratic form in the precision matrix $\boldsymbol{\Sigma}^{-1}$. See Appendix B for a discussion of matrices, including quadratic forms and inverse matrices.

$$f(x_1, x_2) = \frac{1}{2\pi\sqrt{\sigma_1^2\sigma_2^2 - \sigma_{12}^2}} \exp\left\{\frac{-1}{2(\sigma_1^2\sigma_2^2 - \sigma_{12}^2)} [\sigma_2^2(x_1 - \mu_1)^2 - 2\sigma_{12}(x_1 - \mu_1)(x_2 - \mu_2) + \sigma_1^2(x_2 - \mu_2)^2]\right\}$$

$$f(x_1, x_2) = \frac{1}{2\pi\sigma_1\sigma_2\sqrt{1 - \rho_{12}^2}} \exp\left\{\frac{-1}{2(1 - \rho_{12}^2)} \left[\left(\frac{x_1 - \mu_1}{\sigma_1}\right)^2 - 2\rho_{12}\left(\frac{x_1 - \mu_1}{\sigma_1}\right)\left(\frac{x_2 - \mu_2}{\sigma_2}\right) + \left(\frac{x_2 - \mu_2}{\sigma_2}\right)^2\right]\right\} \quad \text{(C.4.9)}$$

Here the five parameters defining the distribution are the means (μ_1, μ_2), the variances (σ_1^2, σ_2^2), and the covariance (σ_{12}). In the second formulation σ_{12} is replaced by ρ_{12}, the correlation coefficient, given as $\sigma_{12}/\sigma_1\sigma_2$, as in (C.3.19).

If **X** is distributed as the multivariate normal distribution and the random variables $X_1, X_2, \ldots, X_m$ are mutually independent, then

$$f(x_1 x_2 \cdots x_m) = f_1(x_1) f_2(x_2) \cdots f_m(x_m) \quad \text{(C.4.10)}$$

where $f_j(x_j)$ is the scalar normal distribution as in (C.4.2). The multivariate normal distribution reduces to this case if the covariance matrix $\mathbf{\Sigma}$ is a diagonal matrix, in which case

$$f(\mathbf{x}) = \prod_{j=1}^{m} \frac{1}{\sqrt{2\pi}\,\sigma_j} \exp\left[-\frac{1}{2}\frac{(x_j - \mu_j)^2}{\sigma_j^2}\right] \quad \text{(C.4.11)}$$

so the multivariate normal distribution (C.4.7) reduces to a product of univariate normal distributions. Thus, for the normal distribution a diagonal covariance matrix guarantees independence, so zero covariance is equivalent to independence. This property does *not* hold, however, for any arbitary distribution, as discussed after (C.3.18).

If $\mathbf{X} \sim N(\boldsymbol{\mu}, \mathbf{\Sigma})$, then if **a** is a given $r \times 1$ column vector and **B** is a given $r \times m$ matrix,

$$\mathbf{a} + \mathbf{BX} \sim N(\mathbf{a} + \mathbf{B}\boldsymbol{\mu}, \mathbf{B\Sigma B}'). \quad \text{*(C.4.12)}$$

In particular, any linear function of multivariate normally distributed random variables is itself multivariate normally distributed. Furthermore, there exists a triangular matrix **C** such that

$$\mathbf{C}(\mathbf{X} - \boldsymbol{\mu}) \sim N(\mathbf{0}, \mathbf{I}) \quad \text{(C.4.13)}$$

where $\mathbf{\Sigma}^{-1} = \mathbf{C}'\mathbf{C}$. Here $N(\mathbf{0}, \mathbf{I})$ is the standard *multivariate normal distribution*, with zero means, unit variances, and zero covariances. This standard distribution is, in the univariate case of (C.4.1), a normal distribution with zero mean and unit variance.

According to the *Lindeberg-Levy central limit theorem* the average of independent identically distributed random m vectors converges stochastically to the multivariate normal distribution. More specifically, if $\{\mathbf{X}_i\}$ form a sequence of independent n-dimensional random variables distributed identically with mean vector $\boldsymbol{\mu}$ and covariance matrix $\boldsymbol{\Sigma}$, then

$$\frac{1}{\sqrt{r}} \sum_{i=1}^{r} (\mathbf{X}_i - \boldsymbol{\mu}) \to N(\mathbf{0}, \boldsymbol{\Sigma}) \qquad \text{as } r \to \infty \tag{C.4.14}$$

so the limiting distribution is multivariate normal.

Consider a set of r independent random variables $Z_1, Z_2, \ldots, Z_r$, each of which is distributed as a univariate standardized normal distribution–with zero mean and unit variance. The random variable consisting of the sum of squares of these random variables is distributed as the χ^2 *(chi-square) distribution* with r degrees of freedom:

$$\chi^2 = \sum_{i=1}^{r} Z_i^2 \sim \chi^2(r). \tag*{*(C.4.15)}$$

For example, assuming a parent normal population, if s^2 is the sample variance, defined in (C.3.27), then $(n-1)s^2/\sigma^2$ is distributed as χ^2 with $n-1$ degrees of freedom (since it sums only $n-1$ independent terms). The χ^2 distribution is a positively skewed distribution defined over nonnegative values. The mean is r, the number of degrees of freedom, and the variance is $2r$. From the central limit theorem, as r increases, the distribution of $\chi^2(r)$ approaches that of the normal distribution. Furthermore, from (C.4.13), if $\mathbf{X} \sim N(\boldsymbol{\mu}, \boldsymbol{\Sigma})$ is an r-dimensional vector distributed as the multivariate normal with mean $\boldsymbol{\mu}$ and covariance matrix $\boldsymbol{\Sigma}$, then

$$(\mathbf{X} - \boldsymbol{\mu})'\boldsymbol{\Sigma}^{-1}(\mathbf{X} - \boldsymbol{\mu}) \sim \chi^2(r). \tag{C.4.16}$$

The sum of a finite number of independent χ^2 distributions is also distributed as χ^2, with the number of degrees of freedom equal to the sum of the degrees of freedom of the underlying distributions.

If Z is distributed as a standardized normal with zero mean and unit variance $N(0, 1)$, and $\chi^2(r)$ is independently distributed as the chi-square distribution with r degrees of freedom, then the ratio of Z to the (positive) square root of $\chi^2(r)$, deflated by r, is distributed as the *t distribution* with r degrees of freedom:

$$t = \frac{Z}{\sqrt{\chi^2(r)/r}} \sim t(r). \tag*{*(C.4.17)}$$

For example, again assuming a parent normal population, if $\bar{x}$ is the sample mean, defined in (C.3.25), and s^2 is the sample variance, defined in (C.3.27), then $(\bar{x} - \mu)/(s/\sqrt{n-1})$ is distributed as the t distribution with $n-1$ degrees of freedom. The t distribution is a symmetric distribution for which the mean is zero and the variance is $r/(r - 2)$ (for $r \neq 2$). The distribution has wider tails than the normal distribution, but it approaches the normal distribution $N(0, 1)$ as $r \to \infty$. In fact, for $r > 30$ the t distribution does not differ appreciably from the normal distribution.

If $\chi^2(r)$ is distributed as the chi-square distribution with r degrees of freedom and $\chi^2(s)$ is distributed independently as the chi-square distribution with s degrees of freedom, then the ratio of these two, after deflating each for the number of degrees of freedom, is distributed as the *F distribution* with r and s degrees of freedom:

$$F = \frac{\chi^2(r)/r}{\chi^2(s)/s} \sim F(r, s). \qquad *(\text{C.4.18})$$

For example, yet again assuming a parent normal population, if s_i^2 is the variance from a sample of size n_i, then the ratio s_1^2/s_2^2 is distributed as the F distribution with $(n_1 - 1)$ and $(n_2 - 1)$ degrees of freedom. The F and t distributions are related by

$$\sqrt{F(1, s)} = \frac{Z}{\sqrt{\chi^2(s)/s}} = t(s) \qquad *(\text{C.4.19})$$

which is the t distribution with s degrees of freedom. The F distribution is a positively skewed distribution defined over nonnegative values. As $s \to \infty$, the ratio $\chi^2(s)/s$ approaches unity in the probability limit, so $F(r, s)$ approaches $\chi^2(r)/r$. As both r and $s \to \infty$, $F(r, s)$ approaches unity in the probability limit.

BIBLIOGRAPHY

Anderson, T. W. (1958), *An Introduction to Multivariate Statistical Analysis.* New York: John Wiley & Sons, Inc.

Cramer, H. (1946), *Mathematical Methods of Statistics.* Princeton, N.J.: Princeton University Press.

De Groot, M. (1969), *Optimal Statistical Decisions.* New York: McGraw-Hill Book Company.

Feller, W. (1968), *An Introduction to Probability Theory and its Applications,* 3rd Ed. New York: John Wiley & Sons, Inc.

Fisz, M. (1963), *Probability Theory and Mathematical Statistics.* 3rd Ed. New York: John Wiley & Sons, Inc.

Fraser, D. A. S. (1958), *Statistics: An Introduction.* New York: John Wiley & Sons, Inc.

Graybill, F. A. (1961), *An Introduction to Linear Statistical Models.* New York: McGraw-Hill Book Company.

Hoel, P. G. (1971), *Introduction to Mathematical Statistics,* 4th Ed. New York: John Wiley & Sons, Inc.

Kendall, M. G., and A. Stuart (1958), *The Advanced Theory of Statistics*. New York: Hafner Publishing Co.

Mood, A. M., and F. A. Graybill (1963), *Introduction to the Theory of Statistics*, 2nd Ed. New York: McGraw-Hill Book Company.

Mood, A. M., F. A. Graybill, and D. C. Boes (1974), *Introduction to the Theory of Statistics*, 3rd Ed. New York: McGraw Hill Book Company.

Raiffa, H. C. (1968), *Decision Analysis*. Reading, Mass.: Addison-Wesley Publishing Co.

Rao, C. R. (1965), *Linear Statistical Inference and its Applications*. New York: John Wiley & Sons, Inc.

Savage, L. J. (1954), *The Foundations of Statistics*. New York: John Wiley & Sons, Inc.

Scheffé, H. (1959), *The Analysis of Variance*. New York: John Wiley & Sons, Inc.

Searle, S. R. (1971), *Linear Models*. New York: John Wiley & Sons, Inc.

Wilks, S. S. (1962), *Mathematical Statistics*. New York: John Wiley & Sons, Inc.

Table C.1 The Normal Distribution

$$Z = \frac{X - \mu}{\sigma} \quad \text{(Standardized normal)}$$

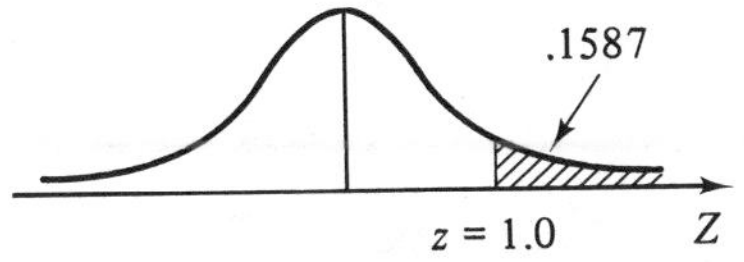

z	.00	.01	.02	.03	.04	.05	.06	.07	.08	.09
0.0	.5000	.4960	.4920	.4880	.4840	.4801	.4761	.4721	.4681	.4641
0.1	.4602	.4562	.4522	.4483	.4443	.4404	.4364	.4325	.4286	.4247
0.2	.4207	.4168	.4129	.4090	.4052	.4013	.3974	.3936	.3897	.3859
0.3	.3821	.3783	.3745	.3707	.3669	.3632	.3594	.3557	.3520	.3483
0.4	.3446	.3409	.3372	.3336	.3300	.3264	.3228	.3192	.3156	.3121
0.5	.3085	.3050	.3015	.2981	.2946	.2912	.2877	.2843	.2810	.2776
0.6	.2743	.2709	.2676	.2643	.2611	.2578	.2546	.2514	.2483	.2451
0.7	.2420	.2389	.2358	.2327	.2296	.2266	.2236	.2206	.2177	.2148
0.8	.2119	.2090	.2061	.2033	.2005	.1977	.1949	.1922	.1894	.1867
0.9	.1841	.1814	.1788	.1762	.1736	.1711	.1685	.1660	.1635	.1611
1.0	.1587	.1562	.1539	.1515	.1492	.1469	.1446	.1423	.1401	.1379
1.1	.1357	.1335	.1314	.1292	.1271	.1251	.1230	.1210	.1190	.1170
1.2	.1151	.1131	.1112	.1093	.1075	.1056	.1038	.1020	.1003	.0985
1.3	.0968	.0951	.0934	.0918	.0901	.0885	.0869	.0853	.0838	.0823
1.4	.0808	.0793	.0778	.0764	.0749	.0735	.0721	.0708	.0694	.0681
1.5	.0668	.0655	.0643	.0630	.0618	.0606	.0594	.0582	.0571	.0559
1.6	.0548	.0537	.0526	.0516	.0505	.0495	.0485	.0475	.0465	.0455
1.7	.0446	.0436	.0427	.0418	.0409	.0401	.0392	.0384	.0375	.0367
1.8	.0359	.0351	.0344	.0336	.0329	.0322	.0314	.0307	.0301	.0294
1.9	.0287	.0281	.0274	.0268	.0262	.0256	.0250	.0244	.0239	.0233
2.0	.0228	.0222	.0217	.0212	.0207	.0202	.0197	.0192	.0188	.0183
2.1	.0179	.0174	.0170	.0166	.0162	.0158	.0154	.0150	.0146	.0143
2.2	.0139	.0136	.0132	.0129	.0125	.0122	.0119	.0116	.0113	.0110
2.3	.0107	.0104	.0102	.0099	.0096	.0094	.0091	.0089	.0087	.0084
2.4	.0082	.0080	.0078	.0075	.0073	.0071	.0069	.0068	.0066	.0064
2.5	.0062	.0060	.0059	.0057	.0055	.0054	.0052	.0051	.0049	.0048
2.6	.0047	.0045	.0044	.0043	.0041	.0040	.0039	.0038	.0037	.0036
2.7	.0035	.0034	.0033	.0032	.0031	.0030	.0029	.0028	.0027	.0026
2.8	.0026	.0025	.0024	.0023	.0023	.0022	.0021	.0021	.0020	.0019
2.9	.0019	.0018	.0018	.0017	.0016	.0016	.0015	.0015	.0014	.0014
3.0	.0013	.0013	.0013	.0012	.0012	.0011	.0011	.0011	.0010	.0010

Source Based on ***Biometrika Tables for Statisticians***, Vol. 1, 3rd ed. (1966), with the permission of the *Biometrika* trustees.

NOTE The table plots the cumulative probability $Z \geqslant z$.

Table C.2 The χ^2 Distribution

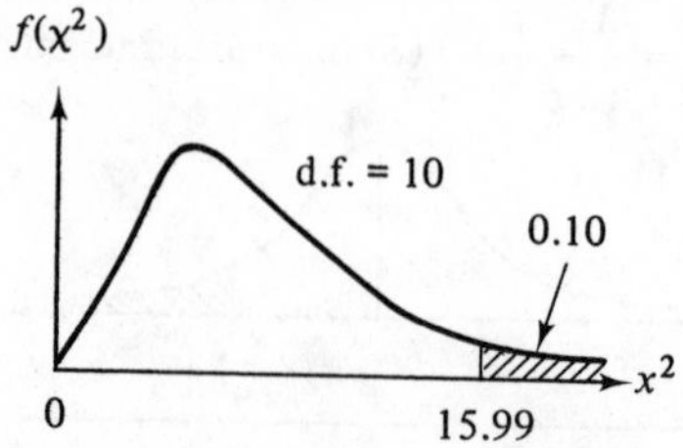

Degrees of Freedom	Probability of a Value at Least as Large as the Table Entry								
	0.90	0.75	0.50	0.25	0.10	0.05	0.025	0.01	0.005
1	0.0158	0.102	0.455	1.323	2.71	3.84	5.02	6.63	7.88
2	0.211	0.575	1.386	2.77	4.61	5.99	7.38	9.21	10.60
3	0.584	1.213	2.37	4.11	6.25	7.81	9.35	11.34	12.84
4	1.064	1.923	3.36	5.39	7.78	9.49	11.14	13.28	14.86
5	1.610	2.67	4.35	6.63	9.24	11.07	12.83	15.09	16.75
6	2.20	3.45	5.35	7.84	10.64	12.59	14.45	16.81	18.55
7	2.83	4.25	6.35	9.04	12.02	14.07	16.01	18.48	20.3
8	3.49	5.07	7.34	10.22	13.36	15.51	17.53	20.1	22.0
9	4.17	5.90	8.34	11.39	14.68	16.92	19.02	21.7	23.6
10	4.87	6.74	9.34	12.55	15.99	18.31	20.5	23.2	25.2
11	5.58	7.58	10.34	13.70	17.28	19.68	21.9	24.7	26.8
12	6.30	8.44	11.34	14.85	18.55	21.0	23.3	26.2	28.3
13	7.04	9.30	12.34	15.98	19.81	22.4	24.7	27.7	29.8
14	7.79	10.17	13.34	17.12	21.1	23.7	26.1	29.1	31.3
15	8.55	11.04	14.34	18.25	22.3	25.0	27.5	30.6	32.8
16	9.31	11.91	15.34	19.37	23.5	26.3	28.8	32.0	34.3
17	10.09	12.79	16.34	20.5	24.8	27.6	30.2	33.4	35.7
18	10.86	13.68	17.34	21.6	26.0	28.9	31.5	34.8	37.2
19	11.65	14.56	18.34	22.7	27.2	30.1	32.9	36.2	38.6
20	12.44	15.45	19.34	23.8	28.4	31.4	34.2	37.6	40.0

Source Based on *Biometrika Tables for Statisticians*, Vol. 1, 3rd ed. (1966), with the permission of the *Biometrika* trustees.

Table C.3 The t Distribution

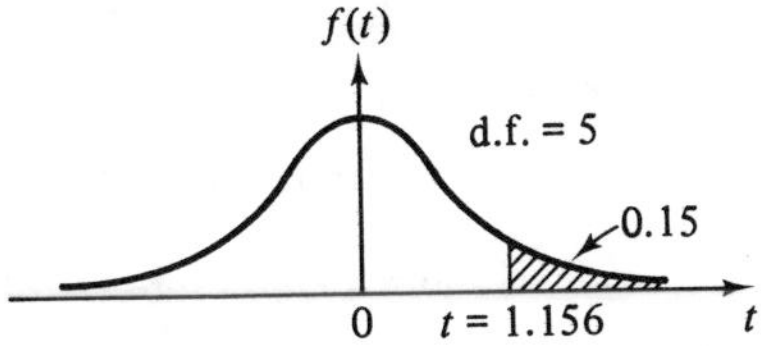

Degrees of Freedom	Probability of a Value at Least as Large as the Table Entry					
	0.15	0.1	0.05	0.025	0.01	0.005
1	1.963	3.078	6.314	12.706	31.821	63.657
2	1.386	1.886	2.920	4.303	6.965	9.925
3	1.250	1.638	2.353	3.182	4.541	5.841
4	1.190	1.533	2.132	2.776	3.747	4.604
5	1.156	1.476	2.015	2.571	3.365	4.032
6	1.134	1.440	1.943	2.447	3.143	3.707
7	1.119	1.415	1.895	2.365	2.998	3.499
8	1.108	1.397	1.860	2.306	2.896	3.355
9	1.100	1.383	1.833	2.262	2.821	3.250
10	1.093	1.372	1.812	2.228	2.764	3.169
11	1.088	1.363	1.796	2.201	2.718	3.106
12	1.083	1.356	1.782	2.179	2.681	3.055
13	1.079	1.350	1.771	2.160	2.650	3.012
14	1.076	1.345	1.761	2.145	2.624	2.977
15	1.074	1.341	1.753	2.131	2.602	2.947
16	1.071	1.337	1.746	2.120	2.583	2.921
17	1.069	1.333	1.740	2.110	2.567	2.898
18	1.067	1.330	1.734	2.101	2.552	2.878
19	1.066	1.328	1.729	2.093	2.539	2.861
20	1.064	1.325	1.725	2.086	2.528	2.845
21	1.063	1.323	1.721	2.080	2.518	2.831
22	1.061	1.321	1.717	2.074	2.508	2.819
23	1.060	1.319	1.714	2.069	2.500	2.807
24	1.059	1.318	1.711	2.064	2.492	2.797
25	1.058	1.316	1.708	2.060	2.485	2.787
26	1.058	1.315	1.706	2.056	2.479	2.779
27	1.057	1.314	1.703	2.052	2.473	2.771
28	1.056	1.313	1.701	2.048	2.467	2.763
29	1.055	1.311	1.699	2.045	2.462	2.756
30	1.055	1.310	1.697	2.042	2.457	2.750
(Normal) ∞	1.036	1.282	1.645	1.960	2.326	2.576

Source Reprinted from Table IV in Sir Ronald A. Fisher, ***Statistical Methods for Research Workers***, 14th ed. (copyright © 1972 by Hafner Press, a Division of Macmillan Publishing Co., Inc.) with the permission of the publisher and the late Sir Ronald Fisher's Literary Executor.

Table C.4 The *F* Distribution

5% (Roman Type) and 1% (Boldface Type) Points for the Distribution of *F*

n_2	n_1 degrees of freedom for numerator											
	1	2	3	4	5	6	7	8	9	10	11	12
1	161	200	216	225	230	234	237	239	241	242	243	244
	4,052	**4,999**	**5,403**	**5,625**	**5,764**	**5,859**	**5,928**	**5,981**	**6,022**	**6,056**	**6,082**	**6,106**
2	18.51	19.00	19.16	19.25	19.30	19.33	19.36	19.37	19.38	19.39	19.40	19.41
	98.49	**99.00**	**99.17**	**99.25**	**99.30**	**99.33**	**99.34**	**99.36**	**99.38**	**99.40**	**99.41**	**99.42**
3	10.13	9.55	9.28	9.12	9.01	8.94	8.88	8.84	8.81	8.78	8.76	8.74
	34.12	**30.82**	**29.46**	**28.71**	**28.24**	**27.91**	**27.67**	**27.49**	**27.34**	**27.23**	**27.13**	**27.05**
4	7.71	6.94	6.59	6.39	6.26	6.16	6.09	6.04	6.00	5.96	5.93	5.91
	21.20	**18.00**	**16.69**	**15.98**	**15.52**	**15.21**	**14.98**	**14.80**	**14.66**	**14.54**	**14.45**	**14.37**
5	6.61	5.79	5.41	5.19	5.05	4.95	4.88	4.82	4.78	4.74	4.70	4.68
	16.26	**13.27**	**12.06**	**11.39**	**10.97**	**10.67**	**10.45**	**10.27**	**10.15**	**10.05**	**9.96**	**9.89**
6	5.99	5.14	4.76	4.53	4.39	4.28	4.21	4.15	4.10	4.06	4.03	4.00
	13.74	**10.92**	**9.78**	**9.15**	**8.75**	**8.47**	**8.26**	**8.10**	**7.98**	**7.87**	**7.79**	**7.72**
7	5.59	4.74	4.35	4.12	3.97	3.87	3.79	3.73	3.68	3.63	3.60	3.57
	12.25	**9.55**	**8.45**	**7.85**	**7.46**	**7.19**	**7.00**	**6.84**	**6.71**	**6.62**	**6.54**	**6.47**
8	5.32	4.46	4.07	3.84	3.69	3.58	3.50	3.44	3.39	3.34	3.31	3.28
	11.26	**8.65**	**7.59**	**7.01**	**6.63**	**6.37**	**6.19**	**6.03**	**5.91**	**5.82**	**5.74**	**5.67**
9	5.12	4.26	3.86	3.63	3.48	3.37	3.29	3.23	3.18	3.13	3.10	3.07
	10.56	**8.02**	**6.99**	**6.42**	**6.06**	**5.80**	**5.62**	**5.47**	**5.35**	**5.26**	**5.18**	**5.11**
10	4.96	4.10	3.71	3.48	3.33	3.22	3.14	3.07	3.02	2.97	2.94	2.91
	10.04	**7.56**	**6.55**	**5.99**	**5.64**	**5.39**	**5.21**	**5.06**	**4.95**	**4.85**	**4.78**	**4.71**
11	4.84	3.98	3.59	3.36	3.20	3.09	3.01	2.95	2.90	2.86	2.82	2.79
	9.65	**7.20**	**6.22**	**5.67**	**5.32**	**5.07**	**4.88**	**4.74**	**4.63**	**4.54**	**4.46**	**4.40**
12	4.75	3.88	3.49	3.26	3.11	3.00	2.92	2.85	2.80	2.76	2.72	2.69
	9.33	**6.93**	**5.95**	**5.41**	**5.06**	**4.82**	**4.65**	**4.50**	**4.39**	**4.30**	**4.22**	**4.16**
13	4.67	3.80	3.41	3.18	3.02	2.92	2.84	2.77	2.72	2.67	2.63	2.60
	9.07	**6.70**	**5.74**	**5.20**	**4.86**	**4.62**	**4.44**	**4.30**	**4.19**	**4.10**	**4.02**	**3.96**
14	4.60	3.74	3.34	3.11	2.96	2.85	2.77	2.70	2.65	2.60	2.56	2.53
	8.86	**6.51**	**5.56**	**5.03**	**4.69**	**4.46**	**4.28**	**4.14**	**4.03**	**3.94**	**3.86**	**3.80**
15	4.54	3.68	3.29	3.06	2.90	2.79	2.70	2.64	2.59	2.55	2.51	2.48
	8.68	**6.36**	**5.42**	**4.89**	**4.56**	**4.32**	**4.14**	**4.00**	**3.89**	**3.80**	**3.73**	**3.67**
16	4.49	3.63	3.24	3.01	2.85	2.74	2.66	2.59	2.54	2.49	2.45	2.42
	8.53	**6.23**	**5.29**	**4.77**	**4.44**	**4.20**	**4.03**	**3.89**	**3.78**	**3.69**	**3.61**	**3.55**

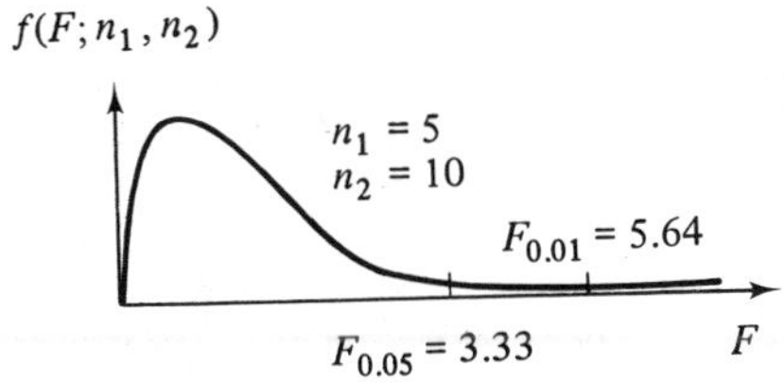

14	16	20	24	30	40	50	75	100	200	500	∞	n_2
245	246	248	249	250	251	252	253	253	254	254	254	1
6,142	**6,169**	**6,208**	**6,234**	**6,258**	**6,286**	**6,302**	**6,323**	**6,334**	**6,352**	**6,361**	**6,366**	
19.42	19.43	19.44	19.45	19.46	19.47	19.47	19.48	19.49	19.49	19.50	19.50	2
99.43	**99.44**	**99.45**	**99.46**	**99.47**	**99.48**	**99.48**	**99.49**	**99.49**	**99.49**	**99.50**	**99.50**	
8.71	8.69	8.66	8.64	8.62	8.60	8.58	8.57	8.56	8.54	8.54	8.53	3
26.92	**26.83**	**26.69**	**26.60**	**26.50**	**26.41**	**26.35**	**26.27**	**26.23**	**26.18**	**26.14**	**26.12**	
5.87	5.84	5.80	5.77	5.74	5.71	5.70	5.68	5.66	5.65	5.64	5.63	4
14.24	**14.15**	**14.02**	**13.93**	**13.83**	**13.74**	**13.69**	**13.61**	**13.57**	**13.52**	**13.48**	**13.46**	
4.64	4.60	4.56	4.53	4.50	4.46	4.44	4.42	4.40	4.38	4.37	4.36	5
9.77	**9.68**	**9.55**	**9.47**	**9.38**	**9.29**	**9.24**	**9.17**	**9.13**	**9.07**	**9.04**	**9.02**	
3.96	3.92	3.87	3.84	3.81	3.77	3.75	3.72	3.71	3.69	3.68	3.67	6
7.60	**7.52**	**7.39**	**7.31**	**7.23**	**7.14**	**7.09**	**7.02**	**6.99**	**6.94**	**6.90**	**6.88**	
3.52	3.49	3.44	3.41	3.38	3.34	3.32	3.29	3.28	3.25	3.24	3.23	7
6.35	**6.27**	**6.15**	**6.07**	**5.98**	**5.90**	**5.85**	**5.78**	**5.75**	**5.70**	**5.67**	**5.65**	
3.23	3.20	3.15	3.12	3.08	3.05	3.03	3.00	2.98	2.96	2.94	2.93	8
5.56	**5.48**	**5.36**	**5.28**	**5.20**	**5.11**	**5.06**	**5.00**	**4.96**	**4.91**	**4.88**	**4.86**	
3.02	2.98	2.93	2.90	2.86	2.82	2.80	2.77	2.76	2.73	2.72	2.71	9
5.00	**4.92**	**4.80**	**4.73**	**4.64**	**4.56**	**4.51**	**4.45**	**4.41**	**4.36**	**4.33**	**4.31**	
2.86	2.82	2.77	2.74	2.70	2.67	2.64	2.61	2.59	2.56	2.55	2.54	10
4.60	**4.52**	**4.41**	**4.33**	**4.25**	**4.17**	**4.12**	**4.05**	**4.01**	**3.96**	**3.93**	**3.91**	
2.74	2.70	2.65	2.61	2.57	2.53	2.50	2.47	2.45	2.42	2.41	2.40	11
4.29	**4.21**	**4.10**	**4.02**	**3.94**	**3.86**	**3.80**	**3.74**	**3.70**	**3.66**	**3.62**	**3.60**	
2.64	2.60	2.54	2.50	2.46	2.42	2.40	2.36	2.35	2.32	2.31	2.30	12
4.05	**3.98**	**3.86**	**3.78**	**3.70**	**3.61**	**3.56**	**3.49**	**3.46**	**3.41**	**3.38**	**3.36**	
2.55	2.51	2.46	2.42	2.38	2.34	2.32	2.28	2.26	2.24	2.22	2.21	13
3.85	**3.78**	**3.67**	**3.59**	**3.51**	**3.42**	**3.37**	**3.30**	**3.27**	**3.21**	**3.18**	**3.16**	
2.48	2.44	2.39	2.35	2.31	2.27	2.24	2.21	2.19	2.16	2.14	2.13	14
3.70	**3.62**	**3.51**	**3.43**	**3.34**	**3.26**	**3.21**	**3.14**	**3.11**	**3.06**	**3.02**	**3.00**	
2.43	2.39	2.33	2.29	2.25	2.21	2.18	2.15	2.12	2.10	2.08	2.07	15
3.56	**3.48**	**3.36**	**3.29**	**3.20**	**3.12**	**3.07**	**3.00**	**2.97**	**2.92**	**2.89**	**2.87**	
2.37	2.33	2.28	2.24	2.20	2.16	2.13	2.09	2.07	2.04	2.02	2.01	16
3.45	**3.37**	**3.25**	**3.18**	**3.10**	**3.01**	**2.96**	**2.89**	**2.86**	**2.80**	**2.77**	**2.75**	

Table C.4 (*continued*)

n_2	n_1 degrees of freedom for numerator											
	1	2	3	4	5	6	7	8	9	10	11	12
17	4.45	3.59	3.20	2 96	2.81	2.70	2.62	2.55	2.50	2.45	2.41	2.3[illegible]
	8.40	**6.11**	**5.18**	**4.67**	**4.34**	**4.10**	**3.93**	**3.79**	**3.68**	**3.59**	**3.52**	**3.4[illegible]**
18	4.41	3.55	3.16	2.93	2.77	2.66	2.58	2.51	2.46	2.41	2.37	2.3[illegible]
	8.28	**6.01**	**5.09**	**4.58**	**4.25**	**4.01**	**3.85**	**3.71**	**3.60**	**3.51**	**3.44**	**3.3[illegible]**
19	4.38	3.52	3.13	2.90	2.74	2.63	2.55	2.48	2.43	2.38	2.34	2.3[illegible]
	8.18	**5.93**	**5.01**	**4.50**	**4.17**	**3.94**	**3.77**	**3.63**	**3.52**	**3.43**	**3.36**	**3.3[illegible]**
20	4.35	3.49	3.10	2.87	2.71	2.60	2.52	2.45	2.40	2.35	2.31	2.2[illegible]
	8.10	**5.85**	**4.94**	**4.43**	**4.10**	**3.87**	**3.71**	**3.56**	**3.45**	**3.37**	**3.30**	**3.2[illegible]**
21	4.32	3.47	3.07	2.84	2.68	2.57	2.49	2.42	2.37	2.32	2.28	2.2[illegible]
	8.02	**5.78**	**4.87**	**4.37**	**4.04**	**3.81**	**3.65**	**3.51**	**3.40**	**3.31**	**3.24**	**3.1[illegible]**
22	4.30	3.44	3.05	2.82	2.66	2.55	2.47	2.40	2.35	2.30	2.26	2.2[illegible]
	7.94	**5.72**	**4.82**	**4.31**	**3.99**	**3.76**	**3.59**	**3.45**	**3.35**	**3.26**	**3.18**	**3.1[illegible]**
23	4.28	3.42	3.03	2.80	2.64	2.53	2.45	2.38	2.32	2.28	2.24	2.20
	7.88	**5.66**	**4.76**	**4.26**	**3.94**	**3.71**	**3.54**	**3.41**	**3.30**	**3.21**	**3.14**	**3.07**
24	4.26	3.40	3.01	2.78	2.62	2.51	2.43	2.36	2.30	2.26	2.22	2.18
	7.82	**5.61**	**4.72**	**4.22**	**3.90**	**3.67**	**3.50**	**3.36**	**3.25**	**3.17**	**3.09**	**3.03**
25	4.24	3.38	2.99	2.76	2.60	2.49	2.41	2.34	2.28	2.24	2.20	2.16
	7.77	**5.57**	**4.68**	**4.18**	**3.86**	**3.63**	**3.46**	**3.32**	**3.21**	**3.13**	**3.05**	**2.99**
26	4.22	3.37	2.98	2.74	2.59	2.47	2.39	2.32	2.27	2.22	2.18	2.15
	7.72	**5.53**	**4.64**	**4.14**	**3.82**	**3.59**	**3.42**	**3.29**	**3.17**	**3.09**	**3.02**	**2.96**
27	4.21	3.35	2.96	2.73	2.57	2.46	2.37	2.30	2.25	2.20	2.16	2.13
	7.68	**5.49**	**4.60**	**4.11**	**3.79**	**3.56**	**3.39**	**3.26**	**3.14**	**3.06**	**2.98**	**2.93**
28	4.20	3.34	2.95	2.71	2.56	2.44	2.36	2.29	2.24	2.19	2.15	2.12
	7.64	**5.45**	**4.57**	**4.07**	**3.76**	**3.53**	**3.36**	**3.23**	**3.11**	**3.03**	**2.95**	**2.90**
29	4.18	3.33	2.93	2.70	2.54	2.43	2.35	2.28	2.22	2.18	2.14	2.10
	7.60	**5.42**	**4.54**	**4.04**	**3.73**	**3.50**	**3.33**	**3.20**	**3.08**	**3.00**	**2.92**	**2.87**
30	4.17	3.32	2.92	2.69	2.53	2.42	2.34	2.27	2.21	2.16	2.12	2.09
	7.56	**5.39**	**4.51**	**4.02**	**3.70**	**3.47**	**3.30**	**3.17**	**3.06**	**2.98**	**2.90**	**2.84**
32	4.15	3.30	2.90	2.67	2.51	2.40	2.32	2.25	2.19	2.14	2.10	2.07
	7.50	**5.34**	**4.46**	**3.97**	**3.66**	**3.42**	**3.25**	**3.12**	**3.01**	**2.94**	**2.86**	**2.80**
34	4.13	3.28	2.88	2.65	2.49	2.38	2.30	2.23	2.17	2.12	2.08	2.05
	7.44	**5.29**	**4.42**	**3.93**	**3.61**	**3.38**	**3.21**	**3.08**	**2.97**	**2.89**	**2.82**	**2.76**
36	4.11	3.26	2.86	2.63	2.48	2.36	2.28	2.21	2.15	2.10	2.06	2.03
	7.39	**5.25**	**4.38**	**3.89**	**3.58**	**3.35**	**3.18**	**3.04**	**2.94**	**2.86**	**2.78**	**2.72**
38	4.10	3.25	2.85	2.62	2.46	2.35	2.26	2.19	2.14	2.09	2.05	2.02
	7.35	**5.21**	**4.34**	**3.86**	**3.54**	**3.32**	**3.15**	**3.02**	**2.91**	**2.82**	**2.75**	**2.69**

14	16	20	24	30	40	50	75	100	200	500	∞	n_2
2.33	2.29	2.23	2.19	2.15	2.11	2.08	2.04	2.02	1.99	1.97	1.96	17
3.35	**3.27**	**3.16**	**3.08**	**3.00**	**2.92**	**2.86**	**2.79**	**2.76**	**2.70**	**2.67**	**2.65**	
2.29	2.25	2.19	2.15	2.11	2.07	2.04	2.00	1.98	1.95	1.93	1.92	18
3.27	**3.19**	**3.07**	**3.00**	**2.91**	**2.83**	**2.78**	**2.71**	**2.68**	**2.62**	**2.59**	**2.57**	
2.26	2.21	2.15	2.11	2.07	2.02	2.00	1.96	1.94	1.91	1.90	1.88	19
3.19	**3.12**	**3.00**	**2.92**	**2.84**	**2.76**	**2.70**	**2.63**	**2.60**	**2.54**	**2.51**	**2.49**	
2.23	2.18	2.12	2.08	2.04	1.99	1.96	1.92	1.90	1.87	1.85	1.84	20
3.13	**3.05**	**2.94**	**2.86**	**2.77**	**2.69**	**2.63**	**2.56**	**2.53**	**2.47**	**2.44**	**2.42**	
2.20	2.15	2.09	2.05	2.00	1.96	1.93	1.89	1.87	1.84	1.82	1.81	21
3.07	**2.99**	**2.88**	**2.80**	**2.72**	**2.63**	**2.58**	**2.51**	**2.47**	**2.42**	**2.38**	**2.36**	
2.18	2.13	2.07	2.03	1.98	1.93	1.91	1.87	1.84	1.81	1.80	1.78	22
3.02	**2.94**	**2.83**	**2.75**	**2.67**	**2.58**	**2.53**	**2.46**	**2.42**	**2.37**	**2.33**	**2.31**	
2.14	2.10	2.04	2.00	1.96	1.91	1.88	1.84	1.82	1.79	1.77	1.76	23
2.97	**2.89**	**2.78**	**2.70**	**2.62**	**2.53**	**2.48**	**2.41**	**2.37**	**2.32**	**2.28**	**2.26**	
2.13	2.09	2.02	1.98	1.94	1.89	1.86	1.82	1.80	1.76	1.74	1.73	24
2.93	**2.85**	**2.74**	**2.66**	**2.58**	**2.49**	**2.44**	**2.36**	**2.33**	**2.27**	**2.23**	**2.21**	
2.11	2.06	2.00	1.96	1.92	1.87	1.84	1.80	1.77	1.74	1.72	1.71	25
2.89	**2.81**	**2.70**	**2.62**	**2.54**	**2.45**	**2.40**	**2.32**	**2.29**	**2.23**	**2.19**	**2.17**	
2.10	2.05	1.99	1.95	1.90	1.85	1.82	1.78	1.76	1.72	1.70	1.69	26
2.86	**2.77**	**2.66**	**2.58**	**2.50**	**2.41**	**2.36**	**2.28**	**2.25**	**2.19**	**2.15**	**2.13**	
2.08	2.03	1.97	1.93	1.88	1.84	1.80	1.76	1.74	1.71	1.68	1.67	27
2.83	**2.74**	**2.63**	**2.55**	**2.47**	**2.38**	**2.33**	**2.25**	**2.21**	**2.16**	**2.12**	**2.10**	
2.06	2.02	1.96	1.91	1.87	1.81	1.78	1.75	1.72	1.69	1.67	1.65	28
2.80	**2.71**	**2.60**	**2.52**	**2.44**	**2.35**	**2.30**	**2.22**	**2.18**	**2.13**	**2.09**	**2.06**	
2.05	2.00	1.94	1.90	1.85	1.80	1.77	1.73	1.71	1.68	1.65	1.64	29
2.77	**2.68**	**2.57**	**2.49**	**2.41**	**2.32**	**2.27**	**2.19**	**2.15**	**2.10**	**2.06**	**2.03**	
2.04	1.99	1.93	1.89	1.84	1.79	1.76	1.72	1.69	1.66	1.64	1.62	30
2.74	**2.66**	**2.55**	**2.47**	**2.38**	**2.29**	**2.24**	**2.16**	**2.13**	**2.07**	**2.03**	**2.01**	
2.02	1.97	1.91	1.86	1.82	1.76	1.74	1.69	1.67	1.64	1.61	1.59	32
2.70	**2.62**	**2.51**	**2.42**	**2.34**	**2.25**	**2.20**	**2.12**	**2.08**	**2.02**	**1.98**	**1.96**	
2.00	1.95	1.89	1.84	1.80	1.74	1.71	1.67	1.64	1.61	1.59	1.57	34
2.66	**2.58**	**2.47**	**2.38**	**2.30**	**2.21**	**2.15**	**2.08**	**2.04**	**1.98**	**1.94**	**1.91**	
1.98	1.93	1.87	1.82	1.78	1.72	1.69	1.65	1.62	1.59	1.56	1.55	36
2.62	**2.54**	**2.43**	**2.35**	**2.26**	**2.17**	**2.12**	**2.04**	**2.00**	**1.94**	**1.90**	**1.87**	
1.96	1.92	1.85	1.80	1.76	1.71	1.67	1.63	1.60	1.57	1.54	1.53	38
2.59	**2.51**	**2.40**	**2.32**	**2.22**	**2.14**	**2.08**	**2.00**	**1.97**	**1.90**	**1.86**	**1.84**	

Table C.4 (*continued*)

n_2	n_1 degrees of freedom for numerator											
	1	2	3	4	5	6	7	8	9	10	11	12
40	4.08	3.23	2.84	2.61	2.45	2.34	2.25	2.18	2.12	2.07	2.04	2.00
	7.31	**5.18**	**4.31**	**3.83**	**3.51**	**3.29**	**3.12**	**2.99**	**2.88**	**2.80**	**2.73**	**2.66**
42	4.07	3.22	2.83	2.59	2.44	2.32	2.24	2.17	2.11	2.06	2.02	1.99
	7.27	**5.15**	**4.29**	**3.80**	**3.49**	**3.26**	**3.10**	**2.96**	**2.86**	**2.77**	**2.70**	**2.64**
44	4.06	3.21	2.82	2.58	2.43	2.31	2.23	2.16	2.10	2.05	2.01	1.98
	7.24	**5.12**	**4.26**	**3.78**	**3.46**	**3.24**	**3.07**	**2.94**	**2.84**	**2.75**	**2.68**	**2.62**
46	4.05	3.20	2.81	2.57	2.42	2.30	2.22	2.14	2.09	2.04	2.00	1.97
	7.21	**5.10**	**4.24**	**3.76**	**3.44**	**3.22**	**3.05**	**2.92**	**2.82**	**2.73**	**2.66**	**2.60**
48	4.04	3.19	2.80	2.56	2.41	2.30	2.21	2.14	2.08	2.03	1.99	1.96
	7.19	**5.08**	**4.22**	**3.74**	**3.42**	**3.20**	**3.04**	**2.90**	**2.80**	**2.71**	**2.64**	**2.58**
50	4.03	3.18	2.79	2.56	2.40	2.29	2.20	2.13	2.07	2.02	1.98	1.95
	7.17	**5.06**	**4.20**	**3.72**	**3.41**	**3.18**	**3.02**	**2.88**	**2.78**	**2.70**	**2.62**	**2.56**
55	4.02	3.17	2.78	2.54	2.38	2.27	2.18	2.11	2.05	2.00	1.97	1.93
	7.12	**5.01**	**4.16**	**3.68**	**3.37**	**3.15**	**2.98**	**2.85**	**2.75**	**2.66**	**2.59**	**2.53**
60	4.00	3.15	2.76	2.52	2.37	2.25	2.17	2.10	2.04	1.99	1.95	1.92
	7.08	**4.98**	**4.13**	**3.65**	**3.34**	**3.12**	**2.95**	**2.82**	**2.72**	**2.63**	**2.56**	**2.50**
65	3.99	3.14	2.75	2.51	2.36	2.24	2.15	2.08	2.02	1.98	1.94	1.90
	7.04	**4.95**	**4.10**	**3.62**	**3.31**	**3.09**	**2.93**	**2.79**	**2.70**	**2.61**	**2.54**	**2.47**
70	3.98	3.13	2.74	2.50	2.35	2.23	2.14	2.07	2.01	1.97	1.93	1.89
	7.01	**4.92**	**4.08**	**3.60**	**3.29**	**3.07**	**2.91**	**2.77**	**2.67**	**2.59**	**2.51**	**2.45**
80	3.96	3.11	2.72	2.48	2.33	2.21	2.12	2.05	1.99	1.95	1.91	1.88
	6.96	**4.88**	**4.04**	**3.56**	**3.25**	**3.04**	**2.87**	**2.74**	**2.64**	**2.55**	**2.48**	**2.41**
100	3.94	3.09	2.70	2.46	2.30	2.19	2.10	2.03	1.97	1.92	1.88	1.85
	6.90	**4.82**	**3.98**	**3.51**	**3.20**	**2.99**	**2.82**	**2.69**	**2.59**	**2.51**	**2.43**	**2.36**
125	3.92	3.07	2.68	2.44	2.29	2.17	2.08	2.01	1.95	1.90	1.86	1.83
	6.84	**4.78**	**3.94**	**3.47**	**3.17**	**2.95**	**2.79**	**2.65**	**2.56**	**2.47**	**2.40**	**2.33**
150	3.91	3.06	2.67	2.43	2.27	2.16	2.07	2.00	1.94	1.89	1.85	1.82
	6.81	**4.75**	**3.91**	**3.44**	**3.14**	**2.92**	**2.76**	**2.62**	**2.53**	**2.44**	**2.37**	**2.30**
200	3.89	3.04	2.65	2.41	2.26	2.14	2.05	1.98	1.92	1.87	1.83	1.80
	6.76	**4.71**	**3.88**	**3.41**	**3.11**	**2.90**	**2.73**	**2.60**	**2.50**	**2.41**	**2.34**	**2.28**
400	3.86	3.02	2.62	2.39	2.23	2.12	2.03	1.96	1.90	1.85	1.81	1.78
	6.70	**4.66**	**3.83**	**3.36**	**3.06**	**2.85**	**2.69**	**2.55**	**2.46**	**2.37**	**2.29**	**2.23**
1000	3.85	3.00	2.61	2.38	2.22	2.10	2.02	1.95	1.89	1.84	1.80	1.76
	6.66	**4.62**	**3.80**	**3.34**	**3.04**	**2.82**	**2.66**	**2.53**	**2.43**	**2.34**	**2.26**	**2.20**
∞	3.84	2.99	2.60	2.37	2.21	2.09	2.01	1.94	1.88	1.83	1.79	1.75
	6.64	**4.60**	**3.78**	**3.32**	**3.02**	**2.80**	**2.64**	**2.51**	**2.41**	**2.32**	**2.24**	**2.18**

Source Based on *Biometrika*, vol. 33 (1943), with the permission of the *Biometrika* trustees.

14	16	20	24	30	40	50	75	100	200	500	∞	n_2
.95	1.90	1.84	1.79	1.74	1.69	1.66	1.61	1.59	1.55	1.53	1.51	40
.56	**2.49**	**2.37**	**2.29**	**2.20**	**2.11**	**2.05**	**1.97**	**1.94**	**1.88**	**1.84**	**1.81**	
.94	1.89	1.82	1.78	1.73	1.68	1.64	1.60	1.57	1.54	1.51	1.49	42
.54	**2.46**	**2.35**	**2.26**	**2.17**	**2.08**	**2.02**	**1.94**	**1.91**	**1.85**	**1.80**	**1.78**	
.92	1.88	1.81	1.76	1.72	1.66	1.63	1.58	1.56	1.52	1.50	1.48	44
.52	**2.44**	**2.32**	**2.24**	**2.15**	**2.06**	**2.00**	**1.92**	**1.88**	**1.82**	**1.78**	**1.75**	
.91	1.87	1.80	1.75	1.71	1.65	1.62	1.57	1.54	1.51	1.48	1.46	46
.50	**2.42**	**2.30**	**2.22**	**2.13**	**2.04**	**1.98**	**1.90**	**1.86**	**1.80**	**1.76**	**1.72**	
.90	1.86	1.79	1.74	1.70	1.64	1.61	1.56	1.53	1.50	1.47	1.45	48
.48	**2.40**	**2.28**	**2.20**	**2.11**	**2.02**	**1.96**	**1.88**	**1.84**	**1.78**	**1.73**	**1.70**	
.90	1.85	1.78	1.74	1.69	1.63	1.60	1.55	1.52	1.48	1.46	1.44	50
.46	**2.39**	**2.26**	**2.18**	**2.10**	**2.00**	**1.94**	**1.86**	**1.82**	**1.76**	**1.71**	**1.68**	
.88	1.83	1.76	1.72	1.67	1.61	1.58	1.52	1.50	1.46	1.43	1.41	55
.43	**2.35**	**2.23**	**2.15**	**2.06**	**1.96**	**1.90**	**1.82**	**1.78**	**1.71**	**1.66**	**1.64**	
.86	1.81	1.75	1.70	1.65	1.59	1.56	1.50	1.48	1.44	1.41	1.39	60
2.40	**2.32**	**2.20**	**2.12**	**2.03**	**1.93**	**1.87**	**1.79**	**1.74**	**1.68**	**1.63**	**1.60**	
.85	1.80	1.73	1.68	1.63	1.57	1.54	1.49	1.46	1.42	1.39	1.37	65
2.37	**2.30**	**2.18**	**2.09**	**2.00**	**1.90**	**1.84**	**1.76**	**1.71**	**1.64**	**1.60**	**1.56**	
.84	1.79	1.72	1.67	1.62	1.56	1.53	1.47	1.45	1.40	1.37	1.35	70
2.35	**2.28**	**2.15**	**2.07**	**1.98**	**1.88**	**1.82**	**1.74**	**1.69**	**1.62**	**1.56**	**1.53**	
.82	1.77	1.70	1.65	1.60	1.54	1.51	1.45	1.42	1.38	1.35	1.32	80
2.32	**2.24**	**2.11**	**2.03**	**1.94**	**1.84**	**1.78**	**1.70**	**1.65**	**1.57**	**1.52**	**1.49**	
1.79	1.75	1.68	1.63	1.57	1.51	1.48	1.42	1.39	1.34	1.30	1.28	100
2.26	**2.19**	**2.06**	**1.98**	**1.89**	**1.79**	**1.73**	**1.64**	**1.59**	**1.51**	**1.46**	**1.43**	
1.77	1.72	1.65	1.60	1.55	1.49	1.45	1.39	1.36	1.31	1.27	1.25	125
2.23	**2.15**	**2.03**	**1.94**	**1.85**	**1.75**	**1.68**	**1.59**	**1.54**	**1.46**	**1.40**	**1.37**	
1.76	1.71	1.64	1.59	1.54	1.47	1.44	1.37	1.34	1.29	1.25	1.22	150
2.20	**2.12**	**2.00**	**1.91**	**1.83**	**1.72**	**1.66**	**1.56**	**1.51**	**1.43**	**1.37**	**1.33**	
1.74	1.69	1.62	1.57	1.52	1.45	1.42	1.35	1.32	1.26	1.22	1.19	200
2.17	**2.09**	**1.97**	**1.88**	**1.79**	**1.69**	**1.62**	**1.53**	**1.48**	**1.39**	**1.33**	**1.28**	
1.72	1.67	1.60	1.54	1.49	1.42	1.38	1.32	1.28	1.22	1.16	1.13	400
2.12	**2.04**	**1.92**	**1.84**	**1.74**	**1.64**	**1.57**	**1.47**	**1.42**	**1.32**	**1.24**	**1.19**	
1.70	1.65	1.58	1.53	1.47	1.41	1.36	1.30	1.26	1.19	1.13	1.08	1000
2.09	**2.01**	**1.89**	**1.81**	**1.71**	**1.61**	**1.54**	**1.44**	**1.38**	**1.28**	**1.19**	**1.11**	
1.69	1.64	1.57	1.52	1.46	1.40	1.35	1.28	1.24	1.17	1.11	1.00	∞
2.07	**1.99**	**1.87**	**1.79**	**1.69**	**1.59**	**1.52**	**1.41**	**1.36**	**1.25**	**1.15**	**1.00**	

Table C.5 The Durbin-Watson Test Statistic *d*

Significance Points of d_L and d_U: 5%

n	$k = 2$		$k = 3$		$k = 4$		$k = 5$		$k = 6$	
	d_L	d_U	d_L	d_U	d_L	d_U	d_L	d_U	d_L	d_U
15	1.08	1.36	0.95	1.54	0.82	1.75	0.69	1.97	0.56	2.21
16	1.10	1.37	0.98	1.54	0.86	1.73	0.74	1.93	0.62	2.15
17	1.13	1.38	1.02	1.54	0.90	1.71	0.78	1.90	0.67	2.10
18	1.16	1.39	1.05	1.53	0.93	1.69	0.82	1.87	0.71	2.06
19	1.18	1.40	1.08	1.53	0.97	1.68	0.86	1.85	0.75	2.02
20	1.20	1.41	1.10	1.54	1.00	1.68	0.90	1.83	0.79	1.99
21	1.22	1.42	1.13	1.54	1.03	1.67	0.93	1.81	0.83	1.96
22	1.24	1.43	1.15	1.54	1.05	1.66	0.96	1.80	0.86	1.94
23	1.26	1.44	1.17	1.54	1.08	1.66	0.99	1.79	0.90	1.92
24	1.27	1.45	1.19	1.55	1.10	1.66	1.01	1.78	0.93	1.90
25	1.29	1.45	1.21	1.55	1.12	1.66	1.04	1.77	0.95	1.89
26	1.30	1.46	1.22	1.55	1.14	1.65	1.06	1.76	0.98	1.88
27	1.32	1.47	1.24	1.56	1.16	1.65	1.08	1.76	1.01	1.86
28	1.33	1.48	1.26	1.56	1.18	1.65	1.10	1.75	1.03	1.85
29	1.34	1.48	1.27	1.56	1.20	1.65	1.12	1.74	1.05	1.84
30	1.35	1.49	1.28	1.57	1.21	1.65	1.14	1.74	1.07	1.83
31	1.36	1.50	1.30	1.57	1.23	1.65	1.16	1.74	1.09	1.83
32	1.37	1.50	1.31	1.57	1.24	1.65	1.18	1.73	1.11	1.82
33	1.38	1.51	1.32	1.58	1.26	1.65	1.19	1.73	1.13	1.81
34	1.39	1.51	1.33	1.58	1.27	1.65	1.21	1.73	1.15	1.81
35	1.40	1.52	1.34	1.58	1.28	1.65	1.22	1.73	1.16	1.80
36	1.41	1.52	1.35	1.59	1.29	1.65	1.24	1.73	1.18	1.80
37	1.42	1.53	1.36	1.59	1.31	1.66	1.25	1.72	1.19	1.80
38	1.43	1.54	1.37	1.59	1.32	1.66	1.26	1.72	1.21	1.79
39	1.43	1.54	1.38	1.60	1.33	1.66	1.27	1.72	1.22	1.79
40	1.44	1.54	1.39	1.60	1.34	1.66	1.29	1.72	1.23	1.79
45	1.48	1.57	1.43	1.62	1.38	1.67	1.34	1.72	1.29	1.78
50	1.50	1.59	1.46	1.63	1.42	1.67	1.38	1.72	1.34	1.77
55	1.53	1.60	1.49	1.64	1.45	1.68	1.41	1.72	1.38	1.77
60	1.55	1.62	1.51	1.65	1.48	1.69	1.44	1.73	1.41	1.77
65	1.57	1.63	1.54	1.66	1.50	1.70	1.47	1.73	1.44	1.77
70	1.58	1.64	1.55	1.67	1.52	1.70	1.49	1.74	1.46	1.77
75	1.60	1.65	1.57	1.68	1.54	1.71	1.51	1.74	1.49	1.77
80	1.61	1.66	1.59	1.69	1.56	1.72	1.53	1.74	1.51	1.77
85	1.62	1.67	1.60	1.70	1.57	1.72	1.55	1.75	1.52	1.77
90	1.63	1.68	1.61	1.70	1.59	1.73	1.57	1.75	1.54	1.78
95	1.64	1.69	1.62	1.71	1.60	1.73	1.58	1.75	1.56	1.78
100	1.65	1.69	1.63	1.72	1.61	1.74	1.59	1.76	1.57	1.78

NOTE n = number of observations; k = number of explanatory variables, including the constant term.

Table C.5 *(continued)*

Significance Points of d_L and d_U: 1%

n	k = 2		k = 3		k = 4		k = 5		k = 6	
	d_L	d_U	d_L	d_U	d_L	d_U	d_L	d_U	d_L	d_U
15	0.81	1.07	0.70	1.25	0.59	1.46	0.49	1.70	0.39	1.96
16	0.84	1.09	0.74	1.25	0.63	1.44	0.53	1.66	0.44	1.90
17	0.87	1.10	0.77	1.25	0.67	1.43	0.57	1.63	0.48	1.85
18	0.90	1.12	0.80	1.26	0.71	1.42	0.61	1.60	0.52	1.80
19	0.93	1.13	0.83	1.26	0.74	1.41	0.65	1.58	0.56	1.77
20	0.95	1.15	0.86	1.27	0.77	1.41	0.68	1.57	0.60	1.74
21	0.97	1.16	0.89	1.27	0.80	1.41	0.72	1.55	0.63	1.71
22	1.00	1.17	0.91	1.28	0.83	1.40	0.75	1.54	0.66	1.69
23	1.02	1.19	0.94	1.29	0.86	1.40	0.77	1.53	0.70	1.67
24	1.04	1.20	0.96	1.30	0.88	1.41	0.80	1.53	0.72	1.66
25	1.05	1.21	0.98	1.30	0.90	1.41	0.83	1.52	0.75	1.65
26	1.07	1.22	1.00	1.31	0.93	1.41	0.85	1.52	0.78	1.64
27	1.09	1.23	1.02	1.32	0.95	1.41	0.88	1.51	0.81	1.63
28	1.10	1.24	1.04	1.32	0.97	1.41	0.90	1.51	0.83	1.62
29	1.12	1.25	1.05	1.33	0.99	1.42	0.92	1.51	0.85	1.61
30	1.13	1.26	1.07	1.34	1.01	1.42	0.94	1.51	0.88	1.61
31	1.15	1.27	1.08	1.34	1.02	1.42	0.96	1.51	0.90	1.60
32	1.16	1.28	1.10	1.35	1.04	1.43	0.98	1.51	0.92	1.60
33	1.17	1.29	1.11	1.36	1.05	1.43	1.00	1.51	0.94	1.59
34	1.18	1.30	1.13	1.36	1.07	1.43	1.01	1.51	0.95	1.59
35	1.19	1.31	1.14	1.37	1.08	1.44	1.03	1.51	0.97	1.59
36	1.21	1.32	1.15	1.38	1.10	1.44	1.04	1.51	0.99	1.59
37	1.22	1.32	1.16	1.38	1.11	1.45	1.06	1.51	1.00	1.59
38	1.23	1.33	1.18	1.39	1.12	1.45	1.07	1.52	1.02	1.58
39	1.24	1.34	1.19	1.39	1.14	1.45	1.09	1.52	1.03	1.58
40	1.25	1.34	1.20	1.40	1.15	1.46	1.10	1.52	1.05	1.58
45	1.29	1.38	1.24	1.42	1.20	1.48	1.16	1.53	1.11	1.58
50	1.32	1.40	1.28	1.45	1.24	1.49	1.20	1.54	1.16	1.59
55	1.36	1.43	1.32	1.47	1.28	1.51	1.25	1.55	1.21	1.59
60	1.38	1.45	1.35	1.48	1.32	1.52	1.28	1.56	1.25	1.60
65	1.41	1.47	1.38	1.50	1.35	1.53	1.31	1.57	1.28	1.61
70	1.43	1.49	1.40	1.52	1.37	1.55	1.34	1.58	1.31	1.61
75	1.45	1.50	1.42	1.53	1.39	1.56	1.37	1.59	1.34	1.62
80	1.47	1.52	1.44	1.54	1.42	1.57	1.39	1.60	1.36	1.62
85	1.48	1.53	1.46	1.55	1.43	1.58	1.41	1.60	1.39	1.63
90	1.50	1.54	1.47	1.56	1.45	1.59	1.43	1.61	1.41	1.64
95	1.51	1.55	1.49	1.57	1.47	1.60	1.45	1.62	1.42	1.64
100	1.52	1.56	1.50	1.58	1.48	1.60	1.46	1.63	1.44	1.65

Source J. Durbin and G. S. Watson, "Testing for Serial Correlation in Least Squares Regression," *Biometrika*, vol. 38 (1951), pp. 159–77. Reprinted with the permission of the authors and the *Biometrika* trustees.

Index